McGRAW-HILL EDUCATION

Essential ESL Dictionary

for Learners of English

New York Chicago San Francisco Athens London Madrid
Mexico City Milan New Delhi Singapore Sydney Toronto

Published by McGraw-Hill Global Education Holdings, LLC © 2014, under license from SM™.

4 5 6 7 8 9 10 DOC 20 19 18 17 16

ISBN 978-0-07-184018-7
MHID 0-07-184018-4

e-ISBN 978-0-07-184019-4
e-MHID 0-07-184019-2

Library of Congress Cataloging-in-Publication Data

McGraw-Hill Education Essential ESL dictionary for learners of English / Editors of McGraw-Hill Education. — Primera edición.
pages ; cm
"Primera edición (basado en My World Learner's Dictionary, SM): mayo 2014."
Includes index.
ISBN 0-07-184018-4
1. English language—Dictionaries. 2. English language—United States—Dictionaries. 3. English language—Textbooks for foreign speakers. 4. Americanisms—Dictionaries. I. McGraw-Hill Education (Firm) II. Title: Essential ESL dictionary for learners of English.
PE1628.M315 2014
423'.1—dc23

2014020212

Coordinación editorial
Yolanda Lozano Ramírez de Arellano

Proyecto editorial
Concepción Maldonado González

Asesoría y revisión
Mike Champion
Lauren Robbins

Autores
Luis Aragonés
Bernadette Maguire
Ramón Palencia

Equipo de redacción
Elisa Ambrogio
Ana Chicote
Liz Dilley
Jana García
Pilar García
Alba Gil
Malcolm Greenwood
Teresa Gutiérrez
María Clara Henríquez
Serafín Hernández
Laura Mesanza
Matilde Pérez

Edición técnica
Marlene Díaz
Elena Díaz-Plaza

Ilustración
Archivo SM
Escletxa
Nacho Rúa
Rugoma Cartografía

Fotografía
Javier Calbet, Sonsoles Prada, Sergio Cuesta, José Manuel Navia/Archivo SM; Pedro Carrión; Montse Fontich; Christiam Musat/iSTOCKPHOTO.COM; Dmitry Maslov, Stephen Meese, Janpietruszka/DREAMSTIME; JUPITER IMAGES/GETTY IMAGES; KEYSTONE; EFE; DIGITAL VISION; PHOTODISC; CREATAS; PHOVOIR; INGIMAGE; THINKSTOCK; BRAND X PICTURES; ABLESTOCK; 123RF; NASA; Documentation Française; Museo Imperial de la Guerra; Museo del Prado

Maquetación
Negra

Diseño
Mario Dequel
Maritxu Eizaguirre
Patricia Fernández
Diego García

Diseño Guía de conversación
Bernal Prieto

Diseño de cubierta
Maritxu Eizaguirre

This book is printed on acid-free paper.

Contents

Preface

McGraw-Hill Education: Essential ESL Dictionary for Learners of English is an English dictionary especially designed for students who are studying English at elementary and intermediate levels. Its **approach** guarantees that all of the terms appearing in the subjects that are taught in English are contained in this dictionary, so that any lexical doubt which students may have regarding these subjects can be easily solved by consulting their dictionary. In addition, it contains **40 pages of thematic illustrations** especially designed to help students to learn vocabulary in a significant and contextualized way and to reinforce the key vocabulary and concepts found in their textbooks.

It also has many **usage notes** and **grammar boxes** which explain and clarify the main doubts and difficulties which arise for students in their English language learning process, and is supplied with a large number of illustrations to facilitate lexicon acquisition.

The dictionary also includes a **Conversation guide** which provides the user with examples of common conversations that occur in specific contexts, showing the vocabulary and language structures that students need to learn. This guide will help students to tackle successfully a wide range of communication situations.

User's Guide

This sign indicates the most common words – the first you need to learn.

+**breakfast** /'brek.fəst/ [countable noun] The first meal of the day: *I always have breakfast in bed on Sundays.*

Key terms for the study of school courses in English

calyx /'keɪ.lɪks/ [countable noun] The sepals which together form the layer that protects a flower in bud: *The calyx is the outer part of the flower.* ■ The plural is "calyces" or "calyxes". ■ Compare with "corolla" (The petals which form the inner envelope of a flower).

Phonetic transcription and pronunciation notes. (All phonetic symbols are listed on page 11.)

volcano US: /vɑːl'keɪ.noʊ/ UK: /vɒl'keɪ.nəʊ/ [countable noun] A hole where very hot rock comes out: *The volcanoes of the United States are located along the West Coast.* ■ Be careful with the pronunciation of this word! "ca" rhymes with "day". ■ The plural is "volcanoes".

Grammatical category is shown in brackets and not abbreviated. Headwords with different grammatical functions are separated by numbers.

+**answer**[1] US: /'ænt.sɚ/ UK: /'ɑːnt.səʳ/ [countable noun] The response to a question: *I've asked you a question and I want an answer.*

answer[2] [verb] **1** To say something to somebody who has asked you a question: *I asked her about Jim but she didn't answer.* **2** **to answer the door** To open the door in answer to a knock or ring: *I had to ring twice before they answered the door.* **3** **to answer the telephone** To pick up the telephone in answer to a call: *Can you answer the phone, Mark? I'm in the bathroom.*

Clear and simple definitions separated by a number and with examples

compass /'kʌm.pəs/ [countable noun] **1** An instrument that shows direction: *A compass has a pointer that always points north.* **2** A metal or plastic instrument which is used for drawing circles: *If you change the angle of the compass, you can draw circles of different size.* ■ In this use, we also say "compasses". ■ The plural is "compasses". See page 456.

stave [countable noun] The five parallel lines on which musical notes are written in a score: *The music teacher wrote the tune of the song on a stave on the whiteboard.* See page 460.

Irregular verbs with their forms

+**forget, forgot, forgotten** /fər'get/, /fɔr-/ [verb] Not to remember something: *Don't forget we're having a test on Monday.*

†**call**[2] US: /kɑːl/ UK: /kɔːl/ [verb] **1** To attract somebody's attention by shouting: *Somebody called my name from the other end of the room.* **2** To telephone: *I called Jane to invite her to go to the movies with me but she wasn't in.* **3** to be called To have a name: *What is this animal called in English?* **4** to call collect On the phone, to ask the person you are calling to pay for the call: *When I was in Europe this summer I called collect every week to talk to my parents.* ■ In British English they say "reverse the charges". ▸ **PHRASAL VERBS** · **to call back** To return a telephone call or to call again: *He said he'd call me back when he got home.* · **to call on** To visit: *We'll call on you tomorrow evening.* · **to call off** To stop something that had been planned: *As it was raining, we had to call off the game.*

Clear distinction between idioms and phrasal verbs

†**people** /ˈpiː.pl̩/ [plural noun] More than one person: *How many people shall we invite to the party?* ■ Be careful! "People" is a countable noun. We say: "There are many people here". (We don't say: "There is many people here").

Notes to avoid poor translations or incorrect usage

†**library** /ˈlaɪ.brər.i, -bri/ [countable noun] A place where you can borrow or read books: *The library in our school has all kinds of books.* ■ The plural is "libraries". ■ Compare with "bookstore" (a shop where you can buy books). 👁 **See picture at street.**

†**tooth** /tuːθ/ [countable noun] **1** One of the hard parts in your mouth: *I'm going to have one of my back teeth taken out tomorrow.* **2** tooth decay The process of going bad of a tooth: *Eating too many candies can cause tooth decay.* ■ The plural is "teeth".

Information about the plural and comparative forms

†**big** /bɪg/ [adjective] Large or important: *An elephant is big, a mouse is small.* ■ The comparative form is "bigger" and the superlative form is "biggest". 👁 **See pictures at opposite and a piece of...**

chemist's /ˈkemɪst/ [countable noun] See **pharmacy**. ■ This word is British English.

Notes about British English

viviparous /vɪˈvɪp.ər.əs/ US: /-ɚ-/ [adjective] Giving birth to live young that have developed inside the body of the mother: *Mammals are all viviparous.* ■ Compare with "oviparous" (born from an egg outside the mother). 👁 **See page 427.**

Notes with other important information

Illustrations index

Grammar and usage boxes index

Symbols

▮	Separates different grammatical categories
®	Trademarks
■	Notes
/ /	Phonetic transcription
👁	See a picture or a illustration
↑	Most common words

Phonetic Symbols

VOWEL SOUNDS

/æ/	**a**t,	**a**ccident	
/e/	**e**gg,	**e**very	
/ɪ/	**i**n,	d**i**d,	k**i**t
/ɒ/	**o**n,	**o**ff,	t**o**p
/ʊ/	p**u**t,	b**oo**k	
/ʌ/	**u**s,	s**u**n,	b**u**s
/i/	ver**y**,	bab**y**	
/ə/	**a**go,	b**a**lloon	
/ɑ:/	**ar**m,	c**ar**,	f**a**ther
/i:/	**ea**t,	m**e**,	f**ee**l
/ɜ:/	s**i**r,	h**er**,	l**ear**n
/ɔ:/	**or**,	h**or**se,	s**aw**
/u:/	y**ou**,	bl**ue**,	bedr**oo**m
/eɪ/	d**ay**,	**a**ge,	**ei**ght
/aɪ/	**I**,	b**y**,	b**i**ke
/ɔɪ/	b**oy**,	t**oy**,	**oi**l
/əʊ/	**o**pen,	g**o**,	c**o**at
/oʊ/	l**ow** *(US)*		
/aʊ/	ab**ou**t,	h**ou**se,	n**ow**
/ɪə/	**ea**r,	y**ea**r,	h**e**re
/eə/	**air**,	h**air**,	wh**ere**
/ʊə/	p**ure**,	h**ou**r	
/aɪə/	f**ire**,	h**ire**	
/aʊə/	o**ur**,	fl**our**,	sh**ower**

CONSONANTAL SOUNDS

/b/	**b**ad,	**b**ye,	ver**b**
/d/	**d**ay,	sa**d**	
/dʒ/	**j**ust,	a**g**e	
/f/	**f**ine,	i**f**	
/g/	**g**o,	ba**g**	
/h/	**h**appy,	**h**ouse,	**h**e
/j/	**y**es,	**y**ou	
/k/	**c**at,	ba**ck**,	**k**ey
/l/	**l**eg,	**l**ike	
/m/	**m**e,	ti**m**e,	**m**ap
/n/	**n**ot,	ca**n**	
/ŋ/	ri**ng**,	sa**ng**	
/p/	**p**et,	hel**p**	
/r/	**r**ead,	d**r**y	
/s/	**s**it,	pre**ss**	
/ʃ/	**sh**e,	fi**sh**	
/t/	**t**en,	bi**t**	
/t̬/	be**tt**er *(US)*		
/tʃ/	**ch**ip,	**ch**eap,	ri**ch**
/v/	**v**iew,	dri**v**e	
/w/	**w**e,	**w**indow	
/z/	**z**oo,	cra**z**y	
/ʒ/	plea**s**ure,	divi**s**ion	
/ð/	**th**is,	**th**ey,	mo**th**er
/θ/	**th**in,	**th**ink,	ba**th**

Dictionary

a[1] /eɪ/ The first letter of the alphabet: *The name "Albert" begins with an "A".*

†**a**[2] /eɪ, ə/ [article] **1** Not a particular one: *A spider is an insect.* **2** One: *I need a hundred dollars.* **3** Each: *I normally go to the movies twice a month.* ■ See box on the following page.

A /eɪ/ [countable noun] The sixth musical note of the scale of C major: *The music teacher asked me to play an A.* ■ The plural is "As" or "A's". 👁 **See page 460.**

†**abandon** /əˈbæn.dən/ [verb] **1** To leave somebody or something: *The sailors had to abandon the ship when it hit the iceberg.* **2** To stop doing something: *I had no money, so I had to abandon the idea of going to India.*

abbey /ˈæb.i/ [countable noun] A building where Christian monks or nuns live: *Westminster Abbey is the most famous abbey in Britain.*

abbreviation /əˌbriː.viˈeɪ.ʃᵊn/ [countable noun] A short form of a word: *UN is an abbreviation for United Nations.* ■ See box on the following page.

ABCs [plural noun] All the letters of a language: *Do you know your ABCs, Jamie?* ■ Be careful. "ABCs" is always written with the first three letters in capitals. ■ The same meaning: "alphabet".

abdomen /ˈæb.də.mən/ [countable noun] The part of the body where the stomach, bowels and reproductive organs are to be found: *The abdomen is the part of the body where food is digested.*

abdominal /æbˈdɒmɪnəl/ [adjective] Referring to the abdomen: *Exercise strengthens the abdominal muscles.* 👁 **See page 423.**

†**ability** /əˈbɪl·ɪ·t̬i/ [noun] **1** The capacity or knowledge to do something: *Jack's abilities are more academic than mine; I prefer sports myself.* **2** Being able to do something well: *His ability with the guitar is amazing.* ■ The plural is "abilities". ■ The same meaning: "skill".

ablaze [adjective] On fire: *He dropped a cigarette in the wastepaper basket and set it ablaze.*

†**able** /ˈeɪ.bl̩/ [adjective] Good at doing something: *John is a very able goalkeeper.* ■ "Be able to" is used as the infinitive of "can": "I'd like to be able to sing well". ■ See box at **can**.

aboard /əˈbɔrd/, /-ˈbourd/ [preposition and adverb] **1** On a ship, airplane, train or bus: *The ship will leave when everyone is aboard.* **2** Onto a ship, airplane, train or bus: *Let's go aboard!*

abolish /əˈbɑl·ɪʃ/ [verb] To end a practice by law: *Slavery was abolished in the 19th century.*

abolition /ˌæb.əˈlɪʃ.ᵊn/ [uncountable noun] The ending of a practice by law: *Many people are in favor of the abolition of capital punishment.*

Aborigine /ˌæb.əˈrɪdʒ.ᵊn.i/ [countable noun] One of the original inhabitants of Australia: *The Aborigines had*

a b c d e f g h i j k l m n o p q r s t u v w x y z

been living in Australia for centuries before the first Europeans arrived. ■ Be careful! "Aborigine" has a capital "A".

+**about[1]** /ə'baʊt/ [preposition] On the subject of something: *This book is about the adventures of a girl in the jungle.*

about[2] /ə'baʊt/ [adverb] **1** Approximately: *He's about six feet tall.* **2 to be about** To be on the subject of: *This book is really interesting. It's about the Lewis and Clark expedition.* **3 to be about to** To be going to do something very soon: *We were just about to have dinner when you arrived.* **4 how about** An expression used for making a suggestion: *How about having something to eat? I'm hungry.*

+**above[1]** /ə'bʌv/ [preposition] **1** Higher than something: *The temperature was above 90 ºF.* **2 above all** Especially: *Work hard, but above all, have a good time.* See picture at **over**.

above[2] /ə'bʌv/ [adverb] At a higher point: *High above, the vultures circled in the sky.*

+**abroad** /ə'brɔːd/ [adverb] In or to another country: *We're going abroad for our vacation this summer.* ■ Be careful. We always say: "We're going abroad". (We don't say: "We're going to abroad").

abrupt /ə'brʌpt/ [adjective] **1** Sudden and unexpected: *Mark's trip came to an abrupt end when his car crashed.* **2** Not polite: *Barbara is sometimes quite abrupt, but I think she's nice really.*

abruptly [adverb] In a sudden and unexpected manner: *The door swung open abruptly and there, to our surprise, was the principal.*

+**absence** /'æb.sᵊnts/ [noun] **1** Not being present: *Everybody at the party noticed Sheila's absence.* **2 in the absence of** The lack of something: *They gave us water to drink in the absence of anything else.*

absent /'æb.sᵊnt/ [adjective] Not present: *Rosemary was absent from school on Monday because she was ill.*

a* and *an
We use ***a*** before words beginning with a consonant sound, like *b*, *d*, or *k*, or before words beginning with *y* or *eu*. We use ***an*** before words beginning with a vowel sound. Note that in some words beginning with an *h* the *h* is silent. We use ***an*** before these words.

a	an
a balloon	*an airplane*
a dog	*an octopus*
a kite	*an American singer*
a European country	*an hour*
a yard	

absent-minded /ˌæb.sᵊnt'maɪn.dɪd/ [adjective] Often forgetting things or forgetting what you are doing: *Mary is so absent-minded that she once came to school with her pajamas on!*

+**absolute** /ˌæb.sə'luːt/ [adjective] Total, without any limit: *The dictator had absolute power over his country.*

+**absorb** /əb'zɔrb/, /-'sɔrb/ [verb] To take in liquid: *Sponges absorb water.*

abstract /'æb.strækt/ [adjective] **1** Not concrete: *All his ideas are very abstract and nobody understands them.* **2** Not showing something as it is: *Abstract art is difficult to understand.*

absurd /əb'sɜrd/, /æb-/, /-'zɜrd/ [adjective] Strange and ridiculous: *The idea that I would steal the money is absurd.*

abundant /ə'bʌn.dᵊnt/ [adjective] Available in generous quantities: *In the tree you can see abundant quantities of apples.* ■ Compare with "sparse" (widely scattered).

abuse[1] /ə'bjuːs/ ▌[noun] **1** The wrong or bad use of something: *Drug abuse is a very serious problem.* ▌[uncountable noun] **2** Being cruel to somebody: *Child abuse is a terrible crime.* **3** Rude or insulting words: *When Arthur saw us, he started shouting abuse at us.*

+**abuse[2]** /ə'bjuːz/ [verb] **1** To use something in a wrong or bad way: *Bad politicians often abuse their power.* **2** To treat somebody with cruelty: *It is a terrible problem when parents abuse their children.* **3** To insult: *That man stands there all day abusing people with bad language.*

academic[1] /ˌækə'demɪk/ [adjective] Referring to study, mainly at a university: *At our school we only do academic subjects like Geography; I'd like to learn cooking, too.*

+**academic[2]** /ˌækə'demɪk/ ▌[countable noun] **1** A university teacher: *Yale academics wear black gowns when they give lectures.* ■ In British English they say "lecturer". ▌[plural noun] **2** School subjects: *My brother is better at academics than at sports.*

academy /ə'kæd.ə.mi/ [countable noun] A school specialized in a particular field: *The boys began their training in the military academy at the age of eighteen.* ■ The plural is "academies".

accelerate /ɪk'sel·əˌreɪt/, /æk-/ [verb] To go faster: *The car in front of us accelerated and left us far behind.*

+**accent** /'æk.sᵊnt/ [countable noun] **1** A particular way of pronouncing a language, characteristic of a particular place or social class: *Pierre still speaks English with a slight French accent.* **2** A small sign over a letter: *Normally there are no accents in English.* **3** A special emphasis given to a musical note or

Abbreviations

AD	*in the year of our Lord (d.de C.)*	mg	*milligram(s)*
AIDS	*Acquired Immune Deficiency Syndrome (sida)*	Miss	*a single woman*
a.m.	*before noon*	mm	*millimeter*
Ave	*Avenue*	mph	*miles per hour*
b.	*born*	Mr.	*a man*
BA	*Bachelor of Arts (a university degree)*	Mrs.	*a married woman*
BC	*before Christ (a.de C.)*	Ms.	*a woman*
BCE	*Before de Common Era*	N	*north*
BS	*Bachelor of Science*	NATO	*North Atlantic Treaty Organization*
oC	*centigrade, Celsius*	NE	*northeast*
ca.	*approximately*	NW	*northwest*
CD	*compact disc*	OK	*all correct*
CE	*Common Era*	oz	*ounce*
cf.	*compare*	p.	*page or pence*
cm	*centimeter*	PE	*Physical Education*
Corp.	*corporation*	pl.	*plural*
d.	*died*	p.m.	*afternoon*
dept.	*department*	PO	*Post Office*
div.	*division*	Prof.	*Professor*
Dr.	*doctor*	PS	*an extra note at the end of a letter*
E	*east*	PTO	*please turn over (the page)*
e.g.	*for example*	Rd	*road*
et al.	*and other people*	RIP	*rest in peace (descanse en paz)*
etc.	*and all the rest*	rpm	*revolution(s) per minute*
EU	*European Union*	RSVP	*please reply*
oF	*Fahrenheit*	$	*dollar*
FBI	*Federal Bureau of Investigation*	S	*south*
FM	*Frequency Modulation*	sci-fi	*science fiction*
ft	*foot, feet*	SE	*southeast*
g	*gram*	sq.	*square*
GB	*Great Britain*	Sr.	*senior*
GMT	*Greenwich Mean Time*	St	*Saint or street*
GNP	*Gross National Product*	SW	*southwest*
Hz	*Hertz*	3-D	*three-dimensional*
i.e.	*that is*	TV	*television*
Inc.	*incorporated*	UFO	*unidentified flying object (ovni)*
in/ins	*inch*	UK	*United Kingdom*
IQ	*Intelligence quotient*	UN	*United Nations*
Jr	*junior*	US, USA	*United States of America*
kg	*kilogram*	v	*consult*
km	*kilometer*	vol.	*volume(s)*
£	*sterling pound*	vs.	*versus*
lb	*pound (measure of weight)*	VCR	*video cassette recorder*
Ltd.	*Limited*	W	*west*
m	*mile or meter*	WHO	*World Health Organization (OMS)*
M.D.	*Doctor of Medicine*	yd	*yard*

You will see that not all abbreviations have a period [.] in English.

chord: *Musical accents are often indicated by a mark.* **See page 460.**

†**accept** /ək'sept/ [verb] **1** To say yes to an offer or an invitation: *I invited Mary to my party and she accepted.* **2** To receive or to permit something: *I can't accept such an expensive present.*

†**acceptable** /ək'sep.tə.bḷ/ [adjective] That is considered good enough: *Mr. Petty said that my history project was not acceptable.*

acceptance /ək'sep.tᵊnts/ [noun] Saying yes to an offer or an invitation: *My sister applied to Harvard University and she's still waiting for her letter of acceptance.*

†**access** /'æk.ses/ [uncountable noun] **1** A way of getting into a place: *Access to the gym is from the long hallway.* **2** The possibility of getting something or using it: *The older students have access to a computer at school.*

accessible /ək'ses.ə.bḷ/ [adjective] That is easy to get to or to obtain: *The castle is not accessible by car, so you'll have to go up on foot.*

†**accident** /'æk.sɪ.dᵊnt/ [countable noun] **1** Something bad that happens by chance or through carelessness: *I had an accident on my bike and broke my leg.* **2** by accident Without wanting to: *I read Bill's letter by accident because I thought it was for me.*

ACCIDENT

†**accidental** /ˌæk·sə'dent·ə·l/ [adjective] Happening by chance: *Our meeting was quite accidental.*

†**accommodation** /əˌkɑm·ə'deɪ·ʃən/ [uncountable noun] A place to live or to stay in: *I'm looking for accommodations for a group of twenty Japanese tourists.* ■ This word is more common in the plural.

accompaniment /ə'kʌm.pᵊn.ɪ.mənt/ [noun] Music to accompany a singer or another instrument: *I usually sing to the accompaniment of a piano.*

†**accompany** /ə'kʌm.pə.ni/ [verb] **1** To go somewhere with somebody: *Julia's mother accompanied us to the airport.* **2** To back a singer or another musician with a musical instrument: *Rick sings and his brother accompanies him on the guitar.* ■ Be careful with the spelling of these forms: "accompanies", "accompanied".

accomplice /ə'kɑm·plɪs/ [countable noun] A person who helps somebody in a crime: *He robbed the bank with two accomplices.*

accomplish /ə'kʌmplɪʃ/ [verb] To do something very well: *How did Mozart accomplish so much in such a short lifetime?*

accordance /ə'kɔːdəns/ in accordance with In agreement: *The rules were drawn up in accordance with the team requirements.*

according according to As somebody says or writes: *According to my opinion you should already go to bed.*

†**according to** /ə'kɔːdɪŋtuː/ [preposition] As somebody says or writes; as stated by somebody: *According to Barbara, her brother is very intelligent.*

accordion /ə'kɔr·di·ən/ [countable noun] A musical instrument that you pull and push: *You have to squeeze the accordion to get a sound out of it.*

†**account** /ə'kaʊnt/ [countable noun] **1** A description of an event: *Mark's account of his vacation made everybody laugh.* **2** An arrangement with a bank to keep money in it: *I have very little money in my bank account at the moment.* **3** bank account See "bank account" in the word **bank**[1]. **4** on account of Because of: *The game was cancelled on account of the bad weather.*

accountant /ə'kaʊn·tə·nt/ [countable noun] A person whose job is to keep accounts: *Tim's mother works as an accountant for a big company.*

accounts /ə'kaʊnts/ [plural noun] Written records of money: *We have an accountant to keep the accounts and see how much we earn and spend.*

accumulate /ə'kjuː.mjʊ.leɪt/ [verb] To collect a number or quantity of something over a period of time: *My uncle accumulated a small fortune over his lifetime.*

accurate /'æk.jʊ.rət/ [adjective] Correct, exact: *Can you give me an accurate description of the bag you lost?*

accusation /ˌæk.jʊ'zeɪ.ʃᵊn/ [countable noun] Saying that somebody has done something wrong: *You shouldn't make accusations if you don't have any evidence.*

†**accuse** /ə'kjuːz/ [verb] To charge somebody with having done something: *Tom accused me of cheating in the test.*

accustomed /ə'kʌs.təmd/ [adjective] That is used to something: *Six o'clock! I'm not accustomed to getting up so early.* ■ Be careful with the pronunciation of the end of this word! The "e" is not pronounced. ■ Be careful. We always say: "to be accustomed to (something)". The verb after "to" is in the "-ing" form.

ace /eɪs/ [countable noun] **1** The most important playing card: *Who's got the ace of diamonds?* **2** In tennis, a service which your opponent cannot return: *He served an ace that the other player had no chance of reaching.* **3** A person who is very good at something: *Tom is a basketball ace and everybody wants to play in his team.*

ache[1] /eɪk/ [countable noun] A pain that doesn't stop: *I have an ache in a tooth in the right side of my mouth that stops me sleeping.*

ache[2] /eɪk/ [verb] To feel a regular pain: *My legs ached all afternoon after the run yesterday.*

achieve /ə'tʃiːv/ [verb] To succeed in doing something: *Poor Arthur! He couldn't achieve his ambition of being the best climber in the world.*

achievement /ə'tʃiːv.mənt/ [countable noun] Something difficult that has been done very well: *Going around the world in a small boat in such a short time was a great achievement.*

Achilles' heel /əˌkɪl.iːz'hiːl/ [noun] Weak point or small fault: *Although he passed all his tests, Mathematics still were his Achilles' heel.*

Achilles' tendon /əˌkɪl.iːz'ten.dən/ [countable noun] The tendon attaching the calf muscles to the heel: *He had to give up the football league because of a ruptured Achilles' tendon.*

acid /'æs.ɪd/ [noun] **1** A chemical substance that may destroy things: *That acid is very dangerous and you can get burned if any of it goes on your skin.* **2** acid rain Rain that is polluted by acid: *Acid rain destroys forests in some parts of Canada.*

acknowledge /ɪk'nɑl·ɪdʒ/, /æk-/ [verb] To recognize to somebody that something is true: *Sheila acknowledged her mistake.*

acorn /'eɪ·kɔrn/, /-kərn/ [countable noun] The fruit of an oak tree: *Pigs love eating acorns.*

acoustic /ə'kuː.stɪk/ [adjective] Referring to sound: *The acoustic nerve is in the ear.*

acoustics /ə'kuː.stɪks/ [plural noun] The sound quality of a place: *The acoustics in the concert hall is perfect.* ■ It is usually used with a singular verb.

acquaintance /ə'kweɪn.tᵊnts/ [countable noun] A person that you know slightly: *They're not really my friends; they're just acquaintances.* ■ Compare with "friend" (somebody who you know well, get on well with and feel loyal to).

acquainted /ə'kweɪn·tɪd/ [adjective] **1** Knowing somebody: *I don't know George at all, but I'm slightly acquainted with his brother.* **2** to get acquainted with (somebody) To get to know somebody: *They had a party to get acquainted with the new neighbors.* ■ Be careful with the pronunciation of the end of this word. The "e" is pronounced like the "i" in "did". ■ We always say: "acquainted **with** (somebody)".

acquire /ə'kwaɪər/ [verb] **1** To get something or to buy it: *I have just acquired a new car.* ■ We usually say "buy" or "get". **2** To develop something: *When I was in England, I acquired the habit of drinking a lot of tea.*

acquisition /ˌæk.wɪ'zɪʃ.ᵊn/ [countable noun] Something which has been acquired: *A cellphone is a useful acquisition.* ■ We usually say "buy".

acre /'eɪ·kər/ [countable noun] A unit of land area equal to 2.59 square kilometers: *He owns ten acres of land.*

acrobat /'æk.rə.bæt/ [countable noun] An entertainer who does difficult exercises: *She works as an acrobat in a traveling circus.*

across[1] /ə'krɒs/ [preposition] **1** From one side to the other: *I have to walk across the road to go to Ben's house.* **2** On the other side of something: *Ben lives across the road.* ■ See picture on the following page. 👁 See picture at **preposition**.

across[2] /ə'krɒs/ [adverb] **1** From one side to the other: *The river near our house is about 30 feet across.* **2** On or to the other side of something: *Come on! See if you can jump across.*

act[1] /ækt/ [countable noun] Something which is done: *What you did was an act of kindness.*

act[2] /ækt/ [verb] **1** To play a part in a play or in a movie: *Sara is acting in the school musical of "Grease" which is on next week.* **2** To do something: *We have to act before it's too late.* **3** to act as To do a job on certain occasions: *George acts as the secretary at school meetings.*

▶ **PHRASAL VERBS** · **to act out** **1** To express thoughts or feelings in actions rather than in words: *Can you act out for us what you felt?.* **2** To behave badly especially as a way of expressing frustration or painful emotions: *My brother started acting out when my dad didn't buy him a toy and we had to leave the store.*

acting /'æk.tɪŋ/ [uncountable noun] The work done by an actor or an actress: *My sister loves acting and belongs to a theater group.*

action /'æk.ʃᵊn/ [noun] **1** Something that a person does: *Norman's quick action in calling the firefighters saved us all.* **2** in action In the process of doing something: *Serena Williams was in action at Wimbledon yesterday.*

active /'æk.tɪv/ [adjective] **1** Energetic, busy: *He's always doing something; he's so active.* **2** Involved in a job or an organization: *She plays a very active role in Greenpeace.* **3** Referring to volcanoes, that can still erupt: *The Pacific is an area of active volcanoes.*

activity /æk'tɪv·ɪ·t̬i/ ▮ [countable noun] **1** A planned action that you can do: *There are lots of cultural activities in Denver.* ▮ [uncountable noun] **2** Being active: *There was a lot of activity in the classroom.* ■ The plural is "activities".

actor /'æk·tər/ [countable noun] A person who acts in movies or in plays: *Keanu Reeves is my favorite actor.*

actress /ˈæktrəs/ [countable noun] A woman who acts in movies or in plays: *Julia Roberts is a famous American actress.* ■ The plural is "actresses". ■ A man who acts is an "actor". When we don't want to specify the person's sex, we say "actor".

†**actual** /ˈæk.tʃu.əl, -tju-, -tʃʊl/ [adjective] Real, true: *They said the trip would cost $425, but the actual cost was $550.*

†**actually** /ˈæk.tʃu.ə.li, -tju-, -tʃʊ.li/ [adverb] **1** Really, in fact: *He says he's English, but actually he's Scottish.* **2** A polite way of saying that something is wrong: *Actually, I'm from Boston and not from New York.*

ad /æd/ [countable noun] See **advertisement**.

Adam's apple [countable noun] The part that stands out at the front of the neck: *The Adam's apple moves up and down when one talks or swallows.*

adapt /əˈdæpt/ [verb] **1** To make something suitable for a new use: *This wheelchair has been adapted to go over stony ground.* **2** To become adjusted to a new situation or condition: *John was able to adapt quickly to his new school.*

†**add** /æd/ [verb] **1** To join numbers: *Add two and three and you get five.* **2** To join things: *I think you need to add some water to the soup because it's too thick.* **3** To say or to write something more:

ACROSS AND *THROUGH*

We use "across" to say that we go from one side to another of a surface: *I walked **across** the street to Ben's house.*

We use "through" to say that we go from one side to another in a three-dimensional space or in a space that contains obstacles: *We went **through** a tunnel.*

He finished the list of invitations, and then added Joe's name.

◗ **PHRASAL VERBS** · **to add up** To join several numbers: *Add up all the numbers and you'll have the solution.*

addict /'æd.ɪkt/ [countable noun] A person who needs to do something that is usually harmful to himself or herself: *His life improved greatly after he stopped being a drug addict.*

addicted /ə'dɪktɪd/ [adjective] Being dependent on something: *People can become addicted to legal as well as illegal drugs.* ■ We say: "addicted **to** (something)".

addictive /ə'dɪk.tɪv/ [adjective] When talking about some substances, that makes you dependent on them: *Drugs are addictive. They contain substances which make you want to take them again and again.*

†**addition** /ə'dɪʃ.ᵊn/ ▮ [uncountable noun] **1** In mathematics, joining numbers: *You have to do the additions on page 4 for homework.* ▮ [countable noun] **2** A person or thing that is added: *Baby Tom is the new addition to the family.* **3 in addition to** Also, added to something: *In addition to football, the children play baseball and basketball.*

additional /ə'dɪʃ.ᵊn.ᵊl/ [adjective] Added to the basic package: *There will be an additional bus service to the airport on Sundays.*

†**address**[1] US: /'ædres/ UK: /ə'dres/ [countable noun] **1** The specific location of an apartment or a house: *My address is 2060, Second Avenue.* **2** A formal speech: *The principal gave an address on the first day of school.* ■ The plural is "addresses".

address[2] /ə'dres/ [verb] **1** To write an address on an envelope: *Don't forget to address the letter.* **2** To speak to a group of people: *She climbed to a balcony and addressed the demonstrators.*

†**adequate** /'æd.ə.kwət/ [adjective] Enough, sufficient: *Many old people do not have adequate heating in their houses in winter.*

adhesive[1] /əd'hiː.sɪv/ [countable noun] Substance used for sticking things together: *Quick-drying adhesives can be used for models.*

adhesive[2] /əd'hiː.sɪv/ [adjective] Able to stick firmly to something: *She bought adhesive plastic to cover her books.*

adjectival /ˌædʒɪk'taɪvəl/ [adjective] Relating to adjectives or like an adjective: *Nouns can sometimes have an adjectival function.*

†**adjective** /'ædʒ.ek.tɪv/ [countable noun] A word that describes a noun: *"Good" is an adjective in the sentence: "That book is good".*

†**adjust** /ə'dʒʌst/ [verb] **1** To change something slightly: *Can you adjust the color of the television?* **2** To get used to something: *It takes time to adjust to a new situation.*

administer /əd'mɪnɪstər/ [verb] **1** To control or manage a business or an organization: *The Jamaican colony was administered by the British government.* **2** To apply or give a remedy or a drug: *The doctor administered antibiotics to the patient.*

administration /ədˌmɪn.ɪ'streɪ.ʃᵊn/ ▮ [uncountable noun] **1** The management of the work of an organization: *Administration involves a lot of paperwork.* ▮ [countable noun] **2** In some countries, the government: *The Kennedy administration did much for human rights in the early 1960's.*

administrative /əd'mɪn·əˌstreɪ·t̬ɪv/, /æd-/ [adjective] Referring to the managing of a business or an organization: *She works as an administrative assistant of the company.*

administrator /əd'mɪnɪstreɪtər/ [countable noun] A person who administers public interests, a business or an organization: *The administrator called a meeting of the beneficiaries.*

admirable /'æd.mɪ.rə.bl̩/ [adjective] Excellent, something that should be admired: *He has an admirable sense of humor.*

admiral /'æd.mɪ.rəl/ [countable noun] The top officer in the navy: *George Dewey was a famous United States admiral during the Spanish-American War.*

†**admiration** /ˌæd.mɪ'reɪ.ʃᵊn/ [uncountable noun] A feeling of respect and pleasure: *I am filled with admiration for what she has achieved.*

†**admire** /əd'maɪər/ [verb] **1** To have a lot of respect for somebody: *I admire people who fight for their ideas.* **2** To look at somebody or something with pleasure: *We all admired his new electric guitar.*

admission /əd'mɪʃ.ᵊn/ [noun] Entrance, usually to a show or a party: *On the door it said, "Admission by invitation only".*

†**admit** /əd'mɪt/ [verb] **1** To recognize that something, usually negative, is true: *He admitted he had stolen the book.* **2** To allow admission to a place: *We don't admit anybody after 1 a.m.* ■ Be careful with the spelling of these forms: "admitted", "admitting".

adolescence /ˌædəl'esəns/ [countable noun] The period of time during which a child develops into an adult: *John spent his adolescence listening to music and reading poetry.*

adolescent[1] /ˌædəl'esənt/ [countable noun] A young person between about twelve and fifteen years old: *Adolescents usually like all kinds of pop music.*

adolescent[2] /ˌædəl'esənt/ [adjective] Referring to a young person: *Some adolescent boys are very shy.*

✝adopt /əˈdɑpt/ [verb] To take a baby or a child into your family: *They adopted Terry after his parents died.*

adore /əˈdɔr/, /əˈdour/ [verb] To love somebody very much: *He adores his wife.*

adorn /əˈdɔrn/ [verb] To make somebody or something look beautiful: *We adorned Bert's room with paper flags for his birthday.*

✝adult[1] US: /əˈdʌlt/ UK: /ˈædʌlt/ [countable noun] A person or an animal that is no longer a child: *I'd like to be an adult to do what I want.*

adult[2] US: /əˈdʌlt/ UK: /ˈædʌlt/ [adjective] **1** No longer a child: *There are some new adult elephants on the reserve.* **2** Mature: *His behavior could be described as adult.*

adulthood /ˈæd.ʌlt.hʊd, əˈdʌlt-/ [uncountable noun] The condition of being an adult: *Adulthood brings many responsibilities.*

advance[1] /ədˈvɑːns/ [countable noun] **1** Forward movement: *The army made an advance into enemy territory.* **2 in advance** Before a particular time or event: *You should book tickets for the concert well in advance.*

✝advance[2] /ədˈvɑːns/ [verb] **1** To move forward: *They advanced across the Sahara desert to Timbuktu.* **2** To make progress: *Science has advanced a lot in the last century.*

✝advanced /ədˈvænst/, /æd-/ [adjective] **1** Something that is nearly finished or has progressed substantially: *The building of the new school is quite advanced.* **2** Of a high level: *Louise is in the advanced French group.* ■ Be careful with the pronunciation of the end of this word. The "e" is not pronounced.

✝advantage /ədˈvæn·tɪdʒ/, /æd-/ [noun] **1** Something that is helpful for you: *Being able to speak languages is a tremendous advantage.* **2 to take advantage of (something)** To benefit from an opportunity: *If you want to buy a computer, take advantage of the special offers in the January sales.* ■ Be careful with the pronunciation of this word. The last "a" is pronounced like the "i" in "did".

✝adventure /ədˈven·tʃər/, /æd-/ [noun] A dangerous or exciting experience: *She told us about her adventures in the jungle.*

adventurous /ədˈven·tʃər·əs/ [adjective] Who likes doing dangerous or exciting things: *John's grandfather was an adventurous man who traveled all over China.*

✝adverb /ˈæd·vɜrb/ [countable noun] A word that describes a verb, an adjective or another adverb: *"Well" is an adverb in the sentence: "He sings well".* ■ See box at **frequency**.

adverbial /ædˈvɜr·bi·əl/ [adjective] Relating to adverbs or like an adverb: *The suffix -ly is adverbial.*

✝advertise /ˈæd·vərˌtɑɪz/ [verb] **1** To give information about something for sale: *We wanted to sell the puppies, so we advertised in the local paper and sold them the next day.* **2** To give publicity to a public event: *They are advertising the latest Spielberg movie on television.*

advertisement US: /ˈæd.vɝː.taɪz.mənt/ UK: /ədˈvɜː.tɪs.mənt/ [countable noun] Words or pictures that give information about something, usually for sale: *I found my mountain bike through an advertisement in the newspaper.* ■ "Ad" is short for "advertisement".

✝advice /ədˈvaɪs/ [uncountable noun] A suggestion about what somebody should do: *When I have a problem I ask my brother for advice.* ■ Be careful! We don't say "an advice". We say "some advice" or "a piece of advice".

advisable /ədˈvaɪ.zə.bl̩/ [adjective] Something that is a good idea to do: *It's advisable to wear sunglasses when you go skiing.*

✝advise /ədˈvaɪz/ [verb] To suggest, to recommend: *The doctor advised him to do more exercise.*

aerial /ˈer·i·əl/, /ˈær-/ [countable noun] An apparatus that receives television or radio signals: *They installed a new aerial in the roof of my home.* ■ The same meaning: "antenna".

aerobics /eəˈroʊ·bɪks/ [uncountable noun] Fast gymnastic exercises accompanied by music: *Jane does aerobics every morning to be fit.* ■ It is usually used with a singular verb.

aeroplane UK: /ˈeə.rə.pleɪn/ [countable noun] See **airplane.** ■ This is a British English spelling.

aerosol US: /ˈer.ə.sɑːl/ UK: /ˈeə.rəʊ.sɒl/ [countable noun] A can with liquid that comes out in a spray: *What an awful smell; pass me the aerosol.*

aesthetic /esˈθetɪk/ [adjective] **1** Concerned with beauty and its appreciation: *Her work fully agrees with aesthetic standards.* **2** Showing great beauty: *This ancient piece of furniture is both aesthetic and practical.*

aesthetics /esˈθetɪks/ [uncountable noun] Branch of philosophy concerned with the study of beauty and its appreciation: *She teaches aesthetics at the university.*

✝affair /əˈfeər/ [countable noun] **1** A matter or a concern: *It's no affair of yours.* **2** An event or a series of events: *The party turned into a very noisy affair.*

✝affect /əˈfekt/ [verb] To influence, to produce a change to: *Drugs are dangerous and can affect your mind.*

✝affection /əˈfek.ʃən/ [noun] The feeling of liking somebody: *I feel great affection for my grandfather.*

affectionate /əˈfek.ʃən.ət/ [adjective] That feels or shows affection: *Simon sent me a very affectionate letter on my birthday.*

affirm /əˈfɜrm/ [verb] To state that something is true: *A police spokesman affirmed that a suspect had been arrested in connection with the murder.*

+**affirmative** /ə'fɜr·mə·t̬ɪv/ [adjective] When talking about a statement, which is not in the negative: *"The cat is a graceful animal" is an affirmative sentence.*

+**afford** /ə'fɔrd/, /ə'fourd/ [verb] To have enough money to buy something: *I can't afford a new computer.*

+**afraid** /ə'freɪd/ [adjective] **1** Frightened or feeling fear: *I am afraid of spiders.* See picture at **emotions.** **2 I'm afraid** A polite way of saying "I'm sorry": *I'm afraid I don't have any money with me.*

African[1] [countable noun] A person from Africa: *Africans speak many different languages.* ■ Be careful! "African" has a capital "A".

African[2] /'æfrɪkən/ [adjective] Referring to Africa: *Nigeria is an African country.* ■ Be careful! "African" has a capital "A".

African-American or **Afroamerican** /ˌæfrəʊə'merɪkən/ [countable noun] An American with African ancestors: *The mayor of this town is an African-American.* ■ Be careful! "African-American" and "Afroamerican" are always written with capital letters.

+**after**[1] /'ɑːftər/ [preposition] **1** Later than: *I always brush my teeth after lunch.* **2** Behind: *Run after Jane and tell her she's forgotten her bag.* **3 after all** In spite of everything, in spite of expectations: *I know Richard can be naughty sometimes but he's only little after all.* ■ Compare with "afterwards" ("After" is always "after something").

after[2] /'ɑːftər/ [conjunction] Later than something: *We'll do our homework after I talk to Denise.*

afterbirth US: /'æf.tɚ.bɝːθ/ UK: /'ɑːf.tə.bɜːθ/ [countable noun] The material which is pushed out of the mother's womb just after giving birth: *The afterbirth consists of the placenta and other fetal membranes.*

+**afternoon** /ˌæf·tər'nun/ [noun] **1** The part of the day between midday and about five o'clock: *My father always takes a short nap in the afternoon, after lunch.* ■ Be careful! We say: "**in** the afternoon". **2 good afternoon** A greeting that is used in the afternoon: *Good afternoon, Charles. How are you today?.*

afterwards US: /'æf.tɚ.wɚdz/ UK: /'ɑːf.tə.wədz/ [adverb] At a later time: *What are you going to do afterwards?* ■ Compare with "after[1]" ("Afterwards" is always "after the time mentioned").

again /ə'gen/, /ə'geɪn/ [adverb] **1** One more time: *Can you say that again, please?* **2 again and again** Many times: *I've told you again and again to stop using my bike.*

against /ə'genst/, /ə'geɪnst/ [preposition] **1** Next to something and touching it: *Push those chairs against the wall.* **2** Opposing the other side in a game or in a fight: *We're playing against Broughton High on Saturday.* **3** Opposed to something: *I'm against the death penalty.*

+**age** /eɪdʒ/ [noun] **1** The amount of time that somebody has lived: *My grandmother doesn't look her age.* **2 for ages** For a long time: *I've known Anne for ages.*

aged /eɪdʒd/, /'eɪ.dʒɪd/ [adjective] At the age of: *They have two children, aged five and three.* ■ Be careful with the pronunciation of this word! The "e" is not pronounced.

+**agency** /'eɪ.dʒᵊnt.si/ [countable noun] A company that does things for people: *We booked our vacation through a travel agency.* ■ The plural is "agencies".

agenda /ə'dʒen.də/ [countable noun] A list of things to discuss: *One of the points on the agenda was a new swimming pool for the school.*

+**agent** /'eɪ.dʒᵊnt/ [countable noun] A person who does things for other people: *Lucy's mom is an estate agent who sells houses and apartments for other people.*

+**aggressive** /ə'gres.ɪv/ [adjective] **1** Violent, likely to attack: *Many animals become aggressive when they're hungry.* **2** Likely to disagree violently: *He always gets aggressive when that subject is mentioned.*

agile /'ædʒ·əl/, /-ɑɪl/ [adjective] **1** That can move fast and without effort: *Monkeys are extremely agile.* **2** That can think quickly: *Sheila has a very agile mind.*

aging [uncountable noun] The process of becoming older: *Skin wrinkles usually appear as a result of the aging process.*

agitate /'ædʒɪteɪt/ [verb] **1** To shake a liquid: *You must agitate the solution to dissolve the mixture.* **2** To make somebody feel anxious or troubled: *You will agitate him if you tell him the truth.* **3** To protest to move public concern about an issue: *The students are agitating against the cuts in public services.*

agitated /'ædʒ·əˌteɪ·t̬ɪd/ [adjective] Nervous and worried: *My mom gets agitated whenever I'm late.* ■ Be careful with the pronunciation of this word! The "e" is pronounced like the "i" in "did".

agitation /ˌædʒɪ'teɪʃən/ [uncountable noun] A state of worry and anxiety: *The working conditions have increased the agitation of the staff.*

+**ago** /ə'goʊ/ [adverb] Before now: *I started learning English three years ago.* ■ "Ago" goes after the period of time it refers to: "two weeks ago" (hace dos semanas).

agony /'æg.ə.ni/ [noun] Great pain or suffering: *I was in agony for nearly an hour when I broke my arm.* ■ The plural is "agonies".

+**agree** /ə'griː/ [verb] **1** To think the same as another person: *Sheila agreed with me that it's a good movie.* **2** To say that you will do something that somebody has asked you to do: *I have agreed to sing at her party.* ■ Be careful! We say: "I agree". We don't say: "I am agree".

†**agreement** /ə'griː.mənt/ [countable noun] **1** An arrangement made by two or more people: *The politicians have tried to reach an agreement all week.* **2 in agreement** Having the same opinion: *We were all in agreement about having a dog.*

agricultural /ˌægrɪ'kʌltʃərəl/ [adjective] Referring to agriculture: *Rearing cattle and growing crops are agricultural activities.*

agriculture /'æg·rɪˌkʌl·tʃər/ [uncountable noun] Growing plants or keeping animals for food: *In Africa, most people work in agriculture.*

†**ahead** /ə'hed/ [adverb] **1** In front of somebody or something: *Nick and Mary were ahead of us in the line.* **2 straight ahead** Forwards without turning, towards: *Go straight ahead and you'll see the bank on your left.*

†**aid** /eɪd/ [uncountable noun] **1** Help: *Next Sunday there's a concert in aid of African refugees.* **2 first aid** See "first aid" in the word **first²**. **3 first aid box** See "first aid box" in the word **first²**.

AIDS /eɪdz/ [uncountable noun] A disease that destroys the body's capacity to fight other diseases: *With medical help, many people with AIDS are able to survive for years.* ■ Be careful! "AIDS" is always written in capital letters. ■ "AIDS" is an abbreviation for "Acquired Immune Deficiency Syndrome". ■ See box at **abbreviations**.

†**aim¹** /eɪm/ [countable noun] A plan or a goal: *My aim in life is to help those who suffer.*

aim² /eɪm/ [verb] **1** To direct an object towards somebody or something: *Don't aim that gun at me.* **2** To have a plan: *She aims to finish her studies by the time she's 21.*

aimless /'eɪmləs/ [adjective] Without any purpose or direction: *Unemployed people can find themselves living an aimless life.*

†**air** US: /er/ UK: /eəʳ/ [uncountable noun] **1** The gases that we breathe: *In industrial areas, the air is polluted.* **2** The space above the ground: *He threw the ball in the air and then headed it.* **3 by air** By airplane: *Send the parcel by air; it's more expensive but faster.* **4 hot air** See **hot air.** **5 in the open air** See "in the open air" in the word **open¹**.

airbag /'eəbæg/ [countable noun] A device in a car which inflates itself quickly to protect the driver and passengers if the vehicle gets involved in an accident: *The airbag saved the driver from hitting his head on the steering wheel.*

air-conditioning [uncountable noun] A system of controlling the temperature in a building: *We need air-conditioning in our house because it's very hot in the summer.*

†**aircraft** US: /'er.kræft/ UK: /'eə.krɑːft/ [countable noun] A machine that can fly: *There were all kinds of aircrafts at the fair like airplanes and helicopters.* ■ The plural is also "aircraft".

aircraft carrier [countable noun] A large ship which carries aircraft: *Aircraft carriers have a long flat area where planes can take off and land.*

airfield /'eə.fiːld/ US: /'er-/ [countable noun] A piece of land where airplanes can take off and land: *The plane made an emergency landing on a small airfield.* ■ "Airfields" are smaller than "airports".

air force [countable noun] The part of the armed forces that fights in the air: *The United States Air Force is an essential part of the US Army.*

airline /'er·laɪn/, /'ær-/ [countable noun] A company that runs flights: *American Airlines is the United States national airline.*

airliner US: /'erˌlaɪ.nɚ/ UK: /'eəˌlaɪ.nəʳ/ [countable noun] A large airplane that carries passengers: *The Concorde was the fastest airliner in the world of its time.*

airmail /'er·meɪl/, /'ær-/ [uncountable noun] Mail carried by air: *She sent the present by airmail.*

airplane /'eərˌpleɪn/ [countable noun] A machine with wings that can fly: *I like seeing the clouds when I'm in an airplane.* ■ We also say "plane". ■ The British English spelling is "aeroplane". 👁 See picture at **transport**

†**airport** US: /'er.pɔːrt/ UK: /'eə.pɔːt/ [countable noun] The place where airplanes land or take off: *The plane took off from Gatwick airport at 11.45.*

†**alarm** /ə'lɑrm/ ▮ [countable noun] **1** A light or a sound telling you that something is wrong: *When the thief tried to get in, the alarm went off.* ▮ [uncountable noun] **2** A feeling of fear: *A problem at the nuclear plant caused public alarm.* **3 alarm clock** See "alarm clock" in the word **clock.** **4 fire alarm** See **fire alarm.**

albatross /'æl.bə.trɒs/ US: /-trɑːs/ [countable noun] A large, white seabird: *Albatrosses live in the Pacific and the South Atlantic.* ■ The plural is "albatrosses".

album /'æl.bəm/ [countable noun] **1** A book for keeping photographs, stamps and so on: *George keeps an album with postcards of all the countries he's visited.* **2** A musical record: *Have you heard the latest U2 album?*

†**alcohol** /'æl·kəˌhɔl/ [uncountable noun] A drink that can make people drunk: *It is bad for you to drink too much wine or any other kind of alcohol.*

alcoholic¹ /ˌælkə'hɒlɪk/ [adjective] That contains alcohol and can make you drunk: *I don't drink alcoholic drinks like wine or whisky.*

†**alcoholic²** /ˌælkə'hɒlɪk/ [countable noun] A person who is addicted to alcoholic drinks: *Alcoholics Anonymous is an organization that helps people who drink too much.*

alert /ə'lɜrt/ [adjective] Lively and watchful: *He's such an alert baby.*

algebra /ˈæl.dʒə.brə/ [uncountable noun] A type of mathematics: *In algebra, letters can represent numbers.*

alibi /ˈælɪbaɪ/ [countable noun] Proof that you were somewhere else when a crime was committed: *His alibi was that he was in Boston when the bank was robbed in Chicago.*

alien[1] /ˈeɪliən/ [adjective] Foreign, different: *That type of music is completely alien to me.*

alien[2] /ˈeɪliən/ [countable noun] A creature from another planet: *Last night I saw a movie about aliens invading the earth.*

alike[1] /əˈlaɪk/ [adjective] Similar: *Sarah and Brenda are not twins but they look alike.*

alike[2] /əˈlaɪk/ [adverb] The same: *I treat all my friends alike.*

alimentary canal [countable noun] The passage for the digestion of food in animals: *The alimentary canal includes all of the organs in the digestive tract.*

⁺**alive** /əˈlaɪv/ [adjective] Living, that is not dead: *The sheriff offered 10,000 dollars for him, dead or alive.* ■ The same meaning: "living[2]".

all[1] /ɔːl/ [pronoun] Everything or everyone: *All you need is love.* ■ See box at **every**.

⁺**all**[2] [adjective] **1** Every one of a group: *All my friends came to the party.* **2** The whole amount: *Give me all your money!.*

all[3] /ɔːl/ [adverb] **1** Completely: *She was dressed all in red.* **2 all over 1** In all parts: *It rained so hard that there were floods all over the country.* **2** Finished: *It's all over, Jane and I don't want to see you again.* **3 all right 1** Good enough: *That painting is all right, but Frank could do better.* **2** Safe, well: *He fell off a tree but he was all right.* **3** An expression used to say "yes": *Can you lend me some money? Oh, all right.* ■ For "all right" you can also spell "alright".

allergic /əˈlɜr·dʒɪk/ [adjective] That is affected by a certain food or thing: *Some people are allergic to cats.*

allergy /ˈæl·ər·dʒi/ [countable noun] A disease in which a certain food or thing makes you ill: *I've got an allergy to some kinds of food.* ■ The plural is "allergies".

alley /ˈæl.i/ [countable noun] A very narrow street or path: *There's a little alley between Ohio Street and Michigan Avenue.* ■ The plural is "alleys".

alliance /əˈlaɪ.ᵊnts/ [countable noun] An agreement to work together: *The two countries made an alliance.*

alligator /ˈæl·ɪˌgeɪt̬·ər/ [countable noun] A large reptile, similar to a crocodile: *Alligators live in tropical rivers in North and South America.* 👁 **See page 430**

⁺**allow** /əˈlaʊ/ [verb] To let somebody do something: *My parents don't allow me to get home after 10 p.m.*

almond /ˈɔ·mənd/, /ˈɔl-/, /ˈɑ·mənd/, /ˈɑl-/ [countable noun] A type of oval shaped nut that can have a sweet or bitter taste: *Candies made from almonds are absolutely delicious.*

almond or **almond tree** /ˈɑːmənd/ [countable noun] A tree which bears almonds: *Almond trees have white or pale pink flowers.* 👁 **See page 434**

⁺**almost** US: /ˈɑːl.moʊst/ UK: /ˈɔːl.məʊst/ [adverb] Nearly, not quite: *Tim is almost as tall as his father.*

⁺**alone** /əˈloʊn/ [adjective and adverb] Without any other person: *Elizabeth sometimes likes to be alone.* ■ Compare with "lonely" (alone and sad because of it).

⁺**along**[1] /əˈlɒŋ/ [preposition] From one end towards the other: *They were walking along the street when they saw the accident.* 👁 See picture at **preposition.**

along[2] /əˈlɒŋ/ [adverb] **1** Forward: *Drive along slowly and you'll see the hospital on the right.* **2** With somebody: *Come along with me and I'll show you the way.* ■ This use is informal.

⁺**alongside** US: /əˈlɑːŋ.saɪd/ UK: /əˌlɒŋˈsaɪd/ [preposition and adverb] By the side of something: *The car was parked alongside the wall.*

⁺**aloud** /əˈlaʊd/ [adverb] In a voice that people can hear, not silently: *I don't like reading aloud.*

⁺**alphabet** /ˈæl.fə.bet/ [countable noun] All the letters of a language: *The English alphabet has twenty six letters.* ■ The same meaning: "ABCs".

⁺**alphabetical** /ˌæl.fəˈbet.ɪ.kəl/ US: /-ˈbet̬-/ [adjective] In the order of the letters of the alphabet: *The words in this dictionary are in alphabetical order because they are easier to find that way.*

⁺**already** /ɔːlˈred.i/ [adverb] Before now, before expected: *"I've read that book already". "Have you finished already?" "That was really fast.".* ■ See box on the following page.

alright /ɔlˈraɪt/, /ˈɔl·raɪt/ [adverb] See **all**[3].

⁺**also** US: /ˈɑːl.soʊ/ UK: /ˈɔːl.səʊ/ [adverb] Too, as well: *Ken speaks French and Spanish, and he's also studying German.* ■ "Too", "as well" and "also" have the same meaning. "Too" and "as well" go at the end of a sentence. "Also" usually goes in the middle of a sentence. ■ See box on the following page.

⁺**alter** US: /ˈɑːl.t̬ɚ/ UK: /ˈɒl.təʳ/ [verb] To change something: *The museum was closed, so we had to alter our plans.*

alteration /ˌɔl·təˈreɪ·ʃən/ [countable noun] A small change: *There's an alteration to the schedule and History is now first period on Mondays.*

alternate /ˈɔl·tərˌneɪt/ [verb] To do something by turns: *The Bradley family alternate stays in Florida with trips to Mexico.*

⁺**alternative** US: /ɑːlˈtɝː.nə.t̬ɪv/ UK: /ɒlˈtɜː.nə.tɪv/ [countable noun] A choice between two things; another possibility: *There are two alternatives: going to Aspen or going to Vail.*

a b c d e f g h i j k l m n o p q r s t u v w x y z

ᐩalthough US: /ɑːl'ðoʊ/ UK: /ɔːl'ðəʊ/ [conjunction] **1** But: *Betty studies very hard, although she doesn't get good grades.* **2** In spite of: *Although he lived in France when he was a child, he doesn't speak French.*

altitude /'æl·tɪˌtud/ [countable noun] The distance in height from the sea level: *The plane flew across the Atlantic at an altitude of 25,000 feet.*

ᐩaltogether US: /ˌɑːl.tə'geð.ɚ/ UK: /ˌɔːl.tə'geð.əʳ/ [adverb] **1** Completely, on the whole: *What Sebastian told you wasn't altogether true.* **2** In total: *How much is it altogether?*

aluminum [uncountable noun] A light metal that is of a silver color: *Aluminum is used for making window frames.*

alveolus /ˌæl.vi'əʊ.ləs/ US: /æl'viː.ə-/ [countable noun] Any of the tiny air bags found in the lungs: *Oxygen passes into the blood through the very thin walls of the alveoli.* ■ The plural is "alveoli". 👁 **See page 425**

ᐩalways /'ɔl·weɪz/, /-wiz/ [adverb] Every time, all the time: *She always walks to school.* ■ "Always" usually goes before the main verb and after auxiliary verbs like "be", "do" or "have": "James is always late". ■ See box at **frequency**.

also*, *too* and *as well
• We use ***also*** in the middle of a sentence, before a main verb or after an auxiliary verb: - *Sarah plays the piano and she also sings.* • We use ***too*** and ***as well*** at the end of a sentence: - *Sarah plays the piano and she sings too.* - *She plays the piano and she sings as well.*

ᐩa.m. /ˌeɪ'em/ [adverb] Between midnight and 12 o'clock in the morning: *School starts at 9.30 a.m.* ■ "a.m." is an abbreviation for "ante meridiem", a Latin expression that means "before noon". When you use "a.m.", you don't say "o'clock". ■ Compare with "p.m." (between 12 o'clock in the day and midnight). ■ See box at **abbreviations**.

am /æm, əm/ [verb] See **be**.

amateur[1] /'æmətər/ [countable noun] Somebody who does something for pleasure, not for money: *Richard is a very good amateur football player and is going to become a professional.*

amateur[2] /'æmətər/ [adjective] That doesn't do something very well: *I didn't think much of the play which was very amateur.*

ᐩamaze /ə'meɪz/ [verb] To surprise somebody: *Sheila always amazes me with her brightly colored hats.*

amazement /ə'meɪz.mənt/ [uncountable noun] A feeling of great surprise: *When he saw me in costume, he looked at me in amazement.*

ᐩamazing /ə'meɪ.zɪŋ/ [adjective] Pleasantly surprising: *It was an amazing movie! What fantastic photography!* ■ Be careful with the pronunciation of this word! The second part "maz" rhymes with "days".

ambassador /æm'bæs·ə·dər/ [countable noun] A person who represents a country abroad: *Mr. Zuidema is the Dutch ambassador here.*

ᐩambition /æm'bɪʃ.ən/ [noun] **1** Something that you really want to do or to have: *My ambition is to travel to India.* **2** A strong desire to be successful: *You could be an international tennis player if you had more ambition.*

ambitious /æm'bɪʃ.əs/ [adjective] With a strong desire to be successful: *He's very ambitious and wants to become Managing Director.*

already* and *yet
• In **affirmative sentences** we normally use *already*: - *I've already seen that movie.* - *They have already finished their work.* • In **negative sentences** we use *yet*: - *I haven't seen that movie yet.* - *They haven't finished their work yet.* • In **questions** we normally use *yet*: - *Have you seen that movie yet?* - *Haven't you finished yet?* • But in **affirmative questions** it is possible to use either *yet* or *already*, although the meaning is different: - *Have you finished already?* (Expresses surprise that you have finished before expected.) - *Have you finished yet?* (Suggests that it is time to finish or that you are being a little slow.)

ambulance /'æm.bjʊ.lənts/ [countable noun] A vehicle for taking people to hospital: *They put the injured people in an ambulance and took them to hospital.*

ambush [noun] A surprise attack from a hidden position: *The soldiers walked into an ambush laid for them by the enemy.*

American[1] /ə'mer.ɪ.kən/ [countable noun] **1** A person from the United States: *Many Americans have relatives in other countries such as Ireland, Italy, Poland and Mexico.* **2** A person from America: *People from Mexico, Peru, Argentina or Colombia are all Americans.* ■ Be careful! "American" has a capital "A".

American[2] /ə'merɪkən/ [adjective] **1** Referring to the United States of America: *American football is different from rugby.* **2** Referring to North, Central or South America: *They traveled all the way down the American continent from Alaska to Tierra Del Fuego.* ■ Be careful! "American" has a capital "A".

American Indian [noun and adjective] See **Native American.** ■ Be careful! "American Indian" has capital letters.

ammunition /,æm.jʊ'nɪʃ.ən/ [uncountable noun] Bullets and other explosives: *The soldiers had to surrender because they had no ammunition left.*

amnesty /'æm.nɪ.sti/ [noun] A pardon for convicted criminals: *The government gave an amnesty to political prisoners.* ■ The plural is "amnesties".

amniotic sac [countable noun] The sac in which the fetus develops: *The amniotic sac protects the fetus while it is growing.*

amoeba [countable noun] A unicellular organism: *The amoeba moves by continually changing its body shape.*

among or **amongst** /ə'mʌŋ or ə'mʌŋst/ [preposition] **1** Surrounded by things: *Jungle Jim lived among the trees of the Amazon jungle.* **2** Divided by more than two people: *They divided the prize among the four winners.* 👁 See picture on the following page and at **preposition.**

amount /ə'maʊnt/ [countable noun] A quantity: *They spend a huge amount of money on books.*

amphibian /æm'fɪb.i.ən/ [countable noun] An animal which lives both in water and on land: *Frogs, toads and salamanders are amphibians.* 👁 **See pages 431 and –**

amphitheater [countable noun] A circular or oval building without a roof where public events take place: *The Romans built amphitheaters throughout the empire.*

amplifier /'æm·plə,fɑɪ·ər/ [countable noun] A machine that makes sounds louder: *She connected her guitar to the amplifier so that everybody could hear.*

amuse /ə'mju:z/ [verb] **1** To make people smile or laugh: *Why are you laughing? Did I say something that amused you?* **2** To keep somebody busy and happy: *In the evenings I amuse myself arranging the stamps in my collection.*

amusement /ə'mju:z.mənt/ ▮ [uncountable noun] **1** The feeling of being amused: *To everyone's amusement, he started imitating Charlie Chaplin.* ▮ [countable noun] **2** An enjoyable activity: *The bad thing about this town is that there are no amusements for young people.*

amusing /ə'mju:.zɪŋ/ [adjective] That makes people smile or laugh: *The clowns in the circus in the square are very amusing.*

an /ən, æn/ [article] See **a**[2]. ■ See box at **a**.

analysis /ə'næl.ə.sɪs/ [noun] An examination of something: *A careful analysis was made of the school's finances.* ■ The plural is "analyses".

analyze or **analyse** /'ænəlaɪz/ [verb] To study something closely and in detail: *The company will have to analyze the problem in order to solve it.* ■ "Analyze" is the British English spelling.

AMBULANCE

a b c d e f g h i j k l m n o p q r s t u v w x y z

a b c d e f g h i j k l m n o p q r s t u v w x y z

anatomy [uncountable noun] The science of the structure of animals or plants: *the anatomy of the human body.*

ancestor /ˈæn,ses·tər/, /-səs-/ [countable noun] A member of your family who lived a long time ago: *My ancestors came from Scotland.*

anchor /ˈæŋ·kər/ [countable noun] A metal hook dropped to the bottom of the sea that stops a ship moving: *The ship dropped anchor at the entry to the harbor.*

†**ancient** /ˈeɪn.tʃənt/ [adjective] Belonging to the distant past, very old: *He's an expert on Ancient Egypt.*

†**and** /ænd, ənd, ən/ [conjunction] **1** Also: *Pat plays the guitar and the violin.* **2** Then, afterwards: *She opened the door and went out.*

anemone /əˈnem.ə.ni/ [countable noun] **1** A plant similar to the buttercup which has brightly colored flowers: *The girl is planting anemones in the backyard.* **2** sea anemone A predatory marine animal which looks like a plant: *Sea anemones have an adhesive foot called basal disc.*

angel /ˈeɪn.dʒəl/ [countable noun] **1** A celestial being, usually shown with wings: *Angels are said to be messengers from God.* **2** A loving person: *Laura's such an angel.*

†**anger** /ˈæŋ·gər/ [uncountable noun] A very strong feeling of annoyance: *I felt real anger when I saw Mark hitting his brother.*

†**angle**[1] /ˈæŋ.gl̩/ [countable noun] **1** The space between two lines where they meet: *When a vertical line meets a horizontal line they form an angle of 90º.* **2** right angle An angle of 90º: *All the angles in a square are right angles.*

angle[2] /ˈæŋgl/ [verb] To fish: *I love to angle at the weekends.*

†**angry** /ˈæŋ.gri/ [adjective] That feels anger against somebody or something: *My mom got very angry when she saw the state of my room.* ■ The same meaning: "cross[3]". See picture at **emotions.**

anguish /ˈæŋ.gwɪʃ/ [uncountable noun] Great suffering: *The mother's anguish at the death of her daughter was terrible to see.*

†**animal** /ˈæn.ɪ.məl/ [countable noun] A living thing that breathes and moves: *There are different kinds of animals: amphibians, fish, reptiles, birds and mammals.* **See pages 426-431.**

†**ankle** /ˈæŋ.kl̩/ [countable noun] The part of the body where the foot joins the leg: *She fell and sprained her ankle.* **See page 422.**

†**anniversary** /ˌæn·əˈvɜr·sə·ri/ [countable noun] An annual celebration of a past event: *My parents are soon going to celebrate their fifteenth wedding anniversary.* ■ The plural is "anniversaries".

AMONG AND *BETWEEN*

We normally use "among" when we are talking about three or more people or things:

The dog is ***among*** *people.*

When we are talking about only two people or things, we use "between":

The dog is ***between*** *two people.*

announce /ə'naʊnts/ [verb] To make something public: *He announced the news of his daughter's wedding to Paul.*

announcement /ə'naʊnt.smənt/ [noun] A written or spoken message to make something public: *The headmaster said he had an important announcement to make.*

announcer /ə'naʊn·sər/ [countable noun] A person who describes and comments a sports event: *The announcer on last Friday football game was the captain's father.*

annoy /ə'nɔɪ/ [verb] To make somebody a little angry: *My brother annoys me when he wears my clothes.*

annoyance /ə'nɔɪ.ᵊnts/ [uncountable noun] State of being annoyed: *She showed her annoyance by slamming the door.*

annoyed /ə'nɔɪd/ [adjective] Angry and very irritated: *She is annoyed with me for not going to her party.* See picture at **emotions.**

annoying /ə'nɔɪ.ɪŋ/ [adjective] That makes somebody angry: *The noise the neighbors are making upstairs is quite annoying.*

annual /'ænjuəl/ [adjective] Happening once a year: *They hold an annual art competition at the local Art Gallery.*

anonymous /ə'nɑn·ə·məs/ [adjective] Who is not known: *I received a letter telling me that I had an anonymous admirer in my class.*

anorak /'æn.ᵊr.æk/ [countable noun] A short and warm jacket: *Put on your anorak, Jane. It's cold and wet outside.*

another[1] [adjective] **1** One more: *Can you give me another sandwich?* **2** Several more: *We have to wait another three months.* ■ Be careful! We say "another" not "an other". ■ This word is always used without the definite article. Don't say: "The another girls came late". ■ Compare with "other" (as the thing or person already mentioned).

another[2] /ə'nʌðər/ [pronoun] A different one: *I don't like this bike. I want another.*

answer[1] US: /'ænt.sɚ/ UK: /'ɑːnt.səʳ/ [countable noun] The response to a question: *I've asked you a question and I want an answer.*

answer[2] [verb] **1** To say something to somebody who has asked you a question: *I asked her about Jim but she didn't answer.* **2** **to answer the door** To open the door in answer to a knock or ring: *I had to ring twice before they answered the door.* **3** **to answer the telephone** To pick up the telephone in answer to a call:

ANIMAL NOISES

These are some of the noises that animals make:

*Cows **moo** in the fields.*

*Ducks **quack**.*

*A dog **barks**.*

*A cock **crows** at dawn.*

*Sheep **bleat** when they're hungry.*

*Cats **meow** when they want something and **purr** when they are stroked.*

*A lion **roars**.*

a b c d e f g h i j k l m n o p q r s t u v w x y z

a b c d e f g h i j k l m n o p q r s t u v w x y z

Can you answer the phone, Mark? I'm in the bathroom.

answering machine or **answerphone** [countable noun] A machine that records telephone calls: *When I got home, there were three messages on the answering machine.*

ant /ænt/ [countable noun] A small insect that lives in groups: *Some ants live in holes in the ground.* See page 431.

ANT

antacid /ˌæn'tæs.ɪd/ [uncountable noun] A substance which helps to prevent or decrease stomach acidity: *Whenever we have a heavy meal we take an antacid.*

antarctic /ænt'ɑrk·tɪk/, /-'ɑr·t̬ɪk/ [adjective] Referring to the regions around the South Pole: *The Antarctic Circle is the line of latitude 66º 30' South.*

antelope /'æn·tə·lˌoʊp/ [countable noun] An animal with horns, similar to a deer: *Antelopes can run very fast.*

antenna /æn'ten.ə/ [countable noun] **1** The long and thin part on the heads of some animals: *Insects use their antennae for feeling.* **2** An apparatus that receives television or radio signals: *We couldn't see the image clearly because the antenna was broken.* ■ In this use, the same meaning: "aerial". ■ The plural is "antennae".

anthem /'ænt.θəm/ [countable noun] See **national anthem**.

anthropoid [countable noun] Resembling a human being: *Monkeys, apes and gorillas are anthropoids.*

anti- US: /æntɑɪ/ UK: /ænti-/ [prefix] An addition to the beginning of a word that usually means "against": *She's in the antinuclear energy movement.*

antibiotic /ˌænt·i·bɑɪ'ɑt̬·ɪk/, /ˌæn·tɑɪ-/ [noun] A drug used to cure infections: *The doctor gave him an antibiotic for his sore throat.* ■ Be careful with the pronunciation of this word! The third syllable "bi" rhymes with "by".

antibody /'ænti,bɒdi/ [countable noun] A protein produced in the blood to defend the body against bacteria and viruses: *Our blood produces antibodies when we catch an infection.* ■ The plural is "antibodies".

˄**anticipate** /æn'tɪs.ɪ.peɪt/ [verb] To act because you see something is about to happen: *With Mr. Johnson, it's always easy to anticipate the test questions.*

antique[1] /æn'tiːk/ [countable noun] An object that is old and valuable: *Antiques can obtain very high prices at auctions.*

antique[2] [adjective] Old and usually valuable: *They sold an antique vase for $4,300.*

antiseptic /ˌænti'septɪk/ [noun] A substance that is used to prevent a wound from getting infected: *Put some antiseptic on that cut.*

anus /'eɪnəs/ [countable noun] The opening at the end of the alimentary canal through which excretions leave the body: *Suppositories are inserted up into the anus.* See page 424.

anvil /'æn.vɪl/ [countable noun] An iron block on which heated metals are beaten into shape: *John hammers the horseshoes on the anvil.*

ANTENNA

anxiety /æŋˈzaɪ·ɪ·t̬i/ [uncountable noun] A feeling of worry: *The test results caused great anxiety in our family.* ■ The plural is "anxieties".

anxious /ˈæŋk.ʃəs/ [adjective] **1** Worried: *My parents get anxious when I go out at night.* **2** With a strong wish to do something: *I'm anxious to start music lessons.*

any[1] [adjective] **1** "some" in questions: *Have you brought any tapes?* **2** "some" in negative sentences: *There isn't any butter in the fridge.* **3** One of a group: *You can get the book in any bookstore.* ■ See box at **some**.

any[2] /ˈeni , əni/ [pronoun] **1** "some" in questions: *I don't have any money. Do you have any?* **2** "some" in negative sentences: *There are some apples on this tree, but there aren't any on that one.* **3** No special one: *"Which newspaper do you want?" "Oh, any of them will do.".* ■ See box at **some**.

anybody /ˈen·iˌbɑd·i/, /-bə·di/ [pronoun] **1** Any person: *Has anybody seen my glasses?* **2** No special person: *With time and a smile, anybody can learn a foreign language.* ■ The same meaning: "anyone". ■ "Anybody" is used in questions and negative sentences. In positive sentences we usually use "somebody". ■ See box below.

anyhow /ˈen.i.haʊ/ [adverb] See **anyway**.

anyone /ˈen.i.wʌn/ [pronoun] See **anybody**. ■ "Anyone" is used in questions and negative sentences. ■ See box bellow.

anything /ˈen.i.θɪŋ/ [pronoun] **1** Any object: *There isn't anything in the box; it's empty.* ■ In this use "anything" is used in questions and negative sentences. **2** No special thing: *What would you like to eat? Oh, anything.*

anyway /ˈen.i.weɪ/ [adverb] **1** In any case: *You can keep your bike; I don't need it anyway.* **2** In any way: *If you buy the television you can pay for it anyway you want.* ■ The same meaning: "anyhow".

anywhere /ˈen·iˌhweər/, /-ˌweər/ [adverb] In any place or to any place: *Have you seen my watch anywhere? Are you going anywhere this weekend?*

aorta /eɪˈɔr·t̬ə/ [countable noun] The main artery of the body which carries blood to the rest of the circulatory system: *The aorta passes up from the heart and down the front of the backbone.*

apart /əˈpɑrt/ [adverb] Separated: *Stand with your feet apart and your arms by your sides.*

apartment /əˈpɑrt·mənt/ [countable noun] Rooms that are part of a building and are used as a home: *My sister has a very nice apartment with a view on the park.* ■ In British English they say "flat". 👁 See picture at **house**.

ape /eɪp/ [countable noun] A large monkey without a tail: *Apes are very similar to men in some ways.*

apex /ˈeɪpeks/ [countable noun] The highest point of something: *The lever rests on the apex.* ■ The plural is "apexes" or "apices".

apologize or **apologise** /əˈpɒlədʒaɪz/ [verb] To say that you are sorry for something you have done: *I apologize for my behavior; I won't do it again.*

apology /əˈpɑl·ə·dʒi/ [noun] Something you say to show that you are sorry: *Please, Miss Newsom, accept my apologies for what happened yesterday.* ■ The plural is "apologies".

apostrophe /əˈpɑs·trə·fi/ [countable noun] **1** A mark used in writing to show that something has been left out ['']: *The apostrophe in "isn't" shows that it is short for "is not".* **2** A mark in writing to indicate possession ['']: *You need to use an apostrophe in the sentence "Mark's bike was broken".*

appalling /əˈpɔː.lɪŋ/ US: /-ˈpɑː-/ [adjective] Very bad, horrible: *The movie was appalling, the worst I've seen in years.*

apparatus /ˌæp·əˈræt̬·əs/ [uncountable noun] **1** Equipment: *That store sells breathing apparatus for deep sea diving.* **2** Machines: *We've got test tubes and other apparatus in the laboratory.*

apparel [uncountable noun] A person's clothing: *He came to the party wearing sports apparel.*

apparent /əˈpær·ənt/, /-ˈpeər-/ [adjective] **1** Obvious: *It's quite apparent that you have no interest in Physics at all.* **2** That seems true: *Anne's apparent lack of talent in painting is due to her never having done it before.*

apparently /əˈpær·ənt·li/, /-ˈper-/ [adverb] According to what people say: *I wasn't there, but apparently they had a terrible argument.*

anybody / anyone, everybody / everyone, somebody / someone, nobody / no one

- We use singular verbs with these words:
  - ***Has*** *anyone seen my jacket?*
  - *Why* ***is*** *everyone so quiet today?*
  - *Someone here* ***knows*** *the answer. I am sure.*
- However, after the verb we often use *they*, *them* or *their*. The reason for this is that in this way we avoid having to say *she or he*, *her or him* or *her or his*:
  - ***Is everyone*** *sure that* ***they*** *know what* ***they*** *have to do?*
  - ***Does anyone*** *have* ***their*** *calculator with* ***them****?*
  - ***Someone*** *left* ***their*** *jacket here yesterday.*

†**appeal**[1] /ə'pi:l/ [countable noun] **1** A strong request for something: *The school has launched an appeal for money to build a new gym.* **2 sex appeal** Being attractive to other people: *That actor has a lot of sex appeal.*

appeal[2] /ə'pi:l/ [verb] **1** To like something: *Going swimming in winter doesn't really appeal to me.* **2** To make a strong request for something: *The police are appealing for help to catch the thieves.*

†**appear** /ə'pɪər/ [verb] To come into view: *The bus appeared round the corner.*

†**appearance** /ə'pɪər·əns/ [countable noun] **1** The way a person looks: *Tony's appearance has improved since he started going out with Laura.* **2** The coming of somebody: *The party came to an abrupt end on the appearance of Mary's parents in the house.*

appetite /'æp.ɪ.taɪt/ [noun] A desire for food: *If you eat that chocolate now, you won't have any appetite for lunch.*

applaud /ə'plɔd/ [verb] To clap your hands: *The audience applauded for five minutes at the end of the concert.*

applause /ə'plɔz/ [uncountable noun] Clapping of hands: *Let's give them a big round of applause.*

†**apple** /'æp.l̩/ [noun] **1** A round green or red fruit: *I like all kinds of apples, but especially Granny Smith.* **2 apple pie** A pie made with apples, flour and sugar: *My mom makes the most delicious apple pie you can imagine.* 👁 **See page 436.**

apple tree [countable noun] A tree which bears apples: *My father has planted three apple trees in the orchard.* 👁 **See page 435.**

appliance /ə'plaɪ.ənts/ [countable noun] An electrical machine for doing a job in a house: *They have all the latest domestic appliances: dishwasher, microwave oven and so on.*

†**application** /ˌæp.lɪ'keɪ.ʃən/ [noun] A written request: *If you want to join the club, please fill in the application form.*

†**apply** /ə'plaɪ/ [verb] To make a formal request for something, especially a job: *Ben's going to apply for a job for this summer.* ■ We always say: "to apply **for** (something)".

▶ **PHRASAL VERBS** · **to apply to** To be relevant: *Forget the "Principal's instructions"; they don't apply to us.* ■ Be careful with the spelling of these forms: "applies", "applied".

†**appoint** /ə'pɔɪnt/ [verb] To choose somebody for a job: *Ms. Norton has been appointed director of studies.*

†**appointment** /ə'pɔɪnt.mənt/ ▮ [countable noun] **1** An arrangement to meet your dentist, attorney and so on: *I've got an appointment with the dentist on Tuesday at nine o'clock.* ▮ [noun] **2** The choosing of somebody for a job: *Mr. McFarlane's appointment as head of the local police was a total surprise.*

†**appreciate** /ə'pri:.ʃi.eɪt/ [verb] **1** To be grateful to somebody: *I appreciate what you've done for me, Mr. Tutuola.* **2** To feel the value of something: *She certainly appreciates good music.*

appreciation /əˌpri:ʃi'eɪʃən/ [uncountable noun] **1** Favorable or grateful recognition of something: *Mary gave the gardener a tip in appreciation of his hard work.* **2** Awareness and enjoyment of the good qualities of something: *She shows a great appreciation of good music.*

apprentice /ə'pren·tɪs/ [countable noun] Somebody who is learning a trade: *I'm going to work in my father's factory as an apprentice electrician.*

approach[1] /ə'proʊtʃ/ ▮ [uncountable noun] **1** The act of going near somebody or something: *The animals ran away at our approach.* ▮ [countable noun] **2** A way of doing something: *His approach to problems is always very direct.*

†**approach**[2] /ə'prəʊtʃ/ [verb] To come near: *It's November 18th, winter is approaching.*

†**appropriate** /ə'proʊ·pri·ət/ [adjective] Right: *I don't think this book is appropriate for children.*

†**approval** /ə'pru:.vəl/ [uncountable noun] **1** A good opinion: *We showed our approval of the play by clapping enthusiastically.* **2** Acceptance of a plan or a suggestion: *My plans for becoming an attorney have my parents' approval.*

†**approve** /ə'pru:v/ [verb] **1** To agree with something: *I don't approve of people who eat with their fingers.* ■ Be careful! In this use we always say: "to approve **of** (something)". **2** To accept a plan or a suggestion: *The plans for the new building have not been approved.*

†**approximate** /ə'prɑk·sə·mət/ [adjective] Not exact: *The approximate number of students at my school is 700.*

approximately /ə'prɒksɪmətli/ [adverb] More or less, in a not completely exact way: *Approximately fifty people came to the party.*

apricot /'æp·rˌkɑt/, /'eɪ·pr-/ [countable noun] A small fruit like a peach: *Apricots have a soft, orange or yellow skin.* ■ Be careful with the pronunciation of this word! The "a" is pronounced like the "a" in "volcano".

†**April** /'eɪ.prəl/ [noun] **1** The fourth month of the year: *April is usually a very rainy month.* **2 April Fools' Day** April 1st, when people play tricks: *On April Fools' Day we hid the teacher's books and she couldn't find them anywhere.* ■ Be careful! "April" has a capital "A". 👁 See picture at **calendar.**

apron /'eɪ.prən/ [countable noun] A piece of clothing that covers the front of the body: *Tom always puts an apron on when he's cooking.*

aquarium /ə'kweər·i·əm/ [countable noun] A glass container to keep fish: *Anthony has an aquarium with a lot of tropical fish.*

Aquarius /ə'kweər·i·əs/ [noun] A sign of the zodiac: *If your birthday is between January 21st and February 19th, you're an Aquarius.* ■ Be careful. "Aquarius" has a capital "A".

aquatic /ə'kwæt̬·ɪk/ [adjective] Referring to water: *Scuba diving is an aquatic activity.*

aqueduct /'æk.wɪ.dʌkt/ [countable noun] A structure for carrying water overland that looks like a bridge with many arches: *The aqueduct brings water from the river to the town.*

aquifer US: /'ɑːkwə.fɚ/ UK: /'æk.wɪ.fər/ [countable noun] An underground water source: *The men drilled down into the rock until they found the aquifer.*

Arab /'ær·əb/ [noun and adjective] A member of a people living in the Middle East and North Africa, whose first language is Arabic: *The Arabs have a great tradition of hospitality.* ■ Be careful! "Arab" has a capital "A".

Arabic[1] [adjective] Referring to Arab culture: *Arabic numbers were introduced in Europe in the 12th century.* ■ Careful! "Arabic" has a capital "A".

Arabic[2] /ˌær·ə·bɪk/ [uncountable noun] The language spoken by Arabs: *Arabic is written from right to left.* ■ Be careful. "Arabic" has a capital "A".

arachnid /ə'ræk.nɪd/ [countable noun] Any of a class of arthropods similar to insects but with four pairs of legs: *Spiders and scorpions are arachnids.*

arch US: /ɑːrtʃ/ UK: /ɑːtʃ/ [countable noun] **1** A part of a building that is curved: *The new church has many arches.* **2** A monument that is curved at the top: *The Gateway Arch in Saint Louis was built as a monument to westward expansion of the United States.*

archaeological or **archeological** [adjective] Referring to the study of human history through the analysis of physical remains: *The students visited the archeological museum of Athens.* ■ The British English spelling is "archaeological".

archaeologist or **archeologist** /ˌɑːki'ɒlədʒɪst/ [countable noun] A person who studies human history through the analysis of physical remains: *The archeologists found some graves with human bones and broken pottery inside.* ■ The British English spelling is "archaeologist".

archaeology or **archeology** /ˌɑr·ki'ɑl·ə·dʒi/ [uncountable noun] The study of human history through the study of physical remains: *Archeology investigates the way people lived in the past.* ■ The British English spelling is "archaeology".

archbishop /ˌɑːtʃ'bɪʃ.əp/ [countable noun] A very important priest: *The Archbishop of Los Angeles receive the faithful on Sunday in the Cathedral of Our Lady of the Angels.*

archery US: /'ɑr.tʃɚ.i/ UK: /'ɑː.tʃə.ri/ [uncountable noun] The sport of shooting arrows with a bow: *Archery is an Olympic sport.*

archipelago US: /ˌɑːr.kɪ'pel.ə.goʊ/ UK: /ˌɑː.kɪ'pel.ə.gəʊ/ [countable noun] A group of small islands: *The islands of the Caribbean make up an archipelago.* 👁 **See page 444.**

architect /'ɑr·kɪˌtekt/ [countable noun] A person who designs buildings: *Eero Saarinen was a famous architect who designed The Gateway Arch in Saint Louis, Missouri.*

architectural /ˌɑːkɪ'tektʃərəl/ [adjective] Referring to the design of buildings: *The architectural style of this cathedral is Gothic.*

architecture US: /'ɑːr.kɪ.tek.tʃɚ/ UK: /'ɑː.kɪ.tek.tʃəʳ/ [uncountable noun] **1** The activity of designing buildings: *Modern architecture uses metal and glass.* **2** The style of a building: *Greek architecture was very elegant.*

arctic [adjective] Referring to the regions around the North Pole: *The Arctic Ocean is partly covered by sea ice.*

are /ɑːʳ/, /ɑːʳ/ [verb] See **be.**

ᐩ**area** /'eər·i·ə/ ▮ [countable noun] **1** A part of a place: *Jamie lives in a poor area of Tucson.* ▮ [noun] **2** Space, measure of the unit of something: *The area of this room is 12 square feet.* ■ Be careful with the pronunciation of this word. The "e" is pronounced like the "i" in "did".

aren't US: /ɑːrnt/ UK: /ɑːnt/ The contraction of "are not".

Argentinian[1] [adjective] Referring to Argentina: *The tango is an Argentinian dance.* ■ Be careful! "Argentinian" has a capital "A".

Argentinian[2] [countable noun] A person from Argentina: *My uncle is married to an Argentinian and they live in Buenos Aires.* ■ Be careful! "Argentinian" has a capital "A".

†**argue** /'ɑr·gju/ [verb] **1** To quarrel, disagree: *Craig and his sister don't get on very well; they're always arguing with each other.* ■ We say: "argue **with** (somebody)". **2** To give an opinion: *Susan argues that girls are more intelligent than boys.*

†**argument** /'ɑr·gjə·mənt/ [countable noun] **1** An angry disagreement: *When Paul said he wasn't going to wash up, his sister started a big argument about it.* **2** A reason for something or against it: *The best argument against racism is that we are all different from one another.*

Aries US: /'er.iːz/ UK: /'eə.riːz/ [noun] A sign of the zodiac: *If your birthday is between March 21st and April 20th, you're an Aries.* ■ Be careful. "Aries" has a capital "A".

†**arise, arose, arisen** /ə'raɪz/ [verb] To appear or to happen: *If more problems arise, we'll have to put the trip off until next month.*

arisen Past participle of **arise.**

aristocracy /ˌærɪ'stɒkrəsi/ [countable noun] The highest social class: *The aristocracy is mainly made up of members of royalty and nobility.* ■ The plural is "aristocracies".

aristocrat /ə'rɪs·təˌkræt/, /'ær·ə·stə-/ [countable noun] A person with a title of nobility: *Counts and dukes are aristocrats.*

arithmetic /ə'rɪθ·məˌtɪk/ [uncountable noun] Calculations with numbers: *Children at elementary school do reading, writing and arithmetic.*

†**arm** US: /ɑːrm/ UK: /ɑːm/ [uncountable noun] **1** The part of the body between the shoulder and the hand: *Alfred's mom broke her right arm and she can't drive.* 👁 **See page 421.** **2 arm in arm** With your arm around somebody else's arm: *Julie and Peter walked arm in arm down the street.*

armband /'ɑːmbænd/ [countable noun] **1** Band worn around the upper arm as a sign of something or to hold up the shirt sleeve: *He wears an armband which identifies him as a member of the first aid team.* **2** Plastic ring filled with air that children wear on the upper arm to help them float: *Thomas has to wear armbands at the swimming pool because he is still learning to swim.*

armchair US: /'ɑːrm.tʃer/ UK: /'ɑːm.tʃeəʳ/ [countable noun] A big and comfortable chair: *My dad always sits in the armchair in front of the TV.* 👁 See pictures at **chair** and **living room.**

†**armed** US: /ɑːrmd/ UK: /ɑːmd/ [adjective] **1** That has a weapon: *The thieves were armed with small guns.* **2 armed robbery** A robbery in which weapons are used: *They were convicted of armed robbery and sent to jail for five years.* **3 the armed forces** See "the armed forces" in the word **force**[1] **4 the armed services** See "the armed services or the services" in the word **service** ■ Be careful with the pronunciation of the end of this word. The "e" is not pronounced.

armor [uncountable noun] A metal protection worn by medieval soldiers: *Some knights wore armor from head to toe.*

armpit /'ɑrmˌpɪt/ [countable noun] The part of the body under the arm where the arm joins the shoulder: *I put deodorant on my armpits every day.*

†**army** /'ɑr·mi/ [countable noun] The part of the armed forces that fights on land: *When he was in the army, he drove a tank.* ■ The plural is "armies".

arose /ə'roʊz/ Past tense of **arise.**

around[1] /ə'raʊnd/ [adverb and preposition] **1** Moving in a circle: *The earth takes 365 days to go around the sun.* **2** On all sides of something: *Mr. Leech lives in a house with high walls all around.* **3** In different places or to different places: *Mike is never at home. He's always traveling around.* **4** Near, in the area nearby: *There is a pharmacy around here somewhere.* ■ In British English they say "round".

†**around**[2] /ə'raʊnd/ [preposition] **1** On all sides of something: *There is a fence all around the house.* **2** In different places or to different places: *We spent the summer traveling around the United States.* **3** Approximately: *There were around 20 people at the party.*

†**arrange** /ə'reɪndʒ/ [verb] **1** To make plans: *Susan and I have arranged to play tennis on Sunday.* **2** To put something in a particular way or order: *The books are arranged in alphabetical order.* **3 to arrange to meet** To agree on the details of where to get together with somebody: *We've arranged to meet at 7.30, outside the gym.*

†**arrangement** /ə'reɪndʒ.mənt/ ▮ [noun] **1** An agreement to do something: *I have a special arrangement with my brother to take it in turns to wash up.* ▮ [countable noun] **2** A group of things organized in a particular way: *We changed the arrangement of the desks to do some group work.*

arrangements /ə'reɪndʒmənt/ [plural noun] Plans: *We've made arrangements to go to swimming on Sunday.*

†**arrest**[1] /ə'rest/ [noun] **1** The act of making somebody a prisoner: *The police have made a number of arrests in connection with the bank robbery.* **2 to**

be under arrest To be kept by the police as a prisoner: *My neighbor is under arrest; he was caught robbing a bank.*

arrest[2] /ə'rest/ [verb] To make somebody a prisoner: *The thieves were arrested by the police as they came out of the house.*

†**arrival** /ə'raɪ.vəl/ [uncountable noun] The act of getting to a place: *His arrival was so unexpected that we were still in bed.*

†**arrive** /ə'raɪv/ [verb] To get to a place: *The bus broke down, so we didn't arrive in Boston before 10 p.m.* ■ Be careful with the pronunciation of this word! "rri" rhymes with "my". ■ Be careful. We say: "to arrive **in** a country, city, town and so on". We say: "to arrive **at** a building, station, airport and so on".

arrogant /'ær·ə·gənt/ [adjective] Proud, considering yourself superior: *Stuart is so arrogant that he thinks nobody will get better grades than him.*

†**arrow** US: /'er.oʊ/ UK: /'ær.əʊ/ [countable noun] **1** A stick with a point at the end: *She took the bow and shot the arrow close to the target.* **2** A sign that indicates direction: *Follow the arrows and you'll get to the exit.*

†**art** US: /ɑːrt/ UK: /ɑːt/ [uncountable noun] **1** Painting, drawing, music and so on: *In Art class we are now doing a huge wall painting.* **2 arts and crafts** Artistic and practical skills: *an arts and crafts festival.* **3 fine arts** The creation of works of art: *In France, the government spends a lot of money on the fine arts: music, the movies and so on.*

artery /'ɑr·t̬ə·ri/ [countable noun] **1** A tube which circulates oxygenated blood from the heart: *The arteries get thicker with age.* **2** A traffic route between two population centers: *The road and rail arteries connect the capital with the suburbs.* ■ The plural is "arteries".

arthropod US: /'ɑːr.θrə.pɑːd/ UK: /'ɑː.θrə.pɒd/ [countable noun] An invertebrate animal with an external skeleton, a segmented body and joint legs: *Spiders and crustaceans are arthropods.*

artichoke US: /'ɑːr.t̬ɪ.tʃoʊk/ UK: /'ɑː.tɪ.tʃəʊk/ [noun] A vegetable with big and dark green leaves: *Artichokes are often eaten with a sauce.*

†**article** /'ɑrt̬·ɪ·kəl/ [countable noun] **1** A piece of writing in a newspaper or magazine: *I'm going to write an article on China for the school magazine.* **2** A type of word that goes with nouns: *"A", "an" and "the" are articles in English.* **3 definite article** See **definite article.** **4 indefinite article** See **indefinite article.**

articulate /ɑr'tɪk·jə,leɪt/ [verb] **1** To express one's feelings or opinions clearly: *Tom wasn't able to articulate his feelings.* ■ This use is formal. **2** To pronounce syllables or words clearly: *She has hearing difficulties, so please articulate thoroughly.*

articulated /ɑː'tɪkjəleɪtɪd/ [adjective] With sections connected by joints: *An articulated vehicle can turn more easily.*

†**artificial** /,ɑr·t̬ə'fɪʃ·əl/ [adjective] That is not natural or real: *We always have an artificial Christmas tree and once it's decorated, it looks great.*

artisan US: /'ɑːrtəzən/ UK: /,ɑːtɪ'zæn/ [countable noun] A skilled, manual worker: *The interior of the theater was constructed by artisans in the 16th century.*

†**artist** US: /'ɑːr.t̬ɪst/ UK: /'ɑː.tɪst/ [countable noun] A person who creates works of art: *Some people think Picasso was the greatest artist of all times.*

†**artistic** /ɑr'tɪs·tɪk/ [adjective] That is good at creating works of art: *Alice is very artistic. She paints and plays the piano.*

artwork US: /'ɑːrt.wɝːk/ UK: /'ɑːt.wɜːk/ [uncountable noun] Illustrations that accompany a story: *The story wasn't very good, but the artwork was excellent.*

†**as** /əz, æz/ [adverb and preposition] **1** In the same way: *Do as Mr. Blundell told you and you'll pass.* **2** When: *I saw John as he was going to school.* **3** Doing the job or function of: *He's got a job as a secretary.* ■ Be careful! We don't use "as" when we are giving examples or making noun comparisons. We say: "singers **like** Whitney Houston, Mariah Carey"; "a house **like** yours". Compare with "like[2]" (in the same way or manner as). **4** While: *I normally listen to the radio as I work.* **5** Because: *As he didn't get permission, he couldn't go on the trip.* **6 as... as** A way of showing that two people or things are equal: *My younger brother is as tall as I am.* **7 as long as** On condition that: *I'll let you come with me as long as you promise to be good.*

ash /æʃ/ ▮ [uncountable noun] **1** The powder you get when you burn something: *The ashtray was full of cigarette ash.* ▮ [countable noun] **2** A beautiful tree from northern countries: *An ash is gray and has long, thin leaves.*

a b c d e f g h i j k l m n o p q r s t u v w x y z

†**ashamed** /ə'ʃeɪmd/ [adjective] That feels bad or embarrassed, usually about something wrong that they have done: *Don't be ashamed. Everybody makes mistakes when they're learning a language.* ■ Be careful with the pronunciation of this word. The "e" is not pronounced. See picture at **emotions.**

ashore /ə'ʃɔr/, /ə'ʃoʊr/ [adverb] Onto the land from water: *Tomorrow the ship will stop at Pireus so that we can go ashore to visit the Acropolis.*

ashtray /'æʃ.treɪ/ [countable noun] A small dish for cigarette ash: *Please put your cigarettes out in the ashtray, not on the floor.*

Asian[1] [countable noun] **1** A person from Asia: *Genghis Khan was a famous Asian emperor.* **2** A person of Asian origin: *Many Asians in United States work in small family businesses.* ■ Be careful! "Asian" has a capital "A".

Asian[2] /'eɪʒən/ [adjective] Referring to Asia: *China is an Asian country.* ■ Careful! "Asian" has a capital "A".

†**aside** /ə'saɪd/ [adverb] On one side: *Move aside to let people come in.*

as if [conjunction] In a way that suggests that something is true: *He talks as if he were the boss.*

†**ask** US: /æsk/ UK: /ɑːsk/ [verb] **1** To put a question to somebody: *Can I ask you something? How old are you?* **2** To request: *Jane asked me to help her with her Math homework.* **3 to ask for (something)** To make a request for something: *Tom is always asking me for money.*
▶ **PHRASAL VERBS** · **to ask to** To invite: *Mom, I've asked Carol to tea. Is that all right?*

†**asleep** /ə'sliːp/ [adjective] **1** Sleeping: *Don't make a noise! The baby's asleep.* ■ Be careful! We don't use "asleep" before a noun. We say: "The **sleeping** child". **2 fast asleep** Sleeping very deeply: *He didn't hear the thieves; he was fast asleep.* **3 to fall asleep** See "fall asleep" in the word **fall**[2].

asparagus /ə'spær·ə·gəs/ [uncountable noun] A long, thin and green vegetable: *Asparagus is one of my favorite dishes.* See page 437.

†**aspect** /'æs.pekt/ [countable noun] Characteristic, side: *One good aspect of learning languages is that you can communicate with people from other countries.*

aspirin® /'æs.pɪ.rɪn/ [noun] A medicine that is used against pain: *I always take an aspirin when I have a headache.*

ass /æs/ [countable noun] An animal of the horse family: *An ass is smaller than a horse.* ■ The plural is "asses".

assassinate /ə'sæs.ɪ.neɪt/ [verb] To kill an important person: *Gandhi was assassinated in 1948.*

assassination /ə,sæs.ɪ'neɪ.ʃən/ [noun] The murder of an important person: *I saw a movie about President Kennedy's assassination on television.*

assault /ə'sɔlt/ [verb] To attack somebody or something: *The robbers assaulted the bank and stole half a million dollars.*

assemble /ə'sem.bl/ [verb] **1** To put the parts of something together: *It's easy to assemble the kite if you follow the instructions.* **2** To get together: *In United States, all the teachers and students of a school assemble every morning before classes.*

assembly /ə'sem.bli/ [noun] A meeting of all the teachers and students of a school: *The Principal told us at assembly that classes would stop at midday.* ■ The plural is "assemblies".

assess /ə'ses/ [verb] **1** To estimate or judge the quality or quantity of a person or thing: *We have an oral test tomorrow to assess our spoken English.* **2** To calculate how much something is worth: *The estate agent assesses the value of a property.*

†**assist** /ə'sɪst/ [verb] To help: *The surgeon performed the operation, assisted by two nurses.*

†**assistance** /ə'sɪs.tənts/ [uncountable noun] Help: *I think I need some assistance with my homework.*

†**assistant** /ə'sɪs.tənt/ [countable noun] A person who helps another to do a job: *Dr. Burton's assistant sees patients on Mondays.*

†**associate** /ə'soʊ·ʃi,eɪt/, /-si-/ [verb] To connect ideas in your mind: *I always associate good weather with vacation.*

†**association** /ə,soʊ·ʃi'eɪ·ʃən/, /-si-/ ▮ [countable noun] **1** An organization: *Lucy's a member of the Association of Young Artists.* ▮ [noun] **2** A connection of ideas in your mind: *The seaside has pleasant associations for me.*

†**assume** /ə'sum/ [verb] To think that something is true: *I assume I'll pass Science without any problems.*

assurance /ə'ʃʊər·əns/ [countable noun] A promise: *She gave us an assurance that she wouldn't be late again.*

†**assure** /ə'ʃʊər/ [verb] **1** To say that something is certainly true: *I can assure you that this meat is first quality.* **2** To promise: *Johnny assured me that he wouldn't wear my jeans again.*

asterisk /'æs·tər,ɪsk/ [countable noun] A mark like a star [*] used in writing: *In my English textbook, new words have been marked with an asterisk.*

asteroid /'æs·tə,rɔɪd/ [countable noun] A very small planet, particularly one of many between Mars and Jupiter: *The spaceship passed through the group of asteroids.*

astonish /ə'stɑn·ɪʃ/ [verb] To surprise somebody very much: *He astonished everyone when he said he was going to live in China.*

astonishment /ə'stɑn·ɪʃ·mənt/ [uncountable noun] Surprise: *To my astonishment, Rebecca played extraordinarily well.*

astrologer /ə'strɒl.ə.dʒər/ US: /-'strɑː.lə.dʒɚ/ [countable noun] A person who studies the influence of stars and planets: *An astrologer told me once that I'd be famous.*

astrology /ə'strɑl·ə·dʒi/ [uncountable noun] The study of the influence of stars and planets: *I'm interested in astrology; what's your sign of the zodiac?*

astronaut /'æs·trəˌnɔt/, /-ˌnɑt/ [countable noun] A person who travels in space: *The Soviet Union was the first country to send astronauts into space.*

astronomer /ə'strɑn·ə·mər/ [countable noun] A person who studies stars and planets: *Nowadays, astronomers can watch the sky with powerful telescopes.*

astronomy /ə'strɑn·ə·mi/ [uncountable noun] The study of stars and planets: *Astronomy is the oldest science of all.*

as well [adverb] Too, also: *I'd like to be rich, and I'd like to be famous as well.* ■ "Too", "as well" and "also" have the same meaning. "Too" and "as well" go at the end of a sentence. "Also" usually goes in the middle of a sentence. ■ See box at **also**.

asylum /ə'saɪ.ləm/ [uncountable noun] Protection to somebody who has had to leave their country for political reasons: *The Cuban refugees were given asylum in United States.*

⁺**at** /æt, ət/ [preposition] **1** Used to show a point in space: *I'll be waiting for you at home.* **2** Used to show an exact point in time: *We can meet at 10 o'clock.* **3** Used to show price, frequency or speed: *The train was going at 100 miles an hour.* **4** Used when you say which number house somebody lives at in a street: *Mark lives at 3245 Grand Canyon Road, and Peter at number 3249.* ■ See box at **time: prepositions**. 👁 See picture at **preposition.**

ate /et, eɪt/ Past tense of **eat**.

athlete /'æθ.liːt/ [countable noun] A person who does athletics: *Some athletes run; others jump or throw things.*

athletics /æθ'let̬·ɪks/ [uncountable noun] **1** Sports and physical games: *Mary participates in high school athletics.* **2** See **track and field.** ■ This use is British English.

atlas /'æt.ləs/ [countable noun] A book of maps: *I like looking up places in an atlas.* ■ The plural is "atlases".

ATM [countable noun] A machine from which you can get money: *I withdrew some cash from the ATM.* ■ "ATM" is an abbreviation for "Automatic Teller Machine". ■ The same meaning: "cash dispenser".

⁺**atmosphere** /'æt·məˌsfɪər/ [noun] **1** The gases that surround a planet: *The Earth's atmosphere is made up of different gases.* 👁 **See page 449. 2** The air in a place: *Has somebody been smoking? It's impossible to breath in this atmosphere.* **3** The feeling created in a place: *The atmosphere in the English class is excellent.*

atmospheric /ˌætməs'ferɪk/ [adjective] Referring to the atmosphere: *The rocket was launched into space when the atmospheric conditions were right.*

⁺**atom** /'æt̬·əm/ [countable noun] The smallest part of a substance: *Scientists learnt how to split the atom in the 1920's.*

atrium /'eɪtriəm/ [countable noun] The central court of a building with rooms opening off it: *The atrium was filled with light from the sun which flooded in.*

⁺**attach** /ə'tætʃ/ [verb] **1** To join one thing to another: *You have to attach a photo to your application form.* **2** to be attached to (somebody or something) To be very close to somebody or something: *James is very attached to his dog.*

attachment /ə'tætʃmənt/ [countable noun] Something which is attached to something else: *The document accompanies the e-mail as an attachment.*

⁺**attack**[1] /ə'tæk/ [noun] A violent attempt to hurt somebody or to destroy something: *They made an attack on the castle.*

attack[2] /ə'tæk/ [verb] To try to hurt somebody or to destroy something: *The army attacked the Presidential Palace.*

⁺**attempt**[1] /ə'tempt/ [countable noun] An effort made to do something: *It was his second attempt to escape from prison.*

attempt[2] /ə'tempt/ [verb] To make an effort to do something: *He attempted to walk across Illinois in a month.*

⁺**attend** /ə'tend/ [verb] **1** To go to an event: *Many people attended the meeting to organize the school club.* **2** To look after somebody: *He's being attended by a doctor.*

attendance /ə'ten.dᵊnts/ [noun] Being present: *His record of school attendance is very good.*

⁺**attention** /ə'ten.tʃᵊn/ [uncountable noun] **1** Looking or listening carefully: *Can I have your attention, please?* **2** to pay attention See "pay attention" in the word **pay**[2].

attentive /ə'ten·tɪv/ [adjective] Watching and listening carefully: *I am always attentive to what my teacher says.*

attic /'æt̬·ɪk/ [countable noun] A room in the roof of a house: *I keep all my old toys in the attic.* 👁 See picture at **house.**

⁺**attitude** US: /'æt̬.ɪ.tuːd/ UK: /'æt.ɪ.tjuːd/ [noun] Your feelings or opinions about somebody or something: *She adopted an attitude of superiority.*

⁺**attorney** US: /ə'tɜːni/ [noun] A person whose job is to help with legal problems: *My aunt is an attorney in a big law firm.* ■ The same meaning: "lawyer".

⁺**attract** /ə'trækt/ [verb] **1** To make somebody or something come near: *Honey attracts bears.* **2** To provoke interest or admiration: *I was attracted by her intelligence.*

†**attraction** /ə'træk.ʃᵊn/ ▮ [uncountable noun] **1** The ability to make people like something: *I can't see the attraction in watching football.* ▮ [countable noun] **2** Something interesting to do or to visit: *The castle is one of the main tourist attractions in Edinburgh.*

†**attractive** /ə'træk.tɪv/ [adjective] **1** Good-looking: *That actor is very attractive.* **2** Interesting: *They had very attractive plans for the vacation.*

aubergine /'əʊ.bə.ʒiːn/ US: /'oʊ.bɚ-/ [noun] See **eggplant.** ■ This word is British English.

auction¹ /'ɔːkʃən/ [noun] A public sale: *Mr. Hamnett paid $4,000 for that painting at an auction in New York.*

auction² [verb] To sell by auction: *The Duchess auctioned her collection of paintings.*

†**audience** /'ɔ·di·əns/, /'ɑ·di-/ [noun] The people who listen or watch at a concert, play and so on: *The audience watched the play with great enjoyment.*

AUDIENCE

audio-visual /ˌɔːdiəʊ'vɪʒuəl/ US: /ˌɑːdioʊ-/ [adjective] Describing something that combines sound and vision: *English is taught using audio-visual techniques.*

audition /ɔ'dɪʃ·ən/ [countable noun] A session to see if a singer or an actor is good: *I've got an audition for a part in a movie on Tuesday.*

auditory /'ɔ·dɪˌtɔr·i/, /-ˌtoʊr·i/ [adjective] Referring to hearing: *The ears are our auditory organs.*

†**August** /'ɔ·gəst/ [noun] The eighth month of the year: *The Browns always go on vacation in August.* ■ Be careful with the pronunciation of this word. The beginning is pronounced like the "aw" in "saw". ■ Be careful! "August" has a capital "A". 👁 See picture at **calendar**.

†**aunt** US: /ænt/ UK: /ɑːnt/ [countable noun] Your father's or mother's sister, or your uncle's wife: *I like going to aunt Liza's because she lets me play her piano.* ■ "Auntie" is informal for "aunt". 👁 See picture at **family**.

auntie US: /ænt/ UK: /ɑːnt/ [countable noun] See **aunt.** ■ This word is informal.

au pair /ˌəʊ'peər/ [countable noun] A foreign person usually young, who lives with a family and helps in the house: *We had a young German au pair who came here to learn the language.*

Australian¹ [adjective] Referring to Australia: *Kangaroos and koalas are famous Australian animal.* ■ Be careful! "Australian" has a capital "A".

Australian² [countable noun] A person from Australia: *There are two Australians staying at our hotel.* ■ Be careful! "Australian" has a capital "A".

authentic US: /ɑː'θen.t̬ɪk/ UK: /ɔː'θen.tɪk/ [adjective] Real, genuine: *That's not an authentic Versace. It's a copy.*

†**author** US: /'ɑː.θɚ/ UK: /'ɔː.θər/ [countable noun] A person who writes books: *Jules Verne is my favorite author.* ■ Be careful with the pronunciation of this word. The beginning is pronounced like the "aw" in "saw".

authoritarian¹ [countable noun] A person who demands complete obedience and gives no freedom: *At military training the officers are usually strict authoritarians.*

authoritarian² /əˌθɔr·ə'teər·i·ən/, /-əˌθɑr-/ [adjective] Demanding strict obedience to authority: *As the situation grew worse, the President became more and more authoritarian.*

†**authority** US: /ə'θɔːr.ɪ.t̬i/ UK: /ɔː'θɒr.ɪ.ti/ ▮ [uncountable noun] **1** The power to do something: *The principal is the only person with the authority to expel students.* ▮ [countable noun] **2** A person who knows a lot about a subject: *Mrs. Hoggs is an authority on Art.* ■ The plural is "authorities".

authorization or **authorisation** /ˌɔːθəraɪ'zeɪʃən/ [countable noun] Official permission: *The family were given authorization to put fencing around their land.*

authorship /'ɔ·θərˌʃɪp/ [uncountable noun] The origin of a book or other work: *The authorship of the document was traced back to the previous century.*

autobiography /ˌɔt̬·ə·baɪ'ɑg·rə·fi/ [countable noun] The story of a person's life told by himself or by herself: *Have you read Gandhi's autobiography?* ■ The plural is "autobiographies".

autograph US: /'ɑː.t̬ə.græf/ UK: /'ɔː.tə.grɑːf/ [countable noun] A signature, usually of a famous person: *I have Serena William's autograph in my collection.*

†**automatic** /ˌɔ·t̬ə'mæt̬·ɪk/ [adjective] That works by itself: *After take-off, the captain put the plane in automatic pilot.*

automobile /'ɔ·t̬ə·moʊˌbil/, /ˌɔ·t̬ə·moʊ'bil/ [countable noun] A vehicle which is able to move independently: *The automobile climbed the hill without any effort.*

autonomous /ɔː'tɒnəməs/ [adjective] Able to function independently: *The regional government was completely autonomous.*

a b c d e f g h i j k l m n o p q r s t u v w x y z

autonomy /ɔ'tɑn·ə·mi/ [uncountable noun] The ability to operate independently: *Autonomy was the objective of the independence movement.*

†**autumn** US: /'ɑː.ṭᵊm/ UK: /'ɔː.təm/ [noun] The season of the year between summer and winter: *In the autumn, the leaves of the deciduous trees change color and fall.* ■ The same meaning: "fall[1]". 👁 **See page 448.**

auxiliary[1] /ɔg'zɪl·jə·ri/ [countable noun] A person whose job is to help other workers with their work: *Mary started as an auxiliary.*

auxiliary[2] /ɔg'zɪl·jə·ri/ [adjective] Assisting in the carrying out of a task: *Auxiliary nurses help the nursing staff.*

auxiliary verb [countable noun] A verb that is used with the main verb of the sentence to show tense, a question form and so on: *"Be", "have" and "do" are auxiliary verbs.*

†**available** /ə'veɪ.lə.bḷ/ [adjective] That is free to be used or obtained: *There are still seats available for the trip to Segovia.*

avalanche /'æv·əˌlæntʃ/ [countable noun] The sudden fall of a lot of snow down a mountain: *The party of climbers was trapped by an avalanche.*

Ave A written abbreviation for **avenue.** ■ Be careful! "Ave" has a capital "A". It is only used when the name of the avenue is mentioned. ■ See box at **abbreviations.**

avenue /'æv·ənˌju/, /-əˌnu/ [countable noun] A wide street: *Fifth Avenue is one of the main streets in New York.* ■ The abbreviation "Ave" is only used in written language. ■ See box at **abbreviations.**

†**average[1]** /'æv·rɪdʒ/, /-ər·ɪdʒ/ [countable noun] The result of dividing a total by the number of the different quantities: *The average of 10, 5 and 30 is 15.* ■ Be careful with the pronunciation of this word. The last "a" is pronounced like the "i" in "did".

average[2] /'ævərɪdʒ/ [adjective] Ordinary: *He's not as tall as you think; just average height.* ■ Be careful with the pronunciation of this word. The last "a" is pronounced like the "i" in "did".

avocado or **avocado pear** /ˌævə'kɑːdəʊ/ [noun] A yellow fruit with a green skin: *I love avocado in salads.*

†**avoid** /ə'vɔɪd/ [verb] **1** To prevent something from happening: *My little brother always tries to avoid wash the dishes.* **2** To keep away from a person: *Rachael has been trying to avoid me all week.*

await /ə'weɪt/ [verb] To wait for: *Dear Sirs, I wrote to you last month but I am still awaiting your reply.* ■ This word is formal. We usually say "wait".

†**awake[1]** /ə'weɪk/ [adjective] Not asleep: *It was 3 a.m. and the children were still awake.*

†**awake[2]**, awoke, awoken /ə'weɪk/ [verb] To wake from sleep: *He awoke suddenly.*

†**award[1]** /ə'wɔːd/ [countable noun] A prize: *I'd like to win an award for best actor.*

award[2] /ə'wɔːd/ [verb] To give a prize: *Anne was awarded the prize for the best original drawing.*

†**aware** /ə'weər/ [adjective] Knowing something or understanding it: *Are you completely aware of the problem?* ■ Be careful. We always say: "to be aware **of** (something)".

awareness /ə'weənəs/ [uncountable noun] A state of consciousness or knowledge of one's surroundings: *Blind people have a special awareness of their environment.*

†**away** /ə'weɪ/ [adverb] **1** Not at home: *When I phoned Margaret, she was away.* **2** In another place or to another place: *This summer we're going away to Argentina.* **3** Distant: *I live twenty miles away from Houston.* **4 to put (something) away** See "put (something) away" in the word **put.**

awesome [adjective] **1** Causing feelings of admiration or fear: *When he accepted the new job, he took an awesome responsibility.* **2** Extremely good or extraordinary: *Last night we had an awesome time at the party.*

†**awful[1]** /'ɔːfəl/ [adjective] Terrible, horrible: *What awful weather!*

awful[2] [adverb] Very: *She's been gone an awful long time, do you think she's coming back?* ■ This word is informal.

awfully /'ɔf·li/, /'ɔ·fə·li/ [adverb] Very: *I'm awfully sorry.* ■ This word is informal.

awkward US: /'ɑː.kwɚd/ UK: /'ɔː.kwəd/ [adjective] **1** Embarrassing: *It's very awkward at a meeting when nobody says anything.* **2** Clumsy: *He made an awkward movement and dropped his glass on the floor.*

ax /æks/ [countable noun] An instrument with a sharp metal head for cutting up wood: *I learnt how to use an axe at summer camp.* ■ The British English spelling is "axe".

axe /æks/ [countable noun] See **ax.** ■ This is a British English spelling.

axis /'æk.sɪs/ [countable noun] The imaginary line around which a body rotates: *The Earth rotates on its axis.* ■ The plural is "axes".

axle /'æksl/ [countable noun] A bar that connects two wheels: *Bicycles, cars and trucks have several axles.*

axon [countable noun] Long, thin part of a neuron which conducts impulses to other cells: *Neurons have only one axon.*

B

b

b /biː/ The second letter of the alphabet: *The name "Barbara" begins with a "B".*

b. Referring to a date when somebody came into the world: *Mary Smith (b. 8 November 1979, Pittsburgh).* ■ "b." is an abbreviation for "born". ■ See box at **abbreviations**.

B /biː/ [countable noun] The seventh musical note of the scale of C major: *Play a B on the guitar, please.* ■ The plural is "Bs" or "B's". **See page 460.**

BA Referring to a first college degree in the arts or social sciences, or somebody who has this degree: *Michael has a BA in History from the University of Arizona.* ■ "BA" is an abbreviation for "Bachelor of Arts". Compare with "BS" (an abbreviation for "Bachelor of Science"). ■ See box at **abbreviations**.

↑**baby** /ˈbeɪ.bi/ [countable noun] A very young child: *Mary's going to have a baby.* ■ The plural is "babies".

baby-sit /ˈbeɪ.bi.sɪt/ [verb] To look after children while their parents are out: *Jenny baby-sits on Friday nights.*

babysitter /ˈbeɪ·biˌsɪt̬·ər/ [countable noun] A young person who looks after children when their parents are out: *Jenny is our children's babysitter.*

bachelor /ˈbætʃ·ə·lər/ [countable noun] **1** A man who is not married: *John wants to stay a bachelor for the rest of his life.* ■ See box at **abbreviations**.

↑**back**[1] /bæk/ [countable noun] **1** The part of the body that goes from the neck to the bottom: *You will hurt your back if you carry that heavy case.* **2** The opposite side from the front: *The kids are playing basketball at the back of the house.* **3 back to front** The wrong way round: *You're wearing your jumper back to front.* **4 behind (somebody's) back** To do or to say something without a person knowing it: *She's always talking about me behind my back.*

back[2] /bæk/ [adjective] **1** Situated behind something: *The dog's sitting in the backyard.* ■ Compare with "frontal" (being at the front). **2 back door** The door that is at the back of a house: *When you go into the yard, close the back door behind you.*

↑**back**[3] /bæk/ [adverb] **1** In the direction that is behind you: *Move back, please; give him some space.* **2** To where somebody or something was before: *I'll be back at five.* **3** Again: *Call me back as soon as you can.*

back[4] /bæk/ [verb] **1** To make something go backwards: *She backed the car into the driveway.* **2** To support: *The organization is backed by the United Nations.*

◗ **PHRASAL VERBS** · **to back away** To walk back from somebody or something: *The child was frightened and backed away from the bulldog.* · **to back (somebody) up** To support: *Don't worry, I'll back you up if Louise tells your father.*

backache /'bæk.eɪk/ [noun] A pain in the back: *After the game, John had a terrible backache.*

backbone /'bæk,boʊn/ [countable noun] The line of bones that goes down the back: *The lion killed the zebra by breaking its backbone.* ■ The same meaning: "spine".

↑**background** /'bæk.graʊnd/ ▮ [countable noun] **1** A person's education, family, and experience of life: *I feel ashamed of my background.* ▮ [uncountable noun] **2** The back part in a picture: *This photograph was taken against a red background.* ■ Compare with "foreground" (that part of a view which is closest to the viewer).

backing /'bæk.ɪŋ/ [uncountable noun] Help or support: *Our team has a lot of backing and they say it helps them to play better.*

backpack /'bæk.pæk/ [countable noun] A bag that you carry on your back: *We couldn't get very far carrying our tents and backpacks in the heavy rain.* ■ In British English they say "rucksack".

BACKPACK

backstroke /'bæk·stroʊk/ [uncountable noun] A style of swimming in which you swim on your back: *The Russians won the backstroke last year.*

↑**backward** /'bæk·wərd/ [adjective] In the direction that is behind you, that moves towards the back: *She took a backward look at her town before she left it for the last time.*

backwards /'bæk·wərdz/ [adverb] **1** Towards the back, towards behind you: *Be careful you don't fall backwards.* **2** With the end first: *Can you say the alphabet backwards, from Z to A?*

BACKWARDS

backyard [noun] A piece of land behind a house and belonging to it: *They grow vegetables in their backyard.*

bacon /'beɪ.kᵊn/ [uncountable noun] Smoked or salted meat from a pig: *A lot of people like bacon for breakfast.*

↑**bacteria** /bæk'tɪər·i·ə/ [noun] Very small living things: *Some bacteria can cause diseases.* ■ This word is always plural.

bacterial [adjective] Referring to bacteria: *The infection is bacterial.*

↑**bad** /bæd/ [adjective] **1** Not good: *We're having bad weather these days.* **2** Damaging to somebody or something: *Doctors say smoking is bad for your health.* **3** Serious: *His parents had a bad accident on the road to Seattle.* **4 to go bad** To become unpleasant or unhealthy to eat: *We can't eat the fish because it's gone bad.* **5 not bad or not so bad** Quite good: *The movie on TV yesterday wasn't bad.* ■ The comparative form is "worse" and the superlative form is "worst".

bade Past tense of **bid²**.

badge /bædʒ/ [countable noun] A piece of metal or plastic that you wear on clothes: *He wears the club badge on his blazer.*

badger /'bædʒ·ər/ [countable noun] A black and white animal that lives in holes: *Badgers hunt at night.*

badly /'bæd.li/ [adverb] **1** Not well: *He plays tennis really badly.* **2** Seriously: *She was badly hurt in a car crash last week.* **3** Very much: *Your friend badly needs a shave.* ■ The comparative form is "worse" and the superlative form is "worst".

badminton /'bæd.mɪn.tᵊn/ [uncountable noun] A game like tennis with a very light ball that has feathers: *My sister's good at badminton.*

badtempered /'bæd'tem·pərd/ [adjective] Annoyed or angry: *Why is that kid always so badtempered?*

a b c d e f g h i j k l m n o p q r s t u v w x y z

†**bag** /bæg/ [countable noun] **1** A container that people use for carrying things: *We need a large bag to carry the fruit.* **2** sleeping bag See **sleeping bag**.

†**baggage** /'bæg.ɪdʒ/ [uncountable noun] Bags that you use when traveling: *Help me put the baggage in the car, please.* ■ Be careful with the pronunciation of this word. The last "a" is pronounced like the "i" in "did".

baggy /'bæg.i/ [adjective] Fitting loosely: *Those pants are much too baggy for me.* ■ This word is informal. ■ The comparative form is "baggier" and the superlative form is "baggiest".

bagpipes /'bæg.paɪps/ [plural noun] A musical wind instrument made of an air sack attached to pipes: *Bagpipes are popular in Scotland.* ■ We can also use "bagpipe" with a singular meaning: "to play the bagpipe".

BAGPIPES

†**bake** /beɪk/ [verb] To cook food in an oven: *Bake the bread for thirty minutes.*

baker /'beɪ·kər/ [countable noun] A person who makes and sells bread and cakes: *The baker in our street sells very good bread.*

bakery [countable noun] A store that sells bread and cakes: *Sheila's gone to the bakery to buy a loaf of bread.* 👁 See picture at **market**.

†**balance**[1] /'bæl.ᵊnts/ [uncountable noun] **1** The ability to stay in one position without falling: *Her balance wasn't very good and she fell.* **2** A situation in which two or more things have the same importance: *People need to find a balance between work and play.* **3** to lose your balance To become unsteady: *If you try to carry those heavy things, you'll lose your balance and fall.*

balance[2] /'bæləns/ [verb] To keep or to stay in one position without falling: *I bet you can't balance this ball on your head.*

balcony /'bæl.kə.ni/ [countable noun] An open or glass covered area on the outside wall of a building: *We spent the evening talking on the balcony.* ■ The plural is "balconies".

bald US: /bɑːld/ UK: /bɔːld/ [adjective] With no hair on your head: *My father's been bald since he was thirty.* 👁 See picture at **hair**.

†**ball** US: /bɑːl/ UK: /bɔːl/ [countable noun] **1** A round object used in games: *Helen hits the ball really hard when she's playing tennis.* **2** Anything that is round: *I'll need another ball of wool to finish the sweater.* **3** A big party where people can dance: *Lucy and Mark went to a New Year's ball last year.*

ballet /bæ'leɪ/ [uncountable noun] **1** Dancing and music that tells a story: *My favorite ballet is "Swan Lake".* **2** ballet dancer A person who dances ballet: *Nureyev was a great ballet dancer.*

balloon /bə'luːn/ [countable noun] **1** A rubber bag filled with air or gas: *Let's get some balloons for the party.* **2** A big bag filled with gas that can fly, carrying passengers: *The hot-air balloon moved slowly across the valley.* 👁 See picture at **transport**.

BALLOON

ballpoint [countable noun] A pen with a small ball at the end: *My ballpoint has no ink left.* ■ We also say "ballpoint pen". ■ In British English they say "biro".

ballpoint pen /ˌbɔːlpɔɪnt'pen/ [countable noun] See **ballpoint**.

bamboo /bæm'buː/ [noun] A tall, strong, tropical plant: *Pandas eat bamboo.*

†**ban**[1] /bæn/ [countable noun] A law or a rule that says that you must not do something: *There's a ban on smoking in hospitals.*

ban[2] /bæn/ [verb] To make a law or a rule that says that something must not be done: *Governments should ban nuclear tests.* ■ Compare with "forbid" (to tell somebody that you do not allow them to do something).

banana /bəˈnæn·ə/ [noun] A long, yellow fruit: *I like bananas for dessert.* **See page 436.**

banana tree [countable noun] A plant which produces bananas and has very large leaves: *The banana tree grows in tropical or subtropical regions.* **See page 435.**

band /bænd/ [countable noun] **1** A thin, narrow piece of material for holding things together: *Try tying your pencils together with this rubber band.* **2** A group of people who play music together: *He plays the drums in the town band.* **3** A group of people who act together: *A band of thieves have stolen three cars in this street.*

bandage[1] /ˈbændɪdʒ/ [countable noun] A piece of cloth that covers a wound: *The bandage round my arm's a bit loose now.* ■ Be careful with the pronunciation of this word. The last "a" is pronounced like the "i" in "did".

bandage[2] /ˈbændɪdʒ/ [verb] To tie a piece of cloth round a wound: *The nurse is going to bandage his arm.* ■ Be careful with the pronunciation of this word. The last "a" is pronounced like the "i" in "did".

B&B [countable noun] See **bed and breakfast.** ■ Be careful. "B&B" is always written in capital letters.

bandit /ˈbæn.dɪt/ [countable noun] An armed robber, usually in a wild place: *The bandits attacked the travelers in the mountains and took everything they had.*

bang[1] /bæŋ/ [countable noun] **1** A loud noise: *Pete always closes the door with a bang.* **2** A sharp blow: *Sharon had a bang on her left leg.*

bang[2] /bæŋ/ [verb] **1** To make a loud noise when you close something: *Don't bang the door when you go out.* **2** To hit something: *Tom fell and banged his head against the table.*

banger /ˈbæŋ.ər/ US: /-ɚ/ [countable noun] **1** See **firecracker.** **2** See **sausage.** ■ This word is British English.

bangs /bæŋz/ [plural noun] The front part of somebody's hair, cut so that it hangs over the forehead: *The hairdresser only cut her bangs a little.* ■ In British English they say "fringe". See picture at **hair.**

banish /ˈbæn.ɪʃ/ [verb] To send somebody away from their country: *Napoleon was banished to the island of Elba.*

banister /ˈbæn·ə·stər/ [countable noun] The rail at the side of a staircase: *Hold onto the banister so you don't fall down.*

bank /bæŋk/ [countable noun] **1** A place where people keep money: *My aunt has a lot of money in the bank.* **2** The land along the side of a river or of a lake: *We'll put up our tent on the river bank.* **3** A place where something is stored: *Hospital blood banks save a lot of lives.* **4** **bank account** An arrangement with a bank to keep money in it: *I haven't got much money in my bank account.*

banker /ˈbæŋ·kər/ [countable noun] A person who is in charge of a bank: *Talk to a banker if you need a loan.*

banking /ˈbæŋ.kɪŋ/ [uncountable noun] The activity of directing a bank: *He's an expert in international banking.*

bankrupt[1] /ˈbæŋkrʌpt/ [adjective] Unable to pay your debts: *Mr. Fowler went bankrupt and had to sell his house.*

bankrupt[2] /ˈbæŋkrʌpt/ [verb] To make somebody or something very poor so that they are unable to pay their debts: *Bad management bankrupted the company.*

banner /ˈbæn·ər/ [countable noun] **1** A long flag: *Our club banner is black and yellow.* **2** A long piece of cloth or paper with words on it: *The banners said: "Stop nuclear tests!".*

banquet /ˈbæŋ.kwɪt/ [countable noun] A large, formal meal: *The wedding banquet will take place at the Hilton.*

baptize or **baptise** /bæpˈtaɪz/ [verb] To formally admit somebody to the Christian church: *They've baptized the child with the name of George.*

bar US: /bɑːr/ UK: /bɑːʳ/ [countable noun] **1** A place where people go to drink: *Shall we go to the bar for a drink.* **2** A piece of soap, chocolate and so on: *Don't eat that bar of chocolate before dinner.* See picture at **a piece of...** **3** A long piece of straight metal: *They put iron bars on that house after the robbery.* **4** Any of the segments of time into which a piece of music is divided: *Each bar is marked with a vertical line on the stave.*

barbecue[1] /ˈbɑr·bɪˌkju/ [countable noun] **1** A grill in the open air: *My parents have bought a barbecue so*

BANK

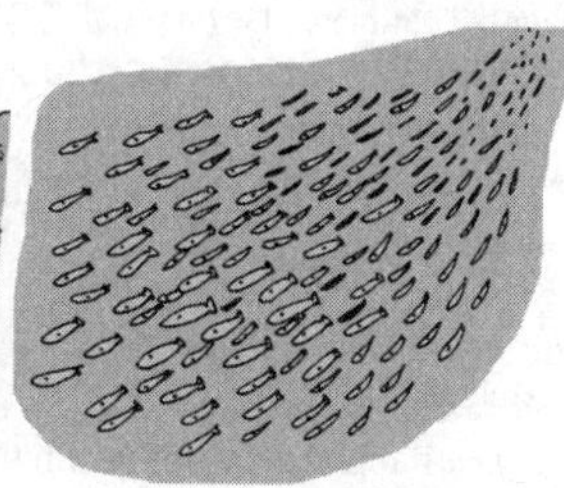

that we can eat in the backyard. **2** A party where food is eaten in the open air: *My cousins came to the barbecue last night.* ■ Be careful with the pronunciation of this word! The "ue" is pronounced as "you".

barbecue² [verb] To cook food on a barbecue: *We will barbecue meat and vegetables for the party.* See picture at **cook**.

barber US: /ˈbɑːr.bɚ/ UK: /ˈbɑː.bəʳ/ [countable noun] A man who cuts men's hair: *The barber washed Tim's hair before cutting it.* ■ Compare with "hairdresser" (a person who cuts and arranges hair).

barber's US: /ˈbɑːr.bɚz/ UK: /ˈbɑː.bəz/ [countable noun] The place where a barber works: *Jason is at the barber's getting a haircut.*

bare US: /ber/ UK: /beəʳ/ [adjective] **1** When we talk about parts of the body, without clothing: *When they saw his bare arms, they were amazed at his tattoos.* **2** Empty: *Our living room is still very bare; we've got just two chairs and a small table.*

barefoot /ˈbeərˌfʊt/ [adverb] Without any shoes on: *Sandra's playing barefoot on the lawn.*

barely /ˈbeər·li/ [adverb] Very little: *There's barely any sugar left.*

bargain¹ /ˈbɑr·gən/ [countable noun] Something that you buy cheap: *This electric guitar was a bargain.*

bargain² /ˈbɑːgɪn/ [verb] To argue about the price of something: *You can't bargain in this store; all the prices are fixed.*

barge¹ US: /bɑːrdʒ/ UK: /bɑːdʒ/ [countable noun] A long river or canal boat: *The barges crossing the river are full of tourists in summer.*

barge² /bɑːdʒ/ **to barge in** To rush in somewhere, interrupting something: *The door opened suddenly and the children barged in.*

bark¹ US: /bɑːrk/ UK: /bɑːk/ ▮ [countable noun] **1** The noise that a dog makes: *Don't be afraid of Boxer, his bark is worse than his bite.* See picture at **animal.** ▮ [uncountable noun] **2** The outer part of a tree: *They're collecting pieces of bark to start the fire.*

bark² /bɑːk/ [verb] To make a noise like a dog: *Kate's dog always barks at children.*

barley /ˈbɑr·li/ [uncountable noun] A cereal that is used for food and for making some drinks: *Whisky and beer are made from barley.*

barman /ˈbɑː.mən/ US: /ˈbɑːr-/ [countable noun] A man who serves drinks in a bar or in a pub: *The barman is busy and can't bring the drinks now.* ■ The plural is "barmen". ■ A woman who serves drinks is a "waitress".

barn US: /bɑːrn/ UK: /bɑːn/ [countable noun] A large farm building: *We keep the food for the pigs in the barn.*

barometer /bəˈrɑm·ɪ·t̬ər/ [countable noun] An instrument that says what the weather will be like: *According to the barometer, the weather will be very cold tomorrow.*

barrel /ˈbær.əl/ [countable noun] A large, round container for liquids: *Whisky is kept in oak barrels.*

barrier /ˈbær·i·ər/ [countable noun] A fence that is an obstacle: *The police have put up barriers to control the traffic.*

basalt /bəˈsɔlt/, /ˈbeɪ·sɔlt/ [uncountable noun] A dark, volcanic rock which can form columns: *The columns in the cave were of basalt.*

base¹ /beɪs/ [countable noun] **1** The lowest part of something: *The base of this bottle is cracked.* **2** The place from which something is controlled: *The organization United Nations has its main base in New York.* **3** A military camp: *People think the air base is too close to the town.* ■ Be careful with the pronunciation of this word!

base² /beɪs/ [verb] To use something as a starting point: *The movie is based on an old Chinese tale.* ■ Be careful with the pronunciation of this word! ■ We say: "based **on** (something)".

baseball /ˈbeɪsˌbɔl/ [uncountable noun] An American sport played with a bat and a ball: *In baseball, when you hit the ball you have to run around a field.* See picture at **sport**.

basement /ˈbeɪ.smənt/ [countable noun] A room that is under the ground: *I'm going to put the old papers in the basement.* ■ The same meaning: "cellar".

basic /ˈbeɪ.sɪk/ [adjective] Simple and necessary: *Helen's learning the basic vocabulary of Spanish.*

basically /ˈbeɪ.sɪ.kli/ [adverb] A word used when you say what you think is the most important thing about somebody or something: *Basically, I think Fred's rather shy.*

basil US: /ˈbeɪzəl/ UK: /ˈbæzəl/ [uncountable noun] An aromatic herb used to add flavor to food: *Italians use basil in the tomato sauce on their pasta.*

basis /ˈbeɪ.sɪs/ [countable noun] **1** The foundation or support for an idea: *Making profit is the basis for the capitalist economy.* **2** The starting point for something: *Governments agreed on the basis for negotiations.* ■ The plural is "bases". **3 on a {daily/weekly/regular} basis** The way in which something is arranged: *During the illness she will visit the Doctor on a weekly basis.*

basket US: /ˈbæs.kɪt/ UK: /ˈbɑː.skɪt/ [countable noun] A container made of thin sticks: *We put all the dirty clothes in a basket.*

basketball US: /ˈbæs.kɪt.bɑːl/ UK: /ˈbɑː.skɪt.bɔːl/ [uncountable noun] A sport played by two teams of five players who throw a ball into a high net: *Pau Gasol is my favorite basketball player.* See picture at **sport**.

bass /beɪs/ ▮ [noun] **1** The deepest tone in which a male voice can sing: *The bass sings a solo number.* **2** The instrument that produces a deep sound: *She plays the bass at the chamber orchestra.* ■ The plural is "basses". ▮ [countable noun] **3** A fish that can live in the sea or in a river: *Mom prepared bass with onion and lemon for dinner.* ■ Be careful with the pronunciation of this word! "a" is pronounced "ei". "Bass" rhymes with "face". ■ The plural is also "bass".

bass drum [countable noun] A large drum with a low pitch: *The bass drum is often used to mark or keep time.* ■ Be careful with the pronunciation of this word! "Bass" rhymes with "face". 👁 **See page 459.**

bass guitar [countable noun] A guitar that makes a deep sound: *Rick plays the bass guitar in our group.*

bassoon [noun] A musical instrument with a long wooden tube and metal keys which gives a very low sound: *He plays the bassoon in the local orchestra.*

bat /bæt/ [countable noun] **1** A small animal that flies at night: *Bats live in caves and feed on fruit and insects.* **2** An instrument for hitting a ball in a cricket, baseball and other sports, usually made of wood: *Careful! If you hit the bat against the table you will damage it.*

BAT

*__bath[1]__ US: /bæθ/ UK: /bɑːθ/ [countable noun] **1** See **bathtub**. ■ This use is British English. **2** Water for a bath: *Your bath will be ready in a few minutes.* **3** The act of washing your body in a large container: *Isn't it about time you had a bath, Peter?*

bath[2] US: /bæθ/ UK: /bɑːθ/ [verb] To wash all over in a large container: *My dad always baths before going to bed.* ■ We usually say: "to take a bath". ■ Compare with "bathe" (to wash part of your body).

bathe /beɪð/ [verb] **1** To wash part of your body: *She bathed her sore feet in hot water.* ■ Compare with "bath[2]" (to wash the whole body in a long container). **2** To swim: *The kids shouldn't bathe in very deep water.*

bathing suit [countable noun] A piece of clothing worn for swimming, usually by women and girls: *Don't forget your bathing suit for the vacation.*

*__bathroom__ /ˈbæθˌrum/, /-ˌrʊm/ [countable noun] A room with a bathtub and a sink: *Linda's in the bathroom taking a shower.* ■ In British English they say also "toilet". 👁 See picture on the following page and at **house**.

bathtub [countable noun] A long container for washing your body: *Jessica's been in the bathtub for half an hour.* ■ "Tub" is short for "bathtub". ■ In British English they say "bath". 👁 See picture at **bathroom**.

*__battery__ US: /ˈbæt̬.ɚ.i/ UK: /ˈbæt.ᵊr.i/ [countable noun] A closed container that produces electricity: *Your radio needs new batteries.* ■ The plural is "batteries".

*__battle__ /ˈbæt̬·ə·l/ [noun] **1** A fight between armed forces: *Admiral Nelson died in the Battle of Trafalgar.* **2** Any fight: *Scientists are winning the battle against cancer.*

*__bay__ /beɪ/ [countable noun] An area of sea partly surrounded by land: *The Bay of San Francisco is between Oakland City and San Francisco City.* 👁 **See page 444.**

*__be,__ was, been /biː, bi/ [verb] **1** Used to show a permanent or temporary quality: *The room is cold.* **2** Used to refer to situations or locations: *I was at the races last Saturday, but where were you?* **3** To happen: *The concert was last night.* **4** Used to refer to measures: *The lake is two seven feet deep.* **5** Used to refer to distance: *The mountains are very far away.* **6** Used to refer to age: *My brother is eighteen years old.* **7** To feel (sensation): *Have some water if you are thirsty.* **8** Used with other verbs in order to form continuous tenses: *"I am reading a magazine" is an example of the Present Continuous tense.* **9** Used with other verbs in order to form passive tenses: *"The rocket was launched at eight o'clock" is an example of the past passive tense.* **10** **to be afraid** To feel fear: *I am afraid of snakes.* **11** **to be lucky** To have good fortune: *Carol was lucky when she went to Paris because she had great weather.* **12** **to be on** To be shown on television or at a movie theater, a theater and so on: *What's on at the Roxy theater at the moment?* **13** **to be right** To be the one who is correct, or to have the correct answer: *You are right.* **14** **to be wrong** To be the one who is not correct, or to have the incorrect answer: *I am afraid you are wrong.* ■ See box on the following page.
▸ **PHRASAL VERBS** · **to be into (something)** To like something a lot: *I am really into chess.* · **to be up to (something)** To do something, often mis-

BATHROOM

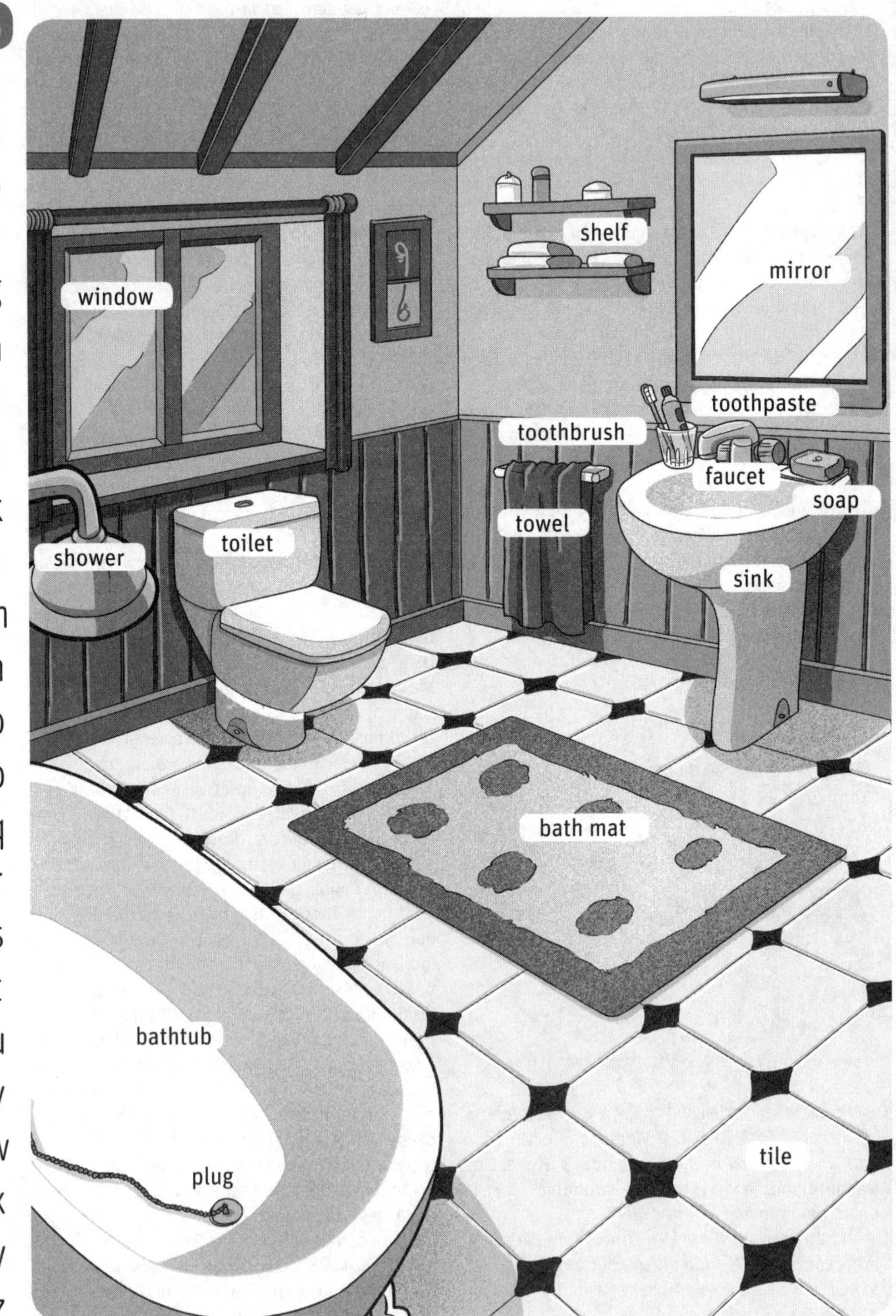
shelf
mirror
window
toothpaste
toothbrush
faucet
soap
towel
toilet
shower
sink
bath mat
bathtub
tile
plug

chievous or in secret: *I think the two children are up to something, they are being so quiet.*

†**beach** /biːtʃ/ [countable noun] An area of sand next to the sea: *The beaches were full of tourists last summer.* **See page 444.**

†**beak** /biːk/ [countable noun] The hard part of a bird's mouth: *Parrots have big, curved beaks.*

beaker /ˈbi·kər/ [countable noun] A plastic glass with a lip that makes it easy to pour, used in chemistry: *You can use the beaker to measure out the chemicals.* **See page 440.**

beam /biːm/ [countable noun] A line of light: *We can see the beam of the lighthouse from the beach.*

bean /biːn/ [countable noun] **1** The seed of some plants, that are eaten as a vegetable: *We never have beans for dinner.* **See page 437.** **2** A seed of some plants from which food or drink is made: *Those coffee beans come in tins.* **3 baked beans** White beans cooked in a tomato sauce and tinned: *We had fried eggs and baked beans for lunch.*

†**bear**[1] US: /ber/ UK: /beəʳ/ [countable noun] A very large, strong animal with thick fur: *Bears are fond of honey.* ■ Be careful with the pronunciation of this word! It is pronounced like "air". **See page 428.**

bear[2], **bore, born** /beər/ [verb] **1** To support weight: *That seat won't bear the weight of two people.* **2** To be able to tolerate somebody or something: *I can't bear noisy places.* ■ Be careful with the pronunciation of "bear". It is pronounced like "air".

†**beard** US: /bɪrd/ UK: /bɪəd/ [countable noun] The hair on a man's face: *You'll look older with a beard.*

beast /biːst/ [countable noun] **1** A large animal or creature: *Have you seen "Beauty and the Beast"?* ■ We usually say "animal". **2** A cruel, unpleasant person: *Don't be such a beast! Let me go!*

beat[1] /biːt/ [countable noun] **1** A regular sound: *After he ran up the hill, his heart beat was very fast.* **2** A regular measure in music: *He tapped his foot in time to the beat of the music.*

†**beat**[2], **beat, beat** /biːt/ [verb] **1** To defeat somebody: *She beats me at tennis most of the time.* **2** To hit somebody or something many times: *The wind's beating against the windows.* **3** To move many times: *His heart beats faster every time he sees Karen.*

beaten /ˈbi·tə·n/ Past participle of **beat**.

beautician /bjuːˈtɪʃ.ᵊn/ [countable noun] A person who gives beauty treatments to your face or your body: *My sister is studying to be a beautician.*

†**beautiful** /ˈbju·ţɪ·fəl/ [adjective] Very pleasing to look at: *That's a beautiful picture!* ■ When we use "beautiful" for people, this is usually to talk about girls and women. For men we usually say "handsome" or "good-looking".

†**beauty** /ˈbju·ţi/ [uncountable noun] The state of being beautiful: *The Lake District is an area of great natural beauty.* ■ The plural is "beauties".

beaver /ˈbi·vər/ [countable noun] A small animal with fur that lives near water: *Beavers have strong teeth and heavy tails.*

became /bɪˈkeɪm/ Past tense of **become**.

†**because** /bɪˈkəz/, /bɪˈkəz/ [conjunction] **1** For the reason that: *I'll take a taxi because I'm in a hurry.* **2 because of** By reason of: *His plane couldn't land because of the fog.*

†**become, became, become** /bɪˈkʌm/ [verb] **1** To grow or to change into something: *Janet became a doctor after years of studying.* **2** To happen to: *What will become of you if you don't finish your*

to be: auxiliary verb

We sometimes use the verb ***to be*** as an auxiliary verb (this is a verb that is used with the main verb of the sentence). ***To be*** is used in the following ways:

- **Continuous tenses:**
  to be + *-ing* form of main verb:
  - *They're playing football.*
  - *I was walking through the park when I found a book.*
  - *How long have you been watching television?*
- **The passive form:**
  to be + past participle of main verb:
  - *English is spoken in Australia.*
  - *Cars are repaired in garages.*

to be

- **Present tense**

affirmative	contractions	negative	questions
I am	I'm	I'm not	am I?
you are	you're	you're not	are you?
he /she / it is	he's / she's / it's	he / she / it isn't	is he / she / it?
we are	we're	we aren't	are we?
you are	you're	you're not	are you?
they are	they're	they aren't	are they?

- **Past tense**

affirmative	negative	questions
I was	I wasn't	was I?
you were	you weren't	were you?
he / she / it was	he / she / it wasn't	was he / she / it?
we were	we weren't	were we?
you were	you weren't	were you?
they were	they weren't	were they?

- **Present participle**
  being
- **Past participle**
  been

a **b** c d e f g h i j k l m n o p q r s t u v w x y z

studies? ■ Be careful. In this use we say: "to become of".

***bed** /biː'ed/, /biː'ed/ [noun] **1** A piece of furniture for sleeping on: *We need a room with two beds.* **2** to make a bed To tidy the sheets and blankets on a bed: *Andrew always makes his bed in the mornings.* 👁 See picture at **bedroom**.

bed and breakfast [countable noun] A small family hotel: *At a bed and breakfast they give you a bed for the night and breakfast the next morning.* ■ "B&B" is a written abbreviation for "bed and breakfast".

bedclothes /'bed,klouz/, /-,klouðz/ [plural noun] Sheets and blankets for making the bed: *I won't get into a bed with such dirty bedclothes.*

bedrock /'bedrɒk/ [uncountable noun] A solid layer of rock lying under loose earth and sand: *The archeologists got down to the granite bedrock.*

***bedroom** /'bed.rʊm/ [countable noun] A room for sleeping in: *I've got posters of all my favorite groups on my bedroom walls.* 👁 See picture at **house**.

bedside /'bed.saɪd/ [noun] The side of a bed: *She's got a small lamp by her bedside.*

bedside table [countable noun] A small low table which is placed next to a bed: *Tom always has a book on his bedside table.* ■ The same meaning: "night table", "side table". 👁 See picture at **bedroom**.

bee /biː/ [countable noun] A flying insect that makes honey: *If you disturb the bees they'll sting you.* 👁 **See page 431.**

beech or **beech tree** /biːtʃ/ [noun] A large, northern tree: *The leaves of beech trees fall in winter.*

***beef** /biːf/ [uncountable noun] The meat from a cow: *We had roast beef for lunch on Sunday.* ■ Compare with "cow" (large female farm animal bred to produce meat and milk).

beehive /'biː.haɪv/ [countable noun] A small wooden box in which bees live: *The beehives must be full of honey by now.* ■ We also say "hive".

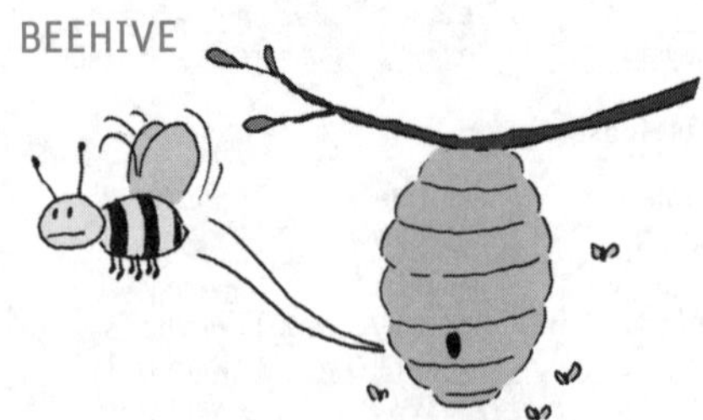

been /biːn/ Past participle of **be**.

***beer** US: /bɪr/ UK: /bɪəʳ/ [noun] **1** An alcoholic drink made from grain: *Too much beer makes you sleepy.* **2** A glass, a can or a bottle of beer: *Will you buy us a beer?*

beetle /'bit̬.ə.l/ [countable noun] An insect with a hard black cover: *Beetles are harmful to plants.* 👁 **See page 431.**

beetroot /'biː.truːt/ [noun] A sweet dark red vegetable: *Yesterday I only had a beetroot salad for lunch.*

before[1] /bɪ'fɔːr/ [adverb] **1** Earlier: *Why didn't she come before?* **2** In front: *Look at the page before.*

***before**[2] /bɪ'fɔːr/ [preposition] **1** In front of: *Don't talk like that before the kids.* **2** Earlier than: *She came home before eleven last night.* **3** Ahead of: *The gas station's one hundred yards before the bank.*

before[3] /bɪ'fɔːr/ [conjunction] Earlier than the time when: *Think before you talk.*

beg /beg/ [verb] **1** To ask for money or for food: *A lot of people live through begging in the big cities.* **2** To ask somebody strongly to do something: *Mark begged me not to tell anybody.* ■ Be careful with the spelling of these forms: "begged", "begging".

began /bɪ'gæn/ Past tense of **begin**.

beggar /'beg.ər/ [countable noun] A person who lives by asking for money: *Many beggars sleep in the streets.*

***begin,** began, begun /bɪ'gɪn/ [verb] **1** To start: *Come quickly; the movie's beginning.* **2** to begin with At first: *To begin with he was angry, but soon he smiled.*

beginner /bɪ'gɪn.ər/ [countable noun] A person who is starting to learn something: *I think John is very good at baseball considering he's only a beginner.*

***beginning** /bɪ'gɪn.ɪŋ/ [countable noun] The first part of something: *A good beginning makes for a good ending.*

begun /bɪ'gʌn/ Past participle of **begin**.

behalf /bɪ'hɑːf/ on behalf of (somebody) For somebody: *I talked to the boss this morning on your behalf.*

***behave** /bɪ'heɪv/ [verb] **1** To act in a particular way: *Why did Mike behave so strangely at the party?* **2** behave oneself To act in a correct way: *Please behave yourself, Tom; you're old enough to know better.*

behavior [uncountable noun] A way of acting: *Her behavior at school has improved in the last year.*

behind[1] /bɪ'haɪnd/ [adverb] **1** At or towards the further back of somebody or something: *If you walk too fast you'll leave us behind.* **2** Late: *I think Jim's behind with his homework.*

***behind**[2] /bɪ'haɪnd/ [preposition] **1** At the back of: *There's somebody talking behind the door.* **2** Less advanced than somebody: *We are behind the Americans in technology.* 👁 See picture at **preposition**.

a b c d e f g h i j k l m n o p q r s t u v w x y z

BEDROOM

ceiling
picture
closet
lamp
wall
crib
pillow
bed
sheet
blanket
bedside table
rug
dresser

a b c d e f g h i j k l m n o p q r s t u v w x y z

beige /beɪʒ/ [noun and adjective] A very pale brown color: *Our school uniform is beige.*

⁺**belief** /bɪˈliːf/ [noun] **1** An opinion that you feel sure about: *It's my belief that the thief broke in after we all left.* **2** The feeling that something is true: *My aunt has very strong religious beliefs.*

⁺**believe** /bɪˈliːv/ [verb] **1** To think something is true: *I believe what you say.* **2** To be of the opinion: *I don't believe we have met before.* **3** To be sure that something is real: *I don't believe in ghosts.*

⁺**bell** /bel/ [countable noun] **1** A device that makes a sound when you press it: *He rang the bell twice but there was no answer.* **2** A metal object that makes a sound when it is hit: *Church bells call people to Mass.*

belly /ˈbel.i/ [countable noun] The part of your body just below your chest: *Tom's dad has a really big belly.* ■ This word is informal. ■ The plural is "bellies".

belly-button [countable noun] The small hollow in the middle of the stomach where the cord attaching a baby to its mother used to be: *The girl has her belly-button pierced.* ■ This word is informal. ■ The same meaning: "navel".

⁺**belong** /bɪˈlɒŋ/ [verb] **1** To be owned by: *Those keys belong to me.* **2** To be a member of: *Her sister belongs to the Red Cross.*

belongings /bɪˈlɒŋ·ɪŋz/ [plural noun] Small things that you own: *I put all my belongings in a trunk.*

below[1] /bɪˈləʊ/ [adverb] To a lower level: *In winter the temperature often goes twenty Fahrenheit degrees.*

⁺**below**[2] /bɪˈləʊ/ [preposition] Lower than: *Yesterday the temperature was five degrees below zero.*

⁺**belt** /belt/ [countable noun] **1** A piece of leather or other material that goes round your body at your waist: *You need to tighten your belt or your pants will fall down.* 👁 See picture at **clothes**. **2** safety belt See **safety belt**.

bench /bentʃ/ [countable noun] A long seat, for example in a park: *Let's sit on this bench for a minute.* ■ The plural is "benches".

bend[1] /bend/ [countable noun] A curve: *Mountain roads often have very sharp bends.*

bend[2], bent, bent /bend/ [verb] To curve: *That iron bar will never bend.*

▸ **PHRASAL VERBS** · **to bend down** To move down the top of your body: *She bent down to take her shoes off.*

⁺**beneath** /bɪˈniːθ/ [preposition] Under: *They sat beneath the apple tree and read poetry.*

beneficial /ˌben.ɪˈfɪʃ.ᵊl/ [adjective] Helpful: *Rain forests are beneficial to the environment.*

⁺**benefit**[1] /ˈbenɪfɪt/ [noun] A profit, an advantage: *The new conditions will be to everyone's benefit.*

benefit[2] /ˈbenɪfɪt/ [verb] To get an advantage: *Unemployed people will benefit from the new laws.*

bent /bent/ Past tense and past participle forms of **bend**[2].

beret US: /bəˈreɪ/ UK: /ˈber.eɪ/ [countable noun] A round cloth cap: *Soldiers often wear berets.* 👁 See picture at **hat**.

Bermuda shorts or **Bermudas** [plural noun] A pair of shorts that go to the knees: *Where are my Bermuda shorts? I'm going to the beach.* ■ Be careful! "Bermuda shorts" and "Bermudas" have a capital "B".

berry /ˈber.i/ [countable noun] A small fruit with seeds: *Strawberries and blackberries are kinds of berries.* ■ The plural is "berries".

⁺**beside** /bɪˈsaɪd/ [preposition] At the side of: *My grandparents used to live beside the sea.*

besides[1] /bɪˈsaɪdz/ [preposition] In addition to: *Besides your sister, who else is with you in the photo?*

besides[2] /bɪˈsaɪdz/ [adverb] Also: *I didn't like the movie; besides, it was too long.*

⁺**best**[1] /best/ [noun and adjective] **1** The superlative form of **good**[1]. **2** all the best Words you use when you say goodbye: *I'll see you after the vacation; all the best.* **3** best wishes Words you write at the end of an informal letter: *I look forward to hearing from you, best wishes, Hugh.* **4** do your best To do as well as you can: *I know the test is very difficult but just do your best.*

⁺**best**[2] /best/ [adverb] The superlative form of **well**[2].

best man [noun] The man who helps the bridegroom at a wedding: *George is going to be best man at his brother's wedding.*

bestseller /ˌbestˈselər/ [noun] A book that sells a large number of copies: *"Peter Pan" has been a bestseller for many years.*

⁺**bet**[1] /bet/ [countable noun] An agreement to risk money: *Let's make a bet on the result of the Cup final.*

bet[2], bet, bet /bet/ [verb] **1** To risk money on a race and so on: *He's always betting money on horses.* **2** I bet I am sure: *I bet you'll get lost if you go without a map.* ■ Be careful with the spelling of this form: "betting".

betray /bɪˈtreɪ/ [verb] To be disloyal, to aid an enemy: *Judas betrayed Jesus Christ for thirty silver coins.*

⁺**better**[1] /ˈbet̬·ər/ [adjective] The comparative form of **good**[1].

⁺**better**[2] /ˈbet̬·ər/ [adverb] **1** The comparative form of **well**[2]. **2** had better Should, ought to: *You'd better tell him what's happening.*

⁺**between** /bɪˈtwiːn/ [preposition] **1** In the middle of two people or things: *She always sits between Paul and me.* **2** To and from two places: *There's a ferry* *between Staten Island and Manhattan.* **3** More than one thing but less than another: *The tickets will cost between ten and fifteen dollars.* **4** After one time and before another time: *It rained between 4 and 6 this morning.* **5** Shared or divided in two: *We paid the bill between us last night.* 👁 See pictures at **among** and **preposition.**

beware /bɪˈweər/ [verb] To be careful: *Beware of the dog!* ■ Be careful. We always say: "beware **of** (something)".

beyond[1] /biˈjɒnd/ [preposition] On the other side of something: *The bakery is beyond the bookstore.*

beyond[2] /biˈjɒnd/ [adverb] Further than something: *The Duke owned the land as far as those hills and even beyond.*

Bible /ˈbaɪ.bl̩/ [noun] The sacred book of Christians and Jews: *In the Christian Church, the Bible consists of the Old Testament and the New Testament.* ■ Be careful. "Bible" has a capital "B".

bicarbonate [uncountable noun] An acid salt used as an antacid or for baking: *He relieves his stomach-ache with a spoonful of bicarbonate.*

biceps /ˈbaɪ.seps/ [countable noun] The muscle which bends the elbow: *The biceps have grown stronger with exercise.* ■ The plural is also "biceps". 👁 **See page 423.**

*__bicycle__ /ˈbaɪ.sɪ.kl̩/ [countable noun] A vehicle with two wheels and pedals: *David could ride a bicycle when he was four.* 👁 **See page 441.**

*__bid__[1] /bɪd/ [countable noun] An offer of money to buy something: *Portland Timbers made a high bid for a Dutch international player.*

bid[2]**,** bade, bid /bɪd/ [verb] To offer money to buy something: *The company bid one million dollars for the building.* ■ Be careful with the spelling of this form: "bidding".

*__big__ /bɪg/ [adjective] Large or important: *An elephant is big, a mouse is small.* ■ The comparative form is "bigger" and the superlative form is "biggest". 👁 See pictures at **opposite** and **a piece of...**

big toe [countable noun] The largest toe on the foot: *Be careful! You have just stepped on my big toe.*

*__bikini__ /bɪˈkiː.ni/ [countable noun] Swimming costume in two pieces, for women: *I bought a great bikini yesterday.* 👁 See picture at **clothes.**

bile /baɪl/ [countable noun] A bitter, alkaline fluid which aids digestion: *The liver secretes bile.*

bilingual /baɪˈlɪŋ.gwəl/ [adjective] **1** Able to speak two languages fluently: *John is bilingual in Spanish and English.* **2** Spoken or written in two languages: *Use this bilingual dictionary to do your translation.*

*__bill__ /bɪl/ [countable noun] **1** A piece of paper showing how much money somebody must pay in a restaurant: *Tell the waiter to bring the bill.* ■ The same meaning: "check[1]". **2** A piece of paper showing how much money somebody must pay for services and so on: *The phone bill was very high this month.* **3** A piece of paper money: *Can you change this 50 dollar bill?*

BILL

billfold US: /ˈbɪlfəʊld/ [noun] A small container, often made of leather, for holding bills or other documents: *The pickpocket got away with my billfold.* ■ The same meaning: "wallet".

billiards US: /ˈbɪl.jɚdz/ UK: /ˈbɪl.i.ədz/ [uncountable noun] A game in which balls are hit by sticks across a table: *Are you good at billiards?* ■ This word is singular. ■ The same meaning: "pool".

billion /ˈbɪl.jən/ [noun] A thousand million: *In figures, one billion is written 1,000,000,000.* ■ In the past this word was used to mean one million million. Compare with "trillion" (one million million).

*__bin__ /bɪn/ [countable noun] A container for garbage: *Put this soup tin in the bin, please.*

binary /ˈbaɪnəri/ [adjective] Consisting of two elements: *A binary code alternates 0 and 1.*

bind, bound, bound /baɪnd/ [verb] To tie something with rope or string: *They bound the luggage together before putting it on top of the bus.*

binder /ˈbaɪn·dər/ [countable noun] A cover for holding paper, magazines and so on: *Nelly keeps all her notes in a binder.*

binding /ˈbaɪn.dɪŋ/ [countable noun] The cover of a book: *I really like the binding of this dictionary.*

bingo /ˈbɪŋ·goʊ/ [uncountable noun] A game played by covering numbers on a card: *Ron goes to play bingo every week.*

binoculars /bəˈnɑk·jə·lərz/, /baɪ-/ [plural noun] Double glasses for seeing long distances: *I like watching birds through my binoculars.*

biography /baɪˈɑg·rə·fi/ [countable noun] The written story of a person's life: *She's working on a biography of President Abraham Lincoln.* ■ The plural is "biographies".

a b c d e f g h i j k l m n o p q r s t u v w x y z

biological [adjective] Referring to the scientific study of living things: *He works in a biological paper about genetic diseases.*

biologist /baɪˈɑl·ə·dʒɪst/ [countable noun] A person who studies biology: *Linnaeus was a famous biologist of the eighteenth century.*

✦**biology** /baɪˈɑl·ə·dʒi/ [uncountable noun] The science of living things: *We're studying underwater plants in Biology at the moment.* ■ Be careful with the pronunciation of this word! "Bi" rhymes with "my".

biomass /ˈbaɪ·oʊ,mæs/ [countable noun] The total quantity of living material in a given ecosystem: *Biomass may be converted into energy.*

✦**bird** US: /bɝːd/ UK: /bɜːd/ [countable noun] An animal with wings and feathers: *Birds lay eggs in nests.* 👁 See pages 426 and 429.

biro UK: /ˈbaɪərəʊ/ [noun] See **ballpoint**. ■ This word is British English.

✦**birth** US: /bɝːθ/ UK: /bɜːθ/ [noun] **1** The act of being born: *Mr. and Mrs. Davies flew back to Denver for the birth of their grandson.* **2 to give birth to (somebody)** To have a baby: *She gave birth to twins.*

✦**birthday** /ˈbɜrθ,deɪ/ [countable noun] **1** The anniversary of the day when somebody was born: *Fran gave me a wallet for my birthday.* **2 Happy Birthday!** Greetings said on a birthday: *In her telegram Laura wished me Happy Birthday.* ■ Be careful. "Happy Birthday" has capital letters.

biscuit /ˈbɪs.kɪt/ [countable noun] See **cookie**. ■ Be careful with the pronunciation of this word. The ending "cuit" is pronounced the same as the word "kit". ■ This word is British English.

bishop /ˈbɪʃ.əp/ [countable noun] **1** An important priest: *Several bishops will meet the Pope at the airport.* **2** A chess piece: *Bishops move diagonally.* 👁 See picture at **chess**.

✦**bit**[1] /bɪt/ [countable noun] **1** A small piece of something: *Last night she only ate some bread and a bit of cheese.* **2** A small amount of something: *We were in New York City doing a bit of shopping on Friday.*

bit[2] /bɪt/ Past tense of **bite**[2].

bitch /bɪtʃ/ [countable noun] A female dog: *"What sex is your dog?" It's a bitch.*

bite[1] /baɪt/ [countable noun] **1** A wound that is made by biting: *His hands are covered with insect bites.* **2** A mouthful: *I took a big bite of cake.*

✦**bite**[2], **bit, bitten** /baɪt/ [verb] **1** To cut something with your teeth: *A small dog bit him on the ankle yesterday.* **2** To sting: *Mosquitoes bit her face and arms during the night.*

bitten /ˈbɪt.ən/ Past participle of **bite**.

✦**bitter**[1] /ˈbɪtər/ [adjective] **1** With a hard taste, that can be unpleasant: *Black coffee without sugar tastes bitter.* **2** With resentment, angry: *He feels very bitter about how he was treated.* **3** Very cold: *A bitter wind from the North is affecting most of the country.*

bitter[2] US: /ˈbɪt̬.ɚ/ UK: /ˈbɪt.əʳ/ [uncountable noun] A brown beer: *Another pint of bitter, please.*

bivalve /ˈbaɪ.vælv/ [countable noun] Mollusk with a double shell: *A bivalve has two parallel bodies enclosed in joined shells.*

bizarre /bɪˈzɑr/ [adjective] Very strange: *His bizarre clothing amuses everyone.*

✦**black**[1] /blæk/ [noun and adjective] The opposite of white: *Black is the color of night.*

black[2] /blæk/ [adjective] **1** Who has a dark skin: *Many black people in the United States now prefer to be called Afroamericans.* **2** Without milk, when you are talking about tea or coffee: *I can't drink black coffee; it's too strong for me.* **3** Bad: *Accidents often make Sundays a black day on the roads.* **4 in black and white** Containing only black and white colors: *We saw an old movie in black and white on the television last night.*

blackberry /ˈblæk.bər.i/ US: /-ber-/ [countable noun] A small black fruit that grows on a bush: *You'll get sick if you eat too many blackberries.* ■ The plural is "blackberries".

blackbird /ˈblæk.bɜːd/ US: /-bɝːd/ [countable noun] A small black bird: *Blackbirds eat insects and seeds.*

blackboard /ˈblæk,bɔrd/, /-,boʊrd/ [countable noun] A board with a black surface on which you write with chalk: *The teacher wrote the instructions on the blackboard.* ■ Compare with "whiteboard" (a board on which you write with a special marker). 👁 See picture at **classroom**.

blackcurrant /,blækˈkʌr.ənt/ US: /ˈblæk.kɝː-/ [countable noun] A very small, round black fruit with a sharp taste: *I had some bread and blackcurrant jam for breakfast this morning.*

black eye [countable noun] A dark mark around your eye caused by a blow: *Did you get that black eye in a fight?*

black magic [uncountable noun] Magic that is used in a bad way: *Some people believe that you can actually kill people using black magic.*

blackmail /ˈblæk.meɪl/ [verb] To get money from somebody by telling them you will tell their secrets if they don't pay you: *The banker was blackmailed by the Mafia.*

blackout [countable noun] Lack of illumination caused by an electrical power failure: *A blackout in the building caused the elevator to stop abruptly.*

blacksmith [countable noun] Somebody who works with iron: *The number of blacksmithers is much smaller now.*

bladder /'blædər/ [countable noun] A membrane sac in the body which contains urine: *Urine is produced by the kidneys and held in the bladder.* 👁 **See page 424.**

†**blade** /bleɪd/ [countable noun] The cutting part of an instrument: *Careful! That knife has a very sharp blade.*

†**blame** /bleɪm/ [verb] To feel and to say that somebody is responsible for something bad: *Nobody can blame Jenny for the accident.*

bland /blænd/ [adjective] With very little taste: *I think the soup's too bland.*

blank[1] /blæŋk/ [adjective] **1** With nothing written or drawn on it: *You must fill in the blank spaces on the form.* **2** Empty, without expression: *You look blank; is there something you don't understand?*

blank[2] /blæŋk/ [countable noun] An empty space: *Fill in the blanks in the following exercise.*

blanket /'blæŋ.kɪt/ [countable noun] A thick covering used on a bed: *She needs two blankets to keep warm at night.* 👁 See picture at **bedroom**.

blast US: /blæst/ UK: /blɑːst/ [countable noun] **1** A sudden movement of air: *The blast of wind made the doors bang.* **2** An explosion: *How many people were hurt in the blast?*

blast-off US: /'blæst.ɑːf/ UK: /'blɑːst.ɒf/ [uncountable noun] The moment when a spacecraft leaves the ground: *Ten, nine, eight... two, one, blast-off!*

blaze[1] /bleɪz/ [countable noun] A large and dangerous fire: *The blaze quickly destroyed the building.*

blaze[2] /bleɪz/ [verb] To burn strongly: *The logs blazed in the fireplace.*

blazer /'bleɪ·zər/ [countable noun] A formal jacket: *Our school blazer is navy blue with the school badge on the pocket.*

bleach[1] /bliːtʃ/ [uncountable noun] Substance which takes the color out of something: *Put some bleach in the water when you are washing white sheets.*

bleach[2] /bliːtʃ/ [verb] **1** To make something clean or white: *I bleached the sheets yesterday morning.* **2** To make something white or pale: *The sun bleached her hair last summer.*

bleak /bliːk/ [adjective] Cold, unpleasant: *The weather's very bleak up here in the mountains.*

bleat /bliːt/ [verb] To make the sound that sheep make: *I can hear the sheep bleating in the barn.* 👁 See picture at **animal**.

bled /bled/ Past tense and past participle forms of **bleed**.

bleed, bled, bled /bliːd/ [verb] To lose blood: *Her hand is still bleeding from the dog's bite.*

blend[1] /blend/ [countable noun] A mixture: *My grandma's favorite blend of coffee is ice coffee.*

blend[2] /bliːd/ [verb] **1** To mix: *Blend the sugar and butter together before adding the flour.* **2** To go well together: *The flute and the violin blend beautifully in that piece of music.*

blender /'blen·dər/ [countable noun] A small electric machine used for making solid foods into liquid: *I used the blender to make some fresh apple juice.*

bless /bles/ [verb] **1** To ask for God's protection: *The bishop's going to bless our new chapel.* **2 bless you** Words you say when somebody has sneezed: *"Bless you!" said my grandfather.* ■ Be careful with the spelling of the 3rd person singular present tense form: "blesses". ■ "Bless" also has regular past and past participle forms: "blessed".

blew /bluː/ Past tense of **blow**[2].

†**blind**[1] /blaɪnd/ [adjective] Not able to see: *His aunt has been blind since birth.*

blind[2] /blaɪnd/ [countable noun] The covering over a window: *If we pull the blinds down, we'll keep the light out.*

blindfold /'blaɪnd,fould/ [verb] To cover somebody's eyes with cloth: *Wendy was blindfolded by the pirates.*

blink /blɪŋk/ [verb] To close and open your eyes quickly: *The morning sunshine makes me blink.*

blister /'blɪs·tər/ [countable noun] A swelling under the skin with water underneath: *My new shoes are giving me blisters on my feet.*

blizzard /'blɪz·ərd/ [countable noun] A bad storm with strong winds and snow or sand: *Blizzards are very dangerous for car drivers.*

†**block**[1] /blɒk/ [countable noun] **1** A large piece of something solid: *The monument is made of blocks of stone.* 👁 See picture at **a piece of...** **2** A group of buildings: *Her office is only two blocks away.* 👁 See picture at **house**. **3 block capitals** or **block letters** Letters written in their big form: *Write your name in block capitals, please.*

block[2] /blɒk/ [verb] To stop somebody or something from going forward: *The truck crashed into a tree and blocked the road.*

†**blond** [adjective] Having hair that is yellow in color: *Tim is a tall boy with blond hair.*

†**blonde** US: /blɑːnd/ UK: /blɒnd/ [noun and adjective] Referring to females, having hair that is yellow in color: *Angela has dyed her hair blonde.*

†**blood** /blʌd/ [uncountable noun] The red liquid inside people's bodies: *After he fell in the playground, his knees were covered with blood.* ■ Be careful with the pronunciation of this word. The vowel sound here is pronounced the same as in "sun".

bloodstream /'blʌd.striːm/ [noun] The flow of blood round the body: *She's got a bad infection of the bloodstream.* ■ Be careful with the pronunciation of this word. The vowel sound in "blood" is pronounced the same as in "sun".

blood vessel [countable noun] Any of the tubes that transport blood through the body tissues and organs: *There are three types of blood vessels: arteries, capillaries and veins.*

bloody /ˈblʌd.i/ [adjective] **1** With a lot of blood on it: *Craig had a very bloody nose after the fight.* **2** With much violence: *The battle was very bloody.* **3** A word used for giving force to what you say: *You're a bloody liar!* ■ In this use "bloody" is a swear word. ■ Be careful with the pronunciation of this word. The vowel sound here is pronounced the same as in "sun". ■ The comparative form is "bloodier" and the superlative form is "bloodiest".

bloom /bluːm/ [verb] To have flowers: *Monica's rose trees bloom twice a year.*

blossom US: /ˈblɑː.sᵊm/ UK: /ˈblɒs.ᵊm/ [verb] To have flowers: *The roses are blossoming earlier this year.*

blot /blɒt/ [countable noun] The result of spilling ink: *The paper had a single blot at the top.*

blouse US: /blaʊs/ UK: /blaʊz/ [countable noun] A woman's shirt: *That belt doesn't go very well with your blouse.*

blow[1] US: /bloʊ/ UK: /bləʊ/ [countable noun] A hard stroke: *The blow made him fall off the bike.*

↑**blow[2], blew, blown** US: /bloʊ/ UK: /bləʊ/ [verb] **1** To send air out of your mouth: *He took a deep breath and blew as hard as he could.* **2** To move in the wind: *Be careful! The wind will blow your cap away.* **3 to blow your nose** To clean your nose by blowing it into a handkerchief: *Take a handkerchief and blow your nose.*
▶ **PHRASAL VERBS** · **to blow down** To fall down because of the wind: *The trees were blown down by the strong winds.* · **to blow (something) out** To stop something burning by blowing on it: *Blow out the candles on your birthday cake.* · **to blow (something) up 1** To destroy in an explosion: *The terrorist group has blown the bridge up.* **2** To fill something with air: *Will you help me blow these balloons up?*

blowhole US: /ˈbloʊ.hoʊl/ UK: /ˈbləʊ.həʊl/ [countable noun] An opening used for breathing: *Whales have a blowhole on the top of their head.*

blown US: /bloʊn/ UK: /bləʊn/ Past participle of **blow[2]**.

↑**blue** /bluː/ [noun and adjective] The color of the sky on a fine day: *I like your new blue jeans.*

blueish [adjective] See **bluish**.

bluff[1] /blʌf/ [countable noun] An attempt to deceive somebody: *We all thought it was a bluff, but when he showed his cards they were excellent.*

bluff[2] /blʌf/ [verb] To pretend, to attempt to deceive somebody: *You don't really know how to repair computers; you're just bluffing.*

bluish [adjective] Slightly blue: *My new dress is bluish-grey.*

blunt /blʌnt/ [adjective] **1** Not sharp: *That knife is so blunt that it can't cut anything.* **2** Direct, not polite: *Don't ask him such blunt questions.*

blur US: /blɝː/ UK: /blɜːʳ/ [verb] To make something difficult to see: *Tears blurred my eyes.* ■ Be careful with the spelling of these forms: "blurred", "blurring".

blurry [adjective] Difficult to see clearly: *The photo was blurry.*

blush /blʌʃ/ [verb] To become red in the face because of embarrassment: *He couldn't help blushing at her compliments.*

boar US: /bɔːr/ UK: /bɔːʳ/ [countable noun] **1** A male pig used for breeding: *Tina's uncle has a boar on the farm.* **2** A wild pig: *The boar ran into the forest.*

↑**board[1]** /bɔːd/ ▮ [countable noun] **1** A long, thin piece of wood: *We need some boards to repair the shelves.* **2** A flat surface on which somebody writes: *They've put the prices up on the board.* **3** A flat, thin piece of wood, cardboard or other material that is used for a particular purpose: *In this game you throw a dice to move around the board.* ▮ [noun] **4** A group of people who run a company: *The board of directors will discuss the problem at tomorrow's meeting.* ■ Be careful with the pronunciation of this word! The "a" is not pronounced.

board[2] /bɔːd/ [verb] **1** To get on a plane, train or ship: *The passengers had to wait two hours to board the Airbus.* **2 on board** On a plane, train or ship: *Look! Jack's already on board the train.* ■ Be careful. In this use we say: "on board the ship". We don't say: "on board **of** the ship".

board game [countable noun] A game played on a square board: *Chess and checkers are popular board games.*

BOARD GAME

boarding card [countable noun] See **boarding pass.** ■ This word is British English.

boarding pass [countable noun] A card that passengers show before getting on a plane: *You must show* *your boarding pass at Gate Five.* ■ In British English they say "boarding card".

boarding school [countable noun] A school where students live while they are studying: *Clive's parents sent him to an expensive boarding school when he was fourteen.*

boast US: /boʊst/ UK: /bəʊst/ [verb] To talk about something with exaggerated pride: *She never boasts about her family even though they're all wonderful musicians.*

boastful /ˈboʊst·fəl/ [adjective] Expressing too much pride in things you have done or in yourself: *Tom's very boastful; he's always talking about the new motorcycle he's bought.*

↑**boat** US: /boʊt/ UK: /bəʊt/ [countable noun] **1** A vehicle used on water, particularly a small one: *We always rent a sailing boat for the summer.* **2** **power boat** See **power boat.** ■ Be careful with the pronunciation of this word! "boa" rhymes with "go". ■ A "boat" is usually smaller than a "ship" or travels shorter distances. Sometimes however in spoken English, "boat" is used for a big ship.

↑**body** US: /ˈbɑː.di/ UK: /ˈbɒd.i/ [countable noun] **1** All the physical parts of a person or an animal: *We're studying the human body in Biology.* **2** A dead person: *The police found the body in a van.* **3** The main part of a person or an animal: *He got a wound in his leg and two more in his body.* ■ The plural is "bodies". 👁 **See page 421.**

bodyguard US: /ˈbɑː.di.gɑːrd/ UK: /ˈbɒd.i.gɑːd/ [countable noun] Somebody who goes with and protects an important person: *The President has a lot of bodyguards.*

body piercing [noun] See **piercing.**

↑**boil** /bɔɪl/ [verb] **1** To heat a liquid until it becomes steam: *Water boils at 100 ºC.* **2** To cook something in very hot water: *Boil this egg for four minutes.*

▶ **PHRASAL VERBS** · **to boil over** Referring to a liquid, to rise and go out of the container: *Careful! The milk's boiling over.* 👁 See picture at **cook.**

boiling point [countable noun] It is the temperature at which a liquid becomes a gas: *The boiling point of water is 100ºC.*

bold /bəʊld/ [adjective] Brave, confident, not afraid: *I am Sir Brian, as bold as a lion.*

Bolivian[1] [adjective] Referring to Bolivia: *Cochabamba is a Bolivian city.* ■ Be careful! "Bolivian" has a capital "B".

Bolivian[2] [countable noun] A person from Bolivia: *My aunt is a Bolivian.* ■ Be careful! "Bolivian" has a capital "B".

bolt US: /boʊlt/ UK: /bəʊlt/ [countable noun] **1** A metal bar used for keeping a door closed: *We've put a bolt on the back door.* **2** A screw that is used with a metal ring to hold things together: *We fixed the two boards together with nuts and bolts.*

↑**bomb**[1] US: /bɑːm/ UK: /bɒm/ [countable noun] A metal container filled with explosives: *Fortunately, nobody was injured when the bomb went off.* ■ Be careful with the pronunciation of this word! The "b" is silent.

bomb[2] /bɒm/ [verb] To attack a place with bombs: *London was bombed during the Second World War.*

↑**bone** US: /boʊn/ UK: /bəʊn/ [noun] **1** One of the hard parts of a person's body: *Lynn's broken a bone in her arm.* **2** One of the hard parts of an animal's body: *I can't eat this fish, it's got too many bones.*

bonfire US: /ˈbɑːn.faɪr/ UK: /ˈbɒn.faɪəʳ/ [countable noun] An open air fire: *Bonfires are forbidden in clean air zones.*

bonnet US: /ˈbɑː.nɪt/ UK: /ˈbɒn.ɪt/ [countable noun] **1** A small round hat for babies: *That baby's wearing a lovely bonnet.* **2** See **hood.** ■ This use is British English.

bonus /ˈboʊ·nəs/ [countable noun] Extra money: *We're getting a bonus at Christmas.* ■ The plural is "bonuses".

bony /ˈboʊ·ni/ [adjective] Extremely thin: *My grandfather has long bony fingers.*

boo /buː/ [verb] To make a sound because you don't like something: *The spectators booed the basketball players after they lost by twenty points.*

boob tube [noun] See **television.** ■ This word is informal.

↑**book**[1] /bʊk/ [countable noun] A set of pages fastened together for reading: *What's your favorite book?* 👁 See picture at **classroom.**

book[2] /bʊk/ [verb] To reserve a seat, a table and so on: *Have you booked the airplane tickets for our trip yet?*

a b c d e f g h i j k l m n o p q r s t u v w x y z

bookcase /ˈbʊk.keɪs/ [countable noun] A piece of furniture with shelves for books: *This bookcase is full of interesting books.* 👁 See picture at **living room**.

booking /ˈbʊk.ɪŋ/ [noun] A reservation of seats, places and so on: *We'll make the bookings for the concert tomorrow.*

bookshelf /ˈbʊk.ʃelf/ [countable noun] A shelf for books: *Could you please put this book back on the bookshelf?* ■ The plural is "bookshelves". 👁 See picture at **classroom**.

bookshop /ˈbʊkʃɒp/ [countable noun] See **bookstore**. ■ This word is British English.

bookstore [countable noun] A shop where books are sold: *I bought this paperback at the new bookstore.* ■ Compare with "library" (a place where you can read and borrow books). ■ In British English they say "bookshop".

boom /buːm/ [verb] To make a loud, deep sound: *The principal's voice boomed across the hall: "Why are you late?".*

booster /ˈbuːstər/ [countable noun] **1** The increase in power or strength given by additional resources: *The international assistance was a morale booster for the soldiers.* **2** The extra amount of vaccine or drug given to increase or renew the effect: *The resistance to this illness is increased by a booster.*

↑**boot** /buːt/ [countable noun] **1** A strong shoe that covers the ankle: *Please don't take your boots off in the dining room.* 👁 See picture at **clothes**. **2** See **trunk**. ■ This use is British English.

↑**border** US: /ˈbɔːr.dɚ/ UK: /bɔː.dəʳ/ [countable noun] **1** A line between two countries, provinces and so on: *They live near the border between the United States and Mexico.* **2** An edge: *That tablecloth has a beautiful, colored border.*

↑**bore¹** /bɔːr/ [countable noun] An uninteresting person or thing: *She's a bore; her conversation is always about what she saw on television last night.*

bore² /bɔːr/ [verb] To make somebody feel tired and uncomfortable: *Watching TV all evening really bores me.*

bore³ Past tense of **bear²**.

↑**bored** US: /bɔːrd/ UK: /bɔːd/ [adjective] Tired, not interested: *I'm bored of his jokes; they're always the same.* ■ Be careful with the pronunciation of the end of this word. The "e" is not pronounced. ■ Compare with "boring" (that makes you feel bored). ■ See box on the following page. 👁 See picture at **emotions**.

↑**boring** US: /ˈbɔːr.ɪŋ/ UK: /ˈbɔː.rɪŋ/ [adjective] Something that makes you bored: *The game we saw on Saturday was very boring.* ■ Compare with "bored" (that feels bored). ■ See box on the following page.

↑**born** /bɔːn/ **1** Past participle of **bear**. **2 to be born** To come into the world: *Tom was born in Greenfield, Indiana in 1985.* ■ See box at **abbreviations**.

borne US: /bɔːrn/ UK: /bɔːn/ Past participle of **bear**.

↑**borrow** US: /ˈbɑː.roʊ/ UK: /ˈbɒr.əʊ/ [verb] To take or to use something belonging to somebody else for some time: *Can I borrow your car tonight, mom?* ■ Compare with "lend" (to let somebody use something that you own).

↑**boss** US: /bɑːs/ UK: /bɒs/ [countable noun] A person who is in charge of others: *I'll ask the boss if we can go on vacation next week.* ■ The plural is "bosses".

bossy US: /ˈbɑː.si/ UK: /ˈbɒs.i/ [adjective] Who is always giving orders: *Your sister is rather bossy.* ■ The comparative form is "bossier" and the superlative form is "bossiest".

botanical /bəˈtænɪkəl/ [adjective] Referring to botany: *The plants they found were separated into botanical groups.*

botany /ˈbɑt·ə·n·i/ [uncountable noun] The study of plants: *Botany is a branch of biology.*

↑**both** US: /boʊθ/ UK: /bəʊθ/ [adjective and pronoun] **1** The two together: *They both like cooking.* ■ "Both" usually goes before ordinary verbs: "They both like tennis". It goes after auxiliary verbs: "They can both cook". **2 both... and...** At the same time: *Both Canada and United States are in North America.*

bother¹ /ˈbɒðər/ [uncountable noun] Trouble, worry: *The baby never gives me any bother.*

bother² /ˈbɒðər/ [verb] **1** To give trouble: *Don't bother me with silly questions.* **2** To take trouble: *She never bothers to take her medicine.* **3 can't be bothered** Not wanting to try: *I can't be bothered to do the dishes now.*

↑**bottle¹** US: /ˈbɑː.t̬l̩/ UK: /ˈbɒt.l̩/ [countable noun] A glass or a plastic container for liquids: *There are some bottles of lemonade in the fridge.*

bottle² /ˈbɒtl/ [verb] To put into bottles: *This wine was bottled in 1970.*

↑**bottom¹** US: /ˌbɑː.t̬əm/ UK: /ˌbɒt.əm/ [countable noun] **1** The lowest part of anything: *Something has fallen to the bottom of the swimming pool.* **2** The part of the body that is used for sitting: *I fell and hurt my bottom.*

bottom² /ˈbɒtəm/ [adjective] Lowest, last: *Her boyfriend's sitting in the bottom row.*

bought US: /bɑːt/ UK: /bɔːt/ Past tense and past participle forms of **buy**. ■ Be careful with the pronunciation of this word. It rhymes with "fort".

bounce /baʊnts/ [verb] To make something come back by throwing it: *The neighbor often bounces his ball against my wall.*

bound¹ /baʊnd/ [adjective] **1** Obliged: *He is bound by the rules to attend the meeting.* **2** Certain, very likely: *That team can't possibly win; you're bound to lose your bet.* **3** Intending to go: *This class is* *designed for college bound students.* ■ Be careful. We say: "to be bound to (do something)".

bound[2] /baʊnd/ Past tense and past participle forms of **bind**.

boundary /ˈbaʊn.dᵊr.i/ [countable noun] A line that divides one area from another: *They've moved the town boundary to include the old cottages.* ■ The plural is "boundaries".

bouquet /bʊˈkeɪ/ [countable noun] A bunch of flowers that is arranged in an attractive way: *The singer received a bouquet of roses.*

bourgeois /ˈbʊər·ʒwɑ/, /bʊərˈʒwɑ/ [adjective] Referring to the middle class: *During the recent centuries, bourgeois citizens form a social class characterized by their possession of capital and their related culture.*

bourgeoisie /ˌbʊər·ʒwɑˈzi/ [uncountable noun] The social class which has economic power in a capitalist society: *The bourgeoisie holds the reins of society.*

boutique /buːˈtiːk/ [countable noun] A small store that sells fashionable things: *Jane buys her dresses in a boutique.*

bow[1] /baʊ/ [countable noun] **1** A weapon made of wood and string: *In the Middle Ages soldiers fought with bows and arrows.* 👁 See picture at **arrow**. **2** A knot used for decorations and for tying your shoes: *She tied a bow in her hair.*

bow[2] /baʊ/ [verb] To bend the head or the body to show respect: *Everyone bows to the king and the queen.*

bowel /baʊəl/ [countable noun] The lower part of the alimentary canal: *The bowel is found below the stomach.*

bowl US: /boʊl/ UK: /bəʊl/ [countable noun] A round, plastic or wooden container: *Give the cat a bowl of milk.* 👁 See picture at **plate**.

bowling /ˈboʊ·lɪŋ/ [uncountable noun] **1** A game in which balls are rolled: *Bowling is my favorite pastime.* **2 bowling alley** A building with tracks for bowling: *We meet our friends at the bowling alley.*

box[1] /bɒks/ [countable noun] **1** A square or rectangular container with a lid: *There's a box of matches on the shelf over there.* 👁 See picture at **container**. **2** A small balcony room in a theater: *They gave us seats in a box so that we could see the play in comfort.* **3** An empty square or rectangle on a form in which you have to write something: *You have to write your family name in the box below.* ■ The plural is "boxes". **4 boom box** A large portable cassette player, with speakers: *Roy carries his boom box on his shoulder, playing loud reggae music.* ■ This word is informal. **5 first aid box** See "first aid box" in the word **first[2]**.

box[2] /bɒks/ [verb] To fight in a boxing ring: *Have you ever seen Mike Tyson box?*

boxer US: /ˈbɑːk.sɚ/ UK: /ˈbɒk.səʳ/ [countable noun] A man who boxes: *Muhammad Ali was a famous boxer who became world champion three times.*

boxing /ˈbɑk·sɪŋ/ [uncountable noun] A sport in which two men fight: *Boxing is fought with gloves.*

box number [countable noun] A box in the post office where somebody receives letters: *Please, reply to the box number that you'll find below.*

box office [countable noun] The place in a movie theater, theater or concert hall where tickets are bought: *I'll phone the box office to book our seats.*

boy /bɔɪ/ [countable noun] A male child or a male adolescent: *Clive used to be very fat as a boy, but now he's slim.* ■ Be careful! Many people feel it is offensive to call a man a "boy" after he has become an adult.

boyfriend /ˈbɔɪ.frend/ [countable noun] The male companion of somebody: *She's been to Hawaii with her boyfriend.*

Boy Scout [countable noun] See **Scout**. ■ Be careful! "Boy Scout" has capital letters.

bra /brɑː/ [countable noun] A piece of woman's underwear for supporting the breasts: *She took off her bra before getting into bed.*

bracelet /ˈbreɪ.slət/ [countable noun] A chain or a band that you wear on your wrist as an ornament: *Rosie wears a silver bracelet on her left wrist.* 👁 See picture at **jewelry**.

bored / boring

- There are many pairs of adjectives that end in *-ed* and *-ing*:
  - *bored*
  - *boring*
  - *interested*
  - *interesting*
  - *surprised*
  - *surprising*
  - *frightened*
  - *frightening*
  - *excited*
  - *exciting*
- The two words do not mean the same thing (if something is *-ing*, it makes you *-ed*):
  - *If a movie is **boring**, it makes you **bored**.*
  - *If a movie is **frightening**, it makes you **frightened**.*

  Examples:
  - *I am **bored**, I have nothing to do.*
  - *I don't like Pat, he's **boring**. The only thing he talks about is car racing.*
  - *Is that an **interesting** book you are reading?*
  - *Are you **excited** about your trip to New York?*

braces /'breɪ.sɪz/ [plural noun] **1** Orthodontic treatment with wire and small metallic or porcelain pieces over the teeth to correct and straighten them: *After they took off his braces, he had a perfect smile.* **2** See **suspenders.** ■ This use is British English.

brackets /'brækɪts/ [plural noun] A pair of marks like these ( ), used in writing: *This (word) is written in brackets.*

brag /bræg/ [verb] To boast: *Stop bragging about how clever you are.* ■ Be careful with the spelling of these forms: "bragged", "bragging".

braid /breɪd/ [countable noun] Hair which is intertwined: *Braids are an important part of afro-hairstyles.* 👁 See picture at **hair.**

Braille /breɪl/ [uncountable noun] Special printing for blind people: *Blind people read Braille by touching raised dots with their fingers.* ■ Be careful. "Braille" has a capital "B".

+**brain** /breɪn/ [countable noun] The part inside the head that thinks and feels: *The brain controls all your body's movements.*

brainstem [countable noun] The brain's central trunk which continues to form the spinal cord: *The cerebrum and the cerebellum are set on the brainstem.*

brainy /'breɪ.ni/ [adjective] Intelligent, especially at school work: *His sister gets good grades because she's quite brainy.* ■ The comparative form is "brainier" and the superlative form is "brainiest".

brake[1] /breɪk/ [countable noun] A device for stopping a vehicle: *You need to use your brakes when you take this curve.* 👁 **See page 441.**

brake[2] /breɪk/ [verb] To stop a vehicle by putting on the brakes: *Ralph braked quickly when his tire burst.*

+**branch** US: /bræntʃ/ UK: /brɑːntʃ/ [countable noun] **1** The part of a tree that comes out of the trunk: *The branches are full of leaves now.* 👁 **See pages 432 and 434.** **2** An office or a store that is part of a big business: *Our company has branches all over the world.*

+**brand** /brænd/ [countable noun] A product with a particular commercial name: *She's using a new brand of perfume.*

brand-new [adjective] Completely new: *Ann has a brand-new watch which she got for her birthday last week.*

brandy /'bræn.di/ [noun] A strong alcoholic drink: *Would you like a brandy after your coffee?* ■ The plural is "brandies".

brass US: /bræs/ UK: /brɑːs/ [uncountable noun] A bright yellow metal: *This store sells brass rings and bracelets.* ■ The plural is "brasses".

brass instrument [countable noun] A wind instrument which is usually made of brass: *Trumpets and trombones are brass instruments.*

+**brave** /breɪv/ [adjective] Ready to do something dangerous: *You were very brave to go into the cave on your own.*

bravery /breɪv/ [uncountable noun] The quality that allows you to do something dangerous: *The firefighters showed great bravery during the fire.*

Brazilian[1] [adjective] Referring to Brazil: *Brazilian Carnival is famous all around the world.* ■ Be careful! "Brazilian" has a capital "B".

Brazilian[2] [countable noun] A person from Brazil: *There are two Brazilians staying at our hotel.* ■ Be careful! "Brazilian" has a capital "B".

+**bread** /bred/ [uncountable noun] Food made of baked flour: *I've bought a loaf of bread for sandwiches.* ■ Be careful! We say "a piece of bread", "a slice of bread" or "a loaf of bread".

BREAD

breadth /bredθ/, /bretθ/ [uncountable noun] The distance between two sides of something: *What's the breadth of that swimming pool?*

+**break**[1] /breɪk/ [countable noun] **1** A short rest: *Let's have a break for lunch.* **2** See **recess.** ■ This use is British English. **3** An opening: *You can see their pool through a break in the wall.*

break[2], broke, broken /breɪk/ [verb] **1** To make something go into pieces: *The child's broken your key ring.* **2** To go into small pieces: *If the mirror falls it'll break.* **3** To stop something working: *You're going to break my watch.* **4** **to break the law** To do something against the law: *If you break the law you could end up in prison.*

▶ **PHRASAL VERBS** · **to break down** In machines, to stop working: *Our car broke down on the way to Paris.* · **to break (something) down** To destroy:

a b c d e f g h i j k l m n o p q r s t u v w x y z

Nobody answered the door, so the police broke it down. · **to break in** To get into a place by force: *A thief broke in and stole their television.* · **to break off** To get a piece of something by breaking it: *Can you break off another piece of bread for me?* · **to break out** To start suddenly: *Most fires here break out in summer.* · **to break out of (something)** To escape from a place: *There was a riot at the prison and twenty prisoners broke out of their cells.* · **to break up 1** To separate: *Sharon and Paul broke up two weeks ago.* **2** To come to the end of term: *When does school break up?*

breakable /ˈbreɪ.kə.bl̩/ [adjective] Easy to break: *Don't let the kid play with that glass; it's breakable.*

breakdown /ˈbreɪk.daʊn/ [countable noun] A time when a vehicle or other machine stops: *They had a breakdown on the way home.*

*breakfast** /ˈbrek.fəst/ [countable noun] The first meal of the day: *I always have breakfast in bed on Sundays.*

*breast** /brest/ [countable noun] **1** Part of a woman's body that produces milk when she has a baby: *She had her baby at her breast.* **2** The front of the top part of the body of a person or animal: *Can I have chicken breast and french fries, please?* **3 breast stroke** A style of swimming: *You do the breast stroke swimming on your front in the water.*

breastbone /ˈbrest.bəʊn/ US: /-boʊn/ [countable noun] A thin and flat bone which is in the middle of the chest: *The breastbone is connected to the ribs.* ■ The same meaning: "sternum".

*breath** /breθ/ [uncountable noun] **1** The air that goes in and out of your lungs: *After running so quickly I have no breath left.* **2 breath of fresh air** The clean air outside: *It's too hot in here; let's go out for a breath of fresh air.* **3 to hold your breath** To stop breathing for a short time: *I held my breath when the phone rang last night.* **4 out of breath** Quick, difficult breathing: *I'm still out of breath from running for the bus.*

*breathe** /briːð/ [verb] To take air in and out of your lungs: *Open the windows because nobody can breathe in here.*

breathless /ˈbreθ.ləs/ [adjective] Out of breath: *We were breathless after climbing so many stairs.*

bred /bred/ Past tense and past participle forms of **breed²**.

breed¹ /briːd/ [countable noun] A particular race of animal: *Their cows are a new breed imported from Australia.*

breed², bred, bred /briːd/ [verb] **1** To produce young animals: *Canaries breed in cages without any problem.* **2** To keep animals to make young ones: *Mike breeds rabbits as a hobby.*

breeze /briːz/ [countable noun] A light wind: *This breeze is coming from the sea.*

breve /briːv/ [countable noun] A musical note which has the time value of two semibreves: *Breves are often represented as a square.* 👁 **See page 460.**

brew /bruː/ [verb] To prepare tea or coffee: *He's brewing coffee in the kitchen.*

bribe /braɪb/ [verb] To offer money to persuade somebody to be dishonest: *They tried to bribe the journalist to stop her publishing the article.*

*brick** /brɪk/ [countable noun] A hard block used for building: *Their cottage is made of red bricks.*

BRICK

bride /braɪd/ [countable noun] A woman on her wedding day: *The bride looks very pretty in her white dress.* ■ A man on his wedding day is a "bridegroom".

bridegroom /ˈbraɪd.grʊm/, /ˈbraɪd.grʊm/ [countable noun] A man on his wedding day: *The bridegroom's wearing a top hat.* ■ "Groom" is short for "bridegroom". A woman on her wedding day is a "bride".

bridesmaid /ˈbraɪdz.meɪd/ [countable noun] A girl who helps a bride at a wedding: *The bride's sister will be one of the bridesmaids.*

*bridge** /brɪdʒ/ [countable noun] A structure that goes over a road, river and so on: *They've built a new bridge over the highway.* 👁 **See page 445.**

*brief** /briːf/ [adjective] **1** Short: *His letters are usually brief.* **2 in brief** In a few words: *In brief, what exactly happened?*

briefcase /ˈbriːf.keɪs/ [countable noun] A small case for carrying papers, books and other things, usually to work: *I've got some brochures here in my briefcase.*

brigade /brɪˈgeɪd/ [countable noun] A military formation comprising three battalions: *A brigade forms part of a division.*

*bright** /braɪt/ [adjective] **1** With a shining light: *The sun's bright and hot here in summer.* ■ Compare with "dark¹" (with very little light). **2** With a strong color: *Lisa's eyes are bright green.* **3** Clever at learning: *Mandy's a very bright kid, she already knows how to multiply.* **4** Happy, cheerful: *There's always a bright smile on his face.*

brighten /ˈbraɪ·tə·n/ [verb] To look or to feel happier than before: *Her face brightened when she saw Tom.*

brightness [uncountable noun] **1** The strength of a light: *The brightness of the car headlights illuminates the road.* ■ Compare with "darkness" (the state of being dark). **2** The strength of a color: *I like the brightness of your dark green dress.* **3** The strength of a sound: *The architectural conditions of the theater favors the brightness of sounds.*

†**brilliant** /'brɪl.i.ənt/ [adjective] **1** Very bright: *Yesterday the sky was a brilliant blue.* **2** Very intelligent: *Your sister always has some brilliant ideas.* **3** Very good: *I think that movie is brilliant.*

brim /brɪm/ [countable noun] An edge: *That glass is full to the brim with milk.*

†**bring, brought, brought** /brɪŋ/ [verb] **1** To carry something to the place where the speaker is: *Bring your books to the lessons, please.* **2** To come to a place with somebody: *Paul's bringing his sister to the party.* ◗ **PHRASAL VERBS** · **to bring (something) back 1** To return something: *When is she going to bring our car back?* **2** To make you remember: *That photo brings back memories of my school days.* · **to bring (somebody) up** To take care of a child and educate him or her: *Jane's mother died when she was little, so she was brought up by her grandparents.* · **to bring (something) up** To mention: *Don't bring politics up when my father is in the house.*

brisk /brɪsk/ [adjective] Quick, active: *We went for a brisk walk and soon warmed up.*

British /'brɪt̬·ɪʃ/ [adjective] Referring to Great Britain: *British milk tastes delicious.* ■ Be careful! "British" has a capital "B". For people, the singular is "a British man", "a British woman" or "a Briton" and the plural is "the British".

Briton /'brɪt·ə·n/ [countable noun] A person from Great Britain: *There are three Britons staying at the hotel.* ■ Careful! "Briton" has a capital "B". We usually say "British people".

broach [countable noun] An ornament that you wear on your clothes: *She's wearing a silver broach on her blouse.* 👁 See picture at **jewelry**.

†**broad** US: /brɑːd/ UK: /brɔːd/ [adjective] Wide: *The street is very broad in front of the church.*

broadcast[1] US: /'brɑːd.kæst/ UK: /'brɔːd.kɑːst/ [countable noun] A radio or a television program: *The game broadcast will be at nine o'clock.*

broadcast[2] /'brɔːdkɑːst/ [verb] To send out programs by radio or on television: *The CNN broadcasts news to many different countries.*

broccoli /'brɑ·kə·li/, /'brɑk·li/ [uncountable noun] A plant with green flower heads, eaten as a vegetable: *Do you like broccoli?* 👁 **See page 437.**

brochure US: /broʊ'ʃʊr/ UK: /'brəʊ.ʃəʳ/ [countable noun] A very thin book with advertising: *I'll get some travel brochures on skiing vacation.*

broil US: /brɔɪl/ [verb] To grill food: *She broiled the chicken.*

broke[1] /brəʊk/ **to be broke** To be without money, bankrupt: *I lent Keith some money because he was broke.* ■ This expression is informal.

broke[2] /brəʊk/ Past tense of **break**[2].

†**broken**[1] /'brəʊkən/ [adjective] **1** In pieces, damaged: *Careful! There's some broken glass on the floor.* **2** Not working: *This calculator must be broken again.*

broken[2] /'brəʊkən/ Past participle of **break**[2].

bronchial /'brɒŋ.ki.əl/ US: /'brɑːŋ-/ [adjective] Referring to the bronchi: *Bronchial asthma provokes coughing and shortness of breadth.*

bronchitis US: /brɑːŋ'kaɪ.t̬ɪs/ UK: /brɒŋ'kaɪ.tɪs/ [uncountable noun] Swelling affecting the lungs: *Bronchitis left her feeling very weak.*

bronchus /'brɒŋ.kəs/ US: /'brɑːŋ-/ [uncountable noun] The tube that conducts air into the lungs: *Oxygen reaches the lungs through the trachea and then the two bronchi.* ■ The plural is "bronchi". 👁 **See page 425.**

bronze US: /brɑːnz/ UK: /brɒnz/ [uncountable noun] A hard, brown metal: *Church bells are made of bronze.*

broom /bruːm/, /brʊm/ [countable noun] A brush with a long handle: *Take this broom and sweep the floor, please.*

broomstick /'bruːm.stɪk/, /'brʊm.stɪk/ [countable noun] The long handle of a broom: *In the story, the witch flew away on her broomstick laughing wildly.* 👁 See picture at **witch**.

†**brother** /'brʌð·ər/ [countable noun] **1** A boy or a man who has the same parents as you: *Peter and Bill are brothers.* ■ Be careful. When you ask somebody if they have any brothers or sisters, in English you have to say "brothers and sisters". If you only say "brothers" you are only asking about the male relatives: "How many brothers and sisters do you have?". **2 brother-in-law 1** The brother of your husband or your wife: *Hugh's brother-in-law is going to help him to get a job.* **2** The husband of your sister: *My sister and my brother-in-law have gone to live in Argentina.* ■ The plural of "brother-in-law" is "brothers-in-law". 👁 See picture at **family**.

brought US: /brɑːt/ UK: /brɔːt/ Past tense and past participle forms of **bring**. ■ Be careful with the pronunciation of this word. It rhymes with "fort".

†**brown** /braʊn/ [noun and adjective] The color of coffee with milk: *In the fall the leaves turn brown, yellow and red and fall off the trees.*

Brownie /'braʊ.ni/ [countable noun] A girl who is a Girl Scout in the grades second through third: *Jenny's daughter became a Brownie when she was seven.* ■ Be careful! "Brownie" has a capital "B".

a b c d e f g h i j k l m n o p q r s t u v w x y z

brownish [adjective] Referring to a color, that is approximately brown, or that has a brown element to it: *Do you think that this water is OK to drink? It looks a little brownish.*

bruise[1] /bru:z/ [countable noun] A mark produced by a blow: *How did you get that bruise on your arm?*

bruise[2] [verb] To get marks from a blow: *He bruised his legs after falling off his bike.*

*****brush**[1] /brʌʃ/ [countable noun] An instrument with a handle for cleaning: *We need a larger brush to paint the wall.* ■ The plural is "brushes".

brush[2] /brʌʃ/ [verb] To clean with a brush: *Jim brushes his teeth after every meal.*

Brussels sprout /ˌbrʌs.ᵊlz'spraʊt/ [countable noun] See **sprout**.

brutal /'bru·t̬ə·l/ [adjective] Violent, cruel: *The movie began with a brutal murder.*

BS Referring to a first level university degree in science: *a BS in geology.* ■ "BS" is an abbreviation for "Bachelor of Science". Compare with "BA" (an abbreviation for "Bachelor of Arts"). ■ See box at **abbreviations**.

bubble[1] /'bʌbl/ [countable noun] A ball of air surrounded by liquid: *This soap makes the water full of bubbles.*

bubble[2] /'bʌbl/ [verb] To make bubbles: *The coffee's bubbling in the pot.*

bubblegum [uncountable noun] A kind of chewing gum that you can make into a bubble and burst: *Sue always has some bubblegum in her mouth, she loves it.*

buck /bʌk/ [noun] See **dollar**. ■ This word is informal.

bucket /'bʌk.ɪt/ [countable noun] A round, open container with a handle: *We can't carry all this paint in just one bucket.*

buckle /'bʌk.l̩/ [countable noun] A piece of metal that fastens a belt: *He wears a belt with a silver buckle.*

bud /bʌd/ [countable noun] **1** A leaf or flower before it opens: *The rose trees are already covered with buds.* **2** See **buddy**. ■ This word is informal.

Buddhism /'bʊd.ɪ.zᵊm/ [uncountable noun] The religion founded by Buddha: *Buddhism began in India in the 6th century BC.* ■ Be careful. "Buddhism" has a capital "B".

Buddhist /'bʊd.ɪst/ [noun and adjective] Referring to Buddhism or a follower of Buddhism: *In China there are many beautiful Buddhist temples.* ■ Be careful. "Buddhist" has a capital "B".

buddy [countable noun] A friend: *Bye, mom, I'm going out with my buddies.* ■ The plural is "buddies". ■ This word is informal.

*****budget**[1] /'bʌdʒɪt/ [countable noun] A plan of how much money you can spend: *We've only got a small budget for our vacation this year.*

budget[2] /'bʌdʒɪt/ [verb] To plan how to spend money: *We can't buy any more games, we have only budgeted for two.*

buffalo /'bʌf·əˌloʊ/ [countable noun] A large wild animal similar to a cow: *Buffaloes have long horns.* ■ The plural is "buffaloes" or "buffalo".

buffet /'bʌf.ɪt/ US: /bə'feɪ/ UK: /'bʊf.eɪ/ [countable noun] A self-service meal: *There will be a cold buffet at the reception.*

bug /bʌg/ [countable noun] **1** A small insect: *Bugs live in dirty places.* **2** A kind of illness that is not serious: *Bob has caught the flu bug.*

*****build,** built, built /bɪld/ [verb] To construct: *They're building the stadium next to the school.* ■ Be careful with the pronunciation of this word. The beginning is pronounced the same as the word "bill".

builder /'bɪl·dər/ [countable noun] A person who makes buildings: *I'll talk to the builder about the cracks in the ceiling.* ■ Be careful with the pronunciation of this word. The beginning is pronounced the same as the word "bill".

*****building** /'bɪldɪŋ/ [countable noun] A structure with a roof and walls: *The church is the oldest building in the town.* ■ Be careful with the pronunciation of this word. The beginning is pronounced the same as the word "bill".

built Past tense and past participle forms of **build**.

BRUSH

hairbrush

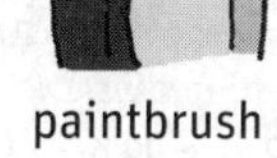

paintbrush

toothbrush

bulb /bʌlb/ [countable noun] **1** The central, round glass part of a lamp: *That bulb gives very poor light.* ■ We can also say "light bulb". **2** The round, underground part of a plant: *Those tulip bulbs were planted last spring.*

BULB

light bulb onion bulb

bulky /'bʌl.ki/ [adjective] Large, difficult to move: *That box is too bulky for you to carry.* ■ The comparative form is "bulkier" and the superlative form is "bulkiest".

bull /bʊl/ [countable noun] The male of the cow family: *My uncle has a bull and three cows in his farm.*

bulldog /'bʊl·dɔg/ [countable noun] A strong, fierce kind of dog: *A bulldog guards the entrance to the house.*

bulldozer /'bʊlˌdoʊ·zər/ [countable noun] A large machine that moves dirt and rocks: *They're using bulldozers to make the new road.*

↑**bullet** /'bʊl.ɪt/ [countable noun] A piece of metal that is fired from a gun: *The bullet went through the cowboy's hat, just missing his head.*

bulletin board [countable noun] A board that gives information about something: *There were some advertisements for summer jobs on the bulletin board this morning.* ■ In British English they say "noticeboard".

bullfight /'bʊl.faɪt/ [countable noun] An entertainment in which a person fights a bull: *There were thousands of people at the bullfight.*

bull's-eye /'bʊl.zaɪ/ [countable noun] The small, round area at the center of a target: *If you hit the bull's-eye you win a doll.*

bully[1] /'bʊl.i/ [countable noun] A person who frightens, hurts or imposes their will on weaker people: *A bully is always a coward.* ■ The plural is "bullies".

bully[2] /'bʊli/ [verb] To frighten, hurt or impose your will on somebody weaker than you: *Simon's always bullying smaller children.* ■ Be careful with the spelling of these forms: "bullies", "bullied".

bumblebee /'bʌm.bl̩.biː/ [countable noun] A large, hairy bee: *Careful! That bumblebee may sting you!*

bump[1] /bʌmp/ [countable noun] A small swelling on the surface of something: *She banged her head against the shelf and she has an enormous bump on it now.*

bump[2] /bʌmp/ [verb] To hit something while you are moving: *Alan bumped into a car with his new bike yesterday.* ■ Be careful! We say: "bump **into** (somebody or something)".

bumper /'bʌmpər/ [countable noun] A bar at the front and at the back of a car: *His car's got a dent in the front bumper.* 👁 **See page 441.**

bumpy /'bʌm.pi/ [adjective] With a rough surface: *The road was very bumpy after all the heavy rains.* ■ The comparative form is "bumpier" and the superlative form is "bumpiest".

bun /bʌn/ [countable noun] **1** A small sweet cake: *Have a bun with your tea.* **2** Hair gathered and fastened in a small round shape at the back of the neck: *She wears a bun right on top of her head.*

↑**bunch** /bʌnʃ/ [countable noun] A number of things that are put together: *I sent Susan a bunch of flowers on her birthday.* 👁 See picture at **a piece of...**

bundle /'bʌn.dl̩/ [countable noun] A number of things that you wrap or tie together: *Why don't you make the old newspapers into a bundle and take them to be recycled?*

bungalow /'bʌŋ·gəˌloʊ/ [countable noun] A house with one floor: *The Browns are going to rent a bungalow in July.*

bungee jumping /'bʌn.dʒiˌdʒʌm.pɪŋ/ [uncountable noun] An adventure activity that consists in jumping off a bridge or other high structure, on the end of an elastic rope: *I thought I wouldn't be brave enough to go bungee jumping, but in the end I did it and it was great!*

bunk /bʌŋk/ [countable noun] **1** A narrow bed on a ship or train with another above or below it: *There were no bunks left on the night train to Edinburgh.* **2** See **bunk bed**.

bunk bed [countable noun] A bed formed by two beds one on top of the other: *Our room is small, so my brother and I have to sleep in a bunk bed.* ■ We say also "bunk".

bunny /'bʌni/ [countable noun] A child's word for a rabbit: *Bunnies love eating carrots.* ■ The plural is "bunnies".

buoyancy /'bɔɪənsi/ [uncountable noun] **1** The ability to float: *The principle of buoyancy is called Archimedes's Principle.* **2** Rise or high level of success: *Prices have shown no buoyancy during the last two years.* **3** Cheerful and confident character: *Sheyla recovers quickly from disappointments due to her buoyancy.*

burden /'bɜr·də·n/ [countable noun] A heavy load: *The refugees walked for miles carrying enormous burdens.*

bureaucracy /bjʊ'rɑk·rə·si/ [noun] An administrative system full of rules: *A lot of people are tired of bureaucracy.* ■ The plural is "bureaucracies".

burger US: /ˈbɝː.gɚ/ UK: /ˈbɜː.gəʳ/ [countable noun] See **hamburger.**

burglar US: /ˈbɝː.glɚ/ UK: /ˈbɜː.gləʳ/ [countable noun] A thief who breaks into houses: *The burglars broke in when we were away on vacation.*

BURGLAR

burglary /ˈbɜr·glə·ri/ [noun] The crime of entering a house to steal things: *We bought an alarm after the last burglary.* ■ The plural is "burglaries".

burial /ˈber.i.əl/ [noun] The ceremony of putting a dead body into the ground: *A lot of people are coming to her grandmother's burial.*

burlap /ˈbɜr·læp/ [uncountable noun] A rough kind of fabric: *Sails are normally made of burlap.* ■ In British English they say "hessian".

burn[1] /bɜːn/ [countable noun] A mark made with fire or heat: *He got burns on his hands from the boiling water.*

burn[2] US: /bɝːn/ UK: /bɜːn/ [verb] **1** To be on fire: *I can smell the meat burning in the oven.* **2** To destroy with fire: *They've burned all their old papers.*
▶ **PHRASAL VERBS** · **to burn down** Referring to a building, to be destroyed by fire: *Lots of houses burned down after the earthquake.*

burrow US: /ˈbɝː.oʊ/ UK: /ˈbʌr.əʊ/ [countable noun] A hole that small animals make in the ground: *Rabbits live in burrows.*

burst, burst, burst /bɜːn/ [verb] To break open suddenly: *Your suitcase will burst if you put too many clothes in it.*

bury /ˈber.i/ [verb] To put a dead person or something into a hole in the ground: *Ann's going to bury her dog in the backyard.* ■ Be careful with the spelling of these forms: "buries", "buried". Note also the pronunciation of this word. It is pronounced like "merry".

bus /bʌs/ [countable noun] **1** A large road vehicle that carries passengers: *Can I take a bus to get to downtown?* 👁 See picture at **transport. 2 bus stop** The place where buses stop: *We'll get off at the next bus stop.* ■ The plural is "buses". 👁 See picture at **street.**

bush /bʊʃ/ [countable noun] **1** A small tree with many branches: *There's a bird singing in that bush.* **2 the bush** Wild land in Africa or in Australia: *When we visited Australia we went for a car ride in the bush.* ■ The plural is "bushes".

bushy /ˈbʊʃ.i/ [adjective] Growing thick, when you are talking about hair: *My cat has a wonderful bushy tail.* ■ The comparative form is "bushier" and the superlative form is "bushiest".

business /ˈbɪz.nɪs/ ▮ [uncountable noun] **1** Commerce, trade: *Her uncle's in the car business.* ▮ [countable noun] **2** A firm or a store: *His parents own two different businesses.* ■ In this use the plural is "businesses". ■ Be careful with the pronunciation of this word. The first part, "busi", rhymes with "is". **3 mind your own business** To pay attention to your own affairs and not to put your nose in somebody else's: *Why don't you mind your own business and leave me alone?* **4 none of your business** It's not your concern: *My personal life is none of your business.* **5 on business** For the purposes of your job: *I'm here on business, not for pleasure.*

businessman /ˈbɪz.nɪs.mən/ [countable noun] A man who works in business: *Her uncle makes a lot of money because he's a good businessman.* ■ The plural is "businessmen". ■ A woman is a "businesswoman".

businesswoman /ˈbɪz.nɪsˌwʊm.ən/ [countable noun] A woman who works in business: *His mother's a businesswoman in New York.* ■ The plural is "businesswomen". ■ A man is a "businessman".

busy /ˈbɪz.i/ [adjective] **1** Occupied, with a lot of things to do: *Emma can't come because she's busy.* **2** With a lot of activity: *This street's busy today.* **3** A word that means that a telephone line or a restroom is being used and that you can't use it: *I telephoned several times but the number was busy.* ■ In this use, in British English we say "engaged".

but[1] /bʌt, bət/ [conjunction] **1** A word that you use to indicate that something is different from what might be expected: *Gary drives well, but he has a lot of accidents.* **2** However, in spite of this: *He was extremely ill, but he stayed cheerful.*

but[2] /bʌt, bət/ [preposition] Except: *I like all sports but basketball.*

butcher /ˈbʊtʃər/ [countable noun] A person who sells meat: *The butcher I know sells very good beef.*

butcher's [countable noun] A store that sells meat: *I'm just going to the butcher's to get something for dinner.* 👁 See picture at **market.**

butler /ˈbʌt·lər/ [countable noun] The chief male servant in a house: *In many old thrillers, the butler is responsible for the crime.*

a b c d e f g h i j k l m n o p q r s t u v w x y z

butter[1] US: /ˈbʌt̬.ɚ/ UK: /ˈbʌt.əʳ/ [uncountable noun] A soft yellow food made from cream: *I ate bread and butter for breakfast.*

butter[2] /ˈbʌtər/ [verb] To spread butter on bread: *Can you butter my toast, please?*

buttercup /ˈbʌtəkʌp/ [countable noun] A plant with small yellow flowers: *Buttercups grow in grass.*

butterfly /ˈbʌt̬·ərˌflɑɪ/ [countable noun] An insect with colorful wings: *Some butterflies can travel thousands of miles.* ■ The plural is "butterflies". **See page 431.**

buttock /ˈbʌtək/ [countable noun] One of the two round and fleshy protuberances at the base of the back: *The buttocks are also known as the gluteus maximus.*

button[1] /ˈbʌtən/ [countable noun] **1** A small, round object for fastening clothes: *I can't undo these coat buttons.* **2** A small object or piece of apparatus that is pressed to start a machine: *Put the money in here and when you are ready to start, press this button.*

button[2]
PHRASAL VERBS · **to button up** To fasten an article of clothing: *Button your coat up before you go out.*

buttonhole US: /ˈbʌt̬.ᵊn.hoʊl/ UK: /ˈbʌt.ᵊn.həʊl/ [countable noun] A hole for a button: *Your buttonholes are too big for these buttons.*

buy, bought, bought /baɪ/ [verb] To get something by paying money: *She'll buy David a computer at Christmas.*

buzz /bʌz/ [verb] To make a sound like a bee: *My ears are buzzing from the cold.*

buzzard /ˈbʌz·ərd/ [countable noun] A kind of bird of prey: *Buzzards hunt at night.*

by[1] /baɪ/ [preposition] **1** Used to show who or what did something: *That music was composed by Chopin.* **2** Not later than: *I should finish the book by Friday.* **3** Using: *Lisa came home by taxi last night.* **4** Used to show how you do something: *He makes a living by selling cars.* **5** **by the way** Words to show that you have just remembered something you want to say to the person you are talking to: *By the way, when are you going to pay me back?*

by[2] /baɪ/ [adverb] **1** Past: *She's just gone by without looking.* **2** Near: *My cousins live by the sea.*

bye [interjection] An informal way of saying goodbye: *I'll see you on Monday. Bye!* ■ This word is informal.

c /siː/ The third letter of the alphabet: *The name "Carol" begins with a "C".*

C¹ /siː/ A written abbreviation for **centigrade.**

C² /siː/ [countable noun] The first musical note of the scale of C major: *The musician played the song in the key of C.* ■ The plural is "Cs" or "C's". 👁 **See page 460.**

cab /kæb/ [countable noun] A car that takes you somewhere if you pay: *It's late. Let's get a cab.* ■ The same meaning: "taxi".

cabbage /ˈkæb.ɪdʒ/ [noun] A round vegetable with big leaves: *Mom is boiling some cabbage for lunch.* ■ Be careful with the pronunciation of this word. The last "a" is pronounced like the "i" in "did". 👁 **See page 437.**

cabin /ˈkæb.ɪn/ [countable noun] **1** A room on a ship: *We had a cabin with two beds.* **2** A small house made of wood: *We spent the night in a cabin in the mountains.*

↑**cabinet** /ˈkæbɪnət/ [countable noun] A piece of furniture in which you can keep things: *There's a cabinet in our living room with lots of antiques in it.*

↑**cable** /ˈkeɪ.bl̩/ [noun] A wire that carries an electric signal, that can be used in various ways: *The lamp needs a new cable.* ■ Be careful with the pronunciation of this word. It is pronounced like "table".

cable car [countable noun] A system of transport in which carriages hang from a cable that moves: *We took the cable car to the top of the mountain.*

cable television [uncountable noun] A system of sending television programs: *A lot of sports events are broadcasted on cable television.*

cactus /ˈkæk.təs/ [countable noun] A type of plant that grows in deserts: *Cactuses do not need a lot of water.* ■ The plural is "cactuses" or "cacti".

café /ˈkæf.eɪ/ [countable noun] A small restaurant that serves drinks and simple meals: *We had coffee and cake at a café on the Roselle Road.* ■ The same meaning: "diner".

cafeteria /ˌkæf·ɪˈtɪər·i·ə/ [countable noun] A self-service restaurant, usually in a college or store: *I usually have lunch in the college cafeteria.*

caffeine /ˈkæf.iːn/ [uncountable noun] A substance in tea, coffee and coke that makes you feel more active: *If I drink something with caffeine in it at night, I can't sleep.*

cage /keɪdʒ/ [countable noun] A box or a room for keeping animals in: *The parrot escaped from its cage.*

↑**cake** /keɪk/ [countable noun] A sweet food made from flour, eggs, sugar and butter: *My mom baked a chocolate cake for my birthday.*

calamity /kəˈlæm·ɪ·t̬i/ [countable noun] An event that causes great destruction, loss and suffering: *It would be an absolute calamity for these towns if the river flooded again.* ■ The plural is "calamities".

a b c d e f g h i j k l m n o p q r s t u v w x y z

calcium /'kælsiəm/ [uncountable noun] Soft metallic element which occurs naturally in limestone: *Calcium is found in teeth, bones and chalk.*

†**calculate** /'kæl.kjʊ.leɪt/ [verb] To solve a problem by a mathematical operation: *I'm trying to calculate how much we've spent on our vacation.*

†**calculation** /ˌkæl.kjʊ'leɪ.ʃən/ [noun] Finding answers through mathematical operations: *According to my calculations, we've spent $200 on presents.*

calculator /'kæl·kjəˌleɪ·t̬ər/ [countable noun] An electronic machine for doing mathematical operations: *We're learning to use our calculators in Math.*

calendar /'kæl·ən·dər/ [countable noun] A list of the days and months of a year: *According to my calendar, next Tuesday is a vacation.*

calf US: /kæf/ UK: /kɑːf/ ▮ [countable noun] **1** A young cow: *Have you seen the cow with its calf in the field?* ■ Compare with "veal" (the meat from a young cow). **2** Back part of the leg below the knee: *After a work out you should stretch your calves.* ▮ [uncountable noun] **3** Leather made from cow's skin: *We gave mom a calf purse for her birthday.* ■ The plural is "calves".

calf muscle [countable noun] Either of a pair of muscles which are located in the calf: *The calf muscles are connected to the foot by the Achilles tendon.* 👁 **See page 423.**

caliph /'keɪ.lɪf/ [countable noun] Muslim civil and religious ruler: *The Caliph is considered to be the follower of Mohammed.*

caliphate [countable noun] The area ruled over by the Caliph: *The caliphate was the first system of government established in Islam.*

call[1] US: /kɑːl/ UK: /kɔːl/ [countable noun] **1** A shout: *Give me a call at 7.00 tomorrow, mom. I have a test at 9.00.* **2** A telephone conversation: *Give me a call tonight, Pete.*

†**call**[2] US: /kɑːl/ UK: /kɔːl/ [verb] **1** To attract somebody's attention by shouting: *Somebody called my name from the other end of the room.* **2** To telephone: *I called Jane to invite her to go to the movies with me but she wasn't in.* **3** **to be called** To have a name: *What is this animal called in English?* **4** **to call collect** On the phone, to ask the person you are calling to pay for the call: *When I was in Europe this summer I called collect every week to talk to my parents.* ■ In British English they say "reverse the charges".

◗ **PHRASAL VERBS** · **to call back** To return a telephone call or to call again: *He said he'd call me back when he got home.* · **to call on** To visit: *We'll call on you tomorrow evening.* · **to call off** To stop something that had been planned: *As it was raining, we had to call off the game.*

caller US: /'kɑː.lɚ/ UK: /'kɔː.ləʳ/ [countable noun] **1** A person who telephones: *Somebody rang for Julie, but the caller didn't give his name.* **2** A person who comes on a visit: *They had lots of callers who wanted to buy the apartment.*

†**calm**[1] /kɑːm/ [adjective] Quiet and peaceful, still: *She's usually a very calm person.*

calm[2] /kɑːm/ [verb] To make somebody or something quiet: *When the little boy started crying, she tried to calm him.*

◗ **PHRASAL VERBS** · **to calm down** To become quiet or to make somebody quiet: *Paula, please calm down and listen.*

calorie /'kæl·ə·ri/ [countable noun] A unit of heat energy used to show the energy value of food: *Bacon has a lot of calories.*

calyx /'keɪ.lɪks/ [countable noun] The sepals which together form the layer that protects a flower in bud: *The calyx is the outer part of the flower.* ■ The plural is "calyces" or "calyxes". ■ Compare with "corolla" (The petals which form the inner envelope of a flower).

camcorder /'kæmˌkɔr·dər/ [countable noun] A camera for making video movies: *John filmed Alice's birthday party with his camcorder.*

came /keɪm/ Past tense of **come**.

camel /'kæm.əl/ [countable noun] An animal with one or two humps, that lives in deserts: *When we were in Tunisia, we went for a camel ride in the desert.* 👁 **See page 428.**

†**camera** /'kæm.rə/ [countable noun] A machine for taking photographs: *Mary has a tiny camera that takes excellent photos.*

camouflage[1] /'kæm.ə.flɑːʒ/ [uncountable noun] **1** The disguising of soldiers or military vehicles and equipment: *Camouflage is used to hide tanks from enemy aircraft.* **2** The way an animal protects itself with a shape or color matching the surroundings: *The chameleon's green coloring when it is surrounded by vegetation is a natural camouflage.*

camouflage[2] /'kæm.ə.flɑːʒ/ [verb] To hide something or somebody by camouflage: *The crews need to camouflage their tanks with leaves and branches.*

†**camp**[1] /kæmp/ [countable noun] A place where people live in tents or cabins: *I spent last vacation in a summer camp near Boston.*

camp[2] /kæmp/ [verb] **1** To live in a tent, usually during a vacation: *We camped near a river at the entry to the valley.* **2** **to go camping** To spend a vacation living in a tent: *If we have good weather, we'll go camping next week.*

†**campaign** /kæm'peɪn/ [countable noun] **1** Activities organized to achieve an objective: *The school is running a campaign to get funds for sports equipment.* **2** Organized military operations: *Napoleon's*

CALENDAR

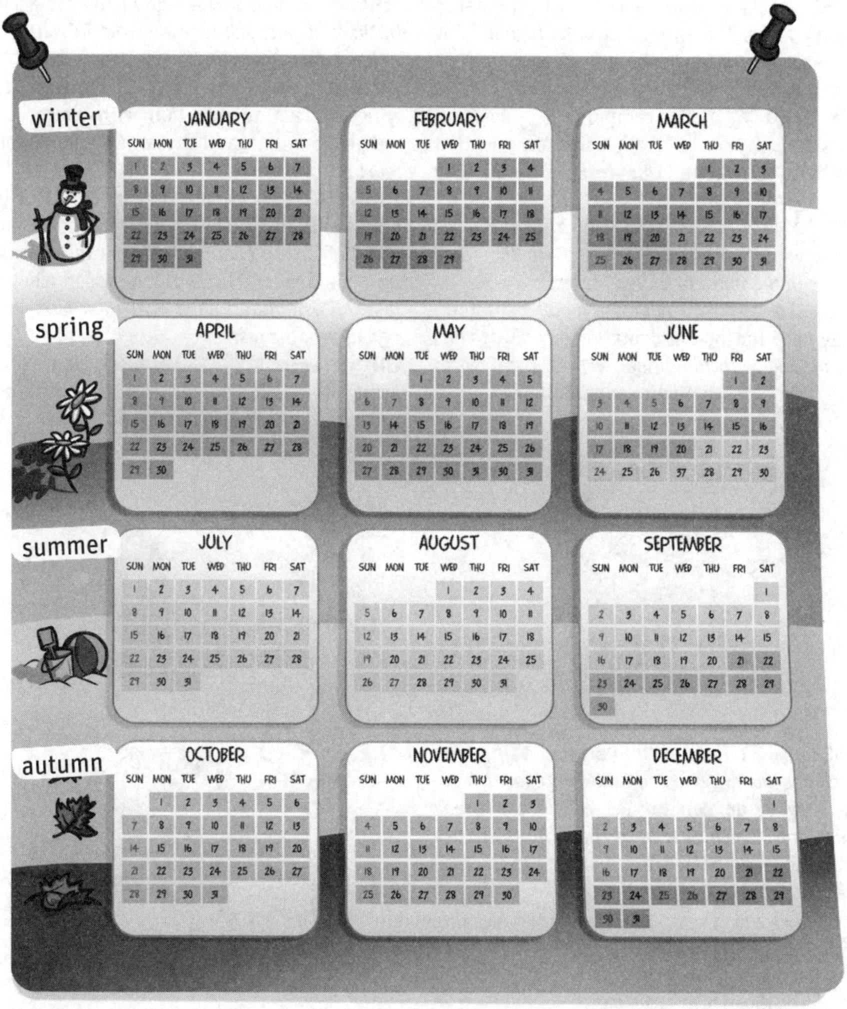

winter
JANUARY
FEBRUARY
MARCH
spring
APRIL
MAY
JUNE
summer
JULY
AUGUST
SEPTEMBER
autumn
OCTOBER
NOVEMBER
DECEMBER
SUN MON TUE WED THU FRI SAT

month
DECEMBER
SUN MON TUE WED THU FRI SAT
week
SUNDAY 23
MONDAY 24
TUESDAY 25
WEDNESDAY 26
THURSDAY 27
FRIDAY 28
SATURDAY 29
holiday
day

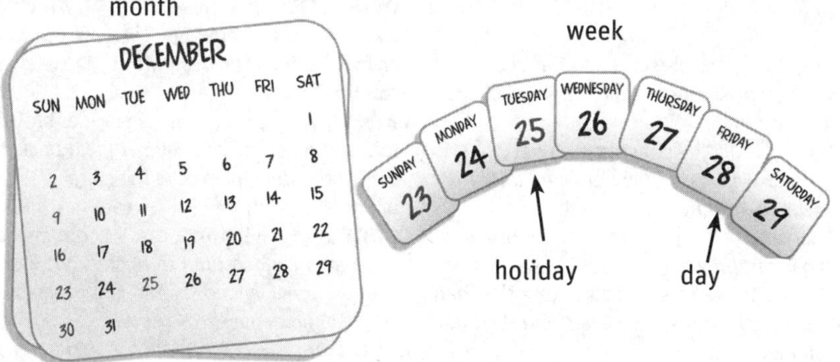

winter campaign in Russia was a disaster because of the bad weather.

camper [countable noun] A small house on wheels that is moved by a car: *There were lots of tents and a few campers at the campsite.* ■ We say also "camper van". ■ In British English they say "caravan".

camper van [countable noun] See **camper**.

†**camping** /'kæm.pɪŋ/ [uncountable noun] Going on vacation with a tent or caravan: *This weekend we're going camping in the mountains.*

campsite /'kæmp.saɪt/ [countable noun] An area for tents and caravans: *Every summer we go to the same campsite in the south of United States.*

can[1] /kæn, kən/ [countable noun] A small metal container, usually used for food or drink: *Jeremy always has a can of Coke with his dinner.* ■ In British English they say "tin". ◉ See picture at **container**.

†**can**[2] /kæn/ [verb] **1** To be able to do something: *Can you tell me the way to the station, please?* **2** To know how to do something: *Wayne can speak Spanish and French.* **3** A word that you use to ask permission to do something: *Can I go to the restroom, please?* ■ In this use, the conditional "could" is often used and is more polite form. ■ Be careful! The verb after "can" is in the infinitive without "to". The past and the conditional form of "can" is "could". ■ See box on the following page.

Canadian[1] [adjective] Referring to Canada: *I love the Canadian landscapes.* ■ Be careful! "Canadian" has a capital "C".

Canadian[2] [countable noun] A person from Canada: *Most Canadians live in southern Canada.* ■ Be careful! "Canadian" has a capital "C".

canal /kə'næl/ [countable noun] An artificial river that is used by boats: *We crossed the Panama Canal from Pacific Ocean to Atlantic Ocean.*

canary /kə'ner·i/ [countable noun] A small yellow bird: *Canaries sing beautifully.* ■ The plural is "canaries".

†**cancel** /'kænt.səl/ [verb] To stop something that had been planned: *All trains have been cancelled due to bad weather.*

cancer /'kænsər/ [noun] A serious disease in which some of the victim's cells increase too fast: *Smoking can produce lung cancer.*

Cancer /'kænsər/ [noun] A sign of the zodiac: *If your birthday is between June 21st and July 20th, you're a Cancer.* ■ Be careful. "Cancer" has a capital "C".

candida /'kæn.dɪ.də/ [uncountable noun] Parasitic fungus which causes an infection with white pimples, mostly in mouth and throat: *Candida is found in most parts of the body.*

†**candidate** /'kæn.dɪ.dət, -deɪt/ [countable noun] **1** A person who wants to be chosen for a job, for a political post and so on: *There were three candidates for the post of mayor of Portland.* **2** A person who takes a test: *All candidates must write their number on every page of the test.*

candle /'kæn.dḷ/ [countable noun] A piece of wax with a string down the middle that you burn to give light: *There was no electricity, so the rooms were lit by candles.*

candlestick /'kæn.dḷ.stɪk/ [countable noun] An object that you can put a candle on: *There was a candlestick on every table of the restaurant.* ◉ See pictures at **candle**.

†**candy** /'kæn.di/ [noun] A small piece of boiled sugar, toffee and so on: *Will you get me a packet of candies at the store, please?* ■ The plural is "candies". ■ In British English they say "sweet".

canned [adjective] Put in a can: *My brother says that he prefers canned tuna to fresh tuna.* ■ Be careful with the pronunciation of the end of this word. The "e" is not pronounced.

cannibal /'kæn.ɪ.bəl/ [countable noun] A person who eats other people: *Some cannibals believed that they* *would receive human qualities, such as courage, from the person they ate.*

*__cannot__ /kə'nɑt/, /'kæn·ɑt/ The negative form of "can". ■ Its contraction is "can't".

canoe /kə'nuː/ [countable noun] A light, thin boat moved with paddles: *We went down the river by canoe.* 👁 See picture at **transport**.

can opener [countable noun] An object used for opening cans: *Oh no! Don't tell me that we've forgotten the can opener!*

can't US: /kænt/ UK: /kɑːnt/ The contraction of "cannot".

canvas /'kæn.vəs/ ▮ [uncountable noun] **1** Cloth made from a strong natural fiber: *The tent is made of canvas.* ▮

can and *could*

This modal verb only has two forms: a present form ***can***, and a past and conditional form, ***could***. The verb that follows it is in the infinitive without *to*:

- *I can ride a bicycle.*
- *I could swim when I was four.*

In other tenses, we use ***to be able to***.

- **Present tense**

affirmative	negative	questions
I can do	I cannot / can't do	can I do?
you can do	you cannot / can't do	can you do?
he / she / it can do	he / she / it cannot / can't do	can he / she / it do?
we can do	we can't do	can we do?
you can do	you can't do	can you do?
they can do	they can't do	can they do?

Examples:

- *I can speak German.*
- *I can't swim.*
- *Can you drive?*

- **Past and conditional tenses**

affirmative	negative	questions
I could do	I couldn't do	could I do?
you could do	you couldn't do	could you do?
he / she / it could do	he / she / it couldn't do	could he / she / it do?
we could do	we couldn't do	could we do?
you could do	you couldn't do	could you do?
they could do	they couldn't do	could they do?

Examples:

- *I could read when I was six.*
- *I couldn't play tennis.*
- *Could you go swimming?*

- **Future tense:** we use ***will be able to***:
  - *Sorry, but I don't think I'll be able to come to your party.*
- **Past participle:** we use ***been able to***:
  - *Margaret is ill. She hasn't been able to finish her homework.*

[countable noun] **2** Cloth for painting on, or the finished picture: *The artist started his oil painting on a large canvas.*

canvass /ˈkænvəs/ [verb] To go around an area looking for political support: *The candidate will canvass next week.*

canyon /ˈkæn.jən/ [countable noun] Depression in the earth which often has a river running through it, or has had in the past: *The Grand Canyon in the USA is world famous.* ■ Be careful with the pronunciation of this word!

†**cap** /kæp/ [countable noun] A type of hat with a part that goes out at the front: *Jockeys wear caps of different colors and patterns.* 👁 See picture at **hat**.

capability /ˌkeɪpəˈbɪləti/ [countable noun] The state of being capable: *This student has the capability of somebody much older.* ■ The plural is "capabilities".

†**capable** /ˈkeɪ.pə.bl̩/ [adjective] **1** Good at what they do: *Liz is a very capable teacher.* **2** That can do something: *I don't think he's capable of any hard work. He's so lazy!*

†**capacity** /kəˈpæs·ɪ·t̬i/ ▮ [noun] **1** The amount of something that a container or a place can hold: *This car has a tank with a capacity of 40 liters.* ▮ [noun] **2** The ability to do something: *Stella has a great capacity for always saying the right word.* ■ The plural is "capacities".

cape /keɪp/ [countable noun] **1** An article of clothing like a coat without sleeves: *Very few people wear capes nowadays.* ■ The same meaning: "cloak". **2** A piece of land that sticks out into the sea: *Sailors used to fear going round the Cape of Good Hope.* 👁 **See page 444.**

capillary /ˈkæp·əˌler·i/ [countable noun] Any of the small blood vessels which form a network through our body: *The capillaries carry blood between the arteries and veins.* ■ The plural is "capillaries".

†**capital** /ˈkæp·ɪ·t̬ə·l/ ▮ [countable noun] **1** The main city of a region, a country or a state: *Washington, D.C. is the capital of the United States of America.* ▮ [uncountable noun] **2** Money that is invested in a business: *This firm's capital is $500,000.* **3 capital letter** A large letter at the beginning of a name or a sentence: *You write people's names with a capital letter, not a small one.*

capitalism /ˈkæpɪtəlɪzəm/ [uncountable noun] An economic system which depends upon private investment for profit: *Capitalism was regulated during the twentieth century to try to reduce inequalities.*

Capricorn /ˈkæp·rɪˌkɔrn/ [noun] A sign of the zodiac: *If your birthday is between December 21st and January 20th, you're a Capricorn.* ■ Be careful. "Capricorn" has a capital "C".

†**captain** /ˈkæp·tən/ [countable noun] **1** The person in charge of a ship or an airplane: *The captain spoke to the passengers after the take-off.* **2** An officer in the army or in the navy: *The captain gave the order to attack.* **3** The leader of a team: *Wendy is the captain of the school volleyball team.* ■ Be careful with the pronunciation of this word! The "a" is not pronounced.

caption /ˈkæp.ʃən/ [countable noun] A text that goes with a picture or a photograph in a book or in a newspaper: *The caption said that the man in the photo was from Chile.*

captivity /kæpˈtɪv·ɪ·t̬i/ [uncountable noun] Not being free to go where you want: *The prisoners were kept in captivity until the end of the war.*

†**capture** /ˈkæp·tʃər/ [verb] **1** To take somebody prisoner: *Anthony's grandfather was captured by the Germans in World War II.* **2** To take control of a place by force: *The Marines captured the island after a long battle.*

†**car** US: /kɑːr/ UK: /kɑːʳ/ [countable noun] **1** A small motor vehicle: *My dad's new car seats seven people.* 👁 See picture at **transport**. **2** A passenger wagon on a train: *The train had an engine and four cars.* ■ In this use, in British English we say "carriage". 👁 **See page 441.**

caravan /ˈkær·əˌvæn/ [countable noun] See **camper**. ■ This word is British English.

carbohydrate /ˌkɑːbəʊˈhaɪdreɪt/ [noun] Energy producing compound of carbon, hydrogen and oxygen: *The carbohydrates in your diet are important for providing you with energy.*

carbon /ˈkɑr·bən/ [uncountable noun] **1** A non-metallic element which is found in all organic compounds: *Carbon occurs naturally like diamonds.* **2 carbon dating** A method of calculating the age of very old objects: *Carbon dating consists of measuring the amounts of different forms of carbon in a particular piece.*

carbon dioxide /ˌkɑːbəndaɪˈɒksaɪd/ [uncountable noun] A gas which is both colorless and odorless: *Carbon dioxide is formed by respiration.*

†**card** US: /kɑːrd/ UK: /kɑːd/ [countable noun] **1** See **postcard**. **2** A small piece of stiff paper with pictures, that is for playing games: *Ron has a new cards to play poker.* **3** A small piece of stiff paper with a person's name and address: *Before leaving, Mr. Clark gave me his card.* **4 pack of cards** See "deck of cards" in the word **deck**.

†**cardboard** US: /ˈkɑːrd.bɔːrd/ UK: /ˈkɑːd.bɔːd/ [uncountable noun] A type of thick paper that is used for making boxes, folders and so on: *My sister keeps all her toys in a cardboard box.*

cardigan /ˈkɑrd·ɪ·gən/ [countable noun] A knitted woolen jacket: *My mother is knitting me a new blue cardigan.*

cardinal[1] /ˈkɑːdɪnəl/ [adjective] Used for numbers that show quantity: *"One", "two" and "ten" are cardinal numbers.*

cardinal[2] /ˈkɑr·də·n·əl/ [countable noun] A very important member of the Catholic Church: *Cardinals elect the Pope.*

†**care** US: /ker/ UK: /keəʳ/ [verb] **1** To feel interest in somebody or something or to worry about them: *Rebecca doesn't care if she fails all her tests.* ■ This use is formal. **2 to take care of (somebody) 1** To look after somebody: *Could you take care of the baby while I prepare lunch?* **2** To do what is necessary: *I'll take care of the tickets.*

◗ **PHRASAL VERBS** · **to care for (somebody)** To look after somebody: *When her mother fell ill, Anne cared for her.*

†**career** /kəˈrɪər/ [countable noun] Professional life: *She said her latest movie was the best movie in her career as an actress.*

†**careful** /ˈkeər·fəl/ [adjective] **1** Thinking about what you do so that you do it well and do not hurt yourself, somebody or something: *He was careful not to break anything.* **2** Made with care: *Joana painted a careful portrait of the vase full of flowers.* **3 to be careful** An expression that tells you that there is a danger: *Be careful if you ride your bike in the rain.* ■ We say "be careful **with** (something/somebody)".

carefully /ˈkeər·fə·li/ [adverb] **1** Not hurting yourself, somebody or something: *We wrapped all the glasses very carefully in tissue paper.* **2** Thoroughly: *Tom was asked to mix the ingredients carefully.*

†**careless** /ˈkeər·ləs/ [adjective] Not thinking about what you do and doing it badly: *He made a lot of careless mistakes.*

caress /kəˈres/ [countable noun] A gentle and loving touch or a kiss: *He gave the ball a caress and put it on the penalty spot.*

caretaker US: /ˈkerˌteɪ.kɚ/ UK: /ˈkeəˌteɪ.kəʳ/ [countable noun] A person who looks after a building: *They reported the broken window to the school caretaker.*

cargo US: /ˈkɑːr.goʊ/ UK: /ˈkɑː.gəʊ/ [noun] Things carried on a ship or on a plane: *The ship had a cargo of bananas from Costa Rica.*

Caribbean /ˌkær·əˈbi·ən/, /kəˈrɪb·i·ən/ [adjective] Referring to a country in the Caribbean Sea: *I'd love to spend my vacation on a Caribbean island.* ■ Be careful! "Caribbean" has a capital "C".

caricature US: /ˈker.ɪ.kə.tʃʊr/ UK: /ˈkær.ɪ.kə.tʃʊəʳ/ [noun] A comic drawing of a person: *There was a funny caricature of the Prime Minister in the newspaper this morning.*

carnation /kɑrˈneɪ·ʃən/ [countable noun] A type of plant with flowers that are usually pink or red: *I gave mom a bunch of red carnations for her birthday.* 👁 **See page 433.**

carnival /ˈkɑr·nə·vəl/ [countable noun] Celebration held prior to Lent in which people wear costumes and masks: *The carnival in Brazil is a popular tourist attraction.*

carnivore /ˈkɑːnɪvɔːr/ [countable noun] An animal which eats meat: *The dog is a carnivore.* ■ Compare with "herbivore" (an animal which only eats plants). 👁 **See page 427.**

carol /ˈkær·əl/ [countable noun] A type of song that people sing at Christmas: *My favorite carol is "Santa Claus is Coming to Town".*

carpal [adjective] Referring to the wrist bones: *The carpal bones are to be found in the wrist.* ■ Compare to "tarsal" (referring to the ankle bones).

car park [countable noun] See **parking lot.** ■ This word is British English.

carpenter US: /ˈkɑːr.pɪn.t̬ɚ/ UK: /ˈkɑː.pɪn.təʳ/ [countable noun] A person who makes wooden things for buildings: *The carpenter had to change all the doors after the burglary.*

†**carpet** /ˈkɑːpɪt/ [noun] A covering for the floor: *There's a beautiful carpet in our living room.*

carpus [countable noun] The small bones between the forearm and the fingers: *The carpus forms the wrist.*

carriage /ˈkær·ɪdʒ/ [countable noun] **1** See **car.** ■ This use is British English. **2** A vehicle pulled by a horse: *Movie stars were the premiere in a carriage drawn by six horses.* ■ Be careful with the pronunciation of this word. The ending is pronounced like the ending of "fridge".

†**carrot** /ˈkær·ət/ [noun] A bright orange vegetable: *Rabbits love carrots.* 👁 **See page 437.**

†**carry** /ˈkær·i/ [verb] **1** To take something from one place to another in your hands or arms, especially something heavy: *Can you carry the bag? I'm tired; I will carry you to the next corner only.* ■ When it is something small or light, we say "take": "I am going to take an apple with me". Incorrect: "I am going to carry an apple". **2** To have with you: *She never carries a lot of money.* **3** To take something from one place to another in a vehicle: *This train doesn't carry passengers.* **4** To involve: *This offence carries a severe penalty.* **5** Referring to sound, to be heard at a distance: *The sound of the festivities carried right across the valley.* **6 to be/get carried away** To lose control of yourself because of excitement: *When he scored the goal I got carried away and started hugging everyone.*

◗ **PHRASAL VERBS** · **to carry (something) forward/over** To include an amount from one calculation in another: *You carry this figure over to the next column.* · **to carry off** To do successfully

a b c d e f g h i j k l m n o p q r s t u v w x y z

something that is difficult: *Her last exercise in the skating competition was very difficult, but she carried it off.* • **to carry on 1** To continue to do something: *Will you please carry on with this exercise while I go to the teacher's room.* **2** To make a lot of noise or to behave in an uncontrolled way: *Will you please stop carrying on like that? I can't concentrate.* • **to carry (something) out** To do something planned: *We carried out the experiment at the laboratory.* • **to carry (something) through** To do something planned or promised, until it is finished: *It was an ambitious project; but she carried it through.* ■ Be careful with the spelling of these forms: "carries", "carried".

cart US: /kɑːrt/ UK: /kɑːt/ [countable noun] **1** A vehicle pulled by a horse: *The farmer put two sacks of potatoes in the cart and to take to the market.* **2** A container on wheels that is used for carrying things: *Let's put everything in the cart. It will be easier to carry.* ■ In this use, in British English we say "trolley". 👁 See picture at **market**.

carton US: /'kɑːr.t̬ən/ UK: /'kɑː.tən/ [countable noun] A cardboard or plastic box, used for food, drinks or cigarettes: *We'll have to buy a carton of milk for breakfast.* 👁 See picture at **container**.

cartoon /kɑr'tun/ [countable noun] **1** A funny drawing: *The first thing I read in the paper is the cartoons.* **2** A movie made of moving drawings: *My favorite cartoon is "Superman".*

CARTOON

cartridge /'kɑr·trɪdʒ/ [countable noun] **1** A case or container that goes in a machine to make it work: *We need a new black ink cartridge for the printer.* **2** A tube with explosives and a bullet: *We need new cartridges for the firing practice.*

cartwheel /'kɑrt·hwil/, /-wil/ [countable noun] A gymnastic movement in which you turn sideways like a wheel: *The clown did two cartwheels and fell into the sand.*

carve US: /kɑːrv/ UK: /kɑːv/ [verb] **1** To cut a solid material to make a figure: *Mr. Norton is carving a statue of Beethoven.* **2** To cut meat into pieces: *My dad likes carving the meat for our Sunday lunch.*

carving /'kɑr·vɪŋ/ [noun] A figure made of wood or stone: *I have an African carving of a giraffe in my room.*

⁺**case** /keɪs/ [countable noun] **1** An example of something: *There was a case of food poisoning last week.* **2** See **suitcase. 3** A box for protecting something: *When he finished playing he put the violin into its case.* **4 in any case** Anyway: *I don't like that movie, and in any case, I don't have any money.* **5 in case** Thinking that something might happen: *I'll make more sandwiches in case Ann and Paul want to come with us.*

⁺**cash[1]** /kæʃ/ [uncountable noun] Money in bills and coins: *You can't use a check to buy a newspaper. You need cash.*

cash[2] /kæʃ/ [verb] To get cash for a check: *I'll cash this check and we'll have money for the weekend.*

cash dispenser [countable noun] A machine from which you can get money: *When we get to the mall I need to go to the cash dispenser to get money to go shopping.* ■ The same meaning: "ATM".

cashier /kæ'ʃɪər/ [countable noun] **1** A person who takes money from customers in a store: *My sister has found a job as a cashier at a supermarket.* **2** A person who takes or gives out money in a bank: *The thief pointed the gun at the cashier and told him to give him all the money.*

cash register [countable noun] A machine in a store in which money is kept: *Let's take the CD to the cash register and pay for it.* ■ We also say "register".

cassette /kə'set/ [countable noun] A small plastic box with a tape, that can be used for listening to or recording sound: *Andrew has a large collection of jazz cassettes.*

⁺**castle** US: /'kæs.l̩/ UK: /'kɑː.sl̩/ [countable noun] **1** An old military building: *When we were in Europe we saw a lot of castles.* **2** A chess piece that looks like a tower: *The castle can move horizontally and vertically.* ■ Be careful with the pronunciation of this word! The "t" is silent. 👁 See picture at **chess**.

casual /'kæʒ.ju.əl/ [adjective] **1** Not serious: *She adopted a casual attitude at the meeting.* **2 casual clothes** Informal clothes: *Sheila likes wearing casual clothes like jeans and sneakers.*

casualty /'kæʒ.ju.əl.ti/ [countable noun] A person hurt or killed in an accident or in a war: *There was a terrible fire at the Odeon theater last week with 160 casualties.* ■ The plural is "casualties".

⁺**cat** /kæt/ [countable noun] **1** A small animal kept as a pet: *Cats are very skillful at catching mice.* **2** The name of a group of animals: *Lions belong to the cat family.* 👁 See picture at **pet**.

catastrophe /kə'tæs.trə.fi/ [countable noun] An event that causes great damage: *The hurricane in the Pacific was a catastrophe.*

catch, caught, caught /kætʃ/ [verb] **1** To get something or somebody that is in movement with your hands: *Here! Catch the ball!* **2** To get on public transport: *It's late, I'll have to catch the last train.* **3** To get an illness: *James has caught the flu.* **4 to catch fire** To begin to burn: *She dropped a match in the waste paper basket and the papers caught fire.*

PHRASAL VERBS · to catch up with (something) To reach somebody or something, or to get on the same level: *Timmy was off school when he was ill, but it didn't take him long to catch up with the rest of the class.*

category /'kæţ.ɪ,gɔr.i/, /-,gour.i/ [countable noun] A group of people or things of the same type: *In libraries, the books are divided into different categories.* ■ The plural is "categories".

caterpillar US: /'kæţ.ə.pɪl.ə/ UK: /'kæt.ə.pɪl.ər/ [countable noun] The young form of an insect that becomes a moth or a butterfly: *Caterpillars eat the leaves of plants.* **See page 431.**

cathedral /kə'θiː.drəl/ [countable noun] A very large church: *In La Paz we went to the Cathedral to hear mass.* ■ Be careful with the pronunciation of this word.

Catholic /'kæθ.əl.ɪk/ [noun and adjective] That belongs to the Roman Catholic Church: *I take my children to a Catholic school.* ■ Be careful with the pronunciation of this word! The "o" is not pronounced. ■ Be careful! "Catholic" has a capital "C". ■ We also say "Roman Catholic".

Catholicism /kə'θɑl.ə,sɪz.əm/ [uncountable noun] The beliefs of the Roman Catholic Church: *Catholicism is an important force in many parts of the world.* ■ Be careful! "Catholicism" has a capital "C".

cattle /'kætl/ [plural noun] Animals of the cow family: *When Craig works on his uncle's farm, he takes the cattle out to the fields.*

caught US: /kɑːt/ UK: /kɔːt/ Past tense and past participle forms of **catch**. ■ Be careful with the pronunciation of this word. It rhymes with "fort".

cauliflower US: /'kɑː.lɪ,flaʊr/ UK: /'kɒl.ɪ,flaʊ.ər/ [noun] A vegetable with a large white head: *There's cauliflower for dinner.*

cause US: /kɑːz/ UK: /kɔːz/ [noun] **1** Something that makes something happen: *The rain and the fog were the causes of the accident.* **2** Something you believe in and you want to help with: *She decided that fighting racism was the most important cause to get involved with.* ■ Be careful with the pronunciation of this word! The "e" is not pronounced.

caution /'kɔ.ʃən/ [uncountable noun] Care or precaution: *The sign said: "Proceed with caution".*

cautious /'kɔ.ʃəs/ [adjective] Careful: *Pat's mom is a very cautious driver.*

cava /'kɑː.və/ [uncountable noun] Sparkling white wine from Spain similar to Champagne: *A glass of cava was given to each guest to toast the couple.*

cave /keɪv/ [countable noun] A large hole in rock: *They got lost in the countryside and had to spend the night in a cave.*

cavity /'kæv.ə.ţi/ [countable noun] The hollow part inside a solid body: *Every tooth has a cavity.* ■ The plural is "cavities".

CD /,siː'diː/ [countable noun] See **compact disc.** ■ See box at **abbreviations.**

CD player [countable noun] See **compact disc player.**

ceiling /'siː.lɪŋ/ [countable noun] The top of a room: *We're painting the walls yellow and the ceiling white.* See picture at **bedroom.**

celebrate /'sel.ɪ.breɪt/ [verb] To do something special to remember or to mark a particular event or day: *Nigel is giving a party to celebrate his birthday.*

celebration /,sel.ɪ'breɪ.ʃən/ [noun] A party to celebrate something: *I've been invited to the celebration of the fiftieth anniversary of the school.*

celebrity [countable noun] A famous person: *There were a lot of celebrities at the party.* ■ The plural is "celebrities".

celery /'sel.ə.ri/ [uncountable noun] A long white or green vegetable, that is usually eaten raw: *Put a stick of celery in the salad.* ■ The plural is "celeries". **See page 437.**

celestial /sə'lestiəl/ [adjective] Referring to heaven or the sky: *The sky is not empty, it is full of celestial bodies.* ■ This word is literary. ■ Compare with "terrestrial" (of the Planet Earth).

cell /sel/ [countable noun] **1** Room in a prison or in a monastery: *The prisoner escaped from his cell by climbing out of the window.* **2** Basic unit of all living things: *Cells are much too small to see.* ■ Be careful with the pronunciation of this word! The "c" is pronounced as an "s".

cellar /'sel.ər/ [countable noun] A room that is underground: *We keep old papers and things like that in the cellar.* ■ The same meaning: "basement".

cello /'tʃel.oʊ/ [countable noun] A large musical instrument with strings: *A cello is much larger than a violin.* ■ "Cello" is short for "violoncello". **See page 458.**

cellophane /'seləfeɪn/ [uncountable noun] Thin and transparent material used for wrapping: *The package was covered in cellophane.*

cellphone /'sel.fəʊn/ US: /-foʊn/ [countable noun] A telephone that you can use wherever you are:

a b c d e f g h i j k l m n o p q r s t u v w x y z

a b c d e f g h i j k l m n o p q r s t u v w x y z

Although Tim was in the Highlands we could speak to him on his cellphone. ■ In British English they say "mobile" or "mobile phone". 👁 **See pages 442 and 443.**

Celsius /ˈsel.si.əs/ [noun and adjective] See **centigrade.** ■ Be careful. "Celsius" has a capital "C".

cement /sɪˈment/ [uncountable noun] A grey powder that becomes hard when mixed with water: *Cement is used in most modern buildings.*

cemetery /ˈsem·ɪˌter·i/ [countable noun] A place where people are buried when they die: *Shelley went to the cemetery to visit her grandpa's grave.* ■ The plural is "cemeteries". Be careful with the spelling of this word.

census /ˈsent.səs/ [countable noun] A survey collecting information on population: *The census is held every ten years.*

cent /sent/ [countable noun] A small coin: *There are a hundred cents in a dollar.*

center /ˈsen·tər/ [noun] **1** The middle area of or the exact middle of something: *Arthur lives in the center of Denver.* **2 leisure center** See **leisure center.** **3 sports center** See **sports center.** ■ Be careful with the pronunciation of this word! The "c" is pronounced as a "s". ■ The British English spelling is "centre".

centigrade /ˈsen·tɪˌgreɪd/ [noun and adjective] A scale for measuring temperature: *On the centigrade scale, water boils at 100 ºC and freezes at 0 ºC.* ■ The abbreviation "C" is only used in written language. With figures we normally write the sign "ºC" instead of writing "centigrade". ■ The same meaning: "Celsius". ■ Compare with "Fahrenheit": water boils at 212 ºF and freezes at 32 ºF. ■ See box at **abbreviations.**

centimeter /ˈsent·əˌmi·t̬ər/ [countable noun] A small unit of length: *There are a hundred centimeters in a meter.* ■ The British English spelling is "centimetre".

centimetre /ˈsentɪˌmiːtər-/ UK: /ˈsen.tɪˌmiː.təʳ/ [countable noun] See **centimeter.** ■ The abbreviation "cm" is only used in written language. ■ This word is British English spelling.

centipede /ˈsent·əˌpid/ [countable noun] Invertebrate with segmented body and many legs: *The centipede is a predator which moves very quickly.* 👁 **See page 431.**

†**central** /ˈsen.trəl/ [adjective] **1** That is in the center of something: *The station is very central.* **2 central heating** A heating system: *Alice's parents want to install central heating in their house.*

central nervous system [uncountable noun] The nerve tissue which controls the body's activities: *The central nervous system comprises the brain and the spinal cord.*

centre UK: /ˈsen.təʳ/ [countable noun] See **center.** ■ The British English spelling is "center". Be careful with the pronunciation of this word! The "c" is pronounced as a "s". ■ This is a British English spelling.

†**century** /ˈsen·tʃə·ri/ [countable noun] **1** A hundred years: *That building is nearly two centuries old.* **2** A period of a hundred years used to measure time: *The year 2000 is the end of the twentieth century.* ■ The plural is "centuries". ■ Be careful with the pronunciation of this word! The "c" is pronounced as a "s".

cephalopod /ˈsef.əl.əʊ.pɒd/ US: /-ə.pɑːd/ [countable noun] Marine mollusk with tentacles around a beaked mouth: *The squid is a cephalopod.*

cephalothorax [countable noun] The combined head and neck of arthropods: *The cephalothorax can be found on crustaceans like crabs.*

ceramics /səˈræmɪks/ [noun] **1** Pots made from clay hardened by heat: *These dishes are a fine example of local ceramics.* **2** The production of pots made from clay hardened by heat: *In the past, ceramics was an important industry in Mexico.*

cereal /ˈsɪər·i·əl/ [noun] **1** A plant that produces grain: *Wheat and barley are cereals.* **2** A grain food, usually eaten for breakfast: *I always have cornflakes or other cereals for breakfast.*

cerebellum /ˌser.əˈbel.əm/ [countable noun] The part of the brain at the rear of the skull coordinating the muscles: *The cerebellum controls the movement of the arms and legs.*

cerebrum /sɪˈriː.brəm/ [countable noun] The main part of the brain at the front of the skull which combines sensory and neural functions: *The cerebrum is where the centers of sight, touch, hearing, taste and smell are located.* ■ The plural is "cerebra".

†**ceremony** /ˈser.ɪ.mə.ni/ [noun] An event used to mark a special occasion: *There was a demonstration while the Nobel Prize ceremony was taking place.* ■ The plural is "ceremonies".

†**certain** /ˈsɜr·tə·n/ [adjective] **1** Having no doubt about something: *They're certain they're going to beat the girls' team but I'm not so sure.* **2** Particular: *There's a certain boy in my class who is always telling jokes.* **3 to make certain** To make sure: *You should make certain that he keeps his promise.*

certainly /ˈsɜr·tə·n·li/ [adverb] **1** Definitely: *It will certainly rain today.* **2** Of course: *Will you help me with my homework? Certainly.*

†**certificate** /sərˈtɪf·ɪ·kət/ [countable noun] A document that proves something: *In Rose's birth certificate it says she was born in Paris.*

cetacean /sɪˈteɪ.ʃən/ [countable noun] A marine mammal with a smooth skin and a blowhole: *Whales and dolphins are cetaceans.*

cf. A word used in writing when you want the reader to make a comparison between two references. ■ "cf." is an abbreviation for "compare". ■ See box at **abbreviations**.

†**chain** /tʃeɪn/ [countable noun] A string of metal rings: *They closed the gate with a chain and a lock.* 👁 **See page 441.**

†**chair** US: /tʃer/ UK: /tʃeəʳ/ [countable noun] **1** A piece of furniture used for sitting on: *Don't sit on that chair. One of the legs is broken.* 👁 See pictures at **classroom** and **living room**. **2** A person in charge of a meeting or the head of a company: *The chair of the company celebrates his 60th birthday this month.*

chairman /'tʃeə.mən/ [countable noun] A man in charge of a meeting or the head of a company: *The chairman welcomed everybody to the meeting.* ■ The plural is "chairmen". ■ A woman is a "chairwoman". When we don't want to say a person's sex, we can use "chair".

chairwoman /'tʃeərˌwʊm·ən/ [countable noun] A woman in charge of a meeting or the head of a company: *"I prefer to be called "chair", because "chairwoman" is discriminatory", she said.* ■ The plural is "chairwomen". ■ A man is a "chairman". When we don't want to say a person's sex, we can use "chair".

chalk US: /tʃɑːk/ UK: /tʃɔːk/ [noun] A white stick used for writing on a blackboard: *Go to Mrs. Booth's class and ask her for a packet of chalks.* 👁 See picture at **classroom**.

challenge[1] /'tʃæl.ɪndʒ/ [noun] **1** Something difficult: *Learning Russian was a challenge for me.* **2** An invitation to do something difficult: *Gabby accepted Megan's challenge to run two miles in under 14 minutes.*

challenge[2] /'tʃæl.ɪndʒ/ [verb] **1** To ask somebody to compete against you: *I challenged him to a boxing match.* **2** To ask somebody to do something difficult: *Peter challenged me to run faster than him.*

chamber /'tʃeɪmbər/ [countable noun] A judge's room for hearing cases that do not need to be heard in court: *The judge called the witnesses to give a statement at the chamber.*

chambers /'tʃeɪm·bərz/ [plural noun] **1** The offices of a legal practice: *Everyday the chambers are busy as the attorneys come and go from the courts.* **2** A Judge's room for hearing cases that must not necessarily be brought into court: *The case will be heard in chambers.*

chameleon /kə'miː.li.ən/ [countable noun] Lizard with a long tongue and a tail that it can grip with: *The chameleon changes its color as camouflage against danger.* ■ Be careful with the pronunciation of this word! 👁 **See page 430.**

champagne /ʃæm'peɪn/ [uncountable noun] A type of sparkling French wine: *My parents had a glass of champagne to celebrate New Year.*

champion /'tʃæm.pi.ən/ [countable noun] The winner of a competition: *The Russians are great chess champions.*

championship /'tʃæm.pi.ən.ʃɪp/ [countable noun] A competition: *I'd like to take part in the tennis championship.*

†**chance** US: /tʃænts/ UK: /tʃɑːnts/ ▮ [noun] **1** Possibility: *I don't have a chance of passing the test. It's too difficult for me.* ▮ [uncountable noun] **2** Luck, fortune: *Work hard, don't leave it to chance!* ▮ [countable noun] **3** An opportunity: *Getting a part in "The Importance of Being Earnest" gave him a real chance to prove how well he could act.* **4 by chance** Accidentally: *I don't know how I did it. I did it by chance.* **5 to take a chance** To try to do something risky: *I haven't studied for the exam so I'll just have to take a chance and hope I pass it.*

change[1] /tʃeɪndʒ/ ▮ [noun] **1** Something different from what was before: *There have been a lot of changes in the football team this year.* ▮ [uncountable noun] **2** The money that you get back when you pay for something: *I paid for the drinks and got 10 cent change.* **3** Money in coins: *I'll have to pay with a five dollar bill because I didn't have any change.* ■ In this use "change" is an uncountable noun. ▮ [countable noun] **4** Going for one bus, train or plane to another as part of a journey: *We had to make a change in London on our flight to New York.* **5 for a change** To do something different: *This summer I'd like to go to the mountains for a change.*

CHAIR

rocking chair

wheelchair

armchair

deckchair

a b c d e f g h i j k l m n o p q r s t u v w x y z

change² /tʃeɪndʒ/ [verb] **1** To become different or to make something different: *The city has changed a lot in the last twenty years.* **2** To get off one train, bus or plane to get another to continue the journey: *We have to change here to the circle line.* **3 to change your mind** See "to change your mind" in the word **mind¹**.

changeable /ˈtʃeɪn.dʒə.bl̩/ [adjective] Which changes often, likely to change: *The weather is very changeable at this time of year.*

changing room [countable noun] The room in a sports center, a swimming pool and so on, where you change your clothes: *John left his new sneakers in the changing room.*

channel /ˈtʃæn.əl/ [countable noun] **1** The part of a sea that is between two areas of land: *We crossed the Florida Channel from Key West to Havana.* **2** A television or radio station: *CNN is my favorite channel.*

chant¹ /tʃɑːnt/ ▮ [countable noun] **1** The repeated shouting of a name or a phrase: *At the demonstration, the crowd's chant was "No more deaths! Stop the war!".* ▮ [noun] **2** A type of song that has no musical accompaniment: *Jazz chants are useful for learning English pronunciation.*

chant² /tʃɑːnt/ [verb] To shout a name or a phrase many times: *The demonstrators chanted slogans against the Prime Minister.*

chapel /ˈtʃæp.əl/ [countable noun] **1** A small church in a building: *We have Bible study in the school chapel.* **2** A part of a large church: *I saw the chapel with the famous paintings in it.*

chapter /ˈtʃæp·tər/ [countable noun] One of the parts in which books are divided: *I'm on chapter four of "The Adventures of Tom Sawyer".*

character US: /ˈker.ɪk.tɚ/ UK: /ˈkær.ɪk.təʳ/ ▮ [noun] **1** The way a person is: *Tony has a very unpleasant character. He's always sarcastic.* ▮ [countable noun] **2** One of the people in a story: *My favorite character in "The Lion King" is Simba.* ■ Be careful with the pronunciation of this word! The "ch" is pronounced as a "k".

characteristic¹ /ˌkærəktəˈrɪstɪk/ [adjective] Typical: *Those houses are very characteristic of this area.* ■ Be careful with the pronunciation of this word! The "ch" is pronounced as a "k".

characteristic² /ˌkærəktəˈrɪstɪk/ [countable noun] A typical quality: *One of the characteristics of modern American movies is their violence.* ■ Be careful with the pronunciation of this word! The "ch" is pronounced as a "k".

characterize or **characterise** /ˈkærəktəraɪz/ [verb] To be a typical feature of something: *Actors have to characterize the part that they play.* ■ Be careful with the pronunciation of this word! The "ch" is pronounced as a "k".

charge¹ /tʃɑːdʒ/ [noun] **1** Money to be paid: *There will be an admission charge of 20 dollars at the School Fair.* **2 in charge of (somebody or something)** Being responsible for somebody or something: *Mrs. Hope left Lucy in charge of the class while she went out for a moment.* **3 to reverse the charges** See "to call collect" in the word **call²**. ■ This use is British English.

charge² /tʃɑːdʒ/ [verb] **1** To ask for money in exchange for something: *Mrs. Hogg charges a lot for private lessons.* **2** To run: *The children charged into the dining room.* **3** To accuse: *The police charged him with murder.*

chariot /ˈtʃær·i·ət/ [countable noun] An open vehicle with two wheels, that was pulled by a horse or horses in ancient times: *In the movie "Ben Hur" there is a famous chariot race.*

charity US: /ˈtʃer.ɪ.t̬i/ UK: /ˈtʃær.ɪ.ti/ [noun] **1** Help given to people who need it: *Nobody likes living on charity.* **2** An organization that collects money for good causes: *My parents always give money to one or two charities at Christmas.* ■ The plural is "charities".

charm¹ /tʃɑːm/ ▮ [noun] **1** The ability to be pleasing and delightful for other people: *Rick has so much charm that everybody likes him.* ▮ [uncountable noun] **2** An object that you think brings you good luck: *I always carry a rabbit foot on me as a charm.*

charm² /tʃɑːm/ [verb] To delight or please somebody: *Annette charmed me the moment I saw her.*

charming /ˈtʃɑr·mɪŋ/ [adjective] That is attractive and pleasant: *Mr. Donaldson is a charming man.*

chart US: /tʃɑːrt/ UK: /tʃɑːt/ [countable noun] A table or a picture with information: *On the bulletin board there's a chart with information on the test results.*

chase /tʃeɪs/ [verb] To run after somebody or something: *The dogs chased the fox down to the river.*

chat /tʃæt/ [verb] To talk in a friendly way: *We were chatting about hundreds of different things until two in the morning.* ■ Be careful with the spelling of these forms: "chatted", "chatting".

chauffeur US: /ʃəʊˈfɜːr/ UK: /ˈʃəʊfər/ [countable noun] A person who drives cars for other people: *Tim's father works as a chauffeur for the director of a big company.*

cheap /tʃiːp/ [adjective] That costs very little or costs little in comparison: *I'll have to buy something cheap. I don't have much money.* 👁 See picture at **opposite**.

cheat¹ /tʃiːt/ [countable noun] A person who uses dishonest means to win: *I don't want to play cards with James because he's a cheat.*

cheat[2] /tʃiːt/ [verb] To win a game by dishonest means: *It's impossible to play chess seriously with Anne; she's always cheating.*

check[1] /tʃek/ [countable noun] **1** An examination to see that something is correct: *I need to take my bike for a check. There's something wrong with the brakes.* **2** A mark [SÍMBOLO VISTO BUENO] made to show that something is correct: *I got ten checks in my notebook today!* ■ In British English they say "tick". **3** A type of note that you can exchange for money at a bank: *Great! Auntie Dora has sent me a check for fifty dollars.* ■ In British English they say "cheque". **4** A piece of paper showing how much money somebody must pay in a restaurant: *What a great dinner, let's pay the check and go home.* ■ In this use, the same meaning: "bill".

†**check**[2] /tʃek/ [verb] To make sure that something is right or that something has been done: *Check your answers when you finish the exercise.*
▶ **PHRASAL VERBS** · **to check in 1** To register in a hotel: *Don't forget that you need to check in before 8 p.m.* **2** To present your ticket and your luggage for a flight: *Hurry up! We have to check in 45 minutes before departure.* · **to check out** To pay your bill when you leave a hotel: *Guests are requested to check out before 12 a.m.*

checkbook [countable noun] A little book with checks: *My mom couldn't find her checkbook and had to pay in cash.* ■ In British English they say "cheque book".

checked /tʃekt/ [adjective] With a square pattern: *I'm going to wear my red, black and white checked shirt today.*

checkers [noun] A game played with counters on a black and white board: *Do you want a game of checkers?* ■ It is usually used with a singular verb. ■ In British English they say "draughts".

checkout /ˈtʃek.aʊt/ [countable noun] The place in a supermarket where you pay: *Don't pay here. You pay for the meat at the checkout.*

check-up /ˈtʃekʌp/ [countable noun] A general medical examination: *My mom wasn't feeling very well, so she went to the doctor for a check-up.*

†**cheek** /tʃiːk/ ▮ [countable noun] **1** The part of your face below your eyes: *Pink cheeks are a sign of health.* ▮ [noun] **2** Not having respect for somebody, often in a funny or not serious way: *What a cheek! She's taken my dessert!*

cheekbone /ˈtʃikˌboʊn/ [countable noun] The bone below the eye: *His cheekbone was broken from the blow.*

cheeky /ˈtʃiː.ki/ [adjective] Behaving without respect: *Wayne is very cheeky. He told Mrs. Green that she was getting fat.* ■ The comparative form is "cheekier" and the superlative form is "cheekiest".

cheer US: /tʃɪr/ UK: /tʃɪəʳ/ [verb] **1** To shout to encourage somebody: *We spent the whole game cheering our team.* **2** **three cheers** An expression you use to ask people to congratulate somebody: *Three cheers for Lesley!*
▶ **PHRASAL VERBS** · **to cheer up** To feel happier: *Cheer up, Rosie. Tomorrow's Saturday.*

†**cheerful** /ˈtʃɪər·fəl/ [adjective] Happy and lively: *Sam is such a cheerful baby! He's always smiling.*

†**cheese** /tʃiːz/ [noun] Solid food made from milk: *Camembert is my favorite cheese.*

cheeseburger /ˈtʃizˌbɜr·gər/ [countable noun] A hamburger with a slice of cheese: *We ordered two cheeseburgers, french fries and two orange drinks.*

cheetah /ˈtʃiːtə/ [countable noun] Animal that looks like a cat with a spotted coat: *The cheetah is the fastest mammal.*

chef /ʃef/ [countable noun] An important cook in a restaurant: *The chef of this restaurant is Colombian.*

chemical[1] /ˈkemɪkəl/ [countable noun] A substance that is used in chemistry or produced by chemistry: *We need a strong chemical to clean this metal surface.* ■ Be careful with the pronunciation of this word! The "ch" is pronounced as a "k".

chemical[2] /ˈkemɪkəl/ [adjective] Referring to chemistry or that is used in chemistry: *We can only do chemical experiments if we are supervised by a teacher.* ■ Be careful with the pronunciation of this word! The "ch" is pronounced as a "k".

†**chemist** /ˈkem.ɪst/ [countable noun] **1** See **pharmacist**. ■ This use is British English. **2** A person who does chemistry: *My mother works as a research chemist at the university.* ■ Be careful with the pronunciation of this word! The "ch" is pronounced as a "k".

†**chemistry** /ˈkem.ɪ.stri/ [uncountable noun] The study of chemical substances: *Chemistry is one of my favorite subjects.* ■ Be careful with the pronunciation of this word! The "ch" is pronounced as a "k". ■ The plural is "chemistries".

chemist's /ˈkemɪst/ [countable noun] See **pharmacy**. ■ This word is British English.

cheque /tʃek/ [countable noun] See **check**[1]. ■ This word is British English.

cheque book /ˈtʃekbʊk/ [countable noun] See **checkbook**. ■ This word is British English.

cherry /ˈtʃer.i/ [countable noun] A small round red or black fruit: *Don't eat too many cherries! You'll get stomach ache.* ■ The plural is "cherries". 👁 **See page 436.**

cherry or **cherry tree** /ˈtʃeri/ [countable noun] A tree which bears cherries: *Heavy rain can easily damage cherry trees.*

chess /tʃes/ [uncountable noun] A game for two people that is played on a black and white board: *Chess is a very difficult game.*

†**chest** /tʃest/ [countable noun] The front part of the body between the neck and the stomach: *He received a blow on his chest and was unconscious for five minutes.*

chestnut[1] /'tʃesnʌt/ [countable noun] **1** A red brown nut: *I love eating roasted chestnuts in the fall.* **2** A tree that gives chestnuts: *Chestnuts are tall trees with broad leaves.*

chestnut[2] [noun and adjective] A color that is between red and brown: *There's a beautiful chestnut horse in that field.*

chest of drawers [countable noun] See **dresser**. ■ This word is British English.

†**chew** /tʃuː/ [verb] To make something soft with your teeth: *This meat is hard to chew.*

chewing gum [uncountable noun] A candy that you keep in your mouth and bite on, but do not swallow: *Could you please take that chewing gum out of your mouth when you're speaking to me?*

chick /tʃɪk/ [countable noun] A very young bird: *Have you seen the new chicks in the barn?*

†**chicken** /'tʃɪkɪn/ ▮ [countable noun] **1** A young hen: *Mrs. McKay keeps chickens at her cottage.* ▮ [uncountable noun] **2** The meat of a young hen: *There's chicken for lunch every Tuesday.*

chickenpox /'tʃɪk·ən,pɑks/ [uncountable noun] A disease that gives you red pimples on your skin: *Three children in our class are absent with chickenpox.*

chickpea /'tʃɪk.piː/ [countable noun] A fat round seed, commonly used as food: *When I go to Mexico I like to eat chickpeas. In United States you don't usually see them.*

chief[1] /tʃiːf/ [countable noun] The most important person in a group of people or organization: *The chief of police spoke to the press about the incidents in the school.*

chief[2] /tʃiːf/ [adjective] Most important: *Violence is one of the chief problems nowadays.*

chiefly /'tʃiː.fli/ [adverb] Mainly: *The accident was chiefly due to the bad weather.*

CHESS

↑child /tʃaɪld/ [countable noun] **1** A young person: *A child should not be left alone at home.* ■ "Child" is used for both girls and boys. **2** A son or a daughter: *Mrs. Higgins has three children.* ■ When we want to say the sex, we use "boy" for "son" and "girl" for "daughter": "Mrs. Higgins has two boys and a girl". The plural is "children".

childbirth /ˈtʃaɪldbɜːθ/ [uncountable noun] The process of giving birth to a child: *The experience of childbirth can be exhausting for the new mother.*

childhood /ˈtʃaɪld.hʊd/ [noun] The time of life when people are children: *Rob had a happy childhood in Australia.*

childish /ˈtʃaɪl.dɪʃ/ [adjective] Always behaving like a child: *Colin is fourteen years old but he's still very childish.*

children /ˈtʃɪl.drən/ The plural of **child**.

Chilean¹ [adjective] Referring to Chile: *Valparaiso is one of the main Chilean tourist destination.* ■ Be careful! "Chilean" has a capital "C".

Chilean² [countable noun] A person from Chile: *My sister is married to a Chilean and the live in Santiago.* ■ Be careful! "Chilean" has a capital "C".

chill /tʃɪl/ [verb] To make something cold: *Put some ice in your drink to chill it.*

chilly /ˈtʃɪl.i/ [adjective] Feeling a little cold: *It's not very cold, but I feel a bit chilly.*

chime¹ [countable noun] The sound made by a bell or clock: *The chime of bells is a pleasant sound.*

chime² /tʃaɪm/ [verb] To sound a bell or a clock: *Listen! The clock is chiming three.*

chimney /ˈtʃɪm.ni/ [countable noun] A stone tube that takes the smoke away from a fire: *Santa Claus gets into houses through the chimney.* ■ Compare with "fireplace" (the place in a room where you can make a fire).

chimpanzee /ˌtʃɪm.pænˈziː/ [countable noun] A type of ape from Africa: *Chimpanzees are very intelligent animals.*

↑chin /tʃɪn/ [countable noun] The part of the face below the mouth: *I fell off my bike and hurt my chin.* 👁 See picture at **face**.

china /ˈtʃaɪ.nə/ [uncountable noun] **1** A type of fine pottery: *English china is of very high quality.* **2** Cups, dishes and plates made of china: *Put the china away but don't break anything.*

↑chip /tʃɪp/ [countable noun] **1** A thin slice of fried potato or other cereals sold in bags: *What do you want corn chips or potato chips?* ■ In British English they say "crisp". ■ This use is more common in the plural. **2** See **french fry**. ■ This use is British English. ■ This use is more common in the plural. **3** A small piece of electronic equipment: *The chip in my new computer is very fast.* ■ In this use, we also say "microchip".

chirp US: /tʃɝːp/ UK: /tʃɜːp/ [verb] To make a sound, some birds and insects: *I love hearing our canary chirp in the morning.*

chlorophyll /ˈklɔr·əˌfɪl/, /ˈkloʊr-/ [uncountable noun] A green substance in plants which provides them with energy: *Photosynthesis is a result of the absorption of light by the chlorophyll.*

↑chocolate /ˈtʃɑk·lət/, /ˈtʃɔk-/ [noun] **1** A brown sweet: *I always have a sandwich and a bar of chocolate for snack.* **2** A small sweet made of chocolate: *I had three boxes of chocolates for my birthday.* ■ Be careful with the pronunciation of this word! The second "o" is not pronounced and the "a" is pronounced as in "ago".

↑choice /tʃɔɪs/ [noun] **1** The act of choosing: *Which cake do you want? Hurry up and make your choice.* **2** The number of things that you can choose from: *There's a very good choice of movies on just now.*

choir US: /kwaɪr/ UK: /kwaɪəʳ/ [countable noun] A group of people who sing together, especially during religious services: *I like singing but I don't sing well enough to be in the school choir.* ■ Be careful with the pronunciation of this word! The "ch" is pronounced as a "k".

choke US: /tʃoʊk/ UK: /tʃəʊk/ [verb] To have difficulties to breathe: *Last Sunday I choked on a fish bone.*

a b c d e f g h i j k l m n o p q r s t u v w x y z

cholera /'kɑl·ər·ə/ [uncountable noun] A serious infectious disease causing severe diarrhea: *A cholera epidemic can cause a large number of deaths.*

↑**choose,** chose, chosen /tʃuːz/ [verb] **1** To take one from several things or people: *Which pants did you choose, the jeans or the black ones?* **2** To decide to do something: *Donald has chosen to go to university.*

↑**chop**[1] /tʃɒp/ [countable noun] A piece of meat on a bone: *I ordered pork chops with sweet and sour sauce.*

chop[2] /tʃɒp/ [verb] To cut into small pieces: *Wendy's father spent the morning chopping wood for the fire.*

chopsticks /'tʃɒpstɪks/ [plural noun] A pair of thin sticks used for eating in oriental countries: *At our local Chinese restaurant you can use chopsticks or a knife and fork.*

choral /'kɔːrəl/ [adjective] Referring to a choir: *The best part of the program was the choral music.* ■ Be careful with the pronunciation of this word! La "ch" is pronounced as a "k" and the first syllable emphasized.

chord US: /kɔːrd/ UK: /kɔːd/ [countable noun] **1** Group of musical notes played together to form a harmony: *The pianist played a major chord.* **2** A line segment joining two points: *During the lesson of geometry the teacher asked us to draw a chord.* ■ Be careful with the pronunciation of this word! The "ch" is pronounced as a "k".

chore US: /tʃɔːr/ UK: /tʃɔːʳ/ [countable noun] A job that has to be done regularly, especially housework: *I hate chores like cleaning up or making the bed.* ■ This word is more common in the plural.

chorus US: /'kɔːr.əs/ UK: /'kɔː.rəs/ [countable noun] **1** A group of singers or dancers in a musical: *The chorus who sang "Aida" was superb!* **2** The part of a song that is repeated: *I don't know the words of the song very well, only the chorus.* ■ Be careful with the pronunciation of this word! The "ch" is pronounced as a "k".

chose US: /tʃoʊz/ UK: /tʃəʊz/ Past tense of **choose**.

chosen /'tʃoʊ·zən/ Past participle of **choose**.

Christ /kraɪst/ [noun] The name of Jesus, the son of God in the Christian religion: *Christ died when he was about 33 years old.* ■ Be careful. "Christ" has a capital "C".

christen /'krɪs.ən/ [verb] **1** To make somebody a member of the Christian church: *We christened our new baby on Saturday.* **2** To give a first name to somebody: *They christened the baby Thomas.*

Christian /'krɪs.tʃən, -ti.ən/ [noun and adjective] Referring to Christianity or a follower of Christianity: *Some of the early Christians were persecuted in Rome.* ■ Be careful! "Christian" has a capital "C".

Christianity /ˌkrɪs·tʃi'æn·ɪ·t̬i/ [uncountable noun] The religion that follows the teachings of Jesus Christ: *Christianity began in the first century AD.* ■ Be careful! "Christianity" has a capital "C".

Christian name [countable noun] See **name**[1].

Christmas /'krɪs.məs/ [noun] A feast on December 25th that celebrates the birth of Jesus Christ: *When I was a child Christmas was the happiest time of the year.* ■ Be careful. "Christmas" has a capital "C". The abbreviation "Xmas" is only used in written language.

chrysalis /'krɪs.əl.ɪs/ [countable noun] The form of a moth or butterfly while it is growing: *The chrysalis turned into a butterfly.* ■ The plural is "chrysalises".

↑**church** US: /tʃɝːtʃ/ UK: /tʃɜːtʃ/ [countable noun] A place where Christians meet to pray: *We usually hear mass at St John's Church.* ■ The plural is "churches".

cigar /sɪ'gɑr/ [countable noun] Tobacco leaves rolled together for smoking: *Havana cigars are famous all over the world.*

↑**cigarette** /ˌsɪg·ə'ret/ [countable noun] Small pieces of tobacco rolled in paper for smoking: *Cigarette smoking causes many kinds of disease.*

↑**cinema** /'sɪn.ə.mə/ [countable noun] See **movie theater**. ■ This word is British English. ■ Be careful with the pronunciation of this word! The "c" is pronounced as a "s".

↑**circle**[1] /'sɜːkl/ [countable noun] **1** A completely round shape: *We formed several circles to dance at the party.* **See page 457.** **2** An area of seats that is upstairs in a theater and so on: *I've booked seats in the front row of the circle.* ■ Be careful with the pronunciation of this word! The first "c" is pronounced as a "s".

circle[2] /'sɜːkl/ [verb] **1** To go around: *The airplane circled the airport for an hour before landing.* **2** To draw a circle around something: *Circle the right answers.*

circuit /'sɜr·kət/ [countable noun] **1** Established route for an activity: *I follow a five miles circuit when I run.* **2** A path along which an electric current flows: *We built a parallel circuit.* ■ Be careful with the pronunciation of this word! The first "c" is pronounced as a "s" and the "u" is not pronounced.

circular US: /'sɝː.kjʊ.lɚ/ UK: /'sɜː.kjʊ.ləʳ/ [adjective] Round: *Wheels are circular.* ■ Be careful with the pronunciation of this word. The first "c" is pronounced like an "s".

circulate /'sɜr·kjəˌleɪt/ [verb] To go or to pass around: *Mrs. Cameron has to take pills to help her blood to circulate well.*

circulation /ˌsɜr·kjəˈlei·ʃən/ [uncountable noun] **1** The movement of blood through the body: *His circulation was affected by his illness.* **2** The passing or spreading of something from one place or person to another: *There was a story in circulation about their differences of opinion.*

circulatory [adjective] Referring to the circulation of blood: *Dizziness is often caused by circulatory problems.*

circulatory system [countable noun] The system which circulates blood or sap: *The circulatory system carries nutrients and oxygen to our cells.*

circumference /sərˈkəm·fər·əns/ [noun] The outside edge of a circle: *The circumference of the earth is about 40,000 kms.*

***circumstance** US: /ˈsɜː.kəm.stænts/ UK: /ˈsɜː.kəm.stɑːnts/ [countable noun] An action or fact that influences something: *In the circumstances we were lucky to come out alive.*

circus /ˈsɜr·kəs/ [countable noun] **1** A show with clowns, acrobats and animals: *I love seeing the clowns at a circus.* **2** A round, open space in a town: *Piccadilly Circus is one of London's most famous tourist attractions.* ■ The plural is "circuses". ■ Be careful with the pronunciation of this word! The first "c" is pronounced as a "s".

***citizen** /ˈsɪṭ·ə·zən/ [countable noun] A person who legally belongs to a country: *People born in Puerto Rico are citizens of the United States.*

***city** /ˈsɪṭ·i/ [countable noun] A large town: *My favorite city is Paris.* ■ The plural is "cities". Be careful with the pronunciation of this word! The "c" is pronounced as an "s".

civil /ˈsɪv.əl/ [adjective] **1** Relating to citizens and their concerns not to religion or the army: *The army should not interfere in the elections as it is a civil matter.* **2** Polite: *Her answer was very civil.*

civilization /ˌsɪv.əl.aɪˈzeɪ.ʃən/ [noun] **1** An advanced stage of social and cultural development: *We are studying ancient civilizations at school.* **2** A society: *Some explorers have discovered the ruins of an ancient American civilization.* ■ This word is also written "civilisation".

civil servant [countable noun] Somebody who works in a government department: *My cousin is a civil servant.*

civil service [noun] The administration of a government: *Sheila's mother has a high post in the civil service.*

***claim**[1] /kleɪm/ [countable noun] **1** Something that you say which you maintain is true: *His claim that I copied his project is totally false.* **2** Something that you ask for because you think you have a right to it: *After the accident, he sent his claim to the insurance company.*

claim[2] /kleɪm/ [verb] **1** To say that something is true: *Liz claimed that she had seen Tom Hanks at the supermarket.* **2** To ask for something that you think you have a right to: *Fred claimed the first prize, but he was only given the second prize.*

clang /klæŋ/ [countable noun] A loud, metallic sound: *The clang of that machine drives me crazy.*

***clap** /klæp/ [verb] To show approval by joining your hands together again and again: *Everyone started clapping when the concert finished.* ■ Be careful with the spelling of these forms: "clapped", "clapping".

clarinet /ˌklærɪˈnet/ [countable noun] A musical instrument which has the shape of a tube and is played by blowing into its top: *The clarinet is considered to be a difficult instrument to play.* 👁 **See page 459.**

clash[1] /klæʃ/ [countable noun] **1** The sound that things make when they hit each other: *When he dropped the box, there was a clash of cutlery.* **2** A battle or a conflict: *There has been a clash between soldiers at the frontier.*

clash[2] /klæʃ/ [verb] **1** To fight: *The demonstrators clashed with the police.* **2** Not to match: *I think the colors of your blouse and your skirt clash.*

***class** US: /klæs/ UK: /klɑːs/ [countable noun] **1** A group of students: *The whole class agreed with the idea of going on an excursion.* **2** A group of people or things of the same kind: *There are many different classes of pine tree.* **3 first class** See **first class**[2]. **4 second class** See **second class**[2]. ■ The plural is "classes".

***classic** /ˈklæs.ɪk/ [countable noun] Something considered as an extremely good example of its kind: *Oliver Twist is a classic of world literature.*

classical /ˈklæs.ɪ.kəl/ [adjective] Traditional, based on an old and established system: *Classical music is OK but I prefer jazz.*

classification /ˌklæsɪfɪˈkeɪʃən/ [countable noun] **1** Arrangement into classes or categories: *The insects belong to different classifications according to their type.* **2** A group or class into which something is put: *Fish come under the classification of biological vertebrate.*

classify /ˈklæs.ɪ.faɪ/ [verb] **1** To grade things by their qualities: *It is best to classify soccer teams by the number of goals.* **2** To place somebody or something in a particular category: *Do they classify his compositions as Baroque Music?* ■ Be careful with the spelling of these forms: "classifies", "classified".

classmate /ˈklæsˌmeɪt/ [countable noun] A student in your class: *I get on well with my classmates.*

a b **c** d e f g h i j k l m n o p q r s t u v w x y z

↑**classroom** /ˈklæsˌrum/, /-ˌrʊm/ [countable noun] A place in a school where lessons are held: *This school is very small. It has only three classrooms.*

clavicle /ˈklæv.ɪ.kl̩/ [countable noun] The bone joining the breastbone and the shoulder blade: *He broke his clavicle in the accident.* ■ The same meaning: "collarbone".

claw US: /klɑː/ UK: /klɔː/ [countable noun] The very sharp nails on the feet of an animal or a bird: *Tigers have very sharp claws.*

clay /kleɪ/ [uncountable noun] A type of soil used to make bricks or pottery: *That ashtray from Morocco is made of clay.*

clean¹ /kliːn/ [adjective] Not dirty: *Colin keeps his house very clean.*

↑**clean²** /kliːn/ [verb] To remove dirt: *Have you cleaned your room today?*

cleaner /ˈkli·nər/ [countable noun] Somebody who cleans: *The mess that was left behind was taken care of by the cleaner.*

cleanse /klenz/ [verb] To clean thoroughly: *The priest cleanses his flock through confession.*

↑**clear¹** /klɪər/ [adjective] **1** That you can see through: *On a clear day, you can see the sea from here.* **2** Easy to read, to hear or to understand: *Mr. Wells' instruc-*

CLASSROOM

tions are not always clear. **3** Obvious: *It was clear that Mr. Moon was joking.*

clear[2] /klɪər/ [verb] To put things away: *Can you clear the table, Ben? I'll wash up.*
◗ **PHRASAL VERBS** · **to clear (something) away** To remove something which is in the way: *Can you clear your books away from the table? I want to use it.* · **to clear up** To find an answer or an explanation: *The disappearance of the test papers was never cleared up.*

clearly /ˈklɪər·li/ [adverb] **1** In a way that is easy to read, to hear or to understand: *You have to speak more clearly, Danny. I never know what you're saying.* **2** Obviously: *The advertiser is clearly not telling the truth about the features of that car.*

clergy /ˈklɜr·dʒi/ [plural noun] The people ordered officially by a Christian church: *The clergy give their opinion on many things.*

clerk US: /klɝːk/ UK: /klɑːk/ [countable noun] **1** A person who does office work: *Susan's mother works as a clerk in a bank.* **2** A person who serves customers in a store: *The store clerk showed me three different jackets, all of them terrible.* ■ In this use, in British English we say "shop assistant".

clever /ˈklev·ər/ [adjective] Intelligent: *She's a very clever girl; she understands everything very quickly.*

cleverness /ˈklev.ə.nəs/ US: /-ɚ-/ [uncountable noun] Intelligence: *The children were delighted by the monkeys' cleverness.*

click /klɪk/ [countable noun] A short, sharp sound: *We heard a click and the door opened.*

client /ˈklaɪ.ᵊnt/ [countable noun] **1** A person or company that asks for the advice or services of a professional: *The architect showed his designs to his client.* ■ Compare with "customer" (a person who buys goods or services). **2** A customer: *He's good client. He's always buying books from us.*

cliff /klɪf/ [countable noun] High, very steep rock on a coast: *Climbing cliffs can be very dangerous.* 👁 **See page 444.**

climate /ˈklaɪ.mət/ [noun] The normal weather of an area: *It's usually hot in tropical climates.*

climax /ˈklaɪ.mæks/ [countable noun] The most exciting part of a story, usually just before the end: *The story reaches its climax when the children find the treasure.* ■ The plural is "climaxes".

climb /klaɪm/ [verb] **1** To go up towards the top of something: *The bus was full and it climbed the road very slowly.* **2** To go up something using hands and feet: *We had to climb a wall to get into the yard.* **3** To go up mountains: *Several men and women have now climbed Everest.* ■ Be careful with the pronunciation of this word. The "b" is silent. This word rhymes with "time".

climber /ˈklaɪmər/ [countable noun] **1** A climbing plant: *The ivy earned its reputation as a climber by covering the front of the house.* **2** A person who climbs: *Climbers use harnesses and picks.*

climbing /ˈklaɪ.mɪŋ/ [uncountable noun] The sport of going up steep rocks: *We're going climbing in the Pyrenees this summer.*

climogram [countable noun] Representation of climate patterns in graphic form: *The climogram showed record rainfall and temperatures.*

clinic /ˈklɪn.ɪk/ [countable noun] A place where you can get specialist medical treatment: *The health clinic will give you information about the dangers of drinking too much alcohol.*

clip /klɪp/ [countable noun] An object made from wire, used for holding things together: *Use a clip or you'll lose all your papers.*

cloak /kləʊk/ [countable noun] An article of clothing like a coat without sleeves, worn over the arms: *Cloaks have become old-fashioned.* ■ The same meaning: "cape".

cloakroom /ˈkloʊkˌrum/, /-ˌrʊm/ [countable noun] A place in a theater or a restaurant where you can leave your coat: *When the play finished, James went to the cloakroom for our coats.*

clock US: /klɑːk/ UK: /klɒk/ [countable noun] **1** An instrument that tells the time, that is on a wall, a shelf and so on: *The school clock is ten minutes fast. It's only five to nine.* ■ Compare with "watch[1]" (carried on your person, usually on your wrist). **2** **alarm clock** A clock that wakes you up: *They set the alarm clock for 6.30.*

CLOCK

a b c d e f g h i j k l m n o p q r s t u v w x y z

clockwise /ˈklak,waɪz/ [adverb] In the direction in which the hands of a clock move: *We had to run clockwise around the yard for 10 minutes.*

clockwork /ˈklɒkwɜːk/ [uncountable noun] Machinery used in clocks and toys: *My little brother got a clockwork train for Christmas.*

close[1] /kləʊz/ [adjective] **1** Near: *Our school is quite close to the local church.* **2** Liking each other: *Barry and I have been close friends for years.* **3** Careful: *After a close examination of the handwriting, Sherlock Holmes realized who the murderer was.*

close[2] /kləʊz/ [adverb] Near: *The boy followed close behind his mother.*

*close**[3] /kləʊz/ [verb] To shut, to change the position of something so that it is not open: *Close the door, please. It's very cold.*

▸ **PHRASAL VERBS** · **to close down** To end an activity or a business: *My uncle's business did so badly last year that he had to close it down.*

closely /ˈkloʊs·li/ [adverb] **1** In a connected and associated way: *The American team worked closely with the Mexican.* **2** In a dense way: *We traveled very closely packed in my uncle's car.* **3** At a short distance: *She has followed that singer's career very closely.*

closet US: /ˈklɒzɪt/ [countable noun] A piece of furniture that is used for keeping clothes in: *Don't leave your clothes around, Tim. Keep them in your closet.* ■ Compare with "cupboard" (used for keeping all kinds of things in). ■ In British English they say "wardrobe". 👁 See picture at **bedroom**.

clot /klɒt/ [countable noun] A lump formed from a coagulated liquid: *The dried blood formed into a clot.*

*cloth** US: /klɑːθ/ UK: /klɒθ/ ▮ [uncountable noun] **1** Material made from cotton, wool and so on: *I need some cloth to make the drapes.* ▮ [countable noun] **2** A piece of material used for cleaning: *You can clean the mess with that cloth over there.*

clothed /kləʊðd/ [adjective] Wearing clothing: *The children were clothed in traditional costumes for the carnival.*

*clothes** US: /kloʊðz/ UK: /kləʊðz/ [plural noun] **1** The things that people wear: *Put your clothes on before you catch cold.* **2** casual clothes See "casual clothes" in the word **casual**.

*clothing** /ˈkloʊ·ðɪŋ/ [uncountable noun] Clothes: *She sells articles of clothing like shirts, blouses and skirts.*

*cloud** /klaʊd/ [noun] A mass of water drops or dust that is in the air: *Look at those black clouds in the sky; it's going to rain.* 👁 **See page 438.**

cloudy /ˈklaʊ.di/ [adjective] That is covered with clouds: *It was so cloudy that we couldn't see the sun.* ■ The comparative form is "cloudier" and the superlative form is "cloudiest".

clown /klaʊn/ [countable noun] A person, usually with funny clothes, who makes people laugh: *I love seeing the clowns at the circus.*

*club** /klʌb/ [countable noun] **1** An organization of people with the same interests: *I'm a member of the skiing club.* **2** A stick used to hit the ball in golf: *I left the clubs at home and we couldn't play golf.* **3** A playing card with black shapes on it: *I've got the Ace of clubs.*

*clue** /kluː/ [countable noun] Something that gives information to solve a problem or a mystery: *The clues for this crossword are very easy.*

clump [countable noun] A small group of plants or trees: *a clump of grass.* 👁 See picture at **a piece of...**

clumsy /ˈklʌm.zi/ [adjective] That is not very skillful with the hands: *That boy is so clumsy! He's always dropping things.* ■ The comparative form is "clumsier" and the superlative form is "clumsiest".

cluster /ˈklʌstər/ [countable noun] A close grouping: *A cluster of mushrooms grew around the roots of the tree.*

clutch[1] /klʌtʃ/ [countable noun] The pedal in a car used to change gear: *You have to press the clutch with your foot when you want to change gears.*

clutch[2] /klʌtʃ/ [verb] To hold something firmly: *He clutched the policeman's hand and was lifted to safety.*

*cm** A written abbreviation for **centimeter**. ■ See box at **abbreviations**.

c/o An abbreviation used in addresses before the name of a person who passes on the letter for another person: *Please send the letter to American Airlines, c/o Human Resources department, PO Box 619612 MD 2400.* ■ "c/o" is a written abbreviation for "care of".

*coach** US: /koʊtʃ/ UK: /kəʊtʃ/ [countable noun] **1** A bus used for long journeys: *Get the coach to Chicago; it's cheaper than the train.* **2** A person who trains sportsmen or sportswomen: *Susan's father is the coach of our school football team.* ■ In this use, the same meaning: "trainer". ■ The plural is "coaches".

coagulate /koʊˈæg·jə,leɪt/ [verb] To clot: *Blood coagulates after a blow to form a bruise.*

*coal** US: /koʊl/ UK: /kəʊl/ [noun] A black mineral used as a fuel: *Burning coal pollutes the atmosphere.* 👁 **See page 439.**

coalminer [countable noun] A person who works in a coal mine: *Five of my uncles were coalminers.*

*coast** US: /koʊst/ UK: /kəʊst/ [countable noun] The land that is next to the sea: *Finlay's parents have a house on the coast.*

coastal /ˈkəʊstəl/ [adjective] Referring to the coast: *Coastal beaches continue for 900 miles in the northeast of Brazil.* 👁 **See page 444.**

CLOTHES

jacket

swimming trunks

bikini

sweatshirt

purse

boot

scarf

sock

T-shirt

suit

sweater

coat

raincoat

hat

jeans

dress

tie

skirt

glove

thong

pants

shorts

shoe

belt

tracksuit

coaster US: /'koʊ.stɚ/ UK: /'kəʊ.stəʳ/ [countable noun] **1** A small protecting mat that you put drink containers on: *The coaster prevents marks from being made on the wooden surface of the table.* **2** A ship that sails from port to port along a coast: *The coaster was used for trade between coastal locations.*

coastline /'koʊst,laɪn/ [noun] The line of the coast: *The coastline of Florida is very irregular.*

ᐩ**coat** US: /koʊt/ UK: /kəʊt/ [countable noun] **1** A piece of clothing with sleeves and buttons that you wear over other clothes when you are cold: *Don't go out without your coat, Jim. It's very cold.* 👁 See picture at **clothes**. **2** **coat hanger** A piece of metal, wood or plastic on which you hang clothes: *Don't leave your jacket on a chair, please. Put it on a coat hanger.* ■ Be careful with the pronunciation of this word! "coa" rhymes with "go".

cobweb /'kɑb,web/ [countable noun] A fine net made by a spider: *The fly was caught in the cobweb.* ■ The same meaning: "spiderweb".

Coca Cola® US: /,koʊ.kə'koʊ.lə/ UK: /,kəʊ.kə'kəʊ.lə/ [noun] A fizzy sweet brown drink: *Sorry, but I don't want a Coca Cola. It's too sweet for me.* ■ Be careful! "Coca Cola" has capital letters. ■ We also say: "Coke".

cochlea /'kɒk.li.ə/ US: /'kɑːk-/ [countable noun] Spiral cavity of the inner ear: *The cochlea sends information to the brain.*

cock US: /kɑːk/ UK: /kɒk/ [countable noun] An adult male chicken: *I like hearing the cocks crow at dawn.*

cockpit /'kɑk·pɪt/ [countable noun] The part in a plane where the pilot is: *The captain invited all the children on board to visit the cockpit.*

cocktail /'kɑk,teɪl/ [countable noun] A drink made by mixing several drinks: *I drank a little champagne cocktail at my sister's wedding.*

cocoa US: /'koʊ.koʊ/ UK: /'kəʊ.kəʊ/ [uncountable noun] A powder used for making hot chocolate: *I always have a cup of cocoa before going to bed.*

coconut /'koʊ·kə,nʌt/ [countable noun] A very large nut from a palm tree: *Coconuts have a hard brown shell, white flesh and a very sweet liquid.* 👁 See **page 436**.

cod US: /kɑːd/ UK: /kɒd/ [noun] A fish with white flesh that is good to eat: *In Portugal they have lots of ways of cooking cod.* ■ The plural is also "cod".

ᐩ**code** US: /koʊd/ UK: /kəʊd/ [noun] **1** A system used to send secret messages: *My sister and I have a code in which we use numbers instead of letters.* **2** A group of rules: *If you want to get a driving license, you have to learn the Highway Code.*

ᐩ**coffee** US: /'kɑː.fi/ UK: /'kɒf.i/ [noun] **1** The beans of a tropical plant that are used to make a drink: *Colombia produces some of the best coffee in the world.* **2** A drink made with coffee beans: *My dad always has coffee after lunch.* ■ We say: "to **make** a coffee". **3** **coffee table** A low table that is usually in the living room: *Mick got some glasses from the kitchen and left them on the coffee table.* ■ "Black coffee" is coffee without milk. "Decaffeinated coffee" is coffee with the caffeine taken out. "Instant coffee" is coffee made simply by adding hot water or milk to coffee powder. Coffee can be "weak" or "strong". 👁 See picture at **living room**.

cogwheel /'kɒg.wiːl/ US: /'kɑːg-/ [countable noun] Wheel with projecting teeth which rotates and interacts with a similar wheel on a different shaft: *The cogwheel transfers power from the drive-shaft to the axle of the car.*

ᐩ**coin** /kɔɪn/ [countable noun] Piece of metal used as money: *I need two quarter coins for the telephone.*

coincidence /koʊ'ɪn·sɪ·də·ns/, /-sə,dens/ [countable noun] Something that happens by chance: *What a coincidence! We were born on the same day!*

Coke® US: /koʊk/ UK: /kəʊk/ [noun] See **Coca Cola®**. ■ Be careful! "Coke®" has a capital "C". ■ Be careful with the pronunciation of this word. The "o" is long, as in "show".

ᐩ**cold**[1] /koʊld/ [adjective] That has a low temperature: *It's very cold, 2 ºC below zero.* ■ "Cold" indicates a lower temperature than "cool" and often a disagreeable one. "Cool" often refers to a pleasant temperature: "a cold winter", "a cool breeze". 👁 See picture at **opposite**.

cold[2] /kəʊld/ ▮ [uncountable noun] **1** A low temperature: *I don't like the cold. It makes it very difficult to get out of bed in the morning!* ▮ [countable noun] **2** An illness that causes a headache, a dripping nose and a slight fever: *I think I've caught a cold. I've got a headache and I feel hot.*

coliseum [countable noun] Large stadium or amphitheater: *The coliseum here is used for big concerts and sport events.*

collage US: /'kɑː.lɑːʒ/ UK: /'kɒl.ɑːʒ/ [noun] A picture made with bits of different things: *James makes funny collages by sticking together photographs from magazines.* ■ Be careful with the pronunciation of this word.

ᐩ**collapse** /kə'læps/ [verb] To fall down: *When he heard the news, he collapsed into a chair, unable to speak.*

collar US: /'kɑː.lɚ/ UK: /'kɒl.əʳ/ [countable noun] **1** The part of a shirt or coat that goes around the neck: *Ed has a shirt with a big blue collar.* **2** A band around the neck of an animal: *I need a collar for my new pet dog.*

collarbone US: /'kɑː.lɚ.boʊn/ UK: /'kɒl.ə.bəʊn/ [countable noun] The bone joining the breastbone and the shoulder blade: *The collarbone is the only long* *bone lying horizontally.* ■ The same meaning: "clavicle".

colleague US: /'kɑː.liːg/ UK: /'kɒl.iːg/ [countable noun] A person who works or studies with you: *Sid's dad and Emma's mom are colleagues at the same company.*

collect /kə'lekt/ [verb] **1** To acquire and keep things as a hobby: *Keep that stamp from Finland for Keith. He collects stamps.* **2** To gather fruit or flowers: *We always used to collect flowers for my mother in spring.*

collection /kə'lek.ʃᵊn/ [countable noun] A group of things of the same kind: *Have you seen Colin's collection of postcards? It's beautiful.*

collective /kə'lektɪv/ [adjective] Of a joint group: *Collective memory is passed from generation to generation.*

collector /kə'lek·tər/ [countable noun] **1** A person who collects something as a hobby: *Eric's uncle is a collector of modern art. He's very rich.* **2** A person whose job it is to collect tickets, taxes, rent and so on: *Get your ticket ready. The ticket collector is coming.*

college US: /'kɑː.lɪdʒ/ UK: /'kɒl.ɪdʒ/ [noun] A place where students go after high school: *I want to go to art college when I finish school.*

collide /kə'laɪd/ [verb] **1** To strike against something violently and suddenly: *The meteor is expected to collide with planet Earth.* **2** To be in disagreement: *The interests of the different political parties collide.*

collision /kə'lɪʒ.ᵊn/ ▮ [noun] **1** Crashing into something: *There was a collision between two buses and five people were injured.* ▮ [countable noun] **2** Strong disagreement of opposing aims, opinions, etc.: *Her strong belief brought her into collision with the law.*

cologne /kə'loʊn/ [uncountable noun] A kind of perfume that is not very strong: *What cologne do you use? It smells good.*

Colombian[1] [adjective] Referring to Colombia: *We're going to the Colombian Pacific coast for our vacation this summer.* ■ Be careful! "Colombian" has a capital "C".

Colombian[2] [countable noun] A person from Colombia: *My Spanish teacher is a Colombian.* ■ Be careful! "Colombian" has a capital "C".

colon US: /'koʊ.lən/ UK: /'kəʊ.lɒn/ [countable noun] A mark [:] used in writing to show that what comes after it is an example or an explanation: *You use a colon in a written dialog before somebody's actual words.*

colonel /'kɜr·nə·l/ [countable noun] An army officer: *A colonel is usually in command of a regiment of soldiers.*

colonization or **colonisation** /ˌkɒl.ə.naɪ'zeɪ.ʃən/ US: /ˌkɑː.lə-/ [uncountable noun] The act of settling in a different country in large numbers in order to control it or benefit from it: *Many countries suffered colonization by the Romans.*

colonize or **colonise** /'kɑl·əˌnaɪz/ [verb] To establish a settlement: *The British settlers arrived to colonize North America.*

colony /'kɑl·ə·ni/ [countable noun] **1** A country that belongs to another country: *Jamaica was a British colony before its independence.* **2** A group of insects that live together: *Yesterday at school we saw a movie about a colony of ants.* ■ The plural is "colonies".

color[1] /'kʌl·ər/ [noun] The quality that makes something look brown, red, blue and so on: *Black is Vanessa's favorite color.* ■ The British English spelling is "colour".

color[2] /'kʌl·ər/ [verb] To paint with color: *Color the rectangles red and the circles blue.* ■ The British English spelling is "colour".

color-blind [adjective] Unable to see the difference between certain colors: *Cyril is color-blind. He sees red as green.*

colorful [adjective] Full of color: *Some butterflies are very colorful.*

colorless /'kʌləlәs/ [adjective] Without color: *Water is a colorless liquid.*

colour[1] /'kʌlər/ [noun] See **color[1]**. ■ This is a British English spelling.

colour[2] /'kʌlər/ [verb] See **color[2]**. ■ This is a British English spelling.

column US: /'kɑː.ləm/ UK: /'kɒl.əm/ [countable noun] A tall post that is used in buildings or to support a statue: *Astoria Column is in Oregon.*

comb[1] /kəʊm/ [countable noun] An object used for arranging your hair: *I need a strong comb because my hair is so curly.* ■ Be careful with the pronunciation of this word. It rhymes with "home".

comb[2] /kəʊm/ [verb] To arrange your hair with a comb: *Wash your face and comb your hair! It's getting late for school.*

combination /ˌkɑm·bə'neɪ·ʃən/ [noun] The putting of different things together: *Steel is a combination of iron and other metals.*

combine /kəm'baɪn/ [verb] To put different things together: *When I travel, I like to combine vacation with studying.*

combustible[1] [uncountable noun] Substance which burns easily: *Gasoline is combustible and should never be close to a naked flame.*

combustible[2] /kəm'bʌs.tɪ.bḷ/ [adjective] Able to catch fire and burn easily: *The wood used to make the fire was very dry and combustible.*

combustion /kəm'bʌstʃən/ [uncountable noun] The act of burning: *Flames are produced as the result of combustion of a fuel.*

a b c d e f g h i j k l m n o p q r s t u v w x y z

+come, came, come /kʌm/ [verb] **1** To move towards the speaker: *"Come here. I want to show you something" "OK, I'm coming".* **2** To arrive: *Have your friends come yet?* **3** To have been born in a place: *Do you come from Mexico?* **4** To have been made in or originate from a place: *This T-shirt comes from Peru.* **5** **to come in** To go inside: *Come in, all the others are here.* **6** **come on!** Used to hurry somebody up to make them go faster: *Come on! I can see the school bus coming.* ■ This use is informal. **7** **to come out** To go outside: *As soon as we started shouting, she came out.* **8** **to come true** To happen in the way you thought, hoped or dreamed: *My dream has come true!*

PHRASAL VERBS · **to come about** To happen, occur: *How did it come about?* · **to come across (somebody or something)** To find somebody or something by chance: *I was looking for a book and I came across a lot of old comics.* · **to come apart** To break into some pieces: *The book was so cheap that it came apart after a few weeks.* · **to come back** To return: *After ten years abroad, he came back to the United States.* · **to come forward** To volunteer to do something, or to go to somebody with information they want: *Many people came forward with information about the missing person.* · **to come into (something)** To inherit: *Janet came into a lot of money when her father died.* · **to come off** **1** To break while it is in your hand: *When I picked up the bag, the handle came off.* **2** Referring to paint or a stain, to be removed, disappear: *This paint won't come off my hand.* **3** Referring to an idea or plan, to be successful: *Our plan came off.* · **to come out** **1** Referring to paint or a mark, to be removed, disappear: *I hope the chocolate stain comes out when this shirt is washed.* **2** To become public knowledge: *In the end the truth came out.* **3** Referring to a flower, to open: *The spring flowers came out early this year.* **4** Referring to a book, to be published: *When does her new book come out?* · **to come round** **1** To visit a friend in their house: *Come round this evening and I'll show you.* **2** To recover consciousness: *Tim fainted but came round again almost immediately.* **3** To be convinced in the end by somebody: *Lisa was against the plan at first, but in the end she came round.* · **to come to** To recover consciousness: *When I came to after the operation I felt very strange.* · **to come up** **1** To come near or towards somebody or something: *He came up to me and asked me to dance.* **2** Referring to a problem or opportunity, to occur: *I'm sorry, something has come up and I have to go.* · **to come up against (a problem or difficulty)** To have an unexpected problem with something: *I have come up against a problem with the new program.* · **to come up with (something)** To suggest something: *Henry came up with the most brilliant idea for the name.*

comedian /kəˈmiː.di.ən/ [countable noun] **1** An entertainer who tells funny stories: *At the party there was a comedian who told jokes.* **2** An actor who does comedies: *Eddy Murphy is my favorite comedian. He's so funny!*

+comedy /ˈkɑm·ə·di/ [countable noun] A funny play or movie: *I prefer comedies to tragedies.* ■ The plural is "comedies".

comet US: /ˈkɑː.mɪt/ UK: /ˈkɒm.ɪt/ [countable noun] Small body of ice and rock that goes around the sun: *As comets orbit the sun they shed a stream of ice and dust.*

+comfort /ˈkʌm·fərt/ [uncountable noun] The feeling of being relaxed and in a pleasant state: *Susie's aunt lives in comfort in Australia and doesn't want to go back to the United States.*

+comfortable /ˈkʌm·fər·t̬ə·bəl/, /ˈkʌmf·tər·bəl/ [adjective] That makes you feel relaxed: *I think the new chairs are very comfortable.*

comforter US: /ˈkʌmfətər/ [countable noun] A bag of soft material used on beds: *In spring we use a lighter comforter than the one we have in the winter.* ■ In British English they say "duvet".

comic[1] /ˈkɒmɪk/ [countable noun] A magazine with illustrated stories: *Superman has been a popular comic for many years.*

comic[2] /ˈkɒmɪk/ [adjective] Funny: *Peter and Jim are preparing a comic act for the end of term show.*

comma US: /ˈkɑː.mə/ UK: /ˈkɒm.ə/ [countable noun] A mark used to separate different parts of a sentence or words in a list [,]: *I always forget to put the commas in my writing.*

+command[1] /kəˈmɑːnd/ ▮ [countable noun] **1** An order: *Soldiers must obey commands.* ▮ [uncountable noun] **2** Ability to do something: *Lucy has never been to France but her command of French is really impressive.*

command[2] /kəˈmɑːnd/ [verb] To tell somebody to do something: *The colonel commanded his soldiers to respect the prisoners.*

commander /kəˈmɑːndər/ [countable noun] **1** The officer who gives the orders in an operation: *The commander ordered his men to get ready to fight.* **2** A senior officer in the navy: *A commander has a high rank in the Royal Navy.*

commemorate /kəˈmem.ə.reɪt/ [verb] To celebrate an event, usually on its anniversary: *The soldiers paraded to commemorate the end of the war.*

commemoration /kəˌmeməˈreɪʃən/ [noun] The act of commemorating an event: *The commemoration is held every year on the same date.*

*__comment__[1] /'kɒment/ [noun] An opinion or an explanation: *Mr. Todd made a comment about me that I considered unfair.*

comment[2] /'kɒment/ [verb] To give an opinion or an explanation: *After the movie, Sarah commented that the actors weren't very good.*

commentary /'kam·ən,ter·i/ [noun] A description of an event: *Since I don't have a television, I have to listen to the football commentaries on the radio.* ■ The plural is "commentaries".

commentator US: /'kɑː.mən.teɪ.t̬ɚ/ UK: /'kɒm.ən.teɪ.təʳ/ [countable noun] A person who gives a commentary on radio or television: *The commentator said he thought the penalty kick was unfair.*

commerce US: /'kɑː.mɝːs/ UK: /'kɒm.ɜːs/ [uncountable noun] The buying and selling of things: *My sister's doing a commerce course at the local community college.*

commercial[1] /kə'mɜːʃəl/ [adjective] **1** Referring to the buying and selling of things: *There's very intensive commercial activity between the United States and the United Kingdom.* **2** That is interested mainly in making money: *The group's new CD is very commercial.*

*__commercial__[2] /kə'mɜːʃəl/ [countable noun] A television or radio advertisement: *Have you seen that new TV commercial for jeans?*

commission[1] /kə'mɪʃ.ən/ ▮ [countable noun] **1** Various people named by the authorities to investigate and report on a specific matter: *The government formed a commission to report on child poverty.* **2** A request for the production of a special piece of work, a design or a work of art: *The architect was given the commission to design the office building.* **3** The award of the rank of officer: *Ray was given a commission in the army as major.* ▮ [noun] **4** Pay that is directly linked to the sales achieved: *For every apartment she sells, she gets 1% commission.*

commission[2] /⊠a⊠ɪðað/, /kə'mɪʃ.ən/ [verb] **1** To give somebody the job of making something: *The sponsor commissioned an advertisement of its products.* **2** To bring an industrial plant or machine into service: *The engineer worked hard to commission the plant by the due date.*

commissioner /kə'mɪʃ·ə·nər/ [countable noun] **1** Somebody appointed to do a specific task: *The actress was appointed as United Nations Commissioner for the region.* **2** A public official of high rank: *My friend's father is a police commissioner.*

*__commit__ /kə'mɪt/ [verb] **1** To do something, usually wrong or illegal: *The prisoner committed three robberies in two weeks.* **2 to be committed** To give a great deal of your time and energy to something, to believe strongly in it: *My sister is very committed to what she does. She works as a missionary in Africa.* ■ Be careful with the spelling of these forms: "committed", "committing".

*__committee__ /kə'mɪt̬·i/ [countable noun] A group of people chosen to do a job: *I'm on the school committee that's preparing the hundredth anniversary celebrations.*

*__common__ US: /'kɑː.mən/ UK: /'kɒm.ən/ [adjective] **1** That exists in large quantities: *Mark and Mary are very common names.* **2** That happens very often: *Unfortunately, road accidents are very common here.* **3** Ordinary: *The common man and woman are not normally particularly interested in complicated scientific developments.* **4** Shared by a number of people or things: *I have my own bedroom but the bathroom is common to all the people who live on this floor.* **5 common sense** Ordinary good sense or judgment: *If you use your common sense, you can find the answer.*

Commonwealth /'kɒmənwelθ/ [noun] A group of countries that were part of the British Empire: *The Commonwealth was created in London in 1931.* ■ Be careful. "Commonwealth" has a capital "C".

*__communicate__ /kə'mjuː.nɪ.keɪt/ [verb] To exchange information or feelings with others: *If you speak English, you can communicate with people from lots of countries.* ■ Be careful! We say: "communicate **with** (somebody)".

*__communication__ /kə,mjuː.nɪ'keɪ.ʃən/ [uncountable noun] The act or the process of communicating: *Television is an important means of communication.*

*__community__ /kə'mju·nɪ·t̬i/ [countable noun] A group of people who live in the same area or have something important in common: *The African-American community has made great progress in American society over the past 30 years.* ■ The plural is "communities".

compact disc [countable noun] **1** A small disc that stores music or information: *I have a whole encyclopedia on a compact disc.* ■ "CD" is an abbreviation for "compact disc". **2 compact disc player** A piece of equipment for listening to the sounds on a compact disc: *Wendy has a new compact disc player.* ■ "CD player" is an abbreviation for "compact disc player".

companion /kəm'pæn.jən/ [countable noun] A person who spends some time with another: *Her dog has been a wonderful companion to Mrs. Moxon for many years.*

*__company__ /'kʌm.pə.ni/ [countable noun] **1** A business: *I'm working for an international company that makes and sells computers.* **2** A group of actors or dancers who work together: *I'm going to join a dance company when I finish college.* **3 to keep (some-**

a b c d e f g h i j k l m n o p q r s t u v w x y z

body) company To be with somebody: *Go and rest in the armchair if you're not feeling well, and I'll come round and keep you company.* ■ The plural is "companies".

comparative /kəm'pær·ət̬·ɪv/ [countable noun] The form of an adjective or adverb that is used to compare two people or things: *"Better" is the comparative of "good" and of "well".*

+compare /kəm'peər/ [verb] To examine one thing or person in relation to another thing or person: *Compare the two pianos. You'll find the Austrian one is better.* ■ See box at **abbreviations**.

+comparison /kəm'pær·ə·sən/ [noun] The act of comparing: *I don't like it when people make comparisons between me and my brother.*

compartment /kəm'part·mənt/ [countable noun] **1** A separate part in a railroad car: *When we went to Chicago we traveled in a first class compartment.* **2** A separate part in a container: *The new fridge has compartments for different types of food.*

compass /'kʌm.pəs/ [countable noun] **1** An instrument that shows direction: *A compass has a pointer that always points north.* **2** A metal or plastic instrument which is used for drawing circles: *If you change the angle of the compass, you can draw circles of different size.* ■ In this use, we also say "compasses". ■ The plural is "compasses". See page 456.

compasses [plural noun] See **compass**.

compel /kəm'pel/ [verb] To force somebody to do something: *They compelled him to resign.* ■ Be careful with the spelling of these forms: "compelled", "compelling".

+compete /kəm'piːt/ [verb] **1** To take part in a competition to see who is the best: *Six people will compete this weekend for the "Best bowler in Montana" trophy.* **2** To try to beat others in a contest over something: *If you want to go to Oxford or Cambridge you no longer have to compete with other students in a special entrance examination.*

competence /'kam·pə·t̬əns/ ▮ [noun] **1** The capability to carry out a task or to do something which requires a certain skill: *This job requires competence in foreign languages.* ■ The same meaning: "competency". ▮ [uncountable noun] **2** The authority of a court or judge to deal with a matter: *That case falls beyond this court's competence.*

competency /'kɒm.pɪ.tənt.si/ US: /'kaːm-/ [uncountable noun] The capability to carry out a task or do something which requires a certain skill: *I do not doubt his competency as a mechanic.* ■ The same meaning: "competence". ■ The plural is "competencies".

competent [adjective] With enough ability, knowledge or training to do something well: *She is a highly competent surgeon.*

+competition /ˌkam·pə'tɪʃ·ən/ ▮ [countable noun] **1** An event to see who is the best at something: *The winner in the skiing competition was Swiss.* ▮ [uncountable noun] **2** A situation in which people try to get the same thing: *There is a lot of competition for every job that becomes available now.*

competitor /kəm'pet̬·ɪ·t̬ər/ [countable noun] **1** Somebody who takes part in a competition: *All the competitors for the marathon have to register with the organizers.* **2** Somebody who is fighting against you over something: *My main competitor for the job was a girl from Portugal.*

+complain /kəm'pleɪn/ [verb] To say that you think something is wrong, unfair or must be changed: *Mr. Robinson is always complaining about the weather.* ■ We say "complain **about** (something)". We say "complain **to** (somebody)".

complementary /ˌkɒmplɪ'mentəri/ [adjective] **1** Being additional to a basic package: *The CD player is complementary to the basic equipment of the car.* **2** Referring to two or more things that are useful or go well together: *Those colors are complementary.*

complete[1] /kəm'pliːt/ [adjective] **1** All of something: *Are you really thinking of reading the complete works of Charles Dickens?* **2** Finished: *This album is complete.*

+complete[2] /kəm'pliːt/ [verb] To finish something: *I just need two stickers to complete my collection.*

completely /kəm'pliːt.li/ [adverb] Totally or in every way: *This book is completely absurd. I can't understand anything at all.*

complex[1] /'kam·pleks/ [countable noun] **1** A set of buildings which comprise a whole: *The complex is made up of a factory, an office building and an exhibition center.* **2** An emotional problem about something caused by illogical fears or worries: *He's got a complex about his height.*

complex[2] /kəm'pleks/, /'kam·pleks/ [adjective] Complicated or involving lots of different elements: *The human body is very complex.*

complexity /kəm'plek·sɪ·t̬i/ [uncountable noun] The number of levels involved, or the degree of complication: *It's a problem of great complexity.* ■ The plural is "complexities".

+complicated US: /'kaːm.plɪ.keɪ.t̬ɪd/ UK: /'kɒm.plɪ.keɪ.tɪd/ [adjective] Difficult to do or to understand: *I can't put the kit together. The instructions are too complicated.* ■ Be careful with the pronunciation of this word. The "e" is pronounced like the "i" in "did".

compliment /'kam·plə·mənt/ [countable noun] Something good you say about a person to that same person: *Mrs. Burns is always paying me compliments: she says I'm intelligent and well-behaved.*

comply /kəm'plaɪ/ [verb] To be in accordance with the requirements: *The courts ordered her to comply with the company's work rules.* ■ Be careful with the spelling of these forms: "complies", "complied".

component /kəm'pəʊnənt/ [countable noun] Part which, together with others, makes up a whole: *The steering wheel is a vital component of the car.*

compose /kəm'poʊz/ [verb] To write music or poetry: *Beethoven composed the "Moonlight" Sonata.*

composer /kəm'poʊ·zər/ [countable noun] Somebody who writes music: *Lennon and McCartney were two famous composers of pop music in the 1960's.*

composition /ˌkɑm·pə'zɪʃ·ən/ [countable noun] A piece of writing: *I have to write a composition on "A day in my life" for English.*

compound /'kɒmpaʊnd/ [countable noun] A combination of two or more elements: *Chemicals are mixed to form a compound.*

comprehension /ˌkɒm.prɪ'hen.tʃən/ US: /ˌkɑːm-/ [uncountable noun] Understanding: *In class we read different texts and then we have to answer comprehension questions to see how much we've understood.*

comprehensive /ˌkɑm·prə'hen·sɪv/ [adjective] That has everything: *This dictionary is very comprehensive. It has phonetic information, grammar notes, definitions, spelling notes and translations.*

compress[1] /'kɑm·pres/ [countable noun] A piece of cloth applied firmly to a part of the body to relieve swelling or pain: *Hold the compress to the side of the head.*

compress[2] /kəm'pres/ [verb] To squeeze into a smaller area: *The sap from the leaves was compressed into cubes.*

comprise /kəm'praɪz/ [verb] To be formed of: *The team comprises eleven players.*

compulsory /kəm'pʌl·sə·ri/ [adjective] That you have to do by law: *It's still compulsory in our school to wear uniform.*

ᐩ**computer** /kəm'pju·t̬ər/ [noun] A machine that can do complicated calculations quickly and can store a lot of information: *Glenda uses her computer to do all her projects.* ■ Be careful with the pronunciation of this word! the "u" is pronounced as "you". 👁 **See pages 442 and 443.**

computer game [countable noun] A game that you play on a computer: *He spends all day long playing computer games.*

computerize or **computerise** /kəm'pjuːtəraɪz/ [verb] **1** To install a computer system: *To computerize the company, the old ways of working need to be changed.* **2** To store information in a computer: *In order to computerize the company records, all of the paper documents need to be put on the computer.*

computer programmer US: /'proʊ.græm.ɚ/ UK: /'prəʊ.græm.ər/ [countable noun] A person who writes programs or other material to use on a computer: *If I were a computer programmer I'd just make games.*

ᐩ**concentrate** /'kɑn·sən,treɪt/ [verb] To direct all your attention to one activity: *I have to concentrate on passing this test.*

concept /'kɑn·sept/ [countable noun] A way of viewing a particular subject: *It is a revolutionary new concept.*

ᐩ**concern**[1] /kən'sɜːn/ [noun] Interest, worry: *We all felt a lot of concern about his illness.*

concern[2] /kən'sɜːn/ [verb] To be of interest to you: *What the principal said at assembly about the trip to Long Beach doesn't concern us because our class isn't going.*

concerned /kən'sɜrnd/ [adjective] Worried about something: *I'm very concerned about Pat's health. She looks ill.* ■ Be careful with the pronunciation of the end of this word. The last "e" is not pronounced.

ᐩ**concert** US: /'kɑːn.sɚt/ UK: /'kɒn.sət/ [countable noun] A musical performance: *Have you seen Elton John in concert? He's great.* ■ Be careful with the pronunciation of this word! The second "c" is pronounced as a "s".

conch US: /kɑːntʃ, kɑːŋk n/ UK: /kɒntʃ, kɒŋk/ [countable noun] The spiral shell of various gastropods: *Conches are found on the seashore.*

ᐩ**conclude** /kən'kluːd/ [verb] To think that something is true because of the evidence: *After listening to all the evidence, the jury concluded that he must be innocent.*

ᐩ**conclusion** /kən'kluː.ʒən/ [noun] An opinion that you have because of certain information: *Mr. Dunne compared the two papers and reached the conclusion that we had not cheated.*

concrete[1] /'kɒŋkriːt/ [adjective] Definite, real: *There's no concrete proof that he did the crime.*

ᐩ**concrete**[2] /'kɒŋkriːt/ [uncountable noun] A material used for building: *Concrete is a mixture of sand, pebbles, cement and water.*

condensation /ˌkɑn·dən'seɪ·ʃən/, /-den-/ [uncountable noun] **1** The combining of two molecules which results in the production of two elements: a new molecule and water: *The condensation process produces a cloud of steam.* 👁 **See page 438.** **2** Drops of water that form on a cold surface when steam or water touches it: *The mirror in the bathroom usually gets covered with condensation when you shower.* **3** The act of pressing together something into a shorter version: *Condensation is needed to make this document more accessible.*

ᐩ**condition** /kən'dɪʃ.ən/ ▮ [uncountable noun] **1** The state that something or somebody is in: *The cottage is in very bad condition. It needs a lot of repairs.* ▮

[countable noun] **2** Something necessary for something else to happen: *I'll lend you my bike on condition that you lend me your skateboard.*

conditional /kən'dɪʃ.ᵊn.ᵊl/ [noun] A form of a verb that is made by adding "would" to the infinitive of a verb: *In the sentence "I would go to the party tonight if I didn't have to finish my essay", the conditional is "would go".* ■ The conditional is used when you want to express that an action depends upon something else happening.

conduct[1] /'kɒndʌkt/ [uncountable noun] Behavior: *Your conduct at my party was absolutely inexcusable.*

conduct[2] /kən'dʌkt/ [verb] **1** To direct an orchestra: *Mrs. Robinson conducts the school orchestra.* **2** To transmit electricity, heat or sound: *Water conducts electricity very well.*

conductor /kən'dʌk·tər/ [countable noun] **1** A person whose job it is to direct orchestras: *William is studying music. He wants to be a conductor.* **2** A material that conducts electricity, heat or sound: *Copper is a good conductor of electricity.*

cone US: /koun/ UK: /kəʊn/ [countable noun] **1** A shape, round at the base and rising to a point: *The clever clown's hat was in the shape of a cone.* **2** fir cone The fruit of a fir tree: *There are lots of fir cones on the ground in this wood.* **3** ice cream cone An ice cream with a cone made of cookie for holding ice cream: *I want a chocolate ice cream cone, please.*

conference /'kɑn·fər·əns/, /-frəns/ [countable noun] A special meeting to talk about a subject: *Sir Nicholas is attending the conference on Human Rights next week.*

confess /kən'fes/ [verb] To admit what you have done wrong: *After an hour at the police station, the thief confessed.*

confession /kən'feʃ.ᵊn/ [noun] Admitting what you have done wrong: *The prisoner signed his confession.*

confidence /'kɑn·fə·dəns/, /-ˌdens/ [uncountable noun] The feeling of being able to do something: *I don't feel much confidence about my test results.*

confident /'kɑn·fə·dənt/, /-ˌdent/ [adjective] Feeling you can do something, feeling sure: *My dad is a very confident driver.*

confirm /kən'fɜrm/ [verb] To say again that something will happen or that something is true: *James confirmed that the trip to Los Angeles would be in the first week of April.*

confirmation /ˌkɑn·fər'meɪ·ʃən/ [noun] An assurance that something is true or will happen: *We've received confirmation of our vacation in Mallorca.*

conflict /'kɑn·flɪkt/ [noun] A fight or disagreement between two things: *There are conflicts in many parts of the world.*

confuse /kən'fjuːz/ [verb] **1** To mix things in your mind so that you are not sure about something: *All the different publications about the assassination of President Kennedy have confused the whole question.* **2** To think that one thing or one person is another: *I always confuse Ralph with his brother.*

confused /kən'fjuːzd/ [adjective] That doesn't understand: *I'm totally confused. What exactly do you want to do?* ■ Be careful with the pronunciation of the end of this word. The "e" is not pronounced.

confusing /kən'fjuː.zɪŋ/ [adjective] That is difficult to understand: *I find our math teacher's explanations a bit confusing.*

conglomerate /kən'glɑm·ər·ət/ [countable noun] A sedimentary rock which consists of round pieces of rock implanted in finer material: *Clay is often part of conglomerate.*

congratulate /kən'græt.jʊ.leɪt/ [verb] To tell somebody that you are pleased with them because of something they have done: *The principal congratulated me on my admission to Harvard.*

congratulations /kənˌgræt.jʊ'leɪ.ʃᵊnz/ [plural noun] An expression that you use to show somebody that you are pleased with them because of something they have done: *Congratulations, Mark! You are the winner.*

Congress /'kɒŋgres/ [noun] The parliament in the United States and some other countries: *The American Congress makes laws in the United States.* ■ Be careful. "Congress" has a capital "C".

conjunction /kən'dʒʌŋk.ʃᵊn/ [countable noun] A word that joins parts of sentences: *The word "and" is the most common conjunction.*

connect /kə'nekt/ [verb] To join: *The secretary's and the principal's offices are connected by telephone.*

connection /kə'nek.ʃᵊn/ [countable noun] Something that joins things, people or events: *Doctors are certain of the connection between smoking and cancer.*

connector /kə'nek.tər/ US: /-tɚ/ [countable noun] Something which joins things together: *A connector is used when joining the two halves of the cable together.*

conquer US: /'kɑːŋ.kɚ/ UK: /'kɒŋ.kəʳ/ [verb] **1** To take by force a country, city and so on: *The crusaders conquered Jerusalem in the late eleventh century.* **2** To achieve something difficult: *Space began to be conquered in the second half of the 20th century.*

conqueror /'kɒŋkərər/ [countable noun] Somebody who conquers: *Pizarro was the conqueror of the Inca Empire in the 16th century.*

conquest /'kɑn·kwest/, /'kɑŋ-/ ▮ [noun] **1** The capturing of something by force: *The United States conquest California in 1848.* ▮ [uncountable noun] **2** A difficult achievement: *Man's conquest of disease will never be complete.*

conscience /'kɑn·ʃəns/ [noun] Your knowledge of right and wrong that governs what you think and do: *My conscience tells me that we should have helped Nora.*

conscious /'kɑn·ʃəs/ [adjective] **1** Awake and with all your senses: *When I saw him after the operation, he was fully conscious.* **2** Aware of something: *Are you conscious of the risk you're taking?*

consciousness /'kɑn·ʃəs·nəs/ [uncountable noun] The capacity of being aware of what is happening around you: *He fainted but recovered consciousness after a few minutes.*

consent /kən'sent/ [verb] To agree to something: *Mrs. Burns consented to our using the music room to practice in.* ■ Be careful. We always say: "consent **to** (something)".

consequence /'kɑn·sɪ·kwəns/, /-ˌkwens/ [countable noun] The result of an action or an event: *This punishment is a consequence of your bad behavior.*

consequently /'kɑn·sɪ·kwənt·li/, /-ˌkwent·li/ [adverb] As a result: *We had to wait for Jim for an hour and consequently missed the beginning of the movie.*

conservation /ˌkɑn·sər'veɪ·ʃən/ [uncountable noun] The protection of nature, wildlife, historic buildings and so on: *Any government should mainly worry about the conservation of natural areas.*

conserve /kən'sɜːv/ [verb] To protect something from harm, loss or destruction: *This organization is campaigning to conserve our local woodland.*

consider /kən'sɪd·ər/ [verb] **1** To think about something carefully: *Consider my proposal and give me an answer tomorrow.* **2** To think that something is true: *I consider that it is a good thing to learn languages.*

considerable /kən'sɪd·ər·ə·bəl/ [adjective] Quite large: *I think he drank a considerable amount of beer.*

consideration /kənˌsɪd.ə'reɪ.ʃən/ [uncountable noun] **1** The careful study of something before you make a decision: *After some consideration, I decided to accept the job.* **2** Caring about other people: *Brian doesn't show any consideration for anybody but himself.*

consist /kən'sɪst/ [verb] To be made of different parts: *This textbook consists of an introduction and twelve units.* ■ Be careful. We always say: "consist **of**".

console [countable noun] A flat surface on which the controls for a machine or electrical equipment are located: *Check the connectors of the computer console before taking it to the technician.*

consonant /'kɑn·sə·nənt/ [countable noun] Some of the letters of the alphabet: *B, c, d, f, g and so on are consonants.*

constant /'kɑn·stənt/ [adjective] **1** That happens all the time: *There is a constant noise in this street.* **2** Faithful: *My dog Roger has been a constant friend.*

constantly [adverb] All the time or without a pause: *It is not nice when you constantly touch your hair while we are sitting at the table.* ■ The same meaning: "continuously", "continually".

constitution /ˌkɑn·stɪ'tu·ʃən/ [countable noun] The basic laws and political principles of a country: *The American constitution says that everybody has the right to a job.*

constitutional /ˌkɑn·stɪ'tju·ʃə·nə·l/ [adjective] Referring to the basic laws of a country: *United States is a constitutional republic.*

construct /kən'strʌkt/ [verb] To make something: *The children have constructed a bridge across the stream with the branches of a tree.*

construction /kən'strʌk.ʃən/ ▮ [uncountable noun] **1** The action of constructing something: *The Government has plans for the construction of a new road.* ▮ [countable noun] **2** The result of the work done by builders: *You can see a massive construction on the other side of the river.* ▮ [noun] **3** The interpretation or understanding of ideas: *His construction of events is very different from mine.*

consult /kən'sʌlt/ [verb] **1** To ask somebody for advice or for their opinion: *I think you should consult a doctor. That wound doesn't look good to me.* **2** To use a book or a map to find information: *We're lost, Jane. We'd better consult the map.*

consume /kən'sum/ [verb] To eat or to drink: *They consumed forty sandwiches and three bottles of lemonade at the party.*

consumer /kən'su·mər/ [countable noun] Person who buys goods or uses services: *Large families are great water consumers.*

consumer research [uncountable noun] Investigation carried out in order to identify customers' needs and habits: *Some newspapers publish consumer research to help their readers become more aware as consumers.*

consumption /kən'sʌmp.ʃən/ [uncountable noun] The habit of buying or using up: *When the economy is doing badly, consumption falls.*

contact[1] /'kɒntækt/ [uncountable noun] Relationship, close communication: *Children need to be in contact with other children to develop properly.*

contact[2] /'kɒntækt/ [verb] To see, speak or write to somebody: *Sean wasn't well while we were at camp so we had to contact his parents.*

contact lens [countable noun] Small piece of plastic that some people put in their eyes to enable them to see better: *I have a new pair of contact lenses. They were very expensive.* ■ When we talk about two

a b c d e f g h i j k l m n o p q r s t u v w x y z

or more "contact lens", we use the word "pairs": "I have two pairs of contact lens".

contagious /kən'teɪ.dʒəs/ [adjective] **1** Referring to a disease that is spread by contact: *The disease is contagious and patients should be isolated.* **2** Spreading easily among people: *Her enthusiasm is contagious.*

✦**contain** /kən'teɪn/ [verb] To have something inside: *This carton contains one liter of orange juice.* ■ Be careful with the pronunciation of this word! "tain" rhymes with "rain".

✦**container** /kən'teɪ·nər/ [countable noun] Something you can use to keep things in: *There are many types of containers: boxes, cartons, tubes.*

contaminate /kən'tæm.ɪ.neɪt/ [verb] To make less pure by adding other substances: *It is illegal to contaminate the seas by dumping waste.*

contamination /kən,tæmɪ'neɪʃən/ [uncountable noun] The introduction of unwanted and harmful material into air, water or soil: *The contamination of the river is mainly due to the dumping of factory waste.*

contemporaneous /kən,tem.pə'reɪ.ni.əs/ [adjective] Occurring at approximately the same time: *These two historical events were contemporaneous.* ■ This word is formal.

contemporary[1] /kən'tem·pə,rer·i/ [countable noun] Somebody or something of the same period: *Douglas MacArthur is a contemporary of George S. Patton.* ■ The plural is "contemporaries".

contemporary[2] /kən'tem·pə,rer·i/ [adjective] Being of the same time or period: *Do you like contemporary art?*

✦**content** /kən'tent/ [adjective] Happy: *Are you content with your test grades?*

contented /kən'ten·tɪd/ [adjective] Happy, satisfied: *I'm not very contented with my way of life. I work too hard.* ■ Be careful with the pronunciation of the end of this word. The last "e" is pronounced like the "i" in "did".

✦**contents** /'kɑn·tents/ [uncountable noun] The things that are part of something or inside something: *If you want to find something quickly, look in the list of contents.* ■ Sometimes the singular form "content" is also used.

✦**contest** /'kɑn·test/ [countable noun] A competition: *I always watch the American Idol Contest.*

contestant /kən'tes.tᵊnt/ [countable noun] Somebody who takes part in a competition: *One of the contestants knew the answers to all the questions.*

✦**continent** US: /'kɑːn.t̬ᵊn.ənt/ UK: /'kɒn.tɪ.nənt/ ▮ [countable noun] **1** A large mass of land: *Asia is the biggest continent on earth.* ▮ [noun] **2** Europe, except for the British Isles: *We're going to spend next summer on the continent.* ■ This use is British only.

continental US: /,kɑːn.t̬ᵊn'en.t̬ᵊl/ UK: /,kɒn.tɪ'nen.tᵊl/ [adjective] Referring to Europe, except for the British Isles: *The continental breakfast is often served at hotels in North America.*

continual /kən'tɪn.ju.əl/ [adjective] Constant: *The continual banging next door is driving me crazy.* ■ Be careful. We use "continual" for actions that are repeated one after another. It's often used to refer to something negative: "The continual banging next door is driving me crazy". We use "continuous" for things that continue without interruption.

continually /kən'tɪn.ju.ə.li/ [adverb] All the time or without a pause: *I'm continually telling Joan not to run in the hallway.* ■ The same meaning: "constantly", "continuously".

✦**continue** /kən'tɪn.juː/ [verb] To go on doing something: *When I went into the library, Mick continued reading without looking up.*

✦**continuous** /kən'tɪn.ju.əs/ [adjective] That goes on without interruption: *A continuous line in the middle of the road means you can't pass.* ■ Be careful. We use "continuous" for things that continue without interruption. We use "continual" for actions that are repeated one after another.

continuously /kən'tɪn.ju.ə.sli/ [adverb] With no interruption: *Liz! You've been watching television continuously since five o'clock.* ■ The same meaning: "constantly", "continually".

contour[1] US: /'kɑːn.tʊr/ UK: /'kɒn.tɔːʳ/ [countable noun] **1** The outer shape of an object or piece of land: *The contour of the mountain range is very rough.* **2 contour line** A line on a map joining points that are the same height above sea level: *From the contour lines you can see that this area is much lower.*

CONTAINER

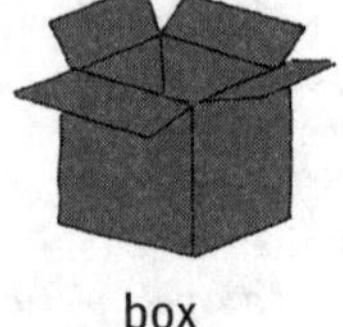
box

can

jar

carton

contour[2] [verb] To outline something: *He has to accurately contour the coastline if he wants the map to be precise.*

contraceptive /ˌkɒntrə'septɪv/ [countable noun] A drug or device which is used to prevent pregnancy: *They stopped using contraceptives because they wanted to have a baby.*

contract /'kɑn·trækt/ [countable noun] A document showing the conditions of a sale or a job: *According to my contract, I have only four weeks' vacation a year.*

contraction /kən'træk.ʃᵊn/ [uncountable noun] The shortened form of a word or words: *"Let's" is a contraction of "let us".*

contradict /ˌkɑn·trə'dɪkt/ [verb] To say the opposite of what another person has said: *That was what happened so don't contradict me!*

contrary /'kɑnˌtrer·i/ [adjective] **1** Opposite: *Do you always have to take the contrary view to what I say?* ■ We usually say "opposite". **2 on the contrary** Certainly not: *I don't think she's stupid. On the contrary, she's very intelligent.*

contrast /'kɑn·træst/ [noun] A clear difference: *I like the contrast of seasons in New England.*

contribute /kən'trɪb·jut/, /-jət/ [verb] To help, usually with money: *Would you like to contribute to our charity?*

contribution /ˌkɑn·trə'bju·ʃən/ [noun] Help, usually with money: *The contributions to the Church Fund have increased this year.*

control[1] /kən'troul/ [verb] To have power over somebody or something: *Mr. Daniels may be Managing Director, but does he really control the company?*

control[2] /kən'trəʊl/ [uncountable noun] **1** Authority or power: *The principal has absolute control in my school.* **2** Ability to guide a machine: *He recovered control of the car just before it reached the cliff.* **3 out of control** That you cannot control: *Dad forgot to put the handbrake on and the car went downhill out of control.* **4 under control** That you can control: *Calm down. The fire is under control.*

controls [plural noun] The buttons or other parts of a machine used to make it work: *The controls of a modern airplane are very complicated.*

convenient /kən'viː.ni.ənt/ [adjective] **1** Good for you: *When is it most convenient for you to come, Philip?* **2** That is well situated for your needs: *The apartment is in a very convenient place, near the shopping center and the bus station.*

convent /'kɑn·vent/, /-vənt/ [countable noun] The place where nuns live: *Daniel's sister left her job and entered a convent.*

converge /kən'vɜrdʒ/ [verb] Referring to lines, roads or rivers that come together: *The traffic on the coast road converges with the traffic on the highway at this point.*

conversation /ˌkɑn·vər'seɪ·ʃən/ [noun] A situation in which two or more people speak to each other: *I had a very interesting conversation with Mr. Jones about India.*

convert /kən'vɜrt/ [verb] To change something into a different thing: *They have converted their house into a hotel.*

convict[1] /'kɒnvɪkt/ [countable noun] Somebody in prison after having being found guilty of something: *In the past, many convicts were sent to forced labor.*

convict[2] /kən'vɪkt/ [verb] To declare somebody guilty of a crime: *The prisoner was convicted of murder.*

convince /kən'vɪnts/ [verb] To make other people believe you: *She spoke to her mother and convinced her that she had not broken the window.*

cook[1] /kʊk/ [countable noun] A person whose job is to prepare food for others: *There's a new cook at The Red Castle.*

cook[2] /kʊk/ [verb] To prepare food: *How do you cook cod, Laurie?*

cooker /kʊk·ər/ [countable noun] See **stove**. ■ This word is British English.

cookie /'kʊk.i/ [countable noun] **1** A flat baked sweet: *These new coconut cookies are delicious.* ■ In British English they say "biscuit". **2 tough cookie** Hard person: *He*

TO COOK

to barbecue

to roast

to grill

to boil

a b c d e f g h i j k l m n o p q r s t u v w x y z

a b c d e f g h i j k l m n o p q r s t u v w x y z

is a tough cookie but a clever one. ■ "Tough cookie" is informal.

cooking [uncountable noun] The art of preparing food: *Peter goes to a cooking class every Wednesday.*

cooktop [countable noun] The flat surface of a device which you put pans on to cook food: *That soup is ready. You can switch off the cooktop.* ■ In British English they say "hob".

†**cool**[1] /kuːl/ [adjective] **1** That has quite a low temperature: *It's very hot during the day, but it gets cool at night.* ■ "Cool" often refers to a pleasant temperature. "Cold" indicates a lower temperature than "cool" and often a disagreeable one: "a cool breeze", "a cold winter". **2** Very nice: *Wow! That jacket is really cool.* ■ This use is informal.

cool[2] /kuːl/ [verb] To reduce the temperature: *Wait until the soup has cooled a little.*
▸ **PHRASAL VERBS · to cool down** To calm down: *Cool down a bit, Alice. There's no need to get so furious.*

cooperate US: /koʊˈɑː.pə.reɪt/ UK: /kəʊˈɒp.ᵊr.eɪt/ [verb] To work together with others: *We all need to cooperate to make this world a better place, don't you think?*

coordinate[1] /koʊˈɔr·də·n·ət/ [countable noun] The two numbers or letters used to fix the position of a point on a graph or map: *10 degrees North is a coordinate on the map.*

coordinate[2] /koʊˈɔr·də·nˌeɪt/ [verb] To organize things or people so that they occur as planned or function together correctly: *We have to coordinate the classes so that they do not clash.*

coordination /kəʊˌɔːdɪˈneɪʃən/ [uncountable noun] The working together of differing elements: *The coordination of the marching bands is only achieved with a lot of practice.*

copper US: /ˈkɑː.pɚ/ UK: /ˈkɒp.əʳ/ [uncountable noun] A metal that is between red and brown in color: *Electric wire is made with copper.*

copy[1] /ˈkɒpi/ [countable noun] **1** One example of a book, magazine, newspaper and so on: *In the school library there are twenty copies of "The Adventures of Tom Sawyer".* **2** Something that is made to look exactly like something else: *We had to make several copies of the play we had written.* ■ The plural is "copies".

†**copy**[2] /ˈkɒpi/ [verb] To do the same as another person: *My younger brother copies everything I do: my clothes, my hair and my hobbies.* ■ Be careful with the spelling of these forms: "copies", "copied".

copy editor [countable noun] The editor that improves the style and accuracy of texts: *At every newspaper staff there are several copy editors.*

copyright /ˈkɑp·iˌrɑɪt/ [noun] The right of an author or inventor not to have their work copied without their permission: *The copyright of the invention must be registered.*

coral /ˈkɔr·əl/, /ˈkɑr-/ [uncountable noun] Structure formed of the skeletons of tiny sea animals in tropical waters: *We went to an island which has a beautiful coral reef.*

cord US: /kɔːrd/ UK: /kɔːd/ [noun] A string: *The child made a train using cardboard and a cord.*

cordon /ˈkɔːdən/ [countable noun] **1** A line of security staff preventing access to a site: *The cordon was set up at some distance from the body.* **2** An ornamental cord or braid: *The cordon is worn over one shoulder.*

corduroys [plural noun] A type of pants: *I've bought a new pair of corduroys for my vacation in Austria.* ■ When we talk about two or more "cords", we use the word "pairs": "I bought three pairs of corduroys".

†**core** US: /kɔːr/ UK: /kɔːʳ/ [countable noun] The center of something: *The core of the Earth is made up of a very hot liquid.* See page 449.

Corinthian /kəˈrɪnt.θi.ən adj/ [adjective] **1** Referring to Corinth in southern Greece: *St Paul wrote letters to the Corinthians communities.* **2** Referring to the most ornate of the three principal classical building styles: *The temple has eight beautiful Corinthian columns.* ■ Compare with "Doric" (the simplest of the building styles) and "Ionic" (with some decoration).

cork US: /kɔːrk/ UK: /kɔːk/ ▮ [uncountable noun] **1** The bark of a particular kind of oak tree: *The floor in my bathroom is made of cork.* ▮ [countable noun] **2** Something that you use to close bottles: *Put the cork in the bottle or the smell will go out.*

corkscrew /ˈkɔrkˌskru/ [countable noun] Something used for pulling corks out of bottles: *You have to screw the corkscrew into the cork and then pull.*

corn US: /kɔːrn/ UK: /kɔːn/ [uncountable noun] A plant that produces yellow seeds that we can eat: *The United States produces a great amount of corn.* ■ Compare with "sweet corn" (the part of the plant that you can eat it as a vegetable). ■ In British English they say "maize".

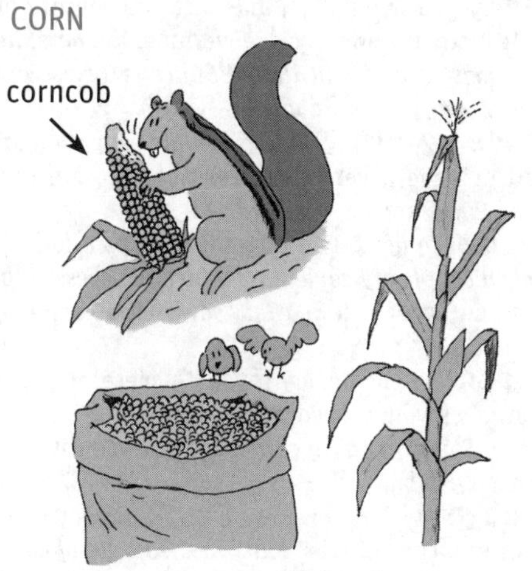

corncob US: /'kɔːrn.kɑːb/ UK: /'kɔːn.kɒb/ [countable noun] The hard central part of the corn to which the grains are attached: *The corncob has a cylindrical shape.* See picture at **corn**.

cornea /kɔr'ni·ə/ [countable noun] The transparent layer which covers the eye: *The cornea protects the eyeball.*

†**corner** US: /'kɔːr.nɚ/ UK: /'kɔː.nəʳ/ [countable noun] The point where two sides meet: *I'll meet you at the corner of Michigan Avenue and Ohio Street.* See picture at **street**.

cornflakes /'kɔːn.fleɪks/ US: /'kɔːrn-/ [plural noun] A type of grain food usually eaten for breakfast: *My only breakfast is a bowl of cornflakes with sugar and milk.*

corolla /kə'rɒl.ə/ US: /-'roʊ.lə/ [countable noun] The petals which form the inner envelope of a flower: *The corolla is to be found inside the flower.* ■ Compare with "calyx" (the sepals which form the outer envelope that protects the flower bud when it is forming).

corporation /ˌkɔr·pə'reɪ·ʃən/ [countable noun] A big company: *Corporations are sometimes made up of a group of companies.* ■ See box at **abbreviations**.

†**correct**[1] /kə'rekt/ [adjective] Right: *I had ten correct answers in the school quiz.*

correct[2] /kə'rekt/ [verb] To make right something that was wrong: *Mrs. King corrects our homework in red.*

correction /kə'rek.ʃən/ [noun] The correct form or answer for something that was wrong: *The correction of homework is one of a teacher's duties.*

correspond US: /ˌkɔːr.ɪ'spɑːnd/ UK: /ˌkɒr.ɪ'spɒnd/ [verb] **1** To write letters to each other: *Our class corresponds with a group of students in Sydney.* **2** To match: *Norman's description of the thief did not correspond with the one the police had.* ■ Be careful. We say: "correspond **with** (somebody)".

correspondence /ˌkɔr·ə'spɑn·dəns/, /ˌkɑr-/ [uncountable noun] Letters: *I receive very little correspondence, only one or two letters a month.*

correspondent /ˌkɔr·ə'spɑn·dənt/, /ˌkɑr-/ [countable noun] Somebody who reports for a newspaper, a radio or on television: *The article was signed by their correspondent in Canada.*

corridor US: /'kɔːr.ɪ.dɚ/ UK: /'kɒr.ɪ.dɔːʳ/ [countable noun] A passage in a building: *The secretary's office is at the end of the corridor, on the right.* ■ The same meaning: "hallway".

cosmetic[1] /kɑz'meţ·ɪk/ [countable noun] A product to make somebody look nicer: *Our local store sells practically everything from candies to cosmetics.*

cosmetic[2] /kɑz'meţ·ɪk/ [adjective] Referring to a product or treatment which is intended to improve the appearance of somebody: *She used cosmetic powder for her skin to look more velvety.*

†**cost**[1] /kɒst/ [uncountable noun] **1** The price of something: *What is the cost of your school trip?* **2 at all costs** At any price or effort: *I must get that bike at all costs. It's fantastic!*

cost[2], **cost, cost** /kɒst/ [verb] To be priced: *How much does that magazine cost?*

costly /'kɔs·tli/ [adjective] Expensive: *My parents say we can't have another costly vacation this year.*

costume US: /'kɑː.stuːm/ UK: /'kɒs.tjuːm/ [noun] **1** The clothes that are typical of a certain country or period: *The kimono is one of Japan's national costumes.* **2** The clothes worn by actors in a play: *All the actors were dressed in 19th century costumes.* **3** Clothes that make somebody look different or very difficult to recognize: *My Halloween costume this year will be Darth Vader.* ■ In this use, the same meaning: "disguise[1]".

cot US: /kɑːt/ UK: /kɒt/ [countable noun] See **crib**. ■ This use is British English.

cottage US: /'kɑː.ţɪdʒ/ UK: /'kɒt.ɪdʒ/ [countable noun] A small country house: *My grandparents rent a cottage in Vermont for their vacations.* ■ Be careful with the pronunciation of this word. The "a" is pronounced like the "i" in "did".

†**cotton** /'kɒtən/ [uncountable noun] **1** A tall tropical plant which produces a soft white fiber: *They grow a lot of cotton in India.* **2** A thread or material made

a b **c** d e f g h i j k l m n o p q r s t u v w x y z

a b c d e f g h i j k l m n o p q r s t u v w x y z

from this fiber: *I like wearing cotton shirts. They are very comfortable.* **3** A piece of this material used for cleaning wounds: *I'll go and get some cotton and some antiseptic to clean your wound.*

couch /kaʊtʃ/ [countable noun] A long seat for two or more people: *Get off that couch! You've been lying there for hours.* ■ The same meaning: "sofa".

†**cough**[1] /kɒf/ [countable noun] An illness that makes you cough: *I don't like that cough. You should see a doctor.* ■ Be careful with the pronunciation of this word.

cough[2] /kɒf/ [verb] To make a noise with your throat: *Susan caught a cold and spent the night coughing.*

†**could** /kʊd, kəd/ See **can**[2]. ■ Be careful! The verb after "could" is in the infinitive without "to". ■ See box at **can**.

couldn't /ˈkʊd.ᵊnt/ The contraction of "could not".

†**council** /ˈkaʊnt.sᵊl/ [countable noun] The people who run a town or a county: *The elections for the town council will be held next month.*

councilor [countable noun] A person elected as a member of a council: *Councilor Atney is in charge of education.*

count[1] /kaʊnt/ [countable noun] A man with a special noble title: *Have you read "The Count Dracula"?* ■ A woman is a "countess".

†**count**[2] /kaʊnt/ [verb] **1** To say numbers in order: *Can you count to a hundred?* **2** To find how many there are of something: *I counted the people at the party and there were thirty of us.*

◗ **PHRASAL VERBS** · **to count on (somebody)** To feel that you can trust and depend on somebody: *If there are any problems, you can count on me, George.*

countable /ˈkaʊn·tə·bəl/ [adjective] That can be counted: *Apples are countable because you can have one apple, two apples and so on.*

countdown /ˈkaʊnt.daʊn/ [noun] A counting backwards to the starting moment of something: *We all listened to the countdown and watched as the spaceship took off.*

counter /ˈkaʊn·tər/ [countable noun] **1** A kind of table in a store or in a bar: *I put the bottle of milk on the counter while I looked for the money.* **2** A small round thing that you use for board games: *To play this game you need four counters and a dice.*

countess /ˈkaʊn.tes/ US: /-t̬əs/ [countable noun] A woman with a special noble title: *We watched a movie about a countess with no money.* ■ A man is a "count".

†**country** /ˈkʌn.tri/ ▮ [countable noun] **1** An area with its own government, laws, army and so on: *India and China are Asian countries.* ▮ [uncountable noun] **2** Land outside towns and cities: *Which do you prefer, living in the city or in the country?* **3 developing country** See **developing country**. ■ The plural is "countries".

countryside /ˈkʌn.trɪ.saɪd/ [uncountable noun] Land outside towns and cities that is used for farms, tourism and so on: *The countryside in Madison is very beautiful.*

county /ˈkaʊnt·i/ [countable noun] One part of a country or state with its own local government: *The state with most counties in United States is Texas with 254.* ■ The plural is "counties".

†**couple** /ˈkʌp.l̩/ [countable noun] **1** Two people who are married or have a very close relationship: *Mr. and Mrs. Page are an old married couple who live next-door to us.* **2** Two of something or a few of: *Only a couple of people have joined the chess club.* **3 a couple of** A few: *I last saw him a couple of months ago.*

coupon /ˈku·pɑn/, /ˈkju-/ [countable noun] A piece of paper that gives you a discount or points to get something: *Some brands of cornflakes give you coupons to get a free bowl.*

†**courage** /ˈkɜr·ɪdʒ/, /ˈkʌr·ɪdʒ/ [uncountable noun] Bravery, the ability to control fear: *Mary needed a lot of courage to go up to Mr. Donnelly and tell him everything.* ■ Be careful with the pronunciation of this word. The "a" is pronounced like the "i" in "did".

courgette /kɔːˈʒet/ US: /ˈkʌv.ər.ɪŋ/ [countable noun] See **zucchini**. ■ This word is British English.

†**course** US: /kɔːrs/ UK: /kɔːs/ [countable noun] **1** A series of lessons: *Sheila is doing a course on local history.* **2** A part of a meal: *For first course there's soup and for second course, hamburger and french fries.* **3** The place where some sports are played: *The race car went off the course out of control.* **4** Direction: *Which course do we have to follow? North?* ■ Be careful with the pronunciation of this word. It rhymes with "horse". **5 to change course** To go in a different direction: *The ship had to change course to avoid the rocks.* **6 golf course** See **golf course**. **7 of course** Certainly: *Of course I'm American!*

†**court** US: /kɔːrt/ UK: /kɔːt/ [countable noun] **1** The place where the judge sees cases: *They took him to court for stealing a car.* **2** A place where you play tennis or other games: *In the new sports center there are two indoor tennis courts and four badminton courts.*

courtyard US: /ˈkɔːrt.jɑːrd/ UK: /ˈkɔːt.jɑːd/ [countable noun] An open space surrounded by buildings: *Prisoners can walk in the courtyard for an hour every day.*

†**cousin** /ˈkʌz.ᵊn/ [countable noun] The son or the daughter of your uncle and aunt: *I like visiting uncle Paul because I can play with my two cousins.* ■ This word can be used for both boys and girls. 👁 See picture at **family**.

cover[1] /ˈkʌvər/ [countable noun] A thing you put over something else: *Rose has a beautiful red cover on her bed.* 👁 See picture at **book**.

†**cover**[2] /ˈkʌvər/ [verb] To put something over something else: *The painters covered the furniture with plastic sheets before they started work.*

coveralls [plural noun] A suit made from one piece, worn to protect the other clothes while you are working: *My brother wears coveralls at the garage where he works.*

COVERALLS

†**covering** /ˈkʌv.ər.ɪŋ/ US: /-ɚ-/ [countable noun] Something that covers or hides: *They put a plastic covering on the table.*

†**cow** /kaʊ/ [countable noun] **1** The adult female of cattle: *Some cows can give four or five liters of milk a day.* ■ Compare with "beef" (the meat from a cow). 👁 **See page 428. 2 mad cow disease** See "mad cow disease" in the word **mad**.

coward US: /ˈkaʊ.ɚd/ UK: /ˈkaʊ.əd/ [countable noun] Somebody who gets frightened easily and cannot control their fear: *I'm a coward about going to see the dentist.*

cowardly /ˈkaʊ·ərd·li/ [adjective] Easily frightened, lacking courage: *Fred's cowardly behavior took us all by surprise.*

cowboy /ˈkaʊ.bɔɪ/ [countable noun] A man who looks after a large group of cattle: *Nowadays, American cowboys follow the cattle in cars.*

cowshed /ˈkaʊ.ʃed/ [countable noun] A shed where cows are kept in winter or at night: *After the heavy rains, a hole has appeared in the cowshed roof.*

cozy [adjective] Warm and comfortable: *My room may not be very big but it's cozy.* ■ The comparative form is "cozier" and the superlative form is "coziest".

crab /kræb/ [noun] An animal with a hard shell that lives near the water: *Crabs walk sideways.* 👁 See picture at **shellfish**.

crack[1] /kræk/ [countable noun] A thin break: *This plate has a crack in it.*

†**crack**[2] /kræk/ [verb] To break: *The ice cracked while Irene was skating on it and she fell in the lake.*

cracker /ˈkræk·ər/ [countable noun] **1** A flat baked food made of flour and water: *Would you like crackers with cheese for snack?* **2** A small cardboard tube covered with colored paper, that makes a bang when pulled: *Crackers are usually pulled at Christmas.*

cradle /ˈkreɪ.dl̩/ [countable noun] A bed for a baby that moves from side to side: *She put the baby in the cradle and rocked it gently.* ■ Compare with "crib" (a bed that doesn't move from side to side).

†**craft** US: /kræft/ UK: /krɑːft/ [noun] Work in which you make things with your hands: *Pottery is a very relaxing craft.*

craftsman /ˈkræfts·mən/ [countable noun] An expert whose job is to make or repair things with his hands: *Nowadays there are very few craftsmen who repair pianos.* ■ The plural is "craftsmen". ■ A woman is a "craftswoman".

craftswoman /ˈkræfts,wʊm·ən/ [countable noun] An expert whose job is to make or repair things with her hands: *This basket was made by a craftswoman who has a stall in the market.* ■ The plural is "craftswomen". ■ A man is a "craftsman".

crane /kreɪn/ [countable noun] A machine that can lift heavy objects: *They had to use a crane to put the statue on the roof of the building.*

crank[1] /kræŋk/ [countable noun] A bar with a handle in the shape of an L, used for converting movement backwards and forwards into circular movement: *The pedals of a bicycle are attached to a crank.*

crank[2] /kræŋk/ [verb] To start a car or machine by rotating a handle: *The only way to start his vintage car is by cracking it.*

cranky [adjective] Badtempered or easily angry: *His illness made him a cranky person.*

†**crash**[1] /kræʃ/ [countable noun] **1** An accident when a vehicle hits something at high speed: *The crash was horrific but fortunately no one was hurt.* ■ The plural is "crashes". **2 crash helmet** A hard hat that you wear on your head for protection when you ride a

bike: *You shouldn't ride on a motorcycle without a crash helmet.*

crash² /kræʃ/ [verb] To hit something at high speed: *He crashed against a lamp-post and had to be taken to hospital.*

crate /kreɪt/ [countable noun] A large box, usually made of wood: *A crate of fruit fell off the truck.*

crater /'kreɪ·t̬ər/ [countable noun] A round cavity left by a bomb or a volcano eruption: *The bomb left a crater where it exploded.* ■ Be careful with the pronunciation of this word! The syllable "cra" rhymes with "day".

crawl¹ /krɔːl/ [uncountable noun] A style of swimming in which you swim on your front and stretch out each arm alternately: *The crawl is one of the fastest swimming styles.*

crawl² /krɔːl/ [verb] To move on hands and knees: *The Lawrences' baby has started crawling.*

crayon /'kreɪ·ɑn/ [countable noun] A stick of colored wax used for drawing with: *Jamie needs a new box of crayons for school.*

⁺**crazy** /'kreɪ.zi/ [adjective] **1** Mad: *She laughs so strangely that people think she's crazy.* **2** Foolish: *That boy's crazy. He's climbed to the top of that tree.* **3 to be crazy about (somebody or something)** Liking somebody or something very much: *Patrick's crazy about Isabel.*

creak /kriːk/ [verb] To make the sound that wood often makes: *I get frightened when the floorboards creak at night.*

⁺**cream** /kriːm/ [uncountable noun] **1** A thick liquid that you make from milk: *I love strawberries with cream.* **2** Smooth paste: *My father uses shaving cream.*

⁺**create** /kri'eɪt/ [verb] To make something: *The Bible says that God created the world in six days.*

creation /kri'eɪ.ʃən/ ▮ [noun] **1** The act of making something: *There are different theories about the creation of the world.* ▮ [countable noun] **2** Something that you have made: *Have you seen my painting? I'm very proud of my creation!*

creative¹ /kri'eɪ·t̬ɪv/ [countable noun] Person whose job is to apply their imagination and artistic ability to their work: *The creatives at the advertising agency came up with a completely new campaign.*

creative² /kri'eɪtɪv/ [adjective] **1** Original and imaginative: *Christine is very creative.* **2 creative writing** Poetry, plays, novels and short stories, or the writing of them: *At creative writing classes Tom is learning how to write better poems.*

creativity /ˌkri·eɪ'tɪv·ɪ·t̬i/, /ˌkri·ə-/ [uncountable noun] The ability to create and to be imaginative: *Creativity is important in many jobs.*

⁺**creature** /'kri·tʃər/ [countable noun] A living being that is not human: *St Francis of Assisi loved all creatures.*

⁺**credit** /'kred.ɪt/ [uncountable noun] A special arrangement in which you buy something now and pay for it later: *I'm going to buy a new computer on credit.*

⁺**credit card** [countable noun] A card that you can use to buy on credit: *When my father has no cash, he uses his credit card.*

creek [countable noun] A small stream: *In spring we always play in the creek behind our house.*

creep, crept, crept /kriːp/ [verb] **1** To move quietly so that no one hears or sees you: *Susan gave me a fright when she crept into my room.* **2** To move with your body close to the ground: *The soldiers crept across the field to surprise the enemy.*

creepy /'kriː.pi/ [adjective] That makes you feel rather nervous and frightened: *The deserted property at the end of the road is a creepy place.* ■ This word is informal. ■ The comparative form is "creepier" and the superlative form is "creepiest".

cremate US: /'kriː.meɪt/ UK: /krɪ'meɪt/ [verb] To burn a dead body: *I want to be cremated when I die.*

crème brûlée [noun] A yellow sweet made with eggs, milk and burned sugar on top: *Would you like a crème brûlée?*

crept /krept/ Past tense and past participle forms of **creep**.

crest /krest/ [countable noun] **1** The top of a slope or hill: *Selena surfed on the crest of the wave.* **2** A row of feathers running along the head of a bird: *The bird has a distinctive crest.*

crew /kruː/ [countable noun] A group of people who work on a ship or an airplane: *The Captain was from Australia but the rest of the crew were Americans.*

crib /krɪb/ [countable noun] **1** A bed for a baby: *My little sister sleeps in a crib.* ■ Compare with "cradle" (a bed that moves from side to side). ■ In British English they say "cot". 👁 See picture at **bedroom**. **2** A thing dishonestly used to help somebody remember something in a dishonest way: *She cheated in the test using a crib.* ■ This use is informal.

cricket /'krɪk.ɪt/ ▮ [uncountable noun] **1** A game for two teams, played with bats and a ball: *Sri Lanka surprised people when they won the cricket world championship in 1996.* ▮ [countable noun] **2** A small, jumping insect: *I like listening to crickets singing on very hot days.* 👁 **See page 431.**

⁺**crime** /kraɪm/ [countable noun] An action that is against the law: *If you drive at high speed in a city, you are committing a crime.* ■ Compare with "murder¹" (the killing of somebody).

criminal¹ /'krɪmɪnəl/ [adjective] Referring to crime: *Inspector Wexford is in charge of the criminal investigation department.*

⁺**criminal²** /'krɪmɪnəl/ [countable noun] A person who does something against the law: *The police arrested the* *two criminals and took them to the police station.* ■ Compare with "murderer" (a person who kills another person).

crimson /ˈkrɪm.zᵊn/ [noun and adjective] A deep red color: *Cardinals wear crimson cloaks.*

†**crisis** /ˈkraɪ.sɪs/ [noun] A difficult moment: *Sue is going through a real crisis. She doesn't know whether to go to university or not.* ■ The plural is "crises".

†**crisp**[1] UK: /krɪsp/ [countable noun] See **chip**. ■ This word is British English. ■ This word is more common in the plural.

crisp[2] /krɪsp/ [adjective] That is hard but breaks easily: *These crackers are very tasty; they're nice and crisp, too.*

criterion /kraɪˈtɪər·i·ən/ [countable noun] A standard by which something is judged: *She believes that the sole criterion for success is hard work.* ■ The plural is "criteria".

critic /ˈkrɪt̬·ɪk/ [countable noun] A person who is paid to give his or her opinion on movies, books and so on: *Some authors pretend that they don't read what the critics say about their books.*

†**critical** /ˈkrɪt̬·ɪ·kəl/ [adjective] Having a bad opinion of somebody or something: *David is always too critical of his teachers.*

†**criticism** /ˈkrɪt·əˌsɪz·əm/ [noun] Saying what is bad about somebody or something: *I thought his criticism was totally unfair.*

criticize or **criticise** /ˈkrɪtɪsaɪz/ [verb] To say what you think is bad about somebody or something: *I was criticized for not going to Beckie's birthday party.*

critique /krɪˈtiːk/ [countable noun] An extensive analysis of a situation, or of somebody's work or ideas, usually containing a negative judgment on it: *The professor wrote a critique of the author's new book.*

croak US: /kroʊk/ UK: /krəʊk/ [verb] To make the sound that a frog makes: *Frogs croak when they are on land.*

crockery /ˈkrɑk·ə·ri/ [uncountable noun] Plates, cups and saucers: *Leave the dirty crockery in the sink; we'll wash it up later.* ■ Compare with "cutlery" (knives, forks and spoons). ■ The plural is "crockeries".

crocodile /ˈkrɑk·əˌdaɪl/ [countable noun] A large reptile with strong jaws: *Crocodiles attack people when they're hungry.* 👁 **See page 430.**

crooked /ˈkrʊk.ɪd/ [adjective] **1** Bent: *To get to the castle you have to go up a long crooked road.* **2** Dishonest: *There are too many crooked politicians in the world.* ■ Be careful with the pronunciation of the end of this word! The "e" is pronounced like the "i" in "did".

crop US: /krɑːp/ UK: /krɒp/ [countable noun] A plant that is grown for food: *In Africa they need to grow crops like wheat to prevent famines.*

†**cross**[1] /krɒs/ [verb] To go across something: *I've crossed the Atlantic twice by plane.*
▸ **PHRASAL VERBS** · **to cross out** To make a mark with a cross on something written: *I didn't have an eraser, so I just crossed out the mistake.* ■ Be careful with the spelling of the 3rd person singular present tense form: "crosses".

cross[2] /krɒs/ [countable noun] The shape of two lines crossing each other: *The cross is one of the symbols of Christianity.* ■ The plural is "crosses".

cross[3] /krɒs/ [adjective] That feels anger against somebody or something: *Susan was very cross with me when I lost her book.* ■ The same meaning: "angry".

crossing US: /ˈkrɑː.sɪŋ/ UK: /ˈkrɒs.ɪŋ/ [countable noun] The act of going across something: *The channel crossing was very rough.*

crossroads US: /ˈkrɑːs.roʊdz/ UK: /ˈkrɒs.rəʊdz/ [countable noun] A place where one road crosses another: *This crossroads is quite dangerous. There have been lots of accidents here lately.* ■ The plural is "crossroads".

crosswalk [countable noun] A place on the road where pedestrians can cross: *Many crosswalks are controlled by stoplights.* ■ In British English they say "pedestrian crossing", "zebra crossing". 👁 See picture at **street**.

crossword /ˈkrɒswɜːd/ [countable noun] A puzzle in which you complete blanks with words: *I can't finish this crossword. I don't know the words for these two clues.*

crotchet US: /ˈkrɑː.tʃət/ UK: /ˈkrɒtʃ.ət/ [countable noun] A musical note which has the time value of half a minim: *Crotchets are represented by a filled-in oval head with a stem.* 👁 **See page 460.**

crouch /kraʊtʃ/ [verb] To bend down: *When we found the baby, she was crouching behind the kitchen door, hiding from us.*

crow[1] /krəʊ/ [countable noun] A large black bird: *Look at the crows on that tree.*

crow[2] /krəʊ/ [verb] To make the sound that a cock makes: *Cocks crow at dawn.* 👁 See picture at **animal.**

†**crowd** /kraʊd/ [countable noun] A large group of people: *Crowds in football stadiums always make me feel nervous.* 👁 See picture at **groups.**

crowded /ˈkraʊ.dɪd/ [adjective] With many people for the space available: *The hall was crowded. Many people had to wait outside.* ■ Be careful with the pronunciation of this word. The "e" is pronounced like the "i" in "did".

†**crown** /kraʊn/ [countable noun] An object that kings or queens wear on their heads: *In the United Kingdom, when the Queen opens parliament she always wears her crown.*

a b c d e f g h i j k l m n o p q r s t u v w x y z

✝**cruel** /ˈkruː.əl, krʊəl/ [adjective] That causes suffering: *I think that fox hunting is a very cruel sport.*

cruelty /ˈkru·əl·ti/ [noun] Deliberately making people or animals suffer: *He was taken to court for cruelty to his horses.* ■ The plural is "cruelties".

cruise /kruːz/ [countable noun] **1** A long journey by boat: *How long does the cruise from New Jersey to Quebec take?* **2** A vacation on a ship stopping at several ports: *This summer my parents are going on a cruise around the Mediterranean.*

crumb /krʌm/ [countable noun] A tiny piece of bread or cake: *We can feed these crumbs to the pigeons.* 👁 See picture at **a piece of...**

crumble /ˈkrʌm.bl̩/ [verb] To break into pieces: *The farmer had to repair the wall where it was crumbling.*

crumple /ˈkrʌm.pl̩/ [verb] To crush or to make something to become wrinkled: *He crumpled up the sheets of paper in disgust.* ■ We always say: "crumple (something) **up**".

crunch /krʌntʃ/ [verb] To eat something with a noise: *Frances sat watching television and crunching cookies.*

crusade /kruːˈseɪd/ [countable noun] A medieval war between Christians and Muslims for possession of the Holy Land: *In the Children's Crusade of 1212 thousands of children set off from Europe to go to Jerusalem; many never arrived.*

✝**crush** /krʌʃ/ [verb] To press something very hard and injure or break it: *I didn't see his paper castle on the chair and I crushed it when I sat down.*

crust /krʌst/ [noun] **1** The outside part of bread: *I like the crust of a loaf because it's so crisp.* **2** The outside part of the Earth: *Land and sea form the Earth's crust.* 👁 **See page 449.**

crustacean /krʌsˈteɪ.ʃən/ [countable noun] Any animal with a hard shell that mostly lives in water: *Crabs, shrimps and lobsters are examples of crustaceans.*

crutch /krʌtʃ/ [countable noun] A stick that you use when you cannot walk well: *When I broke my leg I had to use crutches for two months.*

✝**cry** /kraɪ/ [verb] **1** To weep, usually because you are unhappy: *She cried when she heard the news of her brother's accident.* **2** To shout: *"I didn't break it", she cried.* ■ Be careful with the spelling of these forms: "cries", "cried".

crystal /ˈkrɪs.tᵊl/ [uncountable noun] **1** A transparent mineral or chemical with a particular regular shape: *Sugar crystals are like little brown rocks.* **2** Glass of a very high quality: *Be careful with that crystal vase.*

cub /kʌb/ [countable noun] A very young wolf, lion or bear: *It's dangerous to approach a wolf when she's with her cubs.*

Cub /kʌb/ [countable noun] A boy who is a junior Scout: *Danny became a Cub when he was eight.* ■ Be careful! "Cub" has a capital "C".

Cuban¹ [adjective] Referring to Cuba: *My father loves Cuban music.* ■ Be careful! "Cuban" has a capital "C".

Cuban² [countable noun] A person from Cuba: *There are two Cubans in my baseball team.* ■ Be careful! "Cuban" has a capital "C".

cube /kjuːb/ [countable noun] **1** A shape with six square faces: *A dice is a cube.* **2 ice cube** See **ice cube**.

cuckoo /ˈkʊk.uː/ [countable noun] A gray European bird: *Cuckoos lay their eggs in other birds' nests.*

cucumber /ˈkju·kʌm·bər/ [noun] A long green vegetable: *Cucumber is very nice in salads.*

cuddle /ˈkʌdl/ [verb] To hold somebody affectionately in your arms: *When I see Joanna's baby I always like to cuddle her.*

cuisine /kwɪˈziːn/ [uncountable noun] A style of cooking: *I love French cuisine.* ■ This word is formal.

cul-de-sac [countable noun] A street closed at one end: *Her house was set at the end of a cul-de-sac.*

cultivate /ˈkʌl·tə,veɪt/ [verb] To grow crops: *In Brazil they cultivate a lot of coffee.*

cultivation /,kʌl·təˈveɪ·ʃən/ [uncountable noun] The activity of growing crops: *The cultivation of rice is highly developed in Japan.*

✝**cultural** /ˈkʌl·tʃər·əl/ [adjective] Referring to culture: *It's interesting to find out about cultural differences.*

✝**culture** /ˈkʌl·tʃər/ ▮ [uncountable noun] **1** The arts: *The Ministry of Culture gives a prize every year to the best artists and writers.* ▮ [noun] **2** The way of life of a community: *Do movies give a good picture of American culture?* ■ Be careful with the pronunciation of this word. The first part, "u", is pronounced like the "u" in "cup", and the ending "ture" is pronounced like the "cher" in "butcher".

cunning /ˈkʌnɪŋ/ [adjective] Clever: *Arthur is good at inventing cunning plans to make money.*

✝**cup** /kʌp/ [countable noun] A small round container with a handle used for drinking hot drinks: *I brought the cups but I forgot the coffee.* ■ Compare with "mug" (a tall straight cup).

CUP

cup

mug

cupboard /ˈkʌb·ərd/ [countable noun] A piece of furniture where you keep things in: *If you need glasses, there are a lot in the cupboard in the kitchen.* ■ Compare with "closet" (used for keeping clothes in). 👁 See picture at **kitchen**.

cupcake /ˈkʌp.keɪk/ [countable noun] A small iced cake which is baked in a cup-shaped container: *The cupcake is one of my favorite sweets.*

cupful /ˈkʌp.fʊl/ [countable noun] The quantity of something that you can get into a cup: *To make an apple pie you need one and a half cupfuls of sugar.*

curb [countable noun] The edge of a sidewalk: *You parked your car a long way from the curb.* ■ In British English they say "kerb".

cure[1] /kjʊər/ [countable noun] A remedy: *Do you know of a cure for flu?*

cure[2] /kjʊər/ [verb] To make somebody ill better: *How did you cure your cold?*

curiosity US: /ˌkjʊr.iˈɑː.sə.t̬i/ UK: /ˌkjʊə.riˈɒs.ɪ.ti/ [uncountable noun] A strong desire to know something: *I've always felt curiosity about how television works.* ■ The plural is "curiosities".

curious /ˈkjʊər·i·əs/ [adjective] **1** Wanting to know: *We were curious to know where Tanya was from.* **2** Strange or odd: *That's curious. I didn't know that George went to our school.*

curl US: /kɝːl/ UK: /kɜːl/ [noun] A piece of hair that curves: *He has really beautiful hair. Such lovely curls!*

curly /ˈkɜr·li/ [adjective] That has natural curls: *He's very good looking: blue eyes, dark, curly hair.* ■ The comparative form of is "curlier" and the superlative form is "curliest". 👁 See pictures at **hair** and **opposite**.

currant /ˈkɜr·ənt/, /ˈkʌr·ənt/ [countable noun] A sweet, dried grape: *My father makes wonderful currant buns.*

currency /ˈkɜr·ən·si/, /ˈkʌr·ən-/ [noun] The money used in a country: *United States currency is the dollar.* ■ The plural is "currencies".

current[1] /ˈkʌrənt/ ▮ [countable noun] **1** The movement of water in a river or ocean: *The current took the boat away.* ▮ [noun] **2** The electricity going through a wire: *Use this switch to turn the current off completely.*

current[2] /ˈkʌrənt/ [adjective] Of the present time: *Today in History, we talked about the current situation in the Middle East.*

curry /ˈkɜr·i/, /ˈkʌr·i/ [noun] A hot, spicy meal: *In India you can eat meat, fish or vegetable curries.* ■ The plural is "curries".

curse US: /kɝːs/ UK: /kɜːs/ [countable noun] An appeal for something bad to happen to somebody: *In stories, witches sometimes put curses on people.*

curtain US: /ˈkɝː.t̬ən/ UK: /ˈkɜː.tən/ [countable noun] See **drape**. ■ This word is British English.

curvature US: /ˈkɝː.və.tʃɚ/ UK: /ˈkɜː.və.tʃər/ [noun] The state of being curved: *The curvature of the earth can only be seen from space.*

curve US: /kɝːv/ UK: /kɜːv/ [countable noun] A bending line: *This road is dangerous. It has lots of curves.*

cushion /ˈkʊʃ.ən/ [countable noun] A cloth bag filled with soft material that people have on chairs or sofas: *Sit on that cushion and you'll be more comfortable.*

custard /ˈkʌs·tərd/ [uncountable noun] A sweet yellow liquid made from milk, eggs and sugar: *Do you want some hot custard on your apple pie, Jane?*

custom /ˈkʌs.təm/ [noun] **1** A tradition: *I like the custom of giving presents at Christmas.* **2** Something that a person does regularly: *George has the custom of having a short nap after lunch.*

customer /ˈkʌs·tə·mər/ [countable noun] A person who buys: *They closed the store because they didn't have any customers.* ■ Compare with "client" (a person or company who receives services of a professional). 👁 See picture at **market**.

customs /ˈkʌs.təmz/ [plural noun] The place at a border where they control imports: *They stopped James at customs and opened his suitcase.*

cut[1] /kʌt/ [countable noun] **1** An opening made with a sharp thing: *He has a cut on his finger.* **2** A reduction in amount, size and so on: *The government have announced a cut in spending on defense.*

cut[2], cut, cut /kʌt/ [verb] To break something evenly with a knife or scissors: *Can you cut the bread, Sue?*
▸ **PHRASAL VERBS** · **to cut (something) down** To make something fall to the ground by cutting it: *They cut down the tree on the corner.* · **to cut off** To separate from other things or people: *The whole town was cut off by the snow.* · **to cut (something) out** **1** To remove or to stop: *You ought to cut out all those candies you eat.* **2** To remove something by cutting: *I'm going to cut the photo of the gorilla out of the newspaper.* · **to cut (something) up** To cut something into pieces: *Let's cut the cake up and start eating.* ■ Be careful with the spelling of this form: "cutting".

cute /kjuːt/ [adjective] **1** Attractive in an amusing or a pretty way: *What a cute little puppy!* **2** Clever or wanting to appear clever: *Be careful with him. He's very cute.* ■ This use is informal. Be careful with the pronunciation of this word.

cutlery /'kʌt·lə·ri/ [uncountable noun] Knives, forks and spoons: *When you've dried the cutlery, put it away in that drawer, please.* ■ The plural is "cutleries". ■ Compare with "crockery" (plates, cups and saucers).

CUTLERY

cut-out [countable noun] **1** A shape cut out of paper, wood, etc.: *He made a large cut-out in the shape of a cat.* **2** A device which automatically disconnects the electricity supply: *The cut-out stopped the supply of power to the computer.*

cutting /'kʌtɪŋ/ [countable noun] Small piece of paper cut out of a newspaper or a magazine: *I have a lot of press cuttings about this actor.*

cuttlefish /'kʌt.l̩.fɪʃ/ US: /'kʌţ-/ [countable noun] A cephalopod mollusk with ten arms which expels a fluid that looks like ink: *The cuttlefish repels its predators with ink.*

cycling /'saɪ.klɪŋ/ [uncountable noun] Riding a bicycle as a sport: *Lance Armstrong is famous for his victories in cycling in the Tour of France.* 👁 See picture at **sport**.

cyclist /'saɪ.klɪst/ [countable noun] A person who rides a bicycle: *Professional cyclists can ride up to 160 miles in a day.*

cylinder /'sɪl·ən·dər/ [countable noun] A long, round shape like a tube: *A pencil or a bottle are examples of cylinders.*

cymbals /'sɪmbəl/ [countable noun] A pair of round metal plates used as an instrument: *I play the cymbals in the school band.* 👁 **See page 459.**

cypress /'saɪ.prəs/ [countable noun] A type of tall, thin tree: *Cypresses do not lose their leaves in winter.* ■ The plural is "cypresses".

cytoplasm /'saɪ·ţəˌplæz·əm/ [uncountable noun] The inside part of a cell surrounding the nucleus: *The cell is filled with cytoplasm.*

D

d

d /diː/ The fourth letter of the alphabet: *The name "David" begins with a "D".*

d. Referring to a date of the death of somebody: *Peter Wright (d. 19 August 1992, Louisville, Alabama).* ■ "d." is an abbreviation for "died". ■ See box at **abbreviations**.

D /diː/ [countable noun] The second musical note of the scale of C major: *The music teacher asked me to play a D.* ■ The plural is "Ds" or "D's". 👁 **See page 460.**

dad or **daddy** /dæd or 'dædi/ [countable noun] See **father**. ■ These words are informal. 👁 See picture at **family**.

daffodil /'dæf.ə.dɪl/ [countable noun] A yellow spring flower: *In May the yards in Chicago are filled with daffodils.*

dagger /'dæg·ər/ [countable noun] A short, sharp knife: *Pirates used to carry daggers in their belts.*

†**daily**[1] /'deɪli/ [adjective] Happening every day: *"The New York Times" is a United States daily newspaper.*

daily[2] /'deɪli/ [adverb] Every day: *We feed our cat twice daily.*

dainty /'deɪn·ti/ [adjective] Delicate or elegant: *The furniture for the old dolls' house was beautiful and dainty.* ■ The comparative form is "daintier" and the superlative form is "daintiest".

dairy /'deəri/ [countable noun] A place where milk products are made: *Cheese, butter and yoghurt are made in a dairy.* ■ The plural is "dairies".

daisy /'deɪ.zi/ [countable noun] A small white and yellow flower: *Daisies often grow wild in the grass.* ■ The plural is "daisies".

dalmatian /dæl'meɪ.ʃən/ [countable noun] A white dog with black spots: *"A Hundred and One Dalmatians" is one of my favorite movies.*

dam /dæm/ [countable noun] A wall blocking a river or lake: *Hoover Dam on the border between Arizona and Nevada is a major tourist attraction, nearly a million people tour the dam each year.* 👁 **See page 445.**

†**damage**[1] /'dæmɪdʒ/ [uncountable noun] The harm done to things: *Hurricanes sometimes cause a lot of damage in the Caribbean.* ■ Be careful with the pronunciation of this word. The last "a" is pronounced like the "i" in "did".

damage[2] /'dæmɪdʒ/ [verb] To harm something: *The fire damaged the building so badly that it had to be pulled down.* ■ Be careful with the pronunciation of this word. The last "a" is pronounced like the "i" in "did".

damn /dæm/ [noun] A word that people say when they are angry: *Damn! I've forgotten my keys.* ■ This word is a swear word. ■ Be careful with the pronunciation of this word! The "n" is silent.

a b c d e f g h i j k l m n o p q r s t u v w x y z

↑**damp** /dæmp/ [adjective] A little wet: *The weather is usually quite damp in the fall.* ■ "Damp" is often a negative word. Compare with "moist" (is usually a positive word: "You must keep the earth moist for this plant").

dance[1] /dɑːns/ [noun] The movements that people do to music: *The waltz is my grandfather's favorite dance and he dances it very well.*

↑**dance[2]** /dɑːns/ [verb] To move to music: *My mom and dad dance very well together.*

↑**dancer** US: /ˈdænt.sɚ/ UK: /ˈdɑːnt.səʳ/ [countable noun] A person who dances: *My cousin is a very good ballet dancer.*

dandelion /ˈdæn·də·lˌɑɪ·ən/ [countable noun] A yellow flower: *Dandelions grow wild in the countryside.*

↑**danger** /ˈdeɪn·dʒər/ [noun] The possibility that something bad may happen: *There's a danger that the giant panda may become extinct.* ■ Be careful with the pronunciation of this word! "da" is pronounced as "day".

↑**dangerous** /ˈdeɪn·dʒər·əs/, /ˈdeɪndʒ·rəs/ [adjective] That can cause injury, death or something else bad: *Don't go near the railroad; it's dangerous!* ■ Be careful with the pronunciation of this word! "Da" is pronounced as "day".

↑**dare** /deər/ [verb] **1** To be brave enough to do something: *Peter wanted to ask Anne to go out with him but he didn't dare.* **2 I daren't** Words that you say when you don't want to do something because you are afraid of somebody or something: *I daren't tell the teacher what we did.*

daring /ˈdeərɪŋ/ [adjective] Brave enough to do dangerous things: *You have to be quite daring to go up in a balloon.*

↑**dark[1]** /dɑːk/ [adjective] With very little light: *It's a dark night tonight because there's no moon.* ■ Compare with "bright" (with a shining light).

↑**dark[2]** /dɑːk/ [uncountable noun] **1** The absence of light: *Bats usually hunt in the dark.* **2 after dark** After the sun goes down: *Don't go out after dark!*

darkness /ˈdɑrk·nəs/ [uncountable noun] The state of being dark: *The room was in complete darkness.* ■ Compare with "brightness" (the strength of a light).

darling /ˈdɑr·lɪŋ/ [noun and adjective] A word for somebody you love: *Are you happy tonight, darling?*

dart[1] /dɑːt/ [verb] To move very quickly: *The lizard darted across the yard.*

dart[2] /dɑːt/ [countable noun] An object like a small arrow: *They shot a special dart into the tiger to make it sleep.*

darts /dɑːts/ [countable noun] A game that you play by throwing darts at a board: *In United States, people often play darts in pubs.*

dash[1] /dæʃ/ [countable noun] A mark used to separate information in a sentence [–]: *Some people consider that it is usually better to use commas than dashes.*

dash[2] /dæʃ/ [verb] To hurry: *I must dash, or I'll be late.*

↑**data** /ˈdeɪ·t̬ə/, /ˈdæt̬·ə/, /ˈdɑt̬·ə/ [uncountable noun] Facts, information: *I have enough data to do the experiment.* ■ Be careful with the pronunciation of this word! This word can be used with either a singular or a plural verb: "The data is/are being checked".

database [countable noun] A large amount of information which is stored in a computer: *You can modify and update the information in the database.*

↑**date** /deɪt/ [countable noun] **1** A particular day of the month or year: *"What's the date today?" "It's the 20th of October".* **2** An arrangement to see somebody: *My brother's got a date with Marie tonight.* **3** A small, very sweet brown fruit of some palm tree: *At Christmas we eat a lot of dates.* **4 out of date** Unfashionable, that you can use no longer: *That style of skirt is very out of date.* **5 up to date** Modern, with all the latest information: *Is this telephone directory up to date?*

↑**daughter** US: /ˈdɑː.t̬ɚ/ UK: /ˈdɔː.təʳ/ [countable noun] **1** Somebody's female child: *My teacher's daughter is very clever.* **2 daughter-in-law** The wife of somebody's son: *Their daughter-in-law is Colombian.* ■ The plural of "daughter-in-law" is "daughters-in-law". 👁 See picture at **family**.

dawn US: /dɑːn/ UK: /dɔːn/ [noun] The time when the sun rises: *Farmers have to get up at dawn.* ■ Be careful with the pronunciation of this word. The beginning of this word is pronounced like "door".

↑**day** /deɪ/ ▮ [countable noun] **1** A period of twenty-four hours: *There are 365 days in a year.* 👁 See picture at **calendar**. ▮ [noun] **2** The time when it is light: *Owls sleep during the day and hunt at night.* **3 one day** On a certain day: *One day, Little Red Riding Hood went for a walk in the woods.* **4 some day** At some time in the future: *Some day I'll be a famous opera singer.* **5 the day after tomorrow** The day that follows tomorrow: *If today is Monday, the day after tomorrow is Wednesday.* **6 the day before yesterday** The day that came before yesterday: *If today is Monday, the day before yesterday was Saturday.* **7 these days** Now, in the present age: *These days it's quite normal to have a computer in your home.*

daybreak /ˈdeɪ.breɪk/ [uncountable noun] The early morning when the sun rises: *At daybreak, the birds always start singing.*

day care [countable noun] Nursery where babies can be left while their parents are at work: *My mother leaves my sister in the day care every morning.*

daydream [verb] To imagine good things happening to you: *Stop daydreaming and pay attention!*

daylight /'deɪ.laɪt/ [uncountable noun] The light of day: *My dad prefers to drive in daylight rather than at night.*

day off [countable noun] An extra day when you don't go to school or to work: *Take a day off. You'll feel better tomorrow.*

daytime /'deɪ.taɪm/ [uncountable noun] The time when it is light: *Our new baby brother likes to sleep in the daytime.*

+**dead** /ded/ [adjective] **1** Not living: *Both my grandfathers are dead.* **2** Very: *That movie is dead good.* ■ This use is informal.

dead end [countable noun] A street with no way out: *Don't go down there. It's a dead end.*

dead heat [countable noun] A race with two winners: *They crossed the finishing line together; the judges declared the race a dead heat.*

deadline /'ded.laɪn/ [countable noun] A time limit: *Our teacher told us that Friday was the deadline for finishing our project on the Amazon.*

deadly /'ded.li/ [adjective] That kills: *That snake's bite is nearly always deadly.* ■ The comparative form is "deadlier" and the superlative form is "deadliest".

+**deaf** /def/ [adjective] Not able to hear: *The accident left him deaf in one ear.*

deafen /'def.ᵊn/ [verb] To make somebody unable to hear because of a loud noise: *The explosion nearly deafened us.*

+**deal**[1] /diːl/ [countable noun] **1** A commercial agreement: *The businessmen made a deal with their clients.* **2 a good deal** A large quantity: *My brother eats a good deal.* **3 a great deal of** A lot of: *I spent a great deal of time studying for this test so I deserved to pass.* ■ We use "a great deal of" with uncountable nouns.

deal[2], **dealt, dealt** /diːl/ [verb] To hand out: *It's my turn to deal the cards.*

▸ **PHRASAL VERBS · to deal with (something)** To organize things in order to solve a problem or to resolve a situation: *Mom parked the car while dad dealt with the theater tickets.*

dealer /'di·lər/ [countable noun] A person who buys and sells things: *My aunt is a secondhand car dealer.*

dealt /delt/ Past tense and past participle forms of **deal**[2].

+**dear** US: /dɪr/ UK: /dɪəʳ/ [adjective] **1** Loved: *His grandma was very dear to him.* **2** A word that goes at the beginning of a letter: *Dear Jane, thank you for the lovely present.* **3 oh dear!** An expression of irritation: *Oh dear! I've spilt ink all over my exercise book.*

+**death** /deθ/ [noun] The end of life: *The old man's death upset us all.*

+**debate** /dɪ'beɪt/ [noun] A public discussion about something important: *There was an interesting debate on the television last night.* ■ Be careful with the pronunciation of this word.

+**debt** /det/ [noun] Money that must be paid back: *My brother is in debt because he owes the bank about five thousand dollars.* ■ Be careful! We say: "to be **in** debt". Note also the pronunciation of this word. The "b" is not pronounced.

+**decade** /'dek.eɪd, -'-/ [countable noun] Period of ten years: *The 1960's was a decade of great changes in technology.*

decay[1] [uncountable noun] **1** The process of going bad or falling apart: *Many of the houses in my father's town are in advanced state of decay.* **2 tooth decay** See "tooth decay" in the word **tooth**.

+**decay**[2] /dɪ'keɪ/ [verb] To go bad, to fall apart: *Pollution causes some buildings to decay.*

+**deceive** /dɪ'siːv/ [verb] To make somebody believe something that is not true: *Jim tried to deceive me by saying he didn't know who broke my racket.*

+**December** /dɪ'sem·bər/ [noun] The last month of the year: *Winter begins in December.* ■ Be careful! "December" has a capital "D". 👁 See picture at **calendar**.

deception /dɪ'sepʃən/ [uncountable noun] The act of deceiving or misleading: *Illusionists practice the art of deception.*

+**decide** /dɪ'saɪd/ [verb] To choose after thinking about something: *Mary decided to buy the blue dress instead of the green one.* ■ Be careful with the pronunciation of this word! The first "e" is pronounced like the "i" in "did", the "i" rhymes with "my" and the second "e" is not pronounced.

deciduous /dɪ'sɪd.ju.əs/ [adjective] **1** Losing its leaves every year: *The maple and the oak are both deciduous.* ■ Compare with "evergreen" (having green leaves all through the year). **2 deciduous tree** Tree that loses its leaves annually: *Many deciduous trees flower during the period when they are leafless as this increases the effectiveness of pollination.* 👁 **See page 434.**

decimal system [noun] A system of mathematics based on the number 10: *Most countries use a decimal system for counting their money.*

+**decision** /dɪ'sɪʒ.ᵊn/ [countable noun] A choice that you make after thinking about something: *The referee's decision to send the player off made the spectators very angry.* ■ We say **make a decision**.

deck /dek/ [countable noun] **1** The floor of a ship: *On the last day of the cruise, the passengers and crew all had a party on deck.* **2 deck of cards** A set of playing cards: *Get the deck of cards out and we'll have a game.*

a b c d e f g h i j k l m n o p q r s t u v w x y z

deckchair /'dek.tʃeər/ US: /-tʃer/ [countable noun] A folding chair that is used outside: *We rented some really comfortable deckchairs on the beach.* See picture at **chair**.

declaration /ˌdek.lə'reɪ.ʃən/ [countable noun] A formal announcement: *The United States of America made their Declaration of Independence from British rule in 1776.*

+**declare** /dɪ'kleər/ [verb] To announce something very clearly: *United States declared war on Mexico in 1846.*

+**decline** /dɪ'klaɪn/ [verb] **1** To refuse an offer: *She declined Paul's invitation to his birthday party.* **2** To get worse: *Old Mrs. Conroy's health is declining slowly.*

decompose /ˌdiːkəm'pəʊz/ [verb] To make or become rotten or decayed: *Bodies of animals and plants begin to decompose soon after death.*

decomposer /ˌdiː.kəm'pəʊz.ər/ US: /'poʊz.ɚ/ [countable noun] A living organism which contributes to the process of decomposition: *Decomposers such as bacteria and mould, break down the remains of other living things.*

decomposition /ˌdiˌkɑm·pə'zɪʃ·ən/ [uncountable noun] The act of becoming rotten: *After death the body is subject to a process of decomposition.*

decompression /ˌdiː.kəm'preʃ.ən/ [uncountable noun] The release of pressure: *As they come up from under the water, divers go through a process of decompression.*

+**decorate** /'dek.ə.reɪt/ [verb] **1** To put beautiful things on something: *The children decorated the room for the party.* **2** To paint a room or to put paper on the walls: *Everyone helped and we decorated the apartment in one weekend.*

decoration /ˌdek.ə'reɪ.ʃən/ [countable noun] **1** The process of decorating something: *He is very good at interior decoration.* **2** Something that adorns or decorates: *Paint and wall paper are used as decoration of the living room.* **3** A medal awarded as an honor: *All of the soldiers who took part in the war received a decoration.*

decorations /ˌdekə'reɪʃən/ [countable noun] Beautiful objects that you put on something: *The Christmas decorations in the Michigan Avenue look fantastic this year.*

+**decrease** /'diː.kriːs/ US: /'diː.kriːs/ UK: /dɪ'kriːs/ [verb] To become less or smaller: *Cigarette smoking is decreasing among young people.*

dedicate /'ded.ɪ.keɪt/ [verb] To offer something to a particular cause or person: *Francis of Assisi dedicated his life to the poor.*

deed /diːd/ [countable noun] An action: *Many authors have written about Seventh Calvary heroic deeds.* ■ We usually say "action".

+**deep** /diːp/ [adjective] Profound: *Don't go in the deep end of the swimming pool because you can't swim well enough.*

deep-freeze [countable noun] A refrigerator for frozen food: *Put this chicken in the deep-freeze and we'll eat it next week.*

deer US: /dɪr/ UK: /dɪəʳ/ [countable noun] A wild animal with large horns: *Deer can run very fast.* ■ The plural is also "deer". ■ A female deer is a "doe". **See page 428.**

defeat /dɪ'fiːt/ [verb] To win a game or a battle: *Boston Celtics defeated Chicago Bulls 92-87 in the basketball game yesterday.*

defect /dɪ'fekt/, /'diː.fekt/ [countable noun] A fault: *There's a defect in the motor of this car.*

+**defence** /dɪ'fents/ [noun] See **defense.** ■ This is a British English spelling.

+**defend** /dɪ'fend/ [verb] To protect: *The navy defended the beach.*

defender /dɪ'fen·dər/ [countable noun] Player in a position of defense: *The defender stopped the ball going into the net with his head.* See picture at **soccer**.

+**defense** /dɪ'fens/ [noun] Resistance against an attack: *Many female animals will fight to the death in defense of their young.* ■ The British English spelling is "defence".

+**define** /dɪ'faɪn/ [verb] To say what a word means: *Can you define the word "science"?*

+**definite** /'def.ɪ.nət/ [adjective] Very clear or sure: *Give me a definite answer by tomorrow.*

definite article [countable noun] The word "the": *The definite article "the" is one of the most common words in the English language.*

+**definition** /ˌdef.ɪ'nɪʃ.ən/ [countable noun] An explanation of the meaning of a word: *All the definitions in the dictionary "Horizon" have examples.*

defy /dɪ'faɪ/ [verb] To refuse to obey a person or a law: *He defied the policeman's order to stop.* ■ Be careful with the spelling of these forms: "defies", "defied".

+**degree** /dɪ'griː/ [countable noun] **1** A course of a study at a university or the qualification you get if you finish it: *My cousin has a degree in Biology.* **2** A scientific measurement for angles: *A circle has 360 degrees.* **3** A scientific measurement for temperatures: *Today the temperature is forty five Fahrenheit degrees.*

+**delay**[1] /dɪ'leɪ/ [noun] A situation where you have to wait because something does not happen as it should or normally does: *There was a delay of twenty minutes before the train left.*

delay[2] /dɪ'leɪ/ [verb] **1** To make somebody late: *I'm late because I was delayed in a gridlock.* **2** To decide not to do something until a later time: *In the* end we have been forced to delay our vacation until September.

deliberate /dɪ'lɪb·ər·ət/ [adjective] Planned or not accidental: *That kick was deliberate.*

delicate /'del.ɪ.kət/ [adjective] Easy to damage or to hurt, very fine: *Be careful with these glasses because they are very delicate.*

delicatessen /ˌdel.ɪ.kə'tes.ən/ [countable noun] A store that sells special and unusual food: *In United States you buy certain foreign foods in a delicatessen.*

delicious /dɪ'lɪʃ.əs/ [adjective] Good to eat: *Let's go to the new Italian restaurant; the food there is delicious.*

delight[1] /dɪ'laɪt/ [noun] Great happiness: *Our cat's greatest delight is sleeping in front of the fire.*

delight[2] /dɪ'laɪt/ [verb] To give great happiness: *The young musicians' concert delighted everyone, especially the parents.*

delighted /dɪ'laɪ·t̬ɪd/ [adjective] Very happy: *The girls were delighted to see each other again after such a long time.* ■ Be careful with the pronunciation of this word. The last "e" is pronounced like the "i" in "did". See picture at **emotions.**

delightful /dɪ'laɪt.fəl/ [adjective] Charming: *What a delightful person Maggie is!*

deliver /dɪ'lɪv·ər/ [verb] To take something to its destination: *They say that they will deliver the pizza to us within half an hour.*

delivery /dɪ'lɪv·ə·ri/ [noun] Taking something to a place or to a person: *There are only two postal deliveries a week here.* ■ The plural is "deliveries".

delta /'del·tə/ [countable noun] A triangular area of flat land where a river divides into several smaller rivers before entering the sea: *Have you ever been in Nile Delta, in Northern Egypt?*

deltoid[1] [countable noun] Triangular shoulder muscle: *The deltoid muscle is used when the arm is raised.* **See page 423.**

deltoid[2] [adjective] Triangular in shape: *This aircraft has deltoid wings.*

de luxe /dɪ'lʌks/ [adjective] Of high quality: *The de luxe model camera is too expensive.*

demand /dɪ'mænd/ [verb] To ask for something strongly: *The customer demanded to see the store manager.*

demanding /dɪ'mæn·dɪŋ/ [adjective] Expecting or requiring a great deal of attention, effort of skill: *My mother has a very demanding job and when she comes home she is very tired.*

demisemiquaver [countable noun] A musical note which has the time value of half a semiquaver: *Demisemiquavers have three tails on the stem.* **See page 460.**

democracy /dɪ'mɑk·rə·si/ [countable noun] A country in which people vote for their leaders: *Democracy was established in Poland in 1989.* ■ The plural is "democracies".

democratic /ˌdem·ə'kræt̬·ɪk/ [adjective] Referring to a political system or decision making process in which all the people living in that country or society participate: *A government is democratic when freely elected by a majority of voters.*

demolish /dɪ'mɑl·ɪʃ/ [verb] To destroy a building in a controlled way: *The old building was demolished and a bingo hall was built there.*

demolition /ˌdem.ə'lɪʃ.ən/ [noun] The controlled destruction of a building: *The new plans involved the demolition of several houses.*

demonstrate /'dem.ən.streɪt/ [verb] **1** To show clearly: *The mechanic demonstrated how the machine worked.* **2** To show your opinion about something in public: *A large crowd of people demonstrated against the war outside the embassy.*

demonstration /ˌdem.ən'streɪ.ʃən/ ▮ [noun] **1** Showing how to do something: *The salesman gave a demonstration of the new computer.* ▮ [countable noun] **2** A protest march or meeting: *There was an antinuclear demonstration in downtown yesterday.*

demonstrative /dɪ'mɒnstrətɪv/ [adjective] **1** That shows feelings openly, especially affection: *He was really demonstrative when meeting his parents at the airport.* **2** Referring to an adjective or pronoun, that indicates the person or thing referred to: *In "That is my house", "that" is a demonstrative pronoun.* **3** That serves to point out or indicate: *The possession of books is demonstrative of an interest in reading.* ■ This use is formal.

demonstrator /'dem·ənˌstreɪ·t̬ər/ [countable noun] A person who demonstrates: *Two hundred demonstrators were arrested during the march.*

dendrite /'den·draɪt/ [countable noun] Part of the cytoplasm of the neurons that receives stimulation from other neural cells: *The dendrites carry messages to the nerve cells.*

denim /'den.ɪm/ [uncountable noun] **1** A thick kind of cotton cloth: *Jeans are made of denim.* **2** See "denim jacket" in the word **jacket**.

dense /dents/ [adjective] Thick: *There was a dense fog in the city.* ■ We usually say "thick".

density /'den·sɪ·t̬i/ [noun] The degree of compactness of a substance, or the number of objects or people within a particular space: *In Physics, density is defined as weight per unit volume, and the symbol for it is "ρ".* ■ The plural is "densities".

dent /dent/ [countable noun] A hollow part in a flat surface: *He must have gotten that dent in his car when he was parking.*

DENT

↑**dentist** /'den·tɪst/ [countable noun] A person who looks after people's teeth: *I go to the dentist every six months.*

↑**deny** /dɪ'naɪ/ [verb] To say that something is not true: *Anne denied that she had stolen the money.* ■ Be careful with the spelling of these forms: "denies", "denied".

deodorant /di'oʊ·də·rənt/ [noun] A liquid that prevents bad smells: *Don't forget to use a deodorant after your shower.*

depart /dɪ'pɑrt/ [verb] To leave: *The train to Denver departs from platform six at 10.50.* ■ This word is formal. We usually say "leave".

↑**department** /dɪ'pɑrt·mənt/ [countable noun] A part of a school, bank, company and so on: *Kevin's mom has just got a job as head of the languages department in our school.* ■ See box at **abbreviations**.

department store [countable noun] A very large shop: *Enormous shops like Harrods are called department stores.* ■ We also say "store".

↑**departure** /dɪ'pɑr·tʃər/ [noun] Leaving a place: *What is your departure time?*

↑**depend** /dɪ'pend/ [verb] **1** To need somebody or something: *Children depend on their parents especially when they are very small.* **2** To trust somebody: *I know that I can depend on Margaret to help me.* **3** To be decided by things that are not sure: *"Shall we play tennis tomorrow?" "That depends on the weather".* ■ Be careful! We say: "depend **on** (somebody or something)".

dependent /dɪ'pen.dənt/ [adjective] Needing something or somebody: *Young kangaroos are completely dependent on their mothers for many months.* ■ Be careful! We say: "dependent **on** (somebody or something)".

depict /dɪ'pɪkt/ [verb] To represent with an image or in writing: *The intention of the play is to depict the main character as vain and selfish.*

depletion /dɪ'pliːʃən/ [noun] A reduction in number or strength: *Cuts in spending will result in a depletion of parts of the armed forces.* ■ This word is formal.

depose /dɪ'pəʊz/ [verb] To remove from office: *It is the intention of the demonstrators to depose the President.*

deposit[1] /dɪ'pɒzɪt/ [countable noun] Money that you pay to reserve something: *I put a deposit on a new bike last week and I'm going to collect it today.*

↑**deposit**[2] /dɪ'pɒzɪt/ [verb] To put money or other valuable objects into a bank or building society: *My mother deposited some money in the bank for me to start saving for my vacation.*

depot [countable noun] A building that is used for keeping things: *We saw old steam engines when we visited the train depot in Durango, Colorado.* ■ The same meaning: "storehouse".

↑**depress** /dɪ'pres/ [verb] To make somebody very unhappy: *All the terrible news on the television really depresses me.* ■ Be careful with the spelling of the 3rd person singular present tense form: "depresses".

↑**depressed** /dɪ'prest/ [adjective] Very unhappy: *Old Mr. Williams has been very depressed since his dog died.* ■ Be careful with the pronunciation of the end of this word. The last "e" is not pronounced.

↑**depressing** /dɪ'pres.ɪŋ/ [adjective] Making you feel very sad: *The end of the movie is very depressing.*

depression /dɪ'preʃ.ən/ [uncountable noun] A feeling of great unhappiness: *Depression can sometimes be a serious illness.*

↑**depth** /depθ/ [noun] The distance down: *What's the depth of the swimming pool?*

deputy /'dep·jə·ţi/ [countable noun] Person second in importance: *My uncle is the deputy sheriff of our town.* ■ The plural is "deputies".

dermis /'dɜː.mɪs/ US: /'dɝː-/ [uncountable noun] The part of the skin of vertebrates that is connective tissue, thicker than the epidermis: *The dermis is the layer of tissue beneath the epidermis.* ■ The plural is also "dermis".

descend /dɪ'send/ [verb] **1** To go down: *It's sometimes more difficult to descend a mountain than it is to go up it.* ■ This use is formal. We usually say "go down". **2** To come from somebody who lived before: *My family descends from Irish immigrants.*

descendant /dɪ'sen.dənt/ [countable noun] A person directly related to a previous person in their family tree: *She is descendant of Native Americans.*

↑**describe** /dɪ'skraɪb/ [verb] To say what somebody or something is like: *Can you describe the suitcase that you have lost?*

↑**description** /dɪ'skrɪp.ʃən/ [noun] A picture in words: *The description of the battle was horrific.*

†**desert** /dɪˈzɜrt/ [noun] A large, very dry, sandy area of land: *The Sahara desert is in North Africa.* ■ Compare with "dessert" (the sweet dish at the end of a meal).

†**deserted** /dɪˈzɜr·t̬ɪd/ [adjective] Empty of people: *It was four o'clock in the morning and the streets were deserted.* ■ Be careful with the pronunciation of the end of this word. The last "e" is pronounced like the "i" in "did".

desert island [countable noun] An island with no people: *Which book would you take to a desert island if you had to choose?*

†**deserve** /dɪˈzɜrv/ [verb] To earn something by the way you behave: *You deserve a long vacation after all those tests.*

†**design**[1] /dɪˈzaɪn/ [countable noun] **1** A plan or a drawing: *What do you think of the designs for the new school?* **2** A pattern or a drawing: *I like the design on that T-shirt.* ■ Be careful with the pronunciation of this word!

design[2] /dɪˈzaɪn/ [verb] To make a plan, to invent and develop: *Our Lady of the Angels' Cathedral was designed by Rafael Moneo in the 20th Century.* ■ Be careful with the pronunciation of this word!

designer /dɪˈzaɪ·nər/ [countable noun] A person who designs: *Marc Jacobs is a very famous American fashion designer.* ■ Be careful with the pronunciation of this word!

desire /dɪˈzaɪər/ [noun] A strong wish for something: *I have a great desire to travel the world.*

†**desk** /desk/ [countable noun] A table for writing: *Leave the papers on my desk.* 👁 See picture at **classroom**.

despair[1] /dɪˈspeər/ [uncountable noun] A feeling of having no hope: *Anne-Marie was in despair when she failed all her tests.*

despair[2] /dɪˈspeər/ [verb] To lose hope: *Don't despair! Some day you will get a job.* ■ Be careful. We say: "despair **of** (doing something)".

†**desperate** /ˈdes·pər·ət/ [adjective] **1** Almost without hope, willing to do almost anything: *She was desperate after her application for the job was turned down.* **2** Very serious: *The situation in Bangladesh is getting desperate because of the floods.*

despise /dɪˈspaɪz/ [verb] To hate or to have a very bad opinion of somebody: *You shouldn't despise somebody just because they are different from you.*

†**despite** /dɪˈspaɪt/ [preposition] In spite of: *We played football yesterday despite the wind and the rain.*

†**dessert** /dɪˈzɜrt/ [noun] The sweet food at the end of a meal: *I always like an ice cream for dessert.* ■ Compare with "desert" (a large, very dry, sandy area of land).

destination /ˌdes.tɪˈneɪ.ʃən/ [countable noun] The place where somebody is going: *After a terrible journey they finally reached their destination.*

destiny /ˈdes.tɪ.ni/ [countable noun] Fate, the things that happen to somebody in the future: *Her destiny was to die young.* ■ The plural is "destinies".

†**destroy** /dɪˈstrɔɪ/ [verb] To ruin completely: *Bombs destroyed the United States naval base at Pearl Harbor.*

†**destruction** /dɪˈstrʌk.ʃən/ [uncountable noun] Great damage: *The Great Fire of Chicago caused enormous destruction in 1871.*

destructive /dɪˈstrʌktɪv/ [adjective] **1** Causing destruction or serious damage: *Drinking, smoking and taking drugs are destructive habits.* **2** Wanting or tending to destroy: *That boy shows a really destructive behavior.*

detach /dɪˈtætʃ/ [verb] To separate: *Detach this part of the receipt and take it back to the store where you bought the radio.*

†**detail** /dɪˈteɪl/, /ˈdi·teɪl/ ▮ [countable noun] **1** One of the small facts about something: *I will not go into details.* ▮ [noun] **2** Information: *I'm going to phone the travel agent to get all the details about this special flight to Paris.*

detect /dɪˈtekt/ [verb] To notice or to discover something that is difficult to see: *After his death, the police detected poison in his body.*

detective /dɪˈtek.tɪv/ [countable noun] A policeman who investigates crimes: *The detective discovered the murderer after questioning several suspects.*

detergent /dɪˈtɜr·dʒənt/ [noun] A chemical that is used for washing: *How much detergent shall I put in the washing machine?*

deteriorate /dɪˈtɪr·i·əˌreɪt/ [verb] To get worse: *His grandpa's health deteriorated rapidly.*

†**determination** /dɪˌtɜr·məˈneɪ·ʃən/ [uncountable noun] A strong intention to do something: *My grandmother is very ill. However, she has great determination and I think she'll get better.*

determine /dɪˈtɜr·mən/ [verb] **1** To decide upon: *The role of the judge is to determine the sentence to be passed.* **2** To find out or establish: *The job of the commission is to determine the facts of the case.*

determined /dɪˈtɜr·mənd/ [adjective] Having firmly decided to succeed: *He is determined to learn to play the piano.* ■ Be careful with the pronunciation of the end of this word. The last "e" is not pronounced.

detest /dɪˈtest/ [verb] To hate: *I detest going to the dentist.*

detour [countable noun] Sending cars, planes and so on a different way: *There's a detour here because of an accident at Kenilworth.*

devastate /ˈdev.ə.steɪt/ [verb] To destroy completely: *Fire devastates enormous areas of forest every summer.*

a b c d e f g h i j k l m n o p q r s t u v w x y z

↑**develop** /dɪˈvel.əp/ [verb] **1** To grow: *In a few months, the kitten developed into a big cat.* **2** To make something bigger and better: *The old downtown has been developed; now it has a shopping mall, a theater and a movie theater.* **3** To make a photograph with chemicals: *I've had the vacation photographs developed.*

developing country [countable noun] A country that is becoming more modern: *The government has promised to send more money to help the developing countries.* ■ The plural is "developing countries".

↑**development** /dɪˈvel.əp.mənt/ ▮ [uncountable noun] **1** Slow growth: *There's been a lot of development of the town in recent years.* ▮ [countable noun] **2** A new event: *There have been some new developments in the crisis between Israel and Palestine.*

deviation /ˌdiːviˈeɪʃən/ [uncountable noun] An action or behavior which differs from what is usual or expected: *The winds resulted in a deviation from the route.*

↑**device** /dɪˈvaɪs/ [countable noun] A small thing invented for a specific purpose or a way of achieving a particular purpose: *I have a device on my phone that lets me speak to two people at the same time.*

devil /ˈdev.əl/ ▮ [countable noun] **1** An evil spirit: *The priest tried to force the devils to abandon the body of the person they were inhabiting.* ▮ [noun] **2** The most powerful evil spirit, according to Christians: *In the book "The portrait of Dorian Gray", the main character sells his soul to the Devil.* ■ Be careful! In this use "Devil" has a capital "D". This use has no plural.

↑**devote** [verb] To give a lot of time, energy and so on to somebody or something: *My cousin is a missionary and she devotes all her time to working with orphans.*

dew US: /duː/ UK: /djuː/ [uncountable noun] The water that forms at night on objects in the open air: *The drops of dew on the roses look so beautiful in the morning.*

diagnose US: /ˌdaɪ.əgˈnoʊz/ UK: /ˈdaɪ.əg.nəʊz/ [verb] To identify the nature of a problem, especially an illness: *The mechanic needs to diagnose what is wrong with the car.*

diagnosis /ˌdɑɪ·ɪgˈnoʊ·sɪs/ [noun] The identification of the nature of a problem: *The doctor makes a diagnosis after studying the symptoms.* ■ The plural is "diagnoses".

diagonal /daɪˈæg.ən.əl/ [adjective] Going from one corner to the opposite one: *If you draw a diagonal line from one corner of a square to another you get two equal triangles.*

↑**diagram** /ˈdaɪ.ə.græm/ [countable noun] A plan or a picture that explains an idea: *A diagram can show how a machine works.*

dial[1] /daɪəl/ [countable noun] The round part of a machine with numbers or letters: *Look! The dial is indicating that there is almost no gas left.*

dial[2] /daɪəl/ [verb] To use a dial: *In the United States you dial 911 in an emergency.*

dialect /ˈdaɪ.ə.lekt/ [noun] A local form of a language: *The Cajun is a famous Louisiana dialect.*

dialog [noun] A conversation between two people: *I like movies that have interesting dialogs in them.* ■ The British English spelling is "dialogue".

dialogue UK: /ˈdaɪ.ə.lɒg/ [noun] See **dialog**. ■ This is a British English spelling.

diameter /daɪˈæmɪtər/ [noun] Line that goes through the center of a circle and divides it in two equal parts: *The diameter of a circle is twice its radius.*

↑**diamond** /ˈdaɪə.mənd/ ▮ [noun] **1** A very hard, transparent stone that is very valuable: *Diamonds are very expensive.* ▮ [countable noun] **2** A playing card with red diamond shapes on it: *Who's got the King of Diamonds?*

diaper /ˈdɑɪ·pər/, /ˈdɑɪ·ə·pər/ [countable noun] A piece of cloth or paper that covers a baby's bottom: *Can you help me change the baby's diaper, please?* ■ In British English they say "nappy".

diaphragm /ˈdaɪəfræm/ [countable noun] **1** A muscular membrane which separates the thorax from the abdomen: *The diaphragm performs an important function in respiration.* **2** A thin piece of plastic or rubber that prevents sperm entering into the womb of a woman during sex: *The diaphragm is fitted over the narrow part of the womb.*

diarrhea [uncountable noun] An illness in which a person has to go to the bathroom too often: *I have to drink a lot of lemon juice because I've got diarrhea.*

↑**diary** US: /ˈdaɪr.i/ UK: /ˈdaɪə.ri/ [countable noun] A record of what somebody has done during the day: *Anne Frank kept a fascinating diary while she was hiding during the Second World War.* ■ The same meaning: "journal". ■ The plural is "diaries".

diastole /dɑɪˈæs·tə·li/ [countable noun] The period separating two contractions of the heart: *The heart muscle relaxes during the diastole and in this way allows it to be filled with blood.* ■ Compare with "systole" (a single heart contraction).

dice /daɪs/ [countable noun] A small cube with dots: *Dice are used to play many different games.* ■ The plural is also "dice".

DICE

dictate /ˈdɪk·teɪt/, /dɪkˈteɪt/ [verb] To speak to somebody who writes your words down: *The President dictated his speech to the secretary.*

dictation /dɪkˈteɪ.ʃᵊn/ [countable noun] Words that one person speaks and others write down: *Our teacher is going to give us a dictation today.*

dictator US: /ˈdɪk.teɪ.t̬ɚ/ UK: /dɪkˈteɪ.təʳ/ [countable noun] A person who rules a country alone: *Dictators are usually unpopular with the people in their country.*

dictatorship /dɪkˈteɪ·t̬ər,ʃɪp/ [countable noun] A state or country ruled by a dictator, or this situation: *The dictatorship was abolished after eighteen years.*

⁺**dictionary** /ˈdɪk·ʃəˌner·i/ [countable noun] A book that explains the meaning of words: *Let's look up the word "earthquake" in our "Horizon" dictionary.* ■ The plural is "dictionaries".

did /dɪd/ Past tense of **do**.

⁺**die** /daɪ/ [verb] To stop living: *Peter's grandfather died of a heart attack.* ■ Be careful with the spelling of this form: "dying".

die down /daɪ/ [verb] To come slowly to an end: *The storm went on all night and died down the next morning.*

⁺**diet**[1] /daɪət/ ▮ [noun] **1** The food that somebody eats: *You should eat a balanced diet of meat, vegetables, fruit, cereals and dairy products.* ▮ [countable noun] **2** A special program of eating, usually to lose weight: *I'm getting rather fat so I think that I'll have to go on a diet for a few weeks.* ■ Be careful! In this use we say: "to be or to go **on** a diet".

diet[2] /daɪət/ [verb] To follow a special program of eating, usually to lose weight: *You've lost some weight. Have you been dieting?*

differ /ˈdɪf·ər/ [verb] **1** To be different from something else: *Cats differ from dogs in that they are usually very independent.* ■ Be careful! We say: "differ **from** (somebody or something)". **2** To disagree with the opinion of somebody else: *Scientists differ about the cause of the phenomenon.* ■ This use is formal.

⁺**difference** /ˈdɪf·rəns/, /-ər·əns/ [noun] The way that things are not the same: *There is an age difference of two years between Mark and Paul.*

⁺**different** /ˈdɪf·rənt/, /-ər·ənt/ [adjective] Not the same: *Living in a town is very different from living in a city.* ■ Be careful. We say: "different **from** (something)". We don't say: "different **of** (something)".

differentiate /ˌdɪf.əˈren.tʃi.eɪt/ [verb] To find or make differences between things: *It is not easy to differentiate between these two species of primates.*

⁺**difficult** /ˈdɪf.ɪ.kᵊlt/ [adjective] Not easy, needing a lot of skill or effort: *My piano exam was so difficult that I don't think I passed it.*

⁺**difficulty** /ˈdɪf·ɪ·kəl·ti/, /-ˌkʌl·ti/ [countable noun] A problem: *I have difficulty understanding mathematics.* ■ The plural is "difficulties".

dig, dug, dug /dɪg/ [verb] To make a hole in the ground: *The prisoner dug a tunnel from his cell to outside the prison walls.*

digest /daɪˈdʒest/, /ˈdaɪ.dʒest/ [verb] To absorb food in your stomach: *My grandmother finds it hard to digest some foods.*

digestion /daɪˈdʒes.tʃᵊn/ [noun] Action of turning food into energy: *A quick walk after a meal helps the digestion.*

digestive /daɪˈdʒestɪv/ [adjective] Referring to or helping digestion: *The digestive system processes the food we eat and transforms it into nutrients.* 👁 **See page 424.**

digestive gland [countable noun] An organ which serves the same purpose as the liver and pancreas, found in arthropods, mollusks and fish: *The digestive gland is an organ of the digestive tract.*

digestive system [countable noun] The set of organs in the body which process food: *Food enters the digestive system through the mouth.* 👁 **See page 424.**

digestive tract [countable noun] A pipe in the body along which food travels: *The digestive tract goes from the throat to the anus.*

digital /ˈdɪdʒ·ɪ·t̬ə·l/ [adjective] **1** Based on computer technology and the representation of information by series of the numbers 0 and 1: *Digital television has replaced analogue television.* **2** Related to fingers or toes: *Braille is a digital system which blind people use to read.*

dignified /ˈdɪg.nɪ.faɪd/ [adjective] Calm and serious: *My grandmother is a very dignified old lady.*

dilate /daɪˈleɪt/, /ˈdaɪ·leɪt/ [verb] To become or make something wider, larger or further open: *The womb of women naturally dilate just before giving birth.*

dilation /daɪˈleɪʃən/ [uncountable noun] The process of making an opening or cavity wider: *Dilation of the pupil occurs, for example, when you enter a dark room.*

dilute /daɪˈluːt/ [verb] To add water to another liquid to make it weaker: *You have to dilute this orange juice before you drink it.*

dim /dɪm/ [adjective] Not bright: *The light is too dim to read in here.* ■ The comparative form is "dimmer" and the superlative form is "dimmest".

dime /daɪm/ [countable noun] A ten cents coin: *If you have ten dimes, you have a dollar.*

dimension /ˌdaɪˈmen.tʃᵊn/ [countable noun] The length, width and height of something: *What are the dimensions of this table?*

a b c d e f g h i j k l m n o p q r s t u v w x y z

dimensional /ˌθriːdɪˈmenʃənəl/ [adjective] Having a specified number of dimensions: *We went to the movies and watched a three-dimensional film.*

diner /ˈdaɪ·nər/ [countable noun] **1** Somebody who is eating in a restaurant: *This restaurant seats twenty diners.* **2** A small restaurant that serves drinks and simple meals: *We had soda and a sandwich at a diner on the Second Avenue.* ■ The same meaning: "café".

dinghy /ˈdɪŋ.gi/ [countable noun] A small sailing boat: *The children played on the lake in the rubber dinghy.* ■ The plural is "dinghies".

dining room [countable noun] A room for eating in: *Our dining room is next to the backyard so we can watch the birds while we eat.*

dining table [countable noun] A table usually located in a dining room at which meals are served: *My grandmother loves joining the family at the dining table.* See picture at **living room**.

+**dinner** /ˈdɪn·ər/ [noun] The most important meal of the day: *In my family we always eat dinner together.*

dinosaur /ˈdaɪ·nəˌsɔr/ [countable noun] A reptile that lived a very long time ago: *Not all dinosaurs were big; one kind was only two feet long.*

dioxide [uncountable noun] An oxide with two atoms of oxygen which are not linked to an atom of another element: *Carbon dioxide is a naturally occurring chemical compound.*

dip¹ [noun] A sauce to put food in it and take it out to eat: *We have corn chips and spinach or artichoke dip for watching the game.*

dip² /dɪp/ [verb] To put something in liquid and then take it out: *I like dipping my cookie in my hot chocolate.* ■ Be careful with the spelling of these forms: "dipped", "dipping".

diploma /dəˈploʊ·mə/ [countable noun] A certificate: *Helen got her diploma when she passed her test.*

diplomat /ˈdɪp.lə.mæt/ [countable noun] A person who represents his or her country: *Bernard's mother is a diplomat.*

direct¹ US: /daɪˈrekt/ UK: /dɪˈrekt/ [verb] **1** To tell somebody how to go somewhere: *I got lost in the downtown but a policeman directed me to the store.* **2** To manage or to control something: *Captain Athey directed the rescue operation and all the mountaineers were saved.*

+**direct²** US: /daɪˈrekt/ UK: /dɪˈrekt/ [adjective] **1** Straight or immediate, without break: *Is there a direct route from here to Chicago?* **2** Clear and plain: *I'd like you to give me a direct answer to my question.*

+**direction** /daɪˈrek.ʃᵊn/ [countable noun] The way a person is moving or looking: *You're going in the wrong direction.*

directions /daɪˈrek.ʃᵊnz/ [plural noun] Instructions on how to go somewhere: *The boys got lost, so they had to ask for directions.*

directly /daɪˈrekt.li/ [adverb] **1** In a direct line or manner without deviation: *The bus takes you directly to the downtown.* **2** At once, immediately: *He did not answer directly, he needed a little time to think.* **3** Just, exactly: *They live directly opposite us.*

+**director** /daɪˈrek.təʳ/ [countable noun] **1** A person who directs: *Mrs. Rhys has been the director of our local theater for years.* **2** managing director See **managing director**.

+**dirt** US: /dɝːt/ UK: /dɜːt/ [uncountable noun] An unclean substance like mud or earth: *Clean the dirt off your shoes before you come in.*

+**dirty** US: /ˈdɝː.t̬i/ UK: /ˈdɜː.ti/ [adjective] Not clean, with dirt: *If you play in the mud you'll get dirty.*

dis- /dɪs-/ [prefix] An addition to the beginning of a word that gives it the opposite meaning: *"Dishonest" is the opposite of "honest".*

disability /ˌdɪs·əˈbɪl·ɪ·t̬i/ [noun] A physical or a mental state that makes you unable to use part of your body: *Somebody who is deaf has a disability.* ■ The plural is "disabilities".

+**disabled** /dɪˈseɪ.bl̩d/ [adjective] Not able to use a part of the body well: *Yesterday I watched a basketball game for disabled players.* ■ Be careful with the pronunciation of this word. The "e" is not pronounced.

+**disadvantage** /ˌdɪs·ədˈvæn·tɪdʒ/ [noun] A thing that makes a situation difficult for one side: *The football team was at a disadvantage because their best player was ill.* ■ Be careful with the pronunciation of this word. The last "a" is pronounced like the "i" in "did".

+**disagree** /ˌdɪs.əˈgriː/ [verb] Not to agree: *I disagree with the way you are doing that math problem.*

disagreeable /ˌdɪs.əˈgriː.ə.bl̩/ [adjective] Unpleasant: *The trip was disagreeable because the sea was very rough.*

+**disagreement** /ˌdɪs.əˈgriː.mənt/ [noun] Lack of agreement, dispute: *They had a disagreement about money.*

disallow /ˌdɪs.əˈlaʊ/ [verb] Not to allow or accept something: *The referee disallowed a goal in the last minute.*

+**disappear** /ˌdɪs·əˈpɪər/ [verb] To go out of sight: *The ship disappeared slowly over the horizon.*

disappearance /ˌdɪs·əˈpɪər·əns/ [noun] Not being there: *The child's disappearance worried the parents terribly.*

+**disappoint** /ˌdɪs.əˈpɔɪnt/ [verb] To be worse than expected and hoped: *The latest cartoon movie really disappointed me.*

↑**disappointed** /ˌdɪs·əˈpɔɪn·tɪd/ [adjective] Sad because something is worse than expected: *Our teacher said that she was very disappointed by the compositions we had written.* ■ Be careful with the pronunciation of the end of this word. The "e" is pronounced like the "i" in "did".

↑**disappointing** /ˌdɪs·əˈpɔɪn·tɪŋ/ [adjective] Making you feel disappointed: *My mom said that she found the exhibition disappointing.*

↑**disappointment** /ˌdɪs.əˈpɔɪnt.mənt/ [uncountable noun] Sadness because something is worse than expected: *The result of the football game caused great disappointment in the town.*

disapprove /ˌdɪs.əˈpruːv/ [verb] To think that something is bad or morally wrong: *My grandfather disapproves of boys with long hair.* ■ Be careful. We say: "He disapproves **of** (somebody)". We don't say: "He disapproves (somebody)".

↑**disaster** /dɪˈzæs·tər/ [countable noun] A catastrophe, natural or produced by people: *Earthquakes and hurricanes are examples of natural disasters.*

↑**disc** /dɪsk/ [countable noun] **1** A round, flat object: *He said the UFO was shaped like a disc.* **2** A record: *The latest Taylor Swift disc is fantastic.*

↑**discipline** /ˈdɪs.ə.plɪn/ [uncountable noun] Control and order: *There's no discipline at that school.*

disc jockey [countable noun] A person who plays records on the radio or in discotheques: *Some disc jockeys are as famous as the music they play.* ■ "DJ" is an abbreviation for "disc jockey".

disco /ˈdɪs·koʊ/ [countable noun] A place for dancing: *The music is usually very loud in discos.* ■ Be careful with the pronunciation of this word! The "o" is pronounced as in "go". ■ "Disco" is short for "discotheque".

discomfort /dɪˈskʌmfət/ ▮ [uncountable noun] **1** Slight pain or an uncomfortable feeling, physical or mental: *The patient suffered some discomfort after the operation.* ▮ [countable noun] **2** Something that causes slight pain or makes somebody uncomfortable: *Old people suffer more the discomforts of travel.*

disconnect /ˌdɪs.kəˈnekt/ [verb] To stop the supply of electricity to something: *The telephone will be disconnected if you don't pay the bill.*

discotheque /ˈdɪs.kə.tek/ [countable noun] See **disco**.

↑**discount** /ˈdɪs.kaʊnt/, /dɪˈskaʊnt/ [countable noun] A reduction in price: *There's a ten per cent discount on the price of all books this month.*

discourage /dɪˈskɜr·ɪdʒ/, /-ˈskʌr-/ [verb] To try to stop somebody from doing something: *She became discouraged after she was turned down for the job.* ■ Be careful with the pronunciation of this word. The "a" is pronounced like the "i" in "did".

↑**discover** /dɪˈskʌv·ər/ [verb] To find something for the first time: *Christopher Columbus discovered America in 1492.*

↑**discovery** /dɪˈskʌv·ə·ri/ [noun] Finding something: *The discovery of penicillin changed many people's lives.* ■ The plural is "discoveries".

discriminate /dɪˈskrɪm.ɪ.neɪt/ [verb] To treat differently: *Companies should not discriminate against women.* ■ Be careful. We say: "discriminate **against** (somebody)".

discrimination /dɪˌskrɪm.ɪˈneɪ.ʃən/ [uncountable noun] Treating some people worse than others: *Religious, racial and sexual discrimination are illegal.*

discus /ˈdɪskəs/ [countable noun] A round, flat metallic object that is thrown: *The athlete broke the record for throwing the discus.*

↑**discuss** /dɪˈskʌs/ [verb] To talk about something: *Some people love discussing politics.* ■ Look at the spelling of the 3rd person singular present tense form: "discusses".

↑**discussion** /dɪˈskʌʃ.ən/ [noun] A period of talking about something: *There was a very interesting discussion about music on the radio last night.*

↑**disease** /dɪˈziːz/ [noun] An illness: *Cholera can be a terrible disease.* ■ Compare with "illness" ("Disease" is used when we talk about a specific illness. "Illness" is used when we talk about the general state of being ill and the time during which you are ill).

disgrace /dɪsˈgreɪs/ [uncountable noun] A state of shame or loss of respect: *The boy had stolen money from his classmates and the teacher sent him home in disgrace.*

disgraceful /dɪsˈgreɪs.fəl/ [adjective] Very bad, wrong: *His behavior was completely disgraceful.*

disguise[1] /dɪsˈgaɪz/ [noun] Clothes that make somebody look different or very difficult to recognize: *Some famous people go out in disguise so that nobody can recognize them.* ■ The same meaning: "costume".

disguise[2] /dɪsˈgaɪz/ [verb] To change your appearance: *John disguised himself as a Red Indian to go to Patricia's party.*

↑**disgust** /dɪsˈgʌst/ [uncountable noun] A strong feeling of dislike: *The movie was so bad that she walked out of the theater in disgust.*

disgusted /dɪsˈgʌstɪd/ [adjective] Feeling intense dislike or anger about something: *I was disgusted when I saw the fly on the soup.* 👁 See picture at **emotions**.

↑**disgusting** /dɪsˈgʌs.tɪŋ/ [adjective] Causing strong dislike: *I think that blood sports are disgusting.*

↑**dish** /dɪʃ/ [countable noun] **1** A plate: *Will you wash the dishes, please?* **2** A particular preparation of food: *That meat dish certainly looks nice.* ■ The plural is "dishes". 👁 See pictures at **dishwasher** and **plate**.

a b c d e f g h i j k l m n o p q r s t u v w x y z

dishcloth /'dɪʃ.klɒθ/ US: /-klɑːθ/ [countable noun] A cloth used for washing or drying dishes: *Wipe the tables with this dishcloth.*

†**dishonest** /dɪs'ɑn·əst/ [adjective] Not honest: *You can't trust him; he's dishonest.*

dishwasher /'dɪʃ,wɑʃ·ər/, /-wɔ·ʃər/ [countable noun] A machine that washes dishes, cups and so on: *Put these plates in the dishwasher, please.* See picture at **kitchen**.

DISHWASHER

disinfect /,dɪs.ɪn'fekt/ [verb] To clean something with a substance that kills germs: *Pure alcohol is used to disinfect wounds.*

disinfectant /,dɪs·ɪn'fek·tənt/ [noun] A liquid that kills germs: *My mother always puts disinfectant down the bathroom.*

†**disk** /dɪsk/ [countable noun] **1** A flat, round object used in computers: *A disk can contain a lot of information.* **2 hard disk** The part inside a computer that stores information: *There's no space available on the hard disk.*

†**dislike**[1] /dɪ'slaɪk/ [uncountable noun] The feeling of not liking somebody or something: *I have a strong dislike for anything connected with fashion.*

dislike[2] /dɪ'slaɪk/ [verb] Not to like: *I dislike his way of laughing.*

disloyal /,dɪs'lɔɪ.əl/ [adjective] Not loyal: *We are no longer friends. He was disloyal and I haven't forgiven him.*

†**dismiss** /dɪ'smɪs/ [verb] To make a person leave his or her job: *He was dismissed from his job because he always arrived late.* ■ Be careful with the spelling of the 3rd person singular present tense form: "dismisses".

dismount /dɪ'smaʊnt/ [verb] To get off a horse or a bike: *When I tried to dismount, I fell off.*

disobedient /,dɪs·ə'bid·i·ənt/ [adjective] Not obeying, not wanting to obey: *What a disobedient girl you are!*

disobey /,dɪs·ə'beɪ/ [verb] Not to obey: *You shouldn't disobey your teacher.*

disorder /dɪs'ɔr·dər/ ▮ [uncountable noun] **1** Lack of order: *My paper are always in a state of complete disorder.* ▮ [countable noun] **2** Violent behavior by many people: *The police were brought in to prevent disorder in the streets.*

disorganized or **disorganised** /dɪs'ɔr·gə,naɪzd/ [adjective] Untidy: *Your composition is quite good but it's rather disorganized.* ■ Be careful with the pronunciation of the end of this word. The "e" is not pronounced.

disperse /dɪ'spɜrs/ [verb] To scatter in different directions, to separate: *The soldiers had to disperse in order to reduce casualties.*

display[1] /dɪ'spleɪ/ [noun] A show or exhibition of things: *Did you see the firework display last night?*

display[2] /dɪ'spleɪ/ [verb] To show something for somebody to see: *Next year's fashions are already being displayed in the store windows.*

disposable /dɪ'spoʊ·zə·bəl/ [adjective] Which can be thrown away after use: *I've bought some disposable plastic plates for the party.*

dispute /dɪ'spjuːt, 'dɪs.pjuːt/ [noun] A conflict: *Work stopped because of a dispute over pay.*

disqualify /dɪs'kwɑl·ə,faɪ/ [verb] To decide that somebody cannot do something: *Mr. Jones was found guilty of drunken driving and was disqualified from driving for a year.* ■ Be careful with the spelling of these forms: "disqualifies", "disqualified". Be careful. We say: "He was disqualified **from** doing (something)".

dissatisfied /dɪs'sæt̬·əs,fɑɪd/ [adjective] Not happy with something: *My parents were dissatisfied with the food in the hotel they stayed at in Florence.*

†**dissolve** /dɪ'zɑlv/ [verb] To break up and disappear in a liquid: *Sugar dissolves quickly in hot water.*

†**distance** /'dɪs.tᵊnts/ [noun] **1** The space between two places: *What distance is there between our house and yours?* **2 in the distance** Far away: *I can see a river in the distance.*

distant /'dɪs.tᵊnt/ [adjective] Far away: *From our hotel room we have a distant view of the sea.*

distinct /dɪ'stɪŋkt/ [adjective] **1** Clear: *David has a distinct British accent.* **2** Different: *There are several distinct languages in this Country.*

†**distinguish** /dɪ'stɪŋ.gwɪʃ/ [verb] **1** To notice the difference between things or people: *How do nurses distinguish between babies when they are all together in the nursery?* **2** To see with difficulty: *It was so dark that I could hardly distinguish her face.*

distinguished /dɪˈstɪŋ.gwɪʃt/ [adjective] Famous, highly respected: *John Wayne was a distinguished American actor.* ■ Be careful with the pronunciation of the end of this word. The "e" is not pronounced.

distract /dɪˈstrækt/ [verb] To attract somebody's attention away from something: *Don't distract me while I'm working.*

distress /dɪˈstres/ [uncountable noun] Great sadness: *Their mother's death caused them great distress.*

†**distribute** /dɪˈstrɪb·jut/, /-jət/ [verb] To give things to many people: *He distributed the pamphlets outside the school.*

distribution /ˌdɪs.trɪˈbjuː.ʃᵊn/ [noun] **1** The act of providing and delivering: *She uses a van for the distribution of her goods.* **2** The way in which something is divided or shared: *The distribution of riches is very unequal.*

†**district** /ˈdɪs.trɪkt/ [countable noun] An area: *My mother works in the financial district of New York.*

†**disturb** /dɪˈstɜrb/ [verb] **1** To interrupt somebody or something: *Don't disturb me while I'm on the phone.* **2** To upset or worry somebody: *The news about the accident disturbed us all.*

disturbance /dɪˈstɜr·bəns/ [noun] A disturbing noise that people make: *I was woken by a tremendous disturbance in the street.*

ditch /dɪtʃ/ [countable noun] A long, narrow hole next to a road: *When I tried to avoid a rabbit on the road I drove the car straight into the ditch.*

ditto US: /ˈdɪt̬.oʊ/ UK: /ˈdɪt.əʊ/ [countable noun] A mark used in writing to show that the same thing is to be repeated: *Ditto is written ".*

dive, dove, dived /daɪv/ [verb] **1** To jump into water, head first: *The children dove into the sea off the rocks.* **2** To go under the water: *They dove for several hours but were unable to find the sunken boat.*

diver /ˈdaɪ·vər/ [countable noun] A person who works underwater: *The police use divers in their investigations when they want to examine what's in a lake.*

diversity US: /dɪˈvɝː.sə.t̬i/ UK: /daɪˈvɜː.sɪ.ti/ [uncountable noun] Difference or variety within something: *An important aspect of an ecosystem is the diversity of the species it contains.*

divert US: /dɪˈvɝːt/ UK: /daɪˈvɜːt/ [verb] To send cars, planes and so on a different way: *The flights to Washington were diverted to Baltimore airport because of fog.*

†**divide** /dɪˈvaɪd/ [verb] To separate into parts: *If you divide eight by two, you get four.*

divine /dɪˈvaɪn/ [adjective] Connected to God: *The prophets were divine messengers.*

division /dɪˈvɪʒ.ᵊn/ ▮ [noun] **1** The process of dividing one number by another number: *Division is an element of arithmetic.* **2** Disagreement or different opinion: *There is a division of opinion about this within the community.* ▮ [countable noun] **3** A military force made up of several brigades: *The Fourth Division was able to hold off the enemy.* **4** A part of a large organization: *The number of people working in the Sales Division has increased.* ■ See box at **abbreviations**.

†**divorce** /dɪˈvɔrs/, /-ˈvoʊrs/ [noun] The legal separation of a husband and wife: *If a person gets a divorce, he or she can marry again.*

dizzy /ˈdɪz.i/ [adjective] Feeling that everything is spinning round: *I felt very dizzy after I went on the roller coaster.* ■ The comparative form is "dizzier" and the superlative form is "dizziest".

DJ /ˌdiːˈdʒeɪ/ [countable noun] See **disc jockey**. ■ Be careful. "DJ" is always written in capital letters.

†**do, did, done** /duː, də/ [verb] **1** To act: *What did you do this morning?* ■ See box on the following page. **2** To carry out a particular task or activity: *I will do the project this week.* ■ See box at **make**. **3** An auxiliary verb used to form negative sentences and questions, or to form answers in a shortened form: *"Did you find the keys?" "Yes, I did."*. ■ See box on the following page. **4** To be satisfactory, to be good enough: *I hope that my work will do.* **5** To be good for somebody: *I could do with a little help here.* **6** **to do badly (at something)** To have problems in a subject or class: *He did badly at math last year, but this year he has improved.* **7** **to do damage** To break or spoil something or somewhere: *The storm did a lot of damage.* **8** **to do one's best** To do the best you are capable of, to try hard: *I promise that I will do my best.* **9** **to do the dishes** To clean the plates and other items used in a meal: *It's your turn to do the dishes.* **10** **to do well (at something)** To be successful in a subject or class: *She is doing well at school this year.* **11** **to have nothing to do with (something or somebody)** To be something that a particular person does not have responsibility for, or not be relevant: *That has nothing to do with me; I wasn't here.* **12** **How do you do?** Words that you say when meeting somebody for the first time: *"How do you do?" "Pleased to meet you."*. **13** **What do you do?** Words for asking about somebody's job: *"What do you do?" "I'm an electrician"*.

▶ **PHRASAL VERBS** · **to do away with (something)** To not have something: *They have done away with the drinks machines at school.* · **to do (somebody) in** To make somebody very tired: *This math problem is doing me in: can you help me?* ■ This use is informal. · **to do (something) up** **1** To fasten an article of clothing: *Do your coat up before you go out.* **2** To improve something and make

a b c d e f g h i j k l m n o p q r s t u v w x y z

it look better: *My brother's new apartment looks old and not very nice but he is going to do it up.* · **to do without (something or somebody)** To not have something: *The team can do without him, he is not essential.*

dock US: /dɑːk/ UK: /dɒk/ [countable noun] Artificial harbor: *The ship arrived at the dock, and the passengers got off.*

†**doctor** US: /'dɑːk.tɚ/ UK: /'dɒk.təʳ/ [countable noun] A person who looks after people's health: *Malcolm felt so ill that he had to call the doctor in the middle of the night.* ■ The abbreviation "Dr." is only used in written language. ■ See box at **abbreviations**.

†**document** /'dɑk·jə·mənt/ [countable noun] An important paper: *My father left the documents on the train on his way to a meeting!*

to do

• **Present tense**

affirmative	negative	questions
I do	I don't	do I?
you do	you don't	do you?
he / she/ it does	he / she / it doesn't	does he / she / it?
we do	we don't	do we?
you do	you don't	do you?
they do	they don't	do they?

• **Past tense**
did

• **Past participle**
done

***to do*: auxiliary verb**

We sometimes use the verb ***to do*** as an auxiliary verb (this is a verb that is used with the main verb of the sentence). *To do* is used in this way, without any meaning:

- In negative sentences, with ordinary verbs:
  - *Susan* ***doesn't*** *like reading much.*
  - *I* ***didn't*** *see Tony at the party.*
- In questions, with ordinary verbs:
  - ***Do*** *you have school on Saturdays?*
  - *What time* ***do*** *you usually get up?*
- In short answers:
  - ***Do*** *you like playing tennis? Yes, I* ***do****.*
- When we do not want to repeat a verb or part of a sentence:
  - *Jeremy went swimming yesterday, but Charles* ***didn't*** *(= didn't go swimming).*

†**dog** US: /dɑːg/ UK: /dɒg/ [countable noun] An animal that people often keep as a pet and sometimes keep for protection: *My dog barks if anybody comes near the house.* 👁 See picture at **pet**.

doghouse [countable noun] A small house for a dog: *My dog is accustomed to sleeping in the doghouse.* ■ In British English they say "kennel".

doll /dɒl/ [countable noun] A toy that looks like a person: *My sister collects dolls from different countries.*

†**dollar** US: /'dɑː.lɚ/ UK: /'dɒl.əʳ/ [countable noun] Money used in the United States: *There are a hundred cents in a dollar.* ■ "Buck" is informal for "dollar". ■ See box at **abbreviations**.

†**dolphin** /'dɑl·fən/, /'dɔl-/ [countable noun] An intelligent sea animal with a wide mouth: *Although you might think they are fish, dolphins are mammals.* 👁 See page 428.

domain /dəʊ'meɪn/ [countable noun] **1** An area of interest or activity: *The backyard is my husband's domain.* **2** An area of land which is controlled by a particular person or government: *This region was added to his domains.* ■ This use is more common in the plural. **3** An area of the internet which is controlled by a particular organization or person: *Before the website is designed a domain has to be obtained.*

dome US: /doʊm/ UK: /dəʊm/ [countable noun] A round, arched roof: *One of the identifying features of the Kremlin is its domes.*

†**domestic** /də'mes.tɪk/ [adjective] **1** Referring to the home: *I don't really like doing domestic jobs but we all have to help in the house.* **2** Not wild: *Domestic animals are kept at home or on a farm.*

domesticate /də'mes.tɪ.keɪt/ [verb] To train an animal to live or work for persons: *It would be difficult to domesticate a lion.*

domesticated /də'mes·tɪˌkeɪ·t̬ɪd/ [adjective] Referring to an animal, that has been trained: *Cats and dogs are among the most popular domesticated animals.*

†**dominate** /'dɑm·əˌneɪt/ [verb] To control something: *The Chicago Bulls dominated the game.*

Dominican[1] [adjective] Referring to Dominican Republic: *Santo Domingo is the Dominican capital.* ■ Be careful! "Dominican" has a capital "D".

Dominican[2] [countable noun] A person from Dominican Republic: *There are a Dominican in our baseball team.* ■ Be careful! "Dominican" has a capital "D".

dominoes US: /'dɑː.mɪ.noʊz/ UK: /'dɒm.ɪ.nəʊz/ [countable noun] A game played with small, flat pieces that have dots on them: *My dad says that to play dominoes well you have to do math to know which piece to use next.* ■ It is usually used with a singular verb.

donate US: /ˈdoʊ.neɪt/ UK: /dəʊˈneɪt/ [verb] To give something to people who need it: *She donated a lot of her fortune to charity.*

done[1] /dʌn/ Past participle of **do**.

done[2] /dʌn/ [adjective] Finished: *Her work done, she returned to her room to listen to some music.*

donkey /ˈdɑŋ·ki/, /ˈdʌŋ-/, /ˈdɔŋ-/ [countable noun] An animal like a horse with long ears: *Baby donkeys are very cute.* **See page 428.**

donor US: /ˈdoʊ.nɚ/ UK: /ˈdəʊ.nəʳ/ [countable noun] A person who gives something to somebody who needs it: *My mother is a regular blood donor at the local hospital.*

don't US: /doʊnt/ UK: /dəʊnt/ The contraction of "do not".

donut® /ˈdoʊ·nʌt/, /-nət/ [countable noun] A small round cake: *Donuts are cooked in oil.* ■ The British English spelling is "doughnut".

doodle /ˈduː.dl̩/ [verb] To draw lines or figures while you are thinking about something else: *She always doodles while she is talking on the phone.*

door US: /dɔːr/ UK: /dɔːʳ/ [countable noun] The way into a room or a building: *Open the door, please; I'm on the phone.*

DOOR

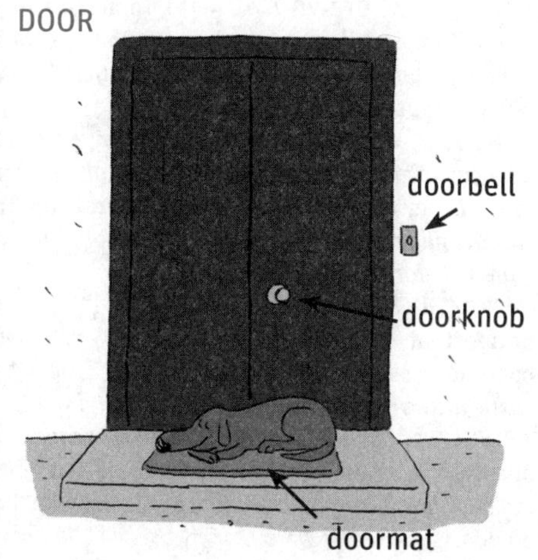

doorbell /ˈdɔrˌbel/, /ˈdoʊr-/ [countable noun] A bell outside a door: *She rang the doorbell, but nobody answered.* See picture at **door**.

doorknob US: /ˈdɔːr.nɑːb/ UK: /ˈdɔː.nɒb/ [countable noun] A small round handle for opening or closing the door: *The thief turned the doorknob quietly and went in.* See picture at **door**.

doormat /ˈdɔrˌmæt/, /ˈdoʊr-/ [countable noun] A small mat in front of a door: *Robert wiped his feet on the doormat.* See picture at **door**.

doorstep /ˈdɔrˌstep/, /ˈdoʊr-/ [countable noun] A step in front of a door: *Be careful when you come in because the doorstep is quite high.*

Doric /ˈdɒr.ɪk/ US: /ˈdɔːr-/ [adjective] Referring to the simplest of the building styles in Ancient Greece: *Doric pillars are topped by a plain capital and stand directly on the sidewalk, without a separate base.* ■ Compare with "Ionic" (with some decoration) and "Corinthian" (the most ornate).

dormitory /ˈdɔr·məˌtɔr·i/, /-ˌtoʊr·i/ [countable noun] **1** A big room with beds in a school, hostel and so on: *The girls slept in a lovely dormitory at the summer camp.* **2** A building with rooms for university students to live in: *That university has a great dormitory at the campus.* ■ The plural is "dormitories".

dorsal /ˈdɔː.səl/ US: /ˈdɔːr-/ [adjective] Referring to the back of a person, animal or fish: *Fish have a dorsal fin.* **See page 423.**

dot US: /dɑːt/ UK: /dɒt/ [countable noun] A small round mark: *The Braille alphabet uses dots to represent each letter of the alphabet.*

dotted line [countable noun] A line of several dots: *Please sign on the dotted line.*

double[1] /ˈdʌbl/ [adjective] **1** Twice as much or two of: *I'd like a double ice cream, please.* **2** Made for two people: *My parents sleep in a double bed.*

double[2] /ˈdʌbl/ [verb] To multiply by two: *The sales in my aunt's store have doubled over the past three months.*

double bass [countable noun] A very big instrument like an enormous violin: *Andrew plays the double bass in the school orchestra.* **See page 458.**

double-decker bus /ˌdʌb.l̩.dek.əˈbʌs/ US: /-ɚ-/ [countable noun] A bus with two levels: *Many cities have double-decker buses for the tourists to see the city and learn about its main buildings and attractions.*

doubt[1] /daʊt/ [noun] **1** A feeling of not being sure: *Jack had doubts about the answer to the question.* **2 in doubt** Not sure: *If you are in doubt about something, just ask the teacher.* **3 no doubt** Almost certainly: *No doubt they'll telephone you when they arrive.* ■ Be careful with the pronunciation of this word! The "b" is not pronounced.

doubt[2] /daʊt/ [verb] To think that something is probably not the case: *I doubt if they'll be in.* ■ Careful with the pronunciation of this word! The "b" is not pronounced.

doubtful /ˈdaʊt.fəl/ [adjective] Not certain, unlikely: *Cecil is a bit doubtful about entering the competition.* ■ Careful with the pronunciation of this word! The "b" is not pronounced.

dough US: /doʊ/ UK: /dəʊ/ [noun] A mixture made mainly with flour and water: *Bread is made by cooking dough.*

a b c d e f g h i j k l m n o p q r s t u v w x y z

a b c d e f g h i j k l m n o p q r s t u v w x y z

doughnut UK: /'dəʊ.nʌt/ [countable noun] See **donut®**. ■ This is a British English spelling.

dove[1] /dʌv/ [countable noun] A white bird of the pigeon family: *A dove is often used as a symbol of peace.*

dove[2] Past tense of **dive**.

down[1] /daʊn/ [adjective] **1** Lower: *The price of the dollar is down today.* **2** Sad, unhappy: *You're looking a bit down today.*

✝down[2] /daʊn/ [adverb and preposition] In or towards a lower place: *The anchor went down to the bottom of the sea.* 👁 See picture at **preposition**.

downhill /ˌdaʊn'hɪl/ [adverb] To the bottom of a hill: *The cyclists went downhill at an incredible speed.*

✝downstairs /'daʊn'steərz/ [adverb] On a lower floor or to a lower floor: *Tommy went downstairs to make breakfast.*

downtown [adjective and adverb] In or to the central area or main business area of a city: *You can see the highest buildings of downtown Denver from the distance.*

downward [adjective] Towards the ground, in a down direction: *She indicated yes with a downward movement of the head.*

✝downwards /'daʊn·wərdz/ [adverb] Towards the ground, in a down direction: *Lily fell asleep face downwards under the apple tree.*

doze /dəʊz/ [verb] To sleep lightly: *Grandmother dozed in the chair for a few minutes after lunch.*

✝dozen /'dʌz.ᵊn/ [countable noun] Twelve: *Go and buy a dozen eggs from the farm.* ■ Be careful. We always say: "a dozen eggs". We don't say: "a dozen of eggs".

✝Dr. A written abbreviation for **doctor**. ■ See box at **abbreviations**.

✝draft US: /dræft/ UK: /drɑːft/ [countable noun] **1** The first form of a piece of writing: *Sally made a draft of her composition before giving it to the teacher.* **2** Current of air: *Shut that door, please! There's an awful draft in here.* ■ In this use, in British English we say "draught".

drag[1] /dræg/ [noun] A person or a thing that is a bore: *Shopping is a real drag.*

drag[2] /dræg/ [verb] To pull something along the ground: *Sandra dragged the box into the room.*

dragon /'dræg.ᵊn/ [countable noun] A legendary animal which breathes fire: *The dragon in the story had wings and lived in a cave.*

dragonfly /'dræg.ᵊn.flaɪ/ [countable noun] A colorful flying insect with a long thin body: *Some dragonflies can fly at fifty miles an hour.* ■ The plural is "dragonflies".

drain[1] /dreɪn/ [countable noun] A metal cover with holes, in the street, which carries dirty water away: *The drains are blocked with leaves.*

drain[2] /dreɪn/ [verb] To let liquid flow away: *Wash the mushrooms and drain them. Then cut them up.*

drainpipe /'dreɪn.paɪp/ [countable noun] A pipe on the outside of a building: *The thieves climbed up the drainpipe and got in through the bedroom window.*

✝drama UK: /'drɑː.mə/ US: /'dræm.ə/ ▮ [countable noun] **1** A serious play for the theater or television: *People have said that Shakespeare's dramas are a mirror of life.* ▮ [uncountable noun] **2** Acting and plays: *My sister Sheila went to drama school and is now an actress.* ▮ [noun] **3** Excitement: *There was a big drama when one of the children got lost on the trip.*

✝dramatic /drə'mæt̬·ɪk/ [adjective] Exciting: *The movie had a dramatic ending.*

drank /dræŋk/ Past tense of **drink**.

drape /dreɪp/ [noun] Material used for covering a window or door: *One of the girls hid behind the drapes.* ■ In British English they say "curtain". 👁 See picture at **living room**.

draught /drɑːft/ [countable noun] See **draft**. ■ This word is British English.

draughts US: /dræfts/ UK: /drɑːfts/ [noun] See **checkers**. ■ This word is British English. ■ It is usually used with a singular verb.

draw[1] /drɔː/ [countable noun] See **tie[1]**. ■ This word is British English.

✝draw[2], drew, drawn /drɔː/ [verb] **1** To make a picture with a pencil, a pen and so on: *The little boy drew a picture of a snowman for his mother.* **2** See **tie[2]**. ■ This use is British English.

◗ **PHRASAL VERBS** · **to draw (something) out** To take something out: *I'm going to the bank to draw some money out for the vacation.* · **to draw up** To stop: *A huge car drew up outside the hotel and a man with dark glasses got out.*

drawbridge /'drɔː.brɪdʒ/ US: /'drɑː-/ [countable noun] A bridge that can be raised or lowered, to allow boats to pass, or to permit entry to a castle: *The castle drawbridge was lowered on market days.*

✝drawer US: /drɑː/ UK: /drɔːʳ/ [countable noun] Compartment of a desk or a table which slides out: *My new writing desk has four drawers in it.* ■ Be careful with the pronunciation of this word.

DRAWER

†**drawing** /ˈdrɔ·ɪŋ/ ▮ [countable noun] **1** A picture done with a pencil, a pen and so on: *The Museum of Modern Art in New York has the best drawings of the twentieth century.* ▮ [uncountable noun] **2** The art of making pictures with a pencil, a pen and so on: *Peter is very good at drawing, isn't he?* 👁 See **page 456.**

drawing pin [countable noun] See **thumbtack.** ■ This word is British English.

drawn US: /drɑːn/ UK: /drɔːn/ Past participle of **draw.**

dread /dred/ [verb] To be very afraid of something: *Harry dreaded telling Jane that her dog had died.*

dreadful /ˈdred.fᵊl/ [adjective] Horrible: *I had a dreadful day today; everything went wrong.*

†**dream**[1] /driːm/ [countable noun] **1** Something that you imagine while you are asleep: *I had a lovely dream last night.* **2** Something nice that you would like to happen: *My dream is to meet Tom Hanks.*

†**dream**[2], **dreamt, dreamt** /driːm/ [verb] **1** To imagine things while you are asleep: *Last night, I dreamt I went to Manderley again.* **2** To want something nice to happen: *I often dream about going to the Himalayas one day.* ■ "Dream" also has regular past and past participle forms: "dreamed".

†**dress**[1] /dres/ [countable noun] An article of woman's clothing with a top and a skirt in one: *What a beautiful dress!* ■ The plural is "dresses". 👁 See picture at **clothes.**

†**dress**[2] /dres/ [verb] **1** To put clothes on: *Sam dressed quickly and went out.* **2** To put clothes on somebody: *I dressed the baby while Peter prepared the stroller.* **3** To wear something: *Lewis always dresses in black.*

▸ **PHRASAL VERBS** · **to dress up 1** To wear unusual clothes: *Let's dress up as Romans for Anne's party on Saturday.* **2** To wear elegant clothes: *They were all dressed up for the wedding.* ■ Be careful with the spelling of the 3rd person singular present tense form: "dresses".

dresser [countable noun] A piece of furniture which has drawers where you can keep clothes: *Please, put these shirts in the dresser in your bedroom.* ■ In British English they say "chest of drawers". 👁 See picture at **bedroom.**

dressing /ˈdres.ɪŋ/ [countable noun] **1** A covering that you put on a wound: *You'll have to wear that dressing for a week and then come back and see the doctor.* **2** A liquid that goes with salads: *My friend Hannah has shown me how to make a delicious salad dressing.*

dressing gown [countable noun] See **robe.** ■ This word is British English.

dressmaker /ˈdresˌmeɪ.kər/ US: /-kɚ/ [countable noun] A person who makes women's clothes: *I'm going to ask the dressmaker to alter this dress.* ■ A person who makes men's clothes is a "tailor".

drew /druː/ Past tense of **draw.**

drier [countable noun] See **dryer.**

drill[1] /drɪl/ [countable noun] **1** A tool for making holes: *Dentists use small drills in their work.* **2** An exercise where people practice many times till they know well what to do: *At my school we have fire drills and tornado drills.*

drill[2] /drɪl/ [verb] To make a hole using a drill: *Ron drilled a hole in the wall for the picture.*

drink[1] /drɪŋk/ [noun] A liquid that is suitable for swallowing: *Chocolate milk makes a tasty drink for children.*

†**drink**[2], **drank, drunk** /drɪŋk/ [verb] **1** To swallow liquid: *You should drink at least one liter of water a day.* **2 drinking water** Clean water for drinking: *The water from this tap is for washing only; it is not drinking water.*

drip /drɪp/ [verb] To fall in drops: *Water drips through the roof of our classroom when it rains.* ■ Be careful with the spelling of these forms: "dripped", "dripping".

drive[1] /draɪv/ [countable noun] A journey in a car: *They went for a drive in the countryside.*

†**drive**[2], **drove, driven** /draɪv/ [verb] To make a motor vehicle travel: *She drove all the way to Santa Fe in one day.*

driven /ˈdrɪv.ᵊn/, /ˈdrɪv.ᵊn/ Past participle of **drive**[2].

†**driver** /ˈdraɪ·vər/ [countable noun] A person who drives: *The driver stopped for half an hour to drink a cup of coffee.*

driver's license [countable noun] A card showing that you can drive: *You need a special driver's license to drive a bus.*

driveway [countable noun] A short road from a street to a house: *He parked the car in the driveway and went to the house.*

drizzle[1] [uncountable noun] A fine and light rain: *We had drizzle in the morning but the rest of the day it was sunny.*

drizzle[2] [verb] To rain in small drops: *It has been drizzling all morning.*

drop[1] /drɒp/ [countable noun] A small quantity of liquid: *My eyes are very red so I am going to use some eye drops.* 👁 See picture at **a piece of...**

†**drop**[2] /drɒp/ [verb] **1** To let something fall: *Patsy dropped the eggs and broke them all.* **2** To go down rapidly: *Sales always drop considerably in February.*

▸ **PHRASAL VERBS** · **to drop in** To pay a short visit: *I'll drop in and see you on the way to school.* ■ Be careful with the spelling of these forms: "dropped", "dropping".

dropper US: /'drɑː.pɚ/ UK: /'drɒp.ər/ [countable noun] A short tube used to measure out liquids by drops: *The nurse used a dropper to dispense the medicine.* 👁 **See page 440.**

drought /draʊt/ [noun] A long time with no rain: *Africa often suffers from droughts.* ■ Be careful with the pronunciation of this word. It rhymes with "out".

drove /drəʊv/ Past tense of **drive**.

drown /draʊn/ [verb] To die in water because you cannot breathe: *The ship sank and twenty people drowned.*

✝**drug** /drʌg/ [countable noun] **1** A chemical that is used as a medicine: *There are very many new drugs against cancer these days.* **2** An addictive substance which people use for pleasure or excitement: *Drugs can affect your health.*

✝**drugstore** /'drʌgˌstɔr/, /-ˌstoʊr/ [countable noun] A store that sells medicines: *I went to the drugstore to get some cough medicine.* ■ The same meaning: "pharmacy". ■ In British English they say "chemist's".

✝**drum** /drʌm/ [countable noun] A hollow musical instrument that you hit: *She plays the drum in the local band.* 👁 **See page 459.**

drunk[1] /drʌŋk/ Past participle of **drink[2]**.

✝**drunk[2]** /drʌŋk/ [adjective] Having had too much alcohol: *You should never drive when you are drunk.*

✝**dry[1]** /draɪ/ [adjective] **1** Not wet: *The clothes that you hang outside are already dry.* 👁 See picture at **opposite**. **2** Without rain: *The ground was very dry because of the drought.* ■ The comparative form is "drier" and the superlative form is "driest".

dry[2] /draɪ/ [verb] **1** To become dry: *Our laundry is drying very well in the sun.* **2** To make something dry: *Dry the dishes, please.*
▶ **PHRASAL VERBS** · **to dry out** To dry completely: *Don't worry; your coat will have dried out by tomorrow morning.* ■ Be careful with the spelling of these forms: "dries", "dried".

dry cleaner's or **cleaners** US: /'draɪ 'kli·nər/ [countable noun] A place where you take clothes to be cleaned with chemicals, not in water: *I'm going to take this silk dress to the dry cleaner's. Do you have anything else to take?*

dryer [countable noun] A machine that make something dry: *You can use the clothes dryer to save time in the laundry.* ■ This word is also written "drier".

duchess /'dʌtʃ.es/ [countable noun] A woman with a special noble title: *The Duchess of Kent presents the cup at Wimbledon every year.* ■ A man with a special title is a "duke".

duck[1] /dʌk/ [countable noun] A bird that lives near water: *You can often see ducks on lakes in parks or farms.* 👁 **See page 429.**

duck[2] /dʌk/ [verb] To move down quickly to avoid something: *John ducked just in time so the ball didn't hit him.*

duckling /'dʌk.lɪŋ/ [noun] A baby duck: *The mother duck and her ducklings swam down the river together.*

✝**due** US: /duː/ UK: /djuː/ [adjective] **1** Expected: *When is the baby due to be born?* **2** Having to be paid: *Our rent is due within the first five days of every month.* **3** **due for** Ready for something: *I'm due for a visit to the dentist quite soon.* **4** **due to** Because of something: *Due to repair work, the theater will have to be closed for the rest of the season.*

duet /du'et/ [countable noun] A song or a piece of music for two: *Rachel and Emma played a marvelous duet on the piano.*

duffle coat /'dʌf.l̩ˌkəʊt/ US: /-ˌkoʊt/ [countable noun] A thick coat with a hood: *Duffle coats are usually very warm.*

dug /dʌg/ Past tense and past participle forms of **dig**.

duke US: /duːk/ UK: /djuːk/ [countable noun] A man with a special noble title: *Some dukes received their title from their king.* ■ A woman with a special title is a "duchess".

✝**dull** /dʌl/ [adjective] **1** Not bright, gray: *It's a very dull day today.* **2** Not interesting: *The game was so dull that we went home after an hour or so.*

dumb /dʌm/ [adjective] Not intelligent: *Don't start making dumb comments again.* ■ Be careful with the pronunciation of this word. The "b" is silent.

dummy /'dʌmi/ [countable noun] **1** A model of a person used to show clothes in a store: *There were four dummies in the shop window.* **2** See **pacifier**. ■ This use is British English. ■ The plural is "dummies".

dump[1] /dʌmp/ [countable noun] A place to put garbage: *Throw that old box on the garbage dump.*

✝**dump[2]** /dʌmp/ [verb] **1** To throw something away: *Some factories just dump their waste in the sea.* **2** To leave a thing somewhere carelessly: *Don't just dump your school bag in the middle of the floor like that. Put it away.*

dune US: /duːn/ UK: /djuːn/ [countable noun] A hill or wave of sand: *Dunes are usually to be found near the sea.*

duplex [countable noun] A house joined to another house on one side: *Many people in New York live in a duplex with a small yard to the back and the front.* 👁 See picture at **house**.

✝**during** US: /'dʊr.ɪŋ/ UK: /'djʊə.rɪŋ/ [preposition] **1** All the time that something is going on: *Smoking is not allowed during the flight.* **2** At some point when something is going on: *Dad became ill during the night.*

✝**dust[1]** /dʌst/ [uncountable noun] Dirt that is like fine powder: *The furniture in the old house was covered in dust.*

dust[2] /dʌst/ [verb] To clean the dust: *Dust those shelves quickly before the visitors come.*

dustbin /'dʌst.bɪn/ [countable noun] See **trash can.** ■ This word is British English.

duster /'dʌs.tər/ US: /-tɚ/ [countable noun] A thing that removes dust: *Take the duster and clean the whiteboard, please.*

Dutch[1] /dʌtʃ/ [adjective] Referring to Holland: *I think Dutch cheese is delicious.* ■ Be careful! "Dutch" has a capital "D".

Dutch[2] [uncountable noun] The language of Holland and other countries: *Do you speak Dutch?* ■ Careful! "Dutch" has a capital "D".

†**duty** US: /'duː.t̬i/ UK: /'djuː.ti/ [noun] **1** Something that you have to do: *It's my duty to feed our dog and cat.* **2** A tax that you have to pay if you bring certain things into the country: *Do I have to pay duty on this CD player?* **3 off duty** Not working: *Night nurses are off duty during the day.* **4 on duty** Working or at work: *Dr. Barnes is on duty at the hospital between three and six o'clock.* ■ The plural is "duties".

duty-free /'du·t̬i 'fri/ [adjective] Without duty: *There are duty-free stores at airports and on boats.*

duvet /'duː.veɪ/ US: /-'-/ [countable noun] See **comforter.** ■ This word is British English.

dwarf /dwɔːf/ [countable noun] A very small person: *Have you seen the movie of "Snow White and the Seven Dwarves"?* ■ The plural is "dwarves" or "dwarfs".

dwell, dwelt, dwelt /dwel/ [verb] To live or to stay: *This animal dwells in a forest.* ■ This use is formal. We usually say "live".

◗ **PHRASAL VERBS · to dwell on (something)** To think, to speak or to write about something for a long time: *Try not to dwell on how you did in the test. Wait until you get the results.*

dwelt Past tense and past participle forms of **dwell.**

dye /dwɔːf/ [verb] To change the color of something: *She dyed her T-shirt red.*

dynamic /daɪ'næm.ɪk/ [adjective] Active and interesting: *We need a dynamic person to take charge of this summer camp.*

dynamite /'daɪ.nə.maɪt/ [uncountable noun] A chemical used as an explosive: *Dynamite is used for getting rocks out of the ground.* ■ Be careful with the pronunciation of this word! "dy" rhymes with "my".

dynamo /'daɪ·nə,moʊ/ [countable noun] A machine which converts mechanical energy into electrical energy: *A dynamo is often used on a bicycle to power its lights.*

E

e

e /iː/ The fifth letter of the alphabet: *The name "Elizabeth" begins with an "E".*

E /iː/ [countable noun] The third musical note of the scale of C major: *This song has been composed in the key of E.* ■ The plural is "Es" or "E's". 👁 **See page 460.**

†**each** /iːtʃ/ [adjective] **1** Every person or thing: *Each student has to bring an exercise book and a pencil to class.* **2 each other** Words that show that people do the same thing or feel the same way: *My grandparents love each other.* ■ The same meaning: "one another".

eager /ˈi·gər/ [adjective] Enthusiastic: *June is always eager to help.*

eagle /ˈiː.gl/ [countable noun] A large fierce bird with a sharp beak: *Eagles live in mountain areas and hunt small animals for food.*

†**ear** US: /ɪr/ UK: /ɪəʳ/ [countable noun] A part of the head that is used for hearing: *Indian elephants have enormous ears.* 👁 See picture at **face**.

earache US: /ˈɪr.eɪk/ UK: /ˈɪə.reɪk/ [noun] A pain in the ear: *Earache is one of the worst pains you can have.*

eardrum /ˈɪədrʌm/ [countable noun] The membrane of the middle ear: *The eardrum can be damaged by excess noise.*

†**early** /ˈɜr·li/ [adverb] **1** Before time: *The bus arrived five minutes early.* **2** Near the beginning of a period of time: *Harry gets up early every day.* ■ The comparative form is "earlier" and the superlative form is "earliest". ■ Compare with "soon" (in a short time in the future).

†**earn** US: /ɝːn/ UK: /ɜːn/ [verb] **1** To get money by working: *My uncle earns a lot.* **2** To get something because you deserve it: *Why don't you have a break now? You've earned it.* ■ Compare with "win" (to reach an objective).

earnings /ˈɜr·nɪŋz/ [plural noun] Money that you get for working: *My brother spent his first earnings on a motorcycle.*

earphones US: /ˈɪr.foʊnz/ UK: /ˈiə.fəʊnz/ [plural noun] Things that you put over your ears to listen to music and so on: *Sally had her earphones on so she couldn't hear me.* 👁 **See page 442.**

earring US: /ˈɪr.ɪŋ/ UK: /ˈɪə.rɪŋ/ [countable noun] Something you wear on your ears for decoration: *What unusual earrings! Where did you get them?* 👁 See picture at **jewelry**.

†**earth** /ɜːθ/ [uncountable noun] **1** The planet that we live on: *The earth looks blue when it is seen from space.* 👁 **See pages 446 and 448.** **2** Soil; the substance in which plants grow in: *Barbara planted the seeds in the earth.*

earthquake /ˈɜrθˌkweɪk/ [countable noun] A sudden shaking of the earth: *There was a terrible earthquake in Mexico a few years ago.*

earthworm US: /ˈɝːθ.wɜːrm/ UK: /ˈɜːθ.wɜːm/ [countable noun] A common type of worm which burrows in the ground: *The earthworm is capable of regenerating parts of itself.*

ease[1] /iːz/ [uncountable noun] A lack of difficulty: *Monkeys climb trees with ease.*

ease[2] /iːz/ [verb] **1** To make something less painful: *Cold water eases the pain of a burn.* **2 to be at ease** or **to feel at ease** To feel relaxed: *My grandmother is such a nice person that everyone feels at ease with her.*

easel /ˈiː.zəl/ [countable noun] A frame to hold a picture that is being painted: *Artists use easels when they do a painting.*

easily /ˈiː.zɪ.li/ [adverb] **1** With no difficulty: *We can easily finish the picture this morning.* **2** By far: *My sister is easily the best at bread baking.* **3** At least: *You must have been walking easily for four hours.* **4** Very imaginable: *This could easily have happened to us as well.*

east /iːst/ [noun, adjective and adverb] **1** The direction you look to see the sun rise: *My cousins live in the East Coast of the United States.* ■ See box at **abbreviations**. **2 the Far East** China, Japan, Indonesia and other countries to the east of India: *Naomi is always going for vacations in the Far East.* **3 the Middle East** Countries situated at the point where Europe, Africa and Asia meet: *Many of the biggest oil producing countries are in the Middle East.* ■ Be careful! "Far East" and "Middle East" have capital letters.

Easter /ˈi·stər/ [noun] **1** A Christian feast celebrating Jesus' return to life: *Easter is always in March or April.* **2 Easter egg** A chocolate egg eaten at Easter: *My aunt always gives us a huge Easter egg at Easter.* ■ Be careful! "Easter" has a capital "E".

eastern /ˈi·stərn/ [adjective] Of the east: *The eastern coast of United States is the most populated.*

easy /ˈiːzi/ [adjective] **1** Not difficult: *The homework was so easy I did it in five minutes.* ■ The comparative form is "easier" and the superlative form is "easiest". **2 to go easy** To be careful with something, not to use too much of something: *She should go easy on the cigarettes; she smokes too much.* ■ We say "go easy **on** or **with** something".

eat, ate, eaten /iːt/ [verb] To take food in through your mouth, chew and swallow it: *Come on, eat your dinner!*

▶ **PHRASAL VERBS** · **to eat out** To eat in a restaurant: *We often eat out on Sundays.*

eaten Past participle of **eat**.

eater /ˈiːtər/ [countable noun] **1** Person or animal that eats: *We have no meat eaters in the family.* **2 big eater** Person who eats a lot: *My cousin has a reputation for being a big eater.*

e-book [countable noun] A book which can be read on a computer or a special electronic device: *This book is available as an e-book or paperback.*

echinoderm /ɪˈkaɪ.nəʊ.dɜːm/ US: /-dɝːm/ [countable noun] A marine invertebrate with a shell and tube feet: *The starfish is an echinoderm.*

echo /ˈek·oʊ/ [countable noun] A sound that is repeated back to you: *You can often hear an echo in a cave or a tunnel.*

eclipse /ɪˈklɪps/ [countable noun] A time when the light from the sun or from the moon is hidden by the moon or by the earth: *We all stayed up to watch the eclipse of the moon.*

ecological /ˌi·kəˈlɑdʒ·ɪ·kəl/, /ˌek·ə-/ [adjective] Relating to or concerned about the environment: *The Green Party is an ecological movement.*

ecology /ɪˈkɑl·ə·dʒi/ [uncountable noun] The study of living things and where they live: *My sister is very interested in ecology and works on a forest conservation project at the weekends.* ■ The plural is "ecologies".

economic /ˌɪ·kəˈnɑm·ɪk/, /ˌek·ə-/ [adjective] Referring to finance: *The Financial Times is a newspaper that specializes in economic news.*

economics /ˌɪ·kəˈnɑm·ɪks/, /ˌek·ə-/ [uncountable noun] The study of money, trade and industry: *Jim is studying Economics at university.* ■ It is usually used with a singular verb.

economy /ɪˈkɑn·ə·mi/ [countable noun] A country's financial situation: *They say that the economy is improving but I don't see it!* ■ The plural is "economies".

ecosystem /ˈi·koʊˌsɪs·təm/, /ˈek·oʊ-/ [countable noun] The collection of biological organisms with a particular physical environment and how they interact: *The Amazonian rainforest is an example of an ecosystem.*

eczema /ˈeksmə/ [uncountable noun] A swelling of the skin: *Eczema causes itching.*

edge /edʒ/ [countable noun] The limit of something: *We went to the edge of the canyon and looked down.*

edible /ˈed.ɪ.bl/ [adjective] Suitable to be eaten: *Many sea creatures are edible.*

edit /ˈed.ɪt/ [verb] To prepare a text or a movie for publication or printing: *When I edited our class magazine, I asked Anna to do all the pictures.*

a b c d e f g h i j k l m n o p q r s t u v w x y z

edition /ɪˈdɪʃ.ᵊn/ [countable noun] A book or a newspaper that comes out at a particular time: *The news was too late for the early morning editions of the newspapers.*

editor /ˈed·əṭ·ər/ [countable noun] **1** Somebody who edits material for publication or broadcasting: *The editor has the last word on what goes into the newspaper.* **2** A function which corrects text or data you put on the computer: *He decided to work without the text editor as it did not recognize many new words.* **3** copy editor The person responsible for correcting the style of written material accepted for publishing: *She has been offered a job as copy editor in the publishing house.*

editorial[1] /ˌed·əˈtɔr·i·əl/, /-ˈtoʊr-/ [countable noun] A newspaper article giving the opinion of the newspaper on a current issue: *The editorial establishes the tone for the newspaper.*

editorial[2] /ˌedɪˈtɔːriəl/ [adjective] Referring to the editing of a publication: *Editorial responsibility is a question of choosing what to publish.*

educate /ˈed.jʊ.keɪt/ [verb] To teach, to instruct: *Andrea was educated at a girls' school in Portland.*

education /ˌed.jʊˈkeɪ.ʃᵊn/ [noun] **1** Teaching and learning: *If Aristotle is to be believed, "The roots of education are bitter, but the fruit is sweet".* **2** higher education See **higher education.**

eel /iːl/ [countable noun] A long, thin fish like a snake: *Eels swim long distances to have their young.*

effect /ɪˈfekt/ [noun] **1** The result of something: *Global warming is having a very negative effect on the environment.* **2** to take effect To begin applying a rule, to begin working: *The agreement will take effect in June.*

effective /ɪˈfek.tɪv/ [adjective] That works well, that produces the desired result: *The library system is very effective. It's easy to find what you want.*

efficiency /ɪˈfɪʃ.ᵊnt.si/ [uncountable noun] Good functioning: *We need to improve the efficiency of this machine.* ■ The plural is "efficiencies".

efficient /ɪˈfɪʃ.ᵊnt/ [adjective] Able to work well and without waste: *The waiters are very efficient here; they've already taken our order.*

efficiently [adverb] Competently and effectively, minimizing effort and waste: *She did the job very efficiently.*

effort /ˈef·ərt/ [noun] The use of energy or determination to do something: *Fred made an enormous effort to get everything ready for the children's birthday party.*

e.g. /iːˈdʒiː/ A written abbreviation for **for example.** ■ "e.g." is an abbreviation for "exempli gratia", a Latin expression that means "for example". ■ See box at **abbreviations**.

egg /eg/ [countable noun] **1** A fragile object that contains a baby bird or reptile: *The hen has laid six eggs today.* **2** scrambled eggs See **scrambled eggs**.

eggplant /ˈeg·plænt/, /ˈeɪg-/ [countable noun] A vegetable with a purple skin: *Fried eggplant is one of my favorite dishes.* ■ In British English they say "aubergine". **See page 437.**

eight /eɪt/ [noun, adjective and pronoun] The number 8: *Four plus four makes eight.*

eighteen /eɪˈtiːn/ [noun, adjective and pronoun] The number 18: *You can vote at the age of eighteen in the United States.*

eighteenth /eɪˈtiːnθ/ [noun and adjective] Referring to eighteen: *Hugh's birthday is on the eighteenth of January.* ■ "Eighteenth" can also be written "18th".

eighth /eɪtθ/ [noun and adjective] Referring to eight: *August is the eighth month of the year.* ■ "Eighth" can also be written "8th".

eightieth /ˈeɪṭ·i·əθ/ [noun and adjective] Referring to eighty: *It's my grandfather's eightieth birthday today.* ■ "Eightieth" can also be written "80th".

eighty /ˈeɪṭ·i/ [noun, adjective and pronoun] The number 80: *I will be eighty years old on June 15th 2065.*

either /ˈi·ðər/, /ˈɑɪ-/ [adjective and pronoun] **1** One of two things or people: *You can have either the blue one or the red one.* ■ Note that we say: **"either ... or ..."**. **2** Both: *There are flowers on either side of the path.* **3** Used with a negative sentence, it means "also": *Alfred doesn't like football and I don't either.* ■ In this use, "either" goes at the end of the sentence and is used with a negative verb. "Neither" is used with a positive verb.

elastic[1] /ɪˈlæstɪk/ [adjective] That stretches easily: *My mom gave me a new swimsuit for Christmas. It is very elastic.*

elastic[2] /ɪˈlæstɪk/ [uncountable noun] **1** A material that stretches easily: *Socks have elastic in them so that they don't fall down.* **2** elastic band A thin piece of rubber that we use to hold things together: *Let's* *put an elastic band around these cards so that we don't lose them.*

elasticity /ˌɪlæsˈtɪsəti/ [uncountable noun] The condition of being able to be stretched: *Let's test the elasticity of this material.*

elbow /ˈelbəʊ/ [countable noun] The part of your arm where it bends: *She gave me a push with her elbow to warn me that the teacher was coming.* See page 421.

elder /ˈel·dər/ [countable noun] The comparative form of **old**. ■ It is used when people's ages are compared, especially the ages of members of a family. It cannot be used with "than", and if it is used with a noun it always goes in front of the noun: "My elder brother is a singer".

elderly /ˈel·dər·li/ [adjective] Old: *They've just opened a home for elderly people in our street.*

eldest /ˈel.dɪst/ [adjective] The superlative form of **old**. ■ It is used when people's ages are compared, especially the ages of members of a family. It cannot be used with "than", and if it is used with a noun it always goes in front of the noun: "Martin is the eldest member of the family".

elect /ɪˈlekt/ [verb] To choose by voting: *The new parliamentary was elected on Tuesday.*

election /ɪˈlek.ʃən/ [noun] **1** A time when leaders are chosen by voting: *In the USA, an election to choose a president is held every four years.* **2 general election** See **general election.**

electric /ɪˈlek.trɪk/ [adjective] Referring to something moved or worked by electricity: *We have a very good electric stove.*

electrical /ɪˈlek.trɪ.kəl/ [adjective] Referring to electricity: *My aunt is an electrical engineer.*

electrically /ɪˈlek.trɪ.kli/ [adverb] By means of or with electricity: *The vacuum cleaner is powered electrically.*

electrician /ˌɪl.ekˈtrɪʃ.ən/ [countable noun] A person who puts in or repairs with electrical systems: *The lights are not working properly, so we'll have to call the electrician.*

electricity /ɪˌlekˈtrɪs·əṭ·i/ [uncountable noun] A form of energy that produces light, heat and movement: *There was a tremendous storm the other day and the electricity was cut off.*

electromagnetism /ɪˌlek.trəʊˈmæg.nə.tɪ.zəm/ US: /-troʊ-/ [uncountable noun] Magnetism produced by an electrical current, or the science relating to it: *Electromagnetism is a feature of electric motors, hard drives and many other devices.*

electronic /ɪˌlekˈtrɑn·ɪk/ [adjective] Using electric impulses: *We use electronic calculators at school.* See page 442.

electronic mail [uncountable noun] See **e-mail.**

electronics /ɪˌlekˈtrɑn·ɪks/ [uncountable noun] The technology of using microchips to make radios, computers and so on: *The electronics industry is one of the most important in the world.* ■ It is usually used with a singular verb.

elegant /ˈel.ɪ.gənt/ [adjective] With good style or grace: *She was wearing an elegant black dress.*

element /ˈel.ɪ.mənt/ [countable noun] **1** A part of something: *Chance is an important element in this game.* **2** A simple substance: *Oxygen is one of the elements in air.*

elementary /ˌel·əˈmen·tri/, /-ˈmen·tə·ri/ [adjective] Simple and basic: *I'm doing an elementary course of practical mathematics.*

elementary school [countable noun] A school for children from five to eleven years old: *My sister is at elementary school.* ■ The same meaning: "primary school".

elephant /ˈel.ɪ.fənt/ [countable noun] A large, gray animal with a very long nose: *Elephants live wild in Africa and Asia.* See page 428.

elevation /ˌelɪˈveɪʃən/ ▌[noun] **1** The process of raising something: *The elevation of the nails was produced by magnetism.* **2** The angle of something in relation to the horizontal plane: *The elevation of the gun barrel is 15 degrees.* ▌[countable noun] **3** The height of a place, especially above sea level: *The city is at an elevation of 6,000 feet.* **4** A scale drawing of the front or side of a building: *The architect prepared a drawing of the front elevation of the building.*

elevator /ˈel·əˌveɪ·ṭər/ [countable noun] A machine that takes people up and down a building: *The elevator is broken, so you'll have to use the stairs.* ■ In British English they say "lift". See picture at **escalator.**

eleven /ɪˈlev.ən/ [noun, adjective and pronoun] The number 11: *There are eleven players in a soccer team.*

eleventh /ɪˈlev.ənθ/ [noun and adjective] Referring to eleven: *November is the eleventh month of the year.* ■ "Eleventh" can also be written "11th".

eliminate /ɪˈlɪm.ɪ.neɪt/ [verb] **1** To remove somebody or something that is not wanted or needed: *They eliminated Florida as a possible vacation choice because of the cost.* **2** To lose a game or round in a competition and not take part any more: *George was eliminated in the second stage of the competition.*

elm or **elm tree** /elm/ [noun] A large tree with broad leaves: *Many elms have died in recent years from a strange disease which originated in Holland.* See page 435.

else /els/ [adverb] **1** More: *Would you like anything else to eat?* **2** Other: *If you don't want pizza you can*

a b c d e f g h i j k l m n o p q r s t u v w x y z

a b c d e f g h i j k l m n o p q r s t u v w x y z

have something else. ■ "Else" is used after words formed with "any-", "no-", "some-", and after question words.

†**elsewhere** /ˈelsˌhweər/, /-ˌweər/ [adverb] To another place or in another place: *If you don't like this burger bar, we can always go elsewhere.*

'em /əm/ The contraction of "them". ■ This word is informal.

e-mail /ˈiː.meɪl/ [countable noun] Mail that is sent or received through a computer: *You can read my e-mail if you want.* ■ "E-mail" is an abbreviation for "electronic mail".

†**embarrass** /ɪmˈbær·əs/ [verb] To make somebody feel uncomfortable or ashamed: *My mother always embarrasses me by making me play the piano when her friends come.*

embarrassed /ɪmˈbær·əst/ [adjective] Uncomfortable or ashamed: *Dan felt embarrassed when he slipped and fell down in the school hall.* ■ Be careful with the pronunciation of the end of this word. The last "e" is not pronounced. 👁 See picture at **emotions.**

†**embarrassing** /ɪmˈbær·ə·sɪŋ/ [adjective] Making you feel uncomfortable or ashamed: *It was so embarrassing when I couldn't remember his name!*

†**embarrassment** /ɪmˈbær·əs·mənt/ [noun] A person or a thing that makes you uncomfortable or ashamed: *It was a great embarrassment to me when I dropped the bottle.*

embassy /ˈem.bə.si/ [countable noun] A place with the official representative of a foreign country: *If you're abroad and lose your passport, you should contact the embassy of your country in the place you're visiting.* ■ The plural is "embassies".

embroider /ɪmˈbrɔɪ·dər/ [verb] To decorate cloth using thread: *My grandmother embroiders all her sheets and towels.*

embryo /ˈem·briˌoʊ/ [countable noun] An unborn baby or animal in its early stages: *The embryo is going to grow into a fetus.* ■ The plural is "embryos".

emerald /ˈem.ə.rəld/ [noun] A precious green stone: *In North Carolina you can visit the emerald mines.*

emerald green [noun and adjective] Bright green: *The water of the lake was emerald green.*

†**emerge** /ɪˈmɜrdʒ/ [verb] To come out: *At last, the baby birds emerged from the egg.*

†**emergency** /ɪˈmɜr·dʒən·si/ [noun] A sudden, dangerous situation requiring help: *The emergency room in a hospital is where patients are taken if they are very ill.* ■ The plural is "emergencies".

emigrant /ˈem.ɪ.grənt/ [countable noun] A person who emigrates: *An emigrant leaves behind many things.*

emigrate /ˈem.ɪ.greɪt/ [verb] To go and live in a foreign country: *Many Italians emigrated to Argentina in the early 20th century.* ■ The same meaning: "migrate".

emigration /ˌemɪˈgreɪʃən/ [uncountable noun] The act of leaving one's own country and going to live in a foreign country: *Emigration has always been a characteristic of human history.*

emit /ɪˈmɪt/ [verb] To send out (heat, noise, smell, gas): *Light bulbs tend to emit heat.* ■ Be careful with the spelling of these forms: "emitting", "emitted".

†**emotion** /ɪˈmoʊ·ʃən/ [noun] A strong feeling: *Sometimes it is difficult to describe emotions.*

†**emotional** /ɪˈmoʊ·ʃə·nə·l/ [adjective] Having, showing or causing strong feelings: *Brian is a very emotional person.*

emperor /ˈem·pər·ər/ [countable noun] A man who rules a number of countries, not just one: *Julius Caesar was probably the most famous Roman Emperor.* ■ A woman who rules a number of countries is an "empress".

†**emphasis** /ˈemp.fə.sɪs/ [noun] Force, stress: *He put great emphasis on the need for a big final effort.*

†**empire** /ˈem·paɪər/ [countable noun] A group of countries ruled by an emperor: *The eastern part of the Roman Empire, known as Byzantium, survived until 1453.*

†**employ** /ɪmˈplɔɪ/ [verb] To give somebody a job: *The car industry in Brazil employs thousands of people.*

†**employee** /ɪmˈplɔɪ.iː/ [countable noun] Somebody who is employed by another person or by a company: *Every employee in my mother's company got a present at Christmas.*

†**employer** /ɪmˈplɔɪ·ər/ [countable noun] Person who gives work to people and pays them: *Mr. Amis is a very good employer, he treats his workers very well.*

†**employment** /ɪmˈplɔɪ.mənt/ [uncountable noun] Paid work: *It is quite difficult to find employment these days.*

empress /ˈem.prəs/ [countable noun] An emperor's wife, or a woman who rules a number of countries: *Britain's Queen Victoria was made Empress of India in 1877.* ■ A man who rules a number of countries is an "emperor".

emptiness /ˈemp.tɪ.nəs/ [uncountable noun] An area or a space that has nothing in it: *I feel an emptiness now that she has gone.*

†**empty** /ˈemp.ti/ [adjective] With nothing inside: *Take those empty bottles back to the store.* 👁 See picture at **opposite.**

†**enable** /ɪˈneɪ.bl/ [verb] To make something possible: *Computers enable you to store information in a very small space.* ■ Be careful with the pronunciation of this word. It is pronounced like "table".

enchanting /ɪnˈtʃæn·tɪŋ/ [adjective] Very beautiful or magical: *What an enchanting evening we had at the theater!*

EMOTIONS

happy  | delighted  | pleased  | relaxed

proud  | shy  | sad  | miserable

disgusted  | embarrassed 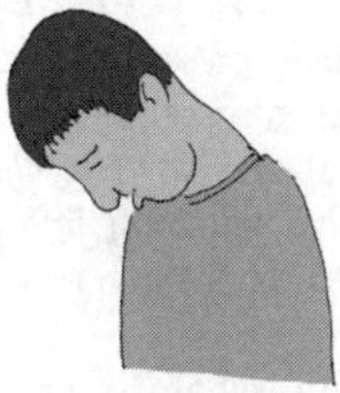 | ashamed  | bored

tense  | nervous  | afraid  | worried

shocked  | annoyed  | angry  | furious

enclose /ɪn'kloʊz/ [verb] To put an object inside something: *I'm enclosing a photo of my new baby sister with this letter.*

encore US: /'ɑːŋ.kɔːr/ UK: /'ɒŋ.kɔːʳ/ [countable noun] A call to play more music at the end of a concert: *Bruce Springsteen played "Born in the USA" for an encore.*

✦**encourage** /ɪn'kɜr·ɪdʒ/, /-'kʌr·ɪdʒ/ [verb] To give somebody help and confidence: *My parents have always encouraged me to learn languages.* ■ Be careful with the pronunciation of this word. The "a" is pronounced like the "i" in "did".

encouragement /ɪn'kɜr·ɪdʒ·mənt/, /-'kʌr·ɪdʒ-/ [noun] Something that gives help and confidence to somebody: *Little children need a lot of help and encouragement when they are learning to read and write.*

encouraging /ɪn'kɜr·ə·dʒɪŋ/, /-'kʌr·ə-/ [adjective] Making somebody feel hopeful: *Eight out of ten for the math test; now that's encouraging!*

encyclopaedia or **encyclopedia** /ɪn,saɪ.klə'piː.di.ə/ [countable noun] A book or series of books that give information about an enormous range of things: *If you want to know about Shakespeare's life, look it up in an encyclopedia.*

encyclopedia or **encyclopaedia** /ɪn,saɪ.klə'piː.di.ə/ [countable noun] A book, or set of articles, giving information on a great number of subjects or a great amount on one subject: *The Encyclopedia Britannica is an extensive source of information.* ■ Be careful with the pronunciation of this word! "cy" rhymes with "my".

✦**end**[1] /end/ [countable noun] **1** The point where something finishes: *At the end of the class we all went out for a break.* **2** **end to end** One behind the other: *The cars were end to end on the highway almost without moving.* **3** **at the end of (something) or in the end** At last: *Janet was going to buy a computer but in the end she decided not to.* ■ We do not use "in the end" to refer to the end of something specific. We say: "at the end of the page". We don't say: "In the end of the page". **4** **on end** Continuously: *The movie seemed to go on for hours on end.*

end[2] /end/ [verb] To stop: *The movie ended with everybody living happily.*

▸ **PHRASAL VERBS** · **to end up** To finish in a particular way: *The stove broke down last night so we ended up going out for a hamburger with french fries.*

endangered /ɪn'deɪn·dʒərd/ [adjective] In danger: *The giant panda is an endangered species; it needs protection or there will soon be none left.* ■ Be careful with the pronunciation of the end of this word. The last "e" is not pronounced.

✦**ending** /'en.dɪŋ/ [countable noun] The final part of a story or a movie: *I don't like the ending of the movie, it's depressing.*

endless /'end.ləs/ [adjective] Appearing to have no end: *The journey was so long that it seemed endless.*

endoscope /'en.dəʊ,skəʊp/ US: /-doʊ,skoʊp/ [countable noun] An instrument used by a surgeon for examining the inside of the body: *The endoscope is inserted down the throat in order to examine the chest cavity.*

✦**enemy** /'en.ə.mi/ [countable noun] **1** A person who is bitterly opposed to you: *Andrew has a very difficult character and he often makes enemies.* **2** A country that is opposed to another in a war: *United States and Japan were enemies during the Second World War.* ■ The plural is "enemies".

energetic /,en·ər'dʒeṭ·ɪk/ [adjective] Full of energy: *Violet is very energetic and she never seems to rest.*

✦**energy** /'en·ər·dʒi/ [uncountable noun] **1** The ability to be active: *Greg has so much energy that he can play football all day without feeling tired.* **2** Power, force: *Solar energy will probably be used in hot countries in the future.* ■ The plural is "energies".
👁 **See page 439.**

enforce /ɪn'fɔrs/, /-'foʊrs/ [verb] **1** To make sure that laws and regulations are obeyed: *I think traffic police helps enforcing road safety.* ■ Be careful! In this use we say: "to enforce something **on/against** something/somebody". **2** To make something happen by force or authority: *The teacher tried to enforce silence.*

✦**engaged** /ɪn'geɪdʒd/ [adjective] **1** Having agreed to get married: *Sam and Jenny got engaged last month.* ■ We say: "to get engaged" or "to be engaged". **2** See **busy**. ■ This use is British English. ■ Be careful with the pronunciation of this word. The last "e" is not pronounced.

engagement /ɪn'geɪdʒ.mənt/ [countable noun] An official agreement to get married: *My grandparents had a very long engagement before their wedding.*

✦**engine** /'en.dʒɪn/ [countable noun] **1** A machine that makes something move: *My mom's car is old but it has a new engine.* ■ "Engine" is usually used for vehicles. Compare with "motor" (usually used for electrical appliances). **2** The part of the train that pulls the cars: *I prefer to sit at the front of the train, near the engine.* **3** **engine driver** A person who drives a train: *Engine drivers often have to spend the night away from home.* ■ Be careful with the pronunciation of this word! The final "e" is not pronounced.

✦**engineer** /,en·dʒə'nɪər/ [countable noun] **1** A person who plans and makes machines, bridges, roads and so on: *My mother's an engineer; she helped to design* the bridge over the river near our house. **2** A person who runs a train: *The engineer blew the whistle so the cow would move away from the tracks.*

†**engineering** /ˌen·dʒəˈnɪər·ɪŋ/ [uncountable noun] The science of making machines, bridges, roads and so on: *My brother hopes to study engineering when he finishes school.*

English[1] /ˈɪŋglɪʃ/ [adjective] **1** Referring to England: *Cricket is an English game.* ■ Be careful! "English" has a capital "E". When referring to people, the singular is "an Englishman" or "an Englishwoman" and the plural is "the English"."English" does not refer to people from Wales, Scotland or Northern Ireland! **2 the English Channel** The channel between England and France: *Every year people attempt to swim across the English Channel and some succeed.* ■ Careful! "English Channel" has capital letters.

English[2] /ˈɪŋglɪʃ/ [uncountable noun] The language of the USA, Britain and many other countries: *Do you speak English?* ■ Careful! "English" has a capital "E". 👁 **See pages 454 and 455.**

†**enjoy** /ɪnˈdʒɔɪ/ [verb] **1** To feel happy doing something: *I really enjoy going for walks in the countryside.* ■ The verb immediately after "enjoy" is in the "-ing" form. **2 to enjoy oneself** To have a good time: *Betty enjoyed herself tremendously at the party.*

†**enjoyable** /ɪnˈdʒɔɪ.ə.bl̩/ [adjective] Very pleasant: *What an enjoyable day we had at the seaside!*

†**enjoyment** /ɪnˈdʒɔɪ.mənt/ [uncountable noun] Pleasure: *My father is a gardener and he gets a lot of enjoyment from his job.*

enlarge /ɪnˈlɑrdʒ/ [verb] To make something bigger: *Do they enlarge photographs in that store?*

†**enormous** /ɪˈnɔr·məs/ [adjective] Very big: *Some dinosaurs were enormous: some were 72 feet long and 20 feet tall!*

†**enough** /ɪˈnʌf/ [adjective and adverb] **1** Sufficient, as much as you need: *Have you got enough money?* ■ "Enough" usually goes before a noun ("He has enough money") or after an adjective ("I'm not old enough to go to discos"). **2** Sufficiently: *Put another sweater on if you are not warm enough.* **3 to have had enough** To be tired of somebody or something: *I've had enough of your bad behavior.*

enquire /ɪnˈkwaɪər/ [verb] See **inquire**. ■ This word is British English.

enrol /ɪnˈrəʊl/ [verb] See **enroll**. ■ This is a British English spelling.

enroll [verb] To enter your name on a list: *I'm going to enroll for a summer course in San Diego.* ■ Be careful with the spelling of these forms: "enrolled", "enrolling". ■ The British English spelling is "enrol".

†**ensure** /ɪnˈʃʊər/ [verb] To make sure: *Please ensure that you turn off the computer when you finish.*

†**enter** /ˈen·tər/ [verb] To go in or to come in: *Do not enter without permission.* ■ Be careful! We say: "enter a building". We don't say: "enter **in** a building". ■ "Enter" is a little formal. It is more usual to say "go in" or "come in".

enterprise /ˈen·tərˌprɑɪz/ ▮ [countable noun] **1** A difficult and interesting project: *The object of the enterprise was to reach the mountain peak without using oxygen.* ▮ [noun] **2** A business activity: *Private enterprise is the engine of the capitalist system.* ▮ [uncountable noun] **3** The ability, desire and energy to start new projects: *Enterprise is rewarded in this company.*

†**entertain** /ˌen·tərˈteɪn/ [verb] To give somebody a good time: *My grandpa entertained us with stories about his childhood.*

†**entertainer** /ˌen·tərˈteɪ·nər/ [countable noun] A person who entertains: *My cousin's got a summer job as a children's entertainer in a summer camp.*

†**entertaining** /ˌen·tərˈteɪ·nɪŋ/ [adjective] Interesting or amusing: *The movie was short but really entertaining.*

†**entertainment** /ˌen·tərˈteɪn·mənt/ [noun] Something that entertains people: *There's always a lot of entertainment in a big city.*

†**enthusiasm** /ɪnˈθu·ziˌæz·əm/ [uncountable noun] Great interest in doing something: *My brother didn't show much enthusiasm when I asked him for help with the computer.*

†**enthusiastic** /ɪnˌθu·ziˈæs·tɪk/ [adjective] Keen, very interested in something: *Patty is very enthusiastic about her new school.* ■ Be careful. We say: "to be enthusiastic **about** (something)".

†**entire** /ɪnˈtɑɪər/ [adjective] Complete: *The entire class went to the party together.*

†**entrance** /ˈen.trənts/ ▮ [countable noun] **1** The way into a place: *The entrance to the museum is round the corner.* ▮ [noun] **2** Going into a place: *The President and his wife made their entrance into the hall.* **3 entrance examination** An examination to enter a particular school or college: *The ACT in an entrance examination used by many American universities.*

†**entry** /ˈen.tri/ ▮ [uncountable noun] **1** The right to go into a place: *You can't go in there; it says "No Entry".* **2** The way into a place: *I'll meet you at the entry to the market.* ▮ [countable noun] **3** One item of written information in a dictionary, diary, accounts book and so on: *How many entries do you think this dictionary has?* ■ The plural is "entries".

†**envelope** US: /ˈɑːn.və.loʊp/ UK: /ˈen.və.ləʊp/ [countable noun] A paper covering for a letter: *Mary put the letter in the envelope and sent it off.*

a b c d e f g h i j k l m n o p q r s t u v w x y z

a b c d e f g h i j k l m n o p q r s t u v w x y z

envious /'en.vi.əs/ [adjective] Wishing you had something belonging to somebody else, feeling bad because of what they have: *I felt really envious when I saw Penny's new mountain bike.*

✦**environment** /ɪn'vaɪ·rən·mənt/, /-'vaɪ·ərn-/ [noun] **1** The world around us: *Not enough people realize how important it is to look after the environment.* **2** The conditions in which you live or work: *Sarah was brought up in a very comfortable environment.*

environmental /ɪn,vaɪ·rən'men·tə·l/, /-,vaɪ·ərn-/ [adjective] **1** Referring to nature and the environment: *The environmental impact of the proposed road will be assessed.* **2** Referring to a person's environment: *Brain development is influenced by environmental factors.*

envy[1] /'envi/ [uncountable noun] The feeling of wanting something belonging to somebody else: *She was filled with envy when she saw Anne's new bracelet.*

envy[2] /'envi/ [verb] To wish you had something that somebody else has: *I envy her so much; she seems to have everything she wants!* ■ Be careful with the spelling of these forms: "envies", "envied".

epicenter /'ep·ɪ,sent·ər/ [countable noun] The place on the earth's surface directly above the focus of an earthquake: *The epicenter had its epicenter several miles from the coast.*

epidemic /,ep.ɪ'dem.ɪk/ [countable noun] An infectious disease affecting many people at the same time: *There was an epidemic of cholera in India last year.*

epidermis /,ep·ɪ'dɜr·məs/ [uncountable noun] The outer layer of the skin: *The epidermis is sensitive to the sun's rays.*

episode /'ep·ə,soʊd/ [countable noun] One part of a story on television, in a newspaper and so on: *I want to watch the last episode of Jane Eyre on the television tonight.*

equal[1] /'iːkwəl/ [verb] **1** To be exactly the same: *Two and two equals four.* **2** To be as good as: *Nobody can equal Julian as a pianist; he's absolutely marvelous!* ■ Be careful with the spelling of these forms: "equalled", "equalling".

✦**equal**[2] /'iːkwəl/ [adjective] The same in size, number or value: *All people are equal and we should treat them all in the same way.*

equality /ɪ'kwɑl·ə·t̬i/ [uncountable noun] The same rights: *Martin Luther King fought for equality between black and white people.* ■ The plural is "equalities".

equator /ɪ'kweɪ·t̬ər/ [noun] An imaginary line round the earth: *It is very hot in the countries that are nearest the equator.* 👁 **See page 449.**

equip /ɪ'kwɪp/ [verb] To give a person the necessary things for something: *Before you go mountaineering you have to equip yourself properly.* ■ Be careful with the spelling of these forms: "equipped", "equipping".

✦**equipment** /ɪ'kwɪp.mənt/ [uncountable noun] The things that you need for doing something: *The equipment that you need for deep sea diving is very expensive.*

✦**equivalent** /ɪ'kwɪv.ᵊl.ᵊnt/ [noun and adjective] Having the same value: *One mile is equivalent to 1,609 meters.*

era US: /'ɪr.ə/ UK: /'ɪə.rə/ [countable noun] A distinct period of time: *This piece of furniture is from the Victorian era.*

eradicate /ɪ'ræd.ɪ.keɪt/ [verb] To completely destroy or eliminate: *The plague has been eradicated.*

erase /ɪ'reɪs/ [verb] To remove writing, sounds or images: *It is very easy to erase and edit texts on this computer.*

✦**eraser** [noun] A small object used to remove something written in pencil: *Can I borrow your eraser for a minute, please?* 👁 **See page 456.**

erect[1] /ɪ'rekt/ [adjective] Standing straight: *Try to sit with your back straight and your head erect.*

erect[2] /ɪ'rekt/ [verb] To build: *They erected a sports center just outside the town.* ■ We usually say "build" or "construct".

Erlenmeyer flask [countable noun] A glass container used in laboratories, which has a conical body and a narrow cylindrical neck: *The Erlenmeyer flask was named after a German chemist.* 👁 **See page 440.**

ermine /'ɜː.mɪn/ US: /'ɝː-/ [uncountable noun] The fur of the stoat in winter that is white with dark spots: *Members of the House of Lords wear ermine robes on ceremonial occasions.* ■ Compare with "stoat" (small animal with brown fur that turns mainly white in winter).

erode /ɪ'roʊd/ [verb] To wear away very gradually: *The waves erode the coast over the years.*

erosion /ɪ'rəʊʒən/ [uncountable noun] **1** The process of wearing away: *Soil erosion is a major problem in countries where deforestation has occurred.* **2** The gradual reduction or destruction: *The political crisis has led to an erosion of the President's authority.*

✦**error** /'er·ər/ [noun] A mistake: *There's been an error of calculation here and we've paid too much.*

erupt /ɪ'rʌpt/ [verb] To explode: *When the volcano Vesuvius erupted in Roman times, the town of Pompeii was buried in ash.*

eruption /ɪ'rʌp.ʃᵊn/ [noun] An explosion of a volcano: *The city of Pompeii was buried in the eruption of Mt Vesuvius.*

escalator /'es·kə,leɪ·t̬ər/ [countable noun] Moving stairs: *Most airports have escalators so that people don't have to carry their luggage up stairs.*

✦**escape**[1] /ɪ'skeɪp/ [noun] Getting free from some people or something: *"The Great Escape" is a movie about prisoners who organize a big escape from a prisoner of war camp.*

escape[2] /ɪ'skeɪp/ [verb] To get free from some people or something: *The prisoners escaped by climbing over the wall in the middle of the night.*

escort /ɪ'skɔːt/ [verb] To accompany somebody: *The bodyguards escorted the President to his car.*

Eskimo /'es·kəˌmoʊ/ [countable noun] See **Inuit**. ■ Be careful! The word "Eskimo" is now considered insulting by many because it means "raw meat eater". It is better to say "Inuit".

esophagus /ɪ'sɒf.ə.gəs/ US: /ɪ'sɑː.fə-/ /ɪ'sɑf·ə·gəs/ [countable noun] The part of the alimentary canal which goes from the mouth to the stomach: *The esophagus is a muscular tube.* See page 424.

especially /ɪ'speʃ.əl.i/ [adverb] **1** In particular: *I love going on vacation, especially to the beach.* **2** Very much: *Traveling by boat is especially enjoyable.* **3** For a particular purpose: *Pat has brought a present especially for me because it's my birthday.* ■ In this use it is also written "specially".

†**essay** /'es.eɪ/ [countable noun] A piece of writing: *Yesterday at school we had to write two essays.*

†**essential** /ɪ'sen.tʃəl/ [adjective] Very important, vital: *It is essential that you read all the instructions before doing this exercise.*

†**establish** /ɪ'stæb.lɪʃ/ [verb] To start something: *The chocolate factory here was established in 1892.*

establishment /ɪ'stæb.lɪʃ.mənt/ [uncountable noun] **1** The act of establishing: *The establishment of the new bus service has been a success.* **2 the establishment** The important and powerful people in society, seen as a group that is resistant to change: *The newspapers there are on the side of the establishment.*

†**estate** /ɪ'steɪt/ [countable noun] **1** A large piece of land, usually in the country: *The Duke has a large stable on his estate in Yorkshire.* **2 estate agent** See **realtor**. ■ This use is British English.

estimate[1] /'estɪmət/ [countable noun] **1** A calculation of something: *According to our teacher's estimate, only 50% of us will pass the test.* **2** A calculation of the cost of something: *My parents asked the builders for an estimate before deciding.*

†**estimate**[2] /'estɪmeɪt/ [verb] To give an opinion on the number of something: *It is estimated that 500 people attended the actor's wedding.*

et al. Used to refer the list of names of people who have written something together: *The book is written by Davidson et al.* ■ "et al." is an abbreviation for "et alia", a Latin expression that means "and other people". ■ See box at **abbreviations**.

etc. /et'setərə/ And so on: *When I started at my new school, my parents had to buy me the uniform, a new sports gear, etc.* ■ "etc." is an abbreviation for "et cetera", a Latin expression that means "and other things". ■ See box at **abbreviations**.

eternal /ɪ'tɜr·nə·l/, /i-/ [adjective] Never ending: *The movie went on for so long that it seemed eternal.*

ethnic /'eθ.nɪk/ [adjective] Of a particular race or country: *Many different ethnic groups live in New York.*

EU Used to refer to the countries that belong to the European Union: *the EU countries.* ■ "EU" is an abbreviation for "European Union". ■ See box at **abbreviations**.

eucalyptus or **eucalyptus tree** /ˌjuː.kəl'ɪp.təs,triː/ [noun] A tall evergreen tree native to Australia: *The*

a b c d e f g h i j k l m n o p q r s t u v w x y z

a b c d e f g h i j k l m n o p q r s t u v w x y z

koala feeds on the leaves of the eucalyptus tree. ■ The plural is "eucalyptus" or "eucalyptuses".

euro /ˈjʊərəʊ/ [countable noun] The official unit of money used in most countries of the European Union: *Britain is one of the European countries that don't use the euro.*

European[1] [countable noun] A person from Europe: *People from Greece, Norway, Poland or Spain are all Europeans.* ■ Be careful. "European" has a capital "E".

European[2] /ˌjʊərəˈpiːən/ [adjective] Referring to one or more of the countries of Europe: *Several countries wish to join the European Union.* ■ Careful! "European" has a capital "E".

euthanasia /ˌjuːθəˈneɪ.ʒə/ [uncountable noun] The painless killing of somebody with a disease that has no cure, to end suffering: *Euthanasia is illegal in most countries.*

evacuate /ɪˈvæk.ju.eɪt/ [verb] To take people away from a place or area: *The authorities evacuated the area because of the floods.*

evaluate [verb] To estimate the value, quality or importance of something: *They must evaluate the benefits of the project.*

evaporate /ɪˈvæp·əˌreɪt/ [verb] To change or to turn liquid into gas or steam: *When water is heated it evaporates into steam.* **See page 438.**

evaporation /ɪˌvæpəˈreɪʃən/ [uncountable noun] **1** The transformation of a liquid into vapor: *Evaporation takes place, for example, when you boil water.* **See page 438.** **2** The loss or disappearance of something: *There was a 70% evaporation of their voters overnight.*

eve /iːv/ [noun] The day before a particular day: *Christmas Eve is on 24th December, the day before Christmas Day.*

even[1] /ˈiːvən/ [adjective] **1** Flat and smooth: *You'll have to put something under one table leg because the floor is not even.* **2** Equal: *Last year our school won the game but this year their team did, so now we're even!* **3 even number** A number that can be exactly divided by two: *2, 4, 6, 8 are all examples of even numbers.* ■ Compare with "odd number" (a number that can't be divided by two).

⁺**even[2]** /ˈiːvən adverb/ [adverb] **1** Surprisingly: *Grandfather was feeling much better today; he even wanted to play a game of cards.* **2** A word that gives more importance to the following word or expression: *I didn't like her last movie but this one is even worse!* **3 even if** Nothing changes if: *Even if you leave immediately you won't arrive in time for the beginning of the movie.* **4 even though** Although: *Even though he says he can't dance, I'm sure he can.*

⁺**evening** /ˈiːv.nɪŋ/ [noun] **1** The part of the day between the afternoon and the night, more or less between six o'clock and midnight: *I'll see you tomorrow evening at about 6.30.* ■ Be careful. We say: "**in** the evening". **2 good evening** A greeting that is used in the evening: *Good evening, Martha. I'm sorry I'm late.* ■ Compare "good evening" with "good night" (an expression that you use before going to bed).

evenly /ˈiː.vᵊn.li/ [adverb] Equally: *Divide those candies evenly between you, please.*

⁺**event** /ɪˈvent/ [countable noun] **1** Something that happens: *The most important event in our family last year was the birth of my baby brother.* **2** A race or a competition: *The next event is the five miles running.*

eventual /ɪˈven.tju.ᵊl/ [adjective] Final, happening at last: *The eventual failure of the business was no surprise to anybody, what was surprising was that it had survived so long.*

eventually /ɪˈven.tju.ᵊl.i/ [adverb] After a time: *After walking for hours we eventually found the store.*

⁺**ever** /ˈev·ər/ [adverb] **1** At any time: *Have you ever been to Argentina?* **2 ever since** During all the time since something happened: *Karen and I have been friends ever since we were at school together.* **3 for ever** For always: *I'll love you for ever!* ■ Be careful! We use "ever" with a negative verb.

evergreen /ˈevəgriːn/ [adjective] **1** Having green leaves all through the year: *Pine trees are evergreen.* ■ Compare with "deciduous" (losing its leaves every year). **2 evergreen tree** A tree that has leaves throughout the year: *The jack pine is an evergreen tree.* **See page 434.**

⁺**every** /ˈev.ri/ [adjective] **1** All the things or people in a group: *I go to see my aunt every day.* ■ When we want to say "todos", we use "every" with a singular noun: "I speak to her every day". **2** Used to say how often something happens: *The medicine has to be taken every two hours.* ■ See box on the following page.

everybody /ˈev·riˌbɒd·i/, /-ˌbʌd·i/ [pronoun] Every person, all the people: *Is everybody ready? Then we will begin.* ■ Be careful! We use "everybody" with singular verbs. ■ The same meaning: "everyone". ■ See box at **anybody**. ■ For the difference in use with the word "all", see box at **every**.

everyday /ˈev.ri.deɪ/ [adjective] Ordinary: *My dad gave me a good book about everyday life in Rome.* ■ Be careful. Don't confuse this word with "every day".

everyone /ˈev.ri.wʌn/ [pronoun] **1** Every person, all the people: *Give my greetings to everyone at school.* **2 everyone else** All the other people: *Everyone else but me has gone to the party.* ■ Be careful! We use "everyone" with singular verbs. ■ The same meaning: "everybody". ■ See box at **anybody**.

■ For the difference in use with the word "all", see box at **every**.

⁺**everything** /'ev.ri.θɪŋ/ [pronoun] All things: *Let's put everything away so that we have room to play table tennis.* ■ Be careful. We use "everything" with singular verbs. ■ See box at **every**.

⁺**everywhere** /'ev·ri,hwer/, /-,wer/ [adverb] In all places: *I've looked everywhere but I can't find my watch.* ■ Be careful. We use "everywhere" with singular verbs.

⁺**evidence** /'ev.ɪ.dənts/ [uncountable noun] A proof of what happened: *There was no evidence of the thieves' entry into the house.*

evident /'ev.ɪ.dənt/ [adjective] Clear and easy to understand: *It is quite evident that you have studied a lot.*

⁺**evil** /'iː.vəl/ [adjective] Very bad, harmful: *In the movie, the witch has an evil influence over the king.*

evolution /,iː.və'luː.ʃən, ,ev.ə-/ [uncountable noun] **1** The way living things change and develop over a very long time period: *Evolution is responsible for mankind having progressed to its present stage of development.* **2** A process of change and gradual development: *Astronomers are trying to understand the evolution of the sun.*

⁺**exact** /ɪg'zækt/ [adjective] Totally correct, precise: *Can you tell me the exact time, please?*

exactly /ɪg'zæktli/ [adverb] **1** Precisely: *What exactly did he say?* **2** Expression used to emphasize or agree with what has been said: *"Did you say that you were going on vacation to California?" "Exactly".*

⁺**exaggerate** /ɪg'zædʒ·ə,reɪt/ [verb] To make something seem bigger, better or worse than it is: *Don't exaggerate; there were only 30 or 40 people at the party, not hundreds!*

⁺**exam** /ɪg'zæm/ [countable noun] A written, spoken or practical test: *You may now look at your exam papers.* ■ We can also say "examination".

⁺**examination** /ɪg,zæm.ɪ'neɪ.ʃən/ [countable noun] **1** See **exam.** **2** A careful look at somebody or something: *My mother had to have a medical examination because she didn't feel well.*

⁺**examine** /ɪg'zæm.ɪn/ [verb] **1** To look carefully at something: *The policeman examined my bag to see if I had any stolen goods.* **2** To give somebody an exam: *The teacher examined the children on the last five chapters of their book.*

⁺**example** /ɪg'zæm·pəl/ [countable noun] **1** Something that is typical of the group of which it forms a part: *Katie's composition is a good example of how to write well.* **2** A person to be copied: *Janet's kindness is an example to us all.* **3 for example** Words that you use to introduce an example of something: *There are many very interesting places to visit in New York City: for example, the Statue of Liberty, the Empire State Building and Ellis Island.* ■ The

every, all

- ***all, everyone / everybody, everything***

  We do not normally use *all* to mean *everyone / everybody* or *everything*:
  - We say: *Everyone enjoyed the day at the seaside.* (We don't say: *All enjoyed the day.*)
  - We say: *They explained everything to us.* (We don't say: *They explained all to us.*)

  All can be used with *about*:
  - *They told us **all about** their experience.*

- ***all, every*** with time words:

  When we use *all* with time words, it means "the complete ___":
  - *all year* (the complete year)
  - *all morning* (the complete morning)

  When we use *every* with time words, we are saying how often something happens:
  - *every year* (each year)
  - *every morning* (each morning)

  Examples:
  - ***Every year** we go to the beach for our vacation.*
  - *Last year I was lazy, but this year I have worked hard **all year**.*

to take an exam

to pass an exam

to fail an exam

a b c d e f g h i j k l m n o p q r s t u v w x y z

abbreviation "e.g." is only used in written language. See box at **abbreviations**.

excavate /'ek.skə.veɪt/ [verb] **1** To dig a hole in the ground: *The builders need to excavate the site before laying the foundations.* **2** To remove soil to look for archaeological remains: *When the archeologists excavated that area they found the remains of a Roman house.*

excavation /ˌekskə'veɪʃən/ [noun] **1** The act of excavating: *Once the excavation was complete, the foundations were laid.* **2** The act of removing earth to look for archeological remains: *Many interesting objects were found in the excavation.*

exceed /ɪk'siːd/ [verb] To do more than what is allowed or necessary: *Drivers should not exceed the speed limit.*

+**excellent** /'ek.sᵊl.ᵊnt/ [adjective] Very good: *That was an excellent meal!*

+**except** /ɪk'sept/ [preposition] Apart from: *All the boys went on the excursion except Bill, who was ill.*

+**exception** /ɪk'sep.ʃᵊn/ [noun] Somebody or something that is not included or that is different: *With the exception of Emily, we all had a good time.*

exceptional /ɪk'sep.ʃᵊn.ᵊl/ [adjective] **1** Extremely good: *All the students' results were good, but Rose's were exceptional.* **2** Not usual: *The weather is exceptional for this time of year.*

excess /ɪk'ses/ [adjective] More than usual: *You have to pay $20 per kilo for excess baggage.*

+**exchange** /ɪks'tʃeɪndʒ/ [verb] To change one thing for another: *We exchanged addresses after the vacation.*

+**excite** /ɪk'saɪt/ [verb] To make somebody have strong feelings: *Movies sometimes excite children so much that they can't sleep.*

+**excited** /ɪk'saɪ·t̬ɪd/ [adjective] **1** Feeling very happy about something that is going to happen, not calm: *I'm so excited about seeing my cousin again!* **2** Feeling strongly, nervous and agitated: *You don't have to get so excited! I was only joking!* ■ Be careful with the pronunciation of this word. The last "e" is pronounced like the "i" in "did". ■ See box at **bored**.

+**excitement** /ɪk'saɪt.mənt/ [noun] State of being excited: *There was enormous excitement in the house as the great day approached.*

+**exciting** /ɪk'saɪ·t̬ɪŋ/ [adjective] Making you feel excited: *"Star wars" is a very exciting movie.* ■ See box at **bored**.

exclaim /ɪk'skleɪm/ [verb] To say something suddenly: *"Wow!" exclaimed Bob.*

exclamation /ˌek.sklə'meɪ.ʃᵊn/ [countable noun] **1** A sound, word or phrase that expresses surprise, anger or other emotion: *I heard her exclamation in the next room: "Johnny! What are you doing here?".* **2** **exclamation mark** A mark in writing to indicate an exclamation [!]: *You should have put an exclamation mark at the end of that sentence.*

+**exclude** /ɪk'skluːd/ [verb] To prevent entry, not to include: *Those horrible children always exclude Oliver from their games.*

+**excluding** /ɪk'skluː.dɪŋ/ [preposition] Without, not including: *There were forty-five people on the plane, excluding the crew.*

excrement /'ekskrəmənt/ [uncountable noun] Waste matter which is eliminated through the anus: *There was dogs' excrement on the sidewalk.* ■ The same meaning: "feces".

excretion /ɪk'skriːʃən/ [noun] A waste substance expelled by an organism as a result of the metabolic process: *Sweat is an excretion.*

excretory [adjective] Referring to the process of excretion: *The elimination by plants of carbon dioxide is an excretory process.* 👁 **See page 424.**

excretory system [countable noun] The system which carries and expels waste matter: *The excretory system filters waste substances.* 👁 **See page 424.**

excursion /ɪk'skɜr·ʒən/ [countable noun] A short journey for fun: *We went on a fantastic excursion to Boston.*

+**excuse**[1] /ɪk'skjuːz/ [countable noun] An explanation for your behavior: *You've missed the game again. What's your excuse this time?*

excuse[2] /ɪk'skjuːz/ [verb] **1** To forgive somebody: *Please excuse me for being so rude to you yesterday!* **2** To give permission to somebody to miss something: *Can I be excused from the swimming class today? I'm not feeling well.* **3** **excuse me** Words that you use if you interrupt somebody: *Excuse me! May I come through here, please?* ■ We normally say "excuse me" before we disturb or interrupt somebody. Compare with "sorry" (used for apologizing) and "pardon[1]" (used when somebody has not heard something).

execute /'ek.sɪ.kjuːt/ [verb] To kill a person as a punishment: *Many people were executed during the Civil War in United States.*

executive[1] /ɪɡ'zek·jə·t̬ɪv/ [countable noun] **1** Somebody with management responsibility in a business or organization: *An executive has to take decisions.* **2** **the executive** The part of government responsible for putting into operation laws and decisions: *The executive has prepared a summary of the new regulations.*

executive[2] /ɪɡ'zek·jə·t̬ɪv/ [adjective] **1** Referring to the function of putting into operation plans, decisions and laws: *The tax office is an executive body responsible for the collection of taxes.* **2** Related to, or designed for, a person with a managerial or professional job: *This is an executive leather briefcase.*

+**exercise**[1] /'ek·sər,saɪz/ [noun] **1** Physical activity: *Swimming is very good exercise.* **2** A movement that you do to keep well: *My grandfather has to do exercises every day for his back.* **3** Something that you do for practice: *We did exercises three and four in class.*

exercise[2] /'ek·sər,saɪz/ [verb] To make your body work hard: *The doctor told my dad to exercise more.*

exert /ɪg'zɜːt/ [verb] **1** To use or apply a quality, skill or pressure: *He exerted all his skills of persuasion to make them accept his application.* **2 to exert oneself** To make a big or constant effort: *You will have to exert yourself if you want to achieve your goals.*

exhalation /,eks.hə'leɪ.ʃən/ [noun] The act of breathing out: *With each exhalation, stretch a little more.* ■ Compare with "inhalation" (the act of breathing in).

exhale /eks'heɪl/ [verb] To expel air through the nose or mouth: *Exhale slowly and relax.* ■ Compare with "inhale" (to breath in).

exhaust /ɪg'zɔst/ [verb] To make somebody very tired: *The long journey exhausted the children.*

+**exhibit** /ɪg'zɪb.ɪt/ [verb] To show something to the public: *The painter exhibited his work in a small gallery in the town.*

+**exhibition** /,ek.sɪ'bɪʃ.ᵊn/ [noun] A public display: *There's a great exhibition of steam engines at the Railway Museum this month.*

exile /'ek.saɪl, 'eg.zaɪl/ ▮ [uncountable noun] **1** Having to live away from your country: *Trotsky was a leader of the Russian Revolution, but he later lived in exile in Mexico.* ▮ [countable noun] **2** A person who has to live away from his or her country: *There are thousands of political exiles living in the United States.*

+**exist** /ɪg'zɪst/ [verb] To be: *Some people believe that life exists on other planets.*

+**existence** /ɪg'zɪs.tᵊnts/ [uncountable noun] Being: *Do you believe in the existence of God?*

existing /ɪg'zɪs.tɪŋ/ [adjective] Present at the moment: *There are plans to build a new disco because the existing disco is very small.*

+**exit** /'eksɪt/ [countable noun] The way out: *The emergency exit is down there on the left.*

exotic /ɪg'zɑt̬·ɪk/ [adjective] Strange and interesting: *These beautiful exotic flowers come from Peru.*

+**expand** /ɪk'spænd/ [verb] To become bigger: *Water expands into ice when it is frozen.*

expansion /ɪk'spæn.tʃᵊn/ [noun] Growth: *The company opened a new factory because of the expansion of its business.*

+**expect** /ɪk'spekt/ [verb] **1** To believe that something will happen: *I expect they'll arrive at about 5 o'clock this afternoon.* ■ We use "expect" when we have reasons to think that something will happen: "I expect I'll work in my father's store when I'm older". Compare with "hope[2]" (to want something to happen). **2** To be pregnant: *My wife is expecting twins!* **3 I expect so** Words that you say when you think that something will happen: *"Do you think you'll pass the test?" "I expect so!".*

expectancy /ɪk'spektənsi/ [uncountable noun] **1** The state of expecting or hoping: *The children looked at their aunt with an air of expectancy, because she normally brought presents.* **2** Something expected, as a result of the usual or average case: *Life expectancy in this country is now eighty years.*

expedition /,ek.spə'dɪʃ.ᵊn/ [countable noun] **1** A long and difficult journey: *Captain Scott led his first expedition to Antarctica in 1901.* **2 shopping expedition** Going somewhere specifically to do shopping: *I went on a shopping expedition with my cousin to buy clothes.*

expel /ɪk'spel/ [verb] To throw somebody out of a school or club: *The principal expelled the students for smoking.*

+**expense** /ɪk'spents/ [uncountable noun] The cost of something: *Vacation in Mexico? Now that would be a big expense!*

+**expensive** /ɪk'spent.sɪv/ [adjective] Costing a lot of money: *That coat is very expensive. Why don't you buy a cheaper one?* See picture at **opposite**.

+**experience** /ɪk'spɪər·i·əns/ ▮ [countable noun] **1** Something that happens to a person: *That car accident was a terrible experience.* ▮ [uncountable noun] **2** Practice in doing something and the skill or knowledge acquired from doing it: *Have you had much skiing experience?* ■ In this use "experience" is an uncountable noun.

experienced /ɪk'spɪər·i·ənst/ [adjective] Having experience at something: *My mother's a very experienced teacher.* ■ Be careful with the pronunciation of the end of this word. The last "e" is not pronounced.

+**experiment**[1] /ɪk'sperɪmənt/ [noun] A test, usually scientific, to find out about something: *Experiments with new drugs are often done on animals before they are used with people.*

experiment[2] /ɪk'sperɪment/ [verb] To do experiments with something: *At the moment they are experimenting with a completely new type of car.*

experimentation /ɪk,sperɪmen'teɪʃən/ [uncountable noun] The process of doing experiments or trying different things: *Experimentation is an essential part of research and development.*

*__expert__ /'ek·spɜrt/, /ɪk'spɜrt/ [noun and adjective] **1** A person who knows a lot about something: *He is an expert on reggae music.* **2** A person who is good at doing something: *I'm an expert at solving problems on the computer.*

*__explain__ /ɪk'spleɪn/ [verb] To make something clear: *Can you explain this math problem to me?* ■ Be careful! We say: "explain (something) **to** somebody": "explain it to me" (not "explain it me".).

*__explanation__ /ˌek.splə'neɪ.ʃᵊn/ [noun] **1** Making something clear: *After listening to her explanation, I understand the law of gravity very well.* **2** A reason for something: *Tammy didn't give an explanation for being late.*

*__explode__ /ɪk'sploʊd/ [verb] To burst with a loud noise and lots of force: *The bomb exploded, killing seven people.*

exploration /ˌekspləˈreɪʃən/ [noun] **1** The act of traveling to somewhere new, of discovering: *Exploration of the Antarctic continues.* **2** The act of examining something thoroughly in order to see how it is, especially in medicine: *They are carrying out a full exploration to discover what is causing the problem.*

*__explore__ /ɪk'splɔr/, /-'sploʊr/ [verb] **1** To travel around an unknown place in order to learn about it: *Livingstone explored large areas of Africa in the 19th century.* **2** To analyze or discuss something in detail in order to learn more about it: *The consequences of atmospheric pollution are still being explored.* **3** To touch something thoroughly in order to examine it: *The doctor explored the affected area.*

explorer /ɪk'splɔr·ər/, /-'sploʊr-/ [countable noun] A person who explores: *The great explorers often brought back unknown plants and animals that they found on their travels.*

*__explosion__ /ɪk'sploʊ·ʒən/ [noun] The act of exploding: *The explosion we heard was caused by a gas leak in the Washington Street.*

explosive /ɪk'sploʊ·sɪv/ [adjective] Capable of exploding or blowing up: *It's dangerous to smoke near explosive material.*

export[1] /'ekspɔːt/ [noun] Something that is sold and sent to another country: *Argentina's exports include beef and wine.*

*__export__[2] /ɪk'spɔːt/ [verb] To sell and send things to other countries: *Japan exports thousands of cars every year.*

exporter /ek'spɔr·t̬ər/, /-'spoʊr-/ [countable noun] A person or a company that exports things: *Mr. Mann is a cotton exporter.*

*__express__[1] /ɪk'spres/ [adjective] Fast: *Some highways have an express lane for vehicles with two or more occupants.*

express[2] /ɪk'spres/ [verb] To show what you think or feel: *She is very good at expressing her ideas.* ■ Be careful with the spelling of the 3rd person singular present tense form: "expresses".

*__expression__ /ɪk'spreʃ.ᵊn/ [countable noun] **1** A look on somebody's face: *Hilda had a rather sad expression when we met her.* **2** A phrase that has a particular meaning: *"To be broke" is an expression that means "not to have any money".*

expressive /ɪk'spres.ɪv/ [adjective] **1** Full of expression, communicating a lot: *He gave his girlfriend an expressive look which said more than a thousand words.* **2 to be expressive of something** To show a particular feeling: *Her words are expressive of great sincerity.* ■ This use is formal.

expulsion /ɪk'spʌl.ʃᵊn/ [noun] **1** The act of forcing somebody to leave a place: *The teacher threatened the students with expulsion from class when they refused to listen to him.* **2** The act of expelling something from the body: *The expulsion of the feces takes place through the anus.* **3 expulsion order** Arrangement made by an official institution for an illegal citizen to leave the country: *Mohammed was given an expulsion order by the Courts.*

*__extend__ /ɪk'stend/ [verb] **1** To make something longer or bigger: *We extended our visit to two weeks.* **2** To go on or to continue: *My uncle's land extends as far as the eye can see.*

*__extension__ /ɪk'sten.tʃᵊn/ ▮ [noun] **1** A continuation of something: *My parents built an extension onto their house to make a big kitchen.* ▮ [countable noun] **2** A telephone line: *Can you put me through to extension 2289, please?* ■ In this use, "x" is a written abbreviation for "extension".

*__extensive__ /ɪk'stent.sɪv/ [adjective] Large: *Our science teacher also has an extensive knowledge of music.*

*__extent__ /ɪk'stent/ [uncountable noun] **1** The size or degree of something: *What was the extent of the damage?* **2 to what extent** How much: *To what extent are you willing to put up with Harry's behavior?*

*__exterior__ /ek'stɪər·i·ər/ [countable noun] The outside of something: *The exterior of the house had to be repaired.*

external /ek'stɜr·nə·l/ [adjective] Referring to the outside of something: *This cream is for external use only.*

extinct /ɪk'stɪŋkt/ [adjective] Not existing anywhere any more: *Every year many species of wildlife become extinct.*

extinction /ɪk'stɪŋk.ʃᵊn/ [uncountable noun] The act of making extinct: *Extinction was the fate of the dinosaurs.*

extinguish /ɪk'stɪŋ.gwɪʃ/ [verb] To put out a fire: *The firefighters managed to extinguish the forest fire after a few days.*

extinguisher /stɪŋ·gwɪ·ʃər/ [countable noun] See **fire extinguisher**.

†**extra** /'ek.strə/ [adjective] More than normal: *This bicycle will cost you an extra ten dollars.*

extracurricular /ˌek·strə·kə'rɪk·jə·lər/ [adjective] An activity which is not included in a school or college course: *Playing an instrument is an extracurricular activity.*

†**extraordinary** /ɪk'strɔr·də·nˌer·i/ [adjective] Very strange or unusual, special: *We are having extraordinary weather this year.*

extravagant /ɪk'stræv.ə.gᵊnt/ [adjective] **1** Spending or costing too much: *He is very extravagant and he owes a lot of money.* **2** Not controlled or wild: *She's very extravagant in the way she dresses.*

†**extreme** /ɪk'striːm/ [adjective] **1** Very great: *She's under extreme pressure at work at the moment.* **2** Furthest away, at the very end or beginning: *They live in the extreme tip of South America.*

extrovert /'ek.strə.vɜːt/ US: /-vɝːt/ [noun and adjective] A person who is open and sociable in character: *Lenny is very extrovert; he finds it very easy to make friends.*

†**eye** /aɪ/ [countable noun] **1** What you see with: *My cat has beautiful green eyes.* 👁 See picture at **face**. **2 to keep an eye on** To look after, to watch: *Will you keep an eye on the house while we're on vacation?*

EYE

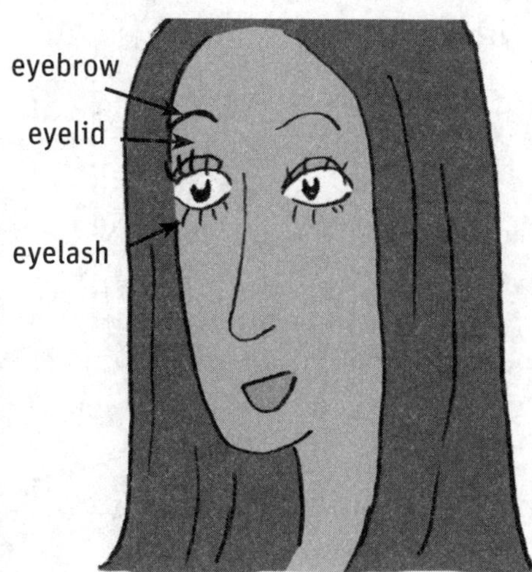

eyeball /'aɪbɔːl/ [countable noun] **1** The round structure of the eye, that can be covered by the eyelids: *The eyeball has three parts: the iris, the pupil and the retina.* **2 eyeball to eyeball** Face to face: *They had an eyeball to eyeball debate.*

eyebrow /'aɪ.braʊ/ [countable noun] The row of hairs above your eye: *He has very thick eyebrows.* 👁 See pictures at **eye** and **face**.

eyelash /'aɪ.læʃ/ [countable noun] One of the hairs that grow on your eyelids: *She has beautiful long eyelashes.* 👁 See picture at **eye**.

eyelid /'aɪ.lɪd/ [countable noun] The skin that protects the eye: *My eyelids are very sore because I didn't sleep very well last night.* 👁 See picture at **eye**.

eyesight /'aɪ.saɪt/ [uncountable noun] The ability to see: *I have very bad eyesight and I have to wear very thick glasses.*

f /ef/ The sixth letter of the alphabet: *The name "Frank" begins with an "F".*

F[1] /ef/ A written abbreviation for **Fahrenheit**.

F[2] /ef/ [countable noun] The fourth musical note of the scale of C major: *Play an F on the guitar, please.* ■ The plural is "Fs" or "F's". **See page 460.**

fable /ˈfeɪ.bl̩/ [noun] A story that teaches a lesson: *"The tortoise and the hare" is a well-known fable.* ■ Be careful with the pronunciation of this word. It is pronounced like "table".

fabric /ˈfæb.rɪk/ [noun] Material: *Silk and woolen fabrics are soft to the touch.*

fabulous /ˈfæb.jʊ.ləs/ [adjective] Wonderful: *We had a fabulous time at John's party.*

face[1] /feɪs/ [countable noun] **1** The part of the body that includes your eyes, nose and mouth: *He had a scar on his face, near his mouth.* **2 to make faces** To make strange gestures with your eyes, mouth and so on: *When the baby tasted the food, it began to make faces.*

FACE

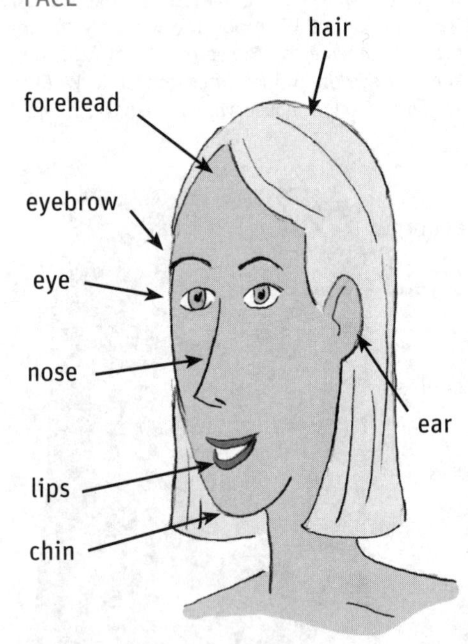

face[2] /feɪs/ [verb] To look towards, to have the front in the direction of: *Our house faces the market.*

facial[1] /ˈfeɪ.ʃəl/ [countable noun] Treatment of the face given by a beautician: *The lady was given a facial.*

facial[2] /ˈfeɪ.ʃəl/ [adjective] Referring to the face: *His facial expression did not change when he heard the news.*

facilities [plural noun] Places and equipment for people to use: *The sports facilities in George's school are excellent.*

†**facility** /fəˈsɪl·ɪ·t̬i/ [noun] Ease: *He has a great facility for learning languages.* ■ The plural is "facilities".

†**fact** /fækt/ [noun] **1** Something that is true: *It is a fact that the sun rises in the east and sets in the west.* **2 in fact** Actually or really: *I thought Peter was fifteen, but in fact he's only thirteen.*

factor /ˈfæk·tər/ [countable noun] **1** Something which contributes to a result: *Many factors are responsible for her success.* **2** Any number, except 1, by which a larger number can be divided: *2, 4 and 8 are factors of 16.*

†**factory** /ˈfæk·tə·ri/, /ˈfæk·tri/ [countable noun] A place where things are manufactured: *Liz's father works in a car factory.* ■ The plural is "factories".

fade /feɪd/ [verb] **1** To lose color: *Don't wash that blouse in hot water or it will fade.* **2** To disappear gradually: *The sound of the music from the band faded as the train moved slowly out of the station.*

Fahrenheit /ˈfær.ᵊn.haɪt/ [uncountable noun] A scale for measuring temperature: *On the Fahrenheit scale water boils at 212 ºF and freezes at 32 ºF.* ■ Be careful. "Fahrenheit" has a capital "F". ■ With figures we normally write the sign "ºF" instead of writing "Fahrenheit". ■ Compare with "centigrade" and with "Celsius": water boils at 100 ºC and freezes at 0 ºC. ■ See box at **abbreviations**.

†**fail** /feɪl/ [verb] **1** Not to manage to do something: *He tried hard but he failed to get tickets for the basketball game.* ■ Be careful. We say: "fail **to** do (something)". **2** Not to pass a test: *Sonia didn't have time to study and failed her math test.* 👁 See picture at **exam**.

†**failure** /ˈfeɪl·jər/ [noun] Not being successful: *His attempt to become a pop star was a total failure.*

faint[1] /feɪnt/ [adjective] Difficult to see or to hear because it is not strong or clear: *We could hear a faint noise coming from the attic, but we didn't know what it was.*

faint[2] /feɪnt/ [verb] To lose consciousness: *Alf felt so weak that he fainted.*

†**fair**[1] /feər/ [countable noun] A place in the open air with entertainments and stalls: *Every year in May there is a fair in my town.*

fair[2] /feər/ [adjective] **1** Just, reasonable: *Mr. Wells is very fair with his grades.* **2** Light yellow: *Amanda has fair hair and blue eyes.*

fairly /ˈfeər·li/ [adverb] Quite but not very: *Susan is fairly tall, about 1.75m.* ■ See box.

fairy US: /ˈfer.i/ UK: /ˈfeə.ri/ [countable noun] **1** A small supernatural being who does magic: *Fairies are usually very small and have wings.* ■ The plural is "fairies". **2 fairy tale** See "fairy tale" in the word **tale**. ■ The plural is "fairies".

†**faith** /feɪθ/ [uncountable noun] **1** The feeling that you can trust somebody or something: *She has absolute faith in her brothers and sisters.* **2** A religious belief: *Her Christian faith has helped her through her difficulties.*

†**faithful** /ˈfeɪθ.fᵊl/ [adjective] **1** Loyal: *James is a very faithful friend.* **2 yours faithfully** An expression used at the end of formal letters when the person to whom the letter is addressed is not named: *The letter ends: "Yours faithfully, Robert Burton".* ■ We use "yours faithfully" when the person to whom the letter is addressed is not named. Compare with "yours sincerely" (used at the end when the person to whom the formal letter is addressed has name).

fake /feɪk/ [countable noun] A copy of something made to deceive people: *Arthur thought he had a real Picasso, but it was a fake.*

falcon /ˈfæl·kən/, /ˈfɔl-/ [countable noun] A hunting bird with pointed wings and a long tail: *The falcon hunts small mammals.*

falconer US: /ˈfɑːl.kə.nɚ n/ UK: /ˈfɒl.kən.ər/ [countable noun] Somebody who trains falcons: *The falconer has to work many hours with the falcon.*

falconry /ˈfɒl.kən.ri/ US: /ˈfɑːl-/ [uncountable noun] The art of breeding and training falcons: *Falconry is an ancient art.*

fall[1] /fɔːl/ [noun] The season of the year between summer and winter: *Most trees lose their leaves in the fall.* ■ The same meaning: "autumn".

†**fall**[2], **fell, fallen** /fɔːl/ [verb] **1** To drop down towards the ground: *She slipped out of the tree, fell and broke her leg.* **2** To become less or lower: *The temperature has fallen a lot today.* **3 to fall asleep** To become asleep: *He was so tired he fell asleep while watching TV.* **4 to fall in love with (somebody)** See "to fall in love with (somebody)" in the word **love**[1].

▸ **PHRASAL VERBS** · **to fall apart** To break into pieces: *These shoes are falling apart. I need a new pair.* · **to fall behind** To do something too slowly: *James, you're falling behind with your English. You should be on lesson 5.* · **to fall over** To be standing

fairly, quite, rather, pretty,* and *very

We use *fairly*, *quite*, *rather*, *pretty*, and *very* with some adjectives to modify their meaning:

1,70 m	1,80 m	1,87 m
fairly / quite tall	*rather / pretty tall*	*very tall*

(This use of the word *pretty* is informal.)

a b c d e f g h i j k l m n o p q r s t u v w x y z

and then fall to the ground: *Richard fell over and cut his knee when he was running for the bus yesterday.* • **to fall through** To fail to happen: *Our plans fell through because we didn't have any money.*

fallen /ˈfɔ·lən/ Past participle of **fall²**.

Fallopian tube /fəˌləʊ.pi.ənˈtjuːb/ US: /-ˌloʊ.pi.ənˈtuːb/ [countable noun] One of the two tubes in women's bodies in which ova travel along: *The Fallopian tube connects the ovaries to the uterus.* See page 425.

+**false** US: /fɑːls/ UK: /fɒls/ [adjective] **1** Not true: *Read the sentences and say if they are true or false.* **2** Not real; artificial: *Alice's grandpa has false teeth.*

+**fame** /feɪm/ [uncountable noun] Being well-known: *Some stars say that they don't enjoy their fame very much.*

+**familiar** /fəˈmɪl·jər/ [adjective] **1** Well-known to you: *That boy looks familiar. Maybe he goes to the same school as me.* **2 to be familiar with (something)** To know something well: *Are you familiar with this word processor?*

familiarity /fə·mɪlˈjær·ɪ·ţi/, /-ˌmɪl·iˈær-/ [uncountable noun] **1** The state of being familiar with something or having a good knowledge of it: *Familiarity with a range of subjects is necessary for a substitute teacher.* ■ Be careful! In this use we always say: "familiarity **with** (something)". **2** Friendliness or informality in the way of acting: *Jeff's familiarity to us was very nice.* ■ We always say: "familiarity **to** or **towards** (somebody)". ■ The plural is "familiarities".

+**family** /ˈfæm.əl.i/ [noun] **1** A group of people who are related to each other: *We're a very close family and we try to help each other as much as possible.* ■ The plural is "families". **2 family tree** A plan that shows the relationship between the people in a family: *I have drawn a family tree which includes five generations.*

family name [countable noun] See **name¹**.

famine /ˈfæm.ɪn/ [noun] A period when there is not enough food in an area or a country: *In Africa some countries have regular famines and thousands of people die.* ■ Compare with "hunger¹" (the need and desire for food).

+**famous** /ˈfeɪ.məs/ [adjective] Well-known: *The Beatles are the most famous pop group of all times.*

+**fan** /fæn/ [countable noun] **1** A supporter of a team or a pop group: *Lee is a fan of the Denver Broncos.* **2** A thing that moves the air around you to make you cooler: *When we lived in India, we had fans in all the rooms.*

+**fancy** /ˈfænt.si/ [verb] **1** To like somebody as your boyfriend or girlfriend: *I quite fancy Mark; he's very handsome.* **2** To want to do something: *I fancy going dancing tonight.* ■ Be careful with the spelling of these forms: "fancies", "fancied". The verb immediately after "fancy" is in the "-ing" form.

fang /fæŋ/ [countable noun] A long, sharp tooth: *A snake can inject poison through his fang.*

fantastic /fænˈtæs.tɪk/ [adjective] **1** Difficult to believe: *He writes fantastic stories about life on other planets.* **2** Very good: *The movie was absolutely fantastic.*

fantasy /ˈfæn.tə.si/ [noun] Something that you imagine, but is not real: *Don't believe a word of what he says; the whole thing is a fantasy.* ■ The plural is "fantasies".

far¹ /fɑːr/ [adverb] **1** At a long distance from somebody or something or a long distance to it: *Do you have to travel far to school?* ■ The comparative form is "farther" or "further" and the superlative form is "farthest" or "furthest". **2 as far as 1** Until a certain place: *To get to Lucy's house, go down the road as far as the hospital and then turn right.* **2** A phrase used to introduce a statement or opinion: *As far as I know, she still lives in Sydney.* **3 far away** At a long distance from somebody or something or a long distance to it: *I don't want to go to the movie theater; it's too far away.* **4 how far** To what degree: *I don't know how far to believe him.* **5 so far** Until now: *So far we haven't had any problems with the car.*

+**far²** /fɑːr/ [adjective] That is at a long distance, not near: *We can't walk to the sports center; it's too far.* ■ The comparative form is "farther" or "further" and the superlative form is "farthest" or "furthest".

+**fare** US: /fer/ UK: /feəʳ/ [countable noun] The money you pay to travel on a bus, train and so on: *Does anybody know why airplane fares change so much?*

+**farm** US: /fɑːrm/ UK: /fɑːm/ [countable noun] A place used for growing crops or keeping animals: *George's father has a huge farm with pigs, cows and sheep.*

+**farmer** US: /ˈfɑːr.mɚ/ UK: /ˈfɑː.məʳ/ [countable noun] A person who owns or works on a farm: *The farmer showed us his baby pigs.*

farmer's market [countable noun] A market that sells fruit, vegetables and other farm products: *Where's the nearest farmer's market?* See picture at **market**.

farmhouse /ˈfɑrm,haʊs/ [countable noun] The house on a farm where the farmer lives: *We had coffee with the farmer in the farmhouse.*

+**farming** /ˈfɑː.mɪŋ/ US: /ˈfɑːr-/ [uncountable noun] The job of growing crops or keeping animals to sell: *Farming is a very hard job.*

farmyard US: /ˈfɑːrm.jɑːrd/ UK: /ˈfɑːm.jɑːd/ [countable noun] An open space next to a farmhouse: *There was a*

RICK'S FAMILY

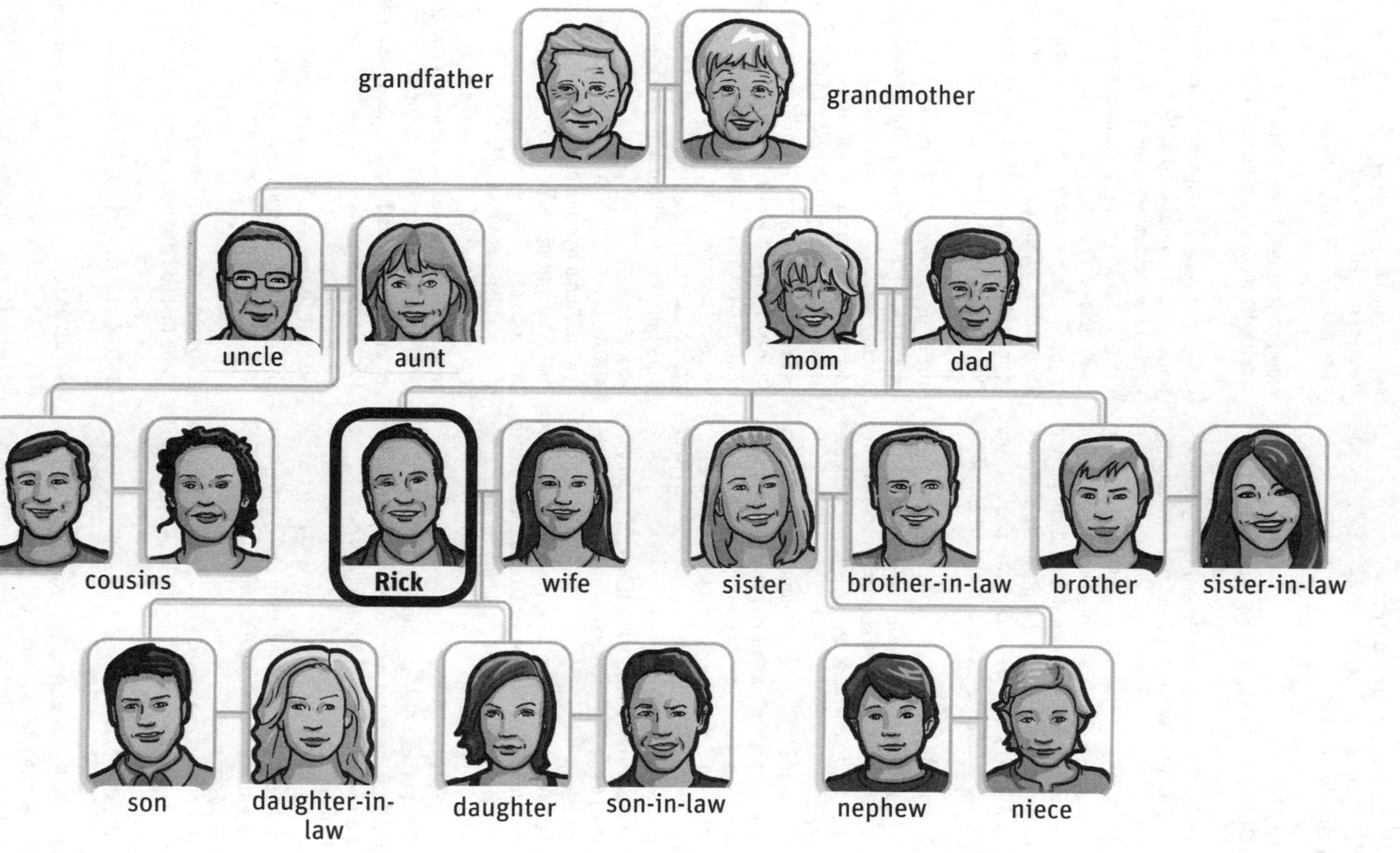

a b c d e f g h i j k l m n o p q r s t u v w x y z

tractor, a van and a car in the farmyard as well as chickens, ducks, geese and a cat!

ᐩ**farther** US: /ˈfɑːr.ðɚ/ UK: /ˈfɑː.ðəʳ/ [adjective and adverb] The comparative form of **far**.

farthest /ˈfɑr·ðəst/ [adjective and adverb] The superlative form of **far**.

fascinate /ˈfæs.ɪ.neɪt/ [verb] To interest greatly or attract somebody: *India fascinates me.*

fascinating /ˈfæs·əˌneɪ·t̬ɪŋ/ [adjective] That greatly interests or attracts people: *Mexico is a fascinating country.*

ᐩ**fashion** /ˈfæʃ.ᵊn/ [noun] **1** The style of something that is popular at a certain time: *These kind of pants were the fashion in the sixties.* **2 in fashion** Popular at that moment: *I think short hair is in fashion now.* **3 out of fashion** Not popular any more: *My brother says that ties are out of fashion now.*

ᐩ**fashionable** /ˈfæʃ.ᵊn.ə.bl̩/ [adjective] That is in fashion: *Jason likes wearing fashionable clothes.*

fashion show [countable noun] A show where clothes are shown: *In Milan there are very famous fashion shows.*

ᐩ**fast**[1] /fɑːst/ [adjective and adverb] Quick, rapid: *James is very fast; he can run a yard in eleven seconds.* ■ Compare with "quick" ("Quick" is usually used to refer to length of time, while "fast" refers to speed. We say "a quick visit" not "a fast visit", and "a quick decision" not "a fast decision").

fast[2] /fɑːst/ [adverb] **1** Firmly fixed: *Make the boat fast to the dock.* **2 fast asleep** See "fast asleep" in the word **asleep**.

ᐩ**fasten** US: /ˈfæs.ᵊn/ UK: /ˈfɑː.sᵊn/ [verb] To tie or to join something firmly: *Ladies and Gentlemen: please fasten your seat belts. We're going to land.* ■ Be careful with the pronunciation of this word. The "t" is not pronounced.

fastener US: /ˈfæs.ᵊn.ɚ/ UK: /ˈfɑːs.ᵊn.əʳ/ [countable noun] Something used for tying or joining things: *I've got a new red coat with metal fasteners.* ■ Be careful with the pronunciation of this word. The "t" is not pronounced.

fast food [uncountable noun] Food that can be prepared very quickly: *I love pizzas, hamburgers and all types of fast food.*

fast forward /ˌfɑːstˈfɔːwəd/ [verb] To make a tape go forward quickly: *Fast forward the tape, I don't like this song.* ■ "ff" is an abbreviation for "fast forward". ■ Compare with "rewind" (to make a tape go back towards the beginning).

ᐩ**fat**[1] /fæt/ [adjective] With a big, round body: *If you keep eating like that, you'll get fat.* ■ The comparative form is "fatter" and the superlative form is "fattest".

fat[2] /fæt/ [uncountable noun] The greasy substance under the skin of animals and people: *You can cut the fat off the meat if you don't like it.*

fatal /ˈfeɪ·t̬ə·l/ [adjective] **1** That causes death: *There was a fatal accident on the road to Portland this morning; four people were killed.* **2** That has bad results: *We made a fatal mistake and we're paying for it.*

fate /feɪt/ [uncountable noun] A mysterious force that some people believe controls what happens: *I think it's not just a coincidence that we've met today. It's fate.*

ᐩ**father** /ˈfɑð·ər/ [countable noun] **1** A male parent: *My father's name is Charles.* ■ "Dad" and "daddy" are informal for "father". See picture at **family**. **2 father-in-law** When you are married, your wife's or your husband's father: *My sister's father-in-law is Italian.* ■ The plural of "father-in-law" is "fathers-in-law".

ᐩ**faucet** US: /ˈfɔːsɪt/ [countable noun] A device to let liquid out of a tube, pipe and so on: *The bathtub faucet is leaking.* ■ In British English they say "tap". See pictures at **bathroom** and **kitchen**.

ᐩ**fault** US: /fɑːlt/ UK: /fɒlt/ ▮ [countable noun] **1** Something that is wrong: *I think there's a fault in the television set. It doesn't work.* ▮ [noun] **2** Responsibility for something not good that happens: *It's your own fault if you don't pass your tests.*

faulty US: /ˈfɑːl.t̬i/ UK: /ˈfɒl.ti/ [adjective] That doesn't work well: *This television is faulty; the image is not very clear.*

fauna /ˈfɔ·nə/ [uncountable noun] All of the animal life of a region: *Fauna refers to birds, fish, reptiles, insects and other animals.* ■ The plural is "faunas" or "faunae". ■ Compare with "flora" (the plants that grow in a particular region or period).

ᐩ**favor** /ˈfeɪ·vər/ [uncountable noun] **1** Something you do to help somebody: *James, do me a favor and close the window, please.* **2 to be in favor of (something)** To think that something is a good idea: *I'm in favor of abolishing nuclear arms.* ■ The British English spelling is "favour".

favorable /ˈfeɪ·vər·ə·bəl/ [adjective] Good for something: *I think we should wait for a favorable moment to tell Mr. Menzies about our plans.* ■ The British English spelling is "favourable".

ᐩ**favorite** /ˈfeɪ.vər.ɪt/ [adjective] The person or the thing that you like best: *Red is my favorite color.* ■ The British English spelling is "favourite".

ᐩ**favour** UK: /ˈfeɪ.vəʳ/ [uncountable noun] See **favor**. ■ This is a British English spelling.

favourable UK: /ˈfeɪ.vᵊr.ə.bl̩/ [adjective] See **favorable**. ■ This is a British English spelling.

ᐩ**favourite** /ˈfeɪ.vᵊr.ɪt/ [adjective] See **favorite**. ■ This is a British English spelling.

fax[1] /fæks/ [countable noun] **1** A machine that produces copies of documents via the telephone line: *George's father has got a fax in his office.* **2** A copy of a document sent by a fax machine: *Alice sent me a fax with all the information I needed.* ■ The plural is "faxes".

fax[2] /fæks/ [verb] To send a document by fax: *Fax me a copy, please.* ■ Be careful! We say: "fax (somebody) (something)".

ᐩ**fear**[1] /fɪər/ [noun] The feeling that you have when you think you are in danger: *When Arthur saw the snake, he started shaking with fear.*

fear[2] /fɪər/ [verb] To anticipate with anxiety, to be frightened of somebody or something: *When the mountain rescue team couldn't find her, they started to fear the worst.*

fearless /ˈfɪər·ləs/ [adjective] Without fear: *You must be fearless in order to work as a trapeze artist.* ■ We always say "fearless **of** (something)".

feast /fiːst/ [countable noun] **1** A large meal to celebrate a special occasion: *Medieval warriors used to celebrate their victories by having enormous feasts.* **2** A time people come together to celebrate a particular occasion, especially one with a religious base: *Christmas Day is the feast when Christians celebrate Jesus' birth.* ■ In this use, the same meaning: "festival".

feat /fiːt/ [countable noun] Something difficult or dangerous to do: *Swimming from Nassau to The Bahamas is a great feat.*

ᐩ**feather** /ˈfeð·ər/ [countable noun] One of the small things that cover a bird's body: *My canary's feathers are yellow and green.*

FEATHER

ᐩ**feature** /ˈfi·tʃər/ [countable noun] **1** One of the different parts of your face: *He had peculiar features: small eyes, big ears.* **2** An important part or quality of something: *The best feature of my new bike is its speed.*

ᐩ**February** /ˈfeb·juˌer·i/, /ˈfeb·ru-/ [noun] The second month of the year: *February is usually a very cold month.* ■ Be careful! "February" has a capital "F". 👁 See picture at **calendar**.

feces /ˈfiːsiːz/ [plural noun] Solid waste matter expelled out of the body through the anus: *Feces are the waste product of the digestive system.* ■ This word is formal. ■ The same meaning: "excrement".

fed /fed/ Past tense and past participle forms of **feed**.

ᐩ**federal** /ˈfed·ər·əl/ [adjective] Referring to a system where a group of semi-independent states exist under a central government: *The United States of America is a federal republic.*

ᐩ**fee** /fiː/ [countable noun] The money that somebody pays for a service: *The fees at private schools can be very high.*

feeble /ˈfiː.bl̩/ [adjective] Very weak, inadequate: *That was a very feeble effort. Now, try again.*

ᐩ**feed, fed, fed** /fiːd/ [verb] **1** To give food to: *I like feeding the ducks in the park.* **2** To put something into a computer or other machine: *He fed information into the computer.* **3 to be fed up** To be bored or unhappy about something: *I'm fed up with watching TV. I'm going out.* ■ Be careful! In this use we usually say: "be fed up **with** (something)".

feedback /ˈfiːd.bæk/ [uncountable noun] Information returned about the results of something: *They need to get feedback from customers about the new washing machines.*

ᐩ**feel, felt, felt** /fiːl/ [verb] **1** To have a certain sensation or emotion: *I feel great affection for my parents.* **2** To touch something with your fingers: *Feel this sweater. Isn't it soft?* **3 to feel like (something) or feel like doing (something)** To want something: *I feel like something to drink.*

▶ **PHRASAL VERBS** · **to feel for (something)** To try to find something with your fingers: *He felt for the keys in his pocket.*

ᐩ**feeling** /ˈfiː.lɪŋ/ [noun] **1** Something that you feel mentally or physically: *I had a great feeling of happiness when I saw Mary.* **2** The ability to feel: *I have had no feeling in that finger since the accident.*

feet /fiːt/ The plural of **foot**.

fell /fel/ Past tense of **fall**[2].

ᐩ**fellow**[1] /ˈfeləʊ/ [countable noun] A man or a boy: *Jamie is a very nice fellow.* ■ This word is informal.

fellow[2] /ˈfeləʊ/ [adjective] That belongs to the same group: *He went out to celebrate with his fellow workers.*

felt /felt/ Past tense and past participle forms of **feel**.

felt-tip pen or **felt pen** [countable noun] A pen with a soft tip made of felt: *Felt-tip pens are used for drawing in different colors.*

a b c d e f g h i j k l m n o p q r s t u v w x y z

female[1] /ˈfiːmeɪl/ [adjective] **1** Referring to women and girls: *I prefer female company.* **2** Referring to the sex that gives birth: *I have two female hamsters.*

†**female**[2] /ˈfiːmeɪl/ [countable noun] The sex of an animal or human that gives birth: *The zoo has one male zebra and two females.*

feminine /ˈfem.ɪ.nɪn/ [adjective] With qualities traditionally considered appropriate to women or typical of women: *Pat says that her new hairstyle makes her look more feminine.*

femur /ˈfiː.mər/ US: /-mɚ/ [countable noun] The thigh bone in the leg: *The femur is the bone between the hip and the knee.* ■ The plural is: "femurs" or "femora". 👁 **See page 422.**

†**fence** /fents/ [countable noun] A wooden or metal barrier between two pieces of land or around a field: *There's a small wooden fence between the Browns' backyard and ours.*

fencing /ˈfent.sɪŋ/ [uncountable noun] **1** A series of fences or the material used to make fences: *I asked the gardener to put some fencing to prevent foreign dogs from coming in.* **2** The sport of fighting with blunt swords: *In fencing you have to score points against your rival according to certain rules.*

ferment[1] /ˈfɜːment/ [uncountable noun] **1** A fungal substance used in making beer and wine or to make bread rise: *The ferment is added to the dough.* **2** A state of agitation and excitement: *The country is in a state of ferment.*

ferment[2] /fərˈment/ [verb] To cause something to change chemically and to expel gases, through the action of yeast or bacteria: *Milk is fermented to make yoghurt.*

fermentation /ˌfɜːmenˈteɪʃən/ [uncountable noun] The process of changing something chemically by the action of a living organism: *Microorganisms break down a substance to bring about fermentation.*

fern US: /fɝːn/ UK: /fɜːn/ [countable noun] A green plant with big leaves and no flowers: *Ferns grow in wet places.*

ferocious /fəˈroʊ·ʃəs/ [adjective] Fierce, savage: *Some hungry dogs can become ferocious animals.*

ferry /ˈfer.i/ [countable noun] A boat or a ship that carries people and vehicles across the water: *Every week we take the ferry from New Yersey to New York.* ■ The plural is "ferries". 👁 See picture at **transport**.

fertile US: /ˈfɝː.t̬əl/ UK: /ˈfɜː.taɪl/ [adjective] Good for growing plants: *The land is so fertile that they can grow two crops a year.*

fertilization or **fertilisation** /ˌfɜːtɪlaɪˈzeɪʃən/ [uncountable noun] The process of making fertile: *Fertilization makes plants productive.*

fertilize or **fertilise** /ˈfɜːtɪlaɪz/ [verb] **1** To introduce pollen into a plant so that it develops seeds or sperm into an egg or a female animal so that a young animal develops inside: *One single sperm cell is enough to fertilize an ovum.* **2** To make soil fertile by adding natural or chemical substances: *You can fertilize your garden in the fall.* ■ The British English spelling is "fertilise".

fertilizer or **fertiliser** /ˈfɜːtɪlaɪzər/ [noun] A substance used to help plants grow: *This plant is nearly dead. It needs some fertilizer.* ■ The British English spelling is "fertiliser".

†**festival** /ˈfes.tɪ.vəl/ [countable noun] **1** A time when there are cultural events of the same kind: *In Chicago there's a famous blues festival every year.* **2** A time people come together to celebrate a particular occasion, especially one with a religious base: *The main Christian religious festivals in Britain are Christmas and Easter.* ■ In this use, the same meaning: "feast".

festivity /fesˈtɪvəti/ ▮ [uncountable noun] **1** Celebration, happiness and enjoyment at a party, festival or other event: *That wedding was an occasion of great festivity.* ▮ [countable noun] **2** Celebration of a special event held in honor of something or somebody: *The town festivities are held every year on the same date.* ■ The plural is "festivities". This use is more common in the plural.

†**fetch** /fetʃ/ [verb] To go to get somebody or something: *I have to fetch my little brother from school every Monday and Wednesday.*

fête /feɪt/ [countable noun] An outdoors party with games and things to buy: *My school is holding a fête on Saturday to get money for a trip to California.*

fetus /ˈfi·t̬əs/ [countable noun] The unborn human or animal that has developed past a certain stage within its mother's body or in an egg: *The ultrasound image showed that the fetus was developing well.*

feudal /ˈfjuːdəl/ [adjective] Referring to the pre-capitalist social system in the Middle Ages in Europe, which was based on rank: *feudal society.*

†**fever** /ˈfi·vər/ [noun] A high body temperature and fast pulse: *I have a fever. I think I've caught a cold.*

†**few** /fjuː/ [adjective] **1** Not many: *Very few people live in the interior of Greenland.* **2 a few** Some: *We need a few volunteers to help us move some chairs.* ■ See box on the following page.

ff [verb] See **fast forward**.

fiancé US: /ˌfiː.ɑːnˈseɪ/ UK: /fiˈɑ̃ːn.seɪ/ [countable noun] A man who is engaged to get married: *My sister's fiancé is Puerto Rican.* ■ A woman is a "fiancée".

fiancée US: /ˌfiː.ɑːnˈseɪ/ UK: /fiˈɑ̃ːn.seɪ/ [countable noun] A woman who is engaged to get married: *He is very much in love with his fiancée.* ■ A man is a "fiancé".

fib /fɪb/ [countable noun] A small lie: *George is always telling fibs.* ■ This word is informal.

fiber /ˈfaɪ·bər/ [uncountable noun] A substance in some foods that helps your digestion: *Cereals and vegetables are rich in fiber.* ■ The British English spelling is "fibre".

fibre /ˈfaɪbər·/ UK: /ˈfaɪ.bəʳ/ [uncountable noun] See **fiber.** ■ This is a British English spelling.

fibrous /ˈfaɪ.brəs/ [adjective] Of or resembling fiber: *The connective tissue in the body is a fibrous tissue.*

fibula /ˈfɪb.jʊ.lə/ [countable noun] The smaller of the two bones connecting the knee and the ankle: *The fibula is the outer bone in the leg between the knee and the ankle.* ■ The plural is "fibulas" or "fibulae". 👁 **See page 422.**

†**fiction** /ˈfɪk.ʃᵊn/ [uncountable noun] An invented story, books that are invented stories: *Roald Dahl wrote fiction for children.*

†**field** /fiːld/ [countable noun] A piece of land: *My uncle has a field where he keeps cows.*

fierce US: /fɪrs/ UK: /fɪəs/ [adjective] Wild, aggressive and frightening: *The Driscolls' dog is so fierce that I daren't go near their house.*

fiery /ˈfaɪəri/ [adjective] **1** Having an appearance similar to fire: *He has fiery red hair.* **2** Becoming quickly or easily angry: *When working under pressure, he is a fiery man.* **3** Intense, with passion: *The speaker's fiery speech produced a rapid response.* **4** Producing a burning sensation in the throat: *He cooked a fiery Mexican meal for us.*

fifteen /ˌfɪfˈtiːn/ [noun, adjective and pronoun] The number 15: *You have fifteen minutes to finish the test.*

fifteenth /ˌfɪfˈtiːnθ/ [noun and adjective] Referring to fifteen: *Jane was born on May the fifteenth.* ■ "Fifteenth" can also be written "15th".

fifth /fɪfθ/ [noun and adjective] Referring to five: *I'm the fifth boy in my family.* ■ "Fifth" can also be written "5th".

fiftieth /ˈfɪf.ti.əθ/ [noun and adjective] Referring to fifty: *My grandparents celebrated their fiftieth wedding anniversary last month.* ■ "Fiftieth" can also be written "50th".

fifty /ˈfɪf.ti/ [noun, adjective and pronoun] The number 50: *They have a country house about fifty miles from Denver.*

fig /fɪg/ [countable noun] A soft sweet brown fruit grown in warm countries: *Figs are green or yellow inside and have lots of seeds.* 👁 **See page 436.**

†**fight¹** /faɪt/ ▮ [countable noun] **1** Two or more people trying to hurt each other: *A fight broke out during recess between Rick and Paul.* ▮ [uncountable noun] **2** An attempt to stop something or to achieve something despite the difficulties: *The fight against cancer must go on.*

fight², fought, fought /faɪt/ [verb] **1** To try to hurt another person: *I wouldn't like to have to fight in a war.* **2** To quarrel: *Sue and her brother are always fighting.*

◗ **PHRASAL VERBS** · **to fight for (something)** To try to do something or to get something: *Native Americans in the USA are still fighting for their rights.*

fighter /ˈfaɪ·t̬ər/ [countable noun] **1** A person who fights: *She's a fighter. She doesn't give in easily.* **2** A fast airplane used to attack other airplanes: *The F-18 is a famous United States Air Force fighter.*

†**fighting** /ˈfaɪt̬·ɪŋ/ [uncountable noun] A conflict that is more than one isolated incident, or that has no clear end: *The fighting continues along the border of the two countries.*

†**figure** /ˈfɪg·jər/ [countable noun] A symbol we use for writing numbers: *Please write these numbers in figures, not in words.*

filament /ˈfɪl.ə.mənt/ [countable noun] A very fine, thread-like fiber: *Light bulbs contain a filament which heats up and gives off light.*

†**file¹** /faɪl/ [noun] **1** A box or a folder for papers, the contents of it: *I keep all my school projects in a file.* **2** A metal tool with very small teeth used for cutting or making something smooth: *The prisoner escaped by cutting through the bars with a file.*

file² /faɪl/ [verb] **1** To put papers in files: *Mom files all our school reports.* **2** To make something smooth with a file: *My sister is always filing her nails.*

†**fill** /fɪl/ [verb] **1** To make something full: *Can you fill this bottle with water, please?* ■ Be careful. We say: "fill something **with** (something)". **2** To become full: *Entry to see the show was free, so the seats filled very quickly.*

> ***few* and *a few***
>
> Note the difference between *few* and *a few:*
>
> - ***Few*** has a negative connotation:
>   - *Few people came to the party. It was boring.*
>   - *He has few friends.*
>   - *I have very few CDs. I'm going to buy some more when I have the money*
> - ***A few*** has a more positive connotation:
>   - *Can you lend me a few CDs?*
>   - *I'm going to the movies tonight with a few friends.*
>   - *I've been to the new swimming pool a few times. It's really big.*
>
> This is a difference of attitude, not a difference in amount.
>
> Exactly the same principle applies with ***little*** and ***a little***.

a b c d e f g h i j k l m n o p q r s t u v w x y z

▸ **PHRASAL VERBS** · **to fill (something) in** To write answers or information in a questionnaire or form: *We have to fill in a school form with our personal details.* · **to fill (something) up** To fill something completely: *"Fill up the tank, please" "How much gas do you want?".*

filling /ˈfɪlɪŋ/ ▮ [noun] **1** The food inside a sandwich, a cake and so on: *I like cakes with cream fillings.* ▮ [countable noun] **2** Something that a dentist puts in holes in teeth: *The dentist said Beckie needed three fillings.*

↑**film**[1] /fɪlm/ ▮ [noun] **1** A story made for the movie theater or for television: *My favorite films are westerns.* ▮ [countable noun] **2** The material used for making films or for taking photographs: *I need a film for my camera.* **3 film star** A famous movies actor or actress: *Marilyn Monroe was a big film star of the 1950's.*

film[2] /fɪlm/ [verb] To make a film of something: *My father likes filming all our birthday parties.*

filter /ˈfɪl·tər/ [countable noun] Something used for separating solid substances from liquids or from gases: *We need a new filter for the coffee machine.*

filthy /ˈfɪl.θi/ [adjective] Very dirty: *Our playing clothes were really filthy after the game.* ■ The comparative form is "filthier" and the superlative form is "filthiest".

fin /fɪn/ [countable noun] The thin parts of a fish's body that help them move in the water: *Some fish have very large colorful fins.* ■ Compare with "flipper" (part of the body of some sea animals, not fish).

final[1] /ˈfaɪnəl/ [adjective] Last: *I didn't like the final part of the movie.*

↑**final**[2] /ˈfaɪnəl/ [countable noun] The last game in a competition: *The Super Bowl final this year is between Giants and Patriots.*

finally /ˈfaɪ.nə.li/ [adverb] **1** In the end, after some time or effort: *We talked about the party for some time and finally agreed to have it on Friday.* **2** Lastly: *We had salad, steak and finally ice cream.*

↑**finance**[1] /ˈfaɪnæns/ [uncountable noun] The management of money: *The Minister of Finance has promised more money for education.*

finance[2] /ˈfaɪnæns/ [verb] To provide money for something: *She can't find anybody to finance her movie.*

↑**financial** /faɪˈnæn.tʃəl, fɪ-/ [adjective] That is connected with money: *Alice's father is a financial expert.*

↑**find, found, found** /faɪnd/ [verb] **1** To get or to see something you are looking for: *I found my keys in the end: they were in my other jacket; Can you find Wally in this picture?; I found the store in the end, after walking around for 20 minutes.* **2** To look for and locate somebody: *The police found him in the park.* ■ Compare with "meet" (to see somebody by chance). **3** To produce a particular sensation for somebody: *I found the movie really interesting.* **4 to find it difficult** To have difficulty doing something: *I find it difficult to understand her sometimes.*

▸ **PHRASAL VERBS** · **to find (something) out** To discover a fact or hear a particular piece of news: *I don't know Mary's address, but I can find it out; Today I found out that one of my classmates is Iker's nephew.* · **to find (somebody) out** To reveal the truth about somebody: *The Japans found him out because of his accent: they realized that he was American.*

fine[1] /faɪn/ [countable noun] Money that you pay when you break the law: *Dad was given a fine for parking on the corner.*

↑**fine**[2] /faɪn/ [adjective] **1** Well, in good health: *I'm fine, thank you.* **2** Very good: *Lawrence is a fine violinist.* **3** All right: *That's fine. I don't want more french fries.* **4** Thin: *I need a fine pencil for my drawing class.*

↑**finger** /ˈfɪŋgər/ [countable noun] **1** One of the five parts at the end of your hands: *The middle finger is the longest finger.* ■ Compare with "toe" (at the end of your feet). 👁 See picture at **hand**. **2 keep your fingers crossed** To wish that something will happen as you want: *I hope my dad says "yes". Keep your fingers crossed.*

fingernail /ˈfɪŋ·gərˌneɪl/ [countable noun] The hard white part that grows at the end of your fingers: *Mary always has very long, red fingernails.* ■ Compare

FINGER

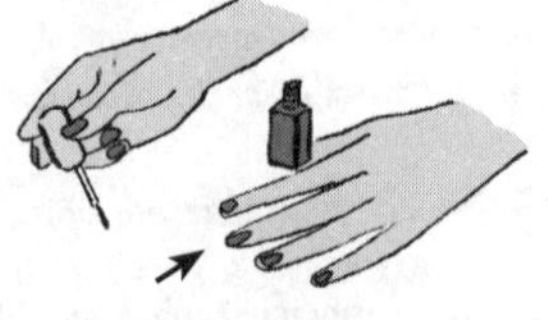
fingernails

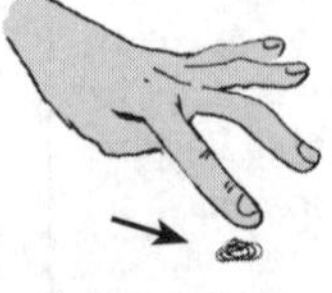
fingerprint

fingertip

with "toenail" (at the end of your toes). See picture at **finger**.

fingerprint /'fɪŋ·gər,prɪnt/ [countable noun] The mark that a finger makes on something: *The police took his fingerprints before putting him into jail.* See picture at **finger**.

fingertip /'fɪŋ·gər,tɪp/ [countable noun] The end part of your fingers: *You just have to press the computer keys with your fingertips.* See picture at **finger**.

finish /'fɪn.ɪʃ/ [verb] To end: *The movie finishes at eight o'clock.* ■ The verb after "finish" is in the "-ing" form: "When you finish doing that, call me".

PHRASAL VERBS · **to finish (something) off** To eat the last part of something: *Mary finished off all the french fries.* · **to finish with (somebody)** Not to want to see a person any more: *I've finished with Bob; we are not going out any more.*

finishing line [countable noun] The line that marks the finishing point of a race: *The Jamaican athlete crossed the finishing line in first place.*

fire¹ /faɪər/ [noun] **1** The heat and the light produced when something burns: *We made a fire with some wood to cook the fish.* **2 to be on fire** To be burning: *Look! That car is on fire.* **3 to catch fire** To begin to burn: *He put his socks so near the fireplace that they caught fire.* **4 to put out a fire** To stop a fire: *When the firefighters came they put out the fire very quickly.* **5 to set fire to (something)** To make something burn: *Did you hear that somebody set fire to the shopping mall last night?*

fire² /faɪər/ [verb] **1** To shoot a gun: *The thieves fired twice before they ran away.* **2** To dismiss from a position: *His bosses were not happy with his productivity, so they fire him.* ■ This use is informal.

fire alarm [countable noun] A warning bell that rings when there is a fire: *When we heard the fire alarm, we quickly left the building.*

fire brigade [countable noun] The people whose job is to put fires out: *John called the fire brigade when he saw the flames.*

firecracker [countable noun] A small firework that explodes with a short loud noise: *The kids bought some firecrackers for the celebrations.* ■ In British English they say "banger".

fire engine [countable noun] A vehicle with equipment for putting out fires: *When my class visited the fire station I got on a fire engine and rang the bell.*

fire escape [countable noun] The stairs on the outside of a building that are used for escape if there is a fire: *If you hear the fire alarm, go quickly to the fire escape.*

fire extinguisher [countable noun] A special container with water or chemicals that is used to put out a fire: *Stuart pointed the fire extinguisher at the fire and put it out.* ■ We also say "extinguisher".

firefighter /'faɪə,faɪ.təʳ/ [countable noun] A person whose job is to control and put out fires: *There were many firefighters trying to stop the large fire.* ■ We used to say "fireman" or "firewoman". Most people now prefer to say "firefighter" because it can be used for either a man or a woman.

firefly /'faɪər,flaɪ/ [countable noun] A beetle with a soft body, a member of the glow-worm family: *The firefly is also known as the glow-worm.* ■ The plural is: "fireflies".

fireman /'faɪər·mən/ [countable noun] See **firefighter.** ■ The plural is "firemen". ■ A woman is a "firewoman".

fireplace /'faɪər·pleɪs/ [countable noun] The place in a room where you can make a fire: *I like reading next to the fireplace; it's so warm and comfortable.* ■ Compare with "chimney" (a stone tube that takes the smoke away from a fire). See picture at **living room.**

fire station [countable noun] A building where firefighters wait for calls for help: *The firefighters were having a cup of coffee in the fire station when the call came through.*

firewoman [countable noun] See **firefighter.** ■ The plural is "firewomen". ■ A man is a "fireman".

firewood /'faɪər,wʊd/ [uncountable noun] Wood used for fires: *My dad chopped some firewood for the fire.*

firework /'faɪəwɜːk/ [countable noun] Something that makes a loud noise and/or colored lights in the sky: *There was a beautiful display of fireworks during the festival.* ■ This word is more common in the plural.

firm¹ /fɜːm/ [countable noun] A company: *Gary's mother works for a computer firm.*

firm² /fɜːm/ [adjective] Strong and difficult to move: *Be careful with that rock. It's not very firm and it might fall over.*

fir or **fir tree** /fɜːr/ [countable noun] A tall evergreen tree with leaves that look like needles: *Firs are used as Christmas trees.* **See page 435.**

first¹ /'fɜːst/ [noun and adjective] Referring to one: *Christine lives on the first floor.* ■ "First" can also be written "1st".

first² /'fɜːst/ [adverb] **1** Before everybody else or everything else: *She always finishes first.* **2** For the first time: *I first went to the United States in 1995.* **3** Before doing anything else: *Read the instructions first.* **4 at first** At the beginning: *At first, Mary wasn't very happy at her new school.* **5 first aid** The medical help that a person gets immediately after an accident: *We were taught how to do some first aid at school.* **6 first aid box** A box containing medicines for first aid: *There's a first aid box in the changing rooms.* **7 first of all** Before anything else: *I'd like to visit the whole town, but first of all we should eat something.*

first class[1] /ˌfɜːstˈklɑːs/ [adjective] Of the best type: *In this school the food is first class.*

first class[2] [noun and adverb] In the most comfortable and expensive part of a train, plane or other vehicle: *George's mother always travels first class.*

first name [countable noun] The name or names that go before the family name: *My mom's first names are Wendy Sue but like most people she only uses one name, Wendy.* ■ The same meaning: "Christian name".

fish[1] /fɪʃ/ [noun] **1** A class of animals that live in water: *I have some beautiful fish in my aquarium.* ■ The plural is usually "fish", not "fishes". 👁 **See pages 426 and 430.** **2** A class of animals that live in water used as food: *Would you like a piece of fish?* ■ In this use "fish" is an uncountable noun. We say "some fish" or "a piece of fish".

fish[2] /fɪʃ/ [verb] To try to catch fish: *I go fishing at a river near my house.*

fishbone [noun] Bone in a fish: *Fishbones can be dangerous if they get stuck in your throat.*

fisherman /ˈfɪʃ·ər·mən/ [countable noun] A man who fishes: *Some fishermen spend three months at sea.* ■ The plural is "fishermen".

fish finger /ˌfɪʃˈfɪŋ.gər/ [countable noun] A small, finger shaped piece of fish covered for example in flour: *We're having fish fingers for lunch.*

fishing rod US: /ˈfɪʃ·ɪŋ ˌrɑd/ [countable noun] A special long stick with a line, used for fishing: *Get your fishing rod, Jane. We're going fishing.*

fissure /ˈfɪʃ·ər/ [countable noun] A long, narrow crack: *A fissure opened up during the earthquake.*

fist /fɪst/ [countable noun] A closed hand: *The baby had its fist closed around my finger.*

fit[1] /fɪt/ [adjective] **1** Healthy and active: *Arthur goes jogging every morning to keep fit.* **2** Attractive or sexy: *Lisa came to the party with a fit guy.* ■ This use is informal. ■ The comparative form is "fitter" and the superlative form is "fittest".

↑**fit**[2] /fɪt/ [verb] To be the right size: *I think those shoes are your size; they fit you perfectly.* ■ Be careful with the spelling of these forms: "fitted", "fitting".

fitness /ˈfɪt.nəs/ [uncountable noun] State of health of the body: *You must improve your physical fitness if you want to be in the team.* ■ We also say "physical fitness".

fitting room [countable noun] The room in a clothing store where you try on clothes before you buy them: *The fitting rooms are over there.*

↑**five** /faɪv/ [noun, adjective and pronoun] The number 5: *We have five fingers on each hand.*

↑**fix** /fɪks/ [verb] **1** To repair something: *I have to fix my bicycle; the brakes don't work.* **2** To put something firmly in place so that it won't move: *She fixed the picture on the wall with some drawing pins.*

fizzy /ˈfɪz.i/ [adjective] That has gas that makes bubbles: *I don't like lemonade or any other type of fizzy drinks.* ■ The comparative form is "fizzier" and the superlative form is "fizziest".

fjord or **fiord** /fjɔːd/ US: /fjɔːrd/ [countable noun] A long narrow strip of sea between high cliffs: *In Norway you can visit the beautiful fjords where the Opera House is located.*

↑**flag** /flæg/ [countable noun] A piece of cloth fixed to a pole: *Our sports club has a special flag.*

flagpole /ˈflæg,poʊl/ [countable noun] A stick from which flags are hung: *Outside the embassy there's a flagpole with the national flag.*

flake /fleɪk/ [countable noun] A small thin piece of something: *Through the window we watched the flakes of snow slowly falling.*

↑**flame** /fleɪm/ [noun] A tongue of fire: *The candle gave out a steady flame.*

flamingo /fləˈmɪŋ·goʊ/ [countable noun] A large pink bird with thin legs that lives near water: *Flamingos live in big groups.* ■ The plural is "flamingos" or "flamingoes". 👁 **See page 429.**

flan /flæn/ [countable noun] A thick custard covered with caramel sauce: *My mom makes flan with condensed milk and it's very sweet.*

flap /flæp/ [verb] To move something flat up and down or from side to side: *The bird flapped its wings and took off.* ■ Be careful with the spelling of these forms: "flapped", "flapping".

flash[1] /flæʃ/ [countable noun] **1** A brief bright light: *The firework exploded in a big flash of red and white light.* **2** An apparatus used to take photos when it is dark: *I'll have to use the flash or the picture won't come out.* ■ The plural is "flashes".

flash[2] /flæʃ/ [verb] **1** To give out a light quickly: *The police car flashed its lights to warn other drivers.* **2** **flash past** To move quickly: *The motorcycle flashed past all the cars.*

flashlight /ˈflæʃ.laɪt/ [countable noun] A small, portable electric light: *Don't forget to take your flashlight* *with you when you go camping.* ■ In British English they say "torch".

flask /flɑːsk noun [☒]/ [countable noun] A glass container for liquids used in laboratories, or for keeping liquids: *The scientist kept a sample of the soil in a flask.* 👁 See page 440.

*__flat¹__ /flæt/ [countable noun] See **apartment**. ■ This word is British English.

flat² /flæt/ [adjective] **1** With no parts higher than others, level: *Holland is famous for being very flat.* **2** Referring to a musical sound which is lower than the true or normal pitch: *The opera singer was singing slightly flat.* ■ The comparative form is "flatter" and the superlative form is "flattest".

flat³ /flæt/ [countable noun] A musical note which is lowered a semitone lower than the specified pitch: *The orchestra played piece in C flat.*

flatten /ˈflæt·ə·n/ [verb] To make flat: *Don't put that bag on the cardboard boxes or you will flatten them.*

flatter US: /ˈflæṱ.ɚ/ UK: /ˈflæt.əʳ/ [verb] To say something nice about somebody because you want to please them or because you want something from them: *John flattered me by saying how nice I looked in my new dress.*

*__flavor__ /ˈfleɪ·vər/ [countable noun] Taste: *I love the flavor of chocolate ice cream.* ■ The British English spelling is "flavour".

*__flavour__ UK: /ˈfleɪ.vəʳ/ [noun] See **flavor**. ■ This is a British English spelling.

flea /fliː/ [countable noun] A small, jumping insect that drinks blood: *Jeremy's dog has fleas.*

fled /fled/ Past tense and past participle forms of **flee**.

flee, fled, fled /fliː/ [verb] To run away from something dangerous: *They managed to flee just before the soldiers arrived.*

fleece¹ /fliːs/ ▮ [noun] **1** The coat of a sheep or goat after it has been cut: *The fleece was placed on a pile by the person in charge of shaving the sheep.* ▮ [countable noun] **2** A soft warm material, or a jacket made from this material: *When I go to the mountains, I always wear a fleece.*

fleece² [verb] To get money from somebody by dishonest or unfair means: *Some local stores really fleece the tourists.* ■ This use is informal.

fleet /fliːt/ [countable noun] A group of ships or other vehicles: *The fleet came into the harbor in perfect formation.*

*__flesh__ /fleʃ/ [uncountable noun] The soft part of the body of an animal or a person: *Flesh that is eaten is called meat.*

flew /fluː/ Past tense of **fly²**.

flexible /ˈflek.sɪ.bl̩/ [adjective] **1** Able to be bent without breaking: *The palm tree is flexible whenever the wind blows.* **2** Willing and able to change or adapt to different circumstances or situations: *If you are flexible about the seats, last minute tickets will cost you less money.* ■ Compare with "inflexible" (unwilling to change or adapt).

*__flight__ /flaɪt/ [countable noun] A journey by airplane: *The flight from Denver to New York lasts about four hours.*

flight attendant [countable noun] A person who helps passengers on flights: *The flight attendant told me to fasten my seat belt.*

flint /flɪnt/ ▮ [noun] **1** A hard, gray stone which occurs naturally in chalk: *Flint played an important role in human progress as a tool and as a source of fire.* ▮ [countable noun] **2** A small piece of a hard metal used to produce a spark in a cigarette lighter: *The flints in old cigarette lighters often need to be replaced.*

flip-flop /ˈflɪp,flɒp/ [countable noun] See **thong**. ■ This word is British English.

flipper /ˈflɪp·ər/ [countable noun] **1** The part of the body of some sea animals that they use for swimming: *Seals use their flippers for moving in the water and on land.* ■ Compare with "fin" (part of a fish's body, not part of a sea animal's body). **2** A kind of long shoes that swimmers put on their feet to help them swim: *When you swim with flippers, you go much faster.*

flirt US: /flɝːt/ UK: /flɜːt/ [verb] To play at attracting and being attracted by somebody for amusement: *He's always flirting with the women in the office.*

*__float__ US: /floʊt/ UK: /fləʊt/ [verb] To stay on top of a liquid or in the air: *I've made a boat from a piece of paper, and look, it floats!*

flock /flɒk/ [countable noun] A group of animals, especially birds: *In spring, flocks of swallows pass this way towards the north.*

*__flood¹__ /flʌd/ [noun] A large amount of water that suddenly covers land that is usually dry: *The rain has caused floods in towns and fields.* ■ Be careful with the pronunciation of this word. The vowel sound here is pronounced the same as in "sun".

flood² /flʌd/ [verb] To cover dry land with water: *The fields by the river are flooded each winter.* ■ Be careful with the pronunciation of this word. The vowel sound here is pronounced the same as in "sun".

*__floor__ US: /flɔːr/ UK: /flɔːʳ/ [countable noun] **1** The surface in a room on which you walk: *Most houses in the United States have carpets on the floor.* **2** Each of the horizontal parts of a building: *The highest skyscraper in this city has 120 floors.* **3** **ground floor** The part of a building that is at street level: *You don't need to take the elevator. My office is on the ground floor.*

a b c d e f g h i j k l m n o p q r s t u v w x y z

a b c d e f g h i j k l m n o p q r s t u v w x y z

floorboard US: /ˈflɔːr.bɔːrd/ UK: /ˈflɔː.bɔːd/ [countable noun] A piece of wood used for the floor of a room: *When the floorboards make a creaking sound at night, I always think there's somebody in the house.*

flop /flɒp/ [noun] Not a success, a disaster: *The new play was a complete flop.*

flora US: /ˈflɔːr.ə/ UK: /ˈflɔː.rə/ [uncountable noun] The plants that grow in a particular region or period: *The Amazon rainforest has a wide variety of flora species.* ■ Compare with "fauna" (all of the animal life of a region).

florist /ˈflɔr·ɪst/, /ˈflɑr-/ [countable noun] A person who works in a store that sells flowers: *The florist made a beautiful bouquet.*

florist's [countable noun] A store that sells flowers and indoor plants: *Is there a florist's near here?*

↑**flour** US: /flaʊɚ/ UK: /flaʊəʳ/ [uncountable noun] A powder made from wheat that is used for making bread, cakes, sauces and so on: *Add a bit of flour to make the sauce thicker.*

flourish /ˈflɜr·ɪʃ/, /ˈflʌr-/ [verb] To do well and grow: *The business is flourishing. We've made $10,000 this month.*

flow¹ /fləʊ/ [countable noun] A movement of liquid, air, people and so on: *The flow of people into the gallery has been continuous all morning.*

flow² /fləʊ/ [verb] To move smoothly: *I like sitting by the river and watching the water flow.*

↑**flower**¹ /flaʊər/ [countable noun] The colored part of a plant: *The flower of the almond tree is small and white or pink.* **See page 433.**

flower² /flaʊər/ [verb] To produce flowers: *Most trees flower in spring.*

flowerpot /ˈflaʊ·ərˌpɑt/, /ˈflaʊər-/ [countable noun] A container used for growing plants individually: *Mrs. Gardner has lots of flowerpots on her balcony.* See picture at **pot**.

flown US: /floʊn/ UK: /fləʊn/ Past participle of **fly**².

↑**flu** /fluː/ [uncountable noun] An illness like a very bad cold: *We were all ill with flu last week.* ■ "Flu" is short for "influenza".

fluent /ˈfluː.ənt/ [adjective] That speaks or writes a language easily and well: *Victoria speaks fluent French.*

fluid /ˈfluː.ɪd/ [noun] A substance that can flow like a liquid or a gas: *After I had the accident I could only take fluids like soup and fruit juice.*

fluoride /ˈflɔːraɪd/ [uncountable noun] A mixture of chemicals that contains fluorine: *Fluoride is added to toothpaste to help prevent tooth decay.*

fluorine /ˈflʊə.riːn/ US: /ˈflʊ-/ [uncountable noun] A yellow chemical element: *Symbol of fluorine at the chemical table is "F".*

flute /fluːt/ [countable noun] A musical instrument with holes in that you play by blowing into it: *The Pied Piper of Hamelin played a flute to take the children away.* **See page 459.**

fly¹ /flaɪ/ [countable noun] A small insect with two wings: *I hate jokes about flies in your soup.* ■ The plural is "flies". **See page 431.**

↑**fly**², **flew**, **flown** /flaɪ/ [verb] To travel through the air: *Most but not all birds can fly.*

flying saucer [countable noun] A flying object with the shape of a saucer: *Wendy says she saw a flying saucer over her house the other day.*

FM Referring to a radio system or broadcasting which produces a very clear sound: *FM radio station.* ■ "FM" is an abbreviation for "frequency modulation". ■ See box at **abbreviations**.

foal US: /foʊl/ UK: /fəʊl/ [countable noun] A very young horse: *Robert's mare had a foal last week.*

foam US: /foʊm/ UK: /fəʊm/ [uncountable noun] Small bubbles on the surface of a liquid: *This soap produces a lot of foam.*

↑**focus**¹ /ˈfəʊkəs/ [countable noun] Center of attention: *Sue's baby is the focus of everyone's interest wherever she goes.*

focus² /ˈfəʊkəs/ [verb] **1** To adjust something to see clearly: *You have to focus the camera before you take the photo.* **2** To concentrate: *You just need to focus on what your doing and your grades will improve.* **3 to be in focus** To be able to be seen clearly: *I think you are in focus now. I'll take the photo.*

foe US: /foʊ/ UK: /fəʊ/ [countable noun] Enemy: *Darth Vader was Luke Skywalker's foe in "Star Wars".* ■ This word is formal.

fog US: /fɑːg/ UK: /fɒg/ [noun] Clouds close to the ground: *We couldn't see a thing because of the fog.* ■ Compare with "mist" ("mist" is thinner than "fog").

foggy US: /ˈfɑː.gi/ UK: /ˈfɒg.i/ [adjective] Covered in fog: *It was so foggy that the airplanes couldn't land.* ■ The comparative form is "foggier" and the superlative form is "foggiest".

foil¹ /fɔɪl/ [uncountable noun] **1** A very thin, very light sheet of metal used mainly for covering food: *Foil is used in cooking to wrap meat or fish to preserve flavor.* **2** A thin sword used in fencing: *When you are ready, raise your foil and salute your opponent.*

foil² /fɔɪl/ [verb] To frustrate or defeat a plan, attempt or attack: *The defending army foiled the enemy attack.*

fold US: /foʊld/ UK: /fəʊld/ [verb] To bend something on itself: *To make a paper airplane you just need to fold a sheet of paper in a special way.*

folder US: /'foʊl.dɚ/ UK: /'fəʊl.dəʳ/ [countable noun] Something used for keeping papers in, usually made of cardboard: *James keeps his school projects in a folder.*

FOLDER

folk US: /foʊk/ UK: /fəʊk/ [noun] People: *Town folk like this part of the countryside.* ■ This word is informal.

folk song US: /'foʊk ˌsɔŋ/ [countable noun] A song that is popular and traditional: *"Oh Susannah!" is an American folk song.*

***follow** US: /'fɑː.loʊ/ UK: /'fɒl.əʊ/ [verb] **1** To go behind somebody: *The head waiter asked us to follow him.* **2** To come after something: *Spring follows winter.* **3** To understand: *Sorry, could you repeat that? I don't quite follow you.* ■ In this use, we usually say "understand".

follower US: /'fɑː.loʊ.ɚ/ UK: /'fɒl.əʊ.əʳ/ [countable noun] A person who follows or supports a particular belief, leader and so on: *Gandhi still has followers today.*

***following** /'fɑl·oʊ·ɪŋ/ [adjective] Next: *We arrive in Rome on Sunday and the following morning we leave for Florence.*

fond US: /fɑːnd/ UK: /fɒnd/ [adjective] **1** Affectionate or pleasant: *I have fond memories of my time in Pakistan.* ■ We usually say "happy" or "affectionate". **2 to be fond of (somebody or something)** Like somebody or something very much: *I think Cindy is very fond of Rick.*

***food** /fuːd/ [noun] What people, animals and plants eat to grow and live: *Some people in Africa die because they don't have any food.*

fool[1] /fuːl/ [countable noun] A stupid person: *He's a fool. He never knows when to keep quiet.*

fool[2] /fuːl/ [verb] To trick somebody: *She fooled us into giving her some money.*

▶ **PHRASAL VERBS · to fool around** To behave in a stupid way: *Some students are always fooling around instead of paying attention.*

foolish /'fuː.lɪʃ/ [adjective] Silly, that behaves like a fool: *It's foolish to try to pretend you haven't broken the window, George. We saw you.*

foosball [countable noun] Game often played in bars in which you move players on bars on a table: *I am useless at foosball.* ■ The same meaning: "table soccer".

***foot** /fʊt/ [countable noun] **1** The part of a person's or an animal's body at the end of the leg: *He stepped on my foot and almost broke my toe.* 👁 **See page 421.** **2** A unit of length: *A foot has 12 inches.* ■ The abbreviation "ft" is only used in written language. See box at **abbreviations**. **3 on foot** Walking: *Richard goes to school on foot.* ■ The plural is "feet".

***football** /'fʊtˌbɔl/ [uncountable noun] **1** In the USA, a game for two teams who try to take a ball behind a line: *Football players wear lots of special clothing for protection.* ■ In British English they say "American football". **2** See **soccer.** ■ This use is British English.

footpath /'fʊtˌpæθ/ [countable noun] A small road where you can only go on foot: *There's a footpath along the river which will take you to the town.*

footprint /'fʊt.prɪnt/ [countable noun] The mark that your feet leave: *We found Susie very easily. We just had to follow her footprints in the snow.*

footstep /'fʊt.step/ [countable noun] The sound of somebody walking: *Hearing footsteps in the middle of the night can be frightening.*

***for** US: /fɔːr/ UK: /fɔːʳ/ [preposition] **1** Showing purpose or use: *I need a lamp for reading.* **2** Intended for somebody or something: *I think mom has got some presents for us.* **3** During a length of time: *We've been walking for two hours now. I'm tired.* ■ See box below. **4** Showing distance: *We haven't seen a house for miles.* **5** Going to: *Excuse me, is this the bus for Boston?* **6** In favor of: *How many of you are for the idea of having the party on Saturday?* **7** Showing price: *I've bought a jazz CD for only $3.* **8** Showing the reason for something: *He was sent to prison for robbing a bank.* ■ Be careful! The verb after "for" is in the "-ing" form.

for and since

We use *for* and *since* with the present perfect or the present perfect continuous to talk about actions that we started doing in the past and that we are still doing in the present.

- ***for***

  We use *for* with periods of time: *hours, one week, two months, three years.*

  - *Carmen has been studying English **for three years**.*
  - *She has been working in the library **for hours.***

- ***since***

  We use *since* with starting points in time: *yesterday, last week, two months ago, September, 1975, their wedding day*, the last time that we saw them...

  - *Sally has been working in this bank **since 1994**.*
  - *I haven't seen Sally and Jim **since their wedding day**.*

a b c d e **f** g h i j k l m n o p q r s t u v w x y z

forbade Past tense of **forbid**.

forbid, forbade, forbidden /fə'bɪd/ [verb] To tell somebody that you do not allow them to do something: *Smoking is forbidden at our school.* ■ Compare with "ban[2]" (to make a law or a rule that says that something must not be done).

forbidden /fər'bɪd·ə·n/, /fɔr-/ Past participle of **forbid**.

+**force**[1] /fɔːs/ ▮ [uncountable noun] **1** Power: *Only judges have the legal force to send somebody to prison.* **2** Strength: *If you try to throw me out by force, you'll be sorry.* ▮ [countable noun] **3** An organized group of people: *Each county in United States has its own police force.* **4 the armed forces** The army, navy and air force: *Rita wants to be a member of the armed forces when she grows up.* ■ In this use, the same meaning: "the armed services", "the services".

force[2] /fɔːs/ [verb] To make somebody do something: *Our teacher forced us to play soccer even though it was snowing.*

forearm [countable noun] The part of the arm between the wrist and the elbow: *The forearm contains two long bones, the radius and the ulna.*

+**forecast**[1] /'fɔːkaːst/ [countable noun] A prediction: *The weather forecast for this weekend is excellent: sunny and warm.*

forecast[2]**,** forecast, forecast /'fɔːkaːst/ [verb] To say what you think that will happen in the future: *Some people forecast that in the 21st century we will be able to visit the planet Mars.* ■ "Forecast" also has regular past and past participle forms: "forecasted".

foreground /'fɔr,graʊnd/, /'foʊr-/ [noun] That part of a view or image which appears to be closest to the viewer: *In the foreground of the picture there is a small farmhouse.* ■ Compare with "background" (the back part in a picture).

forehead US: /'fɑː.rɪd/ UK: /'fɒr.ɪd/ [countable noun] The part of the face between your hair and your eyes: *They say that a wide forehead is a sign of intelligence.* 👁 See picture at **face**.

+**foreign** /'fɔr·ən/, /'fɑr-/ [adjective] Belonging to another country: *It's not easy to speak a foreign language.*

foreigner US: /'fɔːr.ə.nɚ/ UK: /'fɒr.ə.nəʳ/ [countable noun] A person from another country: *There are very few foreigners living in China.*

foreman /'fɔr·mən/, /'foʊr-/ [countable noun] A man who is responsible for a group of workers: *The foreman gave instructions to his workers before they started work.* ■ The plural is "foremen". ■ A woman is a "forewoman".

+**forest** /'fɔr·əst/, /'fɑr-/ [noun] A large area of land covered with trees: *Forests are bigger than woods.*

FOREST

forestry /'fɒrɪstri/ [uncountable noun] The science and practice of planting, looking after and managing forests: *The forestry commission is working on the reforestation of the burned area.*

+**forever** US: /fɔː'rev.ɚ/ UK: /fə're.vəʳ/ [adverb] Always: *I'll remember you forever, Brenda.*

forewoman /'fɔr,wʊm·ən/, /'foʊr-/ [countable noun] A woman who is responsible for a group of workers: *The forewoman told the carpenter and the electrician what they should do.* ■ The plural is "forewomen". ■ A man is a "foreman".

forgave /fər'geɪv/, /fɔr-/ Past tense of **forgive**.

+**forget,** forgot, forgotten /fər'get/, /fɔr-/ [verb] Not to remember something: *Don't forget we're having a test on Monday.*

forgetful /fər'get·fəl/, /fɔr-/ [adjective] That forgets easily: *My girlfriend is very forgetful. She never remembers my birthday.*

+**forgive,** forgave, forgiven /fər'gɪv/, /fɔr-/ [verb] To pardon somebody for something: *Forgive me for breaking your guitar.*

forgiven Past participle of **forgive**.

forgot /fə'gɒt/ Past tense of **forget**.

forgotten /fə'gɒtən/ Past participle of **forget**.

+**fork** US: /fɔːrk/ UK: /fɔːk/ [countable noun] **1** An instrument with several points at one end used for eating: *Charles, use your fork. Don't pick up your food with your hands.* ■ Remember! You eat soup with a spoon, you eat french fries with a fork and you cut cakes with a knife. 👁 See picture at **cutlery**. **2** A large instrument with several points at one end that is used for gardening: *Shona used the garden fork to dig out the weeds.*

a b c d e f g h i j k l m n o p q r s t u v w x y z

form US: /fɔːrm/ UK: /fɔːm/ [countable noun] **1** A type: *Swimming is a very good form of exercise.* **2** A paper with questions: *Please, fill in the form at home and give it to me next week.*

†**formal** /'fɔr·məl/ [adjective] **1** Official: *You need formal permission to leave school before three.* **2** Done according to certain social rules: *My parents wore formal clothes for the Christmas party.*

formation /fɔr'meɪ·ʃən/ [uncountable noun] The forming of something: *The formation of the verbs in English is not difficult.*

former US: /'fɔːr.mɚ/ UK: /'fɔː.məʳ/ [adjective] Previous: *In former times people traveled on horses or in carriages.*

†**formula** /'fɔr·mjə·lə/ [countable noun] **1** A rule in science or mathematics that is written with symbols and numbers: *Who knows the mathematical formula for calculating the circumference of a circle?* **2** A list of substances necessary for making something: *The formula of Coca Cola is secret.*

fort US: /fɔːrt/ UK: /fɔːt/ [countable noun] A building like a castle, built to protect the people inside: *In the American Far West, soldiers lived in wooden forts.*

fortieth /'fɔr·t̬i·əθ/ [adjective] Referring to forty: *I'm the fortieth in the list of admissions to the University.* ■ "Fortieth" can also be written "40th".

fortify /'fɔr·t̬əˌfaɪ/ [verb] To strengthen: *More soldiers were brought in to fortify the defenses of the town.* ■ We say: "to fortify something **with** something": "cereal fortified with extra vitamins". ■ Be careful with the spelling of these forms: "fortifies", "fortified".

fortnight /'fɔrtˌnaɪt/, /'fourt-/ [countable noun] Two weeks: *This summer we're going to Florida for a fortnight.* ■ This word is a contraction of "fourteen nights".

fortunate /'fɔr·tʃə·nət/ [adjective] Lucky: *Those children are fortunate to live in such a beautiful place.*

†**fortune** /'fɔr·tʃən/ ▮ [countable noun] **1** A large amount of money: *Mr. Thomson made his fortune selling secondhand cars.* ▮ [uncountable noun] **2** Good luck: *They had the good fortune of being selected for the trip to Italy.* **3** Fate: *Sara can read your fortune in the Tarot cards.*

forty US: /'fɔːr.t̬i/ UK: /'fɔː.ti/ [noun, adjective and pronoun] The number 40: *Ali Baba was the leader of a gang of forty thieves.*

†**forward**[1] /'fɔːwəd/ [adjective] In the direction that is in front of you: *In American football, you can make forward passes.*

forward[2] **or forwards** /'fɔːwəd/ [adverb] Towards the front, towards in front of you: *Please move forwards because there are lots of free seats at the front.*

forward[3] /'fɔːwəd/ [countable noun] Player in an attacking position: *I play as a forward in the school team.* 👁 See picture at **soccer**.

fossil US: /'fɑː.sᵊl/ UK: /'fɒs.ᵊl/ [countable noun] The remains of a prehistoric plant or animal changed into stone through centuries: *A one million year old fossil was found during the excavations.*

fought US: /fɑːt/ UK: /fɔːt/ Past tense and past participle forms of **fight**[2]. ■ Be careful with the pronunciation of this word. It is pronounced like the word "fort".

foul[1] /faʊl/ [adjective] Very dirty or unpleasant: *Tim is always using foul language. I don't know where he's picked it up.*

foul[2] /faʊl/ [countable noun] An action in sport that is not permitted: *Stopping the ball with your foot in hockey is a foul.*

†**found** /faʊnd/ Past tense and past participle forms of **find**.

†**foundation** /faʊn'deɪ.ʃᵊn/ [uncountable noun] The act of founding something: *The university has been famous for medical studies ever since its foundation.*

foundations /faʊn'deɪʃən/ [plural noun] The base of a building: *If the foundations are solid, the house won't fall down.*

fountain /'faʊn.tɪn/ [countable noun] A construction from which water comes out, usually in a yard or a park: *Chicago has some beautiful fountains.*

fountain pen [countable noun] A pen that you fill with ink: *Some writers don't like using computers. They only write with fountain pens.*

†**four** US: /fɔːr/ UK: /fɔːʳ/ [noun, adjective and pronoun] The number 4: *Dogs have four legs.*

fourteen /ˌfɔː'tiːn/ [noun, adjective and pronoun] The number 14: *James has got ten marbles and I've got fourteen.*

fourteenth /ˌfɔː'tiːnθ/ [noun and adjective] Referring to fourteen: *The fourteenth of July is my birthday.* ■ "Fourteenth" can also be written "14th".

fourth US: /fɔːrθ/ UK: /fɔːθ/ [noun and adjective] Referring to four: *The Fourth of July is Independence Day in the USA.* ■ "Fourth" can also be written "4th". Be careful! When we speak about proportions, we usually say "a quarter" not "a fourth": "I'll be finished in a quarter of an hour". "I ate one quarter of the pizza".

fox US: /fɑːks/ UK: /fɒks/ [countable noun] A wild animal of the dog family, with pointed ears and a bushy tail: *The fox is a mammal.* ■ The plural is "foxes".

fraction /'fræk.ʃᵊn/ [countable noun] **1** A part of a whole number: *1/3 is a fraction.* **2** A small amount: *I closed my eyes for a fraction of a second and he disappeared.*

fractious /'fræk.ʃəs/ [adjective] Disobedient, bad tempered: *You are very fractious today. What is the*

a b c d e f g h i j k l m n o p q r s t u v w x y z

matter with you? ■ This word is usually used when you refer to a child.

fragile US: /ˈfrædʒ.əl/ UK: /ˈfrædʒ.aɪl/ [adjective] **1** That breaks or gets damaged easily: *Glass is quite difficult to transport. It's very fragile.* **2** Delicate or unhealthy: *I was feeling fragile and the doctor prescribed me some vitamins.*

fragility /frəˈdʒɪləti/ [uncountable noun] **1** The state of being easily damaged or broken: *Due to its fragility, the figure needs to be packed carefully.* **2** The state of not being strong and healthy: *The doctor says that her fragility now is normal.*

fragment /frægˈment/, /ˈfræg.mənt/ [countable noun] A small part of something: *Be careful! There are still fragments of glass on the floor.*

frail /freɪl/ [adjective] Weak and delicate: *Mrs. Hawkins is a frail woman. She's always ill.*

↑**frame** /freɪm/ [countable noun] **1** A structure that surrounds pictures, mirrors and other objects: *I like that picture frame. It's simple and not too big.* 👁 See picture at **glasses**. **2** A structure on which something is built: *In Scandinavia many houses have a wooden frame.*

framework /ˈfreɪm,wɜrk/ [countable noun] The basic structure on which something is built or in which something is based: *The framework burned down in the fire and the roof collapsed.*

frank /fræŋk/ [adjective] Open, sincere: *He's a very frank person. He always says what he thinks.*

fraternity /frəˈtɜr·nɪ·ṭi/ [uncountable noun] Friendship or support for other people: *There was a great feeling of fraternity among the people running in the marathon.* ■ The plural is "fraternities".

fraud US: /frɑːd/ UK: /frɔːd/ ▮ [noun] **1** A dishonest action to get money: *He's been in prison twice for fraud.* ▮ [uncountable noun] **2** Somebody who is not what they say they are: *He said he was the king of an Asian country, but he was a fraud.*

freckle /ˈfrek.l̩/ [countable noun] A small, brown spot on your skin: *Children with freckles always look naughty.*

↑**free**[1] /friː/ [adjective] **1** Able to do what you like, without restriction: *Slaves were not free. They had to do what their masters told them.* **2** That does not cost any money: *Hurry up! They're giving away free tickets for the circus.* **3** That is not doing anything: *Are you free tonight, Peter? I'd like you to do me a little favor.* **4** **free from (something)** That doesn't have or suffer from something unpleasant: *I'd like to live in a place free from pollution.* **5** **free speech** The right to free expression: *Free speech is an important characteristic of modern democracies.* **6** **free time** The time when you are not at school or at work: *Do you do any sport in your free time?* **7** **to set free** To let somebody or something go from a prison or from a cage: *The children opened the cage and set free all the doves.*

free[2] /friː/ [verb] To make somebody or something free: *The government has decided to free all political prisoners.*

↑**freedom** /ˈfriː.dəm/ [noun] **1** The right or power to do what you like, the state of being free: *Since I bought the scooter I've had much more freedom of movement.* **2** **freedom of speech** The right to free expression: *Freedom of speech is an important characteristic of modern democracies.*

freelance /ˈfri,læns/ [adjective and adverb] Independent, not employed by one particular company: *My ambition is to be a freelance photographer.*

freely /ˈfriː.li/ [adverb] **1** Without control, limit or obligation: *Contributions to charity are given freely.* **2** Openly: *You can speak freely to me.* **3** Willingly: *I freely admit that I'm jealous.* **4** Liberally: *He spends his money very freely.* **5** Loosely, in a free way: *You have translated this part very freely.*

free-range /ˌfriːˈreɪndʒ/ [adjective] From a farm, not a factory, when talking about eggs, chickens and so on: *I only eat free-range eggs.*

freeway /ˈfriː.weɪ/ [countable noun] A very wide road that goes directly from one town to another: *If you take the freeway, it only takes two hours to get to the city.* ■ In British English they say "motorway".

↑**freeze, froze, frozen** /friːz/ [verb] To become solid at a low temperature: *You can freeze many types of food to preserve them for a period of time.*

freezer /ˈfri·zər/ [countable noun] A large fridge where you can keep food for a few months: *My parents buy large amounts of food and keep it in the freezer.* 👁 See picture at **kitchen**.

freezing /ˈfriː.zɪŋ/ [adjective] Very cold: *Turn on the heating, Paul. It's freezing.*

freight car [countable noun] An open carriage pulled by a train: *That train has 15 freight cars of coal.* ■ In British English they say "wagon, truck".

French[1] [uncountable noun] The language of France and other countries: *Do you speak French?* ■ Be careful! "French" has a capital "F".

French[2] /frentʃ/ [adjective] Referring to France: *Vanessa has a French penpal who lives in Marseilles.* ■ Careful! "French" has a capital "F". For people the singular is "a Frenchman" or "a Frenchwoman" and the plural is "the French".

french fry [countable noun] Small, thick piece of potato cooked in oil: *Do you want french fries with your* *hamburger?* ■ This use is more common in the plural "french fries". ■ Compare with "potato chip" (a thin slice of fried potato sold in packets). ■ In British English they say "chip".

frequency /ˈfriː.kwənt.si/ [noun] How often something happens: *People catch colds with great frequency at this time of year.* ■ The plural is "frequencies". ■ See box below.

frequent /ˈfriː.kwᵊnt/ [adjective] Often happening: *There are frequent storms there in the summer.*

fresh /freʃ/ [adjective] **1** Made or picked a short time ago: *I love fresh bread.* **2** Not tinned or frozen: *Fresh vegetables have more vitamins than frozen ones.* **3** Clean or new: *Let's give the cat some fresh water.* **4** Cool: *By the seaside there's always a fresh breeze.*

freshman [countable noun] A student in the first year of high school or college: *This year she is in 8th grade and next year she'll be a freshman in high school.*

freshwater /ˈfreʃˌwɔt̬·ər/, /-ˌwɑt̬·ər/ [adjective] Of rivers or lakes, not of the sea: *Trout are freshwater fish.*

Friday /ˈfraɪ.deɪ/ [noun] **1** The sixth day of the week: *Friday is between Thursday and Saturday.* **2 Good Friday** See **Good Friday**. ■ Be careful! "Friday" has a capital "F". Be careful with the pronunciation of this word. "fri" rhymes with "my". 👁 See picture at **calendar**.

fridge /frɪdʒ/ [countable noun] A machine for keeping drinks and food cold: *Don't forget to put the bottle of milk in the fridge.* ■ The same meaning: "refrigerator". 👁 See picture at **kitchen**.

fried /fraɪd/ [adjective] That has been cooked in hot oil or fat: *How do you want your eggs, fried or boiled?*

friend /frend/ [countable noun] **1** Somebody who you know well, get on well with and feel loyal to: *Brian is my best friend. I've known him for over ten years.* **2 to make friends with (somebody)** To become friends: *After two weeks at school I had made friends with most of my classmates.* ■ Compare with "acquaintance" (a person that you know slightly). ■ Be careful with the pronunciation of this word. "friend" rhymes with "end".

friendly /ˈfrend.li/ [adjective] **1** That is helpful, open and welcoming: *John is a very friendly boy. He gets on well with everyone.* **2 to be friendly with** Be friend with somebody: *Sue is friendly with nearly everybody in the hockey team.*

friendship /ˈfrend.ʃɪp/ [noun] The relationship with a friend: *Brian and I have kept our friendship for years.*

fright /fraɪt/ [uncountable noun] A feeling of fear: *Hearing the telephone call in the middle of the night always gives me a fright.*

frighten /ˈfraɪ.tᵊn/ [verb] To make somebody feel fear: *I don't want to frighten you. But there's a policeman asking for you.*

frightened /ˈfraɪ.tᵊnd/ [adjective] That is afraid of something: *Don't be frightened. These snakes are not poisonous.* ■ Be careful with the pronunciation of this word. The last "e" is not pronounced. ■ See box at **bored**.

frightening /ˈfraɪ.tᵊn.ɪŋ/ [adjective] That makes you feel fear: *It was a frightening scene: rats all over the place.* ■ See box at **bored**.

fringe /frɪndʒ/ [countable noun] **1** See **bangs**. ■ This use is British English. **2** An ornamental border or edge on cloths, carpets or a piece of cloth, consisting of loose threads or cords: *The carpet at home has thick fringes.* **3** The outer edge of an area, a group or an activity: *The quieter areas are on the fringes of town.*

Frequency adverbs

- We use ***always***, ***usually***, ***often***, ***sometimes***, ***rarely*** and ***never*** to talk about how often we do something:
  - *How often do you sleep eight hours a night?*

....	*always*
....	*usually*
....	*often*
....	*sometimes*
... .	*rarely*
	never

- These words usually go before the main verb:
  - *Susan always walks to school.*
- They go after auxiliary verbs like *to be*, *to do* or *to have*:
  - *James has often been late for school.*

a b c d e f g h i j k l m n o p q r s t u v w x y z

frisbee /'frɪz.bi/ [countable noun] A round thin plastic object that spins when you throw it: *If you throw it right, the frisbee comes back to you.*

frog US: /frɑːg/ UK: /frɒg/ [countable noun] A small green animal with big back legs for jumping: *Frogs live on land but lay their eggs in water.* **See page 431.**

from US: /frɑːm/ UK: /frɒm/ [preposition] **1** Showing where somebody was born: *Irene is from Peru.* **2** Showing the origin of something: *This flight comes from New York.* **3** Showing the time something starts: *I work from nine to five.* **4** Showing the material used to make something: *I have a model boat made from wood.* **5** Because of: *They died from malaria.*

front /frʌnt/ [countable noun] **1** The forward part of something: *Sue's father once hit the wall with the front of his car.* **2** **front door** The door that is at the front of a building or an apartment: *She went in through the front door and out by the back door.* See picture at **house.** **3** **front row** The first row: *Some people like sitting in the front row at the theater.* **4** **in front of (somebody)** **1** Ahead of you, before you in position: *There are just three girls in front of us in the line.* **2** Outside the forward part of something: *Wait for me in front of the library.* See picture at **preposition.**

frontal /'frʌntəl/ [adjective] Being at the front: *Among the skull bones you may find: frontal, parietal and occipital.* ■ Compare with "rear²" (back) and "back²" (situated behind something).

frontier /frʌn'tɪər/ [countable noun] The line between two countries: *The Rio Grande marks the frontier between Mexico and the USA.*

frost US: /frɑːst/ UK: /frɒst/ [noun] Fine covering of ice that forms on things in very cold weather: *In winter, there's frost on the car windshield in the morning.*

frown /fraʊn/ [verb] To make a gesture with your forehead to show that you are angry or surprised: *When I told him I had seen Tom at the movie theater, he frowned.*

froze US: /froʊz/ UK: /frəʊz/ Past tense of **freeze.**

frozen /'froʊ·zən/ Past participle of **freeze.**

fruit /fruːt/ [noun] **1** The soft and often juicy part of some plants or trees that you can eat: *I always have an orange or other fruit for dessert.* ■ This word is usually an uncountable noun. We say "some fruit" or "a piece of fruit". **2** **fruit juice** The liquid you get by pressing some fruits: *I don't drink alcohol, only fruit juice.* ■ Be careful with the pronunciation of this word. The ending is pronounced the same as the word "root". **See page 436.**

fry¹ /fraɪ/ [verb] To cook food in hot oil or butter: *I'm going to fry some peppers.* ■ Be careful with the spelling of these forms: "fries", "fried".

fry² /fraɪ/ [noun] See **french fry.** ■ This use is more common in the plural: "fries".

frying pan [countable noun] A shallow pan used for frying food: *Do not put too much oil in the frying pan.* ■ The same meaning "skillet". See picture at **pan.**

ft A written abbreviation for **foot.** ■ See box at **abbreviations.**

fuel /fjʊəl/ [noun] A substance that can be burned for light or heat: *Gas is the cleanest fuel but it can be dangerous.*

fulcrum /'fʊl.krəm/ [countable noun] The point at which a lever is placed to gain purchase: *Placing the lever at the fulcrum point gives maximum stability.* ■ The plural is "fulcrums" or "fulcra".

fulfill /fʊl'fɪl/ [verb] **1** To do or to complete your duty, plans or promises successfully: *Daniel always fulfills his promises.* **2** To make something you wish for true: *I'd like to fulfill my ambition to become an attorney.*

full /fʊl/ [adjective] **1** Holding or containing the maximum: *Sorry, you can't go in. The room is full.* See picture at **opposite.** **2** **full up** With no room for anything or anybody else: *I can't eat any more. I'm full up.* **3** **in full** Completely: *Write your name in full, please.*

full stop [countable noun] See **period.** ■ This word is British English.

full-time /,fʊl'taɪm/ [adjective and adverb] All the time: *If you want to become a doctor, you'll have to study full-time.*

fun¹ /fʌn/ [adjective] Enjoyable: *It was fun climbing the mountain, but very tiring.* ■ Compare with "funny" (that makes you laugh).

fun² /fʌn/ [uncountable noun] **1** Enjoyment, amusement: *Riding a mountain bike is good fun.* **2** **to have fun** To have a good time: *Bye children! Have fun at the party.* **3** **to make fun of (somebody)** To laugh at somebody: *I don't think you should make fun of other people.*

function¹ /'fʌŋkʃən/ [countable noun] The job or the intended purpose of somebody or something: *The function of a teacher is to help students learn.*

function² /'fʌŋkʃən/ [verb] To work: *This computer doesn't function properly.*

fund¹ /fʌnd/ [countable noun] An amount of money, usually for some special purpose: *At school we're trying to start a fund for a new laboratory.*

fund² [verb] To give money for something: *This environmental project is funded by an important company.*

funeral /'fju·nər·əl/ [countable noun] The ceremony of burying or cremating a dead person: *When Mrs. Nelson died, the whole class went to her funeral.*

funfair /'fʌn.feər/ US: /-fer/ [countable noun] See **amusement**

park in the word **park**[1]. ■ This word is British English.

fungus /'fʌŋ.gəs/ [countable noun] One of a group of spore-producing organisms which feed on organic matter: *This fungus is a mushroom.* ■ The plural is "fungi".

funnel /'fʌnəl/ [countable noun] **1** A kind of tube opening into a wide mouth, used for pouring liquids into bottles: *Use the funnel to fill the bottle or you will spill the water.* **2** The chimney on a ship: *As the ship left the harbor, a column of smoke came out of its funnel.*

funny /'fʌn.i/ [adjective] **1** That makes you laugh: *The joke that she told was so funny that we couldn't stop laughing for ten minutes.* **2** Strange: *That boy is crazy. He behaves in such a funny way.* ■ The comparative form is "funnier" and the superlative form is "funniest". ■ Compare with "fun[1]" (enjoyable).

fur US: /fɝː/ UK: /fɜːʳ/ [noun] The hairy coat of an animal: *Cats have very soft fur.*

fur coat [countable noun] A coat made of the skin of an animal: *There were lots of fur coats in the store window.*

furious /'fjʊər·i·əs/ [adjective] Very angry: *My aunt Maggie was furious when they stole her new car.* 👁 See picture at **emotions**.

furniture US: /'fɝː.nɪ.tʃɚ/ UK: /'fɜː.nɪ.tʃəʳ/ [uncountable noun] The objects you find in a house, such as chairs, tables and so on: *Mom has seen some very nice furniture for our new house.* ■ Be careful! We don't say "a furniture". We say "some furniture" or "a piece of furniture".

furry US: /'fɝː.i/ UK: /'fɜː.ri/ [adjective] **1** Being covered in fur: *Bears are furry creatures.* ■ The comparative form is "furrier" and the superlative form is "furriest". **2** Being covered by hair resembling fur: *The teddy bear was soft and furry to the touch.*

further[1] /'fɜːðər/ [adverb] The comparative form of **far**.

further[2] /'fɜːðər/ [adjective] **1** The comparative form of **far**[2]. **2** Something else: *The library is closed until further notice.*

furthest /'fɜr·ðəst/ [adjective and adverb] The superlative form of **far**.

fury US: /'fjɝː.i/ UK: /'fjʊə.ri/ **to be in a fury** Be in a state of great anger: *Mr. Burns is in a fury because a cow has eaten his roses.*

fusion [countable noun] A combination of elements to form a single thing: *The music of my favorite group is a fusion of different styles.*

fuss /fʌs/ [uncountable noun] **1** A lot of excitement about something that is not very important: *Come on, Linda! Don't make so much fuss over a few cents.* **2** **to make a fuss of somebody** Pay a lot of attention to somebody: *I love aunt Emily. She always makes a fuss of me.*

fussy /'fʌs.i/ [adjective] That gives too much importance to details: *He's very fussy about his clothes. They have to be perfectly clean and ironed.* ■ The comparative form is "fussier" and the superlative form is "fussiest".

future /'fju·tʃər/ [countable noun] The time that will come: *No one knows what will happen in the future.*

future tense [countable noun] A form of a verb that shows that something is going to happen in the time that will come: *In the sentence "I will see you tomorrow", the future tense is "will see".* ■ The future tense is formed by adding "will" to the infinitive of a verb.

G

g

g[1] /dʒiː/ The seventh letter of the alphabet: *The name "George" begins with a "G".*

g[2] /dʒiː/ A written abbreviation for **gram.** ■ See box at **abbreviations**.

G [countable noun] The fifth musical note of the scale of C major: *The opera singer sang a G.* ■ The plural is "Gs" or "G's". See page 460.

gain[1] /geɪn/ [noun] An increase of possessions or profit: *This year the gains have exceeded the losses for the first time.*

gain[2] /geɪn/ [verb] **1** To get something useful: *Lee's gained a lot of experience abroad.* **2** To increase weight, speed and so on: *My dad's gained three kilos in a month and says he's going on a diet.*

galaxy /ˈgæl.ək.si/ [countable noun] A very large system of stars and planets: *The Milky Way is a galaxy.* ■ The plural is "galaxies".

gale /geɪl/ [countable noun] A very strong wind: *The sailors were frightened by the gale.*

galleon /ˈgæl.i.ən/ [countable noun] A large sailing ship with several masts, used in the past for trade and in war: *The galleon was used by the explorers of America.*

gallery /ˈgæl·ə·ri/ [countable noun] A building where people can see paintings: *In Florence we spent a whole day looking at paintings in galleries.* ■ The plural is "galleries".

↑**gallon** /ˈgæl.ən/ [countable noun] A unit of capacity equal to 3.785 liters: *My car does a hundred kilometers to the gallon.* ■ In British English a gallon is equal to 4.5 liters.

gallop /ˈgæl.əp/ [verb] To ride a horse very fast: *She galloped across the valley.*

gamble[1] /ˈgæmbl/ [countable noun] A risk that you take: *It's a gamble going on a picnic on such a cloudy day.*

↑**gamble**[2] /ˈgæmbl/ [verb] **1** To play for money at cards, on the horses and so on: *Uncle Robert lost all his money gambling on horses.* **2** To take a risk to get something: *They're gambling all they have on the new store they are opening.* ■ Be careful. We say: "gamble **on** (something)".

gambler /ˈgæm·blər/ [countable noun] A person who tries to win money on cards, races and so on: *Mr. Ballard is a real gambler; he gambles on anything.*

gambling /ˈgæm.blɪŋ/ [uncountable noun] The act of betting money on cards, horses and so on: *My aunt likes gambling on the lottery.*

↑**game** /geɪm/ ▮ [countable noun] **1** An activity or sport with special rules: *Chess is my favorite game.* **2** Part of a match in tennis and other sports, won by gaining a certain number of points: *Tony won the first game easily, but lost the second and the third.* ▮ [uncountable noun] **3** Wild animals that people hunt: *It is forbidden to shoot game in the National Parks.* ■ In this use "game" is an uncountable noun. **4 board game** See **board game.**

game park [noun] A large area of land used as a reserve for wild animals: *In our trips to Kenya we visited two game parks and saw lots of elephants.*

gang /gæŋ/ [noun] A group of people who act together: *A gang of soccer hooligans were arrested by the police after the game.*

gangster /ˈgæŋ·stər/ [noun] A violent criminal who belongs to a gang or leads it: *Al Capone was a famous gangster who lived in Chicago in the 1920's.*

gaol /dʒeɪl/ [noun] See **jail.** ■ This word is pronounced the same as "jail". ■ This word is British English.

***gap** /gæp/ [noun] **1** A hole: *The cats come into our backyard through a gap in the wall.* **2** An empty space: *Write words in the gaps to complete the exercise.* **3** An interval: *There's a gap of two years between the brothers.*

***garage** US: /gəˈrɑːʒ/ UK: /ˈgær.ɑːʒ/ [noun] **1** A room where you can keep your car: *She puts her car in the garage at night.* 👁 See picture at **house. 2** A place where you take your car for gas or for repairs: *We need to find a garage. I don't know what the red light on the panel means.* ■ Compare with "gas station" and "service station" (only to buy gas and other things, not for repairs).

***garbage** /ˈgɑr·bɪdʒ/ [uncountable noun] Things or material that you don't need and that you throw away: *Please put this garbage in the trash can.* ■ Be careful with the pronunciation of this word. The last "a" is pronounced like the "i" in "did". ■ The same meaning: "trash". ■ In British English they say "rubbish".

***garden** /ˈgɑr·də·n/ [noun] **1** An open space where flower or plants are grown: *This town has beautiful gardens in which you can walk.* **2** A piece of land where vegetables or flowers are cultivated: *This spring we are going to plant strawberries in our garden.* **3 zoological garden** See **zoo.**

gardener US: /ˈgɑːr.dᵊn.ɚ/ UK: /ˈgɑː.dᵊn.əʳ/ [noun] A person who works in a garden: *The gardener is watering the plants.*

garlic /ˈgɑr·lɪk/ [uncountable noun] **1** A small plant with a very strong smell and taste: *Helen has put too much garlic in the soup.* **2 clove of garlic** An individual segment of a garlic bulb: *I need a clove of garlic for this dish.* 👁 **See page 437.**

garment [countable noun] An article of clothing: *This shop sells women's garments.*

***gas** /gæs/ [noun] **1** A substance like air, not a solid or a liquid: *Oxygen is a gas.* 👁 **See page 438. 2** A substance that is used for heating and cooking: *Put the coffee pot on the gas, please.* 👁 **See page 439. 3** See **gasoline.**

gaseous US: /ˈgæ.si.əs/ UK: /ˈgeɪ.si.əs/ [adjective] Of gas, or like gas: *Saturn is a gaseous planet.*

gasoline /ˈgæs.əl.iːn/ [noun] A liquid that is used in motor vehicles for producing power: *A snowstorm is coming, make sure you have enough gasoline in your car.* ■ We also say "gas". ■ In British English they say "petrol".

gasp[1] [noun] A short, quick breath because of surprise, sudden cold and so on: *She gave a gasp when she saw the phone bill.*

gasp[2] /gɑːsp/ [verb] To take a short, quick breath: *Kevin gasped when he felt the cold water.*

gas station [noun] A place where you can buy gasoline and other things for your car: *We stopped at the gas station and filled up with gas for the journey.* ■ The same meaning: "service station". ■ Compare with "garage" (also por repairs).

gastric /ˈgæstrɪk/ [adjective] Referring to the stomach: *Gastric flu can make you very ill.*

gastropod /ˈgæs·trəˌpɑd/ [countable noun] A mollusk with a shell which moves itself using a single foot: *Snails are gastropods.*

***gate** /geɪt/ [countable noun] **1** A small door in a wall or in a fence: *If you leave the gate open, the dog will get out into the road.* **2** A door at an airport: *Passengers must wait at gate three.*

GATE

gateau US: /gæṱˈoʊ/ UK: /ˈgæt.əʊ/ [noun] A large decorated cake with cream: *We're going to buy a gateau for my birthday tea.* ■ The plural is "gateaux" or "gateaus".

***gather** /ˈgæð·ər/ [verb] **1** To come together in a group: *A crowd of people gathered around the ambulance.* **2** To bring things together: *Lisa gathered her books before leaving the room.*

gathering /ˈgæð·ə·rɪŋ/ [noun] An assembly or a meeting: *They had a family gathering yesterday.*

gauze US: /gɑːz/ UK: /gɔːz/ [countable noun] A thin, transparent cloth used mainly to cover wounds: *Gauze is made from silk or cotton.*

gave /geɪv/ Past tense of **give**.

gaze[1] [noun] A deliberate look: *I was so embarrassed that I couldn't return her gaze.*

gaze[2] /geɪz/ [verb] To look at something for a long time: *She sat at the window gazing silently at the view.*

gazelle /gəˈzel/ [noun] A small antelope: *Gazelles live in Africa and Asia.*

↑**gear** US: /gɪr/ UK: /gɪəʳ/ ▮ [noun] **1** In a machine, a set of round pieces with teeth which control the speed: *You have to change gear to go up a hill.* ▮ [uncountable noun] **2** Special equipment or clothes for a sport or a job: *Are you going to take your fishing gear with you?*

geese /giːs/ The plural of **goose**.

Gemini /ˈdʒem.ɪ.naɪ/ [noun] A sign of the zodiac: *If your birthday is between May 21st and June 20th, you're a Gemini.* ■ Be careful. "Gemini" has a capital "G" and doesn't finish in "s".

gender /ˈdʒen·dər/ ▮ [countable noun] **1** The classification of nouns: *Nouns are classified by gender into masculine, feminine and neuter.* ▮ [noun] **2** The condition of being male or female: *Domestic violence is a gender issue.*

gene [countable noun] A part of a cell that determines the characteristics of a living thing: *If the children are red-haired, one of their parents must have a gene for red hair.*

genealogical /ˌdʒi·ni·əˈlɑdʒ·ɪ·kəl/ [adjective] Referring to the study of the history of families: *The family prepared a genealogical tree showing their ancestors.*

↑**general**[1] /ˈdʒenərəl/ [adjective] **1** Affecting many people or things: *The principal's illness was a matter of general concern for parents and students.* **2** Not in detail, describing only the main points: *Give us a general idea of your plan.*

general[2] /ˈdʒenərəl/ [noun] A very important officer in the army: *The generals are inspecting the new tanks.*

general election [noun] An election in which people choose a government: *The general election will be held in March.*

general knowledge [noun] What you know about many different subjects: *We had a general knowledge quiz in class today and I won!*

general practitioner [noun] A family doctor: *General practitioners treat all kinds of illnesses.* ■ "GP" is an abbreviation for "general practitioner".

↑**generate** /ˈdʒen·əˌreɪt/ [verb] To make heat, electricity, power and so on: *The new power station generates electricity for the whole city.*

↑**generation** /ˌdʒen.əˈreɪ.ʃᵊn/ [countable noun] **1** People born at about the same time: *It's hard for old people to understand the younger generation.* **2** A stage in family history: *Look at this photo of me, my mom, my grandma and my great-grandmother: four generations of MacMillan women.*

generator /ˈdʒenəreɪtər/ [countable noun] A machine which converts mechanical energy into electrical energy, or any machine which converts one kind of energy into another: *The generator has broken down.*

generosity /ˌdʒen·əˈrɑs·ət̬·i/ [noun] The quality of being generous: *Aunt Margaret always shows us great generosity, giving us money on our birthdays.*

↑**generous** /ˈdʒen·ə·rəs/ [adjective] **1** Ready, quick to give money, time or other help: *Jonathan's very generous with his money.* **2** Large: *Lady Atholl has made a generous contribution to our school.*

genius /ˈdʒiː.ni.əs/ [noun] An extremely talented person: *Picasso was a genius who made a great contribution to twentieth century art.*

↑**gentle** /ˈdʒen·tə·l/ [adjective] Kind, calm and unaggressive: *The new doctor has a gentle voice.*

↑**gentleman** /ˈdʒen·tə·l·mən/ [countable noun] **1** A polite way of saying "man": *"A gentleman at the door is waiting to see you".* **2** A man who is polite and behaves well to others: *He doesn't behave like a gentleman at all.* ■ The plural is "gentlemen".

↑**genuine** /ˈdʒen.ju.ɪn/ [adjective] Real, true: *This ring is made of genuine gold.*

geographical /ˌdʒiːəʊˈɡræfɪkəl/ [adjective] Referring to geography: *a geographical report.*

↑**geography** /dʒiˈɑɡ·rə·fi/ [noun] The study of the countries of the world, their rivers, mountains, populations and so on: *We're studying the geography of Asia at the moment.* ■ The plural is "geographies".

geological /ˌdʒiːəʊˈlɒdʒɪkəl/ [adjective] Referring to the scientific study of the surface part of the Earth, especially the rocks and soil: *The geological survey of the area took months to complete.*

geology /dʒiˈɑl·ə·dʒi/ [noun] The study of rocks: *They've sent up a satellite to study the geology of Mars.* ■ The plural is "geologies".

geometric or **geometrical** /ˌdʒiːəʊˈmetrɪk/ [adjective] **1** Made up of regular shapes: *She prefers geometric designs.* **2** Referring to geometry: *geometric studies.*

geometry /dʒiˈɑm·ə·tri/ [noun] The study of lines, shapes, curves and so on: *Children learn about squares and circles in geometry.* ■ The plural is "geometries".

geosphere [countable noun] The interior of the Earth and the part of the Earth's surface which is not water: *The geosphere is mainly made up of rock.* 👁 **See page 449.**

geranium /dʒəˈreɪ.ni.əm/ [countable noun] A plant with bright red, pink or white flowers: *Geraniums are very common in the Mediterranean region.* 👁 **See page 433.**

germ US: /dʒɝːm/ UK: /dʒɜːm/ [noun] A very small living thing that causes illness: *Flu is spread by germs.*

German[1] /ˈdʒɜːmən/ [adjective] Referring to Germany: *Beethoven was German.* ■ Be careful! "German" has a capital "G".

German[2] ▮ [countable noun] **1** A person from Germany: *My aunt is married to a German and they live in Bonn.* ▮ [uncountable noun] **2** The language of Germany and other countries: *Robert speaks German fluently.* ■ Be careful! "German" has a capital "G".

Germanic /dʒəˈmæn.ɪk/ US: /dʒɚ-/ [adjective] Referring to Germans, Germany or the German language: *The Germanic tribes invaded Hispania in the 5th century.*

germinate /ˈdʒɜːmɪneɪt/ [verb] To begin to grow, or to cause a seed to grow: *The gardener's main job in spring was to germinate the flowers.*

germination /ˌdʒɜːmɪˈneɪʃən/ [countable noun] The act of germinating: *If you put seeds in warm damp conditions, you are encouraging germination.*

gerund /ˈdʒer.ənd/ [countable noun] The form of a verb used to describe a continuing action, which can also become an adjective: *"Running" is the gerund of the verb "to run".*

gesture /ˈdʒes·tʃər/ [noun] A movement of your head or your hand to show feeling: *Fanny made a gesture indicating that she wanted us to go and join her.*

*****get,** got, gotten /get/ [verb] **1** To buy or to obtain something: *Who will get the tickets for the play?; You won't get any help from him.* **2** To receive something: *Jim got a parcel from Canada yesterday; I got your message.* **3** Used with "have", to possess: *Mike wasn't very happy when he changed schools but now he has got plenty of new friends.* ■ This use only has two forms: "has gotten" or "has got" and "have gotten" or "have got". **4** To bring or to pick up something: *Get me a glass of water, please.* **5** To become: *My grandfather's getting old and can't remember names; It's getting dark: we should go.* **6** To come, to arrive: *How long will it take to get to Miami?; I will phone you when we get to the hotel.* **7** To understand an explanation, joke or instructions: *OK, I get it.* **8** To cause something to happen or be done: *I must get this watch repaired.* **9** When followed by a past participle or an adjective, to be the person that something happens to or that achieves a certain state: *I got stopped by the police yesterday on my motorcycle; I got angry when I saw the results.* **10** To take a bus, taxi, train and so on: *Let's get a bus. It's too far to walk.* **11** To catch an illness: *If you don't wear a jacket you'll get a cold.* **12** **Get out!** Words you use when you think what the other person says can't be true **13** **Got you!** **14** **to be getting on** To be on the way to being late: *It's getting on: we should go now.* ■ See box on the following page.

▶ **PHRASAL VERBS** · **to get away** **1** To escape: *The thief got away with her purse.* **2** To go away somewhere for a break, or to leave somewhere early: *My father is going to get away early this Friday, so that we can all go to the beach.* · **to get away with (something)** To do something wrong or something cheeky, and avoid punishment: *You won't get away with it!* · **to get back** **1** To return to your house, city or base: *My sister's gone on a school trip and she won't get back till next week.* **2** To move away from something, especially something dangerous: *Get back! The firework could still explode.* · **to get (something) back** To be returned something that is yours: *I lent Jason my bike gloves but I expect to get them back on Monday.* · **to get behind** To be late with something: *You're getting behind with your work.* · **to get by** **1** To manage, to survive: *Thanks for all your help; I'd never get by without my friends.* **2** To be able to do what is necessary in another language: *I don't have a good level, but I can get by in French.* · **to get down** To return to the ground from something higher up: *I don't know how to get down from this tree!* · **to get down to (something)** To start doing something: *When are you going to get down to your homework?* · **to get in** **1** Referring to a form of transport on a scheduled journey, to come to a place: *What time does the train get in?* **2** To enter a car or a taxi: *Hurry up, get in the car! We're going to be late!* · **to get off** **1** To leave a train, bus or other vehicles, except car or taxi: *We get off at the last stop.* **2** To stop being on something or somebody: *Get off me, you are too heavy!* · **to get on** **1** To progress: *How are you getting on with your English?* **2** To climb into a vehicle, except a car or a taxi: *You can't get on the bus with all those bags.* **3** To climb onto a horse, donkey, camel and so on: *I got on the camel and hung on as it stood up.* · **to get on well with (somebody)** To have a good, friendly relationship with somebody: *I get on very well with my father.* · **to get out** **1** To leave a car or a taxi: *Kate got out of the car in a hurry.* **2** To leave a room, building, elevator and so on: *We got out of the elevator and walked to the front door, and suddenly...* · **to get over (something)** To recover from bad news, a shock, a blow or a disappointment, or to become well again: *He still hasn't gotten over his friend's death.* · **to get around to (doing something)** To find time to do something, especially something that you don't like doing: *When are you going to get around to put in order your room?* · **to get through** **1** To arrive at the end of something or to finish something: *Jane can't get through all that work alone.* **2** To pass: *Don't worry, you'll get through your test all right.* **3** To survive: *Their relationship was greatly affected by what happened, but they got through it.* · **to get through (to somebody)** **1** To make contact: *I tried to phone my grandmother but I couldn't get through.* **2** To make somebody understand you or respond to you: *I have tried to explain to him, but it's impossible to get through to him because he doesn't want to listen.* · **to get up** **1** To rise to a standing position, to get out of bed: *Ron usually gets up at six o'clock in the morning.* **2** To reach the top of something: *Help your little brother get up the slide.* · **to get up to (something)** To do something naughty or bad: *What has Bobby got up to now?* ■ In British English the past participle of "get" is "got". ■ See box below.

> ***to get***
>
> The verb ***to get*** is used in many senses in English and can be confusing at times. Here is a list of the main uses of *to get* with simple explanations and example sentences:
>
> - **Possession:**
>   - *I have got a lot of books.*
> - **Obligation:**
>   - *You have got to go to the bank this morning to sign some papers.*
> - **Movement** (*to get* + adverb / preposition):
>   - *I have to get back before 10 p.m.*
>   - *The door was locked so we couldn't get in.*
>   - *The thief managed to get away because he could run very fast.*
>   - *When the house caught fire, we had to get out through the window.*
>   - *The burglars got over the wall and into the house.*
> - **Obtaining, receiving:**
>   - *You got a package in the mail this morning.*
> - **Becoming:** (*to get* + adjective)
>   - *Hurry up! Your lunch is getting cold*
> - **Passive:** (*to get* + past participle)
>   - *I must get my hair cut this afternoon.*
>
>   When translating this use of the verb *to get* into Spanish, we usually use the reflexive verb:
>   - *to get one's hair cut*
> - **Arrive:**
>   - *I got home late last night.*

getaway /ˈget̬·əˌweɪ/ [noun] An escape: *The prisoners made a quick getaway.*

geyser US: /ˈgaɪ.zɚ/ UK: /ˈgiː.zər/ [countable noun] A hot-water spring which discharges steam and water intermittently: *The geyser sprays a column of hot water.*

ghost US: /goʊst/ UK: /gəʊst/ [noun] **1** The spirit of a dead person: *I don't believe in ghosts.* **2** **ghost buster** Somebody who tries to remove ghosts from a place: *Have you seen the movie "Ghost busters"?* ■ Be careful with the pronunciation of this word! "gho" is pronounced like "go".

†**giant**[1] /ˈdʒaɪənt/ [noun] An enormous person: *She read the children a story about a giant and a dwarf.*

giant[2] /ˈdʒaɪənt/ [adjective] Very large: *Ford is a giant car company.*

gibe /dʒaɪb/ [noun] See **jibe**.

†**gift** /gɪft/ [countable noun] **1** A present: *I'll give Lynn a puppy as a gift.* ■ The same meaning: "present[2]". **2** A special ability: *Neil has a gift for telling stories.*

gift certificate [countable noun] A card that you can use to buy certain things: *The first prize for the literary competition was a gift certificate for twenty-five dollars.*

gig /gɪg/ [noun] A pop, rock or jazz concert: *I went to a great gig last weekend.* ■ This word is informal.

gigantic /dʒaɪˈgæn·tɪk/ [adjective] Very big: *The Eiffel Tower is gigantic.*

gill /gɪl/ [countable noun] The respiratory organ in many aquatic animals, which can be internal or external: *The gills on a fish are in a slit on the side of its head.*

gin /dʒɪn/ [noun] A colorless alcoholic drink: *Maggie ordered a gin and bitter lemon.*

ginger /ˈdʒɪn·dʒər/ [adjective] Having an orange brown color: *I know the girl with the ginger hair.*

gingerbread /ˈdʒɪn·dʒərˌbred/ [uncountable noun] A cake or cookie flavored with ginger: *Gingerbread is made with syrup.*

giraffe /dʒəˈræf/ [noun] An African animal with a very long neck and spotted skin: *Giraffes are tall enough to eat the leaves from trees.* 👁 **See page 428.**

†**girl** US: /gɝːl/ UK: /gɜːl/ [noun] A female child or a female adolescent: *They have two children: a boy and a girl.* ■ Be careful! Many people feel it is offensive to call a woman a "girl" after she has become an adult.

†**girlfriend** /ˈgɜrl·frend/ [noun] The female romantic companion of somebody, a female friend: *Jim's coming to lunch today with his girlfriend.*

Girl Guide [noun] See **Girl Scout**. ■ Be careful! "Girl Guide" has capital letters. ■ This word is British English.

Girl Scout [countable noun] A girl who belongs to a youth group: *I belong to the Girl Guides and we go to a different camp every summer.* ■ Be careful! "Girl Scout" has capital letters. ■ Boys belong to a similar youth group called the "Scouts". ■ In British English they say "Girl Guide".

†**give, gave, given** /gɪv/ [verb] **1** To let somebody have something, to present somebody with something: *Give me your telephone number, please.* **2** To do an action: *She gave a cry when she burned her fingers.* **3** To make somebody feel something: *The wound's giving Gary a lot of pain.* **4** Referring to a material, to be a little flexible: *These new shoes are a bit tight but I am sure they will give a little.* **5** Referring to a person's attitude, to be a little more flexible: *You are very strict with Jamie, why don't you give a little.* **6 give and take** Exchange between two or more people: *The secret for a relationship is give and take: sometimes you do what you want, sometimes let your friend do what he wants.* **7 Oh, give up!** Words you use when you are tired of somebody complaining, arguing or telling stories you don't believe: *Oh, give up! Stop complaining.* **8 to give way to (somebody)** See "to give way to (somebody)" in the word **way**.
▸ **PHRASAL VERBS** · **to give (somebody) away** To show somebody's real feelings or identity when they are trying to hide them: *Her expression gave her away.* · **to give (something) away** **1** To make a present of something that is yours: *My uncle gave away all his money to the poor.* **2** To make known something that was supposed to be secret: *We were planning a surprise party for my parents, but my little brother gave the secret away.* · **to give (something) back** To return something: *Nicola still has my tennis racket. When is she going to give it back to me?* · **to give in** To surrender, to admit that you are beaten or that you don't know the answer: *Don't give in to James if you think you are right.* · **to give off (something)** To produce a smell, smoke or gas: *That cigarette is giving off a terrible smell.* · **to give (something) out** To distribute: *The teacher gave out the test papers and told us to start.* · **to give up** To abandon the attempt: *I give up! Tell me the answer.* · **to give (something) up** To stop doing something, especially a habit or a difficult enterprise: *My dad has just given up smoking.*

given /ˈgɪv.ᵊn/ Past participle of **give**.

glacier US: /ˈgleɪ.si.ɚ/ UK: /ˈglæs.i.əʳ/ [noun] A large mass of land ice: *Glaciers move slowly down mountains.*

†**glad** /glæd/ [adjective] Pleased and happy: *Martin's glad to be back home again.* ■ Be careful! We don't use "glad" before a noun. We say: "a happy person", not "a glad person".

gladiator /ˈglæd·iˌeɪt̬·ər/ [countable noun] Somebody who fights in an arena with a weapon against other men or wild animals: *Fighting between gladiators was a popular entertainment during the Roman Empire.*

glance[1] /glɑːns/ [noun] A quick look: *I can tell at a glance that you're doing that wrong.*

glance[2] /glɑːns/ [verb] To have a quick look: *I always glance at the newspaper headlines in the morning.*

gland /glænd/ [countable noun] An organ of the body which produces and secretes chemical substances: *Some glands secrete directly into the bloodstream.*

glandular [adjective] Referring to the glands: *She was very ill due to glandular fever.*

glare US: /gler/ UK: /gleəʳ/ **to glare at (somebody)** To look angrily at somebody: *She glared at the man who was smoking in the bus.*

†**glass** US: /glæs/ UK: /glɑːs/ ▮ [uncountable noun] **1** A hard, transparent material: *Glass is used for making windows, bottles and many other things.* ■ In this use "glass" is an uncountable noun. ▮ [countable noun] **2** A container made of glass: *Let's have a glass of champagne and drink to the New Year.* ■ In this use the plural is "glasses".

†**glasses** US: /ˈglæs.ɪz/ UK: /ˈglɑː.sɪz/ [plural noun] Lenses in a frame that help some people to see better: *You'll see better when you've got your new glasses.* ■ When we talk about two or more "glasses", we use the word "pairs": "I have two pairs of glasses".

GLASSES

a b c d e f g h i j k l m n o p q r s t u v w x y z

a b c d e f g h i j k l m n o p q r s t u v w x y z

glide /glaɪd/ [verb] To move in a smooth and silent way: *We watched the eagle gliding slowly over the cliffs.*

glider /ˈglaɪ·dər/ [noun] An airplane without an engine: *Flying in a glider would be an exciting experience!*

glimpse /glɪmps/ [verb] To see somebody or something for a brief moment: *I glimpsed her doing the shopping as I went past the store.*

glitter US: /ˈglɪţ.ɚ/ UK: /ˈglɪt.əʳ/ [verb] To shine with bright flashes: *All that glitters is not gold.*

↑**global** /ˈgloʊ·bəl/ [adjective] Including the whole world: *Scientists say that there will be global climate changes.*

globe US: /gloʊb/ UK: /gləʊb/ [countable noun] **1** A model of the world: *The teacher's using the globe to show Asia to his students.* **2** The earth: *The CNN can be heard all over the globe.* ■ In this use we usually say "earth".

gloomy /ˈgluː.mi/ [adjective] **1** Dark: *What a gloomy morning!* **2** Unhappy, without hope: *Her future looks gloomy.* ■ The comparative form is "gloomier" and the superlative form is "gloomiest".

glorious /ˈglɔr·i·əs/, /ˈgloʊr-/ [adjective] **1** Beautiful, splendid: *We had a glorious day in the mountains.* **2** Having great fame and honor: *The army achieved a glorious victory against the invaders.*

glossary /ˈglɑs·ə·ri/, /ˈglɔ·sə-/ [noun] An alphabetical list with explanations of certain words found in a text: *There's a glossary of scientific terms at the end of the book.* ■ The plural is "glossaries".

↑**glove** /glʌv/ [noun] A covering for your hand: *Put your gloves on because the weather's cold.* 👁 See picture at **clothes**.

glow /gləʊ/ [verb] To shine with a steady light: *A small lamp always glows at their door.*

↑**glue**[1] /gluː/ [noun] A substance that sticks things together: *You'll need some glue to mend that broken cup.* 👁 **See page 456.**

glue[2] /gluː/ [verb] To stick things together: *Oh no, we've broken the fruit bowl! Let's try and glue the pieces together.*

gluteus [countable noun] One of three muscles in the buttock: *The gluteus maximus is the largest muscle in the buttock.* ■ The plural is "glutei". 👁 **See page 423.**

GMT /ˌdʒiː.emˈtiː/ [noun] The time at an imaginary line in Greenwich, an area of London, which divides the earth into east and west: *The times in the rest of the world are determined in relation to the GMT.* ■ "GMT" is an abbreviation for "Greenwich Mean Time". ■ See box at **abbreviations**.

GNP The total value of goods and services produced by a country in one year: *the GNP of the United States.* ■ "GNP" is an abbreviation for "Gross National Product". ■ See box at **abbreviations**.

go[1] US: /goʊ/ UK: /gəʊ/ [noun] **1** A try: *My brother has had several goes at the driving test.* ■ The plural is "goes". **2 in one go** In one try, in one period without break: *Blow out the candles in one go.*

↑**go**[2], **went, gone** US: /goʊ/ UK: /gəʊ/ [verb] **1** To travel a short distance or a long one: *My parents have gone to Canada. I'm going to the movies this evening.* ■ In this meaning, "go" is often used with prepositions like "away", "off" and "over". **2** To travel in a particular direction: *Go along the road until you get to the park, then turn left. We went up the stairs.* **3** To leave a place: *We can't go now because it's raining.* **4** To work, to function: *This CD player won't go.* ■ This use is informal. **5** To become: *Stop playing tricks on him or he'll go crazy.* **6** To result: *How did the meeting go?* **7** To disappear: *Look! My purse's gone!* **8** Referring to time, or to a road, river or canal, to pass: *In the test, the hour went very fast.* **9** Referring to a melody or rhythm, to be in a particular way: *Listen, it goes like this.* **10** To do an activity, usually a free time activity: *Have you ever gone climbing?* ■ In this use, the word after "go" is in the "-ing" form. **11 as you go** Deciding or inventing something in the moment, improvising: *We can decide the other things as we go.* **12 Go for it!** Words you use to encourage somebody to try something or to buy something. **13 going to 1** An expression that shows what you are planning to do: *She's going to get married next week.* **2** An expression that shows what you believe will happen: *Our team is going to lose the game; look how badly they are playing.* **14 to go far** To be successful: *I am sure that she will go far, she has a lot of talent.*

▸ **PHRASAL VERBS** · **to go ahead** To continue with a plan: *Shall we go ahead with the plans with our vacation?* · **to go around 1** To travel around the outside of something, or in a curve or circle: *We had to go around the park because it was closed, and it took us longer.* **2** To have enough for everybody: *Is there enough lemonade to go around?* **3** To visit somebody or something: *Let's go around to Jim's house for a chat.* · **to go away** To leave: *Go away! I'm busy!* · **to go back** To return to a place: *I really enjoyed our vacation in Orlando this year. Can we go back next year?* · **to go by 1** To pass in time or space: *Do you go by the post office on the way to school?* **2** To miss (an opportunity): *Don't let this opportunity go by.* · **to go down 1** To descend: *She went down the stairs slowly, smiling at the photographers.* **2** To fall: *House prices are going to go down this year.* **3** Referring to a vehicle, to sink at sea or to fall out of the sky: *The ship went down in the middle of the Atlantic.* • **to go down with (something)** To become ill: *All the children went down with chickenpox at the same time.* • **to go in** To enter: *Let's buy some popcorn before we go in.* • **to go into something** To explain or look at something more: *You don't need to go into the reasons.* • **to go off 1** To explode: *Don't let that firework go off in your hand!* **2** Referring to something to eat or to drink, to become bad: *We can't eat the cheese because it's gone off.* **3** Referring to lights, to stop working: *All the lights went off suddenly.* **4** Referring to an event, to result: *How did the party go off?* ■ This use is informal. • **to go on 1** To continue: *I can't go on without you; Let's go on with the game.* **2** To happen: *What's going on here?* **3** Words that you use to encourage somebody: *Go on, have another sandwich.* **4** Referring to lights, to start working: *I saw the lights go on in the house opposite.* **5** To talk too long about something: *Stop going on about it. It's only one day!* **6** To have a ride on something in a park or amusement park: *Are you going to go on the roller coaster?* • **to go out 1** To leave: *Bob's gone out to have something to eat.* **2** To stop shining or burning: *The fire had gone out by the time we returned.* • **to go over 1** To cross a mountain pass, a bridge or other thing that is above something else: *We went over the bridge.* **2** To examine for errors or problems something you have done, or to look at the steps of a plan again: *The teacher asked me to go over my homework again.* • **to go through 1** To cross a tunnel, a wood, a crowd of people or other obstacle: *When the train went through the tunnel it went dark.* **2** To suffer, to experience: *The children have gone through a lot since their mother died.* **3** To examine carefully: *If you go through your pockets you'll find the tickets.* • **to go up 1** To go higher: *For the children's department, go up to the second floor.* **2** To increase: *Prices will go up at Christmas.* **3** To approach somebody or something: *She went up to the singer and asked for an autograph.* • **to go with 1** To accompany somebody: *I will go with you to the bus stop.* **2** To taste or look good with something else: *The drapes don't go with the armchairs.*

↑**goal** US: /goʊl/ UK: /gəʊl/ [countable noun] **1** A point in football: *Arsenal won the game by three goals to one.* **2** The space between the posts in games like football: *The ball hit the post and went into the goal.* 👁 See picture at **soccer**. **3** An aim or purpose you have: *His goal in life is to become an astronaut.*

goalie /ˈgəʊli/ [noun] See **goalkeeper**. ■ This word is informal.

goalkeeper US: /ˈgoʊlˌkiː.pɚ/ UK: /ˈgəʊlˌkiː.pəʳ/ [noun] The football or hockey player who defends the goal: *The goalkeeper saved two goals in five minutes.* ■ "Goalie" is informal for "goalkeeper". 👁 See picture at **soccer**.

goat US: /goʊt/ UK: /gəʊt/ [noun] A domestic animal with horns and a beard: *Goats give us milk.* 👁 **See page 428.**

↑**god** /gɒd noun/ [countable noun] **1** A superior being that people believe in: *Some religions have more than one god.* **2** The creator of the universe according to Christians, Jews and Muslims: *Do you believe in God?* ■ Be careful. In this use "God" has a capital "G".

goddess US: /ˈgɑː.des/ UK: /ˈgɒd.es/ [noun] A female god: *Diana was the Roman goddess of the moon and the hunt.* ■ The plural is "goddesses".

godfather US: /ˈgɑːdˌfɑː.ðɚ/ UK: /ˈgɒdˌfɑː.ðəʳ/ [noun] A male godparent: *Ray, my dad's best friend, is my brother's godfather.*

godmother US: /ˈgɑːdˌmʌð.ɚ/ UK: /ˈgɒdˌmʌð.əʳ/ [noun] A female godparent: *My sister's godmother is auntie Beryl.*

godparent US: /ˈgɑːdˌper.ᵊnt/ UK: /ˈgɒdˌpeə.rənt/ [noun] A person that takes secondary responsibility for a child when they are baptized: *My aunt Jean and uncle John are my godparents.* ■ This word is more common in the plural.

goggles US: /ˈgɑː.gl̩z/ UK: /ˈgɒg.l̩z/ [plural noun] Special glasses used for swimming or for protection against dust: *Divers wear goggles to see under water.* 👁 See picture at **glasses**.

go-kart /ˈgəʊkɑːt/ [noun] A very small racing car used for fun: *We went to the go-kart races on Sunday.*

gold[1] /gəʊld/ [adjective] With the color of gold: *The sign is written in gold letters.* ■ The same meaning: "golden".

↑**gold**[2] /gəʊld/ [noun] A very valuable, yellow metal: *Sally wears gold earrings.*

golden /ˈgoʊl·dən/ [adjective] **1** Made of gold: *Debbie's mother wore a golden broach at the opera last night.* **2** With the color of gold: *This cup has a golden rim.* ■ In this use, the same meaning: "gold[1]".

goldfish /ˈgoʊldˌfɪʃ/ [noun] A small orange fish: *Who's going to feed my goldfish when I'm away?* 👁 See picture at **pet**.

golf US: /gɑːlf/ UK: /gɒlf/ [noun] A game played with a small hard ball and long sticks: *I like playing golf.*

golf course [noun] The place where people play golf: *The new golf course has eighteen holes.*

gone US: /gɑːn/ UK: /gɒn/ Past participle of **go**[2]. ■ Be careful. When somebody has gone to a place and has returned, we usually use "has been" not "has gone". We say: "Mark has been to Italy several times". (We don't say: "Mark has gone to Italy several times".).

gonna US: /'gɑː.nə/ UK: /'gə.nə/ [verb] A way of saying "going to": *I'm gonna call the police.* ■ This word is informal.

good[1] /gʊd/ [adjective] **1** Of a high quality: *Frank went to a very good school.* **2** Able to do something well: *My father's a good cook.* **3** Right, suitable: *These pills will be good for your stomach problem.* **4** Pleasant or enjoyable: *Have a good day!* **5** Obedient, well-behaved: *The kids have been good.* **6** Healthy: *Grandma still has very good hearing.* **7 to be good at (something)** To be skillful or successful at doing something: *Ron's good at math.* **8 for good** For the last time, for ever: *He's leaving the town for good.* ■ The comparative form is "better" and the superlative form is "best".

good[2] /gʊd/ [noun] A profit or advantage: *She did it for the good of her country.*

good afternoon [expression] See **afternoon**.

↑**goodbye** /'gʊd.baɪ, 'gʊb-, ˌ-'-/ [interjection] An expression that you say when you leave a place: *It's late, it's time to say "goodbye".* ■ "Bye" is an informal way of saying "goodbye".

good evening [expression] See **evening**.

Good Friday [noun] The Friday before Easter Sunday: *Christians remember the death of Christ on Good Friday.* ■ Be careful. "Good Friday" has capital letters.

good-looking /ˌgʊd'lʊk.ɪŋ/ [adjective] Attractive: *Paul's a good-looking boy.* ■ The same meaning: "handsome". When we use "good-looking" for people, this is usually to talk about boys and men. For women we usually say "beautiful" or "pretty".

good morning [expression] See **morning**.

good natured /ˌgʊd'neɪtʃəd/ [adjective] Kind: *Mary won't get angry because she's a good natured girl.* ■ Be careful with the pronunciation of "natured". The "e" is not pronounced.

goodness[1] /'gʊdnəs/ [noun] Kindness, virtue: *He's a perfect example of human goodness.*

goodness[2] [interjection] A word that shows you are surprised or angry: *My goodness! I've forgotten the keys!*

good night [expression] See **night**.

↑**goods** /gʊdz/ [plural noun] Things that you buy or sell: *Robert stood looking at the goods in the store window.*

goose /guːs/ [noun] A bird with a long neck, that looks like a large duck: *My uncle keeps geese and turkeys on his farm.* ■ The plural is "geese". See **page 429**.

gooseberry /'gʊz.bᵊr.i/ [noun] **1** A small green fruit used in cooking for jam, pies and so on: *You'll need some gooseberries for the pie.* ■ The plural is "gooseberries". **2 to play gooseberry** To be the third person in company of a girlfriend and boyfriend who want to be alone: *I am tired of playing gooseberry. Why don't you two go out without me tonight?*

gorgeous /'gɔr·dʒəs/ [adjective] Very nice, very beautiful: *The weather was gorgeous over the weekend.* ■ This word is informal.

gorilla /gə'rɪl.ə/ [noun] A very large and strong animal of the monkey family: *Gorillas live in forests in Africa.*

gosh US: /gɑːʃ/ UK: /gɒʃ/ [interjection] A word you say when you are surprised: *"Gosh! That's a lot of money!".*

gossip[1] /'gɒsɪp/ ▮ [uncountable noun] **1** Talk about other people or about their private lives: *Don't believe all the gossip you hear.* ■ In this use "gossip" is an uncountable noun. ▮ [countable noun] **2** A person who talks about other people or about their private lives: *Don't tell him anything because he's a gossip.*

gossip[2] /'gɒsɪp/ [verb] To talk about other people or about their private lives: *They're gossiping about the Royal Family again.*

got US: /gɑːt/ UK: /gɒt/ Past tense and past participle forms of **get**. ■ The past participle form is also "gotten".

gotta US: /'gɑː.t̬ə/ UK: /'gɒt.ə/ [verb] A way of saying "have got to" or "have got a": *I gotta go now or I'll be late.* ■ This word is informal.

gotten US: /'gɑː.t̬ᵊn/ UK: /'gɒt.ᵊn/ Past participle of **get**. ■ In British English they say "got".

↑**govern** /'gʌv·ərn/ [verb] To control and rule a country, province and so on: *Spain governed California for many years.*

↑**government** /'gʌv·ərn·mənt/, /-ər·mənt/ [noun] The people who control a country: *The government is going to raise the price of gasoline.*

↑**governor** /'gʌv·ə·nər/, /-ər·nər/ [countable noun] A person who governs a state: *Before he become President of the United States, Bill Clinton was Governor of Arkansas.*

gown /gaʊn/ [noun] A long dress: *She looked so pretty in her wedding gown.*

GP /ˌdʒiː'piː/ [noun] See **general practitioner**. ■ Be careful. "GP" is always written in capital letters.

GPS [uncountable noun] A system which uses signals from satellites to show the position of something or somebody: *Follow the directions of the GPS to get to the final address.* ■ Be careful. "GPS" is always written in capital letters. "GPS" is an abbreviation for "Global Positioning System".

grab /græb/ [verb] To take something quickly and roughly: *The policeman grabbed the thief by the arm and took him away.* ■ Be careful with the spelling of these forms: "grabbed", "grabbing".

grace /greɪs/ [noun] A fine way of moving: *Martha dances with tremendous grace.*

graceful /ˈgreɪs.fəl/ [adjective] Attractive and elegant in movement: *Gazelles are very graceful animals.*

↑**grade**[1] /greɪd/ [countable noun] **1** Year of a school course: *I am in fifth grade and my sister is in seventh.* **2** A mark that a student gets in a test: *Lee got poor grades in his math test.* ■ In British English they say "mark". **3** A level, a quality: *Which grade of gas do you want?*

grade[2] /greɪd/ [verb] **1** To arrange or order things by size, kind and so on: *They grade the fruit by size.* **2** To read a piece of work to say how good it is: *The teacher graded our tests and we all passed.* ■ In this use, the same meaning: "mark[2]".

↑**gradual** /ˈgræd.jʊ.əl, ˈgrædʒ.ʊ.əl/ [adjective] Slow, progressive: *There's been a gradual increase in the number of Hispanics in the United States in the last few years.*

gradually /ˈgræd.jʊ.li, ˈgrædʒ.ʊ.li/ [adverb] Little by little, slowly: *His health should improve gradually.*

graduate[1] /ˈgrædʒuət/ [noun] A person with a university degree: *She's a graduate of Harvard University.*

graduate[2] /ˈgrædjueɪt/ [verb] To receive an academic diploma or degree: *Philip graduated in psychology.*

graduated cylinder [countable noun] A glass cylinder with lines printed on its side which is used by scientists to measure the volume of a liquid: *The chemistry teacher told his students to pour exactly 50 ml of alcohol into the graduated cylinder.* 👁 **See page 440.**

graffiti /grəˈfiːt̬.i/ [uncountable noun] Words or pictures that people paint on walls: *The walls of the subway station were covered with colorful graffiti.*

↑**grain** /greɪn/ [uncountable noun] **1** The seeds of a cereal: *The birds are eating the grains of corn.* **2** A small, hard piece of something: *Some grains of sand got in my camera when I took photos on the beach.*

gram /græm/ [noun] A very small unit of weight: *I need 100 grams of sugar for the cake.* ■ The abbreviation "g" is only used in written language. See box at **abbreviations**. ■ The British English spelling is "gramme".

↑**grammar** /ˈgræm.ər/ [noun] The rules of a language: *English grammar isn't especially difficult.*

grammatical /grəˈmæt̬.ɪ.kəl/ [adjective] According to the rules of grammar: *There were many grammatical errors in the letter he wrote.*

gramme /græm/ [noun] See **gram.** ■ This is British English spelling.

gramophone /ˈgræməfəʊn/ [countable noun] Old-fashioned term for record player: *We found my grandfather's old gramophone in the basement.* 👁 **See page 443.**

gran /græn/ [noun] See **grandmother.** ■ This word is informal.

↑**grand** /grænd/ [adjective] Very important or large: *Ian has got grand ideas for the future.*

grandad /ˈgrændæd/ [noun] See **grandfather.** ■ This word is informal.

↑**grandchild** /ˈgrænd.tʃaɪld/ [noun] The child of your son or your daughter: *My grandpa says she loves having her grandchildren around her.* ■ This word is more common in the plural: "grandchildren".

↑**granddaughter** /ˈgræn,dɔt̬.ər/ [noun] The daughter of your son or your daughter: *Mr. and Mrs. Allen's granddaughter was born in May.*

↑**grandfather** /ˈgrænd,fɑð.ər/ [noun] The father of your mother or father: *Andy's grandfather is 85 years old today.* ■ "Grandad" and "grandpa" are informal for "grandfather". 👁 See picture at **family**.

grandma /ˈgrænd.mɑː, ˈgræm-/ [noun] See **grandmother.** ■ This word is informal.

↑**grandmother** /ˈgrænd,mʌð.ər/ [noun] The mother of your father or mother: *My grandmother doesn't like living alone.* ■ "Gran", "grannie", "granny" and "grandma" are informal for "grandmother". 👁 See picture at **family**.

grandpa /ˈgrænd.pɑː, ˈgræm-/ [noun] See **grandfather**. ■ This word is informal.

grandparent /ˈgrænd,peərənt/ [noun] The parent of your father or your mother: *My grandparents are coming to a barbecue tomorrow.* ■ This word is more common in the plural.

↑**grandson** /ˈgrænd.sʌn/ [noun] The son of your son or your daughter: *Her grandson is only two years old.*

granite /ˈgræn.ɪt/ [uncountable noun] A hard, igneous rock: *Granite is used a lot in building.*

grannie or **granny** /ˈgræn.i/ [noun] See **grandmother.** ■ This word is informal.

grant[1] /grɑːnt/ [noun] Money that you get from the Government or other institution to study or for a particular purpose: *Mark's been given a grant to go and do research at Boston University. My school got a grant to buy new computers.*

grant[2] /grɑːnt/ [verb] To give somebody something they have asked for: *The principal granted us permission to take the day off.* ■ This word is formal.

grape /greɪp/ [noun] A small green or purple fruit: *Wine is made from grapes.* 👁 **See page 436.**

a b c d e f g h i j k l m n o p q r s t u v w x y z

grapefruit /ˈgreɪp.fruːt/ [noun] A yellow fruit that looks like a large orange: *She drinks grapefruit juice for breakfast every morning.* See page 436.

graph /grɑːf, græf/ [noun] A mathematical diagram with information: *This graph shows the pass rate in the standardized state standars test at this school.*

graphic[1] /ˈgræfɪk/ [countable noun] Picture, drawing or design that is made using geometric figures and signs: *The Managing Director showed some graphics in order to explain the company's financial development.*

graphic[2] /ˈgræf.ɪk/ [adjective] **1** Referring to visual arts: *The description of the scene was graphic.* **2** Clear and powerful, easy to imagine: *She gave a graphic account of the incident.*

grasp US: /græsp/ UK: /grɑːsp/ [verb] **1** To hold something firmly: *Uncle Cecil grasped my hand warmly when he saw me.* **2** To understand something: *The teacher tried several times to explain the idea to us, but nobody could grasp it.* ■ In this use we usually say "understand".

†**grass** /grɑːs/ [uncountable noun] **1** A green plant that grows in yards and fields: *Cows eat grass.* **2** A piece of ground covered in grass: *Keep off the grass.* See page 432.

grasshopper US: /ˈgræs,hɑː.pɚ/ UK: /ˈgrɑːs,hɒp.əʳ/ [noun] An insect with long legs: *Grasshoppers move by giving long jumps.* See page 431.

grassy US: /ˈgræs.i/ UK: /ˈgrɑː.si/ [adjective] Covered with grass: *There's a grassy area all around the swimming pool.*

grate /greɪt/ [verb] To rub food into small pieces using a metal tool: *She's grating some carrot for the salad.*

†**grateful** /ˈgreɪt.fᵊl/ [adjective] Feeling or showing thanks to somebody: *I'm very grateful to you for all your help.*

gratitude US: /ˈgræt̬.ə.tuːd/ UK: /ˈgræt.ɪ.tjuːd/ [noun] The feeling of being grateful: *He showed me his gratitude by inviting me to lunch.*

grave[1] /greɪv/ [adjective] Very serious: *He's had a grave illness but he's much better now.*

†**grave**[2] /greɪv/ [noun] A hole in the ground for a dead person: *She visits her mother's grave every week.*

graveyard /ˈgreɪv,jɑrd/ [noun] A piece of land where dead people are buried: *Graveyards are often found near a church.*

gravity /ˈgræv·ɪ·t̬i/ [noun] The force that makes things fall to the ground: *The scientist Isaac Newton discovered the law of gravity.*

gravy /ˈgreɪ.vi/ [noun] A brown sauce for meat: *Would you like some gravy on your roast beef?* ■ The plural is "gravies".

†**gray** /greɪ/ [noun and adjective] The color between black and white: *His hair went gray as he grew old.* ■ In British English they say "grey".

graze /greɪz/ [verb] **1** To eat grass: *The horses are grazing in the field.* **2** To cut yourself slightly: *The child grazed his knee on the fence.*

grease[1] /griːs/ [uncountable noun] **1** A thick oily substance: *You'll have to put some grease in the lock.* **2** The fat from an animal: *There's too much grease in this soup.*

grease[2] /griːs/ [verb] To put grease on something: *You have to grease the dish before you put the meat in it.*

greasy /ˈgriː.si/ [adjective] With a lot of grease on it: *Don't come near me with those greasy fingers.*

†**great** /greɪt/ [adjective] **1** Very large: *The Great Fire of Chicago destroyed the city in 1871.* **2** Important or famous: *Humphrey Bogart was one of the greatest American actors.* **3** Very good: *He's a great cook.* **4** Wonderful, splendid: *We had a great day at the zoo.* **5 a great many** A large number of: *A great many people will see the game.* **6 a great deal of** A large amount of: *She spent a great deal of time cleaning her bike.* ■ Be careful with the pronunciation of this word! The last part "eat" rhymes with "eight".

great-grandfather [noun] The grandfather of your father or mother: *My great-grandfather died in the Second World War.*

great-grandmother [noun] The grandmother of your father or mother: *Her great-grandmother was Polish.*

greed /griːd/ [noun] The desire to have too much: *Jimmy, you've eaten a whole packet of cookies. That's pure greed!*

greedy /ˈgriː.di/ [adjective] Wanting too much, wanting more than you really need: *Henry looked at the steak with greedy eyes.*

Greek[1] [adjective] Referring to or from Greece: *My sister went to the Greek islands last summer and met a Greek boy.* ■ Be careful! "Greek" has a capital "G".

Greek[2] ▮ [countable noun] **1** A person from modern or ancient Greece: *The ancient Greeks built cities in most corners of the Mediterranean.* ▮ [uncountable noun] **2** The language of Greece: *My uncle has been living in Athens for five years and he speaks Greek quite well.* ■ Be careful! "Greek" has a capital "G".

†**green**[1] /griːn/ [noun and adjective] The color of grass: *My mother dressed me in the dark green coat.* ■ The comparative form is "greener" and the superlative form is "greenest".

green[2] /griːn/ [countable noun] An area of grass: *The children ran across the green when they came out of school.*

greenhouse /ˈgriːn.haʊs/ [noun] A glass building for plants: *Craig's watering the roses in the greenhouse.*

GREENHOUSE

greenish [adjective] Referring to a color, that is approximately green, or that has a green element to it: *Are you OK? Your face is a little greenish.*

greens /griːnz/ [plural noun] Vegetables: *Eat up your greens, please.*

greet /griːt/ [verb] To meet somebody with words or actions: *Richard greeted me with a big smile.*

greeting /ˈgri·t̬ɪŋ/ [noun] Something that you say or do when you meet somebody: *Our neighbor never returns our greeting.*

greetings [plural noun] Good wishes: *The birthday card I got from Mary said: "Greetings on this special day".*

grew /gruː/ Past tense of **grow**.

†**grey** /greɪ/ [noun and adjective] See **gray**. ■ This word is British English.

grid /grɪd/ [countable noun] **1** A metal or wooden frame with parallel bars: *Drains are often covered by metal grids.* **2** A pattern of horizontal and vertical lines which form a series of squares: *In drawing class we use paper marked with a grid.* **3** The lines which mark the starting point of a motor race: *The cars line up on the grid ready for the start.* **4** The electricity supply system: *The grid ensures that electricity is supplied to the whole country.* **5** **grid reference** Network of squares on a map, numbered for reference: *The grid reference shows the location on the map.*

gridlock /ˈgrɪdlɒk/ [noun] A situation where there are so many vehicles in the intersection of streets that they can't move: *We had to wait for half an hour because of a gridlock caused by an accident and we were late to school.*

GRIDLOCK

grief /griːf/ [uncountable noun] Great sadness following a loss: *Karen was ill with grief after her mother died.*

grieve /griːv/ [verb] To feel very sad after a loss: *She's still grieving for that silly boyfriend she had.*

grill[1] /grɪl/ [noun] A special metal frame for cooking: *Put the hamburger on the grill.*

grill[2] /grɪl/ [verb] To cook food on a metal frame: *My mother's grilling beef for dinner.* See picture at **cook**.

grim /grɪm/ [adjective] **1** Severe, serious: *Jennifer has a grim sense of humor.* **2** Unpleasant: *We had some grim weather on our trip to Holland.*

grin[1] [noun] A big smile: *Nigel greeted us with a grin.*

grin[2] /grɪn/ [verb] To smile widely: *The little girl grinned when she saw the kite.* ■ Be careful with the spelling of these forms: "grinned", "grinning".

grind, ground, ground /graɪnd/ [verb] To crush something to small pieces or to powder: *He ground some coffee for breakfast.*

grip /grɪp/ [noun] A firm hold: *The handle's wet and I can't get a grip on it.*

grit /grɪt/ [uncountable noun] **1** Very small pieces of stone: *Can you help me get a piece of grit out of my eye?* **2** Determination, courage: *Everybody admires her grit.*

grizzly bear /ˈgrɪz·li ˌbeər/ [noun] A fierce North American bear: *When we went to the National Park we saw several grizzly bears.*

groan[1] [noun] A deep, sad sound of disapproval or pain: *The whole class let out a groan when the teacher said we had a test.*

groan[2] /grəʊn/ [verb] To make a sad sound of disapproval or pain: *I heard you groaning in your sleep last night.*

grocer US: /ˈgroʊ.sɚ/ UK: /ˈgrəʊ.səʳ/ [noun] A person who sells food: *The grocer on the corner sells very cheap packets of potato chips.*

†**groceries** /ˈgroʊ·sə·riz/, /ˈgroʊs·riz/ [plural noun] Food from a grocer's store: *Her shopping bag's full of groceries.*

GROUPS: COLLECTIVE NOUNS

Collective nouns are words that describe a group of people, animals or things:

*a **crowd** of people*

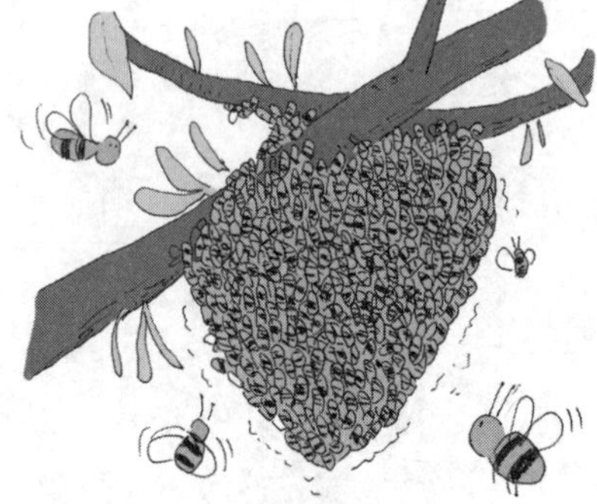

*a **swarm** of bees*

*a **herd** of cows*

*a **herd** of pigs*

*a **herd** of sheep*

*a **pack** of wolves*

*a **herd** of elephants*

grocery store [noun] A store that sells food, particularly canned food, and other things for the house: *Can you go to the grocery store and get some cornflakes and sliced bread, please?* See picture at **market**.

groom /gru:m/ [countable noun] See **bridegroom**.

grope US: /group/ UK: /grəʊp/ [verb] To look for something with your hands: *He groped for the flashlight when the lights went out.*

†**ground**[1] /graʊnd/ [uncountable noun] **1** The surface of the earth: *Golden eagles often hunt in areas of high ground.* **2** Soil, earth: *The ground was too wet for us to lie on.* **3** A piece of land used for a particular purpose: *Smoking is forbidden on school grounds.*

ground[2] /graʊnd/ Past tense and past participle forms of **grind**.

ground beef [noun] Meat that is cut into very small pieces: *My mother makes hamburgers with ground beef.* ■ In British English they say "mince".

ground floor [noun] The part of a building that is at street level: *The apartments on the ground floor don't get much light.*

group /gru:p/ [countable noun] **1** A number of people or things together: *The tourists usually come to the museum in groups.* **2** People who play music together: *My sister plays in a pop group.*

†**grow, grew, grown** US: /grou/ UK: /grəʊ/ [verb] **1** To become bigger: *Those plants grow very quickly.* **2** To look after plants: *My uncle grows vegetables.* **3** To let your hair get longer: *He's growing a beard because he wants to look older.* **4** To become: *Let's go before it grows dark.*

▶ **PHRASAL VERBS** · **to grow into (something)** To get bigger and become something: *These small plants will eventually grow into tall trees.* · **to grow out of (something)** To become too small to wear something: *Ann's grown out of all her old clothes.* · **to grow up** To become an adult: *I want to be an astronaut when I grow up.*

growl /graʊl/ [verb] To make an angry vibrating sound: *Their dog growls at everyone who walks past.*

grown US: /groun/ UK: /grəʊn/ Past participle of **grow**.

grown-up /ˈgroun,ʌp/ [noun] An adult: *My younger sister says that all grown-ups are too serious.* ■ We usually say "adult".

†**growth** US: /grouθ/ UK: /grəʊθ/ [noun] The act of growing or getting bigger: *Children's growth varies at different ages.*

grub /grʌb/ [noun] Food: *The grub at the summer school wasn't very good.* ■ This word is informal.

grumble /ˈgrʌm.bl/ [verb] To complain in a quiet but bad tempered way: *He's always grumbling about his job.* ■ We usually say "complain".

grunt /grʌnt/ [verb] To make a rough noise like a pig: *Don't grunt when I ask you a question. Answer me properly!*

†**guarantee**[1] /,gærənˈti:/ [countable noun] **1** A promise made by a company that it will repair a machine if it does not work: *This television has a one year guarantee.* **2** A promise that something will be done: *Can you give us a guarantee that the goods will arrive on time?*

guarantee[2] /,gærənˈti:/ [verb] **1** To promise to repair a machine if it does not work: *This car is guaranteed for three years.* **2** To say that something will happen: *I can guarantee that you'll have a great time at the summer camp.*

†**guard**[1] /gɑ:d/ [noun] **1** A person who watches over somebody or something: *A primary role for honor guards in the United States is to provide funeral honors for fallen soldiers.* **2** **on guard** Prepared against attack or surprise: *The police were on guard at the airport when the President arrived.* ■ Be careful with the pronunciation of this word! The "u" is not pronounced.

guard[2] /gɑ:d/ [verb] **1** To give protection to somebody or something: *The White House is guarded day and night.* **2** To watch over in order to prevent from escaping: *Two armed men guard the gangster's cell.*

guardian /ˈgɑr·di·ən/ [noun] A person who looks after a child: *Rosemary's grandparents became her guardians when her parents died.*

Guatemalan[1] [adjective] Referring to Guatemala: *The Guatemalan currency is the quetzal.* ■ Be careful! "Guatemalan" has a capital "G".

Guatemalan[2] [countable noun] A person from Guatemala: *My mother is Guatemalan.* ■ Be careful! "Guatemalan" has a capital "G".

guerrilla or **guerilla** [noun] A member of a group which fights against a government: *The guerrillas attacked the government buildings at night.*

†**guess**[1] /ges/ [noun] An estimate or opinion: *It's not a promise, it's a guess.* ■ The plural is "guesses". ■ Be careful with the pronunciation of this word! The "u" is not pronounced.

guess[2] /ges/ [verb] **1** To estimate: *I would guess that there are fifty people here.* **2** To get the right answer by luck: *Guess who's coming to dinner.* ■ Be careful with the spelling of the 3rd person singular present tense form: "guesses". ■ Be careful with the pronunciation of this word! The "u" is not pronounced.

†**guest** /gest/ [countable noun] **1** A person invited somewhere: *How many guests came to the wedding?* **2** A person who stays in a hotel: *Not many guests*

come to this hotel during the winter. ■ Be careful with the pronunciation of this word! The "u" is not pronounced.

guidance /ˈgaɪ.dᵊnts/ [noun] Help and advice: *You should ask your teacher for guidance about how to improve your technique.*

guide¹ /gaɪd/ [countable noun] A person who shows tourists where to go: *They had a guide when they visited Turkey.*

guide² /gaɪd/ [verb] To lead or to show: *My friend guided us through the town of Parker.*

guide-book /ˈgaɪd.bʊk/ [noun] A book that tells tourists about a place: *She's got a guide-book to New York.*

guild /gɪld/ [countable noun] An association of people with similar jobs, interests or aims: *The guild exists to represent the interests of its members.*

guilt /gɪlt/ [uncountable noun] **1** The terrible feeling that somebody has after doing wrong: *It was guilt that made him admit that he'd broken Anne's model.* **2** The fact of having broken a law: *There was no doubt about the guilt of the accused man.*

guilty /ˈgɪl·ti/ [adjective] **1** Showing or feeling unhappiness about doing something wrong: *Laura feels guilty about having lied to her sister.* **2** Having broken a law: *The jury declared her guilty.*

guinea pig /ˈgɪni,pɪg/ [countable noun] **1** A small, fat, furry animal: *Annie keeps a guinea pig as a pet.* **2** A person or an animal that is used in an experiment: *Animals are often used as guinea pigs to test new drugs.*

guitar /gɪˈtɑr/ [countable noun] **1** A musical instrument with six strings: *Helen played her guitar at the party.* See page 458. **2** **bass guitar** See **bass guitar**.

gulf¹ /gʌlf/ [noun] A large area of sea that is partly surrounded by coast: *The Gulf of Mexico lies to the south of the United States.*

gulf² /gʌlf/ [noun] Wide difference in points of view: *There is a huge gulf between my dad's opinions on music and mine.*

gull /gʌl/ [noun] See **seagull**.

gulp [noun] A quick swallow: *He drank the glass of beer in one gulp.*

gum /gʌm/ [noun] **1** A thick substance that sticks things together: *Give me some gum to stick these labels onto the packets.* **2** **chewing gum** See **chewing gum**.

gun /gʌn/ [countable noun] **1** A weapon that fires bullets: *The robber wounded two policemen with his gun.* **2** **machine gun** See **machine gun**.

gunman /ˈgʌn.mən/ [noun] A man who shoots other people: *The policeman was shot in the chest by a gunman.* ■ The plural is "gunmen".

gunpowder /ˈgʌn,paʊ·dər/ [noun] An explosive substance in the form of a powder: *Gunpowder is used in fireworks.*

gutter US: /ˈgʌt̬.ɚ/ UK: /ˈgʌt.əʳ/ [countable noun] **1** A tube that carries away rain water: *We could hear the rain coming down the gutter all night.* **2** A narrow inclined area at the edge of a road: *You shouldn't throw candy packets into the gutter.*

guy /gaɪ/ [noun] A man or a boy: *I think your brother's a nice guy.* ■ This word is informal.

gym /dʒɪm/ [noun] A large room for doing exercise: *Sean goes to the gym every Thursday.* ■ "Gym" is short for "gymnasium".

gymnasium /dʒɪmˈneɪ.zi.əm/ [noun] See **gym**.

gymnast /ˈdʒɪm.næst/ [noun] A person who is trained in gymnastics: *The Russian gymnasts won two gold medals.*

gymnastics /dʒɪmˈnæs.tɪks/ [noun] Exercises to make the body stronger and more agile: *He's broken his leg and can't do gymnastics for the next three months.* ■ It is usually used with a singular verb.

gypsum /ˈdʒɪp.səm/ [uncountable noun] A white or gray mineral: *Gypsum is used in the building industry and also for making plaster.*

Gypsy [noun] Member of a wandering race: *The Gypsies attach great importance to the family.* ■ Be careful! "Gypsy" has a capital "G". ■ The plural is "Gypsies".

h /eɪtʃ/ The eighth letter of the alphabet: *The name "Helen" begins with an "H".*

↑**habit** /ˈhæb.ɪt/ [countable noun] Something that you do very often: *She has the bad habit of always slamming the door behind her.*

habitat /ˈhæb.ɪ.tæt/ [noun] The place where animals or plants live: *Africa is the natural habitat of the gorilla.*

habitual /həˈbɪtʃ.u.əl/ [adjective] **1** Done regularly or as a habit: *They are habitual clients of this restaurant.* ■ Compare with "rare" (unusual and often valuable). **2** Done constantly: *He is a habitual gambler.* **3** Considered as characteristic or typical of somebody: *Tom soon recovered his habitual smile.*

had /hæd, həd, əd/ [verb] See **have**.

haddock /ˈhæd.ək/ [noun] A sea fish similar to cod: *We had haddock for dinner yesterday.* ■ The plural is also "haddock".

hadn't /ˈhæd.ᵊnt/ The contraction of "had not".

hail /heɪl/ [uncountable noun] Small balls of icy rain: *The hail has destroyed the crops.*

↑**hair** US: /her/ UK: /heəʳ/ ■ [countable noun] **1** One of the many thin things that grow on people and animals: *That dog's left a lot of hairs all over the armchair.* ■ [uncountable noun] **2** The mass of hair on a person's head: *Winston has curly, black hair.* 👁 See picture at **face**.

hairbrush /ˈheərˌbrʌʃ/ [countable noun] A brush for keeping your hair tidy: *Here's a hairbrush for you to get ready for the picture.* 👁 See picture at **brush**.

haircut /ˈherˌkʌt/ [countable noun] The act or the way of cutting your hair: *When are you going to have a haircut?*

↑**hairdresser** US: /ˈherˌdres.ɚ/ UK: /ˈheəˌdres.əʳ/ [countable noun] A person who cuts and arranges hair: *The hairdresser always washes my hair before he cuts it.* ■ Compare with "barber" (a man who only cuts men's hair).

hairdryer US: /ˈherˌdraɪ.ɚ/ UK: /ˈheəˌdraɪ.əʳ/ [countable noun] A machine that dries your hair: *I never use a hairdryer on my hair.*

hairpin /ˈheə.pɪn/ US: /ˈher-/ [countable noun] A bent piece of wire used to keep hair in place: *My hair's a mess. Can you give me a hairpin?* 👁 See picture at **pin**.

hairstyle /ˈheərˌstaɪl/ [countable noun] The way in which your hair is arranged: *Her new hairstyle makes her look older.* 👁 See picture on the following page.

hairy US: /ˈher.i/ UK: /ˈheə.ri/ [adjective] **1** Covered with hair: *Monkeys have long, hairy arms.* **2** Worryingly or excitingly dangerous: *It was rather hairy driving down through the mountains in the fog.* ■ This use is informal. ■ The comparative form is "hairier" and the superlative form is "hairiest".

HAIRSTYLE

straight

curly

wavy

spiky

ponytail

braid

short

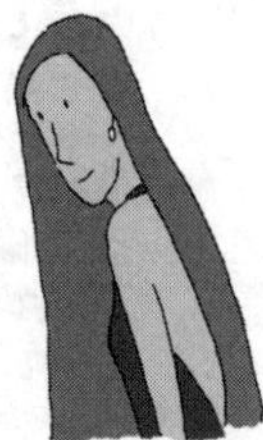
long

bangs

bob

bald

Haitian¹ [adjective] Referring to Haiti: *Port-au-Prince is the Haitian capital.* ■ Be careful! "Haitian" has a capital "H".

Haitian² [countable noun] A person from Haiti: *There is a Haitian in my class.* ■ Be careful! "Haitian" has a capital "H".

+half US: /hæf/ UK: /hɑːf/ [countable noun] **1** One of two equal parts of something: *Do you want half of my apple?* ■ The plural is "halves". **2 in half** Into two equal parts: *The little girl broke the pencil in half.* **3 half past** Thirty minutes after an hour: *The movie starts at half past five.*

half-time US: /ˈhæf.taɪm/ UK: /ˌhɑːfˈtaɪm/ [uncountable noun] A break in the middle of a game: *We were winning 3-0 at half-time.*

halfway /ˈhæfˈweɪ/ [adverb] In the middle: *Their car broke down halfway between Atlantic City and Baltimore.*

+hall US: /hɑːl/ UK: /hɔːl/ [countable noun] **1** A large room or a building for meetings, concerts and so on: *The principal met all the parents in the school hall.* **2** The room next to the front door: *Hang your coat up in the hall and come into the living room.*

hallo /hælˈəʊ/ US: /-ˈoʊ/ [interjection] See **hello**.

Halloween or **Hallowe'en** /ˌhæləʊˈiːn/ [noun] The night of October 31st when witches and ghosts are said to walk about the streets: *Some people wear costumes on Halloween.* ■ Be careful. "Halloween" has a capital "H".

hallway [countable noun] A passage in a building: *My teachers always supervise the hallways during passing period.* ■ The same meaning "corridor".

halt US: /hɑːlt/ UK: /hɒlt/ [verb] To stop: *"Halt! Who is there?" the soldier demanded.*

halve US: /hæv/ UK: /hɑːv/ [verb] To divide something into two equal parts: *Let's halve the pizza between us.*

ham /hæm/ [noun] Salted meat from a pig: *Would you like a ham sandwich?* ■ Compare with "jam¹" (a soft food made with fruit and sugar).

+hamburger /ˈhæmˌbɜr·gər/ [countable noun] A flat, round piece of meat eaten in a bread roll: *This hamburger is very dry. It's horrible.* ■ "Burger" is short for "hamburger".

+hammer¹ /ˈhæmər/ [countable noun] A tool with a metal head used to bang nails into things: *I need a hammer and a bag of nails to hang up the picture.*

hammer² /ˈhæmər/ [verb] **1** To hit something with a hammer: *It's difficult to hammer nails into this wood.* **2** To hit something several times: *Somebody's hammering on the wall, perhaps the music's too loud.*

hammock /ˈhæm.ək/ [countable noun] A kind of informal bed made from fabric or rope: *A hammock can be used anywhere where there are two hooks or trees.*

hamster /ˈhæm·stər/ [countable noun] A small animal like a mouse: *I've bought Jessica a hamster as a pet.* 👁 See picture at **pet**.

+hand¹ /hænd/ [countable noun] **1** The part of your body at the end of your arm: *Give me your hand. I'm going to read your palm.* 👁 **See page 421.** **2** One of the indicators on a clock or a watch: *The minute hand on my watch is broken.* **3 by hand** Not using a machine: *He's doing the washing by hand.* **4 hand to mouth** A way of life in which you have hardly enough food or money to live on: *He's been living from hand to mouth for years.* **5 on the one hand... on the other hand** An expression used for comparing different things or ideas: *On the one hand, my new school is quite far from where I live, but on the other hand there is a bus that goes straight there.* ■ Note that you can make adjectives for manual skill using "hand" and a past participle: "hand-painted", "hand-built", "hand-knitted" and so on.

HAND

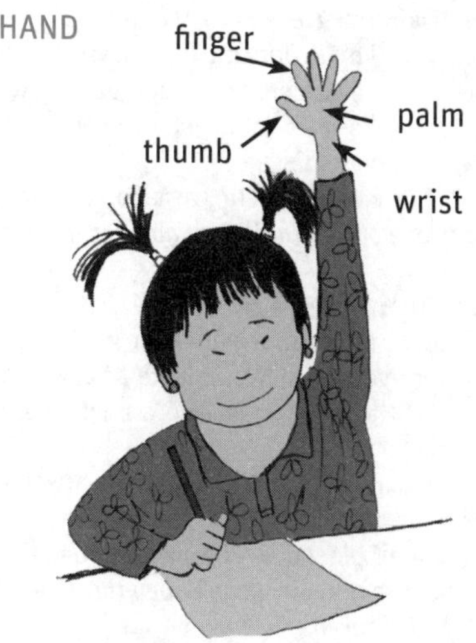

hand² /hænd/ [verb] To give something using your hand: *Hand me that knife, please.*

▶ **PHRASAL VERBS** · **to hand (something) back** To return something to somebody: *The teacher handed the test papers back to us.* · **to hand (something) in** To give something to somebody in a position of authority: *We handed the exercise books in at the end of the class.* · **to hand out (something)** To give one thing to each person: *A woman stood on the corner handing out leaflets to all people passing by.*

handbag /ˈhænd.bæg/ [countable noun] See **purse**. ■ This word is British English.

a b c d e f g **h** i j k l m n o p q r s t u v w x y z

handball /'hænd.bɔːl/ US: /-bɑːl/ [uncountable noun] A game where each team attempts to throw the ball into a goal: *Handball can be played by seven or eleven players.*

handbook /'hænd.bʊk/ [countable noun] A short book that gives instructions and information: *The computer comes with a handbook.*

handbrake or **hand brake** [countable noun] A brake in a vehicle which is operated by hand: *If the main brakes fail, use the handbrake.* See page 441.

handful /'hænd.fʊl/ [countable noun] **1** A small number of things or people: *Only a handful of people came to the show.* **2** The amount that you can hold in your hand: *Put a handful of rice into the bowl, please.*

handicap /'hæn.dɪ.kæp/ [countable noun] Something that stops you doing things: *Not being able to use a computer will be a great handicap in the future.*

handicapped /'hæn.dɪ.kæpt/ [adjective] Having a physical disability: *Tracy is competing in a sports competition for handicapped children.* ■ The word "disabled" is now considered more appropriate. ■ Be careful with the pronunciation of the end of this word. The "e" is not pronounced.

handicrafts [plural noun] Artistic work done by hand: *Weaving is one of the traditional handicrafts of the Indians of Peru.*

handkerchief /'hæŋ·kər·tʃəf/, /-tʃɪf/, /-ˌtʃif/ [countable noun] A square piece of cloth or paper for wiping your nose or your eyes: *Take this handkerchief and dry your tears.* ■ "Hankie" and "hanky" are informal for "handkerchief".

handle¹ /'hændl/ [countable noun] **1** The part of an object that you hold in your hand: *The handle of that knife is made of plastic.* **2** The part of something that you hold to open it: *I can't open the door. The door handle is broken.*

↑**handle²** /'hændl/ [verb] **1** To hold or to touch something: *Handle those cups with care!* **2** To control somebody or something: *The police found the situation difficult to handle.*

handlebars /'hændlbɑːz/ [plural noun] The part at the front of a bicycle or a motorcycle that you put your hands on: *You must hold onto the handlebars firmly when you ride a mountain bike.* See page 441.

handmade /ˌhænd'meɪd/ [adjective] Made by hand: *Handmade shoes can be very expensive.*

handshake /'hænd.ʃeɪk/ [countable noun] Greeting when you take somebody's hand and shake it: *When he introduced me to Neela, she gave me a firm handshake.*

handsome /'hæn.səm/ [adjective] Attractive: *Roy is quite handsome.* ■ The same meaning: "good-looking". When we use "handsome" for people, this is usually to talk about boys and men. For women we usually say "beautiful" or "pretty".

handstand /'hænd.stænd/ **do a handstand** To balance on your hands with your feet in the air: *Anne showed me how to do a handstand yesterday.*

handwriting /'hændˌraɪṱ·ɪŋ/ [uncountable noun] The way you write: *I can't understand your handwriting very well.*

handy /'hæn.di/ [adjective] **1** Useful: *This pocketknife is very handy.* **2** Easy to find, within easy reach: *I always keep a notepad handy by the telephone.*

↑**hang, hung, hung** /hæŋ/ [verb] **1** To suspend, to fasten something from above: *You can hang your coat in the hall.* **2** To kill somebody using a rope around their neck: *They rescued the innocent man before the crowd could hang him.* ■ Be careful! In this use "hang" has regular past and past participle forms: "hanged".

▶ **PHRASAL VERBS** · **to hang about/around 1** To stay in a place doing nothing in particular: *He's always hanging about in the shopping mall with his friends.* **2** To spend some time with somebody: *We were hanging around with him the whole day.* · **to hang on** To wait: *Hang on a moment, please.* · **to hang out** To spend some time with somebody: *Last night, I was hanging out with my friends.* · **to hang up** To end a telephone conversation: *Liz hung up because she heard somebody calling at the door.* ■ In this use, the same meaning: "ring off".

hanger or **coat hanger** /'hæŋ·ər/, /'koʊt ˌhæŋ·ər/ [countable noun] A piece of wood, plastic or wire, with a hook at the top, used for hanging clothes: *Put your shirt on a hanger and put it in the closet.*

hang glider [countable noun] A kind of big kite on which a person can fly: *Hang gliders move with wind currents.*

hang gliding [uncountable noun] Sport of flying on a kind of big kite: *We went hang gliding in the mountains at the weekend.*

hangman /'hæŋ.mən, -mæn/ [countable noun] **1** A person whose job is hanging criminals: *Hangmen used to wear hoods over their heads so that they would not be recognized.* ■ The plural is "hangmen". **2** A word game: *In "hangman" each wrong letter you say adds a bit to the drawing of a man being hanged.*

hankie or **hanky** /'hæŋki/ [countable noun] See **handkerchief.** ■ These words are informal.

↑**happen** /'hæp.ᵊn/ [verb] To take place: *What happened to Carol yesterday?*

a b c d e f g h i j k l m n o p q r s t u v w x y z

happening /ˈhæp.ᵊn.ɪŋ/ [countable noun] An event: *There have been some strange happenings in this house.* ■ We usually use the verb "happen": "Some strange things have happened in this house".

†**happiness** /ˈhæp.ɪ.nəs/ [uncountable noun] The state of being happy: *Her recovery brought great happiness to her family.*

†**happy** /ˈhæp.i/ [adjective] Very pleased, content: *I'm happy to be here with you.* ■ The comparative form is "happier" and the superlative form is "happiest". 👁 See picture at **emotions**.

harbor [countable noun] Safe place where ships can tie up to load, unload and wait before going back to sea: *During the storm the ships stayed in the harbor.* ■ The same meaning: "port".

†**hard**[1] /hɑːd/ [adjective] **1** Firm and solid, not soft: *This cake is as hard as a rock.* **2** Difficult to do or to understand: *This translation is very hard.* **3 hard disk** See "hard disk" in the word **disk**.

hard[2] /hɑːd/ [adverb] A lot, very much and with energy: *Take an umbrella with you because it's raining hard.* ■ Compare with "hardly" (only just or almost not).

hardback /ˈhɑrdˌbæk/ [countable noun] A book with a hard cover: *Hardbacks are nice, but much more expensive than paperbacks.* 👁 See picture at **book**.

harden /ˈhɑr·də·n/ [verb] To become hard: *With this cold wind, the snow's hardening very quickly.*

hardly /ˈhɑrd·li/ [adverb] Almost not; only just: *There's hardly any milk left in the fridge.* ■ Be careful! "Hardly" is not the adverb form of "hard". Compare with "hard[2]" (a lot, very much and with energy).

hardness /ˈhɑrd·nəs/ [uncountable noun] **1** The quality of being solid and not soft: *The hardness of metal makes it difficult to work with.* **2** The quality of being difficult to do or to take: *Everybody agreed about the hardness of the test.* ■ Compare with "softness" (the quality being tender, springy, smooth, gentle, delicate, mild or light).

hardware [uncountable noun] **1** The physical equipment and parts of a computer: *The technician advised me to buy some new hardware for my computer.* **2** Metal equipment, tools and items used in a house: *I will go to the shopping center to get some hardware for gardening.*

hard-working /ˈhɑrdˈwɜr·kɪŋ/ [adjective] Who works a lot: *Tom's a hard-working student.*

hare US: /her/ UK: /heəʳ/ [countable noun] An animal like a big rabbit: *Hares move by jumping.*

†**harm**[1] US: /hɑːrm/ UK: /hɑːm/ [uncountable noun] Damage: *My dog would never do any harm to a child.*

harm[2] /hɑːm/ [verb] To hurt somebody or something: *This storm will harm the trees.*

harmful /ˈhɑrm·fəl/ [adjective] Causing damage to somebody or something: *Eating candies is harmful for your teeth.*

harmless /ˈhɑrm·ləs/ [adjective] Not dangerous: *That dog is harmless; its bark is worse than its bite.*

harmony /ˈhɑr·mə·ni/, /ˈhɑr·mə·ni/ ▮ [uncountable noun] **1** The state of agreement in ideas and feelings: *There's perfect harmony between the two sisters.* ▮ [noun] **2** A pleasant arrangement of sounds or colors: *The choir sang in perfect harmony.* ■ The plural is "harmonies".

harness[1] /ˈhɑːnɪs/ [countable noun] **1** A set of leather straps and metal parts put around the horses's head and body so that it can be controlled and fastened to a cart: *The harness was placed on the horse and they left.* **2** A set of straps for fastening something to a person's body or for controlling a small child: *He needed a harness for the parachute.* **3 to get back in harness** To get back in the routine of one's usual work or activity: *The whole family got back in harness after the summer vacation.*

harness[2] /ˈhɑr·nəs/ [verb] **1** To attach a horse with leather straps: *They harnessed the horse to the cart.* **2** To control and use the power of a natural resource: *Hydroelectric dams harness the force of the river to generate electricity.*

harp US: /hɑːrp/ UK: /hɑːp/ [countable noun] A very large musical instrument with strings that are plucked with the fingers: *Who taught Rebecca to play the harp?* 👁 **See page 458.**

harsh US: /hɑːrʃ/ UK: /hɑːʃ/ [adjective] Rough and unpleasant; cruel: *He spoke in a harsh voice.*

harvest /ˈhɑːvɪst/ ▮ [noun] **1** The time of year when crops are picked: *Peter helps on the farm during the harvest.* ▮ [countable noun] **2** The amount of food collected during this time: *This wonderful weather means there'll be a good harvest.*

harvester [countable noun] **1** A person who cuts and gathers a crop: *The harvesters picked all the grapes.* **2** A machine used in the fields to collect a crop: *The harvester was used to bring in the crop.*

has /hæz, həz, əz/ [verb] See **have**.

hash mark [countable noun] The symbol SÍMBOLO DE ALMOHADILLA: *In some social networks, hash marks are usually added before keywords.* ■ The same meaning: "pound sign".

hasn't /ˈhæz.ᵊnt/ The contraction of "has not".

haste /heɪst/ [uncountable noun] The state of doing things too quickly: *In her haste, she forgot the keys.*

hasty /ˈheɪ.sti/ [adjective] Done quickly and without thinking enough: *That hasty decision was a big mistake.* ■ The comparative form is "hastier" and the superlative form is "hastiest".

a b c d e f g h i j k l m n o p q r s t u v w x y z

†hat /hæt/ [countable noun] A thing that somebody wears on their head: *Take your hat off before you go in.* 👁 See picture at **clothes.**

hatch /hætʃ/ [verb] To come out of an egg or to cause to come out: *Three chickens have already hatched.*

†hate /heɪt/ [verb] Not to like something or somebody at all: *I hate getting up early.* ■ The verb after "hate" is in the "-ing" form.

hatred /ˈheɪ.trɪd/ [uncountable noun] A strong feeling of dislike: *He's full of hatred for the man who killed his dog.*

haunt US: /hɑːnt/ UK: /hɔːnt/ [verb] **1** To be and to appear in a place, when you are talking about ghosts: *They say that ghosts haunt the castle.* **2** To come into your head and stay there, usually something negative: *Her screams still haunt me at night.*

haunted US: /ˈhɑːn.t̬ɪd/ UK: /ˈhɔːn.tɪd/ [adjective] Lived in or visited by ghosts: *Is this house haunted?*

†have, had, had /hæv, həv, əv/ [verb] **1** To own or to be given in life: *George has a new computer; I have two brothers.* ■ See box on the following page. **2** An auxiliary verb that goes with another verb to say that something happened in the past: *Anita and Tony have seen that movie; I have spoken to her about it.* ■ See box on the following page. **3** Used with "got", to own or to be given in life: *My uncle has got a house in Scotland.* ■ This use is always in the present tense. This use is British English. **4** Used with "got", to feel: *I've got a pain in my leg.* ■ This use is always in the present tense. **5** Used with food and drink nouns, to consume: *What time do you have dinner?; I'm going to have a ham sandwich.* **6** Used with many nouns, to talk about doing something: *Do you have a break after lunch?* **7** To receive: *When did Lee have the call from Chile?* **8** To organize that somebody do something: *I'll have him do the laundry.* **9 have to** To be obliged to, must: *I have to finish the work this weekend; You have to take the test, it's compulsory.* ■ "Have to" and "must" have very similar meanings. "Have to" is used generally for external obligation and facts: regulations, the law and so on. "Must" is used mainly for personal opinions (See box at **must**). **10 to have (something) done** Make somebody do something for you: *We'll have the kitchen painted next week.* **11 to have had it** To be about to break or collapse; or to have reached the point where you can't continue: *I think that chair has had it: let's remove it before somebody has an accident.* **12 to have it in for somebody** To dislike somebody and be determined to criticize or harm them: *She has had it in for me ever since I made that joke about her.* **13 to have nothing to do with (somebody or something)** To not be the responsibility of somebody, or not be relevant: *I had nothing to do with it: it was Sam's idea.* ■ When "have" is used to help another verb, it is called an "auxiliary". "Have" is an auxiliary in uses 1, 3, 4 and in the expression "to have (something) done". ■ See box on the following page.

▸ **PHRASAL VERBS** · **to have something back** To recover something that is yours: *Can I have it back on Monday.* · **to have on 1** To wear: *The thief had on a black coat and jeans.* **2** To have on your schedule: *What do you have on next week?* · **to have somebody over** To invite somebody to your house: *I'm having some friends over on Friday.*

haven't /ˈhæv.ᵊnt/ The contraction of "have not".

hawk US: /hɑːk/ UK: /hɔːk/ [countable noun] A bird that catches small animals for food: *Hawks have very good eyesight.*

hay /heɪ/ [countable noun] Dry grass that is food for cattle: *Farmers keep hay in barns so that they can feed the cows in winter.*

hay fever [uncountable noun] An allergy which is caused by breathing in pollen: *I suffer from hay fever every spring.*

hazelnut /ˈheɪ.zᵊl.nʌt/ [countable noun] A small round nut: *Squirrels love eating hazelnuts.*

hazy /ˈheɪ.zi/ [adjective] Not clear: *The day began hazy, but later it became hot and clear.* ■ The comparative form is "hazier" and the superlative form is "haziest".

†he /hiː, hi, i/ [pronoun] The male person or animal being talked about: *John isn't here today because he's ill.*

†head¹ /hed/ [countable noun] **1** The part of your body above your neck: *Be careful you don't bang your head*

HAT

hat

beret

wooly hat

baseball cap

when you go through the tunnel. See page 421. **2** Your brain: *Use your head! If you think a little you will find the solution.* **3** The most important part of something: *Who's going to sit at the head of the table?* **4** The most important person: *Mrs. McIntyre became the head of our department last year.* **5** See **headteacher**. **6 heads or tails** Words that you say when you throw a coin to decide who wins: *Let's toss a coin; heads you win, tails you lose.*

head[2] /hed/ [verb] To hit a ball with your head: *Soccer player headed the ball into the net and shouted: "Goal!".*

▸ **PHRASAL VERBS · to head for** To go towards: *He is heading for Phoenix.*

†**headache** /ˈhed.eɪk/ [countable noun] A pain in your head: *I have a headache so I am going to take an aspirin.*

headband /ˈhed.bænd/ [countable noun] A band of fabric or plastic worn around the head: *Some headbands are decorative, and others help to soak up sweat when you are doing sport.*

heading /ˈhed.ɪŋ/ [countable noun] The words at the top of a piece of writing: *The heading at the top of the page says "Private report".*

headlight /ˈhed.laɪt/ [countable noun] A light at the front of a car: *You won't see the road if you don't switch your headlights on.* See page 441.

headline /ˈhed.laɪn/ [countable noun] Words at the top of a newspaper story: *The headlines announced the news of the Prime Minister's illness.*

headmaster US: /ˈhedˌmæs.t̬ɚ/ UK: /ˌhedˈmɑː.stəʳ/ [countable noun] A man who is in charge of a school in Great Britain or of a private school: *The headmaster had a meeting with the teachers during the recess.* ■ It is now more common to say: "head teacher". ■ A woman who is in charge of a private school is a "headmistress".

headmistress /ˈhedˌmɪs·trəs/, /ˌhedˈmɪs-/ [countable noun] A woman who is in charge of a school in Great Britain or of a private school: *Sally's going to talk to the headmistress about her test results.* ■ It is now more common to say: "head teacher". ■ A man who is in charge of a school is a "headmaster".

head office [noun] The most important office of a firm: *The company's head office is now in Los Angeles.*

headphones /ˈhedˌfoʊnz/ [plural noun] Things that you put over or in your ears to listen to music: *Put on my headphones and listen to this, it's great.*

headquarters /ˈhedˌkwɔr·t̬ərz/ [noun] The most important office of a business or other organization: *This company has its headquarters in New York.* ■ This word can be used with either a singular or a plural verb: "The headquarters is/are in London". "HQ" is an abbreviation for "headquarters".

headteacher UK: /ˌhedˈtiːtʃər/ [countable noun] A person who is in charge of a school in great Britain or of a private school: *The headteacher sent Jack home for continually being noisy.* ■ "Head" is short for "headteacher".

†**heal** /hɪəl/ [verb] To become or to make something healthy again: *Her leg healed quickly after the accident.*

†**health** /helθ/ [uncountable noun] **1** The state of the body when it is well and there is no sickness: *His health is amazing for somebody who is 90 years*

to have: auxiliary verb

To have is used as an auxiliary verb in perfect tenses (*to have* + past participle of main verb):

- *I have never been to China.*
- *When I arrived at the station, the train had already left.*
- *I should have studied harder.*

to have

- **Present tense**

affirmative	contractions	negative	questions
I have	I've	I haven't	have I?
you have	you've	you haven't	have you?
he / she / it has	he's / she's / it's	he / she / it hasn't	has he / she it?
we have	we've	we haven't	have we?
you have	you've	you haven't	have you?
they have	they've	they haven't	have they?

- **Past tense**
  had
- **Past participle**
  had

a b c d e f g h i j k l m n o p q r s t u v w x y z

old. **2** The general condition of your body: *Health is more important than wealth.*

†**healthy** /'hel.θi/ [adjective] **1** Not ill, physically strong: *The best way to stay healthy is by doing exercise and eating fresh food.* **2** In good condition: *Her baby's small but healthy.* ■ The comparative form is "healthier" and the superlative form is "healthiest".

heap[1] /hi:p/ [countable noun] A number of things on top of each other: *When are you going to sort out that heap of photos?*

heap[2] /hi:p/ [verb] To put a number of things on top of each other: *He always heaps his clothes on his bedroom chair.*

HEAP

†**hear, heard, heard** US: /hɪr/ UK: /hɪəʳ/ [verb] **1** To receive sounds through your ears: *Be quiet, everybody! I can't hear the news on the radio.* ■ Compare with "listen" (to pay attention in order to hear somebody or something). **2** To be informed about something: *Have you heard about Laura's operation?*

▸ **PHRASAL VERBS** · **to hear from (somebody)** To get news from somebody: *I haven't heard from Penny for two weeks.* · **to hear of (somebody or something)** To know about somebody or something: *My dad's never heard of the group E.17.*

heard Past tense and past participle forms of **hear**.

†**hearing** US: /'hɪr.ɪŋ/ UK: /'hɪə.rɪŋ/ [uncountable noun] The ability to hear: *Grandma's hearing is getting worse every day.*

†**heart** US: /hɑːrt/ UK: /hɑːt/ ▮ [countable noun] **1** The part of the body that makes the blood flow: *Julie's father is going to have a heart transplant.* ▮ [noun] **2** Your feelings: *Liza has a big heart, she is one of the most generous people I know.* **3** The middle: *Central Park is in the heart of Manhattan.* **4** A playing card with red heart shapes on it: *The Queen of Hearts is a character in "Alice in Wonderland".* **5 by heart** By memory: *I can't learn all those phone numbers by heart.* **6 heart attack** An illness that affects the heart: *Jessica's father had a heart attack yesterday and he is now in hospital.*

heartbeat /'hɑrt,bit/ [countable noun] One complete pulsation of the heart: *The future mother could hear the heartbeat of the baby from inside her belly.*

heartbreak /'hɑrt,breɪk/ [countable noun] Deep sadness or distress: *Their breakup was a heartbreak for him.*

†**heat**[1] /hi:t/ ▮ [noun] **1** The feeling given by something that is hot: *The heat from the fire will dry the towels.* **2** A system for keeping rooms warm: *It's very cold. Could you turn up the heat, please?* ■ The same meaning: "heating". ▮ [countable noun] **3** Eliminating round in a competition: *He won his heat and went through to the semi-finals.*

heat[2] /hi:t/ [verb] To make something hot: *Put your dinner in the microwave to heat it up.*

heater /'hi·t̬ər/ [noun] A machine for heating something: *Is the water heater on?*

heath /hi:θ/ [noun] A big piece of open land: *Very few trees and bushes grow on heaths.*

†**heating** /'hit ,weɪv/, /'hi·t̬ɪŋ/ [uncountable noun] **1** A system for keeping rooms warm: *It's cold in here because the heating's off.* ■ The same meaning: "heat". **2 central heating** See "central heating" in the word **central**.

heatwave /'hi:tweɪv/ [noun] A period of exceptionally hot weather: *There was a heatwave last summer and we went to the swimming pool every day.*

heave /hi:v/ [verb] To lift and pull something heavy: *We all heaved the piano into the living room.*

†**heaven** /'hev.ᵊn/ [noun] A place where some people believe God lives: *Your grandma has gone to heaven.* ■ Be careful! "Heaven" does not have the same meaning as "sky".

heavenly /'hev.ᵊn.li/ [adjective] **1** Divine, of heaven: *He had a heavenly vision.* **2** Of or located in space: *The Sun, the Moon and the Stars are heavenly bodies.* **3** Very pleasant: *The meal was perfect; in fact it was heavenly.* ■ This use is informal.

†**heavy** /'hev.i/ [adjective] **1** With a lot of weight: *The sofa's too heavy to be moved.* 👁 See picture at **opposite**. **2** Great in amount or in force: *The traffic's always heavy at Christmas.* ■ The comparative form is "heavier" and the superlative form is "heaviest".

heavy metal [noun] A type of very loud rock music: *Heavy metal's always played on electric guitars and drums.*

hectare /'hekteər·/ [noun] A unit of land area: *There are 10,000 square meters in a hectare.*

he'd /hi:d/ The contraction of "he had" or "he would".

hedge /hedʒ/ [noun] A line of bushes at the side of a field or yard: *The horse jumped over the hedge.*

†**heel** /hɪəl/ [noun] Back part of the foot: *I hurt my heel when I jumped off the rock.* 👁 **See page 421.**

†**height** /haɪt/ [noun] The measurement of how tall or high something is: *The height of the Empire State*

Building is 381 meters. ■ Be careful with the pronunciation of this word. It is pronounced like the word "high" with a "t" sound at the end.

held /held/ Past tense and past participle forms of **hold.**

helicopter /'hel·ɪˌkɑp·tər/, /'hi·lə-/ [noun] A kind of small aircraft with a large propeller on top: *They took the wounded men to hospital by helicopter.* 👁 See picture at **transport**.

helium /'hiːliəm/ [uncountable noun] A colorless, inactive gas: *Helium is used in balloons.*

†**hell** /hel/ [uncountable noun] **1** A place where some people think the devil lives: *In the museum I saw a beautiful medieval painting of heaven and hell.* **2** A miserable situation: *It was hell in the refugee camp. There was no food and no hope.*

he'll /hiːl/ The contraction of "he will".

†**hello** /he'loʊ/, /hə-/ [interjection] **1** A word that you say when you meet somebody: *Hello, David, how are you?* ■ "Hi" is informal for "hello". **2** A word you say when you are speaking on the telephone: *Hello, who's that speaking?* ■ We also say "hallo".

helm /helm/ [countable noun] **1** The wheel or handle which controls the direction a ship goes: *The Captain is at the helm.* **2 to be at the helm** To be leading or in control of something: *With the new Managing Director at the helm of the company, the future looks better.*

helmet /'hel.mət/ [noun] A hat that protects your head: *Firefighters wear helmets to protect themselves from falling objects.*

†**help**[1] /help/ [uncountable noun] **1** The action of making things easier for somebody or of being of use to them: *I need some help with the shopping.* **2** A person or a thing that makes something easier: *He wasn't much of a help.*

help[2] /help/ [verb] **1** To do something for somebody: *Can you help me take the books upstairs?* **2 help yourself** To take what you want: *Help yourself to a little more fruit.*

†**helpful** /'help.fᵊl/ [adjective] That helps: *This map's very helpful if you want to find your way around Chicago.*

helping /'hel.pɪŋ/ [noun] An amount of food: *Have another helping of cake.*

hemisphere /'hem·əˌsfɪər/ [noun] A half of the earth's globe: *Everything north of the equator is in the northern hemisphere.* 👁 **See page 449.**

hen /hen/ [noun] A female chicken: *Farmers keep hens for their eggs.* 👁 **See page 429.**

†**her**[1] /hɜːr, hər, ər/ [pronoun] A word used for "she", usually when it is the object of a sentence: *I'm looking for Julie because I need her to help me.*

her[2] [adjective] Of her; belonging to her: *Lynn's cleaning her glasses.*

herb US: /ɝːb/ UK: /hɜːb/ [noun] A plant that is used for medicine or in food: *These herbs are good for curing colds.*

herbivore /'hɜː.bɪ.vɔːr/ US: /'hɝː.bə.vɔːr/ [countable noun] An animal which only eats plant material: *Cows, sheep and goats are all herbivores.* ■ Compare with "carnivore" (an animal which eats meat). 👁 **See page 427.**

herd US: /hɝːd/ UK: /hɜːd/ [noun] A group of animals of the same kind: *A herd of cows was blocking the road.* ■ Be careful! When we talk about sheep or birds, we say "flock", not "herd". 👁 See picture at **groups.**

†**here** US: /hɪr/ UK: /hɪəʳ/ [adverb] **1** At this place, to this place: *Come here a minute, please.* **2 here and there** In different places: *Mike left his comics here and there all over the house.* **3 here you are** Words that you say when you give something to somebody: *Here you are; my phone number.* ■ See box below.

hereditary /hə'red.ɪ.tri/ [adjective] Something that passes from parent to child: *Is that disease hereditary?*

heritage /'her·ə·t̬ɪdʒ/ [countable noun] **1** Elements of a particular society, such as works of art, language, buildings and customs, which have been passed on from earlier generations: *Ernest Hemingway forms part of United States literary heritage.* **2** Something inherited at birth, including personal characteristics, rank or status: *The title is part of her heritage.*

†**hero** US: /'hɪr.oʊ/ UK: /'hɪə.rəʊ/ [noun] **1** A boy or a man who has done something very important or brave: *George S. Patton is still a hero for older people in the United States.* **2** The most important boy or man in a book or a movie: *Tom Hanks is the hero of that movie.* ■ The plural is "heroes". A woman is a "heroine".

> ***here***
>
> - In sentences beginning with ***here*** where the subject is a pronoun, the verb is placed after the subject, not before:
>   - *Here it is, on the chair.*
>   - *Here she comes, look!*
> - When the subject is a noun, the verb comes before the subject:
>   - *Here comes the train!*
>   - *Here is the money you asked for.*

a b c d e f g **h** i j k l m n o p q r s t u v w x y z

heroin /ˈher·oʊ·ɪn/ [noun] A hard drug that has the appearance of sugar: *My cousin's friend died at age 20. He was a heroin addict.* ■ Compare with "heroine" (a girl or a woman who is admired for having done something important).

heroine /ˈher·oʊ·ɪn/ [noun] **1** A girl or a woman who has done something very important or brave: *Eleanor Roosevelt was a United States heroine.* **2** The most important girl or woman in a book, movie and so on: *I cried when the heroine died at the end of the movie.* ■ A man is a "hero". ■ Compare with "heroin" (a hard drug).

heron /ˈher.ən/ [countable noun] A wading bird with long legs: *The heron has a long neck.*

herpes /ˈhɜr·piz/ [uncountable noun] A disease that causes painful pimples on the skin: *Herpes is a viral infection.* ■ The same meaning: "shingles".

herring /ˈher.ɪŋ/ [noun] **1** A small sea fish: *We're going to have herrings for dinner.* **2 red herring** See **red herring**.

†**hers** US: /hɝːz/ UK: /hɜːz/ [pronoun] Belonging to her: *Is that Nicola over there? These glasses are hers.*

†**herself** /hərˈself/ [pronoun] **1** A word that refers to a girl or a woman who is the subject of a sentence: *Sadie cut herself with the knife and had to go to the doctor's.* **2** A word that underlines that she is the person the verb refers to: *She'll drive the van herself.* **3 by herself 1** Alone: *She lives by herself.* **2** Without help: *My aunt's painted the kitchen by herself.* ■ Be careful! The plural of "herself" is "themselves".

he's /hiːz/ The contraction of "he is" or "he has".

†**hesitate** /ˈhez.ɪ.teɪt/ [verb] To stop for a moment before you do something: *Lee hesitated before crossing the street because the traffic was so heavy.*

hesitation /ˌhez.ɪˈteɪ.ʃᵊn/ [noun] A short pause before you do something: *He answered the question after a moment's hesitation.*

hessian /ˈhes.i.ən/ [uncountable noun] See **burlap**. ■ This word is British English.

heterogeneous /ˌhet̬·ər·əˈdʒi·ni·əs/, /-dʒin·jəs/ [adjective] Different and varied, not of the same type: *The alliance is made up of a heterogeneous group of parties.* ■ This word is formal. ■ Compare with "homogeneous" (of the same type).

†**hi** /haɪ/ [interjection] See **hello.** ■ This word is informal.

hibernate /ˈhaɪbəneɪt/ [verb] To spend the winter months sleeping: *Tortoises have to hibernate for several months each year.*

hiccups or **hiccoughs** [plural noun] Sudden breathing in resulting in a sound in your throat: *You'll get hiccups if you eat so quickly.*

hid Past tense of **hide**.

hidden Past participle of **hide**.

†**hide, hid, hidden** /haɪd/ [verb] **1** To deliberately put something where it cannot be seen: *We can't open the drawer because Keith's hidden the keys.* **2** To go where people cannot see you: *The dog's hiding under the bed.* **3** Not to tell or show people something: *Kate hides her emotions. You never know what she is feeling.* **4 hide-and-seek** A children's game: *In hide-and-seek a child looks for other children who are hiding.*

hieroglyphs [plural noun] Writing that uses picture symbols, used for example by the Ancient Egyptians: *Early hieroglyphs used figures of animals, objects and people.*

†**high**[1] /haɪ/ [adjective] **1** Having a great distance between the top and the bottom: *I like standing on top of high mountains.* ■ "High" is used for things that are not alive, and for abstract nouns: "high pollution", "high inflation". Compare with "tall" (mainly used for people, trees and structures). **2** Far from the ground: *That cupboard's too high for a child to reach.* **3** Strong, great: *This train can reach a very high speed.* **4** Not low, when you are talking about sound: *Your uncle speaks in a high voice.* ■ Be careful. We do not use "high" for people. We say: "Susan is very tall". **5 high tide** See "hide tide" in the word **tide**.

high[2] /haɪ/ [adverb] Far above the ground: *How high can you jump?*

higher education [noun] Education at a university or a college: *Tricia wants to go on to higher education after she leaves school.*

highlands /ˈhaɪ.ləndz/ [noun] A region with many hills and mountains: *The Ouachita Mountains in Oklahoma are part of the United States Interior Highlands region.* ■ This word is usually used with a plural verb.

highly /ˈhaɪ.li/ [adverb] **1** To a high degree: *The report was highly critical.* **2** Very favorably: *He thinks very highly of himself.* **3** In a high position: *His father is a highly placed official.*

high school [noun] In the United States, a school for students between 14 and 18 years old: *I studied French in my four years in high school.*

high street [noun] The main street in a town: *You'll find a bank in the High Street.*

hightail /ˈhaɪ.teɪl/ [verb] To go off quickly: *The last time we saw him, he was hightailing it down the street.* ■ This word is informal.

high-tech /ˌhaɪˈtek/ [adjective] With the most advanced equipment or machines: *This store sell high-tech computers.* ■ This is a short form of "high-technology". This word is also written "hi-tech".

high-technology [adjective] See **high-tech.** ■ "High-tech" and "hi-tech" are short for "high-technology".

†**highway** /ˈhaɪ.weɪ/ [noun] Especially in America, a main road: *If we go on the highway, we should avoid the gridlock.*

hijack /ˈhaɪ.dʒæk/ [verb] To take control of a vehicle by force: *The guerrillas hijacked a plane that was on the way to Japan.*

hike /haɪk/ [noun] A long walk in the countryside: *Let's go for a hike in the Lake District this weekend.*

hiking /ˈhaɪ.kɪŋ/ [noun] Walking as a relaxation or hobby: *One of the advantages of hiking is that you get to know new places.*

hilarious /hɪˈleər·i·əs/ [adjective] Very funny, making you laugh a lot: *It was hilarious when the policeman walked into the lamp-post.*

†**hill** /hɪl/ [noun] A rise in the land: *Let's walk to the top of the hill and look at the view.* 👁 **See page 445.**

†**him** /hɪm, ɪm/ [pronoun] A word used for "he", usually when it is the object of a sentence: *I'll talk to him later, OK?*

†**himself** /hɪmˈself/ [pronoun] **1** A word that refers to a boy or a man who is the subject of a sentence: *Jim's old enough to look after himself.* **2** A word that underlines that "he" is the person the verb refers to: *I couldn't see Dr. MacKean himself, but I spoke to Dr. Reed.* **3 by himself 1** Alone: *He lives by himself.* **2** Without help: *He mended the bicycle by himself.* ■ Be careful! The plural of "himself" is "themselves".

hind /haɪnd/ [adjective] Referring to the legs of an animal with four legs, located at the rear: *The hind legs of a horse are the most powerful.* ■ Be careful: this adjective has no comparative or superlative forms.

Hindu /ˈhɪn.duː/ [noun and adjective] Referring to Hinduism or a follower of Hinduism: *Most Hindus live in northern India.* ■ Be careful! "Hindu" has a capital "H".

Hinduism /ˈhɪn.duː.ɪ.zᵊm/ [noun] An Indian religion: *There are many gods in Hinduism.* ■ Careful! "Hinduism" has a capital "H".

hinge /ˈhɪndʒ/ [noun] A metal fastener that allows something to swing: *If you oil the hinges, the door won't make that noise.*

hint[1] /hɪnt/ [noun] An indirect suggestion: *If you can't answer the question I'll give you a hint.*

hint[2] /hɪnt/ [verb] To make an indirect suggestion: *Your father hinted that we weren't telling the truth.*

†**hip** /hɪp/ [noun] The side of your body above the legs: *He stood there waiting with his hands on his hips.*

hippo /ˈhɪpəʊ/ [noun] See **hippopotamus.** ■ This word is informal.

hippopotamus /ˌhɪp·əˈpɑt̬·ə·məs/ [noun] A large African animal with a thick skin: *Hippopotamuses live near rivers.* ■ The plural is "hippopotamuses" or "hippopotami". ■ "Hippo" is informal for "hippopotamus". 👁 **See page 428.**

hire /haɪər/ [verb] To give work or a job in exchange of pay: *My mom's business is growing and she's hiring two software designers.*

his[1] [adjective] Of him; belonging to him: *Mark's broken his glasses.*

†**his**[2] /hɪz/ [pronoun] Belonging to him: *Give this comic to Philip, it's his, you know.*

hiss[1] [noun] A sound like a continuous "s": *Can you hear that hiss coming from the pressure cooker?*

hiss[2] /hɪs/ [verb] To make a continuous "s" sound: *The play was a disaster; the audience hissed and threw tomatoes at the actors.* ■ Be careful with the spelling of the 3rd person singular present tense form: "hisses".

hissy or **hissy fit to throw a hissy or to throw a hissy fit** To show silly or childish anger in an uncontrolled way: *As usual, Lisa threw a hissy when she heard the news.*

historian /hɪˈstɔr·i·ən/, /-ˈstour-/ [countable noun] Somebody who dedicates himself to the study of history: *The historians do not agree about the causes of the war.*

historic /hɪˈstɔr·ɪk/, /-ˈstɑr-/ [adjective] So important that it will be remembered: *The arrival of the first person on the moon, on 20 July 1969, was a historic event.*

†**historical** /hɪˈstɔr·ɪ·kəl/, /-ˈstɑr-/ [adjective] Of the past or about the past: *Hemingway's "The Old Man and the Sea" is a historical play.*

†**history** /ˈhɪs·tə·ri/, /-tri/ [uncountable noun] **1** The study of things that happened in the past: *History is her favorite subject at school.* **2** Things that happened in the past: *The fall of the Berlin Wall was a key moment in history.* ■ The plural is "histories". ■ Compare with "story" (a description of a series of events).

†**hit**[1] /hɪt/ [countable noun] **1** A touch with a lot of force: *Jim got a hit on his head when he was playing football yesterday.* **2** A successful song or play: *The new Sting album will be a hit in no time.*

hit[2], hit, hit /hɪt/ [verb] To touch somebody or something with a lot of force: *If you hit me again, I'll tell the teacher.* ■ Be careful with the spelling of this form: "hitting".

hitchhike /ˈhɪtʃ.haɪk/ [verb] To travel by getting free rides in cars: *Last summer we hitchhiked across the United States.*

hi-tech /ˌhaɪˈtek/ [adjective] See **high-tech.** ■ This is a short form of "high-technology".

hive /haɪv/ [noun] See **beehive.**

hoarse US: /hɔːrs/ UK: /hɔːs/ [adjective] Rough in voice: *Kevin's voice is hoarse because he has a very bad cold.*

hoax US: /hoʊks/ UK: /həʊks/ [noun] A trick which makes somebody believe something which isn't true: *They played a hoax on him.* ■ The plural is "hoaxes".

hob UK: /hɒb/ [countable noun] See **cooktop.** ■ This word is British English.

+**hobby** US: /ˈhɑː.bi/ UK: /ˈhɒb.i/ [noun] Something that you do regularly in your free time: *My favorite hobby is playing chess.* ■ The plural is "hobbies".

hobo US: /ˈhoʊ.boʊ/ UK: /ˈhəʊ.bəʊ/ [noun] Somebody who has no home and no job and moves from place to place: *He gave his old coat to a hobo.* ■ The plural is "hobos" or "hoboes".

hockey US: /ˈhɑː.ki/ UK: /ˈhɒk.i/ [noun] A game for two teams that try to hit a ball into a goal with sticks: *Hockey is played on grass or on ice.* See picture at **sport.**

+**hold, held, held** /həʊld/ [verb] **1** To have something in your hands: *Can you hold these books a moment while I open the door, please?* **2** To put part of the body in a certain way: *Hold your head up while I take the photo.* **3** To be able to contain: *This car holds five people.* **4** To have a meeting, party or other event: *They're holding a party upstairs.* **5** To have a title or a record: *She holds the record for the long jump.* **6** To support something, to resist pressure: *That will hold it for a while.* **7 to get hold of (somebody or something)** To find somebody or something: *I need to get hold of Helen to tell her the news.* **8 to hold hands** To have somebody else's hand in your hand: *They walked down the street holding hands.*

PHRASAL VERBS · to hold (somebody or something) back 1 To stop somebody or something from moving forwards: *The police couldn't hold the crowd back; Nothing can hold back the sea.* **2** To keep for yourself or for a later time: *I had to hold back the tears in front of them, but I was really hurt with the way they talked to me.* **3** To not reveal some information: *What are you holding back?* · **to hold off 1** To resist an attack: *They managed to hold off the enemy attack.* **2** To wait or postpone: *They had to hold off the celebration until grandpa got out of the hospital.* · **to hold on 1** To wait: *Hold on a moment while I take my coat off.* ■ In this use, "hold on" is often used in telephone conversations. **2** To grip something or somebody to avoid falling: *Hold on to me. The bus is going very fast.* · **to hold out** To resist or to last: *The people in the castle held out for months.* · **to hold (something) out** To extend your hand, or to put something in your hand and extend it: *He held out his hand.* · **to hold (somebody or something) up 1** To try to rob: *The robbers held up the train.* **2** To lift up: *Hold up your hand.* **3** To detain or delay: *An accident is holding up traffic on this road.*

holder US: /ˈhoʊl.dɚ/ UK: /ˈhəʊl.dəʳ/ [countable noun] **1** Somebody who owns or controls something: *She is the holder of that bank account.* **2** A device for supporting a particular object: *The cup is placed in the drink holder when the driver is at the wheel.*

hold-up /ˈhoʊld,ʌp/ [countable noun] **1** A delay: *I'm late because there was a hold-up on the freeway.* **2** A robbery: *A passer-by was wounded in the hold-up in South London yesterday.*

+**hole** /həʊl/ [noun] An empty space in something: *I lost the money because there was a hole in my pocket.*

+**holiday** /ˈhɑl·ɪˌdeɪ/ ▮ [countable noun] **1** A day for celebration when many people rest from work or school: *July 4th is always a holiday in United States.* See picture at **calendar.** ▮ [countable noun] **2** See **vacation.** ■ This use is British English. **3 on holiday** See **on vacation.** ■ This use is British English.

holler US: /ˈhɒlər/ [verb] To shout out: *We could hear grandma hollering for me from the window.*

+**hollow** US: /ˈhɑː.loʊ/ UK: /ˈhɒl.əʊ/ [adjective] With an empty space inside: *Pipes are hollow.*

holly US: /ˈhɑː.li/ UK: /ˈhɒl.i/ [noun] A tree which has dark green leaves with sharp points: *Holly is often used to decorate houses at Christmas.* ■ The plural is "hollies".

+**holy** /ˈhoʊ·li/ [adjective] **1** Sacred: *The priest blessed the baby with holy water.* **2** Serving God: *She is a very holy person.*

+**home**[1] /həʊm/ ▮ [noun] **1** The place where somebody lives: *I'm bored. I'm going home.* ■ Be careful! With direction verbs like "go", "come" and "arrive" we don't use the preposition "to", "in" or "at". We say: "go home" (We don't say "go to home"). ▮ [uncountable noun] **2** A place where they look after people: *Keith lived in a children's home when his parents died.* **3** A place where a thing comes from: *America is the home of baseball.* **4 at home** In your house: *My parents play cards at home every Wednesday night.* **5 single-family home** A house for one family that stands apart or by itself: *They live in a single-family home.* See picture at **house.**

home[2] /həʊm/ [adjective] Of your home or country: *The home team's losing the game.*

homeless /ˈhoʊm·ləs/ [adjective] **1** With nowhere to live: *There are lots of homeless people in the cities who sleep in the streets.* **2 the homeless** People with nowhere to live: *I saw a report on TV last night about the homeless in New York.*

home-made /ˌhəʊmˈmeɪd/, /ˌhoʊm-/ [adjective] Made at home, not in a factory or store: *Is this soup home-made?*

homesick /ˈhoʊmˌsɪk/ [adjective] Sad because you want to go home: *When I heard this song in Canada, it made me feel homesick.*

*****homework** US: /ˈhoʊm.wɝːk/ UK: /ˈhəʊm.wɜːk/ [uncountable noun] The school work that you have to do at home: *The teacher asked me to finish the calculations for homework.* ■ Be careful! We don't say "a homework". We say "some homework" or "a piece of homework". ■ We say **do** your homework.

homogeneous US: /ˌhoʊməˈdʒiːniəs/ UK: /ˌhɒməˈdʒiːniəs/ [adjective] Of the same type, or with the same appearance: *The result of the process is a homogeneous mixture.* ■ This word is formal. ■ Compare with "heterogeneous" (diverse and varied).

Honduran[1] [adjective] Referring to Honduras: *The Honduran currency is the Lempira.* ■ Be careful! "Honduran" has a capital "H".

Honduran[2] [countable noun] A person from Honduras: *My brother is married to an Honduran and they live in Tegucigalpa.* ■ Be careful! "Honduran" has a capital "H".

*****honest** US: /ˈɑː.nɪst/ UK: /ˈɒn.ɪst/ [adjective] **1** That tells the truth, that doesn't cheat or deceive: *She's the most honest person I know.* **2** Frank: *Be honest; do you think I can pass the test?*

honesty /ˈɑn·ə·sti/ [noun] Being honest: *He's got a reputation for honesty.*

honey /ˈhʌn.i/ ▮ [uncountable noun] **1** A sweet substance that bees make: *If you've got a bad throat, drink hot milk with honey in it.* ▮ [countable noun] **2** A word used when speaking to somebody you love: *Hurry up, honey, we're going to be late.*

honeymoon /ˈhʌn.i.muːn/ [noun] A vacation just after a wedding: *My sister is going to Majorca for her honeymoon.*

honk /hɒŋk/ [verb] To make a noise like a car horn or a goose: *The street was full of cars honking their horns.*

*****honor** /ˈɑn·ər/ [noun] Great respect and pride: *I won't do it. It's a question of honor.* ■ Be careful with the pronunciation of this word! The "h" is silent. ■ The British English spelling is "honour".

*****honour** UK: /ˈɒn.əʳ/ [noun] See **honor.** ■ This is a British English spelling.

hood /hʊd/ [noun] **1** A covering for your head: *Your ears won't get cold if you wear a hood.* **2** A device used for removing smoke and odors when cooking: *In the kitchen, hoods usually hang above the stove.* 👁 See picture at **kitchen.** **3** The metal cover for the front of a car: *There's a dent on the hood of your new car.* ■ In this use, in British English we say "bonnet".

hoodie or **hoody** [countable noun] **1** A sweatshirt with a hood on it: *Tom loves wearing hoodies.* **2** A person who wears a hoodie: *Can you see that hoodie out there? He's my friend Mike.* ■ This word is informal. ■ The plural is "hoodies".

hoof /huːf/ [noun] The hard foot of some animals: *We could hear the horse's hooves in the distance.* ■ The plural is "hooves".

*****hook** /hʊk/ [noun] A piece of metal or plastic for hanging things on: *Hang your cap on this hook.*

hooligan /ˈhuː.lɪ.gᵊn/ [noun] A violent young person: *There were problems with soccer hooligans after the game.*

hoop /huːp/ [noun] A large ring of plastic, wood or metal: *Wendy's outside playing with a hoop.*

hooray /hʊˈreɪ, hə-/ [interjection] An expression of great pleasure: *Hooray! I've passed my driving test.* ■ We also say: "hurrah, hurray".

hoover[1] /ˈhuːvər/ [noun] See **vacuum cleaner.** ■ This word is British English.

hoover[2] [verb] See **vacuum[2]**. ■ This word is British English.

HOOK

a b c d e f g h i j k l m n o p q r s t u v w x y z

a b c d e f g h i j k l m n o p q r s t u v w x y z

hop US: /hɑːp/ UK: /hɒp/ [verb] **1** To jump on one foot: *Let's hop as far as the lamp-post.* **2** To jump with both feet, when you are talking about a bird: *Can you see that bird hopping on the lawn.* ■ Be careful with the spelling of these forms: "hopped", "hopping".

hope[1] /həʊp/ ▮ [noun] **1** A feeling or desire that something good will happen: *There's still a lot of hope for her recovery.* ▮ [countable noun] **2** A person or a thing that can make something happen: *Please talk to her; you're my only hope.*

↑**hope[2]** /həʊp/ [verb] To want something to happen: *"Are you going to the concert?" "I hope so".* ■ Compare with "expect" (to believe that something will happen).

hopeful /ˈhoʊp·fəl/ [adjective] Feeling confident that something will happen: *I'm hopeful about passing the geography test.*

hopeless /ˈhoʊp·ləs/ [adjective] **1** Very bad: *She's hopeless at tennis.* **2** Useless: *It's hopeless to ask him for money.*

hopscotch US: /ˈhɑːp.skɑːtʃ/ UK: /ˈhɒp.skɒtʃ/ [noun] Children's game in which you hop over marked squares on the ground: *In hopscotch you throw a stone onto squares with numbers.*

horizon /həˈraɪ.zən/ [noun] The line where the sky meets the earth: *The sun's setting on the horizon.*

↑**horizontal** US: /ˌhɔːr.ɪˈzɑːn.t̬əl/ UK: /ˌhɒr.ɪˈzɒn.təl/ [adjective] Parallel to the ground: *If you are lying down, you are in a horizontal position.*

horizontally [adverb] In a parallel position to the ground, or to the bottom of a page: *First draw a line horizontally.* ■ Compare with "vertically" (in a vertical position or direction).

↑**horn** US: /hɔːrn/ UK: /hɔːn/ [countable noun] **1** A hard pointed thing on an animal's head: *Bulls have longer horns than cows.* **2** A thing in a car or a vehicle that makes a loud sound: *When you are driving, you shouldn't sound your horn in front of the hospital.*

horoscope US: /ˈhɔːr.ə.skoʊp/ UK: /ˈhɒr.ə.skəʊp/ [noun] A prediction based on the stars: *Tell me your date of birth and I'll read you your horoscope.*

horrible /ˈhɒr·ə·bəl/, /ˈhɑr-/ [adjective] Very unpleasant: *I had a horrible day yesterday; everything went wrong.*

horrific /həˈrɪf.ɪk/ [adjective] Shocking, terrible: *There was a horrific murder on this street last year.*

horrify /ˈhɒr·əˌfaɪ/, /ˈhɑr-/ [verb] To shock somebody: *That kind of haircut horrifies me.* ■ Be careful with the spelling of these forms: "horrifies", "horrified".

↑**horror** US: /ˈhɔːr.ɚ/ UK: /ˈhɒr.əʳ/ [noun] A feeling of fear or shock: *Some people have a horror of snakes.*

↑**horse** US: /hɔːrs/ UK: /hɔːs/ [noun] A big beautiful animal that can carry people: *Can any of you ride a horse?*

horseback riding [noun] The sport of riding a horse: *They often go horseback riding on the beach.*

horseman [countable noun] A man who rides a horse: *My uncle is an excellent horseman.* ■ The plural is "horsemen". ■ A woman is a "horsewoman".

horseshoe /ˈhɔrsˌʃu/ [noun] A piece of iron that goes on a horse's foot: *Some people think that horseshoes bring good luck.*

horsewoman [countable noun] A woman who rides a horse: *The famous horsewoman won the riding competition.* ■ The plural is "horsewomen". ■ A man is a "horseman".

hose US: /hoʊz/ UK: /həʊz/ [noun] A long, flexible tube for water: *I'm going to use the hose to water the plants.*

↑**hospital** US: /ˈhɑː.spɪ.t̬əl/ UK: /ˈhɒs.pɪ.təl/ [noun] A place where sick people are treated: *Jim's father has been in the hospital since his heart attack.*

hospitality US: /ˌhɑː.spɪˈtæl.ə.t̬i/ UK: /ˌhɒs.pɪˈtæl.ə.ti/ [noun] Friendly, welcoming behavior towards guests: *Oh, dear! I forgot to thank Neil's uncle for his hospitality before I left.*

↑**host** US: /hoʊst/ UK: /həʊst/ [noun] A person who invites and receives visitors: *Paul was our host at the party last night.* ■ For a woman we can also say "hostess".

hostage US: /ˈhɑː.stɪdʒ/ UK: /ˈhɒs.tɪdʒ/ [noun] A person kept as a prisoner until somebody or some group get what they want: *The gangsters held three hostages until they got the money.* ■ Be careful with the pronunciation of this word. The "a" is pronounced like the "i" in "did".

hostel US: /ˈhɑː.stəl/ UK: /ˈhɒs.təl/ [noun] A cheap hotel for students, for young people or for the homeless: *Tom slept in youth hostels when he went to San Francisco last year.*

hostess US: /ˈhoʊ.stɪs/ UK: /ˈhəʊ.stes/ [noun] A woman who invites and receives visitors: *Mrs. Roberts is an amazing hostess: really welcoming and a fantastic cook!* ■ We can also say "host".

hostile US: /ˈhɑː.stəl/ UK: /ˈhɒs.taɪl/ [adjective] Unfriendly: *The President's comments had a hostile reception in Congress.*

hostility US: /hɑːˈstɪl.ə.t̬i/ UK: /hɒsˈtɪl.ɪ.ti/ [noun] Unfriendly behavior, feeling of strong dislike: *Although he didn't say anything, I could sense his hostility to the idea.* ■ The plural is "hostilities".

↑**hot** US: /hɑːt/ UK: /hɒt/ [adjective] **1** That has a high temperature: *Don't touch the kettle; it's hot.* ■ "Hot" often refers to a temperature that is too high to be pleasant. "Warm" usually refers to a temperature which is pleasant. See picture at **opposite**. **2** With a strong, burning taste: *That curry's too hot for me.* ■ The comparative form is "hotter" and the superlative form is "hottest".

hot air [noun] False promises: *Lucy's words are all just hot air.*

hot dog US: /'hɑːt.dɑːg, 'hɒt.dɒg/ [noun] A sausage in a bread roll: *I'd like my hot dog with mustard, please.*

hotel /hoʊ'tel/ [noun] A place where you pay to stay and to eat: *We're going to stay at a fantastic hotel near the beach.*

hour US: /aʊr/ UK: /aʊəʳ/ [countable noun] **1** Sixty minutes: *It took us two hours to get to Brussels by train.* **2** A particular time of day or night: *My journey to school takes me an hour.* **3 for hours** For a long time: *I've been waiting here for hours.* ■ The abbreviation "hr" is only used in written language. ■ Be careful. We say: "At what time?" and "What time is it?" (We don't say: "At what hour?" or "What hour is it?").

hourglass US: /'aʊr.glæs/ UK: /'aʊə.glɑːs/ [countable noun] A device with two connected glass containers and sand: *The sand in an hourglass takes exactly one hour to pass from one container to the other.*

house[1] /haʊs/ [noun] A building where people live: *My uncle lives in a house with three floors.* See picture on the following page.

house[2] /haʊz/ [verb] To give accommodation to somebody or something: *The government is housing the refugees in temporary accommodations.*

housewife /'haʊs.waɪf/ [noun] A woman who works for her family in the house: *My mother prefers working to being a housewife.* ■ The plural is "housewives".

housework /'haʊsˌwɜrk/ [uncountable noun] The cooking, cleaning and other work that you do at home: *Housework is very tiring.* ■ Be careful! We don't say "a housework". We say "some housework" or "a piece of housework".

housing /'haʊ.zɪŋ/ [uncountable noun] **1** Apartments and houses for people to live in: *The Government should build more housing for young people.* **2 housing development** Land with a group of houses, built at the same time: *My aunt lives on a housing development in Lake Forest.*

hovercraft US: /'hɑː.vɚ.kræft/ UK: /'hɒv.ə.krɑːft/ [noun] A special boat that travels on a cushion of air: *The best way to see around the Florida Everglades is by taking one hovercrafts rides.*

how /haʊ/ [adverb] **1** In what way or by what way: *How did you find the street?* **2** A word used in questions about time: *How old is your brother?* **3** A word used in questions about amount: *How much money did you spend?* **4** A word used in questions about size: *How big is your room?* **5** A word that you use to ask about somebody's health: *How's your mother today?* **6** A word that you use to show surprise: *How cold the weather is today!* **7 how about** Words that you use when you make a suggestion: *How about going out for dinner this evening?* **8 how are you?** Words that you use to greet people you know: *"How are you?" "Fine, thanks".* **9 how do you do?** Words that you say when you meet somebody for the first time: *"I'm Paul Warner. How do you do?" "How do you do? I'm Jenny Cox".* ■ Be careful! When somebody asks you "How do you do?" you answer with "How do you do?". Often you shake hands when these words are exchanged.

however /haʊ'ev·ər/ [adverb] **1** Nevertheless, in spite of this: *Later in the evening, however, Jane told us the truth.* **2** It does not matter how: *However late it is, I'll go.*

howl /haʊl/ [verb] To make a long, loud and sad sound: *The dog is howling because it's been outside all night.*

HQ /ˌeɪtʃ'kjuː/ [noun] See **headquarters**. ■ Be careful. "HQ" is always written in capital letters.

hr A written abbreviation for **hour**. ■ The plural is "hrs".

hubbub [uncountable noun] A lot of loud noise: *Stop making such a hubbub!*

hug[1] /hʌg/ [verb] To put your arms around somebody and squeeze: *Rachel hugged her mother before she got on the train.* ■ Be careful with the spelling of these forms: "hugged", "hugging".

hug[2] /hʌg/ [countable noun] The acting of putting your arms around somebody: *She was so happy to hear the news that she started giving hugs to everybody.*

huge /hjuːdʒ/ [adjective] Very large: *My neighbors have a huge dog, it's almost as big as me.*

hula hoop [noun] A wide plastic ring that you move around with your hips: *In PE we use the hula hoop and I learn how to move my body to keep it going.*

hull[1] /hʌl/ [countable noun] **1** The main part of a ship, which sits in the water: *The hull is the first part of a ship to be constructed.* **2** The outer covering of peas, beans or other vegetables, or the green part at the base of some fruit: *The ring of leaves attached to a strawberry is called the hull.*

hull[2] /hʌl/ [verb] To remove the casing from fruit or vegetables: *We had to hull the peapods to get the peas.*

hum /hʌm/ [verb] **1** To make a low, continuous sound: *The traffic outside hums all day and then stops at about ten in the evening.* **2** To sing with

HOUSE

TYPES OF HOUSES:

single-family home

duplex

townhouses

apartment building

your lips closed: *Stop humming that song, please.* ■ Be careful with the spelling of these forms: "hummed", "humming".

human[1] /'hjuːmən/ [adjective] Referring to people, not to other animals: *Terrorists have no respect for human rights.*

humanity /hju'mæn·ɪ·t̬i/ [noun] All people: *Nuclear weapons are a danger to humanity.*

human[2] or **human being** /'hjuːmən/ [noun] A person: *Are there creatures like human beings somewhere out in space?*

humble /'hʌm.bl̩/ [adjective] **1** Not proud, not believing you are more important than others: *He's a naturally humble person, even though he's become a famous actor.* **2** Simple or poor: *She comes from humble origins.*

humerus /'hjuː.mə.rəs/ [countable noun] The bone in the upper arm: *The end of the humerus is popularly known as the "funny-bone".* ■ The plural is "humeri". See page 422.

humidity /hju'mɪd·ɪ·t̬i/ [uncountable noun] The amount of water that is in the air: *There's a lot of humidity in this part of the country.* ■ "Humidity" is only used to describe the state of the air. ■ The plural is "humidities".

humiliate /hjuː'mɪl.i.eɪt/ [verb] To make somebody feel ashamed and small: *He humiliated his sister by laughing at her in front of her friends.*

hummingbird /'hʌm·ɪŋ,bɜrd/ [countable noun] A small bird which eats plant nectar: *The hummingbird flaps its wings faster than any other bird and can fly backwards and upside down.*

humor /'hju·mər/ [noun] The ability to find things funny or do funny things: *Don't play tricks on Jim; he has no sense of humor.* ■ The British English spelling is "humour".

humorous /'hjuː.mə.rəs/ [adjective] Funny: *It's quite a humorous book.*

humour /'hjuː.mər/ US: /-mɚ/ UK: /'hjuː.məʳ/ [noun] See **humor.** ■ This is British English spelling.

hump /hʌmp/ [countable noun] **1** A large lump: *Camels have humps on their backs.* **2** A bump in the ground: *Let's go on the highway; the old road has too many humps.*

humus /'hjuː.məs/ [countable noun] The part of the soil which is organic: *Humus is formed from decomposing plants.*

hundred /'hʌn.drəd/ [noun, adjective and pronoun] The number 100: *The movies was invented just over a hundred years ago.* ■ Be careful! We say: "two hundred dollars" (We don't say: "two hundreds dollars").

hundredth /'hʌn.drətθ/ [noun and adjective] Referring to a hundred: *Atomic watches can measure time to a hundredth of a second.* ■ "Hundredth" can also be written "100th".

hung /hʌŋ/ Past tense and past participle forms of **hang.**

hunger[1] /'hʌŋ·gər/ [uncountable noun] The need and desire for food: *Hunger is one reason why babies cry.* ■ Be careful! We say: "I am hungry" (We don't say: "I have hunger"). Compare with "famine" (a period when there is not enough food).

hunger[2]

▸ **PHRASAL VERBS** · **to hunger for (something)** To have a strong desire for something: *She really hungers for adventure.*

hungry /'hʌŋ.gri/ [adjective] Wanting or needing to eat: *I'm always hungry after a swim.* ■ Be careful! We always say: "I am hungry" (We don't say: "I have hungry"). Note also the pronunciation of this word.

hunt[1] /hʌnt/ [noun] Chasing and trying to kill animals for sport or food: *The hunt wasn't very successful, they didn't come back with any deer.*

hunt[2] /hʌnt/ [verb] To chase and try to kill animals for sport or food: *Lions hunt in groups.*

hunter /'hʌn·tər/ [noun] A person or an animal that hunts: *Cats are very good hunters.*

hurrah or **hurray** /hə'rɑː/ [interjection] See **hooray.**

hurricane /'hɜr·ə,keɪn/, /'hʌr·ə-/ [noun] A storm with a very strong wind: *There are hurricanes in the Caribbean every year.*

hurry /'hɜr·i/, /'hʌ·ri/ [verb] **1** To move or do something quickly: *If you don't hurry I'll go without you.* **2 in a hurry** Quickly, tried to finish quickly: *You always do your homework in a hurry.*

▸ **PHRASAL VERBS** · **to hurry up** To move or do something more quickly: *Don't hurry me up, there's plenty of time.* ■ Be careful with the spelling of these forms: "hurries", "hurried".

hurt, hurt, hurt /hɜːt/ [verb] **1** To cause pain to: *I hurt my arm when I fell.* **2** To feel pain: *My finger still hurts.* **3** To make somebody sad to cause somebody emotional pain: *Her words hurt him.*

husband /'hʌz.bənd/ [noun] The man to whom a woman is married: *Margaret's husband is a banker.* ■ The woman to whom a man is married is his "wife".

hut /hʌt/ [noun] A small building usually made of wood: *Does anybody live in that hut in the wood?*

hydrate [verb] To combine with water: *The drinking of water is vital to hydrate the organism.*

hydraulic [adjective] Referring to or operated by the pressure of a liquid: *The Romans were experts at building hydraulic systems.* See page 439.

hydroelectric /,haɪdrəʊɪ'lektrɪk/ [adjective] Using the power of water that is flowing fast to produce electricity: *The hydroelectric power station was built thirty years ago.*

hydrogen /'haɪ.drɪ.dʒən/ [uncountable noun] **1** A colorless, tasteless and odorless gas: *Hydrogen is the lightest element and occurs in water.* **2** **(hydrogen) peroxide** A solution used to kill bacteria or to dye hair blonde: *Hydrogen peroxide is used for healing open wounds.* ■ In this use, the same meaning: "peroxide".

hydrosphere /'haɪ·drəˌsfɪər/ [countable noun] The liquid part of the Earth: *Rivers, lakes, seas and oceans make up the hydrosphere.*

hyena /haɪ'iː.nə/ [noun] A fierce animal like a large dog: *Hyenas eat the flesh of dead animals.*

hygiene /'haɪ.dʒiːn/ [noun] Keeping yourself and your things clean: *Hygiene is important if you want to stay healthy.* ■ Be careful with the spelling of this word!

hygienic /haɪ'dʒiːnɪk/ [adjective] Clean and not likely to cause disease: *The conditions in this restaurant are not hygienic.*

hymn /hɪm/ [noun] A religious song: *Let's sing a hymn in praise of God.*

hypha [countable noun] A long, branching filament which, together with many others, forms the basic structure of a fungus and some bacteria: *Hyphae can be found in the filaments of fungi.* ■ The plural is "hyphae".

hyphen /'haɪ.fᵊn/ [noun] A short line that joins two words or parts of words: *"Well-known" has a hyphen in it.*

hypodermic /ˌhaɪ·pə'dɜr·mɪk/ [adjective] **1** Referring to a medical instrument, used for putting a drug into the body beneath the skin: *The nurse has used a hypodermic needle in order to administer the drug.* **2** Relating to the area immediately under the skin: *The patient was given a hypodermic injection.*

hypodermis [countable noun] The inner, thickest layer of the skin: *Injections are given into the hypodermis.*

hypothesis /haɪ'pɑθ·ə·sɪs/ [countable noun] A theory or suggestion based on known facts but not proven: *You must design an experiment to test your hypothesis.* ■ The plural is "hypotheses".

hypothetical /ˌhaɪ·pə'θet̬·ɪ·kəl/, /ˌhaɪ.pə'θet.ɪ.kəl/ [adjective] Based on possible ideas or situations which are not necessarily true: *"Let's think of a hypothetical example", said the teacher.*

hysterical /hɪ'ster.ɪ.kᵊl/ [adjective] In a state of uncontrollable nerves, excitement or anger: *He showed his nerves in hysterical laughter.*

ꜛi /aɪ/ The ninth letter of the alphabet: *The name "Ian" begins with an "I".*

ꜛI /aɪ/ [pronoun] When you speak, the word you use to refer to yourself: *I like painting landscapes.* ■ Be careful! "I" is always written with a capital letter.

ꜛice /aɪs/ [uncountable noun] Frozen water: *Driving is difficult when there's ice on the roads.* ■ Be careful! We don't say "an ice". We say "some ice", "a piece of ice" or "an ice cube". 👁 See picture on the following page.

iceberg /'aɪs·bɜrg/ [countable noun] A very large piece of ice in the sea: *Icebergs are a danger to ships.* ■ Be careful with the pronunciation of this word. 👁 See picture on the following page.

ꜛice cream [noun] A sweet, frozen food made from milk and eggs: *Would you like a strawberry ice cream?* 👁 See picture at **ice**.

ice cube [countable noun] A small piece of ice, used mainly to make a drink cold: *Can I have an ice cube in my lemonade, please?* 👁 See picture on the following page.

ice lolly [countable noun] See **popsicle®**. ■ This word is British English. ■ We also say "lolly".

ice skate[1] [countable noun] A boot with a horizontal piece of metal under it: *I got a new pair of ice skates for my birthday.* ■ We also say "skate".

ice skate[2] [verb] To move on ice wearing special boots: *Last winter we ice skated on the river.* ■ We also say "skate". 👁 See picture at **ice**.

icing sugar [uncountable noun] Very fine sugar for covering cakes: *How much icing sugar do you need for the cake?*

icy /'aɪ.si/ [adjective] **1** Very cold: *There's an icy wind today.* **2** Covered with ice: *Drive slowly if the road's icy.* ■ The comparative form is "icier" and the superlative form is "iciest".

I'd /aɪd/ The contraction of "I had" or "I would".

ID /ˌaɪ'diː/ See **identification.** ■ Be careful. "ID" is always written in capital letters.

ꜛidea /aɪ'dɪə/ [countable noun] A plan, concept or a thought in the mind: *My idea is to save money.* ■ Be careful with the pronunciation of this word! The "i" is pronounced like the person "I".

ꜛideal /aɪ'dɪəl/ [adjective] The best, perfect: *This hotel is the ideal place for a vacation.* ■ Be careful with the pronunciation of this word.

identical /aɪ'den·tɪ·kəl/ [adjective] Exactly the same: *Those two sisters have identical voices.*

identification /aɪˌdent·ə·fɪ'keɪ·ʃən/ [uncountable noun] Something that shows your identity: *The police are checking people's identification.* ■ "ID" is an abbreviation for "identification".

ꜛidentify /aɪ'dent·əˌfaɪ/ [verb] To recognize and to say who somebody is or what something is: *She identified him as the man who had stolen her purse.* ■

Be careful with the spelling of these forms: "identifies", "identified".

identikit [countable noun] An invented drawing of a person's face: *They made the identikit of the thief from the girl's description.*

†**identity** /aɪ'den·tɪ·t̬i/ [noun] Who somebody is or what something is: *No one knows the identity of the bank robber.* ■ The plural is "identities".

idiom /'ɪd.i.əm/ [countable noun] A group of words with a particular meaning: *"To hit the roof" is an idiom that means "to be very angry".*

idiot /'ɪd.i.ət/ [countable noun] A silly or stupid person: *Don't be an idiot! He'll never believe that story!*

idle /'aɪdl/ [adjective] **1** Lazy: *He's too idle to do his homework.* **2** Not doing any work: *Because of problems with supplies, the machines have been idle for a week.* ■ Be careful with the pronunciation of this word.

idol /'aɪ.dᵊl/ [countable noun] **1** A famous person who somebody admires and loves: *This actor is my sister's idol.* **2** Something that people worship as a god: *The tribe the author studied had many different idols.*

i.e. /ˌaɪ'iː/ That is to say: *This hostel is for males, i.e. boys and men, only.* ■ "i.e." is an abbreviation for "id est", a Latin expression that means "that is". ■ See box at **abbreviations**.

†**if** /ɪf/ [conjunction] **1** On condition that: *If she calls, tell her I'm out.* **2** Used to show a choice between possible actions: *Ask her if she'll come to dinner.*

if only [interjection] A phrase used when you strongly want something that will never happen or will probably not happen: *If only I had more money!* ■ The same meaning: "I wish...!".

igloo /'ɪg.luː/ [countable noun] A house made of ice: *Inuits used to live in igloos, but nowadays many of them live in houses.*

igneous /'ɪg.ni.əs/ [adjective] Formed as the result of volcanic activity: *Igneous rock can be found all around the island.*

ignorance /'ɪg·nər·əns/ [uncountable noun] Not knowing: *His complete ignorance of geography is surprising.*

ignorant /'ɪg·nər·ənt/ [adjective] Not knowing much: *Many people are ignorant of their rights.*

†**ignore** /ɪg'nɔr/, /-'noʊr/ [verb] To take no notice of somebody: *Linda always ignores me when she passes by.*

iguana /ɪ'gwɑː.nə/ [countable noun] A lizard native to tropical America: *The iguana has a spiny crest along its back.*

†**ill** /ɪl/ [adjective] **1** Physically or mentally not well: *Louise is ill; she's got flu.* ■ Be careful. We don't use "ill" before a noun. We always say: "a sick person". (We don't say: "an ill person".). **2** Bad: *His sudden promotion caused a lot of ill feeling in the office.* ■ In this use we usually say "bad".

I'll /aɪl/ The contraction of "I will" or "I shall".

†**illegal** /ɪ'liː.gᵊl/ [adjective] Against the law: *It's illegal to park in this area.*

illegally [adverb] In a manner that is against the law: *The immigrant crossed the border illegally.* ■ Compare with "legally" (in a manner that is within the law).

illegible /ɪ'ledʒ.ə.bl̩/ [adjective] That cannot be read: *When you take a test, you have to be careful that your writing is not illegible.*

illiteracy /ɪ'lɪt̬·ə·rə·si/ [uncountable noun] Lack of ability to read and write: *Governments should face the high levels of illiteracy in Africa.* ■ Compare with "literacy" (the ability to read and write).

illiterate /ɪ'lɪt̬·ər·ət/ [adjective] Not able to read or to write: *The number of people who are illiterate is decreasing.*

†**illness** /'ɪl.nəs/ [uncountable noun] Being ill: *She had the illness for over a month.* ■ The plural is "illnesses". ■ Compare with "disease" ("Illness" is normally used when we talk about the general state of being ill and the time during which you are ill. "Disease" is used when we talk about a specific illness).

illogical /ɪ'lɑdʒ·ɪ·kəl/ [adjective] Not logical: *It's illogical to smoke if you are a keen athlete.*

ill-treat /ˌɪl'triːt/ [verb] To do cruel things to people or to animals: *Although people's attitudes are changing, animals are still frequently ill-treated.*

illuminate /ɪ'luː.mɪ.neɪt/ [verb] To give light to something: *The yard was illuminated by the moonlight.*

ICE

iceberg

ice cream

ice cube

ice skate

a b c d e f g h i j k l m n o p q r s t u v w x y z

illusion /ɪ'luː.ʒᵊn/ [noun] Something that is not really as you see it, a false belief: *He thinks he's the best player in the team but it's an illusion. He's one of the worst.*

⁺**illustrate** /'ɪl.ə.streɪt/ [verb] To add pictures to something: *The book is illustrated with drawings of ships.*

illustration /ˌɪl.ə'streɪ.ʃᵊn/ [noun] A picture: *This dictionary has a lot of color illustrations.*

I'm /aɪm/ The contraction of "I am".

⁺**image** /'ɪm.ɪdʒ/ [countable noun] **1** An idea or mental picture that a person has of somebody or something: *I have an image of your uncle as kind and cheerful.* **2** A copy: *That child is the image of her mother.* **3** A picture or description in a book, movie, painting and so on: *The final image of the movie is very beautiful.* ■ Be careful with the pronunciation of this word. The "a" is pronounced like the "i" in "did".

⁺**imaginary** /ɪ'mædʒ·əˌner·i/ [adjective] Not real, existing only in the mind: *The stories about Captain Nemo are imaginary legends.*

⁺**imagination** /ɪˌmædʒ.ɪ'neɪ.ʃᵊn/ [noun] The ability to make pictures or ideas in your mind: *Children have a lot of imagination.*

imaginative /ɪ'mædʒ·ə·nə·t̬ɪv/ [adjective] Able to have new, different, or attractive ideas: *Paul is very imaginative.*

⁺**imagine** /ɪ'mædʒ.ɪn/ [verb] **1** To make a picture or idea of somebody or something in your mind: *Can you imagine the teacher without his beard?* **2** To believe something: *I imagine my cousin Helen will bring her car.*

imitate /'ɪm.ɪ.teɪt/ [verb] To copy somebody or something: *Karen's always imitating her older sister.*

imitation /ˌɪm.ɪ'teɪ.ʃᵊn/ [countable noun] A copy: *Bob gave a good imitation of a dog's bark.*

immature /ˌɪm·ə'tʃʊər/, /-'tʊər/ [adjective] Not behaving in a grown-up way: *Mary is seventeen years old but she's very immature.*

⁺**immediate** /ɪ'miː.di.ət/ [adjective] Done at once: *I need an immediate solution to my problem.*

immense /ɪ'ments/ [adjective] Very big: *The house is surrounded by immense yards.*

immigrant /'ɪm.ɪ.grənt/ [countable noun] A person who has come to live in a foreign country: *Life is very difficult for many immigrants in United States.*

immigration /ˌɪm.ɪ'greɪ.ʃᵊn/ [uncountable noun] Coming to live in a foreign country: *The new immigration law will be considered by the United States Supreme Court.*

immobilize or **immobilise** /ɪ'moʊ·bəˌlaɪz/ [verb] To prevent something from moving or operating normally: *To immobilize the car all you need to do is turn the key.*

⁺**immoral** /ɪ'mɔr·əl/, /ɪ'mɑr-/ [adjective] Morally wrong: *Torture is immoral.*

immovable /ɪ'muː.və.bl̩/ [adjective] That can't be moved or changed: *That old tree weighted a lot and was absolutely immovable.* ■ Compare with "movable" (able to be moved).

⁺**impact** /'ɪm.pækt/ [countable noun] A hard blow: *The impact of the accident caused my mom's neck injury.*

⁺**impatient** /ɪm'peɪ.ʃᵊnt/ [adjective] Not able to or not wanting to wait: *Don't be so impatient! Wait a minute.*

imperative /ɪm'per·ə·t̬ɪv/ [noun] The form of a verb that tells somebody to do something: *"Be quiet!" is an imperative.*

implant¹ /'ɪm·plænt/ [countable noun] Something which is inserted into a part of the body: *The dog has a microchip implant.* ■ Compare with "transplant¹" (the act of removing an organ from one person and putting it into another person).

implant² /ɪm'plænt/ [verb] **1** To insert into the body: *The dentist implanted the new tooth.* ■ Compare with "transplant²" (to remove an organ or tissue from one person and putting it into another person). **2** To introduce or fix ideas into a person's mind: *Political beliefs should not be implanted in young children.*

implement¹ /'ɪmplɪmənt/ [countable noun] A tool or utensil: *Chimpanzees use sticks and stones as implements.*

implement² /'ɪm.plɪ.mənt/ [verb] To put a decision into practice: *We need to implement the plan.*

impolite /ˌɪm.pᵊl'aɪt/ [adjective] Rude: *It's very impolite to talk with your mouth full.*

⁺**import¹** /ɪm'pɔːt/ [uncountable noun] Something that you bring from abroad to sell in your country: *The teacher said that car imports have increased this year.*

import² /ɪm'pɔːt/ [verb] To bring things from abroad to sell in your country: *Canada imports a lot of wine.*

⁺**importance** /ɪm'pɔr·tə·ns/ [uncountable noun] Big value, significance or power: *Clean air is of great importance to our lives.*

⁺**important** /ɪm'pɔr·tə·nt/ [adjective] **1** With a big value: *Do you think it's important to dress well?* **2** Powerful: *Linda's mother is an important attorney.*

⁺**impose** /ɪm'poʊz/ [verb] To force somebody to accept something they do not want: *A new tax will be imposed on cigarettes.* ■ Be careful. We say: "to impose (something) **on** (somebody)".

impossibility /ɪmˌpɑs·ə'bɪl·ɪ·t̬i/ [noun] Being impossible: *Given the impossibility of getting tickets, I'm going to watch the concert on TV.* ■ The plural is "impossibilities".

a b c d e f g h i j k l m n o p q r s t u v w x y z

⁺**impossible** /ɪm'pɑs·ə·bəl/ [adjective] Not possible, that cannot be done: *It's impossible for me to finish this book by tomorrow, there isn't time.*

⁺**impress** /ɪm'pres/ [verb] To fill somebody with admiration: *She really impressed me with her singing.* ■ Be careful with the spelling of the 3rd person singular present tense form: "impresses".

⁺**impression** /ɪm'preʃ.ᵊn/ [countable noun] A feeling or idea that you have about somebody or something: *His words made a great impression on the audience.*

⁺**impressive** /ɪm'pres.ɪv/ [adjective] Causing admiration: *The volcanoes in Ecuador are very impressive.*

imprison /ɪm'prɪz.ᵊn/ [verb] To send somebody to prison: *He was imprisoned for theft.*

imprisonment /ɪm'prɪz.ᵊn.mənt/ [noun] Being in prison: *He was sentenced to six years' imprisonment.*

improbable /ɪm'prɑb·ə·bəl/ [adjective] Not probable, not likely: *The idea that Maggie stole the money is improbable.* ■ Compare with "probable" (likely to happen or exist).

⁺**improve** /ɪm'pruːv/ [verb] To make something better: *How can I improve my tennis?*

⁺**improvement** /ɪm'pruːv.mənt/ [noun] A change for the better: *They've changed the cafeteria at school. It's a big improvement.*

impulse /'ɪm.pʌls/ [countable noun] **1** A short electrical signal in a nerve or wire, that causes a reaction: *An electric impulse makes the doors open at the airport.* **2** A sudden wish or decision to do something: *When I'm shopping I always have an impulse to buy myself something.*

impulsive /ɪm'pʌl.sɪv/ [adjective] Doing something without stopping to think: *His impulsive actions get him into trouble.*

⁺**in**[1] /ɪn/ [preposition] **1** A word that shows position inside a place: *She lives in an apartment.* **2** A word that shows position at a place: *They work in San Francisco.* **3** A word that says when something happens: *At school we play soccer in summer and basketball in winter.* **4** A word that says how somebody or something is: *She is in a terrible state.* **5** A word that shows the way you do something: *They were speaking in Spanish.* **6** A word that shows somebody's activity or somebody's job: *My brother is in the navy.* **7** A word that shows what clothes somebody wears: *Dave, you can't come to work in shorts.* **8** A word that shows the end of a period of time: *They'll be back in an hour.* ■ See box at **time: prepositions.** See picture at **preposition.**

in[2] /ɪn/ [adverb] **1** To the inside of a place or a thing: *You can't go in now; they're busy.* **2** When used with the verb "to be", at home or at work: *My mother is not in at the moment.*

in[3] A written abbreviation for **inch.** ■ See box at **abbreviations.**

in- /ɪn-/ [prefix] An addition to the beginning of a word that usually gives a word the opposite meaning: *"Inaccurate" means "not accurate".*

⁺**inability** /ˌɪn·ə'bɪl·ɪ·t̬i/ [uncountable noun] Being unable to do something: *I'm surprised by your complete inability to cook.* ■ The plural is "inabilities".

inaccurate /ɪn'æk·jər·ət/ [adjective] Not correct, not exact: *The details you gave me are inaccurate.*

inactive /ɪn'æktɪv/ [adjective] Not active: *After years of political involvement, now he is inactive.*

inadequate /ɪ'næd.ɪ.kwət/ [adjective] Not enough; not good enough: *The amount of studying you do is quite inadequate.*

inappropriate /ˌɪn·ə'proʊ·pri·ət/ [adjective] Not suitable: *What you did was not wrong, but you chose an inappropriate moment to do it.*

Inc. /es/ A written abbreviation for incorporated company, that is written after a name to show that it is a business: *He received an offer from Biker and Baxter Inc. to work in their marketing department.* ■ See box at **abbreviations.**

incapable /ɪn'keɪ.pə.bl̩/ [adjective] Unable to do something: *Jim is incapable of hurting anybody.*

incentive /ɪn'sen·tɪv/ [noun] Something that makes somebody more active: *I don't need any incentive to study because luckily I like studying.*

⁺**inch** /ɪntʃ/ [countable noun] A small unit of length equal to 2.5 centimeters: *There are 12 inches in a foot.* ■ The abbreviations "in" and "ins" are only used in written language. See box at **abbreviations.**

⁺**incident** /'ɪnt.sɪ.dᵊnt/ [countable noun] Something that happens that is of concern or interest: *There was an incident outside the disco last night.*

incidentally /ˌɪn·sə'den·tə·l·i/, /-'dent·li/ [adverb] By the way: *Incidentally, where were you when I phoned this morning?*

inclination /ˌɪn.klɪ'neɪ.ʃᵊn/ [noun] **1** A feeling that makes somebody want to do something: *My inclination is to say yes, but...* **2** The degree of slope: *Be careful with the inclination you will find behind this wall.*

inclined /ɪn'klaɪnd/ [adjective] **1** Ready and wanting to do something: *I'm not inclined to go to Sally's party. She's not really a friend of mine.* **2 to be inclined** To be likely to do something: *We mustn't tell mom about the bike accident. You know that she is inclined to get nervous.* ■ We say: "to be inclined **to** (do something)".

⁺**include** /ɪn'kluːd/ [verb] **1** To contain something as a part of a whole: *The price of the trip includes airplane tickets, hotel stay and breakfast daily.* **2** To make somebody or something part of a whole:

They can't include Matthew. He's not tall enough for a basketball team.

†**including** /ɪn'klu:.dɪŋ/ [preposition] A word that shows that something or somebody is part of a group: *Everybody was at home, including Julie.*

†**income** /'ɪn.kʌm/ [noun] The money that you get from work: *They live on a monthly income of two thousand dollars.*

incomplete /ˌɪn.kəm'pli:t/ [adjective] Not complete, not finished: *This letter to your friend is incomplete. Why don't you finish it?*

incomprehensible /ɪnˌkɑm·prɪ'hen·sə·bəl/ [adjective] Impossible to understand: *His German accent is practically incomprehensible.*

inconvenience /ˌɪn.kən'vi:.ni.ᵊnts/ [noun] Trouble; difficulty: *Would it cause any inconvenience if we have the meeting at our house?*

inconvenient /ˌɪn.kən'vi:.ni.ᵊnt/ [adjective] Not appropriate for somebody: *Four o'clock is an inconvenient time for me because I have to go to the doctor's.*

incorrect /ˌɪn·kə'rekt/ [adjective] Wrong: *Those answers are incorrect.*

†**increase**[1] /ɪn'kri:s/ [noun] A rise in number or amount: *There is an increase in world population every year.*

increase[2] /ɪn'kri:s/ [verb] To become bigger or to make something bigger: *Car prices have increased a lot.*

†**incredible** /ɪn'kred.ɪ.bl̩/ [adjective] **1** Amazing: *Cars go along this road at an incredible speed.* **2** Hard to believe: *Her story sounded a little incredible to me.*

†**indeed** /ɪn'di:d/ [adverb] **1** A word used to agree that something is certainly or really the case: *They told me that "Citizen Kane" was a very good movie, and indeed, it is.* **2** A word that is used with an adjective or an adverb to make it stronger: *This room is very cold indeed.*

indefinite /ɪn'def.ɪ.nət/ [adjective] Not certain, not clear: *I'm afraid your teacher is ill and will be off school for an indefinite period.*

indefinite article [countable noun] The word "a" and the word "an": *You say "a mouse" but "an elephant".*

†**independence** /ˌɪn.dɪ'pen.dᵊnts/ [uncountable noun] **1** Not needing anybody else: *Young people need independence from their parents.* **2** Freedom from the control of another country: *The 4th of July is the day United States celebrates its independence.*

†**independent** /ˌɪn.dɪ'pen.dᵊnt/ [adjective] **1** Not under the control of anybody else: *My older brother wants to live in his own house and be independent.* **2** Free from the rule of another country: *The Americans wanted to be independent of England.*

†**index** /'ɪn.deks/ [countable noun] An alphabetical list of words in a book: *Where's the index in this atlas?* ■ The plural is "indexes" or "indices".

index finger [countable noun] The finger that is next to your thumb: *The teacher pointed to the place on the map with his index finger.*

Indian /'ɪn.di.ən/ [noun and adjective] **1** See **Native American.** **2** Referring to India: *I have an Indian penpal who lives in Delhi.* ■ Be careful! "Indian" has a capital "I".

†**indicate** /'ɪn.dɪ.keɪt/ [verb] To show or to point out: *These lines indicate no parking.*

indicator US: /'ɪn.dɪ.keɪ.tɚ/ UK: /'ɪn.dɪ.keɪ.təʳ/ [countable noun] Something that indicates or gives information: *The indicator showed that we were almost out of gas.*

indignant /ɪn'dɪg.nənt/ [adjective] Feeling offended and angry: *Wendy was indignant at Simon's refusal to let her listen to his tapes.*

†**individual**[1] /ˌɪndɪ'vɪdʒuəl/ [adjective] Single; different: *The children all have individual rooms.*

individual[2] /ˌɪndɪ'vɪdʒuəl/ [countable noun] A single person: *I think your neighbor is a rather strange individual.*

individually /ˌɪn.dɪ'vɪd.ju.ə.li/ [adverb] **1** Separately: *Please get the cheeses individually wrapped.* **2** For or by an individual: *He decided to make a contribution individually.*

†**indoor** /'ɪnˌdɔr/, /-ˌdour/ [adjective] Happening inside a building: *I've bought some indoor plants for the living room.*

†**indoors** /ˌɪn'dɔrz/, /-'dourz/ [adverb] Inside a building: *Let's stay indoors and watch TV.*

†**industrial** /ɪn'dʌs.tri.əl/ [adjective] With a large number of factories: *Detroit is an industrial city.* ■ Be careful with the pronunciation of this word. The vowel sound here is pronounced the same as in "sun".

†**industry** /'ɪn.də.stri/ [uncountable noun] All manufacturing processes: *The car industry in America is very important.* ■ The plural is "industries".

inexpensive /ˌɪn.ɪk'spent.sɪv/ [adjective] Not expensive, cheap: *I want to buy a bike, but an inexpensive one.*

inexperienced /ˌɪn·ɪk'spɪər·i·ənst/ [adjective] Not having experience at something: *My brother is still an inexperienced driver.* ■ Be careful with the pronunciation of the end of this word. The last "e" is not pronounced.

infancy /'ɪn.fənt.si/ [uncountable noun] **1** The early years of a child: *In her infancy she wouldn't sleep without her teddy bear.* **2** in {something/somebody's} infancy The early stage of the development or growth of something: *That branch of science is still in its infancy.*

infant /'ɪn.fənt/ [countable noun] A very young child: *Infants should not have cow's milk until they're one year old.*

infantile /'ɪn·fən,taɪl/ [adjective] **1** Occurring among babies or young children: *German measles and chickenpox are infantile diseases.* ■ This use is formal. **2** Typical of a small child, not of the relevant person's real age: *His behavior could only be described as infantile.*

↑**infect** /ɪn'fekt/ [verb] To make somebody or something ill: *My uncle was infected with malaria when he went to Africa.*

↑**infection** /ɪn'fek.ʃᵊn/ [noun] An illness caused by germs: *My sister's got a serious ear infection.*

↑**infectious** /ɪn'fek.ʃəs/ [adjective] **1** That passes from one person to another: *Flu is infectious.* **2** That influences other people: *Naomi has a very infectious laugh.*

inferior /ɪn'fɪər·i·ər/ [adjective] Not as good as: *Mark's racket is inferior to mine.*

infertile US: /ɪn'fɜːrtəl/ UK: /ɪn'fɜːtaɪl/ [adjective] Incapable of fertilization, unproductive: *This land is infertile since the chemical spill.*

infinite /'ɪn.fɪ.nət/ [adjective] Without end: *You need infinite patience to look after babies.*

infinitive /ɪn'fɪn·ə·t̬ɪv/ [countable noun] The basic form of a verb, often used with "to": *"To swim" "to go" and "to eat" are examples of infinitives.*

inflate /ɪn'fleɪt/ [verb] To fill something with air or with gas: *Can you help me inflate this tire, please?*

↑**inflation** /ɪn'fleɪ.ʃᵊn/ [uncountable noun] State of the economy where prices rise continually: *Inflation is now over five per cent.*

inflexible /ɪn'flek.sɪ.bl̩/ [adjective] **1** Unwilling to change or adapt: *She used to be obstinate and inflexible about her decisions.* **2** Difficult or impossible to be bent: *These shoes will hurt your feet. They are made of inflexible material.* ■ Compare with "flexible" (willing and able to change).

↑**influence**[1] /'ɪnfluəns/ [noun] The power to make somebody or something change: *My father says that television has too much influence on people.*

influence[2] /'ɪnfluəns/ [verb] To make somebody or something change: *Don't be influenced by what your sister says. Decide for yourself!*

influential /,ɪn.flu'en.tʃᵊl/ [adjective] Having the power to make others change: *Virginia Woolf is one of the most influential writers of the twentieth.*

influenza /,ɪn.flu'en.zə/ [uncountable noun] See **flu**.

↑**inform** /ɪn'fɔrm/ [verb] To give information to somebody: *They informed me that the movie was not suitable for children.*

↑**informal** /ɪn'fɔr·məl/ [adjective] Friendly, with no fixed rules: *The minister had an informal meeting with the press.* ■ Be careful with the pronunciation of this word.

↑**information** /,ɪn·fər'meɪ·ʃən/ [uncountable noun] Details about something: *In the college they gave me information about their summer courses.* ■ Be careful! We don't say "an information". We say "some information" or "a piece of information".

informative /ɪn'fɔr·mə·t̬ɪv/ [adjective] Giving you information: *Some TV programs are very informative.*

infrastructure /'ɪnfrə,strʌktʃər/ [countable noun] The supporting structures and facilities needed by a country or other entity to function efficiently: *Before the new houses could be occupied, the road infrastructure needed to be built.*

↑**ingredient** /ɪn'griː.di.ənt/ [countable noun] One of the things in a mixture: *What ingredients did you use to make this cake?*

inhabit /ɪn'hæb.ɪt/ [verb] To live in a place: *I wish I had been alive when dinosaurs inhabited the earth.*

inhabitant /ɪn'hæb.ɪ.tᵊnt/ [countable noun] A person who lives in a place: *Some people think that there are inhabitants on Mars.*

inhalation /,ɪn.hə'leɪ.ʃən/ [noun] The act of breathing in: *Inhalation of this gas is dangerous.* ■ Compare with "exhalation" (the act of breathing out).

inhale /ɪn'heɪl/ [verb] To breath in: *You need to inhale the medicine if you want to cure your bronchitis.* ■ Compare with "exhale" (to expel air).

inherit /ɪn'her.ɪt/ [verb] To be left something by somebody after they have died: *Jeremy inherited his grandfather's gold watch.*

inheritance /ɪn'her.ɪ.tᵊnts/ [noun] The things or property that a person leaves you when they die: *The movie was about a family arguing about their grandfather's inheritance.*

initial[1] /ɪ'nɪʃəl/ [adjective] First: *Our initial idea was to go to Paris, but in the end we went to Mexico.*

initial[2] /ɪ'nɪʃəl/ [countable noun] The first letter of the name of a person or an organization, used as an abbreviation: *"UN" are the initials of the "United Nations".*

inject /ɪn'dʒekt/ [verb] To put a liquid into somebody using a special needle: *A nurse injected me with an antibiotic.*

injection /ɪn'dʒek.ʃᵊn/ [noun] An amount of liquid that is put into somebody with a special needle: *They gave her an injection against the flu.*

↑**injure** /'ɪn·dʒər/ [verb] To hurt a person or an animal: *Be careful! You're going to injure the baby with that pin.*

↑**injury** /'ɪn·dʒə·ri/ [noun] Harm or hurt done to a person: *Most people escaped from the fire without injuries.* ■ The plural is "injuries".

injustice /ɪn'dʒʌs.tɪs/ [noun] Not being right or just: *If we lose this game, it'll be an injustice.*

†**ink** /ɪŋk/ [noun] A liquid used for writing: *I have to buy some ink for my fountain pen.*

inland[1] /ˈɪnlənd/ [adjective] In the center of a country, not on the coast: *Inland areas will have less rain in the next few days.*

inland[2] /ˈɪnlænd/ [adverb] To the center of a country: *When we went to Sweden we traveled inland from the coast in a rented car.*

inn /ɪn/ [noun] A pub or small hotel in the country: *We spent our vacation at an inn near a lake.*

†**inner** /ˈɪn·ər/ [adjective] Inside: *An inner door led to the store basement.*

innocence /ˈɪn.ə.sənts/ [uncountable noun] The state of being right, of being free from guilt: *The jury believed in the innocence of the accused.*

†**innocent** /ˈɪn.ə.sənt/ [adjective] Not having done wrong: *The young man was innocent of the murder.*

inorganic /ˌɪnɔːˈgænɪk/ [adjective] **1** Not being a living organism or of a living organism: *Rocks and minerals are inorganic substances.* **2** In chemistry, being a substance with no or very little carbon: *an inorganic compound.*

inquire /ɪnˈkwaɪər/ [verb] To ask for information: *The police inquired about the motives which led to the school shooting.* ■ In British English they say "enquire".

inquiry US: /ˈɪŋ.kwɚ.i/ UK: /ɪnˈkwaɪə.ri/ [noun] A question about something: *He is making inquiries about his missing uncle.* ■ The plural is "inquiries".

inquisitive /ɪnˈkwɪz·ə·t̬ɪv/ [adjective] With a lot of curiosity, asking many questions about other people: *My parents are always rather inquisitive about my friends.*

ins A written abbreviation for **inches.** ■ See box at **abbreviations.**

insane /ɪnˈseɪn/ [adjective] Mad, crazy: *You must be insane to take Daniel to the party.* ■ The same meaning: "mad".

†**insect** /ˈɪn.sekt/ [countable noun] A very small animal with no bones: *Butterflies are insects.* 👁 **See pages 426 and 431.**

insecure /ˌɪn·sɪˈkjʊər/ [noun] Not safe: *This bookshelf looks very insecure. Who made it?*

insecurity /ˌɪn·sɪˈkjʊər··t̬i/ [noun] The feeling of not being safe: *She's depressed by the insecurity of her job.*

insensitive /ɪnˈsen·sə·t̬ɪv/ [adjective] Not sensitive: *He's such an insensitive man. He has no tact at all.*

†**insert** /ɪnˈsɜrt/ [verb] To put something inside something else: *Insert a coin in the machine if you want to make a call.*

†**inside[1]** /ˌɪnˈsaɪd/ [countable noun] **1** The inner part of something: *These gloves have fur on the inside.* **2 inside out** With what should be on the inside on the outside: *You're putting your sweater on inside out.*

inside[2] /ˌɪnˈsaɪd/ [adjective] In the inner part: *The inside door is always open.*

inside[3] /ˌɪnˈsaɪd/ [adverb] To the inner part: *Let's go inside because it's cold out here.*

†**insist** /ɪnˈsɪst/ [verb] To say something firmly: *She insisted on helping me to paint my bike.* ■ We say "insist **on** (something)".

inspect /ɪnˈspekt/ [verb] To examine something: *The principal inspected the damage to the school gym.*

inspection /ɪnˈspek.ʃən/ [noun] Examining something: *The engineers did an inspection of the bridge.*

inspector /ɪnˈspek.tər/ [countable noun] **1** A person who examines something: *The bus inspector asked for our tickets.* **2** A police officer: *Inspector Grant's investigating the crime.*

inspiration /ˌɪn.spɪˈreɪ.ʃən/ [noun] Somebody or something that gives you ideas: *Poets find their inspiration in different things.*

inspire /ɪnˈspaɪər/ [verb] To give somebody ideas to do things: *His novels were inspired by the sea.*

instability /ˌɪn·stəˈbɪl·ɪ·t̬i/ [uncountable noun] The lack of stability: *Due to the political instability in the country, many foreigners left.*

†**install** /ɪnˈstɔl/ [verb] To put something in, ready for use: *They've installed a drink machine in the school.*

†**instance** /ˈɪn.stənts/ **for instance** For example: *Do something! Put this milk in the fridge, for instance.*

†**instant[1]** /ˈɪnstənt/ [noun] A moment: *Harry hesitated for an instant and then threw the ball.*

instant[2] /ˈɪnstənt/ [adjective] **1** Happening very quickly: *This cream gives instant relief.* **2** Quick and easy to do: *Let's make a cup of instant coffee.*

†**instead** /ɪnˈsted/ [adverb] In place of somebody or something: *If you can't get Sandra on the phone, talk to her sister instead.*

instead of [preposition] In place of somebody or something: *I'm going to have coffee instead of orange juice for a change.* ■ The verb after "instead of" is in the "-ing" form: "Instead of watching TV, let's go and play tennis".

instinct /ˈɪn.stɪŋkt/ [noun] A feeling that makes you do things not using reason: *Dogs chase cats by instinct.*

†**institute** /ˈɪn·stɪˌtut/ [countable noun] A society for a special type of activity: *The United States Naval Institute was founded in 1873.* ■ Compare with "secondary school" (a school for students between 11 and 18 years old).

†**institution** /ˌɪn·stɪˈtu·ʃən/ [countable noun] A large official organization: *The Bank of America is a very old institution.*

a b c d e f g h i j k l m n o p q r s t u v w x y z

instruct /ɪn'strʌkt/ [verb] **1** To teach: *Are you going to instruct me how to use this camera?* **2** To order: *The policeman instructed him to park somewhere else.*

instructions /ɪn'strʌk.ʃᵊnz/ [plural noun] Words that tell you how to use something: *Read the instructions before you plug the electric razor in.*

instructor /ɪn'strʌk·tər/ [countable noun] A person who teaches you how to do something: *There's a new karate instructor at our local gym.*

↑instrument /'ɪn.strə.mənt/ [countable noun] **1** A tool: *A corkscrew is an instrument for opening bottles.* **2** A thing for making musical sounds: *There are a lot of instruments in an orchestra.* 👁 **See pages 458 and 459.**

insulate /'ɪn.sjʊ.leɪt/ [verb] To protect against heat loss, noise or electrical current: *The room had to be insulated against noise from the club in the basement.*

insulating [adjective] Giving protection against heat loss, noise or electrical current: *Electrical charges cannot pass easily through insulating materials such as plastic.*

insulator /'ɪn·sə,leɪ·t̬ər/ [countable noun] Material or device which insulates: *An insulator was used to separate the two wires.*

↑insult[1] /ɪn'sʌlt/ [countable noun] A rude thing that you say to somebody, a rude action: *His insults made me very angry at the party last night.* ■ Be careful with the pronunciation of this word! "su" is pronounced as in "sun".

insult[2] /ɪn'sʌlt/ [verb] To say or to do unpleasant things to somebody: *When I suggested he was lying, he became angry and insulted me.*

↑insurance /ɪn'ʃʊər·əns/, /'ɪn,ʃər-/ [uncountable noun] An agreement with a company for them to pay money to you in case of accident, robbery and so on: *My mom pays her car insurance through the bank every year.*

insure /ɪn'ʃʊər/ [verb] To pay money to a company so that it will give you money in case of accident, robbery and so on: *My mother has insured her jewels against theft.*

integrate /'ɪntɪgreɪt/ [verb] **1** To combine things in such a way that they finally become a unified whole: *Sert's architecture integrates really well with the landscape.* **2** To become part of a social group and be accepted into it: *Children integrate easily with a new culture.* ■ We always say: "integrate (somebody/something) **with** (something)".

integration /,ɪntɪ'greɪʃən/ [uncountable noun] The act of combining things, or people in a group, in such a way that they finally become part of each other: *The integration of a new child in a class usually does not take a long time.*

↑intelligence /ɪn'tel.ɪ.dʒᵊnts/ [uncountable noun] The ability to learn and to understand things well: *Dolphins have a very high level of intelligence.*

↑intelligent /ɪn'tel.ɪ.dʒᵊnt/ [adjective] Clever; quick at learning: *Fiona is very intelligent.*

↑intend /ɪn'tend/ [verb] **1** To plan to do something: *We intend to go to Rome by car.* **2 to be intended for** To be planned, meant or made for a particular person or purpose: *This book is intended for children under ten.*

intense /ɪn'tents/ [adjective] **1** Strong, great: *The intense cold has made everybody stay at home this weekend.* **2** Serious, concentrated: *Brother and sister got into an intense discussion.*

intensity [uncountable noun] The quality of being intense: *The intensity of his feelings was evident.* ■ The plural is "intensities".

↑intention /ɪn'ten.ʃᵊn/ [noun] A purpose: *My intention is to go camping with friends this summer.*

intentional /ɪn'ten.ʃᵊn.əl/ [adjective] Done on purpose: *I think her parents' arrival during the party was intentional.*

interact /,ɪn·tər'ækt/ [verb] To communicate with each other, or act on each other: *These two chemicals interact in a surprising way.* ■ We say: "interact **with** (something/somebody)".

interaction /,ɪn·tər'æk·ʃən/ [countable noun] Action or communication between two or more people or things: *The interaction between the communities led to greater understanding.*

interactive /,ɪn·tə'ræk·tɪv/ [adjective] **1** Acting reciprocally on each other: *The communities became interactive.* **2** Allowing continuous transfer of information in both directions between a device and its user: *Computers, TV and video are some interactive media.*

intercostal /,ɪn.tə'kɒs.təl/ US: /-t̬ɚ'kɑː.stəl/ [adjective] Between the ribs: *the intercostal muscles.* 👁 **See page 423.**

↑interest[1] /'ɪntrəst/ ■ [uncountable noun] **1** Curiosity about somebody or something, desire to know more: *Karen is now taking a real interest in history.* ■ [countable noun] **2** A thing you like doing very much: *Kevin's only interest is rock music.*

interest[2] /'ɪntrəst/ [verb] To call somebody's attention or create a desire to know more: *That book was what first interested me in Buddhism.*

↑interested /'ɪn·trə·stɪd/, /'ɪn·tə,res·tɪd/ [adjective] Curious, wanting to know more: *I'm interested in trains.* ■ We say "interested **in**". This word is not used before a noun. Be careful with the pronunciation of the end of this word. The last "e" is pronounced like the "i" in "did". ■ See box at **bored**.

†interesting /ˈɪn·trə·stɪŋ/, /ˈɪn·təˌres·tɪŋ/ [adjective] Making you feel curious: *The book I read about underwater plants was very interesting.* ■ See box at bored.

†interfere /ˌɪn·tərˈfɪər/ [verb] **1** To try to help somebody when they do not need you: *You shouldn't interfere between Peter and his sister.* **2** To stop something happening: *You shouldn't let your karate interfere with your studies.*

interference /ˌɪn·tərˈfɪər·əns/ [uncountable noun] The act of interfering: *Your interference in our friendship has caused a lot of problems.*

†interior /ɪnˈtɪər·i·ər/ [noun and adjective] The inside of something: *The interior of the theater has been beautifully decorated.*

intermediate /ˌɪn·tərˈmid·i·ət/ [adjective] In the middle of two people or things: *This grammar book is intended for intermediate level students.*

†internal /ɪnˈtɜr·nə·l/ [adjective] Inside: *The stomach is an internal organ.*

†international /ˌɪn·tərˈnæʃ·ə·nə·l/ [adjective] Between different nations: *Soccer is an international sport.* ■ Compare with "national" (belonging to one country).

†internet /ˈɪntənet/ [noun] An international system of communication by computer: *I receive a movie magazine on my computer each month through the internet.*

†interpret /ɪnˈtɜr·prɪt/ [verb] **1** To translate something spoken from one language into another: *He interpreted for the foreign visitors.* **2** To explain the meaning of something: *How do you interpret this passage? I don't understand it.*

interpretation /ɪnˌtɜr·prɪˈteɪ·ʃən/ [noun] The understanding one person has of the meaning of an event or a work of art: *What is your interpretation of what occurred yesterday.*

interpreter /ɪnˈtɜr·prɪ·t̬ər/ [countable noun] A person who translates from one language into another: *An Arab interpreter helped us when we were in Cairo.*

interrogate /ɪnˈter.ə.geɪt/ [verb] To question somebody thoroughly: *The inspector interrogated the witnesses about the murder.*

†interrupt /ˌɪn·təˈrʌpt/ [verb] To stop something happening: *Don't interrupt me when I'm talking on the phone.*

†interruption /ˌɪn·təˈrʌp·ʃən/ [noun] A break: *I can't study with so many interruptions.*

intersection [countable noun] A place where one street crosses another: *When you get to the intersection, turn left.*

†interval /ˈɪn·tər·vəl/ [countable noun] A short period of time between things: *I've got to make a phone call during the interval.*

intervene /ˌɪn·tərˈvin/ [verb] To come between people or groups in a conflict: *I don't know why the referee doesn't intervene.*

intervention /ˌɪn·tərˈven·ʃən/ [noun] Coming between people or groups: *They sold the car thanks to my father's intervention.*

†interview[1] /ˈɪntəvjuː/ [countable noun] A meeting where somebody asks you questions: *The actor gave an interview to some journalists.*

interview[2] /ˈɪntəvjuː/ [verb] To ask somebody questions in an interview: *They interviewed Bill Gates on television last week.*

intestinal US: /ɪnˈtestɪnəl/ UK: /ˌɪntesˈtaɪnəl/ [adjective] Referring to the intestines: *She has an intestinal infection.*

intestine /ɪnˈtes.tɪne/ [countable noun] **1** The lowest part of the alimentary canal, between the stomach and the anus, made up of the small and large intestines: *The small intestine is the longest part of the digestive tract.* **2 large intestine** The final part of the intestine in which water is absorbed from digested food and solid waste is expelled out of the body: *The large intestine is shorter and wider than the small intestine.* **3 small intestine** The first, upper, part of the intestine, which goes from the stomach to the large intestine: *Most of the absorption of digested food takes place in the small intestine.* **See page 424.**

†into /ˈɪn.tuː/ [preposition] **1** To the inside: *Come into the kitchen for a drink.* **2** To a different state: *This armchair can be turned into a bed.* **3** Showing division: *Five into ten goes two.* See picture at **preposition**.

intonation /ˌɪn.təˈneɪ.ʃən/ [noun] The rise and fall in the sound of the voice: *A good intonation helps people to understand you in a foreign language.*

intranet /ˈɪntrənet/ [countable noun] A closed internet system: *The content of the company intranet is not accessible to outsiders.*

†introduce /ˌɪn·trəˈdus/ [verb] **1** To present a person to somebody for the first time: *My cousin introduced me to her friends at the party.* **2** To make something known for the first time, to establish: *Europeans introduced Christianity in America.*

†introduction /ˌɪn.trəˈdʌk.ʃən/ [countable noun] **1** The act of presenting something: *The introduction of computers has changed the world completely.* **2** The act of introducing one person to another: *The hostess made the introductions and everyone shook hands.* **3** The part at the beginning of a book that tells you what it is about: *The introduction to that book consists of five pages.* ■ Be careful with the pronunciation of this word! The "u" is pronounced like the "u" in "cup".

a b c d e f g h i j k l m n o p q r s t u v w x y z

introvert /ˈɪn.trə.vɜːt/ US: /-vɝːt/ [countable noun] A quiet person concerned with their own thoughts and feelings: *Mary's a real introvert, she never wants to go to parties.*

Inuit /ˈɪn.ju.ɪt/ [countable noun] One of a people who live in the Arctic region: *Inuits used to live in igloos and fish in frozen waters.* ■ Be careful! "Inuit" has a capital "I".

invade /ɪnˈveɪd/ [verb] To enter a country or region by force: *The United States invaded Irak in 2003.*

invader /ɪnˈveɪ.dər/ US: /-dɚ/ [countable noun] Somebody or something that invades: *The Viking invaders not only stole and destroyed wherever they went but also established themselves in certain areas.*

invalid /ˈɪnvəlɪd/ [countable noun] A person who is very ill or disabled and needs help: *Her uncle is an invalid and uses a wheelchair.*

invasion /ɪnˈveɪ.ʒən/ [noun] The act of entering a country or region by force: *The Second World War began with the invasion of Poland.*

↑**invent** /ɪnˈvent/ [verb] To make something that didn't exist before: *Edison invented the electric light bulb.*

↑**invention** /ɪnˈvent.ʃən/ [noun] The making of something that didn't exist before: *The invention of the car changed a lot of people's lives.* 👁 **See page 443.**

inventor /ɪnˈven·tər/ [countable noun] A person who makes something that hasn't existed before: *J. L. Baird was the inventor of television.*

invertebrate /ɪnˈvɜː.tɪ.brət/ US: /-ˈvɝː.t̬ə-/ [countable noun] A creature without a backbone: *Worms, insects, crabs and spiders are all invertebrates.* ■ Compare with "vertebrate" (a creature with a backbone). 👁 **See page 427.**

↑**invest** /ɪnˈvest/ [verb] To put money into buying something: *My father now says that he is going to invest in the telephone company.*

↑**investigate** /ɪnˈves.tɪ.geɪt/ [verb] To examine carefully, when talking about an event: *The police is going to investigate the train robbery.*

↑**investment** /ɪnˈvest.mənt/ [noun] The money that you put into buying something: *This house should be a good investment.*

invisible /ɪnˈvɪz.ɪ.bl̩/ [adjective] That cannot be seen: *Her face was invisible behind the mask.*

↑**invitation** /ˌɪn.vɪˈteɪ.ʃən/ [noun] Asking somebody to go somewhere or do something with you: *The party is by invitation only, I'm afraid.*

↑**invite** /ɪnˈvaɪt/ [verb] To ask somebody to go somewhere with you: *I'd like to invite Jackie to lunch.* ■ We do not generally use "invite" in direct speech. We say: "Let me buy you a drink". (We don't say: "I invite you to a drink".).

↑**involve** /ɪnˈvɑlv/, /-ˈvɔlv/ [verb] **1** To bring somebody or something into a situation or scheme, to concern: *Three cars were involved in the crash.* **2** To make necessary: *Going on vacation usually involves a lot of organization.*

inward [adverb] Towards the inside of something: *All the windows here open inward.*

inwards /ˈɪn.wəd/ [adverb] Towards the inside of something: *All the windows here open inwards.*

ionic /ɑɪˈɑn·ɪk/ [adjective] Referring to an atom or group of atoms that are electrically charged: *The rate of electric charge to the radius of an ion is called the ionic potential.*

Ionic /ɑɪˈɑn·ɪk/ [adjective] Referring to classical Greek architecture, the building style characterized by columns standing on a base and having more decoration than the Doric style: *In Ionic architecture the columns are decorated with scroll shapes at the top.* ■ Compare with "Doric" (the simplest of the building styles) and "Corinthian" (the most ornate).

IQ /aɪˈkjuː/ [noun] A supposed measure of human intelligence: *She has a very high IQ.* ■ "IQ" is an abbreviation for "intelligence quotient", the relation between a person's age and their mental age. "IQ" is always written in capital letters. ■ See box at **abbreviations**.

iris /ˈaɪ.rɪs/ [countable noun] **1** The colored diaphragm that controls the amount of light entering the eye: *The iris has a circular opening in its center.* **2** A tall plant with large purple, white or yellow flowers: *We gave her some irises.*

Irish [adjective] Referring to Ireland: *I think Irish landscapes are beautiful.* ■ Be careful! "Irish" has a capital "I".

↑**iron**[1] /aɪən/ ▮ [uncountable noun] **1** A hard metal: *The balcony railings are made of iron.* ▮ [countable noun] **2** An electrical instrument with a flat bottom, used to make clothes smooth: *Don't start using the iron until it's hot.*

IRON

iron² /aɪən/ [verb] To press clothes with a hot iron: *Don't go out without ironing your pants.*

ironing /ˈaɪ·ər·nɪŋ/ [uncountable noun] Pressing clothes with an iron: *My father does all the ironing at home.*

ironing board [countable noun] A folding narrow table used for ironing clothes: *This ironing board isn't big enough to iron the drapes on.*

irregular /ɪˈreg·jə·lər/ [adjective] **1** Not having an order, uneven: *Our house is rather irregular in shape.* **2** Not following the usual rules: *"To buy" is an irregular verb; the past tense is "bought" and not "buyed".*

irreversible /ˌɪrɪˈvɜːsəbl/ [adjective] Not able to be changed back to the initial state: *The Judge's sentence is irreversible.*

irrigate /ˈɪr.ɪ.geɪt/ [verb] To water land: *Farmers in some areas have to irrigate their fields to make crops grow.*

irrigation /ˌɪr.ɪˈgeɪ.ʃən/ [uncountable noun] The watering of crops: *The irrigation of the fields is carried out before the sun rises and after it sets.*

ᐩ**irritate** /ˈɪr.ɪ.teɪt/ [verb] **1** To make somebody a little angry and nervous: *It really irritates me when you take my pen without saying anything.* **2** To make part of your body painful or sore: *Don't rub your eyes or you'll irritate them.*

irritation /ˌɪr.ɪˈteɪ.ʃən/ [noun] Something that annoys or hurts: *Smoking causes irritation to your throat.*

is /ɪz, z, s/ [verb] See **be**.

Islam /ˈɪz.lɑːm, -læm/ [uncountable noun] The religion that follows the teachings of the Koran: *Islam teaches that Allah is the only God.* ■ Be careful! "Islam" has a capital "I".

Islamic /ɪzˈlæm.ɪk, -ˈlɑː.mɪk/ [adjective] Belonging to Islam: *The Koran is the holy Islamic book.* ■ Careful! "Islamic" has a capital "I".

ᐩ**island** /ˈaɪ.lənd/ [countable noun] **1** A piece of land surrounded by water: *Puerto Rico is an island.* ■ Be careful with the pronunciation of this word. The first part "is" is pronounced like "eye". ■ Compare with "isle" (used especially in the name of places). 👁 **See page 444.** **2 desert island** See **desert island.**

isle /aɪl/ [countable noun] A piece of land surrounded by water: *My cousins were both born on the Isle of Wight.* ■ This word is generally used with the names of places. In other cases we say: "island". Compare with "island" (used as a geographical term).

isn't /ˈɪz.ənt/ The contraction of "is not".

isolated /ˈaɪ·səˌleɪ·t̬ɪd/ [adjective] Away from other people or places: *This is an isolated place.* ■ Be careful with the pronunciation of this word. The "e" is pronounced like the "i" in "did".

ᐩ**issue¹** /ˈɪʃuː/ [countable noun] **1** A problem or question: *My mother is always arguing about politics, ecology and other issues with our neighbor.* **2** An edition of a newspaper or magazine: *Today's issue of the Guardian has the winning lottery numbers.*

issue² /ˈɪʃuː/ [verb] To provide somebody with something: *The soldiers were issued with rations and ammunition.*

ᐩ**it** /ɪt/ [pronoun] The thing being talked about: *Pick up the key and give it to me.* ■ Remember that sentences in English usually have a subject. We say: "It's raining". (We don't say: "Is raining".).

Italian¹ /ɪˈtælɪən/ [adjective] Referring to Italy: *I love Italian food.* ■ Be careful! "Italian" has a capital "I".

Italian² ▮ [countable noun] **1** A person from Italy: *My mother is an Italian.* ▮ [uncountable noun] **2** The language of Italy: *I think Italian is a beautiful language.* ■ Careful! "Italian" has a capital "I".

italics /ɪˈtæl.ɪks/ [plural noun] Letters leaning to the right: *The examples in this dictionary are printed in italics.*

itch¹ /ɪtʃ/ [countable noun] An irritating feeling in the skin: *I've got an awful itch on my arm.*

itch² /ɪtʃ/ [verb] To have a feeling in the skin that makes you scratch it: *My arms itch a lot from the mosquito bites I got the other day.*

itchy /ˈɪtʃ.i/ [adjective] Making you want to scratch it: *I know I shouldn't scratch it, but it's very itchy.*

it'd /ˈɪt̬·əd/ The contraction of "it had" or "it would".

ᐩ**item** /ˈaɪ·t̬əm/ [countable noun] **1** One of a group of things: *Check the items on the shopping list to see if I've forgotten something.* **2 news item** A piece of news: *Are there any interesting news items in the paper this morning?*

itinerary /aɪˈtɪn·əˌrer·i/ [countable noun] A detailed route, with planned stopping points: *The itinerary was planned in advance.* ■ The plural is "itineraries".

it'll /ˈɪt̬·ə·l/ The contraction of "it will".

ᐩ**its** /ɪts/ [adjective] Of it; belonging to it: *The school has its own sports field.* ■ Compare with "it's" (short form of "it is" or "it has").

it's /ɪts/ The contraction of "it is" or "it has". ■ Be careful! Compare with "its" (belonging to something that has already been mentioned).

ᐩ**itself** /ɪtˈself/ [pronoun] **1** A word that refers to the thing or animal that is the subject of the sentence: *The dog has been scratching itself all morning.* **2** A word that underlines the thing the verb refers to: *The town itself is ugly but the people are very friendly.* **3 by itself 1** Alone: *The monastery stands by itself on the hill.* **2** Without being controlled by a person: *They say that this robot can cook a meal by itself!* ■ The plural is "themselves".

I've /aɪv/ The contraction of "I have".

ivory /ˈaɪ·və·ri/, /ˈaɪv·ri/ [uncountable noun] A hard substance from the tusks of animals: *This bracelet is made of ivory.* ■ The plural is "ivories".

ivy /ˈaɪ.vi/ [noun] Plant which climbs up walls and trees: *That wall is covered with ivy.* ■ The plural is "ivies".

J

j

j /dʒeɪ/ The tenth letter of the alphabet: *The name "John" begins with a "J".*

jab[1] /dʒæb/ [countable noun] A quick, hard blow: *He just gave me a jab in the shoulder.*

jab[2] /dʒæb/ [verb] To push something pointed quickly and roughly at something else or somebody: *Rachel jabbed at the balloon with a pin and it burst.*

jackal /ˈdʒæk.əl/ [countable noun] A wild animal like a dog: *Jackals are usually solitary animals.*

↑jacket /ˈdʒæk.ɪt/ [countable noun] **1** A short coat: *Your tie doesn't go with your jacket.* **2 denim jacket** A jacket made of the same material as jeans: *Clare, is this you denim jacket or mine?* **3 leather jacket** A jacket made of leather: *I really like Dave's leather jacket.* See picture at **clothes**.

JACKET

leather jacket denim jacket

jack-of-all-trades /ˌdʒæk·əvˌɔlˈtreɪdz/ [countable noun] A person who can do many things: *Rob's father is a jack-of-all-trades, who does everything in the house.*

jackpot /ˈdʒækˌpɑt/ [countable noun] A big prize, an accumulated prize: *My aunt Maggie's very lucky; she won the jackpot in the lottery last year.*

jaguar /ˈdʒæg·wɑr/, /-juˌɑr/ [countable noun] A large wild cat: *Jaguars live in forests and swamps in America.*

jail /dʒeɪl/ [noun] A prison: *The woman was sent to jail for stealing jewelry from a store.* ■ The same meaning: "prison". ■ In British English they say "gaol".

JAIL

↑**jam**[1] /dʒæm/ ▮ [noun] **1** A soft food made from fruit and sugar: *Would you like some strawberry jam on your bread?* ▮ [countable noun] **2** A group of people or things that cannot move: *There was a traffic jam on the highway this morning.* **3** A difficult situation, being in trouble: *I'm in a real jam, I've lost all my school textbooks.* ■ The "j" is pronounced as in the word "John". ■ Compare with "ham" (salted meat from a pig).

jam[2] /dʒæm/ [verb] **1** To push something into a small space: *Susan jammed all her clothes into her bag.* **2** To block something: *The garage doors are jammed so we can't take the car out.*

Jamaican[1] [adjective] Referring to Jamaica: *They spent their vacations in a Jamaican Beach.* ■ Be careful! "Jamaican" has a capital "J".

Jamaican[2] [countable noun] A person from Jamaica: *There are a Jamaican staying at the hotel.* ■ Be careful! "Jamaican" has a capital "J".

janitor [countable noun] Person who cleans a building and maintains it with minor repairs: *There are three janitors in my school and they clean during the evening.*

↑**January** /ˈdʒæn·juˌer·i/ [noun] The first month of the year: *January's a very cold month in Detroit.* ■ Be careful! "January" has a capital "J". 👁 See picture at **calendar**.

jar US: /dʒɑːr/ UK: /dʒɑːʳ/ [countable noun] A container with a wide opening: *There's very little honey left in the jar.* 👁 See picture at **container**.

javelin /ˈdʒæv.lɪn/ [countable noun] A long spear used in sport: *Throwing the javelin is an Olympic sport.*

jaw US: /dʒɑː/ UK: /dʒɔː/ [countable noun] One of the two bones that hold your teeth: *The lion opened its jaws and roared.* ■ The same meaning: "jawbone", "mandible".

jawbone [countable noun] The lower of the two bones that hold your teeth: *The jawbone is also known as the mandible.* ■ The same meaning: "jaw", "mandible". 👁 **See page 422.**

jazz /dʒæz/ [uncountable noun] A kind of music with strong rhythms and parts that are invented at the moment of playing: *In the early twentieth century, African-Americans began playing jazz in the south of the USA.*

↑**jealous** /ˈdʒel.əs/ [adjective] **1** Wanting what somebody else has and feeling bad because you don't have it: *I'm really jealous of Janice. She's clever, beautiful and popular.* **2** Afraid of losing somebody's love: *Stephen's jealous of Karen's male friends.*

jealousy /ˈdʒel.ə.si/ [uncountable noun] Envy: *Jealousy can sometimes be a problem when a small child has a baby brother or sister.* ■ The plural is "jealousies".

↑**jeans** /dʒiːnz/ [plural noun] Pants made of a strong cloth: *Today Emma is wearing blue jeans and a white T-shirt.* ■ When we talk about two or more "jeans", we use the word "pairs": "I bought three pairs of jeans". 👁 See picture at **clothes**.

jeep® /dʒiːp/ [countable noun] A kind of strong car that can go over rough ground: *Neil's father takes his jeep when he goes fishing.*

↑**jelly** /ˈdʒel.i/ [noun] A transparent dessert that shakes when it is moved: *I'd like jelly and ice cream for dessert, please.* ■ The plural is "jellies".

jellyfish /ˈdʒel.i.fɪʃ/ [countable noun] A sea animal with a transparent body: *Some jellyfish are shaped like umbrellas.* ■ The plural is "jellyfish" or "jellyfishes".

jersey /ˈdʒɜr·zi/ [countable noun] A warm piece of clothing with long sleeves: *My soccer jersey has my name and my number on the back.* ■ Be careful with the pronunciation of this word! ■ The same meaning: "jumper", "pullover", "sweater". "Sweater" is the most commonly used word.

jester /ˈdʒes·tər/ [countable noun] A joker employed at court in medieval times: *The job of the jester traditionally was to make people laugh.*

jet /dʒet/ [countable noun] **1** A fast stream of liquid or gas coming out of a small hole: *I've just burned my hand on the jet of steam coming out of the kettle.* **2** A fast airplane: *The jet took off from Heathrow airport at eight o'clock.* **3** jumbo jet See **jumbo jet**.

Jew /dʒuː/ [countable noun] A person who belongs to the religion of Judaism or whose family was originally from ancient Israel: *Saturday is the holy day of the week for practicing Jews.* ■ Be careful! "Jew" has a capital "J".

jewel /ˈdʒuː.əl/ [countable noun] A precious stone: *My mother wore her jewels when she went to the opera last night.*

jeweler /ˈdʒu·ə·lər/, /ˈdʒu·lər/ [countable noun] Person who makes or sells jewelry: *The local jeweler provided*

a b c d e f g h i j k l m n o p q r s t u v w x y z

the rings for the wedding. ■ The British English spelling is "jeweller".

jeweller /ˈdʒuːələ/ UK: /ˈdʒuː.ə.ləʳ/ [countable noun] See **jeweler.** ■ This is a British English spelling.

+**jewellery** /ˈdʒuː.ᵊl.ri/ [uncountable noun] See **jewelry.** ■ Be careful! We don't say "a jewellery". We say "some jewellery" or "a piece of jewellery". ■ This is a British English spelling. ■ The plural is "jewelleries".

+**jewelry** /ˈdʒuː.əl.ri/ [uncountable noun] Valuable ornaments like rings, bracelets and so on: *I keep my jewelry in a special box.* ■ Be careful! We don't say "a jewelry". We say "some jewelry" or "a piece of jewelry". ■ The British English spelling is "jewellery". ■ The plural is "jewelries".

JEWELRY

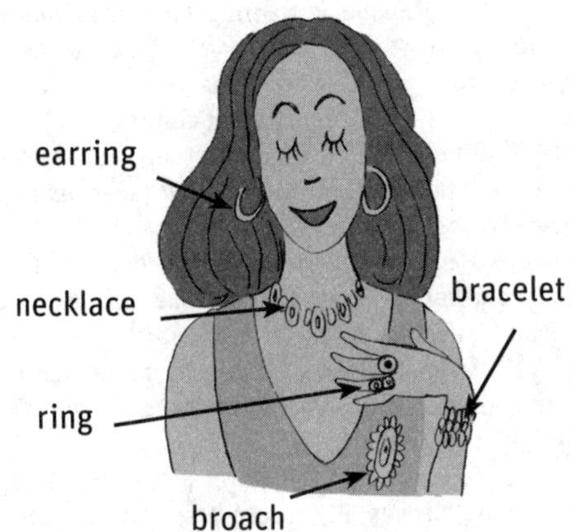

Jewish /ˈdʒuː.ɪʃ/ [adjective] Referring to Jews: *My friend Abraham is Jewish.* ■ Be careful! "Jewish" has a capital "J".

jibe /dʒaɪb/ [countable noun] A remark which makes somebody else look foolish: *That was a cruel jibe. Why are you always so nasty to her?* ■ This word is also written "gibe".

jigsaw or **jigsaw puzzle** /ˈdʒɪgsɔː/ [countable noun] A game in which you put small pieces together to make a picture: *Mark will need a lot of skill and patience to do that jigsaw puzzle.*

jingle /ˈdʒɪŋgl/ [verb] To make a ringing sound: *Timmy thought he heard the jingle of sleigh bells on Christmas Eve.*

+**job** US: /dʒɑːb/ UK: /dʒɒb/ [countable noun] **1** A task that you must do: *Linda's only job here is to look after the plants.* **2** Work that you are paid to do: *Sandra's sister has a job in a travel agency.* **3 out of a job** Without a job: *My sister has been out of a job since January.*

jockey US: /ˈdʒɑː.ki/ UK: /ˈdʒɒk.i/ [countable noun] A person who rides horses in races: *Jockeys have to be very fit and light in weight.*

jog[1] /dʒɒg/ [verb] To run at a slow pace: *A lot of people go jogging to keep fit.*

jog[2] [noun] A slow run: *We went for a jog in the park before breakfast.*

jogging US: /ˈdʒɑː.gɪŋ/ UK: /ˈdʒɒg.ɪŋ/ [uncountable noun] Running at a slow speed for exercise: *My mother likes jogging.*

john US: /dʒɑːn/ UK: /dʒɒn/ [countable noun] Restroom: *I need to go to the john.* ■ This word is informal.

join /dʒɔɪn/ [verb] **1** To connect things: *Join the dots together to make the picture.* **2** To come together: *The two roads join near the bridge.* **3** To become a member of something: *Kevin has just joined the cyclists club.*

▸ **PHRASAL VERBS** · **to join in** To take part in something: *Would you like to join in the darts game?*

joint[1] /dʒɔɪnt/ [countable noun] **1** A place where two things or parts are joined: *The plumber repaired the pipe with a water resistant joint.* **2** Referring to the body, a place where bones meet: *The knee joint is covered by the knee cap.* **3** Piece of meat cooked in the oven: *We had a joint of beef for Sunday lunch.* **4** A cheap place for entertainment: *How can you go to that joint to celebrate her birthday?*

joint[2] /dʒɔɪnt/ [adjective] Together, combined: *The couple opened a joint account.*

joke[1] /dʒəʊk/ [countable noun] **1** Something that you tell or say to make people laugh: *Stop making jokes about my purple socks.* **2 to play a joke on (somebody)** To do something funny to somebody to make people laugh: *They played a joke on Keith by imitating his teacher's voice on the phone.* **3 practical joke** A joke played against somebody: *On April Fools' Day we played a practical joke on Mary.*

joke[2] /dʒəʊk/ [verb] To say funny things against somebody: *I was only joking when I said you ate enough for three people.*

joker US: /ˈdʒoʊ.kɚ/ UK: /ˈdʒəʊ.kəʳ/ [countable noun] A person who makes jokes: *Don't take Jonathan seriously because he's a real joker.*

jolly /ˈdʒɒli/ [adverb] **1** Very: *The comic your brother lent me is jolly good.* **2** Merry, cheerful: *My grandma is very jolly, she's always good fun to be with.* ■ This word is informal.

jot

▸ **PHRASAL VERBS** · **to jot (something) down** To make a quick note of something: *I think I jotted her telephone number down somewhere.* ■ Be careful with the spelling of these forms: "jotted", "jotting".

a b c d e f g h i j k l m n o p q r s t u v w x y z

journal /ˈdʒɜr·nə·l/ [countable noun] **1** A magazine or a newspaper for one particular profession or interest: *The doctor's study was full of medical journals.* **2** A record of what somebody has done during the day: *Philip kept a journal of the things he did during the summer vacation.* ■ In this use, the same meaning: "diary".

journalism /ˈdʒɜr·nə·lˌɪz·əm/ [uncountable noun] The job of writing for magazines or newspapers: *The article about the beginning of the war was a brilliant piece of journalism.*

ᐩ**journalist** /ˈdʒɜr·nə·l·əst/ [countable noun] A person who writes for magazines or newspapers: *Today the Prime Minister is having an interview with foreign journalists.*

ᐩ**journey** /ˈdʒɜːni/ [countable noun] The act of going from one place to another: *Their journey to Reno took a whole day on the car.* ■ Compare with "trip[1]" (a journey involving an activity like business, shopping, sightseeing and so on).

joust[1] [countable noun] An organized combat between two people on horseback with lances: *The knights in armor charged towards each other in the joust.*

joust[2] /dʒaʊst/ [verb] To fight on horseback in a tournament: *In medieval times knights jousted to gain favor.*

joy [noun] Great happiness: *The children jumped for joy when they saw the new.*

joyful /ˈdʒɔɪ.fᵊl/ [adjective] Very happy: *That music is really joyful!* ■ We also say "joyous".

joyous /ˈdʒɔɪ.əs/ [adjective] See **joyful**.

joyride /ˈdʒɔɪ.raɪd/ [countable noun] A ride in a car for pleasure, especially a stolen car driven fast and without care: *They took the car for a joyride and left it on the beach.*

joystick /ˈdʒɔɪ.stɪk/ [countable noun] A special handle used for controlling movement on an airplane, with a computer and so on: *Show me how to use the joystick.*

Judaism /ˈdʒuː.deɪ.ɪ.zᵊm/ [uncountable noun] The religion of the Jews: *Judaism has survived for over 4000 years.* ■ Be careful! "Judaism" has a capital "J".

ᐩ**judge[1]** /dʒʌdʒ/ [countable noun] **1** A person who decides on legal things: *The judge sentenced the robbers to two years' imprisonment.* **2** A person who decides the winner of a competition: *The three judges of the vegetable competition were unanimous in their decision.*

judge[2] /dʒʌdʒ/ [verb] **1** To have an opinion about something: *You should never judge anybody just by their appearance.* **2** To make decisions in a court of law or in a competition: *Who's going to judge the photograph competition tomorrow?*

ᐩ**judgement** /ˈdʒʌdʒ.mənt/ [noun] See **judgment**. ■ This is a British English spelling.

ᐩ**judgment** /ˈdʒʌdʒ·mənt/ ▮ [noun] **1** An opinion: *What should we do, in your judgment?* **2** A decision made by a judge: *Judges have to study cases very carefully before they pronounce judgment.* ▮ [uncountable noun] **3** Common sense: *Stuart showed good judgment when he bought his ticket weeks ago. There are none left now.* ■ The British English spelling is "judgement".

judiciary /dʒʊˈdɪʃ·iˌer·i/, /-ˈdɪʃ·ə·ri/ [countable noun] The collective name for the judges: *The judiciary is responsible for interpreting and applying the laws passed by Congress.*

judo /ˈdʒud·oʊ/ [uncountable noun] A sport in which you wrestle or throw somebody: *Billy does judo at school.*

jug /dʒʌg/ [countable noun] A container for liquids with a handle: *Is there any lemonade left in the jug?*

juggle /ˈdʒʌg.l̩/ [verb] To throw things in the air, catch them and throw them again quickly: *Look! That clown is juggling six eggs.*

juggler /ˈdʒʌg·lər/ [countable noun] A person who juggles: *We saw two excellent jugglers at the circus last week.*

ᐩ**juice** /dʒuːs/ [uncountable noun] The liquid from fruit or vegetables: *Would you like a glass of orange juice with your breakfast?*

juicy /ˈdʒuː.si/ [adjective] Full of juice: *Where did you get these juicy apples?*

jukebox /ˈdʒuk·bɑks/ [countable noun] A machine that plays records in cafés, bars and so on: *Put a coin into the jukebox and it'll play the record you choose.*

ᐩ**July** /dʒʊˈlaɪ/ [noun] The seventh month of the year: *Many schools are closed during July.* ■ Be careful! "July" has a capital "J". 👁 See picture at **calendar**.

jumble[1] /ˈdʒʌmbl/ [noun] A lot of things mixed together in an untidy way: *Everything is in a terrible jumble in my bedroom.*

jumble[2] /ˈdʒʌmbl/ [verb] To mix things in an untidy way: *All my clothes are so jumbled I can't find anything.*

jumbo jet [countable noun] A large airplane: *My brother is arriving on the jumbo jet from New York tomorrow.*

ᐩ**jump[1]** /dʒʌmp/ [countable noun] **1** A quick or sudden movement into the air: *Jenny's last jump was her best.* **2** **high jump** A sport in which people jump over a high bar: *I've never been good at the high jump at school.* **3** **long jump** See "long jump" in the word **long[1]**.

jump[2] /dʒʌmp/ [verb] **1** To move up into the air by using your feet: *If you try to jump over that stream, you're likely to fall into the water.* **2** To move suddenly because something surprises you: *A loud knock at the door made us jump.*

a b c d e f g h i j k l m n o p q r s t u v w x y z

jumper /ˈdʒʌm·pər/ [countable noun] A warm woolen piece of clothing with long sleeves: *Today Nigel's wearing a red jumper and blue jeans.* ■ The same meaning: "jersey", "pullover", "sweater". "Sweater" is the most commonly used word.

jump rope [countable noun] A rope that is used for skipping: *My sister's got a new jump rope with bells in the handles.*

junction /ˈdʒʌŋk.ʃᵊn/ [countable noun] A place where roads meet: *Be careful when you cycle across the junction.*

↑**June** /dʒuːn/ [noun] The sixth month of the year: *Summer begins in June.* ■ Be careful! "June" has a capital "J". 👁 See picture at **calendar**.

jungle /ˈdʒʌŋ.gl/ [noun] A forest in the tropics: *Monkeys and gorillas live in the jungles of Africa and Asia.*

↑**junior**[1] [adjective] **1** Younger: *The older students can have lunch in their classrooms but the junior students use the cafeteria.* ■ See box at **abbreviations**. **2** Less important: *In the army, a colonel is junior to a general.* **3** **junior high or junior high school** In the United States, a school for children between eleven and fourteen years old: *My daughter goes to junior high, she is in 7th grade.* ■ In this use, the same meaning: "middle school".

junior[2] /ˈdʒun·jər/ [countable noun] A student in the third year of high school or college: *My brother is a junior this year so he's studying hard to get good grades for his college application.*

junk food [uncountable noun] Food that is easy and quick to prepare and eat: *Junk food contains a lot of chemicals.*

Jupiter /ˈdʒuːpɪtər/ [countable noun] A planet of the solar system that is fifth in order from the Sun: *Jupiter is the largest planet in the solar system.* 👁 **See page 446-447.**

jurisdiction /ˌdʒʊərɪsˈdɪkʃən/ [uncountable noun] The authority of an official body to administer laws: *That court has no jurisdiction in this kind of case.*

↑**jury** US: /ˈdʒʊr.i/ UK: /ˈdʒʊə.ri/ [countable noun] A group of people who decide if a person is guilty or innocent at a trial: *The jury found him innocent of the murder.* ■ The plural is "juries".

↑**just**[1] /dʒʌst, dʒəst/ [adverb] **1** A very short time ago: *Stephen has just come back from school.* ■ In this use, "just" is normally used with the present perfect tense. **2** Exactly: *This cooking book is just what I need.* **3** At the time when: *The bell rang just as I was taking a shower.* **4** Only, simply: *What you're telling me is just an excuse.* **5** By a small amount: *I just missed the train as it was leaving the station.* **6** **just a minute or just a moment** Words that you say to ask somebody to wait a little: *Just a moment, I think I heard a knock at the door.* **7** **just now** **1** Right now: *I don't have enough money to buy the tickets just now.* **2** A very short time ago: *I gave the keys to your sister just now.*

just[2] /dʒʌst/ [adjective] Fair, morally right: *I think the referee made a just decision.*

↑**justice** /ˈdʒʌs.tɪs/ [uncountable noun] **1** Fair behavior or treatment: *Justice has been done; they've given him his job back.* **2** A system of law: *They took the case to the Indiana Court of Justice.*

K

k

k /keɪ/ The eleventh letter of the alphabet: *The name "Karen" begins with a "K".*

K /keɪ/ A thousand: *My starting salary was $20 K a year.* ■ This word is informal.

kangaroo /ˌkæŋ·gəˈru/ [countable noun] A large Australian animal that moves by jumping on its back legs: *Kangaroos carry their young in a pouch.* 👁 **See page 428.**

karate /kəˈrɑ·t̬i/ [uncountable noun] A sport in which people fight using their hands and feet: *Karate was invented in Japan.* 👁 See picture at **sport**.

kayak /ˈkaɪ.æk/ [countable noun] A light canoe with a covered top: *Kayaks are often made of fiberglass.*

⁺**keen** /kiːn/ [adjective] **1** Enthusiastic, very interested: *Wendy is very keen on tennis.* ■ Be careful. We say: "to be keen **on** (something)". **2** Fine or sharp, when talking about the senses: *She has a keen sense of smell.*

⁺**keep,** kept, kept /kiːp/ [verb] **1** To continue to have something: *Sara keeps all her old clothes.* **2** To continue doing something: *He keeps making noises.* **3** To have something in a particular place: *I keep all my old toys in a closet.* **4** To maintain something in a particular way: *She keeps her room very tidy.* **5** To look after animals, for food: *We have a house in the country where we keep pigs and chickens.* **6** Referring to food, to stay in a good state: *Most food keeps better in the fridge.* **7** To cause somebody to stay: *Many things keep Colin in Colombia, not just his girlfriend.* **8** Referring to the law, a promise or an agreement, to do what it says: *I always keep my promises.* **9** **to keep a secret** Not to reveal a secret that somebody tells you: *Can you keep a secret?* **10** **to keep watch** See "to keep watch" in the word **watch**[1].

▶ **PHRASAL VERBS** · **to keep away** Not to go near something: *Keep away from the dog, he's dangerous.* · **to keep (something) back** **1** To save a part of something, not give all: *I have kept a part of the cake back for Amy, she will arrive much later.* **2** To not tell everything: *I think he is keeping something back Come on, what else you know?* · **to keep (something) down** To retain food, not to vomit it: *With this stomach flu I can't keep any food down.* · **to keep off** Not to go onto something, usually to protect it: *Keep off the grass!* · **to keep on** To continue doing something: *Don't stop! Keep on running.* · **to keep to (something)** To not move away from a line, path, plan or regulation: *We must keep to the original plan.* · **to keep up** To continue doing something well, to maintain a level of effort: *Keep up the good work!* · **to keep up with (somebody or something)** To go as fast as somebody or something: *You're walking too quickly, I can't keep up with you.*

keeper /'ki·pər/ [countable noun] A person who guards or looks after a zoo or a museum: *The keeper has to feed the lions twice a day.*

keep fit /ˌkiːp'fɪt/ [uncountable noun] Physical fitness exercises: *Keep fit classes are very fashionable.*

kennel /'ken.ᵊl/ [countable noun] See **doghouse.** ■ This word is British English.

kept /kept/ Past tense and past participle forms of **keep.**

kerb US: /kɝːb/ UK: /kɜːb/ [countable noun] See **curb.** ■ This word is British English.

ketchup /'ketʃ.ʌp/ [uncountable noun] A sauce made from tomatoes and spices: *I always put ketchup on my hamburgers.*

kettle /'keţ·ə·l/ [countable noun] A container used for boiling water: *Put the kettle on and we'll have tea.*

kettledrum /'ket.l̩.drʌm/ US: /'keţ-/ [countable noun] A large drum which has the shape of a bowl: *Mike plays the kettledrums in the local orchestra.*

ᐩ**key¹** /kiː/ [countable noun] **1** A special shaped piece of metal for opening or closing locks: *Have you got the key for the front door?* **2** One of a group of parts of some musical instruments and machines that you pressed to make them work: *Pianos have many keys.* 👁 **See page 442. 3** A solution or a group of solutions: *The key to the exercises is at the back of the book.*

KEY

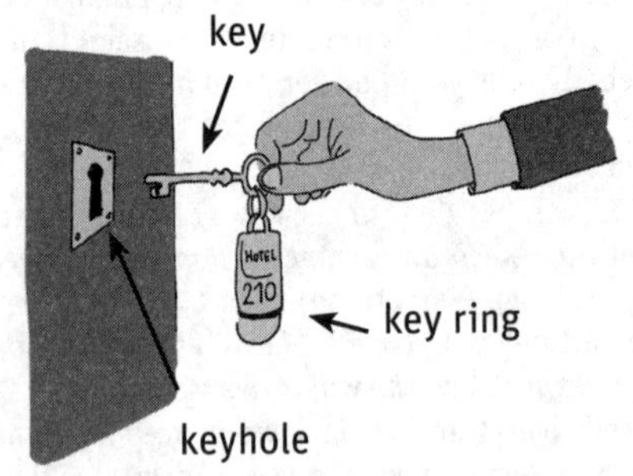

key² /kiː/ [adjective] Very important or necessary: *The key moment in the murder investigation was the discovery of the gun.* ■ Be careful! This word is always used before a noun.

ᐩ**keyboard** /'kiˌbɔrd/, /-ˌbourd/ [countable noun] **1** A set of keys on a piano, typewriter or computer: *I need a new keyboard for my computer.* 👁 **See page 442. 2** An electronic musical instrument: *Sally plays the keyboards in a pop group.*

keyhole /'kiˌhoul/ [countable noun] A hole in which a key goes: *He looked through the door keyhole to see if anybody was in.* 👁 See picture at **key.**

key ring [countable noun] A ring for carrying keys: *I carry all my keys on a key ring.* 👁 See picture at **key.**

kg A written abbreviation for **kilogram.** ■ See box at **abbreviations.**

khaki /'kɑː.ki/ [noun and adjective] A color between yellow and brown: *Soldier's uniforms are often khaki.*

ᐩ**kick¹** /kɪk/ [countable noun] A blow with the foot: *The horse gave him a tremendous kick.*

kick² /kɪk/ [verb] To hit somebody or something with your foot: *He got angry and kicked me.*

kick-off /kɪk , ɔf/ [noun] The start of a soccer game: *The kick-off is at 7.30 pm.*

ᐩ**kid** /kɪd/ [countable noun] **1** A child: *Sara and Tom have three kids.* ■ This use is informal. **2** A young goat: *Look at the goat with her kids.*

kidnap /'kɪd.næp/ [verb] To carry somebody away by force: *His father was kidnapped by the Mafia.* ■ Be careful with the spelling of these forms: "kidnapped", "kidnapping".

kidney /'kɪd.ni/ [countable noun] One of the two body organs used for cleaning the blood: *His kidneys were not working properly and he had to go to the hospital.* 👁 **See page 424.**

ᐩ**kill** /kɪl/ [verb] To make a person or an animal die: *The car ran over the cat and killed it.*

ᐩ**killer** /'kɪl·ər/ [countable noun] A person or animal who kills: *The police caught the killer.*

killing /'kɪl.ɪŋ/ [countable noun] Taking the life of somebody or something, a murder: *He admitted responsibility for the killing.*

kilo /'kɪl·ə/ [countable noun] See **kilogram.**

kilogram /'kɪləʊgræm/ [countable noun] A unit of weight equal to one thousand grams: *In United States people use pounds instead of kilograms.* ■ "Kilo" is short for "kilogram". The abbreviation "kg" is only used in written language. See box at **abbreviations.** ■ The British English spelling is "kilogramme".

kilogramme [countable noun] See **kilogram.** ■ The abbreviation "kg" is only used in written language. ■ This is a British English spelling.

kilometer US: /kɪ'lɑː.mə.ţɚ/ [countable noun] A unit of distance equal to one thousand meters: *In United States people use miles instead of kilometers.* ■ The abbreviation "km" is only used in written language. See box at **abbreviations.** ■ The British English spelling is "kilometre".

kilometre UK: /'kɪl.əˌmiː.təʳ/ [countable noun] See **kilometer.** ■ The abbreviation "km" is only used in written language. ■ This is a British English spelling.

kin /kɪn/ [uncountable noun] **1** The family or relatives of somebody: *He has kin all over the world.* **2** next of kin Somebody's closest relative: *Who is your next of kin?*

†**kind**[1] /kaɪnd/ [adjective] Friendly, helpful, nice: *She's such a kind person, always thinking of others.*

†**kind**[2] /kaɪnd/ [countable noun] A type: *I like reading all kinds of books.*

†**kindness** /ˈkaɪnd.nəs/ [uncountable noun] The quality of being kind: *He showed great kindness to his friends.*

kinetic /kəˈnet̬·ɪk/ [adjective] Referring to movement: *In kinetic art the pieces have moving parts.*

†**king** /kɪŋ/ [countable noun] **1** A man from a royal family who is ruler of a country: *The United States President received the King of Spain in the White House.* ■ A female ruler is a "queen". **2** The most important piece in chess: *Careful! If you lose your king, you lose the game.* See picture at **chess**.

kingdom /ˈkɪŋ.dəm/ [countable noun] A country that has a king or a queen as ruler: *United States is independent of the United Kingdom since 1776.*

kiosk /ˈki·ɑsk/ [countable noun] A small store on the street with an open window through which you buy things: *I went to the station kiosk to buy a newspaper and some chocolate.*

kipper /ˈkɪp.ər/ US: /-ɚ/ [countable noun] A salted and smoked fish: *In Alaska the kipper is excellent.*

†**kiss**[1] /kɪs/ [countable noun] A touch with your lips: *Come on! Be nice and give me a kiss.* ■ The plural is "kisses".

kiss[2] /kɪs/ [verb] To touch with your lips: *She gave him a big kiss.* ■ Be careful with the spelling of the 3rd person singular present tense form: "kisses".

kit /kɪt/ [countable noun] **1** A set of pieces that can be put together to make something: *They built the bookcase from a kit.* **2** Equipment for a particular activity: *He had lots of different screwdrivers in his tool kit.* **3** **first aid kit** Medical supplies for emergencies: *There's a first aid kit in the changing room.*

†**kitchen** /ˈkɪtʃ.ᵊn/ [countable noun] The room where food is cooked: *I usually have breakfast in the kitchen.* See picture on the following page and at **house**.

kite /kaɪt/ [countable noun] A toy with string that flies in the wind: *Veronica enjoys flying her kite at the seaside.*

KITE

kitten /ˈkɪt·ə·n/ [countable noun] A young cat: *Our cat has had five kittens.* See picture at **pet**.

kiwi /ˈkiː.wiː/ [countable noun] **1** A small and hairy fruit: *Kiwis are green inside with lots of black seeds.* **2** A bird from New Zealand that cannot fly: *Kiwis have very long beaks.*

km A written abbreviation for **kilometer**. ■ See box at **abbreviations**.

knack /næk/ [noun] A skillful or particular way of doing something: *There's a knack to opening this door.*

†**knee** /niː/ [countable noun] **1** The part of the leg where it bends: *Craig hurt his knee playing football.* **See page 421.** **2** **on somebody's knee** On a person's legs: *I sat Mary on my knee so that she could see the play better.*

kneel, knelt, knelt /niːl/ [verb] To go down on your knees: *We all knelt down in the church.* ■ "Kneel" also has regular past and past participle forms: "kneeled".

knelt Past tense and past participle forms of **kneel**.

knew US: /nuː/ UK: /njuː/ Past tense of **know**.

knickers /ˈnɪk·ərz/ [plural noun] See **panties**. ■ This word is British English. ■ When we talk about two or more "knickers", we use the word "pairs": "I bought three pairs of knickers".

knick-knack /ˈnɪk.næk/ [countable noun] A small object that is not very useful: *Her room is full of pictures, plants and knick-knacks.* ■ The plural is "knick-knacks".

†**knife** /naɪf/ [countable noun] An object used for cutting things: *Get the knife and cut some bread, please.* ■ The plural is "knives". ■ Remember! You drink soup with a spoon, you eat french fries with a fork and you cut cakes with a knife. See picture at **cutlery**.

knight /naɪt/ [countable noun] **1** A medieval horse soldier: *In the movie "First Knight", Richard Gere is a King Arthur's knight.* **2** A chess piece with a horse's head: *He lost a knight but attacked the queen.* See picture at **chess**.

†**knit** /nɪt/ [verb] To make clothes using two needles: *This woolly scarf was knitted by my granny.* ■ Be careful with the spelling of these forms: "knitted", "knitting".

knitting /ˈnɪt̬·ɪŋ/ [uncountable noun] Material that is being knitted: *She managed to pick up her knitting before the cat got it.* ■ Be careful! We don't say "a knitting". We say "some knitting" or "a piece of knitting".

knob US: /nɑːb/ UK: /nɒb/ [countable noun] A round handle on a door or on a drawer: *All the doors have gold knobs in this hotel.*

†**knock**[1] /nɒk/ [countable noun] A loud sound that is made by

KITCHEN

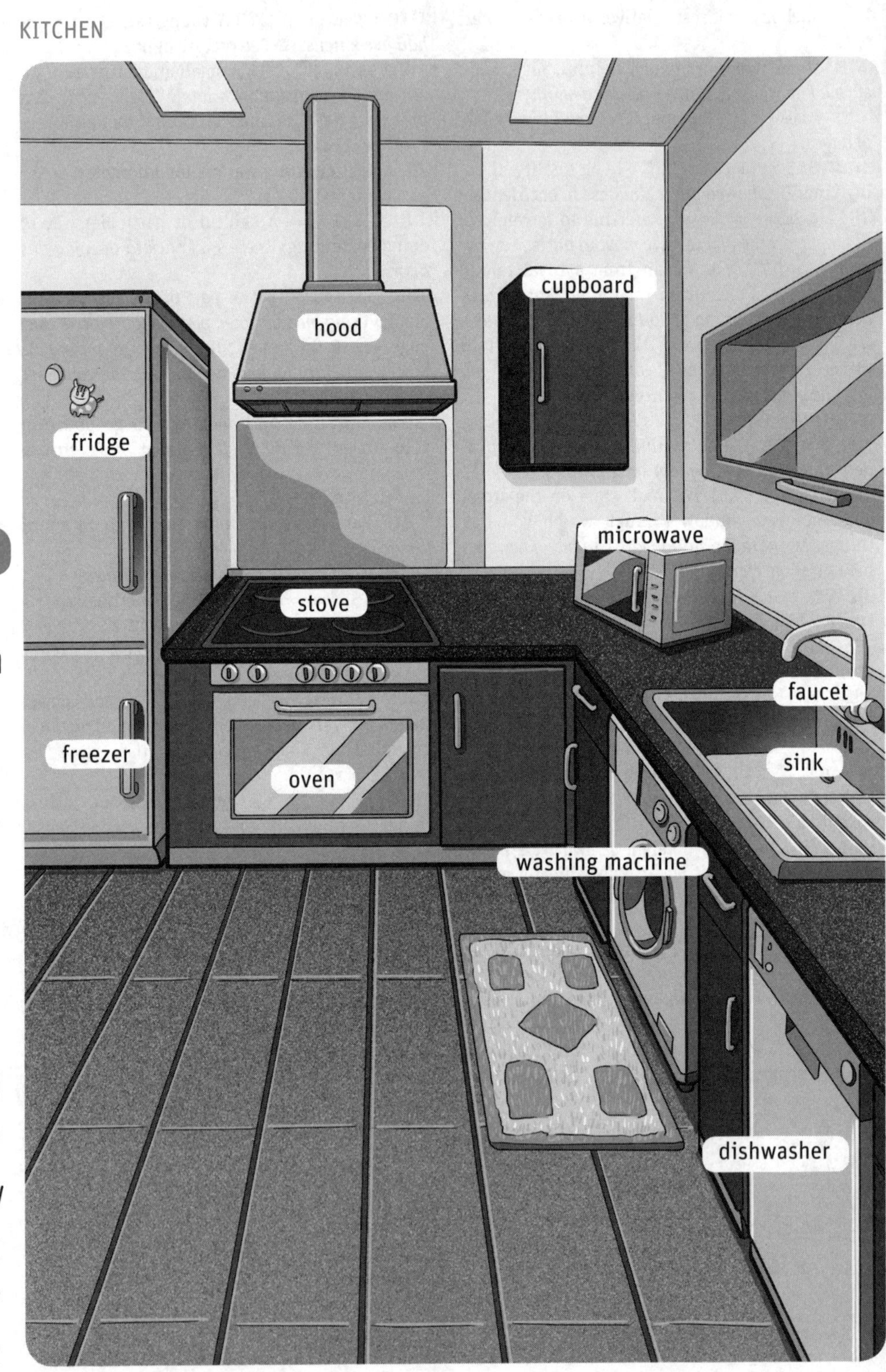
cupboard
hood
fridge
microwave
stove
faucet
freezer
sink
oven
washing machine
dishwasher

hitting something: *Just then, there was a loud knock at the door.*

knock[2] /nɒk/ [verb] **1** To hit or bump somebody: *John knocked Gary by accident.* **2** To hit a door or a window with your hand to call the attention of somebody inside: *The children knocked at the door and ran away.*

◗ **PHRASAL VERBS** · **to knock (somebody) down** To hit somebody and cause them to fall: *He was knocked down by a car.* · **to knock (somebody) out** To hit somebody so that he or she becomes unconscious: *She fell off her bicycle and was knocked out.* · **to knock (something) over** To hit something so that it falls to a horizontal position: *He pushed the table and knocked a vase over.*

*__knot__ US: /nɑːt/ UK: /nɒt/ [countable noun] Part of a rope or ropes where two sections are tied together: *He tied the two pieces of string together in a knot.*

KNOT

*__know,__ knew, known US: /noʊ/ UK: /nəʊ/ [verb] To have information about something: *I know where he lives.*

*__knowledge__ US: /ˈnɑː.lɪdʒ/ UK: /ˈnɒl.ɪdʒ/ [uncountable noun] The things that somebody knows: *His knowledge of science was extraordinary.*

known US: /noʊn/ UK: /nəʊn/ Past participle of **know**.

knuckle /ˈnʌkl/ [countable noun] The parts of your fingers where they join the hand: *I banged the door with my knuckles.*

koala or **koala bear** /kəʊˈɑːlə/ [countable noun] Small Australian animal which carries its young in a pouch: *The koala feeds on eucalyptus leaves.*

Koran /kəˈræn/, /-ˈrɑn/ [noun] The sacred book of Muslims: *the Holy Koran.* ■ Be careful! "Koran" has a capital "K".

l /el/ The twelfth letter of the alphabet: *The name "Linda" begins with an "L".*

lab /læb/ [countable noun] See **laboratory.**

↑**label**^{1} /'leɪ.bəl/ [countable noun] A piece of paper, cloth or plastic attached to an object, that gives information about it: *The label on the hat said "Made in Texas".* ■ Be careful with the pronunciation of this word.

LABEL

label^{2} /'leɪ.bəl/ [verb] To put a label on an object: *Make sure you label your suitcases in case they get lost.* ■ Be careful with the pronunciation of this word.

labor^{1} /'leɪ·bər/ [uncountable noun] Hard physical work: *The house was finished, after months of labor.* ■ We usually say "hard work". ■ The British English spelling is "labour".

labor^{2} /'leɪ·bər/ [verb] To do hard physical work, to struggle to do something: *The miners labored for hours to rescue their friends after the explosion.* ■ We usually say "work hard". ■ The British English spelling is "labour".

↑**laboratory** US: /'læb.rə.tɔːr.i/ UK: /lə'bɒr.ə.tri/ [countable noun] A place or a room where scientists work: *Scientists test new medicines and drugs in the laboratory before using them with patients.* ■ The plural is "laboratories". ■ "Lab" is short for "laboratory". **See page 440.**

laborer /'leɪ·bə·rər/ [countable noun] A person who does hard physical work: *There were twenty-five laborers working on the new road.* ■ The British English spelling is "labourer".

labour^{1} /'leɪbər/ [uncountable noun] See **labor**^{1}. ■ We usually say "hard work". ■ This is a British English spelling.

labour^{2} /'leɪbər/ [verb] See **labor**^{2}. ■ This is a British English spelling.

labourer /'leɪbə·rər·/ UK: /'leɪ.b^{ə}r.ə^{r}/ [countable noun] See **laborer.** ■ This is a British English spelling.

labyrinth /'læb.ə.rɪnθ/ [countable noun] A complicated arrangement of paths: *The palace has a labyrinth of corridors and passages.* ■ The same meaning: "maze".

lace /leɪs/ [countable noun] **1** A kind of string used to tie shoes: *Do your laces up or you'll fall over them.* **2** Fine cloth, with a pattern of small holes: *Lace is often used to decorate ladies' underwear.*

↑**lack**[1] /læk/ [uncountable noun] Not having enough of something: *There's a terrible lack of rain in many parts of Africa.*

lack[2] /læk/ [verb] Not to have something: *Many people in poor countries are lacking in basic things, like food and water.* ■ Be careful. We say: "lack (something)" or "to be lacking **in** (something)".

lacrosse [uncountable noun] A game for two teams in which players hold long sticks with a net for catching, throwing and carrying the ball to score a goal: *Lacrosse is a popular sport in many private schools.*

lad /læd/ [countable noun] A boy or young man: *Robin is a very nice lad.* ■ This word is informal.

ladder /ˈlæd·ər/ [countable noun] Two long, connected pieces of wood or metal, that are used for climbing: *Can you hold the ladder for me while I climb up and clean the windows?*

LADDER

ladle /ˈleɪdl/ [countable noun] A deep, round spoon with a long handle: *David served the soup with the new silver ladle that Mrs. Brown gave us for Christmas.*

↑**lady** /ˈleɪ.di/ [countable noun] **1** A polite way of saying "woman": *Say "Thank you" to the lady, Jenny!* **2** An important title for a woman: *Traditionally, the First Lady of the United States is the president's wife.* ■ The plural is "ladies".

ladybird /ˈleɪ.di.bɜːd/ US: /-bɝːd/ [countable noun] See **ladybug.** ■ This word is British English.

ladybug /ˈleɪ·di,bʌg/ [countable noun] A flying insect which is red or yellow with black spots: *The ladybug flew past and landed on a leaf.* ■ In British English they say "ladybird". 👁 **See page 431.**

lagoon /ləˈguːn/ [countable noun] A lake of salt water separated from the sea by a bar of sand and rock called a reef: *Many tropical islands have lagoons.*

laid /leɪd/ Past tense and past participle forms of **lay**[2].

lain /leɪn/ Past participle of **lie**[3].

↑**lake** /leɪk/ [countable noun] A large area of water with land around it: *Lake Eyre, in Canada, is a curious lake because it sometimes disappears completely in very dry weather.*

lakeside /ˈleɪk.saɪd/ [countable noun] The land around a lake: *The couple bought a house by the lakeside.*

lamb /læm/ ▮ [countable noun] **1** A young sheep: *Twenty lambs were born on our farm this spring.* 👁 **See page 428.** ▮ [uncountable noun] **2** The meat of a young sheep: *We often have lamb for lunch on Sundays.* ■ Be careful with the pronunciation of this word. The "b" is not pronounced. ■ Compare with "sheep" (a farm animal kept for its wool, skin and meat).

lame /leɪm/ [adjective] Not able to walk well: *My dog had an accident in the road last year, and has been lame since then.*

↑**lamp** /læmp/ [countable noun] An object that gives light: *Switch the lamp on; it's getting dark.* 👁 See pictures at **bedroom** and **living room.**

lamp-post /ˈlæmp.pəʊst/ US: /-poʊst/ [countable noun] A tall, thin object in the street that has a light on the top: *Andrew broke his teeth when he bumped into a lamp-post while riding his bike.*

lance[1] /lɑːnts/ US: /lænts/ [countable noun] A long weapon held in the hand, or a knife used in surgery: *The lance used in war had a wooden shaft and a steel point.*

lance[2] US: /lænts/ UK: /lɑːnts/ [verb] To pierce or cut open: *The doctor decided to lance his patient's blister.*

↑**land**[1] /lænd/ [uncountable noun] **1** The part of the earth that is not water: *The sailors were glad to see land again after weeks at sea.* **2** A piece of ground: *My uncle's bought some land in Oregon and is going to build a house on it.*

land[2] /lænd/ [verb] To arrive on the ground after being in the air: *The plane from New York landed at Gatwick Airport at 07.00 hrs.* ■ To go into the air from the ground is "to take off".

landing /ˈlæn.dɪŋ/ [countable noun] **1** The act of arriving on land: *The helicopter made a safe landing in the field.* ■ Compare with "take-off" (the moment when an airplane leaves the ground). **2** The area at the top of the stairs you can walk on: *Go up to the* *landing; the bathroom is on the right.* 👁 See picture at **house.**

landlady /ˈlændˌleɪ.di/ [countable noun] A woman who lets people live in her house for money: *We pay the rent to the landlady every Friday.* ■ A man is a "landlord". ■ The plural is "landladies".

landlord /ˈlændˌlɔrd/ [countable noun] A man who lets people live in his house for money: *The landlord has put a telephone in the hall for the use of everyone who lives here.* ■ A woman is a "landlady".

↑**landscape** /ˈlænd.skeɪp/ [countable noun] A large area of land that you can see from a particular place: *There are some marvelous landscapes in Arizona.* 👁 **See pages 444 and 445.**

landslide /ˈlænd.slaɪd/ [countable noun] The fall of a large amount of earth: *Heavy rain sometimes causes landslides.*

↑**lane** /leɪn/ [countable noun] **1** A small road in the country: *We walked down the lane to the farmhouse.* **2** Part of a big road: *There's a special lane for bicycles on that road.*

↑**language** /ˈlæŋ.gwɪdʒ/ ▮ [uncountable noun] **1** A system of words that people say or write: *Language is what we use to communicate with each other.* ▮ [countable noun] **2** The particular words used by a certain group of people: *They say Chinese is a very difficult language to learn.* **3 bad language** Offensive words: *There's too much bad language in that movie.*

lantern /ˈlæn·tərn/ [countable noun] A glass container for a light: *The pirate lifted the lantern to see the name of the ship.*

lap /læp/ [countable noun] **1** The top of your legs when you are sitting down: *Come and sit on my lap!* **2** Going around once in a running race: *The four yards race is two laps of our sports track.*

laptop or **laptop computer** /ˈlæptɒp/ [countable noun] A small computer that you can carry round with you: *I'd really like a laptop computer for my birthday.*

↑**large** US: /lɑːrdʒ/ UK: /lɑːdʒ/ [adjective] Big, considerable in size: *A Great Dane is a very large dog.*

largely /ˈlɑrdʒ·li/ [adverb] Mostly; for the most part: *The teachers at our school are largely from this town.*

larva /ˈlɑr·və/ [countable noun] The form of an insect after coming out of the egg and before having developed completely: *Larvae look like worms and don't have wings.* ■ The plural is "larvae".

larynx /ˈlær.ɪŋks/ [countable noun] The passage in the throat taking air to the lungs: *The vocal chords are found in the larynx.* ■ The plural is "larynges" or "larynxes". 👁 **See page 425.**

laser /ˈleɪ·zər/ [countable noun] An instrument that makes a very strong line of light: *The laser beam can be used for many different things, from cutting metal to doing very delicate medical operations.* ■ Be careful with the pronunciation of this word! The "a" is pronounced the same as in the word "lake".

lass /læs/ [countable noun] A girl or a young woman: *She's a nice lass.* ■ This word is informal.

↑**last**[1] /lɑːst/ [adjective] **1** After all the others: *Who was the last person to arrive this morning?* **2** Just before now: *Last Saturday, I went to the movie theater to see "Fantasia".* ■ Be careful! We say: "We went to Memphis last year". (We don't say: "We went to Memphis the last year"). "We" only use "the" with "last" when we speak about a period of time up to the present: "I haven't been to school for the last few days". ■ Compare with "latest" (being the newest or most recent or modern. The superlative form of "late"). **3 at last** In the end, after a long time: *Hurray! Vacation is here at last.*

last[2] /lɑːst/ [verb] **1** To continue in time: *How long do you think the concert will last?* **2** To be enough for a certain time: *I hope the food lasts until Saturday; there isn't a store on the campsite.*

↑**late** /leɪt/ [adjective and adverb] **1** After the expected time: *I missed the bus and was late home.* **2** Near the end of a certain time: *My grandmother's marvelous for her age; she's in her late seventies, you know!* **3 later on** At another moment in the near future; after: *We'll have dinner later on.* ■ Be careful! "Latest" does not mean "the most late". See "latest".

↑**latest** /ˈleɪ·t̬ɪst/ [adjective] **1** The superlative form of **late. 2** The last in time in a number of things: *Have you heard their latest song? It's great!* ■ Compare with "last[1]" (after all the others or just before now). **3 at the latest** At the last possible moment: *You must give me your homework by Monday at the latest.*

Latin /ˈlæt·ə·n/ [uncountable noun] A language which was spoken by the people of ancient Rome: *Latin developed into languages like Spanish, Italian and French.* ■ Be careful! "Latin" has a capital "L".

latitude US: /ˈlæt̬.ɪ.tuːd/ UK: /ˈlæt.ɪ.tjuːd/ [noun] A position north or south of the equator that is shown on maps with lines going from east to west: *What latitude is Hawaii on?*

↑**latter** US: /ˈlæt̬.ɚ/ UK: /ˈlæt.əʳ/ [adjective] The second of two things that you have just said: *I study German and Italian, but I think the latter is easier.*

↑**laugh**[1] /lɑːf/ [countable noun] A noise that shows that you think something is funny: *Andrew has a very strange laugh; he sounds like a goat!* ■ Be careful with the pronunciation of this word. It rhymes with "scarf".

laugh[2] /lɑːf/ [verb] **1** To make a noise that shows that you think that something is funny: *James laughed so much that his stomach hurt.* **2 for a**

laugh For fun: *We put a joke cigarette in his packet of cigarettes for a laugh.* **3** to laugh your head off To laugh a lot, loudly: *When the clown ate the man's tie, we laughed our heads off.*

▸ **PHRASAL VERBS** · **to laugh at (somebody or something)** To be amused by something or somebody, often because you think they are ridiculous or stupid: *Don't laugh at him just because he is bald.*

†**laughter** US: /'læf.tɚ/ UK: /'lɑːf.təʳ/ [uncountable noun] The sound of laughing: *There was a lot of laughter coming from the classroom.*

launch[1] /lɔːnʃ/ [countable noun] A small motor boat: *Many people go out on the lake in launches in the summer.*

launch[2] /lɔːnʃ/ [verb] To send a ship into the water or a rocket into space: *Apollo 11 was launched by a Saturn V rocket from Kennedy Space Center.*

launderette or **laundrette** US: /'lɔːndrəmæt/ UK: /ˌlɔːndər'et/ [countable noun] See **laundromat.** ■ This word is British English.

laundromat /'lɔn·drəˌmæt/, /'lɑn-/ [countable noun] A place where you take dirty clothes to wash them in machines: *In the US, students often take their dirty clothes to the laundromat.* ■ In British English they say "launderette or laundrette".

†**laundry** [countable noun] The clothes that you are going to wash or that you have washed: *We hang the laundry to dry in our backyard.* ■ In British English they say "washing".

†**law** US: /lɑː/ UK: /lɔː/ [noun] **1** A rule made by a government: *The law says that all people are equal.* **2** against the law Prohibited, something that you must not do: *Fast driving along country roads is against the law.* **3** to break the law To disobey the law: *If a person breaks the law he or she may have to go to prison.*

lawful /'lɔ·fəl/ [adjective] Permitted by the law: *In Illinois, it is not lawful to sell alcoholic drink to somebody under 21.* ■ We usually say "legal".

lawn US: /lɑːn/ UK: /lɔːn/ [noun] An area of short grass: *We had our sandwiches sitting on the lawn in the park.*

lawnmower US: /'lɑːnˌmoʊ.ɚ/ UK: /'lɔːnˌməʊ.əʳ/ [countable noun] A machine that is used to cut the grass: *My mom's just bought a very light lawnmower which is very easy to use.*

lawsuit US: /'lɑː.suːt/ UK: /'lɔː.sjuːt/ [countable noun] A legal case: *My school is preparing a lawsuit against the driver who crashed his truck into the playground.*

lawyer US: /'lɑː.jɚ/ UK: /'lɔɪ.əʳ/ [countable noun] A person whose job is to help with legal problems: *The suspect demanded to see his lawyer.* ■ The same meaning: "attorney".

lay[1] Past tense of **lie**[3].

†**lay**[2], laid, laid /leɪ/ [verb] **1** To put something down: *She laid the book down on the desk.* **2** to lay an egg To produce an egg: *The hen laid four eggs this morning.* **3** to lay the table To place the plates, knives, forks and so on, on the table before you eat: *Richard, don't forget to lay the table for three.* ■ In this use, the same meaning: "to set the table".

†**layer** /'leɪ·ər/ [countable noun] Something horizontal that is between two other things: *That cake is delicious; it's got a layer of jam in the middle and a layer of cream on top.*

layout /'leɪ.aʊt/ [countable noun] **1** The way things are placed and organized in a particular site: *The layout of the new sports center was shown on the plans.* **2** The way edited material is organized on the page: *The magazine didn't change its cover layout.*

laziness /'leɪ.zɪ.nəs/ [uncountable noun] Not doing something because you don't want to make an effort: *Get out of bed right now; I've never seen such laziness!*

†**lazy** /'leɪ.zi/ [adjective] Not wanting to make an effort: *David is a very lazy boy; he never does his homework.* ■ The comparative form is "lazier" and the superlative form is "laziest".

lb A written abbreviation for the measure of weight **pound.** ■ "Lb" comes from "libra", a Latin expression. The plural is "lbs".

lead[1] /liːd/ ▮ [uncountable noun] **1** A gray metal that is very heavy: *Water pipes used to be made of lead but now they are usually made of copper.* ▮ [noun] **2** The center part of a pencil, that is used for writing: *The lead of my pencil broke, right in the middle of the test!* ■ Be careful. "Lead[1]" and "lead[2]" are not pronounced the same way.

lead[2] /liːd/ ▮ [noun] **1** Being in front or being first: *Maureen is in the lead and I think she is going to win the race.* ▮ [countable noun] **2** See **leash.** ■ This use is British English. ■ Be careful. "Lead[1]" and "lead[2]" are not pronounced the same way.

lead[3], led, led /liːd/ [verb] **1** To go in front of somebody and show the way: *You know the way, so you lead and we'll follow.* **2** To be the first or to be the best in a competition: *Janice led for most of the cycle race.* **3** To go somewhere: *This road leads straight to Denver.* ■ Be careful. "Lead[1]" and "lead[3]" are not pronounced the same way.

†**leader** /'li·dər/ [countable noun] **1** A person who directs other people: *Martin Luther King was a great human rights leader.* **2** A person who is in front of the others in a race: *The leader was ten meters ahead of the rest.*

a b c d e f g h i j k l m n o p q r s t u v w x y z

leadership /ˈli·dər,ʃɪp/ [uncountable noun] The ability to direct other people: *My father says that Mr. Smith has great qualities of leadership.*

*leading** /ˈliː.dɪŋ/ [adjective] The most important in a group: *Picasso was one of the leading artists of his time and of all time.*

lead singer [countable noun] The person in a group who sings most of the songs: *Sean is the lead singer in a very famous pop group.*

*leaf** /liːf/ [countable noun] **1** One of the flat green parts of a plant or a tree: *Some trees lose their leaves in fall.* ■ The plural is "leaves". **See pages 432 and 434.** **2 to turn over a new leaf** To begin to behave much better: *She promised to turn over a new leaf.*

leaflet /ˈliː.flət/ [countable noun] A piece of paper that gives information about something: *We gave out some leaflets in our street to tell people about our school concert.*

*league** /liːg/ [countable noun] **1** A group of teams that play sports against each other: *Our school football team is top of the league, at the moment.* **2** A union of people or countries: *The League of Nations was set up after the first World War to try to keep world peace.*

leak[1] /liːk/ [countable noun] A hole that allows liquid or gas to go through: *The explosion was caused by a gas leak.*

leak[2] /liːk/ [verb] **1** To have a hole that allows liquid or gas to go through: *The pipes have leaked and there's water everywhere.* **2** To go out through a hole: *The vinegar has leaked all over the shopping.*

lean[1] /liːn/ [adjective] With no fat or very little fat: *Runners have to be strong and lean.*

*lean**[2]**, leant, leant** /liːn/ [verb] **1** To put your body and its weight against something: *Don't lean against the wall; it's just been painted.* ■ Be careful! In this use we say: "lean **against** (something)" or "lean **on** (something)". **2** Not to be straight: *The post leans to the right.* **3** To put an object against something: *Lean your bike against the tree; it will be all right there.*

▶ **PHRASAL VERBS · to lean out of** To put the top part of your body out of something: *If you lean out of the window you can see who is ringing at the door downstairs.* ■ "Lean" also has regular past and past participle forms: "leaned".

leant Past tense and past participle forms of **lean**[2].

leap[1] /liːp/ [countable noun] A big jump: *The cat gave a big leap onto the table.*

leap[2]**, leapt, leapt** /liːp/ [verb] To give a big jump: *The wall was very high, but the dog leaped over it.* ■ "Leap" also has regular past and past participle forms: "leaped".

leapt Past tense and past participle forms of **leap**[2].

leap year [countable noun] A year in which February has 29 days: *Leap years occur every four years.*

*learn, learnt, learnt** US: /lɝːn/ UK: /lɜːn/ [verb] To get to know about something or how to do something by studying or practicing it: *I want to learn how to play the guitar.* ■ "Learn" also has regular past and past participle forms: "learned".

learner US: /ˈlɝː.nɚ/ UK: /ˈlɜː.nər/ [countable noun] A person who is getting to know about something or how to do it: *Colette is a very quick learner.*

learning /ˈlɜr·nɪŋ/ [uncountable noun] Gaining knowledge of something: *The learning of a language is a difficult thing.*

learnt Past tense and past participle forms of **learn**.

lease[1] [verb] To rent a building, office and so on: *It is very common to see signs in buildings that say "For lease".*

lease[2] [countable noun] The use of something for money: *The lease on this apartment finish the next year.*

leash [countable noun] A chain or a rope that controls a dog when it walks with a person: *Dogs should always be on a leash when they are out in the street.* ■ In British English they say "lead".

least[1] [adjective] **1** The superlative form of **little**[1]. **2** The smallest quantity of something: *It's not fair! I always get the least amount of candies!*

*least**[2] [adverb] **1** Less than all the others. The superlative form of **little**[2].: *The person who speaks the least in this class is Ray.* **2 at least** Not less than, a minimum of: *I'd like to spend at least two weeks by the sea with my cousin this year.* **3 least of all** Especially not: *You don't deserve to go out to play, least of all you, Daniel.* **4 not in the least** Not at all: *I'm not in the least worried about the test.*

*leather** /ˈleð·ər/ [uncountable noun] **1** The skin of an animal that is used to make shoes, bags and so on: *My mother gave me a pair of leather boots for my birthday.* **2 leather jacket** See "leather jacket" in the word **jacket**.

leave[1] /liːv/ [uncountable noun] A number of days' vacation for people who work: *My parents have taken a few days' leave for when we move into the new house.*

*leave**[2]**, left, left** /liːv/ [verb] **1** To go away from somebody or something: *Richard leaves home at half past seven in the morning every day.* **2** To let somebody or something stay in the same place: *Don't leave your shoes in the middle of the floor, please!* **3** Not to bring something with you: *Oh no! I've left my sneakers at home again.* **4** To give something to somebody after your death: *When my grandmother died, she left me her diamond*

ring. **5** **to leave (somebody) alone** To stop disturbing somebody: *Please, leave me alone because I want to finish this book.* **6** **to leave (something) alone** To stop touching something: *If you don't leave my bike alone, I'm going to get very angry.*
▸ **PHRASAL VERBS** · **to leave off** To stop doing something: *I can't remember where I left off reading in this book.* · **to leave (somebody or something) out** Not to include somebody or something: *The coach has left Richard out of the team for this game.*

lecture[1] /ˈlektʃər/ [countable noun] A formal talk to a group of people: *My mother went to a lecture on the new discoveries about the planet Mars on Saturday.*

lecture[2] /ˈlektʃər/ [verb] To give a talk or series of talks to a group of people: *Our neighbor lectures on pure mathematics at different universities.* ■ We say: "to lecture **on** (something)".

lecturer /ˈlek·tʃər·ər/ [countable noun] See **academic**[2]. ■ This word is British English.

led /led/ Past tense and past participle forms of **lead**.

ledge /ledʒ/ [countable noun] A narrow area at the bottom of a window: *My mother always puts plants on the window ledge.*

leek /liːk/ [countable noun] A long white and green vegetable which tastes like an onion: *The leek is an ingredient in salads and other healthy recipes.*

left[1] /left/ [adjective and adverb] **1** The opposite of right: *Go to the end of the street and turn left.* **2** **on the left hand side** On the left side: *Your heart is on the left hand side of your body.* **3** **left-handed** Using your left hand more than your right: *These scissors are specially for left-handed people.*

left[2] /left/ [noun] The side of your body that contains your heart, the direction towards this side: *In Britain and some other countries, people drive on the left, not on the right.* ■ Be careful! We always say: "**on** the left" (a la izquierda).

left[3] /left/ Past tense and past participle forms of **leave**[2].

leftover US: /ˈlefˌt̬oʊ.vɚ/ UK: /ˈleftˌəʊ.vəʳ/ [adjective] Remaining unused: *Can you give me a bag for the leftover food? I'm going to give it to my dog.*

leftovers [countable noun] Food that was no eaten during a meal and that is serve at another meal: *After Thanksgiving dinner we have leftovers for almost one week.*

left-wing /ˌleftˈwɪŋ/ [adjective] Believing in greater social changes: *My older brother is left-wing.*

leg /leg/ [countable noun] **1** A part of the body that you use for walking: *Ostriches have very long legs.* 👁 **See page 421.** **2** One of the parts of a table or a chair that enable it to stand: *That table is very original; it only has three legs.*

legal /ˈliː.gəl/ [adjective] Permitted by the law: *Did you know that in California it is legal to get married when you are 16?* ■ Be careful with the pronunciation of this word.

legally [adverb] As established by the law: *The business was set up legally.* ■ Compare with "illegally" (in a manner that is against the law).

legend /ˈledʒ.ənd/ [noun] A story from the past that is perhaps not true: *The story of Robin Hood is one of the most famous legends in history.*

legendary /ˈledʒəndəri/ [adjective] Sufficiently famous to be the subject of legend or to be much talked about: *Robin Hood is a legendary figure from the 12th century.*

leggings /ˈleg.ɪŋz/ [plural noun] Very tight elastic pants: *My mom gave me some lovely leggings to wear at my ballet class.*

legible /ˈledʒ.ɪ.bl̩/ [adjective] Clear enough to read: *Make sure that your answers are in legible writing.* ■ Be careful with the pronunciation of this word.

legislature /ˈledʒ·əsˌleɪ·tʃər/ [countable noun] The body which makes and changes laws: *The legislature decides what taxes people must pay.*

leisure US: /ˈliː.ʒɚ/ UK: /ˈleʒ.əʳ/ [uncountable noun] Free time: *I spend a lot of my leisure time reading.*

leisure center [countable noun] A place where you can do exercise or other activities: *They've opened a new leisure center in town.*

lemon /ˈlem.ən/ [noun] A yellow fruit with a very sharp taste: *Lemons need a warm climate to grow in.* 👁 **See page 436.**

lemonade /ˌlem.əˈneɪd/ [uncountable noun] A sweet drink with a lemon flavor: *Lemonade is very refreshing when you're hot.*

lemon juice [uncountable noun] The liquid that is inside the lemon: *Lemon juice is believed to be very good for colds because it contains a lot of vitamin C.*

lend, lent, lent /lend/ [verb] To let somebody have something that they will give you back later: *Can you lend me a dollar, please?* ■ Compare with "borrow" (to take or use something belonging to somebody else).

length /leŋkθ/ ▮ [noun] **1** How long something is: *The Brooklyn Bridge is 1595.5 feet in length.* ▮ [countable noun] **2** A piece of something long: *He tied it with a length of string.*

lengthen /ˈleŋk.θən/ [verb] To make something longer: *You'll have to lengthen the sleeves of that dress; they're too short.*

lengthy /ˈleŋk.θi/ [adjective] Very long, or too long: *My teacher said that my composition was rather lengthy.*

lens /lenz/ [countable noun] **1** A special piece of glass in cameras, glasses, microscopes and so on: *The* *lenses in Tom's glasses are very thick.* 👁 See picture at **glasses. 2** contact lens See **contact lens.** ■ The plural is "lenses".

lent /lent/ Past tense and past participle forms of **lend.**

lentil /'len·tə·l/ [countable noun] A small, dry seed commonly used as food: *Lentils can be cooked in many different ways.*

Leo /'li·oʊ/ [noun] A sign of the zodiac: *If your birthday is between July 21st and August 22nd, you're a Leo.* ■ Be careful! "Leo" has a capital "L".

leopard /'lep·ərd/ [countable noun] A big yellow cat with spots: *Leopards live in Africa and Asia.* 👁 See page 428.

*less[1] [adjective and pronoun] **1** The comparative form of **little**: *I have a little time for practicing my guitar, but Sue has less.* ■ This word is usually used with uncountable nouns. With countable nouns in the plural we use "fewer", the comparative of "few". **2** A smaller quantity or size of something: *My younger brother gets less pocket money than I do.*

less[2] /les/ [adverb] **1** Not so much: *My grandma says that it seems to snow less now than before.* **2** less and less Continuing to be smaller: *I don't like mathematics and I understand it less and less.*

lessen /'les.ᵊn/ [verb] To make something less, to become less: *Take some aspirin; it will lessen the pain.*

*lesson /'les.ᵊn/ [countable noun] A period when you learn something with a teacher: *We have six lessons a day at school.*

*let, let, let /let/ [verb] **1** To allow somebody to do something: *Will you let me go to the party tonight?* **2** to let go of To stop holding something: *James let go of the balloon and it floated away.* **3** to let (somebody) know To tell a person something: *When Lucy came, she phoned her parents to let them know that she was at my house.* **4** let's A word that you use for suggestions: *Let's go for a picnic.* ■ The verb after "let's" is in the infinitive without "to". "Let's" is a contraction of "let" and "us". ▸ **PHRASAL VERBS · to let (somebody) off** To give somebody no punishment: *The thief was very young and the judge let him off with a warning.*

*letter US: /'let̬.ɚ/ UK: /'let.əʳ/ [countable noun] **1** A piece of paper with a message written on it, usually sent in an envelope: *I got a letter from Jane today!* **2** A sign in writing that represents a sound: *There are twenty-six letters in the English alphabet.* **3** capital letter See "capital letter" in the word **capital.**

letterbox US: /'let̬.ɚ.bɑːks/ UK: /'let.ə.bɒks/ [countable noun] See **mailbox.** ■ This word is British English.

lettuce /'let̬·əs/ [noun] A plant with big, pale green leaves that are usually eaten in salads: *Lettuce is delicious with oil and vinegar.* ■ Be careful with the pronunciation of this word. The last part "tuce" rhymes with "kiss". 👁 See page 437.

level[1] /'levəl/ [adjective] Flat, horizontal: *The table has to be level for us to play ping-pong.*

*level[2] /'levəl/ [countable noun] A particular height or position in a scale: *In a bungalow, the rooms are all on the same level.*

lever US: /'levər/ UK: /'liːvər/ [countable noun] **1** A stick or bar for lifting heavy things: *The men used a lever to move the rock.* **2** A handle that is used to make a machine work: *Pull this lever to start the machine.*

liaison /li'eɪ,zɑn/, /'li·ə-/ ▮ [uncountable noun] **1** A working association, links: *There is a close liaison between the school and the parents.* ▮ [countable noun] **2** A short relationship: *His liaison with her was soon over.*

liar /'lɑɪ·ər/ [countable noun] A person who does not tell the truth: *I never believe a word that Brian says, he's such a liar.*

liberal /'lɪb·ər·əl/ [adjective] Generous, tolerant: *Our teacher is very liberal and he lets us say what we think about everything.*

liberate /'lɪb·ə,reɪt/ [verb] To make somebody or something free: *The soldiers liberated the city from the enemy.*

liberty /'lɪb·ər·t̬i/ [uncountable noun] Being free: *When he was released from prison he celebrated his liberty with his family.* ■ The plural is "liberties". We usually say "freedom".

Libra /'liː.brə/ [noun] A sign of the zodiac: *If your birthday is between September 23rd and October 22nd, you're a Libra.* ■ Be careful. "Libra" has a capital "L".

librarian /lɑɪ'breər·i·ən/ [countable noun] A person who looks after a place where books are borrowed: *If you want to know where to find a particular book, ask the librarian.*

*library /'laɪ.brər.i, -bri/ [countable noun] A place where you can borrow or read books: *The library in our school has all kinds of books.* ■ The plural is "libraries". ■ Compare with "bookstore" (a shop where you can buy books). 👁 See picture at **street.**

lice /lɑɪs/ The plural of **louse.**

*licence /'laɪ.sᵊnts/ [countable noun] See **license.** ■ This is a British English spelling.

*license [countable noun] A paper that gives a person official permission for something: *You need a special license to drive a truck.* ■ The British English spelling is "licence".

license plate [countable noun] A sign at the front and the back of a car, that identifies it: *We couldn't see the car's license plate in the dark.* ■ In British English they say "number plate". 👁 See page 441.

lick[1] /lɪk/ [countable noun] An upwards touch with the tongue: *The little boy gave the popsicle one lick and threw it away.*

lick[2] /lɪk/ [verb] To touch with the tongue: *The dog jumped up at me and started to lick my face.*

lid /lɪd/ [countable noun] The top part of a container that can be taken off: *I can't get the lid off this tin of paint.*

lie[1] /laɪ/ [countable noun] Something that is not true: *Every time he told a lie, Pinocchio's nose grew.*

lie[2], **lied, lied** /laɪ/ [verb] To say things that are not true: *Don't lie to me; I know you didn't go to the party!*

lie[3], **lay, lain** /laɪ/ [verb] **1** To be in a horizontal position: *Graham lay on the sofa watching television.* **2** To put something in a horizontal position: *Michael lay the kitten carefully on the bed.*

▸ **PHRASAL VERBS** · **to lie down** To get into a horizontal position: *Lie down on the sofa for a while if you're not feeling well.*

lied Past tense and past participle forms of **lie**[2].

life /laɪf/ [noun] **1** The ability to grow, to breathe and to feel: *Some people think that life exists on other planets.* **2** The time from when somebody is born to when they die: *She's had a long and busy life.* **3** Being alive: *1,513 people lost their lives when the "Titanic" went down in the Atlantic Ocean.* ■ The plural is "lives". **4 full of life** Having a lot of energy: *Those kids are so full of life that they never seem to get tired.*

lifeboat /ˈlaɪfˌboʊt/ [countable noun] A boat for saving people from danger at sea: *The lifeboat could only take ten people so the rest had to swim ashore.*

life expectancy [uncountable noun] The average period a member of a particular group or sex is likely to live: *Life expectancy varies from one country to another.*

lifeguard /ˈlaɪfˌgɑrd/ [countable noun] Person who rescues people who get into difficulties while swimming: *Is there a lifeguard on this beach?*

life jacket [countable noun] A jacket without sleeves that you put on in case of danger at sea: *Life jackets can be inflated, so that they float.*

lifetime /ˈlaɪf.taɪm/ [noun] The time that a person lives: *My grandmother says that she has seen a lot of things in her lifetime.*

lift[1] /lɪft/ [countable noun] **1** See **elevator.** ■ This use is British English. **2 to give (somebody) a lift** To offer somebody a journey in your car: *Can I give you a lift?*

lift[2] /lɪft/ [verb] To move something or somebody up: *Help me lift the sofa so that I can vacuum behind it.*

lift-off /ˈlɪftˌɔf/ [noun] The moment when a rocket goes up into the air: *The lift-off will take place in ten seconds. Ten...nine...eight.*

ligament /ˈlɪg.ə.mənt/ [countable noun] A strip of tissue which connects bones and acts as support: *The ligament is a flexible connection.*

light[1] /laɪt/ ▮ [uncountable noun] **1** The force that makes us able to see things: *There isn't much light in this room, is there?* ▮ [countable noun] **2** Something that gives us light: *I can't see very well. Can you switch on the light, please?* **3** A use of a match or lighter, to light a cigarette or cigar: *Can you give me a light?*

light[2] /laɪt/ [adjective] **1** Not dark in color, pale: *What a lovely light blue blouse you're wearing!* **2** Not heavy: *The good thing about these sneakers is that they are very light.* 👁 See picture at **opposite.** **3** Not very much: *I'm very hungry this evening because I only had a light lunch.*

light[3], **lit, lit** /laɪt/ [verb] **1** To make a cigarette, a candle or a fire begin to burn: *Oh dear! The electricity has been cut off. Let's light the candles.* **2** To focus lights on, to illuminate: *At night the castle walls are lit from below.* **3 to set light to (something)** To make something burn: *They made a big pile with the wood and set fire to it.*

light bulb [countable noun] See **bulb.**

lighten /ˈlaɪ·tə·n/ [verb] **1** To make something less heavy: *I took the books out of the bag to lighten it.* **2** To make something less dark: *Have you seen Christine's hair? She's lightened it.*

lighter /ˈlaɪ·t̬ər/ [countable noun] An object used to light cigarettes: *We gave uncle Ron a silver lighter for his birthday.*

light-hearted /ˌlaɪtˈhɑː.tɪd/ US: /-ˈhɑːr.t̬ɪd/ [adjective] Happy, not serious: *I love light-hearted movies.* ■ Be careful with the pronunciation of this word. The first "e" is not pronounced and the last "e" is pronounced like the "i" in "did".

lighthouse /ˈlaɪt.haʊs/ [countable noun] A tall building next to the sea with a lamp to guide ships: *I've always wanted to live in a lighthouse.* 👁 **See page 444.**

lighting /ˈlaɪ·t̬ɪŋ/ [uncountable noun] The system of electric light: *The lighting in this street is very bad.*

lightning /ˈlaɪt.nɪŋ/ [uncountable noun] Flash of electricity in the sky, followed by thunder: *The lightning hit a tree and broke it in two.*

like[1] /laɪk/ [adjective] The same as: *Look, their school uniform is like ours.*

like[2] /laɪk/ [preposition] **1** In the same way as: *Karen stood like a statue until the wasp flew away.* **2 what is (somebody or something) like** Used to ask for information about somebody or something: *What is Tim like?* ■ Be careful! "Like" is used for comparisons. We don't use "like" when we talk about the job or role somebody really has or had. We say: "She worked **as** a teacher for two years". Compare with "as" (used in comparisons to refer to the degree of something).

like[3] /laɪk/ [verb] To have positive feelings about somebody or something: *I really like John. He's a very good friend.*

likeable /'laɪ.kə.bl̩/ [adjective] Friendly and nice: *What a likeable person your mom is!*

likely /'laɪ.kli/ [adjective] Probable or expected: *Dad's likely to be very angry if you borrow that money without asking.* ■ The comparative form is "more likely" and the superlative form is "most likely". Be careful. We always say: "to be likely to".

lilac[1] /'laɪ.lək/ [noun] A shrub or small tree: *The lilac has aromatic, purple or white flowers.*

lilac[2] /'laɪ.lək/ [noun and adjective] A pale purple or pinkish color, like the flower of the lilac tree: *She wore a lilac blouse.*

lily /'lɪl.i/ [countable noun] A tall plant with flowers that grows from a bulb: *Lilies are often white but they are sometimes other colors.* ■ The plural is "lilies".

limb /lɪm/ [countable noun] An arm or a leg: *If you fall out of that tree, you'll break a limb.*

lime /laɪm/ ▮ [noun] **1** A small, green fruit: *Lemon and lime juice is a popular drink in United States in the summer.* ▮ [uncountable noun] **2** A white chemical: *Farmers often put lime on the earth to fertilize it.*

lime or **lime tree** /laɪm/ [countable noun] A large deciduous tree which bears limes: *The leaves of the lime tree have the shape of a heart.*

limestone /'laɪm,stoʊn/ [uncountable noun] A sedimentary rock mostly made of calcium carbonate: *Limestone is used in building and to make cement.*

limit[1] /'lɪmɪt/ [countable noun] The most that is permitted or possible: *The speed limit on this road is 55 miles per hour.*

limit[2] /'lɪmɪt/ [verb] To put a limit on: *Please limit your projects to a maximum of ten pages.*

limp[1] /lɪmp/ [noun] The way of walking of a person who has one bad leg: *Anne had an accident when she was a baby and now she walks with a limp.*

limp[2] /lɪmp/ [verb] To walk with a limp: *Simon limped slowly off the playing field.*

line[1] /laɪn/ [countable noun] **1** A long, thin mark: *Draw a line under the title and the date.* 👁 **See page 457.** **2** A number of people or things behind each other: *The line of people waiting to buy tickets was very long.* ■ In British English they say "queue". **3** A string or rope: *It's starting to rain and there are clothes on the line!* **4** A railway track: *There was a heavy fall of snow and the lines were blocked.* **5** The cable or connection for telephones or electricity: *I've phoned Janet but the line's bad and I can't hear her.* **6** Rows of writing: *I thought I'd write a few lines to you to tell you about my vacation.*

line[2] /laɪn/ [verb] **1** To cover something on the inside: *Sheila lined the drawers of her dresser with pretty paper.* **2** To form or to stand in a line: *They lined for the bus for half an hour before it arrived.* ■ In this use, we also say "line up". ■ In this use, in British English we say "queue".

linen /'lɪn.ɪn/ [noun] **1** A kind of cloth: *People wear linen in the summer because it's very cool.* **2** Things like sheets, table cloths, towels and so on: *My grandmother always bought her linen at the same store.*

liner /'laɪ·nər/ [countable noun] See **ocean liner**.

linesman [countable noun] In sport, a man who assists the referee or the umpire: *The linesman raise his flag to mark the offside.* ■ The plural is "linesmen". ■ A woman is a "lineswoman".

lineswoman [countable noun] In sport, a woman who assists the referee or the umpire: *The referee consulted the lineswoman and show a yellow card to the player.* ■ The plural is "lineswomen". ■ A man is a "linesman".

linguistic /lɪŋ'gwɪstɪk/ [adjective] Referring to language or the study of language: *Linguistic abilities are important in today's world.*

lining /'laɪ.nɪŋ/ [countable noun] The material on the inside of a piece of clothing: *I love wearing my gray coat with the red lining.*

link[1] /lɪŋk/ [countable noun] **1** Something that holds two things together: *Some companies used to seek partners to form a link between two companies.* **2** One of the pieces in a chain: *A link in my bracelet broke and I've lost it.*

link[2] /lɪŋk/ [verb] To bring two things together: *Hercules Poirot linked all the facts together and discovered that the murderer was the butler.*

lion /'laɪ.ən/ [countable noun] A large wild animal of the cat family: *The male lion has a large mane of hair around its neck.* ■ A female lion is a "lioness". 👁 **See page 428.**

lioness [countable noun] A female lion: *The lioness took her cubs to a safe place.*

lip /lɪp/ [noun] One of the two outside parts of your mouth: *They kissed each other on the lips.* 👁 See picture at **face**.

lipstick /'lɪp.stɪk/ [noun] A substance that gives color to your lips: *We put lipstick on before we went to act on stage.*

liquid[1] /'lɪkwɪd/ [noun] A substance that flows like water, milk or oil: *You should drink a lot of liquids when you have the flu.* 👁 **See page 438.**

liquid[2] /'lɪkwɪd/ [adjective] In a form like water: *Have you tried this liquid yoghurt? it's delicious.*

liquorice /'lɪk.ər.ɪs/, /-ɪʃ/ US: /-ɚ-/ [uncountable noun] A black sweet: *When my grandparents were children, liquorice was one of the few sweet things they had.*

list[1] /lɪst/ [countable noun] A number of things that are written down, one after the other: *Anthony made a list of what they needed and went shopping.*

list[2] /lɪst/ [verb] To write things down in a list: *The teacher listed the names of all those who wanted to be in the choir.*

listen /ˈlɪs.ᵊn/ [verb] To pay attention in order to hear somebody or something: *Listen to that music! Isn't it beautiful?* ■ Be careful with the pronunciation of this word! The "t" is not pronounced. ■ Compare with "hear" (to receive sounds through your ears). ■ Note that we always say: "listen **to** (somebody or something)".

listening [adjective] Referring or related to the action of paying attention to sound: *The job of the people in the listening post is to monitor telephone and internet traffic.*

lit /lɪt/ Past tense and past participle forms of **light**[3].

liter /ˈli·t̬ər/ [countable noun] A unit of capacity for liquids: *My brother drinks two liters of milk a day.* ■ The British English spelling is "litre".

literacy /ˈlɪt̬·ər·ə·si/ [uncountable noun] Ability to read and write: *Levels of literacy are relatively high in United States.* ■ Compare with "illiteracy" (the inability to read and write).

literature US: /ˈlɪt̬.ɚ.ɪ.tʃɚ/ UK: /ˈlɪt.ᵊr.ɪ.tʃəʳ/ [uncountable noun] Writing of a high quality: *I really enjoy literature classes, especially when we read poetry.*

litre UK: /ˈliː.təʳ/ [countable noun] See **liter**. ■ This is a British English spelling.

litter[1] /ˈlɪtər/ [uncountable noun] **1** Garbage thrown on the ground: *Look at all that litter in the playground.* **2** **litter bin** Container for garbage in the street: *There were a lot of litter bins on the campsite.*

litter[2] /ˈlɪtər/ [verb] To throw garbage on the ground: *The office was littered with papers.*

little[1] /ˈlɪtl/ [adjective] **1** Small, not large: *My little brother is very naughty sometimes.* ■ In this use, the comparative form is "smaller" and the superlative form is "smallest". **2** Not much: *My mom only takes a little sugar in her tea.* ■ In this use, the comparative form is "less" and the superlative form is "least". ■ Be careful with the difference between "little", that is negative, and "a little" that is positive. ■ See box at **few**.

little[2] /ˈlɪtl/ [adverb] **1** Not much: *I've got tests this month, so I'm going out very little.* **2** **a little** Quite, rather: *I'm getting a little tired of your silly jokes.* ■ The comparative form is "less[2]" and the superlative form is "least[2]". ■ See box at **few**.

little finger [countable noun] The smallest finger of the hand: *The little finger is furthest from the thumb.*

little toe [countable noun] The smallest toe of the foot: *These shoes hurt my little toes.*

live[1] /laɪv/ [adjective] Not dead: *This truck transports live animals.*

live[2] /laɪv/ [adverb] Not recorded, happening at that moment: *My aunt Jane saw Frank Sinatra live at Radio Music Hall in New York.*

live[3] /lɪv/ [verb] **1** Not to be dead: *My grandmother lived until she was eighty-eight.* **2** To have your home: *I used to live in the country, but now I live in New York City.* **3** To spend your life in a certain way: *My aunt's a pilot and she lives a very exciting life.*

lively /ˈlaɪv.li/ [adjective] Active and full of life: *Young children are usually very lively.*

liver /ˈlɪv·ər/ [noun] The organ of the body that cleans the blood: *Drinking alcohol is harmful to the liver.* **See page 424.**

livestock /ˈlaɪvˌstɑk/ [noun] Animals that live on a farm: *Farmers buy and sell livestock at fairs.*

living[1] /ˈlɪvɪŋ/ [uncountable noun] The way a person makes money to live: *My father made his living working on a ship when he was young.*

living[2] /ˈlɪvɪŋ/ [adjective] Alive, that is not dead: *Who is the world's greatest living writer?* ■ The same meaning: "alive".

living room [countable noun] The main room in a house where people sit and relax: *We usually sit in our living room in the evening and play board games or watch TV.* ■ The same meaning: "sitting-room". ■ Compare with "lounge" (a comfortable room to sit in). See picture on the following page.

lizard /ˈlɪz·ərd/ [countable noun] A small, often green, reptile with a long tail and short legs: *It is said that lizards have been on the earth for 180 million years.* **See page 430.**

load[1] /ləʊd/ [countable noun] **1** Something heavy that you have to carry: *The truck was going very slowly because its load was very heavy.* **2** Plenty, lots: *We've loads of time.*

load[2] /ləʊd/ [verb] **1** To put things in a car, a boat or other vehicle, to be carried to another place: *The children helped to load the car with everything that we needed for the vacation.* **2** To put a film into a camera: *This is a great camera; it's so easy to load.*

loaf US: /loʊf/ UK: /ləʊf/ [countable noun] A big square or round piece of bread: *Go and get two loaves from the bakery.* ■ The plural is "loaves". See picture at **bread**.

loan /ləʊn/ [countable noun] Money that a person or a bank lets you have for a period of time: *My parents got a loan from the bank to pay for our new car.*

lobster US: /ˈlɑːb.stɚ/ UK: /ˈlɒb.stəʳ/ [noun] A sea animal with a shell, a long body and eight legs: *Lobster is my favorite seafood.* See picture at **shellfish**.

LIVING ROOM

picture
bookcase
drape
lamp
fireplace
television
armchair
coffee table
rug
sofa
chair
dining table

↑local /ˈloʊ·kəl/ [adjective] Near where you live: *We all go to the local school.*

↑locate /ˈloʊ·keɪt/, /loʊˈkeɪt/ [verb] To find where something is: *We couldn't locate where the noise was coming from.*

↑location /loʊˈkeɪ·ʃən/ [countable noun] A place: *The hotel is in a lovely location; you can see the lakes from the yard.*

↑lock[1] /lɒk/ [countable noun] A metal object inside a door that keeps it closed: *Oh dear! We'll have to change the lock because I've lost the key.*

lock[2] /lɒk/ [verb] To close something using a key: *Don't forget to lock the door!*
▸ PHRASAL VERBS · **to lock up** To close a building by locking all the doors and windows: *The janitor locks up the school at about six o'clock every evening.*

locker US: /ˈlɑː.kɚ/ UK: /ˈlɒk.əʳ/ [countable noun] A small closet in a school, swimming pool and so on, that you can lock: *I keep my textbooks and binders in my locker.*

locomotive[1] US: /ˌloʊ.kəˈmoʊ.t̬ɪv/ UK: /ˌləʊ.kəˈməʊ.tɪv/ [countable noun] An engine which pulls a train of cars: *A locomotive can be powered by steam, gas or electricity.*

locomotive[2] [adjective] Referring to locomotion: *locomotive power.*

lodge /lɒdʒ/ [verb] To pay money to live in a room in somebody's house: *When I go to college in Fresno, I'm going to lodge with a friend of my mom's.*

lodger US: /ˈlɑː.dʒɚ/ UK: /ˈlɒdʒ.əʳ/ [countable noun] A person who lodges with somebody: *When all her children grew up and left home, my aunt took in a lodger.*

loft US: /lɑːft/ UK: /lɒft/ [countable noun] The space under the roof: *All my old comics are kept in the loft.*

log /lɒg/ [countable noun] A big piece of wood: *Put another log on the fire.*

logic /ˈlɒdʒɪk/ [uncountable noun] The process of reasoning about something: *Logic is used to get to a decision.*

lollipop US: /ˈlɑː.li.pɑːp/ UK: /ˈlɒl.i.pɒp/ [countable noun] A large candy on a stick: *They sell delicious strawberry lollipops in that store.* ■ "Lolly" is short for "lollipop".

lolly US: /ˈlɑː.li/ UK: /ˈlɒl.i/ [countable noun] **1** See **popsicle®**. ■ This use is short for "ice lolly". ■ This use is more common in British English. **2** See **lollipop**. ■ The plural is "lollies". ■ This use is British English.

loneliness /ˈloʊn·li·nəs/ [uncountable noun] A feeling of sadness because you are alone: *Many old people suffer from loneliness.*

lonely /ˈloʊn·li/ [adjective] Alone and sad because of it: *Since my grandpa died, my grandma has been very lonely.* ■ Compare with "alone" (without other people).

↑long[1] /lɒŋ/ [adjective] **1** With a big distance between one end and the other: *Holly has beautiful, long, red hair.* 👁 See pictures at **hair** and **opposite**. **2** **long jump** A sport where you try to jump as far as possible: *Grace is fantastic at the long jump.* **3** **no longer** See "no longer" in the word **no**[1]. **4** **not any longer** See "not any longer" in the word **not**.

long[2] /lɒŋ/ [adverb] **1** For a lot of time: *I haven't been in this school long, only about two months.* **2** **as long as** If: *You can go to the party as long as you come back before ten o'clock.* **3** **long ago** A lot of time in the past: *Long ago, people used to travel everywhere on foot or by horse.* **4** **how long?** What length of time?: *How long is the lesson? One hour or two hours?*

long[3] /lɒŋ/ [verb] To want something very much: *I'm longing for my birthday to arrive.* ■ Be careful. We say: "to long **for** (something)".

long-distance /ˈlɔŋ ˈdɪs·t̬əns/ [adjective] Going from one place to another that is far away: *My mother made a long-distance phone call to her sister to tell her about our new baby.*

longing /ˈlɔŋ·ɪŋ/ [uncountable noun] A feeling of wanting something very much: *I sometimes have a longing for chocolate. Usually every five minutes!*

longitude US: /ˈlɑːn.dʒə.tuːd/ UK: /ˈlɒn.dʒɪ.tjuːd/ [noun] A position east or west on the earth that is shown on maps with lines going from north to south: *The Greenwich meridian, an imaginary line that passes through London, has a longitude of 0 degrees.*

↑look[1] /lʊk/ [verb] **1** To turn your eyes to something so that you can see it: *Look at Mary. She is beautiful in her new dress, isn't she?* **2** To have your eyes directed at something and be paying attention to it: *What are you looking at?; I am looking at that shirt: maybe I am going to buy it.* ■ Be careful! We say: "look **at** (somebody or something)". Note also that with television we say: "I watch television". (We don't say: "I look at television"). Compare with "see" (to watch around). ■ See box at **watch**. **3** To seem to be: *You don't look very well. Are you feeling all right?; That looks difficult.* **4** To have a particular appearance: *He looks great in that jacket; She looks terrible.* **5** **to look like (somebody or something)** **1** To be similar to somebody or something: *Oliver looks just like his father.* **2** To seem to be: *That looks like a nice place for a picnic.* **6** **What does (somebody) look like?** Words that you say when you want to know about somebody's appearance: *What does Emma look like? Is she tall, dark, pretty?* **7** **to look the other way** To pretend that you don't see or know about something that should not happen: *It's not okay to look the other*

a b c d e f g h i j k l m n o p q r s t u v w x y z

way if you know they are bullying somebody in your class, tell your teacher.

▸ **PHRASAL VERBS** · **to look after** To take care of somebody or something: *Will you look after my hamster while I'm on vacation?* · **to look down on (somebody)** To think that somebody is less important than you, and treat them accordingly: *She looks down on Danny because he doesn't speak any languages.* · **to look for** To try to find somebody or something: *I'm looking for my school bag.* · **to look forward to (something)** **1** To feel happy or enthusiastic about something that is going to happen in the future: *I am really looking forward to the summer vacations; I am looking forward to seeing that movie.* **2** *I look forward to hearing from you.* ■ This phrase is used at the end of letters and formal emails. · **to look into (something)** To investigate a problem or matter: *Don't worry, I'll look into it.* · **to look out** **1** To be careful: *Look out! There is a truck coming!* **2** Referring to a window, room or part of a building, to face: *My bedroom window looks out onto the lake.* · **to look out for (somebody or something)** **1** To pay attention in order to see: *Can you look out for the mailman?* **2** To be careful of somebody or something: *Look out for the traffic coming round the corner.* · **to look (something) up** To look for information in a reference book or web site: *If you don't understand a word, look it up in your dictionary.* · **to look up to (somebody)** To admire and respect somebody you know: *She really looks up to her cousin.*

look[2] /lʊk/ [countable noun] **1** Turning your eyes to something to see it: *The teacher gave me a very surprised look when I said that I didn't know the answer.* **2** The way somebody or something appears: *I don't like the look of our cat, so I'm taking her to the vet.*

looks /lʊks/ [plural noun] How somebody's face and figure is: *Kate has everything, including good looks and intelligence.*

†**loose** /luːs/ [adjective] **1** Not well fixed: *The radio is not working very well. Maybe there's a loose wire.* **2** Not close to the body: *Loose dresses are very comfortable in hot weather.*

loosen /ˈluː.sᵊn/ [verb] To make something looser: *Loosen your tie if you are hot.*

†**lord** /lɔːd/ [countable noun] A man with a special title: *Lord Fairfax has a beautiful castle in Yorkshire.*

†**lorry** /ˈlɒr·i/ [countable noun] See **truck.** ■ This word is British English. ■ The plural is "lorries".

†**lose, lost, lost** /luːz/ [verb] **1** To stop having or not be able to find something: *I've lost the new pen that my dad gave me for Christmas; We are going to lose our teacher next year: she is retiring.* ■ Be careful! We say: "to miss the bus". We don't say: "to lose the bus". **2** To be beaten in a game or a competition: *We lost the game the other day.* **3** To have less of something that you had before: *He is losing his hair.* **4** To stop feeling interest, confidence or patience: *He lost his confidence after his girlfriend left him.* **5** **to get lost** To go somewhere and be unable to find your way: *They got lost on the way back.* **6** **Get lost!** Words you say when you want somebody to stop bothering you: *Get lost! I don't have time to listen your silly stories.* **7** **to lose it** To not be able to continue controlling anger, tears or laughter: *When my friend looked at me I just lost it: I couldn't stop laughing.* ■ This use is informal. **8** **to lose the thread** To be unable to follow a conversation or text because you can't see how it connects: *I have lost the thread: what were we talking about?* **9** **to lose the plot** To behave in a very strange way because you have lost your way in life: *Vince has lost the plot, he is always fighting.* ■ This use is informal. **10** **to lose track** To not remember something, or to no longer know what is happening: *I have lost track of the number of times I have seen that movie.* **11** **to lose weight** To become lighter or thinner: *The doctor says I need to lose some weight.* **12** **to lose your temper** See "lose your temper" in the word **temper.** **13** **you've got nothing to lose** Words you say when you want somebody to try something they think is hard to get: *You should try out for the school play, you've got nothing to lose.*

▸ **PHRASAL VERBS** · **to lose out** To not have a benefit or advantage that others have: *Terry often loses out because he is not allowed to go out at the weekend.*

loser /ˈlu·zər/ [countable noun] A person who does not win: *Frank is a very bad loser.*

†**loss** US: /lɑːs/ UK: /lɒs/ [noun] **1** Losing something: *It was a terrible loss to the family when their grandmother died.* **2** Less money coming in: *My mom's store made a loss this year and she is very worried about it.* ■ The plural is "losses".

lost[1] /lɒst/ [adjective] Not found: *I'm lost. I don't know where I am.*

lost[2] /lɒst/ Past tense and past participle forms of **lose.**

lost and found [uncountable noun] Objects that people have lost: *There are five umbrellas in the school lost and found.* ■ In British English they say "lost property".

lost property [uncountable noun] See **lost and found.** ■ This word is British English.

†**lot** US: /lɑːt/ UK: /lɒt/ [adverb] **1** Often or very much: *You have to practice a lot to be a good pianist.* **2** a

lot of Many or a large amount of something: *Harry's got a lot of books about dinosaurs.*

lotion /ˈloʊ·ʃən/ [noun] A liquid that you put on your skin or your hair: *You should always put sun lotion on if you sunbathe.*

lottery /ˈlɑt̬·ər·i/ [countable noun] A game where people buy a ticket with a number that could win a prize: *Jonathan's uncle won a lot of money on the National Lottery.* ■ The plural is "lotteries".

†**loud** /laʊd/ [adjective] Having a sound which is very easily heard: *Uncle Jim has got a very loud voice.*

loudspeaker US: /ˈlaʊdˌspiː.kɚ/ UK: /ˌlaʊdˈspiː.kəʳ/ [countable noun] A machine that makes sound loud: *Our record-player needs a new speaker.* ■ The same meaning: "speaker".

lounge /laʊndʒ/ [countable noun] A comfortable room to sit in: *The adults sat in the lounge of the hotel, while we went to play ping-pong.* ■ Compare with "living room" (the main room in a house).

louse /laʊs/ [countable noun] A small insect that lives on animals and people: *Many years ago, children often used to get lice.* ■ The plural is "lice".

lovable /ˈlʌv.ə.bl̩/ [adjective] Very nice and easy to love: *Hamish is one of the most lovable people I know.*

love[1] /lʌv/ [uncountable noun] **1** A strong emotion of liking somebody or something: *My love for you will last for ever.* **2** Somebody that you love: *Love is one of the main arguments in Hollywood.* **3** In tennis, a score of zero: *She was winning the match 40-love when rain stopped the game.* **4 to be in love with (somebody)** To love somebody in a romantic way: *My brother is in love with the girl who lives in the house next-door.* **5 to fall in love with (somebody)** To begin to love somebody in a romantic way: *My brother says that he fell in love with Melissa the first moment he saw her.* **6 with love from** How you end a letter to a friend: *"Hope everything is OK with you, with love from Lewis".*

†**love**[2] /lʌv/ [verb] **1** To have a feeling of love for somebody or something: *The husband told his wife he loved her more than any one in the world.* **2** To like something very much: *My little brother loves football.*

lovely /ˈlʌv.li/ [adjective] Beautiful or very nice: *"Gone with the Wind" is a lovely movie.*

†**lover** /ˈlʌv·ər/ [countable noun] A person who loves somebody in a romantic way: *Cleopatra and Mark Anthony were famous lovers.*

loving /ˈlʌv.ɪŋ/ [adjective] Feeling love and showing it: *Beatrice has got a very loving grandfather.*

†**low** US: /loʊ/ UK: /ləʊ/ [adjective] **1** Near the ground: *My bed is very low.* **2** Not loud: *He has such a low voice that it's quite difficult to hear what he says sometimes.* **3** Less than usual: *The prices in the sales are very low this year.* **4 to low tide** See "low tide" in the word **tide**.

low-calorie /ˌləʊˈkæləri/ [adjective] With few calories: *This is a low-calorie meal.*

lower US: /ˈloʊ.ɚ/ UK: /ˈləʊ.əʳ/ [verb] To put something nearer the ground or to make something quieter: *Lower your voices, please!*

low-fat /ˌləʊˈfæt/ [adjective] With little fat: *We always have low-fat milk in our house.*

lowland /ˈloʊ·lənd/, /-ˌlænd/ [countable noun] Land which is low and relatively flat: *Flooding can be a problem in the lowlands.*

†**loyal** /ˈlɔɪ.əl/ [adjective] Not changing in friendship or love: *Maria has always been a loyal friend to me.*

loyalty /ˈlɔɪ·əl·ti/ [uncountable noun] Being loyal: *Dogs usually show great loyalty to their owners.* ■ The plural is "loyalties".

Ltd. A written abbreviation for limited company, that is written after a name to show that it is a business: *Wainwright Ltd. have just bought that building. They are going to use it as a factory.* ■ See box at **abbreviations**.

†**luck** /lʌk/ [uncountable noun] **1** Something that brings you good or bad things in your life, by chance: *Some people believe that your luck depends on the stars.* ■ Be careful. We don't say "a luck". We say "some luck" or "a piece of luck". **2 good luck** Words you say to wish somebody success: *Good luck with your test!*

†**lucky** /ˈlʌk.i/ [adjective] Having or bringing good luck: *Alex is very lucky to be going to Disneyland.* ■ The comparative form is "luckier" and the superlative form is "luckiest".

†**luggage** /ˈlʌg.ɪdʒ/ [uncountable noun] Suitcases and bags that you take with you on a trip: *Before you get on a plane, you have to check in your luggage at the desk.* ■ Be careful with the pronunciation of this word. The "a" is pronounced like the "i" in "did".

lullaby [countable noun] A short poem or song for young children: *When I was young, my mother used to sing to me lullabies.* ■ The plural is "lullabies". ■ The same meaning "nursery rhyme".

†**lump** /lʌmp/ [countable noun] **1** A hard piece of something: *We always take some sugar lumps for the horses when we go to the farm.* **2** A swollen part of your body: *The baby had a lump on her forehead where she had bumped into the table.*

lunar /ˈluːnər/ [adjective] Referring to the moon: *The first lunar landing took place in 1969.*

lunatic /ˈlu·nəˌtɪk/ [countable noun] Somebody who behaves in a mad, foolish way: *Monica's brother drives like a lunatic.*

+**lunch** /lʌntʃ/ [noun] **1** A meal that you have in the middle of the day: *My dad made me some delicious sandwiches for my lunch today.* **2 lunch break** A time when you stop work or study to eat your lunch: *Our lunch break is at 12.30.* **3 lunch hour** A time when you stop work to rest and to eat your lunch: *My mom always does her shopping in her lunch hour.* **4 lunch time** The time when you have lunch: *Isn't it lunch time yet? I'm hungry!*

+**lung** /lʌŋ/ [countable noun] One of the two parts of the body inside your chest that you use for breathing: *Smoking is very bad for the lungs.* See page 425.

lute /luːt/ [countable noun] A stringed musical instrument with a flat front part and round back: *The lute was popular in the 17th century.*

luxurious /lɘg'ʒʊr·i·ɘs/, /lɘk'ʃʊr-/ [adjective] Comfortable and very expensive: *Michelle lives in a luxurious house in the middle of Edinburgh.*

luxury /'lʌk·ʃɘr·i/, /'lʌg·ʒɘr·i/ ▮ [countable noun] **1** Something expensive but not necessary: *It's a real luxury to have a swimming pool in the backyard.* ▮ [uncountable noun] **2** Great comfort: *Some people live in luxury while others are very poor.* ■ The plural is "luxuries".

lynx /lɪŋks/ [countable noun] A kind of wild cat: *Lynxes are about one meter long and live in the forest.*

lyrics /'lɪr.ɪks/ [plural noun] The words of a song: *Who wrote the lyrics of this song?*

m[1] The thirteenth letter of the alphabet: *The name "Martin" begins with an "M".*

m[2] **1** A written abbreviation for **meter.** ■ See box at **abbreviations**. **2** A written abbreviation for **mile.** ■ See box at **abbreviations**.

mac /mæk/ [countable noun] See **raincoat.** ■ This word is British English.

macaroni /ˌmæk·əˈroʊ·ni/ [uncountable noun] An Italian food, made of short thick tubes of pasta: *On Thursdays we have macaroni at school.*

macaw /məˈkɔː/ US: /-ˈkɑː/ [countable noun] A bird of the parrot family native to Central and South America: *The macaw has brightly colored feathers.*

†**machine** /məˈʃiːn/ [countable noun] An instrument that does a specific job: *A washing machine is used to wash clothes.*

machine gun [countable noun] A gun that fires continuously: *This machine gun fires a hundred bullets a second.*

machinery /məˈʃi·nər·i/ [uncountable noun] A group of machines or the parts of a machine: *The machinery of a clock is very complicated.* ■ The plural is "machineries".

†**mad** /mæd/ [adjective] **1** Mentally ill to an extreme degree: *The psychiatrist concluded that she was mad.* ■ The same meaning: "insane". **2** Very angry: *He was mad because his friend arrived late.* **3** **to be mad about** Be very keen on somebody or something: *Fred is mad about football.* **4** **mad cow disease** An illness that kills cows: *Sales of beef fell in March 1996 when scientists said that mad cow disease might be the cause of an illness in people.*

madam /ˈmæd.əm/ [noun] A polite way of speaking to a woman: *Excuse me, madam, can I help you?* ■ This word is formal.

made /meɪd/ Past tense and past participle forms of **make.**

†**magazine** /ˌmæg.əˈziːn/ [countable noun] A thin publication with lots of photos or drawings that has stories or articles: *Peter buys a football magazine every week.*

magenta /məˈdʒen.tə/ [noun and adjective] A color in between dark pink and red: *Magenta is one of the three colors of ink used by a printer.*

maggot /ˈmæg.ət/ [countable noun] A small worm: *Fishermen use maggots to catch fish.*

magic[1] /ˈmædʒɪk/ [adjective] **1** That has special powers: *In the story, the old man gave the boy some magic beans.* **2** Referring to magic: *Rob can do magic tricks.*

†**magic**[2] /ˈmædʒɪk/ [uncountable noun] **1** An unnatural power to make happen what you want: *In the play, the witch stopped the rain by magic.* **2** Extraordinary

a b c d e f g h i j k l m n o p q r s t u v w x y z

tricks that people do to surprise others: *The clown performed magic at the party.*

magical /ˈmædʒ.ɪ.kəl/ [adjective] **1** Mysterious and exciting: *Stonehenge is a magical place.* **2** That appears to use magic or produce it: *In the story, the fairy has magical powers.*

magician /məˈdʒɪʃ.ən/ [countable noun] A person who performs magic: *Magicians are very popular at children's parties.*

magistrate /ˈmædʒɪstreɪt/ [countable noun] A judge in a lower court: *The magistrate hears minor cases and preliminary hearings.*

magma /ˈmæg.mə/ [uncountable noun] A semi-fluid material beneath the surface of the Earth: *Magma flows from volcanoes at very high temperatures.*

magnate /ˈmægneɪt/ [countable noun] Somebody who is very rich and powerful, especially in business: *A financial magnate is able to influence governments.*

magnesium /mægˈniːziəm/ [uncountable noun] A metallic element, that has a silver color: *Magnesium is used for making light alloys.*

magnet /ˈmæg.nət/ [countable noun] A piece of metal that attracts metal things: *We have lots of magnets on our fridge door.*

magnetic /mægˈnetɪk/ [adjective] **1** Having the properties of a magnet: *A magnetic field affects metal objects within its area.* **2** Having great power of attraction: *She has a magnetic personality.*

magnetism /ˈmæg·nəˌtɪz·əm/ [uncountable noun] The property of producing magnetic attraction: *Magnetism is a form of attraction and repellence.*

magnificent /mægˈnɪf.ɪ.sənt/ [adjective] Extremely good; wonderful: *This town has some magnificent buildings.*

magnify /ˈmæg.nɪ.faɪ/ [verb] To make things look bigger than they are: *If you magnify this insect with the microscope you'll be able to see it more clearly.* ■ Be careful with the spelling of these forms: "magnifies", "magnified".

mahogany /məˈhɑ·gə·ni/ [uncountable noun] A dark wood used for making furniture: *The desk in my parent's room is made of mahogany.* ■ The plural is "mahoganies".

maid /meɪd/ [countable noun] A woman who cleans or does similar work in a hotel or a house: *The maid cleans the hotel rooms at 12.00 p.m. every day.*

maiden /ˈmeɪ.dən/ [adjective] **1** Referring to an unmarried woman: *My maiden aunt has never got married.* **2** Referring to the first time an event happens or an act is done by a particular person: *The Prime Minister's maiden speech was well received.*

maiden[1] /ˈmeɪdən/ [countable noun] A young unmarried woman: *Maiden is a term used in poetry to refer to innocent young women.* ■ A young unmarried man is a "youth". This word is now old-fashioned.

maiden name [countable noun] The last name that a woman had before she got married: *Mrs. Robinson's maiden name was Jones.* ■ In Britain and the United States when a woman marries, the custom is to take her husband's last name.

✦**mail**[1] /meɪl/ [uncountable noun] Anything that you send by post: *Yesterday I received ten letters and two parcels in the mail.*

mail[2] [verb] To send something by mail: *Didn't you get the birthday card I mailed you?*

mailbox /ˈmeɪlˌbɑks/ [countable noun] **1** A box in the street to put letters in: *The mailboxes in US are blue.* ■ In this use, in British English we say "postbox". **2** An opening in the door for letters: *When you've finished with the book, put it through my mailbox.* ■ In this use, in British English we say "letterbox".

mailman [countable noun] A man who takes letters and so on to people's houses: *What time does the mailman come?* ■ The plural is "mailmen". ■ A woman is a "mailwoman". ■ In British English they say "postman".

mailwoman [countable noun] A woman who takes letters and so on to people's houses: *The mailwoman brought this parcel for you this morning.* ■ The plural is "mailwomen". ■ A man is a "mailman". ■ In British English they say "postwoman".

✦**main** /meɪn/ [adjective] Most important: *The main road in the city is always busy.*

mainland /ˈmeɪnlənd/ [noun] The main part of a country or continent, not the islands which are near: *The ferry connects the islands with the mainland.*

mainly /ˈmeɪn.li/ [adverb] For the most part, principally: *Cows mainly eat grass.* ■ The same meaning: "mostly".

✦**maintain** /meɪnˈteɪn/ [verb] **1** To keep something in good condition: *My uncle's car is old but he maintains it well.* **2** To continue doing or having something: *Her horse took the lead at the start and maintained it until the end of the race.* **3** To look after somebody financially: *He has maintained his parents since they retired.*

maintenance /ˈmeɪn.tɪ.nənts/ [uncountable noun] Keeping something in good condition: *The maintenance of sports cars is quite expensive.*

maize /meɪz/ [uncountable noun] See **corn.** ■ This word is British English.

✦**major**[1] /ˈmeɪdʒər/ [adjective] Very important: *The major cities in most developed countries are connected by highways.*

major[2] /ˈmeɪdʒər/ [countable noun] An army officer: *The major led the attack on the enemy.*

+majority /mə'dʒɔr·ɪ·ţi/, /-'dʒɑr-/ [noun] The largest part of a group: *In the near future the majority of people will own a computer.* ■ The plural is "majorities".

make¹ /meɪk/ [countable noun] The name of the company that produced something: *What make and year is your car?*

+make², made, made /meɪk/ [verb] **1** To build or to create something: *They made a boat from wood.* ■ See box below. **2** To force somebody to do something: *She made him clean his shoes.* **3** To do something: *Can you make some tea?* **4** To earn money: *Dee makes $100,000 a year working as a singer.* **5** **to make a bed** See "to make a bed" in the word **bed.** **6** **to make sure** To be certain: *Before going to a restaurant make sure you have enough money to pay.*

PHRASAL VERBS · **to make it** To arrive in time: *I missed the bus and so I did not make it to the movies.* · **to make out** To understand or to see something that is not clear: *The telephone line was so bad that I could only just make out what she was saying.* · **to make (something) up** To invent something: *He made up so many stories that finally nobody believed anything he said.* · **to make up with (somebody)** To become friends again: *Has John made it up with Pam or are they still not talking to each other?*

make-up /'meɪk.ʌp/ [uncountable noun] A substance used on your face to make yourself look more attractive: *I only use make-up that has not been tested on animals.*

malaria /mə'leər·i·ə/ [uncountable noun] A disease caused by a mosquito bite: *In tropical countries you have to take pills to avoid getting malaria.*

male¹ /meɪl/ [adjective] **1** Referring to men and boys: *My school has a male voice choir.* **2** Referring to the sex that doesn't give birth: *Male lions have very beautiful manes.*

+male² /meɪl/ [countable noun] The sex of an animal or human that does not give birth: *Our new dog is a male. It's called Elvis.*

mall US: /mɑːl/ UK: /mɔːl/ [countable noun] A large and covered shopping area for pedestrians only: *We bought his birthday present at the mall.* ■ We also say "shopping mall", "shopping center".

mallet /'mæl.ɪt/ [countable noun] A hammer with a large head, usually made of wood: *Use the mallet to bang the stakes into the ground.*

mammal /'mæm.əl/ [countable noun] An animal that is fed on its mother's milk when young: *Humans, dogs, cats and whales are mammals.* See pages 426 and 428.

mammoth [countable noun] A large, extinct elephant: *The mammoth had a hairy coat and curved tusks.*

+man /mæn/ [countable noun] An adult human male: *There is a man with a beard waiting to see you.* ■ The plural is "men". An adult human female is a "woman".

+manage /'mæn.ɪdʒ/ [verb] **1** To direct and control a company or part of a company: *Jane has managed the family business since her father died.* **2** To succeed in doing something that is difficult: *Paul managed to move the tree that was blocking the road.* ■ Be careful with the pronunciation of this word. The last "a" is pronounced like the "i" in "did".

+management /'mæn.ɪdʒ.mənt/ [uncountable noun] **1** The activity of managing: *When I leave school, I would like to work in management.* **2** A group of people who control a company: *The management are discussing the new salaries with the workers.*

+manager /'mæn·ɪ·dʒər/ [countable noun] **1** A person who controls part of a company, or manages a store or restaurant: *She's the sales manager in an important publishing company.* ■ A woman is a "manageress". **2** A person who trains a team: *The manager bought two foreign players for the basketball team.*

manageress /ˌmænɪdʒə·r'es/ US: /'mænɪdʒərɪs/ [countable noun] A woman who manages a store or restaurant: *The manageress of the store agreed to give back the customer's money.* ■ A man is a "manager".

managing director [countable noun] The top manager in a company: *My cousin Helen is the managing director of her company.*

mandatory [adjective] Required by law or rule: *Wearing a helmet while riding a motorcycle should be mandatory.* ■ The same meaning: "obligatory".

to make* and *to do

These two words have very similar meanings but they are used differently:

- We use ***do*** when we talk about activity in general:
  - *The children aren't doing anything.*
- We use ***to make*** when we talk about building or creating something:
  - *Let's make a model airplane.*

to do	to make
to do an exam	*to make a bed*
to do good	*to make a coffee*
to do harm	*to make an excuse*
to do better	*to make money*
to do someone a favor	*to make a noise*
to do business	*to make an offer*
to do a good turn	*to make a phone call*
to do physical exercise	*to make war*
to do your best	*to make peace*
to do your homework	*to make a trip*

mandible /ˈmæn.dɪ.bəl/ [countable noun] **1** The lower of the two bones holding your mouth: *Mammals and fish have mandibles.* ■ The same meaning: "jaw", "jawbone". **2** In insects or animals, mouth parts used for biting or seizing: *Crabs have two mandibles.*

mane /meɪn/ [countable noun] The long hair on or around some animals' necks: *Philip held on to the horse's mane when he was riding.*

mango /ˈmæŋ·goʊ/ [noun] A large tropical fruit with yellow flesh and a big seed: *They sell wonderful mangoes in this market.* ■ The plural is "mangoes" or "mangos". See page 436.

mankind /mænˈkaɪnd/ [uncountable noun] The human race: *It is thought that mankind originally developed in Africa.*

*****manner** /ˈmæn·ər/ [noun] The way or the form of doing something: *I don't like it when you answer me in that manner.*

manners /ˈmæn·ərz/ [plural noun] The way of behaving in public: *The teacher complained about the bad manners of the students who were talking during his explanation.*

mantle /ˈmæn·tə·l/ [noun] **1** The role and responsibilities of somebody, that comes with a position: *She was asked to take on the mantle of Managing Director.* ■ This use is formal. **2** A covering of something: *The mountains were covered by a mantle of snow.* **3** The layer between the crust and the core of the Earth: *The earth's mantle is a rocky shell about 1,700 miles thick.* See page 449.

manual[1] /ˈmæn.ju.əl/ [adjective] Done with your hands: *Manual work is hard work.*

manual[2] /ˈmæn.ju.əl/ [countable noun] A book about how to do something: *Even after reading the manual, Peter still could not operate the machine.*

*****manufacture** /ˌmænjəˈfæktʃər/ [verb] To make things with machines: *They manufacture five hundred televisions a day in the factory.*

*****many** /ˈmen.i/ [adjective] **1** A large number: *There weren't many people on the train so it was easy to find a seat.* **2 as many as** The same number as: *I've got as many books as you.* **3 how many** Words that are used to ask about quantity with countable nouns: *How many rooms are there in this house?* ■ "Many" is used with countable nouns. Compare with "much" (used with uncountable nouns). "Many" is normally used in negative sentences and questions. For affirmative sentences we usually use "a lot of": "There were a lot of people on the train". ■ The comparative form is "more" and the superlative form is "most".

*****map** /mæp/ [countable noun] A drawing of the surface of a town, an area, a country and so on: *If you look at a map of the world you can see where all the different countries are.* See pages 450-455.

maple /ˈmeɪ.pl̩/ [noun] A tree with leaves that have five points: *The maple leaf is the national symbol of Canada.*

maraca [countable noun] A musical instrument which has a handle and a hollow container filled with beans or pebbles: *You must shake the maracas to make them sound.* See page 459.

marathon /ˈmær·əˌθɑn/ [countable noun] **1** A long distance race: *My brother once ran a marathon in two hours fifty minutes.* **2** An activity that is long and tiring: *Hugh said that the test was so long that it was like a marathon.*

marble /ˈmɑr·bəl/ ▮ [uncountable noun] **1** An expensive type of stone: *The floor and walls of the bank were solid marble.* ▮ [countable noun] **2** A small ball of glass or stone for playing with: *The children played marbles on the sidewalk.*

*****march**[1] /mɑːtʃ/ [countable noun] An organized walk in a group to protest about something: *Thousands of people attended a march through the city yesterday against the new law.*

march[2] /mɑːtʃ/ [verb] To walk with regular steps: *The soldiers marched five miles in one hour.*

*****March** /mɑːtʃ/ [noun] The third month of the year: *Sometimes Easter is in March and sometimes is in April.* ■ Be careful! "March" has a capital "M". See picture at **calendar**.

mare US: /mer/ UK: /meəʳ/ [countable noun] An adult female horse: *On the excursion we saw a beautiful mare running in a field.*

margarine /ˈmɑr·dʒə·rɪn/ [uncountable noun] A food made from vegetable oils, that is used instead of butter: *Some people prefer margarine to butter. They think it's healthier.* ■ Be careful with the pronunciation of this word.

margin /ˈmɑr·dʒɪn/ [countable noun] **1** The blank space on the sides of a page: *The teacher wrote the corrections in the margin.* **2** The extra amount added to something: *The trip normally takes one hour but we should allow a margin of an extra 20 minutes in case the traffic is bad.*

marine[1] /məˈriːn/ [countable noun] **1** A member of a military force trained to fight on land or at sea: *In the USA a marine is a member of a special force.* **2 the merchant marine** A country's commercial ships together with the people working on them: *The merchant marine can also be called the merchant navy.*

marine[2] /məˈriːn/ [adjective] Referring to the sea: *Marine life is endangered as a result of pollution.*

maritime /məˈriːn/ [adjective] Referring to the sea, to ships or to sailing: *The United States has a brilliant maritime history.*

mark[1] /mɑːk/ [countable noun] **1** A spot or a stain: *Jane returned the shirt to the store because it had a mark on it.* **2** See **grade1.** ■ This use is British English.

mark[2] /mɑːk/ [verb] **1** To read a piece of work to say how good it is: *The teacher spent the whole weekend marking the tests.* ■ The same meaning: "grade[2]". **2** To leave a spot or a stain on something: *James touched the wet paint with his arm and marked his shirt.*

marker US: /ˈmɑːr.kɚ/ UK: /ˈmɑː.kəʳ/ [countable noun] **1** Something used for marking a place: *The marker showed the distance from the starting point.* **2** A pen that draws thick lines: *You can point out that sentence underlining it with a marker.* **See page 456.**

market[1] /ˈmɑːkɪt/ [countable noun] **1** A building or open place where people buy and sell things: *Every Sunday there is a market in our town where you can buy anything from books to animals.* **2** An area in which there is a demand for something: *We are looking for a new market to sell our products.*

market[2] /ˈmɑːkɪt/ [verb] To promote the sale of something: *Large companies use famous people to market their products.*

marmalade /ˈmɑr·məˌleɪd/ [uncountable noun] A kind of jam made from sugar and oranges, lemons or limes: *I always have orange marmalade on toast for my breakfast.*

maroon /məˈruːn/ [verb] To abandon or leave somebody in an isolated place: *The sailors were marooned on a remote island by the storm.*

marriage /ˈmær·ɪdʒ/ ■ [noun] **1** Being married: *She has two children from her first marriage.* ■ [countable noun] **2** The ceremony when a man and a woman get married: *The marriage took place in a small church.* ■ In this use we usually say "wedding". ■ Be careful with the pronunciation of this word. The ending is pronounced like the ending of "fridge".

married /ˈmær·id/ [adjective] **1** Having a husband or a wife: *He is not married. He is single.* **2 to get married** To become husband and wife: *Sarah and Philip got married when they were 25 years old.*

marrow /ˈmær·oʊ/ [uncountable noun] Soft interior of bones: *bone marrow transplants.*

marry /ˈmær·i/ [verb] **1** To become somebody's husband or wife: *I've heard your sister is going to marry a famous singer.* ■ Be careful. We say: "to marry (somebody)". We don't say: "to marry **with** (some-

MARKET

body)". **2** To join two people as husband and wife: *The same priest who married John and Julie is going to marry Andrew and Rachel.* ■ Be careful with the spelling of these forms: "marries", "married".

Mars /mɑːz/ [countable noun] A planet of the solar system that is fourth in order from the Sun: *Mars is often called "the red planet" because of its reddish appearance.* 👁 **See page 446.**

marsh US: /mɑːrʃ/ UK: /mɑːʃ/ [noun] An area of land that is soft and wet: *There are many forms of animal life that live in marshes.*

marshmallow [noun] A soft and white sweet food made of sugar and eggs: *We go camping we like to roast marshmallows on the fire.*

Martian /ˈmɑːʃən/ [countable noun] Creature from the planet Mars: *Last night we watched a movie about the invasion of earth by Martians.* ■ Be careful! "Martian" has a capital "M".

marvel[1] /ˈmɑːvəl/ [countable noun] A wonderful thing: *The computer is a marvel of modern technology.*

marvel[2] /ˈmɑːvəl/ [verb] To wonder at: *The crowd marveled at the skill of the goalkeeper when he saved the penalty.*

marvelous [adjective] Wonderful: *The concert was marvelous.*

mascot /ˈmæs·kɑt/ [countable noun] An object, person or animal that people think brings good luck: *Our team mascot is a toy giraffe.* ■ Compare with "pet" (an animal that you have in the house).

masculine /ˈmæs.kjʊ.lɪn/ [adjective] With qualities traditionally considered appropriate to men or typical of men: *My grandmother likes that singer because she says he is very masculine.*

mash /mæʃ/ [verb] To crush and mix something until it is soft: *Can you mash the potatoes for me, please?*

mashed potato [uncountable noun] Potato that is cooked and then crushed and mixed until soft: *Mashed potato is usually eaten with meat.*

mask /mɑːsk/ [countable noun] Something that covers the face: *The robbers wore masks so that nobody could recognize them.*

mason /ˈmeɪ.sən/ [countable noun] A person who cuts or builds with stone: *A mason is a skilled worker.*

†**mass** /mæs/ ▮ [countable noun] **1** A large quantity of something: *A mass of people blocked the road for a while after the football game.* **2** A solid piece of something: *A mass of rock fell from the mountain and blocked the road.* ▮ [noun] **3** A religious ceremony for Catholics: *Many Catholics go to mass every Sunday.* **4 mass media** See **media**. ■ The plural is "masses".

massacre[1] /ˈmæsəkər/ [countable noun] The killing of a large number of people or animals: *The bombs were responsible for the massacre of two thousand innocent people.*

massacre[2] [verb] To kill a large number of people or animals: *The soldiers of the retreating army were massacred.*

massage[1] US: /məˈsɑːdʒ/ UK: /ˈmæsɑːdʒ/ [noun] Rubbing and pressing the body to take away pain or tension: *After typing for a long time Jane always needs a massage to relieve her backache.* ■ Be careful with the pronunciation of this word.

massage[2] [verb] To rub and to press the body to take away pain and tension: *After he massaged her neck she felt no pain at all.* ■ Be careful with the pronunciation of this word!

masseur /mæˈsɜr/ [countable noun] A man who gives massages: *The masseur cured my father's shoulder problem.* ■ A woman who gives massages is a "masseuse".

masseuse /mæˈsuz/ [countable noun] A woman who gives massages: *She's a great masseuse. She has wonderful hands.* ■ A man who gives massages is a "masseur".

†**massive** /ˈmæs.ɪv/ [adjective] Very big: *There was a massive crowd outside the movie theater.*

mast US: /mæst/ UK: /mɑːst/ [countable noun] A tall post that supports the sails on a boat: *The wind was so strong that the mast broke.*

†**master**[1] /ˈmɑːstər/ [countable noun] **1** A man who is the owner of an animal: *The dog goes for a walk with its master every day.* **2** A person who is very good at something: *This painting is the work of a master.*

master[2] /ˈmɑːstər/ [verb] To become good at something: *He had mastered three languages by the time he was fifteen.*

mastermind /ˈmæs·tərˌmaɪnd/ [countable noun] A person who develops a plan: *The mastermind of the robbery was put in jail for twenty years.*

masterpiece /ˈmæs·tərˌpis/ [countable noun] An extremely good book, painting, sculpture and so on, which is considered to be one of the best: *"Citizen Kane" is a masterpiece of the movies.*

mat /mæt/ [countable noun] **1** A piece of strong material that covers a part of the floor, for example next to a door: *We had to wipe our feet on the mat before entering the house.* **2** A small piece of material that is put under plates or glasses on a table: *Put that hot plate on a mat. Don't put it directly on the table.*

†**match**[1] /mætʃ/ [countable noun] **1** A game between two sides: *What time did the volleyball match start?* **2** A small thin stick of wood that produces a flame: *We'll need a match to light the candles on the cake.* ■ In this use, "match" is short for "matchstick". ■ The plural is "matches".

match[2] /mætʃ/ [verb] To go with or to make something go with something else: *Those armchairs don't match the drapes.*

matchstick /'mætʃ.stɪk/ [countable noun] See **match**[1].

†**mate** /meɪt/ [countable noun] A friend or somebody you work or study with: *My mates have all got computers.* ■ This word is British English. ■ This word is informal.

†**material** /mə'tɪr·i·əl/ [countable noun] **1** Something which can be used for making something: *What materials do you need to make the chair?* **2** Cloth: *I have bought some beautiful material to make a skirt.*

math [uncountable noun] See **mathematics**.

mathematical /ˌmæθ·ə·'mæt̬·ɪ·kəl/ [adjective] Referring to mathematics: *She is a mathematical genius.*

mathematician /ˌmæθəmə'tɪʃən/ [countable noun] Somebody who teaches or does research in mathematics: *The mathematician is at home in the abstract world of numbers.*

mathematics /ˌmæθ·ə'mæt̬·ɪks/ [uncountable noun] The science of numbers and measurements: *He is studying mathematics.* ■ "Math" is short for "mathematics".

†**matter**[1] /'mætər/ ▮ [countable noun] **1** A subject or a situation that you must think about and give your attention to: *There are several important matters we should discuss.* ▮ [noun] **2** All physical substances: *Matter can be divided into solids, liquids or gases.*

matter[2] /'mætər/ [verb] To be important: *Does it matter if I am a little late tomorrow?*

mattress /'mæt.rəs/ [countable noun] The soft part of a bed on which we sleep: *We need a new mattress. The springs in this one make too much noise.* ■ The plural is "mattresses".

mature /mə'tʃʊr/, /-'tʊr/ [adjective] Fully developed, with an adult attitude: *Although she is young, she is very mature for her age.*

†**maximum** /'mæk.sɪ.məm/ [countable noun] The largest possible quantity: *$75 is the maximum I'm willing to pay for those sneakers.*

may /meɪ/ [verb] **1** A word that is used to say that something is possible but not certain: *I don't know what I'm going to do tonight, but I may go out.* ■ The same meaning: "might[1]". **2** A word that is used to ask for permission and give it: *May I go to the restroom, Mr. Norton?* ■ See box below.

†**May** /meɪ/ [noun] The fifth month of the year: *The fields are covered with flowers in May.* ■ Be careful! "May" has a capital "M". 👁 See picture at **calendar**.

†**maybe** /'meɪ.bi, ˌ-'-/ [adverb] Perhaps: *Maybe I'll do it, but I need to think it over.*

mayday /'meɪ.deɪ/ [noun] International call for help over the radio: *The ship sent a Mayday message when it hit the rock.*

mayonnaise /ˌmeɪ.ə'neɪz/ [uncountable noun] A cold yellow sauce made with eggs: *I love eating asparagus with mayonnaise.*

†**mayor** US: /mer/ UK: /meəʳ/ [countable noun] The leader of a town or a city council: *The mayor is coming to open the new city theater.* ■ A woman leader of a town or a city council can also be called a "mayoress". ■ Be careful with the pronunciation of this word! The "y" is not pronounced.

mayoress US: /'mer.ɪs/ UK: /ˌmeə'res/ [countable noun] A woman who is the leader of a town or city council, or the wife of the leader: *The mayoress opened the new school.*

maze /meɪz/ [countable noun] A complicated arrangement of paths: *When we visited Longleat, James got lost in the maze.* ■ The same meaning: "labyrinth".

M.D. Referring to somebody who has a degree to work as a doctor: *William Stosur, MD.* ■ "M.D." is an abbreviation for "Doctor of Medicine". ■ See box at **abbreviations**.

†**me** /miː, mɪ/, /miː/ [pronoun] A word used for "I", usually when it is the object of a sentence: *Rajiv phoned me and told me the whole story.*

mead /miːd/ [uncountable noun] An alcoholic drink made from fermented honey and water: *Mead was a popular drink in the Middle Ages.*

meadow /'med·oʊ/ [noun] A field of grass: *The farmer took his cows to graze in a meadow.*

†**meal** /mɪəl/ [countable noun] Each of the times when we normally have food: *Breakfast, lunch and dinner are the usual meals.* ■ Be careful! Do not confuse with "meat" (the flesh from animals that we eat).

mean[1] /miːn/ [adjective] That is not generous, unkind: *She's really mean. She never buys her brother anything for his birthday.*

†**mean**[2], **meant, meant** /miːn/ [verb] **1** To say what the meaning of something is: *"Butterfly" means "Mariposa" in Spanish.* **2** To plan or to want to do something: *I think he means to give a surprise party.* **3 to mean a lot to (somebody)** To be very important to somebody: *Paul means a lot to me. He's my best friend.*

meander[1] /mi'ændər/ [verb] **1** Talking of a river or road, to have lots of curves or changes of direction: *The river meanders through the valley.* **2** To walk slowly, in no particular direction: *We meandered through the town admiring the view.*

may* and *might

May and ***might*** do not change in form. The verb that follows them is in the infinitive without *to*:

- *You might not pass your exam.*
- *May I go to the restroom?*

meander[2] [countable noun] The curve of a river: *Meanders are formed when a river erodes alternate sections of its banks.* 👁 **See page 445.**

ᐩ**meaning** /'miː.nɪŋ/ [noun] What something means or refers to: *Do you know the meaning of "yacht"?*

ᐩ**means** /miːnz/ [noun] **1** A way of doing something: *Is there any means of knowing when they will come?* ■ This use is formal. We usually say "way" or "method". **2** Money: *My family doesn't have the means to send me to Europe in the summer.* **3 by means of (something)** Using something: *They managed to get out of the burning building by means of a rope.* **4 by no means** In no way at all: *It is by no means clear what we'll do tomorrow.* **5 means of transport** A way of going somewhere: *The train is my favorite means of transport.* ■ The plural is "means".

meant /ment/ Past tense and past participle forms of **mean**[2].

meantime /'miːn.taɪm/ **in the meantime** In the time between two events: *I'd like to go to college, but in the meantime I've got a job at a gas station.*

ᐩ**meanwhile** /'miːn.waɪl/ [adverb] At the same time that something else is happening: *Have a wash. Meanwhile, I'll set the table.*

measles /'miː.zl̩z/ [uncountable noun] An infectious disease that causes red pimples on your skin: *When Cindy had measles, she had to stay in bed for two weeks.*

measure[1] /'meʒər/ [noun] **1** A way of showing the length, size and so on of something: *The mile is still a measure for distance in United States.* **2 tape measure** See **tape measure**.

ᐩ**measure**[2] /'meʒər/ [verb] **1** To find out the length, size and so on of something: *We'll have to measure that table. I think it's too big for our living room.* **2** To have a certain length: *How much does that bed measure?*

ᐩ**measurement** /'meʒ·ər·mənt/ [countable noun] The length, size and so on of something: *We need to know the measurements of the furniture.*

ᐩ**meat** /miːt/ [uncountable noun] The flesh from animals, that we eat: *Vegetarians do not eat meat.* ■ Be careful! Do not confuse with "meal" (each of the times when we normally have food).

meatball /'mit,bɔl/ [countable noun] Food made of ground meat shaped like balls: *My brother makes wonderful meatballs.*

mechanic /mə'kæn.ɪk/ [countable noun] A person who repairs machinery: *The mechanic said that there was something wrong with the engine.*

mechanical /mə'kæn.ɪ.kəl/ [adjective] That works with machinery: *When I was a kid I had lots of mechanical toys.*

mechanize or **mechanise** /'mek.ə.naɪz/ [verb] To introduce machines: *The management of the factory decided to mechanize the production process.*

medal /'med.əl/ [countable noun] A piece of metal that is given as a prize to somebody: *I won a silver medal at the swimming championship.*

ᐩ**media** /'miː.di.ə/ [noun] Means of communication like newspapers, television and radio, which reach a large number of people: *Television is the most popular media of all.* ■ Be careful with the pronunciation of this word! ■ This word can be used with either a singular or a plural verb: "The media is/are often criticized". ■ We also say "mass media".

medical /'med.ɪ.kəl/ [adjective] Referring to health treatment: *Spike is a medical student.*

ᐩ**medicine** /'med.ɪ.sən/ ▮ [uncountable noun] **1** The treatment of illness: *Medicine has advanced a lot in the last twenty years.* ▮ [noun] **2** A substance that is used to cure an illness or to relieve symptoms: *Take this medicine three times a day.*

medieval /ˌmed.i'iː.vəl/ [adjective] Referring to the Middle Ages: *Cathedrals like Chartres, York or Burgos were among the greatest achievements of medieval civilization.* ■ Be careful with the pronunciation of this word.

Mediterranean /ˌmed.ɪ.tə'reɪ.ni.ən/ [adjective] Referring to the Mediterranean Sea or to the region around it: *Spain and Italy are Mediterranean countries.* ■ Be careful! "Mediterranean" has a capital "M". Be careful with the pronunciation of this word! "ran" is pronounced like "rain".

ᐩ**medium** /'miː.di.əm/ [adjective] Average or middle: *She's not very tall. She's medium height.*

ᐩ**meet, met, met** /miːt/ [verb] **1** To get together with another person or other persons: *The class representatives met last week to discuss the new discipline rules.* **2** To get to know somebody: *I'd like to meet somebody famous; I first met Sarah two years ago.* **3** To see somebody by chance: *We met Tom and Bruce in the movie theater yesterday, and they were very surprised to see us.* ■ Compare with "find" (to look for and locate somebody). **4** To join: *The angle where two pieces meet should be 90º.* **5** Referring to needs, requirements, conditions or demands, to satisfy, achieve or fulfill: *The government refused to meet the trade unions' demands.* **6 to meet your match** To be good at something but to have to compete with somebody who is better than you: *Christine is good at tennis but she has met her match with Jane, Jane beats everyone.*

ᐩ**meeting** /'mi·t̬ɪŋ/ [countable noun] A gathering of people: *At the meeting, the class representatives decided not to accept the new rules.*

megalith /'meg.ə.lɪθ/ [countable noun] A large, upright stone placed as a monument: *In the neolithic era* *people made large stone monuments called megaliths, some of which were used as tombs.*

melody /ˈmel.ə.di/ [noun] A song or a tune: *Tchaikovsky wrote great melodies.* ■ The plural is "melodies".

melon /ˈmel.ən/ [noun] A very large fruit that is green or yellow outside: *Melon is my favorite fruit in the summer.* 👁 **See page 436.**

melt /melt/ [verb] To change something from solid to liquid by heating it: *First you melt the butter and then you add the flour.*

melting [uncountable noun] The transformation of a solid into liquid: *the melting of ice.* 👁 **See page 438.**

†**member** /ˈmem·bər/ [countable noun] Somebody who belongs to a group or category: *We are going to start a campaign to get more members for our skating club.*

†**membership** /ˈmem·bərˌʃɪp/ [uncountable noun] The act of belonging to a club: *Membership of the swimming club gives you the right to two free sessions a month.*

membrane /ˈmembreɪn/ [countable noun] An organic tissue that covers an organ or acts as a separation between two cavities: *The membrane serves as the boundary.*

memorial /məˈmɔr·i·əl/, /-ˈmoʊr-/ [countable noun] A monument built in honor of an important event or person: *Have you seen the Walter Scott Memorial in Edinburgh?*

†**memory** /ˈmem·ər·i/ ▮ [noun] **1** The power to remember things: *I can't remember where I've seen her before. I have a really bad memory for faces.* ▮ [countable noun] **2** Something from the past that you remember: *I have wonderful memories of the vacation I spent in France.* ■ The plural is "memories".

men /men/ The plural of **man**.

menace /ˈmen.ɪs/ [countable noun] **1** Something that can be a danger: *I wouldn't like to live with the menace of invasion from space.* **2** Somebody who is a trouble: *That boy is a menace! He destroys everything.* ■ This use is informal.

mend /mend/ [verb] To repair: *Can you mend these shoes?*

menhir [countable noun] A tall, upright stone, often carved: *In Prehistoric times the menhir served as a monument.*

meningitis /ˌmenɪnˈdʒaɪtɪs/ [uncountable noun] An illness that produces a swelling of the tissues around the brain and the spinal cord: *Meningitis is caused by an infection.*

meninx [countable noun] One of the membranes surrounding the central nervous system: *The main function of the meninges is to protect the central nervous system.* ■ The plural is: "meninges".

†**mental** /ˈmen·tə·l/ [adjective] Referring to the mind, in the mind: *My dad is great at mental arithmetic.*

†**mention** /ˈmen.tʃən/ [verb] **1** To refer to somebody or something in a conversation, speech, article and so on: *Mr. Thomson mentioned Paul and Sheila in his speech.* **2 don't mention it** A polite way of answering when somebody says "thank you": *"Thanks for your help". "Don't mention it".*

†**menu** /ˈmen.juː/ [countable noun] **1** A list of the food and drinks served in a restaurant or a café: *Waiter, can you bring us the menu, please?* **2** A list of choices in a computer program, shown on the screen: *To get the menu on your screen press this key.* ■ Be careful with the pronunciation of this word.

meow [verb] To make the sound that a cat makes when for example it wants something: *I can't sleep well. There are always cats meowing.* 👁 See picture at **animal**.

merchant /ˈmɜr·tʃənt/ [countable noun] A person who sells something, usually in large quantities: *Sarah's uncle is a very rich coal merchant.*

merciful /ˈmɜr·sɪ·fəl/ [adjective] That is kind or forgiving to people who are in a bad situation or who have done wrong: *He was a very merciful Priest.*

Mercury /ˈmɜːkjəri/ [countable noun] A planet of the solar system that is first in order from the Sun: *Mercury is the smallest planet in the solar system.* 👁 **See page 446.**

mercy /ˈmɜr·si/ [uncountable noun] Being kind or forgiving to people who are in a bad situation or who have done wrong: *The main character in the movie showed no mercy to his enemies.* ■ This word is usually singular. ■ The plural is "mercies".

†**mere** US: /mɪr/ UK: /mɪəʳ/ [adjective] Only, simple: *It was a mere coincidence that we both bought the same type of pants.*

merely /ˈmɪəli/ [adverb] Simply, only: *Giving your name and ID number at the entrance is merely a formality.*

merge US: /mɝːdʒ/ UK: /mɜːdʒ/ [verb] To join together: *The two soccer clubs in my town are going to merge into one.*

meridian[1] /məˈrɪd.i.ən/ [countable noun] **1** An imaginary line on a map which goes from the north to the south pole: *The meridian helps to establish location.* 👁 **See page 449.** **2** In astronomy, an imaginary circle connecting the pole stars: *The meridian was used to determine the route of sea voyages.* **3** The peak or zenith of something: *the meridian of her success.* ■ This use is formal.

meridian[2] [adjective] **1** Referring to a meridian: *meridian points.* **2** Referring to midday: *the meridian hour.* ■ This word is formal.

meringue /məˈræŋ/ [noun] A type of very light sweet made of eggs and sugar: *There was a thick layer of*

a b c d e f g h i j k l m n o p q r s t u v w x y z

meringue on top of the cake. ■ Be careful with the pronunciation of this word! The ending "ringue" rhymes with "kang" in "kangaroo".

merit /'merɪt/ [noun] The quality of deserving praise, something good: *I don't think there's any merit in doing this puzzle. It's so easy.*

mermaid /'mɜr,meɪd/ [countable noun] An imaginary being, half girl and half fish: *Have you seen the statue of the Little Mermaid in Copenhagen?*

merrily [adverb] **1** Done in an openly happy way: *They walked merrily down the road, singing a song.* **2** Done without thinking or worrying about possible consequences: *He has been merrily driving his truck for years without any lights.*

merry /'mer.i/ [adjective] Happy, cheerful: *Terry's family are a merry group of people.* ■ It is now more common to say: "happy" or "good fun" except in the expression "Merry Christmas".

merry-go-round /'mer·i·goʊ,raʊnd/ [countable noun] A fair ride on which children go round on wooden horses, cars and so on: *When I was 4 years old, I spent a whole afternoon going round on a merry-go-round.*

MERRY-GO-ROUND

mesosphere [uncountable noun] The layer of the atmosphere which is above the stratosphere: *The mesosphere starts at about 30 miles above the earth's surface.* See page 449.

†**mess[1]** /mes/ [uncountable noun] **1** Something dirty or untidy: *Your room is a mess, John. Tidy it up.* **2** A situation full of problems: *I'm in a mess. My girlfriend's left me and I've failed all my tests.*

MESS

mess[2] **1 to mess around** To spend your time without doing anything useful or serious: *Stop messing around and do some work.* **2 to mess (something) up** To spoil something or to make it untidy: *Vanessa, you've messed up all our plans by arriving so late!*

†**message** /'mes.ɪdʒ/ [countable noun] Information sent to somebody: *I've got a message for you from Louise.* ■ Be careful with the pronunciation of this word. The "a" is pronounced like the "i" in "did".

messenger /'mes·ən·dʒər/ [countable noun] The person who carries a message: *The Captain sent a messenger to the General telling him to send more soldiers.*

messy /'mes.i/ [adjective] That is dirty or untidy: *I had to do my homework again because it was a bit messy.* ■ The comparative form is "messier" and the superlative form is "messiest".

met /met/ Past tense and past participle forms of **meet**.

metacarpal[1] [adjective] Referring to the metacarpus: *The pain in her hand was diagnosed as metacarpal.*

metacarpal[2] [countable noun] Any of the five bones of the hand between the wrist and the phalanges: *Metacarpals are flat at the back of the hand and bowed on the palm.*

metacarpus [countable noun] Five long bones that form the part of the hand between the phalanges and the carpus: *The equivalent of the metacarpus in the foot is the metatarsus.* ■ The plural is: "metacarpi".

†**metal** /'met̬·ə·l/ [noun] A hard substance like iron or gold for example: *Metal is used a lot in industry.*

metallic /mə'tæl.ɪk/ [adjective] **1** Referring to metal: *His new guitar makes a very metallic sound.* **2** Like a metal in appearance: *My mother's car is metallic blue.*

metallurgical /,met.əl'ɜː.dʒɪ.kəl/ US: /,met̬.əl'ɜːr-/ [adjective] Referring to the scientific study of metals: *Metallurgical engineers study the properties and uses of metals.*

metalworker [countable noun] Somebody who works with metal: *The number of metalworkers is much smaller now.*

metamorphic /,met̬·ə'mɔr·fɪk/ [adjective] Relating to a change into a very different form: *metamorphic rocks.*

metamorphosis /,metə'mɔːfəsɪs/ [countable noun] The change into something very different in form or nature: *the metamorphosis of the tadpole into a frog.*

metatarsal /,met.ə'tɑː.səl/ US: /,met̬.ə'tɑːr-/ [adjective] Referring to the metatarsus: *A metatarsal fracture is a common problem for runners.*

metatarsus [countable noun] The five bones in the foot located between the tarsal bones and the phalanges of the toes: *The metatarsus forms one end of the arch of the foot.* ■ The plural is "metatarsi".

meteor [countable noun] A piece of rock that burns and shines in the sky when it comes in contact with the earth's atmosphere from outer space: *On August nights when there is a meteor shower you can see many shooting stars.*

meteorite /ˈmi·t̬i·əˌrɑɪt/ [countable noun] A fragment of rock or metal which is the remains of a meteor that has fallen to earth: *If a meteor burns up completely, no meteorite reaches earth.*

meteorology [uncountable noun] The study of the processes and phenomena of the earth's atmosphere: *Meteorology is used to forecast the weather.*

†**meter** /ˈmi·t̬ər/ [countable noun] **1** A unit of length: *There are a thousand meters in a kilometer.* ■ The abbreviation "m" is only used in written language. See box at **abbreviations**. ■ In this use, the British English spelling is "metre". **2** An instrument for measuring the quantity that somebody has used of something: *The electricity company reads the meters every three months.*

†**method** /ˈmeθ.əd/ [countable noun] A way of doing something: *What's your method for learning vocabulary so quickly?*

†**metre** UK: /ˈmiː.təʳ/ [countable noun] See **meter**. ■ This is a British English spelling. ■ The abbreviation "m" is only used in written language. Be careful with the pronunciation of the last syllable of this word. The "e" is not pronounced.

metric /ˈmet.rɪk/ [adjective] Referring to a system of measurement that is based on the number ten: *Meters, liters and kilograms are part of the metric system.*

Mexican[1] [adjective] Referring to Mexico: *I love Mexican food.* ■ Be careful! "Mexican" has a capital "M".

Mexican[2] [countable noun] A person from Mexico: *My uncle is married to a Mexican and they live in Villahermosa.* ■ Be careful! "Mexican" has a capital "M".

mg A written abbreviation for **milligram**. ■ See box at **abbreviations**.

mice /maɪs/ The plural of **mouse**.

micro- /maɪkrəʊ-/ [prefix] An addition to the beginning of a word that usually means "small": *"Microchip" and "microwave" are words that contain the prefix "micro-".* ■ Be careful with the pronunciation of this word! "mi" rhymes with "my".

microbe /ˈmɑɪ·kroʊb/ [countable noun] A very small living thing that can only be seen with a microscope: *Some microbes are extremely dangerous.* ■ Be careful with the pronunciation of this word! "mi" rhymes with "my" and the second "e" is not pronounced.

microchip /ˈmaɪkrəʊtʃɪp/ [countable noun] See **chip**.

microorganism /ˌmɑɪ·kroʊˈɔr·gəˌnɪz·əm/ [countable noun] A microscopic organism: *Bacteria and viruses are microorganisms.* ■ Be careful with the pronunciation of this word! "mi" rhymes with "my".

microphone /ˈmɑɪ·krəˌfoʊn/ [countable noun] An instrument for making sound louder or for recording sounds: *If you use the microphone, we'll hear you better.* ■ "Mike" is informal for "microphone".

microscope /ˈmɑɪ·krəˌskoʊp/ [countable noun] An instrument for seeing very small things: *At school today we studied drops of blood through the microscope.* 👁 **See pages 440 and 443.**

microscopic /ˌmaɪkrəˈskɒpɪk/ [adjective] So small that it cannot be seen with the eye alone: *Microscopic objects can only be seen when magnified.*

microwave or **microwave oven** /ˈmaɪkrəʊweɪv/ [countable noun] An oven that cooks food very quickly: *In a microwave oven you can heat a meal in two minutes.* 👁 See picture at **kitchen**.

†**midday** /ˌmɪdˈdeɪ/ [uncountable noun] Twelve o'clock a.m.: *This lesson finishes at midday.*

middle[1] /ˈmɪdl/ [adjective] Central, half way between two things: *Patsy is the middle daughter.*

†**middle**[2] /ˈmɪdl/ [noun] **1** The central part of something, in or near the center: *The table was in the middle of the room.* **2 to be in the middle of** Being busy doing something: *I'm in the middle of preparing dinner. Can you phone back later?* **3 the Middle Ages** The period in European history between about 1000 and 1500 CE: *Many castles were built in the Middle Ages.* ■ Be careful! "the Middle Ages" has capital letters. **4 middle school** In the United States, a school for children between eleven and fourteen years old: *Sixth, seventh, and eighth grades are the grades you are in middle school.* ■ In this use, the same meaning: "junior high", "junior high school".

middle-aged /ˌmɪd.l̩ˈeɪdʒd/ [adjective] A person who is between 40 and 60 years old: *I think Joan's parents are middle-aged. Her dad must be about 45.*

middle finger [countable noun] The third finger of the hand: *The middle finger is the longest one.*

middle name [countable noun] A name between somebody's first name and their last name: *She won't tell anybody her middle name because she doesn't like it, but I think it's Agnes.*

midfield player [countable noun] Player in a middle position of the sports field: *He plays as a midfield player in the school team.*

†**midnight** /ˈmɪd.naɪt/ [uncountable noun] Twelve o'clock at night or p.m.: *You can have a party at home, but only until midnight.*

midwife /ˈmɪd.waɪf/ [countable noun] A person trained to help women give birth: *Our neighbor is a midwife.* ■ The plural is "midwives".

†**might**[1] /maɪt/ [verb] A word that is used to say that something is possible but not certain: *I might go*

to the movies tonight if I finish my homework. ■ Be careful! The verb after "might" is in the infinitive without "to". ■ The same meaning: "may". ■ See box at **may**.

might[2] /maɪt/ [uncountable noun] Power, force: *He fought with all his might to try to beat his opponent.*

mighty /ˈmaɪ·t̬i/ [adjective] Powerful: *Genghis Khan was a mighty king.* ■ The comparative form is "mightier" and the superlative form is "mightiest".

migrate US: /ˈmaɪgreɪt/ UK: /maɪˈgreɪt/ [verb] **1** Referring to animals, to move from one place to another because of the climate or possibilities of finding food: *Some birds migrate enormous distances every year.* **2** Referring to groups of people, to move from one place to another temporarily: *In times of crisis, many people migrate in search of work.* ■ In this use, the same meaning: "emigrate".

migratory US: /ˈmaɪgrətɔːri/ UK: /ˈmaɪgreɪtəri/ [adjective] Related to the habit of moving from one place to another: *Migratory birds travel to different countries, or continents, according to the season.*

mike /maɪk/ [countable noun] See **microphone.** ■ This word is informal.

↑**mild** /maɪld/ [adjective] **1** Not hot, not cold: *We had very mild weather last December.* **2** Gentle, not aggressive: *That child has a very mild nature.* **3** Not too hot, when talking about spicy food: *I like mild curries, I don't like hot ones.*

↑**mile** /maɪl/ [countable noun] A unit of length: *There are 1,609 meters in a mile.* ■ The abbreviation "m" is only used in written language. See box at **abbreviations**.

↑**military** /ˈmɪl·ɪˌter·i/ [adjective] Referring to the armed forces: *All the injured soldiers were taken to a military hospital.*

↑**milk**[1] /mɪlk/ [uncountable noun] **1** The white liquid produced by female mammals to feed their young: *Milk contains a lot of protein.* **2 skimmed milk** Low fat milk: *I always drink skimmed milk.*

milk[2] /mɪlk/ [verb] To take milk from an animal, usually a cow, sheep or goat: *The farmer gets up at six in the morning to milk the cows.*

milkman /ˈmɪlk.mən/ [countable noun] A man who delivers milk and other basic products to homes from a van: *Our milkman brings us milk and eggs each morning.* ■ The plural is "milkmen".

milk shake /ˈmɪlkʃeɪk/ [noun] A drink made from milk and flavors: *Strawberry milk shake is my favorite.*

mill /mɪl/ [countable noun] **1** A place where grain is crushed and made into flour: *The farmer sent two bags of wheat to the mill.* **2** A large factory for making paper, wood, steel and so on: *When he was younger he worked in a steel mill in Minnesota.*

milligram /ˈmɪlɪgræm/ [countable noun] A mass unit that is equal to one thousandth of a gramme: *Half a gram is equivalent to five hundred milligrams.* ■ The abbreviation "mg" is only used in written language. See box at **abbreviations**. ■ The British English spelling is "milligramme".

milligramme /ˈmɪl.ɪ.græm/ [countable noun] See **milligram.** ■ This is a British English spelling.

millimeter /ˈmɪlɪˌmiːtər/ [countable noun] A very small unit of length: *There are a thousand millimeters in a meter.* ■ The abbreviation "mm" is only used in written language. See box at **abbreviations**. ■ The British English spelling is "millimetre".

millimetre /ˈmɪl.ɪˌmiː.tər/ US: /-t̬ɚ/ UK: /ˈmɪl.ɪˌmiː.təʳ/ [countable noun] See **millimeter.** ■ This is a British English spelling.

↑**million** /ˈmɪl.jən/ [countable noun, adjective and pronoun] A thousand times one thousand: *New York has eight million inhabitants.* ■ Be careful! We say: "seven million" and not "seven millions".

millionaire /ˌmɪl·jəˈneər/ [countable noun] A very rich person: *Danny's cousin found oil in one of his fields and became a millionaire.*

millionth /ˈmɪl.jəntθ/ [noun and adjective] Referring to a million: *It's the millionth time I've told you.*

mime[1] [countable noun] Acting without words: *There's a group of actors doing "Cinderella" in mime at the local theater.*

mime[2] /maɪm/ [verb] To act without words: *Jane's very good at miming film titles.*

mimic /ˈmɪm.ɪk/ [verb] To imitate somebody: *Some comedians mimic famous people.*

mince /mɪnts/ [uncountable noun] See **ground beef.** ■ This word is British English.

mince pie [countable noun] A small pie filled with a mixture of apples, spices, raisins and so on, eaten at Christmas: *Hot mince pies are wonderful!*

↑**mind**[1] /maɪnd/ [countable noun] **1** The part of the body that thinks: *Exercise your mind as well as your body!* **2 to change your mind** To change your opinion or your intentions: *If you change your mind about going to the beach, give me a call.* **3 to make up your mind** To make a decision about something: *Come on, make up your mind. We don't have all day.*

mind[2] /maɪnd/ [verb] **1** To care: *I don't mind what she has said about me. I know she doesn't really mean it.* **2 do you mind? or would you mind?** Words that you use to ask somebody to do something in a polite way: *Do you mind opening the window? It's very hot in here.* **3 to mind your own business** See **business**. **4 never mind** Don't worry: *"Sorry, I don't have any money". "Never mind. I'll ask Paula".*

mine[1] /maɪn/ [pronoun] Belonging to me: *That pen is mine.*

mine[2] /maɪn/ [countable noun] A place from which minerals are taken out: *There are very large emerald mines in North Carolina.*

miner /ˈmaɪ·nər/ [countable noun] A person who works underground, digging for minerals: *The miners in the gold mines in Brazil work in terrible conditions.*

mineral /ˈmɪn.ᵊr.ᵊl/ [countable noun] A natural substance found in the earth, like iron and gold: *Some minerals like iron and copper are very useful for industry.*

mineral salt [uncountable noun] A simple, inorganic chemical which is a nutrient needed by living organisms: *Mineral salts are absorbed in soluble form.*

mini- /mɪni-/ [prefix] An addition to the beginning of a word that usually means "short" or "small": *We went to Indianapolis in the school minibus.*

miniature /ˈmɪnətʃər/ [adjective] That is a small copy or version of something: *Ron has got a fantastic collection of miniature cars.*

minibus /ˈmɪn.ɪ.bʌs/ [countable noun] A kind of a little bus that takes a small number of passengers: *Only twelve students wanted to go on the trip, so we went on the school minibus.*

minim /ˈmɪn.ɪm/ [countable noun] A musical note which has the time value of half a semibreve: *Minims are represented by an oval ring with a stem.* See page 460.

minimize or **minimise** /ˈmɪnɪmaɪz/ [verb] To reduce to a minimum: *We have to minimize our expenses to stay within budget.*

minimum /ˈmɪn.ɪ.məm/ [countable noun] The smallest possible quantity: *To play poker you need a minimum of three players.*

minister /ˈmɪn·ə·stər/ [countable noun] **1** A person who directs a ministry: *In the United States, the finance minister is called the Secretary of the Treasury.* **2** A Protestant priest: *Ronald's father is a minister in the Church of Utah.*

ministry /ˈmɪn.ɪ.stri/ [countable noun] A government department: *The Ministry of Education makes all decisions concerning schools, colleges and universities.* ■ The plural is "ministries".

minor[1] /ˈmaɪnər/ [adjective] Not very important: *He has to go to hospital for a minor operation.*

minor[2] /ˈmaɪnər/ [countable noun] Somebody who is not yet legally an adult: *In most countries, minors cannot be sent to prison.*

minority /məˈnɔr·ɪ·t̬i/, /maɪ-/, /-ˈnɑr-/ ▮ [noun] **1** A small part of a group: *A minority of people in the class didn't want to go to the art gallery.* ▮ [countable noun] **2** A group of people of a particular race or religion who live where most people are of a different race or religion: *Ethnic minorities in Canada have their own radio programs.* ■ The plural is "minorities".

mint /mɪnt/ ▮ [uncountable noun] **1** A plant that has a strong scent: *Mint leaves are used in cooking.* ▮ [countable noun] **2** A place where money is manufactured: *In a mint there are machines that make thousands of coins every day.*

minus /ˈmaɪ.nəs/ [preposition] A word that is used in subtractions: *Ten minus three equals seven.*

minute /ˈmɪn.ɪt/ [countable noun] **1** Sixty seconds: *The train will leave in five minutes.* **2 in a minute** Very soon, in a short space of time: *I can't help you now, but I will in a minute.* ■ Be careful with the pronunciation of this word! The "u" is pronounced like the "i" in "did".

miracle /ˈmɪr.ɪ.kl̩/ [countable noun] Something wonderful that you cannot explain: *It was a miracle that nobody was hurt in the accident.*

miraculous /mɪˈræk.jʊ.ləs/ [adjective] That is wonderful and you cannot explain: *John made a miraculous recovery from his illness.*

mirror /ˈmɪr·ər/ [countable noun] A piece of glass where you can see yourself: *I can't comb my hair if I don't look at myself in a mirror.* See picture at **bathroom**.

misbehave /ˌmɪs.bɪˈheɪv/ [verb] To behave badly: *Mrs. King's children always misbehave when she's not present.*

mischief /ˈmɪs.tʃɪf/ [uncountable noun] Actions that you enjoy but that other people think are bad: *Vanessa is always making mischief.*

mischievous /ˈmɪs.tʃɪ.vəs/ [adjective] That does things that are fun that people think are bad: *Danny is a very mischievous child.*

misconduct /mɪsˈkɑn·dʌkt/ [uncountable noun] Bad behavior: *Bob has been sent home twice for misconduct.*

miserable /ˈmɪz·ər·ə·bəl/ [adjective] Very unhappy or sad: *He was miserable when she didn't write to him.* See picture at **emotions**.

miserably /ˈmɪzərəbli/ [adverb] **1** In a very unhappy way: *She looked miserably out of the window at the rain.* **2** In a very poor way: *He was miserably dressed.* **3** In a very ineffective, depressing way: *The team failed miserably to score.*

misery /ˈmɪz·ər·i/ [noun] Suffering, unhappiness: *Her life was a misery.* ■ The plural is "miseries".

misfortune /mɪsˈfɔr·tʃən/ [noun] Bad luck: *It was his misfortune to be stopped by the bus inspector the day that he had left his ticket at home.*

mislead, misled, misled /mɪsˈliːd/ [verb] To provide with false information: *To mislead the photographers, the singer's publicist told them that she was traveling to Paris instead of Hamburg.*

miss /mɪs/ [verb] **1** To fail to catch a train or other transport: *We missed the last bus and had to walk*

a b c d e f g h i j k l **m** n o p q r s t u v w x y z

home. **2** To fail to arrive in time to see somebody: *You've just missed Lucy. She left a minute ago.* **3** To fail to hit somebody or something: *He threw a snowball at me but missed; Chris took the penalty, but unfortunately he missed.* **4** To be sad about somebody or something that is not with you: *When I was in Europe this summer, I missed my family.* **5** To notice that you don't have something: *I didn't miss my cell phone until I went to check if I had any messages and saw that it was not my jacket.* **6** To avoid or omit something: *If we leave a little later, maybe we will miss the rush hour traffic.* **7** Not to be able to do, to see or to play in something: *I missed their last concert because I was ill; Serena will miss the first part of the movie if she doesn't arrive soon.* **8 to miss an opportunity** Not to take an opportunity: *Jill missed a great opportunity to go to New York with her aunt.* **9 to miss the point** Not to understand the important thing about what somebody says: *You are missing the point: the problem is not that it's expensive, it's that my parents say I can't go.*

PHRASAL VERBS · to miss out 1 Not to do or include something: *Jane always misses out most of her punctuation; You have missed out a line of the text.* **2** Not to be able to have something that others are enjoying: *It is great that you can come this time to the barbecue, I didn't want you to miss out.* ■ Be careful with the spelling of the 3rd person singular present tense form: "misses".

Miss /mɪs/ [noun] A title used for a woman who is not married: *Miss Parker is very elegant.* ■ Be Careful! This word is normally used with a last name. Some people consider that "Miss" is discriminatory and prefer to use "Ms.". ■ "Miss" has a capital "M". ■ See box at **abbreviations**.

missile /ˈmɪs·əl/ [countable noun] A weapon that is thrown through the air: *The fighters shot four missiles at the ship and sank it.*

missing /ˈmɪs.ɪŋ/ [adjective] Not in the normal or right place, lost: *They've found the missing boy in a cave in the mountains.*

missionary /ˈmɪʃ·əˌner·i/ [countable noun] Somebody who tries to teach Christianity to people of other religions or with no religion: *The two missionaries in the town were in charge of the church and a hospital.* ■ The plural is "missionaries".

mist /mɪst/ [noun] A cloud close to the ground: *The fields were covered in mist and it was difficult to see where the animals were.* ■ Compare with "fog" ("fog" is thicker than "mist").

mistake[1] /mɪˈsteɪk/ [countable noun] **1** Something that is incorrect: *How many mistakes did you make in the dictation?* ■ We say **make** a mistake. **2 by mistake** Without wanting to: *I went into Jenny's bedroom by mistake.*

mistake[2], **mistook, mistaken** /mɪˈsteɪk/ [verb] **1** Confuse one person or thing for another: *I mistook Craig for his brother. They are so alike.* **2 to be mistaken** To be wrong, to have a wrong idea: *If you think that I'm going to Sue's party, you are mistaken.*

mistaken /mɪˈsteɪ.kᵊn/ Past participle of **mistake**[2].

mister [noun] See **Mr.**

mistook /mɪˈstʊk/ Past tense of **mistake**[2].

mistrust[1] /ˌmɪsˈtrʌst/ [verb] To be suspicious of somebody: *I mistrust Joanne. I don't think she's very loyal.*

mistrust[2] [uncountable noun] Being suspicious of somebody: *He has a great mistrust of people.*

misty /ˈmɪs.ti/ [adjective] **1** Having clouds of tiny drops of water, that makes it difficult to see: *The morning was misty.* **2** Affected by tiny drops of water: *My glasses are misty.* ■ The comparative form is "mistier" and the superlative form is "mistiest".

misunderstand, misunderstood, misunderstood /mɪsˌʌn·dərˈstænd/ [verb] To understand wrongly: *I misunderstood Roger. I thought he said he didn't want to come.*

misunderstood Past tense and past participle forms of **misunderstand.**

misuse /ˌmɪsˈjuːz/ [verb] To use something in the wrong way: *It's a pity to see Felicity misusing her great talent doing this kind of work.*

mix /mɪks/ [verb] To put several things together: *If you mix white and black, you get gray.*

PHRASAL VERBS · to mix (somebody or something) up To think that one person or one thing is a different person or thing: *I always mix her up with her sister.*

mixture /ˈmɪks·tʃər/ [countable noun] Something made from different things put together: *They communicated in a mixture of English and Spanish.*

mm A written abbreviation for **millimeter.** ■ See box at **abbreviations**.

moan US: /moʊn/ UK: /məʊn/ [verb] **1** To make a low sad sound when in pain or suffering: *The sick sheep were moaning all night.* **2** To complain: *Charles is always moaning about his grades.*

moat US: /moʊt/ UK: /məʊt/ [countable noun] A wide channel with water in it, surrounding a castle: *In the movie, the soldiers fell off the tower into the moat.*

mobile US: /ˈməʊbəl/ UK: /ˈməʊbaɪl/ [adjective] **1** That can be moved or transported: *The mobile crane can travel around the site.* ■ Compare with "stationary" (not moving). **2 mobile home** A static caravan: *Some camping sites allow mobile homes.*

mobile or **mobile phone** US: /'məʊbəl/ UK: /'məʊbaɪl/ [countable noun] See **cellphone.** ■ Be careful with the pronunciation of this word! The "o" in mobile is a long o, as in the English word "no". "Bi" rhymes with "my". ■ This word is British English.

mobility US: /moʊ'bɪl.ə.ṭi/ UK: /məʊ'bɪl.ɪ.ti/ [uncountable noun] The ability to get from place to place to improve position: *Mobility is a vital aspect of modern life.*

mock /mɒk/ [verb] To make fun of somebody: *It's very unpleasant to be mocked.*

modal [adjective] **1** Referring to mode or form: *Modal analysis determines the way in which structures vibrate.* **2** In grammar, referring to a special kind of auxiliary verb: *"Would" is a modal verb which indicates that the accompanying verb is conditional.*

modal verb /'məʊdəl,vɜːb/ [countable noun] A verb that is used with other verbs to express possibility, permission, necessity and so on: *"Can" and "might" are examples of modal verbs.*

mode [countable noun] **1** A manner of doing something: *an unusual mode of expression.* **2** A kind or type: *modes of transport.*

*__model__[1] /'mɒdəl/ [countable noun] **1** A small version of something: *Patrick has a wonderful collection of model airplanes.* **2** A person who wears clothes to show them to other people: *Claudia Schiffer is one of the most famous fashion models.*

model[2] [adjective] Ideal or perfect: *Linda is a model friend. She's always willing to help.*

moderate /'mɑd·ər·ɪt/ [adjective] That is not extreme: *I enjoy moderate heat, but I can't stand it when it's very hot.*

*__modern__ US: /'mɑː.dɚn/ UK: /'mɒd.ən/ [adjective] That belongs to the present or to recent time: *Computers are a very modern invention.*

modernization or **modernisation** /ˌmɒdənaɪ'zeɪʃən/ [uncountable noun] The updating of something, or the renovation of the appearance of something: *The modernization of the hotel was well done.*

modest US: /'mɑː.dɪst/ UK: /'mɒd.ɪst/ [adjective] That does not talk about the things that he or she does well: *He's very modest. Although he has four gold medals he doesn't talk about them.*

modesty /'mɑd·ə·sti/ [uncountable noun] Not talking about the things that you do well: *You should learn a bit of modesty, Jane. You are always boasting.*

modification /ˌmɒdɪfɪ'keɪʃən/ [noun] The act of modifying: *She proposed a modification to the process.*

modify /'mɑd·əˌfɑɪ/ [verb] To alter or adjust: *In the end it was decided to modify the law, not abolish it.* ■ Be careful with the spelling of these forms: "modifies", "modified".

moist /mɔɪst/ [adjective] Damp, slightly wet: *You should always plant seeds in moist earth.* ■ "Moist" is usually a positive word. Compare with "damp" (is often a negative word: "The weather has been damp and cold all this week").

moisturizing or **moisturising** /'mɔɪs.tʃər.aɪ.zər/ [adjective] That makes the skin softer, by preventing it from being too dry: *I use a moisturizing lotion after I take a shower.*

mold[1] [uncountable noun] A container that is used to make something in a particular shape: *Pour the mixture into a round mold and then put it in the oven.*

mold[2] [verb] To make something into a particular shape: *At school the children molded clay into different shapes.*

mole US: /moʊl/ UK: /məʊl/ [countable noun] A small animal with dark fur that lives in the ground: *Moles like living in the dark because they have very poor eyesight.*

MOLE

molecule /'mɑl·əˌkjul/ [countable noun] The smallest independent part of a substance: *Everything is made of lots of tiny molecules.*

mollusk or **mollusc** US: /'mɑː.ləsk/ UK: /'mɒl.əsk/ [countable noun] An invertebrate animal that has soft body and is often covered by a hard shell: *Oysters, snails and octopuses are mollusks.* ■ The British English spelling is "mollusc".

molten /'moʊl·tə·n/ [adjective] Referring to metal, rock or glass, that is melted by heat: *Molten lead is used to make shot for guns.*

*__mom__ [countable noun] See **mother.** See picture at **family**.

*__moment__ /'moʊ·mənt/ [countable noun] **1** A very short period of time: *Can you hold this for me for a moment?* **2** **at the moment** That is happening now: *My biggest problem at the moment is the math test.* **3** **in a moment** Very soon: *Don't be impatient. You'll see it in a moment.* **4** **just a moment!** Wait a little!: *"Have you finished yet?" "Just a moment, I'm writing the last line!".* ■ Be careful! We say: "just a moment!". We don't say: "one moment".

mommy [countable noun] See **mother.** ■ This use is informal and normally used by or to children. ■ The plural is "mommies".

a b c d e f g h i j k l **m** n o p q r s t u v w x y z

monarch US: /'mɑː.nɚk/ UK: /'mɒn.ək/ [countable noun] A king or a queen: *The monarch attended the ceremony in parliament.*

monarchy /'mɑn·ər·ki/ [uncountable noun] A political system in which a king or a queen is the head of state: *In America there are no monarchies; all the countries are republics.* ■ The plural is "monarchies".

monastery US: /'mɑː.nə.ster.i/ UK: /'mɒn.ə.stri/ [countable noun] A place where monks live and work: *Last Sunday we visited a monastery in a remote valley.* ■ The plural is "monasteries".

†**Monday** /'mʌn.deɪ/ [noun] The second day of the week: *Monday is between Sunday and Tuesday.* ■ Be careful! "Monday" has a capital "M". See picture at **calendar**.

†**money** /'mʌn.i/ [uncountable noun] **1** Bills and coins that people use to buy things: *Money is not the most important thing in life.* **2** **to make money** To get money for your work: *Mr. Robinson has made a lot of money working in Saudi Arabia.* **3** **pocket money** See **pocket money**.

money box [countable noun] A box or other container which you put money into to save: *My money box is full.*

†**monitor** US: /'mɑː.nɪ.t̬ɚ/ UK: /'mɒn.ɪ.təʳ/ [countable noun] **1** The part of a computer where you can see your work: *I'm going to get an another flat monitor.* **1** **2** An older boy or girl who helps the teachers: *The monitors wouldn't let us go into the school building until the bell rang.*

monk /mʌŋk/ [countable noun] A man who lives in a religious community: *Saint Bernard Abbey is a monastery of Catholic Benedictine monks in Alabama.*

monkey /'mʌŋ.ki/ [countable noun] An animal that has a long tail, hands and feet, and that lives in trees: *Monkeys jump from branch to branch.* **See page 428.**

monopoly /mə'nɑp·ə·li/ [countable noun] An area of business that belongs to one company only: *They have the monopoly of electrical parts.* ■ The plural is "monopolies".

monotheistic /ˌmɒn.əʊ.θiː'ɪs.tɪk/ US: /ˌmɑː.noʊ-/ [adjective] Believing in one god only: *The three principal monotheistic religions are Judaism, Christianity and Islam.* ■ Compare with "polytheistic" (believing in more than one god).

monotonous /mə'nɑt·ə·nəs/ [adjective] Boring: *I find a lot of modern classical music very monotonous. It all sounds the same to me.*

monster US: /'mɑːnt.stɚ/ UK: /'mɒnt.stəʳ/ [countable noun] **1** A large, horrible being: *In Greek mythology there were monsters with one eye.* **2** A very bad person: *That man is a monster! The way he treats animals is terrible.*

monstrous /'mɑn·strəs/ [adjective] That is strange and frightening: *We saw a science fiction movies in which some monstrous creatures from space invaded the earth.*

†**month** /mʌntθ/ [countable noun] One of the twelve parts of a year: *August is my favorite month. It's when we go on vacation.* See picture at **calendar**.

monthly /'mʌnt.θli/ [adjective] That happens every month or once a month: *I buy a monthly magazine on computers.*

monument /'mɑn·jə·mənt/ [countable noun] **1** An old building or statue: *Washington D.C. is full of beautiful monuments.* **2** A building or statue in honor of somebody or something: *Lincoln Memorial in Washington D.C. is a monument was dedicated to honor President Abraham Lincoln.*

moo [verb] To make the sound that a cow makes: *When they saw the farmer, the cows started mooing.* See picture at **animal**.

†**mood** /muːd/ [countable noun] **1** The way that you are feeling: *Be careful! Mr. MacCarthy is in a bad mood today.* **2** **in the mood for** To want to do or have something: *Switch off the radio, please. I'm not in the mood for music.*

†**moon** /muːn/ [countable noun] **1** A natural satellite that goes around a bigger planet: *Saturn has ten moons.* **See page 448.** **2** The natural satellite that moves round the earth: *It takes the moon one month to go round the earth.* **3** **full moon** The moon when it is a circle: *I think we'll have plenty of light tonight. There's a full moon.* **4** **new moon** The moon when it is a thin line, at the beginning of its cycle: *Nights with a new moon are very dark.* **5** **over the moon** Words used to say that you feel very happy: *The soccer player said that he was over the moon about the goal.*

moonlight /'muːn.laɪt/ [uncountable noun] The light of the moon: *I like going for walks in the moonlight.*

moor[1] /mɔːr/ [countable noun] Open land with grass and bushes: *Moors are not very good for growing crops.*

moor[2] [verb] To make a boat still: *Most people moor their yachts in bad weather.*

mop[1] /mɒp/ [noun] A long stick with strips of cloth or a sponge on the end, that is used for cleaning floors: *With a mop and a little water you can clean the kitchen floor in five minutes.*

mop[2] /mɒp/ [verb] To clean a floor with a mop or a cloth and a little water: *At home we mop the kitchen floor everyday.*

moped /'moʊˌped/ [countable noun] A small, not very powerful, motorcycle: *The good thing about mopeds is that you can use the pedals if you have no gas.*

†**moral**[1] /'mɒrəl/ [adjective] Referring to right or wrong: *Who is responsible for the development of our moral sense?*

moral² /ˈmɒrəl/ [countable noun] The lesson taught by a story: *I don't understand the moral of this story.*

morale /məˈrɑːl/ [uncountable noun] The confidence that you feel in a difficult or important situation: *When the opposing team scored a goal, the morale of our team went right down.*

†**more** US: /mɔːr/ UK: /mɔːʳ/ [adjective and pronoun] **1** The comparative form of **much** and **many**: *Why don't you do it? You have more time than I do.* **2** The comparative form of **very¹**: *That book's okay, but this one is more interesting.* **3 more and more** A greater amount all the time: *More and more people are careful about what they eat.* **4 more or less** Approximately: *She's more or less twenty.* **5 not any more** Not any longer: *I tell you that he does not live here any more.* **6 once more** One other time, again: *Come on, mom! Tell us the story once more!*

†**morning** /ˈmɔːnɪŋ/ [noun] **1** The part of the day until midday: *We have three lessons in the morning and then we have a break for lunch.* ■ Be careful. We say: "**in** the morning". **2 good morning** A greeting that is used in the morning: *Our teacher always says "Good morning" when she comes into the classroom.*

mortal¹ US: /ˈmɔːr.t̬əl/ UK: /ˈmɔː.təl/ [countable noun] A being, that lives and dies: *Human beings are mortals.*

mortal² US: /ˈmɔːr.t̬əl/ UK: /ˈmɔː.təl/ [adjective] Leading to or causing death: *During the Roman Empire, games were held in which gladiators engaged in mortal combat.*

mosaic¹ /moʊˈzeɪ·ɪk/ [countable noun] A design made using many small stones or pieces of glass: *This Roman mosaic represents a scene of a banquet.*

mosaic² [adjective] Relating to a mosaic or looking like one: *The mosaic pattern on your bathroom wall is very original.*

Moslem US: /ˈmɑːz.lem/ UK: /ˈmʊz.lɪm/ [noun and adjective] See **Muslim.** ■ Be careful! "Moslem" has a capital "M".

mosque US: /mɑːsk/ UK: /mɒsk/ [countable noun] A place where Muslims meet to pray: *Mohammed's father goes to the mosque once a day.*

mosquito /məˈski·t̬oʊ/ [countable noun] A small insect that feeds on blood from animals and people: *Mosquitoes spread many serious diseases.* ■ The plural is "mosquitoes".

moss US: /mɑːs/ UK: /mɒs/ [noun] A very small green or yellow plant, which grows on surfaces: *Moss grows on trees, on the ground and on rocks.*

†**most** US: /moʊst/ UK: /məʊst/ [adjective and pronoun] **1** The superlative form of **much** and **many**: *I have more books than John, but Sue has the most of us all. She has hundreds.* **2** The superlative form of **very**: *The new Star Wars movie is the most exciting of them all.* **3 at most** As a maximum: *I don't know how much money I have, but at most I have $20.* **4 to make the most of** To use something in the best and fullest way: *We have to try to make the most of our trip to Mexico.*

mostly /ˈmoʊst·li/ [adverb] In most cases: *My friends are mostly of my age.* ■ The same meaning: "mainly".

moth US: /mɑːθ/ UK: /mɒθ/ [countable noun] A kind of butterfly that usually flies at night: *Open the window so that the moth can fly out.*

†**mother** /ˈmʌð·ər/ [countable noun] **1** A female parent: *My cousin Barbara became a mother last week.* ■ "Mom" and "mommy" are informal for "mother". 👁 See picture at **family.** **2 mother-in-law** When you are married, your wife's mother or your husband's mother: *Joan is living at her mother-in-law's house until their house is ready.* ■ The plural of "mother-in-law" is "mothers-in-law".

mother tongue [countable noun] A person's native language: *His mother tongue is French.*

motion /ˈmoʊ·ʃən/ [noun] Movement: *This week we're going to study the motion of the planets.*

motive US: /ˈmoʊ.t̬ɪv/ UK: /ˈməʊ.tɪv/ [countable noun] A reason for doing something: *I can't understand his motives for wanting to come and see us every day.*

†**motor** US: /ˈmoʊ.t̬ɚ/ UK: /ˈməʊ.təʳ/ [countable noun] Machine, large or small, which causes motion: *The motor of the vacuum cleaner is broken.* ■ "Motor" is usually used for electrical appliances. Compare with "engine" (usually used for vehicles).

motorbike /ˈmoʊ·t̬ərˌbɑɪk/ [countable noun] A motorcycle: *Accidents on motorbikes are quite often fatal.* ■ The same meaning: "motorcycle". 👁 See picture at **transport.**

motor boat [countable noun] A boat that is moved by a small engine: *There's a motor boat that crosses to the island every two hours.* 👁 See picture at **transport.**

motorcycle /ˈmoʊ·t̬ərˌsɑɪ·kəl/ [countable noun] A vehicle with an engine that goes on two wheels: *The Harley Davidson is the most famous motorcycle of all times.* ■ The same meaning: "motorbike".

motorist /ˈmoʊ·t̬ər·ɪst/ [countable noun] A car driver: *There is a campaign to encourage motorists not to drink and drive.* ■ This word is a little formal. We usually say "driver".

motor racing [uncountable noun] A sport in which cars race: *Motor racing is one of the most spectacular sports you can watch.*

motorway /ˈmoʊ·t̬ərˌweɪ/ [countable noun] See **freeway.** ■ This word is British English.

mound /mɑʊnd/ [countable noun] **1** A hill: *From the mound we could see the whole town below and all the boats in the sea.* **2** A pile of something: *There's a* *mound of earth and a big hole in their yard. Are they going to plant a tree?*

↑**mount¹** /maʊnt/ [verb] To get on a horse or a bike: *The cowboys all mounted their horses and galloped across the valley.*

mount² /maʊnt/ [noun] See **Mt.** ■ The abbreviation "Mt" is only used in written language.

↑**mountain** /ˈmaʊn·tə·n/ [countable noun] A piece of land that goes very high: *The mountains in central Asia are the highest in the world.* ■ Be careful with the pronunciation of this word! The "a" is not pronounced. 👁 **See pages 444 and 445.**

mountain bike [countable noun] A special kind of bike with thick wheels, used for riding in the country: *With a mountain bike you can go over very rough ground.*

mountaineer /ˌmaʊn.tɪˈnɪər/ US: /-tənˈɪr/ [countable noun] Somebody who climbs mountains: *The mountaineer reached the summit.*

mountaineering /ˌmaʊn.tɪˈnɪə.rɪŋ/ US: /-tənˈɪr.ɪŋ/ [uncountable noun] A sport in which you climb mountains: *Mountaineering is not a dangerous sport if you are careful.*

mountainous /ˈmaʊn·tə·n·əs/ [adjective] **1** Having many mountains: *The landscape in this area is very mountainous.* **2** Being very big: *a mountainous pile of garbage.*

mourn US: /mɔːrn/ UK: /mɔːn/ [verb] To be sad for somebody who has died: *They mourned their grandpa's death.*

mourning /ˈmɔr·nɪŋ/, /ˈmoʊr-/ [uncountable noun] Feeling or showing sadness for somebody who has died: *They're in mourning for their grandmother.* ■ Be careful! We say: "to be **in** mourning".

↑**mouse** /maʊs/ [countable noun] A small animal with a long tail: *Jackie screamed when she saw the mouse.* ■ The plural is "mice". 👁 **See page 442.**

↑**mouth** /maʊθ/ [countable noun] The part of the body that you use for eating and talking: *Don't talk with your mouth full!* ■ Be careful with the pronunciation of this word! The vowel sound of this word is pronounced the same as in "cow".

mouthful /ˈmaʊθ.fʊl/ [countable noun] The amount of food you can get in your mouth in one go: *She ate a whole sandwich in two mouthfuls.*

mouthorgan [countable noun] A small musical instrument that you play by moving it across your lips while you are blowing: *I would like to play the mouthorgan.*

movable or **moveable** /ˈmuːvəbl/ [adjective] Able to be moved: *The back of the chair is movable.* ■ Compare with "immovable" (that cannot be moved).

move /muːv/ [verb] **1** To change place or position: *I'm going to take a photo. Don't move now.* **2** To make somebody feel sad, happy and so on: *I was so moved by the story that I started crying.*
◗ **PHRASAL VERBS** · **to move into** To go and live in a new apartment or house: *We're moving into our new apartment in September.* · **to move out** To leave an apartment or a house: *We're moving out of our present address at the end of the month.*

↑**movement** /ˈmuːv.mənt/ [noun] A changing of position or place: *There was a movement behind the drapes.*

↑**movie** /ˈmuː.vi/ [countable noun] **1** A film: *The latest Disney movie isn't very good.* **2 the movies** The showing of films at a movie theater: *I'm going to the movies this evening.* ■ In this use, in British English we say "the pictures".

↑**movie theater** [countable noun] A place for showing films: *The movie theaters in my town always show the latest Hollywood films.* ■ In British English they say "cinema". 👁 See picture at **street**.

mow, mowed, mown US: /moʊ/ UK: /məʊ/ [verb] To cut grass or cereals: *How often do you mow your lawn?*

mown Past participle of **mow**.

↑**Mr.** [noun] A title used for a man: *Mr. Johnson teaches us Science.* ■ Be careful! This word is normally used with a last name, when the first name is not mentioned. ■ See box at **abbreviations**.

↑**Mrs.** /ˈmɪs.ɪz/ [noun] A title used for a married woman: *Mrs. Harrison is one of the school teachers.* ■ Be careful! This word is normally used with a last name, when the first name is not mentioned. ■ See box at **abbreviations**.

↑**Ms.** /məz, mɪz/ [noun] A title used for a woman: *When a woman doesn't want to say if she's single or married, she uses "Ms.".* ■ Be careful! This word is normally used with a last name, when the first name is not mentioned. ■ See box at **abbreviations**.

Mt An abbreviation for "Mount" that goes before the name of a mountain: *Mt Everest is the highest mountain in the world.*

↑**much** /mʌtʃ/ [adjective and pronoun] **1** A lot of something: *Hurry up! I don't have much time.* **2 as much as** The same quantity as: *He doesn't know as much math as me.* **3 how much** Words used to ask about quantity with uncountable nouns: *How much butter is there in the fridge?* ■ "Much" is used with uncountable nouns like "time" or "water". Compare with "many" (used with countable nouns). "Much" is normally used in negative sentences and questions. In affirmative sentences we use "a lot of". ■ The comparative form is "more" and the superlative form is "most".

↑**mud** /mʌd/ [uncountable noun] Wet soil: *When it rains the road to the farmhouse gets covered in mud.*

a b c d e f g h i j k l m n o p q r s t u v w x y z

muddy /ˈmʌd.i/ [adjective] Covered in mud: *Clean your boots before coming into the house; they're very muddy.* ■ The comparative form is "muddier" and the superlative form is "muddiest".

muesli /ˈmjuːzli/ [uncountable noun] A breakfast cereal: *Muesli is made from grain, dried fruit and nuts.*

mug /mʌg/ [countable noun] A tall straight cup: *I've bought some new coffee mugs.* ■ Compare with "cup" (a small round container used for drinking hot drinks). 👁 See picture at **cup**.

mule /mjuːl/ [countable noun] An animal similar to a donkey: *Mules are the cross of female horses and male donkeys.*

multi- /mʌlti-/ [prefix] An addition to the beginning of a word that means "many": *Something that is multicolored has many colors.*

multicellular /ˌmʌl·tiˈsel·jə·lər/, /ˌmʌl·tɑɪ-/ [adjective] Having more than one cell: *Every living creature is multicellular except the single-cell amoeba.*

multilingual /ˌmʌltiˈlɪŋgwəl/ [adjective] That uses several languages: *Multilingual guides have information in several languages.*

multiply /ˈmʌl·təˌplɑɪ/ [verb] **1** To add the same number several times: *If you multiply five by three, it is the same as adding five three times.* **2** To grow in number: *Rabbits multiply very quickly.* ■ Be careful with the spelling of these forms: "multiplies", "multiplied".

mummy /ˈmʌm.i/ [countable noun] The body of a person who died a long time ago but is still well preserved: *The Egyptian mummies are fascinating.* ■ The plural is "mummies". Be careful with the pronunciation of this word! The vowel sound here is pronounced the same as in "sun".

mumps /mʌmps/ [uncountable noun] An infectious disease in which your neck swells: *I had mumps when I was a kid.* ■ It is usually used with a singular verb.

municipal /mjuːˈnɪs.ɪ.pəl/ [adjective] Of, or relating to, a town or city: *The library and the baths are municipal.*

municipality /mjʊˌnɪs·əˈpæl·ɪ·t̬i/ [countable noun] A town which has its own local government: *The residents of the municipality elect their representatives.* ■ The plural is "municipalities".

murder[1] /ˈmɜːdər/ [noun] The killing of somebody: *There has been a murder in a bank in Kansas City.* ■ Compare with "crime" (an illegal action).

murder[2] /ˈmɜːdər/ [verb] To kill somebody: *She murdered him by putting poison in his tea.*

murderer US: /ˈmɝː.dɚ.ɚ/ UK: /ˈmɜː.dər.ər/ [countable noun] A person who kills another person: *The police caught the girl's murderer when he was trying to go abroad.* ■ Compare with "criminal[2]" (somebody who does something against the law).

murmur[1] /ˈmɜːmər/ [countable noun] A soft continuous sound: *There was a murmur of approval when the principal presented his plans for the new school.*

murmur[2] /ˈmɜːmər/ [verb] To talk in a very low voice: *She murmured something into my ear but I couldn't understand what she said.*

Murphy's Law US: /ˌmɝː.fizˈlɑː/ UK: /ˌmɜː.fizˈlɔː/ [uncountable noun] A humorous principle that states that if anything can go wrong, it will: *Murphy's Law says that for example if you drop a piece of bread and butter, it will always fall butter side down.* ■ Be careful! "Murphy's Law" has capital letters. ■ This phrase is informal.

muscle /ˈmʌs.l̩/ [noun] One of the parts of the body that cause movement: *The muscles move the bones and allow us to move all parts of the body.* ■ Be careful with the pronunciation of this word! 👁 **See page 423.**

muscular /ˈmʌs·kjə·lər/ [adjective] **1** Having well-developed muscles: *He is very muscular because he goes to the gym regularly.* **2** Relating to muscles: *muscular contractions.* 👁 **See page 423.**

musculature /ˈmʌs.kjʊ.lə.tʃər/ US: /-tʃɚ/ [uncountable noun] The muscular system: *The bat's wing musculature is enviable.* 👁 **See page 423.**

museum /mjuːˈziː.əm/ [countable noun] A building that has interesting objects for people to look at: *In the Museum of Natural History you can learn a lot about the origins of man.*

mushroom /ˈmʌʃ.ruːm, -rʊm/ [countable noun] A plant that has no leaves, flowers or roots: *You can eat some mushrooms but others are poisonous.* 👁 **See page 437.**

music /ˈmjuː.zɪk/ [uncountable noun] **1** Sounds arranged to sound pleasant: *I like different types of music.* **2** The written or printed symbols that represent sounds in a song or symphony: *I can't read music. I play by ear.*

MUSIC

musical[1] /ˈmjuːzɪkəl/ [adjective] Referring to music: *Can you play a musical instrument?* 👁 **See pages 458-460.**

a b c d e f g h i j k l **m** n o p q r s t u v w x y z

†**musical²** /ˈmjuːzɪkəl/ [countable noun] A play or a movie that has songs and dances: *I went to see the musical "Grease" yesterday.*

†**musician** /mjuːˈzɪʃ.ᵊn/ [countable noun] A person who plays or writes music: *There are twenty musicians in the school orchestra.*

Muslim US: /ˈmɑː.zlem/ UK: /ˈmʊz.lɪm/ [noun and adjective] Referring to Islam or a follower of Islam: *In most Arab countries, the people are Muslims.* ■ Be careful! "Muslim" has a capital "M". ■ We also say "Moslem".

mussel /ˈmʌsəl/ [countable noun] A bivalve mollusk with an oval shell: *Mussels live in the sea and are often consumed as food.*

†**must** /mʌst, məst, məs/ [verb] **1** A word that you use to say that it is necessary to do something: *You must listen to me when I speak to you!* **2** A word that you use to show that you think something is true: *She must be a foreigner. She doesn't understand English.* ■ See box below.

must* and *have to

- The verb ***must*** only has one form. The verbs that follow it are in the infinitive without *to*:
  - *You must be more punctual, James.*
  - *I mustn't forget Mom's birthday.*
  - *I must go now.*

  Must is used with a present or future meaning.

- For other tenses, we use ***have to***:
  - past tense: *When I was 14, I had to be home at 10.*
  - present perfect: *They have had to wait years for this opportunity.*

  Have to can be used in any tense.

Negative forms: Note that the negative of *must* (*must not/musn't*) and the negative of *have to* (*have not to*) have completely different meanings:

- ***Must not/musn't*** means that it is imperative that you do not do something:
  - *You must not smoke in the chemistry laboratory. You could start a fire.*
  - *You must not move when the dentist's drill is in your mouth.*
- ***Don't have to*** means that you are not obliged to do something, you can decide to do it or not:
  - *You don't have to come shopping with us. You can stay at home if you want.*
  - *I don't have to finish this homework tonight. I can do it tomorrow night.*

mustache [countable noun] Hair that men have above the mouth: *My great uncle had a very long mustache.*

mustard /ˈmʌs·tərd/ [uncountable noun] A spicy sauce made from the seeds of a plant: *I love hot dogs with mustard.*

mustn't /ˈmʌs.ᵊnt/ The contraction of "must not".

must've The contraction of "must have".

mute [adjective] Not able to speak: *Deaf and mute people often communicate by using a special sign language.*

mutter US: /ˈmʌţ.ɚ/ UK: /ˈmʌt.əʳ/ [verb] To speak in a low voice, often expressing disagreement: *She muttered something but I couldn't hear her.*

mutton /ˈmʌt·ə·n/ [uncountable noun] The meat from an adult sheep: *Anne prepared a leg of mutton with herbs.*

†**my** /maɪ/ [adjective] Of me; belonging to me: *This is my sister Nellie.*

myriapod [countable noun] Any invertebrate which has a body with many segments and legs: *Centipedes and millipedes are myriapods.*

†**myself** /maɪˈself/ [pronoun] **1** A word that refers to "me" when I am the subject of a sentence: *I hurt myself with the bread knife.* **2** A word that underlines that I am the person the verb refers to: *I myself am not very keen on pizza.* **3 by myself 1** Alone: *I go to school by myself.* **2** Without help: *I made this kite all by myself.*

†**mysterious** /mɪˈstɪər·i·əs/ [adjective] That is strange and difficult to explain: *Every night we hear mysterious noises coming from the attic.*

†**mystery** /ˈmɪs·tə·ri/ [noun] Something that is strange and difficult or impossible to explain: *It is still a mystery to me how George could pass Math.* ■ The plural is "mysteries".

myth /mɪθ/ ▮ [countable noun] **1** A story from an ancient civilization: *Do you know the myth of King Midas?* ▮ [noun] **2** Untrue, but commonly believed: *The idea that money or a good job will make you happy is a myth.*

mythical /ˈmɪθ.ɪ.kᵊl, ˈmɪθ.ɪ.k/ [adjective] **1** Referring to a story from an ancient civilization: *A mermaid is a mythical creature.* **2** Untrue, not existing: *He invented a mythical uncle in South America.*

mythological /ˌmɪθəlˈɒdʒɪkəl/ [adjective] Referring to myths: *Many mythological characters from Greek myths are well-known even today.*

mythology /mɪˈθɑl·ə·dʒi/ [uncountable noun] The body of myths from a particular culture, or the study of these myths: *The study of Greek mythology is necessary to understand classical painting.* ■ The plural is "mythologies".

N

n

n /en/ The fourteenth letter of the alphabet: *The name "Nicholas" begins with an "N".*

↑**nail[1]** /neɪl/ [countable noun] **1** The hard part at the end of your fingers or your toes: *I need to cut my nails.* **2** A thin piece of metal with a point: *Would you pass me the hammer and the nails?*

nail[2] /neɪl/ [verb] To fix things with a nail: *I'm going to nail the shelf to the wall.*

↑**naked** /ˈneɪ.kɪd/ [adjective] Without clothes on: *He was alone and swam naked in the sea.* ■ Be careful with the pronunciation of this word. The "e" is pronounced like the "i" in "did".

↑**name[1]** /neɪm/ [countable noun] **1** The word that you use to refer to a person or a thing: *That little girl's name is Lesley.* **2 Christian name** The name or names that go before the family name: *My Christian name is Ruth.* ■ Be careful! "Christian name" has a capital "C". ■ The same meaning: "first name". **3 family name or last name** The name that you share with other people in your family: *My teacher's family name is "Jones".* ■ In this use, the same meaning: "surname".

name[2] /neɪm/ [verb] To give a name to somebody or something: *They're going to name their dog "Momo".*

namely /ˈneɪm.li/ [adverb] That is to say: *Only one student, namely Sarah, is missing this morning.*

nanny /ˈnæn.i/ [countable noun] A woman who looks after the children of a family: *The Smiths need a nanny for the summer vacation.* ■ The plural is "nannies".

nap /næp/ [countable noun] A short sleep: *I felt tired so I took a nap on the sofa.*

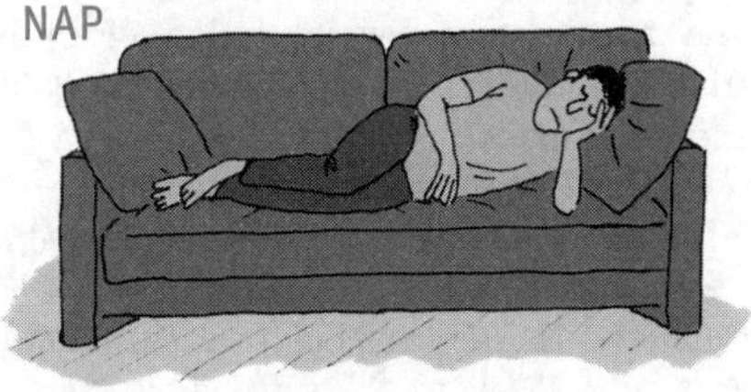
NAP

napkin /ˈnæp.kɪn/ [countable noun] A piece of cloth or paper to clean your hands or lips when you are eating: *Put a napkin beside each plate, please.* ■ The same meaning: "serviette".

nappy /ˈnæp.i/ [countable noun] See **diaper**. ■ This word is British English. ■ The plural is "nappies".

narrate /nəˈreɪt/ [verb] To relate a story or commentary: *The radio presenter narrated the wedding.*

↑**narrow** /ˈnær·oʊ/ [adjective] Not wide, with a short distance from side to side: *This road is very narrow and passing is difficult.* ■ Compare with "wide" (that is large from one side to another).

a b c d e f g h i j k l m n o p q r s t u v w x y z

nasal /ˈneɪ.zᵊl/ [adjective] Referring to the nose: *His voice is quite nasal because he has a cold.*

nasty US: /ˈnæs.ti/ UK: /ˈnɑː.sti/ [adjective] Unpleasant, unkind: *There's a nasty smell coming from the bathroom.* ■ The comparative form is "nastier" and the superlative form is "nastiest".

†**nation** /ˈneɪ.ʃᵊn/ [countable noun] A country and its people: *Canada is an American nation.*

†**national** /ˈnæʃ.ᵊn.ᵊl, ˈnæʃ.nəl/ [adjective] Belonging to one country: *Tomorrow is a national vacation and we're going to the seaside for the day.* ■ Compare with "international" (between different nations).

national anthem [countable noun] The official piece of music of a country: *"The Star-Spangled Banner" is the national anthem of the United States of America.* ■ We also say "anthem".

nationality /ˌnæʃ·əˈnæl·ɪ·t̬i/ [noun] The state of belonging to a country: *What's your friend's nationality? He's Chilean.* ■ The plural is "nationalities". ■ See box on the following page.

native[1] /ˈneɪtɪv/ [adjective] Belonging to the place where you were born: *Her grandmother's native land is Norway.*

native[2] /ˈneɪtɪv/ [countable noun] A person who was born in a particular place: *The girl you met yesterday is a native of California.*

Native American [noun and adjective] Referring to the native people of America: *The Native Americans lost almost all of their land to the white man.* ■ Be careful! "Native American" has capital letters. ■ We also say "American Indian, Indian".

Nativity [uncountable noun] **1** The birth of Jesus Christ: *This play shows the Nativity story.* **2 Nativity scene** A miniature representation of Christ's birth scene: *Crowds of people visited the Nativity scene at Christmas.*

NATO Referring to an international military organization consisting of the US, Canada and many European countries: *NATO members will be meeting this Tuesday in Belgium to discuss the incident.* ■ "NATO" is an abbreviation for "North Atlantic Treaty Organization". ■ See box at **abbreviations**.

†**natural** /ˈnætʃ·ər·əl/ [adjective] **1** Made by nature: *Our new stove works on natural gas.* **2** Usual, normal: *It's natural to be nervous on the first day of school.*

naturally /ˈnætʃ·ər·ə·li/ [adverb] **1** Normally: *Please, try to behave naturally when you see the Princess.* **2** By nature: *Tigers are naturally aggressive.* **3** As you would expect, of course: *Naturally, I hope you'll join us for the trip to Russia.*

†**nature** /ˈneɪ·tʃər/ [uncountable noun] **1** Everything that is not made by man: *One of the best things about living in the country is being able to observe nature day by day.* **2** The qualities of a person or a thing: *Jack would never hurt anybody; it's not in his nature.*

nature reserve [countable noun] An area of land which is protected and managed in order to maintain its flora and fauna: *Nature reserves are an important aspect of conservation.*

naught [countable noun] The number 0: *0.9 is normally read "naught point nine".*

naughty US: /ˈnɑː.t̬i/ UK: /ˈnɔː.ti/ [adjective] Bad in behavior: *If you're naughty I won't buy you an ice cream.* ■ This word is normally used when we talk about a child or to a child. The comparative form is "naughtier" and the superlative form is "naughtiest".

nautical /ˈnɔ·t̬ɪ·kəl/, /ˈnɑt̬·ɪ-/ [adjective] Referring to sailing: *Old sailors love to tell nautical stories.*

naval /ˈneɪ.vᵊl/ [adjective] Belonging to a navy: *The US Navy beat Spain in the naval battle in 1888.*

navel /ˈneɪ.vᵊl/ [countable noun] The small hollow in the middle of the stomach where there used to be the cord attaching a baby to his mother: *He shows a small navel where the Doctor cut the umbilical cord at his birth.* ■ The same meaning: "belly-button".

navigate /ˈnæv.ɪ.geɪt/ [verb] To guide or direct a ship or an aircraft: *Stars and compasses were used by early sailors to navigate their way from one part of the world to another.*

navigation /ˌnævɪˈgeɪʃən/ [uncountable noun] The act of navigating: *Navigation is difficult in these waters because of the currents.*

†**navy** /ˈneɪ.vi/ [noun] The part of the armed forces that fights at sea: *My grandfather served in the navy during the war.* ■ The plural is "navies".

navy blue [noun and adjective] Dark blue: *Our team now wears navy blue shirts and socks.*

†**near**[1] /nɪər/ [adjective] Not far: *The nearest bus station is next to the church.* ■ Be careful! "Near" is not used before a noun except in the comparative and superlative forms ("nearer" and "nearest"). "Nearby" can be used before a noun.

†**near**[2] /nɪər/ [adverb] Not far: *We can go on foot because Lee lives very near.* ■ Be careful! We say "near a place". (We don't say "near to a place").

†**near**[3] /nɪər/ [preposition] Not far from: *The cat's sleeping on the carpet near the fire.* ■ Careful. We say "near the table". (We don't say "near of the table").

nearby[1] /ˌnɪəˈbaɪ/ [adjective] Not far away: *They stay at a nearby hotel when they come to see us.*

nearby[2] /ˌnɪəˈbaɪ/ [adverb] Not far away: *They have put a new bus stop nearby.*

nearly /ˈnɪər·li/ [adverb] Almost: *My parents nearly missed their plane yesterday.*

neat /niːt/ [adjective] Tidy, carefully arranged: *Make sure that your uniforms look neat and clean for the concert this evening.*

Nationalities

country	adjective	person from the country
Algeria	*Algerian*	*Algerian*
Argentina	*Argentinian*	*Argentinian*
Australia	*Australian*	*Australian*
Bolivia	*Bolivian*	*Bolivian*
Brazil	*Brazilian*	*Brazilian*
Bulgaria	*Bulgarian*	*Bulgarian*
Canada	*Canadian*	*Canadian*
Chile	*Chilean*	*Chilean*
China	*Chinese*	*Chinese*
Colombia	*Colombian*	*Colombian*
Cuba	*Cuban*	*Cuban*
Dominican Republic	*Dominican*	*Dominican*
Egypt	*Egyptian*	*Egyptian*
El Salvador	*Salvadoran*	*Salvadoran*
France	*French*	*Frenchman, Frenchwoman*
Germany	*German*	*German*
Greece	*Greek*	*Greek*
Guatemala	*Guatemalan*	*Guatemalan*
Haiti	*Haitian*	*Haitian*
Honduras	*Honduran*	*Honduran*
India	*Indian*	*Indian*
Iran	*Iranian*	*Iranian*
Iraq	*Iraqi*	*Iraqi*
(the) Irish Republic	*Irish*	*Irishman, Irishwoman*
Israel	*Israeli*	*Israeli*
Italy	*Italian*	*Italian*
Jamaica	*Jamaican*	*Jamaican*
Japan	*Japanese*	*Japanese*
Mexico	*Mexican*	*Mexican*
(the) Netherlands	*Dutch*	*Dutchman, Dutchwoman*
New Zealand	*New Zealand*	*New Zealander*
Panama	*Panamanian*	*Panamanian*
Paraguay	*Paraguayan*	*Paraguayan*
Peru	*Peruvian*	*Peruvian*
Puerto Rico	*Puerto Rican*	*Puerto Rican*
Portugal	*Portuguese*	*Portuguese*
Russia	*Russian*	*Russian*
Saudi Arabia	*Saudi, Saudi Arabian*	*Saudi, Saudi Arabian*
South Africa	*South African*	*South African*
Spain	*Spanish*	*Spaniard*
Turkey	*Turkish*	*Turk*
(the) United Kingdom	*British*	*Brit*
(the) United States of America	*American*	*American*
Uruguay	*Uruguayan*	*Uruguayan*
Venezuela	*Venezuelan*	*Venezuelan*

The plural for the person from a particular country is usually formed by adding *-s*. But words ending in *-ese* stay the same (for example, *the Japanese*), and words like *Frenchman* or *Frenchwoman* become *Frenchmen* or *Frenchwomen*.
Be careful! We always begin these words with a capital letter: we write *Mexican* (and not *mexican*).

neatness /ˈniːt.nəs/ [uncountable noun] The quality of being tidy: *The content of your compositions is of course very important, but don't forget neatness, too!*

↑**necessary** /ˈnes.ə.ser.i/ [adjective] What is needed: *I'm not feeling very well today but I don't think it's necessary to call the doctor.*

necessity /nəˈses·ɪ·t̬i/ [uncountable noun] Something that is needed: *We'll only borrow his car in case of necessity.* ■ The plural is "necessities".

↑**neck** /nek/ [countable noun] The part of your body between the head and the shoulders: *Giraffes have very long necks.* 👁 **See page 421.**

necklace /ˈnek.ləs/ [countable noun] A piece of jewelry that goes round your neck: *My aunt sometimes wears an emerald necklace around her neck.* 👁 See picture at **jewelry**.

need[1] /niːd/ [uncountable noun] **1** Something that is necessary: *There is great need for food in many parts of the world.* **2 in need of** Lacking in something: *A lot of African countries are in need of doctors.*

↑**need**[2] /niːd/ [verb] To require or to be necessary: *You need to do more exercise if you want to keep fit.* ■ This verb can be a modal verb.

↑**needle** /ˈniːdl/ [countable noun] **1** A small thin piece of metal used for sewing: *Here's a needle and thread; sew the button on your coat.* **2** A long thin piece of metal or plastic used for knitting: *I had to use a pair of very fine needles to make this tiny sweater for my sister's baby.*

needless /ˈniːd.ləs/ [adjective] Not necessary: *Needless to say, Patsy told Dana about the problem.*

needn't /ˈniː.dᵊnt/ The contraction of "need not".

negation /nɪˈɡeɪʃən/ [uncountable noun] The act of denying: *Negation of the facts will get you nowhere.*

↑**negative**[1] /ˈneɡətɪv/ [adjective] Indicating "no", "not", "never" and so on: *"They didn't go shopping" is a negative sentence.*

negative[2] /ˈneɡətɪv/ [countable noun] A piece of film from which you can make a photograph: *Keep the negatives in case you need more copies.*

neglect[1] /nɪˈɡlekt/ [uncountable noun] A failure to give attention to somebody or something: *The local church is in a terrible state of neglect.*

neglect[2] /nɪˈɡlekt/ [verb] To give little attention to somebody or something: *Some people have pets and when they get tired of them they neglect them.*

neigh [verb] To make the sound that a horse makes: *The pony started neighing when it saw the field.*

↑**neighbor** [countable noun] A person who lives near you: *She always says "Hello" to the neighbors when she meets them in the elevator.*

↑**neighborhood** [countable noun] The area round the place where you live: *The neighborhood is becoming affected by the increase in street violence.* ■ We usually say "area".

neighboring [adjective] Being near: *We tried to hitchhike to the neighboring town but nobody stopped to pick us up.*

neither[1] US: /ˈniːðər/ UK: /ˈnaɪðər/ [adverb] **1** Not: *Peter never makes his bed, and neither does his brother.* **2 neither... nor...** Not and not: *As it was raining yesterday we played neither soccer nor tennis.* ■ Be careful! We use "neither" with a positive verb and "either" with a negative verb.

neither[2] US: /ˈniːðər/ UK: /ˈnaɪðər/ [adjective and pronoun] Not one and not the other of two people or things: *Neither team scored any goals in the game yesterday.* ■ Be careful! We use "neither" with a positive verb and "either" with a negative verb.

↑**nephew** /ˈnef.juː, ˈnev-/ [countable noun] The son of your brother or sister: *My nephew is only seven years old and he can play the piano beautifully.* ■ We say "niece" for a girl. 👁 See picture at **family**.

Neptune /ˈneptjuːn/ [countable noun] A planet of the solar system that is eighth in order from the Sun: *Neptune is the farthest planet from the Sun.* 👁 **See page 447.**

↑**nerve** US: /nɝːv/ UK: /nɜːv/ ▮ [countable noun] **1** One of the long thin parts of the body that carries feelings to your brain and messages from it: *Messages travel along the nerves as a series of tiny electrical impulses.* ▮ [uncountable noun] **2** Courage: *She showed a lot of nerve under pressure.* **3** The cheek or lack of shame necessary to do something rude or outrageous: *She had the nerve to ask me to lend her $20, after insulting me in front of my friends.*

nerves US: /nɝːvz/ UK: /nɜːvz/ [plural noun] The state of being worried or afraid: *My grandma says that grandpa has suffered with his nerves ever since the car accident he had last year.*

↑**nervous** /ˈnɜr·vəs/ [adjective] **1** Worried or afraid: *The mysterious phone calls made everyone in the house nervous.* 👁 See picture at **emotions**. **2** Belonging to the nerves in the body: *The nervous system controls the activities of your body.*

Nessie [noun] A popular nickname for a monster that is supposed to live in a lake in Scotland: *If you ever go to Loch Ness, Nessie may give you a fright.* ■ Be careful! "Nessie" has a capital "N".

↑**nest** /nest/ [countable noun] A place built by birds or small animals to live in: *Birds lay their eggs in nests.*

↑**net** /net/ [noun] A material made of crossed over string, rope and so on, with holes: *Margaret must have been nervous in the tennis game because she kept hitting the ball into the net.*

nettle /ˈnet.l̩/ US: /ˈnet̬-/ [countable noun] A wild plant with stinging leaves: *Be careful with those nettles when you walk through this part of the field.*

network /'net,wзrk/ [countable noun] A system of people or things that are linked together over some distance: *Internet is a large computer network.*

neuron /'njʊərɒn/ [countable noun] A nerve cell that connects the brain to another part of the body: *Neurons transmit impulses.*

neuter [adjective] In certain languages, of the gender which is neither masculine nor feminine: *a neuter noun.*

neutral /'nu·trəl/ [adjective] **1** Not committed to one side or the other: *Switzerland remained neutral during the Second World War.* **2** In chemistry, neither acid nor alkali: *Some substances, like water, are neutral.* **3** In physics, having no charge, neither positive nor negative: *Neutrons are neutral atoms.* **4** Having no particular or strong characteristics: *a neutral color.*

*****never** /'nev·ər/ [adverb] Not at any time: *My father never takes the car when he goes to the city center.* ■ "Never" usually goes before the main verb and after auxiliary verbs like "be", "do" or "have". We don't use "never" with a negative verb. ■ See box at **frequency**.

*****nevertheless** /ˌnev·ər·ðə'les/ [adverb] Despite that, however: *He feels down but nevertheless he says that he is going to continue in the race.*

*****new** US: /nuː/ UK: /njuː/ [adjective] **1** Recently made, bought for the first time: *Come home with me and I'll show you my new CD player.* 👁 See picture at **opposite**. **2** Seen or met for the first time: *I saw the new teacher in the supermarket this morning.* **3** New Year's Day See "New Year's Day" in the word **year**. **4** New Year's Eve See "New Year's Eve" in the word **year**.

newly US: /'nuː.li/ UK: /'njuː.li/ [adverb] Recently: *Don't touch the door because it's newly painted.*

*****news** US: /nuːz/ UK: /njuːz/ [uncountable noun] Information about new events: *There is no interesting news in today's paper.* ■ Be careful! We don't say "a news". We say "the news", "some news" or "a piece of news".

newsagent /'njuːzˌeɪ.dʒənt/ US: /'nuːz-/ [countable noun] A person who has a store that sells newspapers: *I always have a little conversation with the newsagent when I go to buy the newspaper.*

newsagent's UK: /'njuːzˌeɪdʒənt/ [countable noun] See **newsstand**. ■ This word is British English.

*****newspaper** US: /'nuːzˌpeɪ.pɚ/ UK: /'njuːzˌpeɪ.pəʳ/ [countable noun] Sheets of printed paper with news, opinion, pictures and so on: *Have a look at the weather report in the newspaper.* ■ The same meaning: "paper".

newsstand [countable noun] A store that sells newspapers: *I'm going to buy a magazine at the newsstand.* ■ In British English they say "newsagent's". 👁 See picture at **street**.

*****next**[1] /nekst/ [adjective] **1** Coming after this one, the following: *Turn right at the next crossroads and you'll see the shopping center on your left.* **2** next to Beside: *If you want to make a phone call you'll find a call box next to the bookstore.* ■ Be careful! We say: "I'd like to go to Italy next year". We don't say: "I'd like to go to Italy the next year". 👁 See picture at **preposition**.

next[2] /nekst/ [adverb] Coming after something: *I've done the exercise, Miss Furlow. What shall I do next?*

next-door [adjective] In the next building: *Our next-door neighbors are very nice.*

nib /nɪb/ [countable noun] The pointed end of a fountain pen: *I have a special pen with a gold nib.*

*****nice** /naɪs/ [adjective] **1** Pleasant, good: *We had very nice weather during our stay in Majorca.* **2** Kind, friendly: *Be nice to your brother because he's nervous about his tests.* ■ The comparative form is "nicer" and the superlative form is "nicest".

nickel /'nɪk.l/ ▮ [uncountable noun] **1** A shiny metal with a special color that is white with a little silver: *Nickel occurs naturally and is used in steel-making.* ▮ [countable noun] **2** A five cents coin: *The storekeeper gave me back a nickel.*

nickname /'nɪk.neɪm/ [countable noun] An informal name used instead of your real name, especially by friends and family: *William F. Cody's nickname was "Buffalo Bill" because he was a buffalo hunter.*

*****niece** /niːs/ [countable noun] The daughter of your brother or sister: *Mrs. Brown's niece is coming to spend Christmas with her.* ■ We say "nephew" for a boy. 👁 See picture at **family**.

*****night** /naɪt/ [noun] **1** The part of the day when it is dark: *Nights are shorter in summer than in winter.* **2** good night An expression that you use before going to bed: *Say "good night " and go to bed.* ■ Compare "good night" with "good evening" (a greeting that is used in the evening).

nightclub /'naɪt.klʌb/ [countable noun] A place for entertainment that opens at night: *My parents went to a nightclub to see a musical show yesterday.*

nightdress /'naɪt.dres/ [countable noun] A kind of thin dress that women wear in bed: *They gave me a beautiful nightdress with pink spots.* ■ The same meaning: "nightgown". "Nightie" is informal for "nighdress".

nightgown [countable noun] A kind of thin dress that women wear in bed: *My sister prefers pajamas to nightgown.* ■ The same meaning: "nightdress".

nightie /'naɪ.ti/ US: /-t̬i/ [countable noun] See **nightdress.** ■ This word is informal.

nightingale /'naɪ.tɪŋ.geɪl/ US: /-t̬ɪŋ-/ [countable noun] A small bird that is known for its beautiful singing: *Nightingales usually sing at night.*

nightmare /'naɪt,meər/ [countable noun] A bad dream: *Last night I had a nightmare about Dracula running after me.*

night table [countable noun] A small low table which is placed next to a bed: *Mary switched off the alarm clock on her night table.* ■ The same meaning: "bedside table", "side table".

night-time /'naɪt.taɪm/ **night-time** The time when it is dark: *We saw a lot of bats near the river at night-time.*

nil /nɪl/ [uncountable noun] Nothing; zero: *Houston won the game by one goal to nil.* ■ We usually say "nil" in scores in sport.

↑**nine** /naɪn/ [noun, adjective and pronoun] The number 9: *I've done nine of the ten parts of the exercise. One more and I've finished.*

nineteen /,naɪn'tiːn/ [noun, adjective and pronoun] The number 19: *My sister is nineteen years old.*

nineteenth /,naɪn'tiːntθ/ [noun and adjective] Referring to nineteen: *Queen Victoria lived in the nineteenth century.* ■ "Nineteenth" can also be written "19th".

ninetieth /'naɪn·ti·əθ/ [noun and adjective] Referring to ninety: *They're celebrating their grandmother's ninetieth birthday tomorrow.* ■ "Ninetieth" can also be written "90th".

ninety /'naɪn·ti/ [noun, adjective and pronoun] The number 90: *The post office building is ninety years old.*

ninth /naɪntθ/ [noun and adjective] Referring to nine: *The company offices are on the ninth floor.* ■ "Ninth" can also be written "9th".

nitrogen /'naɪtrədʒən/ [uncountable noun] A gaseous element which makes up 80 per cent of the atmosphere: *Nitrogen is an essential part of biological molecules.*

↑**no**[1] /nəʊ/ [adverb] **1** The opposite of yes: *"Do you speak German?" "No, I don't".* **2 no longer** Not any more, in a past time but not now: *I no longer go swimming every morning; with the tests there's no time.*

↑**no**[2] [adjective] **1** Not any, zero: *No animals were hurt in the fire at the zoo last week.* ■ See box at **some. 2** A word that shows you cannot do something: *The sign on the wall says "No parking".*

nobility US: /noʊ'bɪl.ə.t̬i/ UK: /nəʊ'bɪl.ɪ.ti/ [uncountable noun] Members of society belonging to a high rank: *The nobility lost a lot of its power after the Industrial Revolution.*

noble[1] /'nəʊbl/ [countable noun] A member of the aristocracy: *In the past, the nobles were the ruling class.*

noble[2] /'noʊ·bəl/ [adjective] **1** Morally fine, unselfish and admirable: *It was a very noble gesture.* **2** Having a high social rank: *She has noble origins.*

nobleman /'nəʊblmən/ [countable noun] A male member of the nobility: *The nobleman ruled over his properties.* ■ The plural is "noblemen". ■ A female member of the nobility is a "noblewoman".

noblewoman /'nəʊbl,wʊmən/ [countable noun] A female member of the nobility: *The main role of a noblewoman in the Middle Ages was to give her husband a son.* ■ The plural is "noblewomen". ■ A male member of the nobility is a "nobleman".

↑**nobody** US: /'noʊ.bɑː.di/ UK: /'nəʊ.bə.di/ [pronoun] No person: *There's nobody you can speak to just now.* ■ The same meaning: "no one". ■ Be careful! We use "nobody" with a positive verb. ■ "Nobody" is used with a singular verb. ■ See box at **anybody**.

nocturnal /nɒk'tɜːnəl/ [adjective] Of the night or that takes place or is active at night: *The owl is a nocturnal bird.*

nod US: /nɑːd/ UK: /nɒd/ [verb] To move your head up and down: *Don't just nod when I ask you a question. Answer properly.* ■ This word describes an action with a positive meaning. ■ Look at the spelling of these forms: "nodded", "nodding".

↑**noise** /nɔɪz/ [noun] An unpleasant or load sound: *This vacuum cleaner makes a lot of noise.*

↑**noisy** /'nɔɪ.zi/ [adjective] Making lots of noise, very loud: *Our street is very noisy on weekdays.* ■ The comparative form is "noisier" and the superlative form is "noisiest".

nomad /'noʊ·mæd/ [countable noun] A member of a tribe which does not live in one fixed place, moving around, or an individual who does the same: *In the paleolithic era the people were nomads and lived by hunting, fishing and gathering wild plants.*

non- /nɒn-/ [prefix] An addition to the beginning of a word that changes a word's meaning into its opposite: *A "non-alcoholic drink" is a drink that does not contain alcohol.*

↑**none** /nʌn/ [pronoun] Not one; not any: *None of my friends can run faster than me.*

↑**nonsense** US: /'nɑːn.sents/ UK: /'nɒn.sᵊnts/ [uncountable noun] Foolish or silly things: *Don't talk nonsense!*

non-stop US: /,nɑːn'stɑːp/ UK: /,nɒn'stɒp/ [adjective and adverb] Without a stop: *They flew non-stop from Boston to Tokyo.*

noon /nuːn/ [uncountable noun] Midday, twelve o'clock in the midday: *The sun is at its highest at noon.*

↑**no one** [pronoun] See **nobody.** ■ Be careful! We use "no one" with a positive verb. ■ "No one" is used with a singular verb. ■ See box at **anybody**.

↑**nor** US: /nɔːr/ UK: /nɔːʳ/ [conjunction] **1** And not also: *I like neither football nor basketball.* **2** Not either: *I do* *not know how to use this computer and nor do you.* ■ "Nor" is used after phrases with "neither" or "not".

normal /ˈnɔr·məl/ [adjective] Usual; common: *Storms are quite normal in summer around here.*

north US: /nɔːrθ/ UK: /nɔːθ/ [uncountable noun, adjective and adverb] The direction on your left when the sun rises: *You'll find the lake if you keep going north.* ■ See box at **abbreviations**.

northeast [uncountable noun] In between the north and the east: *Brazil's a very large country in the northeast of South America.* ■ See box at **abbreviations**.

northern US: /ˈnɔːr.ðɚn/ UK: /ˈnɔː.ðən/ [adjective] Of the north: *There are a lot of lakes in northern United States.*

North Pole [noun] The most northern place of the earth: *The Norwegian Explorer Roald Amundsen reached the North Pole in 1926.* ■ Be careful! "North Pole" has capital letters.

northwest [uncountable noun] In between the north and the west: *Oregon is in the northwest of United States.* ■ See box at **abbreviations**.

nose US: /noʊz/ UK: /nəʊz/ [countable noun] **1** The part of your face that is just above your mouth: *Tommy fell off his bike and broke his nose.* See picture at **face**. **2 to blow your nose** To blow air through your nose to clean it: *You make a lot of noise when you blow your nose.* **3 to turn your nose up at (something)** To think that something is not good enough for you or to refuse it because you don't like it: *Why did you turn your nose up at the tie I bought you?*

nostalgia /nɑˈstæl·dʒə/, /nə-/, /nəˈstɑl-/ [uncountable noun] A longing for things that happened before: *I often feel nostalgia for where I lived before.* ■ Be careful with the pronunciation of this word!

nostril US: /ˈnɑː.strəl/ UK: /ˈnɒs.trəl/ [countable noun] One of the two holes in the nose that admit air and smells: *My left nostril is blocked.* **See page 425.**

not US: /nɑːt/ UK: /nɒt/ [adverb] **1** A word that makes another word negative: *She's not happy here.* **2 not any longer** Not any more, in a past time but not now: *He doesn't live there any longer. He has moved house.* **3 not at all 1** Not even, a little: *I don't remember his face at all.* **2** A polite way of answering when somebody says "thank you": *Thanks for your help. "Not at all".* ■ In this use, the same meaning: "you're welcome".

note[1] /nəʊt/ [countable noun] **1** Written words that help your memory: *He made a note of the things he had to buy for the trip.* **2** A written message: *I'm going to leave a note for my mom to say I'll be back at six.* **3** A sound in music: *Tracy can't sing a note.* **See page 460. 4 to take notes** To make notes: *He took a lot of notes at the lecture.*

note[2] /nəʊt/ [verb] **1** To give attention to something: *I noted from her tone of voice that Marie seemed to be rather depressed.* **2 to note (something) down** To write something to help your memory: *I'll just note down your telephone number.*

notebook /ˈnoʊtˌbʊk/ [countable noun] A small book where you make notes: *She keeps all her friends' addresses in a notebook.* See picture at **book**.

notepad /ˈnəʊtpæd/ [countable noun] Pieces of paper joined together where you make notes: *You'll find a notepad next to the telephone.*

notepaper US: /ˈnoʊtˌpeɪ.pɚ/ UK: /ˈnəʊtˌpeɪ.pəʳ/ [uncountable noun] Paper for writing letters: *I need some notepaper to write to Pat.*

nothing /ˈnʌθɪŋ/ [pronoun] **1** Not anything: *There's nothing we can do but wait until he calls.* ■ Be careful! We say: "I have nothing" or "I haven't anything". (We don't say: "I haven't nothing"). **2 for nothing** For no money: *Simon gave me the comics for nothing.*

notice[1] /ˈnəʊtɪs/ [countable noun] A public announcement: *The notice says "Visitors must not feed the animals".*

notice[2] /ˈnəʊtɪs/ [verb] **1** To see and note somebody or something: *Have you noticed the new tablecloth?* **2 to take no notice** To give no attention: *She took no notice of what I told her at lunch.*

noticeable /ˈnoʊ·t̬ɪ·sə·bəl/ [adjective] Easy to notice: *The woman we met had a noticeable French accent.*

noticeboard US: /ˈnoʊ.t̬ɪs.bɔːrd/ UK: /ˈnəʊ.tɪs.bɔːd/ [countable noun] See **bulletin board**. ■ This word is British English.

NOTE

†**noun** /naʊn/ [countable noun] A word by which you name somebody or something: *"Pamela" and "ship" are nouns.*

†**novel** US: /ˈnɑː.vᵊl/ UK: /ˈnɒv.ᵊl/ [countable noun] A book that tells a story about people or things: *What's your favorite novel?*

novelist [countable noun] Somebody who writes novels: *Many novelists now write on the computer, but not all.*

†**November** US: /noʊˈvem.bɚ/ UK: /nəʊˈvem.bəʳ/ [noun] The eleventh month of the year: *November has thirty days.* ■ Be careful! "November" has a capital "N". See picture at **calendar**.

†**now**[1] /naʊ/ [adverb] **1** At the present moment: *I can't say anything now.* **2** A word that you use to introduce a request, an explanation, a new subject and so on: *Now listen here!* **3** **from now on** After this moment: *From now on I'll walk to school alone.* **4** **now and then** Sometimes: *Uncle Fred comes to visit us now and then.*

now[2] /naʊ/ [conjunction] Since it is the case: *Now that he's poor, he has very few friends.*

nowadays /ˈnaʊ.ə.deɪz/ [adverb] At the present time: *Nowadays almost everybody has a television set.*

†**nowhere** US: /ˈnoʊ.wer/ UK: /ˈnəʊ.weəʳ/ [adverb] To no place or in no place: *You'll be going nowhere this evening because you have to study for your test on Monday.* ■ Be careful! We use "nowhere" with a positive verb.

†**nuclear** US: /ˈnuː.kliː.ɚ/ UK: /ˈnjuː.klɪəʳ/ [adjective] Using the power of atomic energy: *Nuclear tests are a danger to the environment.* **See page 439.**

nucleus /ˈnu·kli·əs/ [countable noun] **1** The central part of an atom or a cell: *The nucleus controls the cell.* **2** The most important part of a group, around which other parts or people cohere: *Julie and Anne form the nucleus of the drama group.* ■ The plural is "nuclei".

nude US: /nuːd/ UK: /njuːd/ [adjective] Without any clothes on: *Look! The children are bathing nude in the pool!*

nuisance /ˈnu·səns/ [noun] Somebody or something that annoys you: *Don't be a nuisance. I'm trying to do some work.*

†**number**[1] /ˈnʌmbər/ ▮ [countable noun] **1** A word or a figure that is used in counting: *Seven is the favorite number of many people.* ▮ [noun] **2** An amount: *A large number of people visit New York City every year.*

number[2] /ˈnʌmbər/ [verb] To give a number to: *We should number all these rows from 1 to 20.*

numbered [adjective] **1** With a number: *The tickets in this movie theater are numbered.* **2** That cannot go on for long: *The days of the manual typewriter are numbered, in the future there will only be electronic typewriters.* ■ Be careful with the pronunciation of the end of this word. The last "e" is not pronounced.

number plate [countable noun] See **license plate.** ■ This word is British English.

numerous /ˈnu·mər·əs/ [adjective] A lot of: *I've seen that movie on television on numerous occasions.*

nun /nʌn/ [countable noun] A woman who lives in a religious community: *Her aunt is a nun and lives in a convent.*

†**nurse**[1] /nɜːs/ [countable noun] A person who looks after sick people: *A nurse put a bandage on my ankle after I fell off my bicycle.*

nurse[2] /nɜːs/ [verb] To look after people who are sick or hurt: *The patients here are nursed by Red Cross members.*

nursery /ˈnɜr·sər·i/ [countable noun] **1** A place where children are looked after: *Tim goes to a nursery while his parents are at work.* **2** A room where young children play and sleep: *Debbie is playing with her toys in the nursery.* **3** A place where young trees and plants are grown and sold: *Let's go to the nursery and buy some plants for the backyard.* ■ The plural is "nurseries".

nursery rhyme [countable noun] A short poem or song for young children: *When I was young, my mother used to sing to me the nursery rhyme "Cackle, cackle".* ■ The plural is "nursery rhymes". ■ The same meaning "lullaby".

nursery school [countable noun] A school for children between three and five years old: *Helen's brother still goes to nursery school.* ■ The plural is "nursery schools".

†**nut** /nʌt/ [countable noun] **1** A dry kind of fruit that consists of a seed inside a hard shell: *You shouldn't crack those nuts with your teeth.* **2** A small piece of metal with a big hole in the middle: *Use a wrench for turning that nut!* **3** A word you use to say that somebody is mentally disturbed: *Quentin is a bit of a nut; he's always doing mad things.* ■ This use is informal.

nutrient /ˈnu·tri·ənt/ [countable noun] Substance that helps living things to develop and grow: *Mother's milk is rich in nutrients.*

nutrition /nuˈtrɪʃ·ən/ [uncountable noun] The process of taking in and assimilating food, or the study of this: *There is a new guide about health and nutrition during pregnancy.*

nylon /ˈnaɪlɒn/ [uncountable noun] A strong material that is used for making clothes: *I hate the nylon shirts that my mother buys me.*

O US: /oʊ/ UK: /əʊ/ **1** The fifteenth letter of the alphabet: *The name "Oliver" begins with an "O".* **2** A way of saying the number zero: *"My telephone number is: seven six two five o three". "Let me see...762503".*

oak or **oak tree** US: /oʊk/ UK: /əʊk/ [countable noun] **1** A large tree that produces acorns: *Oak was used in the past to build the hull and masts of sailing ships.* **2** **oak forest** A big group of these trees: *We went for a walk in the oak forest.* **See page 435.**

oar US: /ɔːr/ UK: /ɔːʳ/ [countable noun] A long piece of wood that you use to make rowboats move: *You take one oar and I'll take the other.*

oasis /oʊˈeɪ·sɪs/ [countable noun] A place in a desert where there is water: *Palm trees and plants can grow in an oasis.* ■ The plural is "oases".

oats US: /oʊts/ UK: /əʊts/ [plural noun] A kind of cereal plant: *She feeds her horse with oats.*

obedience /oʊˈbid·i·əns/ [uncountable noun] Being obedient: *Army officers expect obedience from lower rank soldiers.*

obedient /oʊˈbid·i·ənt/ [adjective] Ready to do what you are told: *We are trying to teach our dog to be obedient.*

↑**obey** /oʊˈbeɪ/ [verb] To do what people tell you to do: *If you don't obey the doctor's orders you'll never get better.*

↑**object**[1] /ˈɒbdʒɪkt/ [countable noun] **1** A thing that you can see or touch: *Can you see that strange object on top of the mountain?* **2** An aim, a purpose: *His object is to climb the mountain alone.* **3** The person or the thing that is affected by the action in a sentence: *In the sentence "Janet threw the ring out of the window", "the ring" is the object.*

object[2] /əbˈdʒekt/ [verb] To be against something: *Many people object to the new law.*

objection /əbˈdʒek.ʃən/ [countable noun] A reason against doing something: *They have no objection to our joining them on their expedition.*

↑**objective** /əbˈdʒek.tɪv/ [countable noun] A purpose towards which you work: *What's your real objective in life?*

obligation /ˌɑb·ləˈgeɪ·ʃən/ [countable noun] What you must do: *It's your obligation to study hard.*

obligatory [adjective] Required by law or rule: *It is obligatory to show your passport to go through customs.* ■ The same meaning: "mandatory".

oblige /əˈblaɪdʒ/ [verb] To make somebody do something: *The PE teacher obliged us to run around the playing field twenty times.*

oboe US: /ˈoʊ.boʊ/ UK: /ˈəʊ.bəʊ/ [countable noun] A musical instrument which has the shape of a tube and is played by blowing into its top: *The oboe has a distinctive sound.* ■ Be careful with the pronunciation of this word! "Boe" rhymes with "go". **See page 459.**

a b c d e f g h i j k l m n o p q r s t u v w x y z

⁺observation /ˌɑb·zər'veɪ·ʃən/ [countable noun] An examination: *They took the stones to the laboratory for observation.*

⁺observe /əb'zɜrv/ [verb] To watch or examine somebody or something: *I sometimes observe the stars through my telescope at night.*

obstacle /'ɑb·stə·kəl/ [countable noun] Something that stops or delays you: *She didn't let her physical disability be an obstacle to her success.*

obstinate /'ɑb·stə·nət/ [adjective] Not willing to change your mind: *She'll never apologize because she's very obstinate.*

obstruct /əb'strʌkt/ [verb] To be in the way of somebody or something: *The neighbor's van often obstructs our garage door.*

obstruction /əb'strʌk.ʃᵊn/ [countable noun] A thing that stops something moving freely: *There's an obstruction in the sink.*

⁺obtain /əb'teɪn/ [verb] To get something: *My brother obtained a diploma after doing a swimming course.*

⁺obvious /'ɑb·vi·əs/ [adjective] Easy to see or to understand: *It's quite obvious that Stephen isn't as tall as his sister.*

⁺occasion /ə'keɪ.ʒᵊn/ [countable noun] **1** A particular time: *We have already talked to the principal about the gym on three occasions.* **2** A special event: *Dad's fiftieth birthday will be quite an occasion.*

occasional /ə'keɪ.ʒᵊn.ᵊl, -'keɪʒ.nəl/ [adjective] Happening sometimes: *We have occasional conversations about football with our teacher.*

occipital [adjective] Relating to the back of the head: *He received a blow in the occipital area.*

occupant /'ɑk·jə·pənt/ [countable noun] Somebody who occupies a place or a seat, or lives in a particular room or house: *The occupants of the car were saved by their seat belts.*

occupation /ˌɑk·jə'peɪ·ʃən/ [countable noun] **1** Job, area of work: *"What's your father's occupation?" "He's a clerk.".* **2** Pastime: *Reading is Jim's favorite occupation.*

occupied /'ɑk·jəˌpɑɪd/ [adjective] **1** Busy: *I am very occupied at the moment. Can you call me back later tonight?* **2** Taken: *The back row of the movie theater is mostly occupied by young people.*

⁺occupy /'ɑk·jəˌpɑɪ/ [verb] **1** To live or to be in a place: *Who occupies the spare bedroom?* **2** To fill space or time: *This table occupies most of the kitchen.* **3** To invade a place: *The Germans occupied Poland in 1939.* ■ Be careful with the spelling of these forms: "occupies", "occupied".

⁺occur /ə'kɜr/ [verb] **1** To happen: *The fire occurred when there was no one in the store.* **2** To come into your mind suddenly: *The idea for the song occurred to me while I was taking my bath.* ■ Be careful with the spelling of these forms: "occurred", "occurring".

⁺ocean /'oʊ·ʃən/ [uncountable noun] A very large extension of sea: *The Pacific Ocean is between Asia and America.* 👁 **See page 444.**

oceanic /ˌoʊ·ʃi'æn·ɪk/ [adjective] Referring to the ocean: *The oceanic currents vary constantly.*

ocean liner [countable noun] A large ship that carries people across oceans: *Have you ever been on an ocean liner?* ■ We also say "liner".

⁺o'clock /ə'klɑk/ [adverb] A word that you use for telling the time: *Wendy starts school at nine o'clock.* ■ Be careful! "O'clock" is only used with full hours. We say: "5 o'clock". We don't say: "5.20 o'clock".

⁺October US: /ɑːk'toʊ.bɚ/ UK: /ɒk'təʊ.bəʳ/ [noun] The tenth month of the year: *My mother's birthday is in October.* ■ Be careful! "October" has a capital "O". 👁 See picture at **calendar**.

octopus US: /'ɑːk.tə.pəs/ UK: /'ɒk.tə.pəs/ [countable noun] A sea creature with eight arms: *They fish for octopuses in the Atlantic Ocean.* ■ The plural is "octopuses" or "octopi".

⁺odd¹ /ɒd/ [adjective] **1** Strange: *I don't think she's mad but she's certainly odd.* **2** **odd number** A number that can't be divided by two: *1, 3, 5, 7 are all odd numbers.* ■ Compare with "even number" (a number that can be exactly divided by two).

odd² [adverb] Approximately, more or less: *I got a postcard from Philip twenty odd days ago.*

odd man out [uncountable noun] One that is not like the others: *"Castle", "chair", "cottage", "house"; which is the odd man out?*

odor US: /'oʊ.dɚ/ [countable noun] A distinctive smell: *There was a strong odor of cigarette smoke in the room.* ■ The British English spelling is "odour".

odorless /'oʊ·dər·ləs/ [adjective] Without a smell: *They gave us an odorless liquid to drink.* ■ Compare with "scented" (having a pleasant smell).

odour /'əʊdər/ [countable noun] See **odor.** ■ This is a British English spelling.

⁺of US: /ɑːv/ UK: /əv/ [preposition] **1** Belonging to something: *The end of the movie is a bit surprising.* **2** Containing: *There's another bottle of milk in the fridge.* **3** Indicating quantity: *I bought five liters of lemonade for the children's party.* **4** Indicating what something is made from: *Mom gave us another bar of chocolate.* **5** Indicating a date: *They're opening the new shopping center on the first of June.* **6** Indicating a cause: *My grandfather died of cancer last summer.* **7** About: *What did you think of the story she told us?* 👁 See picture at **preposition**.

off¹ /ɒf/ [adjective] Not fresh: *Don't cook that fish because it's a bit off.* ■ Be careful! "Off" never goes before a noun.

off[2] /ɒf/ [adverb and preposition] **1** Away from a place or down from a place: *The town we're looking for is still ten miles off.* **2** Not on, not being used: *It's cold in the house because the heat is off.* **3** Free: *We have two weeks off at Easter.* **4** No longer fresh: *That meat's gone off.* See picture at **preposition**.

offence /ə'fents/ [countable noun] **1** Something that goes against the law: *Drug dealing is a serious offence.* **2 to take offence** To be angry: *He takes offence if you don't say "Hello" to him.*

offend /ə'fend/ [verb] To make somebody angry or unhappy: *Her words offended everybody at the party.*

offensive [adjective] **1** Insulting: *offensive remarks.* **2** Disgusting: *an offensive smell.*

offer[1] /'ɒfər/ [countable noun] **1** Something that you propose to do or give to help somebody: *Thanks for your offer to help with the dishes.* **2** Something that you propose to give somebody to get something: *Tim made me an offer for my surfboard this morning.*

offer[2] /'ɒfər/ [verb] **1** To be willing to give somebody something they need: *She offered me her new racket because mine was broken.* **2** To be willing to help somebody: *My father offered to take us to the game.*

office US: /'ɑː.fɪs/ UK: /'ɒf.ɪs/ [countable noun] **1** A room or a building where people do business, clerical work and so on: *Tom's mother works in a big office.* **2 head office** See **head office**.

officer US: /'ɑː.fɪ.sɚ/ UK: /'ɒf.ɪ.səʳ/ [countable noun] **1** A person with authority in the armed forces or the police: *The soldiers opened fire when the officer gave the order.* **2** A person who does a public job with some responsibility: *The prison officers took him down to his cell.*

official[1] /ə'fɪʃəl/ [adjective] Done or approved by the government or another authority: *The news of the President's illness became official two days ago.*

official[2] /ə'fɪʃəl/ [countable noun] A person in a position of authority in a public organization: *Mrs. Montfort is an important official in the Civil Service.*

offline /ɒf'laɪn/ [adjective and adverb] Not connected to the internet or to a central system: *an offline system.* ■ Compare with "online[1]" (connected to the internet or to a computer).

offshore /ˌɒf'ʃɔːr/ [adjective] **1** Situated at sea at some distance from the coast: *An offshore platform was built by the oil company.* **2** Referring to the wind, blowing from the land towards the sea: *Offshore winds tend to occur in the early evening, when the air over the ocean is warmer than the air over land.* **3** Based in a different country, which offers tax advantages: *Offshore accounts are popular among people who do not want to pay taxes.*

offside [adjective] In some sports, especially in soccer and hockey, in a position which is not allowed by the rules between the ball and the opponents' goal: *The goal was disallowed because the player was offside.*

offspring /'ɒfsprɪŋ/ [countable noun] The children or descendants of an individual, or the young of an animal: *Their offspring all go to good schools.* ■ The plural is also "offspring".

often /'ɔ·fən/, /'ɔf·tən/, /'ɑf·ən/, /'ɑf·tən/ [adverb] Many times, frequently: *I often meet my friends at the bowling alley.* ■ "Often" usually goes before the main verb and after auxiliary verbs like "be", "do" or "have": "I'm often late for school". ■ See box at **frequency**.

oh US: /oʊ/ UK: /əʊ/ [interjection] An expression of surprise, disagreement, pleasure or when you suddenly remember something: *Oh no, not the phone again!*

oil[1] /ɔɪl/ [uncountable noun] **1** A greasy liquid that is used in cooking: *This salad needs a little more oil.* **2** A greasy liquid that comes from under the ground: *Put some oil into the engine.* **3 oil painting** A picture painted in oil colors: *We saw many beautiful oil paintings at the MoMA last year.*

oil[2] [verb] To grease something with oil: *You should oil your bike from time to time.*

oily /'ɔɪ.li/ [adjective] Like oil or covered with oil: *This fish is very oily.* ■ The comparative form is "oilier" and the superlative form is "oiliest".

OK /'oʊ'keɪ/, /ˌoʊ'keɪ/, /'oʊˌkeɪ/ A written abbreviation for **okay**. ■ Be careful! "OK" is always written in capital letters. ■ See box at **abbreviations**.

okay /'oʊ'keɪ/, /ˌoʊ'keɪ/, /'oʊˌkeɪ/ [adjective and adverb] **1** Yes; all right: *"Let's have a coke". "Okay".* **2** All right; well: *Is your sister okay this morning?* ■ The abbreviation "OK" is only used in written language.

old US: /oʊld/ UK: /əʊld/ [adjective] **1** That has lived a long time: *Diana's grandmother is very old.* See picture at **opposite**. **2** Made a long time ago: *The town church is very old.* **3** Known for a long time: *The doctor is an old friend of my parents.* **4** Of age: *Lynn is fifteen years old.* ■ The comparative form is "older" and the superlative form is "oldest". When people's ages are compared, especially the ages of members of a family, "elder" and "eldest" can be used: "John is the elder of the two". "Ann is my eldest sister".

older [adjective] The comparative form of **old**.

oldest [adjective] The superlative form of **old**.

old-fashioned /'oʊld'fæʃ·ənd/ [adjective] Not in use any more, belonging to former times: *The music my brother likes is a bit old-fashioned.* ■ Be careful with the pronunciation of this word. The "e" is not pronounced.

a b c d e f g h i j k l m n **o** p q r s t u v w x y z

olfactory US: /ɑːl'fæk.ter.i/ UK: /ɒl'fæk.tər.i/ [adjective] Referring to the sense of smell: *The olfactory sense is very powerful in dogs.* ■ This word is formal.

olive US: /'ɑː.lɪv/ UK: /'ɒl.ɪv/ [countable noun] A small black or green fruit which produces oil and is used as food: *Those olives taste very bitter.*

olive oil [uncountable noun] Oil made from olives: *Fry the fish in olive oil for ten minutes.*

Olympic [adjective] Relating to the Olympic Games: *She is an Olympic gold medalist.*

Olympic Games or **Olympics** /ə'lɪmpɪkˌgeɪmz/ [plural noun] An international sports competition: *The Olympic Games are held every four years.* ■ Be careful! "Olympic Games" has capital letters.

omelette US: /'ɑː.mə.lət/ UK: /'ɒm.lət/ [countable noun] Eggs that you beat and fry in oil: *My father often makes us an omelette for breakfast.*

omit /oʊ'mɪt/ [verb] **1** To leave something out: *Let's omit the last verse of the song.* **2** Not to do something: *She omitted to put her address on her application form.* ■ Be careful with the spelling of these forms: "omitted", "omitting".

omnivore US: /'ɑːm.nɪ.vɔːr/ UK: /'ɒm.nɪ.vɔːr/ [countable noun] An animal which is both herbivore and carnivore: *Chimpanzees and chickens are omnivores.* 👁 **See page 427.**

↑**on** US: /ɑːn/ UK: /ɒn/ [adverb and preposition] **1** Showing position: *Nicola sat on the teacher's desk.* **2** Showing direction: *You'll see the underground entrance on your left.* **3** Showing when: *We're going to a rock concert on Saturday.* **4** Being used, working: *The lights are still on in my parents' bedroom.* **5** Inside a bus, train, boat or plane: *She saw a movie on the plane.* **6** At the time of: *On leaving the museum, Mr. Thomas remembered that he had to go and pick up his coat from the dry-cleaner's.* **7** Covering a part of your body: *Timothy had his new sneakers on.* **8** Showing that something continues: *She read on through the morning.* **9** About: *At the moment I'm reading a book on astronomy.* **10** Taking place; happening: *What's on at the movies this week?* **11** **on and on** Without stopping: *Richard talks on and on and never lets you speak.* ■ See box at **time: prepositions**. 👁 See picture at **preposition**.

↑**once**[1] /wʌns/ [adverb] **1** One time: *Take these pills once a day.* **2** At one time in the past: *She only brought her car here once.* **3** **at once** **1** Immediately: *Stop making that noise at once!* **2** At the same time: *Don't all get into the car at once.* **4** **once upon a time** The words that are often used at the beginning of a story: *Once upon a time there were three little pigs.*

once[2] /wʌns/ [conjunction] As soon as: *I'll relax once I've found the keys.*

↑**one**[1] [noun and adjective] **1** The number 1: *She's got a big number one on her T-shirt.* **2** A single thing or person: *There's only one disco in the town.* **3** Some: *One day I'll be a famous rock singer.* **4** Only: *I've found the one book I need: "How To Do Everything".*

one[2] /wʌn/ [pronoun] **1** A word that represents a person or a thing already mentioned: *I don't want the blue tie. Give me the red one.* **2** Anybody: *One must always help a friend in need.* **3** **one another** Words that show that people do the same thing or feel the same way: *They always kiss one another when they meet.* ■ In this use, the same meaning: "each other".

oneself /ˌwʌn'self/ [pronoun] **1** A word that refers to a person in general when "one" is the subject of a sentence: *One never knows oneself very well.* **2** A word that makes "one" stronger: *It would be easier to do it oneself.* **3** **by oneself** **1** Alone: *It doesn't sound like fun to spend a whole week camping by oneself.* **2** Without help: *It is difficult to do these math problems by oneself.*

↑**onion** /'ʌn.jən/ [countable noun] A root vegetable with a strong taste and smell: *You've put too much onion in this salad.* 👁 **See page 437.**

online[1] US: /ˌɑːn'laɪn/ UK: /ˌɒn'laɪn/ [adjective] **1** Connected to or controlled by a computer: *an online system.* ■ Compare with "offline" (not connected to the internet or to a central system). **2** On the internet: *Many people like online shopping.*

online[2] US: /ˌɑːn'laɪn/ UK: /ˌɒn'laɪn/ [adverb] **1** Do on the internet, or buy from it: *All the members of the team work online.* **2** **to {go/come} online** Referring to a system, start operating: *The new factory went online last month.*

only[1] /'əʊnli/ [adjective] Being one and no more: *Be careful with it. It's the only skateboard I have.*

↑**only**[2] /'əʊnli/ [adverb] **1** With nothing or no one else: *There are only two customers in the supermarket.* **2** Used to show that something happened very recently: *They came from Tokyo only this morning.*

only[3] /'əʊnli/ [conjunction] But: *I'd buy the video, only it's a bit expensive.*

onomatopoeia /ˌɑn·əˌmɑt̬·ə'pi·ə/, /-mæt̬·ə-/ [countable noun] The formation of a word which resembles the sound which it names: *"Splash" is an onomatopoeia.*

onomatopoeic /ˌɒn.əʊˌmæt.ə'piː.ɪk/ US: /ˌɑː.noʊˌmæt̬.oʊ-/ [adjective] Referring to the use of a word which resembles the sound it names: *"Vroom" is an onomatopoeic word.*

↑**onto** US: /'ɑːn.tu/ UK: /'ɒn.tu/ [preposition] To a position on something or on somebody: *The cat jumped* *onto the table in a flash.* 👁 See picture at **preposition.**

onwards US: /ˈɑːn.wɚdz/ UK: /ˈɒn.wədz/ [adverb] **1** Ahead, in a forward direction: *Keep moving onwards.* **2** After a particular moment: *From then onwards they were friends.*

opal /ˈəʊ.pəl/ US: /ˈoʊ-/ [countable noun] A precious stone made of a compound similar to quartz: *Opal changes color depending on your position.*

opaque /oʊˈpeɪk/ [adjective] **1** That you cannot see through, the opposite of transparent: *A film applied to windows protects them against the sun by making them opaque from outside.* ■ Compare with "transparent" (that you can see through). **2** Unclear, difficult to understand: *a very opaque explanation.*

open¹ /ˈəʊpən/ [adjective] **1** In a position that allows passage, not closed: *It's cold in here because the windows have been open all morning.* 👁 See picture at **opposite**. **2** Ready for customers or visitors: *The supermarket isn't open on Monday afternoons.* **3** Not covered: *The best way to see Miami is from an open bus.* **4** **in the open air** Out of doors, outside: *I like doing exercise in the open air.*

⁺**open²** /ˈəʊpən/ [verb] **1** To move something so that it is not covered or closed: *Open the car door when I tell you, please.* **2** To become open: *The windows opened with the wind last night.* **3** To make a place open to the public: *They've opened a new computer store very near here.*

opener US: /ˈoʊ.pᵊn.ɚ/ UK: /ˈəʊ.pᵊn.əʳ/ [countable noun] **1** An instrument that opens something: *There's a bottle opener in the kitchen cupboard.* **2** **can opener** See **can opener**.

⁺**opening** US: /ˈoʊp.nɪŋ/ UK: /ˈəʊ.pᵊn.ɪŋ/ [countable noun] **1** A hole or a gap in something: *The neighbors' children come in through an opening in the wall.* **2** A beginning: *Hardly anybody came to the opening of the new bookstore.*

opera US: /ˈɑː.pɚ.ə/ UK: /ˈɒp.ᵊr.ə/ [countable noun] A musical play where the actors sing the words: *"Carmen" is a famous opera by Bizet.*

⁺**operate** US: /ˈɑː.pə.reɪt/ UK: /ˈɒp.ᵊr.eɪt/ [verb] **1** To work, when talking about a machine or instrument: *This stove operates on both gas and electricity.* **2** To control a machine: *Do you know how to operate this camera?* **3** To cut open somebody's body in order to make part of it healthy again: *Doctor Green operated on my leg after the accident.* ■ Be careful! We say: "operate **on** (somebody or something)".

⁺**operation** /ˌɑp.əˈreɪ.ʃən/ [countable noun] The act of cutting a person's body to make part of it healthy again: *I had an operation on my elbow last month.*

operator US: /ˈɑː.pə.reɪ.t̬ɚ/ UK: /ˈɒp.ᵊr.eɪ.təʳ/ [countable noun] **1** A person who controls a machine: *My uncle is a computer operator.* **2** A person who connects telephone calls: *Call the operator if you need Karen's phone number.*

⁺**opinion** /əˈpɪn.jən/ [countable noun] An idea or a belief about something: *What's your opinion of the new Math teacher?*

⁺**opponent** /əˈpoʊ·nənt/ [countable noun] A person who is against you in something: *Our opponents deserved their victory because they played better than we did.*

⁺**opportunity** US: /ˌɑː.pɚˈtuː.nə.t̬i/ UK: /ˌɒp.əˈtjuː.nə.ti/ [countable noun] A chance, possibility: *I'll give you an opportunity to beat me at chess.* ■ The plural is "opportunities".

⁺**oppose** /əˈpoʊz/ [verb] To go against something: *All the neighbors are opposed to the loss of the park.*

⁺**opposite¹** /ˈɒpəzɪt/ [adjective] Completely different: *"Hot" is the opposite word of "cold".*

⁺**opposite²** /ˈɒpəzɪt/ [countable noun] Somebody or something that is completely different: *The opposite of black is white.* 👁 See picture on the following page.

⁺**opposite³** /ˈɒpəzɪt/ [preposition] In a position directly on the other side of somebody or something: *The girl sitting opposite us is Luke's girlfriend.* 👁 See picture at **preposition**.

optic¹ /ˈɑp·tɪk/ [countable noun] A device which is attached to a bottle of spirits: *The optic releases a specific quantity of spirit when pressed.*

optic² /ˈɑp·tɪk/ [adjective] Referring to the eye: *the optic nerve.*

optical /ˈɑp·tɪ·kəl/ [adjective] **1** Referring to the sense of sight: *Glasses are fitted with optical lenses.* **2** **optical fiber** A long, thin cable made of glass, that is used to communicate data: *The data sent in optical fiber is in the form of light.* **3** **optical illusion** Something that you think you see, which is not really there: *I thought I saw a castle on the other side of the lake, but it was only an optical illusion.*

optician /ɑpˈtɪʃ·ən/ [countable noun] A person who sells glasses and contact lenses: *You should see an optician if you can't see the screen from here.*

optimist /ˈɑp·tə·mɪst/ [countable noun] A person who always has positive views about things: *An optimist tends to see the best in other people.* ■ Compare with "optimistic" (adjective).

optimistic /ˌɑp·təˈmɪs·tɪk/ [adjective] Seeing the best in things: *Stuart is now much more optimistic about his future.* ■ Compare with "optimist" (noun).

⁺**option** /ˈɑp·ʃən/ [countable noun] A choice: *I don't have any option; I have to go.*

OPPOSITES

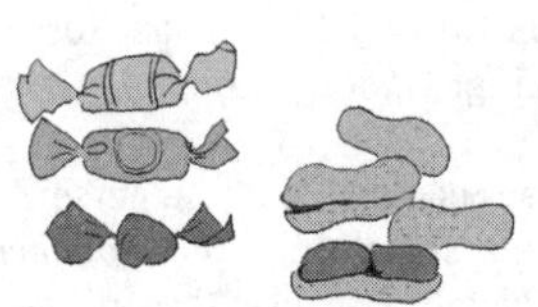

sweet – salty

hot – cold

heavy – light

short – tall

wet – dry

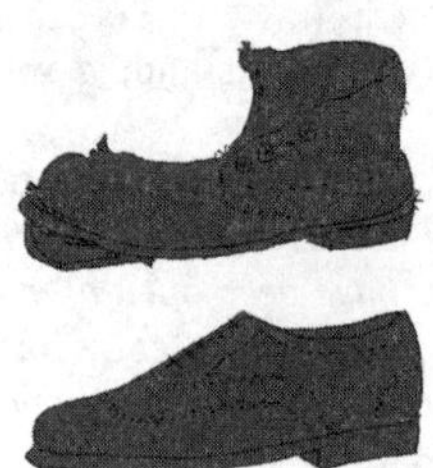

old – new

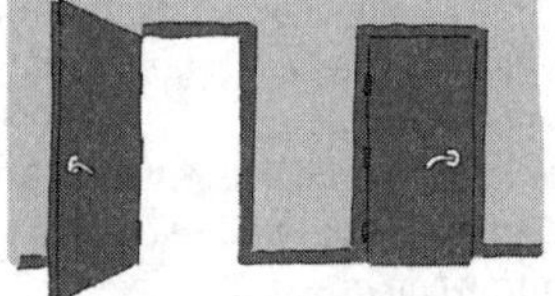

open – closed

big – small

short – long

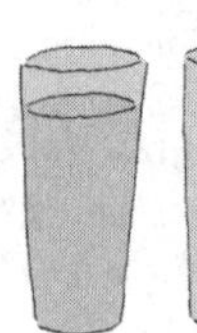

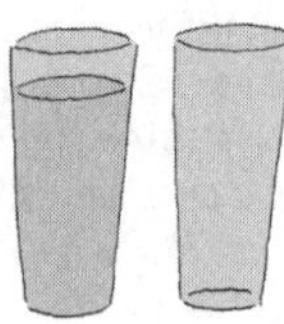

full – empty

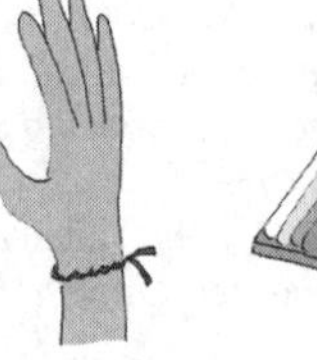

expensive – cheap

tidy – untidy

curly – straight

optional /ˈɑp·ʃə·nə·l/ [adjective] That you can choose: *Medieval history is an optional subject in my school.*

†**or** /ɔːʳ/ [conjunction] A word showing a choice: *Is your friend coming by train or by bus?*

oral US: /ˈɔːr.əl/ UK: /ˈɔː.rəl/ [adjective] Spoken, not written: *The teacher told us to do the oral exercises in pairs.*

orange[1] /ˈɒrɪndʒ/ [countable noun] A round fruit: *I'd like an orange for dessert, please.* ■ Be careful with the pronunciation of this word! The "a" is pronounced as the "i" in "did". See page 436.

†**orange**[2] /ˈɒrɪndʒ/ [noun and adjective] With a color between red and yellow: *The sun is often orange at sunset.* ■ Be careful with the pronunciation of this word! The "a" is pronounced as the "i" in "did".

orange tree [countable noun] An evergreen tree which bears oranges: *Orange trees are very common in warm regions.* See page 435.

orbit /ˈɔr·bɪt/ [countable noun] The curved route of an object moving through space: *The earth's orbit around the sun takes 365 days.*

orbiting [adjective] Revolving around a larger object: *An orbiting spacecraft travels on a closed, curved course.*

orchard US: /ˈɔːr.tʃɚd/ UK: /ˈɔː.tʃəd/ [countable noun] A place with a lot of fruit trees: *They've planted some apple trees in their orchard.*

orchestra /ˈɔr·kə·strə/, /-kes·trə/ [countable noun] A group of people who play musical instruments: *The orchestra's going to play music by Beethoven this evening.* ■ Be careful with the pronunciation of this word! The "ch" is pronounced as a "k".

orchid /ˈɔr·kɪd/ [countable noun] A flower with beautiful, bright colors: *There are some rare orchids in the lower areas of Ecuador.* See page 433.

†**order**[1] /ˈɔːdər/ [noun] **1** The way in which things are arranged: *All the words in this dictionary are in alphabetical order.* **2** A command: *The officer gave the soldiers the order to attack the enemy lines.* **3** A request: *When will the waiter come to take our order?* **4** in order to With the intention of, to make possible: *She went to Chile in order to visit her cousin.* **5** out of order Not working, not in operation: *We'll have to walk up to the seventh floor because the elevators are out of order.*

order[2] /ˈɔːdər/ [verb] **1** To give instructions to somebody: *She ordered Nigel to be quiet.* **2** To tell somebody to make or bring you something: *I'm going to order lamb chops with vegetables.*

†**ordinary** /ˈɔr·də·nˌer·i/ [adjective] Common; normal: *We've had an ordinary day at school.*

†**organ** /ˈɔr·gən/ [countable noun] **1** A part of the body with a special purpose: *The heart is an organ that makes the blood flow around the body.* **2** A musical instrument like a piano, with tubes: *There's an organ concert in the cathedral this evening.*

organelle [countable noun] A part of a cell: *Organelle is a specialized structure which is a part of a cell.*

organic /ɔrˈgæn·ɪk/ [adjective] **1** Referring to living things, found in or produced by them: *Organic waste must be put in a separate container.* **2** Referring to food production, without the use of chemicals: *These vegetables are organic.* **3** Referring to an illness, affecting the structure of an organ or part of the body: *Biology studies organic diseases, among many other subjects.* **4** In chemistry, referring to a compound that contains carbon: *organic compounds.*

organism /ˈɔr·gəˌnɪz·əm/ [countable noun] A single living being: *All plants and animals are individual organisms.*

organization or **organisation** /ˌɔːgənaɪˈzeɪʃən/ ▮ [countable noun] **1** A group of people who work together for a purpose: *"Greenpeace" is an organization for the defense of the environment.* ▮ [uncountable noun] **2** A way of planning or arranging things: *The organization of the painting exhibition was a disaster.*

organized or **organised** /ˈɔr·gəˌnɑɪzd/ [adjective] **1** Clean and tidy: *Her closet is always well organized.* **2** Efficient and able to do things well: *My sister won't forget my message because she's very organized.* ■ Be careful with the pronunciation of the end of this word. The "e" is not pronounced.

organize or **organise** /ˈɔːgənaɪz/ [verb] To give something a structure or put into good order: *We need to organize ourselves so that we can start to save money.*

oriental US: /ˌɔːr.iˈen.t̬əl/ UK: /ˌɔː.riˈen.təl/ [adjective] Referring to the eastern countries like India, China and so on: *I like oriental food.*

†**origin** /ˈɔr·ə·dʒɪn/, /ˈɑr-/ [noun] The beginning of something: *We know very little about the origin of life on earth.*

†**original** /əˈrɪdʒ.ɪ.nəl/ [adjective] **1** Created for the first time, not a copy: *The original text of the play was written in Latin.* **2** New and different: *The plot of that movie is very original.*

originally /əˈrɪdʒ.ɪ.nə.li/ [adverb] At first: *The Bingo Hall was originally a movie theater.*

originate /əˈrɪdʒəneɪt/ [verb] **1** To come from a particular place or time: *Where did that idea originate?* **2** To start something new: *He originated that phrase on a TV program.*

ornament /ˈɔr·nə·mənt/ [countable noun] Something that is beautiful but not useful: *I have lots of little ornaments on my desk.*

ornate /ɔrˈneɪt/ [adjective] Highly adorned: *The ornate ceilings in the Royal Palace are very impressive.*

a b c d e f g h i j k l m n o p q r s t u v w x y z

orphan /ˈɔr·fən/ [countable noun] A child whose parents are dead: *Pat became an orphan when she was only three years old.*

ostrich US: /ˈɑː.strɪtʃ/ UK: /ˈɒs.trɪtʃ/ [countable noun] A large bird with long legs and a long neck: *Ostriches can run very fast but they cannot fly.*

✦**other** /ˈʌð·ər/ [adjective and pronoun] **1** Different: *There will be other programs on television apart from the football game.* **2** Remaining: *I've just found one sock under the bed, but... where's the other?* ■ Be careful! We say "another", (not "an other"): "I need another piece of paper". Compare with "another[1]" (one more person or thing or an extra amount).

✦**otherwise** /ˈʌð·ər,waɪz/ [adverb] **1** If not: *Call your mother now, otherwise she'll be worried.* **2** In other ways: *The car was a bit old, but it was otherwise in good condition.* **3** In a different way: *No one can make my sister act otherwise.*

otter US: /ˈɑː.t̬ɚ/ UK: /ˈɒt.əʳ/ [countable noun] A small swimming animal with short legs and a long tail: *Otters are playful animals.*

ouch /aʊtʃ/ [interjection] A word you say when you feel sudden pain: *Ouch! You hurt me!*

ought to [verb] **1** Words that you use to show what you think is right: *You ought to take a taxi if you want to get to the concert on time.* **2** Words that you use to show what you think is probable: *Pamela ought to be home by now, let's call her.*

ounce /aʊnts/ [countable noun] A small unit of weight equal to 28.35 grams: *There are 16 ounces in one pound.* ■ The abbreviation "oz" is only used in written language. See box at **abbreviations**.

✦**our** US: /aʊɚ/ UK: /aʊəʳ/ [adjective] Of us; belonging to us: *My brother and I study in our bedroom.*

✦**ours** US: /aʊɚz/ UK: /aʊəz/ [pronoun] Of us; belonging to us: *Their apartment is newer than ours.*

✦**ourselves** /aʊər'selvz/, /ɑr-/ [pronoun] **1** A word that refers to "us" when we are the subject of a sentence: *If we fall off this wall we'll hurt ourselves.* **2** A word that underlines that we are the people the verb refers to: *We're going to repair the bike ourselves.* **3 by ourselves 1** Alone: *We stayed at home by ourselves when our parents went away for the weekend.* **2** Without help: *We'll paint the gate by ourselves.*

✦**out[1]** /aʊt/ [adverb] **1** Outside: *Is there anybody out there?* **2** Away from home or from the place where you work: *You can't see my mother now because she's out.* **3** Aloud: *Read the names out slowly, please.*

out[2] /aʊt/ [adjective] **1** Not lit: *The lights are still out in her bedroom.* **2** In sight: *The sun will be out in a few minutes.* **3** Finished: *We'll travel to Canada before the summer's out.*

outdo /ˌaʊt'duː/ [verb] To do better than: *Keith's project was good, but Dee outdid him, hers was brilliant.*

outdoor /ˈaʊt,dɔr/, /-,dour/ [adjective] Done, happening or kept outside: *Kate doesn't like to be indoors, she prefers outdoor activities.*

✦**outdoors** /ˌaʊt'dɔrz/, /-'dourz/ [adverb] In the open air: *If the weather's fine we'll have dinner outdoors.*

✦**outer** /ˈaʊt·tər/ [adjective] On the outside, further out: *The outer part of an orange is called the peel.*

outer space [uncountable noun] See **space**.

outfit [countable noun] A person's clothing: *Please wear appropriate outfit for the occasion.*

outgrew Past tense of **outgrow**.

outgrow, outgrew, outgrown /aʊt'groʊ/ [verb] To become too big for something: *Jackie needs a new coat now that she's outgrown her old one.*

outgrown Past participle of **outgrow**.

outing /ˈaʊ·t̬ɪŋ/ [countable noun] A short trip for pleasure: *We went on an outing to the beach.*

outlaw /ˈaʊtlɔː/ [countable noun] A person in hiding because he has broken the law: *They announced a $ 5,000 reward for the outlaws.*

outline /ˈaʊtlaɪn/ [countable noun] **1** A line that shows the shape of something: *We saw the outline of a ship on the horizon.* **2** The most important points of something: *He gave the press an outline of his speech.*

✦**out of** /aʊt əv/ [preposition] **1** From: *He made a fire out of bits of wood.* **2** Among: *Ten out of the class stayed at home today with flu.* **3** Without: *They're out of breath from climbing so many stairs.* **4** Away from: *Thanks to the doctors the child is now out of danger.* **5** From: *He did it out of spite.*

out-of-date /ˌaʊtəv'deɪt/ [adjective] No more in use, unfashionable: *Uncle John! Those pants are really out-of-date!*

outrageous /ˌaʊt'reɪ.dʒəs/ [adjective] Shocking, making you very angry: *She tried to charge me $7.00 for an ice cream. It's outrageous.*

✦**outside[1]** /ˌaʊt'saɪd/ [countable noun] The exterior or outer part of something: *The outside of the school's surrounded by huge yards.*

outside[2] /ˌaʊt'saɪd/ [adjective] Out of a building or on its exterior: *The outside walls need painting.*

outside[3] /ˌaʊt'saɪd/ [adverb] Out of a building: *Let's go outside for a bit of fresh air.*

✦**outside[4]** /ˌaʊt'saɪd/ [preposition] Out of a building: *If you're bored wait for us outside the museum.*

outsider /ˌaʊt'saɪdər/ [countable noun] **1** Somebody who does not live in a particular place: *It is difficult for outsiders to understand how people here feel.* **2** Somebody who does not want to be part of a group, or is not accepted by the group: *Mark is very independent: a real outsider.*

outskirts /ˈaʊtˌskɜrts/ [plural noun] The areas on the borders of a town: *There's a large shopping center on the outskirts of Sheffield.*

outstanding /ˌaʊtˈstæn.dɪŋ/ [adjective] Excellent, better than the rest: *Neil's mother is an outstanding pianist.*

outstretched /ˌaʊtˈstretʃt/ [adjective] Extended: *I took his outstretched hand and shook it.*

outward /ˈaʊt·wərd/ [adjective and adverb] Towards the outside: *You can't open this door outward.*

oval /ˈəʊvəl/ [adjective] Shaped like an egg: *There's an oval mirror in their hall.*

ovary /ˈoʊ·vər·i/ [countable noun] The female reproductive organ: *The ovary is the part of the female body which produces eggs.* ■ The plural is "ovaries". **See page 425.**

↑**oven** /ˈʌv.ən/ [countable noun] **1** A heated box for cooking food or making pottery: *The fish is baking in the oven.* **2 microwave oven** See **microwave**. See picture at **kitchen**.

over[1] /ˈəʊvər/ [adverb] **1** Above and across: *Don't jump over until I tell you.* **2** Above the top of something and down: *Look! The milk's boiling over.* **3** More than: *The book has over two hundred pages.*

↑**over**[2] /ˈəʊvər/ [preposition] **1** Above and across: *There's a new bridge over the river.* **2** On top of: *She put on*

OVER AND *ABOVE*

Sometimes "above" and "over" have the same meaning:

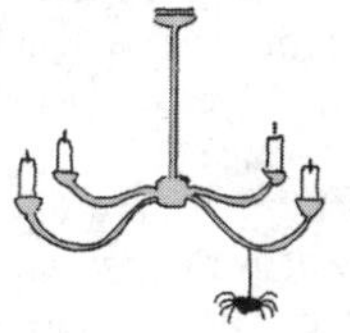

*The lamp is hanging **over/above** your head.*

When there is movement, we normally use "over":

*The airplane flew **over** the houses.*

When one thing is not directly over another, we use "above":

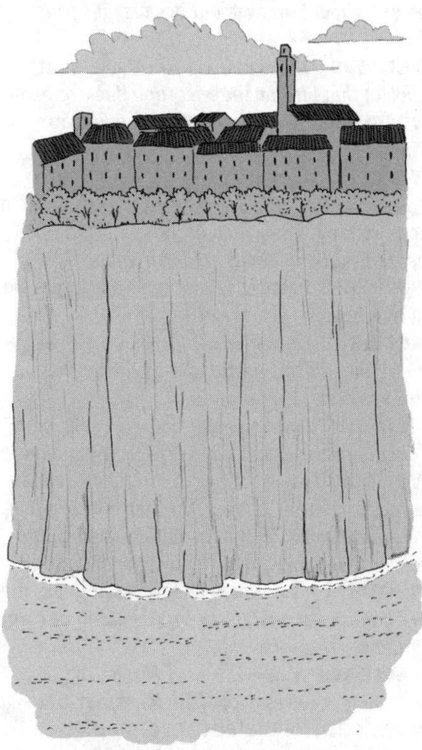

*The village is **above** the lake.*

a sweater over her shirt. **3** To the other side of: *I dare you to jump over that fence.* **4** During: *We painted the kitchen over the weekend.* **5** More than: *This sack weighs over 20 kilos.* **6** When using radio, indicating that you have finished speaking: *"I'm losing fuel rapidly. Where can I land? Over".* **7** **to be over** Be finished: *The lessons are over for today.* **8** **all over** Everywhere: *I've got pimples all over my body.* **9** **over and over** Many times: *Joanna did the exercise over and over again until she did it correctly.* **10** **over there** On the other side, that place: *I think I've put your purse over there.* See picture at **preposition**.

over- /əʊvər/ [prefix] An addition to the beginning of a word that usually means "too much": *To oversleep is to sleep too much or too long.*

overall /'əʊvərɔːl/ [adjective] Total, everything included: *The overall price of the furniture is too high.*

overboard US: /'oʊ.vɚ.bɔːrd/ UK: /'əʊ.və.bɔːd/ [adverb] Over the side of a boat and into the water: *She nearly fell overboard when the storm began.*

overcoat US: /'oʊ.vɚ.koʊt/ UK: /'əʊ.və.kəʊt/ [countable noun] A heavy coat that you wear when it is cold: *Don't go out without an overcoat because it's freezing today.*

overhead[1] /ˌəʊvə'hed/ [adjective] Above your head: *Look at that bird on the telegraph line overhead.*

overhead[2] /ˌəʊvə'hed/ [adverb] Above your head: *There are some black clouds flying overhead.*

overhear, overheard, overheard US: /ˌoʊ.vɚ'hɪr/ UK: /ˌəʊ.və'hɪəʳ/ [verb] To hear other persons talking when they do not see you: *She overheard us talking about her boyfriend.*

overheard Past tense and past participle forms of **overhear**.

overland[1] /'oʊ·vərˌlænd/, /-lənd/ [adjective] By land: *We're making an overland trip to the West Coast this summer.*

overland[2] /'oʊ·vərˌlænd/, /-lənd/ [adverb] By land: *My cousin traveled overland to Greece last summer.*

overlook /ˌəʊvə'lʊk/ [verb] **1** To have a view of something from above: *The balcony overlooks a very large yard.* **2** Not to notice something: *The teacher overlooked a mistake in the dictation.*

overnight /'oʊ·vər'nɑɪt/ [adjective] Lasting one night: *We had an overnight stay in Vienna on our way to Istanbul.*

overseas /ˌəʊ.və'siːz/ [adjective] Across the sea: *This university receives a lot of students from overseas.*

oversleep, overslept, overslept /ˌoʊ·vər'slip/ [verb] To sleep more than you had planned: *I overslept and missed the morning train.*

overslept Past tense and past participle forms of **oversleep**.

overtake, overtook, overtaken /ˌəʊvə'teɪk/ [verb] To pass somebody or something that is slower than you: *My mom looks in the mirror before she overtakes the car in front.*

overtaken Past participle of **overtake**.

overtime /'oʊ·vərˌtɑɪm/ [uncountable noun] Extra hours that you do at work: *My mother is working overtime to pay for the new apartment.*

overtook /ˌoʊ·vər'tʊk/ Past tense of **overtake**.

overweight /'oʊ·vər'weɪt/ [adjective] Too fat: *Gary is overweight because he eats too many chocolates.*

overwhelm /ˌoʊ·vər'hwelm/, /-'welm/ [verb] To defeat somebody in a crushing way, to be too much for: *Bears overwhelmed Patriots in the Super Bowl.*

overwork US: /ˌoʊ.vɚ'wɝːk/ UK: /ˌəʊ.və'wɜːk/ [verb] **1** To work too hard: *If you overwork you'll make yourself ill.* **2** To make somebody or something work too hard: *Don't overwork your muscles; we can work tomorrow as well.*

oviparous [adjective] Born from an egg outside the mother: *All birds are oviparous.* ■ Compare with "viviparous" (developing inside the mother's body before being born). **See page 427.**

ovule /'ɑv·jul/, /'oʊv-/ [countable noun] A mature female reproductive cell: *The ovule is the part of the plant where the seed is formed.* ■ The same meaning: "ovum". **See page 433.**

ovum /'oʊ·vəm/ [countable noun] A mature female reproductive cell: *The ovum is produced by the ovary.* ■ The plural is "ova". ■ The same meaning: "ovule".

†**owe** US: /oʊ/ UK: /əʊ/ [verb] **1** To have to give back sometime money that you have borrowed: *My parents still owe the bank a lot of money.* **2** To be grateful to somebody for something they have done to help you: *I owe you everything.*

owing to /əʊɪŋ tuː/ [preposition] Because of: *We couldn't play tennis owing to the rain.* ■ We usually say "because of".

owl /aʊl/ [countable noun] A big bird with large eyes that hunts at night: *Owls can see very well in the dark.*

†**own**[1] /əʊn/ [adjective and pronoun] **1** Belonging to a particular person or a thing: *Sean has his own computer in his room.* **2** **on your own** **1** Alone: *I like going shopping on my own.* **2** Without help: *Can you lift that armchair on your own?*

own[2] /əʊn/ [verb] To possess something: *They own a little cottage in Canada.*

†**owner** US: /'oʊ.nɚ/ UK: /'əʊ.nəʳ/ [countable noun] A person who possesses something: *Does anybody know who is the owner of this dog?*

ox US: /ɑːks/ UK: /ɒks/ [countable noun] A male animal of the cattle family kept for its meat and for doing heavy work on a farm: *That animal pulling the cart is an ox.* ■ The plural is "oxen".

oxidation /ˌɑk·sɪˈdeɪ·ʃən/ [uncountable noun] The process of combining with oxygen to form another substance: *Metal changes color with oxidation.*

oxide /ˈɑk·sɑɪd/ [uncountable noun] A chemical compound of oxygen and another element: *The oxide stains on the iron staircase are due to the rain.* ■ The same meaning: "rust[1]".

oxygen /ˈɑk·sɪ·dʒən/ [uncountable noun] A gas in the air: *Animals and plants need oxygen in order to live.*

oyster /ˈɔɪ·stər/ [countable noun] A shellfish that you can eat: *Pearls are sometimes found in oysters.*

OYSTER

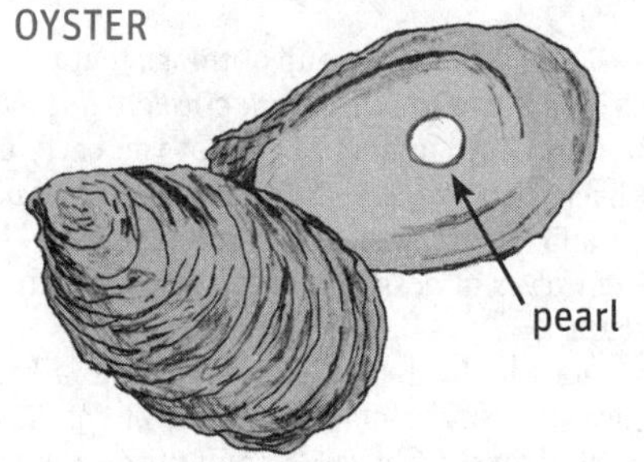

oz A written abbreviation for **ounce**. ■ See box at **abbreviations**.

ozone US: /ˈoʊ.zoʊn/ UK: /ˈəʊ.zəʊn/ [uncountable noun] A type of oxygen: *Ozone is in the atmosphere above the surface of the earth.*

ozone layer [uncountable noun] A layer of gas in the atmosphere: *The ozone layer protects us from the sun's harmful rays.* **See page 449.**

P

p

p /piː/ The sixteenth letter of the alphabet: *The name "Penelope" begins with a "P".*

p. **1** A written abbreviation for **page**. **2** A written or spoken abbreviation for **penny** or **pence**. ■ See box at **abbreviations**.

†**pace**[1] /peɪs/ [countable noun] A step: *Go forward two paces.* ■ We usually say "step".

pace[2] /peɪs/ [verb] To walk backwards and forwards: *Mr. Powell paced the floor, wondering what to do.*

pacifier [countable noun] A rubber or plastic device for babies to suck or bite: *The baby goes to sleep sucking its pacifier.* ■ In British English they say "dummy".

†**pack**[1] /pæk/ [countable noun] **1** A group of things that go together: *I'm going to buy a pack of colored pencils at the store.* **2** A bundle or bag that you carry on your back: *Don't forget to take your pack with you.* **3** A group of animals that hunt together: *The pack of wolves attacked the sheep.* 👁 See picture at **groups**.

pack[2] /pæk/ [verb] **1** To put your clothes in a bag, suitcase or other container for traveling: *Have you packed for the trip yet?* **2** To put things into a container: *The store assistant packed the glasses carefully into the box.*

†**package** /ˈpæk.ɪdʒ/ [countable noun] **1** A number of things packed together firmly, a parcel: *He was very happy when the large package of books arrived.* ■ Be careful with the pronunciation of this word. The last "a" is pronounced like the "i" in "did". **2 package tour or vacation package** A vacation with everything included in the price: *We went on a vacation package to Mexico and had a great time!*

†**packaging** /ˈpæk.ɪ.dʒɪŋ/ [uncountable noun] The paper, string, plastic and so on that is used for wrapping: *Products in supermarkets often have too much packaging.*

†**packet** /ˈpæk.ɪt/ [countable noun] A small container with things in it: *Get me a packet of fruit candies at the store, please.*

pad /pæd/ [countable noun] **1** A thick piece of soft material: *In cricket, you wear pads to protect your legs because the ball is very hard.* **2** Sheets of paper stuck together at one end: *Where's the pad for telephone messages? It should be here by the phone.*

paddle[1] /ˈpædl/ [countable noun] A wooden object with a large wide end that moves a boat through water: *You use a paddle to move a canoe through the water.*

paddle[2] /ˈpædl/ [verb] **1** To move a boat through water using a paddle: *The children really enjoyed paddling up the canal.* **2** To walk in shallow water: *We took our shoes and socks off and paddled in the river.*

paella /paɪ'el.ə/ US: /pɑː'jel-/ [countable noun] A typical Spanish dish: *Paella is usually made with rice, saffron and seafood or chicken.*

↑**page** /peɪdʒ/ [countable noun] A sheet of paper in a book: *Turn page 109.* ■ The abbreviation "p." is only used in written language. See box at **abbreviations**. 👁 See picture at **book**.

paid /peɪd/ Past tense and past participle forms of **pay**[2].

↑**pain** /peɪn/ [noun] **1** A feeling of hurt: *I've got an awful pain in my stomach.* **2** Sadness, emotional hurt: *Mrs. MacDonald's death caused her husband a lot of pain.*

↑**painful** /'peɪn.fəl/ [adjective] Giving pain: *This bruise on my arm is rather painful.*

painkiller /'peɪn,kɪl·ər/ [countable noun] A drug that takes away pain: *When I have a headache, my dad gives me a painkiller.*

painless /'peɪn.ləs/ [adjective] Without pain: *The dentist gave me an injection so that it would be painless.*

↑**paint**[1] /peɪnt/ [uncountable noun] A thick liquid that is used to color things: *We need a can of blue paint.*

PAINT

paint[2] /peɪnt/ [verb] **1** To put paint on something: *We've painted the old chair blue and it looks great.* **2** To make a picture with paint: *Hugh painted a beautiful portrait of my mother.*

paintbox /'peɪnt.bɒks/ US: /-bɑːks/ [countable noun] A small container with blocks of paint: *Aunt Jane gave me a big paintbox on my birthday.*

paintbrush /'peɪnt.brʌʃ/ [countable noun] A brush for painting: *You can buy paintbrushes in different sizes.* 👁 See picture at **brush**.

↑**painter** /'peɪn·tər/ [countable noun] **1** A painter of pictures: *Joe Coleman is one of the greatest painters in America.* **2** A person who paints buildings: *We'll have to call the painter when the wet patch on the ceiling dries.*

↑**painting** /'peɪn·tɪŋ/ [countable noun] **1** A picture done with paint: *My favorite painting is Guernica, by Picasso.* **2** **oil painting** See "oil painting" in the word **oil**[1].

↑**pair** US: /per/ UK: /peər/ [countable noun] **1** Two things that are almost the same and are used together: *Kitty's got four pairs of shoes in her closet.* **2** An object that has two identical parts: *Can you lend me a pair of scissors? I want to cut something out of the newspaper.* **3** Two people or animals that are closely connected with each other: *The pair from Cincinnati won the dancing competition.* **4** **in pairs** In groups of two: *Do this exercise in pairs.* **5** **pair up with (somebody)** To form into a pair to do something together: *He was paired up with my sister in the tennis tournament.*

pajamas [plural noun] Pants and a jacket that you wear in bed: *Put your pajamas on and get into bed.* ■ The British English spelling is "pyjamas".

pal /pæl/ [countable noun] Friend: *My dad's going to meet his old pals from school tonight.* ■ This word is informal.

↑**palace** /'pæl.ɪs/ [countable noun] A big and luxurious house, especially where a king or a queen lives: *The Palace of Fine Arts in San Francisco is one of the most beautiful buildings in California.*

↑**pale** /peɪl/ [adjective] **1** Light in color: *Pale blue is my favorite color.* **2** Without color in your face: *You look pale. Are you ill, or just tired?*

palm /pɑːm/ [countable noun] The flat part of your hand: *Some people think you can tell somebody's future by studying the lines on their palms.* 👁 See picture at **hand**.

palm or **palm tree** /pɑːm/ [countable noun] A tall, tropical tree: *Dates and coconuts come from palm trees.* **👁 See page 435.**

pamphlet /'pæm.flət/ [countable noun] A small thin book with a paper cover that contains information: *Have you got a pamphlet about vacations in Mexico?*

↑**pan** /pæn/ [countable noun] A container for cooking in: *Don't forget to take the pan off the heat when the potatoes are ready.*

PAN

a b c d e f g h i j k l m n o **p** q r s t u v w x y z

Panamanian¹ [adjective] Referring to Panama: *Panama City is the Panamanian Capital.* ■ Be careful! "Panamanian" has a capital "P".

Panamanian² [countable noun] A person from Panama: *The storekeeper of this grocery store is Panamanian.* ■ Be careful! "Panamanian" has a capital "P".

pancake /ˈpæn.keɪk/ [countable noun] A thin cake made with eggs, flour and milk: *My mom makes delicious pancakes, that we eat with maple syrup.* ■ Be careful with the pronunciation of this word! "cake" rhymes with "make".

pancreas /ˈpæŋ.kri.əs/ [countable noun] A gland close to the stomach: *The pancreas provides substances which help in digestion.* 👁 **See page 424.**

panda /ˈpæn.də/ [countable noun] A large black and white animal like a bear: *Pandas mainly eat bamboo but they sometimes eat other plants too.*

⁺panel /ˈpæn.ᵊl/ [countable noun] **1** A long flat piece on a door: *Let's paint the outside of the door brown and the panel yellow.* **2** The part of a machine where the controls are: *What a lot of buttons there are on this control panel!*

panic¹ /ˈpænɪk/ [uncountable noun] A feeling of great fear: *In a fire, panic can be more dangerous than the flames.*

panic² /ˈpænɪk/ [verb] To suffer from panic: *Don't panic! Stay calm!* ■ Be careful with the spelling of these forms: "panicked", "panicking".

pant /pænt/ [verb] To breathe quickly: *The dog came in panting after his run on the hills.*

panther /ˈpæn·θər/ [countable noun] A large wild animal of the cat family, black in color: *Panthers can run very fast.* 👁 **See page 428.**

panties /ˈpæn·tiz/ [plural noun] An article of woman's clothing that is worn under other clothes between the waist and the top of the leg: *Annie says that she only likes white panties.* ■ When we talk about two or more "panties", we use the word "pairs": "I bought three pairs of panties". ■ In British English they say "knickers".

pantomime /ˈpæn·təˌmaɪm/ [countable noun] A particular kind of funny, musical play produced at Christmas: *It's quite traditional to go to see a pantomime at Christmas.*

pantry /ˈpæn.tri/ [countable noun] A small room where food is kept: *Go and get the bread out of the pantry.* ■ The plural is "pantries".

⁺pants /pænts/ [plural noun] **1** See **underpants**. **2** A piece of clothing that you wear on the lower part of your body: *I've bought a new pair of pants.* ■ In this use, in British English we say "trousers". ■ When we talk about two or more "pants", we use the word "pairs": "I bought three pairs of pants". 👁 See picture at **clothes**.

pantyhose [plural noun] A piece of clothing that girls and women wear on their legs: *Do you like these new shiny pantyhose that I've bought for the Christmas Party?* ■ When we talk about two or more "pantyhose", we use the word "pairs": "I bought three pairs of pantyhose".

⁺paper /ˈpeɪ·pər/ [noun] **1** A material that you can write on: *We should try not to waste paper so that we don't have to cut down so many trees.* ■ In this use "paper" is an uncountable noun. We say "some paper", "a piece of paper" or "a sheet of paper". (We don't say: "a paper"). **2** A newspaper: *Have you bought the paper today?* **3** A piece of written schoolwork: *What was the chemistry paper like?* **4** toilet paper See **toilet paper**. **5** wrapping paper See **wrapping paper**.

paperback /ˈpeɪ·pərˌbæk/ [countable noun] A book with a paper cover: *Paperbacks are much cheaper.* 👁 See picture at **book**.

paperclip [countable noun] A small wire object that holds papers together: *Where are those colored paperclips that were on my desk yesterday?*

papers /ˈpeɪ·pərz/ [plural noun] Pieces of paper that have information written on them, often important or official: *May I see your papers, please?*

paperwork /ˈpeɪ·pərˌwɜrk/ [uncountable noun] The work of reading and writing letters, filling in forms, preparing reports and so on: *I've lots of paperwork to do, but I don't want to do it!*

parachute /ˈpærəʃuːt/ [countable noun] A thing that is used when you jump out of a plane: *She thought that her parachute was never going to open when she jumped out of the plane.*

parade /pəˈreɪd/ [countable noun] A procession that people watch: *There are lots of musical bands in the Saint Patrick's parade in New York.*

paradise /ˈpær·əˌdaɪs/, /-ˌdaɪz/ [noun] **1** An ideal or beautiful place: *Lying on a beautiful beach is my idea of paradise.* **2** Heaven: *According to the Bible, Adam and Eve lived in paradise.*

paraffin /ˈpær.ə.fɪn/ US: /ˈper-/ [uncountable noun] An oil used for cooking and heating: *Open the window, please; the gas from that paraffin stove is giving me a headache.*

paragraph US: /ˈper.ə.græf/ UK: /ˈpær.ə.grɑːf/ [countable noun] A few lines of writing without a break: *I had to write a paragraph describing somebody I admired.*

Paraguayan¹ [adjective] Referring to Paraguay: *Trinidad is a Paraguayan city.* ■ Be careful! "Paraguayan" has a capital "P".

Paraguayan² [countable noun] A person from Paraguay: *There are three Paraguayan staying at our hotel.* ■ Be careful! "Paraguayan" has a capital "P".

parakeet [countable noun] A bird like a small parrot: *My aunt's kept a parakeet for years.* 👁 **See page 429.**

parallel[1] /'pær·ə,lel/, /-ləl/ [adjective] That run side by side in exactly the same direction: *A rectangle has two sets of parallel lines.* 👁 **See page 457.**

↑**parallel**[2] /'pær·ə,lel/, /-ləl/ [countable noun] **1** Any of the imaginary lines on a map which are parallel to the equator: *Parallels help to establish latitude on the Earth's surface.* 👁 **See page 449. 2** A similar case: *I can't see any parallel between the two situations.*

paralysis /pə'ræləsɪs/ [uncountable noun] The state of being unable to move your body or part of it: *Paralysis is a result of damage to the motor nerves.* ■ The plural is "paralyses".

parasite /'pærəsaɪt/ [countable noun] An organism which lives on another one and feeds from it: *Some climbing plants are parasites.*

↑**parcel** /'pɑr·səl/ [countable noun] A thing or things wrapped in paper and tied to be sent or carried to somebody: *She took the parcel and began to tear off the wrapping paper.*

pardon[1] /'pɑːdən/ [countable noun] A word used when a person has not heard something: *Pardon? Did you say "5 o'clock" or "9 o'clock"?* ■ Compare with "excuse me" (used before we interrupt somebody) and "sorry" (used for apologizing).

pardon[2] /'pɑːdən/ [verb] To forgive somebody and release them from punishment: *In some countries it is traditional to pardon one prisoner on one particular day of the year.*

↑**parent** US: /'per.ᵊnt/ UK: /'peə.rənt/ [countable noun] **1** A mother or a father: *My parents have gone away for the weekend.* **2 parents-in-love** When you are married, your wife's parents or your husband's parents: *His parents-in-love live next-door to him.* ■ This word is more common in the plural.

↑**park**[1] /pɑːk/ [countable noun] **1** A place with trees and grass where people can relax or play: *I often play with my friends in the park near my house.* **2 amusement park** A place in the open air with rides and stalls: *I like amusement park. It's great.* ■ In this use, in British English we say "funfair". 👁 See picture at **street**.

park[2] /pɑːk/ [verb] To put and leave a car, truck or other vehicle somewhere: *It's difficult to park in the center of town on Saturday mornings.*

parka [countable noun] A warm coat with a hood: *My mom bought me a new parka for winter.*

parking /'pɑr·kɪŋ/ [uncountable noun] Leaving a car, truck or other motor vehicle somewhere: *It says "no parking" here so we'll have to look for a parking lot.* ■ Compare with "parking lot" (an area or building for parking cars).

parking lot [countable noun] An area or building for parking cars: *The hospital staff usually park their vehicles at the parking lot.* ■ Compare with "parking" (leaving a vehicle somewhere). ■ In British English they say "car park". 👁 See picture at **street**.

↑**parliament** /'pɑr·lə·mənt/ [noun] The group of people who are responsible for making the laws in some countries: *The equivalent of the British and Canadian parliaments in the United States is the Congress.*

parliamentary /,pɑːlə'mentəri/ [adjective] Referring to the group of people who govern a country: *Parliamentary debate is an essential part of democratic government.*

parrot /'pær·ət/ [countable noun] A large, colorful bird: *Parrots live in tropical forests and eat seeds and fruit.* 👁 **See page 429.**

parrot-fashion /'pær.ət,fæʃ.ən/ US: /'per-/ [adverb] Repeating something without understanding it: *Think about things; don't just learn everything parrot-fashion.*

parsley /'pɑr·sli/ [uncountable noun] A herb used in cooking: *One of my favorite dishes is fish with parsley sauce.*

parsnip /'pɑr·snɪp/ [countable noun] A vegetable consisting of a long white root: *On Sunday we had roast lamb with potatoes and parsnips for dinner.*

↑**part**[1] /pɑːt/ [noun] **1** Some, but not all; a piece of a whole: *I liked the first part of the program but the rest of it was boring.* **2** A piece of a machine: *It's difficult to get parts for this make of car. It's very old.* **3** A character in a play or a film: *Who's got the part of Hamlet in the school play?* **4 to take part in** To participate: *Our school is taking part in a sponsored walk for the local hospital.*

part[2] /pɑːt/ [verb] To separate: *We parted in Dallas; she went west and I went to the south coast.*

participant /pɑr'tɪs·ə·pənt/ [countable noun] A person who does something with other people: *How many participants are there in the swimming race?*

participate /pɑr'tɪs·ə,peɪt/ [verb] To do something with other people: *Five schools participated in the sports competition.*

particle /'pɑːtɪkl/ [countable noun] An extremely small piece of matter: *Often particles can only be seen with a microscope.*

↑**particular** US: /pɚ'tɪk.jə.lɚ/ UK: /pə'tɪk.jʊ.ləʳ/ [adjective] **1** Special: *Have you got a particular friend you'd like to bring to the party?* **2** One only: *On that particular day I was going to meet Patricia.* **3** Difficult to please: *Don't be so particular. The pizza's not so bad!* **4 in particular** More than the others: *Henry likes all sports, football in particular.*

particularly US: /pɚ'tɪk.jə.lɚ.li/ UK: /pə'tɪk.jʊ.lə.li/ [adverb] Especially: *I don't particularly like Ann, she's rather mean.*

a b c d e f g h i j k l m n o p q r s t u v w x y z

partly /ˈpart·li/ [adverb] To some extent: *It's partly my fault that she's so angry, because I said she was cheating.*

partner US: /ˈpɑːrt.nɚ/ UK: /ˈpɑːt.nəʳ/ [countable noun] **1** A person who does something with you: *Vincent was always my partner in the dancing class.* **2** A husband, wife, boyfriend or girlfriend: *My cousin Bob and his partner Hazel are coming to stay with us for a week.* **3** One of the people who owns a business: *My mom has just been made senior partner in a law firm.*

part of speech [countable noun] A type of word in grammar like noun, adjective, verb and so on: *It is sometimes difficult to know what part of speech a particular word is.*

partridge /ˈpɑː.trɪdʒ/ US: /ˈpɑːr-/ [countable noun] A wild bird with red legs: *I think partridges are delicious.*

part-time /ˈpartˈtaɪm/ [adjective] For part of the working week: *My mom had a part-time job as a waitress when she was a student.*

party /ˈpɑːti/ [countable noun] **1** A meeting of friends, with food and drink: *We had a party to celebrate the end of the school year.* **2** A group of people with similar political ideas: *Clive's dad is the secretary of the local Republican Party.* **3** A group of people doing something together: *The waiter had a table ready for a party of five.* **4** **the Democratic Party** One of the main political parties in the United States of America that originally supported the interests of the working people: *Barack Obama is one of the most famous leaders the Democratic Party has had in recent times.* ■ Be careful! "the Democratic Party" and "the Republican Party" have capital letters. ■ The plural is "parties". **5** **the Republican Party** One of the main political parties in the United States of America, that supports the free market and is against state intervention: *Reagan and Bush were important figures in the Republican Party.*

pass[1] /pɑːs/ [countable noun] **1** A success in an exam: *There were only ten passes in a class of forty students.* **2** Kicking or throwing a ball to somebody in a game: *He's a great player! What a brilliant pass that was!* **3** A card that lets you go somewhere: *You need a special pass to get into that disco.* **4** A very high mountain road: *After two days of snow, the pass was completely blocked.* ■ The plural is "passes".

pass[2] /pɑːs/ [verb] **1** To go past something: *When you go to the station, you pass the market on your left.* **2** To give something to somebody: *Pass me the ketchup, please.* **3** To be successful in an exam: *Hurray! I've passed my piano exam!* 👁 See picture at **exam.** **4** To kick or to throw the ball to somebody in a game: *Larry passed the ball to Stuart, who then got the winning goal.* **5** To go by: *Our conversation was so interesting that the time passed very quickly.* **6** To spend time: *He just sits there in the park, passing the time.*

◗ **PHRASAL VERBS** · **to pass (something) on** To give something you receive to another person: *Can you pass the message on to Martha, please?* · **to pass through** To go through a place: *The Boston to New York train passes through Waterbun but it doesn't always stop there.* ■ Be careful with the spelling of the 3rd person singular present tense form: "passes".

passage /ˈpæs.ɪdʒ/ [countable noun] **1** A narrow way in a building or outside: *I don't like going along that passage at night; it's too dark.* **2** Part of a text: *Read the passage on page 35 of the text book and then answer the questions on it.* ■ Be careful with the pronunciation of this word. The last "a" is pronounced like the "i" in "did".

passenger /ˈpæs·ən·dʒər/ [countable noun] A person who travels on a train, bus or other means of transport: *A Boeing 747 jumbo jet carries over 530 passengers.*

passer-by /ˈpæs·ərˈbaɪ/ [countable noun] A person in the street who is walking past: *A passer-by helped the old lady to cross the road.* ■ The plural is "passers-by".

passion /ˈpæʃ.ᵊn/ [uncountable noun] A very strong emotion: *Romeo and Juliet loved each other with great passion.*

passive /ˈpæs.ɪv/ [noun] The form of a verb when the action is done to the subject of the sentence: *The verb is in the passive in the sentence "The criminal was arrested by the police".*

passport US: /ˈpæs.pɔːrt/ UK: /ˈpɑːs.pɔːt/ [countable noun] A document that identifies you: *You should take your passport with you when you go abroad.*

password US: /ˈpæs.wɝːd/ UK: /ˈpɑːs.wɜːd/ [countable noun] A secret word: *The other day, I forgot my password and I couldn't get into my computer.*

past[1] /pɑːst/ [adjective] **1** Of a time before the present: *We're not interested in your past behavior.* **2** Last; recent: *I've been feeling ill the past two weeks.*

past[2] /pɑːst/ [uncountable noun] The time before now: *In the past, many children had to work in factories. Can you imagine it?*

past[3] /pɑːst/ [adverb and preposition] A word that tells you the number of minutes after the hour: *"Is it six o'clock?" "No, It's twenty-five past six".* ■ Be careful! We say: "twenty-five past four". We don't say: "four past twenty-five". 👁 See picture at **preposition.**

pasta US: /ˈpɑː.stə/ UK: /ˈpæs.tə/ [uncountable noun] An Italian food made from flour and water: *Spaghetti is my favorite pasta.*

past continuous [uncountable noun] A form of a verb that is made with the past tense of "be" and the "-ing" form: *In the sentence "We were watching the news on TV when she arrived", the past continuous is "were watching".*

paste /peɪst/ [uncountable noun] **1** A soft, wet mixture: *Almond paste is often used for making cakes at Christmas.* **2** A substance that is used for sticking paper: *Put paste on the back of your drawing and stick to the wall.*

pastel[1] [countable noun] A soft, light color, or a stick of this color used for drawing and painting: *The landscape was painted with pastels.*

pastel[2] US: /pæs'tel/ UK: /'pæstəl/ [adjective] With a soft, light color: *Her bedroom has pastel blue walls.*

pastime /'pæs,taɪm/ [countable noun] An activity that you do in your free time: *My favorite pastime is reading.*

past participle [uncountable noun] A form of a verb used after "have" to form perfect tenses or used as an adjective or noun: *"Played", "gone" and "listened" are examples of the past participle.*

past perfect [uncountable noun] A form of a verb that is made with the past tense of "have" and the past participle of the verb: *In the sentence "We had eaten all the cake by the time they finally arrived", the past perfect is "had eaten".*

pastry /'peɪ.stri/ [uncountable noun] A mixture that is used for making pies: *My grandma makes delicious pastry.* ■ The plural is "pastries".

past tense [countable noun] A form of a verb used to describe an action that happened at a time before now: *In the sentence "Yesterday I ate too much", "ate" is the past tense.* ■ The past tense of a regular verb is formed by adding "-ed" to the infinitive: "walk", "walked". But there are many irregular verbs!

pasture US: /'pæs.tʃɚ/ UK: /'pɑːs.tʃəʳ/ [countable noun] A field where animals can eat grass: *These fields make marvelous pastures for our cows.*

pat[1] /pæt/ [countable noun] A gentle touch with the hand: *The old man gave the boy a pat on the shoulder and said "goodbye".*

pat[2] /pæt/ [verb] To give a person or an animal a pat: *Alex patted his dog when he brought him the newspaper.* ■ Be careful with the spelling of these forms: "patted", "patting".

patch[1] /pætʃ/ [countable noun] **1** An area that is different from the rest of something: *Our cat's got a white patch above one eye.* **2** A piece of material added to clothing: *Can you help me sew these patches on my jacket?*

patch[2] /pætʃ/ [verb] To sew a patch on something: *I'm going to patch these jeans with some material left over from when we made the drapes.*

pâté US: /pæt'eɪ/ UK: /'pæteɪ/ [uncountable noun] A paste made from meat, fish and so on: *Have you tried that duck pâté that dad bought the other day?*

⁺**path** US: /pæθ/ UK: /pɑːθ/ [countable noun] A small way for walking on: *Little Red Riding Hood walked along the path through the wood.*

pathogen /'pæθ.ə.dʒən/ [countable noun] Any microorganism which causes a disease: *Bacteria and viruses are pathogens.*

pathogenic /,pæθ.ə'dʒen.ɪk/ [adjective] Referring to pathogens: *pathogenic bacteria.*

⁺**patience** /'peɪ.ʃᵊnts/ [uncountable noun] Being calm when something takes time: *You need to have a lot of patience to learn to play chess well.*

patient[1] /'peɪʃənt/ [adjective] Calm when something takes time: *I have a good English teacher; she explains everything and is very patient with us.*

⁺**patient[2]** /'peɪʃənt/ [countable noun] A person who is being treated by a doctor: *There are about twenty patients on this floor of the hospital.*

patrol /pə'trəʊl/ [verb] To go round a place to protect it: *The guards patrolled the factory to make sure that the thieves didn't break in again.*

patron /'peɪ.trən/ [countable noun] Somebody who gives support to a cause or institution: *Special exhibitions often depend on the support of patrons.*

⁺**pattern** US: /'pæt̬.ɚn/ UK: /'pæt.ᵊn/ [countable noun] **1** A repeated design of colors or shapes: *I love the pattern on your jumper.* **2** A thing that you copy to make something: *Can I borrow the pattern for that skirt you made for the party?*

⁺**pause[1]** [countable noun] A short time when you stop doing something: *He talked for half an hour without a pause.*

pause[2] /pɔːz/ [verb] To stop for a short time in something: *The President paused in the middle of his sentence.*

pavement /'peɪv.mənt/ [countable noun] See **sidewalk**. ■ This word is British English.

paw US: /pɑː/ UK: /pɔː/ [countable noun] The foot of an animal: *My dog always has muddy paws.*

pawn US: /pɑːn/ UK: /pɔːn/ [countable noun] The lowest piece in chess: *Charles thought for a while and then moved his pawn.* 👁 See picture at **chess**.

Pax /pæks/ [uncountable noun] A peace greeting or a call for an end to hostilities: *Children call "Pax!" to stop a fight or a game.*

pay[1] /peɪ/ [uncountable noun] The money that a person receives for working: *My sister bought a dress for my mother with her first week's pay.*

⁺**pay[2], paid, paid** /peɪ/ [verb] **1** To give money for something: *I paid $25 for these sneakers.* **2** To give money to a person for doing something: *My mom paid the painters for painting our house.* ■ Be careful. We say: "to pay somebody **for** something". **3 pay attention** To listen or to watch carefully: *Pay attention everyone because the next step is complicated.* **4 to pay (somebody or something) a visit** To visit: *When is grandma going to pay us a visit?* **5 to pay through the nose** To pay a lot of money for something, much more than is reasonable: *He paid through the nose for the table because he thought it was a valuable antique.*

▸ **PHRASAL VERBS** · **to pay (somebody) back** To return money that you have borrowed: *Can you pay me back the fifty dollars that I lent you last week?* · **to pay off** Referring to an effort made or a risky decision, to have a successful result: *The extra training this month has paid off because our results are improving.* · **to pay (something) off** Referring to a debt, to finish paying the money you owe: *She has finally paid off her debt.* · **to pay (somebody) off 1** To give somebody their last payment because you are not going to continue to employ them: *She was paid off and is now unemployed.* **2** To give somebody money so that they do not talk about something or do not cause trouble: *It is believed that the suspect paid off the person who saw the robbery.* · **to pay out 1** To give the money of a prize: *The lottery paid out over a million dollars in prize money on Saturday.* **2** To spend a lot of money on something: *They had to pay out thousands to repair the barge.*

↑payment /ˈpeɪ.mənt/ [countable noun] An amount of money that somebody pays: *When we make this month's payment on the car, it will be ours.*

PC /ˌpiːˈsiː/ [countable noun] A small computer: *My mom's just bought a new PC and she's learning how to use it.* ■ Be careful. "PC" is always written in capital letters. "PC" is an abbreviation for "personal computer". ■ Be careful with the pronunciation of this word! The "p" is pronounced "pee" and the "c" as "see".

PE /ˌpiːˈiː/ [uncountable noun] Learning how to do athletics and play sports in school: *Great! We've got PE today!* ■ Be careful. "PE" is always written in capital letters. "PE" is an abbreviation for "physical education". ■ See box at **abbreviations**.

pea /piː/ [countable noun] A small, round, green vegetable: *My aunt Carol makes delicious pea and ham soup.* 👁 **See page 437.**

↑peace /piːs/ [uncountable noun] **1** A time when there is no war: *The two countries signed an agreement to live in peace.* **2** A calm, quiet time: *I need some peace if I'm going to do my homework.*

↑peaceful /ˈpiːs.fᵊl/ [adjective] **1** Calm and quiet: *We had a very peaceful Christmas.* **2** Without violence: *The march was peaceful, and there were no problems.* ■ Compare with "violent" (aggressive and harmful).

peach /piːtʃ/ [countable noun] A soft fruit with a red and yellow skin: *Peaches are great with cream.* 👁 **See page 436.**

peach or **peach tree** /piːtʃ/ [countable noun] A deciduous tree which bears peaches: *The peach tree is of Chinese origin.*

peacock /ˈpiˌkɑk/ [countable noun] A large bird with beautiful feathers in its huge tail: *The peacock lives in the jungles and forests of India and China.* 👁 **See page 429.**

↑peak /piːk/ [countable noun] **1** The top of a mountain: *Mount Whitney, whose peak is at 14,400 feet, is the highest mountain in the United States.* **2** The time when something is at its maximum: *You have to pay more money for your flight if you travel during the peak period of the summer.* **3** The part of a hat that goes out in front of your eyes and protects them from the sun: *Baseball players wear a cap with a peak.*

peanut /ˈpiː.nʌt/ [countable noun] A small, popular nut: *I'm going to get a packet of salted peanuts from the store at the corner.*

pear US: /per/ UK: /peəʳ/ [countable noun] A fruit that has a green or a yellow skin and is white inside: *What do you want for dessert, pears or peaches?* 👁 **See page 436.**

pearl US: /pɝːl/ UK: /pɜːl/ [countable noun] A small, round and white thing that grows inside an oyster: *My uncle gave my aunt a beautiful pearl bracelet for her birthday.* 👁 See picture at **oyster**.

pear or **pear tree** /peər/ [countable noun] A tree which bears pears: *Most pear trees are deciduous.*

peasant /ˈpez.ᵊnt/ [countable noun] **1** An agricultural laborer with very low social position and few rights: *Please call Mr. Ramsbottom a "farmer" and not a "peasant" when you speak to him. It's much more polite.* ■ Be careful! We usually use this word to talk about people who lived in the past. **2** A person without education or manners ■ Be careful! This use is an insult.

pebble /ˈpeb.l̩/ [countable noun] A small stone: *The children enjoyed themselves collecting pebbles on the beach.*

pectoral /ˈpek.tər.əl/ US: /-tɔːr-/ [adjective] Referring to the chest: *The pectoral muscles are on each side of the chest.* 👁 **See page 423.**

pectorals or **pecs** /ˈpek.tər.əlz/ US: /-tɔːr-/ [plural noun] Chest muscles: *He goes to the gym to develop his pectorals.*

peculiar /pɪˈkjul·jər/ [adjective] Strange: *What a peculiar person William is. You never know what he's going to do next.*

pedal[1] /ˈpedəl/ [countable noun] A part of a machine that you move with your feet: *My feet don't reach the pedals of this bike.* 👁 **See page 441.**

pedal[2] [verb] To move the pedals on a machine: *You don't have to pedal when you go downhill on a bike.*

pedestal /'pedɪstəl/ [countable noun] **1** The base of a statue: *The column has a pedestal at its base.* **2 to knock somebody off their pedestal** To show people that somebody is not as superior or perfect as they appeared to be: *The scandal has really knocked him off his pedestal.*

pedestrian /pə'des.tri.ən/ [countable noun] A person walking down the street: *They've closed the center of town to traffic and turned it into an area for pedestrians only.*

pedestrian crossing [countable noun] See **crosswalk.** ■ This word is British English.

pediment /'ped.ɪ.mənt/ [countable noun] The triangular section at the top of the horizontal part of a building, common in ancient Greek and Roman architecture: *Pediments are usually supported by columns.*

peel[1] /piːl/ [uncountable noun] The outside part of a fruit or a vegetable: *Please put that orange peel into the garbage.*

peel[2] /piːl/ [verb] **1** To take the peel off a vegetable or a piece of fruit: *Peel those potatoes and then cut them into slices.* **2** To fall off slowly in small pieces: *We'll have to redecorate this room because the paint's beginning to peel off.*

peep[1] [countable noun] A quick look: *The baby's asleep but you can come and have a peep at her if you like.* ■ We say: "to take a peep" or "to have a peep".

peep[2] /piːp/ [verb] To look at something quickly: *We peeped over the backyard wall and saw the old man picking apples.*

peephole [countable noun] A small hole through which you can look: *By looking through the peephole he could see into the room.*

peer US: /pɪr/ UK: /pɪəʳ/ [verb] To look hard, carefully or with effort at something: *The old lady peered at me over her glasses.*

peg /peg/ [countable noun] **1** A small object on the wall to hang things on: *Hang your coats up on the pegs as soon as you come into the classroom.* **2** A wooden or plastic object used for hanging clothes on a line: *Pass me the pegs and I'll hang the sheets up to dry.*

pelican /'pel.ɪ.kən/ [countable noun] **1** A large waterbird which catches and holds fish with the lower part of its beak: *Pelicans eat not only fish but also amphibians and crustaceans.* **2 pelican crossing** A place where pedestrians can stop the traffic and cross the road by pressing a button that controls the stoplights: *It is better to go to the pelican crossing in order to cross this busy road.*

↑**pen** /pen/ [countable noun] **1** An object for writing with: *Can I borrow your pen for a minute?* **2** A small place for animals: *When I stayed on my friend's farm we used to put the animals in a pen every night.* **3 ballpoint pen** See **ballpoint. 4 felt pen or felt tip pen** See **felt pen. 5 fountain pen** See **fountain pen.**

penalty /'pen·ə·l·ti/ [countable noun] **1** A punishment for doing something wrong: *There's a $20 penalty for pulling the emergency cord without a reason.* **2** A punishment in sport in the form of a shot at goal given to the opposite team: *The referee gave us a penalty in the last minute of the game.* ■ The plural is "penalties".

pence /pents/ The plural of **penny.** ■ "p." is an abbreviation for "pence". See box at **abbreviations.**

↑**pencil** /'pent.səl/ [countable noun] **1** An object with a lead center for drawing or writing with: *This is a special soft pencil I use in my drawing class.* 👁 **See page 456.** **2 pencil case** A container for pencils, pens and so on: *What an enormous pencil case. How many pencils does it hold?*

pencil sharpener [countable noun] An object used to sharpen pencils: *Can I borrow your pencil sharpener?*

penetrate /'pen.ɪ.treɪt/ [verb] To go into something: *Unfortunately the glass had penetrated John's leg and we had to take him to the hospital.*

penguin /'peŋ.gwɪn/ [countable noun] A black and white bird that lives in the Antarctic region: *Although penguins can't fly, they are very graceful in water.* 👁 **See page 429.**

penicillin /ˌpen.ə'sɪl.ɪn/ [uncountable noun] A drug that treats infections: *Penicillin began to be used after the Second World War.*

peninsula /pə'nɪn·sə·lə/ [countable noun] An area of land that projects into the sea: *The Iberian Peninsula is surrounded on two sides by the Atlantic and on the other by the Mediterranean.*

penis /'piː.nɪs/ [countable noun] The male reproductive organ: *The penis is used to eliminate urine.* ■ The plural is "penises" or "penes". 👁 **See page 425.**

penknife /'pen.naɪf/ [countable noun] A small knife that you can carry in your pocket: *It's always very useful to have a good penknife with you when you go camping.* ■ The plural is "penknives". ■ The same meaning: "pocketknife".

penny /'pen.i/ [countable noun] The smallest unit of British money, a hundred of which make a pound: *You can't buy anything for one penny these days.* ■ The plural is "pence" or "pennies". We use "pennies" when we are talking about one penny coins. ■ "p." is an abbreviation for "penny".

penpal [countable noun] A person that you write to regularly: *I've been writing to my Italian penpal, Piero, for four years now.*

↑**pension** /'pent.ʃən/ [countable noun] Money that the government gives you when you finally stop working:

a b c d e f g h i j k l m n o **p** q r s t u v w x y z

a b c d e f g h i j k l m n o p q r s t u v w x y z

My grandpa goes to the bank for his pension every month.

pentagon /'pentəgɒn/ [countable noun] A shape with five sides: *The United States military headquarters is a building in the shape of a pentagon.*

***people** /'piː.pl/ [plural noun] More than one person: *How many people shall we invite to the party?* ■ Be careful! "People" is a countable noun. We say: "There are many people here". (We don't say: "There is many people here").

***pepper** /'pep·ər/ [noun] **1** A light brown or black powder that gives food a hot taste: *I like salt and pepper on my meat.* **2** A green, red or yellow vegetable: *Red peppers are good in salads.* **See page 437.**

per /pɚ/ US: /pɝː/ UK: /pɜːʳ/ [preposition] For each: *There is one seat per student.*

perceive /pər'siv/ [verb] To note, see or become aware of: *I think she perceives that I am not happy.*

per cent /pə'sent/ [countable noun, adjective and adverb] Parts in every hundred: *Did you know that the human body is about sixty-five per cent water?* ■ With figures we normally write the sign "%" instead of writing "per cent". Be careful with the pronunciation of this word! The "c" is pronounced like an "s".

percentage US: /pɚ'sen.t̬ɪdʒ/ UK: /pə'sen.tɪdʒ/ [countable noun] Proportion out of a hundred: *The percentage of people who smoke is decreasing.* ■ Be careful with the pronunciation of this word. The "c" is pronounced like an "s" and the "a" is pronounced like the "i" in "did".

perception /pər'sep·ʃən/ [noun] **1** The act of perceiving: *Perception depends on attention, but also on memory and mood.* **2** The way of interpreting or understanding something: *Our perception of the world is constantly changing.*

perch[1] /pɜːtʃ/ [countable noun] A place where a bird rests: *Your canary likes the top perch better than all the others, doesn't he?*

perch[2] /pɜːtʃ/ [verb] To sit on a perch: *The robin flew down and perched on the fence.*

percussion /pə'kʌʃən/ [uncountable noun] A group of musical instruments which are played by hitting them with the hand or with a stick or by shaking them: *Drums, maracas and tambourines are percussion instruments.* **See page 459.**

***perfect** /'pɜr·fɪkt/ [adjective] Without any faults: *The party was a perfect way to end the vacation.*

perfection /pər'fek·ʃən/ [uncountable noun] Being perfect: *My piano teacher is really demanding; she always expects perfection.*

perfect tense [countable noun] **1** A form of a verb with "have" and the past participle of the verb: *"I have seen you" is an example of a verb in a perfect tense.* ■ A perfect tense can describe an action in the past, general present or future. **2 past perfect** See **past perfect. 3 present perfect** See **present perfect.**

perforate [verb] To make a hole or several holes in something: *He uses a hole punch to perforate his sheets of papers.*

***perform** US: /pɚ'fɔːrm/ UK: /pə'fɔːm/ [verb] **1** To appear in a play, concert and so on: *Yehudi Menuhin, the violinist, has performed in many of the world's most famous concert halls.* **2** To function or to do a job: *My computer's not performing very well at the moment. There must be something wrong with it.*

***performance** /pər'fɔr·məns/ [noun] **1** A time when a play or a concert is performed: *We went to Stratford to see the Royal Shakespeare Company's first performance of the season.* **2** How well a person or a thing does something: *My sister's new car has a high performance engine.*

***performer** US: /pɚ'fɔːr.mɚ/ UK: /pə'fɔː.məʳ/ [countable noun] A person who is in a show, play, concert and so on: *What a marvelous performer Charlie Chaplin was.*

perfume US: /pɝː'fjuːm/ UK: /'pɜː.fjuːm/ [uncountable noun] **1** A liquid that you put on to smell nice: *We gave the teacher some perfume for her birthday.* **2** A nice smell: *The perfume from the roses filled the room.*

***perhaps** US: /pɚ'hæps/ UK: /pə'hæps/ [adverb] Maybe, possibly: *Are you coming to the party tonight? Perhaps, I don't know.* ■ This word is more formal than "maybe".

***period** /'pɪər·i·əd/ [countable noun] **1** A length of time: *My family lived abroad for a long period of time when I was a child, so they sent me to a boarding school.* **2** A time in the history of a country: *The nineteenth century was a period of great industrial development in United States.* **3** A mark used at the end of a sentence or after some abbreviations [.]: *Don't forget the periods in your letter.* ■ In this use, in British English we say "full stop".

periodic US: /ˌpɪr.i'ɑː.dɪk/ UK: /ˌpɪə.ri'ɒd.ɪk/ [adjective] **1** Occurring regularly or at intervals: *He has periodic attacks of malaria.* **2 periodic table** A list of the chemical elements organized according to their atomic number and to their chemical properties: *We have to study the periodic table for the next chemistry test.*

peripheral /pə'rɪfərəl/ [adjective] On the outer edge of something, or less important: *With this illness, it is your peripheral vision that is affected first.*

periscope /'per·əˌskoʊp/ [countable noun] A device on a submarine which permits the surface to be seen: *The commander ordered the periscope to be raised.*

***permanent** /'pɜr·mə·nənt/ [adjective] Lasting or intended to last, for a period without end; not temporary: *My mom's got a permanent job in Australia, so we're going to live there.*

ᐩ**permission** /pər'mɪʃ·ən/ [uncountable noun] The allowing a person to do something: *Did you get permission from the teacher to leave early?*

ᐩ**permit**[1] /'pɜːmɪt/ [countable noun] A card or a piece of paper that allows a person to do something: *My friend from Mexico needed a work permit to be able to work in the United States.*

permit[2] /pə'mɪt/ [verb] To allow a person to do something: *Eating in class is not permitted.* ■ Be careful with the spelling of these forms: "permitted", "permitting". ■ This word is formal and is mainly used in written language. We usually say "allow".

peroxide /pə'rɑk,saɪd/ [uncountable noun] A chemical used to kill bacteria and to dye hair blonde: *Household detergents contain peroxide.* ■ The same meaning: "hydrogen peroxide".

perpendicular /,pɜːpən'dɪkjʊlər/ [adjective] Referring to a line or surface, that forms a right angle with another line or surface: *The x axis is perpendicular to the y axis.* 👁 **See page 457.**

persecute /'pɜːsɪkjuːt/ [verb] **1** To pursue somebody continually, in an irritating way: *The journalists persecuted the young woman who had just become famous.* **2** To treat somebody cruelly and unjustly because of their religion, race, beliefs or sexuality: *Religious minorities have been persecuted throughout history.*

persistent /pər'sɪs·tənt/, /-'zɪs-/ [adjective] **1** Being very determined, and not stopping: *She always achieves her goals because she is very persistent.* **2** Continuing, lasting a long time: *There have been persistent gossips about their relationship.*

ᐩ**person** /'pɜr·sən/ [countable noun] A man or a woman: *Vicky is a very nice person.* ■ Be careful! For the plural we usually say "people".

ᐩ**personal** US: /'pɝː.sᵊn.ᵊl/ UK: /'pɜː.sᵊn.ᵊl/ [adjective] **1** Of a person or for a person: *I have my own personal copy of the dictionary.* **2** Private: *Mrs. Carey, may I talk to you about something personal, please?*

personal computer [countable noun] See **PC**.

ᐩ**personality** US: /,pɝː.sᵊn'æl.ə.t̬i/ UK: /,pɜː.sᵊn'æl.ə.ti/ [noun] **1** Somebody's character: *Emily's got a very cheerful personality, hasn't she?* **2** A famous person: *There were a lot of sports and television personalities at the concert.* ■ The plural is "personalities".

perspective /pər'spek·tɪv/ [countable noun] **1** Point of view: *Because I am older, I see things from a different perspective.* **2** A technique in two-dimensional drawing which gives an apparent three-dimensional view: *The perspective of the drawing allows us to imagine how the space would be in real life.*

perspiration /,pɜr·spə'reɪ·ʃən/ [uncountable noun] The action of producing sweat, or the sweat itself: *His forehead was covered in perspiration.*

ᐩ**persuade** /pər'sweɪd/ [verb] To cause somebody to do something by talking to him or her: *Tanya persuaded me to sell her my bike and I regret it now.*

persuasion /pər'sweɪ·ʒən/ [uncountable noun] Persuading or being persuaded: *You'll have to use a lot of persuasion if you want her to go to the party with you!*

Peruvian[1] [adjective] Referring to Peru: *Next Saturday, we'll go to have dinner in a Peruvian Restaurant.* ■ Be careful! "Peruvian" has a capital "P".

Peruvian[2] [countable noun] A person from Peru: *My grandma is Peruvian and lives in Lima.* ■ Be careful! "Peruvian" has a capital "P".

pessimist /'pes.ɪ.mɪst/ [countable noun] A pessimistic person: *Vince is a real pessimist. He always thinks that the worst will happen.*

pessimistic /,pes.ɪ'mɪs.tɪk/ [adjective] Thinking that bad things will happen: *Don't be so pessimistic. You'll pass the test all right.*

pest /pest/ [countable noun] An animal that causes damage to crops or to food: *Some insects are pests that can devastate a farmer's crops.*

ᐩ**pet** /pet/ [countable noun] **1** An animal that you have in the house: *We keep a lot of pets: a cat, two parrots and several hamsters.* ■ Compare with "mascot" (an object, person or animal that people think brings good luck). **2 teacher's pet** A student who is treated as a favorite by a teacher: *Irene gets called on a lot because she's the teacher's pet.*

a b c d e f g h i j k l m n o **p** q r s t u v w x y z

petal /ˈpet·ə·l/ [countable noun] One of the colored parts of a flower: *We played at pulling off the daisy petals.* **See page 433.**

petition /pəˈtɪʃ.ᵊn/ [countable noun] A request that is signed by a lot of people: *My parents have signed a petition for a park in our area.*

†**petrol** /ˈpet.rᵊl/ [uncountable noun] See **gasoline.** ■ This word is British English.

petroleum /pəˈtroʊ·li·əm/ [uncountable noun] **1** A dark, thick oil which is found in the upper layers of the Earth: *Petroleum is treated for use as fuel.* **See page 439. 2 petroleum jelly** Substance obtained from petroleum, used on the skin to grease or moisturize: *Petroleum jelly is often used on the lips.*

pet store [countable noun] A store where you can buy pets: *Last week, we went to the pet store and bought Caruso, our canary.*

phalanx US: /ˈfeɪ.læŋks/ UK: /ˈfæl.æŋks/ [countable noun] **1** A group of people that stand together to form a compact mass: *In Classical times, Macedonian soldiers formed into a phalanx.* **2** In anatomy any of the of the bones of the finger or toes: *Breaking a phalanx is much less painful than breaking a main bone.* ■ The plural is "phalanges" or "phalanxes".

phantom /ˈfæn·təm/ [countable noun] A ghost: *I like the musical "The Phantom of the Opera".*

pharaoh /ˈfeərəʊ/ [countable noun] A ruler in ancient Egypt: *The pharaohs ordered the construction of the pyramids.*

pharmacist /ˈfɑr·mə·sɪst/ [countable noun] A person who prepares and sells medicines: *Can you go to the pharmacist and get my medicine for me?* ■ In British English they say "chemist".

pharmacy /ˈfɑr·mə·si/ [countable noun] A store that sells medicines: *I got some cough syrup at the pharmacy.* ■ The plural is "pharmacies". ■ The same meaning: "drugstore". ■ In British English they say "chemist's".

pharynx /ˈfær.ɪŋks/ [countable noun] The part of the alimentary canal behind the nose and mouth: *The pharynx connects the mouth to the esophagus.* ■ The plural is "pharynges" or "pharynxes". **See page 424 and 425.**

phase /feɪz/ [countable noun] One part or stage in a longer process: *The first phase of the job has been completed.* ■ Be careful with the pronunciation of this word! "pha" rhymes with "day" and the "e" is not pronounced.

pheasant /ˈfez.ᵊnt/ [countable noun] A large bird with a long tail: *Some people hunt pheasants and eat them.*

phenomenon /fɪˈnɑm·əˌnɑn/, /-nən/ [countable noun] A physical event or an especially remarkable thing: *Hot springs are a natural phenomenon.* ■ The plural is "phenomena".

philosopher /fɪˈlɑs·ə·fər/ [countable noun] A person who studies philosophy: *The great philosopher Plato lived in ancient Athens.*

philosophical /ˌfɪl·əˈsɑf·ɪ·kəl/ [adjective] Referring to philosophy: *"What is truth?" is a very philosophical question.*

†**philosophy** /fɪˈlɑs·ə·fi/ [noun] **1** The study of the meaning of life, of ways of thinking and so on: *I find philosophy difficult but interesting.* **2** A person's ideas about how to live: *My philosophy is to do what I feel is right, not what other people think.* ■ The plural is "philosophies".

phloem US: /ˈfloʊ.em/ UK: /ˈfləʊ.em/ [countable noun] A tissue which carries food from the leaves to the rest of the plant: *Phloem cells are connected to one another.* ■ Compare with "xylem" (a tissue which transports water and other nutrients from the roots to the rest of the plant).

phone¹ /fəʊn/ [countable noun] **1** An instrument for talking to somebody over long distances: *Can I use your telephone for a minute?* **2 on the phone** Speaking to somebody on the telephone: *Don't be too long on the phone, will you?* ■ "Phone" is short for "telephone". **See page 443.**

phone² /fəʊn/ [verb] To talk to somebody by telephone: *My father has telephoned to say he isn't coming to dinner tonight.* ■ "Phone" is short for "telephone". ■ In British English they say "to ring".

phone book [countable noun] A book with a list of names and telephone numbers: *Her number is in the phone book, I think.* ■ The same meaning: "telephone directory".

phone booth [countable noun] A public telephone in the street: *Is there a phone booth round here, please?* ■ "Phone booth" is short for "telephone booth". ■ In British English they say "phone box".

phone box [countable noun] See **phone booth.** ■ This word is British English.

phonecard [countable noun] A card used instead of coins in a public phone booth: *This phone box only takes phonecards.*

phone number [countable noun] The number of somebody's telephone: *"Here's my phone number. Now, don't forget to phone me tonight".* ■ "Phone number" is short for "telephone number".

phonetic /fəˈneţ·ɪk/ [adjective] Using a special code to show how you pronounce something: *There are phonetic symbols for all the words in this dictionary.*

†**photo** US: /ˈfoʊ.ţoʊ/ UK: /ˈfəʊ.təʊ/ [countable noun] See **photograph.**

photocopy US: /'foʊ.t̬oʊˌkɑː.pi/ UK: /'fəʊ.təʊˌkɒp.i/ [countable noun] A copy of a piece of paper made by a machine: *I'm going to make a photocopy of this poem and give it to Tommy.* ■ The plural is "photocopies".

photograph US: /'foʊ.t̬oʊ.græf/ UK: /'fəʊ.tə.grɑːf/ [countable noun] A picture taken with a camera: *I have a lovely photograph of my mother when she was young.* ■ "Photo" is short for "photograph". ■ Compare with "photography" (the art or technique of taking photos).

*photographer /fə'tɑg·rə·fər/ [countable noun] A person who takes photos: *The photographer took about fifty photos at my cousin's wedding.*

*photography /fə'tɑg·rə·fi/ [countable noun] The art or technique of taking photos: *We are going to start having photography classes at school.* ■ Compare with "photograph" (a picture taken with a camera). ■ The plural is "photographies".

photosynthesis /ˌfəʊ.təʊ'sɪnt.θə.sɪs/ US: /ˌfoʊ.t̬oʊ-/ [uncountable noun] A process by which green plants and algae use sunlight to get nutrients from carbon dioxide and water: *Photosynthesis is a process which occurs above all in green plants.*

phrasal verb /'freɪ·zəl 'vɜrb/ [countable noun] An expression that consists of a verb and an adverb or preposition: *Phrasal verbs are one of the most difficult aspects of English.*

*phrase /freɪz/ [countable noun] A group of words that go together but are not a complete sentence: *"In the beginning" and "to be or not to be" are phrases.*

physical /'fɪz.ɪ.kəl/ [adjective] Referring to the body: *The doctor says that my father should do more physical exercise.*

physical education [uncountable noun] See **PE**.

physical fitness [uncountable noun] See **fitness**.

physically /'fɪz.ɪ.kli/ [adjective] In a physical way: *Pete is physically similar to his father.*

physician /fɪ'zɪʃ.ən/ [countable noun] A doctor: *The Royal College of Physicians is an association of doctors.* ■ It is now more common to say "doctor".

physicist /'fɪz.ɪ.sɪst/ [countable noun] A person who studies physics: *Marie Curie was a famous physicist who won the Nobel prize in 1911.*

*physics /'fɪz.ɪks/ [uncountable noun] The study of forms of substance and of natural forces: *In physics, we are studying Newton's law of gravity.* ■ It is usually used with a singular verb.

physique /fɪ'ziːk/ [noun] The general appearance of a person's body: *He has a splendid physique.*

pianist /'piː.ən.ɪst/ [countable noun] A person who plays the piano: *Beethoven was a brilliant pianist as well as a composer.*

*piano /pi'æn·oʊ/, /'pyæn·oʊ/ [countable noun] An instrument with black and white keys: *Sarah plays the piano beautifully.* ■ Be careful with the pronunciation of this word! See page 458.

pick[1] /pɪk/ [countable noun] A choice: *There are five different types of cakes. Take your pick.*

pick[2] /pɪk/ [verb] **1** To choose: *We picked James as our class representative on the school council; I picked the red one.* **2** To take a flower or a fruit from where it is growing: *We pick flowers in the woods every spring.* **3 to pick a fight with somebody** To provoke a fight with somebody: *Be careful, he is in a bad mood and wants to pick a fight with somebody.* **4 to pick somebody's brains** To take advantage of somebody's knowledge: *Can I pick your brains? I want to know the best way to...* **5 to pick your nose** To put your finger up your nose to clean it: *Stop picking your nose.*

PHRASAL VERBS · **to pick at (something) 1** To eat only a little of the food you are given, without enthusiasm: *Eric picked at his food and left most of it on the plate.* **2** To touch a pimple or scab repeatedly, trying to remove it: *Stop picking at your pimples!* · **to pick off** To shoot at and eliminate one particular animal, person or object from a group of targets: *Kate picked off the targets in the game one by one.* · **to pick on (somebody)** To choose one particular person to treat badly: *Stop picking on me, you bully!* · **to pick (somebody or something) out** To recognize one person or thing in a group: *I picked my dad out immediately in the photo of his school football team.* · **to pick (something) out** To play a melody slowly on an instrument, note by note: *I can pick out some tunes on the piano but that is all.* · **to pick (something) up 1** To learn something without formal lessons: *Laurent has only been in the United States for about three months and he's already picked up a lot of English.* **2** To buy or obtain something: *I picked up this leather jacket very cheap in a street market.* · **to pick (somebody or something) up 1** To take somebody or something in your hand or arms and lift it up: *She picked up the books which had fallen on the floor; He picked up the phone and dialed the number.* **2** To collect somebody or something from a place: *I'll pick you up from the party at 11 o'clock; My mom is going to pick up my uncle from the airport.*

pickpocket /'pɪkˌpɑk·ɪt/ [countable noun] A person who steals from people's pockets: *Be careful when you go to the fair because there are often pickpockets there.*

pickup or **pickup truck** [countable noun] A motor vehicle with an open-top cargo area in the back: *Many people who fix roofs drive a pickup truck where they transport all their tools.*

a b c d e f g h i j k l m n o p q r s t u v w x y z

picnic /ˈpɪk.nɪk/ [countable noun] A meal outside in the country: *Let's go for a picnic in the woods.*

↑**picture** /ˈpɪk.tʃər/ [countable noun] **1** A painting, a drawing or a photograph: *What a lovely picture! Let's buy it for mom for her birthday.* 👁 See pictures at **bedroom** and **living room**. 👁 **See page 456.** **2 the pictures** See "the movies" in the word **movie**. ■ This word is more common in British English.

pie /paɪ/ [countable noun] A dish made of pastry filled with meat, vegetables or fruit: *Dou you want a slice of pumpkin pie or apple pie?* ■ Be careful with the pronunciation of this word. "Pie" rhymes with "my". ■ Compare with "tart[1]" (a piece of pastry with a sweet food on top).

↑**piece** /piːs/ [countable noun] **1** A part of something: *Do you want a piece of cake?* **2** One single thing, a bit: *She cleaned her bike piece by piece.*

pier US: /pɪr/ UK: /pɪəʳ/ [countable noun] A large wooden or metal structure built out into the sea, that is used as a place of entertainment: *Let's walk to the end of the pier.*

pierce US: /pɪrs/ UK: /pɪəs/ [verb] To make a hole in something: *To kill a vampire you have to pierce its heart with a stake!*

piercing ▮ [uncountable noun] **1** The process of making holes in some parts of the body for wearing jewelry: *She works in a store where they do body piercing.* ▮ [countable noun] **2** A hole made in the body for wearing a piece of jewelry on it: *My grandma doesn't want me to wear piercings.* ■ We also say "body piercing".

↑**pig** /pɪg/ [countable noun] **1** A fat animal with short legs that is kept for its meat: *Pigs will eat almost anything that they can find in the ground.* ■ Compare with "pork" (the meat of a pig). 👁 **See page 428.** **2** A greedy person: *Billy's eaten all the sandwiches. What a pig he is!*

pigeon /ˈpɪdʒ.ən/ [countable noun] A gray bird that often lives in towns: *That old lady feeds the pigeons every day at the same time.* 👁 **See page 429.**

piglet /ˈpɪg.lət/ [countable noun] A young pig: *Have you seen the piglets that the pig had last week?*

pigpen [countable noun] The place where pigs live: *Pigpens usually smell horrible.* ■ The same meaning: "pigsty", "sty".

pigsty /ˈpɪg.staɪ/ [countable noun] The place where pigs live: *Pigsties usually smell horrible.* ■ The plural is "pigsties". ■ The same meaning: "pigpen", "sty".

↑**pile[1]** /paɪl/ [countable noun] A lot of things that are on top of each other: *What a huge pile of laundry there is!*

pile[2] [verb] To put things on top of each other: *Let's pile these chairs up to make more room for everyone to dance.* ■ Be careful! We usually say: "to pile (something) **up**".

pilgrimage /ˈpɪl.grɪ.mɪdʒ/ [countable noun] A journey that people make to a special place for religions or emotional reasons: *Muslims try to go on a pilgrimage to Mecca at least once in their lifetime.* ■ Be careful with the pronunciation of this word. The "a" is pronounced like the "i" in "did".

↑**pill** /pɪl/ [countable noun] A small, round item of medicine: *Don't forget to take your pill after dinner.*

pillar /ˈpɪl.ər/ [countable noun] A column that holds a building up: *The Parthenon, a famous temple on a hill in Athens, has many pillars around it.*

pillow /ˈpɪl.oʊ/ [countable noun] A cushion that you put your head on in bed: *I like sleeping with two pillows.* 👁 See picture at **bedroom**.

↑**pilot** /ˈpaɪ.lət/ [countable noun] A person who flies a plane or guides a boat: *My great-grandfather was a pilot during the Second World War.* ■ Be careful with the pronunciation of this word. The beginning is pronounced like the "pi" in "pipe".

pimple [countable noun] A small mark on a person's skin: *I have a pimple on my nose and it huts a lot.*

↑**pin[1]** /pɪn/ [countable noun] **1** A piece of metal used for fixing things together: *My grandma uses a little cushion to stick her pins in while she sews.* **2 drawing pin** A short pin with a big top used for example to put a notice on the wall: *In class we put our drawings on the walls with drawing pins.* **3 safety pin** A type of bent metal pin whose point goes under a cover so that it is not dangerous: *When my mother was a baby, her diapers were fastened with a safety pin.*

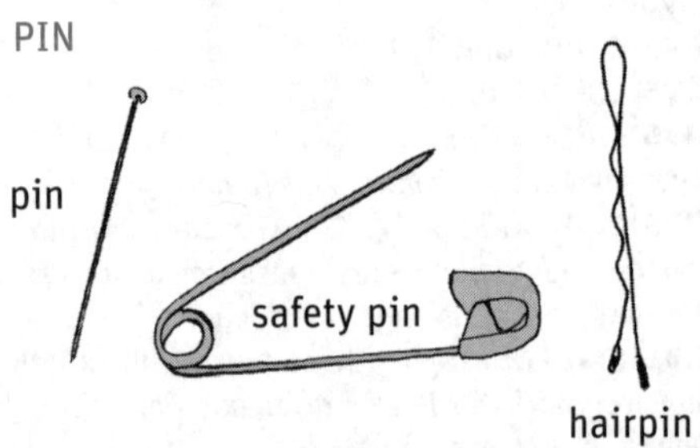

pin[2] /pɪn/ [verb] To stick something together with pins: *I stood on the chair while my grandmother pinned my dress up.* ■ Be careful with the spelling of these forms: "pinned", "pinning".

pincer /ˈpɪnsər/ [countable noun] A tool for gripping or picking something up: *Crabs have two pairs of pincers.*

pinch[1] /pɪnʃ/ [countable noun] **1** Taking something between your thumb and finger: *Peter gave me a really hard pinch while we were playing basketball.*

a b c d e f g h i j k l m n o **p** q r s t u v w x y z

A PIECE OF…

BIG, SOLID

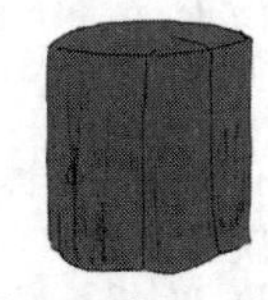

***a piece of** wood*

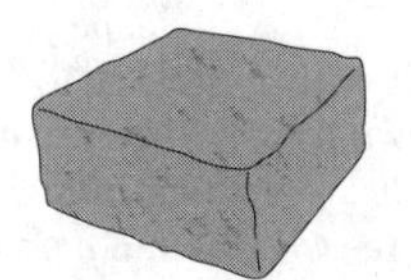

***a block of** stone/wood*

***a clump of** earth*

SMALL, THIN

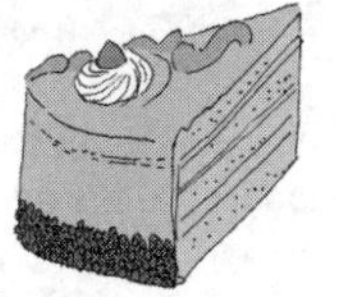

***a slice of** cake*

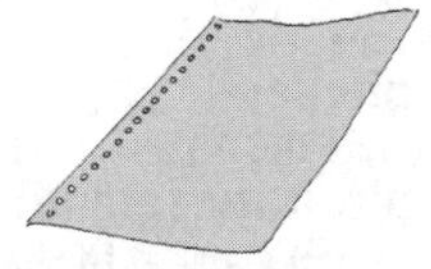

***a piece or sheet of** paper*

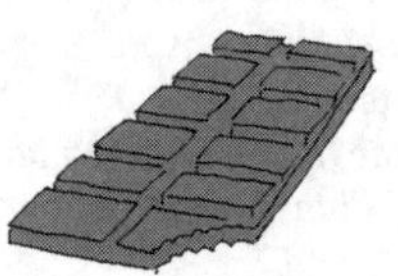

***a bar of** chocolate/soap*

WET

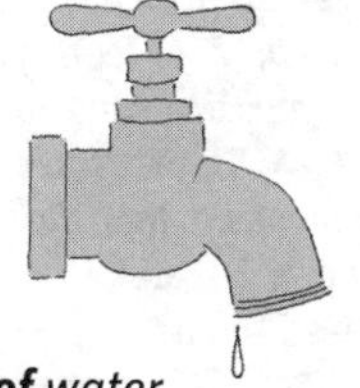

***a drop of** water*

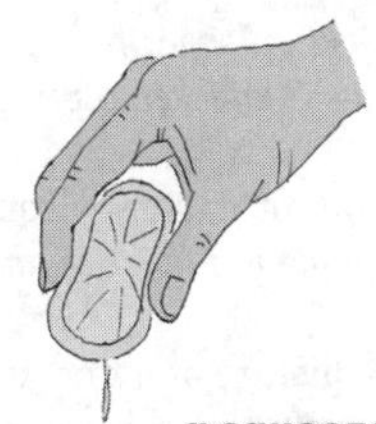

***a squeeze of** lemon*

VERY SMALL

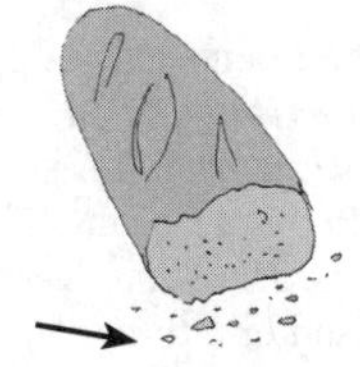

a bread crumb

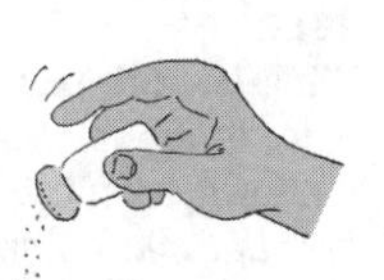

***a pinch of** salt*

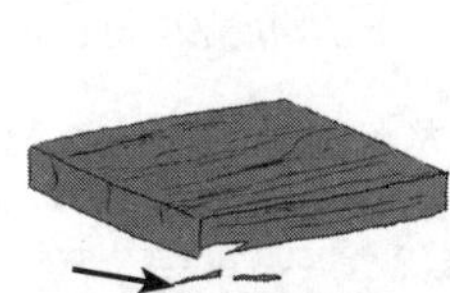

***a splinter of** wood*

a snowflake

BUNCH

***a bunch of** grapes*

***a bunch of** roses*

a b c d e f g h i j k l m n o **p** q r s t u v w x y z

2 A small amount of something: *Put a pinch of salt on the potatoes when you put them on to boil.* 👁 See picture at **a piece of....**

pinch² /pɪnʃ/ [verb] To give somebody a pinch: *Stop pinching me! That hurts!*

pineapple /ˈpaɪn,æp.l̩/ [countable noun] A big fruit with a hard skin that is yellow inside: *Let's buy a fresh pineapple to eat for lunch.* 👁 **See page 436.**

pine or **pine tree** /paɪn/ [countable noun] A tall tree with sharp, fine leaves: *After we'd had a swim in the river, we sat under the pines and had our sandwiches.* 👁 **See page 435.**

ping-pong® /ˈpɪŋ,pɑŋ/, /-,pɔŋ/ [uncountable noun] A game that is played by hitting a ball over a net on a table: *They've put a ping-pong table in the game room. Let's go and have a game.* ■ This word is informal. ■ The same meaning: "table tennis".

⁺pink /pɪŋk/ [noun and adjective] A color made by mixing red and white: *I've bought Pat a bright pink lipstick for her birthday.*

pinkish [adjective] Referring to a color, that is approximately pink, or that has a pink element to it: *What's wrong with your eye? It's pinkish.*

pins [plural noun] Wooden objects placed in a group as a target, in bowling games: *I knocked 6 pins down with my first ball.*

pint /paɪnt/ [countable noun] A unit of capacity equal to 0.568 of a liter: *Ask the milkman to leave an extra pint of milk today.*

pin-up /ˈpɪn.ʌp/ [countable noun] A picture of a famous person, or an attractive person: *I've got pin-ups of all my favorite groups on my bedroom walls.* ■ This word is informal.

pioneer /,paɪ·əˈnɪər/ [countable noun] A person who does something for the first time: *Amelia Earhart was a pioneer of piloting who flew across the Atlantic in 1932.*

pip /pɪp/ [countable noun] The seed of a fruit: *Watermelon pips are black.*

⁺pipe /paɪp/ [countable noun] **1** A long tube used to carry water or gas: *It was so cold last winter that the pipes in our house burst and we had to stay at my grandma's house.* **2** A small object with a bowl at one end for smoking: *Mr. Blair smokes a pipe and it smells terrible!*

pirate US: /ˈpaɪr.ət/ UK: /ˈpaɪ.rət/ [countable noun] A person who attacks ships on the seas: *I was disguised as a pirate with an earring, a colored handkerchief on my head and a plastic parrot on my shoulder.*

Pisces /ˈpaɪ.siːz/ [uncountable noun] A sign of the zodiac: *If your birthday is between February 21st and March 20th, you're a Pisces.* ■ Be careful. "Pisces" has a capital "P".

pistil /ˈpɪs.tɪl n/ [countable noun] The female organs of a flower: *The pistil is made up of the stigma, the style and the ovary.* 👁 **See page 433.**

pistol /ˈpɪs.tᵊl/ [countable noun] A small gun: *We had great fun playing with water pistols on the beach.*

pit /pɪt/ [countable noun] **1** A deep hole in the ground: *The prisoners in the Vietnam war were placed in pits.* **2** A mine: *Many pioneers used to work in a gold pit.* **3** The hard center of some fruits: *Be careful with the pit of that peach; don't swallow it.* ■ In this use, in British English we say "stone".

⁺pitch /pɪtʃ/ [noun] How high or low a sound is on a musical scale: *A cello has a very low pitch.* ■ The plural is "pitches". Compare with "tone" (the quality of a sound).

pitcher [countable noun] A container for liquids with a handle: *Is there any lemonade left in the pitcher?*

pituitary (gland) /pəˈtu·ə,ter·i ,glænd/ [countable noun] A small gland at the base of the brain: *The pituitary gland is essential for growth.* ■ The plural is "pituitaries".

pity¹ /ˈpɪti/ [uncountable noun] **1** Sympathy or sadness for somebody or something who is suffering or in a trouble: *We felt such pity for the kittens that we kept one each.* **2** A feeling of disappointment: *What a pity you can't come to the party!*

pity² /ˈpɪti/ [verb] To feel sorry for somebody: *I pity anybody who has to take the subway at 8 o'clock in the morning.* ■ Be careful with the spelling of these forms: "pities", "pitied".

pizza /ˈpiːt.sə/ [countable noun] A round, flat piece of dough covered with tomato, cheese and so on: *The pizza began in Italy but now it's popular in many other countries.*

⁺place¹ /pleɪs/ [countable noun] **1** Where somebody or something is: *Make sure that everything is back in its place before you leave the classroom.* **2** A particular town, country, building and so on: *What a beautiful place New York is. Have you ever been there?* **3** A space for a person or a thing: *My mom couldn't find a place to park the car, so we had to go to the parking lot.* **4** A position in a competition, race and so on: *Our school finished in third place in the local swimming tournament.* **5** **in place of** Instead of, a substitute for: *Bill played Romeo, in place of Ronnie, who had suddenly fallen ill.* **6** **take place** To happen, usually talking about something that is organized, not accidental: *Is the prize ceremony taking place in the Town Hall again this year?*

place² /pleɪs/ [verb] To put something in a particular place: *Mike placed the coffee tray carefully on the table.*

placenta /plə'sen·tə/ [countable noun] A temporary circular organ that forms in the uterus: *The placenta provides food and support for the fetus until birth.* ■ The plural is "placentas" or "placentae".

plague /pleɪg/ [countable noun] An infectious disease that kills many people: *The Great Plague killed millions of people throughout Europe in the fourteenth century.*

plaice /pleɪs/ [countable noun] A kind of flat sea fish, eaten as food: *We have plaice for dinner.* ■ The plural is also "plaice".

plain[1] /pleɪn/ [adjective] **1** Without pattern or decoration: *I think that plain dress is much nicer than the dress with a pattern.* **2** Simple: *My dad doesn't know how to make complicated dishes but he's great at good, plain cooking.* **3** Clear, easy to understand: *It is quite plain that you haven't studied this new vocabulary at all!* **4** Not pretty: *Some people say that she is rather plain but I think she is attractive.*

plain[2] /pleɪn/ [countable noun] A large flat area of land with few or no trees: *The American Indians hunted buffalo on the plains before the white man came.*

plait [countable noun] Three lengths of hair twisted together: *My little sister had a doll with very long plaits for Christmas.*

↑**plan**[1] /plæn/ [countable noun] **1** Something that you have decided to do: *What's the plan for today?* **2** A map: *We bought a plan of the center of New York to find out where the Guggenheim Museum was.* **3** A drawing of the way something is to be built or constructed: *Have you seen the plans for the new sports center?*

plan[2] /plæn/ [verb] To make plans: *Let's plan my birthday party and decide who we are going to invite.* ■ Be careful with the spelling of these forms: "planned", "planning".

↑**plane** /pleɪn/ [countable noun] An airplane: *The plane to New York leaves at seven in the morning and gets there about seven hours later.*

↑**planet** /'plæn.ɪt/ [countable noun] A large, round object that goes round a sun: *There are nine recognized planets in our solar system: Mercury, Venus, Earth, Mars, Jupiter, Saturn, Uranus and Neptune.*

plank /plæŋk/ [countable noun] A long, flat piece of wood: *They've put a plank across that huge puddle outside the school gate.*

↑**plant**[1] /plɑːnt/ [countable noun] A living thing, usually with green roots in the ground: *It's my turn to water the plants in the classroom this week.* 👁 **See page 432.**

plant[2] /plɑːnt/ [verb] To put something in the ground for it to grow: *We planted some tomato seeds in the school garden so that we could watch them grow.*

plantation /plæn'teɪ·ʃən/ [countable noun] An area of land where cocoa, tobacco, cotton and so on are grown: *There are many large plantations of coffee, cocoa, bananas and nuts in Jamaica.*

plaque US: /plæk/ UK: /plɑːk/ [noun] **1** A flat piece of a hard material which has writing on it: *The silver plaque hangs on the wall.* **2** A deposit which accumulates on teeth: *Plaque contains bacteria which attack the teeth.*

plasma /'plæzmə/ [uncountable noun] A clear fluid which is the part of the blood that contains the blood cells: *Plasma has many nutrients which are necessary for our cells.*

plaster US: /'plæs.tɚ/ UK: /'plɑː.stə^r/ [noun] **1** A light colored, soft substance that is mixed with water and goes hard when it is dry: *I broke my arm playing football and had to have it in plaster for weeks.* **2** A small piece of material that you put on a cut: *Patsy cut her hand when trying to open a tin and had to put a plaster on it.* ■ In this use, we also say "sticking plaster".

↑**plastic**[1] /'plæs.tɪk/ [uncountable noun] A strong, light, synthetic material: *Can I have a plastic bag to put these books in, please?*

plastic[2] [adjective] Made of this material: *Plastic bags used for shopping are a major source of environmental pollution.*

plasticine [uncountable noun] A soft substance often used by children to make figures with: *My little brother made a lots of animals with plasticine today.*

↑**plate** /pleɪt/ [countable noun] A round, almost flat object used for eating: *My little sister always uses a plate with pictures of rabbits on it.*

PLATE

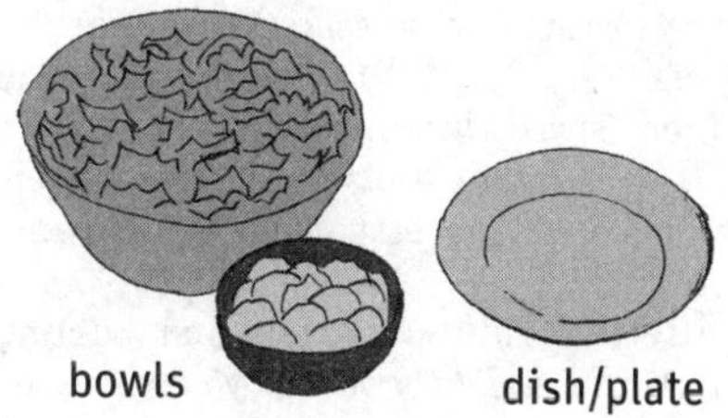

plateau US: /plæ'təʊ/ UK: /'plætəʊ/ [countable noun] A geographical term referring to an area of flat land high above the sea level: *The Andean Plateau covers most of Bolivia.* ■ The plural is "plateaux" or "plateaus".

platelet /plæ'təʊ/ [countable noun] A small, colorless blood cell that helps to stop bleeding: *Platelets are found in large numbers in the blood.*

a b c d e f g h i j k l m n o **p** q r s t u v w x y z

†**platform** /ˈplæt,fɔrm/ [countable noun] **1** The place where you get on or you get off a train: *The train to Chicago will be leaving platform 1 at 4 o'clock.* **2** A place that is raised up: *All the teachers stood on the platform at the prize ceremony.*

PLATFORM

†**play**[1] /pleɪ/ [noun] **1** A story acted in the theater or on television: *Shakespeare wrote different types of plays: comedies, tragedies and historical plays.* **2** Games and playing: *Play time always passes very quickly.*

†**play**[2] /pleɪ/ [verb] **1** To amuse yourself with a game, diversion or toy: *When I was a little girl, I loved playing with cars and dolls.* **2** To participate in a sport: *My brother plays in the local baseball team.* **3** To make music with an instrument: *Hannah played a trumpet solo in the school concert last week.*

†**player** /ˈpleɪ·ər/ [countable noun] **1** A person who plays a game or a sport: *There are five players in a basketball team.* **2** **midfield player** Player in a central position: *Sue's the best midfield player in the school.*

playful /ˈpleɪ.fəl/ [adjective] Active and wanting to play: *Our cat used to be very playful when she was a kitten, but now she sleeps a lot.*

playground /ˈpleɪ.graʊnd/ [countable noun] A place where you play: *We're not permitted to smoke in the playground, but some people do.*

playing card [countable noun] One of a set of cards that are used for playing games with: *Come on, get the playing cards and we'll have a game of cards.*

playing field [countable noun] An area of land for playing sports on: *There are some big playing fields opposite our house.*

playtime /ˈpleɪ.taɪm/ [noun] A time to play: *Our playtime is between 10 o'clock and half past 10.*

plc /,piː.elˈsiː/ A written abbreviation for "public limited company", that is written after a name to show that it is a business: *Sainsbury plc is one of the biggest supermarket companies in Britain.*

plead, pled, pled /pliːd/ [verb] **1** To beg somebody to do something: *Mary pled with her mother to let her go to the party, but she wouldn't let her.* ■ Be careful. We say: "plead **with** (somebody)". **2** To say if you are innocent or guilty: *In court, the man pled guilty to drunk driving.*

†**pleasant** /ˈplez.ənt/ [adjective] Nice or enjoyable: *It's very pleasant to spend a day at the pool, isn't it?*

please[1] /pliːz/ [verb] To make somebody happy: *Don't come with me to the movies just to please me. Come because you want to.*

†**please**[2] [interjection] A word that you say when you ask for something: *Can I borrow your pencil, please?* ■ Be careful! When somebody offers us something, we say: "Yes, please" or "No, thank you". We don't say: "No, please".

†**pleased** /pliːzd/ [adjective] Happy or satisfied: *I was really pleased when my teacher told me that I had passed my tests.* ■ Be careful with the pronunciation of the end of this word! The last "e" is not pronounced. See picture at **emotions**.

†**pleasure** /ˈpleʒ·ər/ [uncountable noun] Happiness or satisfaction: *Old Mrs. Buswell gets great pleasure from having her grandchildren to stay.*

plebeian /pləˈbiː.ən/ [adjective] Referring to the lower social classes: *He was always very proud of his plebeian origins.*

pled Past tense and past participle forms of **plead**.

plentiful /ˈplen·tɪ·fəl/ [adjective] Existing in large quantities: *Cotton is plentiful in hot states like Tennessee and Alabama.*

†**plenty** /ˈplen·ti/ [adverb and pronoun] Lots, more than enough: *There are plenty of candies for everyone.*

pliers /ˈplaɪ·ərz/ [plural noun] An object like strong scissors: *My dad cut the wires with the pliers.* ■ When we talk about two or more "pliers", we use the word "pairs": "I have two pairs of pliers".

plod US: /plɑːd/ UK: /plɒd/ [verb] To walk slowly and heavily: *The old horse plodded home, pulling the cart behind him.* ■ Be careful with the spelling of these forms: "plodded", "plodding".

plot US: /plɑːt/ UK: /plɒt/ [countable noun] **1** The story of a film or a book: *The film was beautiful to look at but the plot was a bit boring.* **2** A secret plan to do something wrong: *The plot to kill the President failed.* **3** A piece of land: *My uncle and aunt have bought a plot of land in the country and are going to build a house on it.*

plough[1] /plaʊ/ [countable noun] See **plow**[1]. ■ This is a British English spelling.

plough[2] [verb] See **plow**[2]. ■ This is a British English spelling.

plow[1] /plaʊ/ [countable noun] A machine used to dig the land: *The farmer asked the bank for a loan to buy a new plow.* ■ The British English spelling is "plough".

plow[2] /plaʊ/ [verb] To use a plow: *Farmers used to plow the land with horses but now they use tractors.* ■ The British English spelling is "plough".

pluck /plʌk/ [verb] **1** To pull the feathers off a bird before cooking it: *We plucked the turkey before cooking it for Christmas Day.* **2** To pull the strings of a guitar or a harp to make a sound: *You need to pluck the strings more gently.*

*****plug**[1] /plʌg/ [countable noun] **1** A round object used to keep water in a sink or bath: *Put the plug in the bathtub and turn the tap on.* See picture at **bathroom**. **2** An object that you put into special holes to get electricity: *The lamp's not working well. I'll ask my mom to change the plug.*

plug[2] /plʌg/ [verb] To block a hole in something: *We had to plug the hole in the wall with cement.*

▶ **PHRASAL VERBS** · **to plug in** To use a plug to connect something to the electricity: *Plug the television in and we'll switch it on for the movie.* ■ Be careful with the spelling of these forms: "plugged", "plugging".

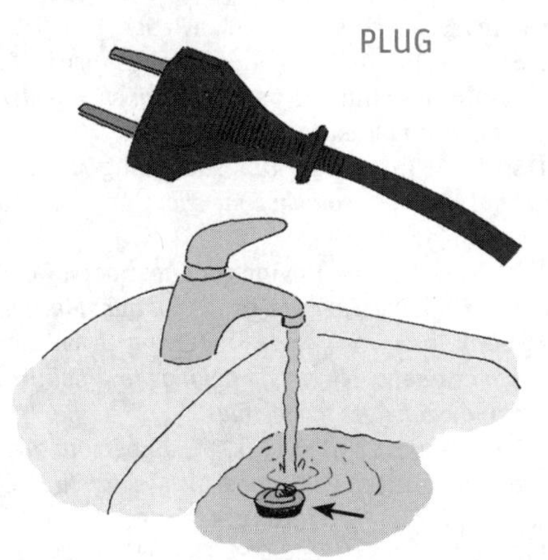

plum /plʌm/ [countable noun] A soft, red or yellow fruit: *There's a tree in our garden that produces wonderful plums.* **See page 436.**

plumber /ˈplʌm·ər/ [countable noun] A person who puts in and repairs water pipes: *The pipes in the bathroom are leaking. We'll have to call the plumber.*

plumbing /ˈplʌm.ɪŋ/ [uncountable noun] The water pipes in a house: *My dad built our house and he did everything himself except the plumbing.*

plum or **plum tree** /plʌm/ [countable noun] A tree which bears plums: *The plum tree loses its leaves every year.*

plump /plʌmp/ [adjective] A little fat but looking nice: *Hasn't the baby got plump legs?*

plural US: /ˈplʊr.əl/ UK: /ˈplʊə.rəl/ [noun and adjective] More than one: *"Feet" is the plural form of "foot".* ■ See box at **abbreviations**.

*****plus** /plʌs/ [preposition] And, or added to: *Two plus three is five.*

plutonium /pluːˈtəʊniəm/ [uncountable noun] A dense, silvery white colored radioactive element: *Plutonium is used to produce nuclear energy and for weapons.*

pluviometer [countable noun] A device for measuring rainfall: *Data from the pluviometer shows rainfall patterns.* ■ The British English spelling is "pluviometre".

pluviometre [countable noun] See **pluviometer.** ■ This is a British English spelling.

*****p.m.** /ˌpiːˈem/ [adverb] Between 12 o'clock in the day and 12 o'clock midnight: *Our train leaves at 4 p.m.* ■ "p.m." is an abbreviation for "post meridiem", a Latin expression that means "after noon". When you use "p.m.", you don't say "o'clock". ■ Compare with "a.m." (between midnight and 12 o'clock in the morning). ■ See box at **abbreviations**.

PO /ˈpoʊst ˌɔ·fɪs/, /ˌɑf·ɪs/ A written abbreviation for **post office.** ■ Be careful! "PO" is always written in capital letters. ■ See box at **abbreviations**.

PO Box [countable noun] A box in the post office where somebody receives letters: *Please send your requests to American Airlines, PO Box 679613 MD 1322, DFW Airport, TX.* ■ Be careful with the capital letters!

*****pocket** US: /ˈpɑː.kɪt/ UK: /ˈpɒk.ɪt/ [countable noun] A small bag in clothes for carrying things: *Put your money in your pocket and don't lose it.*

pocketful /ˈpɑk·ɪtˌfʊl/ [countable noun] The amount that a pocket can hold: *We collected a pocketful of shells on the beach.*

pocketknife [countable noun] A small knife that you can carry in your pocket: *It's always very useful to have a good pocketknife with you when you go camping.* ■ The plural is "pocketknives". ■ The same meaning: "penknife".

pocket money [countable noun] Money that children are given each week: *I'm saving my pocket money to buy a new camera.*

pod [countable noun] The long seed-case of some plants: *There are generally three or four peas in each pod.*

†**poem** US: /ˈpoʊ.əm/ UK: /ˈpəʊ.ɪm/ [countable noun] A piece of writing that says something in a special way: *John sent me a card with a funny poem inside it on Valentine's day.*

poet US: /ˈpoʊ.ət/ UK: /ˈpəʊ.ɪt/ [countable noun] A person who writes poems: *Maya Angelou is a famous poet, born in Saint Louis, Missouri.*

†**poetry** /ˈpoʊ·ɪ·tri/ [uncountable noun] Poems: *My older brother loves poetry; he's always reading it.* ■ The plural is "poetries".

†**point**[1] /pɔɪnt/ [countable noun] **1** The sharp end of something: *Be careful with the point of that pin.* **2** A mark in a game or a sport: *Our team won by ten points.* **3** A reason for something: *The point of our visit to the Abbey is to learn some history.* **4** A moment in time: *Just at that point, Peter sneezed and we all laughed.* ■ Be careful! We say: "at that point". (We don't say: "in that point"). **5** A symbol that is used to separate numbers above and below one: *I got five point five for my composition on Napoleon.* **6 on the point of** About to do something: *I got so angry that I was on the point of shouting at Jenny.*

point[2] /pɔɪnt/ [verb] To show where something is with your finger: *Nancy pointed to the largest cake and said "That's mine".*

▸ **PHRASAL VERBS** · **to point out** To attract somebody's attention to something: *Julie pointed out a bird flying close to the river bank.*

†**pointed** /ˈpɔɪn·tɪd/ [adjective] With a sharp end: *My cat has very pointed ears.* ■ Be careful with the pronunciation of the end of this word. The "e" is pronounced like the "i" in "did".

†**poison**[1] /ˈpɔɪzən/ [uncountable noun] A substance that is harmful to your health: *Some snakes use their natural poison to protect themselves.* ■ Be careful with the pronunciation of this word! "poi" rhymes with "boy".

poison[2] /ˈpɔɪzən/ [verb] To use poison: *Last night I saw a movie about two old ladies who killed their victims by poisoning them!* ■ Be careful with the pronunciation of this word! "poi" rhymes with "boy".

†**poisonous** /ˈpɔɪ.zən.əs/ [adjective] Containing poison: *Some mushrooms are poisonous.*

poke /pəʊk/ [verb] To put a pointed object into something: *Don't poke your finger into your ear; you might hurt yourself.*

poker US: /ˈpoʊ.kɚ/ UK: /ˈpəʊ.kəʳ/ [uncountable noun] A game of cards that people play: *Poker is a game of bluff and skill.*

polar US: /ˈpoʊ.lɚ/ UK: /ˈpəʊ.ləʳ/ [adjective] From or relating to the North or the South Pole: *The polar regions of the world are extremely cold.*

polar bear [uncountable noun] A large white bear: *Polar bears fish in the frozen waters of the North Pole.*

†**pole** US: /poʊl/ UK: /pəʊl/ [countable noun] **1** A long stick: *Pass me the poles, I'm going to put the tent up.* **2** One of the two ends of the earth: *The North Pole is about 420 miles from the tip of Greenland.* ■ Be careful! The "North Pole" and the "South Pole" have capital letters.

†**police** /pəˈliːs/ [uncountable noun] The people whose job is to prevent crime or find criminals: *The police were at the game to make sure there was no fighting.* ■ Be careful with the pronunciation of this word!

policeman /pəˈliːs.mən/ [countable noun] A man who works in the police force: *Let's go and ask that policeman the way.* ■ The plural is "policemen". ■ A woman is a "policewoman".

police station [countable noun] The building where the police work: *The police station is right in the middle of town.*

policewoman /pəˈliːsˌwʊm.ən/ [countable noun] A woman who works in the police force: *My friend's mother is a policewoman.* ■ The plural is "policewomen". ■ A man is a "policeman".

†**policy** /ˈpɑl·ɪ·si/ [uncountable noun] A plan of action, especially of a government: *The Prime Minister's foreign policy is not very popular.* ■ The plural is "policies". ■ The plural is "policies".

polio US: /ˈpoʊ.li.oʊ/ UK: /ˈpəʊliəʊ/ [uncountable noun] See **poliomyelitis.**

poliomyelitis [uncountable noun] A serious infectious disease that affects the central nervous system and can cause paralysis: *Poliomyelitis has appeared again in recent years.* ■ The abbreviation is "polio".

polish[1] /ˈpɒlɪʃ/ [uncountable noun] A substance used for making things shine: *Get some brown shoe polish when you go to the store, please.*

†**polish**[2] /ˈpɒlɪʃ/ [verb] To rub something until it shines: *I just need to polish my shoes and then I'll be ready to go.*

†**polite** /pəˈlaɪt/ [adjective] Having good manners: *Don't forget to be polite when you go to visit aunt Martha.*

†**political** /pəˈlɪt̬·ɪ·kəl/ [adjective] Referring to politics and government: *My cousin belongs to a political party and often goes to meetings.*

†**politician** /ˌpɑl·əˈtɪʃ·ən/ [countable noun] A person who works in politics: *Politicians always try to convince people that their ideas are the best.*

†**politics** /ˈpɑl·əˌtɪks/ [uncountable noun] **1** The activity of governments: *I'm interested in international politics and always watch the news on television.* **2** The study of government: *Tony studied politics, philosophy and economics at Oxford.* ■ It is usually used with a singular verb.

poll[1] /pəʊl/ [countable noun] A survey in which people are asked their opinion of something: *The results of the poll about people's attitude to the environment are very interesting.* ■ See also "polls".

poll[2] US: /poʊl/ UK: /pəʊl/ [verb] To hold an election or opinion survey: *Fifty per cent of the people polled do not recycle.*

pollen /ˈpɒlən/ [uncountable noun] A fine powder produced by the male part of a flower, thus making possible fertilization: *Pollen fertilizes the female ovule.*

pollinate /ˈpɑl·əˌneɪt/ [verb] To pass pollen from the male to the female parts of a flower, thus making possible fertilization: *Flowers and plants are pollinated by insects and by the wind.*

pollination /ˌpɑl·əˈneɪ·ʃən/ [uncountable noun] The act of pollinating: *Pollination is necessary for plants to produce seeds.*

polls [plural noun] The process of voting in a political election or the place where people vote: *More people went to the polls on this occasion.* ■ See also "poll".

pollutant [countable noun] Something which pollutes: *Synthetic material is a pollutant.*

pollute /pəˈluːt/ [verb] To make the air, water or earth dirty and unhealthy: *Airplanes pollute the air with the fuel they use.*

***pollution** /pəˈluː.ʃən/ [uncountable noun] **1** Making the air, water or earth dirty and unhealthy: *Pollution is one of the world's worst problems.* **2** The substances that pollute the air, water or earth: *Some scientists believe that pollution could be the cause of many of today's illnesses.*

polygonal [adjective] With a form that has at least three straight sides and angles: *This museum has some examples of ancient polygonal coins.*

polytheistic /ˌpɒl.ɪ.θiˈɪs.tɪk/ US: /ˌpɑː.lɪ-/ [adjective] Believing in more than one god: *Ancient civilizations such as the Romans, the Greeks and the Egyptians were generally polytheistic.* ■ Compare with "monotheistic" (believing in one single god).

pomegranate /ˈpɑm·ɪˌgræn·ɪt/, /ˈpʌmˌgræn-/ [countable noun] **1** A round fruit with thick skin and many red seeds: *Pomegranate juice can be sweet or sour.* **2 pomegranate tree** The tree that produces this fruit: *Pomegranate trees grow well in India, Armenia, the East Indies and tropical Africa.*

pond US: /pɑːnd/ UK: /pɒnd/ [countable noun] A small pool: *We've got a fish pond in our yard.*

pony /ˈpoʊ·ni/ [countable noun] A small kind of horse: *Isn't Liz lucky? Her grandfather gave her a pony for her birthday.* ■ The plural is "ponies".

ponytail US: /ˈpoʊ.ni.teɪl/ UK: /ˈpəʊ.ni.teɪl/ [countable noun] Long hair tied at the back: *Do you think Pete looks good with that ponytail?* 👁 See picture at **hair**.

***pool** /puːl/ ▮ [countable noun] **1** A natural area of water: *When the tide goes out we'll fish in the pool by the rocks.* **2** See **swimming pool.** ▮ [uncountable noun] **3** A game in which balls are hit by sticks across a table: *Shall we play pool this afternoon?* ■ In this use, the same meaning: "billiards".

pools [plural noun] Gambling where you guess at the results of football games: *My uncle won $1,000 on the pools last week.*

***poor** US: /pʊr/ UK: /pɔːʳ/ [adjective] **1** With very little money: *That man's too poor to buy himself a coat.* **2** A word that you say when you feel sorry for somebody: *Poor Sally! She's very upset about her dog dying.* **3** Not good or not well done: *My French is very poor. I must work harder at it.*

poorly /ˈpʊr·li/ [adjective] Sick, ill: *Granny's been poorly since Christmas.* ■ This word is informal. We usually say "ill" or "sick".

pop[1] /pɒp/ [noun] **1** A type of modern popular music: *I've got about fifty CDs of pop music.* **2** A short, sudden sound: *The cork came out of the bottle with a loud pop.* **3** See **soda or soda pop.**

pop[2] /pɒp/ [verb] **1** To burst with a short, sudden sound: *Look at the dog popping the bubbles we've blown!* **2** To put something somewhere quickly: *Pop those photos on the table for me, please.*

▸ **PHRASAL VERBS** · **to pop in** To go in somewhere for a short time: *Pop in and see me on the way home from school.* · **to pop out** To go out somewhere quickly: *I'm just popping out to the store for a minute.* · **to pop up** To appear suddenly: *Where did you pop up from?* ■ Be careful with the spelling of these forms: "popped", "popping".

popcorn US: /ˈpɑːp.kɔːrn/ UK: /ˈpɒp.kɔːn/ [uncountable noun] White, cooked corn: *We bought some popcorn and ate it while we watched the movie.*

pope US: /poʊp/ UK: /pəʊp/ [countable noun] The head of the Roman Catholic church: *The Pope has traveled to many different countries.*

pop group [countable noun] A musical group who play pop music: *What's your favorite pop group?*

poppy US: /ˈpɑː.pi/ UK: /ˈpɒp.i/ [countable noun] A plant with very thin red or white flowers and round black seeds: *Poppy sap looks like milk.* ■ The plural is "poppies". 👁 **See page 433.**

popsicle® [countable noun] A piece of flavored ice on a stick: *When it's hot, I like to eat popsicles or ice creams.* ■ In British English they say "lolly, ice lolly".

pop star [countable noun] A very famous pop singer: *Dave says he wants to be a pop star when he grows up.*

***popular** US: /ˈpɑː.pjə.lɚ/ UK: /ˈpɒp.jʊ.ləʳ/ [adjective] Liked by many people: *Melissa is the most popular girl in our class.*

popularity US: /ˌpɑː.pjəˈler.ə.t̬i/ UK: /ˌpɒp.jʊˈlær.ə.ti/ [uncountable noun] Being liked by many people: *Some famous people say that they don't really enjoy their popularity.*

a b c d e f g h i j k l m n o p q r s t u v w x y z

populate /'pɒpjəleɪt/ [verb] To live in an area and be part of its population: *These are regions which have densely been populated.*

populated [adjective] Inhabited: *This area is densely populated.*

†**population** /ˌpɑp·jə'leɪ·ʃən/ [uncountable noun] The number of people in a particular place: *The population of this town has gone up a lot over the last thirty years.*

porch [countable noun] A large, open area on the side of a house with a roof but no wall: *I enjoyed reading my book on the porch.*

pore[1] US: /pɔːr/ UK: /pɔːʳ/ [countable noun] A very small opening in a surface or in the skin: *The pores in the skin allow us to sweat.*

pore[2] US: /pɔːr/ UK: /pɔːʳ/

▸ **PHRASAL VERBS** · **to pore over** To study in detail: *The only solution was to pore over the papers to discover what their secrets were.*

pork US: /pɔːrk/ UK: /pɔːk/ [uncountable noun] The meat of a pig: *Followers of the Muslim religion never eat pork.* ■ Compare with "pig" (a farm animal with short legs which is kept for meat).

porridge /'pɔr·ɪdʒ/, /'pɑr-/ [uncountable noun] A food made from oats cooked in milk or water: *I always eat porridge for breakfast on cold mornings.*

†**port** US: /pɔːrt/ UK: /pɔːt/ [countable noun] **1** Safe place where ships can tie up to load, unload and wait before going back to sea: *Let's go to the port and look at the ships.* ■ The same meaning: "harbor". **See page 444.** **2** A town by the sea with a harbor: *Boston is a large port on the northeast coast of the United States.*

portable /'pɔr·t̬ə·bəl/, /'pour-/ [adjective] Which can be carried: *We have a portable TV.*

porter US: /'pɔːr.t̬ɚ/ UK: /'pɔː.təʳ/ [countable noun] A person who carries people's luggage: *When we arrive in London, we'll have to get a porter to help us with all our suitcases.*

portion /'pɔr·ʃən/, /'pour-/ [countable noun] A share of something: *How many portions of pizza shall we ask for?*

portrait US: /'pɔːr.trɪt/ UK: /'pɔː.trət/ [countable noun] A picture of a person: *There's a portrait of Henry VIII hanging in the hall of our school.*

†**pose** US: /pouz/ UK: /pəuz/ [verb] To take a particular physical attitude, as for a photo: *Stop posing, Simon, no one is impressed.*

†**position** /pə'zɪʃ.ən/ [noun] **1** The place where somebody or something is, its arrangement: *Our new house is in a marvelous position; it's practically on the beach.* **2** The way that a person sits or stands: *In my first skiing lessons I learned how to hold the skis in the right position.* **3** Situation, the way things are for a person: *I'm in a very difficult position at the moment at work, because the new boss doesn't like me.* **4** A job or a post: *Mrs. Randall has just got a very good position at the local bank.* ■ This use is formal. **5 in position** In the correct place: *Are you all in position? Ready, steady, go!*

†**positive** US: /'pɑː.zə.t̬ɪv/ UK: /'pɒz.ə.tɪv/ [adjective] **1** Sure of something: *"Are you sure that you want to come to the party with me?" "I'm positive!".* **2** Making you feel hopeful: *My teacher was very positive about my possibilities of passing the test.*

†**possess** /pə'zes/ [verb] To have something: *Does your father possess a telescope?* ■ This word is formal. ■ Be careful with the spelling of the 3rd person singular present tense form: "possesses".

†**possession** /pə'zeʃ.ən/ [countable noun] Something that a person owns: *Poor auntie Sheila lost all her possessions in a fire.* ■ Be careful with the spelling of this word!

possessive /pə'zesɪv/ [adjective] **1** Referring to a word which indicates possession: *"Mine" is a possessive pronoun.* **2** Referring to a person who desires and demands somebody's complete attention and love: *His mother is very possessive and won't let her children out of her sight.* **3** Referring to a person who doesn't like sharing things with other people: *You mustn't be so possessive about your toys.*

†**possibility** US: /ˌpɑː.sə'bɪl.ə.t̬i/ UK: /ˌpɒs.ə'bɪl.ɪ.ti/ [countable noun] Something that may happen: *Is there any possibility of us going to America for the summer this year, mom?* ■ The plural is "possibilities".

†**possible** /'pɑs·ə·bəl/ [adjective] That may happen: *Some people believe that life is possible on other planets.*

†**post**[1] /pəust/ [noun] **1** A tall, strong object put in the ground: *The wind was so fierce that the telephone posts were blown down.* **2** A job: *I'm hoping to get a post as a foreign correspondent when I finish studying.*

post[2] /pəust/ [verb] To send something by post: *Didn't you get the birthday card I posted you?*

post- [prefix] An addition to the beginning of a word that usually means "after": *My older sister is a postgraduate student.*

postage /'pou·stɪdʒ/ [uncountable noun] Money that you pay when you post something: *How much is the postage for a letter to Australia?* ■ Be careful with the pronunciation of this word. The "a" is pronounced like the "i" in "did".

postal /'pəustəl/ [adjective] Referring to the mail service: *The postal service covers every corner of the country.*

postbox US: /'poust.bɑːks/ UK: /'pəust.bɒks/ [countable noun] See **mailbox.** ■ This word is British English.

postcard US: /ˈpoʊst.kɑːrd/ UK: /ˈpəʊst.kɑːd/ [countable noun] A card that you send when you are on vacation: *I must send Joanne a postcard from Disneyland.* ■ "Card" is short for "postcard".

postcode US: /ˈpoʊst.koʊd/ UK: /ˈpəʊst.kəʊd/ [countable noun] See **zip code.** ■ This word is British English.

poster US: /ˈpoʊ.stɚ/ UK: /ˈpəʊ.stəʳ/ [countable noun] A big picture or notice: *Matt's bedroom walls are covered with football posters.* 👁 See picture at **classroom.**

postgraduate /ˌpoʊstˈgrædʒ·u·ɪt/ [countable noun] A student who has finished his or her first degree: *Brendan is a postgraduate at Exeter University where he's studying management.*

postman /ˈpəʊst.mən/ US: /ˈpoʊst-/ [countable noun] See **mailman.** ■ This word is British English. ■ The plural is "postmen". ■ A woman is a "postwoman".

↑**post office** [countable noun] A place where you can send letters from by stamps and so on: *I'm going to take this parcel to the post office.* ■ "PO" is a written abbreviation for "post office", usually in maps.

postpone US: /poʊstˈpoʊn/ UK: /pəʊstˈpəʊn/ [verb] To arrange for something to happen later than originally planned: *It's pouring with rain so we'll have to postpone the game till tomorrow.*

postscript /ˈpoʊstˌskrɪpt/, /ˈpoʊs-/ [countable noun] See **PS.**

posture[1] /ˈpɒstʃər/ [countable noun] **1** The position of the body: *It is difficult to have good posture when you are working on a computer.* **2** The opinion or attitude somebody takes about a particular subject: *When they argue, I always try to adopt a neutral posture.*

posture[2] US: /ˈpɑːs.tʃɚ/ UK: /ˈpɒs.tʃəʳ/ [verb] To behave in an exaggerated or misleading way: *He postures like that for effect.*

postwoman /ˈpəʊstˌwʊm.ən/ US: /ˈpoʊst-/ [countable noun] See **mailwoman.** ■ This word is British English. ■ The plural is "postwomen". ■ A man is a "postman".

↑**pot** /pɒt/ [countable noun] **1** A round container used for cooking: *My grandfather made a big pot of soup for lunch yesterday.* **2** A container for something: *You should warm the pot before you make the chocolate milk in it.*

↑**potato** /pəˈteɪ·t̬oʊ/, /-t̬ə/ [countable noun] A brown root vegetable: *People in the United States eat a lot of potatoes.* ■ The plural is "potatoes". 👁 **See page 437.**

potato chip [countable noun] A thin slice of fried potato sold in a packet: *We had sandwiches and potato chips after the game.* ■ This word is more common in the plural. ■ Compare with "french fry" (a thick piece of potato cooked in oil). ■ In British English they say "crisp".

potion /ˈpoʊ·ʃən/ [countable noun] A drink that is supposed to have healing, poisonous or magical effects: *Juliet drank a potion that made her appear to be dead, but she was just asleep.*

potter[1] US: /ˈpɑː.t̬ɚ/ UK: /ˈpɒt.əʳ/ [countable noun] A person who makes pottery: *The potter has used clay to produce these beautiful painted ceramics.*

potter[2] US: /ˈpɑː.t̬ɚ/ UK: /ˈpɒt.əʳ/ [verb] To be occupied doing unimportant but pleasant things: *He likes to potter about in the backyard now that he's retired.*

pottery /ˈpɑt̬·ə·ri/ [uncountable noun] **1** Objects made out of baked clay, usually used for holding food: *I'm going to take some of this lovely pottery back for my mom.* **2** The art of making plates, cups and so on from baked clay: *We do pottery in art classes at school now, you know.* ■ The plural is "potteries".

pouch /paʊtʃ/ [countable noun] **1** A little bag: *He carried all his money in a little pouch that he attached to his belt.* **2** A special pocket that some animals have: *Kangaroos carry their babies in pouches.*

pounce /paʊnts/ [verb] To jump on somebody or something suddenly: *The lion waited until the deer came nearer and then pounced on it.* ■ Be careful! We say: "pounce **on** (somebody or something)".

↑**pound** /paʊnd/ [countable noun] **1** Money used in Britain: *This jersey cost £25.50, that is, twenty five pounds and fifty pence.* ■ With figures we normally write the sign "£" instead of writing "pound". The "£" sign goes before the figure: "£150". **2** A unit of weight used in Britain and other countries: *A pound equals 0.454 kilos.* ■ In this use, "pound" has an abbrevia-

POT

pot

teapot

flowerpot

a b c d e f g h i j k l m n o p q r s t u v w x y z

tion "lb", used only in written language. ■ See box at **abbreviations**.

pound sign [countable noun] The symbol #: *In some social networks, pound signs are usually added before keywords.* ■ The same meaning: "hash mark".

†**pour** US: /pɔːr/ UK: /pɔːʳ/ [verb] **1** To pass liquid from one container to another: *Shall I pour the orange juice into the glasses?* **2** To rain very heavily: *Oh no! it's pouring again. When is it ever going to stop?*

poverty US: /ˈpɑː.vɚ.t̬i/ UK: /ˈpɒv.ə.ti/ [uncountable noun] Being poor: *There's a lot of poverty in the rich countries of the world.* ■ The plural is "poverties".

†**powder** /ˈpaʊ·dər/ [uncountable noun] A dry substance in the form of small particles: *Soap powder manufacturers always say that their powder washes whiter than any other!*

†**power** US: /paʊɚ/ UK: /paʊəʳ/ [uncountable noun] **1** Strength: *Sailors always say that the power of the sea is a dangerous thing.* **2** The ability to control people: *Having so much power has made you arrogant.* **3** The energy that makes machines work: *Nuclear power can be extremely dangerous if security is faulty.* **4** A very strong country: *Each year the main powers meet and discuss world problems.* **5** **in power** In control, of a country: *This President has been in power for four years.* **6** **in (somebody's) power** The ability to do something: *I'll help you if it's in my power.*

power boat US: /ˈpaʊɚ.boʊt/ UK: /ˈpaʊə.bəʊt/ [countable noun] A very fast and powerful motor boat: *Two power boats raced across the bay.*

†**powerful** /ˈpaʊ·ər·fəl/ [adjective] Having great power or strong in effect: *China is becoming a powerful country.*

powerless /ˈpaʊ·ər·ləs/ [adjective] Without strength or without the capacity to do something: *She is powerless to help us.*

power station [countable noun] A place where electricity is produced: *There's a power station at the end of that street.*

†**practical** /ˈpræktɪkəl/ [adjective] **1** Referring to practice rather than theory: *I love horses but I haven't had any practical experience in looking after them.* **2** Good at doing things with your hands: *My dad's very intelligent but he's not very practical around the house.*

practically /ˈpræk.tɪ.kli/ [adverb] Almost, nearly: *Hold on a minute, I won't be long. I've practically finished my homework.*

†**practice**[1] /ˈpræk.tɪs/ [uncountable noun] **1** Doing something frequently, to try to be good at it: *I like playing tennis but I haven't had much practice yet.* **2** **out of practice** Needing practice: *Janet used to be a good pianist but she's a bit out of practice.*

practice[2] [verb] To do something many times to try to be good: *If you want to be a good musician you have to practice an awful lot.* ■ The British English spelling is "practise".

†**practise** [verb] See **practice**. ■ This is British English spelling.

†**praise**[1] /preɪz/ [uncountable noun] Saying that somebody or something is very good: *The new movie has received a lot of praise from the critics.*

praise[2] /preɪz/ [verb] To say that somebody or something is very good: *My teacher praised me for my test results.*

pram /præm/ [countable noun] A kind of box on wheels for carrying babies: *My mom sometimes lets me push my baby sister's pram.*

prawn US: /prɑːn/ UK: /prɔːn/ [countable noun] **1** A small pink sea animal: *I love eating prawns with mayonnaise.* **2** **king prawn** A large prawn which is usually very expensive: *King prawns are larger and tastier.* 👁 See picture at **shellfish**.

pray /preɪ/ [verb] To talk to God: *We pray for things like world peace at school assembly.*

†**prayer** US: /prer/ UK: /preəʳ/ [countable noun] Words that you say to God: *I sometimes say a prayer when I have a big problem.*

precaution /prɪˈkɔ·ʃən/ [countable noun] Something that you do to avoid something you don't want: *We took the precaution of booking a place in the campsite before we went.*

precious /ˈpreʃ.əs/ [adjective] **1** Very valuable: *Diamonds are beautiful, precious stones.* **2** Very much loved by somebody: *My family and friends are very precious to me.*

precipitation /prɪˌsɪpɪˈteɪʃən/ [uncountable noun] The rain, snow and hail that falls from the sky to the ground: *There was heavy precipitation in the mountains.*

†**precise** /prɪˈsaɪs/ [adjective] Exact and correct: *The teacher gave us precise instructions about how to do the chemical test.*

predator /ˈpred·ə·t̬ər/ [countable noun] An animal which naturally kills and eats other animals: *Lions, leopards and wolves are different species of predators.*

†**predict** /prɪˈdɪkt/ [verb] To say what is going to happen: *My mom predicted that my sister would be a redhead but she's got black hair.*

prediction /prɪˈdɪk.ʃən/ [uncountable noun] Saying what is going to happen: *Unfortunately, my predictions about the weather were quite wrong and we got soaked.*

preface /ˈpref.ɪs/ [countable noun] A piece of writing at the beginning of a book: *Writers often use the preface to express their thanks to people who have helped them.*

†**prefer** /prɪ'fɜr/ [verb] To like one thing more than another: *Which do you prefer, orange or lemon juice?* ■ Be careful with the spelling of these forms: "preferred", "preferring". ■ In the conditional, prefer is followed by the infinitive with "to": "I would prefer to do the shopping tomorrow". Compare with "rather" (followed by the infinitive without "to").

preferable /'pref·ər·ə·bəl/ [adjective] Better or more suitable: *We could go on the train, but the bus is preferable, because it takes us straight to the door.*

†**preference** /'pref·ər·əns/ [countable noun] Something that a person prefers: *My preference is for milk rather than coffee for breakfast.*

prefix /'priː.fɪks/ [countable noun] Letters that you add to the beginning of a word to change its meaning: *With the prefix "un", the word "true" becomes "untrue", which means "false".*

pregnancy /'preg.nənt.si/ [noun] The condition of expecting a baby: *Women sometimes feel a bit sick at the beginning of their pregnancy.* ■ The plural is "pregnancies".

†**pregnant** /'preg.nənt/ [adjective] Expecting a baby: *My cousin June is pregnant and her baby is due in August.*

prehistoric /ˌpriːhɪ'stɒrɪk/ [adjective] **1** Referring to the period before the appearance of writing: *In prehistoric times, many people lived in caves.* **2** Out of date or very old: *Your car is positively prehistoric.*

prejudice /'predʒ.ʊ.dɪs/ [uncountable noun] Not liking somebody or something without a good reason: *A judge should be free from prejudice.*

prejudiced /'predʒ.ʊ.dɪst/ [adjective] Having prejudice against somebody or something: *Don't pay any attention to him, he's prejudiced.*

preliminary /prɪ'lɪm·əˌner·i/ [adjective] Coming before something: *After a few preliminary words from the presenter, the debate began.*

†**preparation** /ˌprep·ə'reɪ·ʃən/ [uncountable noun] **1** Getting something ready: *We'll have to do a lot of preparation for the end of term concert if we want it to be good.* **2 in preparation for** Ready for something: *We all got dressed up in preparation for the party.*

preparations /ˌprep.ər'eɪ.ʃən/ US: /-ə'reɪ-/ [plural noun] Things that you do to get something ready: *My mom is already making preparations for Christmas.*

†**prepare** /prɪ'peər/ [verb] To get ready: *We'll have to start preparing the things for the picnic.*

prepared to [adjective] Willing to do something: *Sandra said she was only prepared to do it if I went with her.* ■ Be careful with the pronunciation of this word. The last "e" is not pronounced.

preposition /ˌprep.ə'zɪʃ.ᵊn/ [countable noun] A word that you put before a noun to show place, direction, time and so on: *In the sentence "She looked through the window", the preposition is "through".* 👁 See picture on the following page.

prepositional /ˌprep.ə'zɪʃ.ən.əl/ [adjective] Having the characteristics of a preposition: *"Behind the door" is a prepositional phrase.*

prerequisite /ˌpriː'rekwɪzɪt/ [countable noun] Something that has to occur or exist before something else is possible: *A passing grade in the first three Spanish courses is a prerequisite to take the advanced Spanish course.*

prescribe /prɪ'skraɪb/ [verb] To advise, especially in writing, which medicine or treatment a patient should have: *The doctor prescribes medicines according to the patient's symptoms.*

prescription /prɪ'skrɪp.ʃᵊn/ [countable noun] A note from a doctor with the name of a medicine on it: *I'm just going to the pharmacy to get this prescription for my grandma.*

†**presence** /'prez.ᵊnts/ [uncountable noun] **1** Being somewhere: *Jennifer makes such a noise that her presence is always noticed.* **2 in the presence of** While somebody was present: *The school prizes were given out in the presence of the Mayor and all the parents.*

†**present**[1] /'prezənt/ [adjective] **1** In a place at the time concerned: *How many people do you think were present at the parents' meeting?* **2** Existing at the moment: *My dad's present post is in Mexico but next year he will be working in Canada.*

†**present**[2] /'prezənt/ [noun] **1** A gift that you give to somebody or receive from somebody: *I got some great games as presents for my birthday.* ■ The same meaning: "gift". **2** The time now: *You can learn about the present by studying the past.*

present[3] /prɪ'zent/ [verb] **1** To give something to somebody: *When our teacher left, we presented her with a lovely watch.* ■ This use is formal. We usually say "give". **2** To introduce somebody or something, particularly a TV or radio show: *She presents the program very badly, she's always forgetting her lines.*

†**presentation** /ˌprez.ᵊn'teɪ.ʃᵊn/ [uncountable noun] Giving something to somebody in public, the manner of presenting something: *The presentation of medals for the sports tournament will be next week in the evening.*

present continuous [uncountable noun] A tense that is made with the present tense of "be" and the "-ing" form: *"I am looking at you" is an example of a sentence in the present continuous.* ■ The present

PREPOSITIONS OF POSITION

continuous is used to describe things that are happening now or to describe things that are going to happen.

presenter /prɪˈzen.tər/ US: /-t̬ɚ/ [countable noun] A person who presents something: *I'd love to be a television presenter when I grow up.*

presently /ˈprez.ᵊnt.li/ [adverb] **1** Soon: *Start doing your exercise; I'll be back presently.* **2** At the moment: *I'm presently going to the local school but my parents want to move me to another one.*

present participle [uncountable noun] A form of a verb made by adding "-ing" to the infinitive: *"Going" is the present participle of the verb "go".*

present perfect [uncountable noun] A form of a verb that is made with the present tense of "have" and the past participle of the verb: *"I have been to America three times" and "We haven't talked about your trip" are examples of sentences in the present perfect.*

present tense [countable noun] A form of a verb that refers to something that is usually true or to something that usually happens: *"I go to the movies every Saturday" is an example of the present tense.* ■ Be careful! In English the present tense is not used to describe something that is happening now.

preservation /ˌprez·ərˈveɪ·ʃən/ [uncountable noun] Keeping something safe from decay, harm or danger: *Unless we do something for its preservation, the tiger could become extinct.*

preserve[1] [noun] A soft food made from fruit and sugar: *I'll have a piece of toast with strawberry preserve.*

†**preserve**[2] /prɪˈzɜrv/ [verb] To keep or to maintain something: *Salt was used to preserve meat on sea journeys before fridges were invented.*

†**president** /ˈprez.ɪ.dᵊnt/ [countable noun] **1** The leader of a government: *Ted knows the names of all of the Presidents of the United States.* **2** The most important person in an organization: *Laura's grandfather is the president of the local golf club.*

†**press**[1] /pres/ [noun] **1** Newspapers and magazines: *The press have published yet another story about the Royal Family.* **2** A machine that prints newspapers, books and so on: *In my work, presses are connected to the computers that journalists write their articles on.* ■ The plural is "presses". 👁 **See page 443.**

press[2] /pres/ [verb] To push something down: *If you want to ring the bell, press this button.* ■ Be careful with the spelling of the 3rd person singular present tense form: "presses".

press-up /ˈpres.ʌp/ [countable noun] See **push-up**. ■ This word is British English.

†**pressure** /ˈpreʃ·ər/ [uncountable noun] The force of something pressing on something else: *We'll have to check the pressure in the tires before we go out on our bikes.*

pressure cooker [countable noun] A type of saucepan with a tight lid, which cooks food rapidly under pressure: *If you cook it in the pressure cooker, it will be done in half the time.* 👁 See picture at **pan**.

†**pretend** /prɪˈtend/ [verb] To try to make people believe something false: *Jan pretends that she's happy about changing schools but I know that she isn't.*

†**pretty**[1] /ˈpeti/ [adjective] Attractive and nice looking: *Sheila is very pretty.* ■ The comparative form is "prettier" and the superlative form is "prettiest". ■ When we use "pretty" for people, this is usually to talk about girls and women. For men we usually say "handsome" or "good-looking".

pretty[2] [adverb] Quite: *I'm pretty sure that George said that he was coming to see us.* ■ See box at **fairly**.

†**prevent** /prɪˈvent/ [verb] To stop something from happening: *The school janitor has to lock up the school at night to prevent vandals from getting in.*

prevention /prɪˈvent.ʃᵊn/ [uncountable noun] Stopping something from happening: *Prevention is better than cure.*

†**previous** /ˈpriː.vi.əs/ [adjective] Happening before now: *Our previous principal was much nicer than the one we have now.*

prey /preɪ/ [uncountable noun] An animal that is hunted by another animal: *Small animals like mice and rabbits are often the prey of larger ones like foxes.*

†**price** /praɪs/ [countable noun] **1** How much something costs: *What is the price of these jeans, please?* **2** **half price** Costing half the usual price: *I know a store where we can buy the video recorder at half price.*

priceless /ˈpraɪ.sləs/ [adjective] Extremely valuable: *The Natural Parks in United States are said to be priceless.*

prick[1] [countable noun] A small, sharp pain: *David felt a prick in his leg when the doctor gave him his injection.*

prick[2] /prɪk/ [verb] To make a very small hole in something: *If you prick the balloon, it will burst.*

†**pride** /praɪd/ [uncountable noun] **1** A feeling of satisfaction with how good something is: *My mom showed everyone my swimming certificate with great pride.* **2** A feeling of superiority: *Tom's worst defect is his pride. He will never say that he's made a mistake.*

†**priest** /priːst/ [countable noun] A person who leads people in their religion, especially Catholics: *Our priest worked in Africa before he came here.* ■ A priest in the church of England is called a "vicar".

a b c d e f g h i j k l m n o p q r s t u v w x y z

†**primary** /'praɪmәri/ [adjective] The most important: *The primary purpose of our visit is to see the Grand Canyon.*

primary color [countable noun] Any of the three colors which can be mixed together in order to obtain any other color: *The three primary colors are red, blue and yellow.*

primary school [countable noun] A school for children from five to eleven years old: *Kathy is at primary school now.* ■ The same meaning: "elementary school".

primate /'praɪmeɪt/ [countable noun] Any member of the most developed group of mammals: *Humans, apes and monkeys are all primates.*

†**Prime Minister** [countable noun] The head of government in some countries: *Prime Minister of Canada is the most politically powerful member of Canadian government.* ■ Be careful! "Prime Minister" has capital letters.

primitive /'prɪm·ɪ·t̬ɪv/ [adjective] Of an early stage in development, simple: *Cave paintings were one of the first artistic expressions of primitive people.*

†**prince** /prɪnts/ [countable noun] A man in a royal family: *There is usually a prince in fairy tales.* ■ A woman is a "princess".

†**princess** /prɪn'ses/ [countable noun] A woman in a royal family: *The wedding of the princess was very spectacular.* ■ The plural is "princesses". A man is a "prince".

†**principal¹** /'prɪnsәpәl/ [adjective] Main or most important: *The journalist asked her what was the principal reason for her success.*

principal² /'prɪnsәpәl/ [countable noun] The head of a school: *The Principal is coming to see you in a minute. He is very angry with the whole class!* ■ "Principal" is written in capital letters when we refer to a particular principal.

†**principle** /'prɪnt.sɪ.pl̩/ [countable noun] A rule that you believe you should always follow: *It's totally against my principles to be cruel to animals.*

print¹ /prɪnt/ [noun] **1** Letters made by a machine on paper: *This print is so small that I can hardly read it.* **2** A mark that has been left: *I can see that the cat's been in here. She's left her prints all over the kitchen floor.*

†**print²** /prɪnt/ [verb] **1** To put words or pictures on paper with a machine: *In this workshop, you learn how to print.* **2** To write letters without joining them: *Please print your name and address clearly on the front page.*

†**printer** /'prɪn·tәr/ [countable noun] **1** A machine that prints: *Have you got a printer for your computer yet?* **See page 442.** **2** A person whose job is to print: *My father is a printer.* **3** A company that prints text or pictures on paper: *When we've finished preparing the book, we'll send it to the printer.*

prior¹ US: /praɪr/ UK: /praɪәʳ/ [countable noun] A monk who is in charge of a priory, or the second in command in a monastery or abbey: *The Prior is away at the moment.* ■ The female equivalent is a "prioress".

prior² /praɪәr/ [adjective] **1** That occurs or exists before something else: *I am afraid you need a prior appointment to see the specialist.* **2** **prior to (something)** Before something: *It was all decided prior to the meeting.*

prioress /'praɪә.res/ US: /'praɪ-/ [countable noun] A nun who is the head of a priory of nuns, or the second in charge in a convent or abbey: *The prioress here is very strict.* ■ The male equivalent is a "prior".

priory [countable noun] A religious house which is under a prior or prioress: *In our trip to France we visited a priory with monks of the Order of St Benedict.* ■ The plural is "priories".

prism [countable noun] A solid figure whose sides are parallel and whose two ends are the same in shape and size: *A hexagonal prism is a prism with hexagonal base.*

†**prison** /'prɪz.әn/ [countable noun] A place where criminals are sent: *Did you know that Sally's uncle has been in prison for five years for robbing a bank?* ■ The same meaning: "jail".

†**prisoner** /'prɪz·ә·nәr/, /'prɪz·nәr/ [countable noun] A person who is in prison: *Prisoners in the United States do not have full rights under the Constitution.*

†**private** /'praɪ.vәt/ [adjective] **1** For a small group of people: *Mr. and Mrs. Turner belong to a private sports club.* **2** Without other people: *We had a private meeting of the club to discuss tactics.* **3** Not belonging to the government: *My cousin went into a private hospital for his operation.* **4** **in private** Without anybody else there: *Can I speak to you in private, please?*

private school [countable noun] A school paid for by the parents: *Neil's cousin goes to a private school.*

privilege /'prɪv.әl.ɪdʒ/ [countable noun] A special right for only one or a few people: *Years ago in United States an education was the privilege of very few people, but now all children go to school.*

†**prize** /praɪz/ [countable noun] A thing that is given to a person for doing something better than others: *Frank got a book prize for winning the essay competition.*

prize or **prise** /praɪz/ [verb] To open, move or separate something by using force: *They prized open the door with a bar.*

probable /'prɒbәbl/ [adjective] Likely to happen or to be true: *It is probable that they will come next weekend.* ■ Compare with "improbable" (not probable, not likely).

probably [adverb] Likely to be true: *We'll probably see you on Sunday.*

†**problem** US: /'prɑː.bləm/ UK: /'prɒb.ləm/ [countable noun] **1** A difficult or worrying situation: *I've got a problem; I want to go to the movies and I don't have any money.* **2** Something that you have to solve: *This mathematical problem is quite easy.*

†**proceed** /prə'sid/, /proʊ-/ [verb] To continue with something: *After lunch we proceeded on our journey up the mountain.* ■ This word is formal. We usually say "continue".

†**process** /'prɑs·es/, /'proʊ·ses/ [countable noun] A number of actions that produce development: *Learning a second language is quite a long process.* ■ The plural is "processes".

procession /prə'seʃ.ᵊn/ [countable noun] A line of people or things moving forward: *We will go to the Grand Mariam Procession in Los Angeles, California.*

proclaim /prəʊ'kleɪm/ [verb] To declare something in a public or official way: *John proclaimed his innocence to the judge.*

produce[1] /'prɒdjuːs/ [uncountable noun] Food that is grown on a farm: *The farmer sells his produce in the local market.*

†**produce**[2] /prə'djuːs/ [verb] **1** To cause something: *That joke is very old, but it always produces a laugh.* **2** To make or to grow something: *This farm produces wheat and potatoes as well as milk and cheese.* **3** To organize or finance a play, a film and so on: *And last but not least, our thanks to Kate's father who produced the play!*.

†**producer** /prə'du·sər/ [countable noun] **1** A country or a company that makes something: *Japan is one of the most important producers of electronic equipment in the world.* **2** A person who organizes or finances a play, a film and so on: *My dad's cousin is a television producer.*

†**product** US: /'prɑː.dʌkt/ UK: /'prɒd.ʌkt/ [countable noun] Something that is made to be sold: *Wool and meat are two of Australia's most important products.*

†**production** /prə'dʌk.ʃᵊn/ [countable noun] Making or growing something: *The furniture production in this workshop has gone up a lot in the last year.*

†**profession** /prə'feʃ.ᵊn/ [countable noun] A job that requires years of study before you can do it: *My father's an attorney by profession.*

†**professional** /prə'feʃ.ᵊn.ᵊl/ [adjective] **1** Referring to a profession, expert: *I think that we should get professional advice from somebody before we buy a new computer.* **2** Doing something for money: *Theresa has been an amateur pianist for many years but now she wants to go professional and do it as a job.*

†**professor** /prə'fes·ər/ [countable noun] The most important teacher of a subject at a university: *He is now Professor at Stanford University.* ■ See box at **abbreviations**.

profile /'proʊ·faɪl/ [countable noun] A person's face or head seen from the side, not the front: *He has an attractive profile.*

†**profit** US: /'prɑː.fɪt/ UK: /'prɒf.ɪt/ [uncountable noun] Money that somebody makes when they sell something for more than what it cost them: *We made $220 profit on the school lottery.*

profitable /'prɑf·ɪ·t̬ə·bəl/ [adjective] Making a profit: *My neighbor had to close the café he opened this summer because it wasn't very profitable.*

profound /prə'faʊnd/ [adjective] Very serious, very deep: *You have my profound sympathy.*

†**program**[1] /'prəʊgræm/ [countable noun] **1** A piece made for television or radio: *My favorite program is on the television tonight.* **2** Written information about a play or a concert: *We read in the program that the play was first performed in 1996.* **3** The instructions that a computer follows: *Some computer programs are more complicated than others.* ■ The British English spelling is "programme".

program[2] /'prəʊgræm/ [verb] To give a set of instructions to a computer: *Terry has got a new job programming computers.* ■ Be careful with the spelling of these forms: "programmed", "programming".

†**programme** /'prəʊgræm/ [countable noun] See **program**. ■ This is a British English spelling.

†**progress**[1] US: /'prɒgres/ UK: /'prəʊgres/ [uncountable noun] Getting better: *I feel as if I'm making progress with my tennis, at last!*

progress[2] /prəʊ'gres/ [verb] **1** To continue: *As my vacation in Paris progressed, I began to feel more confident about my French.* **2** To improve: *The baby's speech is progressing very quickly, isn't it?* ■ Be careful with the spelling of the 3rd person singular present tense form: "progresses".

progressive /prəʊ'gresɪv/ [adjective] **1** That happens or develops in a gradual way: *This illness produces a progressive loss of memory.* **2** In favor of modern ideas or reforms: *The City Council adopted several progressive measures.*

prohibit /prə'hɪb.ɪt/ [verb] To say that something must not be done: *Smoking is prohibited in all areas of the hospital.*

†**project** /prə'dʒekt/ US: /'prɑː.dʒekt/ UK: /'prɒdʒ.ekt/ [countable noun] **1** A plan to do something: *There's a project to build a new sports center at school.* **2** A piece of work for school: *We have to do a project on the Vikings for school so we're going to the museum to get some information.* ■ Be careful! We say: "to do a project **on** (something)".

a b c d e f g h i j k l m n o p q r s t u v w x y z

projector /prə'dʒek·tər/ [countable noun] A device that is used to project movies or images onto a screen: *The projector has a system of lenses and special lighting.*

prom [countable noun] A formal party and dance for high school or college students to celebrate the end of the year: *What are you wearing for the prom?*

†**promise**[1] /'prɒmɪs/ [countable noun] **1** Saying that you will definitely do something: *Anthony and Cleopatra made a promise to love each other for ever.* **2 break a promise** Not to keep a promise: *Thomas said that he'd go with me to the dance but he broke his promise and went with Angela.* ■ Be careful with the pronunciation of this word! "mise" is pronounced like "miss".

promise[2] /'prɒmɪs/ [verb] To say that you will definitely do something: *I promise you that I'll phone you as soon as I get back from my vacation.*

†**promote** /prə'moʊt/ [verb] To give somebody a better job within the same organization: *My mom's just been promoted to manager of the company.*

†**promotion** /prə'moʊ·ʃən/ [countable noun] Moving to a better job within an organization: *My dad is hoping to get a promotion this year.*

†**prompt** US: /prɑːmpt/ UK: /prɒmpt/ [adjective] Quick: *Please send me a prompt answer to my letter.*

†**pronoun** /'proʊˌnaʊn/ [countable noun] A word that takes the place of a noun: *"He", "she", "it" and "they" are all pronouns.*

†**pronounce** /prə'naʊnts/ [verb] To make the sounds of a word: *How do you pronounce "plow"? It rhymes with "cow".*

†**pronunciation** /prəˌnʌnt.si'eɪ.ʃən/ [countable noun] The way somebody pronounces something: *Robert's French pronunciation is very good, isn't it?*

†**proof** /pruːf/ [uncountable noun] A thing that shows that something is true: *The police still haven't found any proof that she committed the crime.*

propeller /prə'pel·ər/ [countable noun] A thing that turns to make a ship, helicopter and so on move: *The propellers started and the boat began to move through the water.*

†**proper** US: /'prɑː.pɚ/ UK: /'prɒp.əʳ/ [adjective] **1** Correct, appropriate: *Make sure that you use the proper paint if you're going to decorate that old chair.* **2** Real: *I'm going to get rid of this old bike and get myself a proper mountain bike.*

†**property** US: /'prɑː.pɚ.t̬i/ UK: /'prɒp.ə.ti/ [noun] **1** Things that somebody owns: *This book is the property of Green Lane Elementary School.* ■ In this use "property" is an uncountable noun. **2** Buildings and land: *Gemma's grandpa has got a lot of property in Colorado.* ■ The plural is "properties".

prophet US: /'prɑː.fɪt/ UK: /'prɒf.ɪt/ [countable noun] A person who gives God's message to people: *Moses, Isaiah and Muhammad were all prophets.*

†**proportion** /prə'pɔr·ʃən/ [countable noun] The amount of something compared to something else: *The proportion of boys to girls in our school is two to one.*

proportional /prə'pɔːʃənəl/ [adjective] That corresponds to something else in size, degree or amount: *The pay there is proportional to the amount of work done.* ■ We say "proportional **to** (something)".

†**proposal** /prə'poʊ·zəl/ [countable noun] A suggestion: *The principal's proposal to build a parking lot on the playing fields was rejected by the parents.*

†**propose** /prə'poʊz/ [verb] To suggest something: *I propose that we give a concert to raise funds for the new gym.*

▶ **PHRASAL VERBS · to propose to (somebody)** To ask somebody to marry you: *Charles proposed to Mary and she immediately refused him!*

prosecute /'prɑs·ɪˌkjut/ [verb] To take legal action against somebody: *The sign in the window said: "Shoplifters will be prosecuted".*

prosper US: /'prɑː.spɚ/ UK: /'prɒs.pəʳ/ [verb] To make money: *Many immigrants who went to the USA prospered and became rich and powerful people.*

prosperity US: /prɑː'sper.ə.t̬i/ UK: /prɒs'per.ɪ.ti/ [uncountable noun] Being rich and successful: *Many people have found prosperity in distant countries.* ■ The plural is "prosperities".

prosperous /'prɑs·pər·əs/ [adjective] Rich and successful: *There are a lot of prosperous people living on Fifth Avenue in New York.*

prostate [countable noun] A gland that surrounds the neck of the bladder in male mammals: *Sperm is carried in the liquid produced by the prostate.*

†**protect** /prə'tekt/ [verb] To guard somebody or something: *This warm coat will protect you from the cold.*

†**protection** /prə'tek.ʃən/ [uncountable noun] Guarding somebody or something: *She bought a guard dog for protection after somebody broke in and took her jewelry.*

protein /'proʊ·tin/ [countable noun] An organic compound that is an essential part of the human diet and is necessary for the body to grow: *Proteins are found in meat, fish, milk, nuts and eggs.*

†**protest**[1] /'prəʊtest/ [uncountable noun] Showing in a strong way that you are against something: *In protest against the war, we are organizing a demonstration.*

protest[2] /'prəʊtest/ [verb] To show that you are against something in a strong way: *Although I protested, I ended up doing what they asked me.*

Protestant /'prɑt̬·ə·stənt/ [countable noun] Referring to a part of the Christian Church that separated from the Roman Catholic Church in the 16th century:

There are many different types of Protestants: over 250 kinds in the United States alone. ■ Be careful! "Protestant" has a capital "P".

*__proud__ /praʊd/ [adjective] **1** Happy and satisfied about something: *She says that she's very proud of her children.* **2** Believing that you are superior to other people: *Laurence is too proud to say sorry.* See picture at **emotions.**

*__prove,__ proved, proven /pruːv/ [verb] To show that something is true: *The police thought that the suspect was guilty, but couldn't prove it.*

proved Past tense of **prove.** ■ Be careful with the pronunciation of this word. The "e" is not pronounced.

proven /'pruː.vᵊn, 'prəʊ-/ Past participle of **prove.**

*__provide__ /prə'vaɪd/ [verb] To give something that is needed: *The school will provide the hall for the party but we have to bring our own food and drink.*

provided /prə'vaɪdɪd/ [conjunction] Only if: *I'll lend you my new skates provided that you promise me you'll bring them back quickly.* ■ Be careful with the pronunciation of this word. The "e" is pronounced like the "i" in "did".

province US: /'prɑː.vɪnts/ UK: /'prɒv.ɪnts/ [countable noun] A part of a country: *Canada has ten provinces.*

provincial /prə'vɪn.tʃᵊl/ [adjective] Referring to a province: *Provincial elections will be held next month.*

provision /prə'vɪʒ.ᵊn/ [countable noun] **1** The act of providing something: *He has made no provisions for his retirement.* **2** Condition in a law or legal document: *Under the provisions of the contract, the agreement finishes after one year.*

provoke /prə'voʊk/ [verb] To annoy somebody: *Don't provoke me! I'm in a bad mood today.*

prowl /praʊl/ [verb] When hunting, to move about quietly, trying not to be seen or heard: *The tiger prowled around the herd of deer waiting to attack them.*

proximity /prɒk'sɪməti/ [uncountable noun] The state of being near in space, time or relationship: *The proximity of her wedding day made her feel nervous.* ■ We say "in the proximity **of** (something)". This word is formal.

prune¹ /pruːn/ [countable noun] A dried plum: *I sometimes have prunes at breakfast.*

prune² /pruːn/ [verb] To cut branches off a tree to improve its shape: *When are you going to prune your rose trees?*

PS /ˌpiː'es/ An abbreviation used at the end of a letter when something is added: *P.S. Don't forget to write back soon!* ■ "PS" is an abbreviation for "postscript". ■ See box at **abbreviations**.

psalm /sɑːm/ [countable noun] A religious song or poem: *King David is said to have written many of the psalms that appear in the Bible.*

psychiatrist /saɪ'kaɪə.trɪst, sɪ-/ [countable noun] A doctor who specializes in illnesses of the mind: *A psychiatrist treated her for depression.*

psychiatry /saɪ'kaɪə.tri/ [uncountable noun] The study of illnesses of the mind: *Psychiatry is a very interesting and difficult subject.* ■ The plural is "psychiatries".

psychologist /saɪ'kɑl·ə·dʒɪst/ [countable noun] A person who specializes in psychology: *A psychologist sometimes comes to our school and gives us tests.*

psychology /saɪ'kɑl·ə·dʒi/ [uncountable noun] The study of the mind and of behavior: *My cousin is studying psychology at Sussex University.* ■ The plural is "psychologies".

PTO To the next page: *Because I didn't notice the PTO at the bottom of the page, I didn't read the information on the back.* ■ "PTO" is an abbreviation for "please turn over". "PTO" is always written in capital letters. ■ See box at **abbreviations**.

*__pub__ /pʌb/ [countable noun] A place where people go to have a drink: *My mom and dad sometimes go to the pub on a Sunday evening.* ■ Be careful with the pronunciation of this word! The "u" is pronounced as in "sun".

puberty /'pjuːbəti/ [uncountable noun] The period during which a person reaches sexual maturity and becomes able to have children: *At puberty, the body changes physically.*

public¹ /'pʌblɪk/ [adjective] **1** For the use of everyone: *I belong to a public library and I get a different book out nearly every week.* **2** Referring to people in general: *Public opinion is very much against the latest cuts in the health service.* ■ Be careful with the pronunciation of this word! The "u" is pronounced as in "sun".

*__public²__ /'pʌblɪk/ [uncountable noun] People in general: *The yards will be open to the public between 3 and 5 o'clock this afternoon.*

*__publication__ /ˌpʌb.lɪ'keɪ.ʃᵊn/ [noun] **1** Printing and selling of a book, magazine and so on: *The publication of a book takes months.* **2** A magazine, a book and so on: *There are many publications on fishing on sale nowadays.*

*__publicity__ /pə'blɪs·ɪ·t̬i/ [uncountable noun] Attracting people's attention to a product, advertising: *There has been a lot of publicity for his new movie.* ■ This word has no plural and you cannot use it with "a" or "an". We say "some publicity" or "a piece of publicity". ■ The plural is "publicities".

publicly [adjective] In public: *After publicly announcing their wedding, the singer and the actor disappeared for a time.*

a b c d e f g h i j k l m n o **p** q r s t u v w x y z

public relations [uncountable noun] Relations between a company and the public: *Peter's father is a public relations officer for a big bank.*

public school [countable noun] A school paid for by the government: *Although his parents are rich he goes to a public school.*

public transport [uncountable noun] The system of buses, trains and so on, that everybody can use: *I go everywhere by public transport.*

↑**publish** /'pʌb.lɪʃ/ [verb] **1** To prepare, print and sell a book, a magazine and so on: *Michael has just written a science fiction novel that is going to be published next year.* **2** To make something known to the public: *The banks publish their accounts after closing the financial year.*

publisher /'pʌb·lɪ·ʃər/ [countable noun] A person or a company that publishes books, magazines and so on: *The publisher of this dictionary is "SM".*

publishing company [countable noun] A company that publishes books, magazines and so on: *"SM" is a large publishing company.* ■ The plural is "publishing companies".

pudding /'pʊd.ɪŋ/ [countable noun] A particular kind of hot dish made principally with flour: *I like to eat Christmas pudding with custard.*

puddle /'pʌd.l̩/ [countable noun] A small pool of water such as one left after rain: *My little sister loves stepping in puddles.*

Puerto Rican[1] [adjective] Referring to Puerto Rico: *Rincon Bay is one of the more popular Puerto Rican beaches.* ■ Be careful! "Puerto Rican" has capital letters.

Puerto Rican[2] [countable noun] A person from Puerto Rico: *Puerto Ricans are US citizens.* ■ Be careful! "Puerto Rican" has capital letters.

puff[1] /pʌf/ [countable noun] A small quantity of wind, smoke or air: *A puff of wind blew all the candles out.*

puff[2] /pʌf/ [verb] To breathe quickly: *I was puffing after running up the hill.*

puffin /'pʌfɪn/ [countable noun] A seabird with a distinctive, brightly colored beak and a large head: *The puffin is to be found in the North Atlantic and the North Pacific.*

pull[1] /pʊl/ [countable noun] Pulling something: *The child gave a pull on my sweater to attract my attention.*

↑**pull**[2] /pʊl/ [verb] **1** To bring somebody or something towards you: *She pulled the chair towards her and sat down.* ■ Be careful! You "pull" something towards you, but you "push" it away from you. **2** To bring something along behind: *Look at that little boy pulling his toy train along the road with a string.* **3** **to pull somebody's leg** To make fun of somebody, for example by telling them something that is not true: *Are you pulling my leg?*

◗ **PHRASAL VERBS** · **to pull down** To destroy a building: *Did you know they're going to pull down the old movie theater and put a Bingo Hall in its place?* · **to pull up** **1** To move something upwards: *Pull up your socks. They're falling down.* **2** To stop a vehicle: *We pulled up at the stoplights.*

pulley /'pʊl.i/ [countable noun] A machine or a tool with a rope used for lifting things: *The workers used a pulley to get the piano up to the third floor.*

pullover /'pʊl,oʊ·vər/ [countable noun] A warm piece of clothing with long sleeves: *My mom gave me this nice blue pullover for my birthday.* ■ The same meaning: "jersey", "jumper", "sweater". "Sweater" is the most commonly used word.

pulmonary /'pʊl·mə,ner·i/ [adjective] Referring to the lungs: *She has a pulmonary infection.*

pulse /pʌls/ [countable noun] Regular beat of the heart: *The nurse took his pulse.*

pump[1] /pʌmp/ [countable noun] A machine that moves a liquid from one place to another: *You get gas from a gas pump in a gas station.*

pump[2] /pʌmp/ [verb] To move liquid with a pump: *My grandpa used to get water by pumping it from a well they had in the back yard.*

pumpkin /'pʌmp.kɪn/ [countable noun] A big yellow vegetable that is orange inside: *People make lanterns out of pumpkins at Halloween.*

↑**punch**[1] /pʌnʃ/ [countable noun] A hit with somebody's fist: *The boxer was knocked out by a very hard punch from his opponent.*

punch[2] /pʌnʃ/ [verb] **1** To hit somebody with your fist: *Boxers punch special bags in their training.* **2** To make a hole in something with a machine: *The ticket collector punched our tickets and told us to get on the train.*

punctual /'pʌŋk.tju.əl/ [adjective] Doing something on time: *Peter's still not here. Why can't he be punctual?*

punctuation /,pʌŋk.tju'eɪ.ʃᵊn/ [uncountable noun] The use in writing of marks like periods and commas: *If you take the punctuation out of a piece of writing, it becomes almost impossible to read.*

puncture /'pʌŋk·tʃər/ [countable noun] A hole made by a sharp object: *My uncle had a puncture on the road to Austin and he didn't know how to change the tire.*

↑**punish** /'pʌn.ɪʃ/ [verb] To make somebody suffer because they have done something wrong: *If you behave like this again I will have to punish you.*

↑**punishment** /'pʌn.ɪʃ.mənt/ [noun] A way in which somebody is punished: *Your punishment will be to pick up all the litter in the playground after recess tomorrow.*

punk /pʌŋk/ [countable noun] A young, rebellious person who dresses in unusual clothes: *There were a number of punks at the disco last night.*

*__pupil__ /ˈpjuː.pᵊl/ [countable noun] **1** Person learning from a teacher: *Our school has about five hundred pupils.* **2** The round black part in the middle of the eye: *The pupil lets light reach the back of the eye.*

puppet /ˈpʌp.ɪt/ [countable noun] A doll with strings or a place for your hand to move it: *We took our little cousins to a puppet show and they really enjoyed it.*

puppy /ˈpʌp.i/ [countable noun] A young dog: *Have you seen the puppies? They're really cute.* ■ The plural is "puppies". See picture at **pet**.

purchase[1] /ˈpɜːtʃəs/ [countable noun] Something that has been bought: *I really like your watch. It was a good purchase.* ■ We usually say "buy".

*__purchase__[2] /ˈpɜːtʃəs/ [verb] To buy something: *Our school has just purchased the building next-door.* ■ This use is formal. We usually say "buy".

*__pure__ US: /pjʊr/ UK: /pjʊəʳ/ [adjective] Not mixed with anything, only: *This is pure orange juice with no artificial flavoring.*

purée US: /pjʊˈreɪ/ UK: /ˈpjʊə.reɪ/ [uncountable noun] Food that has been cooked and made liquid: *Add some tomato purée to the sauce for the pasta.*

*__purple__ /ˈpɜr·pəl/ [noun and adjective] A color made from red and blue: *I've got a new pair of purple jeans.*

*__purpose__ /ˈpɜr·pəs/ [countable noun] **1** The reason for doing or using something, the intention or objective: *The purpose of playing a game should be to have fun, not just to win.* **2 on purpose** Deliberately: *You pushed me on purpose, didn't you?*

purr US: /pɝː/ UK: /pɜː/ [verb] What a cat does when it is happy: *The cat purred happily while I stroked it.* See picture at **animal**.

purse US: /pɝːs/ UK: /pɜːs/ [countable noun] **1** A woman's small bag: *Kate always carries her glasses in her purse.* ■ In British English they say "handbag". See picture at **clothes**. **2** A small bag for money: *My mom took her purse out and gave us all a dollar each.*

*__pursue__ US: /pɚˈsuː/ UK: /pəˈsjuː/ [verb] To go after somebody: *The police pursued the thieves all along the main street.*

push[1] /pʊʃ/ [countable noun] Act of pressing something so that it moves away from you: *They gave the car a push to help it start.*

*__push__[2] /pʊʃ/ [verb] **1** To move something away from you: *Don't push me into the swimming pool!* ■ Be careful! You "push" something away from you, but you "pull" it towards you. **2** To press down on something: *Push the button for service.*

pushchair /ˈpʊʃˌtʃeəʳ/ [countable noun] See **stroller**. ■ This word is British English.

push-up [countable noun] A type of physical exercise: *You do push-ups by lying face down on the floor and pressing down on your arms.* ■ In British English they say "press-up".

pussy /ˈpʊs.i/ [countable noun] An affectionate word for a cat: *Here pussy! Come here!* ■ The plural is "pussies".

pussycat US: /ˈpʊs·iˌkæt/ [countable noun] See **pussy**.

*__put, put, put__ /pʊt/ [verb] **1** Move something to a place: *Put your books on the table.* **2** To place something somewhere: *I have put an ad in the newspaper.* **3** To say or express something: *How can I put it?* **4 I can't put it down** Words you say to express that you are very interested in the book you are reading: *The mystery book you gave me was so good that I couldn't put it down.* **5 to put a stop to something** To make something stop, especially bad or undesirable behavior: *We're all committed to put a stop to bullying in this school.* **6 to put it bluntly** Words you say to indicate that you are going to be very direct: *To put it bluntly I think they were terrible.* **7 to put something behind you** To forget something bad and continue with your life: *It was a bad experience, but you must put it behind you.* **8 to put the blame on somebody** To say that you think it is somebody's fault: *I put the blame on the politicians.*

PHRASAL VERBS · **to put (something) across** To express something you want to say in an effective way: *He is very good at putting his ideas across.* · **to put (somebody) away** To send somebody to prison: *I hope they find the murderer and out him away for a long time.* · **to put (something) away** To return something to its usual place, to put in order: *David, please put your toys away.* · **to put (somebody) down** To criticize or treat somebody as stupid in front of others: *It was so disrespectful when my boss put me down at the meeting.* · **to put (something) down 1** To repress a revolt: *The army put the protesting students down and classes returned to normal.* **2** To end an animal's life because it is old or ill: *We had to have our cat put down.* · **to put (something) down to (something)** To attribute the success or failure of something to a particular thing: *I put his success down to his good looks.* · **to put in (somewhere)** Referring to a boat, to go into a port or bay and stop there: *Let's put in somewhere before the storm starts.* · **to put (somebody) off 1** To make somebody unable to concentrate: *My dad shouted at my sister while she was driving and put her off completely.* **2** To make somebody lose their interest in something: *Linda has put me off going to see the movie. She says it is terrible.* **3** To send somebody away without what they wanted: *We wanted to have everything approved for our school celebration last week, but the principal kept putting us off.* · **to put (something) off** To delay something: *They've put off their wedding until June.* · **to put (something) on 1** To dress: *We all put on our clothes quickly when we came out of the pool because it was cold.* **2** To make a radio, TV, compact disc and so on function: *Let's put the radio on and listen to a concert.* **3** To organize a show or other event **4** To pretend that you are feeling something: *I don't believe that he is so affected, I think that he is putting it on.* · **to put (somebody) out 1** To cause inconvenience to somebody: *I hope that I am not putting you out.* **2** To make somebody feel surprised, angry or upset: *She was put out when she was not chosen.* · **to put (something) out 1** To take out or to extend: *She put out her hand to take the money.* **2** To spread a rumor or some information: *They have put out a gossip that she is going to retire.* · **to put (somebody) through** To connect a telephone caller to the person or extension they want: *Hold on a second, I'm putting you through now.* · **to put (somebody) up** To give somebody a place to stay: *Could you put me up for a few nights, please?* · **to put (something) up** To erect: *Let's put up the tent.* · **to put up with (somebody or something)** To accept or to tolerate: *I'm afraid I can't put up with your friends any longer. They're awful!* ■ Be careful with the spelling of this form: "putting".

puzzle[1] /ˈpʌzl/ [countable noun] **1** A game that makes you think in order to get the solution: *I got a book of puzzles for my birthday.* **2** Something difficult to understand: *Why Jane likes Mick so much is a puzzle to me.*

puzzle[2] /ˈpʌzl/ [verb] To think hard about something trying to get the solution or to understand something: *The mathematical problem was so difficult that we all puzzled over it for hours.*

pyjamas /pɪˈdʒɑː.məz/ [countable noun] See **pajamas.** ■ This is a British English spelling.

pyramid[1] /ˈpɪr.ə.mɪd/ [countable noun] A shape or an object with a square base and four triangular sides which meet in a point at the top: *The ancient Egyptian pharaohs ordered the construction of pyramids to commemorate their lives and to protect their remains.*

pyramid[2] [adjective] Showing the shape of a pyramid: *They were trained for pyramid selling.*

pyrites /paɪˈraɪ.tiːz/ [uncountable noun] A yellowish mineral that contains iron: *In the Victorian era, jewelry made with pyrites was very popular.*

Q

q

q /kjuː/ The seventeenth letter of the alphabet: *The word "Queen" begins with a "Q".*

quack /kwæk/ [verb] To make a noise like a duck: *The ducks ran across the farmyard quacking.* 👁 See picture at **animal**.

quack doctor [countable noun] Person who pretends that they have medical skills or knowledge they don't have: *Quack doctors in the 19th century sold magical medicines that were supposed to cure all illnesses.*

quadrant US: /ˈkwɑː.drənt/ UK: /ˈkwɒd.rənt/ [countable noun] **1** One quarter of a circle or an area: *You must use only one quadrant of the page to do the drawing.* **2** In the past, a device used in ship navigation: *The quadrant measured the height of the stars in the sky.*

quadriceps [uncountable noun] The large, four-part muscle at the front of the thigh: *The quadriceps is essential in walking, running and jumping.* 👁 **See page 423.**

quake /kweɪk/ [verb] To tremble: *In the story, Jack started to quake with fear when he saw the giant coming.* ■ We usually say "shake" or "tremble".

⁺**qualification** /ˌkwal·ə·fɪˈkeɪ·ʃən/ [uncountable noun] Practice, training, knowledge, tests and so on that you need to do a special job: *My sister has got a teaching qualification.*

⁺**qualified** /ˈkwal·əˌfaɪd/ [adjective] Having the right qualifications to do something: *My brother couldn't apply for the job as a nursery school teacher because he wasn't properly qualified.* ■ Be careful with the pronunciation of the ending of this word.

⁺**qualify** /ˈkwal·əˌfaɪ/ [verb] To get the practice, training, knowledge, tests and so on that you need to do a special job: *My mother qualified as a doctor in 1976.* ■ Be careful with the spelling of these forms: "qualifies", "qualified".

⁺**quality** US: /ˈkwɑː.lə.t̬i/ UK: /ˈkwɒl.ɪ.ti/ [uncountable noun] **1** How good something is: *This store only sells the best quality meat.* **2** A characteristic: *Sheila has some very good qualities: patience, intelligence and kindness.* ■ The plural is "qualities".

⁺**quantity** US: /ˈkwɑːn.t̬ə.t̬i/ UK: /ˈkwɒn.tɪ.ti/ [uncountable noun] The amount or number of something: *What quantity of sugar do I need to put in this mixture?* ■ The plural is "quantities".

quarrel[1] /ˈkwar·əl/, /ˈkwɔr-/ [countable noun] An argument, often one that continues in time: *Annie and Alan had a quarrel that lasted more than six months, but it appears to be over now.*

quarrel[2] /ˈkwar·əl/, /ˈkwɔr-/ [verb] To argue: *Will you two stop quarrelling, please?*

quarry /ˈkwɒri/ [countable noun] **1** An animal chased or hunted: *The tiger ran after its quarry but the rabbit* *escaped down a hole.* **2** A place where stone is dug from the earth: *My uncle worked at a quarry once and he says that it's very hard work.* ■ The plural is "quarries".

quarter US: /ˈkwɑː.t̬ɚ/ UK: /ˈkwɔː.təʳ/ [countable noun] **1** One of four equal parts: *Cut the pizza into quarters and we'll have one each.* **2** An area of a town: *The Italian quarter in Manhattan is called "Little Italy".* ■ We usually say "area". **3 quarter past** Fifteen minutes after the hour: *"Shall we meet at quarter past eight outside the library?".* **4 quarter to** 15 minutes before the hour: *The bus goes at quarter to six.*

quarter-final /ˌkwɔːtəˈfaɪnəl/ [countable noun] One of the four games that are played to choose who will play in the semi-final: *Our school tennis team is playing in the quarter-finals which will take place on Saturday.*

quarterly US: /ˈkwɑː.t̬ɚ.li/ UK: /ˈkwɔː.tᵊl.i/ [adverb] Every three months: *My parents pay most of their bills quarterly.*

quartz /ˈkwɔːts/ [uncountable noun] A hard mineral that is usually colorless or white: *Quartz is used to make clocks and watches.*

quaver /ˈkweɪ·vər/ [countable noun] A musical note which has the time value of half a crotchet: *The quaver has a filled-in oval head and a stem with a tail.* **See page 460.**

quay /kiː/ [countable noun] A place in a harbor loaded and unloaded from boats: *Have you seen that yacht at the quay? It belongs to my cousin.* ■ Be careful with the pronunciation of this word.

queen /kwiːn/ [countable noun] **1** A woman from a royal family who is ruler of a country: *Queen Elizabeth the Second is the head of state of Canada.* ■ A male ruler is a "king". **2** A piece in chess: *Thomas made a good move and I lost my queen.* See picture at **chess.**

question[1] /ˈkwestʃən/ [countable noun] **1** Something that you ask: *Do you have any questions?* ■ Be careful. We say: "ask a question". (We don't say: "do/make a question"). **2** A problem that needs to be discussed: *They're going to discuss the question of the new gym at the parents' meeting tonight.* **3 out of the question** Impossible: *A vacation in the Bahamas is out of the question, we don't have the money.* **4 question mark** A mark that you put at the end of a question [?]: *Don't forget to put a question mark at the end of each question.*

question[2] /ˈkwestʃən/ [verb] **1** To ask about something: *The police are questioning the suspects in connection with the bank robbery last week.* **2** To express a doubt about something: *Sean always questions everything our History teacher says.*

questionnaire /ˌkwes·tʃəˈneər/ [countable noun] A number of questions for people to answer: *We made a questionnaire in class today to find out which are the most popular sports in our school.*

queue[1] UK: /kjuː/ [countable noun] See **line**[1]. ■ This word is British English.

queue[2] UK: /kjuː/ [verb] See **line**[2]. ■ This word is British English. ■ We also say "queue up".

quick /kwɪk/ [adjective and adverb] Fast, in a short time: *The train is a quick form of travel.* ■ Compare with "fast[1]" ("Quick" is usually used when we refer to length of time, while "fast" refers to speed. We say "a quick visit" not "a fast visit", and "a quick decision" not "a fast decision").

quid /kwɪd/ [countable noun] When talking about money, a pound: *The CD cost eight quid.* ■ This word is informal. The plural is also "quid".

quiet[1] /kwaɪət/ [adjective] **1** Without making much noise: *Be quiet! I'm trying to listen to this music.* **2** Without a lot of activity: *I was born in a very quiet town just outside St Paul.*

quiet[2] /kwaɪət/ [uncountable noun] Being quiet: *Can I have a bit of peace and quiet while I read my letter, please?*

quit, quit, quit /kwɪt/ [verb] **1** To stop doing something: *My dad has quit smoking.* **2** To leave a job or a place: *She quit her job because she was offered something better.* ■ "Quit" also has regular past and past participle forms: "quitted".

quite /kwaɪt/ [adverb] **1** To some extent but not very: *I think I know this vocabulary quite well but I'm going to study it a little more.* **2** Completely: *Are you quite sure that you want to go to the party?* **3 quite a few** A lot in number: *There are quite a few girls in our soccer team.* **4 quite a lot** A large amount: *I ate quite a lot at lunch time and now I don't feel very well.* ■ See box at **fairly**.

quiz /kwɪz/ [countable noun] **1** A short written or oral test: *We had a quiz in math this morning and I knew all the right answers control.* **2** A game where people try to answer questions: *Did you see the sports quiz on television last night?* ■ The plural is "quizzes".

quotation /kwoʊˈteɪ·ʃən/ [countable noun] Words from a book, play, speech and so on that you repeat: *"To be or not to be: that is the question" is the most famous quotation in the English language.*

quotation marks [noun] The mark used to indicate the beginning and end of words that were spoken [" "]: *He said, "Don't go!".*

r US: /ɑːr/ UK: /ɑːʳ/ The eighteenth letter of the alphabet: *The name "Rachel" begins with an "R".*

rabbit /'ræb.ɪt/ [countable noun] A small animal with long ears and a short tail: *Rabbits love eating carrots.* **See page 428.**

†**race**[1] /reɪs/ [noun] **1** A competition to see who can do things fastest: *No one can say who's going to win this race.* **2** Category to which a group of living things belong that have a series of characteristics in common: *People shouldn't be discriminated against because of their race.* **3** A species of plant or animal: *Many of the most fashionable dogs are the result of a mix of races.*

race[2] /reɪs/ [verb] To take part in a race: *Philip couldn't race last week because of a broken ankle.*

racecourse /'reɪs.kɔːs/ US: /-kɔːrs/ [countable noun] The place where people see horses run: *Would you like to go to the racecourse this Saturday?*

racial /'reɪ.ʃəl/ [adjective] Of race or according to race: *Racial discrimination is against the law in the United States.*

racism /'reɪ.sɪ.zəm/ [uncountable noun] The prejudice that some people are inferior to others because they are of a different race or culture: *We must all fight against racism in our school.*

racist /'reɪ.sɪst/ [countable noun] A person who has the prejudice that some people are inferior to others because they are of a different race or culture: *You mustn't be a racist and speak badly of people who are different from you.*

rack /ræk/ [countable noun] A type of shelf where you can keep things: *Can you put my bag up on the rack before the train leaves?*

racket /'rækɪt/ [countable noun] A bat that is used to hit the ball in tennis, squash or badminton: *I think this tennis racket is too heavy for Helen.* ■ This word is also written "racquet".

racquet /'ræk.ɪt/ [countable noun] See **racket.**

radar /'reɪ·dɑr/ [uncountable noun] A system of discovering the position of ships and planes: *It's difficult to see a plane on a radar screen if it flies too low.*

radiation /ˌreɪdi'eɪʃən/ [uncountable noun] The emission of radiant energy, or the particles emitted: *Radiation can be used to extend the shelf-life of fresh produce.*

radiator /'reɪ·diˌeɪ·t̬ər/ [countable noun] Apparatus containing a hot liquid, that makes rooms hot: *This radiator isn't big enough to heat the living room.*

†**radio** /'reɪ·diˌoʊ/ [countable noun] **1** A machine that receives sound waves and reproduces sounds: *Michelle listens to the sports news on the radio every evening.* **See page 443.** **2** A way of sending out or receiving sounds without connecting wires: *Now the pilot's talking to the control tower by radio.* ■ Be careful with the pronunciation of this word! "ra" rhymes with "day".

radioactive /ˌreɪ·di·oʊ'æk·tɪv/ [adjective] Giving out energy that can be harmful to living things: *Governments have a lot of problems with nuclear radioactive waste.* ■ Be careful with the pronunciation of this word! "ra" rhymes with "day".

radish /'ræd.ɪʃ/ [countable noun] Small red and white root vegetable that is eaten raw: *Let's put some radishes in the salad.* **See page 437.**

radius /'reɪ.di.əs/ [countable noun] The length from the center of a circle to the end: *The radius of a circle is half its diameter.* **See page 422.**

raft US: /ræft/ UK: /rɑːft/ [countable noun] A flat boat made of wood: *The people of the South Pacific traveled long distances on rafts in the past.*

rag /ræg/ [countable noun] A piece of old cloth: *Can you give me a rag to clean the windows with, please?*

rage /reɪdʒ/ [uncountable noun] Great anger: *My sister was in a rage when she saw that somebody had opened her letter.* ■ Be careful. We always say: "to be **in a** rage".

raid[1] /reɪd/ [countable noun] A quick attack into somebody's territory: *The police made a raid on the drug dealers last night.* ■ Be careful. We say: "a raid **on** (somebody or something)".

raid[2] /reɪd/ [verb] To attack a place: *Some robbers raided a bank in Detroit this morning.*

*****rail** /reɪl/ [countable noun] **1** A long piece of wood or metal: *They held onto the rail as they watched the procession from the balcony.* **2 by rail** By train: *I like traveling by rail.*

railings [plural noun] A fence made from metal bars: *They've put new railings up outside the monkeys' cage.*

railroad station [countable noun] A place where trains stop: *Where is the railroad station, please?* ■ The same meaning: "railway station".

railway[1] /'reɪlweɪ/ [countable noun] See **railway line.** ■ Be careful with the pronunciation of this word! "way" rhymes with "day".

railway[2] [adjective] Referring to a train service: *The railway system in Britain is very extensive.*

railway line [countable noun] The line of metal bars on which trains run: *They've built a new railway line that goes through a mountain.* ■ We also say "railway".

railway station [countable noun] A place where trains stop: *The town has a railway station from which trains go to Chicago.* ■ The same meaning: "railroad station".

*****rain[1]** /reɪn/ [uncountable noun] **1** The water falling from the clouds: *I love walking in the rain.* **2 acid rain** See "acid rain" in the word **acid. See page 438.**

rain[2] /reɪn/ [verb] When talking of drops of water, to fall from the sky: *We won't go camping this weekend if it's raining.*

rainbow /'reɪnˌboʊ/ [countable noun] An arch of different colors in the sky: *We might see a rainbow if the sun comes out when the rain stops.*

raincoat /'reɪnˌkoʊt/ [countable noun] A coat that you wear when it rains: *The rain will soak you if you go out without a raincoat.* ■ In British English they say "mac, mackintosh". See picture at **clothes.**

raindrop /'reɪndrɒp/ [countable noun] A single drop of rain: *This photography book contains an image of a raindrop falling.*

rainfall /'reɪnˌfɔl/ [uncountable noun] The amount of rain that falls in a particular place: *The average annual rainfall in Michigan is 32.25 inches.*

rain forest /'reɪn ˌfɔr·əst/, /-ˌfɑr·əst/ [noun] A forest in the tropics that has heavy rain: *We must stop the destruction of the rain forests.*

rainforest /'reɪnˌfɔr·əst/, /-ˌfɑr·əst/ [countable noun] A forest found in tropical zones with heavy rainfall: *The destruction of the rainforest is a threat to the survival of the planet.*

rainy /'reɪ.ni/ [adjective] With a lot of rain: *The climate is rainy in Seattle.*

*****raise** /reɪz/ [verb] **1** To lift somebody or something up: *Please raise your hand if you want to speak in class.* **2** To increase something: *They've raised the price of coffee twice this year.* **3** To get money for a purpose: *We've raised five hundred dollars for our school charity.* **4** To look after a child until it is an adult: *They got married and raised three children.*

raisin /'reɪ.zᵊn/ [countable noun] A dried grape: *Mom's baking a cake with raisins and orange slices.*

rake[1] /reɪk/ [countable noun] A garden tool with a long handle: *Take the rake and clear the leaves from the garden path.*

rake[2] /reɪk/ [verb] To make the ground smooth and free from stones or leaves: *You must rake the soil before planting the seeds.*

ramp /ræmp/ [countable noun] An inclined surface: *The ramp allows wheeled vehicles to enter and leave the building.*

ran /ræn/ Past tense of **run[2].**

ranch US: /ræntʃ/ UK: /rɑːntʃ/ [countable noun] A very large cattle farm in the United States: *Peter's uncle keeps a lot of horses on his ranch in Arizona.*

a b c d e f g h i j k l m n o p q r s t u v w x y z

random /ˈræn.dəm/ [adjective] By chance: *They interviewed a random selection of people for their opinion on the new law.*

rang /ræŋ/ Past tense of **ring**.

*range[1] /reɪndʒ/ [noun] **1** A variety of things of the same kind: *There's a wide range of prices in the new boutique.* **2** The distance somebody or something can see, hear, travel and so on: *This gun has a range of six hundred feet.* **3** A line of hills or mountains: *The Himalayas are the highest mountain range in the world.*

range[2] /reɪndʒ/ [verb] To be between certain limits: *Here the temperature ranges between 5º and 12º centigrade in winter.*

ranger /ˈreɪn·dʒər/ [countable noun] A forest guard: *Rangers are a kind of mounted policeman in country areas.*

*rank /ræŋk/ [noun] Somebody's position in a group of people: *My great-grandfather reached the rank of captain during the war.*

ransom /ˈrænt.səm/ [uncountable noun] The money that you must pay so that a hostage is set free: *The terrorists demanded a ransom of two million dollars for the banker.*

rap /ræp/ [countable noun] **1** A light knock: *She heard a rap at the window and saw that it was her friend.* **2** A kind of music in which singers speak very fast: *This song's fun to sing because it's a rap.*

*rapid /ˈræp.ɪd/ [adjective] Fast; quick: *She made rapid progress, and was soon one of the best swimmers in the school.* ■ We usually say "fast" or "quick".

*rare US: /rer/ UK: /reəʳ/ [adjective] **1** Unusual and often valuable: *These low temperatures are very rare in Montana in the fall.* ■ Compare with "habitual" (usual or repeated). **2** When talking about meat, cooked so that the inside is a little pink: *How do you like your steak: rare, medium or well-done?*

rarely /ˈreər·li/ [adverb] Not often, not frequent: *Gillian and Jane rarely talk to each other.* ■ Be careful. "Rarely" goes before ordinary verbs and after auxiliary verbs: "He rarely comes home before 8 o'clock". "The Queen is rarely seen at soccer games". ■ The same meaning: "seldom". ■ See box at **frequency**.

rash /ræʃ/ [countable noun] An area of the skin with lots of small red pimples, usually caused by an illness or allergy: *He has a rash because he drank milk and he is allergic to dairy products.*

raspberry /ˈræzˌber·i/, /-bə·ri/ [countable noun] A small, very soft red fruit: *If you're hungry have some bread and raspberry jam.* See page 436.

rat /ræt/ [countable noun] An animal like a big mouse: *I've just seen two enormous rats in the subway station.*

*rate /reɪt/ [countable noun] **1** The speed of something or at which something is done: *If we work at a fast rate we'll finish the project by Friday.* **2** The amount of money that you pay or you get for something: *You pay the cheap rate if you phone after six o'clock.* **3** at any rate In any case: *I don't know exactly what the kids said but at any rate, it's not the point.* **4** rate of exchange The relation between the money of two countries: *The rate of exchange today is nearly one and a half euros to the dollar.*

*rather US: /ˈræð.ɚ/ UK: /ˈrɑː.ðəʳ/ [adverb] **1** To some extent: *The video we saw last night was rather boring.* ■ When "rather" is used with a positive word it implies surprise or pleasure on the part of the speaker: "It was rather a nice jacket that they gave me". ■ See box at **fairly**. **2** Used with "would", indicates preference: *I would rather stay at home.* ■ In this use, "rather" is followed by the infinitive without "to": "I would rather do the shopping tomorrow". Compare with "prefer" (followed by the infinitive with "to").

ration /ˈræʃ.ən/ [countable noun] A fixed amount of something that is given out: *The cat's hungry because he hasn't had his rations yet.*

rattle[1] /ˈrætl/ [countable noun] A toy that babies shake: *The baby's playing with the rattle in his crib.*

rattle[2] /ˈrætl/ [verb] To make repeated, banging sounds by shaking something: *The kids are rattling their tins because they want us to put some money in.*

rattlesnake /ˈræt̬·ə·lˌsneɪk/ [countable noun] A poisonous snake: *Rattlesnakes make noises by moving the rings at the end of their tails.*

ravine /rəˈviːn/ [countable noun] A deep, narrow canyon: *Let's go to the ravine.*

*raw US: /rɑː/ UK: /rɔː/ [adjective] **1** Not cooked: *Some people like eating raw fish.* ■ The same meaning: "uncooked". **2** In a natural state: *Factories take raw materials and make them into finished products.*

raw material US: /ˈrɔ məˈtɪər·i·əl/ [uncountable noun] The initial substance which is used to manufacture something: *Companies buy raw materials like coffee and sugar and process them.*

ray /reɪ/ [countable noun] A line of light: *The sun's rays came into the room through an opening in the drapes.*

razor /ˈreɪ·zər/ [countable noun] An instrument for removing hair from your face or body: *My father shaves with an electric razor.*

RAZOR

a b c d e f g h i j k l m n o p q r s t u v w x y z

Rd A written abbreviation for **road.** ■ Be careful. "Rd" has a capital "R". ■ See box at **abbreviations**.

're US: /ɚ/ UK: /ᵊr/ The contraction of "are".

re- /riː-/ [prefix] An addition to the beginning of a word that usually means "again": *"Rewrite" means to write again.*

+**reach** /riːtʃ/ [verb] **1** To arrive at a place: *When we reach New York it'll be dark.* **2** To stretch out your hand to get something: *I can't reach the top shelf.* **3** To extend: *The yard of our house reaches the edge of the road.* **4 out of reach** Too far away to touch: *The medicines are in a closet out of the reach of children.*

+**react** /ri'ækt/ [verb] To act in a particular way when something happens: *How did Jonathan react when he saw you with Louise?*

+**reaction** /ri'æk.ʃᵊn/ [countable noun] The way you act after something has happened: *When Pamela lost the bag her immediate reaction was to call the police.*

+**read, read, read** /riːd, red, red/ [verb] To look at words and understand them: *She read the children the story called "The lion, the witch and the wardrobe".*

▸ **PHRASAL VERBS** · **to read out** To read aloud: *Sam, read out the first paragraph.* ■ Be careful with the pronunciation of the past tense and past participle forms. They are pronunced like the color "red".

+**reader** /'ri·dər/ [countable noun] **1** A person who reads: *My sister's a keen reader of science fiction stories.* **2** A book for reading in class: *We're using two new readers in English.*

readily /'red.ɪ.li/ [adverb] Easily: *This Spanish novel is readily available in Philadelphia.*

reading /'riː.dɪŋ/ [countable noun] **1** The activity or ability to obtain meaning from written texts: *Her reading is improving.* **2** A part of a text that is read out loud: *A reading from the New Testament is part of every church service.* **3** Event where people read poems, a play or book extracts in public: *We attended a poetry reading.* **4** Interpretation: *What is your reading of the situation?*

+**ready** /'red.i/ [adjective] **1** Prepared: *The vegetable soup will be ready in ten minutes.* **2** Happy to do something, willing: *She isn't ready to forgive me yet.* **3 to get ready to (do something)** To become prepared to do something: *Mom's getting ready to take us to the zoo.*

+**real** US: /riː.əl/ UK: /rɪəl/ [adjective] **1** True, actual: *What is that actor's real name?* **2** Genuine, not imitation: *This bracelet is real gold.* **3** Not imaginary: *The story was taken from real life.*

real estate [uncountable noun] Property in the form of land and buildings: *Emily works as a real estate agent.*

realistic /ˌrɪə'lɪstɪk/ [adjective] **1** Seeing and accepting things as they really are, or dealing with them in a practical way: *Let's be realistic about our possibilities of winning.* **2** Appearing to be real, or showing things as they really are or were: *The film gives a realistic picture of the life of a cowboy.*

realize or **realise** /'rɪəlaɪz/ [verb] To come to know or to understand something: *When she arrived at the theater she realized that she had left the tickets at home.*

+**really** /'ri·ə·li/, /'ri·li/ [adverb] **1** Truly, actually: *Do you really need the motorcycle this evening?* ■ In this use "really" goes before a verb. **2** Very: *It's really boring to hear her talking about television programs all the time.* ■ In this use "really" goes before an adjective. **3** A word showing interest, surprise or anger: *"I went to Disneyland when I was in Florida". "Really?".*

realtor US: /'riː.əl.tɔːr/ UK: /'rɪəl.təʳ/ [countable noun] A person who deals with the buying and selling of houses: *My parents have been to see a realtor about selling my grandmother's house.* ■ In British English they say "estate agent".

rear¹ /rɪər/ [countable noun] The back part: *John sits in the rear of the bus each morning.*

rear² /rɪər/ [adjective] Back: *The rear seat of our car only holds two people.* ■ Compare with "frontal" (being at the front).

rear³ /rɪər/ [verb] To bring up animals or children: *Pamela's parents died when she was very small and she was reared by her grandmother.*

rearrange /ˌriː.ə'reɪndʒ/ [verb] To organize things in a new way: *Can you help me to rearrange my bedroom?*

reason /'riː.zᵊn/ [countable noun] **1** A cause that explains something: *The reason I'm calling you is because I want to ask you a favor.* **2** The power to think: *Reason makes people different from animals.*

+**reasonable** /'riː.zᵊn.ə.bl̩/ [adjective] **1** Fair, moderate: *If he's reasonable he'll understand that you can't miss the lessons tomorrow.* **2** Right, sensible: *Peter gave me a reasonable excuse for not coming to my party.*

reasonably /'riː.zᵊn.ə.bli/ [adverb] **1** Quite: *These pants were reasonably cheap.* **2** In a correct way: *I think the referee was acting reasonably when he sent the player off.*

reassurance /ˌri·ə'ʃʊr·əns/ [uncountable noun] Comfort: *Laura found reassurance in her mother's words.*

reassure /ˌri·ə'ʃʊr/ [verb] To stop somebody feeling worried: *My teacher reassured me that the test would not be too difficult.*

rebel[1] /'rebəl/ [countable noun] A person who fights against somebody in authority: *My grandfather says that I'm a rebel because I never do what I'm told.*

rebel[2] /rɪ'bel/ [verb] To fight against somebody in authority: *Kevin always rebels when he thinks something is wrong.*

rebellion /rɪ'bel.i.ən/ [uncountable noun] The disobedience to somebody in authority: *The rebellion failed because of lack of popular support.*

rebuild, rebuilt, rebuilt /ˌriː'bɪld/ [verb] To build something again: *Three months after the earthquake the government began to rebuild the buildings.*

†**receipt** /rɪ'siːt/ [countable noun] A piece of paper showing that you have paid for something: *You'll need the receipt if you want your money back.* ■ Be careful with the pronunciation of this word! The first "e" is pronounced like the "i" in "did".

†**receive** /rɪ'siːv/ [verb] To get something that is sent or given to you: *My father received a fax from the United States yesterday.*

receiver /rɪ'si·vər/ [countable noun] The part of the telephone through which you speak and listen: *Kate put the receiver down when she heard somebody knocking at the door.*

†**recent** /'riː.sənt/ [adjective] That happened not long ago: *There have been a lot of changes in this town in recent years.*

receptacle /rɪ'sep.tə.kl/ [countable noun] A container: *The raindrops fall into the receptacle.*

†**reception** /rɪ'sep.ʃən/ [countable noun] **1** The place where you get information in a hotel or office: *Let's ask at reception if the museum opens on Monday.* **2** A large party: *The wedding reception will take place on Saturday evening.*

receptionist /rɪ'sep.ʃən.ɪst/ [countable noun] The person who receives people at a hotel or office: *The hotel receptionist told us that the airport was closed because of the fog.*

receptor /rɪ'sep·tər/ [countable noun] The end part of a sensory nerve, which responds to a stimulus: *The receptor responds to light and passes a signal along the sensory nerve.*

recess /rɪ'ses/ [countable noun] A short rest during school time: *In school we always have a snack during the morning recess.* ■ In British English they say "break".

recipe /'res.ɪ.pi/ [countable noun] Instructions on how to cook something: *We'll ask Margaret's mother to give us her recipe for apple pie.*

reciprocal /rɪ'sɪprəkəl/ [adjective] Referring to a feeling, attitude or action, that is the same for both of the parties involved: *The feelings of affection between the students and their teacher were reciprocal.*

reckless /'rek.ləs/ [adjective] Dangerous, without care: *I don't like going by car with Jim because he's such a reckless driver.*

†**reckon** /'rek.ən/ [verb] To calculate approximately or to guess: *I reckon we'll be there in half an hour.*

†**recognition** /ˌrekəg'nɪʃən/ [uncountable noun] The act of being identified by somebody when they see you: *I saw her in the street but she didn't show any sign of recognition.*

recognize or **recognise** /'rekəgnaɪz/ [verb] **1** To know somebody or something when you see them again: *Geraldine recognized the singer as soon as she saw him in the supermarket.* **2** To admit that something is true: *Although you may not like it you have to recognize that she is the fastest runner in the school.*

†**recommend** /ˌrek.ə'mend/ [verb] **1** To tell somebody that a person or thing is suitable for something: *I've been recommended a new store to buy cheap jeans. Do you know it?* **2** To suggest or to advise somebody to do something: *The teacher recommended Nicola to see an optician as soon as possible.*

recommendation /ˌrek.ə.men'deɪ.ʃən/ [uncountable noun] Saying that something is good for a particular purpose: *On your recommendation we visited Millennium Park when we went to Chicago.*

record[1] /'rekɔːd/ [countable noun] **1** A round piece of plastic, usually black, that stores music: *I haven't heard Sting's new record yet.* ■ We often say "record" when we mean "C.D.". **2** Written information about something: *She's made a record of everything we saw at the exhibition.* **3** The best result that has been achieved, especially in a sport: *Jeanette broke our school record for the long jump on Saturday.*

record[2] /rɪ'kɔːd/ [verb] **1** To write about things so that you can remember them later: *The students recorded what the writer said in his speech.* **2** To copy sounds or images into a tape: *I'm going to record Mariah Carey's concert tonight.*

record-breaking /'rek·ərdˌbreɪ·kɪŋ/ [adjective] Better than anything done before: *With the rains there'll be a record-breaking potato crop this year.*

recorder /rɪ'kɔr·dər/ [countable noun] **1** A wooden musical instrument with holes: *Lisa played the recorder at the party yesterday.* **2** Instrument that records: *My recorder is broken so I can't record the tape for you.*

†**recording** /rɪ'kɔr·dɪŋ/ [uncountable noun] Sounds or images copied on a tape or on a film: *The CNBC made a recording of Whitney Houston's performance at the Radio City Music Hall last night.*

record-player [countable noun] A machine that plays records: *I've changed my record-player for a new CD player.*

↑**recover** /rɪˈkʌv·ər/ [verb] **1** To get well after an illness: *Margaret has recovered from her ankle operation very quickly.* **2** To get back what you have lost: *My father recovered his wallet at the Lost and Found Office.*

recovery /rɪˈkʌv·ə·ri/ [uncountable noun] **1** The act of becoming well again after an illness: *Adam's made a quick recovery from the flu.* **2** The getting back of what you have lost: *My father was surprised by the quick recovery of his wallet.*

recreation /ˌrek.riˈeɪ.ʃᵊn/ [uncountable noun] A rest from work: *My dad's only recreation is watching football.*

recruit[1] /rɪˈkruːt/ [countable noun] A new member of an organization: *It takes some time for a recruit to get used to army life.*

recruit[2] /rɪˈkruːt/ [verb] To get a new member an organization: *The Navy's trying to recruit young doctors these days.*

recruitment /rɪˈkruːt.mənt/ [uncountable noun] The act of getting new members for an organization: *The recruitment of volunteers for the procession will take some time.*

rectangle /ˈrek.tæŋ.gl̩/ [countable noun] A shape with four straight sides that is longer than it is wide: *A soccer field is a big rectangle of short grass.* 👁 **See page 457.**

rectangular /rekˈtæŋ·gjə·lər/ [adjective] Having a shape like a rectangle: *The pages of this dictionary are rectangular.*

recycle /ˌriːˈsaɪ.kl̩/ [verb] To recover waste material so that it can be used again: *Don't throw all those magazines away. They can be recycled.*

↑**red** /red/ [noun and adjective] **1** The color of blood: *The teacher corrected our tests with a red pen.* **2** **to go red** To become red in the face, to blush: *Lucy went red when Nick told her she looked pretty in her new dress.*

red blood cell [countable noun] Any of the red cells that carry oxygen from the lungs to the rest of the body: *In our blood there are red blood cells and white blood cells, but the red cells are far more common.*

reddish Referring to a color, that is approximately red, or that has a red element to it: *On Saturday I bought a lovely reddish brown sweater.*

redhead /ˈred.hed/ [countable noun] A person who has red hair: *Our English teacher is a redhead from Wisconsin.*

red herring [countable noun] An idea or event which distracts your attention from what is really important: *In this Agatha Christie story there are lots of red herrings.*

↑**reduce** /rɪˈdus/ [verb] To make something less or smaller: *I'll buy the television we saw in the window if they reduce its price.*

↑**reduction** /rɪˈdʌk.ʃᵊn/ [countable noun] The act of making something less or smaller: *The leather jacket she bought had a price reduction of 20%.*

reef /riːf/ [countable noun] A long line of rock in the sea: *Beyond the reef the sea was dark blue.*

reel /riːl/ [verb] To make something go around another thing: *Reel in the line, quick! You have a fish.*

refer /ˈriː.fər/ US: /-fɚ/ [verb] **1** To speak about somebody or something: *My sister wasn't referring to anybody in particular when she talked about the incident.* **2** To mean, to be used to describe: *In the newspaper article the word "butcher" refers to the person who committed all those murders.* **3** To go to something for information or help: *No one knew how to spell the word, so we referred to a dictionary.* ■ Be careful! We always say "to refer **to** (something)". Look at the spelling of these forms: "referred", "referring".

referee /ˌref.əˈriː/ [countable noun] A person who controls a sports game: *The referee blew the whistle and the game was over.* 👁 See picture at **soccer**.

↑**reference** /ˈref·ər·əns/, /ˈref·rəns/ [uncountable noun] **1** The act of looking at something for information: *She always keeps a cook book in the kitchen for reference.* **2** **reference book** A book where you get information about something: *An encyclopedia is a reference book.*

↑**reflect** /rɪˈflekt/ [verb] To send back an image, light, sound or heat: *The river reflected the lights of the city.*

reflection /rɪˈflek.ʃᵊn/ [noun] **1** The sending back an image, light, sound or heat: *Henry could see his reflection in the window.* **2** Thought: *After a little reflection, I decided to tell my friends the truth.*

reforestation /ˌriː.fɒr.ɪˈsteɪ.ʃən/ US: /-fɔːr.ɪ-/ [uncountable noun] The act of planting a forest again: *Reforestation is necessary after a big fire.*

↑**reform**[1] /rɪˈfɔːm/ [countable noun] An improvement: *The government wants to introduce reforms in the educational system.*

reform[2] /rɪˈfɔːm/ [verb] To make something better by changing it: *They say they're going to reform the law.*

reformation /ˌref·ərˈmeɪ·ʃən/ [uncountable noun] The act of reforming something: *The attempted reformation of the Catholic Church in the 16th century resulted in the creation of the Protestant Church.*

refract /rɪˈfrækt/ [verb] To make light or sound change direction or separate: *Light refracts when it moves from air to water.*

refraction /rɪˈfræk.ʃən/ [uncountable noun] The phenomenon that occurs when light or sound is refracted:

a b c d e f g h i j k l m n o p q r s t u v w x y z

Refraction of light takes place because its speed changes.

refresh /rɪ'freʃ/ [verb] To make somebody feel cooler when they are hot and tired: *A cold drink will refresh us after the game.*

refreshing /rɪ'freʃ.ɪŋ/ [adjective] Making you feel cooler when you are hot and tired: *A cold shower is refreshing when it's very hot.*

refreshments /rɪ'freʃ.mənt/ [plural noun] Food and drinks: *We'll make a stop to take some refreshments on our way to the beach.*

*refrigerator** /rɪ'frɪdʒ·ə,reɪ·ṭər/ [countable noun] A machine for keeping drinks and food cold: *Milk should be kept in the refrigerator.* ■ The same meaning: "fridge".

refuge /'ref.juːdʒ/ [countable noun] A place for protection: *If it rains we'll take refuge in the hotel by the lake.*

refugee /,ref.jʊ'dʒiː/ [countable noun] A person who has been forced to leave their country, and goes to another: *A lot of refugees came to America during the Second World War.*

refund /'riːfʌnd/ [uncountable noun] Money that is given back to you: *If you take that dress back to the store they'll give you a refund.*

*refusal** /rɪ'fjuːzəl/ [uncountable noun] The act of saying you will not do something or take part in something: *Charlotte got angry at my refusal to take her to the station.*

refuse /'ref.juːs/ [verb] To say you will not do something or take part in something: *Jonathan refuses to come to the beach with us tomorrow.*

regard[1] /rɪ'gɑrd/ [uncountable noun] **1** A good opinion: *My parents have a high regard for my music teacher.* **2** Consideration for somebody: *She rejected his invitation coldly, with no regard for his feelings.*

regard[2] /rɪ'gɑrd/, /rɪ'gɑːd/ [verb] To consider somebody or something in a specific way: *Matthew is regarded as the best chess player at school.*

*regarding** /rɪ'gɑr·dɪŋ/ [preposition] About, concerning: *Regarding the school trip, do you know how much it will cost?*

regardless /rɪ'gɑrd·ləs/ [adverb] Not caring about: *We're going to buy a new TV set regardless of the price.*

*regards** /rɪ'gɑrdz/ [plural noun] Best wishes: *Please give my regards to your parents.*

regenerate /rɪ'dʒenəreɪt/ [verb] **1** To improve something by making it more vigorous, more active or busier: *We need more tourism to help regenerate the economy of the country.* **2** Referring to a tissue, to grow again after being lost or damaged: *These exercises will help the muscle tissues to regenerate.*

reggae /'reg.eɪ/ [uncountable noun] A type of music originating in Jamaica: *Bob Marley made reggae popular throughout the world.*

regiment /'redʒ.ɪ.mənt/ [countable noun] A large group of soldiers: *The colonel ordered the regiment to attack the enemy forces.*

*region** /'riː.dʒən/ [countable noun] A big area of land: *The North Pole is the coldest region on earth.*

regional /'riː.dʒən.əl/ [adjective] Referring to a region: *The state government is responsible for regional development.*

register[1] /'redʒɪstər/ [countable noun] **1** A list: *Our teacher begins each lesson by calling the register.* **2** See **cash register**.

register[2] /'redʒɪstər/ [verb] **1** To enter a name on a list: *The actress registered at the hotel under a false name.* **2** To show something: *Yesterday morning the thermometer registered twenty five Fahrenheit degrees.*

registration /,redʒ.ɪ'streɪ.ʃən/ [noun] **1** The act of entering a name on a list: *Registration day for next year will be two weeks before the first day of school.* **2 registration number** The license number of a car: *After the crash the truck drove away quickly and nobody could see its registration number.*

regret[1] /rɪ'gret/ [verb] To be sorry about something you have done or haven't done: *I don't regret what I said.*

regret[2] /rɪ'gret/ [uncountable noun] Feeling sorry: *Do you have any regrets about leaving school at sixteen?*

*regular** /'reg·jə·lər/ [adjective] **1** Usual: *Friday is Stuart's regular visiting day.* **2** Always happening at the same time: *My father doesn't have regular working hours.* **3** That follows the usual grammar rules: *"Walk" is a regular verb.*

regularity /,reg·jə'lær·ɪ·ṭi/ [uncountable noun] A state in which things happen again and again: *Our old car breaks down with great regularity.*

regulate /'reg.jʊ.leɪt/ [verb] To control something by using rules and regulations: *Restrictions regulate the speed that vehicles can travel at on the highway.*

*regulation** /,reg.jʊ'leɪ.ʃən/ [noun] A rule: *Do you know all the regulations at school?*

rehearsal /rɪ'hɜr·səl/ [countable noun] The practicing of a play or a concert: *The actors had a lot of rehearsals before the show opened.*

rehearse /rɪ'hɜrs/ [verb] To practice a play or a concert: *Penny rehearsed the songs she had learned at school in front of her parents.*

reign[1] /reɪn/ [countable noun] The time when a king or a queen rules a country: *Independence war in United States was during the reign of George III.* ■ Be careful with the pronunciation of this word! The "g" is silent.

reign[2] /reɪn/ [verb] To rule as a king or a queen: *George III reigned over Great Britain from 1760 to*

a b c d e f g h i j k l m n o p q r s t u v w x y z

1820. ■ Be careful. We say: "reign **over** a country or a people". ■ Be careful with the pronunciation of this word! The "g" is silent.

rein /reɪn/ [countable noun] A length of leather used to control a horse: *The jockey pulled the reins in to stop the horse.* ■ This word is more common in the plural.

reindeer /'reɪn,dɪər/ [countable noun] A big animal of the deer family that lives in Northern Europe: *Santa Claus arrives on a sled pulled by reindeer every Christmas.* ■ The plural is also "reindeer". ◉ See picture at **sled**.

↑reject /rɪ'dʒekt/ [verb] Not to accept something or somebody: *Carol rejected my offer to help her with her homework.*

rejoice /rɪ'dʒɔɪs/ [verb] To feel very happy: *Everybody rejoiced when the peace agreement was announced.*

↑relate /rɪ'leɪt/ [verb] **1** To tell: *We related everything that had happened to the police.* **2** To connect: *Doctors relate heart disease to a poor diet and lack of exercise.* ■ We say "relate **to** (somebody or something)".

related /rɪ'leɪ·t̬ɪd/ [adjective] **1** Belonging to the same family: *Jim's father is related to the school football coach.* **2** Connected: *The detective thinks that the two crimes are related.* ■ Be careful. We say: "to be related **to** (somebody or something)". The verb after "to" is in the "-ing" form. ■ The last "e" is pronounced like the "i" in "did".

↑relation /rɪ'leɪ.ʃᵊn/ [noun] **1** A member of your family: *I only see most of my relations when I go to my grandparents' house at Christmas.* ■ The same meaning: "relative". **2** A connection: *There's a close relation between the Spanish and Italian languages.*

↑relationship /rɪ'leɪ.ʃᵊn.ʃɪp/ [countable noun] **1** Friendship between people or countries: *I have a good relationship with my parents.* **2** The way in which facts or ideas are connected: *The brain controls the relationship between thought and movement.*

↑relative /'rel·ə·t̬ɪv/ [countable noun] A member of your family: *Most of our relatives live in New York.* ■ The same meaning: "relation".

↑relax /rɪ'læks/ [verb] **1** To become less tense: *Don't worry about the test, just lie down a bit and relax.* **2** To have a rest: *When my mother comes home from work she likes to take a shower and relax with her feet up.*

relaxation /,riː.læk'seɪ.ʃᵊn/ [uncountable noun] Rest and recreation: *You study too much; you need some relaxation as well, you know!*

↑relaxed /rɪ'lækst/ [adjective] Calm and tension free: *I felt relaxed once I had finished my tests.* ■ Be careful with the pronunciation of this word. The last "e" is not pronounced. ◉ See picture at **emotions**.

↑relaxing /rɪ'læk.sɪŋ/ [adjective] Making you calm and free: *We had a relaxing swim in the lake after working on the farm all morning.*

relay /,riː'leɪ/ [verb] To receive and to pass on information, radio and television signals, and so on: *Please relay the news to your parents.*

release /rɪ'liːs/ [verb] To set somebody or something free: *If the two nations sign the treaty all the prisoners will be released.*

relevant /'reləvənt/ [adjective] Related to the question discussed, or useful: *That is not relevant to what we are talking about.*

↑reliable /rɪ'laɪə.bl̩/ [adjective] That you can depend on: *Don't ask David to get the movie tickets, because he isn't very reliable.*

↑relief /rɪ'liːf/ [noun] **1** A releasing of tension or pain, comfort: *The aspirin my mother took gave her relief from her backache.* **2** Help to people in need: *The government is sending relief to the people affected by the earthquake.* **3** The difference in height of the terrain in a particular area: *This region has a varied relief with mountains, plains and valleys.*

relieve /rɪ'liːv/ [verb] **1** To reduce pain or trouble: *A massage would relieve your back pain.* **2** To replace somebody on duty: *One of my dad's colleagues relieved him so that he could go to the doctor's.*

↑religion /rɪ'lɪdʒ.ᵊn/ [uncountable noun] A belief in a god or gods: *Sarah says that religion is what gives meaning to her life.*

↑religious /rɪ'lɪdʒ.əs/ [adjective] **1** Related to religion: *The Pope is the religious leader of all the Roman Catholics in the world.* **2** Keeping the rules of a religion, believing very strongly in a religion: *My aunt's a very religious woman.*

reluctant /rɪ'lʌk.tᵊnt/ [adjective] Not wanting to do something, unwilling: *My parents are reluctant to use the car downtown.*

↑rely /rɪ'laɪ/ [verb] To trust in somebody or something: *You can rely on Kate. She knows how to keep a secret.* ■ Be careful! We always say: "rely **on** (somebody or something)". ■ Note the spelling of these forms: "relies", "relied".

↑remain /rɪ'meɪn/ [verb] **1** To be left over: *Although we did a lot of work yesterday, there still remains a lot to be done.* **2** To stay: *My brother remained at home yesterday with a cold.*

remainder /rɪ'meɪn·dər/ [uncountable noun] The rest, the portion that is left of something: *We'll spend the remainder of our vacation at the beach, OK?*

↑remains /rɪ'meɪnz/ [plural noun] The pieces that are left of something: *We gave the remains of our picnic to the dog.*

remark[1] /rɪ'mɑːk/ [countable noun] A comment: *My sister didn't like your remark about her friend.*

remark² /rɪ'mɑːk/ [verb] To comment or to observe: *Sally remarked that she had seen Hugh the other day.*

†**remarkable** /rɪ'mɑr·kə·bəl/ [adjective] Extraordinary: *Paul always does his homework with remarkable speed.*

remedy /'rem.ə.di/ [countable noun] **1** A way of curing pain: *Grandma says that an aspirin and a glass of hot milk is the best remedy for colds.* **2** A solution: *We must find a remedy for this awful situation.* ■ The plural is "remedies".

†**remember** /rɪ'mem·bər/ [verb] To keep in or to bring to your memory people, events or data from the past: *I didn't phone Dick yesterday because I couldn't remember his number.* ■ Compare with "remind" (to say something to somebody to make them remember to do something). ■ Be careful! "Remember" has a different meaning depending on whether it is followed by an infinitive or an "-ing" form of the verb. When it is followed by an infinitive, "remember" refers to an action that has not yet been done: "Remember to turn off the lights when you go to bed". When it is followed by an "-ing" form of the verb, "remember" refers to an action that has already been done: "I remember putting my keys on the table when I came in from school". ■ See box below.

†**remind** /rɪ'maɪnd/ [verb] To say something to somebody to make them remember to do something: *Remind me to get mom a present for Mother's Day.* ■ Compare with "remember" (to keep in or to bring to your memory people, events or data from the past). ■ See box at **remember**.

reminder /rɪ'maɪn·dər/ [countable noun] **1** Something that makes you remember: *This knot in my handkerchief is a reminder that I must take my dictionary to school tomorrow.* **2** Something that makes you think of a particular time: *This Washington D.C. monument is a reminder of the Martin Luther King.*

remote /rɪ'moʊt/ [adjective] Far away: *I'd like to spend a long vacation with some friends on a remote island.*

remote control [countable noun] A device with buttons used to operate a TV, video, toy and so on from a distance: *It's easy to change the TV channels with a remote control even for grandma.*

†**remove** /rɪ'muːv/ [verb] To take away: *We removed the dead tree from the backyard.*

renew /rɪ'nu/ [verb] To make something new again: *We can't go fishing until we renew our fishing license.*

renewable /rɪ'njuːəbl/ [adjective] **1** Referring to anything that can be renewed: *Your library card must be renewed every year.* **2** Referring to a form of energy, that can be replaced or restored by nature: *Wind is a renewable energy source.* 👁 **See page 439.**

†**rent¹** /rent/ [uncountable noun] The money you pay to use something: *How much rent does your uncle pay for the apartment?*

rent² /rent/ [verb] To pay for the use of a house or an apartment, a machine, a vehicle and so on: *We rented a car when we went to Colombia last summer.*

rental [noun] The act of renting: *a car rental.*

repaid /rɪ'peɪd/ Past tense and past participle forms of **repay**.

†**repair¹** /rɪ'peər/ [uncountable noun] Something you do to make an object or a building good and ready for use again: *The museum is closed for repairs.*

repair² /rɪ'peər/ [verb] To put something in good condition again: *When are you going to take the video to be repaired, dad?*

repay, repaid, repaid /ˌriː'peɪ/ [verb] **1** To pay back: *Pat says she can't repay me the money I lent her for the CD until next week.* **2** To do something to thank somebody: *I don't know how to repay you for all you've done for us.* ■ In this use we say: "to repay (somebody) **for** (something)".

†**repeat** /rɪ'piːt/ [verb] To say or to do something again: *Would you mind repeating to me what Rebecca said this morning?*

repel /rɪ'pel/ [verb] **1** To force something to move away or to stop attacking: *The defending forces were able to repel the attack.* **2** To cause a feeling of disgust: *I was repelled by the smell.*

repellent /rɪ'pelənt/ [adjective] Very unpleasant: *The smell coming from the river is repellent.*

repetition /ˌrep.ə'tɪʃ.ən/ [countable noun] The saying or doing of something again: *Pamela learned the common irregular verbs through much repetition.*

remember* and *remind

- Use ***remind*** to indicate that someone has told someone else to do something. Use the phrasal verb *remind of* to indicate that someone or something else reminds you of someone or something else:
  - *Sally reminded me that I had a dentist's appointment.*
  - *You really remind me of someone famous but I can't think who.*

  Remind always takes an object.
- ***Remember*** is used when a person remembers to do something on his or her own. ***Remember*** is also used to express recollections of a past event:
  - *I remembered to buy him a present for his birthday.*
  - *He remembers going to California on vacation when he was very young.*

a b c d e f g h i j k l m n o p q r s t u v w x y z

a b c d e f g h i j k l m n o p q r s t u v w x y z

†**replace** /rɪˈpleɪs/ [verb] **1** To put something back in its proper place: *Please, replace this book where you found it.* **2** To take the place of somebody or something: *Tractors replaced horses on farms years ago.* **3** To put a new thing in the place of another: *If the cup is broken we'll have to replace it immediately.*

replacement /rɪˈpleɪs.mənt/ [countable noun] The act of changing something old or broken: *We're looking for a replacement for our old television.*

†**reply¹** /rɪˈplaɪ/ [countable noun] An answer: *What was her reply when you asked her about her boyfriend?* ■ The plural is "replies".

reply² /rɪˈplaɪ/ [verb] To answer: *You haven't replied to my question yet.* ■ Be careful with the spelling of these forms: "replies", "replied".

†**report¹** /rɪˈpɔːt/ [countable noun] A description prepared for others: *We listened to a brief report of the football results on the radio.*

report² /rɪˈpɔːt/ [verb] **1** To tell somebody about something: *I'll try to report the news as soon as possible.* **2** To complain about somebody or something to an organization of authority: *My uncle reported the theft of his car to the police.*

reporter /rɪˈpɔr·t̬ər/, /-ˈpour·t̬ər/ [countable noun] A person who reports the news in a newspaper, radio or television: *The President had a meeting with reporters after his speech in Congress.*

†**represent** /ˌrep.rɪˈzent/ [verb] **1** To do something on behalf of another person: *In United States, each Member of Senate represents a State.* **2** To be a sign or a symbol of: *On this map the blue lines represent the rivers.*

representation /ˌrep.rɪ.zenˈteɪ.ʃᵊn/ [uncountable noun] **1** The act of representing or being represented: *When the man was arrested, he asked for legal representation.* **2** The description of something in a particular way: *The representation of American society in this novel is very realistic.*

representational /ˌrep.rɪ.zenˈteɪ.ʃən.əl/ [adjective] Referring to representation: *The actor's agent has representational powers.*

†**representative** /ˌrep·rɪˈzen·tə·t̬ɪv/ [countable noun] A person who represents a business, a country and so on: *My uncle's a sales representative for an important car company.*

†**reproduce** /ˌri·prəˈdus/ [verb] **1** To copy something: *The photo of the murderer is going to be reproduced in every newspaper.* **2** To produce new members: *Rabbits reproduce very quickly.*

reproduction /ˌriː.prəˈdʌk.ʃᵊn/ [noun] **1** A copy: *We bought some reproductions of Picasso's most famous paintings when we visited the Museum of Modern Art (MoMA) in New York.* **2** Process by which humans, animals or plants produce new members: *In biology class we are studying animal reproduction.*

reproductive /ˌriːprəˈdʌktɪv/ [adjective] Referring to reproduction: *Pollen plays a vital role in the reproductive cycle of plants.*

reproductive system [countable noun] The set of organs that work together in reproduction: *The reproductive system consists of internal and external organs.* 👁 **See page 425.**

reptile /ˈrep.taɪl/ [countable noun] An animal that has cold blood and scales on its skin: *Snakes, lizards, crocodiles and turtles are all reptiles.* 👁 **See pages 426 and 430.**

republic /rɪˈpʌb.lɪk/ [countable noun] A country that is ruled by a president: *In a republic the government is elected by the people.*

†**reputation** /ˌrep.jʊˈteɪ.ʃᵊn/ [uncountable noun] The opinion that people have about a person: *Carol's mother has a very good reputation as an expert on computers.*

†**request¹** /rɪˈkwest/ [countable noun] Something that you ask for: *Mrs. Willis made a request for an extra two days vacation.*

request² /rɪˈkwest/ [verb] To ask for or demand something: *Our school has requested permission from the local government to open a riding school.*

†**require** /rɪˈkwaɪər/ [verb] To need something: *You will require a map to do this exercise.* ■ We usually say "need".

†**requirement** /rɪˈkwaɪəmənt/ [countable noun] Something that you need: *I think my sister meets all the requirements for taking part in the expedition to the Amazon.*

†**rescue** /ˈres.kjuː/ [verb] To save somebody: *The climbers were rescued from the mountains after the snowstorm with the help of helicopters.*

†**research** /ˈri·sɜrtʃ/, /rɪˈsɜrtʃ/ [uncountable noun] A study to find out new things: *Her latest book about UFO's is the result of many years of research.*

researcher /rɪˈsɜr·tʃər/, /ˈriˌsɜr-/ [countable noun] A person who studies to find out new things: *Researchers are trying hard to discover an effective cure for cancer.*

resemblance /rɪˈzem.blənts/ [uncountable noun] A similarity between people or things: *Do you think there's a family resemblance?*

resemble /rɪˈzem.bl̩/ [verb] To be or to look like somebody or something: *Jackie resembles her sister when she speaks.*

resent /rɪˈzent/ [verb] To be angry about what you consider is bad or unfair: *Laura resents being told what to wear every day.* ■ The verb after "resent" is in the "-ing" form.

resentment /rɪ'zent.mənt/ [uncountable noun] The feeling of being angry and bitter: *I don't feel any resentment about what happened.*

†**reservation** /ˌrez·ər'veɪ·ʃən/ [countable noun] **1** Something that is kept ready for use by a particular person or group: *It's getting a bit late to make the reservations for the train tickets.* **2** A place where a group of people live: *We visited an Indian reservation on our vacation in the United States.*

†**reserve**[1] /rɪ'zɜːv/ [countable noun] **1** An amount of something that is saved for later use: *The water reserves have increased a lot with the recent heavy rain.* **2** A place where wild animals are protected: *The Grand Canyon is a big natural reserve.* **3** Somebody who plays for another in a game: *Graham is first reserve in the school hockey team.* **4** **in reserve** Saved for later use: *We always keep a flashlight in reserve in case the lights go out.*

reserve[2] /rɪ'zɜːv/ [verb] To keep something for later use or to have something kept ready for your use: *We need to reserve the tickets for the concert before they are all sold.*

reservoir /'rez·ərˌvwɑr/, /-ˌvwɔr/ [countable noun] A lake where water is stored: *Reservoirs supply drinking water to cities.* **See page 445.**

residence /'rez.ɪ.dᵊnts/ [noun] **1** The place where somebody lives: *The President's residence in Washington is the White House.* ■ This use is formal. **2** The time during which people live in a place: *She began residence in Italy three years ago.*

†**resident** /'rez.ɪ.dᵊnt/ [countable noun] A person who lives in a place: *My uncle has been a resident of Bogota for many years.*

residual /rɪ'zɪdjuəl/ [adjective] Remaining after the greater part of something has been removed or has gone: *Although many years have passed, he still feels some residual anger.*

residue /'rezɪdjuː/ [countable noun] What remains after the greater part of something has been removed or has gone: *The residues must be eliminated at the end of the production process.*

resign /rɪ'zaɪn/ [verb] To give up a job: *Mr. Roberts, the chemistry teacher, has just resigned. He's going to work in industry.* ■ Be careful with the pronunciation of this word!

resignation /ˌrez.ɪg'neɪ.ʃᵊn/ [countable noun] The act of giving up your job: *His illness led to his resignation from the company.* ■ Be careful with the pronunciation of this word. You must pronounce the "g" in this word.

†**resist** /rɪ'zɪst/ [verb] **1** To oppose or fight against: *The town resisted the enemy attacks night and day.* **2** To keep from doing something: *Joanne couldn't resist the temptation and opened the box of chocolates.*

†**resistance** /rɪ'zɪs.tᵊnts/ [uncountable noun] The act of resisting: *The water resistance of this watch is guaranteed.*

resistant /rɪ'zɪstənt/ [adjective] Not damaged or affected in a negative way by something: *My new watch is water resistant.* ■ We say "(be) resistant **to** (something)".

resolution /ˌrez.ə'luː.ʃᵊn/ [countable noun] A decision: *My mom made a New Year's resolution to give up smoking.* ■ Be careful! We say: "make a resolution".

†**resolve** /rɪ'zɑlv/, /-'zɔlv/ [verb] **1** To solve a problem: *Grandma says that money would solve a lot of my parents' problems.* **2** To decide: *The teacher resolved to postpone the test until the following Monday.*

†**resort** /rɪ'zɔrt/ [countable noun] A place for vacations: *They plan to spend their summer vacation in a fashionable seaside resort.*

resource US: /'riː.sɔːrs/ UK: /rɪ'zɔːs/ [countable noun] The means which are available to achieve an end: *The most important natural resources of this country are coal and petroleum.*

resources US: /'riːsɔːrs/ UK: /rɪ'zɔːs/ [countable noun] The means, materials or skills that a person or a country can use: *Both Argentina and Chile have a lot of natural resources.* ■ It is usually used with a plural verb.

†**respect**[1] /rɪ'spekt/ [uncountable noun] The quality of being polite or having high regard or admiration for somebody: *I think adults talk a lot about respect but don't always show it.*

respect[2] /rɪ'spekt/ [verb] To admire somebody very much or to behave in a polite way towards them: *Nicholas respects his grandmother and always listens to her advice.*

respectable /rɪ'spek.tə.bl̩/ [adjective] Of good character and behavior: *Mrs. Whittington is a very respectable woman; I can't believe she is a drug dealer!*

respiration /ˌrespər'eɪʃən/ [uncountable noun] The act of breathing: *The respiration of clean air is a privilege denied to many.*

respiratory US: /'respərətɔːri/ UK: /rɪ'spɪrətəri/ [adjective] Referring to respiration or to the organs of respiration: *Smoking can cause respiratory illness.* **See page 425.**

respiratory system [countable noun] The set of organs, muscles and tubes which are involved in breathing: *The main function of the respiratory system is to supply the blood with oxygen.* **See page 425.**

†**respond** /rɪ'spɑnd/ [verb] **1** To react: *Jim responded very quickly to the doctor's treatment.* **2** To answer: *I sent Sarah a letter two weeks ago but she hasn't responded yet.* ■ This use is formal. We usually say "answer" or "reply".

a b c d e f g h i j k l m n o p q r s t u v w x y z

†response /rɪ'spɑns/ [countable noun] An answer: *They've had no response to the advertisement they published in the newspaper.*

†responsibility /rɪˌspɑn·sə'bɪl·ɪ·t̬i/ [noun] Something that it is your duty to do or to control: *Taking the dog out in the evening is your responsibility, not mine.* ■ The plural is "responsibilities".

†responsible /rɪ'spɑn·sə·bəl/ [adjective] **1** Reliable: *The company wants a responsible person for the post of night watchman.* **2** **to be responsible for (somebody or something)** **1** To be the cause of a situation: *The fire was responsible for damage to the value of millions of dollars.* **2** In charge of somebody or something: *On a plane the pilot is responsible for the passengers' safety.*

†rest[1] /rest/ [noun] **1** A period of not working and being quiet: *The doctor told my father to take a week's rest from work.* **2** What is left of something: *I took all the paper I needed and threw away the rest.* ■ In this use "rest" is an uncountable noun.

rest[2] /rest/ [verb] **1** To be free from duty, relax: *Let's rest for half an hour before we do our homework.* **2** To place something somewhere: *She rested her head on the pillow and soon went to sleep.*

†restaurant /'res·tər·ənt/, /-təˌrɑnt/ [countable noun] A place where you pay to sit at tables and eat: *My uncle's inviting us to have lunch in a restaurant to celebrate his birthday.*

restful /'rest.fᵊl/ [adjective] Peaceful: *They had a restful morning playing cards and chatting.*

restless /'rest.ləs/ [adjective] Without real rest: *My parents had a restless night at the hotel because it is next to the railway station.*

restore /rɪ'stɔr/, /-'stoʊr/ [verb] To repair something to make it look good again: *My mother has taken the painting to somebody to be restored.*

restriction /rɪ'strɪk.ʃᵊn/ [countable noun] The act of limiting something: *There are strict restrictions on parking in the hospital area.*

restroom US: /'restru:m/ [countable noun] In a public place, a room where toilets are located: *The girls' restroom are down the corridor on the left.* ■ When it is in somebody's house, we say "bathroom". ■ In British English they say "toilet".

†result[1] /rɪ'zʌlt/ [countable noun] **1** The effect of an action: *The dent in my father's car is a result of the accident he had last night.* **2** **as a result** As a consequence of something: *We played very badly and, as a result, we lost the game.*

result[2] /rɪ'zʌlt/ [verb] To end in, to lead to: *Our efforts have resulted in the collection of three hundred dollars for the local children's hospital.*

resume /rɪ'zum/ [verb] To continue after an interruption: *We'll resume work as soon as this noise stops.*

résumé or **resume** [countable noun] List with the studies and work experience of a person: *When you apply for a job you have to send your résumé.*

retail[1] /'ri:.teɪl/ [uncountable noun] The sale of goods in small quantities for personal use or consumption: *The retail business is less profitable today.* ■ Compare with "wholesale" (referring to the trading of goods in large quantities to stores and businesses).

retail[2] /'ri:teɪl/ [verb] To sell in small quantities to people for personal use: *The company retails its products in its store and also online.*

retina /'retɪnə/ [countable noun] An area at the back of the eyeball that sends impulses along the optic nerve to the brain: *The retina is sensitive to light.* ■ The plural is "retinas" or "retinae".

†retire /rɪ'tɑɪər/ [verb] To stop work because you are old or ill: *Mr. Dale, our former principal, retired when he reached the age of 65.*

†retired /rɪ'tɑɪərd/ [adjective] No longer working, because of age or illness: *Our neighbor is a retired army officer.* ■ Be careful with the pronunciation of this word. The last "e" is not pronounced.

†retirement /rɪ'tɑɪər·mənt/ [noun] The time in a person's life when they no longer work: *During his retirement my grandfather spent most of his time fishing and going for long walks in the country.*

retreat /rɪ'tri:t/ [verb] To go back from somebody or something: *The guerrillas retreated into the mountains when the army attacked them.*

retrieval [uncountable noun] The act of recovering something: *The retrieval of the data was not very difficult, in the end.*

†return[1] /rɪ'tɜ:n/ [noun] Coming or going back to somewhere: *We're going to make the return journey by train.*

return[2] /rɪ'tɜ:n/ [verb] **1** To come or to go back to somewhere: *My parents are returning from Italy the day after tomorrow.* **2** To give something back: *When are you going to return the book you borrowed last month?*

reuse[1] [uncountable noun] The act of using something again: *Many stores and supermarkets are promoting the reuse of plastic bags.*

reuse[2] /ˌri:'ju:z/ [verb] To use something again: *Don't throw away that plastic bottle. I will reuse it.*

reveal /rɪ'vi:l/ [verb] To tell a secret or to show something hidden: *My aunt's age is a secret that she won't reveal to anybody.*

revenge /rɪ'vendʒ/ [uncountable noun] Action taken in return for something somebody has done to you that you don't like: *Paul got his revenge on Mary for taking his racket by hiding her tennis shoes.* ■ Be careful! We say: "to get revenge **on** (somebody)" or "to take revenge **on** (somebody)".

reverberation /rɪˌvɜː.bərˈeɪ.ʃən/ US: /-ˌvɝː.bəˈreɪ-/ [countable noun] A sound that echoes and lasts for a while: *Everybody in the valley heard the reverberation caused by the explosion.*

†**reverse** /rɪˈvɜrs/ [verb] To back a car, truck or other vehicle: *My brother bumped into the lamp-post while he was reversing into the parking space the other day.*

reversible /rɪˈvɜr·sə·bəl/ [adjective] That can be turned inside out: *This jacket is reversible. The inside is waterproof.*

†**review**[1] /rɪˈvjuː/ [countable noun] A report about a book, movie and so on: *The new movie by Spielberg got bad reviews in the newspapers, but I enjoyed it.*

review[2] /rɪˈvjuː/ [verb] To write your opinion about a book, film and so on: *That novel you bought was reviewed in last Sunday's newspaper.*

†**revise** /rɪˈvaɪz/ [verb] **1** To study something again: *I spent the weekend revising for the History test on Tuesday.* **2** To change something in order to improve it: *We revised the project and added new photos before we gave it to the teacher.*

†**revision** /rɪˈvɪʒ.ən/ [countable noun] Studying something again: *I always need at least a week for revision before my tests.*

revive /rɪˈvaɪv/ [verb] To make or to become strong, healthy or active again: *When we gave it water, the plant revived immediately.*

revolt /rɪˈvəʊlt/ [verb] To fight against somebody in authority: *The people revolted in Russia in 1917.*

revolting /rɪˈvoʊl·tɪŋ/ [adjective] Very unpleasant: *That movie was revolting.*

†**revolution** /ˌrev.əˈluː.ʃən/ [countable noun] A big change: *The invention of the computer produced a revolution in the working world.*

revolutionary /ˌrev·əˈlu·ʃəˌner·i/ [adjective] Very new, involving great change: *The invention of the light bulb was a revolutionary development.*

revolve /rɪˈvɑlv/, /-ˈvɔlv/ [verb] To turn around a center: *The moon revolves around the earth.*

revolver /rɪˈvɑl·vər/, /-ˈvɔl-/ [countable noun] A small gun: *Wyatt Earp drew his revolver faster than anybody in the Wild West.*

reward[1] /rɪˈwɔːd/ [countable noun] Something given in return for a service: *Ken received a reward for finding the lost dog.*

reward[2] /rɪˈwɔːd/ [verb] To give somebody something in return for a service: *The old lady rewarded George for helping her with the shopping.*

rewind /ˌriːˈwaɪnd/ [verb] To make a tape go back towards the beginning: *Rewind and play the video again, please.* ■ Compare with "fast forward" (to make a tape go forward quickly).

rewrite[1] [countable noun] The act of writing again: *The article was so badly written that it was given a complete rewrite.*

rewrite[2] /ˌriːˈraɪt/ ■ rewrote, rewritten. [verb] To write again: *I am not happy with this so I am going to rewrite it.*

rhino /ˈraɪ·noʊ/ [countable noun] See **rhinoceros.** ■ The plural is "rhino" or "rhinos".

rhinoceros /raɪˈnɒsərəs/ [countable noun] A big animal with a thick skin and one or two horns on its nose: *Rhinoceroses live in Asia and Africa and have traditionally been hunted for their horns.* ■ "Rhino" is short of "rhinoceros". ■ The plural is "rhinoceros" or "rhinoceroses".

rhombus /ˈrɑm·bəs/ [countable noun] A flat shape with four sides that have the same length: *A rhombus has four angles.* ■ The plural is "rhombuses" or "rhombi". **See page 457.**

rhyme[1] /raɪm/ [uncountable noun] Words that finish with the same sound: *Can you think of a rhyme for "table"? Yes, "cable".*

rhyme[2] /raɪm/ [verb] To have words that finish with the same sound: *"Blue" rhymes with "true".*

†**rhythm** /ˈrɪð.əm/ [uncountable noun] A regular movement or sound: *African music has wonderful rhythms.*

rhythmic /ˈrɪð.mɪk/ [adjective] Having a good rhythm or with a regular beat: *The music is so rhythmic that it makes you want to dance.*

rib /rɪb/ [countable noun] One of the curved bones round your chest: *Jason broke two ribs when he fell off the horse.* **See page 422.**

ribbon /ˈrɪb.ən/ [countable noun] A long piece of thin material: *Karen ties her hair back with a red ribbon.*

†**rice** /raɪs/ [uncountable noun] White grains from a plant used as food: *Would you like some chicken and rice for lunch?*

†**rich** /rɪtʃ/ [adjective] **1** With a lot of money: *Vicky's grandfather won the lottery two months ago and now he's a very rich man.* **2** With a large amount of something: *Saudi Arabia is very rich in oil.* **3** When talking about food, that contains a lot of fat, sugar, cream, eggs and so on: *Pumpkin pie is very rich.*

riches /ˈrɪtʃ.ɪz/ [plural noun] A lot of money and expensive things: *Having power and riches won't make you happy.*

rid, rid, rid [verb] **1** To make something free: *A man playing a flute rid the town of Hamelin of rats.* **2** to get rid of (something) To throw something away: *My mother wants to get rid of the old sofa now that we have a new one.*

ridden /ˈrɪd.ən/ Past participle of **ride**[2].

riddle /ˈrɪd.l/ [countable noun] A question with a funny answer: *We spent the afternoon asking each other riddles.*

a b c d e f g h i j k l m n o p q r s t u v w x y z

ride[1] /raɪd/ [countable noun] A journey in a vehicle, on an animal or on an attraction at an amusement park: *When my parents were in India they had a ride on an elephant.*

†**ride**[2], **rode, ridden** /raɪd/ [verb] To travel in a vehicle or on an animal: *My little brother is learning to ride a bike.*

rider /ˈraɪ·dər/ [countable noun] A person who rides a horse, a bicycle or a motorcycle: *My cousin Anna has her own horse and is a great rider.*

ridge /rɪdʒ/ [countable noun] The long, narrow, raised part of something: *Look at the goats walking along the ridge of the mountain.*

†**ridiculous** /rɪˈdɪk.jʊ.ləs/ [adjective] That makes people laugh, absurd: *Miriam, you look ridiculous disguised as a witch.*

rifle /ˈraɪ.fḷ/ [countable noun] A long gun: *The rifle is a very accurate weapon.* ■ Be careful with the pronunciation of this word!

†**right**[1] /raɪt/ [adjective] **1** Correct; true: *Did you get the right answer for number two?* **2** Good; suitable: *It isn't right to talk to your friends like that.* **3** The opposite of left: *There were a lot of trucks parked on the right side of the road.* **4 on the right hand side** On the right side: *The police station is on the right hand side of the road as you go towards town.* **5 right-handed** Using your right more than your left: *Most people are right-handed, aren't they?*

†**right**[2] /raɪt/ [noun] **1** Something that the law or moral justice allows you to do or to claim: *Everyone over 18 has the right to vote in United States.* **2** The side of your body that does not contain your heart, this direction: *You must take the second turning on the right to get to the hotel.* ■ Be careful! In this use we always say: "**on** the right".

right[3] /raɪt/ [adverb] **1** Straight: *Go right along to the end of this street and you'll come to the church.* **2** Completely: *He headed the ball right into the corner of the goal.* **3** Correctly: *I got all the answers right!* **4** Exactly: *I saw Marie the other day. She was sitting right in front of me at the movie theater.* **5 right away** Directly, immediately: *Turn the television off and go to bed right away.* **6 right now** At this moment, exactly now: *He should be getting on the train right now.*

rightly /ˈraɪt.li/ [adverb] Correctly: *If I remember rightly, Paul told me to call him at nine.* ■ We usually say "right" or "correctly".

right-wing /ˌraɪtˈwɪŋ/ [adjective] Having conservative ideas: *Benjamin's uncle is a right-wing politician.*

rigid /ˈrɪdʒ.ɪd/ [adjective] **1** Difficult to bend: *We need some rigid card to make the models.* ■ The same meaning: "stiff". **2** Strict: *There were rigid rules in Mrs. Cameron's private school.*

rim /rɪm/ [countable noun] The edge of something round: *Aren't these cups beautiful? They have a gold rim.*

†**ring**[1] /rɪŋ/ [countable noun] **1** A circle: *The kids stood in a ring around the bonfire.* **2** A round metal band that you wear on your finger: *Why isn't your mother wearing her ring today?* 👁 See picture at **jewelry**. **3** Call on the telephone: *I'll give you a ring tomorrow.*

†**ring**[2], **rang, rung** /rɪŋ/ [verb] **1** To make a sound like a bell: *The doorbell's ringing. Go and answer the door.* **2** See **phone**[2]. ■ In this use we also say "ring up". ■ This use is British English.

▶ **PHRASAL VERBS** · **to ring off** To end a telephone conversation: *Angela was angry so she rang off without saying goodbye.* ■ In this use, the same meaning: "hang up".

ring finger [countable noun] The fourth finger of the hand, between the middle finger and the little finger: *The groom put the wedding ring on the bride's ring finger.*

rink /rɪŋk/ [countable noun] See **skating rink**.

rinse /rɪns/ [verb] To wash something with clear water: *He rinsed the shirt twice before hanging it out on the line.*

riot[1] /raɪət/ [countable noun] A disorder among a crowd of people in the street: *There was a riot after the Cup Final last year.*

riot[2] /raɪət/ [verb] To take part in a riot: *The students rioted because the government was cutting grants.*

rip /rɪp/ [verb] To tear: *I ripped my new pants climbing over the fence.* ■ Be careful with the spelling of these forms: "ripped", "ripping".

RIP Said to express the hope that somebody's spirit has found peace after death. ■ "RIP" is an abbreviation for "rest in peace". ■ See box at **abbreviations**.

ripe /raɪp/ [adjective] Ready to eat: *We can't pick the apples because they aren't ripe yet.*

ripple /ˈrɪpl/ [countable noun] A small repeating wave: *We threw stones into the pool to watch the ripples.*

†**rise**[1] /raɪz/ [countable noun] An increase, especially in money: *My parents say they'll give me a rise in my pocket money this year.*

rise[2], **rose, risen** /raɪz/ [verb] To move up: *When the string broke the child's balloon rose quickly into the sky.*

risen Past participle of **rise**[2].

†**risk**[1] /rɪsk/ [countable noun] **1** A dangerous chance, possible harm: *My brother takes too many risks when he drives.* **2 at risk** In danger: *The baby's at risk playing so near the water.*

risk[2] /rɪsk/ [verb] To take a chance involving possible danger: *Can we risk taking the boat out in this weather?*

risky /ˈrɪs.ki/ [adjective] Dangerous: *It's risky to swim out to those rocks.* ■ The comparative form is "riskier" and the superlative form is "riskiest".

↑**rival** /ˈraɪ.vᵊl/ [countable noun] A person who tries to do better than you in something: *You can still be friends with him even if you're both rivals for the same job.*

rivalry /ˈraɪ.vᵊl.ri/ [uncountable noun] Competition: *There's great rivalry between Mac Donald and Burger King.* ■ The plural is "rivalries".

↑**river** /ˈrɪv·ər/ [countable noun] A large stream of water: *The river that runs through New York is called the River Hudson.* ■ When a particular river is mentioned, we use a capital "R". 👁 **See page 445.**

↑**road** US: /roʊd/ UK: /rəʊd/ [countable noun] **1** A hard path for vehicles in or outside a city: *I like traveling by train more than by road.* ■ Compare with "street" (a road with houses on either side). **2 on the road** Traveling by road: *We were very tired after being on the road for so many hours.* ■ When a particular road is mentioned, we use a capital "R": "The post office is in the High Road". ■ The abbreviation "Rd" is only used in written language. See box at **abbreviations**. ■ Be careful with the pronunciation of this word! It is pronounced as the English word "rode". 👁 **See page 445.**

roam US: /roʊm/ UK: /rəʊm/ [verb] To walk or to travel with no particular purpose or direction: *We spent three days roaming the countryside having picnics and sleeping on the grass.*

roar[1] /rɔːr/ [countable noun] A loud sound like the sound a lion makes: *There was a roar from the crowd when Newcastle scored a goal in the last minute.* 👁 See picture at **animal**.

roar[2] /rɔːr/ [verb] To make a loud, angry sound: *When the lion got caught in the net it roared and frightened everybody.*

roast US: /roʊst/ UK: /rəʊst/ [verb] To cook in an oven: *Dad roasted the leg of lamb for dinner.* 👁 See picture at **cook**.

↑**rob** US: /rɑːb/ UK: /rɒb/ [verb] To take away, usually by force: *A gang of thieves robbed the bank the other day.* ■ Be careful. "Rob" is used when we mention the victim. We say: "They robbed me". (We don't say: "They robbed the money"). Compare with "steal" (it is used when the object taken is mentioned). ■ Look at the spelling of these forms: "robbed", "robbing".

robber US: /ˈrɑː.bɚ/ UK: /ˈrɒb.əʳ/ [countable noun] A thief, usually one who takes something by force: *The robbers were caught as they left the bank.*

robbery /ˈrɑb·ə·ri/ [countable noun] A theft: *This is a quiet neighborhood but there have been quite a few robberies lately.* ■ The plural is "robberies".

robe US: /roʊb/ UK: /rəʊb/ [countable noun] **1** A long, loose dress: *In United States, the judges wear black robes.* **2** An article of clothing that you wear over pajamas: *My sister gave me a lovely robe for my birthday.* ■ In this use, in British English we say "dressing gown".

robin US: /ˈrɑː.bɪn/ UK: /ˈrɒb.ɪn/ [countable noun] A small brown bird with a red breast: *A little robin comes into our backyard every morning.*

robot US: /ˈroʊ.bɑːt/ UK: /ˈrəʊ.bɒt/ [countable noun] A machine that can do the work of a person: *Robots do much of the work in car factories.*

↑**rock**[1] /rɒk/ [countable noun] **1** A large mass of stone: *The railway tunnel goes through solid rock.* **2** A large piece of stone: *We spent the evening sitting on a rock and watching the ships go into the harbor.* **3** A type of modern music: *Bruce Springsteen is my favorite rock singer.*

rock[2] /rɒk/ [verb] To move something from side to side: *She rocked the cradle gently to get the baby to sleep.*

rocket US: /ˈrɑː.kɪt/ UK: /ˈrɒk.ɪt/ [countable noun] **1** A big, extremely fast machine that carries spacecraft or bombs: *The Chinese have launched another rocket to put a satellite into space.* **2** A firework: *When the rocket went off, the sky was lit up with different colors.*

rocking chair [countable noun] A chair that can move backwards and forwards when you are sitting in it: *My grandmother has a wooden rocking chair in her bedroom.* 👁 See pictures at **chair**.

rocky US: /ˈrɑː.ki/ UK: /ˈrɒk.i/ [adjective] Full of rocks: *A rocky path led up to the old church.*

rode US: /roʊd/ UK: /rəʊd/ Past tense of **ride**[2].

rodent /ˈroʊ·də·nt/ [countable noun] A type of small animal which has two long teeth: *Mice and rats are rodents.*

↑**role** US: /roʊl/ UK: /rəʊl/ [countable noun] A character in a play or in a movie: *In that movie Emma Thompson played the role of an attorney.*

roll[1] /rəʊl/ [countable noun] **1** Something rolled into the shape of a cylinder: *I'm going to leave another roll of toilet paper in the bathroom.* **2** A small, round portion of bread: *Would you like a roll with your soup?* 👁 See picture at **bread**.

↑**roll**[2] /rəʊl/ [verb] **1** To move along by turning over and over: *A big rock rolled down the hill and hit a truck.* **2** To wrap something round a thing: *After rolling a cigarette the old man asked my father for a light.*

▸ **PHRASAL VERBS** · **to roll over** To turn your body to a different position: *As he was tired he rolled over on his side and went straight to sleep.* · **to roll (something) up** To put something into the shape of a cylinder: *Let's roll up the rug and put it in the corner.*

a b c d e f g h i j k l m n o p q r s t u v w x y z

roller US: /ˈroʊ.lɚ/ UK: /ˈrəʊ.ləʳ/ [countable noun] **1** A cylinder which rolls on its axis: *I need some paint and a roller to paint the living room.* **2** A small tube used to make curls by rolling the hair around it: *The hairdresser put her hair in rollers.* **3** **roller blind** A window blind with a roller system: *At Eva's house there are roller blinds made of wood.*

roller coaster /ˌrəʊləˈkəʊstər/ [countable noun] A railway at a fair which goes up and down very dramatically: *Let's go on the roller coaster!*

roller-skate[1] [countable noun] A boot with small wheels at the bottom: *Laura often goes to school on her roller-skates.* ■ We also say "skate".

roller-skate[2] [verb] To skate on roller-skates: *Can you roller-skate?* ■ We also say "skate".

Roman /ˈroʊ·mən/ [adjective] Referring to ancient Rome: *The Roman invasion of Britain took place in 49 CE.* ■ Be careful! "Roman" has a capital "R".

Roman Catholic [adjective] See **Catholic.** ■ Be careful! "Roman Catholic" has capital letters.

romance US: /roʊˈmænts/ UK: /rəʊˈmænts/ [countable noun] **1** A relationship between two people in love: *The actress had a secret romance with a famous sportsman.* **2** A love story: *My grandma loves reading romances.*

˄**romantic** US: /roʊˈmæn.t̬ɪk/ UK: /rəʊˈmæn.tɪk/ [adjective] Full of feelings of love, mystery, beauty: *The Brontë sisters wrote very famous romantic novels.*

˄**roof** /ruːf/ [countable noun] The covering of a building: *The rain fell into the bathroom through a hole in the roof.*

˄**room** /ruːm, rʊm/ [noun] **1** One of the divisions of a house: *The biggest room in my house is the living room.* **2** Space: *Let's walk down the stairs. There's no room for us in the elevator.* **3** **dining room** See **dining room.** **4** **living room** See **living room.**

roommate [countable noun] A person who lives in the same room, apartment or house as you: *I'm still in touch with my college roommate, although she lives in Japan.*

roost /ruːst/ [countable noun] A place where birds rest or sleep: *The hens and cocks live in the roost.*

˄**root** /ruːt/ [countable noun] The part of a plant or tree that is under the ground: *The roots of the old oak tree probably reach as far as the road.* 👁 **See pages 432 and 434.**

˄**rope** US: /roʊp/ UK: /rəʊp/ [countable noun] A piece of thick string: *I'm going to get a rope and climb that tree.*

rose[1] /rəʊz/ [countable noun] A beautiful flower: *The smell of roses is sweetest in spring.* 👁 **See page 433.**

rose[2] /rəʊz/ Past tense of **rise**.

rot US: /rɑːt/ UK: /rɒt/ [verb] To go bad: *If we don't pick those apples up off the ground they'll rot.* ■ Be careful with the spelling of these forms: "rotted", "rotting".

rotate US: /ˈroʊ.teɪt/ UK: /rəʊˈteɪt/ [verb] **1** To revolve around an axis: *The Earth rotates on its axis.* **2** To happen in turns: *Intelligent farmers make the most of their land by rotating crops.*

rotation /rəʊˈteɪʃən/ [countable noun] **1** The act of revolving around an axis: *The earth's rotation around the sun causes day and night.* **2** The act of happening in turns: *The workers in this factory work on a rotation system.*

rotten US: /ˈrɑː.tᵊn/ UK: /ˈrɒt.ᵊn/ [adjective] **1** Bad, no longer good to eat: *If you don't put the meat in the fridge it'll go rotten.* **2** Unpleasant, terrible: *My father is always in a bad temper when he's had a rotten day at the bank.*

˄**rough** /rʌf/ [adjective] **1** Not smooth, very uneven: *My skin feels very rough. I'm going to put some lotion on it.* **2** Not gentle or calm: *Why do you play with Jeremy if he's so rough?*

roughly /ˈrʌf.li/ [adverb] **1** About: *There were roughly twenty people in the movie theater last night.* ■ Be careful! In this use "roughly" is not the adverb form of "rough". **2** Not gently: *My grandfather often speaks roughly but he's nice really.*

˄**round[1]** /raʊnd/ [adjective] Like a circle: *There's a round table in the center of the hall.*

round[2] /raʊnd/ [countable noun] **1** A stage in a competition: *I think Tyson won that round.* **2** The drinks for everyone in a group, that one of them pays for: *It's my round. What will you have?* **3** **round trip** A journey made to a place and back: *He made a round trip to Dallas and was back in Houston before dinner time.*

round[3] /raʊnd/ [adverb and preposition] See **around[1]**. ■ This word is British English.

roundabout /ˈraʊnd.ə.baʊt/ [countable noun] **1** See **traffic circle.** ■ This use is British English. **2** A round machine on which children can go in a circle: *Which do you prefer Susie, the swings or the roundabout?*

rounders /ˈraʊndəz/ [countable noun] A British game in which players hit the ball with a bat and run round a circuit: *In the past rounders was a popular children's game similar to American baseball.*

˄**route** /ruːt/ US: /raʊt/ [countable noun] A way: *What route shall we take tomorrow to get to the woods?*

routine[1] /ruːˈtiːn/ [countable noun] **1** A sequence of actions which occur or are done in a regular way: *My daily routine starts with getting up, having breakfast, brushing my teeth and going to school.* **2** Referring to gymnastics or dance, a fixed series of movements: *We will have to practice that routine again before the performance.*

routine[2] /ruːˈtiːn/ [adjective] Normal, not done for any special reason: *The police officers said that it was only a routine control.*

row[1] /rəʊ/ [countable noun] A line: *He has rows and rows of books in his room.* ■ Be careful "row[1]" and "row[2]" are not pronounced the same way! "Row[1]" rhymes with "so".

row[2] /rəʊ/ [countable noun] An argument: *My father has had a row with the neighbor about his dogs.*

row[3] /rəʊ/ [verb] To move a boat with oars: *We spent a quiet afternoon rowing on the lake and fishing.*

rowboat [countable noun] A small boat that is moved by using oars: *There were a few rowboats crossing the river.*

royal /ˈrɔɪ.əl/ [adjective] Referring to a king or a queen: *The royal yacht is very luxurious.*

royalty /ˈrɔɪ·əl·ti/ [uncountable noun] The members of a royal family: *Most of the European royalty were present at the prince's wedding.* ■ The plural is "royalties".

rpm Unit of frequency that accounts for the rotations completed by an object in one minute: *237 rpm.* ■ "rpm" is an abbreviation for "revolution(s) per minute". ■ See box at **abbreviations**.

RSVP Used at the end of a written invitation to ask for reply: *RSVP by December 17th.* ■ "RSVP" is an abbreviation for 'répondez s'il vous plaît', a French expression that means "please reply". ■ See box at **abbreviations**.

rub /rʌb/ [verb] To move something against a surface: *He cleaned the door handles by rubbing them with a cloth.*

▶ **PHRASAL VERBS** · **to rub (something) out** To remove the marks made by a pencil, chalk and so on: *The teacher rubbed out all the writing on the board.* ■ Be careful with the spelling of these forms: "rubbed", "rubbing".

rubber /ˈrʌb·ər/ [noun] An elastic material made from the sap of a tree: *Car tires are made of rubber.*

rubber band [countable noun] A thin ring of rubber: *Here's a rubber band to fasten the pencils together.*

rubber boots [countable noun] Boots that you wear to keep your feet dry: *The farmer put on his rubber boots to go out to the fields.* ■ In British English they say "wellington boots, wellingtons".

rubbish /ˈrʌb.ɪʃ/ [uncountable noun] **1** See **trash** **2** See **garbage.** ■ This word is British English.

rucksack /ˈrʌk.sæk/ [countable noun] See **backpack.** ■ This word is British English.

rude /ruːd/ [adjective] Not kind or polite: *I hate taking friends home because my sister is always so rude to them.*

rug /rʌg/ [countable noun] **1** A small carpet: *My mom has bought a new rug for the living room.* 👁 See pictures at **bedroom** and **living room. 2** A blanket: *She put a rug over her legs because she felt cold in the carriage.*

rugby /ˈrʌg.bi/ [uncountable noun] A game like soccer that is played with an oval ball: *In rugby, players can either kick the ball or carry it in their hands.*

ruin[1] /ˈruːɪn/ [countable noun] A building that is almost destroyed: *The ruin on the top of the hill is an old monastery.*

ruin[2] /ˈruːɪn/ [verb] **1** To destroy something completely: *Bad weather ruined our barbecue last Saturday.* **2** To become very poor: *My grandfather was ruined when his business went bankrupt.*

rule[1] /ruːl/ [verb] To govern a country: *Barak Obama has ruled United States since 2008.*

rule[2] /ruːl/ [countable noun] **1** An order concerning the way you behave: *It's against the rules to eat chewing gum in class.* **2** Government or control: *Some islands in the Pacific Ocean are still under foreign rule.* **3 to rule out** To decide that one choice is out: *My parents haven't ruled out a foreign vacation this year, but it's not very likely.*

ruler /ˈru·lər/ [countable noun] **1** A person who governs a country: *Mrs. Ghandi was ruler of India from 1966 to 1977.* **2** A long piece of wood or plastic with measurements: *You'll need a ruler to draw these parallel lines.* 👁 **See page 456.**

rum /rʌm/ [uncountable noun] A strong alcoholic drink: *They make very good rum in Jamaica.*

ruminant /ˈruː.mɪ.nənt/ [countable noun] An animal that, after swallowing food, brings it back from its stomach into its mouth to chew it again: *Cows, sheep, deer and giraffes are ruminants.*

rumor [countable noun] **1** A piece of news or a story passed from person to person, which may not be true: *I heard a rumor that you had gotten a new job.* **2** General talk or gossip: *Don't listen to rumor.*

run[1] /rʌn/ [countable noun] The act of running: *My aunt goes for a run before work each morning.* ■ Be careful! We say: "go for a run" or "have a run".

run[2], ran, run /rʌn/ [verb] **1** To move quickly on your feet: *We'll have to run to catch that bus; Lisa runs very fast.* **2** Referring to a machine or vehicle, to work: *My motorcycle hasn't run properly since the accident.* **3** Referring to transport, to go, to operate: *There's a train to Boston that runs every half hour.* **4** To organize or to manage a shop, business or club: *Jimmy's father runs the corner store.* **5** To leave in a hurry: *I have to run: I need to be at the library by eight.* **6** To pass: *Two rivers run through the town.* **7** To extend: *The road runs up to the old castle on the top of the hill.* **8** Referring to a tap, to be open, with water coming out: *You have left the tap running!* **9** Referring to somebody's nose, to produce liquid waste: *My nose is running.* **10 to run errands** To go somewhere for somebody to do little jobs: *We can meet Saturday after-*

noon after I run my errands in town.* **11** to be run off one's feet To be in a big rush because you are trying to do many things: *I'm afraid I don't have time now: I'm really run off my feet.* **12** to run rings around somebody To be much better or faster than somebody, especially at a sport: *She ran rings round me at tennis yesterday.*

▸ PHRASAL VERBS · to run away **1** To go away quickly, to escape: *The kid rang our doorbell and then ran away.* **2** Referring to a child, to leave home because they don't want to live there: *He ran away the first time when he was ten.* · to run into (somebody) To meet somebody by accident: *I ran into uncle Frank on Saturday in the park and he looks much better.* · to run into (something) Referring to problems or difficulties, to be faced with them unexpectedly: *We have run into some problems with the new program.* · to run off **1** To go away quickly: *The cat ran off before we could get near it.* **2** To produce or print: *We need to run off one hundred copies of the theater program.* · to run out of (something) To have no more of something left: *Can you go to the shop for me? I've run out of sugar; I'm afraid we have run out of time for today.* · to run over (somebody or something) To drive over somebody or something: *Lynn's dog was run over by a truck yesterday.* · to run over (something) To look at again, especially a plan or something you are going to perform: *Let's run over the sequence one more time.* · to run through (something) **1** To look at again, especially a plan or something you are going to perform: *I think we should run over the game plan again.* **2** To spend or consume: *He ran through the money he inherited in six months.* · to run up To accumulate a debt or bill: *He ran up a very big telephone bill calling every day to Toronto.*

rung[1] /rʌŋ/ Past participle of **ring**[2].

rung[2] /rʌŋ/ [countable noun] A bar of a ladder: *One of the rungs broke and I nearly fell off the ladder.*

*****runner** /ˈrʌn·ər/ [countable noun] A person who runs: *There were over five thousand runners in the marathon last year.*

*****running**[1] /ˈrʌnɪŋ/ [countable noun] Sport in which you move quickly on your feet: *Long distance running is a tough sport.* 👁 See picture at **sport**.

running[2] /ˈrʌnɪŋ/ [adjective] One after another: *Graham has missed the school bus two days running.*

runny /ˈrʌn.i/ [adjective] Containing more liquid than desired: *Your ice cream has gone runny in the heat.*

runway /ˈrʌn.weɪ/ [countable noun] The ground on which airplanes take off and land: *The pilot couldn't see the runway because the weather was foggy.*

*****rural** US: /ˈrʊr.ᵊl/ UK: /ˈrʊə.rəl/ [adjective] Belonging to the country: *A lot of people from rural areas have come to live in cities.*

rush[1] /rʌʃ/ [uncountable noun] **1** A hurry: *I'm in a rush this morning.* ■ Be careful! We say: "be in a rush". (We don't say: "have rush"). **2** the rush hour The time when most people go and come from work: *There are a lot of gridlock in the rush hour.*

rush[2] /rʌʃ/ [verb] To hurry: *A woman rushed out of the store and cried "Stop thief!".*

rust[1] /rʌst/ [uncountable noun] A red brown substance that forms on some metals when attacked by water or air: *After so many days outside there was some rust on Sandra's bike.* ■ The same meaning: "oxide".

rust[2] [verb] To become covered with rust: *If we don't paint the gate it will rust quickly.*

rustler /ˈrʌs·lər/ [countable noun] Horse or cattle thief, particularly in America: *In the movie, the sheriff caught the band of rustlers.*

rusty /ˈrʌs.ti/ [adjective] **1** Covered with rust: *Be careful! Don't prick your finger with that rusty pin.* **2** Almost forgotten, affected by lack of use: *My French is getting a bit rusty nowadays.*

S

S

S /es/ The nineteenth letter of the alphabet: *The name "Susan" begins with an "S".*

sac /sæk/ [countable noun] A part inside a plant or the body of an animal or plant which looks like a bag: *Sacs usually contain liquid or air.*

†**sack** /sæk/ [countable noun] **1** A big bag for carrying things in: *My grandma used to have coal brought to the house in sacks.* **2 to get the sack** To be dismissed from a job: *The factory closed and hundreds of car workers got the sack.* ■ This use is informal.

sacred /'seɪ.krɪd/ [adjective] Holy or belonging to God: *Mosques are the sacred buildings of Muslims.*

sacrifice[1] /'sækrɪfaɪs/ [countable noun] **1** An animal or a person that is killed and offered to a god: *Lambs were often used in sacrifices.* **2** Something important that you permit yourself to lose for a good reason: *Many parents make a lot of sacrifices so that their children can have the best of everything.*

sacrifice[2] /'sækrɪfaɪs/ [verb] To make a sacrifice: *She sacrificed buying clothes and going out so that she could study to be a doctor.*

†**sad** /sæd/ [adjective] Unhappy: *I felt very sad when Oliver told me that his dog had been killed in a road accident.* ■ The comparative form is "sadder" and the superlative form is "saddest". 👁 See picture at **emotions**.

saddle /'sæd.l̩/ [countable noun] **1** A seat on a bicycle: *I'll have to lower the saddle on this bike because my feet don't touch the ground.* **2** A seat that you put on a horse's back: *Hold tight to the saddle when the horse begins to gallop.*

†**sadness** /'sæd.nəs/ [uncountable noun] Feeling sad: *The death of the panda caused great sadness.*

safari /sə'fɑr·i/ [countable noun] A trip to observe or to hunt wild animals: *Dad says that we are going on safari to Kenya this year!*

†**safe** /seɪf/ [adjective] **1** Not dangerous: *The water park is quite safe, you know; there are monitors everywhere.* **2** Not in danger: *Rajah is the gentlest dog I know. The children will be perfectly safe with him.*

†**safety** /'seɪf.ti/ [uncountable noun] Being safe: *Our principal is very concerned about the safety of the new swimming pool.* ■ The plural is "safeties".

safety belt [countable noun] A belt that you wear in a car, plane or other vehicle: *Please, fasten your safety belts. The plane is about to take off.*

saffron /'sæf.rən/ [uncountable noun] **1** An orange powder that adds color and flavor to food: *Saffron is obtained from a flower.* **2** The dark yellow or orange color associated with the central part of the flower of the same name: *Her dress was the color of saffron.*

sag /sæg/ [verb] To hang down: *When you get older, the skin on your face begins to sag!* ■ Be careful with the spelling of these forms: "sagged", "sagging".

a b c d e f g h i j k l m n o p q r **s** t u v w x y z

Sagittarius /ˌsædʒ·ɪ'teər·i·əs/ [uncountable noun] A sign of the zodiac: *If your birthday is between November 22nd and December 20th, you're a Sagittarius.* ■ Be careful. "Sagittarius" has a capital "S".

said /sed/ Past tense and past participle forms of **say**.

†**sail**[1] /seɪl/ [countable noun] A big piece of cloth on a boat, which catches the wind: *We could see the red sail of my uncle's boat from the beach.*

sail[2] /seɪl/ [verb] **1** To travel on the water: *Mary said that she would teach me to sail one weekend.* **2** To start a journey on water: *The boat to Boston sails at half past seven in the evening.* **3** To direct a boat with sails: *I go sailing every summer on the lake near my cousin's house.*

sailboat [countable noun] A boat with sails: *My dad says that if he won the lottery he would buy a sailboat.*

†**sailor** /'seɪ·lər/ [countable noun] A person who works on a ship: *Philip wants to be a sailor in the Merchant Navy when he grows up.*

saint /seɪnt, sᵊnt/ [countable noun] An exceptionally good person, given special respect by the Christian Church: *Saint Patrick day is a big holiday in United States because there are a lot of people at Irish heritage.* ■ The abbreviation "St" is only used in written language. See box at **abbreviations**.

†**sake** /seɪk/ **1 for God's sake or for goodness' shake or for Heaven's shake** Expressions that you use when you are angry, often because of repeated provocation: *For goodness' sake, do as you are told for once!* **2 for (somebody's or something's) sake** For somebody's or something's good or to make them happy: *We moved to Miami for my mother's sake, so that she could be near her elderly sister.*

†**salad** /'sæl.əd/ [countable noun] A cold dish, usually made with raw vegetables: *I love salad with an oil and vinegar dressing and garlic bread.*

salamander /'sæl·əˌmæn·dər/ [countable noun] A small amphibian with a long tail: *There are many different species of salamander.* 👁 **See page 431.**

†**salary** /'sæl·ə·ri/ [uncountable noun] The money that a person receives every month for working, usually for professional or office work and normally in the form of a check: *My mom says that she gets a better salary now than she did when she started working.* ■ The plural is "salaries". ■ Compare with "wages" (the money that a person receives for every week or day he or she works).

†**sale** /seɪl/ [noun] **1** Selling something: *We got $20 for the sale of our old books.* **2** A time when stores sell articles at a lower price: *Some people wait in line for hours outside department stores to be the first to get into the season sales.* **3 for sale** To be sold: *Have you seen that the big house on the corner is for sale?*

salesman /'seɪlz.mən/ [countable noun] A man who works selling things: *Don is a traveling salesman and he says it's very hard work.* ■ The plural is "salesmen". ■ A woman is a "saleswoman".

saleswoman /'seɪlzˌwʊm.ən/ [countable noun] A woman who works selling things: *Jane is a saleswoman in a food firm.* ■ The plural is "saleswomen". ■ A man is a "salesman".

saliva /sə'laɪvə/ [uncountable noun] A liquid which is produced in the mouth: *Saliva helps chewing, swallowing and digestion.*

salivary gland /'sæl·əˌver·i ˌglænd/ [countable noun] Any of the small glands which produce saliva in the mouth: *Most animals and all mammals have salivary glands.*

salmon /'sæm.ən/ [countable noun] A large fish that lives in the sea and in rivers: *Fresh grilled salmon is a delicious dish!* ■ The plural is also "salmon". 👁 **See page 430.**

salmonella /ˌsælmə'nelə/ [uncountable noun] **1** A form of food poisoning, or the bacteria that produces it: *Salmonella usually occurs when contaminated food isn't cooked enough.* **2** Infection caused by this bacteria: *The doctor said that her vomiting and fever were due to the salmonella outbreak.* ■ In this use, the same meaning: "salmonellosis". ■ The plural is "salmonella" or "salmonellae".

salmonellosis [uncountable noun] A form of food poisoning caused by salmonella bacteria: *Salmonellosis can be serious.* ■ The same meaning: "salmonella".

†**salt**[1] US: /sɒlt/ UK: /sɔːlt/ [uncountable noun] A white substance that is found in the sea and other places: *I like a lot of salt and vinegar on my french fries.*

salt[2] US: /sɒlt/ UK: /sɔːlt/ [verb] To add salt to something: *I forgot to salt the potatoes.*

salt water [uncountable noun] Water from the sea, or water with a high content of salt: *Tears are made mainly of salt water.*

†**salty** US: /'sɑːl.t̬i/ UK: /'sɒl.ti/ [adjective] With a lot of salt: *The Dead Sea, which is extremely salty, is the lowest surface in the world.* ■ The comparative form is "saltier" and the superlative form is "saltiest". 👁 See picture at **opposite**.

salute[1] /sə'luːt/ [countable noun] Putting your hand up as a greeting: *The soldiers gave a salute when the General inspected the parade.*

salute[2] /sə'luːt/ [verb] To put your hand up as a greeting: *The soldiers on the door saluted the general as he entered headquarters.*

Salvadoran[1] [adjective] Referring to El Salvador: *San Salvador is the Salvadoran capital.* ■ Be careful! "Salvadoran" has a capital "S".

Salvadoran² [countable noun] A person from El Salvador: *The chef of this restaurant is Salvadoran.* ■ Be careful! "Salvadoran" has a capital "S".

⁺same /seɪm/ [adjective] **1** Not different: *I go to the same school as my cousin.* **2 the same** Very similar in many ways: *My shoes are the same as yours.*

⁺sample /'sæm·pəl/ [countable noun] A small amount of something to try: *They're giving away some free samples of orange juice at the supermarket!*

⁺sand /sænd/ [uncountable noun] The fine ground on the beach: *Sand is really very fine pieces of rock and is also found in the desert.*

sandal /'sæn.dᵊl/ [countable noun] An open shoe for the summer: *I've just bought some lovely white sandals.*

sandcastle /'sænd,kæs·əl/ [countable noun] A small building made of sand: *My little brother loves making sandcastles on the beach.*

⁺sandwich /'sænd·wɪtʃ/ [countable noun] Two slices of bread with something between them: *Let's make the sandwiches for the picnic before everyone comes.* ■ The plural is "sandwiches".

sandy /'sæn.di/ [adjective] With a lot of sand: *I'm really looking forward to my vacation in Morocco; sandy beaches and blue seas.*

sane /seɪn/ [adjective] With a healthy mind, not mad: *No sane person would try to ski down Mount Everest.*

sang /sæŋ/ Past tense of **sing**.

sank /sæŋk/ Past tense of **sink²**.

sap /sæp/ [uncountable noun] The liquid inside a plant: *The sap in a plant or tree contains its food.*

sapphire /'sæfaɪər/ [countable noun] **1** A precious stone which is transparent and usually bright blue: *That woman is wearing a ring with a sapphire on it.* **2 sapphire blue** Bright blue: *The sea is sapphire blue today.*

sarcastic /sɑr'kæs·tɪk/ [adjective] Sharp, often in a cruel way: *Ron has a very sarcastic sense of humor.*

sardine /sɑr'din/ [countable noun] **1** A small fish: *I'm just going to buy a tin of sardines for the picnic.* 👁 **See page 430. 2 like sardines** Very closely packed together: *On the subway this morning we were like sardines.*

sat /sæt/ Past tense and past participle forms of **sit**.

satchel /'sætʃ.ᵊl/ [countable noun] A small bag with a shoulder strap: *That satchel is really heavy. Can't you take something out of it?*

satellite /'sæt·ə·l,ɑɪt/ [countable noun] **1** Something that moves around a planet: *The Earth only has one satellite, the moon, but Jupiter has 16 and Saturn has 17!* **2** An object that is sent into space to send signals: *If you have satellite television you can get programs from all over the world.*

satellite navigation [uncountable noun] A system of satellites and computers which provide information about the position of something or somebody: *Tom's new car is fitted with satellite navigation.* ■ "Satnav" is an abbreviation for "satellite navigation".

⁺satisfaction /,sæt̬·əs'fæk·ʃən/ [uncountable noun] A feeling of happiness because for example you have achieved or got something: *My mom says that she gets great satisfaction from her voluntary job.*

satisfactory /,sæt̬·əs'fæk·tə·ri/ [adjective] OK, just good enough: *The teacher said that my homework wasn't satisfactory. I have to do it again tonight.*

⁺satisfied /'sæt̬·əs,fɑɪd/ [adjective] Pleased and contented: *I am quite satisfied with this drawing. I think it's OK.*

⁺satisfy /'sæt̬·əs,fɑɪ/ [verb] To make somebody happy: *My dad says that his job doesn't really satisfy him.* ■ Be careful with the spelling of these forms: "satisfies", "satisfied".

satnav [uncountable noun] See **satellite navigation.**

⁺Saturday /'sæt̬·ər·deɪ/, /-,di/ [noun] The seventh day of the week: *Saturday is between Friday and Sunday.* ■ Be careful! "Saturday" has a capital "S". 👁 See picture at **calendar.**

Saturn /'sætən/ [countable noun] A planet of the solar system that is sixth in order from the Sun: *Saturn is surrounded by large rings.* 👁 **See page 447.**

⁺sauce US: /sɑːs/ UK: /sɔːs/ [uncountable noun] A thick liquid that you put on food: *My cousin puts tomato sauce on everything!*

saucepan /'sɔs,pæn/ [countable noun] A deep metal container to cook food in: *When you finish drying up, put all the saucepans in the cabinet.* 👁 See picture at **pan.**

saucer US: /'sɑː.sɚ/ UK: /'sɔː.səʳ/ [countable noun] A small plate that goes under a cup: *My aunt's got some lovely cups and saucers with the days of the week written on them.*

sausage US: /'sɑː.sɪdʒ/ UK: /'sɒs.ɪdʒ/ [countable noun] Meat cut up finely, and made into a long, thin shape: *One of my favorite meals is sausages and mashed potatoes.* ■ Be careful with the pronunciation of this word! ■ In British English they say "banger".

SAUSAGE

a b c d e f g h i j k l m n o p q r s t u v w x y z

savage /ˈsæv.ɪdʒ/ [adjective] Wild and aggressive: *The people in that house have a very savage dog.* ■ Be careful with the pronunciation of this word. The last "a" is pronounced like the "i" in "did".

savannah or **savanna** /səˈvæn.ə/ [uncountable noun] A large flat area of land covered with grass, found in tropical and subtropical regions, especially in Africa: *The savannah usually has few trees.*

✝save /seɪv/ [verb] **1** To make somebody or something safe from danger: *The coast guard arrived immediately and saved the children from drowning.* **2** To keep something instead of spending or using it: *I've saved enough money to buy myself a new book.* **3** To use less of something: *At school we're trying to save paper by making sure that we don't waste it.*

savings /ˈseɪ.vɪŋz/ [plural noun] Money that somebody has saved: *Billy has given all his savings to the local children's hospital.*

savor[1] /ˈseɪ.vər/ US: /-vɚ/ [noun] A taste of flavor: *They are enjoying the sweet savor of success.* ■ The British English spelling is "savour".

savor[2] /ˈseɪ·vər/ [verb] To enjoy the taste of a meal or of an experience: *We savored the latest Vietnamese cuisine.* ■ The British English spelling is "savour".

savour[1] /ˈseɪ.vər/ US: /-vɚ/ [noun] See **savor**[1]. ■ This is a British English spelling.

savour[2] /ˈseɪ.vər/ US: /-vɚ/ [verb] See **savor**[2]. ■ This is a British English spelling.

saw[1] /sɔː/ [countable noun] A metal thing for cutting wood: *We used the saw to cut up some wood for the fire.*

saw[2] /sɔː/ Past tense of **see**.

sawdust /ˈsɔˌdʌst/ [uncountable noun] Very small particles of wood which are produced when a saw is used: *Sawdust is often used as fuel.*

sax /sæks/ [countable noun] See **saxophone.** ■ This word is informal.

saxophone /ˈsæk·səˌfoʊn/ [countable noun] A musical instrument made of metal with keys and a turned up end: *The saxophone is a very popular instrument in jazz music.* ■ "Sax" is informal for "saxophone". 👁 **See page 459.**

✝say, said, said /seɪ/ [verb] **1** To speak a word or some words: *Jackie said that she was going to Greece for her vacation; What did you say to him?* ■ Be careful! We say: "She said **to** me he would be late". (We don't say: "She said me he would be late"). ■ Compare with "tell" (to say something to somebody). ■ See box on the following page. **2** Referring to an instrument or meter, to show a particular level or state: *The thermometer says thirty degrees.* **3 say (for example)** Words you use to indicate that you are going to use somebody or something as an example: *Let's look at a composer, say Mahler...* **4 say no** To reject an offer or request: *If you don't want to do it, say no.* **5 say yes** To accept or agree to an offer or request: *If they offer you to be the main character in the play, say yes.* **6 say no more** Words you use to indicate that you have understood or agree with a plan: *Say no more, I know my sister and imagine how your conversation was.* ■ This use is informal. **7 that is to say** Words you use to indicate that you are going to explain something more: *You can go to your friends's house, that is to say if you finish your chores and your homework first.*

saying /ˈseɪ.ɪŋ/ [countable noun] Something significant that people often say: *"Do as you would be done by" is a saying that means you should treat people in the same way as you would like them to treat you.*

scaffolding /ˈskæf.əl.dɪŋ/ [countable noun] A structure on the outside of a building for workers to stand on: *Have you seen the scaffolding outside the town hall? They're going to clean the walls.*

SCAFFOLDING

scald /skɔːld/ [verb] To burn something with boiling water: *I scalded my hand while I was making coffee the other day.*

✝scale /skeɪl/ [noun] **1** A set of marks on something for measurement: *My dad's got a tape measure with a metric scale on one side and feet and inches on the other.* **2** A way of showing distance on a map: *The scale on the map of this area is of two centimeters to the kilometer.* **3** A machine for weighing things or people: *My dad has just bought some speaking weighing scale that actually say how heavy you are!* **4** Small, flat piece of hard material covering some fish or animals: *Remove the fish scales carefully before you put it in the oven to cook.* **5** A series of musical notes up or down from one particular note: *Opera singers need to practice scales every day.*

scampi /ˈskæm.pi/ [plural noun] Large prawns that have been fried in a mixture of flour and milk: *Scampi and french fries is one of my favorite meals.*

scan /skæn/ [verb] **1** To look carefully from a distance: *The police used a helicopter to scan the mountain in search of the lost child.* **2** To read something quickly looking for something in particular: *We scanned the tests results very nervously for our names.* **3** To use a machine to see an image or text in a computer: *The cashier scans the products, except the fruits and vegetables.* ■ Be careful with the spelling of these forms: "scanned", "scanning".

scandal /ˈskæn.dəl/ [uncountable noun] Something that shocks people: *Have you heard the scandal about the Duke running away with the actress?*

scanner /ˈskæn·ər/ [countable noun] A machine that is used to look at the inside of something or to see something in a computer: *Scanners are used in medicine to detect certain types of illnesses.*

scapula /ˈskæp.jʊ.lə/ [countable noun] A flat, triangular bone at the back of each shoulder: *The scapula connects the humerus with the clavicle.* ■ The plural is "scapulas" or "scapulae".

scar[1] /skɑːr/ [countable noun] A mark that is left by a cut: *The pirate had a scar on his cheek and wore a gold earring.*

scar[2] [verb] To leave a scar: *Pamela's face was badly scarred by the riding accident she had last year.* ■ Be careful with the spelling of these forms: "scarred", "scarring".

scarce US: /skers/ UK: /skeəs/ [adjective] Not found in great quantities: *Animals sometimes change their habitat when food starts to get scarce.*

scarcely /ˈskeərs·li/ [adverb] Hardly: *I don't know what's the matter with Jane; she scarcely speaks to me any more.* ■ "Scarcely" goes before ordinary verbs and after auxiliary verbs: "He can scarcely speak two words of German".

scare[1] /skeər/ [countable noun] Making a person or people frightened: *When the monster appeared in the movie it gave him a terrible scare.*

✦**scare**[2] /skeər/ [verb] To frighten somebody: *What a frightening movie that was. It really scared me.*

scarecrow US: /ˈsker.kroʊ/ UK: /ˈskeə.krəʊ/ [countable noun] A figure put in a field to frighten the birds away: *The farmer was very worried about the seed he had just planted and put five scarecrows in the field.*

✦**scared** US: /skerd/ UK: /skeəd/ [adjective] Frightened: *Ever since Frances got bitten by that dog, she's been scared of dogs.* ■ Be careful with the pronunciation of this word! The "e" is not pronounced.

scarf US: /skɑːrf/ UK: /skɑːf/ [countable noun] Something that you wear round your neck or on your head: *I'm knitting my dad a basketball scarf in his team's colors.* ■ The plural is "scarves". See picture at **clothes**.

scarlet [noun and adjective] A bright red color: *I gave my mom a scarlet silk scarf for Christmas.*

scatter US: /ˈskæt̬.ər/ UK: /ˈskæt.əʳ/ [verb] **1** To run in different directions: *All the people scattered when they saw the lion escape from the cage.* **2** To throw things in all directions: *The farmer is scattering seed in the field.*

✦**scene** /siːn/ [countable noun] **1** What you can see in a particular place: *What a lovely scene! The river, the mountains and the swans flying past!* **2** The place where something happens: *The firemen arrived on the scene very promptly and luckily no one was hurt.* **3** A small part of a play or a movie: *I really like the scene where the dog saves the baby from drowning.*

scenery /ˈsi·nə·ri/ [uncountable noun] **1** What you can see in the country: *The scenery in some parts of Arizona*

to say and _to tell_

To say and *to tell* have almost the same meaning, but we use them in different ways:

- We normally use the verb ***to say*** before direct speech:
  - *He said, "Come here."*
- We use the verb ***to say*** without a personal object:
  - *She said that she didn't like fish.*
  - *I said that I was sorry.*
- We normally use ***to tell*** with a personal object:
  - *She told me that she didn't like fish.*
  - *I told them that I was sorry.*
- Here are some expressions:

to say	to tell
to say a word	*to tell a story*
to say a sentence	*to tell the time*
to say your prayers	*to tell the truth*
to say you are sorry	*to tell a secret*
to say goodbye	*to tell a lie*
	to tell a joke
	to tell me

is very wild. ■ In this use, "scenery" is usually a positive word, describing something beautiful or impressive. **2** The things that are on stage during a performance: *The scenery in "Cirque du Soleil" is amazing.* ■ The plural is "sceneries".

scent /sent/ [uncountable noun] **1** A smell, usually a pleasant one perfume: *The scent of those flowers is very strong.* **2** A liquid that makes you smell nice: *Whenever I smell that scent I think of my grandmother.*

scented /ˈsentɪd/ [adjective] Having a pleasant smell: *There was a rose scented ambience at the meeting room.* ■ Compare with "odorless" (without a smell).

†**schedule** US: /ˈskedʒuːl/ UK: /ˈʃedjuːl/ [uncountable noun] **1** A plan that says when somebody is going to do certain things: *I've got my vacation schedule organized so that I know what I'm doing every day.* **2** A timetable: *Have you got the new train schedule from Dallas to Houston?* **3 behind schedule** Late: *I'm a bit behind schedule in my studying, but I'll catch up at the weekend.* **4 on schedule** At the correct time, according to plan: *The building of the new sports center is on schedule, so it should be open by the summer.*

†**scheme** /skiːm/ [countable noun] A plan: *We're trying to think of a scheme to make money for our school trip.*

scholar US: /ˈskɑː.lɚ/ UK: /ˈskɒl.əʳ/ [countable noun] A person who has studied a lot: *Professor Frampton is one of the most important scholars in this field.*

scholarship /ˈskɑl·ərˌʃɪp/ [countable noun] Money given to a student: *Megan has a scholarship to study music at Harvard University.*

†**school** /skuːl/ [countable noun] **1** A place where children learn: *We go to school in the town next to ours.* ◉ See picture at **street**. **2 boarding school** See **boarding school**. **3 elementary school** See **elementary school**. **4 secondary school** See **secondary school**.

†**science** /saɪənts/ [uncountable noun] The study of nature and the world: *Science is one of my favorite subjects at school.* ■ Be careful with the pronunciation of this word! The first syllable rhymes with "my" and the second "e" is not pronounced.

science fiction [uncountable noun] Stories about the future: *I like science fiction movies a lot.* ■ "Sci-fi" is an abbreviation for "science fiction". See box at **abbreviations**.

†**scientific** /ˌsaɪənˈtɪf.ɪk/ [adjective] Referring to science: *My cousin Nancy is doing scientific research at Durham University.* ■ Be careful with the pronunciation of this word! The first syllable rhymes with "my".

†**scientist** /ˈsaɪən.tɪst/ [countable noun] A person who works in science: *Mr. Quentin is a scientist and he works for the Department of Defense.* ■ Be careful with the pronunciation of this word! The first syllable rhymes with "my".

sci-fi /ˈsaɪ.faɪ/ [uncountable noun] See **science fiction**. ■ See box at **abbreviations**.

†**scissors** /ˈsɪz·ərz/ [plural noun] An instrument for cutting paper and so on: *Can you give me some scissors to cut this paper with?* ◉ **See page 456.**

scold US: /skoʊld/ UK: /skəʊld/ [verb] To tell somebody off: *The teacher scolded the children for being disobedient.*

scooter /ˈskuːtər/ [countable noun] **1** A small motorcycle: *My older brother has just bought himself a scooter with his savings.* **2** A board with wheels and a thing to hold onto: *When my mom was little she had a scooter that she shared with her two sisters.*

†**score**[1] /skɔːr/ [countable noun] **1** The number of points or goals in a game: *At half-time the score was 3-2.* **2** A written representation of a piece of music which shows all its notes, parts and instruments: *The piano player had the score of the symphony he was playing in front of him.*

score[2] /skɔːr/ [verb] To get a point or a goal: *In the last minute Frank scored and we won the game.*

scorn[1] /skɔːn/ [uncountable noun] Not having respect for somebody or something: *My uncle Colin always treats our ideas with scorn. He's very negative.*

scorn[2] [verb] To show no respect for somebody or something: *Colonizers often scorned the language and culture of the people they conquered.*

Scorpio US: /ˈskɔːr.pi.oʊ/ UK: /ˈskɔː.pi.əʊ/ [uncountable noun] A sign of the zodiac: *If your birthday is between October 23rd and November 21st, you're a Scorpio.* ■ Be careful. "Scorpio" has a capital "S".

scorpion /ˈskɔr·pi·ən/ [countable noun] A small animal with a sting in its tail: *The sting of some kinds of scorpions can cause death to humans.*

scotch® tape [countable noun] A transparent tape that is used for sticking things together: *Pass me the scotch tape and we'll stick this poster on the wall.* ■ In British English they say "Sello® tape".

Scottish US: /ˈskɑː.t̬ɪʃ/ UK: /ˈskɒt.ɪʃ/ [adjective] Referring to Scotland: *The Scottish countryside is very beautiful.* ■ Be careful. "Scottish" has a capital "S". For people the singular is "a Scot", "a Scotsman" or "a Scotswoman" and the plural is "the Scots".

Scout /skaʊt/ [countable noun] A boy who belongs to a youth group: *It rained every time I went camping with the Scouts.* ■ Be careful! "Scout" has a capital "S". ■ We also say "Boy Scout". ■ Girls belong to a similar youth group called the "Girls Scout" in the United States or "Guides" in Great Britain.

scramble /ˈskræmbl/ [verb] To move quickly but with difficulty: *They scrambled up a tree when they saw the bull.*

scrambled eggs [uncountable noun] Eggs mixed together and stirred as they are cooked in butter: *Let's have some scrambled eggs on toast for breakfast.* See picture at **egg**.

scrap /skræp/ [countable noun] **1** A small piece of something: *I wrote Gerry's address on a scrap of paper and now I've lost it.* **2** A fight: *He got into a scrap.*

scrapbook /ˈskræp.bʊk/ [countable noun] A book where you stick papers and pictures: *I made a scrapbook about my visit to San Francisco.*

scrape /skreɪp/ [verb] **1** To pass an object across something: *I scraped the paint stain on the table with a knife.* **2** To hurt yourself against a rough surface: *I fell off my bike and scraped my knee badly.*

scraps /skræps/ [uncountable noun] Something left over: *We feed our cat on the scraps that we leave after meals.*

†**scratch**[1] /skrætʃ/ [countable noun] A cut made with a sharp thing like a cat's claw: *How did you get that scratch?*

scratch[2] /skrætʃ/ [verb] **1** To cut or to mark something with a sharp thing: *Don't pull the cat's tail or she'll scratch you.* **2** To move your fingernails over part of your skin: *The old man thought for a while and scratched his head.*

scream[1] /skriːm/ [countable noun] A shout in a high voice: *My mom gave a scream when she saw my brother's haircut.*

scream[2] /skriːm/ [verb] To shout in a high voice: *Tessie screamed when she found a spider in the bathtub.*

screech /skriːtʃ/ [verb] To make a loud, high sound: *When he uses the brakes, the car makes a terrible screeching sound.*

†**screen** /skriːn/ [countable noun] **1** A flat thing that you can see images on: *The screen in this movie theater is very big.* **See page 442.** **2** A thin wall that you can move: *When I was taken into hospital the nurses put me in a bed with a screen round it.*

†**screw**[1] /skruː/ [countable noun] A piece of metal in the form of a spiral used to hold two things together: *Just give the screw another turn and it'll be fine!*

screw[2] /skruː/ [verb] **1** To fix two things together with a screw: *Can you help me screw this mirror to the wall?* **2** To turn something round so that it fits another thing: *Make sure you screw the top of that jar on properly.*

screwdriver /ˈskruˌdraɪ·vər/ [countable noun] A tool used for screwing things: *We gave my uncle an electric screwdriver for his birthday.*

scribble /ˈskrɪbl/ [verb] To write marks carelessly on something: *Don't scribble on the whiteboard while I'm out.*

script [countable noun] The plot of a film or any other story: *The writers took three months to develop the script of the film.*

scroll [verb] To move the text or images on a computer screen in a particular direction: *Scroll down the text so that I can see the end of the page, please. You can use the wheel on the mouse to scroll up the photos.*

scrotum US: /ˈskroʊ.t̬əm/ UK: /ˈskrəʊ.təm/ [countable noun] A bag of skin containing the testicles: *The scrotum hangs behind the penis.* ■ The plural is "scrotums" or "scrota".

scrub /skrʌb/ [verb] To rub something hard with a brush and water to clean it: *When we moved into the new house the floors were so dirty that we had to scrub them.* ■ Be careful with the spelling of these forms: "scrubbed", "scrubbing".

scruffy /ˈskrʌf.i/ [adjective] Untidy, dirty looking: *Sam is very scruffy. He looks like he's been through a bush backwards.*

scuba diving /ˈskuː.bəˌdaɪ.vɪŋ/ [uncountable noun] Underwater swimming with an oxygen tank: *My dad takes me scuba diving when we go on vacation.*

sculpt /skʌlpt/ [verb] To create or represent something by carving or molding materials such as wood, stone or clay: *Lynda is sculpting a figure out of wood.*

sculptor /ˈskʌlp·tər/ [countable noun] An artist who makes sculptures: *Michelangelo, one of the greatest artists of all time, was a painter, poet, architect and sculptor.*

sculpture /ˈskʌlp·tʃər/ [countable noun] **1** A shape or figure made from wood, clay or other material: *Have you seen the new sculpture they've put in the town center?* **2** The art of making shapes or figures from wood, clay or other material: *Today's art class was about Roman sculpture.*

†**sea** /siː/ [uncountable noun] **1** The water that surrounds the land on earth: *The sea covers three-quarters of the earth's surface.* **2** A large, salty area of water: *The Baltic Sea is sometimes frozen over.* **3 at sea** Traveling on the sea: *My cousin's a sailor and he spends much of his life at sea.* ■ When we say the name of the sea, for example "the Mediterranean Sea", "sea" is written with a capital "s".

seafood /ˈsiː.fuːd/ [uncountable noun] Sea creatures that you eat: *Whenever we go on vacation to the beach, we eat a lot of seafood.*

seagull /ˈsiː.gʌl/ [countable noun] A large bird that lives near the sea: *Seagulls live off fish that they get* *from the sea.* ■ "Gull" is short for "seagul". See page 429.

sea horse US: /'si,hɔrs/ [countable noun] A small fish which has a head and a neck that look like those of a horse: *The sea horse swims in a vertical position.*

†**seal**[1] /siːl/ [countable noun] A sea animal that lives near cold seas: *All seals are superb swimmers but they are clumsy on land.* See page 428.

seal[2] /siːl/ [verb] To close something firmly: *Letters used to be sealed by putting some hot wax on the back of the envelope.*

seaman /'siːmən/ [countable noun] A sailor: *There are many seamen in port at the moment.* ■ The plural is "seamen".

†**search**[1] /sɜːtʃ/ [countable noun] Looking carefully for somebody or something: *After a two day search, the climbers were found sheltering in a cave.* ■ The plural is "searches".

search[2] /sɜːtʃ/ [verb] To look carefully for somebody or something: *We searched everywhere but couldn't find my mom's ring.*

seashell /'siː.ʃel/ [countable noun] The shell of a small sea animal: *Let's go and look for sea shells and take them home with us.*

seashore /'si,ʃɔr/, /-,ʃoʊr/ [uncountable noun] The land next to the edge of the sea: *I love walking along the seashore early in the morning.*

seasick /'siː.sɪk/ [adjective] Feeling ill because you are on a boat: *I felt very seasick on the boat from Bahamas to Miami.*

seaside /'siː.saɪd/ [uncountable noun] The beach: *My little sister loves the seaside.*

†**season** /'siː.zᵊn/ [countable noun] **1** One of the four parts of the year: *There are four seasons in the year: spring, summer, fall and winter.* **2** A particular period of the year for something: *The soccer season starts in August and finishes in May.*

†**seat** /siːt/ [countable noun] **1** A place to sit: *I offered my seat to an old lady on the bus this morning.* **2** **take a seat** To sit down: *Please come in and take a seat.*

seat belt [countable noun] A belt that you wear in a car: *All new cars are fitted with seat belts.*

seawater [uncountable noun] Water from the sea: *Every kilogram of seawater has approximately 35 grams of salt.*

seaweed /'siː.wiːd/ [uncountable noun] A dark green plant that grows in the sea: *The propeller of our boat got caught in the seaweed and we couldn't move it.*

†**second**[1] [noun and adjective] Referring to two: *February is the second month of the year.* ■ "Second" can also be written "2nd".

second[2] /'sekənd/ [countable noun] **1** A short measure of time: *There are sixty seconds in a minute.* **2** A moment: *Just wait a second.*

secondary /'sek·ən,der·i/ [adjective] **1** Second in importance or position, or happening after something else: *We should forget about secondary issues and solve the main problem first.* **2** Referring to the part of children's education after elementary school: *Children usually start secondary school at the age of eleven.*

secondary school [countable noun] A school for students between eleven and eighteen years old: *Irene's going to secondary school next September.* ■ Compare with "institute" (an organization where people do a particular activity or the buildings used for such activity).

second class[1] /,sekənd'klɑːs/ [adjective] Not of the best or fastest type: *His previous school was second class and he's much happier in his current one.*

second class[2] [noun and adverb] The less comfortable and cheaper part of a train, plane or other vehicle: *We traveled second class from Orlando to Chicago.*

secondhand US: /'sek·ənd'hænd/ [adjective and adverb] Previously owned by somebody else, used: *My car is secondhand.*

secondly /'sek.ᵊnd.li/ [adverb] In second place: *Firstly, they've given me the job, and secondly, we're going to have a party to celebrate!*

†**secret** /'siː.krət/ [countable noun] **1** Something that you don't tell other people: *We're having a party for Teresa's birthday but it's a secret so don't tell anybody.* **2** **to keep a secret** Not to tell anybody a secret: *Don't tell Betty because she can't keep a secret.*

†**secretary** /'sek·rɪ,ter·i/ [countable noun] **1** A person who makes appointments, answers the phone, types letters and so on: *Alison works as a secretary in a big company.* ■ The plural is "secretaries". **2** **Secretary of State** An important member of the government: *The Secretary of State for Agriculture resigned yesterday after a meeting with the Prime Minister.*

†**section** /'sek.ʃᵊn/ [countable noun] A part of something: *The school library has a good reference section.*

sector /'sek·tər/ [countable noun] A distinct part of a society, economy or activity: *Unemployment in the construction sector has grown in the last few years.*

†**secure** /sɪ'kjʊər/ [adjective] **1** Firmly fixed: *We'll have to get that bicycle seat repaired; it's not very secure.* **2** Protected and safe: *Where is a secure place to hide the presents?*

†**security** /sɪ'kjʊər·ɪ·ţi/ [uncountable noun] Being safe: *The police are in charge of the security of the population.*

sediment [uncountable noun] The material that settles at the bottom of a liquid.

sedimentary /ˌsed·əˈmen·tə·ri/, /-ˈmen·tri/ [adjective] Referring to a rock which is made from the sediment that is left by the action of water, ice or wind: *Limestone and sandstone are sedimentary rocks.*

sedimentation /ˌsed.ɪ.menˈteɪ.ʃən/ [uncountable noun] The natural process by which sediment is formed: *Sandstone is a rock formed by sedimentation.*

†see, saw, seen /siː/ [verb] **1** To recognize with your eyes: *I can't see the words on the whiteboard from the back of the classroom.* **2** To watch something: *What film shall we go and see?* ■ Be careful! We say: "I watch television". (We don't say: "I see television"). Compare also with "look[1]" (to turn your eyes to something). ■ See box at **watch**. **3** To understand: *Yes, OK, I see.* **4** To go to somebody or somewhere: *You should see a doctor.* **5 I'll see** An expression that you say when you want to think about something before deciding: *"Ann, can I borrow your jacket?" "Hmmm, I'll see".* **6 Let's see** Something that you say when you are thinking: *Now, what candies shall I buy? Let's see.* **7 Long time no see** Something that you say when you meet somebody that you haven't seen for a long time: *Long time no see, I didn't know you came back from your year abroad!* ■ This use is informal. **8 See you** Goodbye: *Well, I have to go now. See you!* ■ This use is informal. **9 to see that** To ensure that something happens: *See that the windows are closed when you go.*

▶ **PHRASAL VERBS** · **to see (something) in** To celebrate the start of something the moment when it happens: *I will see the New Year in with my family.* · **to see (somebody) off** **1** To go to a train station, airport or harbor to say goodbye to somebody: *I saw him off at the airport.* **2** To get rid of somebody who is an irritant or a threat, or to beat a rival: *She soon saw off the tax inspector.* · **to see to (somebody or something)** To take the responsibility to do something or to attend to somebody: *Can you see to the person who is at the door?; I will see to buying the cake.* · **to see (something) through** To do something even if it is difficult or takes a long time: *Organizing this trip is more complicated than I thought, but I am going to see it through.* · **to see through (somebody)** To perceive what somebody is really like, not what they try to appear: *I saw through him from the start.*

†seed /siːd/ [countable noun] A small thing that a plant grows from: *We planted the seeds in the garden.*

†seek, sought, sought /siːk/ [verb] To look for somebody or something: *Seek the truth!* ■ We usually say "look for".

†seem /siːm/ [verb] To appear to be: *Paul seems nice but he can sometimes be in a very bad mood.*

seen /siːn/ Past participle of **see**.

seesaw /ˈsiˌsɔ/ [countable noun] A long piece of wood or metal with seats at each end that children play on: *You get on one end of the seesaw and I'll get on the other. Come on! Up, down; up, down!*

segment /ˈseg.mənt/ [countable noun] One of the parts that something can be divided into: *All of the segments combined make up the whole.*

seismic /ˈsaɪzmɪk/ [adjective] **1** Referring to or caused by earthquakes: *Seismic activity is monitored by earthquake prediction centers.* **2** Having great, revolutionary or negative effects: *The invention of the wheel was a seismic shift in human development.*

seize /siːz/ [verb] To take hold of somebody or something strongly: *The policeman seized the thief when he came round the corner.*

seldom /ˈsel.dəm/ [adverb] Not often, not frequently: *I have an uncle in Australia, but we seldom hear from him.* ■ "Seldom" goes before ordinary verbs and after auxiliary verbs: "I can seldom go out at weekends". ■ The same meaning: "rarely".

†select /sɪˈlekt/ [verb] To choose somebody or something: *If you could go to any country in the world, which one would you select?*

†selection /sɪˈlek.ʃən/ [countable noun] A number of things that have been selected: *What a fantastic selection of comics they've got in the new store!*

†self /self/ [countable noun] Being or character: *I'm feeling a bit miserable today and I'm not my usual self at all.* ■ The plural is "selves".

self-confident /ˌselfˈkɑn·fə·dənt/ [adjective] Sure of yourself: *It's a good thing to be self-confident when you're learning to speak a language.*

self-evaluation [countable noun] The act of evaluating oneself: *Employees were asked to do a self-evaluation of their work.*

selfish /ˈsel.fɪʃ/ [adjective] Thinking only of yourself: *What a selfish person Thomas is! He never considers anybody else's feelings.*

self-service [countable noun] A place where you take things yourself: *They've changed the system of lunches at school. Now it's a self-service and you just help yourself.*

†sell, sold, sold /sel/ [verb] To give something in exchange for money: *She sold me her mountain bike for $50.*

Sello® tape UK: /ˈseləʊteɪp/ [uncountable noun] See **scotch® tape**. ■ This word is British English. ■ Be careful. "Sello® tape" has a capital "S".

a b c d e f g h i j k l m n o p q r s t u v w x y z

semi- /semi-/ [prefix] An addition to the beginning of a word that usually means "half": *A semicircle is a half of a circle.*

semibreve /'sem.i.briːv/ [countable noun] A musical note which has the time value of two minims: *Semibreves are represented by an oval ring.* See page 460.

semicircle /'sem·i,sɜr·kəl/ [countable noun] Half a circle: *We all stood on stage in a semicircle and sang the song.*

semicolon US: /'sem.i,koʊ.lən/ UK: /,sem.i'kəʊ.lɒn/ [countable noun] A mark [;] used in writing: *You use a semicolon to separate two phrases that are closely connected to each other.*

semi-final /,sem.i'faɪ.nᵊl/ [countable noun] One of the two games played to decide who will be in the final: *If we win this semi-final we will be in the final!*

seminal /'sem.ɪ.nəl/ [adjective] **1** Having great influence on later ideas, developments or creative work: *Frank wrote a seminal article on social networks.* **2** Referring to sperm: *Seminal fluids are produced by the male sexual glands.*

semiquaver [countable noun] A musical note which has the time value of a sixteenth of a semibreve: *Semiquavers have two tails on the stem.* See page 460.

†**Senate** /'sen.ət/ [uncountable noun] One of the houses that forms a government in the United States and other countries: *The Senate House is in a beautiful part of the city.* ■ Be careful. "Senate" has a capital "S".

†**senator** /'senətər/ [countable noun] A member of the Senate: *The visit of the American senators was not a success.* ■ Be careful! "Senator" has a capital "S" when it is followed by a name: "Senator Johnson".

†**send,** sent, sent /send/ [verb] **1** To make a thing go somewhere: *I always send a birthday card to my grandma on her birthday.* **2** To make a person go somewhere: *My mom was sent to an all girls boarding school when she was a child.*
▸ **PHRASAL VERBS** · **to send off 1** To put something in the post: *We'll have to send the letter off today or it won't get there on time.* **2** To make a player go off the field: *Geoffrey was sent off for swearing at the referee.*

sender /'sendər·/ [countable noun] A person who sends something: *I wonder who is writing to Harry; let's look and see if the sender's name is on the envelope.*

†**senior**[1] [adjective] **1** Older: *Sometimes the senior students help the teachers with the younger students in the dining room.* **2** More important: *Mike's father is a senior officer in the Navy.* ■ See box at **abbreviations**.

†**senior**[2] [countable noun] A student in the fourth year of high school or college: *My dad got some scholarships for college when he was a senior in high school.*

senior citizen [countable noun] A person who is over sixty-five years old: *My grandparents have a special bus pass for senior citizens.*

sensation /sen'seɪ.ʃᵊn/ [noun] **1** A feeling: *I always get a strange sensation when I go into that old house.* **2** Interest and excitement: *Molly's new dress caused a sensation at the school party.*

sensational /sen'seɪ.ʃᵊn.ᵊl/ [adjective] Very exciting: *Have you heard the sensational news about the concert?*

†**sense**[1] /sens/ [noun] **1** The ability to see, hear, smell, taste or touch: *We have five senses: hearing, sight, taste, smell and feeling.* **2** The ability to think sensibly: *Polly has got no sense at all. What did she do that for?* **3** The ability to understand something: *Colin has a great sense of justice and always stands up for the younger students.* **4** common sense See "common sense" in the word **common.** **5** to make sense To mean something: *This sentence you wrote doesn't make sense. What do you mean?*

sense[2] /sens/ [verb] To feel something: *We could sense that the teacher was upset.*

†**sensible** /'sent.sɪ.bl̩/ [adjective] Having common sense: *Mary's a very sensible girl. She would never do anything silly.*

†**sensitive** /'sen·sə·t̬ɪv/ [adjective] **1** Easily affected by things: *Don't let Alison see that movie. She's very sensitive and would be upset by it.* **2** Concerned about other people's feelings: *Why did Ray say that about Jane being fat? That wasn't very sensitive of him, was it?*

sensitivity /,sen·sə'tɪv·ɪ·t̬i/ [uncountable noun] **1** The quality of being sensitive: *Tom showed great sensitivity towards his brother in that situation.* **2** The tendency to be offended: *Such sensitivity to people's comments is a problem for him.* ■ We say: "sensitivity **to** (something)". ■ The plural is "sensitivities".

sensory /'sen·sə·ri/ [adjective] Referring to the physical senses: *It is very important to stimulate the baby's sensory perceptions.*

sent /sent/ Past tense and past participle forms of **send.**

†**sentence**[1] /'sentəns/ [countable noun] **1** A group of words ending with a period, a question mark or an exclamation mark: *This example is a sentence.* **2** A punishment given in a court of law: *The man was given a three month prison sentence for robbery.*

sentence[2] /'sentəns/ [verb] To give somebody a punishment in a court of law: *The thief was sentenced to five years imprisonment.*

sepal US: /'siː.pəl/ UK: /'sep.əl/ [countable noun] One of the small green leaves that surround and protect the petals of a flower: *The sepals form the calyx of the flower.* 👁 **See page 433.**

separate[1] /'sepərət/ [adjective] Apart or not together: *When we were at camp, the boys and girls slept in separate dormitories.*

†**separate[2]** /'sepəreɪt/ [verb] **1** To move one thing or one person away from another: *The teacher separated Sophie and me for talking in class.* **2** To stop being together: *Miriam's parents have just separated.* **3** To be between one thing and another: *The Baltic Sea separates Scandinavia and Russia.*

separately /'sep·ər·ət·li/ [adjective] Not together: *Miss Thomas, shall we do this problem together or separately?*

separation /ˌsep·ə'reɪ·ʃən/ [countable noun] The act of moving things or persons apart, or the situation of being apart: *For friends, separation can be painful.*

†**September** /sep'tem·bər/ [noun] The ninth month of the year: *My sister's birthday is in September.* ■ Be careful! "September" has a capital "S". 👁 See picture at **calendar**.

sequence /'siː.kwənts/ [countable noun] **1** A series of related events that occur in a particular order: *Let's move on to the next sequence of exercises.* **2** The order in which a series of related events occur, or are done: *When you do an experiment, you must follow a particular sequence.*

sequoia /sɪ'kwɔɪə/ [countable noun] A large evergreen tree which grows on the west coast of America: *The sequoia is one of the tallest trees on earth.*

sergeant /'sɑr·dʒənt/ [countable noun] An officer in the army or in the police: *Sergeant Robinson is in charge of the drug department in this police station.*

serial /'sɪər·i·əl/ [countable noun] A story that is told in parts: *My dad always listens to a serial on the radio about life in an American town.* ■ Compare with "series" (a number of programs on the radio or television of the same type).

†**series** US: /'sɪr.iːz/ UK: /'sɪə.riːz/ [countable noun] **1** A number of things of the same type: *I'm collecting a series of articles about Hollywood that is being published in the Sunday papers.* **2** A number of programs on the radio or television of the same type: *Are you watching the new Nature series on television?* ■ Be careful with the pronunciation of this word! ■ The plural is also "series". ■ Compare with "serial" (a story that is told in parts).

†**serious** /'sɪr·i·əs/ [adjective] **1** Not funny or joking, solemn: *Jack's a very serious person; he never smiles, does he?* **2** Bad, important, worrying: *Drug taking is a very serious problem in some areas of the country.*

sermon /'sɜr·mən/ [countable noun] A talk that a priest gives: *Father Murphy gave a sermon about the poverty in the world.*

†**servant** /'sɜr·vənt/ [countable noun] A person who works in somebody's house: *Old Mrs. Smith used to be a servant in the Duke's house when she was young.*

†**serve** US: /sɝːv/ UK: /sɜːv/ [verb] **1** To attend customers in a store: *Are you being served, Madam?* **2** To give prepared food to somebody: *Can I serve you some more pudding?* **3** To work actively for a country, the army voluntary organization and so on: *Frank and Anne served as volunteers in the Red Cross last summer.* **4** **it serves you right** Words you say when you think the person deserves something negative that has happened to them: *I told you to listen in class and now you've failed the test. It serves you right for not paying attention.*

†**service** /'sɜr·vɪs/ [noun] **1** Treatment that you receive in a store, restaurant and so on: *The service is not very good in this store, is it?* **2** The work that somebody does in a company: *My grandfather got a gold watch from his company when he retired after fifty years' service.* **3** A religious ceremony: *We went to the early morning service on Christmas Day.* **4** The organization that provides buses, hospitals, schools and so on: *The new Town Council say that they are going to improve the bus service.* **5** **civil service** See **civil service.** **6** **the armed services** or **the services** The army, navy and air force: *There used to be a special radio program for the people in the armed services working in other countries.* ■ In this use, the same meaning: "the armed forces".

service station [countable noun] A place where you can buy gasoline and other things for your car: *We drove into a service station to fill up.* ■ The same meaning: "gas station". ■ Compare with "garage" (also por repairs).

serviette /ˌsɜr·vi'et/ [countable noun] A piece of cloth or paper to clean your hands or lips when you are eating: *Don't forget to buy some paper serviettes when you go to the store.* ■ The same meaning: "napkin".

†**session** /'seʃ.ᵊn/ [countable noun] A time when people meet to do something: *Why don't you bring your guitar along to the music session we're having at my house tonight?*

†**set[1]** /set/ [countable noun] **1** A number of things which go together: *We gave my mom a set of earrings and a necklace for her birthday.* **2** Apparatus for receiving television or radio: *Our television set is broken.*

a b c d e f g h i j k l m n o p q r s t u v w x y z

3 Part of a tennis match, won by gaining a certain number of games: *Sarah won the first set 6-3.*

set², **set**, **set** /set/ [verb] **1** To put something down: *He set the bowl of soup down carefully on the table.* **2** To fix or establish something: *Have they set the date for the meeting?* **3** To give somebody some work: *The teacher set us some very difficult exercises to do for homework.* **4** To go down, when talking about the sun: *The sun rises in the East and sets in the West.* **5** To go solid: *Wait for the jelly to set and then put it into the fridge.* **6** **to set fire to (something)** See "to set fire to (something)" in the word **fire¹**. **7** **to set free** See "to set free" in the word **free¹**. **8** **to set the table** To place on the table the plates, knives, forks and so on before you eat: *You set the table and I'll do the dishes afterwards.* ■ The same meaning: "to lay the table".
▶ **PHRASAL VERBS** · **to set (something) up** To start or to establish something: *This company has set up a new store in San Francisco.* ■ Be careful with the spelling of this form: "setting".

set³ /set/ [adjective] Which cannot be changed: *In my school the meals are at certain set times.*

set-square [countable noun] Instrument to help you draw lines at particular angles: *I need a set-square and a compass for my technical drawing class.* 👁 **See page 456.**

setting /ˈset̬·ɪŋ/ [countable noun] The place where something happens: *They decided that the church in the mountains would be the perfect setting for their wedding.*

⁺**settle** /ˈset̬·ə·l/ [verb] **1** To go and live permanently somewhere: *My dad's friend went to settle in Australia when he was young.* **2** To come to an agreement after a dispute: *Mary and I settled our argument after talking about it.* **3** To come to rest on something: *That robin often settles on the tree outside our window.*
▶ **PHRASAL VERBS** · **to settle down** **1** To become calm and quiet: *Come on. Settle down now, children' said the teacher.* **2** To make oneself comfortable: *The cat settled down in front of the fire for the evening.* **3** To lead a quiet life in one place: *Julia finally settled down in Italy after living in five different countries.*

settlement /ˈset̬·ə·l·mənt/ [countable noun] **1** An agreement: *After very long discussions, the workers and the management reached a settlement.* **2** A place where a group of people have settled: *The towns and cities in the west of the United States started as small settlements.*

settler [countable noun] A person who settles in a country that is being newly populated: *They were among the early settlers on the east coast of America.*

⁺**seven** /ˈsev.ᵊn/ [noun, adjective and pronoun] The number 7: *Seven is a lucky number.*

seventeen /ˌsev.ᵊnˈtiːn/ [noun, adjective and pronoun] The number 17: *My sister Pat is seventeen years old.*

seventeenth /ˌsev.ᵊnˈtiːntθ/ [noun and adjective] Referring to seventeen: *St Patrick's day is on the seventeenth of March.* ■ "Seventeenth" can also be written "17th".

seventh /ˈsev.ᵊntθ/ [noun and adjective] Referring to seven: *July is the seventh month of the year.* ■ "Seventh" can also be written "7th".

seventieth /ˈsev·ə·n·ti·əθ/ [noun and adjective] Referring to seventy: *It's the seventieth anniversary of the death of our local poet, Henry Harris.* ■ "Seventieth" can also be written "70th".

seventy /ˈsev·ə·n·ti/ [noun, adjective and pronoun] The number 70: *My grandfather will be seventy tomorrow.*

⁺**several** /ˈsev·rəl/, /-ər·əl/ [adjective and pronoun] More than a few, but not very many: *Isn't Anna lucky? She's been to Europe several times.*

⁺**severe** /səˈvɪr/ [adjective] **1** Not soft and gentle, hard: *Our teacher is quite severe sometimes but we all like her.* **2** Serious or quite bad: *Maria spent two months ill in bed with a severe lung infection.*

⁺**sew**, **sewed**, **sewn** US: /soʊ/ UK: /səʊ/ [verb] To fix material together with needle and thread: *I'm sewing some buttons on my shirt.* ■ The same meaning: "stitch²".

sewed Past tense of **sew**.

⁺**sewing** /ˈsoʊ·ɪŋ/ [uncountable noun] Something that somebody sews: *Aunt Meg put her sewing down and went to answer the door.*

sewing machine [countable noun] A machine that you sew with: *My grandmother's just bought a new sewing machine.*

sewn /səʊn/ Past participle of **sew**.

⁺**sex** /seks/ [uncountable noun] **1** One of two groups, male or female, into which humans, animals and plants can be divided: *What sex are the kittens? Two are male and one is female.* ■ In this use the plural is "sexes". **2** Making love: *It is much easier to get information about sex now than it was some years ago.* **3** **sex appeal** See "sex appeal" in the word **appeal¹**.

sexual /ˈsek.sjʊəl/ [adjective] Referring to sex or to reproduction: *The uterus is one of the female sexual organs.*

⁺**shade¹** /ʃeɪd/ [uncountable noun] **1** A place where direct sunlight does not reach: *Let's get in the shade under this tree. It's very hot in the sun.* ■ Compare with "shadow" (a dark shape that is made by something blocking the light). **2** A variety of a particular color: *I love that shade of blue.* 👁 See picture at **shadow**.

shade² /ʃeɪd/ [verb] To protect from sunlight: *John shaded his eyes from the sun with his hand.*

†**shadow** /ˈʃæd·oʊ/ [countable noun] A dark shape that is made by something blocking the light: *We made shadows on the wall that looked like different animals.* ■ Compare with "shade[1]" (a place sunlight does not reach).

SHADOW

shadow shade

†**shake, shook, shaken** /ʃeɪd/ [verb] **1** To move something about quickly from side to side: *Shake the can of paint before you open it.* **2** To move from side to side or up and down, to tremble: *Hannah was so afraid that she shook with fear.* **3 to shake hands** To move somebody's hand up and down in greeting or in peace: *Sid shook hands with everyone at the party.* **4 to shake your head** To move your head from side to side: *She shook her head when she heard the question, and said "no".*

shaken Past participle of **shake**.

†**shall** /ʃæl, ʃəl/ [verb] **1** A word that you can use instead of "will", with "I" and "we" only, in the future form: *I shall tell you all about my vacation when I get back.* ■ We usually say "will". **2** A word that you can use instead of "will", with "I" and "we" only, to make suggestions or to ask for suggestions: *Shall we go?* ■ The verb after "shall" is in the infinitive without "to".

†**shallow** /ˈʃæl·oʊ/ [adjective] Not deep: *Stay in the shallow part of the pool because you can't swim very well yet.*

†**shame** /ʃeɪm/ [uncountable noun] **1** A feeling of having done something silly or wrong: *When her mother discovered what she had done, Linda was filled with shame.* **2** A pity: *It's such a shame that you can't come to my party.*

shameful /ˈʃeɪm.fəl/ [adjective] Very wrong: *I think it's shameful the way some people treat animals.*

shampoo /ʃæmˈpuː/ [uncountable noun] A thick liquid used for washing your hair: *That shampoo smells of lemon.*

shamrock /ˈʃæm·rɑk/ [countable noun] A type of small plant with three round leaves on each stem: *The four leaves shamrock is the symbol of good luck.*

shandy /ˈʃæn.di/ [countable noun] A drink made by mixing beer and lemonade: *I'll have a shandy, please.* ■ The plural is "shandies".

shank /ʃæŋk/ [countable noun] **1** The lower part of the leg, from the knee to the ankle: *Jeff has skinny shanks.* **2** The straight, long and narrow part of a tool: *the shank of the anchor.*

shan't US: /ʃænt/ UK: /ʃɑːnt/ The contraction of "shall not".

†**shape[1]** /ʃeɪp/ [uncountable noun] **1** The appearance form of something: *What a beautiful shape that sculpture is.* ■ In this sense, "shape" is much more common in English than "form". 👁 See page 457. **2 in shape** Physically fit: *I haven't been in good shape since I stopped swimming.* **3 out of shape** Not in the correct condition: *My new sweater's all out of shape. I must have put it in the hot wash by mistake.*

shape[2] /ʃeɪp/ [verb] To give something a form: *I shaped the plasticine into an elephant and gave it to the little boy.*

†**share[1]** /ʃeər/ [countable noun] A part of something: *I took my share of the money and went home.*

share[2] /ʃeər/ [verb] **1** To give out something to different people: *We shared the candies between the children.* **2** To have something with somebody else: *My teacher told me to share a desk with Robert.*

shark US: /ʃɑːrk/ UK: /ʃɑːk/ [countable noun] A large and frightening fish: *Sharks have very powerful jaws and teeth but many of them are not dangerous.* 👁 See page 430.

†**sharp[1]** /ʃɑːp/ [adjective] **1** With the ability to cut: *Be careful with that knife because it's very sharp.* **2** Sudden and strong: *I felt a sharp pain in my side as I ran up the hill.* **3** With an acid taste: *That lemonade's a bit sharp for my taste. I'll have to put some sugar in it.* **4** Quick and clever: *My grandma is quite old but she's still extremely sharp.* **5** Referring to a musical sound which is higher than the true or normal pitch: *The opera singer was singing too sharp.*

sharp[2] /ʃɑːp/ [adverb] Exactly, when talking about a time: *The concert will start at 8 o'clock sharp.*

sharp[3] /ʃɑːp/ [countable noun] A musical note which is raised a semitone higher than the specified pitch: *This piece must be played in C sharp.*

sharpen /ˈʃɑr·pən/ [verb] To make something sharp: *He used a stone to sharpen the knife.*

a b c d e f g h i j k l m n o p q r **s** t u v w x y z

sharply [adverb] **1** Suddenly or in a radical way: *Temperatures are expected to drop sharply in the next few days.* **2** Acutely: *She has a sharply developed sense of humor.* **3** Referring to speaking, severely: *My father spoke sharply to us.* **4** Referring to how somebody dresses, well, elegantly: *Terry was sharply dressed at the dinner.*

shatter US: /ˈʃæt̬.ɚ/ UK: /ˈʃæt.əʳ/ [verb] To break into small pieces: *I dropped the mirror and it shattered on the floor.*

+**shave** /ʃeɪv/ [verb] To cut the hair off your face: *My dad shaves every morning at the same time.*

shaver /ˈʃeɪ·vər/ [countable noun] An electric tool to shave with: *We bought my grandfather a new electric shaver for his birthday but he never uses it.*

shaving [countable noun] The act of cutting hair off with a razor: *My father says that shaving is very tedious.*

shavings /ˈʃeɪvɪŋz/ [plural noun] Very thin pieces cut off a piece of wood or metal: *The floor of the carpenter's workshop was covered in shavings.*

shawl US: /ʃɑːl/ UK: /ʃɔːl/ [countable noun] A piece of cloth that goes over a woman's shoulders: *My grandma always wears a shawl in the winter.*

+**she** /ʃiː, ʃi/ [pronoun] The female person or animal being talked about: *How's your mom? She's much better, thank you.*

sheath /ʃiːθ/ [countable noun] A cover for the sharp blade of a knife or sword: *The knight took the sword out of its sheath.*

sheathe [verb] To put a knife or a sword back into a sheath: *The knight sheathed his sword.*

shed /ʃed/ [countable noun] A building used for keeping things in: *My old bike must be in the shed.*

she'd /ʃid, ʃiːd/ The contraction of "she had" or "she would".

+**sheep** /ʃiːp/ [countable noun] A farm animal kept for its wool, skin and meat: *There are two hundred sheep on my uncle's farm.* ■ The plural is also "sheep". ■ Compare with "lamb" (a young sheep or its meat). 👁 **See page 428.**

+**sheet** /ʃiːt/ [countable noun] **1** A large piece of material that you put on a bed: *My grandma's got some beautiful embroidered sheets.* 👁 See picture at **bedroom**. **2** A flat piece of something: *Give out these sheets of drawing paper, please.*

+**shelf** /ʃelf/ [countable noun] A long flat place for keeping books, plates and so on: *Put that book on the shelf, please.* ■ The plural is "shelves". 👁 See picture at **bathroom**.

+**shell** /ʃel/ [countable noun] The hard outside part of eggs, nuts and some animals: *The tortoise went back into its shell.*

she'll /ʃil, ʃiːl/ The contraction of "she will".

shellfish /ˈʃel.fɪʃ/ [uncountable noun] A sea animal that has a shell: *We had a fantastic meal of shellfish and rice on the beach.* ■ The plural is also "shellfish".

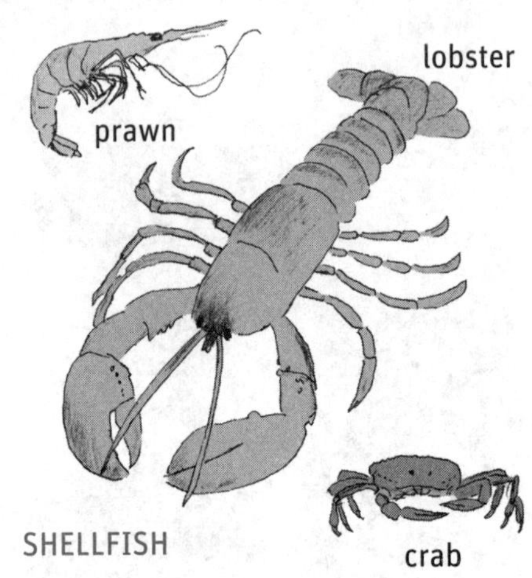

SHELLFISH

+**shelter**[1] /ˈʃeltər/ [countable noun] **1** A place where you go for safety: *In the Second World War, people used to hide from the bombs in special shelters.* **2** Being safe or protected: *We ran into the cave to get shelter from the storm.*

shelter[2] /ˈʃeltər/ [verb] **1** To go somewhere for safety or protection: *We sheltered from the rain under a tree.* **2** To give protection to somebody or something: *My dad's built a high wall to shelter our yard from the sea winds.*

shepherd /ˈʃep·ərd/ [countable noun] A person who looks after sheep: *Shepherds walk long distances taking the sheep from one place to another.*

sheriff /ˈʃer.ɪf/ [countable noun] Chief law officer in a county in the United States, elected by the population: *The sheriff in the cowboy movie chased the horse thieves and caught them.*

she's /ʃiːz, ʃiz/ The contraction of "she is" or "she has".

shield[1] /ʃiːld/ [countable noun] An object to protect somebody or something: *The Roman soldiers held up their shields to protect themselves from the arrows.*

shield[2] /ʃiːld/ [verb] To protect yourself with something: *They shielded themselves from the wind inside the tents.*

shift[1] /ʃɪft/ [countable noun] **1** A change in position or attitude: *There was a shift in public opinion.* **2** A group of people who take turns to do a particular job, or the particular time period they work: *He has to sleep during the day because he is on night shift.* **3** The capitals key on a keyboard: *You have to press shift to write in capitals.* **4** A long straight item of women's underwear: *In the past, many women wore a shift under their dress.*

shift² /ʃɪft/ [verb] **1** To move or to make something or somebody move to a different place: *Please help me to shift these boxes.* **2** To change to a different emphasis, direction or focus: *The war shifted attention away from domestic problems.* ■ We say: "shift (something) **from** somewhere **to** somewhere". **3** To move or leave a place: *That is my seat, so shift yourself!* ■ This use is informal.

†**shine, shone, shone** /ʃaɪn/ [verb] **1** To give light: *The sun was shining when we arrived at the beach.* **2** To be bright: *He polished his boots until they shone.*

shingles /'ʃɪŋ.gl̩z/ [plural noun] A disease that affects the nerves and produces painful pimples on the skin: *The doctor diagnosed the problem as shingles.* ■ The same meaning: "herpes".

shining /'ʃaɪ.nɪŋ/ [adjective] Brilliant: *I have a shining new coin.*

†**shiny** /'ʃaɪ.ni/ [adjective] Bright or polished: *The street was shiny with rain.* ■ The comparative form is "shinier" and the superlative form is "shiniest".

†**ship** /ʃɪp/ [countable noun] A large boat: *I love watching the ships come into harbor.*

shipwreck /'ʃɪp.rek/ [countable noun] An accident at sea: *There was a shipwreck near the coast and several sailors were drowned.*

SHIPWRECK

†**shirt** US: /ʃɝːt/ UK: /ʃɜːt/ [countable noun] An article of clothing: *I bought a really smart shirt for my birthday.*

shiver /'ʃɪv·ər/ [verb] To tremble: *It was so cold at the bus stop that everyone was shivering.*

shoal US: /ʃoul/ UK: /ʃəul/ [countable noun] A large group of fish swimming about: *There were shoals of silver fish in the sea.*

†**shock¹** /ʃɒk/ [countable noun] **1** A bad surprise: *We all had a terrible shock when Grandpa died suddenly.* **2** A pain caused by electricity: *Dry your hands before you touch the plug. You might get a shock.*

shock² /ʃɒk/ [verb] To give somebody a bad surprise: *We were all shocked when the school burned down.*

†**shocking** US: /'ʃɑː.kɪŋ/ UK: /'ʃɒk.ɪŋ/ [adjective] Very wrong and upsetting: *The murder was a shocking crime.*

†**shoe** /ʃuː/ [countable noun] A thing that you wear on your foot: *Do you like my new shoes?* 👁 See picture at **clothes**.

shoelace /'ʃuː.leɪs/ [countable noun] A cord for tying up shoes: *Tie your shoelace up or you'll fall over.*

shoemaker [countable noun] A person who makes or repairs shoes: *I have to take this pair of shoes to the shoemaker.*

shone US: /ʃɑːn/ UK: /ʃɒn/ Past tense and past participle forms of **shine**.

shook /ʃuk/ Past tense of **shake**.

†**shoot, shot, shot** /ʃuːt/ [verb] **1** To send out a bullet, arrow and so on: *The cowboy took out his gun and shot Bad Bill dead.* **2** To move very quickly: *The dog shot past us and ran into the next yard.* **3** To make a movie: *The movie was shot in Italy.*

†**shop¹** /ʃɒp/ [countable noun] A place where you buy things: *My aunt's got a sweet shop in the center of the town.* ■ The same meaning: "store¹".

shop² /ʃɒp/ [verb] To buy things: *My parents always shop in a big supermarket near our house.* ■ Be careful with the spelling of these forms: "shopped", "shopping".

shop assistant [countable noun] See **clerk**. ■ This word is British English.

shoplifter /'ʃɑp,lɪf·tər/ [countable noun] Person who steals things from a shop: *Shops have a big problem with shoplifters.*

†**shopping** US: /'ʃɑː.pɪŋ/ UK: /'ʃɒp.ɪŋ/ [uncountable noun] **1** Buying things: *I'm sorry but I won't be able to meet you this morning. I've got to do the shopping.* **2** The things that you have bought: *John, can you help me put the shopping away?* **3 to go shopping** To go and to buy things: *I really hate going shopping because I get very bored.*

shopping bag [countable noun] A paper or plastic bag used for carrying things: *We put all our shopping in a shopping bag.*

shopping center or **shopping mall** [countable noun] See **mall**.

shop window [countable noun] A window in the front of a shop: *There are some fantastic clothes in that shop window.*

shore /ʃɔːr/ [uncountable noun] The land next to the sea: *My uncle's got a house near the shore.*

†**short** US: /ʃɔːrt/ UK: /ʃɔːt/ [adjective] **1** Not long: *We live a very short distance away from school.* 👁 See pictures at **hair** and **opposite**. **2** Not tall: *Tommy's tall although his parents are short.* 👁 See picture at **opposite**. **3** Not lasting very long: *What a pity that television program is so short because I really enjoy it.* **4 to be short of** Not to have enough of

something: *I'm a bit short of money, so I'll have to wait to buy that CD.* **5** **for short** To use the short way, when saying something: *His name is actually Joseph Patrick, but we all call him Joe for short.*

shortage US: /ˈʃɔːr.t̬ɪdʒ/ UK: /ˈʃɔː.tɪdʒ/ [countable noun] Not enough of something: *There's been such a long drought that there's a shortage of water everywhere.* ■ Be careful with the pronunciation of this word. The "a" is pronounced like the "i" in "did".

shorten /ˈʃɔr·tə·n/ [verb] To make something shorter: *I'm going to ask my aunt to shorten this skirt for me.*

shortly /ˈʃɔrt·li/ [adverb] Soon: *Don't cry, your mom will be here shortly.*

shorts US: /ʃɔːrts/ UK: /ʃɔːts/ [plural noun] Short pants: *I've forgotten my shorts. What can I wear to play soccer?* ■ When we talk about two or more "shorts", we use the word "pairs": "I bought two pairs of shorts". ◉ See picture at **clothes**.

↑**shot**[1] /ʃɒt/ [countable noun] **1** The act of firing a gun: *We all heard the noise of a shot, followed by silence.* **2** A photograph: *Isn't this a great shot of our cat?* ■ This use is informal. **3** A kick, a hit or a throw at goal in a sport: *What a great shot! He's an incredible player.*

shot[2] /ʃɒt/ Past tense and past participle forms of **shoot**.

↑**should** /ʃʊd, ʃəd/ [verb] **1** A word used to say that an action is a good idea or is morally right: *You should go to the doctor if you don't feel well.* **2** A word that you use when you say what you expect to happen: *They should arrive at about eight o'clock.* ■ Be careful! The verb after "should" is in the infinitive without "to".

↑**shoulder** US: /ˈʃoʊl.dɚ/ UK: /ˈʃəʊl.dəʳ/ [countable noun] **1** The part of your body just above your arm: *I hurt my shoulder playing tennis the other day.* ◉ **See page 421.** **2** **shoulder bag** A bag that you hang from one shoulder: *I've got a new shoulder bag. Do you like it?*

should've /ˈʃʊdəv/ The contraction of "should have".

↑**shout**[1] /ʃaʊt/ [countable noun] A word spoken very loudly: *We heard a shout and went outside but there was no one there.*

shout[2] /ʃaʊt/ [verb] To speak very loudly: *Don't shout at me, I can hear you perfectly well.* ■ Be careful! We say "shout **at** (somebody)" when the person shouting is angry or is giving a warning. We say: "shout **to** (somebody)" in other cases: "He shouted to me to come back".

↑**show**[1] /ʃəʊ/ [countable noun] **1** Something that people go and see, like a concert, play and so on: *Are you coming to see the school show?* **2** A number of things together that people go and see: *We're going to see the show of old cars that's on outside the museum next week.* **3** **show business** All the businesses like the films and the theater, that try to entertain people: *My cousin works in a film company in the capital of show business, Hollywood.*

↑**show**[2], showed, shown /ʃəʊ/ [verb] **1** To let a person see something: *I showed my mom and dad my exercise book.* **2** To make something clear: *Can you show me how to do this exercise, please?* **3** To appear or to be noticeable: *John's in love with Sharon and it shows!*

▶ **PHRASAL VERBS** · **to show off** To do something in public so that people will notice and admire you: *Joan always shows off in front of the boys in our class.* · **to show (something) off** To make people look at something you have got that you are proud of: *Albert spent the whole weekend showing off his new bike to everyone.* · **to show up** To arrive: *Harry showed up about half an hour late.*

showed Past tense of **show**[2].

↑**shower** US: /ʃaʊr/ UK: /ʃaʊəʳ/ [countable noun] **1** A place where you stand under running water to wash: *We all went into the showers after the football game.* ◉ See picture at **bathroom**. **2** Washing yourself under water: *I take a shower every morning.* ■ Be careful. We usually say: "to take a shower". **3** A short period of rain: *We waited for the shower to pass and then went out for a walk.*

shown US: /ʃoʊn/ UK: /ʃəʊn/ Past participle of **show**[2].

shrank /ʃræŋk/ Past tense of **shrink**.

shred /ʃred/ [countable noun] A small thin piece of something: *My sock was in shreds when our dog had finished chewing it.*

shriek[1] [countable noun] A noise with a high tone somebody makes when frightened or in pain: *The little boy gave a shriek when he saw the dog running towards him.*

shriek[2] /ʃriːk/ [verb] To make a noise with a high pitch when you are frightened or in pain: *He shrieked when he saw the mouse under the table.*

shrill /ʃrɪl/ [adjective] With a high tone: *The lady who lives next-door to us has got a very shrill voice and we often hear her.*

shrimp /ʃrɪmp/ [countable noun] A very small shellfish with a long tail: *Shrimps can be found all over the world, in shallow and deep waters.*

shrink, shrank, shrunk /ʃrɪŋk/ [verb] To get smaller: *My favorite sweater has shrunk in the wash!*

shrub /ʃrʌb/ [countable noun] A small bush: *My grandpa has all kinds of shrubs in his backyard.* ◉ **See page 432.**

shrug /ʃrʌg/ [verb] To move your shoulders up: *When I asked Anne where she had been, she just shrugged and didn't answer.* ■ Be careful with the spelling of these forms: "shrugged", "shrugging".

a b c d e f g h i j k l m n o p q r s t u v w x y z

shrunk /ʃrʌŋk/ Past participle of **shrink**.

shuffle /ˈʃʌf.l̩/ [verb] **1** To mix cards before you play a game: *Tommy shuffled the cards.* **2** To walk or dance very slowly almost without lifting your feet: *The old man shuffled along the street.*

shut[1] /ʃʌt/ [adjective] Closed: *The store is shut so we'll have to wait until tomorrow.*

ᐩ**shut[2], shut, shut** /ʃʌt/ [verb] **1** To close something: *Can you shut the window, please? It's quite cold in here.* **2** To go into a closed position: *The door shut behind us and we couldn't open it.* **3** To stop something being open: *Mr. Middleton shuts the store at six o'clock every evening.*

▸ **PHRASAL VERBS** · **to shut down** To close and not work any more: *The local glass factory became bankrupt and had to shut down.* · **to shut up** To be quiet: *Can you all shut up and listen!* ■ This expression is informal.

shutter US: /ˈʃʌt̬.ɚ/ UK: /ˈʃʌt.əʳ/ [countable noun] A cover for the outside of a window: *We thought that there was nobody in because all the shutters were closed.*

shuttle /ˈʃʌt̬·ə·l/ [countable noun] A plane or a bus that goes backwards and forwards between two places: *My dad uses the shuttle service between Boston and New York twice a week.*

ᐩ**shy** /ʃaɪ/ [adjective] Uncomfortable with people: *Don't be shy and speak up.* ■ The comparative form is "shyer" and the superlative form is "shyest". 👁 See picture at **emotions**.

shyness /ˈʃaɪ.nəs/ [uncountable noun] Being shy: *You have to try and forget your shyness when you are learning to speak another language.*

ᐩ**sick** /sɪk/ [adjective] **1** Ill: *We had to call the vet to come and look at the sick cows.* **2** **to be sick** To bring up food through your mouth: *My little brother was sick at school and he was sent home.* ■ The same meaning: "to throw up", "to vomit". **3** **to feel sick** To feel that you are going to be sick, to feel ill in your stomach: *I felt sick on the bus on the way to the camp.*

sickness /ˈsɪk.nəs/ [uncountable noun] An illness: *My teacher hasn't been in school this term because of sickness.*

ᐩ**side** /saɪd/ [countable noun] **1** The part of something that is not the top, bottom, front, back or inside: *Go round to the side of the building and you'll see the kitchen entrance on your left.* **2** The edge of something: *There were people selling melons at the side of the road.* **3** One of the surfaces of something: *Turn over the paper and write your paragraph on the other side.* **4** Team: *We all cheered when our side got a goal.* **5** **side by side** Next to each other: *Helen and Anne always sit side by side.*

side table [countable noun] A small low table which is placed next to a bed: *Tom always has a book on his side table.* ■ The same meaning: "night table", "bedside table".

sidewalk /ˈsaɪdˌwɔk/ [countable noun] The part of a street where people walk: *You shouldn't ride your bike on the sidewalk.* ■ In British English they say "pavement". 👁 See picture at **street**.

ᐩ**sideways** /ˈsaɪdweɪz/ [adverb] **1** To one side: *To do this dance, you have to step sideways!* **2** With the side first: *We'll have to try and get the table out of the door sideways.*

sigh[1] [countable noun] A sudden deep breath, showing sadness, relief or other emotion: *"I've got to study for a test tomorrow" said Fred with a sigh.*

sigh[2] /saɪ/ [verb] To take a sudden deep breath because of sadness, relief or other emotion: *Tony sighed with relief when the game was finally over.*

ᐩ**sight** /saɪt/ [countable noun] **1** Something that you see: *Isn't the sun going down over the sea a beautiful sight?* **2** The ability to see: *My mom wears glasses because she's got very poor sight.* **3** **at first sight** As soon as you see something: *My brother says that it was love at first sight when he met Melissa.* **4** **to catch sight** To see something for a short time: *I caught sight of Ken as I was going past his house the other day on the bus.* **5** **the sights** The interesting places to see in a town: *Let's go to Washington D.C. for the day and see the sights.*

sightseeing /ˈsaɪtˌsiː.ɪŋ/ [uncountable noun] Seeing the interesting places: *When we were in Rome we did a lot of sightseeing.*

sign[1] /saɪn/ [verb] To write your name on something: *My dad signed the check and gave it to the bank clerk.* ■ Be careful with the pronunciation of this word! The "i" rhymes with "my".

ᐩ**sign[2]** /saɪn/ [countable noun] **1** A mark with a special meaning: *There are many different signs used in mathematics, like "+".* **2** A thing with words or a picture giving a message: *The road sign says that we have to slow down here.* **3** Something that indicates another thing: *They say that red sky in the morning is a sign of rain.* ■ Be careful with the pronunciation of this word!

ᐩ**signal[1]** /ˈsɪgnəl/ [countable noun] **1** A sign or a gesture: *A green light is a signal that means that we can cross.* **2** Waves that send information: *Cellphones don't work well in places where the signal is weak.*

signal[2] /ˈsɪgnəl/ [verb] To make a signal: *They signaled for us to go to their table.* ■ Be careful with the spelling of these forms: "signalled", "signalling".

ᐩ**signature** /ˈsɪg·nə·tʃər/, /-ˌtʃʊr/ [countable noun] A person's name written by that person: *Can you just put your signature here, please?*

significance /sɪgˈnɪf.ɪ.kənts/ [uncountable noun] The meaning or the importance of something: *They didn't*

a b c d e f g h i j k l m n o p q r **s** t u v w x y z

appreciate the significance of the discovery until many years later.

↑**significant** /sɪɡˈnɪf.ɪ.kənt/ [adjective] **1** Important, big: *There has been a significant change in the bus timetable.* **2** With a special meaning: *I think it's significant that Harriet didn't come to the party.*

sign language [uncountable noun] Signs made with the hands that deaf people use to communicate: *They used sign language to tell each other what had happened.*

signpost /ˈsaɪnpəʊst/ [countable noun] A sign at the side of the road: *I hope we'll see a signpost to Whitby soon.*

↑**silence** /ˈsaɪ.lənts/ [uncountable noun] No noise, complete quiet: *Silence please! The principal has something to say to you.*

↑**silent** /ˈsaɪ.lənt/ [adjective] Without any noise: *The class was silent while they listened.*

silhouette /ˌsɪl.uˈet/ [countable noun] Outline or figure: *We put silhouettes of Christmas characters up on the class windows.*

↑**silk** /sɪlk/ [uncountable noun] A very fine, expensive material: *Silk is made from a fine thread spun by an insect.*

↑**silly** /ˈsɪl.i/ [adjective] Foolish, not sensible, stupid: *Don't be silly; of course you'll pass your test.* ■ The comparative form is "sillier" and the superlative form is "silliest". ■ "Silly" and "stupid" have almost the same meaning, but "stupid" is stronger.

↑**silver** /ˈsɪl·vər/ [uncountable noun] A shiny, gray, precious metal: *This ring is pure silver.*

silvery [adjective] Referring to a color, that is approximately silver, or that has a silver element to it: *The jacket is a silvery gray.*

↑**similar** /ˈsɪm·ə·lər/ [adjective] The same in some ways: *These two paintings are very similar, aren't they?*

similarity /ˌsɪm·əˈlær·ɪ·ṭi/ [uncountable noun] Being the same in some ways: *There are a lot of similarities between Britain and the United States but there are a lot of differences as well.* ■ The plural is "similarities".

↑**simple** /ˈsɪm.pl/ [adjective] **1** Not complicated: *These mathematical problems are quite simple once you understand them.* **2** Without decoration: *Both dresses are nice, but I prefer the simple, white one.*

simplify /ˈsɪm·pləˌfaɪ/ [verb] To make something simpler: *Our teacher tried to simplify the story for us to understand.* ■ Be careful with the spelling of these forms: "simplifies", "simplified".

sin[1] /sɪn/ [countable noun] An action or emotion that your religion tells you is wrong: *It's a sin to kill somebody.*

sin[2] /sɪn/ [verb] To do something that your religion says is wrong: *The priest told us not to sin.* ■ Be careful with the spelling of these forms: "sinned", "sinning".

↑**since[1]** /sɪns/ [adverb] From then until now: *Mary wrote to me last Christmas and I haven't heard from her since.* ■ Be careful with the pronunciation of this word! The "i" is pronounced like the "i" in "did".

↑**since[2]** /sɪns/ [preposition] From a time in the past until now: *I haven't seen you since Monday.* ■ Be careful! "Since" describes the starting point of a period, that is a particular date or a particular action: "We've been walking since one o'clock". "For" describes the duration of a period: "We've been walking for two hours". ■ See box at **for**.

since[3] /sɪns/ [conjunction] **1** From a time when something happened until now: *We haven't eaten since we had breakfast this morning at seven o'clock.* **2** Because: *Since you're so keen on soccer, I thought I'd give you this book about the history of the World Cup.*

↑**sincere** /sɪnˈsɪər/ [adjective] Truthful, honest or real: *Kate is very sincere and always tells you what she thinks.*

sincerely /sɪnˈsɪər·li/ [adverb] **1** In a sincere way: *Were you speaking sincerely when you said that you loved me?* **2 yours sincerely** Words that you put before your signature at the end of a formal letter: *"Yours sincerely, Ron Johnson".* ■ We use "yours sincerely" when the person to whom the letter is addressed is named. Compare with "yours faithfully" (used when the person to whom the letter is addressed is not named).

↑**sing, sang, sung** /sɪŋ/ [verb] To make music with your voice: *Patsy sings in the choir.*

↑**singer** /ˈsɪŋ·ər/ [countable noun] **1** A person who sings: *Molly is a singer in a band.* **2 lead singer** See **lead singer**.

↑**single[1]** /ˈsɪŋɡl/ [adjective] **1** Only one: *There was a single red car waiting for the ferry.* **2** Not married: *Our teacher is single, but he's getting married in June.*

single[2] /ˈsɪŋɡl/ [countable noun] **1** A ticket for a journey to a place but not back again: *I got a single to Boston because my friend's dad was going to bring me back in his car.* **2** A record with only one song on each side: *My mom's got a fantastic collection of Beatles singles.*

singular /ˈsɪŋ·ɡjə·lər/ [noun and adjective] A word in the form that indicates only one: *"Goose" is singular and "geese" is plural.*

↑**sink[1]** /sɪŋk/ [countable noun] **1** A place where dishes are washed: *Put the dishes in the sink and I'll wash them up later.* 👁 See picture at **kitchen**. **2** A container in a bathroom that is used for washing your hands or your face: *Don't leave the soap in the sink, please.* ■ In this use, in British English we say "washbasin". 👁 See picture at **bathroom**.

sink[2], sank, sunk /sɪŋk/ [verb] **1** To go under water: *The fishing boat sank three miles from the Canadian coast.* **2** To make something go under water: *The enemy bombs sank three ships.* **3** To go down: *The sun sank on the horizon.*

sip[1] [countable noun] A very small amount of a drink: *Can I have a sip of your orange juice?*

sip[2] /sɪp/ [verb] To drink little by little: *She sipped her drink slowly.* ■ Be careful with the spelling of these forms: "sipped", "sipping".

†**sir** /sɜːr/ [noun] **1** A polite way of speaking to a man: *Your room is on the second floor, sir.* ■ This use is formal and is now mainly used in letters. **2** A special title for a man: *Sir Winston Churchill was the British Prime Minister during the Second World War.*

siren US: /ˈsaɪr.ən/ UK: /ˈsaɪə.rən/ [countable noun] An instrument that makes a sound to give warning: *Ships use their sirens when they're coming into a harbor.*

†**sister** /ˈsɪs·tər/ [countable noun] **1** A girl or a woman who has the same parents as you: *My sister lives in New York.* **2** **sister-in-law 1** The sister of your husband or your wife: *His sister-in-law teaches at our school.* **2** The wife of your brother: *My brother and sister-in-law live in Rome.* ■ The plural of "sister-in-law" is "sisters-in-law". 👁 See picture at **family**.

†**sit, sat, sat** /sɪt/ [verb] To rest your bottom on something: *Jane sat on the sofa.*

▶ **PHRASAL VERBS** · **to sit down** To sit: *Will you all please sit down!* · **to sit up** To sit when you have been lying down or leaning: *Come on; sit up and have some soup.* ■ Be careful with the spelling of this form: "sitting".

†**site** /saɪt/ [countable noun] A place where something happens or something is: *We visited the site of the Battle of Hastings.*

sitting-room [countable noun] The main room in a house where people sit and relax: *We spent the evening in the sitting-room talking and telling jokes.* ■ The same meaning: "living room".

situated /ˈsɪt.ju.eɪ.tɪd/ US: /-t̬ɪd/ [adjective] In a place: *Our new house is situated just outside the town.* ■ Be careful with the pronunciation of the end of this word. The "e" is pronounced like the "i" in "did".

†**situation** /ˌsɪt.juˈeɪ.ʃən/ [countable noun] Things that are happening in a particular place, position: *My dad's situation is a bit difficult at the moment because he's lost his job.*

†**six** /sɪks/ [noun, adjective and pronoun] The number 6: *Janice has got six sisters.*

sixteen /ˌsɪkˈstiːn/ [noun, adjective and pronoun] The number 16: *There are sixteen girls in my class and only five boys.*

sixteenth /ˌsɪkˈstiːnθ/ [noun and adjective] Referring to sixteen: *Are you going to Alice's sixteenth birthday party?* ■ "Sixteenth" can also be written "16th".

sixth /sɪksθ/ [noun and adjective] Referring to six: *Friday is the sixth day of the week.* ■ "Sixth" can also be written "6th".

sixtieth /ˈsɪk.sti.əθ/ [noun and adjective] Referring to sixty: *It's my grandfather's sixtieth birthday tomorrow.* ■ "Sixtieth" can also be written "60th".

sixty /ˈsɪk.sti/ [noun, adjective and pronoun] The number 60: *I've got about sixty CD's, you know.*

†**size** /saɪz/ [countable noun] **1** How big or small somebody or something is, its measure: *Our classroom is quite a large size.* **2** A particular measurement: *What size shoes do you take?*

skate[1] /skeɪt/ [countable noun] **1** See **roller-skate**[1]. **2** See **ice skate**[1].

skate[2] /skeɪt/ [verb] **1** See **roller-skate**[2]. **2** See **ice skate**[2].

skateboard[1] /ˈskeɪtbɔːd/ [countable noun] A piece of wood or plastic with wheels on: *Pam's really good on her skateboard; she goes very fast.* ■ Be careful with the pronunciation of this word! The first syllable rhymes with "day" and the second "a" is not pronounced.

skateboard[2] [verb] To move using a skateboard: *My friend Anne skateboards very well.*

skating /ˈskeɪ·t̬ɪŋ/ [uncountable noun] The sport that you do with skates on: *Skating is one of the sports that I would really like to be good at.* 👁 See picture at **sport**.

skating rink [countable noun] A place where people go to skate: *Let's go to the skating rink on Saturday morning.* ■ We also say "rink".

skeletal /ˈskelɪtəl/ [adjective] Referring to the skeleton: *One of the main functions of the skeletal system is to provide support.* 👁 **See page 422.**

skeleton /ˈskel·ɪ·tə·n/ [countable noun] The bones that make a person or an animal: *My sister's got a plastic human skeleton hanging up in her bedroom.*

sketch[1] /sketʃ/ [countable noun] A picture that has been drawn quickly: *Some artists' sketches are sold at very high prices.*

sketch[2] /sketʃ/ [verb] To draw something quickly: *The whole class went into the wood and sketched the trees.*

ski[1] /skiː/ [countable noun] One of two long pieces of plastic, wood or other material that you stand on to travel over snow: *People who live in snowy areas often use skis to go from one place to another.*

ski[2] /skiː/ [verb] To travel on snow, using skis: *Last winter we went on a trip to Switzerland and I learned to ski.*

skiing /ˈskiː.ɪŋ/ [uncountable noun] The sport that you do on skis: *My brother goes skiing in Aspen every year.* 👁 See picture at **sport**.

skilful /ˈskɪl.fəl/ [adjective] See **skillful.** ■ This is a British English spelling.

†**skill** /skɪl/ [noun] **1** Being able to do something well: *Water-skiing requires great skill.* **2** Something that

a b c d e f g h i j k l m n o p q r **s** t u v w x y z

a b c d e f g h i j k l m n o p q r s t u v w x y z

you have learned to do: *Speaking languages is a very useful skill.* ■ The same meaning: "ability".

skilled /skɪld/ [adjective] **1** Having the ability to do an activity or job well: *She is a very skilled pianist.* **2** Having the training or experience necessary to do an activity or job: *The staff she works with are highly skilled.*

skillet /'skɪl.ɪt/ [countable noun] A shallow pan used for frying food: *You can use this skillet to fry the steak.* ■ The same meaning: "frying pan".

skillful /skɪl/ [adjective] Good at doing something: *Tanya is a very skillful painter.* ■ The British English spelling is "skilful".

✝**skin** /skɪn/ [countable noun] **1** The covering of a body: *Bertha has a beautiful soft skin.* **2** The covering of some fruit or vegetables: *Throw the banana skins in the garbage, please.*

skinhead /'skɪn.hed/ [countable noun] A young person with a shaved head and aggressive appearance: *Skinheads usually dress in a similar way and go together in a group.*

skinny /'skɪn.i/ [adjective] Very thin: *I don't know how Joe can be so skinny considering he eats so much.* ■ The comparative form is "skinnier" and the superlative form is "skinniest". This word is informal.

skip /skɪp/ [verb] **1** To jump up and down over a rope that you or other people are holding: *The children are skipping in the park.* **2** To give little jumps: *The little girl skipped for happiness when they arrived at the park.* **3** To miss something deliberately: *Jamie skipped a class to go and play soccer with his friends.* ■ Be careful with the spelling of these forms: "skipped", "skipping".

✝**skirt** US: /skɝːt/ UK: /skɜːt/ [countable noun] An article of clothing for a girl or a woman: *Our school uniform skirt is gray.* 👁 See picture at **clothes**.

skull /skʌl/ [countable noun] The bones in the head of a person or an animal: *We've got a sheep's skull in our biology laboratory at school.* 👁 **See page 422.**

✝**sky** /skaɪ/ [uncountable noun] The space above the earth that has air: *The sky is very cloudy today.* ■ Be careful! "Sky" does not have the same meaning as "heaven". ■ The plural is "skies".

skyscraper /'skaɪˌskreɪ·pər/ [countable noun] A very tall building: *The skyscrapers in New York are so tall that you can hardly see the sky.*

slam /slæm/ [verb] **1** To close with a loud noise: *Don't slam the door when you leave!* **2** To put something down with a noise: *He slammed his book down on the table.* ■ Be careful with the spelling of these forms: "slammed", "slamming".

slang /slæŋ/ [uncountable noun] Very informal language, street language: *Slang can be fun to learn but you have to be careful how you use it.*

slap[1] /slæp/ [countable noun] A blow with the open palm of your hand: *His mother gave him a light slap on the face.*

slap[2] /slæp/ [verb] To hit somebody with the open palm of you hand: *The woman slapped the man's face and left angrily.* ■ Be careful with the spelling of these forms: "slapped", "slapping".

slate /sleɪt/ [countable noun] **1** A dark gray rock that can be easily cut, or a small, flat piece of this used to cover a roof: *Some of the slates have fallen off the roof.* **2 to wipe the slate clean** To forget past mistakes, crimes or differences and start something again: *They have agreed to wipe the slate clean in order to work together on the new project.*

slaughter[1] [uncountable noun] The killing of animals or people: *Did you hear about the slaughter of all those people in India!*

slaughter[2] US: /'slɑː.t̬ɚ/ UK: /'slɔː.tər/ [verb] **1** To kill an animal for food: *They slaughter the pigs on the farm.* **2** To kill a lot of people: *How many people were slaughtered in the war?*

slave /sleɪv/ [countable noun] A person who is not free and is forced to work for another person: *Many slaves died on the boats which went from West Africa to America.*

slavery /'sleɪ·və·ri/ [uncountable noun] The system of having slaves: *Slavery was abolished in the United States after the Civil War.*

sled /sled/ [countable noun] A thing that you use to move over snow in, used for carrying loads and for play: *All four of us got on the sled and went speeding down the hill over the snow.* ■ Compare with "sleigh" (a thing that you travel over snow in, usually pulled by a horse). ■ In British English they say "sledge".

sledge /sledʒ/ [countable noun] See **sled.** ■ This word is more common in British English.

sleek /sliːk/ [adjective] **1** Smooth and shiny: *The dog has very sleek fur.* **2** Having an elegant and attractive shape or design: *Their new car is very sleek.*

sleep[1] /sliːp/ [uncountable noun] Being asleep: *What a lovely sleep I had!*

†**sleep**[2], **slept, slept** /sliːp/ [verb] To rest with your eyes closed: *I sleep in the same room as my little brother.*

sleeping bag [countable noun] A bag that you sleep in when you are camping, for example: *We slept in our sleeping bags under the stars.*

sleepless /ˈsliː.pləs/ [adjective] Without sleep: *I spent a sleepless night worrying about my tests.*

sleepy /ˈsliː.pi/ [adjective] Tired and wanting to sleep: *Do you want to go to bed? You look sleepy.*

sleet /sliːt/ [uncountable noun] A mixture of snow and rain: *The weather forecast says there's going to be sleet today.*

†**sleeve** /sliːv/ [countable noun] The part of an article of clothing that covers your arm: *Do you like the sleeves of this dress?*

sleigh /sleɪ/ [countable noun] A thing that you travel over snow in, usually pulled by a horse: *Santa Claus travels in a sleigh pulled by reindeer.* ■ Compare with "sled" (a thing that you use to move over snow in, used for carrying loads and for play). See picture at **sled.**

slender /ˈslen·dər/ [adjective] Slim: *What a lovely slender figure Patricia has.*

slept /slept/ Past tense and past participle forms of **sleep.**

†**slice**[1] /slaɪs/ [countable noun] A piece cut off something: *Would you like a slice of cake?* See pictures at **bread** and **a piece of...**

slice[2] /slaɪs/ [verb] To cut a piece off something: *When we had all sat down dad started to slice the turkey.*

slid Past tense and past participle forms of **slide.**

†**slide**[1] [countable noun] **1** A thing that children play on by sliding down: *Come on, let's go and play on the swings and slides.* **2** A photograph that you show on a screen: *We saw the slides of our teacher's vacation in Greece at school today.*

slide[2], **slid, slid** [verb] To move smoothly over something: *We spent the morning sliding over the ice that had formed on the sidewalk outside.*

†**slight** /slaɪt/ [adjective] Small or not very important: *I've got a slight problem with my math.*

slightly [adverb] A little, in a small amount or degree: *I'm slightly worried about the test.*

slim /slɪm/ [adjective] Thin in an attractive way: *John is very slim and fit.* ■ The comparative form is "slimmer" and the superlative form is "slimmest".

†**slip**[1] /slɪp/ [countable noun] **1** A small mistake: *I made a slip in the math problem and got the wrong answer.* **2** A small piece of paper: *I can't find the slip they gave me in the photographic store.*

slip[2] /slɪp/ [verb] **1** To slide on something by accident: *I slipped on a banana skin and nearly broke my leg.* **2** To move quickly and quietly: *Maggie managed to slip away while nobody was looking.* **3** To put something in a place quickly and quietly: *She slipped the waiter a tip.* ■ Be careful with the spelling of these forms: "slipped", "slipping".

slipper /ˈslɪp·ər/ [countable noun] A light shoe that you wear in the house: *My dog always brings me my slippers when I come in from school.*

slippery /ˈslɪp·ə·ri/ [adjective] Smooth and difficult to hold or to stand on: *The path was very slippery because of the ice.*

slit[1] /slɪt/ [countable noun] A narrow opening: *The rain entered the tent through a slit.*

slit[2], **slit, slit** /slɪt/ [verb] To make a small, straight opening: *He slit the packet open with a knife.*

slither /ˈslɪð·ər/ [verb] To move easily and quickly in a direction by stretching and contracting: *The snake slithered across the ground.*

slogan /ˈsloʊ·gən/ [countable noun] A short and easy to remember phrase used in publicity, demonstrations and so on: *"If you drink, don't drive" is a famous slogan.*

slope[1] /sləʊp/ [countable noun] The side of a hill: *It's quite difficult to skate up a slope, isn't it?* See page 445.

slope[2] /sləʊp/ [verb] To have a slope: *The path slopes a little and then goes round a bend.*

slot US: /slɑːt/ UK: /slɒt/ [countable noun] **1** A thin hole: *Put your money in the slot and then press the button beside the name of the drink you want.* **2 slot machine** A machine that you put money in and pull a handle or press a button to get a price in money: *The hotels in Las Vegas have slot machines all over the halls.*

†**slow**[1] /sləʊ/ [adjective] Not fast: *Daniel is a slow and careful driver.*

slow[2] **to slow down** or **to slow up** To reduce speed or to cause to reduce speed: *Slow down because there are a lot of difficult curves on this road.*

slumber party [countable noun] A party in which a group of friend, especially teenage girls, stay overnight at one's friend home: *In her birthday, she wants to have a slumber party.*

sly /slaɪ/ [adjective] Good at deceiving, not open: *Amelia's a very sly person. The other day she got free tickets for the movies and didn't tell any of us!* ■ The comparative form is "slyer" and the superlative form is "slyest".

a b c d e f g h i j k l m n o p q r **s** t u v w x y z

smack[1] /smæk/ [countable noun] A hit with the flat of the hand: *If you do that again, I'll give you a smack on the bottom!*

smack[2] /smæk/ [verb] To hit somebody with the flat of your hand: *Mom! Jane smacked me!*

†**small** US: /smɑːl/ UK: /smɔːl/ [adjective] Little: *The small boy gave the flowers to the opera singer.* ■ The comparative form is "smaller" and the superlative form is "smallest". 👁 See pictures at **opposite** and **a piece of...**

†**smart** US: /smɑːrt/ UK: /smɑːt/ [adjective] **1** Elegant or well dressed: *Mom wore a smart hat to the wedding.* **2** Clever: *My aunt's a very smart businesswoman.*

smash[1] /smæʃ/ [countable noun] **1** The noise that something makes when it smashes: *We heard the smash of the window and saw the ball come flying into the classroom.* **2 smash hit** A song, movie or musical that is a great success: *Steven Spielberg has had several smash hits.*

†**smash**[2] /smæʃ/ [verb] To break into pieces: *I dropped the mirror and it smashed.*

smashing /'smæʃ.ɪŋ/ [adjective] Marvelous: *What a smashing day for a picnic!*

smash-up /'smæʃ.ʌp/ [countable noun] A violent car accident: *There was a terrible smash-up on the highway last night.*

†**smell**[1] /smel/ [countable noun] **1** Something that you notice with your nose: *What's that awful smell?* **2** The ability to use your nose: *Dogs have a particularly good sense of smell.*

smell[2]**, smelt, smelt** /smel/ [verb] **1** To notice something with your nose: *I could smell the pizza as soon as I opened the door.* ■ In this use, we almost always say "can smell" or "could smell". **2** To have a particular smell: *This jacket smells of smoke.* ■ Be careful! We say: "smell **of** (something)". (We don't say: "smell **to** (something)"). ■ "Smell" also has regular past and past participle forms: "smelled".

smelly /'smel.i/ [adjective] Which gives off an unpleasant smell: *That sweater is a bit smelly. It's time you washed it.* ■ The comparative form is "smellier" and the superlative form is "smelliest".

smelt /smelt/ Past tense and past participle forms of **smell**.

†**smile**[1] /smaɪl/ [countable noun] An expression in your face that shows happiness: *Yolanda walked towards us with a smile on her face.*

†**smile**[2] /smaɪl/ [verb] To show happiness in your face: *Timothy smiled when he saw Janice.*

smoke[1] /sməʊk/ [uncountable noun] The gas you can see when something is burning: *The smoke from the fire could be seen for miles around.*

smoke[2] /sməʊk/ [verb] **1** To use a cigarette, pipe or cigar: *"Do you mind if I smoke?" "I would rather you didn't.".* **2** To make smoke: *The fire is smoking a bit; let's open the window.* **3** To prepare meat or fish by hanging it in smoke: *Smoked salmon is one of my favorite foods.*

smoker US: /'smoʊ.kɚ/ UK: /'sməʊ.kəʳ/ [countable noun] A person who smokes: *Smokers are more likely than other people to die of lung cancer, heart disease and other illnesses.*

†**smoking** /'smoʊ·kɪŋ/ [noun] Using a cigarette, a pipe or a cigar: *Smoking damages your health.*

†**smooth** /smuːð/ [adjective] **1** Completely flat, without obstruction: *My grandma is 80 but her skin is still very smooth.* **2** Gentle: *We had a very smooth flight and arrived on time.*

SMS /esem'es/ [countable noun] A text message sent from one cellphone to another: *He sent an SMS to let his friends know where he was.*

smuggle /'smʌg.l̩/ [verb] To take something into a country illegally: *People in this town smuggled brandy in from Canada in the past.*

snack /snæk/ [countable noun] **1** A small meal: *Let's have a snack in this café before we do our shopping.* **2 snack bar** A place where you have a snack: *They've opened a new snack bar in our school.*

snail /sneɪl/ [countable noun] A small, soft animal with two antennae and a shell on its back: *Snails move very slowly.*

†**snake** /sneɪk/ [countable noun] A long, thin reptile with no legs: *Most snakes move out of sight when they see humans.* 👁 **See page 430.**

snap[1] /snæp/ [countable noun] A photograph: *I really like that snap of you on the beach.*

snap[2] /snæp/ [verb] **1** To break with a noise: *I'm sorry; I've snapped your pencil!* **2** To speak roughly to a person: *Why did you snap at me like that the other day?* **3** To try and bite somebody or something: *The little dog snapped at my feet when I walked past.* ■ Be careful with the spelling of these forms: "snapped", "snapping".

snarl US: /snɑːrl/ UK: /snɑːl/ [verb] To make an aggressive noise lifting the upper lip: *I don't trust that dog because it always snarls at me when it sees me.*

snatch /snætʃ/ [verb] To take something quickly and with force: *The thief came up to her, snatched her bag and ran away.*

sneak[1] /sniːk/ [countable noun] A person who informs on other people in a cowardly manner: *He's a sneak. He tells the teacher everything.* ■ This word is informal.

sneak[2] /sniːk/ [verb] To do something quietly and secretly: *We sneaked out of class without the teacher noticing.*

sneakers US: /'sniːkər/ [plural noun] Sports shoes: *Do you like my new sneakers? I got them in the sales.* ■ When we talk about two or more "sneakers", we use the word "pairs": "I bought three pairs of sneakers". ■ In British English they say "trainers".

sneeze[1] [countable noun] Sending air suddenly out of your nose with a noise: *Pete gave such a loud sneeze that he made me jump.*

sneeze[2] /sniːz/ [verb] To send air suddenly out of your nose with a noise: *You've been sneezing all morning. Maybe you're getting a cold.*

SNEEZE

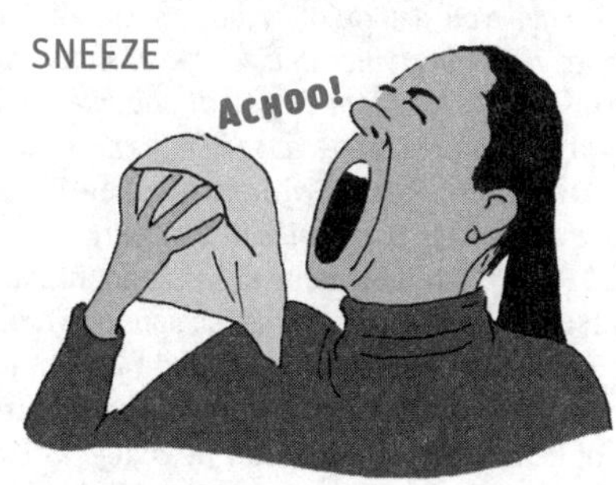

sniff /snɪf/ [verb] **1** To take air in through your nose, making a noise: *I knew that Mary was crying during the movie because I could hear her sniffing.* **2** To smell something: *The dog was sniffing around the shopping bag.*

snore US: /snɔːr/ UK: /snɔːʳ/ [verb] To make a noise while you are asleep: *My aunt was snoring so loudly last night that she woke everyone up in the house.*

snorkel /'snɔr·kəl/ [countable noun] A short tube that is used for breathing under water: *Don't forget to take your snorkel, the water's very clear there.*

snout /snaʊt/ [countable noun] The long nose and mouth of some animals: *The pig uses its snout to dig into the ground to find food.*

†**snow**[1] /snəʊ/ [uncountable noun] A soft, white substance that falls from the sky when it is very cold: *There was about two feet of snow in the yard last winter.* 👁 **See page 438.**

†**snow**[2] /snəʊ/ [verb] When talking of snow, to fall from the sky: *I love it when it snows at Christmas.*

snowball US: /'snoʊ.bɑːl/ UK: /'snəʊ.bɔːl/ [countable noun] A ball made with snow: *Jacqueline threw a snowball at her brother when he came in through the yard gate.*

snowflake /'snoʊˌfleɪk/ [countable noun] A piece of snow as it falls: *Snowflakes are made of different numbers of ice crystals.* ■ Be careful with the pronunciation of this word! The "a" is not pronounced. 👁 See picture at **a piece of...**

snowman /'snəʊ.mæn/ US: /'snoʊ-/ [countable noun] A figure made from snow: *Let's make a snowman in the backyard.* ■ The plural is "snowmen".

snowy /'snoʊ·i/ [adjective] With a lot of snow: *The mountains were still snowy in April this year.* ■ The comparative form is "snowier" and the superlative form is "snowiest".

†**so**[1] /səʊ/ [adverb] **1** Very; very much: *Why are you so nasty to me?* **2** To such a degree: *I was so angry that I couldn't speak to her.* **3** Also: *I'm Argentinian and so was my mother.* **4** That something is the case, when talking about something already mentioned: *"Are you coming to Atlantic City with us tomorrow?" "I think so".* **5 and so on** And other things: *I like sports: football, basketball, hockey and so on.* **6 or so** More or less: *"How much did that book cost?" "About five dollars or so".*

so[2] /səʊ/ [conjunction] **1** Because of what has gone before, for this reason: *The teacher told me to hand in my homework by tomorrow, so I'll have to finish it tonight.* **2** In order that: *I telephoned my aunt so I could tell her that I had passed my test.*

soak US: /soʊk/ UK: /səʊk/ [verb] **1** To leave something in a liquid: *You have to soak the beans in water overnight before cooking them.* **2** To make somebody or something very wet: *We went out in the storm and even though we had our raincoats on we were soaked.*

soaking or **soaking wet** /'səʊkɪŋ/ [adjective] Very wet: *You're sweater is soaking; take it off and we'll dry it in front of the fire.*

so-and-so US: /'soʊ.ənd.soʊ/ UK: /'səʊ.ənd.səʊ/ [countable noun] Somebody, when talking about somebody you don't want to name or whose name you can't remember: *So-and-so did it, you know, the tall boy with red hair.*

†**soap** /səʊp/ [noun] **1** A substance for washing with: *Pass me the soap, please.* **2 soap opera** A long television series about a large group of imaginary people: *"Friends" is one of the most popular United States soap operas.* **3 soap powder** Soap in the form of powder: *You have to put the soap powder in the washing machine before it starts, not after.* 👁 See picture at **bathroom.**

soar US: /sɔːr/ UK: /sɔːʳ/ [verb] **1** To fly high: *The eagle soared high above the valley.* **2** To go up very quickly: *House prices are soaring.*

sob US: /sɑːb/ UK: /sɒb/ [verb] To cry loudly: *What's the matter with Alice? Why is she sobbing in her room?* ■ Be careful with the spelling of these forms: "sobbed", "sobbing".

sober US: /'soʊ.bɚ/ UK: /'səʊ.bəʳ/ [adjective] Not drunk: *Katherine drove after the party because she was the only one sober.*

soccer US: /ˈsɑː.kɚ/ UK: /ˈsɒk.əʳ/ [uncountable noun] A game for two teams who try to kick a ball into a goal: *Los Angeles Galaxy plays in the Major League Soccer.* ■ In British English they say "football". 👁 See picture at **sport**.

sociable /ˈsoʊ·ʃə·bəl/ [adjective] Happy in the company of other people: *Jeff's a very sociable person and enjoys going out with his friends.*

↑**social** /ˈsoʊ·ʃəl/ [adjective] Referring to society: *There are many social problems in big cities, such as crime, poverty and violence.*

social network [countable noun] A website or application through which users communicate with each other: *Social networks are very useful to provide online information.*

social security [uncountable noun] Money that is paid to people by the government when they are ill, out of work and so on: *The right to social security was an important achievement of the workers.*

social worker [countable noun] A person who works with people who have problems: *My friend Kitty's a social worker and she works very long hours.*

↑**society** /səˈsaɪ·ɪ·t̬i/ [noun] **1** People living together, the total of relationships among them: *There are many things wrong with society.* **2** An association: *My dad belongs to the Railway Society and they meet once a week to talk about trains.* ■ The plural is "societies".

↑**sock** /sɒk/ [countable noun] A cotton or woolen article of clothing that you wear on your foot: *These socks have holes in them.* 👁 See picture at **clothes**.

socket US: /ˈsɑː.kɪt/ UK: /ˈsɒk.ɪt/ [countable noun] A place where you put a plug: *There's a socket behind the sofa where you can plug the radio in.*

soda or **soda pop** [countable noun] A drink made from water with bubbles, some flavors and sweetener: *Would you like a soda with your sandwich or just water?* ■ We also say "pop".

sodium /ˈsəʊdiəm/ [uncountable noun] A soft chemical element that is white and is found in salt and food: *Sodium is essential for living organisms.*

↑**sofa** /ˈsoʊ·fə/ [countable noun] A long, comfortable seat: *This sofa is so comfortable that I sometimes fall asleep on it when I'm watching the television.* ■ The same meaning: "couch". 👁 See picture at **living room**.

↑**soft** US: /sɑːft/ UK: /sɒft/ [adjective] **1** Not hard, not resistant to your touch: *This ice cream is very soft, even when you have just taken it out of the freezer.* **2** Gentle and kind: *Old Mr. Jones has a rough manner, but he's soft when you get to know him.* **3** Quiet: *My teacher has a very soft voice and she never shouts at us.* **4** Not bright: *My mom says that she likes soft lighting in the living room because it helps her relax.*

soft drink [countable noun] A drink without alcohol: *There were sandwiches and soft drinks at the party.*

softness [uncountable noun] **1** The quality of being not firm or resistant: *I adore the softness of the cushions at grandma's.* **2** The quality of being smooth and pleasant to touch: *He loved the softness of her skin and hair.* **3** The quality of being delicate, light, low or gentle: *At the concert we enjoyed the softness of the sound when the orchestra played Debussy.* ■ Compare with "hardness" (the quality of being solid and not soft or difficult to do).

↑**software** US: /ˈsɑːft.wer/ UK: /ˈsɒft.weəʳ/ [uncountable noun] Computer programs: *There's a new store near my house that specializes in software.*

↑**soil** /sɔɪl/ [uncountable noun] Earth: *The soil around here is very rich and everything grows really well in it.*

solar US: /ˈsoʊ.lɚ/ UK: /ˈsəʊ.ləʳ/ [adjective] Referring to the sun: *Solar power is obtained directly from the sun.* 👁 **See page 439.**

sold US: /soʊld/ UK: /səʊld/ Past tense and past participle forms of **sell**.

↑**soldier** US: /ˈsoʊl.dʒɚ/ UK: /ˈsəʊl.dʒəʳ/ [countable noun] A person in the armed forces: *The soldiers marched to the top of the hill.*

SOCCER

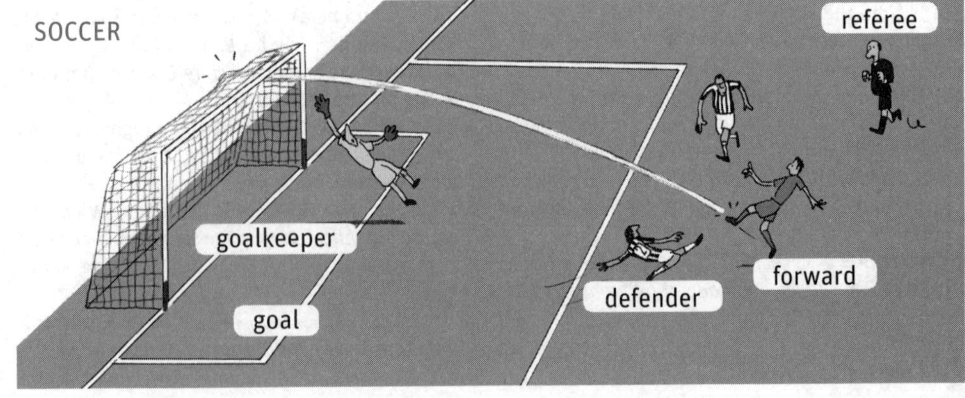

sole¹ /səʊl/ [adjective] Only: *Henry's sole reason for coming here was to be able to meet Linda.* ■ Be careful. This word is always used before a noun.

sole² /səʊl/ [countable noun] The bottom part of a shoe or a foot: *These shoes have leather soles.*

solemn US: /ˈsɑː.ləm/ UK: /ˈsɒl.əm/ [adjective] Serious, grave: *My mother loves solemn music.*

sol-fa [uncountable noun] The names for the notes in an eight-note scale: *In sol-fa, "doh" stands for the note "C".*

solicitor /səˈlɪs·ɪ·t̬ər/ [countable noun] The chief law officer of a city, town or government department: *My cousin was appointed solicitor to represent the federal government before the United States Supreme Court.*

solid¹ /ˈsɒlɪd/ [adjective] **1** Hard; not liquid or gas: *Water becomes solid when you freeze it.* 👁 See picture at **a piece of...** 👁 **See page 438. 2** With no empty space inside: *This bracelet is solid silver.*

ᐩ**solid²** /ˈsɒlɪd/ [countable noun] Not a liquid or a gas: *Most solids are made up of many tiny crystals.*

solidification /səˌlɪd.ɪ.fɪˈkeɪ.ʃən/ [uncountable noun] The act of becoming solid: *With water the solidification process becomes effective at 32 Fahrenheit degrees.* 👁 **See page 438.**

solitary US: /ˈsɑː.lə.ter.i/ UK: /ˈsɒl.ɪ.tri/ [adjective] Alone or liking to be alone: *My uncle Alf is a very solitary person.*

solo¹ /ˈsəʊləʊ/ [adjective and adverb] Alone: *Louis Blériot flew solo across the English Channel on 25 July 1909.*

solo² /ˈsəʊləʊ/ [countable noun] A piece of music for one instrument or one voice: *Mike played a terrific solo on the piano.*

ᐩ**solution** /səˈluː.ʃən/ [countable noun] The answer to a question: *Do you know the solution to problem number 5?*

ᐩ**solve** US: /sɑːlv/ UK: /sɒlv/ [verb] To find the answer to a problem: *The police still haven't been able to solve the mystery of the missing diamonds.*

ᐩ**some** [adjective and pronoun] **1** A number or an amount of something: *Will you get some eggs and some flour for me while you're at the store, please?* **2** Part of something, but not all of it: *I like some classical music, but not all.* **3** A word that you use in a question or an offer when you expect the answer to be "yes": *Would you like some more tea?* ■ See box.

ᐩ**somebody** /ˈsʌmˌbɒd·i/, /-bəd·i/ [pronoun] A person: *There's somebody on the phone for you.* ■ The same meaning: "someone". ■ "Somebody" is used in positive sentences. In negative sentences and questions we usually use "anybody". ■ See box at **anybody**.

ᐩ**somehow** /ˈsʌm.haʊ/ [adverb] In some way: *I'm not sure how I'm going to get there, but I will somehow.*

ᐩ**someone** /ˈsʌm.wʌn/ [pronoun] See **somebody**. ■ "Someone" is used in positive sentences. ■ See box at **anybody**.

somersault /ˈsʌm·ərˌsɔlt/ [countable noun] An action in which you jump up and turn over: *The acrobats did very high jumps and turned somersaults in the air.*

ᐩ**something** /ˈsʌm.θɪŋ/ [pronoun] A thing: *There's something in your bag. What is it, mom?* ■ "Something" is used in positive sentences. In negative sentences and questions we usually use "anything".

sometime /ˈsʌm.taɪm/ [adverb] At a time that you do not know: *Give me a call sometime and we'll meet.*

ᐩ**sometimes** /ˈsʌm.taɪmz/ [adverb] Occasionally: *I sometimes go to see my grandparents on a Sunday.* ■ See box at **frequency**.

ᐩ**somewhere** /ˈsʌm·hwer/, /-weər/ [adverb] At a place, to a place or in a place: *My keys are somewhere in the house but I don't know where.*

ᐩ**son** /sʌn/ [countable noun] **1** Somebody's male child: *Mrs. Moxon has two children; her son is eight and her daughter is five.* ■ Be careful. When you ask somebody if they have any sons or daughters, you have to say "sons and daughters" or "children". If you only say "sons" you are only referring to male children. **2 son-in-law** The husband of somebody's daughter: *Mrs. Frampton's son-in-law is very good to her; he takes her everywhere in the car.* ■ The plural of "son-in-law" is "sons-in-law". 👁 See picture at **family**.

some, any, no...

affirmative	negative	questions
some	(not) any	any
someone	(not) anyone	anyone
somebody	(not) anybody	anybody
something	(not) anything	anything
somewhere	(not) anywhere	anywhere

- *I need some money for the theater.*
- *Do you have any money, John?*
- *I don't have any money.*
- *There's someone jogging in the park.*
- *I don't know anybody who can speak Russian.*
- *Do you have anything for cleaning tables?*
- *I can't find my glasses anywhere.*

• In negative sentences we can also use *no*, *nobody*, *no one*, *nothing*, and *nowhere*. If we use one of these words, the verb is in the affirmative (without *not*):

- *I have no money.*
- *Nobody loves me.*
- *There's nothing on the table.*

a b c d e f g h i j k l m n o p q r s t u v w x y z

†**song** US: /sɑːŋ/ UK: /sɒŋ/ [countable noun] **1** Music with words that you sing: *"Somewhere over the Rainbow" is one of my favorite songs.* **2** The sound that a bird makes: *I love waking up to the birds song, even if it is early in the morning.*

†**soon** /suːn/ [adverb] **1** In a short time in the future: *I'm going out to the stores, but I'll be back soon.* ■ Compare with "early" (before time or near the beginning of a period of time). **2 as soon as** Immediately when: *Write to me as soon as you get there.*

soot /sʊt/ [uncountable noun] The black substance that smoke leaves: *The chimney's full of soot; we'll have to get it cleaned.*

sophomore [countable noun] A student in the second year of high school or college: *My sister is a sophomore and wants to study one year abroad next year.*

†**sore** /sɔːr/ [adjective] Painful: *We walked for miles and my feet ended up being very sore.*

†**sorry** /'sɑr·i/, /'sɔr·i/ [adjective] **1** Sad: *I was very sorry to hear about the death of your grandmother.* **2** A word used for apologizing: *Sorry I'm late!* ■ In this use we normally say "sorry" after we have done something and want to apologize. Compare with "excuse me" (used before we interrupt somebody) and "pardon" (expression used when somebody has not heard something). **3 I'm sorry** Words you use to say that you are sad because you have done something wrong: *I'm very sorry that I said all those horrible things to you.*

†**sort**[1] /sɔːt/ [countable noun] Kind or type: *What sort of things do you like doing in your spare time?*

sort[2] /sɔːt/ [verb] To put things together in groups: *Nowadays a machine sorts letters but before it used to be done by workers.*

▸ **PHRASAL VERBS · to sort (something) out 1** To organize: *Can you help me to sort out these papers?* **2** To solve a problem: *Can you help me sort this problem out?*

so-so US: /ˌsoʊ'soʊ/ UK: /ˌsəʊ'səʊ/ [adjective and adverb] Not very good, not very well: *"How are you feeling today?" "So-so".*

sought US: /sɑːt/ UK: /sɔːt/ Past tense and past participle forms of **seek**.

†**soul** US: /soʊl/ UK: /səʊl/ [noun] **1** The part of a person that is said not to die with the body: *They told her that her grandmother's soul was in heaven.* **2 soul** or **soul music** Afroamerican popular music with a lot of feeling: *My dad's got a great collection of soul.*

†**sound**[1] /saʊnd/ [countable noun] Something that you hear: *I could hear the sound of a dog barking in the distance.*

sound[2] /saʊnd/ [verb] **1** To make something that you can hear: *That CD sounds as if there's something wrong with it.* **2 sound like** To be similar in sound to something, to seem: *This piece of music sounds like Mozart.*

sound[3] /saʊnd/ [adjective] **1** Healthy: *You should always try to have a sound mind in a sound body. That's what my grandpa says!* **2** Good and right: *My mom always gives me sound advice about my friends.*

soundtrack /'saʊnd.træk/ [countable noun] The music of a film: *I didn't like the movie very much but I thought the soundtrack was fantastic.*

†**soup** /suːp/ [uncountable noun] A liquid food: *Sheila makes great tomato soup.*

†**sour** US: /saʊr/ UK: /saʊəʳ/ [adjective] **1** With a sharp taste like lemon juice or vinegar: *I can't eat this yoghurt. It's too sour for me.* **2** In bad condition: *This milk tastes sour. Is it all right?*

†**source** US: /sɔːrs/ UK: /sɔːs/ [countable noun] Where something comes from: *Please write down the source of your information at the bottom of the project.*

†**south** /saʊθ/ [noun, adjective and adverb] The direction on your right when the sun rises: *New Orleans is in the south of the United States.* ■ See box at **abbreviations**.

southeast [uncountable noun] In between the south and the east: *There will be rain all over the southeast this evening.* ■ See box at **abbreviations**.

†**southern** /'sʌð·ərn/ [adjective] Of the south: *The southern part of United States is warmer than the rest.*

South Pole [uncountable noun] The most southern place of the earth: *The South Pole was first reached by an expedition led by Roald Amundsen in December 1911.* ■ Be careful! "South Pole" has capital letters.

southwards or **southward** /'saʊθwədz/ [adverb] Towards the south: *The expedition headed southwards.* ■ We say "southward **of** something".

southwest [uncountable noun] In between the south and the west: *California is in the southwest of United States.* ■ See box at **abbreviations**.

souvenir /ˌsu·və'nɪər/ [countable noun] An object that reminds you of a place: *I bought a Boston Celtics T-shirt as a souvenir of my vacation on Boston.*

sovereign US: /'sɑːv.rən/ UK: /'sɒv.ᵊr.ɪn/ [countable noun] A king or a queen: *Most European sovereigns do not have political power.* ■ Be careful with the pronunciation of this word!

sow, sowed, sown /səʊ/ [verb] To put seed in the ground: *When we were on my cousin's farm we helped to sow the fields with wheat and corn.* ■ "Sow" also has past participle form: "sowed".

sown Past participle of **sow**.

†**space** /speɪs/ ▮ [noun] **1** A place for something: *Look dad, there's a parking space!* ▮ [uncountable noun] **2** The

empty area that is around and beyond the earth: *Space is the area between the stars, or between the planets of the solar system.* ■ We also say "outer space". **3 space shuttle** A spaceship that can come and go between space and the earth: *The space shuttle is able to carry several satellites at once.*

spacecraft /speɪs,kræft/ [countable noun] A vehicle used for travel outside the Earth's atmosphere: *Spacecrafts usually take off from Cape Canaveral.* ■ The plural is also "spacecraft".

spacecraft or **spaceship** /'speɪskrɑːft/ [countable noun] A vehicle for traveling through space: *Astronauts travel in spaceships.*

spaceship /'speɪs.ʃɪp/ [countable noun] A spacecraft which has a crew on board: *The crew of the spaceship will carry out experiments during the flight.*

spade /speɪd/ [countable noun] **1** A tool that is used in gardening: *My mom's digging in the garden with her new spade.* **2** A playing card with black shapes like heart shaped leaves with stems: *There's a great short story called "The Queen of Spades".*

spaghetti /spə'geţ·i/ [uncountable noun] An Italian dish made with long strips of pasta: *Spaghetti is my favorite dish.*

Spaniard /'spæn.jəd/ US: /-jɚd/ [countable noun] A person from Spain: *There were a lot of Spaniards staying at our hotel.* ■ Be careful! "Spaniard" has a capital "S".

spaniel /'spæn.jəl/ [countable noun] A type of dog: *A spaniel has long ears and short legs.*

Spanish[1] /'spænɪʃ/ [adjective] Referring to Spain: *My sister bought some lovely Spanish ceramics when she was in Spain this summer.* ■ Be careful! "Spanish" has a capital "S". For people, the singular is "a Spaniard" and the plural is "the Spanish".

Spanish[2] /speɪn/ [countable noun] The language of Spain and many other countries, especially in Latin America: *I'm learning Spanish at school.* ■ Be careful! "Spanish" has a capital "S".

spanner /'spæn·ər/ [countable noun] See **wrench**. ■ This word is British English.

⁺**spare[1]** /speər/ [adjective] **1** Extra: *We've got a spare room in our house and we rent it out to a student.* **2 spare time** The time when you are not working or at school: *In my spare time I like to read and write poetry.*

spare[2] /speər/ [verb] To afford to give money to somebody or something: *Can you spare some money for our charity?*

spark /spɑːk/ [countable noun] A very short burning of something: *Be careful with that plug; I saw sparks when you plugged it in just then.*

sparkle /'spɑːkl/ [verb] To shine with bright points of light: *The diamond ring on his finger sparkled.*

sparkling /'spɑr·kə·lɪŋ/, /'spɑrk·lɪŋ/ [adjective] When talking about wine or mineral water, with bubbles: *What do you want to drink? Sparkling mineral water, please.*

sparrow US: /'sper.oʊ/ UK: /'spær.əʊ/ [countable noun] A small brown bird: *My dad puts food on a bird table in our backyard and we watch the sparrows come to eat.*

sparse /spɑːs/ [adjective] Existing only in small amounts and usually dispersed over a large area: *Population is very sparse in the Amazon jungle.* ■ Compare with "abundant" (available in generous quantities).

spat /spæt/ Past tense and past participle forms of **spit**.

⁺**speak, spoke, spoken** /spiːk/ [verb] **1** To say words: *Can you speak more loudly, please? I can't hear you.* **2** To know a language: *My mother speaks three languages: French, Spanish and German.* ■ "Speak" has almost the same meaning as "talk". We usually say "talk" when we are referring to a conversation: "We talked for ages". We usually say "speak" when we are referring to the general action: "He speaks a lot. She speaks five languages".

PHRASAL VERBS · **to speak up** To talk louder: *Speak up! I can't hear you!*

⁺**speaker** /'spi·kər/ [countable noun] **1** A person who speaks about something: *We went to a talk on UFO's the other day and the speaker told us that he had seen one!* **2** A machine that makes sound loud: *I got quite a shock when they called my name over the speakers at the station.* ■ In this use, the same meaning: "loudspeaker". **See page 442.**

spear US: /spɪr/ UK: /spɪəʳ/ [countable noun] A long stick with a point at the end that you throw: *In the past, animals were hunted with spears.*

⁺**special** /'speʃ.ᵊl/ [adjective] **1** Important and not ordinary: *We're having a special lunch today to celebrate my mother's birthday.* **2** For a particular person or thing: *Tessie works in a special school for the blind in Cleveland.*

⁺**specialist** /'speʃ.ᵊl.ɪst/ [countable noun] A person who knows a lot about something: *Professor Mansfield is a specialist in dinosaurs.*

specialize or **specialise** /'speʃəlaɪz/ [verb] To know a lot about one particular thing: *Joan specializes in nuclear physics.*

⁺**specially** /'speʃ.ᵊl.i/ [adverb] For a particular purpose: *Look, I've brought a present from Mallorca specially for you!* ■ This word is also written "especially".

species /'spiː.ʃiːz/ [countable noun] A related group of plants or animals: *There are more than a million* *different species of animal in the world.* ■ The plural is also "species".

†**specific** /spəˈsɪf.ɪk/ [adjective] Particular or precise: *What is the specific purpose of this machine?*

specimen /ˈspes.ə.mɪn/ [countable noun] A small amount of something: *I had to have a blood specimen taken, to see if I was ill.*

spectacles /ˈspek.tɪ.kl̩z/ [plural noun] Glasses: *Sherlock Holmes looked at Watson over his spectacles.* ■ We usually say "glasses". ■ When we talk about two or more "spectacles", we use the word "pairs": "I have two pairs of spectacles".

spectacular /spekˈtæk·jə·lər/ [adjective] Dramatic, marvelous to see: *The storm was spectacular, with lightning all over the sky.*

spectator /ˈspek,teɪ·t̬ər/ [countable noun] A person who watches something: *The spectators cheered when the horses crossed the finishing line.*

sped /sped/ Past tense and past participle forms of **speed[2]**.

†**speech** /spiːtʃ/ [noun] **1** A talk that somebody gives: *The Mayor gave a very boring speech when he opened the new Sports Center.* **2** The ability to speak: *Frank's grandfather has had an illness which has affected his speech.*

†**speed[1]** /spiːd/ [uncountable noun] **1** How fast something goes: *Some trains can go at a terrific speed.* **2** **speed limit** The fastest that you are allowed to go: *There's a speed limit of 60 miles per hour on this part of the road.*

speed[2], sped, sped /spiːd/ [verb] **1** To go very fast: *The motorcycle sped down the hill, making a tremendous noise.* **2** To go too fast: *Mr. Trainer was fined for speeding on the highway.* ■ This use can only be used in a continuous tense.

spell[1] /spel/ [countable noun] A state caused by magic or the words used to produce it: *The witch put a spell on the prince and turned him into a frog.*

†**spell[2], spelt, spelt** /spel/ [verb] To use the correct letters when writing a word: *"How do you spell your name?" "J-o-h-n".* ■ "Spell" also has regular past and past participle forms: "spelled".

†**spelling** /ˈspel.ɪŋ/ [countable noun] The correct way of writing a word: *You must make sure that you get your spelling right when you write a formal letter.*

spelling bee [countable noun] A contest in which the participants have to spell words correctly: *I won the spelling bee in my school with the word "spermatozoon".*

spelt /spelt/ Past tense and past participle forms of **spell[2]**.

†**spend, spent, spent** /spend/ [verb] **1** To use money: *I spend most of my pocket money on books and CDs.* **2** To use time: *We spent the summer in Florida.*

spent Past tense and past participle forms of **spend**.

sperm US: /spɝːm/ UK: /spɜːm/ ▮ [countable noun] **1** The reproductive male cell that fertilizes the female's egg: *He has a low sperm count which indicates that he is not very fertile.* ■ The plural is "sperm" or "sperms". ■ The same meaning: "spermatozoon". ▮ [uncountable noun] **2** The thick fluid produced by the male sexual glands which contains spermatozoa: *The seminal vesicles produce sperm.*

spermatozoon US: /ˌspɝː.mə.t̬əˈzoʊ.ɑːn/ UK: /ˌspɜː.mə.təˈzəʊ.ɒn/ [countable noun] The male cell that, combined with a female egg, can develop a young: *A spermatozoon can join an ovum to form an embryo.* ■ The plural is "spermatozoa". ■ The same meaning: "sperm".

sphere US: /sfɪr/ UK: /sfɪəʳ/ [countable noun] A round object like a ball: *The planets and their satellites are spheres.*

†**spice** /spaɪs/ [countable noun] A substance that is used to give taste to food: *Spices can be made from many different things: seeds, leaves and so on.*

†**spicy** /ˈspaɪ.si/ [adjective] When talking about food, with a hot taste: *Indian food is very spicy.*

†**spider** /ˈspaɪ·dər/ [countable noun] A small animal with eight legs: *I like spiders!* ■ Be careful with the pronunciation of this word. "spi" rhymes with "my".
👁 See page 431.

spiderweb [countable noun] A fine net made by a spider: *Spiders use their spiderwebs to catch other insects.* ■ The same meaning: "cobweb".

SPIDERWEB

spied Past tense and past participle forms of **spy[2]**.

spike /spaɪk/ [countable noun] A sharp metal point: *There are spikes on top of the prison wall.*

spiky [adjective] Like a spike or having sharp points: *Tom has short, spiky hair.* 👁 See picture at **hair**.

†**spill, spilt, spilt** /spɪl/ [verb] To let some liquid fall by accident: *Ooops, sorry! I've spilt my orange juice on the carpet.* ■ This verb also has regular past tense and past participle forms: "spilled".

spilt Past tense and past participle forms of **spill**.

*****spin,** spun, spun /spɪn/ [verb] **1** To turn around quickly: *When you skate it is difficult to spin and stay in one place.* **2** To make something turn around quickly: *Spin a coin to decide who goes first.* **3** To make cloth from thread: *My great-grandmother used to work in a factory spinning cloth.* ■ Be careful with the spelling of this form: "spinning".

spinach /ˈspɪn.ɪtʃ/ [uncountable noun] A vegetable with green leaves: *Spinach is very good for you because it has a lot of vitamins and minerals, especially iron.* ■ Be careful with the pronunciation of this word! The "a" is pronounced like the "i" in "did". **See page 437.**

spinal /ˈspaɪnəl/ [adjective] Referring to the spine: *She suffered a spinal injury.*

spinal cord [countable noun] The bundle of nerves which are enclosed in the spine and connect all parts of the body with the brain: *The spinal cord and the brain form the central nervous system.*

spine /spaɪn/ [countable noun] The long line of bones in your back: *Mary fell off her horse and hurt her spine.* ■ The same meaning: "backbone". **See page 422.**

spinning wheel [noun] A wheel that is used to make thread: *Sleeping Beauty pricked her finger on the needle of a spinning wheel.*

spiny /ˈspaɪ.ni/ [adjective] Having spines: *Roses have a spiny stem.* ■ The comparative form is "spinier" and the superlative form is "spiniest".

spiral US: /ˈspaɪr.əl/ UK: /ˈspaɪə.rəl/ [noun and adjective] A shape that goes round and round and up or down: *The staircase in the castle was in the shape of a spiral.* **See page 457.**

spire US: /spaɪr/ UK: /spaɪəʳ/ [countable noun] A pointed tower on a church: *There are a lot of spires in the city of New York that you can see from a distance.*

*****spirit** /ˈspɪr.ɪt/ [noun] **1** The part of a person that is not the body: *In the Dickens story, the spirits appeared to Mr. Scrooge on Christmas Eve.* **2** A strong alcoholic drink: *Whisky, brandy, rum and gin are all spirits.* **3** A humor or a mood: *You're in high spirits today. Have you won the lottery?*

spit, spit, spit /spɪt/ [verb] To send food or liquid out from your mouth with force: *The baby spit out the mouthful of breakfast that his father had just given him.* ■ Be careful with the spelling of this form: "spitting".

*****spite** /spaɪt/ [uncountable noun] **1** Wanting to hurt another person: *Frances didn't invite me to her birthday party out of spite.* ■ In this use, we usually say "out of spite". **2 in spite of** Although something is true: *They went on the walk in spite of the cold and rain.*

splash[1] /splæʃ/ [countable noun] The sound made by somebody or something falling into liquid: *We heard a splash and a shout and realized that somebody had fallen into the river.*

splash[2] /splæʃ/ [verb] **1** To hit a liquid hard making it fall against something: *The car went through a puddle, splashing us as we waited at the bus stop.* **2** To move energetically through the water: *The children splashed around on the water's edge.*

splendid /ˈsplen.dɪd/ [adjective] Very good, fine in appearance: *I think that Velázquez painted some splendid pictures.*

splendor /ˈsplen·dər/ [uncountable noun] Impressive beauty and magnificence: *This is the best place to see the castle in all its splendor.* ■ The British English spelling is "splendour".

splendour /ˈsplen.dər/ US: /-dɚ/ [uncountable noun] See **splendor.** ■ This is a British English spelling.

splinter /ˈsplɪntər/ [countable noun] A very small thin piece of wood: *I've got a splinter in my finger and I can't get it out.* See picture at **a piece of...**

*****split,** split, split /splɪt/ [verb] **1** To break into two parts: *I was very embarrassed when I sat down and split my pants.* **2** To share something: *We split the candies between us.*

▶ **PHRASAL VERBS** · **to split up** To separate: *We were really surprised when Jackie's mom and dad split up.*

*****spoil,** spoilt, spoilt /spɔɪl/ [verb] **1** To damage something or take the joy out of it: *I was caught in the rain and spoilt my new suede jacket.* **2** To give a child too much, affecting its character: *My mom says that my grandpa spoils us by letting us do everything we want to.* ■ "Spoil" also has regular past and past participle forms: "spoiled".

spoilsport /ˈspɔɪl.spɔːt/ US: /-spɔːrt/ [countable noun] A person who stops other people having fun: *Don't be a spoilsport!*

spoilt Past tense and past participle forms of **spoil**.

spoke US: /spoʊk/ UK: /spəʊk/ Past tense of **speak**.

spoken /ˈspoʊ·kən/ Past participle of **speak**.

spokesman /ˈspoʊks·mən/ [countable noun] See **spokesperson.** ■ The plural is "spokesmen". ■ A woman is a "spokeswoman".

spokesperson /ˈspəʊksˌpɜːsən/ [countable noun] A person who speaks for other people: *Mrs. Harris is the spokesperson for the workers who are on strike.* ■ We used to say "spokesman" or "spokeswoman". Most people now prefer to say "spokesperson" because it can be used for either a man or a woman.

spokeswoman /ˈspoʊksˌwʊm·ən/ [countable noun] See **spokesperson.** ■ The plural is "spokeswomen". ■ A man is a "spokesman".

a b c d e f g h i j k l m n o p q r **s** t u v w x y z

sponge /spʌndʒ/ [countable noun] **1** A soft thing that you use to wash with: *I use a sponge shaped like a duck when I take a bath!* **2** A soft yellow cake: *My dad makes a lovely jam sponge.*

spongy /ˈspʌnðʒi/ [adjective] Soft and similar in texture to a sponge: *This moss is spongy.* ■ The comparative form is "spongier" and the superlative form is "spongiest".

sponsor[1] [countable noun] A company or a person that gives money for something: *We're going on a walk for the local children's hospital and we have to look for sponsors.*

sponsor[2] /ˈspɒnsər/ [verb] To give money for something: *Companies often sponsor sports teams so that they can get a lot of publicity.*

spontaneous /spɑnˈteɪ·ni·əs/ [adjective] Happening or done naturally and suddenly and without being planned: *I don't think his reaction was spontaneous, I think he knew.*

spooky /ˈspuːki/ [adjective] Strange and frightening: *The atmosphere there at night is spooky.* ■ The comparative form is "spookier" and the superlative form is "spookiest".

†**spoon** /spuːn/ [countable noun] A round object with a handle that you use to eat soup, yoghurt and so on: *Put the spoons beside the knives, please.* ■ Remember! You drink soup with a spoon, you eat french fries with a fork and you cut cakes with a knife. 👁 See picture at **cutlery**.

spoonful /ˈspuːn.fʊl/ [countable noun] The amount that a spoon holds: *I take two spoonfuls of sugar in my coffee.*

spore US: /spɔːr/ UK: /spɔːr/ [countable noun] A reproductive cell in plants and some simple organisms: *Spores are released by plants and scattered by the wind.*

†**sport** /spɔːt/ [uncountable noun] An activity that you do for exercise and enjoyment: *What sports do you do?*

sports car [countable noun] A very fast car: *My brother is saving up to buy a sports car.*

sports center [countable noun] A building where you can do all kinds of sport activities: *Have you phoned the sports center to see if we can play the volleyball tournament there?* 👁 See picture at **street**.

sporty US: /ˈspɔːr.i/ UK: /ˈspɔː.ti/ [adjective] Good at and very interested in sport and outdoor activities: *She's very sporty, she's always out riding, canoeing or swimming.*

†**spot**[1] /spɒt/ [countable noun] **1** A small mark on a person's skin: *Oh no! I've got a spot on my nose just when I wanted to look nice for the party tonight.* **2** A round mark: *My mom's bought me a lovely new skirt with white spots.* **3** A place: *On the way to California, we stopped at a beautiful spot in the mountains to have our picnic.*

spot[2] /spɒt/ [verb] To see something or somebody suddenly: *Jack spotted his mistake immediately.* ■ Be careful with the spelling of these forms: "spotted", "spotting".

spotted US: /ˈspɑː.ɪd/ UK: /ˈspɒt.ɪd/ [adjective] With spots: *My brother's got an awful spotted tie that he wears all the time!* ■ Be careful with the pronunciation of the end of this word. The "e" is pronounced like the "i" in "did".

spotty US: /ˈspɑː.i/ UK: /ˈspɒt.i/ [adjective] Having spots on your skin: *Having spotty skin is a drag.* ■ The comparative form is "spottier" and the superlative form is "spottiest".

spout /spaʊt/ [countable noun] A tube on a container that the liquid comes out of: *I dropped the teapot and the spout broke off.*

sprain /spreɪn/ [verb] To damage a part of your body for example by moving it too quickly: *My uncle sprained his ankle playing tennis the other day.*

sprang /spræŋ/ Past tense of **spring**[2].

†**spray**[1] /spreɪ/ [uncountable noun] Liquid that comes out of a container in very fine drops: *I'm going to the store to get some hair spray.*

spray[2] /spreɪ/ [verb] To cover something with liquid using a spray: *The rose bushes have gotten bugs; let's spray them before they get everywhere.*

spread[1] /spred/ [uncountable noun] The extension of something: *The Police are worried about the spread of street violence in this town.*

spread[2], spread, spread /spred/ [verb] **1** To cover something with a soft substance: *Tim spread butter and jam on his toast.* **2** To open completely: *Spread the newspaper over the table and then we can all see it.* **3** To move to different places: *The fire spread rapidly to all parts of the building.*

†**spring**[1] /sprɪŋ/ [noun] **1** The season of the year between winter and summer: *If winter comes, can spring be far behind?* 👁 **See page 448.** **2** The beginning of a river: *Pure spring water is the most delicious drink!* **3** A thin, spiral piece of metal: *The spring in my watch is broken and I'll have to take it to be mended.* **4** hot springs or thermal springs A natural spring whose water comes out at a temperature higher than body temperature: *The water of hot springs is heated by geothermal heat.*

spring[2], sprang, sprung /sprɪŋ/ [verb] To jump up quickly: *Mike sprang out of his chair when he saw the mouse.*

springboard /ˈsprɪŋˌbɔrd/, /-ˌboʊrd/ [countable noun] A long piece of wood that people dive into the water from: *Diving into the swimming pool from the springboard doesn't frighten me.*

SPORT

cycling
tennis
soccer
skiing
skating
baseball
swimming
volleyball
hockey
basketball
running
karate

a b c d e f g h i j k l m n o p q r **s** t u v w x y z

sprinkle /ˈsprɪŋ.kl̩/ [verb] To throw a very small amount of a substance on something: *My dad always sprinkles a little salt on his french fries, however salty they already are.*

sprint[1] [countable noun] A very fast race: *Len won the sprint at the school tournament the other day.*

sprint[2] /sprɪnt/ [verb] To run very quickly over a short distance: *Pat sprinted across the road and caught the bus, but I missed it.*

sprout /spraʊt/ [countable noun] A small, round, green vegetable: *In Canada, they often eat sprouts with turkey on Christmas Day.* ■ This is an abbreviation for "Brussels sprout".

sprung /sprʌŋ/ Past participle of **spring**.

spun /spʌn/ Past tense and past participle forms of **spin**.

spy[1] /spaɪ/ [countable noun] A person who gets information in secret: *The spies were important during the Cold War between Russia and the United States.* ■ The plural is "spies".

spy[2] /spaɪ/ [verb] To look at something in secret: *Detectives often have to spy on people to get important information.* ■ Be careful with the spelling of these forms: "spies", "spied".

squad US: /skwɑːd/ UK: /skwɒd/ [countable noun] A group of people who work as a team: *My neighbor works in the police drugs squad.* ■ This word can be used with either a singular or a plural verb: "Has/have the drugs squad arrived yet?".

square[1] /skweər/ [adjective] **1** With four equal sides, or something near to it: *My mom's looking for a square coffee table to go in the living room.* 👁 **See page 457.** **2** The number obtained when you multiply a number by itself: *The square of 4 is 16.*

⁺**square**[2] /skweər/ [countable noun] **1** A shape with four equal sides, or something near to it: *Two squares together make a rectangle.* **2** A place in a town or a village with buildings round it: *Times Square is the most famous square in New York.* ■ See box at **abbreviations**.

squash[1] /skwɒʃ/ [uncountable noun] **1** A fruit drink: *You have to add water to orange squash before you can drink it.* **2** A game where two players hit a ball against a wall: *My cousin teaches squash at the local Sports Center.*

squash[2] /skwɒʃ/ [verb] To press somebody or something very hard: *Don't push! You're squashing me!*

squat US: /skwɑːt/ UK: /skwɒt/ [verb] **1** To crouch until you almost sit on your heels: *He had to squat so as not to be seen.* **2** To live in an uninhabited building without paying and without permission: *They decided to squat in an empty hotel.* ■ Be careful with the spelling of these forms: "squatting", "squatted".

squeak[1] [countable noun] A small, high sound: *We knew the mouse was somewhere in the bedroom because we heard a squeak.*

squeak[2] /skwiːk/ [verb] To make a small, high sound: *My bicycle wheels are squeaking a lot lately, so I'll have to oil them.*

squeal[1] [countable noun] A loud, high sound: *We could hear the squeals of the pigs from the farmhouse.*

squeal[2] /skwiːl/ [verb] To make a loud, high sound: *The little girl squealed when she jumped into the cold water.*

⁺**squeeze**[1] /skwiːz/ [noun] **1** Pushing too much in a small place: *There was a real squeeze on the subway today.* **2** A press between two things: *My dad gave my hand a squeeze and told me not to worry.* 👁 See picture at **a piece of...**

squeeze[2] /skwiːz/ [verb] **1** To press hard between two things: *Squeeze this lemon and add the juice to the mixture.* **2** To push too much into a small place: *My suitcase was too small, but I managed to squeeze all my things in.*

squid /skwɪd/ [countable noun] A sea animal like a small octopus: *We had squid for dinner.*

squirrel /ˈskwɜr·əl/ [countable noun] A small animal with a large tail: *You often find squirrels in parks.* 👁 **See page 428.**

St **1** A written abbreviation for **saint**. ■ See box at **abbreviations**. **2** A written abbreviation for **street**. ■ Be careful! "St" has a capital "S". ■ See box at **abbreviations**.

stab /stæb/ [verb] To push a knife into somebody: *A man was stabbed outside a pub in town the other night.* ■ Be careful with the spelling of these forms: "stabbed", "stabbing".

stable[1] /ˈsteɪbl/ [adjective] Balanced and firmly placed: *That ladder's not very stable; will you hold it for me?*

⁺**stable**[2] /ˈsteɪbl/ [countable noun] A place where horses are kept: *Let's go to the stables and see Caroline's new pony.*

stadium /ˈsteɪ.di.əm/ [countable noun] A place where sports events are held: *Michigan stadium seats about 109,900 people.* ■ The plural is "stadium" or "stadia".

⁺**staff** US: /stæf/ UK: /stɑːf/ [countable noun] The people who work at a place: *The kitchen staff at our school are all very nice.*

staff room /ˈstɑːf.rʊm/, /-ruːm/ US: /ˈstæf-/ [countable noun] The room where teachers go during their breaks: *The students are not allowed to go in the staff room at our school.*

⁺**stage** /steɪdʒ/ [countable noun] **1** The part of a theater where the performers are during a show: *I recognized Emily as soon as she walked on stage.* **2** A particular part of a long event or process: *The next stage of the bicycle race is in the Pyrenees.*

stagger /'stæg·ər/ [verb] To walk with great difficulty: *At the end of the movie the bad was shot, staggered across the bar and fell out of the window.*

stain[1] /steɪn/ [countable noun] A mark made by a substance: *That oil has left a terrible stain on the tablecloth.*

stain[2] /steɪn/ [verb] To make a dirty mark: *Don't leave that glass on the table or it will stain the wood.*

staircase /'steərˌkeɪs/ [countable noun] A set of steps inside a building with rails that you can hold onto: *There are so many staircases in this building that I sometimes get lost.* See picture at **house**.

stairs US: /sterz/ UK: /steəz/ [plural noun] A set of steps: *Be careful carrying those glasses up the stairs.*

stake /steɪk/ [countable noun] A strong pointed stick: *The farmers have to tie tomatoes plants to stakes.*

stale /steɪl/ [adjective] Not fresh: *Take this bread back to the store. It's very stale.*

stalk US: /stɑːk/ UK: /stɔːk/ [countable noun] The part of a plant the flowers and leaves grow out of: *Cut the stalks of those flowers or they'll be too long for the vase.* ■ The same meaning: "stem".

stall US: /stɑːl/ UK: /stɔːl/ [countable noun] A small structure where you can buy things usually in the street: *I bought the lamp at a small stall in the market.*

stamen /'steɪ.mən/ [countable noun] The part of a flower that produces pollen: *The stamen is the male reproductive part of a flower.* **See page 433.**

stamina /'stæm.ɪ.nə/ [countable noun] The capacity to do something for a long time: *Robert has got a lot of stamina. He's very good at long distance running.*

†**stamp**[1] /stæmp/ [countable noun] **1** A small piece of colored paper that you put on an envelope: *The first postage stamp was called the Penny Black and was made in 1840.* **2** A small piece of wood or rubber that makes a particular mark: *I knew that the letter was from school because it had the school stamp on the envelope.*

stamp[2] /stæmp/ [verb] To bang your foot or feet hard on the ground: *She stamped angrily down the stairs and out of the door.*

†**stand**[1] /stænd/ [countable noun] **1** A table that you put things on in an exhibition, fair and so on: *My mom spent the afternoon at the Red Cross stand selling flags.* **2** A thing that you put objects on to use them more easily: *I need a new music stand; mine's broken.* **3** One of the wide steps from which you can watch a football or rugby game: *There was a great atmosphere on the stands.*

stand[2], **stood, stood** /stænd/ [verb] **1** To be on your feet: *We stood in the line for hours to get tickets for the concert.* **2** To get on your feet: *We all stood for the National Anthem.* **3** To be in a particular place: *The castle stands on a hill overlooking the valley.* **4** To move to a particular place while you are on your feet: *Stand in line, please.* **5** **can't stand** To dislike very much: *I can't stand going to the dentist's.*

▸ **PHRASAL VERBS** · **to stand by** To help and support: *Good friends always stand by you when you have problems.* · **to stand for** To mean something: *USA stands for United States of America.* · **to stand out** To be easily seen, to project above the rest: *George is so tall that he always stands out in a crowd.* · **to stand up** To get on your feet: *We stood up when the teacher came into the room with the President.* · **to stand (somebody) up** Not keep a date or an appointment with somebody: *She didn't come! She stood me up.* · **to stand up for (somebody or something)** To defend or to support: *When are you going to stand up for your rights?*

†**standard**[1] /'stændəd/ [adjective] Ordinary, not special: *This is the standard model of bicycle but we do have special mountain bikes with extra gears.*

standard[2] /'stændəd/ [countable noun] A level: *The general standard of work in this class has gone up. Well done, Class 3!*

stang Past tense of **sting**.

stank /stæŋk/ Past tense of **stink**.

stapler /'steɪ·plər/ [countable noun] Hand instrument for attaching papers with a small piece of bent metal: *The stapler doesn't work.*

†**star**[1] /stɑːr/ [countable noun] **1** A large mass in space which you see as a point in the sky at night: *The Sun is a yellow star that gives out heat.* **2** A famous and popular person: *I would like to be a pop star when I grow up.* **3** A shape with five points: *The starfish is a sea animal shaped like a star.*

star[2] /stɑːr/ [verb] To be the main actor in a movie or a show: *Brad Pitt stars in that movie.* ■ Be careful! We say: "star **in** a film".

†**stare** US: /ster/ UK: /steəʳ/ [verb] To look very hard at somebody or something: *I wish Richard wouldn't stare at me like that. It makes me nervous.*

starfish /'stɑr·fɪʃ/ [countable noun] Sea animal shaped like a star: *I found this starfish on the beach last summer.*

†**start**[1] /stɑːt/ [countable noun] The beginning of something: *We were late and we missed the start of the movie.*

start[2] /stɑːt/ [verb] **1** To begin doing something: *Here are your tests; don't start until I tell you to.* **2** To begin to happen: *What time does the movie start?* **3** To make something begin to work: *My dad always has trouble starting our car in the winter.*

starting point /'stɑːtɪŋˌpɔɪnt/ [countable noun] The place where something starts: *The starting point of the marathon will be the Town Hall.*

a b c d e f g h i j k l m n o p q r s t u v w x y z

starve US: /stɑːrv/ UK: /stɑːv/ [verb] **1** To die of hunger: *Thousands of people starved during the terrible drought in Africa this year.* **2** **to be starving** To be very hungry: *When's dinner? I'm starving.* ■ This use is informal.

state[1] /steɪt/ [countable noun] **1** How somebody or something is: *My bedroom is in a terrible state; I need to tidy it up.* **2** A country and its government: *The head of state in the United States is the President.* **3** A region of a country: *Florida is a state of the USA.* **4** **state of mind** How somebody feels, how somebody is mentally: *He's in a rather confused state of mind at the moment.*

state[2] /steɪt/ [verb] To say or to write something important: *The principal stated that the vacations would start earlier this year.*

statement /ˈsteɪt.mənt/ [countable noun] Something that a person has said: *The police spokesperson issued a statement about the road accident.*

statesman /ˈsteɪt.smən/ [countable noun] A very important politician: *Some people think that Sir Winston Churchill was one of the greatest statesmen of the twentieth century.* ■ The plural is "statesmen". ■ A woman is a "stateswoman".

stateswoman /ˈsteɪtˌswʊm.ən/ [countable noun] A very important female politician: *Benazir Bhutto was a stateswoman from Pakistan.* ■ The plural is "stateswomen". ■ A man is a "statesman".

static[1] /ˈstætɪk/ [adjective] Staying in one place for a long time or not changing: *Prices will not stay static for long.*

static[2] /ˈstætɪk/ [uncountable noun] **1** Noise interference on a television, cellphone or radio that is caused by electricity in the air: *There was too much static to hear his message properly.* **2** Electricity that collects on some surfaces as a result of friction: *Static can give you an electric shock.*

station /ˈsteɪ.ʃᵊn/ [countable noun] **1** A place where buses and trains come and go: *I'll meet you at the station at 8 o'clock tomorrow.* **2** A place where certain people work: *They've built a new police station and a fire station in the center of town, very near each other.* **3** A television or a radio company: *Some stations only have one type of program on them, often sports or news.* **4** **railway station** See **railway station.**

stationary /ˈsteɪ·ʃəˌner·i/ [adjective] Not moving: *The bus was stationary so we jumped on it, just in time.* ■ Compare with "mobile" (that can be moved).

stationer /ˈsteɪʃə·nər·/ [countable noun] A person who sells writing materials: *He bought a pen and a pad from the stationer's.*

stationer's /ˈsteɪ.ʃən.əz/ US: /-ɚz/ [countable noun] See **stationery store.** ■ This use is British English.

stationery store [countable noun] A store that sells pens, paper, ink and so on: *I'm going to the stationery store to buy some envelopes, do you want to come?* ■ In British English they say "stationer's".

statistics /stəˈtɪs.tɪks/ [countable noun] Numbers giving information about things: *According to statistics, children who eat well do better at school.* ■ It is usually used with a singular verb.

statue /ˈstætʃ.uː/ [countable noun] A figure of a person made of stone, wood or other material: *There's a statue of William Shakespeare outside our school.*

statute /ˈstætʃ.uːt/ [countable noun] A written law or regulation: *The limited company has statutes which all employees must comply with.*

stave [countable noun] The five parallel lines on which musical notes are written in a score: *The music teacher wrote the tune of the song on a stave on the whiteboard.* See page 460.

stay[1] /steɪ/ [countable noun] A time when you live somewhere: *I really enjoyed my stay in New York this summer.*

stay[2] /steɪ/ [verb] **1** Not to move from a place: *My brothers went out to play but I stayed in the house with my parents.* **2** To live in a place for a short time: *I went to stay in New York with my aunt Sheila.*

PHRASAL VERBS · **to stay up** Not to go to bed: *Last night, I stayed up until three o'clock in the morning, watching a movie.*

steady /ˈsted.i/ [adjective] **1** Stable; not falling: *Little Janet is still not very steady on her feet. She's only eighteen months old.* **2** Constant, not changing: *He's making steady progress in his mathematics.*

steak /steɪk/ [countable noun] A thick piece of meat: *My favorite food is steak and french fries.* ■ Be careful with the pronunciation of this word. It rhymes with "make". (It helps if you remember "steaks make you strong").

steal, stole, stolen /stiːl/ [verb] To take something that is not yours: *Somebody has stolen my purse from my desk.* ■ Be careful! "Steal" is used when the object taken is mentioned, not the victim. We say: "he stole my bag". (We don't say: "he stole me". Compare with "rob" (taking away something illegally).

steam[1] /stiːm/ [uncountable noun] Vapor that water produces when it is very hot: *The power of steam was used in steam engines for trains.*

steam[2] /stiːm/ [verb] To send out steam: *The water is steaming in the bathtub.*

steamboat /ˈstiːm.bəʊt/ US: /-boʊt/ [countable noun] A boat powered by steam: *The steamboat moved slowly up the river.*

steam engine [countable noun] An engine that uses steam to generate power: *The steam engine was* *an essential element during the Industrial Revolution.* 👁 **See page 443.**

↑**steel** /stiːl/ [uncountable noun] A very hard metal: *Steel is used for example in buildings, bridges and trains.*

↑**steep** /stiːp/ [adjective] That rises or falls strongly: *It's impossible to run up this hill; it's too steep.*

↑**steer** US: /stɪr/ UK: /stɪəʳ/ [verb] To direct a vehicle: *We'll row and you can steer the boat.*

steering wheel [countable noun] The wheel inside a car or other vehicle that is used for guiding it: *In the United States, the steering wheel in cars is on the left.* 👁 **See page 441.**

stem /stem/ [countable noun] The part of a plant that leaves and flowers grow out of: *These flowers have very thick stems, haven't they?* ■ The same meaning: "stalk". 👁 **See page 432.**

stencil[1] /ˈstensəl/ [countable noun] A thin piece of cardboard or plastic with a design cut into it: *You can use the stencil to draw the outline of the figure.*

stencil[2] [verb] To draw or paint a design using a stencil: *He stenciled the design onto the T-shirt.*

↑**step**[1] /step/ [countable noun] **1** A movement of your foot in a particular direction: *Take three steps forwards and one step back. Now swing your partner in the dance!* **2** One part of the stairs, particularly when outdoors: *There are three steps up to our front door.* **3** A part of a process: *Follow the steps carefully when making this model.* **4 step by step** Little by little; in the correct order: *You have to learn to play the piano step by step.*

step[2] /step/ [verb] To move your foot in a particular direction: *He stepped forward when the teacher read his name out.*

▸ **PHRASAL VERBS** · **to step in** To begin to take part in a difficult situation in order to help: *When we need help repairing our mountain bikes, uncle John always steps in.* ■ Be careful with the spelling of these forms: "stepped", "stepping".

stepfather /ˈstepˌfɑ·ðər/ [countable noun] A man who is married to your mother but is not your natural father: *My stepfather is always very kind to me.*

stepmother /ˈstepˌmʌð·ər/ [countable noun] A woman who is married to your father but is not your natural mother: *Jackie's stepmother is Colombian.*

stereotype /ˈster.i.ə.taɪp/ [countable noun] A classification of people or things that is not based on observation or experience: *Forget your stereotypes: people are basically the same all over the world.*

sterile /ˈster·əl/ [adjective] **1** Completely clean and without any bacteria: *A sterile bandage is used to cover the wound.* **2** Unable to produce seeds, fruit, young or children: *A mule is a sterile animal.* **3** Unable to produce vegetation: *This is sterile soil. You can't plant any crops here.*

sterling /ˈstɜr·lɪŋ/ [uncountable noun] The money used in Britain: *The value of sterling has fallen.* ■ Be careful. This word is formal. We usually say just "pounds".

stern /stɜːn/ [adjective] Serious and strict: *My teacher is rather stern, but he's a very nice person all the same.*

sternocleidomastoid [countable noun] A muscle found on each side of the neck at the front: *The sternocleidomastoid muscles help to bend and rotate the head.* 👁 **See page 423.**

sternum /ˈstɜː.nəm/ US: /ˈstɝː-/ [countable noun] A flat bone in the center of the chest: *The sternum is an extended, segmented bone that the ribs connect to.* ■ The plural is "sternums" or "sterna". ■ The same meaning: "breastbone". 👁 **See page 422.**

stew US: /stuː/ UK: /stjuː/ [uncountable noun] A dish made from meat and vegetables: *My grandma makes us a fantastic stew whenever we go for lunch.*

steward US: /ˈstuː.ɚd/ UK: /ˈstjuː.əd/ [countable noun] A man who looks after passengers on a plane or a ship: *The steward asked us if we wanted a drink.* ■ A woman who helps passengers is a "stewardess".

stewardess /ˈstjuːədes/ [countable noun] A woman who looks after passengers on a plane or a ship: *My cousin wants to be a stewardess.* ■ The plural is "stewardesses". A man who helps passengers is a "steward".

stick[1] /stɪk/ [countable noun] **1** A long thin piece of wood: *Our dog loves it when you throw a stick for him to fetch.* **2** A thin piece of something: *Pass me a stick of chalk.*

↑**stick**[2]**, stuck, stuck** /stɪk/ [verb] **1** To fix something with glue: *Let's try and stick the vase together before mom gets back!* **2** To put a pointed object into something: *Be careful you don't stick the needle into your finger.* **3** To put something somewhere: *Just stick those books in the corner and we'll sort them out later.* ■ This use is informal. **4** To be fixed and not be able to move: *My finger is stuck in this hole.*

sticker /ˈstɪk·ər/ [countable noun] A piece of paper with a drawing or photo, that you can stick to things: *Rachel's folder is covered with football stickers.*

sticking plaster [countable noun] See **plaster**.

↑**sticky** /ˈstɪk.i/ [adjective] Covered with a substance that sticks: *Spiders' webs have a sticky substance to catch insects in.* ■ The comparative form is "stickier" and the superlative form is "stickiest".

↑**stiff** /stɪf/ [adjective] Difficult to bend: *Get some stiff cardboard and we'll use it to make the masks.* ■ The same meaning: "rigid".

stile /staɪl/ [countable noun] A step device usually found between fields, which permits a fence or wall to be crossed: *Stiles allow people to cross the fence but not animals.*

still[1] /stɪl/ [adjective] Without moving: *I stood completely still and the bee flew away.*

+**still**[2] /stɪl/ [adverb] Until this time: *My dad still enjoys playing with train sets.* ■ See box below.

stimulation /ˌstɪmjə'leɪʃən/ [uncountable noun] Something which causes excitement, development, growth or activity, or the action of doing this: *Babies need stimulation to help them develop.*

stimulus /'stɪmjələs/ [countable noun] **1** Something which produces a reaction in a living thing: *The application of the stimulus to the knee produces a reflex reaction.* **2** Something that encourages activity, growth or a greater effort, etc.: *Stress can provide you with a stimulus to achieve your goals.* ■ The plural is "stimuli".

sting[1] /stɪŋ/ [countable noun] **1** A mark where an insect has stung you: *Those herbs are very good for bee stings.* **2** The part of an insect that can prick you: *Scorpions usually use their stings in self defense.*

sting[2], **stung, stung** /stɪŋ/ [verb] **1** To inject poison, when you are talking about an insect, scorpion and so on: *A wasp stung me last week when I trod on it at the swimming pool.* **2** To feel a sharp pain: *The cigarette smoke in my brother's office makes my eyes sting.*

stink[1] /stɪŋk/ [uncountable noun] A very bad smell: *What a stink there is in this classroom; let's open the windows.*

stink[2], **stunk, stunk** /stɪŋk/ [verb] To smell very badly: *Those eggs must be bad. They stink.* ■ In British English the past can also be "stank".

+**stir** US: /stɝː/ UK: /stɜːʳ/ [verb] **1** To move something round and round: *Jane put two spoons of sugar in her coffee and stirred it.* **2** To move a little: *Our baby sleeps so deeply that she doesn't stir even when we make a noise.* ■ Be careful with the spelling of these forms: "stirred", "stirring".

stirrup /'stɪrəp/ [countable noun] A metal object for resting your foot when you are riding a horse: *Put your foot into the stirrup and mount.*

stitch[1] /'stɪrəp/ [countable noun] The piece of thread that you put in cloth when you sew: *These stitches are big and untidy. We'll have to do them again.* ■ The plural is "stitches".

stitch[2] /'stɪrəp/ [verb] To fix material together with needle and thread: *I need to stitch this button on my coat.* ■ The same meaning: "sew".

stoat US: /stoʊt/ UK: /stəʊt/ [countable noun] Small animal with brown fur that in winter turns mainly white: *Stoats eat other animals.* ■ Compare with "ermine" (the fur of the stoat in winter).

+**stock**[1] /stɒk/ [uncountable noun] **1** Goods that are to be sold or used: *We have a very large stock of sports equipment.* **2 in stock** Ready to be sold: *Have you any smoked salmon in stock, please?* **3 out of stock** Not in the store: *I'm sorry but those shoes are out of stock at the moment.*

stock[2] /stɒk/ [verb] To keep in a store to sell: *We don't stock classical music in our store.*

stocking US: /'stɑː.kɪŋ/ UK: /'stɒk.ɪŋ/ [countable noun] A long, thin article of clothing for the leg: *My mom used to have to wear thick, gray stockings when she went to school.*

stole US: /stoʊl/ UK: /stəʊl/ Past tense of **steal**.

stolen /'stoʊ·lən/ Past participle of **steal**.

+**stomach** /'stʌm.ək/ [countable noun] The part of your body where food goes when you eat it: *My stomach hurts. I must have eaten too much.* 👁 **See pages 421 and 424.**

+**stone** US: /stoʊn/ UK: /stəʊn/ [countable noun] **1** A piece of rock: *Stop throwing stones; it's dangerous.* **2** A type of rock: *I love those little stone houses that*

still	*yet*
• Emphasizes that something continues. • Goes next to the verb. • Is used in affirmative sentences: - *We are still waiting for a reply.* - *That plant still has flowers.* • Is sometimes used in negative sentences to give greater emphasis: - *He hasn't come yet, but it's only ten.* - *It's ten o'clock and he still hasn't come.*	• Asks if something has happened or says that it hasn't. • Goes at the end of the sentence. • Is often used with the present perfect. • Is used in negative sentences: - *We haven't had a reply yet.* - *Tom isn't here yet.*
• In questions, both are possible: - *Is he still here?* - *Hasn't he gone yet?*	

you often see in the country. **3** See **pit.** ■ This use is British English.

stood /stʊd/ Past tense and past participle forms of **stand.**

stool /stuːl/ [countable noun] A small chair with no back: *You sit on the chair and we'll use the kitchen stools.*

stop[1] /stɒp/ [countable noun] **1** A place where a bus or a train stops: *Next stop, Times Square!* **2** **full stop** See **period.** ■ This use is British English.

⁺**stop**[2] /stɒp/ [verb] **1** To finish doing something: *Can you please stop talking and listen to me?* **2** To finish moving: *Does the number 18 bus stop here?* **3** To make something finish: *Stop the bus! I want to get off.* **4** To prevent somebody from doing something: *I'm sorry, but I couldn't stop her from coming in.* ■ Be careful with the spelling of these forms: "stopped", "stopping".

stoplight US: /ˈstɒplaɪt/ [countable noun] Lights that change color to control the traffic on roads: *The stoplights are red. Don't drive on!* ■ This word is more common in the plural. ■ In British English they say "traffic light". 👁 See picture at **street.**

stopover US: /ˈstɑːpˌoʊ.vɚ/ UK: /ˈstɒpˌəʊ.vəʳ/ [countable noun] A stop in a long journey: *We had to have a stopover in Vancouver on the way to New York because of bad weather.*

stop watch /ˈstɒpwɒtʃ/ [countable noun] A watch that is used to time sports events: *Liz Jones was in charge of the stop watch during our athletics tournament.*

⁺**store**[1] /stɔːr/ [countable noun] **1** A place where you buy things: *When I grow up I would like to work in a stationery store.* ■ The same meaning: "shop[1]". 👁 See picture at **market.** **2** See **department store.** **3** Goods that you have for later: *We always have a good store of food in the house, in case something happens.*

store[2] /stɔːr/ [verb] To keep things in order to use them later: *We usually store the apples from our trees in the attic.*

storehouse /ˈstɔrˌhaʊs/, /ˈstoʊr-/ [countable noun] A building that is used for keeping things: *Near where I live there's a storehouse full of computer equipment.* ■ The same meaning: "depot". ■ In British English they say "warehouse".

storekeeper [countable noun] A person who owns a shop: *That storekeeper opens his shop every morning at nine o'clock.*

storey US: /ˈstɔːr.i/ UK: /ˈstɔː.ri/ [countable noun] A floor of a building: *That building has thirty storeys.*

stork US: /stɔːrk/ UK: /stɔːk/ [countable noun] A large bird with long legs and a long beak: *Storks build large nests on the top of churches and other high places.*

⁺**storm** US: /stɔːrm/ UK: /stɔːm/ [countable noun] Bad weather with wind, rain and sometimes thunder: *Did you hear the storm last night?*

stormy /ˈstɔr·mi/ [adjective] With a lot of storms: *The weather forecast says that there will be stormy weather all next week.*

⁺**story** US: /ˈstɔːr.i/ UK: /ˈstɔː.ri/ [countable noun] A description of events that you write, say or listen to: *Tell us a story!* ■ The plural is "stories". ■ Compare with "history" (things that happened in the past).

storyline [countable noun] The plot of a novel, film or any other story: *The writers took three months to develop the storyline of the film.*

⁺**stove** US: /stoʊv/ UK: /stəʊv/ [countable noun] A machine that is used for cooking or heating: *Put the potatoes on the stove and we'll have dinner as soon as possible.* ■ In British English they say "cooker". 👁 See picture at **kitchen.**

⁺**straight**[1] /streɪt/ [adjective] **1** Not bent or curved: *Stand in a straight line, please.* 👁 See pictures at **hair** and **opposite.** **2** Level: *Stand over there and tell me if this picture is straight.*

straight[2] /streɪt/ [adverb] **1** Directly: *Go straight home without stopping on the way.* **2** In a straight line: *Walk straight across the side of the mountain and you'll come across a hut.* **3** **straight ahead** or **straight on** Directly in front of you: *You go straight on for two miles and then turn left at the crossing.* **4** **straight away** Immediately: *Go and see the principal straight away!*

straighten /ˈstreɪt·ə·n/ [verb] To make something straight: *My mom straightened my dad's tie before they went out.*

straightforward /ˌstreɪtˈfɔr·wərd/ [adjective] Not complicated: *You'll find the instructions quite straightforward.*

strain[1] /streɪn/ [uncountable noun] Too much pressure: *The strain of work made my uncle ill.*

strain[2] /streɪn/ [verb] **1** To do something with a great effort: *Don had to strain his eyes to see the whiteboard from where he was sitting.* **2** To hurt yourself trying something too hard: *Don't lift that heavy box on your own; you might strain your back.* **3** To put a substance through an instrument with small holes: *My dad strained the boiled apples for the baby to eat.*

strainer [countable noun] A tool with little holes that lets liquid pass and keeps solids: *Can you use a strainer for my orange juice?*

strait /streɪt/ [countable noun] A narrow area of sea between two pieces of land: *The Magellan Strait is between the southern end of South America and Tierra del Fuego.*

⁺**strange** /streɪndʒ/ [adjective] **1** Unusual, odd: *I think that Christine is a bit strange sometimes.* **2** Not known: *Isn't it interesting to walk around a strange town?*

+**stranger** /ˈstreɪn·dʒər/ [countable noun] A person you do not know: *When I opened the door a complete stranger was standing there.*

strangle /ˈstræŋ.gl̩/ [verb] To kill somebody pressing their neck very hard: *His body was found by the river. He had been strangled.*

strap[1] /stræp/ [countable noun] A narrow piece of material for holding something: *I'll have to buy another watch strap; mine has just broken.*

strap[2] [verb] To fasten something with a strap: *John strapped the books to his bicycle and went off to school.* ■ Be careful with the spelling of these forms: "strapped", "strapping".

+**strategy** /ˈstræt̬·ə·dʒi/ [countable noun] A detailed plan of how to do something: *The generals planned their strategy for the battle.* ■ The plural is "strategies".

stratosphere /ˈstræt̬·əˌsfɪər/ [countable noun] The layer above the troposphere: *The stratosphere extends up to 30 miles above the surface of the earth.* See page 449.

straw US: /strɑː/ UK: /strɔː/ [noun] **1** The dried stems of a plant: *Our rabbit sleeps in a cage with straw in it.* **2** A long, thin tube for drinking through: *Would you like a straw for your drinks?*

strawberry US: /ˈstrɑːˌber.i/ UK: /ˈstrɔː.bᵊr.i/ [countable noun] A soft red summer fruit: *Strawberries are wonderful with cream.* ■ The plural is "strawberries". See page 436.

stray [adjective] Lost and far from home: *We found a stray kitten in the street and took it home with us.*

+**stream[1]** /striːm/ [countable noun] **1** A very small river: *There's a stream opposite our house and we catch frogs in it.* **2** A continuous flow: *There has been a stream of visitors all week to see the new acquisition.*

stream[2] /striːm/ [verb] **1** To flow fast and strongly: *Tears streamed down her face as she held the sick puppy in her arms.* **2** To send to your screen on a continuous basis: *The quickest way to watch an online movie is streaming.*

+**street** /striːt/ [countable noun] A road with houses on either side: *There's a store on the corner of our street.* ■ The abbreviation "St" is only used in written language. See box at **abbreviations**. ■ When a particular street is mentioned, we use a capital "S": "Oxford Street is a famous shopping street in London". ■ Compare with "road" (a hard path for vehicles in or outside a city).

street lamp [countable noun] A light on top of a tall post on a street or road: *Modern street lamps are provided with cells sensitive to light which turn the lamps on at sunset.* ■ The same meaning: "streetlight".

streetlight /ˈstriːt.laɪt/ [countable noun] A light on top of a tall post on a street or road: *The streetlights illuminate the streets when it is dark.* ■ The same meaning: "street lamp". See picture at **street**.

+**strength** /streŋθ/ [uncountable noun] Being strong: *I haven't the strength to lift these boxes; I'll have to get Bob to do it.*

strengthen /ˈstreŋ.θᵊn/ [verb] To make or become stronger or more efficient: *These exercises will strengthen your stomach muscles.* ■ Compare with "weaken" (to make somebody or something weaker).

+**stress[1]** /stres/ [noun] **1** Nervous strain, tension: *He couldn't stand the stress of modern life.* **2** Force, pressure: *Architects need to calculate the stress of a roof on the walls.*

stress[2] /stres/ [verb] **1** To use extra force when pronouncing part of a word: *In the word "station", the first part "sta" is the part stressed.* **2** To give special attention: *My teachers always stress the importance of reading at home to become a good reader.* ■ Be careful with the spelling of the 3rd person singular present tense form: "stresses".

+**stretch[1]** /stretʃ/ [countable noun] An area of land or water: *Now we go through a lovely stretch of woods.*

stretch[2] /stretʃ/ [verb] **1** To pull something to change its size or shape: *Don't put your new sweater in the washing machine or it'll stretch.* **2** To push out your arms, legs and so on as far as possible: *The cat stretched and went out for a walk in the backyard.*

stretcher /ˈstretʃ·ər/ [countable noun] A flat object to carry a sick or injured person on: *The ambulance men carried the injured people on stretchers.*

stricken Past participle of **strike[2]**.

+**strict** /strɪkt/ [adjective] Very firm: *My piano teacher is very strict and makes me practice every day for three hours!*

stridden Past participle of **stride**.

stride, strode, stridden /straɪd/ [verb] To walk or to run with long steps: *We watched Paul striding across the street.*

strike[1] /straɪk/ [noun] Stopping of work by workers, usually because they want a change in conditions: *In the company where my mother works, they are going on strike next week.* ■ Be careful. We always say: "**on** strike".

+**strike[2], struck, stricken** /straɪk/ [verb] **1** To hit somebody or something: *The car struck the barrier and then ran into the wall.* ■ We usually say "hit". **2** In a clock, to ring a bell a particular number of times so that people know what time it is: *The clock in the living room struck seven.*

striker /ˈstraɪ·kər/ [countable noun] **1** A person who plays in a forward position in sports like soccer, hockey

a b c d e f g h i j k l m n o p q r **s** t u v w x y z

and so on: *My brother plays as striker in the school team.* **2** A person who goes on strike: *The strikers asked for an interview with the Secretary.*

ᐩ**string** /strɪŋ/ [countable noun] **1** Thin rope that is used for tying things: *Take this string and finish wrapping the parcel.* **2** A fine wire or fiber that is used on an instrument: *One of my guitar strings broke in the middle of the concert.* 👁 **See page 458.**

string instrument [countable noun] A musical instrument which has strings and produces sounds by making them vibrate: *Guitars, violins and harps are string instruments.*

STREET

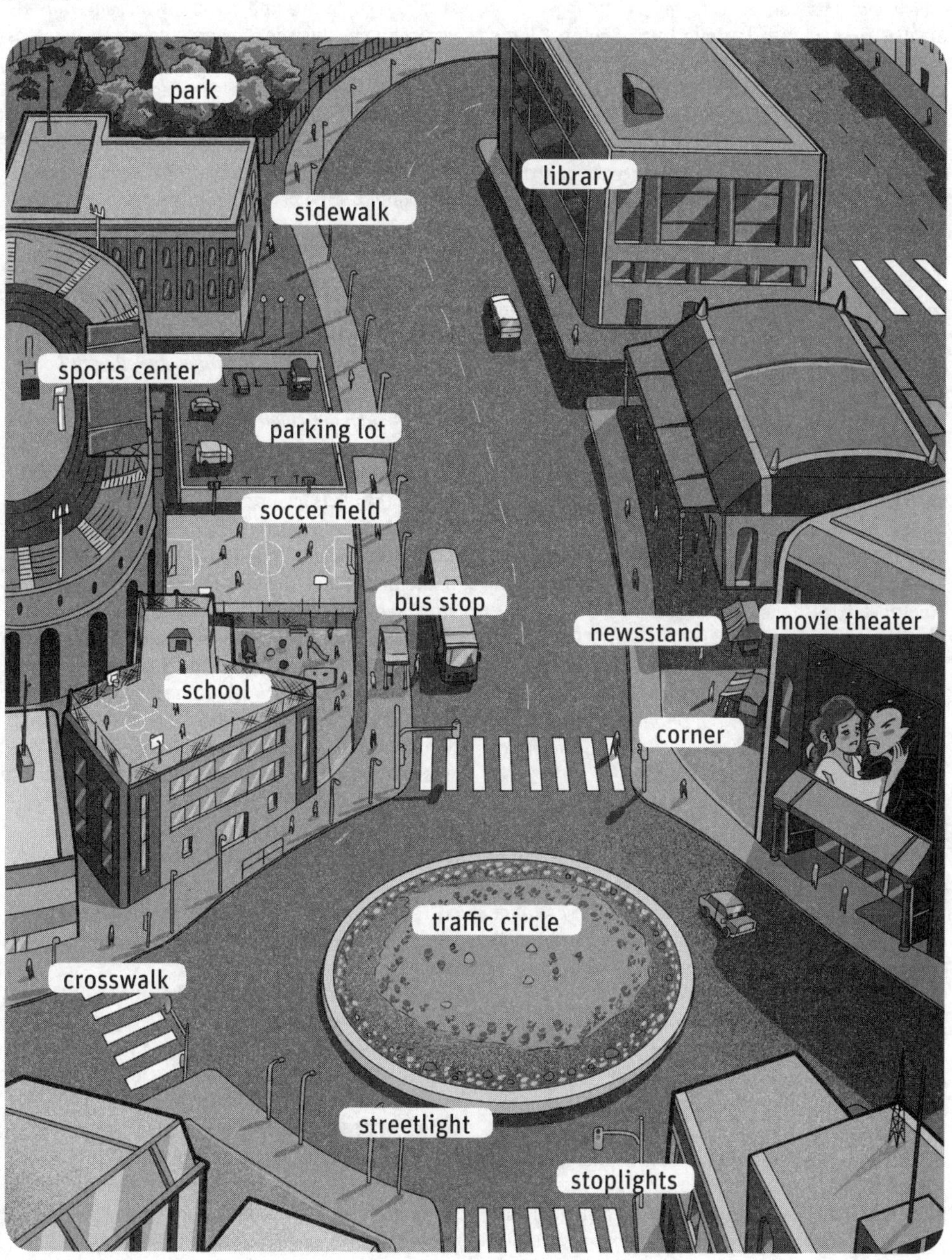

a b c d e f g h i j k l m n o p q r s t u v w x y z

↑**strip**[1] /strɪp/ [countable noun] A long, narrow piece of something: *Cut the paper into strips.*

strip[2] /strɪp/ [verb] **1** To take a covering of something off: *We stripped the wallpaper off the walls and painted them white.* **2** To take all your clothes off: *When we arrived on the beach, we stripped our clothes off and dove into the water.* ■ In this use, the same meaning: "undress". ■ Be careful with the spelling of these forms: "stripped", "stripping".

↑**stripe** /straɪp/ [countable noun] A long line of color: *Zebras have black and white stripes and live in Africa.*

↑**striped** /straɪpt/ [adjective] With stripes: *Do you like my new striped skirt?* ■ Be careful with the pronunciation of this word. The "e" is not pronounced.

strode US: /stroʊd/ UK: /strəʊd/ Past tense of **stride**.

↑**stroke**[1] /strəʊk/ [countable noun] **1** A movement that you make with your arm in a sport: *I can go from one end of the swimming pool to the other in eight strokes.* **2** The sound of a clock: *On the stroke of twelve, the new year starts.* **3** A sudden illness of the brain: *My grandpa died of a stroke last year.*

stroke[2] /strəʊk/ [verb] To move your hand over somebody or something in an affectionate way: *Don't stroke that dog; it looks a bit vicious to me!*

stroll[1] [countable noun] A slow walk: *Let's go for a stroll in the park.*

stroll[2] /strəʊl/ [verb] To walk slowly: *We strolled along the river bank watching the ducks.*

stroller [countable noun] A chair on wheels for a baby: *I'm going to take the baby to the park in the stroller.* ■ In British English they say "pushchair".

↑**strong** US: /strɑːŋ/ UK: /strɒŋ/ [adjective] **1** Physically powerful: *My big brother is very strong. He can lift my mom up.* **2** Difficult to break: *The rope will need to be very strong to lift the piano up.* **3** When we talk about a smell, a taste and so on, powerful or intense: *This coffee is very strong.*

struck /strʌk/ Past tense and past participle forms of **strike**[2].

↑**structure** /ˈstrʌk·tʃər/ [noun] **1** A building or something that has been made: *The new sculpture that they've put outside the Town Hall is a very strange structure, isn't it?* **2** The way that something is made: *We've got a test tomorrow on the structure of the eye.*

struggle[1] /ˈstrʌgl/ [countable noun] A fight: *After a brief struggle the police managed to capture the thieves.*

struggle[2] /ˈstrʌgl/ [verb] To fight or to try very hard: *We struggled to get the armchair out of the living room.*

stuck /stʌk/ Past tense and past participle forms of **stick**[2].

↑**student** /ˈstu·də·nt/, /-dənt/ [countable noun] **1** A person who attends a school or a college: *There are 400 students in my elementary school.* **2** A person who studies something: *This dictionary is for English language students.* 👁 See picture at **classroom**.

studious /ˈstud·i·əs/ [adjective] Keen on studying: *My older sister's very studious, but I prefer going out and enjoying myself.*

study[1] /ˈstʌdi/ [noun] **1** Learning: *When do you finish your studies?* **2** A room where somebody goes to study, read, write and so on: *When my parents work at home, they do it in our study.* ■ The plural is "studies".

↑**study**[2] /ˈstʌdi/ [verb] **1** To learn about something: *My cousin is studying Math at university.* **2** To look at something carefully: *We studied the map but we still couldn't find the name of the town where we were going.* ■ Be careful with the spelling of these forms: "studies", "studied".

↑**stuff**[1] /stʌf/ [uncountable noun] Things, material or substance: *What's all your stuff doing on the living room floor?*

stuff[2] /stʌf/ [verb] **1** To fill something with something: *My school bag is always stuffed with books.* **2** To put something somewhere quickly: *I could hear the teacher coming, so I stuffed the sandwich into my coat pocket.*

stuffing /ˈstʌf.ɪŋ/ [uncountable noun] Something that you put into a thing: *I love roast chicken with bread and onion stuffing.*

stumble /ˈstʌm.bl̩/ [verb] To put your foot down badly and almost fall: *As the kitchen was dark he stumbled over the stool.*

stun /stʌn/ [verb] **1** To make somebody dizzy by hitting them very hard on the head: *Roger was stunned by a cricket ball hitting him on the head while he watched the game.* **2** To shock somebody: *She was stunned when they offered her the job. She was not expecting it at all.* ■ Be careful with the spelling of these forms: "stunned", "stunning".

stung /stʌŋ/ Past participle of **sting**.

stunk /stʌŋk/ Past tense and past participle forms of **stink**[2].

stunning /ˈstʌn.ɪŋ/ [adjective] Very beautiful or impressive: *Your cousin is absolutely stunning. Does she have a boyfriend?*

stunt man [countable noun] A man who does dangerous actions in movies in place of an actor: *The stunt man jumped from the moving train into the car.* ■ The plural is "stunt men". ■ A woman is a "stunt woman".

stunt woman [countable noun] A woman who does dangerous actions in movies in place of an actress: *When the director shouted "Action!" the stunt woman jumped from one roof to another.* ■ The plural is "stunt women". ■ A man is a "stunt man".

stupid /'stu·pɪd/ [adjective] Silly or not clever: *Don't be stupid! Of course you can come to my party.* ■ "Stupid" and "silly" have almost the same meaning, but "stupid" is stronger.

stupidity US: /stuː'pɪd.ə.i/ UK: /stjuː'pɪd.ɪ.ti/ [noun] Being stupid: *I've never seen such stupidity in all my life!* ■ The plural is "stupidities".

stutter US: /'stʌ.ɚ/ UK: /'stʌt.əʳ/ [verb] To speak repeating the same sounds: *"I ddddon't know", he stuttered.*

sty /staɪ/ [countable noun] A place where pigs live: *The sty smells badly, even though it's just been cleaned out.* ■ The plural is "sties". ■ The same meaning: "pigsty", "pigpen".

style /staɪl/ [noun] **1** A particular way of doing something: *I really like his style of dancing.* **2** The form of something: *I like her style of writing, with short and precise sentences.*

subject /səb'dʒekt/, /'sʌb.dʒekt/ [countable noun] **1** Something that you are studying at school: *How many subjects do you study at school?* **2** Something that you are speaking or writing about: *What's the subject of the composition that we have to do for homework?* **3** The person or the thing that does the action in a sentence: *In "The cat sat on the mat", "the cat" is the subject of the sentence.* **4** A person who belongs to a particular country: *My father is a Canadian subject because he was born in Toronto.*

submarine /ˌsʌb.mə'riːn/ [countable noun] A ship that travels under the water: *My brother is in the Navy and works on a submarine.* ■ Be careful with the pronunciation of this word! "sub" is pronounced as in "sun". 👁 See picture at **transport**.

subscription /səb'skrɪp.ʃən/ [countable noun] Money that you pay to receive a magazine or to be in a club: *Have you paid your subscription for the mountaineering club this month?*

subsoil /'sʌb.sɔɪl/ [uncountable noun] The layer of soil which is under the surface level: *The subsoil often includes only partially worked substances like sand and clay that affect the quality of the soil.*

substance /'sʌb.stənts/ [countable noun] A liquid or solid material: *Water is a liquid substance and rock is a solid substance.*

substantial /səb'stæn.ʃəl/ [adjective] Large or important: *There were substantial differences between the two versions of the film.*

substitute[1] /'sʌbstɪtjuːt/ [countable noun] A person or a thing that takes the place of another: *I've been chosen as a substitute for the school football team.*

substitute[2] /'sʌbstɪtjuːt/ [verb] To take the place of somebody or something: *Our teacher was away today and the principal had to substitute for her.*

subterranean /ˌsʌbtər'eɪniən/ [adjective] Under the ground: *The subway trains go through subterranean tunnels.*

subtitles [plural noun] The words sometimes put at the bottom of the screen in a movie: *The only reason I could understand the movie was because there were subtitles.*

subtle /'sʌt̬.ə.l/ [adjective] Not immediately obvious or understandable, delicate: *I don't like the way you said that so directly; you should be more subtle.*

subtract /səb'trækt/ [verb] To take one number away from another: *If you subtract two from four, you get two.*

subtraction /səb'træk.ʃən/ [countable noun] Taking one number from another: *She's only four but she can already do simple addition and subtraction.*

subtropical /sʌb'trɒp·ɪ·kəl/ [adjective] Referring to the regions bordering on the tropics: *Puerto Rico has a subtropical climate.*

suburb /'sʌb·ɜrb/ [countable noun] An area of the city that is outside the center: *We used to live in the center of town until my parents bought a house in a suburb.*

subway /'sʌb.weɪ/ [countable noun] Underground railway: *Let's take the subway station into the Museum of Natural History. It's the quickest way.* ■ In British English they say "underground, tube".

succeed /sək'siːd/ [verb] To achieve what you are trying to do, to achieve recognition or popularity: *At first the baby elephant couldn't stand up, but after lots of trying, she succeeded.* ■ Be careful with the pronunciation of this word. The first "c" is pronounced like a "k" and the second like an "s".

success /sək'ses/ [uncountable noun] Achieving what you want, achieving popularity: *He was a big success in the part of Hamlet.* ■ Be careful with the pronunciation of this word. The first "c" is pronounced like a "k" and the second like an "s".

successful /sək'ses.fəl/ [adjective] Achieving what you want, achieving popularity: *My dad's new store is successful and he's very pleased with it.* ■ Be careful with the pronunciation of this word. The first "c" is pronounced like a "k" and the second like an "s".

succession /sək'seʃ.ən/ [noun] **1** The process of succeeding in genealogical line or time: *The United States presidential succession defines who may become or act as President of the United States upon the incapacity, death, resignation or removal from office.* **2** A number of things or people which follow each other in order or time: *Our teacher showed us a succession of images relating to the history of art in the 20th century.*

such /sʌtʃ/ [adjective] **1** A word that is used to give emphasis: *This is such a nice place that I could stay here for the rest of my life.* **2** **such as** Like; for example: *Janice likes fiction books such as "Star Wars", "Harry Potter" and "Hunger Games".*

suck /sʌk/ [verb] **1** To bring liquid into your mouth: *We went to see the new puppies. They were lying on the floor, sucking milk from their mother's breasts.* **2** To have something in your mouth for a long time: *You're not allowed to suck candies in class.*

sucker /ˈsʌk·ər/ [countable noun] **1** A part on the body of certain animals which enables them to stick to a surface: *Octopus have suckers on their tentacles.* **2** A rubber disc that enable things to be stuck to a surface: *The toy gun fires darts with suckers on the end.* **3** A person who believes everything they are told and so is easily tricked: *I am a real sucker: When Joe told me his dad is a millionaire I believed him.* **4** A person who likes something a lot and does not distinguish between good ones and bad ones, because he likes them all: *I am a sucker for love songs, any love songs.* ■ This use is informal. ■ We say: "to be a sucker **for** something/somebody".

sudden /ˈsʌd.ən/ [adjective] **1** Happening quickly: *Olive's sudden illness gave us all a shock.* **2 all of a sudden** In a quick and unexpected way: *Yesterday I was walking to school when, all of a sudden, a dog jumped out at me from behind a tree.*

suddenly /ˈsʌd.ən.li/ [adverb] In a sudden way: *I was sitting in the park reading when it suddenly began to rain.*

suede /sweɪd/ [uncountable noun] A soft leather: *Do you like my blue suede shoes?*

suffer /ˈsʌf·ər/ [verb] To experience pain, sadness, or loss: *I'm suffering from a very bad flu and I can't go to school.*

suffering /ˈsʌf·ər·ɪŋ/ [uncountable noun] Great pain, sadness or loss: *Human beings often ask themselves why there is so much suffering in the world.*

sufficient /səˈfɪʃ.ənt/ [adjective] Enough: *We didn't really have sufficient time to finish the test.*

suffix /ˈsʌf.ɪks/ [countable noun] Letters that you add to the end of a word to change its meaning: *If you add the suffix "less" to "harm", you get "harmless", which describes something that will not harm you.*

sugar /ˈʃʊg·ər/ [uncountable noun] **1** A substance that makes food sweet: *Several countries in the Caribbean produce and export sugar.* **2 icing sugar** See **icing sugar**.

suggest /səˈdʒest/ [verb] To say what you think should be done: *I suggested to my brother that he tell the teacher about his problem.* ■ We say "suggest **to** (somebody)".

suggestion /səˈdʒes.tʃən/ [countable noun] Saying what you think should be done: *We need some ideas for raising money for the school theater group. Any suggestions?*

suicide /ˈsuː.ɪ.saɪd/ [countable noun] **1** Killing yourself: *Her attempt at suicide was the result of a profound depression.* **2 commit suicide** To kill yourself: *Adolph Hitler committed suicide when he realized that he had lost the war.*

suit[1] /suːt/ [countable noun] **1** A jacket with either pants or a skirt: *My dad has bought himself a new gray suit for my brother's wedding.* See picture at **clothes**. **2** One of the four groups with the same symbol in a pack of cards: *The four suits in United States a pack of cards are: hearts, diamonds, clubs and spades.* ■ Be careful with the pronunciation of this word. It rhymes with "boot".

suit[2] /suːt/ [verb] **1** To look good on you: *I like your new dress; the color really suits you.* **2** To be right: *How about meeting at 8 o'clock? Does that suit you?* ■ Be careful with the pronunciation of this word. It rhymes with "boot".

suitable /ˈsu·t̬ə·bəl/ [adjective] Right or acceptable: *I don't think that movie is really suitable for young children.* ■ Be careful with the pronunciation of this word! The first part of this word rhymes with "boot".

suitcase /ˈsutkeɪs/ [countable noun] A container to carry things in when you travel: *We had to wait a long time for our suitcases to come through at Los Angeles Airport.* ■ Be careful with the pronunciation of this word! The first part of this word rhymes with "boot". ■ "Case" is short for "suitcase".

sulk /sʌlk/ [verb] To be angry and not speak to anybody: *Stop sulking! I'm sorry I said that you're terrible at football.*

sultan /ˈsʌltən/ [countable noun] A Muslim ruler, especially in the past: *The first sultan ruled at the end of the 10th century.*

sum /sʌm/ [countable noun] **1** A simple mathematical operation: *Have you finished your sums yet?* **2** The answer that you get when you add two numbers together: *The sum of fifteen and fifteen is thirty.* **3** An amount of money: *My cousin won a large sum of money in the Lottery.*

summarize or **summarise** /ˈsʌm·əˌraɪz/ [verb] To give a short description of the most important ideas of something: *I usually summarize each chapter of my history book to help me remember it.*

summary /ˈsʌm·ə·ri/ [countable noun] A short description of the most important ideas of something: *We have to write a summary of what we discussed in class today.* ■ The plural is "summaries".

summer /ˈsʌm·ər/ [noun] The season of the year between spring and fall: *When I was smaller, we always used to spend the summer at my uncle's house.* See page 448.

summer resort [noun] A place for organized vacation: *On vacation we're going to a summer resort.*

summit /ˈsʌm.ɪt/ [countable noun] The top of a mountain: *The first successful attempt to reach the summit of Mount Everest was in 1953.* See page 445.

†**sun** /sʌn/ [noun] **1** The round object in the sky that gives light and heat: *Without the energy from the sun, life on earth would be impossible.* See page 446. **2** The light and the heat that the sun gives: *Don't sit in the sun for too long or you'll get burned.* ■ Be careful with the pronunciation of this word! The "u" is pronounced like the "u" in "cup".

sunbathe /ˈsʌn.beɪð/ [verb] To lie in the sun: *Lying down on the beach sunbathing is very boring.* ■ Be careful with the pronunciation of this word! The "u" is pronounced like the "u" in "cup", and "ba" rhymes with "day".

sunburned or **sunburnt** /ˈsʌn.bɜːnt/ US: /-bɝːnt/ [adjective] When talking of people, burnt by being in the sun: *Larry fell asleep on the beach and got sunburned.*

†**Sunday** /ˈsʌn.deɪ/ [noun] The first day of the week: *Sunday is between Saturday and Monday.* ■ Be careful! "Sunday" has a capital "S". See picture at **calendar**.

sunflower /ˈsʌnˌflaʊ·ər/, /-flaʊər/ [countable noun] A tall plant with very large yellow flowers: *The sunflower is grown for its seeds as well as its flowers.* See page 433.

sung /sʌŋ/ Past participle of **sing**.

sunglasses US: /ˈsʌnˌglæs.ɪz/ UK: /ˈsʌŋˌglɑː.sɪz/ [countable noun] Dark glasses to protect your eyes from the sun's rays: *I left my sunglasses on the beach and now I've lost them.* ■ When we talk about two or more "sunglasses", we use the word "pairs": "I have two pairs of sunglasses". See picture at **glasses**.

sunk /sʌŋk/ Past participle of **sink²**.

sunken /ˈsʌŋ.kən/ [adjective] Which is beneath the surface, especially of water: *The bottom of the boat crashed into the sunken rocks.*

sunlight /ˈsʌn.laɪt/ [uncountable noun] The light from the sun: *Let's go in the shade; the sunlight's very bright today.*

sunny /ˈsʌn.i/ [adjective] Bright with the light from the sun: *What a lovely sunny day it is! Let's go on a picnic.* ■ The comparative form is "sunnier" and the superlative form is "sunniest".

sunrise /ˈsʌn.raɪz/ [uncountable noun] When the sun appears in the sky: *My aunt is a farmer and she has to get up at sunrise every day.*

sunset /ˈsʌn.set/ [uncountable noun] When the sun goes down: *Let's get a photograph of this sunset. Isn't it beautiful?*

sunshine /ˈsʌn.ʃaɪn/ [uncountable noun] The light and heat from the sun: *Let's eat our sandwiches outside in the sunshine.*

suntan /ˈsʌn.tæn/ [countable noun] The brown color that you get from sunbathing: *What a fantastic suntan you've got. Have you been on vacation?* ■ "Tan" is short for "suntan".

super /ˈsu·pər/ [adjective] Wonderful: *What a super person Jimmy is. I really like him.* ■ This word is informal.

superb /sʊˈpɜrb/ [adjective] Extremely good: *We had a superb meal in an Italian restaurant.*

superimpose /ˌsuːpərɪmˈpəʊz/ [verb] To place words or images on top of something: *The couple asked the photographer to superimpose some of the wedding photos to form a collage.*

†**superior** /sʊˈpɪər·i·ər/ [adjective] Better than somebody or something: *These shoes are of superior quality to the ones I bought here last year.*

superiority /sʊˌpɪər·iˈɔr·ɪ·t̬i/, /-ˈɑr·ɪ·t̬i/ [uncountable noun] Being superior: *I can't stand Jill's air of superiority when she is answering the teacher's questions.*

superlative /sʊˈpɜr·lə·t̬ɪv/ [noun and adjective] The form of an adjective that indicates its greatest level: *"Highest" is the superlative form of "high".*

†**supermarket** /ˈsu·pərˌmɑr·kɪt/ [countable noun] A large store where food and other things are sold: *My parents always do the week's shopping on Saturdays in the local supermarket.*

supernatural /ˌsu·pərˈnætʃ·ər·əl/ [adjective] Relating to ghosts, spirits and other unnatural forces: *The bad guy of the movie was over nine feet tall and had supernatural powers.*

supersonic /ˌsu·pərˈsɑn·ɪk/ [adjective] Faster than the speed of sound: *Concorde was the world's first supersonic passenger aircraft and first flew in 1969.*

superstition /ˌsu·pərˈstɪʃ·ən/ [countable noun] Something that people believe and that is not based on logic: *There's a superstition that breaking a mirror brings you bad luck.*

supervise /ˈsu·pərˌvɑɪz/ [verb] To watch somebody doing something to make sure that it is done correctly: *The teacher supervised us very carefully while we did the experiment.*

supervision /ˌsu·pərˈvɪʒ·ən/ [uncountable noun] Watching somebody doing something to make sure that it is done correctly: *Little children need supervision at all times.*

supper /ˈsʌp·ər/ [countable noun] A meal that you have late in the evening: *Shall we have supper out or stay at home?*

supply¹ /səˈplaɪ/ [countable noun] An amount of something that you keep: *Have you bought the supplies for the trip?* ■ The plural is "supplies".

†**supply²** /səˈplaɪ/ [verb] To give or to sell something that is needed: *Tim's dad works in a bakery that supplies all the local stores with bread, buns and*

a b c d e f g h i j k l m n o p q r s t u v w x y z

cakes. ■ Be careful with the spelling of these forms: "supplies", "supplied".

↑**support[1]** /sə'pɔːt/ [countable noun] **1** A thing that holds something up: *Be careful with that post. It's the main support of the tent.* **2** Help: *I'd like to thank you for all the support that you have given me.*

support[2] /sə'pɔːt/ [verb] **1** To hold something up: *These pillars support the roof of the building.* **2** To give somebody the things that they need to live: *I don't know how Mrs. Duncan manages. She's got four children and her parents to support.* **3** To be on the side of somebody: *Harry and Bill support New Orleans Saints.*

↑**supporter** /sə'pɔr·t̬ər/, /-'pour·t̬ər/ [countable noun] A fan or a follower: *In our town the football supporters always behave well.*

↑**suppose** /sə'pouz/ [verb] **1** To expect that something will happen: *I suppose that you'll spend Christmas with you grandparents as usual.* **2** **to be supposed to** To be expected to do something: *Come here, please! You're supposed to be helping me!*

supposing [conjunction] In case; if: *Supposing the bus comes before Tom does, what do we do then?*

↑**sure** US: /ʃur/ UK: /ʃɔːʳ/ [adjective] **1** Certain: *I'm sure I saw you at the disco on Saturday.* **2** **to be sure to** To do something for sure: *If you wait outside school at 4 o'clock, you'll be sure to see Sally come out.* **3** **to make sure** To check something to be sure about it: *Make sure you switch off the gas before you leave the house.*

surely /'ʃuər·li/, /'ʃour·li/ [adverb] Certainly, I am sure that: *Surely you're not going to wear that awful dress at the party!*

surf[1] /sɜːf/ [uncountable noun] The white bubbles on top of waves: *Look at all that surf on the waves! It must be very windy.*

surf[2] /sɜːf/ [verb] To ride on the waves with a board: *I tried to learn to surf last summer but I found it very difficult.*

↑**surface** /'sɜr·fəs/ [countable noun] **1** The outside of something: *Make sure you clean the surface of the laboratory bench properly.* **2** The top of the water: *The ball went under the water but then appeared on the surface.* ■ Be careful with the pronunciation of this word! The "a" is pronounced like "i" in "did".

surfboard US: /'sɝːf.bɔːrd/ UK: /'sɜːf.bɔːd/ [countable noun] A board that you use for surfing: *Richard has bought himself a new surfboard and has given me his old one.*

surfing /'sɜr·fɪŋ/ [uncountable noun] The sport of riding on the waves with a board: *Anna won a cup in a surfing competition last year.*

surgeon /'sɜr·dʒən/ [countable noun] A doctor who performs operations: *Kate's aunt is an excellent surgeon whose specialty is doing heart transplants.*

surgery /'sɜr·dʒə·ri/ [countable noun] Cutting somebody's body for medical reasons: *My grandpa has to have heart surgery next month.*

↑**surname** /'sɜr·neɪm/ [countable noun] The name that you share with other people in your family: *My first name is Michael and my surname is Smith.* ■ The same meaning: "family name", "last name".

↑**surprise[1]** /sə'praɪz/ [countable noun] **1** Something that is not expected: *Don't tell Freddie about the present. It's supposed to be a surprise.* **2** The feeling that you have when something unexpected happens: *I was sure that I was going to fail the test, but to my surprise, I passed.*

surprise[2] /sə'praɪz/ [verb] To give a surprise: *Maggie's reaction surprised us all.*

↑**surprised** /sər'prɑɪzd/, /sə-/ [adjective] Feeling or showing surprise: *She was so surprised when she saw him that she dropped her coffee.* ■ See box at **bored**.

↑**surprising** /sər'prɑɪ·zɪŋ/, /sə-/ [adjective] Giving surprise: *We all found the movie surprising. It wasn't what we had expected at all.* ■ See box at **bored**.

surrealistic /səˌrɪə'lɪs.tɪk/ [adjective] Very unusual and strange, not appearing to be real: *The atmosphere in the deserted city was surrealistic.*

surrender /sə'ren·dər/ [verb] To stop fighting, to admit defeat: *The soldiers surrendered and the war came to an end.*

↑**surround** /sə'raʊnd/ [verb] To go or be round something: *Our house is surrounded by trees.*

↑**surroundings** /sə'raʊn.dɪŋz/ [plural noun] The things that surround you: *The hotel that we go to on vacation every year has beautiful surroundings.*

↑**survey** /'sɜr·veɪ/ [countable noun] Asking questions about what people think: *At school we did a survey on the type of music people like.*

survival /sər'vɑɪ·vəl/ [uncountable noun] The state of continuing to live: *They went on a safari and took with them everything they needed for survival.*

↑**survive** /sər'vɑɪv/ [verb] To live through difficult circumstances: *I don't know how Irene survived such a terrible accident.*

survivor [countable noun] A person who survives a disaster: *There were no survivors of the air crash.*

↑**suspect[1]** /'sʌspekt/ [countable noun] A person who the police think has done something wrong: *The police say that they have arrested a suspect.*

suspect[2] /sə'spekt/ [verb] **1** To believe that something may be true: *I suspect that Tom is not coming today. It's 10 o'clock and he hasn't phoned.* **2** To believe that somebody may have done something: *"Who did that drawing on the white-board?" "I suspect George".*

suspend /sə'spend/ [verb] **1** To hang something: *At the circus the best act was an acrobat who was suspended from the top of the tent.* **2** To stop something: *The concert was suspended because one of the singers was ill.*

suspenders /sə'spen·dərz/ [plural noun] Elastic straps to keep your pants up: *My uncle wears red suspenders.* ■ In British English they say "braces".

suspense /sə'spents/ [uncountable noun] A feeling of fear and anxiety while waiting for something to happen: *The suspense in the movie was tremendous.*

suspension /sə'spenʃən/ [uncountable noun] **1** The condition of being stopped temporarily: *The suspension of the building work is the result of problems with the finance.* **2** A form of punishment that consists in not being permitted to attend school or work or to compete in sport: *The player was punished with a three game suspension.* **3** The condition of hanging in the air: *For a climber, suspension on the end of a rope is normal.* **4** In chemistry, the dispersion of solid or liquid particles in a liquid or gas without being mixed: *When flour is added to water, a suspension is produced.* **5** The system by which a vehicle is supported on its wheels and the passengers protected from the shocks: *My father's car is a 4x4 and has independent suspension for each wheel.* **6 suspension bridge** A bridge suspended from steel cables: *We crossed Brooklyn Bridge which is one of the most famous suspension bridges in the world.*

†**suspicion** /sə'spɪʃ.ən/ [countable noun] The belief, without certain proof, that something has happened: *I have a suspicion that Jennifer is in trouble.*

†**suspicious** /sə'spɪʃ.əs/ [adjective] Feeling or giving the idea that something is wrong: *Marilyn Monroe died in suspicious circumstances.*

†**swallow**[1] /'swɒləʊ/ [countable noun] A small bird with a long split tail and special way of flying: *You know that summer is really here when you see the swallows.*

†**swallow**[2] /'swɒləʊ/ [verb] To make food or drink go from your throat to your stomach: *She swallowed her breakfast quickly and ran down the stairs.*

swam /swæm/ Past tense of **swim**.

swamp /swɒmp/ [countable noun] Very wet ground: *There are always a lot of insects near a swamp in summer.*

swan US: /swɑːn/ UK: /swɒn/ [countable noun] A large bird with a long neck: *Swans are beautiful, elegant birds that live on lakes and rivers.*

swap /swɒp/ [verb] To exchange one thing for another: *I like your T-shirt. Will you swap it with me?* ■ Be careful with the spelling of these forms: "swapped", "swapping".

swarm US: /swɔːrm/ UK: /swɔːm/ [countable noun] A large group of insects flying together: *Look at that swarm of bees coming this way!* 👁 See picture at **groups**.

sway /sweɪ/ [verb] To move from side to side: *The palm trees swayed in the wind.*

†**swear, swore, sworn** US: /swer/ UK: /sweəʳ/ [verb] **1** To use rude words: *When he bumped his car into the lamp-post, he swore.* **2** To make a solemn promise: *I swore that I would never speak to her again.* **3 swear word** A rude word: *Don't use those swear words in front of grandma!*

†**sweat**[1] /swet/ [uncountable noun] The liquid that comes out of your skin when you are hot: *He had run for miles and his T-shirt was wet with sweat.*

sweat[2] [verb] To have sweat coming out of your skin: *It was so hot in the room that we were all sweating.*

†**sweater** US: /'swet̬.ɚ/ UK: /'swet.əʳ/ [countable noun] A warm piece of clothing with long sleeves: *Do you like my new sweater?* ■ The same meaning: "jersey", "jumper", "pullover". "Sweater" is the most commonly used word. 👁 See picture at **clothes**.

sweat gland [countable noun] A gland which produces and excretes sweat: *Sweat glands are found beneath the skin.*

sweatshirt /'swet,ʃɜrt/ [countable noun] A sweater made out of thick cotton: *It was so hot that I had to take my sweatshirt off.* 👁 See picture at **clothes**.

†**sweep, swept, swept** /swiːp/ [verb] **1** To clean something by brushing it: *Can you sweep the floor, please?* **2** To move very quickly: *The principal swept through the classroom, telling us all to go to the lunch room.* **3** To push something quickly and smoothly: *She swept the money off the table and into her pocket.*

TO SWEEP

a b c d e f g h i j k l m n o p q r **s** t u v w x y z

⁺**sweet**[1] /swiːt/ [adjective] **1** With sugar: *This cake is too sweet for me.* 👁 See picture at **opposite**. **2** Nice: *What a sweet baby!* **3** Kind and loving: *I was very upset, but the teacher was sweet to me and I felt better.* **4** Smelling good: *Those flowers smell sweet.*

sweet[2] /swiːt/ [countable noun] **1** See **candy**. ■ This use is British English. **2** A sweet dish that you have at the end of a meal: *What would you like for sweet? Fruit or apple pie?* ■ In this use "sweet" is informal.

sweet corn /ˈswiːt.kɔːn/ US: /-kɔːrn/ [uncountable noun] The yellow part of the corn plant: *I love sweet corn with butter.* ■ Compare with "corn" (the plant).

sweetheart /ˈswitˌhɑrt/ [countable noun] Somebody that you love: *My grandma married her childhood sweetheart: my grandfather!*

⁺**swell, swelled, swollen** /swel/ [verb] To get bigger: *I got bitten by a wasp the other day, and my arm swelled like a balloon.*

swelled Past tense of **swell**. ■ Be careful with the pronunciation of the end of this word. The last "e" is not pronounced.

⁺**swelling** /ˈswel.ɪŋ/ [countable noun] A lump on the body: *I went to the doctor's because I had a swelling on my hand.*

swept /swept/ Past tense and past participle forms of **sweep**.

swerve /swɜːv/ [verb] To turn quickly to avoid something: *The car swerved so as not to hit the dog and went off the road.*

swift /swɪft/ [adjective] Fast: *Claire is a very swift player and we're hoping that she'll score some goals for our team.*

swiftly [adverb] In a rapid, easy way: *We swiftly put the tables back in the right place.*

swim[1] /swɪm/ [countable noun] Moving through the water: *Shall we go for a swim?*

⁺**swim**[2], **swam, swum** /swɪm/ [verb] To move through the water: *I swam across the lake in about twenty minutes.* ■ Be careful with the spelling of this form: "swimming".

swim bladder [countable noun] A sac filled with gas which helps fish control their buoyancy: *The swim bladder helps a fish to stay at the depth it wants without wasting energy.*

swimmer /ˈswɪm·ər/ [countable noun] A person who swims: *Mark is an excellent swimmer.*

⁺**swimming** /ˈswɪm.ɪŋ/ [uncountable noun] The sport you do when you swim: *Swimming is my favorite sport.* 👁 See picture at **sport**.

⁺**swimming pool** [countable noun] A place where you can swim: *Let's go to the outdoor swimming pool. It's a really nice day.* ■ We also say "pool".

swimming trunks [plural noun] Short pants that men and boys wear for swimming: *I like your new swimming trunks. Where did you get them?* ■ When we talk about two or more "swimming trunks", we use the word "pairs": "I bought three pairs of swimming trunks". ■ We also say "trunks". 👁 See picture at **clothes**.

swimsuit /ˈswɪmˌsut/ [countable noun] A piece of clothing that women and girls wear for swimming: *Put your swimsuit on and we'll go to the beach.*

swing[1] /swɪŋ/ [countable noun] A suspended seat that moves backwards and forwards: *Let's go and play on the swings in the park.*

⁺**swing**[2], **swung, swung** /swɪŋ/ [verb] **1** To move backwards and forwards while you are hanging from something: *He tied the rope to the branch and swung on it for a long time.* **2** To make something move backwards and forwards: *Swing your arms as you walk and you'll soon get warm.*

swipe [verb] To steal something: *Hey! You've swiped my pencil.* ■ This use is informal.

⁺**switch**[1] /swɪtʃ/ [countable noun] A small object that you press to turn electricity on: *The light switch is on the left as you go in.*

switch[2] /swɪtʃ/ [verb] To change to another thing: *We always used to walk to school but this term we've switched to getting the bus.*

▶ **PHRASAL VERBS** · **to switch off** To press a switch to turn electricity off: *Switch the television off and listen to me.* · **to switch on** To press a switch to turn electricity on: *Switch the light on, please. It's getting dark.*

swollen /ˈswəʊlən/ Past participle of **swell**.

sword US: /sɔːrd/ UK: /sɔːd/ [countable noun] A very long, sharp knife for fighting: *We saw some beautiful swords at the Viking exhibition on Sunday.*

swore US: /swɔːr/ UK: /swɔːʳ/ Past tense of **swear**.

sworn /swɔːn/ Past participle of **swear**.

swum /swʌm/ Past participle of **swim**.

swung /swʌŋ/ Past tense and past participle forms of **swing**.

syllable /ˈsɪl.ə.bl̩/ [countable noun] A part of a word that has one vowel sound: *The word "institution" has four syllables.*

⁺**symbol** /ˈsɪm.bəl/ [countable noun] A sign or an object that represents something: *The dove is the symbol of peace.*

symmetrical /sɪˈmet.rɪ.kəl/ [adjective] That has parts that are in pleasant harmony or that exactly match: *The new arts center building is not symmetrical, it is very unusual.*

symmetry /ˈsɪm.ə.tri/ [uncountable noun] The state where the parts or sides of something are in harmony or exactly match each other: *From the front the aircraft has perfect symmetry.* ■ The plural is "symmetries".

↑**sympathetic** /ˌsɪm·pəˈθet̬·ɪk/ [adjective] Understanding and kind: *Kitty was very sympathetic when my boyfriend left me.*

↑**sympathy** /ˈsɪm.pə.θi/ [uncountable noun] Understanding and kindness: *Everyone showed a lot of sympathy when my father died.* ■ The plural is "sympathies".

symphonic /sɪmˈfɒn.ɪk/ US: /-ˈfɑː.nɪk/ [adjective] Referring to a symphony: *The orchestra played some beautiful pieces of symphonic music.*

symphony /ˈsɪmp.fə.ni/ [countable noun] A long musical composition for an orchestra: *Symphonies usually have four parts.* ■ The plural is "symphonies".

symptom /ˈsɪmp.təm/ [countable noun] A sign of an illness: *All your symptoms make me think that you must have chickenpox.*

synagogue /ˈsɪn·əˌgɑg/ [countable noun] A place where Jews meet to pray: *There are many synagogues in United States.*

synthetic /sɪnˈθet̬·ɪk/ [adjective] False; not natural: *This dress is made of synthetic material.*

syringe /sɪˈrɪndʒ/ [countable noun] A medical instrument for giving injections: *Most hospitals and clinics use disposable syringes.*

syrup /ˈsɪr.əp/ [uncountable noun] **1** A sweet substance made from sugar and juice or water: *I like tinned fruit but I don't like the syrup.* **2** Liquid medicine: *I had some cough syrup last night and I slept great.*

↑**system** /ˈsɪs.təm/ [countable noun] **1** An arrangement of things which work together: *Today we studied the human nervous system at school.* **2** A way of organizing something, a method: *You must tell me what your system is for studying, you always get really good grades.*

systemic /sɪˈstem.ɪk/ [adjective] Referring to or affecting a system, organism or institution as a whole: *Blood poisoning is a systemic infection.*

systole /ˈsɪs·tə·li/ [countable noun] A single heart contraction: *In the course of a systole, blood is pumped into the arteries.* ■ Compare with "diastole" (the period separating two contractions of the heart).

t /tiː/ The twentieth letter of the alphabet: *The name "Thomas" begins with a "T".*

tab[1] /tæb/ [countable noun] **1** A small piece of paper, metal or other material that is attached to something else and used for identification or for fastening: *A tab was attached to each document showing its ID number.* **2** **to keep tabs on somebody / something** To watch somebody or something periodically to check on the situation: *We should keep tabs on him: he could be a real talent.*

tab[2] [verb] To apply identifying strips: *The documents have to be tabbed for identification purposes.* ■ Be careful with the spelling of these forms: "tabbing", "tabbed".

†**table** /ˈteɪbl/ [countable noun] **1** A piece of furniture with a flat top and legs: *We always play dominoes on the kitchen table.* See picture at **living room**. **2** Facts or numbers arranged in columns: *Rachel is busy learning her multiplication tables.* **3** **coffee table** See "coffee table" in the word **coffee**. **4** **set the table** See "set the table" in the word **set**[2].

tablecloth /ˈteɪ·bəlˌklɔθ/ [countable noun] A cloth that you put over a table: *Take that tablecloth off; it's dirty.*

table soccer [countable noun] Game often played in bars in which you move players on bars on a table: *We used to play table soccer in my garage.* ■ The same meaning: "foosball".

tablespoon /ˈteɪ.bḷ.spuːn/ [countable noun] A spoon for serving food: *Don't forget to put tablespoons on the table for the mashed potatoes.*

†**tablet** /ˈtæb.lət/ [countable noun] A small, round piece of medicine: *Take these tablets three times a day.*

table tennis [countable noun] A game that is played by hitting a ball over a net on a table: *Sarah and Andrew are playing table tennis in the garage.* ■ The same meaning: "ping-pong".

tabulator [countable noun] The key of a computer for advancing certain positions: *Please do not use the space bar too often and use the tabulator instead.*

tact /tækt/ [uncountable noun] Acting or speaking carefully so that you do not upset people: *You didn't show much tact when you said that auntie Linda had become fat.*

tactful /ˈtækt.fᵊl/ [adjective] Careful not to do or to say things that upset people: *Be tactful. Don't mention the accident.*

tactic /ˈtæk.tɪk/ [countable noun] Way of doing something in order to be at an advantage: *The coach changed the tactics and the team won the game.*

tactile /ˈtæk.taɪl/ US: /-təl/ [adjective] Referring to the sense of touch: *Modern phones are now provided with a tactile screen.*

tactless /'tækt.ləs/ [adjective] Not careful about upsetting people: *She was tactless when she said that she didn't like their sister.*

tadpole /'tæd,poul/ [countable noun] A small animal with a simple form that lives in water and develops into a frog: *The frog's eggs hatched and produced lots of tadpoles.*

tag /tæg/ [countable noun] A label that gives you information about something: *There's no price tag on the CD so I'm going to ask the store assistant.*

ᐩ**tail** /teɪl/ [countable noun] The long and thin part at the back of an animal: *Monkeys have very long tails.*

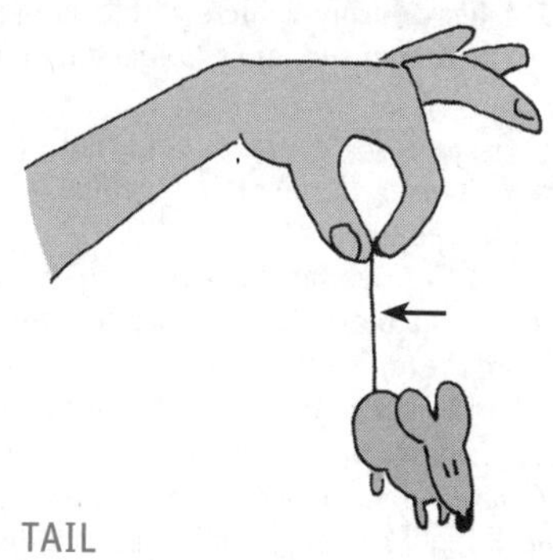

TAIL

tailor[1] [countable noun] A person who makes men's clothes: *My father has his suits made by the local tailor.* ■ A person who makes women's clothes is a "dressmaker".

tailor[2] [verb] To make and fit men's clothes: *He has his suits tailored in New York.*

ᐩ**take**, took, taken /teɪk/ [verb] **1** To carry something: *Take these glasses to the kitchen, please; Don't forget to take your keys.* **2** To remove; to steal: *Somebody has taken my pencil case.* **3** To hold something: *Can you take the baby a minute?* **4** To accompany somebody or drive somebody somewhere: *Who's taking the children to school tomorrow?* **5** To catch a vehicle: *We took the bus to the center; Why don't you take the night plane? It's cheaper.* **6** To occupy a place or space: *Is this seat taken?* **7** To swallow medicine: *He has to take the pills after lunch.* ■ Be careful! We don't use "take" when we talk about food and drink, we use "have". We say "have dinner", "have coffee", and so on. **8** To need time, to last: *The flight from Orlando to Dallas takes two hours. It took me 30 minutes to do the test.* **9** To accept something: *This hotel doesn't take dogs.* **10** To capture a place: *The enemy troops have just taken the town.* **11** To stand: *I can't take this pressure.* **12** To require a quality: *It takes courage to do that.* **13** **to take a look at something** To examine something: *Can you take a look at my drawing and give me some advice?* **14** **to take care of (somebody)** See "to take care of (somebody)" in the word **care.** **15** **to take into account** To consider something when you decide, evaluate or do something: *I will take that into account when I decide.* **16** **to take note** To notice and learn: *I took note of how Joe does it, and I think I know how to do it.* **17** **to take notes** To write down things to help you understand or study something: *I take a lot of notes in that class.* ◗ **PHRASAL VERBS** · **to take after (somebody)** To resemble somebody who is a relation: *The baby really takes after his mother.* · **to take (something) apart** To disconnect the parts of a machine, instrument or piece of furniture: *Help me to take apart this machine.* · **to take (somebody or something) away** **1** To remove, to cause something to disappear: *Here's an aspirin. It will take away the pain; When he had the attack they took him away.* **2** To get prepared food from a place to take home or take to the street: *I want a sandwich to take away.* · **to take (something) back** **1** To return something: *I'm going to take these shoes back to the store. They are too small.* **2** To retract your words, to admit that what you said before was wrong: *I take back what I said, it is a good place.* · **to take (something) down** **1** To take notes of something that is said: *The students took down the teacher's explanation.* **2** To lower something: *They took down the flag.* · **to take (somebody) in** To deceive somebody: *He really took us in. Everyone thought he was a nice guy.* · **to take (something) in** To assimilate ideas or information: *I'm going to stop studying for today. I can't take in any more information.* · **to take off** **1** To go into the air from the ground: *The plane took off at exactly eight o'clock.* **2** To become successful or popular: *Her business has really taken off.* · **to take (something) off** To remove something, especially clothes or accessories: *Take your boots off before you come into the house, please.* · **to take (somebody) on** **1** To begin to employ somebody: *Thirty workers have been taken on at the new factory.* **2** To compete against or fight somebody: *We took on the champions in the semi-final, and beat them.* · **to take (somebody) out** To invite somebody out: *He took me out to dinner.* · **to take (something) out** To remove something from a pocket, bag and so on: *I took out my cell phone.* · **to take over** **1** To get responsibility for: *Mrs. Wallace took over the class while our teacher was ill.* **2** To take control of something: *A German company has taken over the firm my sister works for.* · **to take to (somebody)** To like somebody: *I took to Susie from the start.* · **to**

take up **1** To occupy space or time: *The armchair by the bed takes up a lot of room.* **2** To start in a position: *After three years in the department I think you're ready to take up the manager position.* **3** To start a hobby: *I have taken up chess.*

taken /ˈteɪ.kᵊn/ Past participle of **take**.

take-off /ˈteɪkˌɔf/ [countable noun] The moment when an airplane leaves the ground: *What time is take-off?* ■ Compare with "landing" (the act of arriving on land).

takeout [countable noun] **1** A restaurant that sells food to eat at home or in the street: *How about buying something at the Mexican takeout?* **2** Food for eating at home or in the street: *My father ordered an Indian takeout for lunch last Sunday.*

tale /teɪl/ [countable noun] **1** A story: *I like mystery tales.* **2** A report: *Pat's always telling tales about her classmates.* **3** **fairy tale** A story about magic people or events, usually for children: *"The Beauty and the Beast" is one of my favorite fairy tales.*

↑**talent** /ˈtæl.ᵊnt/ [uncountable noun] A special skill at something: *The teacher says Hannah has a talent for languages.*

talented /ˈtæl·ən·tɪd/ [adjective] Able to do something well: *Everyone agrees that she's a talented actress.* ■ Be careful with the pronunciation of the end of this word. The last "e" is pronounced like the "i" in "did".

talk[1] /tɔːk/ [countable noun] **1** A conversation: *Matthew and I had a long talk on the phone this morning.* **2** A more or less informal speech: *A doctor's giving us a talk about sex this afternoon.*

↑**talk**[2] /tɔːk/ [verb] To speak: *Sarah says she doesn't want to talk to me.* ■ Be careful! We say: "talk **to** somebody" or "talk **about** (something)". ■ "Speak" has almost the same meaning as "talk". We usually say "talk" when we are referring to a conversation: "We talked for ages". We usually say "speak" when we are referring to the general action: "He speaks a lot. She speaks five languages".

talkative US: /ˈtɑː.kə.ɪv/ UK: /ˈtɔː.kə.tɪv/ [adjective] Who talks a lot: *Linda is very talkative in class.*

↑**tall** US: /tɑːl/ UK: /tɔːl/ [adjective] Somebody or something with more than average height: *My cousin James is very tall. He's 6 feet 2 inches.* ■ "Tall" is usually used for people, trees and structures. Compare with "high[1]" (is used for abstract nouns like "tech" or "definition" and for inanimate things). 👁 See picture at **opposite**.

tambourine /ˌtæm.bəˈriːn/ [countable noun] A small, round drum with metal pieces around it: *I play the tambourine in the school band.*

tame[1] /teɪm/ [adjective] Accustomed to human beings: *Our next-door neighbor keeps a tame monkey.*

tame[2] /teɪm/ [verb] To make a wild animal accustomed to human beings: *It took Kim a lot of patience to tame his monkey.*

tan /tæn/ [countable noun] See **suntan**.

tangerine /ˌtæn·dʒəˈrin/ [countable noun] A small orange: *Would you like a tangerine?*

tangram [countable noun] A puzzle originating in China that is made of seven flat pieces: *The pieces of the tangram have to be put together to make different shapes.*

↑**tank** /tæŋk/ [countable noun] **1** A large container for liquids or gases: *We'll have to fill the tank at the next gas station.* **2** A heavy army vehicle with a long gun out front: *The army used tanks to take the rebels' positions.*

tanker /ˈtæŋ·kər/ [countable noun] A large ship that carries oil: *When the tanker hit the rocks it spilled a lot of petroleum into the sea.*

↑**tap**[1] /tæp/ [countable noun] **1** See **faucet**. ■ This use is British English. **2** A light blow: *The dog started barking when it heard the tap on the window.*

tap[2] /tæp/ [verb] To hit something softly: *Tap on the door to see if anybody's in.* ■ Be careful with the spelling of these forms: "tapped", "tapping".

↑**tape**[1] /teɪp/ [countable noun] **1** A long, thin strip of cloth, paper or sticky material: *We used some tape to prepare the parcels.* **2** A thin band of plastic for recording sound or images: *My parents still have some 80's music tapes that they like to play in our car.*

tape[2] /teɪp/ [verb] **1** To fix something with a tape: *You'll have to tape the parcel up before you take it to the post office.* **2** To record music or a film: *Shall we tape the Charlie Chaplin film tonight?*

tape measure [countable noun] A long piece of cloth or metal marked in centimeters or inches, used for measuring: *Do you have a tape measure? I want to measure the length of this shelf.*

tape-recorder [countable noun] A machine that records and plays back sounds: *The journalist prepared her tape-recorder for her interview with the candidate.*

tapestry /ˈtæp.ɪ.stri/ [countable noun] A piece of cloth with a picture on it: *When we visited the White House we saw some beautiful tapestries.* ■ The plural is "tapestries".

tapeworm /ˈteɪpˌwɜrm/ [countable noun] A parasite which lives in the intestines of humans and other animals: *The tapeworm has a long, segmented body and a small head.*

tap or **tap dance** [countable noun] A kind of dance with shoes with metal plates on the heels and toes to make sound with your feet: *We're learning new tap steps for the recital.*

↑**target** /ˈtɑr·gɪt/ [countable noun] An object that you aim at: *The missile just missed the target.*

tarnish /ˈtɑr·nɪʃ/ [verb] To stain something: *The reputation of this actor was tarnished by the scandal.*

tarsal [adjective] Referring to the ankle bones: *He broke his tarsal bones in the accident.* ■ Compare to "carpal" (referring to the wrist bones).

tart[1] /tɑːt/ [countable noun] A piece of pastry with sweet food on top: *Would you like another piece of strawberry tart?* ■ Compare with "pie" (a dish made of pastry filled with meat, vegetables or fruit).

tart[2] /tɑːt/ [adjective] With a sharp or acid taste: *I like candy made with tart lemon flavor and cover with sugar.*

tartan US: /ˈtɑːr.ᵊn/ UK: /ˈtɑː.tᵊn/ [uncountable noun] A woolen cloth with colored squares on it: *In 1998 the US Senate designated 6 April as Tartan Day in recognition of the monumental achievements and invaluable contributions made by Scottish Americans.*

†**task** US: /tæsk/ UK: /tɑːsk/ [countable noun] A job that you must do: *I was given the task of checking that all the younger children crossed the road safely.*

†**taste[1]** /teɪst/ [noun] **1** The ability to appreciate food and recognize flavors: *Taste is one of the five senses.* **2** The particular flavor of food or drink: *Some olives have a very bitter taste.* **3** The ability to choose what is good: *Jenny has great taste in music.* **4** A small quantity of food or drink: *Can I have a taste of your pie?*

taste[2] /teɪst/ [verb] **1** To test the flavor of food or drink: *Can I taste a bit of that cheese to see if I like it?* **2** To have a particular flavor in your mouth: *This soup tastes delicious.*

taste bud US: /ˈteɪst ˌbʌd/ [countable noun] Any of the many nerve endings on the surface of the tongue: *Taste buds allow us to savor food as we eat it.*

tasteful /ˈteɪst.fᵊl/ [adjective] Having good taste: *The clothes Lynn wears are very tasteful.*

tasteless /ˈteɪst.ləs/ [adjective] **1** Without taste: *This soup is tasteless.* **2** Having a bad taste: *Their dining room furniture is completely tasteless.*

tasty /ˈteɪ.sti/ [adjective] Having a pleasant taste: *The pizza we had yesterday was really tasty.* ■ The comparative form is "tastier" and the superlative form is "tastiest".

tattoo /təˈtuː, tætˈuː/ [countable noun] A picture on a person's skin: *He has a tattoo of a dragon on his right arm.*

taught US: /tɑːt/ UK: /tɔːt/ Past tense and past participle forms of **teach**. ■ Be careful with the pronunciation of this word. It rhymes with "fort".

Taurus US: /ˈtɔːr.əs/ UK: /ˈtɔː.rəs/ [noun] A sign of the zodiac: *If your birthday is between April 21st and May 20th, you're a Taurus.* ■ Be careful. "Taurus" has a capital "T".

†**tax** /tæks/ [noun] Money paid to the government: *People pay taxes according to their income.* ■ The plural is "taxes".

†**taxi** /ˈtæk.si/ [countable noun] A car that takes you somewhere if you pay: *We took a taxi to the airport.* ■ The same meaning: "cab".

†**tea** /tiː/ [noun] **1** A drink that is made with hot water and dry leaves: *Mom's making tea in the kitchen.* **2** A plant that you make a drink with: *What sort of tea shall I get, dad?* **3** A light afternoon meal: *My aunt can't come to lunch, but she's coming to tea.* **4** An evening meal: *Will you join us for tea tonight?*

†**teach, taught, taught** /tiːtʃ/ [verb] **1** To give lessons: *My uncle Jim teaches English.* **2** To show somebody how to do something: *My father's going to teach me to make spaghetti.*

†**teacher** /ˈti·tʃər/ [countable noun] A person who gives lessons: *Our history teacher gave us a talk about Abraham Lincoln yesterday.* ■ Be careful! We say: "She is **a** teacher". (We don't say: "She is teacher"). 👁 See picture at **classroom**.

†**teaching** /ˈtiː.tʃɪŋ/ [uncountable noun] A teacher's job or work: *Our new teacher has unusual teaching methods.*

teacup /ˈtiːkʌp/ [countable noun] A cup for drinking tea: *He poured tea into the teacups.*

†**team** /tiːm/ [noun] **1** A group of people who play sport together: *There are eleven players in a soccer team.* **2** A group of people who work together: *The operation was carried out by a team of doctors.*

teamwork /ˈtimˌwɜrk/ [uncountable noun] The work done by a team: *This project requires good teamwork.*

teapot /ˈtiˌpɑt/ [countable noun] A special pot with a handle and a spout for making tea: *I dropped my grandma's best china teapot and broke it.* 👁 See picture at **pot**.

†**tear[1]** /teər/ [countable noun] **1** A drop of water from the eye: *The tears ran down his cheeks as he peeled the onion.* **2 to be in tears** To be crying: *Johnny was in tears when he discovered that his puppy was lost.* **3 to burst into tears** To start crying suddenly and dramatically: *She burst into tears when she heard the news.*

tear[2] /tɪər/ [countable noun] A hole usually in a piece of cloth: *It's time you sewed the tear in your coat.*

†**tear[3], tore, torn** /teər/ [verb] **1** To make a hole in something by pulling: *I tore my sleeve on a wire this morning.* **2** To remove something roughly: *The baby has torn some pages out of this book.*

▶ **PHRASAL VERBS** · **to tear (something) up** To pull paper or cloth into pieces: *I didn't like the photograph so I tore it up.*

tease /tiːz/ [verb] To annoy or to irritate somebody in a joking way: *She teased Adam about his new haircut.*

a b c d e f g h i j k l m n o p q r s **t** u v w x y z

teaspoon /'ti:.spu:n/ [countable noun] A small spoon for putting sugar into drinks and so on: *Pass me a teaspoon, please.*

⁺**technical** /'tek.nɪ.kᵊl/ [adjective] That requires special knowledge: *Books about medicine are difficult to understand because they are full of technical terms.*

technically /'teknɪkəli/ [adverb] **1** In terms of mechanics, applied sciences: *Technically the vehicle is very complicated.* **2** In terms of a specialized knowledge or skill: *Technically she is a fantastic dancer.* **3** Strictly, according to the regulations: *Technically speaking you are not bilingual, but...*

technician /tek'nɪʃ.ᵊn/ [countable noun] A worker with practical skills, particularly in industry or science: *Dad sent for a technician to repair the heat.*

⁺**technique** /tek'ni:k/ [noun] A special way of doing something: *Scientists are trying to find new techniques to cure cancer.*

technological /ˌteknə'lɒdʒɪkəl/ [adjective] Referring to technology: *Technological advances have made the treatment possible.*

⁺**technology** /tek'nɑl·ə·dʒi/ [noun] The knowledge or application of scientific or industrial methods: *Computer technology is advancing very rapidly nowadays.* ■ The plural is "technologies".

teddy or **teddy bear** /'tediˌbeər/ [countable noun] A soft toy bear: *Jason has had his teddy bear since he was a baby.* ■ The plural is "teddies" or "teddy bears".

tee [countable noun] In golf, the spot from which you first hit the ball when playing a hole: *He put the ball on the tee, looked at the hole and hit the ball.*

teenage [adjective] Of, or suitable for, people in their teens: *They have a teenage son.*

teenager /'tinˌeɪ·dʒər/ [countable noun] A person between thirteen and nineteen years old: *The disco on my street is always full of teenagers on Friday nights.*

teens [plural noun] The years of a person's life between the ages of thirteen and nineteen: *She's in her teens.*

tee-shirt [countable noun] See **T-shirt**.

teeth /ti:θ/ The plural of **tooth**.

telecommunications /ˌtelɪkəˌmju:nɪ'keɪʃənz/ [plural noun] Communications by phone, TV or radio, and the related science: *My sister works for a telecommunications company.*

telegram /'tel.ɪ.græm/ [countable noun] A message sent by telegraph: *In his telegram my brother told us to pick him up at the airport.*

telegraph /'tel·əˌgræf/ [uncountable noun] A system of sending messages by radio: *Before the ship sank, the radio operator sent out messages by telegraph.*

⁺**telephone**[1] /'telɪfəʊn/ [countable noun] See **phone**[1].

telephone[2] /'telɪfəʊn/ [verb] See **phone**[2].

telephone booth [countable noun] See **phone booth**.

telephone directory [countable noun] A book with a list of names and telephone numbers: *I've forgotten Simon's number. Pass me the telephone directory, please.* ■ The same meaning: "phone book".

telephone number [countable noun] See **phone number**.

telescope /'tel·əˌskoʊp/ [countable noun] An instrument for looking at distant objects: *If the sky's clear tonight we'll look at the stars through my telescope.*

⁺**television** /'tel·əˌvɪʒ·ən/ [noun] **1** A machine that receives and shows pictures and sound: *My father has bought a new television for the kitchen.* ■ "Boob tube" is informal for "television". 👁 See picture at **living room**. 👁 **See page 443.** **2** A system of sending out pictures and sound: *Did you see the baseball game on television this afternoon?* ■ "TV" is an abbreviation for "television".

⁺**tell,** told, told /tel/ [verb] **1** To make something known in words to somebody: *Louise has told everyone she's got a new hamster.* ■ Be careful. We don't say: "He told that he had no money". We say: "He told **me** that he had no money" or "He said that he had no money". ■ Compare with "say" (to pronounce words o sounds but not directly to somebody). ■ See box at **say**. **2** To give somebody instructions: *Tell him to wash his hands at once.* **3** To recognize something: *Can you tell which horse is in front?* **4** **I told you so** Words that you say when you warned somebody that something was going to happen, and it did: *"I've burned my fingers on the heater again". "I told you so".*

▸ **PHRASAL VERBS** · **to tell (somebody) off** To speak angrily to somebody because of what they have done: *Father will tell you off when he sees what you have done to your jacket.*

temper /'tem·pər/ [noun] **1** A person's mood particularly their capacity to be angry: *Nicola's got a sweet temper. She's always smiling.* **2** **to lose your temper** To become angry: *Wayne loses his temper each time he has to see the doctor.*

tempera /'tem.pər.ə/ US: /-pɚ.ə/ [uncountable noun] A painting method which uses paint combined with egg: *This canvas was painted using tempera.* ■ Compare with "watercolor" (pigment diluted with water).

temperate /'tem·pər·ət/ [adjective] When we talk about the weather, that is neither hot nor cold: *The weather is temperate in the Canary Islands all the year round.*

⁺**temperature** /'tem·pər·ə·tʃər/, /-ˌtʃʊr/ [noun] **1** A degree of heat or cold: *The temperature of the sea water here is cold even in summer.* **2** A body temperature that is above normal: *Mom gave me an aspirin when she found I had a temperature.*

template /ˈtempleɪt/ [countable noun] A pattern to be followed when working with metal or wood, or the model for a computer text: *The use of a template allows each item to be made identically.*

temple /ˈtem.pl̩/ [countable noun] A building where people pray: *Churches are Christian temples and mosques are Muslim temples.*

†**temporary** /ˈtem·pəˌrer·i/ [adjective] Used or held for a short time only: *My brother got a temporary job as a waiter when he went to Sydney.*

tempt /tempt/ [verb] To attract somebody to do something: *The boy was tempted to steal the chocolates from his sister's room.*

temptation /tempˈteɪ.ʃən/ [noun] Something that attracts you: *Philip resisted the temptation to take the money out of his brother's money box.*

tempting /ˈtemp.tɪŋ/ [adjective] Attractive: *The apple tart was so tempting that we couldn't resist having a taste of it before our mother came back.*

tempura US: /ˈtem.pʊ.rɑː/ UK: /temˈpʊə.rə/ [uncountable noun] A Japanese dish made of fish or vegetables lightly covered in batter and deep fried: *I always order tempura when I come to this restaurant.*

†**ten** /ten/ [noun, adjective and pronoun] The number 10: *Two times five equals ten.*

†**tend** /tend/ [verb] To be inclined to do something: *Marty tends to catch cold very easily when he plays outside.*

†**tendency** /ˈten.dənt.si/ [countable noun] The way a person usually behaves: *Sally has a tendency to lose things.* ■ The plural is "tendencies".

tender /ˈten·dər/ [adjective] **1** Easy to cut and to eat: *The steak I had at lunch was really tender.* **2** Kind, loving: *My grandfather is a very tender person.* **3** Hurt, damaged: *I hit my leg with a baseball bat last week and it's still a bit tender.*

tendon /ˈten.dən/ [countable noun] A thin piece of fibrous tissue which attaches muscle to bone: *The Achilles tendon connects the lower leg muscles to the heel bone.*

tennis /ˈten.ɪs/ [uncountable noun] **1** A game in which you hit a ball over a net with a racket: *Sheila always wins when we play tennis.* **2 tennis court** The place where you play tennis: *If the tennis court gets wet we won't be able to play our game.* 👁 See picture at **sport**.

tense[1] /tens/ [noun] A form of a verb that shows when things happen: *"I'll answer the phone" is a sentence in the future tense.*

tense[2] /tens/ [adjective] **1** Nervous, tight, anxious: *I'm always tense at the beginning of a test.* 👁 See picture at **emotions**. **2** Pulled tight: *Kirpal's leg muscles were tense after the game and he had to have a massage.*

†**tension** /ˈtent.ʃən/ [uncountable noun] The state of being tense: *The tension was enormous at the end of the movie.*

†**tent** /tent/ [countable noun] A structure made of strong cloth and poles, that you can sleep in: *We put our tent up under some trees in the field.*

tentacle /ˈten·tɑ·kəl/ [countable noun] A long arm with suckers possessed by some sea creatures, such as the octopus: *Tentacles are used for feeling, holding and feeding.* ■ Be careful with the pronunciation of this word! "cle" is pronounced as in "uncle".

tenth /tentθ/ [noun and adjective] Referring to ten: *The record department in this store is on the tenth floor.* ■ "Tenth" can also be written "10th".

†**term** US: /tɝːm/ UK: /tɜːm/ [countable noun] **1** One of the parts of a year at school: *The spring term always seems the longest one to me.* **2** A period of time: *We all still remember Carol's term of office as President of the student union.* **3** A name or a word with a special meaning: *This engineering book is difficult to understand because it's full of technical terms.* **4 in the long term** In a long period from now or over a long period: *My father says that in the long term, it's better to buy a good camera even if it is quite expensive.* **5 in the short term** For a short period from now: *My plans in the short term are to find any job and a house to rent. Later I will try to find a good job.*

terminal /ˈtɜr·mə·nə·l/ [countable noun] A place where a journey begins or ends: *Don't get off the bus until you get to the terminal.*

terms US: /tɝːmz/ UK: /tɜːmz/ [plural noun] **1** Conditions that tell you what you must do: *Jackie always wants us to play on her terms.* **2** Relations: *I haven't been on good terms with Bob since the summer.*

terrace /ˈter.əs/ [countable noun] A flat surface outside a restaurant where people can eat or drink: *It was such a nice day that we had lunch on the hotel terrace.*

terrain [uncountable noun] An extension of land, considered in terms of its physical characteristics: *The terrain in this area is uneven.*

terrestrial /təˈres.tri.əl/ [adjective] **1** Living or growing on land, not in the sea or in the air: *The elephant is a terrestrial creature.* **2** Of or relating to the planet earth: *These are my terrestrial everyday problems.* **3 terrestrial planet** A planet made mainly of rock, like the earth: *Saturn and Venus are not terrestrial planets, they are gas planets.* ■ Compare with "celestial" (referring to heaven or the sky).

†**terrible** /ˈter.ə.bl̩/ [adjective] **1** Very bad: *We had terrible weather when we visited Minneapolis last sum-*

mer. **2** With very bad consequences, horrible: *They saw a terrible accident on the freeway yesterday.*

terrific /tə'rɪf.ɪk/ [adjective] **1** Very good: *We had a terrific lunch at my aunt's yesterday.* **2** Very great: *The man drove across the junction at a terrific speed.*

terrify /'ter.ə.faɪ/ [verb] To frighten somebody greatly: *The children were terrified by the big rat.* ■ Be careful with the spelling of these forms: "terrifies", "terrified".

terrifying /'ter.ə.faɪ.ɪŋ/ [adjective] Frightening: *Our dog was very nervous last night because of the terrifying storm.*

territory /'ter·ə,tɔr·i/, /-,toʊr·i/ [noun] **1** The land under the control of a government: *The United States was British territory until 1776.* **2** An area dominated by a person or an animal: *We crossed into enemy territory under the cover of darkness.* ■ The plural is "territories".

terror /'ter·ər/ [uncountable noun] Great fear: *The boy ran away from the snake in terror.*

terrorism /'ter·ə,rɪz·əm/ [uncountable noun] The use of violence and murder to achieve political objectives: *Terrorism is a big problem in many countries.*

terrorist /'ter·ə·rəst/ [noun and adjective] A person who uses violence and murder to try to achieve political objectives: *The terrorists announced that they had put a bomb in a garbage can in the main street.*

tertiary [adjective] Relating to the third stage or level of something: *People at university are in tertiary education.*

⁺test[1] /test/ [countable noun] **1** An examination to see if something works well or is healthy: *I'm going to have a blood test.* **2** A short written or practical examination to see what somebody knows: *The teacher's giving us a math test tomorrow.*

test[2] /test/ [verb] **1** To examine or try something to see how it works: *Yesterday I tested my new basketball boots.* **2** To give somebody a short examination: *The teacher tested us in geography today.*

testicle /'testɪkl/ [countable noun] Either one of two male reproductive organs that lie behind the penis: *The testicles produce spermatozoa.* 👁 **See page 425.**

testimony /'tes·tə,moʊ·ni/ [noun] A statement that something is true: *The bank clerk's testimony proved that the robbers knew somebody working at the bank.* ■ The plural is "testimonies".

test tube [countable noun] A small glass tube used in chemical tests or in experiments: *We used test tubes to do an experiment in chemistry this morning.* 👁 **See page 440.**

tetanus /'tetənəs/ [uncountable noun] A disease caused by a specific bacteria: *The symptoms of tetanus are rigidity and paralysis of the muscles, especially around the mouth.*

⁺text[1] /tekst/ [noun] The main part of a book, a message or a newspaper, with writing but not with pictures: *We have to translate this text from Spanish into English for homework.*

text[2] /tekst/ [verb] To send a text message: *Please, text me when you get to the airport.*

textbook /'tekst.bʊk/ [countable noun] A book that students study at school: *You'll find the answer to these questions in your textbook.*

textile[1] /'tek.staɪl/ [countable noun] Woven cloth: *Textiles are used for clothing, for drapes and for many other household items.*

textile[2] [adjective] Referring to cloth or weaving: *The textile industry is mostly concentrated in Asia.*

texture /'teks·tʃər/ [noun] The feel or appearance of a surface or a substance: *This fabric has a wonderful soft texture.*

⁺than /ðæn, ðən/ [conjunction and preposition] A word used when comparing people or things: *Kate is much taller than me.* ■ Be careful! We say: "taller **than** me". (We don't say: "taller **that** me").

⁺thank /θæŋk/ [verb] **1** To say how grateful you are for something: *He thanked Laura for coming to his party.* **2** **thanks to** Because of: *Thanks to Mr. Gibbon, we managed to collect enough money for the new theater.*

Thanksgiving /,θæŋks'gɪvɪŋ/ [noun] A public holiday in the United States and Canada when people give thanks for the food that has been grown that year: *In the United States, Thanksgiving is celebrated on the fourth Thursday in November.* ■ Be careful! "Thanksgiving" has a capital "T".

thank you or **thanks** /'θæŋkju , θæŋks/ [interjection] Words you say to show that you are grateful: *Thanks for the dictionary.* ■ "Thank you" is more formal than "thanks".

⁺that[1] [adjective and pronoun] **1** The person or the thing distant from the speaker: *That boy doesn't live here any more.* **2** The person or the thing more distant from the speaker: *I don't like this dress I'm wearing; pass me that one, please.* ■ The plural is "those".

⁺that[2] /ðæt/ [pronoun] A word that is used instead of "who" or "which": *The ballpoint that you're using is mine.*

that[3] /ðæt/ [adverb] So: *I don't think Janet's mom can be that old.*

that[4] /ðæt, ðət/ [conjunction] A word that is used after certain verbs, nouns and adjectives to introduce a new part of the sentence: *He said that he'd call at a quarter to nine.* ■ Be careful! We say: "older **than** me". (We don't say: "older **that** me").

†**the** /ðiː, ðə/ [article] **1** A word that you use about something or somebody that is already known or has already been mentioned: *There's a book here. Is it the one you sent for?* **2** A word that you use when there is only one of a thing: *Make the earth a better place!* **3** A word that you use to define a group of people: *The old should try to understand the younger generation.* **4** A word that you use before dates: *My sister is getting married on the third of May.* ■ Be careful! We don't use "the" with parts of the body: "My leg hurts".

theater US: /ˈθiː.ə.ɚ/ [noun] **1** A building in which plays are acted: *Shall we go to the theater tonight?* **2** Plays in general: *I want to study theater when I leave school.* ■ The British English spelling is "theatre".

theatre UK: /ˈθɪə.təʳ/ [noun] See **theater**. ■ This is a British English spelling.

theft /θeft/ [noun] The act of stealing, usually without violence and secretly: *The woman was sent to prison for theft.*

†**their** US: /ðer/ UK: /ðeəʳ/ [adjective] Of people or things that have already been named, or belonging to them: *They've lost their ball.*

†**theirs** US: /ðerz/ UK: /ðeəz/ [pronoun] Belonging to them: *This ball isn't ours. It must be theirs.*

†**them** /ðem, ðəm/ [pronoun] A word used for "they", usually when it is the object of a sentence or comes immediately after a preposition: *I saw Sam and Louise at the movie theater last night and told them about the party on Saturday.*

†**theme** /θiːm/ [countable noun] A subject that you write or talk about: *The main theme of the book is life in the Middle Ages.*

theme park [countable noun] A large area with many attractions, usually connected by a main idea: *Disneyland is one of the most popular theme parks.*

†**themselves** /ðəmˈselvz/ [pronoun] **1** A word that refers to the people or things who are the subject of a sentence: *My brothers both hurt themselves when they played football on Saturday.* **2** A word that underlines that they are the people the verb refers to: *They did all the decorating themselves.* **3** **by themselves** **1** Alone: *The children can't stay at home by themselves.* **2** Without help: *My brothers repaired the brakes themselves.*

†**then** /ðen/ [adverb] **1** At that time: *How can I write about what happened in 1960, Mrs. Athey? I wasn't alive then.* **2** After that: *They went shopping and then had lunch.* **3** In that case: *If you don't like this pizza, then don't eat it.*

†**theory** US: /ˈθɪr.i/ UK: /ˈθɪə.ri/ [countable noun] An explanation that tries to prove something: *Einstein's theories caused a revolution in the world of science.* ■ The plural is "theories".

†**there**[1] /ðeər/ [adverb] In that place: *We're going to the seaside on Friday and we'll be staying there until Sunday night.*

there[2] /ðeər, ðər/ [pronoun] **1** Used with the verb "to be", to show that somebody or something exists: *There is plenty of cheese in the fridge; just help yourself.* ■ In this use, "there" can also be used with modal verbs or the verbs "seem" and "appear": "There seems to be a problem". **2** **there you are** Words that you can say when you offer something: *"There you are!" he said, putting the book in my hand.*

†**therefore** US: /ˈðer.fɔːr/ UK: /ˈðeə.fɔːʳ/ [adverb] So, for this reason: *It's not easy for Harriet to make friends. We must therefore make an effort with her.*

thermal /ˈθɜr·məl/ [adjective] Referring to the generation, presence or retention of heat: *Thermal underwear holds in the heat of the body.*

thermometer US: /θɚˈmɑː.mə.ɚ/ UK: /θəˈmɒm.ɪ.təʳ/ [countable noun] An instrument for measuring temperature: *The nurse took my temperature with the thermometer and it was very high.*

thermosphere [uncountable noun] The layer of the atmosphere which is directly above the mesosphere: *The thermosphere is the biggest layer in the atmosphere.* **See page 449.**

†**these** /ðiːz/ The plural of **this**.

†**they** /ðeɪ/ [pronoun] **1** The people or things being talked about: *Wash your hands at once! They're very dirty.* **2** A person who has already been mentioned, when the person's sex is not stated or isn't important: *If there is a doctor on board, would they please come forward?*

they'd /ðeɪd/ The contraction of "they had" or "they would".

they'll /ðeɪl/ The contraction of "they will".

they're US: /ðer/ UK: /ðeəʳ/ The contraction of "they are".

they've /ðeɪv/ The contraction of "they have".

†**thick** /θɪk/ [adjective] **1** Having a large distance between its opposite sides, not thin: *The jewels in the exhibition were protected by thick glass.* **2** Having a lot close together, dense: *There were a lot of road accidents on the roads yesterday because of the thick fog.* **3** Not flowing easily: *This sauce is too thick. Why didn't you add a little more water?* **4** Stupid: *Don't call me thick! I'm just as intelligent as you are.* ■ This use is informal.

†**thickness** /ˈθɪk.nəs/ [noun] Being thick: *The castle wall was about two feet in thickness.*

†**thief** /θiːf/ [countable noun] A person who steals, usually without violence and secretly: *A thief stole my mother's purse while she was in the bus line.* ■ The plural is "thieves".

thigh /θaɪ/ [countable noun] The part of the leg above the knee: *Peter kicked me in the thigh in judo.* 👁 **See page 421.**

†**thin** /θɪn/ [adjective] **1** Not fat: *Sheila eats a lot but she is very thin.* 👁 See picture at **a piece of... 2** Not thick, fine: *The walls were so thin that we could hear the people in the next room talking.* **3** With a lot of water, when talking of a liquid mixture: *I don't like this soup. It's too thin.* ■ The comparative form is "thinner" and the superlative form is "thinnest".

†**thing** /θɪŋ/ [countable noun] **1** An object or an idea: *Put those things back in your bedroom, please.* **2** Something that you do or think: *You mustn't say those things in front of your parents.*

†**think,** thought, thought /θɪŋk/ [verb] **1** To use your mind: *I can't think if you keep talking to me.* **2** To have an opinion about something: *She thinks she can swim faster than me.* **3** I think so Words that you say when you agree with something: *"Danny's coming, isn't he?" "Yes, I think so".*

▶ **PHRASAL VERBS** · **to think about** To consider: *My parents are thinking about buying a second hand car for my sister.* · **to think about (somebody or something)** To have somebody or something in your mind: *I never think about school when I'm on vacation.*

third US: /θɝːd/ UK: /θɜːd/ [noun and adjective] **1** Referring to three: *My grandparents live on the third floor.* ■ "Third" can also be written "3rd". **2** One of three equal parts: *We kept a third of the apple tart for Gillian.*

thirst US: /θɝːst/ UK: /θɜːst/ [uncountable noun] The feeling that you want to drink liquid: *I have such a thirst that I could drink a river dry.* ■ We say "thirst **for** something".

†**thirsty** /ˈθɜr·sti/ [adjective] Wanting or needing to drink: *Have some lemonade if you feel thirsty.* ■ The comparative form is "thirstier" and the superlative form is "thirstiest". Be careful! We always say: "I am thirsty". We don't say: "I have thirsty".

thirteen /ˌθɜrtˈtin/ [noun, adjective and pronoun] The number 13: *A lot of people believe thirteen is an unlucky number.*

thirteenth /ˌθɜrtˈtinθ/ [noun and adjective] Referring to thirteen: *Thirteenth amendment abolished slavery in the United States.* ■ "Thirteenth" can also be written "13th".

thirtieth /ˈθɜr·t̬i·ɪθ/ [noun and adjective] Referring to thirty: *Mary's birthday is on May the thirtieth.* ■ "Thirtieth" can also be written "30th".

thirty US: /ˈθɝː.t̬i/ UK: /ˈθɜː.ti/ [noun, adjective and pronoun] The number 30: *Some months have thirty days.*

†**this** /ðɪs/ [adjective and pronoun] **1** The person or the thing close to or closer to the speaker: *This is my bedroom, and that one over there is my sister's.* **2** When we talk about a period of time, of the present: *My cousin's coming to see us this week.* ■ The plural is "these".

thistle /ˈθɪs.l/ [countable noun] A plant with sharp points: *The thistle is the symbol of Scotland.*

thong US: /θɑːŋ/ UK: /θɒŋ/ [countable noun] **1** A narrow strip of leather: *His sandals are fastened by a thong.* **2** A type of open sandal usually made from plastic or rubber: *The thong has a strap which goes between the toes.* ■ In British English they say "flip-flop". 👁 See picture at **clothes. 3** Minimal piece of underwear or bottom part of a bikini: *Some women prefer a thong when they wear tight pants.*

thorax US: /ˈθɔːr.æks/ UK: /ˈθɔː.ræks/ [countable noun] The part of the body between the neck and the abdomen: *The organs of the thorax are protected by the rib-cage.* ■ The plural is "thoraxes" or "thoraces".

thorn US: /θɔːrn/ UK: /θɔːn/ [countable noun] A sharp point growing from some plants: *Be careful with the thorns when you pick the roses; you might prick your fingers.*

†**thorough** /ˈθɜr·oʊ/, /ˈθʌr-/ [adjective] Careful and complete: *You must give your bedroom a thorough cleaning.*

†**those** US: /ðoʊz/ UK: /ðəʊz/ The plural of **that[1]**.

†**though[1]** /ðəʊ/ [conjunction] **1** Although, even if: *Though he's rich he isn't selfish.* **2 as though** As if: *Lisa behaves as though she knows everything.* **3 even though** See "even though" in the word **even[2]**.

though[2] /ðəʊ/ [adverb] However: *I quite like school, though this year we have to work very hard.*

†**thought[1]** [noun] **1** The act of thinking: *I didn't give much thought to the things she said at the party.* **2** A plan: *She had no thought of buying herself the necklace.*

thought[2] Past tense and past participle forms of **think.**

†**thousand** /ˈθaʊ.zənd/ [noun, adjective and pronoun] The number 1,000: *My father's computer cost about a thousand dollars.*

thousandth /ˈθaʊ.zəndθ/ [noun and adjective] Referring to a thousand: *How many miles can light travel in a thousandth of a second?*

†**thread[1]** /θred/ [noun] A thin line of material used in sewing: *Here's a needle and thread to sew the button on.*

thread[2] /θred/ [verb] To pass a thread through something: *I always thread the needles for grandma because she can't see very well.*

threat [noun] **1** A warning that one is going to hurt or punish somebody: *He will certainly carry out* *his threat to harm you.* **2** A sign of something dangerous or unpleasant which may be, or is, about to happen: *a threat of rain.* **3** A source of danger: *His presence is a threat to our plan.*

threaten /'θret.ᵊn/ [verb] To warn that you may do something unpleasant if somebody doesn't do what you want: *He threatened to call the police.*

three /θriː/ [noun, adjective and pronoun] The number 3: *A triangle has three sides.*

three-dimensional /ˌθriː.daɪ'ment.ʃᵊn.ᵊl/ [adjective] Having length, depth and height, or appearing to: *You need special glasses to see three-dimensional movies.* ■ See box at **abbreviations**.

threw /θruː/ Past tense of **throw**.

thrill[1] /θrɪl/ [countable noun] A feeling of great excitement: *It was such a thrill to compete in the finals of the national youth athletics competition.*

thrill[2] /θrɪl/ [verb] To cause great excitement: *When we were small, my grandpa thrilled us with fantastic stories about his adventures at sea.*

thriller /'θrɪl·ər/ [countable noun] An exciting novel or movie, usually about crime: *I like reading thrillers.*

thrilling /'θrɪl.ɪŋ/ [adjective] Exciting: *What a thrilling movie that was!*

throat US: /θroʊt/ UK: /θrəʊt/ [countable noun] **1** The front part of the neck: *She had a real diamond necklace around her throat.* **2** The part of the body inside your neck: *I've got a really sore throat so I'll have to have a day off school.*

throne US: /θroʊn/ UK: /θrəʊn/ [countable noun] A special seat for a king or a queen: *The king sat on the throne during the ceremony.*

through /θruː/ [adverb and preposition] **1** From one side of something to the other, particularly when there is obstruction: *The train from Reno to Denver has to go through several tunnels.* **2** From the beginning of something to the end: *I looked through the book but I didn't like it much.* **3** Because of somebody: *I heard about the swimming competition through my cousin.* **4 to put (somebody) through** See "to put (somebody) through" in the word **put**. ■ See box at **across**. 👁 See pictures at **across** and **preposition**.

throughout /θruː'aʊt/ [adverb and preposition] **1** In all parts of something: *There has been rain throughout the country today.* **2** From the beginning to the end of something: *Those two boys talked throughout the movie.*

throw[1] /θrəʊ/ [countable noun] The act of sending something through the air from your hand, often a ball: *What a brilliant throw!*

throw[2], threw, thrown /θrəʊ/ [verb] To send something through the air with your hand: *Throw me the ball!*

▶ **PHRASAL VERBS · to throw (something) away** To put something in the garbage: *Why don't you throw that clock away. It's broken.* · **to throw up** To bring up food through your mouth: *Dad, can you stop the car? I feel like I'm going to throw up.* ■ In this use, the same meaning: "to be sick", "to vomit".

thrown Past participle of **throw**.

thrust, thrust, thrust /θrʌst/ [verb] To push somebody or something firmly: *He walked along with his hands thrust into his pockets.*

thud /θʌd/ [countable noun] A sound made by something heavy falling: *We heard a thud upstairs and went up immediately to see what was happening.*

thug /θʌg/ [countable noun] Violent person: *Two thugs pulled up the roses in the park.*

thumb /θʌm/ [countable noun] The short, thick finger at the side of your hand: *Put your thumbs up when you are ready.* ■ Be careful with the pronunciation of this word! The "b" is silent. 👁 See picture at **hand**.

thumbtack [countable noun] A pin with a round flat top: *Get some thumbtacks and put this poster up in the hallway, please.* ■ In British English they say "drawing pin".

thump /θʌmp/ [verb] **1** To hit somebody with your hand closed: *Mom! Peter has just thumped me on the back!* **2** To make a regular, heavy sound: *My heart was thumping as we waited for the teacher to tell us our results.*

thunder[1] /'θʌndər/ [uncountable noun] A loud noise in the sky during a storm: *Did you hear the thunder last night?*

thunder[2] /'θʌndər/ [verb] **1** To produce thunder: *It rained and thundered all day long.* **2** To make a sound like thunder: *His heavy footsteps thundered across the floor.*

thunderstorm /'θʌn·dərˌstɔrm/ [countable noun] A storm with thunder and lightning: *The thunderstorm started in the town next to ours and was soon just above our valley.*

Thursday /'θɜrz·deɪ/, /-di/ [noun] The fifth day of the week: *Thursday is between Wednesday and Friday.* ■ Be careful! "Thursday" has a capital "T". ■ Be careful with the pronunciation of this word. "Thur" rhymes with "her". 👁 See picture at **calendar**.

thus /ðʌs/ [adverb] **1** In this way, like this: *"It is done thus", said the math teacher.* ■ We usually say "like this". **2** Therefore, as a result of this: *My grandfather is only 59 and thus is not old enough to receive a pension.*

tibia /'tɪb.i.ə/ [countable noun] The largest of the two lower leg bones and the one closest to the center: *The tibia extends from the knee to the ankle.* ■ The plural is "tibias" or "tibiae". 👁 **See page 422.**

tick[1] /tɪk/ [countable noun] **1** See **check[1]**. ■ This use is British English. **2** The sound of a clock or a watch: *I could hear the tick of Henry's watch from the other side of the classroom.* **3** A small parasite that sucks blood: *Ticks can transmit many diseases, so it's important to remove then completely.*

tick[2] /tɪk/ [verb] **1** To make a mark showing that something is correct: *My teacher spent her whole break ticking the exercises.* **2** To make a small regularly repeated sound: *I love hearing the old clock ticking when I go to sleep in my gran's house.*

↑**ticket** /ˈtɪk.ɪt/ [countable noun] A small piece of card or paper showing that something has been paid for: *Let's go and get tickets for "Washington Redskins" this evening.*

ticket office [countable noun] A small office where you buy tickets: *There was a long line at the ticket office when we got there.*

tickle /ˈtɪk.l̩/ [verb] To irritate a part of somebody's body lightly: *Stop tickling me! You're making me laugh!*

tide /taɪd/ [countable noun] **1** The movement that the sea makes twice a day: *I like walking along the beach when the tide is low.* **2** **high tide** The time when the sea has reached its highest point up the sand: *At high tide the sea comes up almost as far as those houses.* **3** **low tide** The time when the sea has gone away from the sand: *Let's cross the bay at low tide.*

tidings /ˈtaɪ.dɪŋz/ [plural noun] News and information: *The ship brought glad tidings to the people on the island.* ■ This word is now old-fashioned.

↑**tidy[1]** /ˈtaɪdi/ [adjective] **1** In good order, neat: *What a nice tidy room this is.* **2** Keeping things in good order: *Dave is a very tidy boy.* ■ The comparative form is "tidier" and the superlative form is "tidiest". 👁 See picture at **opposite**.

tidy[2] /ˈtaɪdi/ [verb] To make something ordered: *When you've tidied your room you can watch the television.* ■ Be careful with the spelling of these forms: "tidies", "tidied".

↑**tie[1]** /taɪ/ [countable noun] **1** A long strip of material that men and boys sometimes wear around their neck: *I like wearing a black tie and jacket sometimes.* 👁 See picture at **clothes**. **2** The result of a game when both sides finish equal: *The soccer game ended in a tie so we'll have to play again next week.* ■ In this use, in British English we say "draw".

tie[2] /taɪ/ [verb] **1** To hold something with a rope, piece of string and so on: *We tied the dog's leash to the fence while we went in the store to buy candies.* **2** To end a game without winning or losing: *Amy and Sarah tied in the sack race so they had a prize each.* ■ In British English they say "draw".

▶ **PHRASAL VERBS** · **to tie (somebody or something) up** To fix somebody or something in a certain position, using a rope, piece of string and so on: *They found the dog tied up to a post in the backyard, making a lot of noise.* ■ Be careful with the spelling of this form: "tying".

tiger /ˈtaɪ.gər/ [countable noun] A wild animal with yellow fur and black stripes: *The tiger is the largest of the big cats.* 👁 **See page 428.**

↑**tight** /taɪt/ [adjective] **1** Firmly pulled together: *The knot in these shoelaces is so tight that I can't undo it.* **2** Closely fitting: *This shoe is a bit too tight for me; I think that I should take the next size.*

tighten /ˈtaɪ.tᵊn/ [verb] To make something tight: *Can you help me tighten this screw, please?*

tile /taɪl/ [countable noun] A flat piece of clay used to cover roofs, floors or walls: *My mom has put some lovely Spanish tiles on our bathroom walls.* 👁 See picture at **bathroom**.

↑**till[1]** /tɪl/ [conjunction] Up to when: *I waited till the clock struck ten and then I went home.*

till[2] /tɪl/ [preposition] Up to a particular time: *We are on vacation till the weekend and then we go back to school.*

tilt /tɪlt/ [verb] To lean to one side: *Frances leaned on the table and it tilted and all the books fell off.*

↑**time[1]** /taɪm/ [noun] **1** An amount of minutes, days, years and so on, or their passing: *They played for a really long time. The concert lasted 3 hours.* **2** A certain point in the day: *What time is it?* **3** An occasion: *Do you remember the time we went fishing on the lake and fell in the water?* **4** Experience: *Didn't we have a lovely time the day we went to Bangor?* **5** A particular period: *Grandpa says that in his time, children had more fun.* ■ Be careful! We say: "The weather's good today, it's sunny". (We don't say: "The time's good today"). **6** **at times** Sometimes: *You really are rude, at times!* **7** **for the time being** For the moment: *Our school is in repairs so we are having classes in the gym for the time being.* **8** **from time to time** Occasionally: *I'm not really a football fan but I like to watch a game from time to time.* **9** **in time** **1** Not late for something: *We got to school just in time to hear the bell go for assembly.* **2** After a while, with the passing of time: *I didn't like my new school at first but in time I got used to it.* **10** **on time** Not late or early: *The plane from New York was on time.* **11** **one at a time** Each one separately: *I can't understand a word. Speak one at a time, please!* **12** **spend time** To use time doing something: *I spend a lot of time playing the piano.* **13** **tell the time** To say what time it is by looking at a clock or a watch: *Dar-*

ren has learnt to tell the time at school this week. ■ See box below.

time² /taɪm/ [verb] To measure how much time it takes to do something: *We timed how long it took us to run round the track.*

timeline /ˈtaɪm.laɪn/ [countable noun] A chronological account of events that have happened, or a schedule of planned events, often in diagram form: *The timeline shows the key events in the history of that period.*

times /taɪmz/ [preposition] Multiplied by: *Three times three is nine.*

ᐩ**timetable** /ˈtaɪmˌteɪ.bl̩/ [countable noun] A list of times: *There's a bus timetable over there!*

timid /ˈtɪm.ɪd/ [adjective] Easily frightened, shy: *Jenny's very timid. She doesn't like speaking in public.*

timpani [plural noun] A set of kettledrums: *My cousin plays the timpani in the municipal band.* 👁 **See page 459.**

ᐩ**tin** /tɪn/ [noun] **1** A soft metal: *My dad had some toy soldiers made of tin when he was a little boy.* **2** See **can.** ■ This use is British English.

ᐩ**tiny** /ˈtaɪ.ni/ [adjective] Very small: *What tiny shoes. They must be for a new baby.* ■ The comparative form is "tinier" and the superlative form is "tiniest".

ᐩ**tip¹** /tɪp/ [countable noun] **1** The pointed or thinner end of something: *I've hurt my finger tips playing the guitar for too long.* **2** A small amount of money that you give for example to a waiter: *My mom left a tip for the waiter because he had been so helpful.* **3** A piece of advice: *Let me give you a tip about playing tennis against Laura. Send the balls to her left side.*

tip² /tɪp/ [verb] To make something lean at an angle: *She tipped her school hat to one side so that it would look a bit more fashionable.*

▸ **PHRASAL VERBS** · **to tip (something) over** To make something fall: *Jane tipped her chair over when she got up.* ■ Be careful with the spelling of these forms: "tipped", "tipping".

tiptoe /ˈtɪpˌtoʊ/ [verb] To walk on the tips of your toes: *She tiptoed up the stairs so that her parents wouldn't hear her.*

TO TIPTOE

ᐩ**tire¹** /taɪər/ [countable noun] A thick piece of rubber that fits on a wheel: *If you live in Colorado you need good snow tires for your car in the winter.* ■ The British English spelling is "tyre". 👁 **See page 441.**

ᐩ**tire²** /taɪər/ [verb] To make somebody or something tired: *Working on the computer for a long time tires my eyes.*

ᐩ**tired** US: /taɪrd/ UK: /taɪəd/ [adjective] **1** Needing to rest: *I'm tired. I want to go to bed.* **2 to be tired of (something)** To have had too much of something you don't like: *I'm tired of the way you always ignore me when I see you in the playground.* **3 to be tired out** To be very tired: *I'm tired out after all those tests. I could do with a vacation!* ■ Be careful with the pronunciation of this word. The "e" is not pronounced.

ᐩ**tiring** /ˈtaɪər·ɪŋ/ [adjective] Making somebody tired: *I find trying to speak Chinese extremely tiring.*

tissue /ˈtɪʃ.uː, ˈtɪs.juː/ ▮ [uncountable noun] **1** One of the kinds of substance of which the organs of the body are made: *nervous tissues; muscle tissue.* ▮ [countable noun] **2** A thin piece of soft paper: *Get me some tissues when you go to the store, please. I think I'm getting a cold.*

ᐩ**title** /ˈtaɪ·t̬ə·l/ [countable noun] **1** The name of something: *What is the title of this movie?* **2** A word that goes in front of somebody's name: *"Mrs.", "Dr.", "Lord" and "Duchess" are examples of titles.*

ᐩ**to** US: /tə, t̬ə, tu/ UK: /tuː, tʊ, tu, tə/ [preposition] **1** In the direction of: *Montana is to the north of United States.* **2** A word that shows why you do something: *Mary came to see you the other day but you*

Time: prepositions

in	in the morning, in the afternoon, in the evening in July, in November in (the) spring, in (the) summer in (the) fall, in (the) winter in 1997, in 1992 in recent years in the meantime
on	on January 4th, on July 15th on Monday on Tuesday morning on the first day of term
at	at night at Christmas at Easter at two o'clock at breakfast, at lunch, at dinner

a b c d e f g h i j k l m n o p q r s t u v w x y z

weren't in. **3** A word that you use to compare things: *I prefer Geography to Math.* **4** As far as: *Go to the junction, turn left and follow the signs for Helmsley.* **5** Until: *This store is open from eight in the morning to nine at night.* **6** A word that indicates the number of minutes before the hour: *It's ten to eight. Pete is late.* **7** The word that goes before a verb to indicate the infinitive: *"To be or not to be, that is the question".*

toad US: /toʊd/ UK: /təʊd/ [countable noun] An animal like a big frog: *Toads have rough skins.*

toast[1] /təʊst/ [uncountable noun] A thin piece of bread that has been heated until it is brown: *I always have toast for breakfast.* ■ Be careful with the pronunciation of this word. It rhymes with "most".

toast[2] /təʊst/ [verb] To hold up your glass and drink to somebody or something: *At the end of the dinner, they all toasted the newly married couple.*

toaster US: /'toʊ.stɚ/ UK: /'təʊ.stəʳ/ [countable noun] A machine that toasts bread: *My dad's bought a new toaster that not only toasts the bread but keeps it warm, too!*

tobacco /tə'bæk·oʊ/ [countable noun] Dried leaves of a particular plant that people smoke: *Tobacco was brought to Europe from America in the sixteenth century.*

†**today** /tə'deɪ/ [adverb] **1** This day: *We've got a hockey game against Stoke Park Girls' School today.* **2** At present: *Today, most people believe in equal rights for men and women.*

†**toe** US: /toʊ/ UK: /təʊ/ [countable noun] One of the five parts at the end of your feet: *I broke my big toe skating last year.* ■ Compare with "finger" (at the end of your hands).

toenail /'toʊˌneɪl/ [countable noun] The hard part that grows at the end of your toes: *My mom always paints her toenails in summer.* ■ Compare with "fingernail" (at the end of your fingers).

toffee US: /'tɑː.fi/ UK: /'tɒf.i/ [noun] A small brown sweet that you chew: *My favorite toffee is the one my aunt brings me from Devon.*

†**together** /tə'geð.ər/ US: /-ɚ/ [adverb] **1** With each other: *Patsy and Viv walk home from school together every afternoon.* **2** So that two or more things are mixed or joined: *Mix the eggs and flour together and then add the milk.*

†**toilet** /'tɔɪ.lət/ [countable noun] **1** A seat that you use when you eliminate waste from your body: *You should use this product to clean the toilet.* **2** See **bathroom.** ■ This use is British English. 👁 See picture at **bathroom.**

toilet paper [uncountable noun] Paper that you use to clean yourself after using the toilet: *This toilet paper is very soft.*

token /'toʊ·kən/ [countable noun] **1** A sign of something: *We gave Mrs. Harris a present at the end of the school year as a token of our gratitude.* **2** A piece of plastic, metal and so on that you can use instead of money: *The children have their own store where they buy things with tokens instead of money.*

told US: /toʊld/ UK: /təʊld/ Past tense and past participle forms of **tell.**

tolerant /'tɑl·ər·ənt/ [adjective] Allowing or accepting something that you don't agree with or don't like; with an open mind: *My parents are very tolerant.*

tolerate US: /'tɑː.lə.reɪt/ UK: /'tɒl.ᵊr.eɪt/ [verb] To allow or to accept something that you don't agree with or don't like: *How can you tolerate that noise?*

†**tomato** /tə'meɪ·t̬oʊ/, /-'mɑ-/ [noun] A red fruit that you often eat in salads: *The tomatoes from my grandpa's garden are absolutely delicious.* ■ The plural is "tomatoes". 👁 **See page 437.**

tomb /tuːm/ [countable noun] A stone object where a dead body is buried: *We went to see the tomb of Elvis Presley when we went to Memphis.* ■ Be careful with the pronunciation of this word!

†**tomorrow** /tə'mɑr·oʊ/, /-'mɔr-/ [noun and adverb] The day after today: *I'm so glad that it's Saturday tomorrow.*

†**ton** /tʌn/ [countable noun] A very large unit of weight: *There are 907 kilos in a ton.* ■ In British English a ton equals 1,016 kilograms.

†**tone** US: /toʊn/ UK: /təʊn/ [noun] The quality of a sound: *Marie sings beautifully. Her voice has a lovely tone.* ■ Compare with "pitch" (how high or low a sound is on a musical scale).

tongs /tɒŋz/ [plural noun] An instrument used for picking up objects: *My mom always uses kitchen tongs to turn the food while it is cooking.* 👁 **See page 440.**

†**tongue** /tʌŋ/ [countable noun] The soft and long part inside the mouth that is used for speaking and eating: *Ow! I've just bitten my tongue eating this sandwich!*

tongue twister [countable noun] Something that is difficult to say quickly: *"She sells sea shells on the sea shore" is a tongue twister.*

†**tonight** /tə'naɪt/ [noun] The night of today: *I'm going to the movies with Ron tonight.*

†**tonne** /tʌn/ [countable noun] A very large unit of weight: *There are 1,000 kilos in a tonne.*

†**too** /tuː/ [adverb] **1** Also, in addition: *I really enjoy vacations but I like school, too!* ■ "Too", "as well" and "also" have the same meaning. "Too" and "as well" go at the end of a sentence. "Also" usually goes in the middle of a sentence. ■ See box at **also.** **2** A word used before an adjective or adverb to indicate that they are in excess: *It's too hot today.*

took /tʊk/ Past tense of **take.** ■ Be careful with the pronunciation of this word! "Took" rhymes with "book".

†tool /tuːl/ [countable noun] An object that you use to do a particular job: *My mom likes doing jobs around the house so we gave her a new box of tools for her birthday.*

†tooth /tuːθ/ [countable noun] **1** One of the hard parts in your mouth: *I'm going to have one of my back teeth taken out tomorrow.* **2 tooth decay** The process of going bad of a tooth: *Eating too many candies can cause tooth decay.* ■ The plural is "teeth".

toothache /ˈtuːθ.eɪk/ [uncountable noun] A pain in one or more of your teeth: *I slept very badly last night. I had an awful toothache.*

toothbrush /ˈtuːθ.brʌʃ/ [countable noun] A small brush that you use for brushing your teeth: *I gave my dad an electric toothbrush for his birthday.* 👁 See pictures at **brush** and **bathroom**.

toothpaste /ˈtuːθ.peɪst/ [uncountable noun] A substance that you use for brushing your teeth: *You don't need a lot of toothpaste to brush your teeth, just a little bit.* 👁 See picture at **bathroom**.

toothpick /ˈtuːθ.pɪk/ [countable noun] A small, thin piece of wood used to remove pieces of food caught between the teeth: *Can you give me a toothpick?*

†top[1] /tɒp/ [countable noun] **1** The highest part of something: *We sat at the top of the hill and looked down on the sea.* **2** The cover of something: *I like the picture on the top of this chocolate box.* **3** A piece of clothing that you wear on the top part of your body: *I bought a new top for tomorrow's party. Do you like it?* **4 on top** On the highest part of something: *Here's the cake. Let's put a cherry on top.* **5 on top of** On something or over it: *Look at the clouds on top of the mountain. I think we're going to have rain.*

top[2] /tɒp/ [adjective] Highest: *This book goes on the top shelf. Can you put it back?*

top dog [countable noun] The person in the most important position: *Who is the top dog in your gang?* ■ This word is informal.

†topic US: /ˈtɑː.pɪk/ UK: /ˈtɒp.ɪk/ [countable noun] A subject: *Tomorrow in class, we have to talk for five minutes on a topic related to the environment.*

topographic US: /ˌtɑp·əˈgræf·ɪk/ [adjective] Referring to topography: *The topographic survey provides a detailed representation of the physical features of the region.*

topography US: /təˈpɑg·rə·fi/ [uncountable noun] A detailed description of the physical features of a particular place: *Having studied the topography of the area, we decided on the best place to camp.*

topsoil /ˈtɑpˌsɔɪl/ [uncountable noun] The upper layer of soil: *The gardener adds natural fertilizer to improved the topsoil.*

torch US: /tɔːrtʃ/ UK: /tɔːtʃ/ [countable noun] See **flashlight**. ■ This word is British English. ■ The plural is "torches".

tore US: /tɔːr/ UK: /tɔːʳ/ Past tense of **tear**.

torn US: /tɔːrn/ UK: /tɔːn/ Past participle of **tear[3]**.

tornado US: /tɔːrˈneɪ.doʊ/ UK: /tɔːˈneɪ.dəʊ/ [countable noun] A violent wind that goes round and round: *The winds inside a tornado can reach speeds of up to 180 miles per hour.* ■ Be careful with the pronunciation of this word! "nad" rhymes with "made". ■ The same meaning: "twister".

torrent /ˈtɒrənt/ [countable noun] **1** A very strong, fast stream of rain: *The heavy rain produced a torrent which caused a lot of damage in the town.* **2** A very big, sudden amount of something: *a torrent of insults.*

tortoise US: /ˈtɔːr.əs/ UK: /ˈtɔː.təs/ [countable noun] A reptile with a very hard shell on its back that lives in the sea or on land: *The tortoises of the Galapagos islands can live for over 150 years.* ■ The same meaning: "turtle". In British English "tortoise" is used to refer to this reptile that lives on land, whereas "turtle" is used to refer to this reptile that lives in the sea.

torture[1] [noun] Making somebody feel great pain: *Torture should be prohibited in all countries.*

torture[2] /ˈtɔːtʃər/ [verb] To make somebody feel great pain to get information or just to be cruel: *In the movie, the gangsters tortured the hero but he didn't betray his friends.*

toss /tɒs/ [verb] **1** To throw something quickly: *Jack tossed the orange peel into the trash can.* **2** To throw a coin into the air: *Let's toss a coin to decide who has to go and buy the drinks.* **3** To move quickly up and down: *The donkey tossed its head when we tried to stroke it.* ■ Be careful with the spelling of the 3rd person singular present tense form: "tosses".

†total[1] /ˈtəʊtəl/ [adjective] Complete: *There was total silence as the principal walked into the hall.*

total[2] /ˈtəʊtəl/ [countable noun] The final number that you get after adding numbers together: *A total of three hundred people were at the game.*

toucan /ˈtuː.kən/ US: /-kæn/ [countable noun] A bird found in tropical America that has a very large colored beak: *The toucan eats fruit.*

†touch[1] /tʌtʃ/ [noun] **1** The act of putting part of your body against somebody or something: *I felt a light touch on my arm and turned round and saw Henry smiling at me.* **2** One of the five senses: *Braille writing consists of a pattern of raised dots that can be read by touch.* **3 to get in touch** To establish contact with somebody: *Don't forget to get in touch with me when you arrive in Portland.* **4 to keep in touch** Not to lose contact: *Although my friend left our town at the age of twelve, we still keep in touch.*

a b c d e f g h i j k l m n o p q r s t u v w x y z

touch² /tʌtʃ/ [verb] **1** To put your hand or another part of the body in contact with somebody or something: *Don't touch the pots on this table; they're fragile.* **2** To come into contact with: *This skirt is so long that it touches the ground.*

touching /ˈtʌtʃ.ɪŋ/ [adjective] That produces tender feelings: *It's a very touching movie.*

†**tough** /tʌf/ [adjective] **1** Strong, hard: *Jackie is very tough; she broke her arm riding the other day and didn't even cry.* **2** Difficult: *The math test we had today was really tough.* **3** Not tender: *This steak is so tough that it's practically impossible to cut.*

†**tour** US: /tʊr/ UK: /tʊəʳ/ [noun] **1** A journey where you stop at different places: *We went on a marvelous tour of California last summer.* **2** A visit to a particular place with a guide: *They took us on an interesting tour of The White House.*

tourism /ˈtʊr,ɪz·əm/ [uncountable noun] The vacation industry: *Tourism is very important for our economy.*

†**tourist** US: /ˈtʊr.ɪst/ UK: /ˈtʊə.rɪst/ [countable noun] A person who visits a place on vacation: *There are lots of tourists in New York in the summer.*

tourist office [countable noun] An office where tourists get information: *My cousin speaks several languages and has got a summer job in the local tourist office.*

tournament /ˈtʊr·nə·mənt/, /ˈtɜr-/ [countable noun] A sports competition with several teams or competitors: *There is a basketball tournament in our town next week.*

tow /tʌtʃ/ [verb] To pull a vehicle using a rope or a chain attached to another vehicle: *Our car broke down in the snow and it had to be towed back to town.*

†**towards** or **toward** US: /tʊˈwɔːrdz/ UK: /təˈwɔːdz/ [preposition] **1** In the direction of somebody or something: *They walked towards the house together.* **2** Near a particular time: *I was getting quite bored towards the end of the movie.*

†**towel** /taʊəl/ [countable noun] A piece of material that you use to dry yourself on: *Don't forget to bring your swimsuit and towel with you in case the weather is nice.* 👁 See picture at **bathroom**.

†**tower** US: /taʊɚ/ UK: /taʊəʳ/ [countable noun] A tall, narrow building or part of a building: *Empire State is one of the most famous towers in United States.*

†**town** /taʊn/ [countable noun] A place where people live and work with many streets and buildings: *I was brought up in a small town.*

town hall [countable noun] A building where the local government has its offices: *Our neighbor is a local councilor and he works at the town hall.*

townhouse [countable noun] A house that is part of a continuous row of houses: *Sharon's uncle sold his old townhouse and now he's bought a duplex.* 👁 See picture at **house**.

†**toy** /tɔɪ/ [countable noun] An object that a child plays with: *Paul's favorite toy is his teddy bear.*

trace¹ /treɪs/ [noun] A mark that shows that somebody has been in a place: *The police could find no trace of the murderer.*

trace² /treɪs/ [verb] **1** To look for and find somebody or something: *The bills stolen in the robbery have been traced.* **2** To put transparent paper over something and draw it: *Don't tell me that you drew that dinosaur by yourself. I bet you traced it.*

trachea US: /ˈtreɪ.kiə/ UK: /trəˈkiː.ə/ [countable noun] The passage which carries air from the larynx to the bronchial tubes: *The trachea is also known as the windpipe.* ■ The plural is "tracheas" or "tracheae". 👁 **See page 425.**

†**track¹** /træk/ [noun] **1** A path or a rough road: *We followed the track and ended up near the canal.* **2** A special path or road for races: *The car race will have to be postponed because the track is wet.* **3** A footprint or other mark left on the ground: *We knew that a car had been there because we could see the tire tracks in the sand.*

track² /træk/ [verb] To follow tracks to find somebody or something: *They tracked the murderer to the station and captured him there.*

track and field [countable noun] Sports where people run, jump and so on: *My brother's great at track and field; he can run, jump and throw the javelin.* ■ In British English they say "athletics".

tracksuit /ˈtræk.sjuːt/ US: /-suːt/ [countable noun] A pair of pants and a jacket that you wear for sport: *I got a lovely red tracksuit for Christmas.* 👁 See picture at **clothes**.

tract /trækt/ [countable noun] **1** A large area of land: *Sequoia National Park in California is a tract of land dedicated to natural conservation.* **2** In anatomy, a system of connected tubes: *The digestive tract of the cow includes four stomachs.*

tractor /ˈtræk·tər/ [countable noun] A big vehicle that is used for pulling things on a farm: *My uncle has just bought a new tractor and it saves him a lot of work.*

trade¹ /treɪd/ [noun] **1** Buying and selling: *My dad works in a company that deals with international trade.* **2** A particular kind of business: *June's mom is in the secondhand car trade.* **3** A particular job: *Karen's uncle is a carpenter by trade.* **4** **trade union** See **union**.

trade² /treɪd/ [verb] To buy and to sell things: *The United States trades with many countries.* ■ Be careful with the spelling of this form: "trading".

trademark /ˈtreɪdˌmɑrk/ [countable noun] A mark on a product that shows who made it: *This trademark is taken from the name of the man who founded the company.*

↑**tradition** /trəˈdɪʃ.ᵊn/ [noun] A custom that has existed for a long time: *In United States, it is a tradition for many people to listen to the President's speech on Independence Day.*

↑**traditional** /trəˈdɪʃ.ᵊn.ᵊl, -ˈdɪʃ.nᵊl/ [adjective] Referring to tradition: *I love traditional Spanish food.*

↑**traffic** /ˈtræf.ɪk/ [uncountable noun] Vehicles on a road: *There's always a lot of traffic at this time of the morning.*

traffic circle [countable noun] A place where roads meet and cars move in a circle: *Go to the traffic circle and take the second exit.* ■ In British English they say "roundabout". 👁 See picture at **street**.

TRAFFIC CIRCLE

traffic jam [countable noun] See **gridlock**.

traffic light [countable noun] See **stoplight**. ■ This word is British English. ■ This word is more common in the plural.

traffic policeman [countable noun] A man who makes sure that cars are correctly parked: *The traffic policeman wrote down the numbers of all the cars that were parked in the street.* ■ The plural is "traffic policemen". ■ A woman is a "traffic policewoman". ■ In British English they say "traffic warden".

traffic policewoman [countable noun] A woman who makes sure that cars are correctly parked: *The traffic policewoman wrote down the numbers of all the cars that were parked in the street.* ■ The plural is "traffic policewomen". ■ A man is a "traffic policeman". ■ In British English they say "traffic warden".

traffic sign [countable noun] A sign providing information to drivers: *Speed limits are one kind of traffic sign.*

traffic warden [countable noun] See **traffic policeman**. ■ This word is British English.

tragedy /ˈtrædʒ.ə.di/ [noun] **1** A terrible thing that happens: *The fire was a tragedy. Several people died.* **2** A very serious play with a sad or terrible ending: *The movie "Romeo and Juliet" is based in one of Shakespeare's most famous tragedies.* ■ The plural is "tragedies".

tragic /ˈtrædʒ.ɪk/ [adjective] Very sad, relating to tragedy: *There was a tragic accident on the canal this afternoon. Three people drowned.*

trail[1] /treɪl/ [countable noun] **1** A path in the country: *Just go along that trail and you'll soon come to the river.* **2** A line of marks that shows where somebody or something has been: *We followed the trail of footsteps and soon found where the children had hidden.*

trail[2] /treɪl/ [verb] To pull something along behind you: *That little boy is always trailing an old rag doll behind him.*

trailer /ˈtreɪ·lər/ [countable noun] **1** A vehicle with two wheels that is pulled by a car or by another vehicle: *We couldn't get all our luggage into the trunk so we had to take the trailer with us.* **2** A very short film that is used as publicity for a film that is about to be released: *We saw the trailer for the new Spielberg film when we went to the movies yesterday.* ■ Be careful with the pronunciation of this word!

↑**train**[1] /treɪn/ [countable noun] Cars pulled by an engine along a railway: *My aunt and uncle went all the way to Ottawa by train when they were young.* 👁 See picture at **transport**.

train[2] /treɪn/ [verb] **1** To teach a person or an animal how to do something: *Iris trains dogs for the blind.* **2** To prepare yourself for a competition or for something difficult: *Maggie was determined to do well in the school athletics tournament so she trained very hard.*

trainer /ˈtreɪ·nər/ [countable noun] **1** A person who trains sportsmen and sportswomen: *Tim's the trainer for our local baseball team.* ■ The same meaning: "coach". **2** A person who trains animals: *My cousin is a racehorse trainer.*

trainers [plural noun] See **sneakers**. ■ This word is British English. ■ When we talk about two or more "trainers", we use the word "pairs": "I bought three pairs of trainers".

↑**training** /ˈtreɪ.nɪŋ/ [uncountable noun] Preparing for a sport or job: *We have basketball training every Tuesday and Thursday.*

traitor /ˈtreɪ·t̬ər/ [countable noun] A person who is not loyal to their friends, country and so on, and causes them harm: *Judas was a traitor.*

tramp /træmp/ [countable noun] Somebody who has no home and no job and moves from place to place: *There are a lot of tramps sleeping in the streets in New York.* ■ The same meaning: "hobo".

↑**transfer**[1] [noun] Moving from one place to another: *Pau Gasol has asked for a transfer to another basketball team.*

transfer[2] /trænsˈfɜːr/ [verb] To move somebody or something from one place to another: *My mom* *has been transferred to the Dallas branch of her bank, so we're moving there next month.* ■ Be careful with the spelling of these forms: "transferred", "transferring".

transform /træns'fɔrm/ [verb] To change dramatically: *When he performs he is transformed into another person.* ■ We say "to transform **into** something".

transfusion /træns'fjuː.ʒən/ [countable noun] A medical treatment in which blood is transferred from one person to another: *The blood transfusion saved his life.*

transition /træn'zɪʃən/ [noun] The change from one type or condition to another, or the process when this happens: *The supremacy of the Caucasian in United States is having a transition to a multiracial society.* ■ We say "transition **from** something **into** something".

+**translate** /træns'leɪt, trænz-/ [verb] To put something which is in one language into another language: *He asked me to translate the letter into Spanish.*

+**translation** /træns'leɪ.ʃən, trænz-/ [noun] Saying or writing something in a different language: *I've got a Latin translation to do for tomorrow's class.*

translator /træns'leɪ·t̬ər/, /'træns·leɪ·t̬ər/ [countable noun] Person who translates: *Sarah wants to be a translator so she is studying languages at university.*

translucent /trænz'luːsənt/ [adjective] Semi-transparent: *Fine bone china is almost translucent.*

transmission /trænz'mɪʃən/ [noun] **1** The condition of being transmitted: *The transmission of computer data often occurs nowadays via wi-fi.* **2** A radio or TV broadcast, or the process of transmitting it: *The transmission of the game was interrupted by a newsflash.* **3** The passing of something from one person or place to another: *the transmission of the disease.*

transmit /træns'mɪt/, /trænz-/ [verb] **1** To emit or send out by radio or TV: *Under the terms of its license, the radio station has to transmit twenty four hours a day.* **2** To pass something from one person to another: *Some characteristics are transmitted from parents to children through their genes.* ■ Be careful with the spelling of these forms: "transmitting", "transmitted".

transparency /træn'spærənsi/ ▮ [uncountable noun] **1** The quality of being easy to see through: *The key characteristics of glass is its transparency.* **2** Open communication about actions so that they can be seen and understood: *Transparency is the soul of democratic government, but is very difficult to achieve.* ▮ [countable noun] **3** A slide that is shown using a projector: *The first transparency shown is a photograph taken before the eruption.* ■ The plural is: "transparencies".

+**transparent** /træn'spær·ənt/, /-'speər-/ [adjective] That you can see through: *Glass is used to protect pictures because it is strong and transparent.* ■ Compare with "opaque" (that you cannot see through).

transplant[1] /'trænsplaːnt/ [countable noun] The action of removing an organ from one person and putting it into another person, or the new organ the second person receives: *He had a heart transplant operation.* ■ Compare with "implant[1]" (something which is inserted into a part of the body).

transplant[2] /'trænsplaːnt/ [verb] **1** To remove a plant and plant it at another place: *The gardener explained us that in order to transplant successfully we need to take the plant's roots as well.* **2** To remove an organ or tissue from one person in order to put it into another person: *The surgeon transplants and the patient then needs to accept the transplanted organ.* ■ Compare with "implant[2]" (to insert into the body).

+**transport**[1] /'trænspɔːt/ [uncountable noun] **1** A way of taking people from one place to another: *My dad has a good car but he goes to work by public transport.* **2** **means of transport** See "means of transport" in the word **means**.

transport[2] /'trænspɔːt/ [verb] To take people or things from one place to another: *The horses were transported to the show in horse trailers.*

transportation /ˌtræns·pər'teɪ·ʃən/ [uncountable noun] The act of taking people or things from one place to another: *The transportation of goods by train has many advantages.*

+**trap** /træp/ ▮ [countable noun] **1** An object that is used to catch animals with: *We put mouse traps out on the kitchen floor but we didn't manage to catch any.* **2** A plan to catch somebody: *The detective set a trap for the murderer.* ▮ [noun] **3** Mouth: *Keep your trap shut.* ■ This word is informal.

trapeze /trə'piːz/ [countable noun] A swing used by acrobats: *Mastery of the trapeze takes many years.*

trapezium or **trapezoid** /trə'piː.zi.əm/ [countable noun] **1** A shape with four straight sides, two of which are parallel: *A trapezoid is a geometrical shape.* **2** A bone located in the wrist near the base of the thumb: *The trapezoid is a carpal bone.* ■ The plural is: "trapeziums" or "trapezia". ■ Compare with "trapezius" (large triangular muscle).

trapezius [countable noun] Either of two large, triangular muscles on each side of the top of the back and shoulders: *The trapezius muscles help to rotate the shoulder blades.* ■ The plural is "trapezii". ■ Compare with "trapezium" (a bone located in the wrist). See page 423.

trapezoidal [adjective] Showing a trapezoid form: *They used a sheet with a trapezoidal prism form.*

TRANSPORT

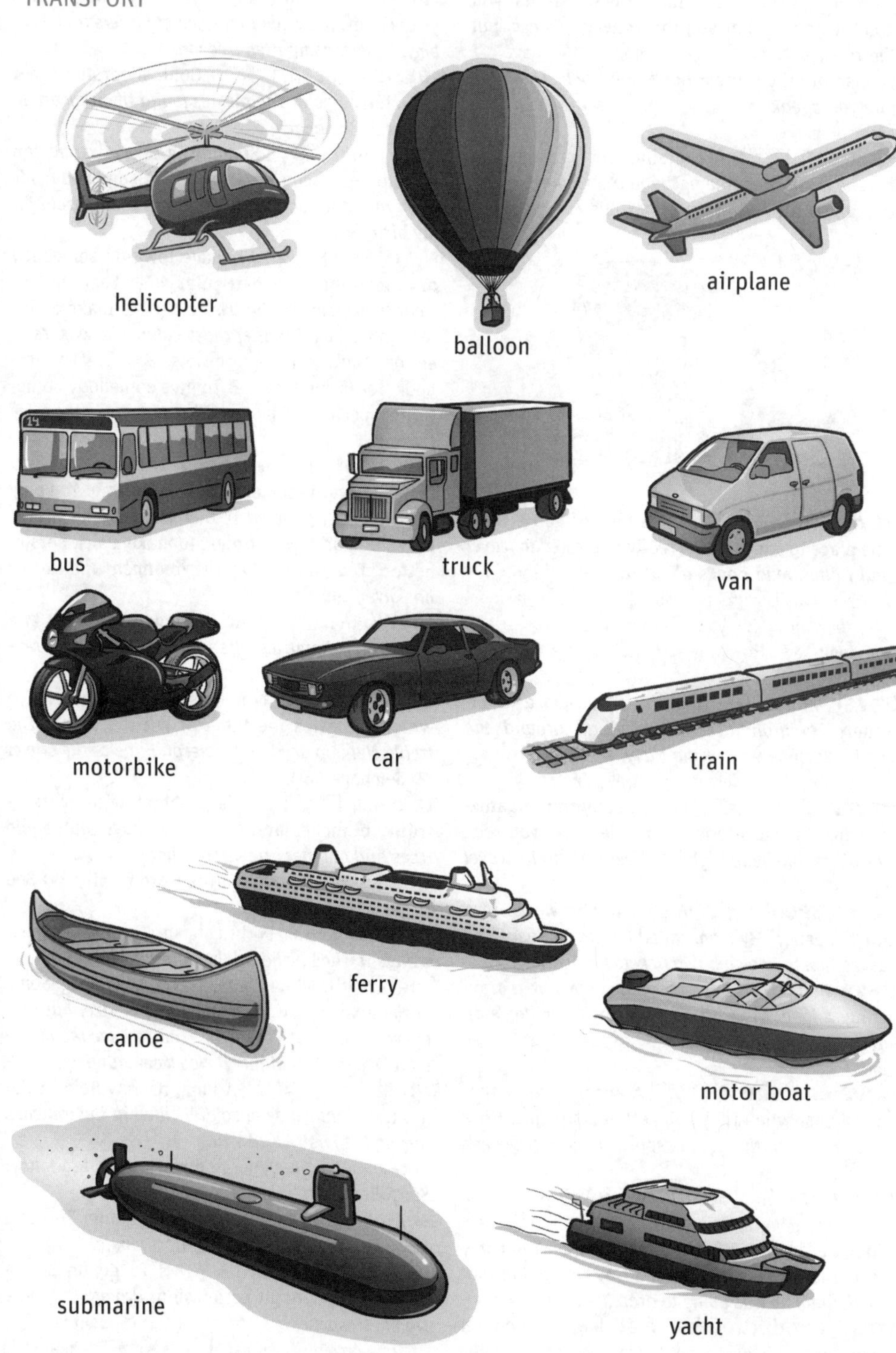

helicopter

balloon

airplane

bus

truck

van

motorbike

car

train

ferry

canoe

motor boat

submarine

yacht

a b c d e f g h i j k l m n o p q r s **t** u v w x y z

trash /træʃ/ [uncountable noun] **1** Things or material that you don't need and that you throw away: *Please, put the trash out.* ■ The same meaning: "garbage". **2** Foolish or silly things: *Don't talk trash! Think before you speak.* ■ In British English they say "rubbish".

trash can [countable noun] A container for garbage: *Put out the trash cans, the garbage truck comes by today.* ■ In British English they say "dustbin".

TRASH CAN

travel[1] /'trævəl/ [uncountable noun] The idea of going from one place to another: *I'm really interested in travel and I often read books about it.* ■ Be careful! This word is not used to talk about specific occasions. (We say: "How was your journey back from Paris?". We don't say: "How was your travel back from Paris?").

⁺**travel[2]** /'trævəl/ [verb] To go from one place to another: *My grandfather traveled all around the world when he was in the Navy.* ■ The British English spelling is "travelled" and "travelling".

travel agency [countable noun] A company that organizes trips and vacations for people: *Have you seen the offers for cheap flights to New York in the travel agency?*

travel agent [countable noun] A person who works in a travel agency: *My mom called her travel agent and asked him to book her two tickets for Acapulco.*

⁺**traveler** [countable noun] A person who travels or is traveling: *A lot of travelers on their way to Oregon stop at this hotel.* ■ The British English spelling is "traveller".

traveler's check [countable noun] A special check that people use when they go to other countries: *Have you got everything? Passport, ticket, traveler's checks?*

⁺**traveller** [countable noun] See **traveler.** ■ This is a British English spelling.

tray /treɪ/ [countable noun] A flat object that is used to carry food and drinks: *The waiter's tray was so full that we thought he was going to drop it.*

tread, trod, trodden /tred/ [verb] To step on something: *Please try not to tread on my feet while we're dancing!*

treason /'triː.zᵊn/ [uncountable noun] A crime that harms your country: *By giving the secret papers to the enemy, the spy committed treason.*

treasure /'treʒ·ər/ [uncountable noun] Gold, silver and other valuable objects: *The pirates found the treasure in a cave on the beach.*

⁺**treat[1]** /triːt/ [countable noun] Something special that you give to somebody or arrange for somebody: *My mom and dad took me to Disneyland as a treat for my birthday.*

treat[2] /triːt/ [verb] **1** To behave towards somebody or something in a particular way: *Some people treat their pets very badly.* **2** To try to make a sick person well again: *After the accident she was treated for shock.* ■ In this use we say: "to treat (somebody) **for** (something)". **3** To give somebody something special: *Come on! I'll treat you to an ice cream!*

⁺**treatment** /'triːt.mənt/ [noun] **1** The way that you behave towards somebody or something: *You only get the best treatment in this hotel!* **2** The things that a doctor does or orders to make a sick person better: *You must follow the treatment the doctor has given you.*

treaty /'tri·t̬i/ [countable noun] An agreement between two countries: *Countries often have commercial treaties.* ■ The plural is "treaties".

treble clef [countable noun] A musical sign on a stave which indicates the pitch of written notes: *The treble clef is placed on the second line of the stave.* 👁 **See page 460.**

⁺**tree** /triː/ [countable noun] **1** A large plant with roots, a trunk, branches and leaves: *We have four apple trees and one pear tree in our back yard.* **2 family tree** See "family tree" in the word **family.** 👁 **See pages 434 and 435.**

tremble /'trem.bl̩/ [verb] To shake: *The dog trembled with fear when he heard the thunder.*

tremendous /trɪ'men.dəs/ [adjective] **1** Very big: *Some of the dinosaurs were tremendous in size, but others were small.* **2** Very good: *Did you see the movie on television last night? It was tremendous!*

trench /trentʃ/ [countable noun] A long, narrow hole in the ground: *Thousands of soldiers died in the trenches during the First World War.*

trend [countable noun] A general direction or tendency: *She follows all the latest trends in fashion.*

trendy /'trendi/ [adjective] Very fashionable: *This is a trendy disco. It plays all the latest music.*

trespass /'tres,pæs/, /-pəs/ [verb] To go on somebody's land without permission: *Private Property. Do not trespass.* ■ Be careful with the spelling of the 3rd person singular present tense form: "trespasses".

⁺**trial** /traɪəl/ [noun] **1** The process in a court of law which establishes if a person is guilty: *The trial lasted for weeks and the suspects were declared guilty of murder.* **2** A period of time when something or somebody is tested: *We've got our new car on trial for a month.*

triangle /ˈtraɪ.æŋ.gl/ [countable noun] **1** A flat shape with three sides and three angles: *How can you calculate the angles in a triangle?* **See page 457.** **2** A musical instrument which consists of a thin metal bar in the shape of a triangle: *One of the angles of the triangle is left open.* **See page 459.**

triangular /traɪˈæŋgjələr/ [adjective] Having the form of a triangle: *Kites usually have a triangular shape.*

tribe /traɪb/ [countable noun] A group of people who live together and who have the same customs and language: *There are still tribes living in the Amazon.*

tributary /ˈtrɪb·jəˌter·i/ [countable noun] A small river that joins a larger one: *The Amazon is the largest river in the world and takes in many tributaries.* ■ The plural is "tributaries".

tribute /ˈtrɪb.juːt/ [noun] Something that is done to show respect for somebody: *There is a large black monument in Washington that was built as a tribute to those who died in the Vietnam war.*

triceps /ˈtraɪ.seps/ [countable noun] The large muscle at the back of the upper arm: *The triceps has three points of attachment.* ■ The plural is also "triceps". **See page 423.**

†**trick**[1] /trɪk/ [countable noun] **1** A clever plan to deceive somebody: *Don't believe him! It's a trick!* **2** Something clever that you do to amuse people: *Richard is a clown in his spare time and he does some wonderful card tricks.* **3 to play a trick on (somebody)** To deceive somebody for a joke: *The children played a trick on their father changing the sugar and the salt.*

trick[2] /trɪk/ [verb] To deceive somebody: *The robber tricked the old man into thinking that he worked for the Town Council.*

trickle[1] /ˈtrɪk.l̩/ [countable noun] A thin line of liquid: *A trickle of gasoline comes out of the car.*

trickle[2] /ˈtrɪk.l̩/ [verb] To flow very slowly: *It rained all afternoon and we sat and watched the water trickle down the windows.*

tricycle /ˈtraɪ.sɪ.kl/ [countable noun] An object like a bicycle, but with three wheels: *My little brother wants a red tricycle for Christmas.*

trident /ˈtraɪ.dənt/ [countable noun] In the past, a weapon like a fork with three points and a long pole: *Neptune carries a trident.*

trifle /ˈtraɪfl/ [noun] A sweet made of jelly, fruit sponge and custard: *What do you want for dessert, trifle or fruit?*

trigger /ˈtrɪg·ər/ [countable noun] A small lever on a gun that makes it fire: *The farmer aimed the gun at the rabbit and pulled the trigger.*

trillion /ˈtrɪl.jən/ [noun] One million million: *In figures, one trillion is written 1,000,000,000,000.* ■ Compare with "billion" (a thousand million).

†**trip**[1] /trɪp/ [countable noun] A journey also involving an activity like business, shopping, sightseeing and so on: *We went on a school trip to Paris last weekend.* ■ Compare with "journey" (the act of going from one place to another).

trip[2] /trɪp/ [verb] To hit your foot against something and fall: *I tripped on the step and fell and hurt my knee.*

PHRASAL VERBS · **to trip (somebody) up** To make somebody fall or nearly fall: *Ken tripped me up when I was just about to score a goal.* ■ Be careful with the spelling of these forms: "tripped", "tripping".

triumph /ˈtraɪ.əmpf/ [countable noun] A great success: *The school football team celebrated their triumph in the league by having a big party.*

triumphant /traɪˈʌmp.fənt/ [adjective] Very happy about a great success: *Robbie was triumphant when he won the art competition.*

trod US: /trɑːd/ UK: /trɒd/ Past tense of **tread**.

trodden US: /ˈtrɑː.dən/ UK: /ˈtrɒd.ən/ Past participle of **tread**.

trolley US: /ˈtrɑː.li/ UK: /ˈtrɒl.i/ [countable noun] See **cart**. ■ This word is British English.

trombone US: /trɑːmˈboʊn/ UK: /trɒmˈbəʊn/ [countable noun] A large musical instrument with a sliding tube: *Sam is learning to play the trombone at school.* **See page 459.**

troops /truːps/ [plural noun] Soldiers: *Troops were sent to the area to try and keep the peace.*

trophy /ˈtroʊ·fi/ [countable noun] A prize for a game or a race: *I keep my swimming trophy on my bedside table.* ■ The plural is "trophies".

†**tropical** /ˈtrɑp·ɪ·kəl/ [adjective] Referring to the tropics: *The coconut is a tropical fruit.*

tropics /ˈtrɒpɪks/ [plural noun] The very hot part of the earth either side of the equator: *The boundaries of the tropics are the tropic of Cancer and the tropic of Capricorn.*

troposphere /ˈtrɑp·əˌsfɪər/, /ˈtroʊ·pə-/ [countable noun] The lowest part of the atmosphere: *The troposphere extends up between 9,000 and 54,000 feet from the surface of the earth.* **See page 449.**

trot US: /trɑːt/ UK: /trɒt/ [verb] To run quickly with small steps: *The horses trotted around the ring at the circus.* ■ Be careful with the spelling of these forms: "trotted", "trotting".

trouble¹ /'trʌbl/ [noun] **1** Problems and difficulties: *My aunt and uncle have had a lot of trouble finding a school for my cousin.* **2** Conflict or violence: *There is sometimes trouble in this area on Saturdays because of the soccer game.* **3** An illness: *My grandfather has got heart trouble.* **4 to get into trouble** To do something that brings problems: *Joseph has got into trouble with the police for drinking and shouting on the town square.*

trouble² /'trʌbl/ [verb] To worry somebody or cause somebody problems: *I'm sorry to trouble you but can you tell me where the hospital is, please?*

troubled /'trʌb.ld/ [adjective] Worried because of problems: *I'm a bit troubled about the situation with Matthew. He doesn't talk to me.*

trousers /'traʊ·zərz/ [plural noun] See **pants.** ■ Be careful with the pronunciation of this word! ■ This word is British English. ■ When we talk about two or more "trousers", we use the word "pairs": "I bought three pairs of trousers".

trout /traʊt/ [noun] A large, spotted fish that lives in rivers: *We went for a meal in a restaurant the other day and I had trout.* ■ The plural is also "trout". See page 430.

truant /'tru:.ənt/ **to play truant** To stay away from school without permission: *How many times have you played truant this term, Jimmy?*

truce /tru:s/ [countable noun] An agreement between enemies to stop fighting for a certain time: *The armies of both countries decided to call a truce.*

truck /trʌk/ [countable noun] **1** A big vehicle for carrying heavy things: *There are a lot of trucks on the roads at this time of year.* ■ In British English they say "lorry". See picture at **transport.** **2** See **freight car.** ■ This use is British English.

trucker [countable noun] A professional driver of a truck: *My uncle is a trucker and spends long periods away from home.*

true /tru:/ [adjective] **1** Right or correct, agreeing with the facts: *Is it true that you are going to America for the Christmas vacations?* **2** Real, not false: *Is this a true story or are you making it up?*

truly /'tru:.li/ [adverb] **1** Really, in truth: *Georgina was truly sorry for having upset her mother.* **2 yours truly** Words that you put before your name at the end of a formal letter: *She finished the letter in the following way: "I look forward to receiving your reply. Yours truly, Penny Davies".*

trumpet /'trʌm.pɪt/ [countable noun] A musical instrument with three buttons: *The great jazz musician Louis Armstrong used to play the trumpet.*

trunk /trʌŋk/ [countable noun] **1** The main part of a tree: *The trunk of the oak tree is so wide that I can't get my arms around it.* See page 434. **2** A large strong box for transporting things when you travel: *Has my trunk arrived yet?* **3** The long nose of an elephant: *Elephants use their trunks for breathing, smelling and sucking up water.* **4** The back part of a car: *Please help me take my luggage out of the trunk.* ■ In this use, in British English we say "boot". See page 441.

TRUNK

trunks /trʌŋks/ [plural noun] See **swimming trunks.**

trust¹ /trʌst/ [uncountable noun] The belief that somebody or something is good or reliable: *A good friendship is based on trust.*

trust² /trʌst/ [verb] To believe that somebody or something is good or reliable: *I don't trust Christine because she tells lies.*

trustworthy /'trʌst,wɜr·ði/ [adjective] Honest and able to be trusted: *There is no problem in letting Ian look after the money. He's very trustworthy.*

truth /tru:θ/ [uncountable noun] **1** Being true: *There is some truth in what you say.* **2 to tell the truth** To say what is true: *Come on, tell the truth. Did you take my pen?*

truthful /'tru:θ.fᵊl/ [adjective] **1** True: *Give me a truthful answer to my question.* **2** Who tells the truth: *Lewis is a very truthful person. He never lies.*

try[1] /traɪ/ [countable noun] An attempt: *I've never been sailing, but I'd love to have a try.*

try[2] /traɪ/ [verb] **1** To attempt to do something: *I tried to open the door but I couldn't.* **2** To test something to see if you like it: *Would you like to try one of these candies?* **3** To ask somebody questions in court: *The prisoner was tried and found guilty.* **4** **to try and (do)** To attempt to do something: *Try and get the little ball into the hole.*

PHRASAL VERBS · **to try (something) on** To put a piece of clothing on to see if you like it: *"Where can I try these jeans on?" "In the changing rooms over there".* ■ Be careful with the spelling of these forms: "tries", "tried".

T-shirt /'tiˌʃɜrt/ [countable noun] An article of clothing made of cotton like a shirt with no collar: *I've got a new T-shirt with my name on the back.* ■ This word is also written "tee-shirt". See picture at **clothes**.

T-square [countable noun] A ruler like the letter "T" form drawing perpendicular lines and right angles: *I need a T-square for my drawing class.*

tsunami /tsu:'nɑ:.mi/ [countable noun] A very big wave, usually caused by an undersea earthquake: *A tsunami devastated the coastal areas of many southeast Asian countries a few years ago.*

tub /tʌb/ [countable noun] **1** A round container: *I'm going to have a tub of ice cream. Do you want one?* **2** See **bathtub**.

tuba /'tju:bə/ [countable noun] A musical instrument which consists of a long, curved metal bent tube: *The tuba produces low notes.* **See page 459.**

tube US: /tu:b/ UK: /tju:b/ [countable noun] **1** A pipe made of metal, plastic and so on: *When you donate blood, the blood goes from your arm along a tube into a bag.* **2** A long, thin container with a hole at one end: *Don't forget to get a tube of toothpaste when you go to the store.* **3** See **subway**. ■ This use is informal. This use is British English. ■ Be careful with the pronunciation of this word. The first part "tu" is pronounced like the word "you" with a "t" in front.

Tuesday /'tuz·deɪ/, /-di/ [noun] The third day of the week: *Tuesday is between Monday and Wednesday.* ■ Be careful! "Tuesday" has a capital "T". ■ Be careful with the pronunciation of this word. The first part, "Tue" sounds like "you" with a "t" in front. See picture at **calendar**.

tug[1] /tʌg/ [countable noun] **1** A hard pull: *The little girl gave her mother's hand a tug.* **2** A small, strong boat: *The tug towed the fishing boat across the harbor.*

tug[2] /tʌg/ [verb] To pull hard and suddenly: *Don't tug at that knot or you'll never get it undone.* ■ Be careful with the spelling of these forms: "tugged", "tugging".

tulip /'tu·lɪp/ [countable noun] A spring flower shaped like a champagne glass: *Holland is famous for its tulips.* ■ Be careful with the pronunciation of this word! **See page 433.**

tumble /'tʌmbl/ [verb] To fall suddenly: *I tripped over the carpet and tumbled down the stairs.*

tummy /'tʌm.i/ [countable noun] Stomach: *I've got an awful tummy ache after eating all those chocolates.* ■ This word is informal. ■ The plural is "tummies".

tumor [countable noun] A mass of dead cells that grows on or in the body: *They operated on him for a brain tumor.* ■ Be careful with the pronunciation of this word.

tuna /'tu·nə/ [noun] A large fish that lives in the sea: *My mom makes a delicious tuna salad.* ■ Be careful with the pronunciation of this word! **See page 430.**

tune[1] /tju:n/ [countable noun] A series of musical notes arranged in a pleasant way: *Can you remember the tune of that song we learnt at school the other day?* ■ Be careful with the pronunciation of this word.

tune[2] /tju:n/ [verb] To make a musical instrument sound correct: *The orchestra tuned their instruments before they began to play.* ■ Be careful with the pronunciation of this word.

tunnel /'tʌn.ᵊl/ [countable noun] A long passage under the ground or water: *The Holland Tunnel in New York was the first underwater tunnel designed for automobiles.* **See page 445.**

turban /'tɜr·bən/ [countable noun] A covering for a man's head: *A turban is made from a very long piece of cloth.*

turbine /'tɜ:baɪn/ [countable noun] A turning engine driven by wind, water or steam: *Turbines are often used to generate energy.*

turkey /'tɜ:ki/ [noun] A large farm bird: *In United States, turkey is the traditional dish for Thanksgiving day.* **See page 429.**

turn[1] /tɜ:n/ [countable noun] **1** Moving something around: *Give the wheel another turn.* **2** A change of direction: *Take a right turn when you get to the stop lights.* **3** Your time to do something: *It's your turn to throw the dice.* **4** **in turns** One after the other: *Let's do the shopping in turns. That's the fairest way.* **5** **to take turns** To do something, one person after the other: *Don't all rush to the table at once. Take turns to serve yourselves.*

turn[2] US: /tɝ:n/ UK: /tɜ:n/ [verb] **1** To go around and around: *The wheels of a vehicle turn as it goes.* **2** To change direction: *When you get to the station, turn left.* **3** To move so that you are facing a different direction: *She turned and waved before she went into school.* **4** To change color or state: *The sea was so bad that Frank turned white and looked*

a b c d e f g h i j k l m n o p q r s t u v w x y z

as if he was going to be sick. **5 to turn the page** To move to the next page: *Please, turn the page and read the first paragraph.*

▸ PHRASAL VERBS · **to turn around 1** To face the opposite direction: *Turn around and look at me!* **2** To make an unsuccessful business successful again: *Our transformation plan helped turn around the company.* ■ The same meaning: "to turn round". · **to turn back** To stop and return in the direction you came from: *They turned back when they saw that it was impossible to continue.* · **to turn (somebody) down** To reject somebody for a job or other thing: *They turned my sister down for the job.* · **to turn (something) down 1** To refuse something: *Gina turned down our offer of help.* **2** To lower the volume: *Turn that music down. I can't concentrate.* · **to turn into (something)** To become different: *Water turns into ice when it freezes.* · **to turn (something) off** To stop something functioning: *Let's turn the television off. I'm fed up of watching it.* · **to turn on (somebody)** To attack or criticize somebody unexpectedly: *After a year of friendship Kathy turned on her best friend after the field trip.* · **to turn (something) on** To start something functioning: *Let's turn on the radio and listen to the eight o'clock news.* · **to turn out 1** To end in a particular way: *The concert didn't start well, but it turned out well in the end.* **2** *It turns out that...* · **to turn (something) over** To move something so that the other side is facing up: *The child turned the pages over slowly looking at the pictures.* · **to turn round** See **to turn around**. · **to turn up 1** To appear, to arrive: *Tammy turned up late as usual; Who turned up at the party?* **2** To increase the volume of something: *Turn the radio up. I can't hear it properly.*

turning /ˈtɜr·nɪŋ/ [countable noun] The place where a road goes to the left or right: *Take the first turning on the right.*

turnip /ˈtɜr·nɪp/ [noun] A round, white vegetable: *My grandma used to make lovely turnip stew when we were little.*

turn signal [countable noun] A light on a car that shows in which direction the driver is intending to turn: *The turn signal shows that the car's going to turn right.* **👁 See page 441.**

turquoise /ˈtɜːkwɔɪz/ [noun] A precious blue stone: *Turquoise is an opaque blue mineral.*

turquoise blue [noun and adjective] The color of a turquoise: *The ocean is a turquoise blue today.*

turtle US: /ˈtɝː.ʈl/ UK: /ˈtɜː.tl/ [countable noun] A reptile with a very hard shell on its back that lives in the sea or on land: *Turtles lay their eggs on land and the babies find their way back to the sea.* ■ The same meaning: "tortoise". In British English "turtle" is used to refer to this reptile that lives in the sea, whereas "tortoise" is used to refer to this reptile that lives on land. **👁 See page 430.**

tusk /tʌsk/ [countable noun] A long tooth that grows outside the mouth of some animals: *Elephants have long tusks which are in fact their teeth.*

tutu [countable noun] A short stiff skirt that the female ballet dancers wear: *My mom bought me a new tutu for my ballet class.*

⁺TV /ˌtiːˈviː/ [noun] See **television**. ■ Be careful! "TV" is always written in capital letters. ■ See box at **abbreviations**.

tweet[1] /twiːt/ [countable noun] **1** A single sound made by a young or small bird: *A bird makes the sound of a tweet.* **2** A contribution to Twitter: *Stephen Fry's tweets are followed by millions of people.*

tweet[2] [verb] **1** To make the sounds young or small birds make: *This morning when I woke up I heard the birds tweeting.* **2** To contribute to Twitter: *You have to tweet frequently if you want people to follow you on Twitter.*

tweezers /ˈtwi·zərz/ [plural noun] A small pair of pincers: *Tweezers are used for handling small objects.*

twelfth /twelfθ/ [noun and adjective] Referring to twelve: *December is the twelfth and last month of the year.* ■ "Twelfth" can also be written "12th".

⁺twelve /twelv/ [noun, adjective and pronoun] The number 12: *There are twelve months in the year.*

twentieth /ˈtwen·ti·ɪθ/ [noun and adjective] Referring to twenty: *It's my sister's twentieth birthday today.* ■ "Twentieth" can also be written "20th".

twenty /ˈtwen·ti/ [noun, adjective and pronoun] The number 20: *There are twenty boys in our class and ten girls.*

⁺twice /twaɪs/ [adverb] Two times: *I liked that movie so much that I saw it twice in one week.*

twig /twɪg/ [countable noun] A very small, thin branch of a tree: *My mom cut off all the twigs that had been damaged by the frost.*

⁺twin /twɪn/ [countable noun] One of two children that are born of the same mother at the same time: *Elizabeth and Margaret are identical twins.*

twinkle /ˈtwɪŋkl/ [verb] To shine with a small light: *"Twinkle, twinkle, little star" is a popular lullaby in United States.*

⁺twist[1] /twɪst/ [countable noun] **1** A hard turn: *Give the lid a twist and see if you can undo it.* **2** A curve: *The road had a lot of twists and turns in it.*

twist[2] /twɪst/ [verb] **1** To turn something strongly: *I twisted my ankle playing hockey the other day.* **2** To turn in different directions: *The road twisted up the hill.* **3** To wind together: *She twisted her hair into a braid.*

twister US: /ˈtwɪstər/ [countable noun] A violent wind that goes round and round: *The village was destroyed by a twister.* ■ The same meaning: "tornado".

†**two** /tuː/ [noun, adjective and pronoun] The number 2: *I've got two sisters and a brother.*

two-way /ˈtuː.weɪ/ [adjective] Going in opposite directions: *This is a two-way street.*

†**type**[1] /taɪp/ [countable noun] A sort or kind of something: *It's a horror movie and I don't like that type of movie.*

type[2] /taɪp/ [verb] To write using a machine: *We are learning to type at school.* ■ Be careful with the spelling of this form: "typing".

typewriter /ˈtaɪpˌraɪ·t̬ər/ [countable noun] A machine that types: *an electronic typewriter.*

†**typical** /ˈtɪp.ɪ.kəl/ [adjective] Showing the qualities of a particular group: *In United States it is typical to eat turkey on Thanksgiving.*

typist /ˈtaɪ.pɪst/ [countable noun] A person who types: *My cousin works as a typist for a publishing company.*

tyrant /ˈtaɪ·rənt/ [countable noun] A very cruel ruler of a country: *Many of the Roman Emperors were tyrants.*

†**tyre** UK: /taɪəʳ/ [countable noun] See **tire**[1]. ■ This is a British English spelling.

u /juː/ The twenty-first letter of the alphabet: *The word "uniform" begins with a "u".*

UFO /ˌju·ef'oʊ/ [countable noun] A strange object seen in the sky: *My uncle said he saw a UFO on the way back from the pub last week.* ■ Be careful! "UFO" is always written in capital letters. "UFO" is an abbreviation for "Unidentified Flying Object". ■ See box at **abbreviations**.

↑**ugly** /'ʌg.li/ [adjective] Not pretty, unpleasant to look at: *What an ugly face you've got when you're angry!* ■ The comparative form is "uglier" and the superlative form is "ugliest".

UK Used to refer to the country of Great Britain and Northern Ireland: *She lives in the UK.* ■ "UK" is an abbreviation for "United Kingdom". ■ See box at **abbreviations**.

ulna /'ʌl.nə/ [countable noun] The thinnest and longest of the two bones in the forearm between the elbow and the hand: *The ulna is on the side opposite the thumb.* ■ The plural is "ulnae" or "ulnas". **See page 422.**

ultrasound /'ʌltrəsaʊnd/ [uncountable noun] **1** Band of special sound with a frequency above the upper limit of human hearing: *Ultrasound is used to examine unborn babies and to test objects for defects.* **2** A scan to examine a baby still inside its mother: *She had an ultrasound at the hospital.*

ultraviolet /ˌʌltrə'vaɪələt/ [adjective] Referring to the spectrum of light beyond that which people can see: *Ultraviolet light is found in sunlight and is the main cause of sunburn and skin cancer.*

umbilical cord /ʌm'bɪlɪkl‚kɔːd/ [countable noun] A flexible tube that is the connection between the fetus and its mother: *The umbilical cord is cut when the baby is born.*

↑**umbrella** /ʌm'brel.ə/ [countable noun] An object that you use to protect yourself from the rain: *Don't forget your umbrella. It looks like rain.*

umpire /'ʌm·paɪər/ [countable noun] The referee in some games, especially tennis and baseball: *The umpire decided that the ball was out.*

un- /ʌn-/ [prefix] An addition to the beginning of a word that usually gives it the opposite meaning: *If you add "un-" to "happy", you get "unhappy", which means "sad".*

UN Used to refer to an international organization that was established in 1945 to keep world peace: *Harry James works for the UN.* ■ "UN" is an abbreviation for "United Nations". ■ See box at **abbreviations**.

↑**unable** /ʌn'eɪ.bl̩/ [adjective] Not able: *I'm sorry, I'm unable to help you at the moment. I'm too busy.* ■ Be careful with the pronunciation of this word! It is pronounced like "table".

unanimous /juːˈnæn.ɪ.məs/ [adjective] With everyone's agreement: *The decision to suspend the game was unanimous.*

unarmed /ʌnˈɑrmd/ [adjective] Without a gun, knife, or other weapon: *Rangers in the National Park are usually unarmed.* ■ Be careful with the pronunciation of the end of this word. The "e" is not pronounced.

unattractive /ˌʌn.əˈtræk.tɪv/ [adjective] Not attractive: *I think that style of blouse is very unattractive.*

unbearable /ʌnˈbeər·ə·bəl/ [adjective] Awful, that you can't tolerate: *What an unbearable movie!*

unbelievable /ˌʌn.bɪˈliː.və.bl/ [adjective] Difficult to believe, very surprising: *What you say is so unbelievable that I think that you must be inventing it.*

⁺**uncertain** /ʌnˈsɜr·tə·n/ [adjective] Not sure: *We were uncertain about which way to go.*

unchain [verb] To remove the chains by which somebody or something is fastened: *She unchained the dog and took him to the car.*

⁺**uncle** /ˈʌŋ.kl/ [countable noun] Your father's or mother's brother, or your aunt's husband: *My aunt and uncle live next-door to us.* ■ Be careful of the pronunciation of this word! "un" is pronounced like "sun". 👁 See picture at **family**.

unclear /ʌnˈklɪər/ [adjective] Not clear, not evident: *The instructions for this computer program are unclear.*

⁺**uncomfortable** /ʌnˈkʌm·fər·t̬ə·bəl/, /-ˈkʌmf·tər·bəl/ [adjective] Not comfortable: *These shoes are very uncomfortable. I think they're too small.*

uncommon /ʌnˈkɑm·ən/ [adjective] Not common, unusual: *That bird is uncommon in this part of the country.*

⁺**unconscious** /ʌnˈkɑn·ʃəs/ [adjective] Not conscious: *Timmy was knocked unconscious when he fell off his bike.*

uncontrollable /ˌʌn·kənˈtroʊ·lə·bəl/ [adjective] Impossible to control: *The children in that class are uncontrollable.*

uncooked [adjective] Not cooked: *I can't eat this meat; it's uncooked in the middle.* ■ Be careful with the pronunciation of the end of this word. The last "e" is not pronounced. ■ The same meaning: "raw".

uncountable /ʌnˈkaʊn·tə·bəl/ [adjective] That cannot be counted: *"Water" is an uncountable noun because you cannot have "one water", you have "some water" or "a glass of water".*

uncover /ʌnˈkʌv·ər/ [verb] **1** To take a cover off something: *We uncovered the birthday cake and showed it to everyone.* **2** To discover a crime or a criminal: *The police uncovered a drug gang in the town next to ours.*

⁺**under** /ˈʌndər/ [adverb and preposition] **1** Below something: *The cat sat under the table.* **2** Less than: *If you are under sixteen, you are not allowed to apply for a driving license.* **3** Subject to the orders or authority of: *My aunt is a manager in a restaurant and she has about twenty people working under her.* 👁 See picture at **preposition**.

underclothes /ˈʌn·dərˌkloʊz/, /-ˌkloʊðz/ [plural noun] Clothes that you wear next to your skin under your other clothes: *I went shopping yesterday with my mom to buy some new underclothes.* ■ The same meaning: "underwear".

undergraduate /ˌʌn·dərˈgrædʒ·u·ət/ [countable noun] A student at university doing a first degree, specially a bachelor's degree: *There's a special dining room for undergraduates and one for postgraduates at the local university.*

⁺**underground**[1] /ˈʌndəgraʊnd/ [adjective and adverb] Under the ground: *We can leave the car in the underground parking lot.*

underground[2] /ˈʌndəgraʊnd/ [noun] See **subway**. ■ This word is British English.

underline /ˈʌn·dərˌlɑɪn/ [verb] To draw a line under something: *Write the title and the date and then underline them.*

⁺**underneath** /ˌʌn·dərˈniθ/ [adverb and preposition] Under something: *Put your bag underneath the chair and then you won't fall over it.*

underpants /ˈʌn·dərˌpænts/ [plural noun] A piece of clothing that a boy or a man wears under his pants: *We gave my dad a pair of underpants with "Angeles Lakers" written on them.* ■ "Pants" is short for "underpants". ■ When we talk about two or more "underpants", we use the word "pairs": "I bought three pairs of underpants".

underprivileged /ˌʌn·dərˈprɪv·lɪdʒd/ [adjective] Very poor, without the advantages of other members of society: *The people in this area of the city are underprivileged.*

undersea /ˌʌn.dəˈsiː/ US: /-dɚ-/ [adjective] Beneath the surface of the sea: *The submarine is an undersea vessel.*

undershirt [countable noun] An article of underwear that you wear on the top part of your body: *Don't forget to put your woolly undershirt on. It's extremely cold today.* ■ In British English they say "vest".

⁺**understand**, understood, understood /ˌʌn·dərˈstænd/ [verb] **1** To know the meaning of something: *I don't understand this word. What does it mean?* **2** To know something because it has been explained to you: *I understand the physics we did in class today now that you have explained it to me.*

⁺**understanding**[1] /ˌʌndəˈstændɪŋ/ [adjective] Kind and sympathetic: *I told my teacher about how I had* *fallen over on the way to school and she was very understanding.*

understanding[2] /ˌʌndəˈstændɪŋ/ [uncountable noun] The ability to understand something: *You must have a good understanding of mathematics to do this physics course.*

understood /ˌʌndəˈstʊd/ Past tense and past participle forms of **understand**.

underwater /ˌʌndəˈwɔːtər/ [adjective and adverb] Under the water: *We had an underwater swimming race from one end of the pool to the other.*

underwear /ˈʌn·dərˌweər/ [uncountable noun] Clothes that you wear next to your skin under your other clothes: *Here are the clean clothes: jeans and shirts in this basket and underwear in the other.* ■ The same meaning: "underclothes".

undid /ʌnˈdɪd/ Past tense of **undo**.

undo, undid, undone /ʌnˈduː/ [verb] To untie or unfasten something: *Help me to undo my shoelaces, please.*

undone /ʌnˈdʌn/ Past participle of **undo**.

undoubtedly /ʌnˈdaʊ·t̬ɪd·li/ [adjective] Without a doubt: *Michelle is undoubtedly the best tennis player we have ever had in this school.* ■ Be careful with the pronunciation of this word. The "b" is silent and the "e" is pronounced like the "i" in "did".

undress /ʌnˈdres/ [verb] To take your clothes off: *I undressed and got in the bathtub.* ■ The same meaning: "strip[2]". ■ Be careful with the spelling of the 3rd person singular present tense form: "undresses".

uneasily /ʌnˈiː.zɪ.li/ [adverb] Showing that you are worried: *We waited uneasily while the teacher went to fetch the principal.*

uneasy /ʌnˈiː.zi/ [adjective] Worried; a little afraid: *Mom and dad always get uneasy when we come home late.*

unemployed /ˌʌn.ɪmˈplɔɪd/ [adjective] Without a paid job: *James lost his job last March and has been unemployed ever since.* ■ Be careful with the pronunciation of the end of this word. The last "e" is not pronounced.

unemployment /ˌʌn.ɪmˈplɔɪ.mənt/ [uncountable noun] The state of not having a paid job, the totally number of unemployed: *The unemployment figures have gone up a lot in this town over the past year.*

uneven /ʌnˈiː.vᵊn/ [adjective] Not level, not regular: *The ground is very uneven in this part of the backyard.*

unexpected /ˌʌn.ɪkˈspek.tɪd/ [adjective] Not expected, surprising: *The test results were totally unexpected. We all thought we would pass.* ■ Be careful with the pronunciation of the end of this word. The last "e" is pronounced like the "i" in "did".

unfair /ʌnˈfeər/ [adjective] Not fair or just: *It's unfair that I have to stay one hour after class.*

unfamiliar /ˌʌn·fəˈmɪl·jər/ [adjective] Not familiar, not seen or known before: *I knew that I had got off the train at the wrong station when everything looked so unfamiliar.*

unfashionable /ʌnˈfæʃ.ᵊn.ə.bl̩/ [adjective] Not fashionable, out of date: *I don't want to wear those clothes. They're so unfashionable.*

unfasten /ʌnˈfæs·ən/ [verb] To undo, to make loose something that was fastened: *Can you unfasten this knot for me? It is very tight.*

unfit /ʌnˈfɪt/ [adjective] **1** Not healthy or strong: *The doctor told my dad that he was unfit and that he should do more exercise.* **2** Not good enough for something: *The inspectors said that the old building was unfit to be used as a school.*

unfortunate /ʌnˈfɔr·tʃə·nət/ [adjective] Unlucky: *My mom has been very unfortunate recently. First she lost her job and then she had a car accident.*

unfriendly /ʌnˈfrend.li/ [adjective] Not friendly: *Mark is a very unfriendly person. He hardly ever smiles.*

ungrateful /ʌnˈgreɪt.fᵊl/ [adjective] Not grateful: *It was very ungrateful of you not to say "Thank you" for the present.*

unhappiness /ʌnˈhæp.ɪ.nəs/ [uncountable noun] The state of being unhappy: *Can you explain the reason for your unhappiness?*

unhappy /ʌnˈhæp.i/ [adjective] Sad, not satisfied: *Stuart says that he was very unhappy at his last school.* ■ The comparative form is "unhappier" and the superlative form is "unhappiest".

unhealthy /ʌnˈhel.θi/ [adjective] **1** Not healthy: *Elaine looks very unhealthy these days. She's very pale and thin.* **2** Not good for you: *Too many potato chips and candies are unhealthy for you.* ■ The comparative form is "unhealthier" and the superlative form is "unhealthiest".

unhelpful /ʌnˈhelp.fᵊl/ [adjective] Not helpful: *The instructions for this computer are very unhelpful.*

unicellular /ˌju·nəˈsel·jə·lər/ [adjective] Referring to an organism, that only has one cell: *An amoeba is unicellular.*

uniform /ˈju·nəˌfɔrm/ [noun] Specially designed clothing that members of a group institution wear: *Our school uniform is a gray skirt or pants and a blue sweater.*

unimportant /ˌʌn·ɪmˈpɔr·tə·nt/ [adjective] Not important, of little importance: *Don't worry about the type of paper you use, that's quite unimportant for the moment.*

uninhabited /ˌʌn.ɪnˈhæb.ɪ.tɪd/ US: /-t̬ɪd/ [adjective] Without people living there: *Some of the small islands off the coast of Alaska are totally unin-*

habited. ■ Be careful with the pronunciation of the end of this word. The "e" is pronounced like the "i" in "did".

uninteresting /ʌn'ɪn.tər.es.tɪŋ/ US: /-tə-/ [adjective] Not interesting: *That book is really uninteresting, isn't it?*

†**union** /'juː.ni.ən/ [noun] **1** An association of workers: *My dad is the representative of his department in the National Union of Teachers.* ■ We also say "trade union". **2** A group of countries or people that get together: *My sister belongs to the Women's Union that meets once a week.* **3** Coming together: *The union of the girls' school with the boys' school took place last year.*

Union Jack [countable noun] The British flag: *The Union Jack is formed by the combined flags of Scotland, Wales and England.* ■ Be careful. "Union Jack" has capital letters.

†**unique** /jʊ'niːk/ [adjective] Not like anybody or anything: *This painting is quite unique in its style.*

†**unit** /'juː.nɪt/ [countable noun] **1** One thing which is complete in itself, although very often part of a series: *The Social Studies textbook we use in class is divided into 10 units.* **2** A measurement: *A "dollar" is a unit of money; a "mile" is a unit of length; and a "pound" is a unit of weight.*

†**unite** /jʊ'naɪt, juː-/ [verb] To bring things together: *Texas and United States united in 1845.*

universal /ˌjuːnə'vɜr·səl/ [adjective] Which is everywhere, which affects everyone: *There was universal excitement when the first person stepped on the moon.*

†**universe** /'ju·nəˌvɜrs/ [noun] The earth, the planets and all the stars: *My uncle is an astronomer and studies the universe.*

†**university** /ˌju·nə'vɜr·sɪ·t̬i/ [noun] A place of higher education: *I would like to study Biology at university.* ■ The plural is "universities".

unkind /ʌn'kaɪnd/ [adjective] Not kind, cruel: *I don't like Susan very much. She's very unkind sometimes.*

†**unknown** /ʌn'noʊn/ [adjective] Not known: *The painter of that picture is unknown.*

unleaded [adjective] Not containing lead: *Our car uses unleaded gas.*

†**unless** /ən'les/ [conjunction] If... not; except if: *Unless you start studying for your test now, you'll never pass it.*

†**unlike**[1] [adjective] Not like something, different from: *This school is unlike my last one.*

unlike[2] /ʌn'laɪk/ [preposition] **1** In contrast to: *Unlike me, my sister is very lively and likes going out. I like reading and listening to music.* **2** Not typical of: *I am very surprised at what you say about Judy. It's unlike her to be cruel.*

unlikely /ʌn'laɪ.kli/ [adjective] Not probable: *It's unlikely that our team will beat Chicago Bulls, but you never know.*

†**unload** /ʌn'ləʊd/ [verb] To take things out of a car, boat or other vehicle: *Can you help me unload the van, please?*

unlock /ʌn'lɑk/ [verb] To open something with a key: *I've lost the key of my suitcase and now I can't unlock it.*

unlucky /ʌn'lʌk.i/ [adjective] Not lucky, with bad luck: *We were very unlucky to lose the game. We were the better team.*

unmarried /ʌn'mær·id/, /-'meər-/ [adjective] Not married: *My uncle is unmarried.*

unnatural /ʌn'nætʃ·ər·əl/ [adjective] Not natural, that is not usual or expected: *It's unnatural for a person never to have any friends.*

unnecessary /ʌn'nes.ə.ser.i/ [adjective] Not necessary: *It's unnecessary to take so much money on a school trip.*

unpack /ʌn'pæk/ [verb] To take your things out of your suitcase or bag after a trip: *When you've unpacked, come down and have something to eat.*

†**unpleasant** /ʌn'plez.ᵊnt/ [adjective] Not pleasant, unfriendly: *Pat was very unpleasant to my friends the other day. It was quite embarrassing.*

unpopular /ʌn'pɒp·jə·lər/ [adjective] Not popular: *Dave is unpopular because he's so rude to people.*

unreasonable /ʌn'riː.zᵊn.ə.bl̩/ [adjective] Not reasonable: *Don't be so unreasonable, mom! Why can't I go to the party?*

unreliable /ˌʌn.rɪ'laɪə.bl̩/ [adjective] Not reliable: *Frank is very unreliable. You can never trust him to do anything.*

unsafe /ʌn'seɪf/ [adjective] Not safe, not dangerous: *That bicycle is unsafe because the brakes don't work very well.*

unsatisfactory /ˌən·sæt̬·əs'fæk·tə·ri/ [adjective] Not satisfactory, not acceptable: *You work is most unsatisfactory. You never pay attention in class.*

unscramble /ʌn'skræm.bl̩/ [verb] To return to a legible state something that has been coded: *We need to unscramble the message to find out what it says.*

unselfish /ʌn'sel.fɪʃ/ [adjective] Not selfish, thinking of others before yourself: *My mother is a very unselfish person and is always doing things for others.*

unskilled /ʌn'skɪld/ [adjective] Without special training: *Unskilled workers often have to do the most tiring jobs in a factory.* ■ Be careful with the pronunciation of the end of this word. The "e" is not pronounced.

unsteady /ʌn'sted.i/ [adjective] Not steady: *That table's very unsteady. Let's put something under one of the legs.*

a b c d e f g h i j k l m n o p q r s t u v w x y z

unsuccessful /ˌʌn.sək'ses.fəl/ [adjective] Not successful: *There were several unsuccessful attempts to climb Everest before a British expedition reached the top in 1953.* ■ Be careful with the pronunciation of this word. The first "c" is pronounced like a "k", the second "c" like an "s".

unsuitable /ʌn'su·t̬ə·bəl/ [adjective] Not suitable: *Those dirty old jeans are quite unsuitable to wear to a wedding.*

unsympathetic /ˌʌn.sɪm.pə'θet.ɪk/ US: /-'θet̬-/ [adjective] Not sympathetic: *My father was quite unsympathetic when I told him that I wasn't feeling well.*

untidy /ʌn'taɪ.di/ [adjective] Not tidy, in disorder: *Karen's room's always untidy, but she seems to like it that way.* ■ The comparative form is "untidier" and the superlative form is "untidiest". 👁 See picture at **opposite**.

untie /ʌn'taɪ/ [verb] To undo a piece of string, shoelace and so on: *Untie your shoes before you take them off, please!* ■ Be careful with the spelling of this form: "untying".

until[1] /ən'tɪl/ [conjunction] Up to the time when: *Wait here on the corner until I finish in the store.*

†**until**[2] /ən'tɪl/ [preposition] Up to a certain time: *The swimming pool doesn't open until 5 o'clock.*

untrue /ʌn'truː/ [adjective] Not true, false: *The story George told you about me is completely untrue.*

unused /ʌn'juːzd/ [adjective] Not used: *We can practice our songs in that unused room at the end of the corridor.* ■ Be careful with the pronunciation of this word. The "e" is not pronounced.

†**unusual** /ʌn'juː.ʒu.əl/ [adjective] Not usual, uncommon, different: *It's unusual for Sean to be so late. I wonder where he is.*

unwelcome /ʌn'wel.kəm/ [adjective] Not welcome: *Old Mr. Harding is an unwelcome guest since he was so rude to my grandma.*

unwell /ʌn'wel/ [adjective] Not well, ill: *My grandfather's been unwell for some time now and we're quite worried about him.*

unwilling /ʌn'wɪl.ɪŋ/ [adjective] Not willing, not wanting to: *Dad says that he's unwilling to accept the new post until he knows more about it.*

unwise /ʌn'waɪz/ [adjective] Not wise, not a good idea: *It would be unwise to drive in this foggy weather.*

†**up** /ʌp/ [adjective, adverb and preposition] **1** To a higher place or in a higher place: *Harry put the book up on the shelf.* **2** Out of bed: *It's twelve o'clock and you're still not up.* **3** Along: *Walk up the street with me to the corner.* **4** Higher: *The bad news is that inflation is up again.* **5** to be up to (something) See "to be up to (something)" in the word **be** **6** to come up See "to come up" in the word **come** **7** to cut up See "to cut up" in the word **cut**[2] **8** to get up See "to get up" in the word **get** **9** to go up See "to go up" in the word **go**[2]. **10** up and down In one direction and then in the other: *Mr. Browning walked up and down the road waiting for his daughter.* **11** up to Until: *We've got up to the end of the month to finish the project.* **12** to use up See "to use up" in the word "use[2]" **13** What's up? Words that you say when you ask somebody what's happening or what's the matter: *What's up with you? Why are you looking so sad?* 👁 See picture at **preposition**.

update /'ʌp.deɪt/, /ʌp'deɪt/ [verb] To bring up to date: *Update me on the news. What's been happening?*

uphill /ʌp'hɪl/ [adverb] Towards the top of a hill: *We walked uphill to the farmhouse.*

†**upon** /ə'pɒn/, /ə'pɔn/ [preposition] On: *The church stands upon a little hill, about two miles from the town.* ■ We usually say "on".

†**upper** /'ʌp·ər/ [adjective] Higher: *The upper part of the mountain is covered in snow.*

upright /'ʌpraɪt/ [adjective and adverb] Straight up, in a vertical position: *Carry that box upright or the contents will be damaged.*

uprising /'ʌpˌraɪ.zɪŋ/ [countable noun] A rebellion: *There was an uprising in United States against British rule in 1776.*

†**upset**[1] /ʌp'set/ [adjective] **1** Sad, angry or otherwise emotionally disturbed: *We were all very upset when the cat was killed in an accident.* **2** Ill: *Brian's not here today because he's got an upset stomach.*

upset[2], upset, upset /ʌp'set/ [verb] **1** To make somebody sad, angry or otherwise emotionally disturbed: *She upset me when she told me that I was fat.* **2** To make something go wrong: *The arrival of Nancy's parents upset our plans for an all night party.* **3** To knock over or to spill something: *I'm sorry! I've just upset the milk all over the table.* ■ Be careful with the spelling of this form: "upsetting".

†**upside down** [adverb] With the top part at the bottom: *You've hung the picture upside down!*

†**upstairs** /'ʌp'sterz/ [adverb] On a higher floor or to a higher floor: *Go upstairs and get my glasses from the bedroom, please.*

up to date /ˌʌptə'deɪt/ [adjective] Modern, having all the latest information: *Jane is always up to date on the latest fashions.*

upward [adverb] Up; towards a higher place: *Look at all those people looking upward. I wonder what they're looking at.*

†**upwards** /'ʌp·wərdz/ [adverb] Up; towards a higher place: *Look at all those people looking upwards. I wonder what they're looking at.*

uranium /jʊə'reɪniəm/ [uncountable noun] A radioactive metallic element which occurs naturally: *Uranium can be used for the production of nuclear energy.*

Uranus /'jʊərənəs/ [countable noun] A planet of the solar system that is seventh in order from the Sun: *Uranus was the first planet discovered with a telescope.* See page 447.

†**urban** /'ɜr·bən/ [adjective] Of a town or a city: *My grandfather says that he could never get used to living in an urban area.*

urchin /'ɜr·tʃən/ [countable noun] **1** A small child that is mischievous, especially a dirty and poor child: *That street urchin is dressed in rags.* ■ This use is now old-fashioned. **2 sea urchin** A small, edible sea creature with a round, spiny shell: *Sea urchins mainly eat algae.*

ureter US: /jʊ'riː.t̬ɚ/ UK: /jʊə'riː.tər/ [countable noun] Either of two vessels in the body which carries urine from the kidneys to the bladder: *The ureters are muscular tubes that push the urine through.* See page 424.

urethra /jʊ'ri·θrə/ [countable noun] A vessel which carries urine from the bladder out of the body: *The urethra carries urine out of the body through the penis.* ■ The plural is "urethras" or "urethrae". See pages 424 and 425.

†**urge**[1] /ɜːdʒ/ [countable noun] A strong desire to do something: *Laurie had a sudden urge to sing and dance.*

urge[2] /ɜːdʒ/ [verb] To try to make somebody do something by strong persuasion: *My teacher urged me to study harder.*

urgency /'ɜr·dʒən·si/ [uncountable noun] The need to do something very quickly: *"Come quickly!" he said with urgency in his voice.* ■ The plural is "urgencies".

†**urgent** /'ɜr·dʒənt/ [adjective] Needing to be done very quickly: *I must call home immediately. I've had an urgent message from my mother.*

urinary /'jʊə.rɪ.nər.i/ US: /'jʊr.ɪ.ner-/ [adjective] Referring to urine, and the vessels which carry or produce it: *Infections of the urinary tract are a common problem.*

urine /'jʊərɪn/ [uncountable noun] A liquid emitted as waste from the body by the kidneys: *Urine is normally pale yellow.*

Uruguayan[1] [adjective] Referring to Uruguay: *The Uruguayan Peso is the currency of Uruguay.* ■ Be careful! "Uruguayan" has a capital "U".

Uruguayan[2] [countable noun] A person from Uruguay: *My cousin is married to a Uruguayan and they live in Montevideo.* ■ Be careful! "Uruguayan" has a capital "U".

†**us** /ʌs, əs/ [pronoun] A word used for "we", usually when it is the object of a sentence or comes straight after a preposition: *Daniel wrote to my sister and me, and asked us to go and visit him.*

USA The United States of America: *Sarah lives in the USA.* ■ "USA" is an abbreviation for "Unites States of America". ■ See box at **abbreviations**.

use[1] /juːs/ [noun] **1** The act or fact of using something: *The whiteboard is not for the use of the students, but for the teacher.* **2 to make use of (something)** To find a use for something: *Can you make use of this umbrella? I've got two.*

†**use**[2] /juːz/ [verb] To do something with an object: *My mom uses a computer at work.*

▶ **PHRASAL VERBS** · **to use up** To use something until it is finished: *We've used up all the firewood. Do we have any more?*

†**used**[1] /juːst/ [adjective] **1** Not new, that has already had one owner: *My mom bought a used car last week and she says it's a bargain.* **2 to be used to** To be accustomed to something: *I am used to getting up early.* **3 to get used to** To become accustomed to something: *My mom is learning to ski and she's finding it very difficult to get used to it.* ■ The verb after "be used to" or "get used to" is in the "-ing" form. ■ Be careful with the pronunciation of this word. The "e" is not pronounced.

used[2] **used to** Words that you use to talk about something that happened often in the past: *My cousin says that when he was little, he used to believe in Santa Claus.* ■ The verb after "used to" is in the infinitive form: "He used to go". ■ Be careful with the pronunciation of this word. The "e" is not pronounced.

†**useful** /'juːs.fᵊl/ [adjective] Good for doing something: *We gave my dad a book about gardening and he says it's very useful.*

†**useless** /'juː.sləs/ [adjective] Not good for doing something: *This pocketknife is useless; it doesn't cut at all.*

†**user** /'ju·zər/ [countable noun] A person who uses something: *Will all the users of the swimming pool please leave the changing rooms as clean as they found them.*

†**usual** /'juː.ʒu.əl/ [adjective] **1** Happening as expected: *Don't worry; it's quite usual for Ben to be late.* **2 as usual** As normally happens: *Then Olive invited us all to her house for coffee, as usual.*

†**usually** /'juː.ʒu.ə.li/ [adverb] Normally, most often: *We usually have our main meal in the evening, but at the weekend we have it at midday.* ■ "Usually" goes before the main verb and after auxiliary verbs like "be", "do" or "have": "I'm usually on time for school". ■ See box at **frequency**.

utensil /juː'ten.sɪl/ [countable noun] An object that you use in the kitchen: *This is where we keep our cooking utensils.* ■ This word is more common in the plural.

uterus /'juːtərəs/ [countable noun] The organ in women and some female animals where the baby is carried before birth: *The uterus is where babies grow before being born.* ■ The plural is "uteri" or "uteruses". ■ The same meaning: "womb". 👁 **See page 425.**

utter[1] /'ʌtər/ [adjective] Complete: *There was utter silence in the exam room when I left.* ■ We usually say "complete".

utter[2] /'ʌtər/ [verb] To say something: *She didn't utter a single word all the time we were there.* ■ We usually say "say".

U-turn [countable noun] A turn, in the shape of the letter U, made by a vehicle in order to reverse his direction: *In this road, U-turns are not permitted.*

v. /viː/ An abbreviation for **versus.** ■ See box at **abbreviations**.

V[1] /viː/ The twenty-second letter of the alphabet: *The name "Victor" begins with a "V".*

V[2] A word used in writing when you want the reader to look something up to get more information. ■ "v" is an abbreviation for "consult". ■ See box at **abbreviations**.

vacancy /ˈveɪ.kᵊnt.si/ [countable noun] **1** A room in a hotel that is not filled: *There are plenty of vacancies in the hotels at this time of year.* **2** A job that is not filled: *There's a vacancy at our school as head of the language department.* ■ The plural is "vacancies".

vacant /ˈveɪ.kᵊnt/ [adjective] **1** Not being used: *Is this chair vacant?* **2** Not filled: *The principal has retired and the post is now vacant.*

⁺**vacation** /veɪˈkeɪ.ʃᵊn/ [noun] **1** A period of time to rest from work or school: *Last year, we spent our summer vacation in Asia.* ■ In this use, in British English we say "holiday". ■ When we speak about a short period we normally say "holidays": "national holidays". **2 on vacation** Not at work or at school: *Hurray! We're on vacation next week!* ■ In this use, in British English we say "on holiday".

vaccinate /ˈvæk.sɪ.neɪt/ [verb] To give somebody an injection to protect them against disease: *We were vaccinated against yellow fever before we went on safari to Africa.*

vaccination /ˌvæk.sɪˈneɪ.ʃᵊn/ [noun] An injection given to somebody to protect them against disease: *My grandma is going to have her flu vaccination today.*

vaccine /ˈvæk.siːn/ [uncountable noun] A substance with a harmless amount from a virus or bacteria, that is given to people to stop them from getting a certain disease: *Vaccines can be given orally or by injection.*

vacuum[1] /ˈvækjuːm/ [countable noun] A completely empty space: *Outer space is not a vacuum, it contains a very small amount of material.*

vacuum[2] /ˈvækjuːm/ [verb] To clean with a vacuum cleaner: *He has vacuumed the whole house.* ■ In British English they say "hoover".

vacuum cleaner [countable noun] A machine that cleans floors by sucking up the dirt: *I quite like cleaning with the vacuum cleaner.* ■ In British English they say "hoover".

vacuum flask [countable noun] A special kind of bottle that keeps drinks hot or cold: *We'll take the vacuum flask with us on the picnic.*

vagina /vəˈdʒaɪ.nə/ [countable noun] The canal connecting the uterus and the vulva: *The vagina functions as the birth canal.* 👁 **See page 425.**

a b c d e f g h i j k l m n o p q r s t u v w x y z

vague /veɪg/ [adjective] Not clear: *I only have a vague memory of my grandmother.*

vain /veɪn/ [adjective] **1** Very proud of yourself: *Kevin is so vain. He thinks he's the prettiest boy in the class.* **2 in vain** Without success: *I tried in vain to learn my vocabulary. There were too many words.*

valentine card or **valentine** /ˈvæl.ən.taɪn/ [countable noun] Card sent to somebody you love on February 14th: *I hope to get at least one valentine card next week on February 14th.*

†**valley** /ˈvæl.i/ [countable noun] Low land between two or more hills: *To get to the next town, you have to cross the valley.*

†**valuable** /ˈvæl.jʊ.bl/ [adjective] **1** Worth a lot of money: *My dad collects stamps and he's got some quite valuable ones.* **2** Very useful: *The police received some very valuable information about the crime from an anonymous phone call.*

†**value**[1] /ˈvælju:/ [noun] **1** The money that something is worth: *It is impossible to calculate the value of the Yosemite National Park.* **2** How much something is worth or how useful it is: *A good telescope is of great value to anybody.* **3 good value** Good for the price: *I got this dress in the sales. It was really good value.*

value[2] /ˈvælju:/ [verb] **1** To think that something is important: *I value your friendship enormously.* **2** To say how much something would cost: *The painting has been valued at $2,000,000.* ■ Be careful with the spelling of this form: "valuing".

valve /vælv/ [countable noun] A device that opens or closes to control liquid or gas: *I can't inflate my bicycle tire because there's something wrong with the valve.*

vampire /ˈvæm·paɪər/ [countable noun] A mythical person who drinks people's blood: *Count Dracula is the most famous vampire ever.*

†**van** /væn/ [countable noun] A vehicle that is used for transporting things: *My uncle has just bought a new van.* See picture at **transport**.

vandal /ˈvændəl/ [countable noun] Somebody who deliberately breaks or damages things in public places: *The vandals destroyed the bus stop.*

vandalism /ˈvæn.dəl.ɪ.zəm/ [uncountable noun] Damage done to people's property for no particular reason: *There is a lot of vandalism in our area these days.*

vane /veɪn/ [countable noun] **1** An object put on top of a building which turns to show wind direction: *The vane indicates that the wind is coming from the north today.* **2** The blade attached to a rotating wheel: *Aircraft propellers and electric fans have vanes.*

vanilla /vəˈnɪl.ə/ [uncountable noun] A plant that is used to give a special taste to sweet food: *Can I have a vanilla ice cream, please?*

vanish /ˈvæn.ɪʃ/ [verb] To disappear suddenly: *The food at the children's party vanished in minutes.*

vanity /ˈvæn·ɪ·t̬i/ [uncountable noun] Being too proud of yourself: *Stop looking at yourself in the mirror. Your vanity is incredible.* ■ The plural is "vanities".

vapor /ˈveɪ.pər/ [uncountable noun] A gas form of a liquid, usually caused by heating: *Mist is a kind of vapor.* ■ The British English spelling is "vapour". See page 438.

vapour /ˈveɪ.pər/ US: /-pɚ/ [uncountable noun] See **vapor**. ■ This is a British English spelling.

variation /ˌveər·iˈeɪ·ʃən/, /ˌvær-/ [countable noun] **1** A change from the usual condition, process or way: *Now that you all know the basic steps, let's introduce some variations.* **2** Fluctuation: *There was a great variation in the price of gasoline this year.* ■ We say "variation **in** or **of** something". **3** Any one of several melodies based on a principal melody in a piece of music: *Bach's Goldberg variations consists of 30 variations on a theme.*

†**variety** /vəˈraɪ·ɪ·t̬i/ [noun] **1** Different things: *They have a great variety in the new clothes store.* ■ In this use "variety" is an uncountable noun. **2** A particular group of different things: *You can get these jeans in a great variety of colors.* **3** A type of something: *There are a lot of varieties of roses.* ■ The plural is "varieties".

†**various** /ˈveər·i·əs/, /ˈvær-/ [adjective] Several different: *There are various types of sweet dishes on the menu.*

†**vary** US: /ˈver.i/ UK: /ˈveə.ri/ [verb] To change: *You should call the airport the day before your flight because flight times can vary.* ■ Be careful with the spelling of these forms: "varies", "varied".

vas [countable noun] An anatomical vessel or duct that contains a fluid: *Blood flows through vasa.* ■ The plural is "vasa".

vas deferens [countable noun] Either one of two vessels which links the testicles to the urethra: *The vasa deferentia take sperm from the testicles to the urethra during ejaculation.* ■ The plural is "vasa deferentia".

vase US: /veɪs/ UK: /vɑ:z/ [countable noun] A container that you put flowers in: *There was a lovely vase of flowers on the table.*

†**vast** US: /væst/ UK: /vɑ:st/ [adjective] Enormous: *The Sahara is a vast desert in North Africa.*

VAT /ˌvi:.eɪˈti:, væt/ [uncountable noun] A kind of tax: *Is VAT included in the bill?* ■ Be careful! "VAT" is always written in capital letters. "VAT" is an abbreviation for "Value Added Tax".

VCR /ˌviˌsiˈɑr/ [countable noun] See **video cassette recorder**. ■ Be careful! "VCR" is always written in capital letters. ■ See box at **abbreviations**.

've /-v, -əv/ The contraction of "have".

veal /viːl/ [uncountable noun] The meat from a young cow: *Shall we have some veal for dinner tonight?* ■ Compare with "calf" (a young cow).

†**vegetable** /'vedʒ.tə.bl̩/ [countable noun] A plant that people eat: *We had vegetable soup for lunch yesterday.* ■ Be careful with the pronunciation of this word! The second "e" is not pronounced. 👁 **See page 437.**

vegetarian /ˌvedʒ·ɪ'teər·i·ən/ [countable noun] A person who does not eat meat: *Paul and Rita are vegetarians so we can't do chicken for dinner.*

vegetation /ˌvedʒɪ'teɪʃən/ [uncountable noun] A collective name for plant life: *The vegetation of the Amazon rainforest is very diverse.*

†**vehicle** /'viː.ɪ.kl̩/ [countable noun] Something that carries things or people from one place to another: *It is forbidden for any vehicle to go into the town center.*

veil /veɪl/ [countable noun] A covering over a woman's face and head: *In some Muslim countries women wear a veil over their head when they go out.*

vein /veɪn/ [countable noun] One of the tubes in the body that carries blood, that appear to be blue in color: *Veins carry blood from different parts of the body to the heart.*

velvet /'vel.vɪt/ [uncountable noun] A very soft, thick material: *My grandma has some beautiful dark red velvet drapes in her living room.*

vena cava /ˌviː.nə'keɪ.və/ [countable noun] One of two veins which carry deoxygenated blood back to the heart: *The heart is supplied by two vena cavae, that bring blood from the top and the bottom part of the body.* ■ The plural is also "vena cavae".

Venezuelan[1] [adjective] Referring to Venezuela: *Caracas is the Venezuelan capital.* ■ Be careful! "Venezuelan" has a capital "V".

Venezuelan[2] [countable noun] A person from Venezuela: *The chef of this restaurant is a Venezuelan.* ■ Be careful! "Venezuelan" has a capital "V".

vengeance /'ven.dʒᵊnts/ [uncountable noun] A punishment you give to somebody for harm done to you: *The film was about a man who took vengeance on a politician for the death of his wife.* ■ Be careful! We say: "to take vengeance **on** (somebody)".

vent /vent/ [countable noun] **1** A small opening which gas or liquid to pass or leave: *Keep the vent open so that the smoke can go out.* **2 air vent** Ducts used in heating, air conditioning or ventilation to deliver and remove air: *Cars are usually provided with air vents.*

ventilate /'ven·tə·lˌeɪt/ [verb] To let fresh air into a place: *Open the window; let's ventilate the classroom.*

ventricle /'ven.trɪ.kl̩/ [countable noun] Either one of two spaces in the heart that move blood to the rest of the body as a result of the pumping action: *The human heart has two ventricles, left and right.*

Venus /'viːnəs/ [countable noun] A planet of the solar system that is second in order from the Sun: *After the Sun and the Moon, Venus is the brightest object in the night sky.* 👁 **See page 446.**

verandah /və'ræn.də/ [countable noun] A large, open area on the side of a house with a roof but no wall: *We sat on the verandah and talked until three in the morning.*

†**verb** US: /vɝːb/ UK: /vɜːb/ [countable noun] **1** A word that tells us what somebody or something does: *"go", "tell", "look" and "run" are all verbs.* **2 auxiliary verb** See **auxiliary verb**. **3 phrasal verb** See **phrasal verb**.

verbal /'vɜr·bəl/ [adjective] **1** That is spoken: *The student was given a verbal warning.* **2** Referring to a verb: *a verbal phrase.*

verdict /'vɜr·dɪkt/ [countable noun] A decision taken by a jury in a court of law: *The jury's verdict was that the prisoner was guilty.*

verse US: /vɝːs/ UK: /vɜːs/ [noun] **1** Poetry: *Shakespeare wrote much of his work in verse.* **2** A group of lines forming a part of a song or a poem: *I know the first verse of the song. Does anybody know the second?*

†**version** /'vɜr·ʒən/ [countable noun] **1** A different form of something made or performed by somebody: *My brother belongs to a pop group and they sing their own versions of popular hits.* **2** A personal view of something: *Bert and Ernie have had an argument. Bert has told me his version but I haven't heard Ernie's yet.*

versus /'vɜr·səs/ [preposition] Against: *Did you see the basketball match last night? White Sox versus Chicago Cubs.* ■ "v." and "vs." are abbreviations for "versus", but "vs." is only used in written language.

vertebra /'vɜr·t̬ə·brə/ [countable noun] Any of the segments of the backbone: *The human backbone is usually made up of 33 vertebrae, but only 24 are movable.* ■ The plural is "vertebras" or "vertebrae". 👁 **See page 422.**

vertebrate /'vɜr·tə·brət/ [countable noun] A creature with a backbone: *Vertebrates make up only 5% of all species found on Earth.* ■ Compare with "invertebrate" (a creature without a backbone). 👁 **See page 427.**

†**vertical** /'vɜr·t̬ɪ·kəl/ [adjective] Going straight up and down: *To get two points in football, you have to kick the ball between the two vertical posts.*

vertically [adverb] That is done in a vertical position or direction: *Helicopters can take off vertically.* ■ Compare with "horizontally" (in a parallel position to the horizon).

a b c d e f g h i j k l m n o p q r s t u v w x y z

†**very¹** /'veri/ [adverb] A word that you use to make another word stronger: *My sister Diane is very tall. She's taller than my father.* ■ The comparative form is **more** and the superlative form is **most**. ■ See box at **fairly**.

very² /'veri/ [adjective] The same or exact: *You are the very person I wanted to talk to.* ■ We usually say "exact".

vesicle [countable noun] A small sac or cavity, especially one that is filled with fluid: *Vesicles are found in plants and animals.*

vessel /'ves.ᵊl/ [countable noun] **1** A hollow container for liquid: *Coffee is drunk from a vessel such as a cup.* **2** A tube in the body that contains liquid: *Veins and arteries are blood vessels.* **3** A ship or boat: *The vessel sets sail at six o'clock.* ■ Be careful with the pronunciation of this word! "el" is pronounced like "le" in "little".

vest /vest/ [countable noun] **1** See **undershirt**. ■ This use is British English. **2** A piece of clothing without sleeves that you can wear under your jacket: *My new suit consists of a jacket, a vest and pants of the same material.* ■ In this use, in British English we say "waistcoat".

vet /vet/ [countable noun] See **veteran**. ■ This word is informal.

veteran /'vetərən/ [countable noun] **1** Somebody with a lot of experience: *The new President is a veteran politician.* **2** A former member of the armed forces: *November 11th is the Veterans Day in memory of the end of World Wars.* ■ "Vet" is short for "veteran".

veterinary or **vet** /vet/ [countable noun] A doctor for animals: *We took our cat to the vet because she hadn't eaten for days.*

†**via** /vaɪə, 'viː.ə/ [preposition] Through, by way of: *The train from Boston to Chicago goes via Cleveland.*

vibrate /vaɪ'breɪt/ [verb] To shake very quickly: *My grandma's house is so near the railway station that the windows vibrate when a train goes by.*

vibration /vaɪ'breɪ.ʃᵊn/ [noun] A continuous, shaking movement: *The soldiers could feel the vibrations from the explosion.*

vicar /'vɪk.ər/ US: /-ɚ/ [countable noun] A priest of the Church of England: *Have you met the new vicar yet? My mom says he's very nice.*

vice /vaɪs/ [countable noun] A bad habit: *Smoking and drinking too much are vices.*

vice- [prefix] A word that goes before a title to show that somebody is second in importance: *My dad is the vicepresident of the town chess club.*

vicious /'vɪʃ.əs/ [adjective] Cruel and bad tempered: *Be careful with that dog. He is vicious.*

†**victim** /'vɪk.tɪm/ [countable noun] A person who suffers from the action of somebody or something: *The victims of the bomb attack are being treated in hospital.*

victorious /vɪk'tɔr·i·əs/, /-'tour-/ [adjective] Winning: *The victorious team wins the Super Bowl.*

†**victory** /'vɪk·tə·ri/, /-tri/ [noun] A win: *Her victory in the judo competition was no surprise.* ■ The plural is "victories".

†**video** /'vɪd·i,oʊ/ [noun] **1** A movie on tape: *I got a great video for my birthday.* **2** See **video cassette recorder**.

videocassette [countable noun] A tape where programs and movies can be recorded: *I erased the videocassette before I recorded the concert.* ■ The same meaning: "videotape¹".

video cassette recorder [countable noun] A machine that records and plays back television programs: *We set the video cassette recorder to record the film at seven o'clock.* ■ "VCR" is an abbreviation for "video cassette recorder". ■ We also say "video" and "video recorder".

video game [countable noun] A game you play on a TV, using a special machine: *I've asked my mom to get me the video game that we were talking about the other day.*

video recorder [countable noun] See **video cassette recorder**.

videotape¹ /'vɪdiəʊteɪp/ [noun] A tape where programs and movies can be recorded: *We need to get some more videotapes if we're going to record all the movies.* ■ The same meaning: "videocassette".

videotape² [verb] To record a television program: *I videotaped yesterday's edition of the series.*

†**view** /vjuː/ [countable noun] **1** What you can see from a certain place: *The view from our hotel room is marvelous.* **2** An opinion: *My grandpa is always giving his views on everything that he sees on television.* **3** **in view of** Considering: *In view of the bad weather we have decided to suspend the game.* **4** **on view** Where everyone can see: *A number of old photographs of our town are on view at the local art gallery.*

viewer /'vju·ər/ [countable noun] A television spectator: *Good evening, viewers, and welcome to our program.*

vignette /vɪ'njet/ [countable noun] A brief episode of writing or section of a movie that gives a picture of something: *The book is composed of a series of vignettes about frontier life.*

vigorous /'vɪg·ər·əs/ [adjective] Active and strong: *My grandpa is seventy-eight but he still does quite vigorous exercise every morning.*

Viking /'vaɪ.kɪŋ/ [countable noun] A person of a race that lived in Scandinavia from the 8th to the 11th centuries: *The Vikings were famous for their long boats.* ■ Be careful! "Viking" has a capital "V".

villa /ˈvɪl.ə/ [countable noun] A vacation house: *My aunt owns a villa in Montreal.*

↑**village** /ˈvɪl.ɪdʒ/ [countable noun] A small place in the country where people live: *My young cousin goes to a village school.* ■ Be careful with the pronunciation of this word. The last "a" is pronounced like the "i" in "did". 👁 **See page 445.**

villager /ˈvɪl·ɪ·dʒər/ [countable noun] A person who lives in a village: *All the villagers were invited to the brother's wedding.*

villain /ˈvɪl.ən/ [countable noun] **1** The bad character in a play or a movie: *I play the part of the villain in the school play.* **2** A criminal: *The villains who robbed the bank were caught as they tried to get away.* ■ This use is informal.

vine /vaɪn/ [countable noun] The plant that grapes grow on: *My mom has planted a vine in a warm part of our yard.*

vinegar /ˈvɪn·ɪ·gər/ [uncountable noun] A liquid with a very sour taste: *I love a lot of salt and vinegar on my salad.*

vineyard /ˈvɪn·jərd/ [countable noun] A place where a lot of vines are grown: *We saw lots of vineyards when we went to California.*

vintage[1] /ˈvɪntɪdʒ/ [countable noun] A fine wine that was made in a particular year: *This is a bottle of the 1973 vintage.*

vintage[2] /ˈvɪntɪdʒ/ [adjective] **1** Of very high quality: *This actress gave a vintage performance as Lady Macbeth.* **2** When talking about a car, that was made between 1919 and 1930: *My grandpa still has a vintage car.*

viola /viˈəʊlə/ [countable noun] A musical instrument that is similar to a violin but is slightly larger: *The viola has a lower pitch than the violin.* 👁 **See page 458.**

↑**violence** /ˈvaɪə.lᵊnts/ [uncountable noun] Aggressive and harmful behavior: *There's a lot of violence in some areas of New York.* ■ Be careful with the pronunciation of this word! "vi" rhymes with "my".

↑**violent** /ˈvaɪə.lᵊnt/ [adjective] Aggressive and harmful: *Some of the soccer fans got violent at the end of the game.* ■ Be careful with the pronunciation of this word! "vi" rhymes with "my". ■ Compare with "peaceful" (without violence).

violently [adverb] **1** Done with violence: *He slammed the door violently.* **2** Extremely, very strongly: *She is violently opposed to the idea.*

violet[1] [noun and adjective] A pale purple color: *Do you like my new violet top?*

violet[2] /ˈvaɪələt/ [countable noun] A small purple flower: *I bought my mom a violet on my way home from school.*

violin /ˌvaɪəˈlɪn/ [countable noun] A musical instrument made of wood that you put on your shoulder to play: *I play the violin in the school orchestra.* 👁 **See page 458.**

violinist /ˌvaɪəˈlɪn.ɪst/ [countable noun] A person who plays the violin: *Yehudi Menuhin was a world-famous violinist.*

violoncello [countable noun] See **cello.**

VIP /ˌviː.aɪˈpiː/ [countable noun] An abbreviation for "very important person": *This area is for VIP's only.* ■ Be careful! "VIP" is always written in capital letters.

viral /ˈvaɪrəl/ [adjective] **1** Relating to, or caused by, a virus: *He is not going to school today because he has a viral infection.* **2** Quickly and widely spread or popularized in the internet, through video sharing websites, social media or e-mail: *Have you seen the viral video of the boy who dances all over the world?*

virgin /ˈvɜr·dʒən/ [adjective] That has not yet been used: *There's still a lot of virgin land in Australia.*

Virgo US: /ˈvɝː.goʊ/ UK: /ˈvɜː.gəʊ/ [noun] A sign of the zodiac: *If your birthday is between August 23rd and September 24th, you're a Virgo.* ■ Be careful. "Virgo" has a capital "V".

virtue /ˈvɜr·tʃu/ [countable noun] A good quality: *Patience is one of my mother's virtues.*

↑**virus** /ˈvaɪ·rəs/ [countable noun] A very small living thing that can give you a disease: *My sister had a virus last year and had to stay in bed for three weeks.* ■ The plural is "viruses". Be careful with the pronunciation of this word! "vi" rhymes with "my".

visa /ˈviː.zə/ [countable noun] Special permission that you need to visit certain countries: *Do you need a visa to go to America?*

↑**visible** /ˈvɪz.ɪ.bl̩/ [adjective] That you can see: *On a clear day the lighthouse is visible from miles away.*

↑**vision** /ˈvɪʒ.ᵊn/ [noun] **1** Sight: *Kitty had an accident last year which damaged her vision.* **2** A dream: *I have this vision of us all living in the country one day.*

↑**visit**[1] /ˈvɪzɪt/ [countable noun] Visiting a person or a place: *We went to give Mr. Jones a visit in hospital.*

visit[2] /ˈvɪzɪt/ [verb] To go and see a person or a place: *Have you ever visited New York?*

↑**visitor** /ˈvɪz·ɪ·t̬ər/ [countable noun] A person who is visiting: *Visitors are requested not to take photographs inside the church.*

visual /ˈvɪʒ.u.əl/ [adjective] Referring to sight: *The visual arts are those that you can look at: painting, sculpture, the movies and so on.*

↑**vital** /ˈvaɪ·t̬ə·l/ [adjective] Very important: *The detective discovered a vital piece of information that helped him to solve the crime.*

vitamin /ˈvaɪ·t̬ə·mɪn/ [countable noun] One of the elements in food that a person needs to live: *Fruit and vegetables contain lots of vitamins.*

a b c d e f g h i j k l m n o p q r s t u **v** w x y z

viviparous /vɪ'vɪp.ər.əs/ US: /-ɚ-/ [adjective] Giving birth to live young that have developed inside the body of the mother: *Mammals are all viviparous.* ■ Compare with "oviparous" (born from an egg outside the mother). 👁 **See page 427.**

↑**vocabulary** /voʊ'kæb·jə,ler·i/ [noun] **1** Words: *Tomorrow we've got an English vocabulary test.* **2** All the words that you know: *Jeremy has got a marvelous vocabulary considering that he is only nine.* ■ The plural is "vocabularies".

vocal /'voʊ·kəl/ [adjective] **1** Referring to the voice: *To learn to sing you need a vocal coach.* **2** Active in expressing an opinion: *Linda is very vocal in her opposition to the planned power station.*

↑**voice** /vɔɪs/ [countable noun] The sounds that you make when you speak or sing: *Olga has got a beautiful singing voice.*

volcanic /vɑl'kæn·ɪk/, /vɔl-/ [adjective] Referring to volcanoes, or to their action or presence: *These rock formations are the result of volcanic action.*

volcano US: /vɑːl'keɪ.noʊ/ UK: /vɒl'keɪ.nəʊ/ [countable noun] A hole where very hot rock comes out: *The volcanoes of the United States are located along the West Coast.* ■ Be careful with the pronunciation of this word! "ca" rhymes with "day". ■ The plural is "volcanoes".

volleyball US: /'vɑː.li.bɑːl/ UK: /'vɒl.i.bɔːl/ [uncountable noun] A game in which you hit a ball over a net with your hands: *I've been chosen for the school volleyball team!* 👁 See picture at **sport**.

volt US: /voʊlt/ UK: /vɒlt/ [countable noun] A measure of electricity: *The current here is 220 volts.*

↑**volume** /'vɑl·jəm/, /-jum/ [uncountable noun] **1** The amount of space that something occupies: *What is the volume of this barrel?* **2** The amount of sound made by something: *Turn the volume up, please. I can't hear the music.* ■ See box at **abbreviations**.

voluntary US: /'vɑː.lᵊn.ter.i/ UK: /'vɒl.ən.tri/ [adjective] **1** Done because somebody wants to do it: *The visit to the theater is voluntary.* **2** Done for no pay: *My mom does voluntary work for the Red Cross.*

volunteer US: /ˌvɑː.lən'tɪr/ UK: /ˌvɒl.ən'tɪəʳ/ [countable noun] A person who offers to do something: *Can I have a volunteer to take these books to the library, please?*

vomit US: /'vɑː.mɪt/ UK: /'vɒm.ɪt/ [verb] To bring up food through your mouth: *After supper I felt ill and began to vomit.* ■ The same meaning: "to be sick", "to throw up".

↑**vote**[1] /vəʊt/ [countable noun] **1** Choosing somebody or something by voting: *We had a vote to decide where to go on the school trip.* **2** A choice by voting: *There were ten votes in favor of Jack and thirteen in favor of Ruth.*

vote[2] /vəʊt/ [verb] To choose somebody or something by raising your hand or putting a piece of paper in a box: *We voted for our class representative today at school.* ■ Be careful with the spelling of this form: "voting".

vowel /vaʊəl/ [countable noun] One of the written or spoken letters, "a", "e", "i", "o", "u": *The English alphabet has twenty-one consonants and five vowels.*

voyage /'vɔɪ.ɪdʒ/ [countable noun] A journey usually by sea or in space: *A voyage from New York to Liverpool used to take weeks.* ■ Be careful with the pronunciation of this word. The "a" is pronounced like the "i" in "did".

vs. A written abbreviation for **versus**. ■ See box at **abbreviations**.

vulture /'vʌl·tʃər/ [countable noun] A large bird that eats the flesh of dead animals: *Vultures are very graceful flyers.*

vulva /'vʌl.və/ [countable noun] The external part of the female reproductive system: *The vulva is the external opening of the vagina and has a double set of lips.* ■ The plural is "vulvas" or "vulvae". 👁 **See page 425.**

W

W /ˈdʌb.l̩.juː/ The twenty-third letter of the alphabet: *The name "Wendy" begins with a "W".*

wade /weɪd/ [verb] To walk through water: *This is the only point where you can wade across the river.*

wafer /ˈweɪ·fər/ [countable noun] Thin sweet cookie eaten with ice cream: *Jenny says the best bit of the ice cream is the wafer.*

wag /wæg/ [verb] To move something from side to side: *Dogs wag their tails when they're playing.* ■ Be careful with the spelling of these forms: "wagged", "wagging".

wage or **wages** /weɪdʒ/ [noun] The money that a person receives for every week or day he or she works: *I'll pay you back on Friday, when I get my wages.* ■ This word is more common in the plural. ■ Compare with "salary" (the money that a person receives every month, usually for professional or office work).

wagon /ˈwæg.ən/ [countable noun] **1** A vehicle pulled by a horse: *Wagons are very useful on farms for carrying heavy loads.* **2** See **freight car.** ■ This use is British English.

wail /ˈvʌl.və/ [verb] To make a long sad noise: *The girl started wailing when she realized that she was lost.*

↑**waist** /weɪst/ [countable noun] The narrow part of the body just above the hips: *She took my waist measurement so that she could make me a skirt.* 👁 **See page 421.**

waistcoat /ˈweɪst.kəʊt/ [countable noun] See **vest.** ■ This word is British English.

wait[1] /weɪt/ [uncountable noun] The act of being in one place until somebody arrives or something happens: *The class had a long wait until they opened the museum.*

↑**wait**[2] /weɪt/ [verb] To stay in one place until somebody arrives or something happens: *I'm waiting for Louise. We're going to the movies.*

↑**waiter** /ˈweɪ·t̬ər/ [countable noun] A man who takes drinks or food to people in a restaurant or a bar: *The waiter brought us two ice creams.* ■ a woman who takes drinks or food to people is a "waitress". ■ Be careful! We say: "He is **a** waiter". (We don't say: "He is waiter").

waiting-room [countable noun] A place where people wait for an appointment or for trains, buses and so on: *There were only two people in Dr. Norton's waiting-room.*

waitress /ˈweɪ.trəs/ [countable noun] A woman who takes drinks or food to people in a restaurant or a bar: *We sat down at a table and asked the waitress for a menu.* ■ The plural is "waitresses". A man who takes drinks or food to people is a "waiter".

a b c d e f g h i j k l m n o p q r s t u v w x y z

↑wake, woke, woken /weɪk/ [verb] **1** To stop sleeping: *What time do you usually wake up on Sundays?* **2** To make somebody stop sleeping: *Don't make so much noise! You'll wake the baby.* ■ It is more common to say "wake up". Be careful. "Wake" cannot be used as an order, for orders we use "wake up!".

walk¹ /wɔːk/ [countable noun] A journey on foot: *Do you want to go for a walk in the park, Alice?*

↑walk² /wɔːk/ [verb] To move on foot: *I walk to school. It only takes five minutes.*

walkie-talkie /ˌwɔːki'tɔːki/ [countable noun] A portable radio system with which you can talk to somebody who is not next to you: *I used the walkie-talkie to speak to my brother who was in the other room.*

↑wall US: /wɑːl/ UK: /wɔːl/ [countable noun] **1** A side of a room or a building: *Mrs. Flannegan has all the walls in her living room covered with paintings.* 👁 See picture at **bedroom**. **2** A construction that surrounds a garden, town, and so on: *The backyard in Martin's house is surrounded by a stone wall.*

wall chart [countable noun] A kind of poster with words and pictures: *In my classroom there's a wall chart with all kinds of dinosaurs.*

↑wallet US: /'wɑː.lɪt/ UK: /'wɒl.ɪt/ [countable noun] A small container, often made of leather, for holding bills or other documents: *Last week I found a wallet with $50 in it.* ■ The same meaning: "billfold".

wallpaper /'wɔːlˌpeɪpər/ [noun] Paper that is used to decorate the walls of a room: *The wallpaper in my room is blue with little pink flowers.*

walnut /'wɔl·nət/, /-ˌnʌt/ [countable noun] A round nut with a hard, light brown shell: *I love eating walnuts.*

waltz US: /wɑːlts/ UK: /wɒlts/ [countable noun] A slow dance in which two people go round and round: *I danced a waltz with my grandpa at my sister's wedding.*

wand US: /wɑːnd/ UK: /wɒnd/ [countable noun] A stick with magical powers: *The fairy touched the mice with her wand and they became horses.*

↑wander US: /'wɑːn.dɚ/ UK: /'wɒn.dəʳ/ [verb] To walk in no special direction and without rush: *We wandered around the town for some time before we looked for somewhere to eat.*

wanna US: /'wɑː.nə/ UK: /'wɒn.ə/ [verb] A way of saying "want to": *Do you wanna come to the dance?* ■ This word is very informal.

↑want US: /wɑːnt/ UK: /wɒnt/ [verb] **1** To wish something: *Claire wants to be an architect.* **2** To need something: *What you want is a good rest.*

↑war US: /wɔːr/ UK: /wɔːʳ/ [noun] **1** Fighting between two or more countries or groups of people: *I wouldn't like to have to go to war against anybody.* **2** A fight against something, usually bad: *The government has declared a war on drugs.* **3 at war** In a state of fighting: *Mexico and United States were at war in the nineteenth century.*

ward US: /wɔːrd/ UK: /wɔːd/ [countable noun] A large room for patients in a hospital: *In ward five there are ten beds.*

warden /'wɔr·dən/ [countable noun] A person whose job it is to look after people in a particular place and to see that its rules are obeyed: *Youth hostels and old people's homes have wardens.*

wardrobe US: /'wɔːr.droʊb/ UK: /'wɔː.drəʊb/ [countable noun] **1** See **closet**. ■ This use is British English. **2** A collection of clothes: *She has a fantastic wardrobe with over 50 dresses and ten coats.*

warehouse /'weəhaʊs/ [countable noun] See **storehouse**. ■ This word is British English.

↑warm¹ /wɔːm/ [adjective] **1** Not too hot: *I like warm weather but I can't stand it when it's hot.* ■ "Warm" often refers to a temperature which is pleasant. "Hot" often refers to a temperature that is too high to be pleasant. **2** Friendly: *We were given a warm welcome at the school.* **3 to be warm** When speaking of clothing, to keep in the heat and protect you from the cold: *I love this coat. It's really warm.*

warm² /wɔːm/ [verb] To make something warm: *Can you warm some milk for the baby?*

▸ **PHRASAL VERBS** · **to warm up** To do some gentle exercise before a game, race and so on: *Athletes always warm up before a competition.*

↑warmth US: /wɔːrmpθ/ UK: /wɔːmpθ/ [uncountable noun] **1** Pleasant heat: *We all sat round the fireplace for warmth.* **2** Friendly or kind behavior: *The warmth of their welcome surprised us.*

↑warn US: /wɔːrn/ UK: /wɔːn/ [verb] To tell somebody about possible danger: *I warned them not to play with the bottles.*

↑warning /'wɔr·nɪŋ/ [noun] Something that tells you about possible danger: *There was a warning at the entrance saying "Beware of the dog!".*

warrior US: /'wɔːr.i.ɚ/ UK: /'wɒr.i.əʳ/ [countable noun] Person who fights in a war: *Cochise was a famous Indian warrior.*

was /wəz/ US: /wɑːz, wəz/ UK: /wɒz/ [verb] See **be**.

wash¹ /wɒʃ/ [noun] The act of cleaning somebody or something with water: *Can you give the car a wash this afternoon.* ■ The plural is "washes".

↑wash² /wɒʃ/ [verb] **1** To clean somebody or something with water: *Children, wash your hands before we have lunch.* **2** To clean yourself with water: *You have to wash every morning, Linda.*

washbasin /'wɒʃˌbeɪ.sən/ US: /'wɑːʃ-/ [countable noun] See **sink¹**. ■ This word is British English.

washing US: /'wɑː.ʃɪŋ/ UK: /'wɒʃ.ɪŋ/ [countable noun] See **laundry**. ■ This word is British English.

washing machine [countable noun] A machine for washing clothes: *Don't wash that blouse in the washing machine. It's too delicate.* 👁 See picture at **kitchen**.

wasn't US: /ˈwɑː.zᵊnt/ UK: /ˈwɒz.ᵊnt/ The contraction of "was not".

wasp US: /wɑːsp/ UK: /wɒsp/ [countable noun] An insect with black and yellow stripes, similar to a bee: *If a wasp stings you, it can be quite painful.*

+**waste[1]** /weɪst/ [uncountable noun] **1** The wrong use of something: *We have to throw away all this food. What a waste!* **2** Garbage or things that cannot be used any more: *One of the problems of nuclear energy is what to do with the waste from power stations.*

waste[2] /weɪst/ [verb] **1** To use more than necessary of something: *Don't waste the soap. You only need a little to do those plates.* **2** Not to make a good use of something: *Don't waste your time waiting for Paula. She's gone home.*

wastebasket [countable noun] A container where you throw away useless papers and other things: *At the end of the day the wastebasket in our classroom is always full.* ■ The same meaning: "wastepaper basket".

wastepaper basket [countable noun] A container where you throw away useless papers: *Please throw all your trash into the wastepaper basket.* ■ The same meaning: "wastebasket".

+**watch[1]** /wɒtʃ/ [noun] **1** An instrument for telling the time that is carried on your person, usually on your wrist: *Have you got a watch? I need to know the time.* ■ Compare with "clock" (that is on a wall, a shelf and so on). 👁 See picture at **clock**. **2 to keep watch** To guard or to look around carefully for signs of danger: *Can you keep watch on the store for a moment? I need to go out for a minute.* ■ The plural is "watches".

+**watch[2]** /wɒtʃ/ [verb] **1** To look at somebody or something that is moving or may move: *How many hours a day do you spend watching television?* ■ See box below. **2** To be careful about something: *Watch where you are going!* **3 to watch out** To be careful: *Watch out! There's ice on the road.*

watchful /ˈwɑtʃ·fəl/, /ˈwɔtʃ-/ [adjective] Watching something carefully: *The cat kept a watchful eye on her kittens.*

watchman /ˈwɒtʃ.mən/ US: /ˈwɑːtʃ-/ [countable noun] A person whose job is to guard a building: *The night watchman goes round the building at night making sure everything is in order.* ■ The plural is "watchmen".

+**water[1]** /ˈwɔːtər/ [uncountable noun] **1** A natural liquid without color that you can drink: *I think we need to drink about a liter of water a day.* **2 tap water** The water that comes from the faucet: *Do you want tap water or bottle water?* 👁 **See page 438.**

water[2] /ˈwɔːtər/ [verb] To give water to plants: *If it doesn't rain soon, we will have to water the backyard plants.*

water closet [countable noun] See **WC.**

watercolor US: /ˈwɑː.t̬ɚˌkʌl.ɚ/ [noun] A paint used by artists which uses a coloring substance diluted with water: *Watercolor painting requires a different technique to oil painting.* ■ Compare with "tempera" (pigment mixed with egg). ■ The British English spelling is "watercolour". 👁 **See page 456.**

watercolour UK: /ˈwɔː.təˌkʌl.əʳ/ [noun] See **watercolor.** ■ This is a British English spelling.

waterfall US: /ˈwɑː.ɚ.fɑːl/ UK: /ˈwɔː.tə.fɔːl/ [countable noun] A cut in a river where the water falls through the air to a lower level: *The Iguazu waterfalls in Brazil are 80 m high.*

waterfowl /ˈwɔ·t̬ərˌfaʊl/, /ˈwɑt̬·ər-/ [plural noun] Birds which like to live around ponds and lakes: *Geese and ducks are waterfowl.*

watering-can [countable noun] A container that is used for watering plants: *Can you fill the watering-can with water, James?*

watermelon /ˈwɔt̬·ərˌmel·ən/, /ˈwɑt̬-/ [noun] A large fruit that is green outside and red inside: *Watermelons are refreshing.* 👁 **See page 436.**

waterproof /ˈwɔ·t̬ərˌpruf/, /ˈwɑt̬·ər/ [adjective] That doesn't let water go through: *These boots are completely waterproof. You can walk through water in them.*

watershed /ˈwɔːtəʃed/ [countable noun] An event that marks an important change; especially in people's lives: *The spring of 2011 was a watershed for many Arab countries.*

water-skiing /ˈwɔːtəskiːɪŋ/ [uncountable noun] A sport in which you move across water on skis, pulled by a boat: *Have you ever done water-skiing? It's not difficult.*

watt US: /wɑːt/ UK: /wɒt/ [countable noun] A unit of electrical power: *I've put a 100 watt bulb in my bedroom.*

to watch, to look at, to see

- We use ***to watch*** when you look at something that moves or may move:
  - *We watched the birds eating the food outside.*
  - *I watched the door to see who was coming in.*
- We use ***to look at*** when you turn your eyes to something or when you observe something that doesn't move, like a painting:
  - *Look at the painting carefully.*
  - *Look at the nice hat that man is wearing!*
- We use ***to see*** when you receive information through your eyes independent of any particular interest or attention:
  - *I can't see anything without my glasses!*
  - *We saw a horrible accident in the street yesterday.*

a b c d e f g h i j k l m n o p q r s t u v w x y z

⁺wave[1] /weɪv/ [countable noun] **1** Moving your hand from side to side to greet somebody: *The President gave a wave as he went past.* **2** A rising and falling movement of water, especially in the sea: *It's dangerous to get into the sea when there are high waves.* **3** A form of energy that travels through air or water: *Radio waves carry sound across very long distances.*

wave[2] /weɪv/ [verb] **1** To move your hand from side to side to say "hello" or "goodbye": *Douglas and Marie waved as they drove off.* **2** To move something from side to side: *She waved her handkerchief at him as the train left the station.*

wavy /ˈweɪ.vi/ [adjective] Having the form of waves: *She has beautiful wavy black hair.* ■ The comparative form is "wavier" and the superlative form is "waviest". 👁 See picture at **hair**.

wax /wæks/ [uncountable noun] The substance used for making candles: *Some candles are made from natural wax made by bees.*

⁺way /weɪ/ [countable noun] **1** A direction, a route: *Look at me! Don't look the other way.* **2** A road: *Excuse me, is this the way to Lancaster?* **3** A manner of doing something: *I don't like the way he talks to his parents.* **4** **by the way** See "by the way" in the word **by**[1]. **5** **to give way to (somebody)** To let somebody go before you: *I think you have to give way at this crossroads.* **6** **in the way** Not letting somebody see something: *I couldn't see half the game. John was in the way all the time.* **7** **out of the way** In a position that lets you go somewhere: *Unless you get your car out of the way, I won't be able to move.* **8** **the Milky Way** White band in the night sky made of many stars: *I can see the Milky Way through my telescope.* **9** **way out** The part where you leave a place: *It's difficult to find the way out in this maze.* ■ Be careful! "Milky Way" has capital letters.

WC /ˌdʌb.l̩.juˈsiː/ [countable noun] A restroom: *Where it says WC, that's a restroom.* ■ Be careful! "WC" is always written in capital letters. "WC" is an abbreviation for "water closet".

⁺we /wiː, wi/ [pronoun] I and somebody else: *We live in Atlanta.*

⁺weak /wiːk/ [adjective] **1** Not having much strength: *Brian has been quite weak since his illness.* **2** Easy to break: *Don't sit on that chair! It's too weak.*

weaken /ˈwiː.kᵊn/ [verb] To make somebody or something weaker: *A cold can weaken you a lot.* ■ Compare with "strengthen" (to make stronger).

⁺weakness /ˈwiːk.nəs/ [noun] **1** Not having power or strength: *I don't understand why I have this sudden weakness in my leg.* **2** Something bad in a person: *I think his weakness is that he is a little lazy.* ■ The plural is "weaknesses".

⁺wealth /welθ/ [uncountable noun] A lot of money and property: *No one knows what the Bill Gates total wealth is but he's got many houses, cars and lands.*

wealthy /ˈwel.θi/ [adjective] Rich: *Some actors are very wealthy people.* ■ The comparative form is "wealthier" and the superlative form is "wealthiest".

⁺weapon /ˈwep.ən/ [countable noun] Something that is used for fighting: *They were defeated because the enemy's weapons were better.*

weaponry /ˈwep.ən.ri/ [countable noun] Weapons: *Modern weaponry is very hi-tech.* ■ The plural is "weaponries".

⁺wear, wore, worn US: /wer/ UK: /weəʳ/ [verb] To have clothes on your body: *When I saw Louise, she was wearing a white blouse and jeans.* ■ In English we often use a continuous tense to talk about the clothes somebody has on: "Tina is wearing red jeans today".

▸ PHRASAL VERBS · **to wear off** To disappear gradually: *I can't read this label. The writing has worn off.* · **to wear out (something)** To make something old and damaged: *Michael wears out his shoes so quickly that he needs a new pair every month.*

⁺weather /ˈweð.ər/ [uncountable noun] The state of the atmosphere: *The weather in Alaska is very cold.*

weathercock /ˈweð.ə.kɒk/ US: /-ɚ.kaːk/ [countable noun] A weather-vane in the shape of a cock: *The weathercock told us that the wind was coming from the North.*

weather forecast [countable noun] Information about the weather for the next few days: *According to the weather forecast, it will be sunny this weekend.*

weave, wove, woven /wiːv/ [verb] To make material by putting threads over and under one another: *An old lady taught us how to weave wool.*

weaving /ˈwiː.vɪŋ/ [noun] Making material by putting threads over and under one another: *Shona is learning weaving at evening classes.*

⁺web /web/ [countable noun] A net of fine threads made by a spider to catch other insects: *Spiders usually live in the center of their webs.*

webcam /ˈwebkæm/ [countable noun] A camera attached to a personal computer: *The webcam allows you to talk with friends online face to face.* 👁 **See page 442.**

website /ˈweb.saɪt/ [countable noun] A section of the internet that is organized by a specific person or organization and that has a unique domain: *Helen is setting up her own website, but it takes a lot of time.*

we'd /wiːd, wid/ The contraction of "we had" or "we would".

wedding /'wed.ɪŋ/ [countable noun] A ceremony in which a man and a woman get married: *The wedding will take place at St John's Church.*

Wednesday /'wenz.deɪ/ [noun] The fourth day of the week: *Wednesday is between Tuesday and Thursday.* ■ Be careful! "Wednesday" has a capital "W". Be careful with the pronunciation of this word! The second "e" is not pronounced. See picture at **calendar**.

weed[1] /wiːd/ [countable noun] A wild plant that you do not want: *Weeds can affect the way a crop grows.*

weed[2] /wiːd/ [verb] To pull out weeds in a yard or a field: *Before planting the seed, you have to weed your backyard.*

week /wiːk/ [countable noun] The seven days that go from Sunday to Saturday: *How many weeks does this term have?* See picture at **calendar**.

weekday /'wiːk.deɪ/ [countable noun] One of the days of a week, except Saturday or Sunday: *We never go to the movies on a weekday; we go only at the weekend.*

weekend /ˌwiːk'end/ [countable noun] Saturday and Sunday: *What are you doing this weekend?*

weekly[1] /'wiːkli/ [adjective] That happens once a week or every week: *The swimming club has weekly meetings.*

weekly[2] /'wiːkli/ [adverb] Once a week or every week: *I have a group of friends who meet weekly.*

weep, wept, wept /wiːp/ [verb] To cry: *They wept when they heard the news.*

weigh /weɪ/ [verb] **1** To measure how heavy somebody or something is: *You have to weigh the parcel to know what the postage is.* **2** To have a certain weight: *How much do you weigh?*

weight /weɪt/ [noun] **1** How heavy somebody or something is: *What's the weight of that parcel?* **2** A heavy object that you lift to make your muscles stronger: *He can lift weights of up to 60 kilos.* **3 to lose weight** To become thinner: *Mr. Palmer has lost a lot of weight with his new diet.* **4 to put on weight** To become fatter: *Tom has put on weight since he stopped playing tennis.*

weird US: /wɪrd/ UK: /wɪəd/ [adjective] Very strange: *My friend Pat has some weird ideas.*

welcome[1] /'welkəm/ [noun] **1** A friendly greeting: *We had such a wonderful welcome that we didn't want to leave.* **2 to be welcome to** To let somebody do or have something: *You're welcome to any book in that box. I have two copies.*

welcome[2] /'welkəm/ [verb] **1** To greet somebody in a friendly way: *We all went out to welcome the Canadian visitors.* **2** To receive something with pleasure: *After a week of rain, we welcomed the sunshine.* **3 to make (somebody) welcome** To make somebody feel at home: *Mrs. Carter made us very welcome when we went to see her in her home.* **4 you're welcome** An expression that you say when somebody thanks you for something: *"Thank you for the chocolates". "You're welcome".* ■ In this use, the same meaning: "not at all".

welcome[3] [interjection] A word that you say to show somebody that you are happy that they are there: *Welcome home!*

we'll /wiːl, wil/ The contraction of "we will" or "we shall".

well[1] /wel/ [countable noun] A hole in the ground to take out water or oil: *If it doesn't rain soon there won't be any water left in the well.*

well[2] /wel/ [adverb] **1** In a good way: *Sarah plays the piano very well.* **2** Very much: *I don't know Pete very well.* ■ The comparative form is "better[2]" and the superlative form is "best[2]". **3 as well** Too: *She plays the piano, and she sings as well.* ■ "Too", "as well" and "also" have the same meaning. "Too" and "as well" go at the end of a sentence. "Also" usually goes in the middle of a sentence. ■ See box at **also**. **4 as well as** Besides: *She speaks English as well as Spanish.* **5 to do (something) well** To do something in a good way: *Sue is doing well in her new job.*

well[3] /wel/ [adjective] In good health: *I'm quite well, thank you.* ■ The comparative form is "better[1]" and the superlative form is "best[1]".

well-behaved /ˌwel.bɪ'heɪvd/ [adjective] Having good behavior, when you are talking about children: *My mother is always telling my younger sister to be well-behaved.* ■ Be careful with the pronunciation of this word. The last "e" is not pronounced.

well-done [adjective] When talking about food, thoroughly cooked: *I like my meat well-done.*

wellington boots or **wellingtons** [countable noun] See **rubber boots.** ■ This word is British English.

well kept /ˌwel'kept/ [adjective] That is well looked after: *They have a well kept yard at the back of the house.*

well-known /ˌwel'nəʊn/ [adjective] That is known by many people: *It is a well-known fact that babies learn to talk by listening to other people talking.* ■ Be careful! We say: "she's a well-known actress". (We don't say: "she's a known actress").

well-off /'wel'ɒf/ [adjective] Rich: *He is poor but the rest of his family is well-off.*

Welsh[1] [adjective] Referring to Wales: *Welsh choirs are famous.* ■ Be careful. "Welsh" has a capital "W". For people the singular is "a Welsh man" or "a Welsh woman" and the plural is "the Welsh".

Welsh[2] /welʃ/ [uncountable noun] The language of Wales: *The street signs in Wales are in Welsh and English.* ■ Be careful. "Welsh" has a capital "W".

a b c d e f g h i j k l m n o p q r s t u v w x y z

a b c d e f g h i j k l m n o p q r s t u v w x y z

went /went/ Past tense of **go**.

wept /wept/ Past tense and past participle forms of **weep**.

we're US: /wɪr/ UK: /wɪəʳ/ The contraction of "we are".

were /wəʳ/ [verb] See **be**.

weren't US: /wɝːnt/ UK: /wɜːnt/ The contraction of "were not".

west /west/ [noun, adjective and adverb] **1** The direction where the sun sets: *My uncle lives in West Chicago.* ■ See box at **abbreviations**. **2 the West** Europe and America: *The way of life in the West is based around the car.*

western[1] /ˈwestən/ [adjective] **1** Of the west: *My cousin Andy lives in Western Nevada.* **2** Referring to the west: *Florence has produced some of the finest art of western civilization.*

western[2] /ˈwestən/ [countable noun] A movie about the American Far West: *John Wayne acted in many westerns.*

wet[1] /wet/ [adjective] **1** That is covered with or soaked in liquid: *Pass me a wet cloth to wipe the table.* See pictures at **opposite** and **a piece of... 2** Rainy: *Which is the wettest season in your country?* ■ The comparative form is "wetter" and the superlative form is "wettest".

wet[2] /wet/ [verb] To cover something with liquid: *Wet the brush a little before using it.* ■ Be careful with the spelling of these forms: "wetted", "wetting".

we've /ˈwiːv, wiv/ The contraction of "we have".

whale /weɪl/ [countable noun] A very large sea mammal: *Most countries have made it illegal to hunt whales.*

wharf US: /wɔːrf/ UK: /wɔːf/ [countable noun] A place in a port where ships can be loaded or unloaded: *In wharves there are storehouses to keep goods.* ■ The plural is "wharves".

what US: /wɑːt/ UK: /wɒt/ [pronoun] **1** A word that is used in questions to ask about things: *What do you want?* ■ Be careful! We use "what" when we refer to one member of a large group. When the group is much more limited, we use "which": "Which one of these is yours?". "What is your favorite food?". **2** The thing or things that: *He doesn't know what he wants.* **3** A word that is used to show your feeling: *What a beautiful animal!* **4 what about...?** An expression used to make a suggestion: *What about going to Coney Island next weekend?* **5 what... for?** Why: *What do you want that thing for?* **6 what is (somebody or something) like** See "what is (somebody or something) like" in the word **like**[2]: *What is Liz like?*

whatever US: /wɑːˈev.ɚ/ UK: /wɒtˈev.əʳ/ [pronoun] Anything that: *Do whatever you want.*

wheat /wiːt/ [uncountable noun] A kind of cereal plant: *Most wheat is used for making flour.*

wheel /wiːl/ [countable noun] A circular object that is used to move vehicles or machines: *Most cars have only four wheels.* **See page 441.**

wheelbarrow /ˈhwilˌbær·oʊ/, /ˈwil-/ [countable noun] A small cart with one wheel at the front and two handles behind: *Wheelbarrows are used by gardeners and builders.*

wheelchair /ˈhwilˌtʃeər/, /ˈwil-/, /-ˌtʃær/ [countable noun] A chair on wheels for people who cannot walk: *Mr. Sherman has been in a wheelchair since the accident.* See picture at **chair**.

wheelie [countable noun] The act of keeping the front wheel of a bicycle or motorcycle in the air for a short time while riding it: *Don't do wheelies on your bike! It can be dangerous!* ■ We say **do** a wheelie.

when[1] /wen/ [adverb] A word that is used to ask about time: *When was television invented?*

when[2] /wen/ [conjunction] At the time that: *I'll tell Sarah when I see her.*

whenever /hwenˈev·ər/, /wen-/, /hwən-/, /wən-/ [conjunction] At any time: *I'll show you my CD collection whenever you want.*

where[1] /weər/ [adverb] A word that is used to ask about place: *Where is Nepal?*

where[2] /weər/ [conjunction] At the place that or in the place that: *He still lives in the house where he was born.*

whereas US: /werˈæz/ UK: /weəˈræz/ [conjunction] On the other hand, while: *I only speak English whereas my brother speaks five languages.*

wherever US: /werˈev.ɚ/ UK: /weəˈrev.əʳ/ [conjunction] In any place or to any place: *I'll find you wherever you are.*

whether /ˈhweð·ər/, /ˈweð-/ [conjunction] If: *We don't know whether they will come.*

which /wɪtʃ/ [pronoun] **1** A word that is used to ask about a particular person or thing: *Which United States president was born in Kentucky?* ■ Be careful! We use "which" when we refer to one member of a small group. When the group is much longer, we use "what": "Which of those sweaters is yours?" "What is your favorite movie?". **2** That: *Have you seen the tie which John has bought for his father?*

whichever /hwɪtʃˈev·ər/, /wɪtʃ-/ [adjective and pronoun] Anything that: *Take whichever book you like.*

while[1] /waɪl/ [uncountable noun] A period of time: *You always have to wait for a while when you go to the dentist.*

while[2] /waɪl/ [conjunction] During the time that: *I'll do it while you wait.*

whip /wɪp/ [countable noun] A piece of leather that is used for hitting animals: *She hit the horse with the whip to make it jump.*

whirlpool /ˈwɜːlpuːl/ [countable noun] **1** A powerful, very fast circular flow in the sea: *Whirlpools are dangerous because they pull things into the center and down into the sea.* **2** A heated pool for relaxing in: *This gym has a whirlpool and a Turkish bath.*

whirlwind /ˈwɜːlwɪnd/ [countable noun] A column of air that goes round and round very fast: *The whirlwind damaged many buildings in the town.*

whisker /ˈhwɪs·kər/, /ˈwɪs-/ [countable noun] A stiff hair near the mouth of some animals: *Cats clean their whiskers after meals.*

whisky /ˈwɪs.ki/ [noun] An alcoholic drink made from barley: *I think Scotch whisky is the best in the world.* ■ The plural is "whiskies".

†**whisper** /ˈhwɪs·pər/, /ˈwɪs-/ [verb] To speak in a very low voice: *If you don't want anybody else to hear, you can whisper in my ear.*

†**whistle**[1] /ˈwɪsl/ [countable noun] A small instrument that makes a sound when you blow it: *The referee blew his whistle to indicate the end of the game.* ■ Be careful with the pronunciation of this word! The "t" is silent.

whistle[2] /ˈwɪsl/ [verb] To make a sound by blowing air through your lips: *Some shepherds direct their dogs by whistling to them.* ■ Be careful with the pronunciation of this word! The "t" is silent.

†**white**[1] [noun and adjective] The color of snow: *The pages of this book are white.*

white[2] /waɪt/ [countable noun] The part of an egg around the yolk: *We just need the white of the egg for the cake.*

white[3] /waɪt/ [adjective] Who has a very light skin: *This movie is about the arrival of the white man in America.*

white blood cell [countable noun] A colorless blood cell: *White blood cells are important in the fight against diseases.*

whiteboard [countable noun] A board with a hard white surface on which you write with a special marker: *In my school there are no blackboards, only whiteboards.* ■ Compare with "blackboard" (a board on which you write with chalk).

whitecollar /ˈhwaɪt ˈkɑl·ər/, /ˈwaɪt/ [adjective] That works in an office: *Not all whitecollar workers are well paid.*

†**who** /huː/ [pronoun] **1** A word that we use instead of "that", when talking about a person: *Rhona is the girl who lent you her ruler.* **2** A word used to ask about people: *Who's that boy in the corner?*

WHO Referring to a department of the United Nations which aims to improve health all over the world and limit the spread of diseases. ■ "WHO" is an abbreviation for "World Health Organization". ■ See box at **abbreviations**.

who'd /huːd/ The contraction of "who had" or "who would".

†**whoever** /huˈev·ər/ [pronoun] Anybody at all: *I think "X" is crazy, whoever he is.*

†**whole** US: /hoʊl/ UK: /həʊl/ [adjective] **1** The total amount of something: *He was so thirsty that he drank a whole bottle of milk.* **2** That is not broken: *I don't want that broken cookie. I want a whole one.* **3 on the whole** In general: *On the whole, I agree with the idea.*

wholemeal /ˈhəʊl.miːl/ US: /ˈhoʊl-/ [adjective] See **whole wheat.** ■ This word is British English.

wholesale /ˈhəʊlseɪl/ [adjective] Referring to the trading of goods in large quantities to stores, not individual consumers: *You can't buy in that place, it only sells wholesale to people who have stores.* ■ Compare with "retail[1]" (the sale of goods in small quantities).

whole wheat [adjective] Made with flour containing all parts of the grain: *Have you tried these whole wheat cookies? They're very tasty.* ■ In British English they say "wholemeal".

who'll /huːl/ The contraction of "who will".

wholly /ˈhoʊl·li/ [adverb] Completely: *I wholly agree with you.*

†**whom** /huːm/ [pronoun] **1** A word that is used to ask about people: *About whom are you speaking?* **2** The person or people that: *Look! That's the boy with whom I'm going out.* ■ This word is formal. We usually say "who" or "that".

who's /huːz/ The contraction of "who is" or "who has".

†**whose**[1] [pronoun] A word that is used to ask about the owner of something: *Whose coat is this? Is it yours?*

whose[2] [adjective] That belongs to that person or those people: *That's the girl whose father is a famous actor.*

†**why** /waɪ/ [adverb] A word used to ask about the reason for something: *Why are you so angry? I haven't done anything wrong.*

wicked /ˈwɪk.ɪd/ [adjective] Morally very bad: *The wicked witch converted the Prince into a frog.* ■ Be careful with the pronunciation of this word. The "e" is pronounced like the "i" in "did".

†**wide** /waɪd/ [adjective] **1** That is large from one side to another: *The Amazon is so wide that you can't see one side from the other.* **2** From one side to the other: *The forest is 5 miles wide.* ■ The comparative form of "wide" is "wider" and the superlative form is "widest". ■ Compare with "narrow" (showing a small distance from one side to the other).

widespread /ˌwaɪdˈspred/ [adjective] That is found or used in many places: *The use of computers is now quite widespread.*

widow /ˈwɪd·oʊ/ [countable noun] A woman whose husband is dead: *She became a widow in World War II.* ■ A man whose wife is dead is a "widower".

widower /ˈwɪd·oʊ·ər/ [countable noun] A man whose wife is dead: *Pat's father has been a widower for many years now.* ■ A woman whose husband is dead is a "widow".

width /wɪtθ, wɪdθ/ [noun] The distance from one side of something to the other: *The width of the park at this point is 1 mile.*

wife /waɪf/ [countable noun] The woman to whom a man is married: *My brother's wife is Japanese.* ■ The plural is "wives". The man to whom a woman is married is her "husband". See picture at **family**.

wig /wɪg/ [countable noun] False hair: *In the 18th century many men wore wigs, it was the fashion.*

wiggle[1] /ˈwɪgl/ [verb] To move from side to side: *You need to wiggle the wire about to get it through the wall.* ■ This use is informal.

wiggle[2] [countable noun] A move which is made from side to side: *With a wiggle or two, he got into the suit.* ■ This use is informal.

wild /waɪld/ [adjective] **1** That lives or grows freely: *I think wild animals shouldn't be in zoos.* **2** Violent: *The Clarks' dog is very wild.*

wildlife /ˈwaɪld.laɪf/ [uncountable noun] Animals and plants that live and grow freely: *We are studying the wildlife of our area.*

will[1] /wɪl/ [noun] **1** A document in which you say to whom you want to give your things when you die: *Mrs. Palumbo has left $3,000 to the school in her will.* **2** The determination to do something: *My dad says that you need a strong will to stop smoking.*

will[2] /wɪl, wəl, əl/ [verb] **1** A word that is used to form the future of verbs: *"I will do" is the future of "do".* **2** A way of asking somebody to do something: *Will you tell Diana that she's going to be late for school?* ■ This is a more direct form than "could" or "would". ■ Be careful! The verb after "will" is in the infinitive without "to".

willing /ˈwɪl.ɪŋ/ [adjective] Prepared to do something: *Are you willing to help?*

willingly /ˈwɪl.ɪŋ.li/ [adverb] With a strong interest: *I would willingly do it if I had the time.*

willpower /ˈwɪl,paʊ·ər/ [uncountable noun] Determination: *If you have willpower, you can achieve anything you want.*

win, won, won /wɪn/ [verb] To be the best in a particular competition, game and so on: *Who do you think is going to win the game?* ■ Compare with "earn" (to get money by working). ■ Be careful with the spelling of this form: "winning".

wind[1] /wɪnd/ [noun] Moving air: *You need some wind to sail properly.* See pages 439 and 459.

wind[2], wound, wound /waɪnd/ [verb] **1** To have a lot of curves: *Be careful. The road winds down the hill quite sharply.* **2** To turn the key of a toy, clock and so on, to make it work: *Don't forget to wind the alarm clock.* **3** To make something go round another thing: *You have to wind the bandage around your wrist.*

windmill /ˈwɪnd.mɪl/ [countable noun] A machine for grinding grain that is moved by the wind: *Danish windmill is one of the most popular and successful tourist attractions in Iowa.*

window /ˈwɪn·doʊ/ [countable noun] An opening in a wall or a roof for light and air: *I looked out of the window and watched the procession in the street.* See picture at **classroom**.

window-ledge or **window-sill** [countable noun] A flat piece of stone, marble and so on just under a window: *She has some flowerpots on the window-sill.*

windpipe /ˈwɪndpaɪp/ [countable noun] The tube in the body which connects the throat to the lungs: *"Windpipe" is the popular name for the trachea.*

windscreen /ˈwɪnd.skriːn/ [countable noun] See **windshield.** ■ This word is British English.

windshield [countable noun] The glass in the front of a car or other vehicle: *This morning the windshield of our car was covered in ice.* ■ In British English they say "windscreen". See page 441.

windsurfing /ˈwɪnd,sɜr·fɪŋ/ [uncountable noun] The sport of sailing on a board with a sail: *It's easier to go windsurfing in a lake than at sea.*

windy /ˈwɪn.di/ [adjective] With a lot of wind: *It was windy on the beach, which was great for flying our kite.* ■ The comparative form is "windier" and the superlative form is "windiest".

wine /waɪn/ [noun] An alcoholic drink made from grapes: *Which do you prefer, white wine or red?*

wing /wɪŋ/ [countable noun] **1** The part of a bird's or an insect's body that they use for flying: *Most insects have four wings.* **2** The part of an airplane that it flies with: *Modern airplanes have two large wings.* **3** An extension of a building: *The new wing of the museum will be finished next year.*

wingspan /ˈwɪŋ.spæn/ [countable noun] Distance from the end of one wing to the end of the other, in birds and aircraft: *The wingspan of the largest kind of vulture can be more than nine feet.*

wink /wɪŋk/ [verb] To close and to open one eye quickly to show friendship or amusement: *Are you winking at me?*

winner /ˈwɪn·ər/ [countable noun] The person or the team that wins a competition or a game: *Who was the winner of that race?*

winter /ˈwɪn·tər/ [noun] The season of the year between fall and spring: *Winter is the best time of the year to go skiing.* See page 448.

wipe /waɪp/ [verb] **1** To clean something with a cloth or with your hand: *Can you wipe the table, please?* **2** To clean something by rubbing it: *Wipe your shoes before coming into the house.*

▸ **PHRASAL VERBS** · **to wipe (something) off** To erase or remove something: *Can you wipe those formulas off the whiteboard?* · **to wipe up** To take away liquid with a cloth: *He wiped up the milk on the floor.* ■ Be careful with the spelling of this form: "wiping".

↑**wire** US: /waɪr/ UK: /waɪəʳ/ [countable noun] A long, thin piece of metal: *Don't touch those wires. They could give you a shock.*

wireless /ˈwaɪələs/ [adjective] Without wires, or which does not need wires: *Do you have wireless internet?*

↑**wise** /waɪz/ [adjective] Knowing what to do in different situations with good sense and judgment: *I think buying this computer was a wise choice, it's very powerful.*

wish[1] /wɪʃ/ [countable noun] Something you would like to happen: *I have only one wish, to visit the Galapagos islands again.* ■ The plural is "wishes".

↑**wish**[2] /wɪʃ/ [verb] **1** To think or to say that you would like something to happen: *She wished me good luck.* **2 I wish...!** A phrase used when you strongly want something that will never happen or will probably not happen: *I wish I was taller!* ■ In formal English only, after "I wish" we use "were", not "was", with "I", "she", "he": "I wish I were able to express my thanks better". ■ The same meaning: "if only...!".

witch /wɪtʃ/ [countable noun] A woman with magic powers: *There are witches in a lot of fairy tales.* ■ The plural is "witches". A man is a "wizard".

witchcraft /ˈwɪtʃˌkræft/ [uncountable noun] Magic powers: *If I could do witchcraft, I would send rain to Africa.*

witch doctor /ˈwɪtʃˌdɒk.təʳ/ US: /-ˌdɑːk.tɚ/ [countable noun] A man in a primitive tribe who appears to cure illnesses by magic: *The witch doctor treated him with herbs and sang a song.*

↑**with** /wɪð/ [preposition] **1** Accompanied by: *I'm going to the movies with some friends tonight.* **2** Using: *He wrote the note with a pencil.* **3** Having: *I live in a building with ten floors.* **4** Together: *Put these tapes with those books.* **5** Because of: *She cried with rage.*

↑**withdraw, withdrew, withdrawn** /wɪθˈdrɔː/, /wɪð-/ [verb] **1** To take something away or remove something: *I need to withdraw some money from my savings account.* **2** To go away: *I thought I didn't have any chance of winning, so I withdrew from the competition.*

withdrawn /wɪθˈdrɔn/, /wɪð-/ Past participle of **withdraw.**

withdrew Past tense of **withdraw.**

↑**within**[1] /wɪˈðɪn/ [preposition] In a particular period of time: *We should be there within a couple of hours.*

within[2] /wɪˈðɪn/ [adverb] Inside: *Shop assistant required. Apply within.*

↑**without** /wɪˈðaʊt/ [preposition] **1** A word that shows that you don't have something: *Louise went to the party without her boyfriend.* **2** A word that shows that you don't do something: *They went away without paying the bill.* ■ The verb after "without" is in the "-ing" form.

↑**witness**[1] /ˈwɪtnəs/ [countable noun] A person who sees something happen and can say what has happened: *Two of the witnesses at the trial identified the murderer.* ■ The plural is "witnesses".

witness[2] /ˈwɪtnəs/ [verb] To see something happen: *I was in the street when the accident happened so I witnessed everything.* ■ Be careful with the spelling of the 3rd person singular present tense form: "witnesses".

witty /ˈwɪt̬.i/ [adjective] Clever and funny: *Clive makes some very witty remarks.* ■ The comparative form is "wittier" and the superlative form is "wittiest".

wizard /ˈwɪz.ərd/ [countable noun] A man believed to have magic powers: *David Copperfield is one of the greatests wizards of our time.* ■ A woman is a "witch".

woke US: /woʊk/ UK: /wəʊk/ Past tense of **wake.**

woken /ˈwoʊ.kən/ Past participle of **wake.**

wolf /wʊlf/ [countable noun] An animal like a large wild dog: *Wolves are excellent hunters.* ■ The plural is "wolves". See page 428.

↑**woman** /ˈwʊm.ən, ˈwɪmɪn/ [countable noun] An adult human female: *I think Rhona will become a very intelligent* *woman.* ■ The plural is "women". ■ An adult human male is a "man".

womb /wu:m/ [countable noun] The organ in women and some female animals where the baby is carried before birth: *The womb is where life begins.* ■ The same meaning: "uterus".

women /ˈwɪmɪn/ The plural of **woman.** ■ Be careful with the pronunciation of this word! The "o" and the "e" are both pronounced like the "i" in "did".

won /wʌn/ Past tense and past participle forms of **win.**

†**wonder** /ˈwʌn·dər/ [verb] **1** To ask yourself: *I wonder why they're not here yet.* **2** To be amazed at something: *I sometimes wonder at his ability with languages.* **3 no wonder** An expression to show that you are not surprised by something: *No wonder she speaks Spanish so well. She lived in Mexico when she was a girl.*

†**wonderful** /ˈwʌn·dər·fəl/ [adjective] Very good: *It was wonderful to be back home again after our awful vacation.*

won't US: /woʊnt/ UK: /wəʊnt/ The contraction of "will not".

†**wood** /wʊd/ [noun] **1** The substance that forms the trunk and branches of a tree: *If you get me some wood, I'll make you a table.* **2** A small area of land covered with trees: *A wood is smaller than a forest.*

†**wooden** /ˈwʊd.ᵊn/ [adjective] Made of wood: *Jamie got a wooden train for his birthday.*

woodland /ˈwʊd.lənd/ [noun] Country covered in woods: *The areas of woodland in United States are amazing.*

woodpecker /ˈwʊd,pek·ər/ [countable noun] A bird which uses its beak to make holes in tree trunks: *The woodpecker taps the tree in search of insects.*

woodwind instrument [countable noun] A wind instrument which can be made of wood, metal or plastic: *The flute is a woodwind instrument.*

woodwork /ˈwʊd,wɜrk/ [uncountable noun] The craft of making things from wood: *Woodwork is a very relaxing activity for me.*

woody /ˈwʊd.i/ [adjective] **1** Covered with trees: *There is a woody area between the two towns.* **2** Similar to wood in hardness or texture: *a woody stem.* ■ The comparative form is "woodier" and the superlative form is "woodiest".

woof¹ /wʊf/ [countable noun] The sound made by a dog: *"Woof!" said the dog.* ■ This word is usually used by young children, or in books for them.

woof² [verb] To bark: *The dog woofed and woofed at the evil magician.* ■ This word is usually used by young children, or in books for them.

†**wool** /wʊl/ [uncountable noun] The hair of sheep that is used for making material: *If you get me some wool, I'll knit you a sweater.*

woolen [adjective] Made of wool: *Tony bought a beautiful woolen jacket at the sales.*

woolly or **wooly** /ˈwʊl.i/ [adjective] Made of wool or like wool: *You need some wooly gloves.*

†**word** US: /wɝːd/ UK: /wɜːd/ [countable noun] **1** The smallest complete unit of a language that has a meaning: *There are thousands of words in this dictionary.* **2 to have a word with (somebody)** To speak to somebody in private: *The principal said she wanted to have a word with me in her office.* **3 in other words** An expression that shows you are going to say the same thing in a different way: *"His parties are always boring". "In other words, you're not going!".* **4 to keep your word** To do something you promised: *If you don't keep your word, you won't be my friend any more.* **5 swear word** See "swear word" in the word **swear.** **6 to take (somebody's) word for it** To believe what somebody says: *OK. This time I'll take your word for it.*

word processor [countable noun] A computer or a computer program that is used for typing texts: *With a word processor, it's very easy to make corrections in a letter.*

wore US: /wɔːr/ UK: /wɔːʳ/ Past tense of **wear.**

†**work¹** /wɜːk/ [uncountable noun] **1** Activity requiring effort that is done for money or because of obligation: *I need work. I don't have any money.* ■ Be careful! We don't say "a work". We say "some work", "a piece of work" or "a job". **2 at work** Doing some work: *There are some men at work in my street.* **3 out of work** Without a job: *Tina's dad has been out of work for three months now.* **4 work of art** A book, piece of music, painting and so on of great artistic quality: *I'd like to be able to create beautiful works of art.*

†**work²** /wɜːk/ [verb] **1** To do a job, a physical task or studying: *Elizabeth's father works as an accountant with a large firm.* **2** To function well: *This video recorder doesn't work. It hasn't recorded the program.* **3 work hard** To work a lot: *Idris works very hard in some subjects but not in others.*

▶ **PHRASAL VERBS** · **to work out 1** To do physical exercise to be fit: *Paula works out for half an hour every day.* **2** To do well, to have a good result: *Our plan didn't work out.* **3** To calculate: *Let's try and work out how to do this mathematical problem.* · **to work (something) out** To solve a problem by thinking: *Are you good at working out puzzles?*

workbook /ˈwɜːk.bʊk/ US: /ˈwɝːk-/ [countable noun] A book with written exercises: *Have you done the exercises in the workbook?*

†**worker** US: /ˈwɝː.kɚ/ UK: /ˈwɜː.kəʳ/ [countable noun] **1** A person who has a job: *That factory employs twenty*

workers. **2** A person who works or studies hard: *You're such a worker! You even study on Sundays.*

working class [countable noun] The social class of people who earn low wages, doing manual or low status work: *The working class, the middle class and the upper class are the three groups that make up our society.*

workman /'wɜrk·mən/ [countable noun] A man who works with his hands: *A workman fixed the gas leak.* ■ The plural is "workmen".

workmate /'wɜːk.meɪt/ US: /'wɝːk-/ [countable noun] Somebody who works with you: *Yesterday one of my mother's workmates came to have dinner with us.*

workshop US: /'wɝːk.ʃɑːp/ UK: /'wɜːk.ʃɒp/ [countable noun] **1** A place where things are made or repaired, in a house or in a place of work: *He is making a table in his workshop.* **2** A special class based on an activity or a discussion: *I'm going to a painting workshop this weekend to improve my technique.*

†**world** US: /wɝːld/ UK: /wɜːld/ [countable noun] **1** The earth: *The world is divided into continents.* **2** People who do the same activity: *It's not easy to get into the world of the movies.*

world-famous /'wɜrld'feɪ·məs/ [adjective] Known in the whole world: *The Beatles were a world-famous pop group of the 1960's.*

worldwide /'wɜːld,waɪd/ [adjective] That is in all parts of the world: *Some scientists say that there will be a worldwide energy crisis in the next century.*

worm US: /wɝːm/ UK: /wɜːm/ [countable noun] A small, long animal that lives in the ground: *Some people use worms for fishing.*

worn[1] [verb] Past participle of **wear**.

worn[2] /wɔːn/ [adjective] That is old because it has been used a lot: *Poor Paul! He always wears worn clothes.*

worn-out /,wɔːn'aʊt/ [adjective] Very tired: *After the game they were so worn-out that they went straight to bed.*

†**worried** /'wɜr·id/, /'wʌr·id/ [adjective] That is anxious about something: *Liz's parents are worried because she went out to a store an hour ago and she hasn't returned yet.* 👁 See picture at **emotions**.

worry[1] /'wʌri/ [uncountable noun] Something that makes you anxious: *My main worry is not being able to finish my project on time.*

†**worry**[2] /'wʌri/ [verb] To be anxious about something: *She always worries a lot about tests.* ■ Be careful with the spelling of these forms: "worries", "worried".

†**worrying** /'wʌr.i.ɪŋ/ US: /'wɝː-/ [adjective] That causes worry: *Her state of health is very worrying.*

†**worse** US: /wɝːs/ UK: /wɜːs/ [adjective and adverb] The comparative form of **bad** and **badly**.

worship[1] [uncountable noun] A feeling of love for God: *A church is a place of worship to God.*

worship[2] /'wɜːʃɪp/ [verb] **1** To show your love for God: *I go to church to worship God.* **2** To think that somebody is wonderful: *Tony worships his History teacher.* ■ Be careful with the spelling of these forms: "worshipped", "worshipping".

†**worst** US: /wɝːst/ UK: /wɜːst/ [adjective and adverb] The superlative form of **bad** and **badly**.

†**worth**[1] /wɜːθ/ [adjective] **1** Having a certain value: *That racket is worth nearly $100.* **2 to be worth** Words you use to recommend doing something: *It's worth reading the book again.*

worth[2] /wɜːθ/ [uncountable noun] The value of something: *We have nothing of worth at home.*

worthless /'wɜrθ·ləs/ [adjective] That has no value or is useless: *That painting is worthless. No one will give you any money for it.*

worthwhile /wɜrθ'hwaɪl/, /-'waɪl/ [adjective] Useful, good to: *I think it's worthwhile making an effort to learn a foreign language.* ■ The verb after "worthwhile" is in the "-ing" form.

†**would** /wʊd, wəd, əd/ [verb] **1** A word that is used to form the conditional of verbs: *"I would do" is the conditional of "do".* **2** A polite way of asking somebody to do something: *Would you mail these letters for me, please?* ■ Be careful! The verb after "would" is in the infinitive form without "to".

wouldn't /'wʊd.ᵊnt/ The contraction of "would not".

would've The contraction of "would have".

†**wound**[1] /wuːnd/ [countable noun] An injury involving a cut or a hole in your body: *The nurse cleaned and dressed the wound.* ■ Be careful with the pronunciation of this word. It rhymes with "soon".

wound[2] /wuːnd/ [verb] Past tense and past participle forms of **wind**[2].

wove US: /woʊv/ UK: /wəʊv/ Past tense of **weave**.

woven /'woʊ·vən/ Past participle of **weave**.

wow /waʊ/ [interjection] A word used to show surprise or admiration: *Wow! I've got all the answers right. I can't believe it!*

†**wrap** /ræp/ [verb] To cover something completely with paper or material: *The clerk wrapped the sweater and put it in a carrier bag.* ■ Be careful with the spelling of these forms: "wrapped", "wrapping".

wrapping paper [uncountable noun] Paper used for covering things: *Stores usually have special wrapping paper at Christmas.*

wreck[1] /rek/ [countable noun] **1** A ship that has sunk: *There are many wrecks in the Caribbean.* **2** Anything that has been badly damaged and can't be used any more: *His car was a total wreck after the accident.*

wreck² /rek/ [verb] To destroy something completely: *You've wrecked my mom's collection of china cups!*

wrench [countable noun] A tool that you use for turning things: *Pass me the wrench and I'll try to tighten this nut.* ■ In British English they say "spanner".

wrestle /ˈres.l̩/ [verb] To fight by trying to throw your opponent to the ground: *The people who wrestle on TV are part athletes, part actors.*

wrestler /ˈres·lər/ [countable noun] A person who practices the sport of wrestling: *The two wrestlers greeted each other before the fight.*

wrestling /ˈres.lɪŋ/ [uncountable noun] A sport in which you fight by trying to throw your opponent to the ground: *Wrestling matches are very dramatic.*

wring, wrung, wrung /rɪŋ/ [verb] To hold something firmly and twist it: *Our socks were so wet that we had to wring them out.*

wrinkle /ˈrɪŋ.kl̩/ [countable noun] A line in a person's skin or in material: *My grandfather has lots of wrinkles on his face.*

↑**wrist** /rɪst/ [countable noun] The part of the body where the arm joins the hand: *Louise injured her wrist playing tennis.* 👁 **See page 421.** 👁 See picture at **hand**.

↑**write,** wrote, written /raɪt/ [verb] **1** To make words or numbers on paper with a pen or a pencil: *We have to write a composition every week.* **2** To create books, music or other written texts: *Charles Dickens wrote excellent books.* ■ Be careful! We say: "written **by** (somebody)". For example: "Oliver Twist" was written by Charles Dickens. **3** To put a letter in writing and send it to somebody: *Have you written your mother?* ■ Be careful! In American English we say: "write somebody", but in British English we say: "write **to** somebody".

▶ **PHRASAL VERBS · to write (something) down** To write something on paper: *I'll write down your telephone number or I'll forget it.*

↑**writer** /ˈraɪ·t̬ər/ [countable noun] A person who writes books: *Mrs. Parnell is a writer. She writes detective stories.*

↑**writing** /ˈraɪ·t̬ɪŋ/ [uncountable noun] **1** Anything that is written, the style in which something is written: *I don't understand your writing. What is this word?* **2 in writing** Written on paper: *I'll wait until I see my grades in writing.*

↑**written** /ˈrɪt·ə·n/ Past participle form of **write.** ■ Be careful with the pronunciation of this word. The "i" is pronounced like the "i" in did and the "e" is not pronounced.

↑**wrong¹** /rɒŋ/ [adjective] **1** Not right, incorrect: *I'm sorry, Charles, but three of your answers are wrong.* **2** Bad: *I think it's wrong to laugh at others.* **3** That doesn't work well: *I think there's something wrong with this computer. It's too slow.* **4 to get (something) wrong** To make a mistake: *I got three answers wrong.*

wrong² /rɒŋ/ [adverb] **1** Not right, incorrect: *You keep getting my name wrong. It's Mark, not Mike.* **2 to go wrong** Not to happen as expected: *Although all our plans for the day went wrong, we still had a good time.*

wrote US: /roʊt/ UK: /rəʊt/ Past tense of **write.**

wrung /rʌŋ/ Past tense and past participle forms of **wring.**

a b c d e f g h i j k l m n o p q r s t u v w x y z

X[1] /eks/ The twenty-fourth letter of the alphabet: *The word "X-ray" begins with an "X".*

X[2] /eks/ A written abbreviation for **extension**.

Xmas /'krɪstməs/ A written abbreviation for **Christmas**.

X-ray[1] /'eksreɪ/ [countable noun] **1** A form of energy that passes through solid things: *X-rays are used in medicine.* **2** A photo of the inside of a person's body: *She had an X-ray taken of her lungs.*

X-ray[2] [verb] To take a photo of the inside of a person's body with an X-ray machine: *She had her ankle X-rayed after her fall.*

xylem /'zaɪ.ləm/ [uncountable noun] A tissue in plants which carries nutrients and water from the roots to the other parts of the plant: *The xylem and the phloem are the main transportation systems in plants.* ■ Compare with "phloem" (the tissue in plants which carries food from the leaves to the rest of the plant).

Y

y

y /waɪ/ The twenty-fifth letter of the alphabet: *The name "Yvonne" begins with a "Y".*

yacht US: /jɑːt/ UK: /jɒt/ [countable noun] A sailing boat: *When I'm a millionaire, the first thing I'll do is buy a yacht.* ■ Be careful with the pronunciation of this word. It rhymes with "not". See picture at **transport.**

yachting US: /ˈjɑː.ɪŋ/ UK: /ˈjɒt.ɪŋ/ [uncountable noun] The sport that you do when you sail a yacht: *I like yachting on the lake in the summer.* ■ Be careful with the pronunciation of the beginning of this word. It rhymes with "not".

†**yard** US: /jɑːrd/ UK: /jɑːd/ [countable noun] **1** A unit of length: *There are around three feet in a yard.* ■ The abbreviation "yd" is only used in written language. **2** An open space surrounded by walls or buildings: *Our house has the biggest yard in our neighborhood.*

†**yawn** US: /jɑːn/ UK: /jɔːn/ [verb] To open and stretch your mouth because you are tired or bored: *The movie was so boring that I couldn't stop yawning.*

yd A written abbreviation for **yard.** ■ See box at **abbreviations.**

†**yeah** /jeə/ [adverb] See **yes.** ■ This word is informal.

†**year** US: /jɪr/ UK: /jɪəʳ/ [countable noun] **1** A period of twelve months: *There are 365 days in a year.* **2 leap year** See **leap year. 3 New Year's Day** The first day of the year: *New Year's Day is a vacation in United States.* **4 New Year's Eve** The last day of the year: *Let's have a party on New Year's Eve.* ■ Be careful! "New Year's Day" and "New Year's Eve" have capital letters.

yearly[1] /jɪəli/ [adjective] That happens once a year: *The school has a yearly summer excursion.*

yearly[2] /jɪəli/ [adverb] Every year; once a year: *We go on vacation twice yearly.*

yeast /jiːst/ [uncountable noun] A substance used to make beer and wine, and that causes bread to rise:

Yeast is used in the fermenting process of alcoholic drinks.

yell /jel/ [verb] To shout: *When I saw them pushing the old man, I yelled at them to stop.*

†**yellow** /ˈjel·oʊ/ [noun and adjective] The color of the sun: *Most canaries are yellow.*

yellowish [adjective] Referring to a color, that is approximately yellow, or that has a yellow element to it: *That bird has a yellowish chest.*

†**yes** /jes/ [adverb] A word used to give affirmative answers: *"Do you live near here?" "Yes, I do".* ■ "Yeah" is informal for "yes".

†**yesterday** /ˈjes·tər·di/, /-deɪ/ [noun and adverb] The day before today: *I did five hours of homework yesterday.*

†**yet**[1] /jet/ [adverb] Before now: *Have you seen the Lakers yet?* ■ See boxes at **already** and at **still**.

yet[2] /jet/ [conjunction] But: *I didn't get very good grades yet I can't complain. I didn't work very hard.*

yet again [adverb] Once more: *Chicago Bulls has won yet again.*

yield [verb] **1** To give up: *He yielded all his possessions to the state.* **2** To let somebody go before you: *At last the door yielded.*

yoghurt or **yogurt** US: /ˈjoʊ.gɚt/ UK: /ˈjɒg.ət/ [noun] Food made from milk with bacteria added to it: *We always have yoghurt for dessert at school.* ■ Be careful with the pronunciation of this word.

yolk US: /joʊk/ UK: /jəʊk/ [countable noun] The yellow part of an egg: *You need to separate the yolk from the white.*

†**you** /juː, jə, jʊ/ [pronoun] When somebody speaks, the word they use to refer to the person or people they are speaking to: *Who are you?*

you'd /juːd/ The contraction of "you had" or "you would".

you'll /juːl/ The contraction of "you will".

†**young**[1] /jʌŋ/ [adjective] Not old: *My dog is still very young, he's only nine months old.*

†**young**[2] /jʌŋ/ [plural noun] The babies of an animal: *In our safari we saw a lioness with her young.*

†**your** /jɔːʳ/, /jɔːʳ/ [adjective] Of you; belonging to you: *Can I borrow your dictionary?*

you're /jɔːʳ/ The contraction of "you are".

†**yours** US: /jʊrz/ UK: /jɔːz/ [pronoun] Belonging to you: *Is this dictionary yours?*

†**yourself** /jɔːˈself/ [pronoun] **1** A word that refers to "you" when you are the subject of a sentence: *Have you hurt yourself?* **2** A word that underlines that you are the person the verb refers to: *Do you do all the work yourself?* **3 by yourself 1** Alone: *Would you like to live by yourself?* **2** Without help: *You'll have to do the laundry by yourself.* ■ The plural is "yourselves".

†**youth** /juːθ/ [noun] **1** The period of a person's life when they are young: *In her youth, she traveled all over South America.* **2** A young person, usually a young man: *He spends a lot of time in the club with other local youths.* ■ In this use "youth" often expresses a negative opinion. **3** Young people: *Do you think today's youth is very different from that of other times?* **4 youth club** A place where young people meet: *We have two pool tables at our local youth club.* **5 youth hostel** A place where young people can stay for a few nights: *We spent our vacation hitchhiking in Arizona and staying in youth hostels.*

you've /juːv, jəv/ The contraction of "you have".

yummy or **yumyum** [interjection] A word used to show that you like a particular food: *Today grandpa is making a chocolate cake for dessert, yumyum!* ■ This word is informal and is usually used by children.

Z

z

z US: /ziː/ UK: /zed/ The twenty-sixth letter of the alphabet: *The word "zoo" begins with a "z".*

zebra /ˈzeb.rə, ˈziː.brə/ [countable noun] An animal like a horse with black and white stripes: *Zebras live in the bush in Africa.* **See page 428.**

zebra crossing [countable noun] See **crosswalk.** ■ This word is British English.

†**zero** US: /ˈzɪr.oʊ/ UK: /ˈzɪə.rəʊ/ [noun, adjective and pronoun] Nothing; the number 0: *His interest in History is zero.*

zigzag /ˈzɪg.zæg/ [noun and adjective] A line that goes right and left alternately: *Follow the zigzag path that goes up the hill if you want to get to the castle.*

zip code [countable noun] System of letters or numbers to indicate the town or the street where somebody lives: *What's your zip code?* ■ In British English they say "postcode".

zipper [noun] A type of metal fastener: *Do your zipper up, Tom.*

zodiac /ˈzoʊd·iˌæk/ [uncountable noun] An imaginary area in the sky that includes the planets and is divided into twelve parts: *"What's her sign of the zodiac?" "Let me see: she was born... under Gemini".*

†**zone** US: /zoʊn/ UK: /zəʊn/ [countable noun] An area with a particular characteristic: *The sign said: "Military zone. No entry".*

zoo /zuː/ [noun] A place where wild animals are kept: *I don't like going to our local zoo. They keep the animals in such small cages.* ■ Be careful with the pronunciation of this word! This word is an abbreviation for "zoological garden".

zoom /zuːm/ [verb] To move very quickly and with a loud noise: *The plane zoomed up into the air.*

zucchini /zʊˈki·ni/ [noun] A long vegetable, green outside and white inside: *How do you cook zucchinis? Can you fry them?* ■ In British English they say "courgette". **See page 437.**

zygote /ˈzaɪ·goʊt/ [countable noun] A cell born from the union between two cells: *The zygote is formed during sexual reproduction.*

the body

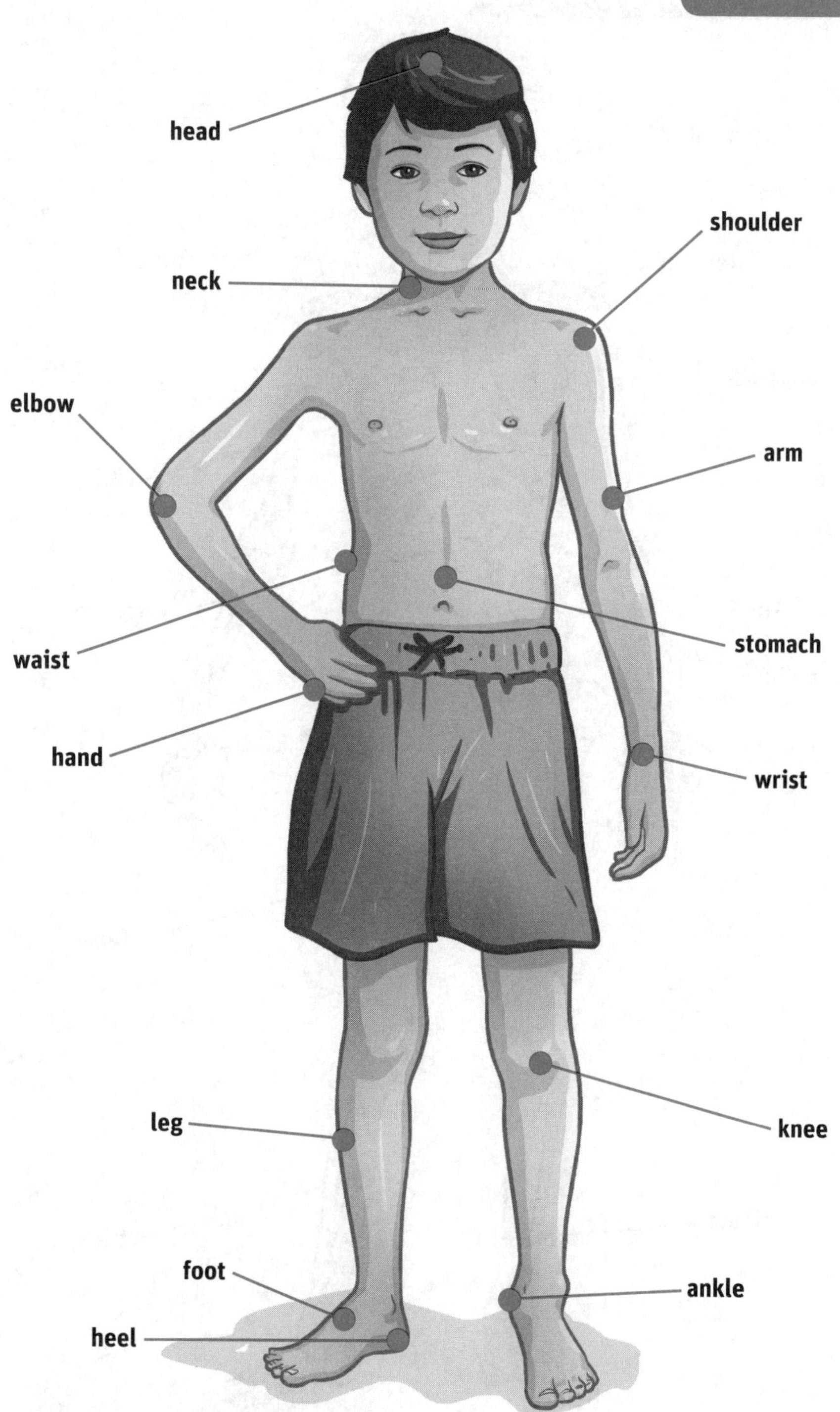
head
shoulder
neck
elbow
arm
waist
stomach
hand
wrist
leg
knee
foot
ankle
heel

the skeletal system

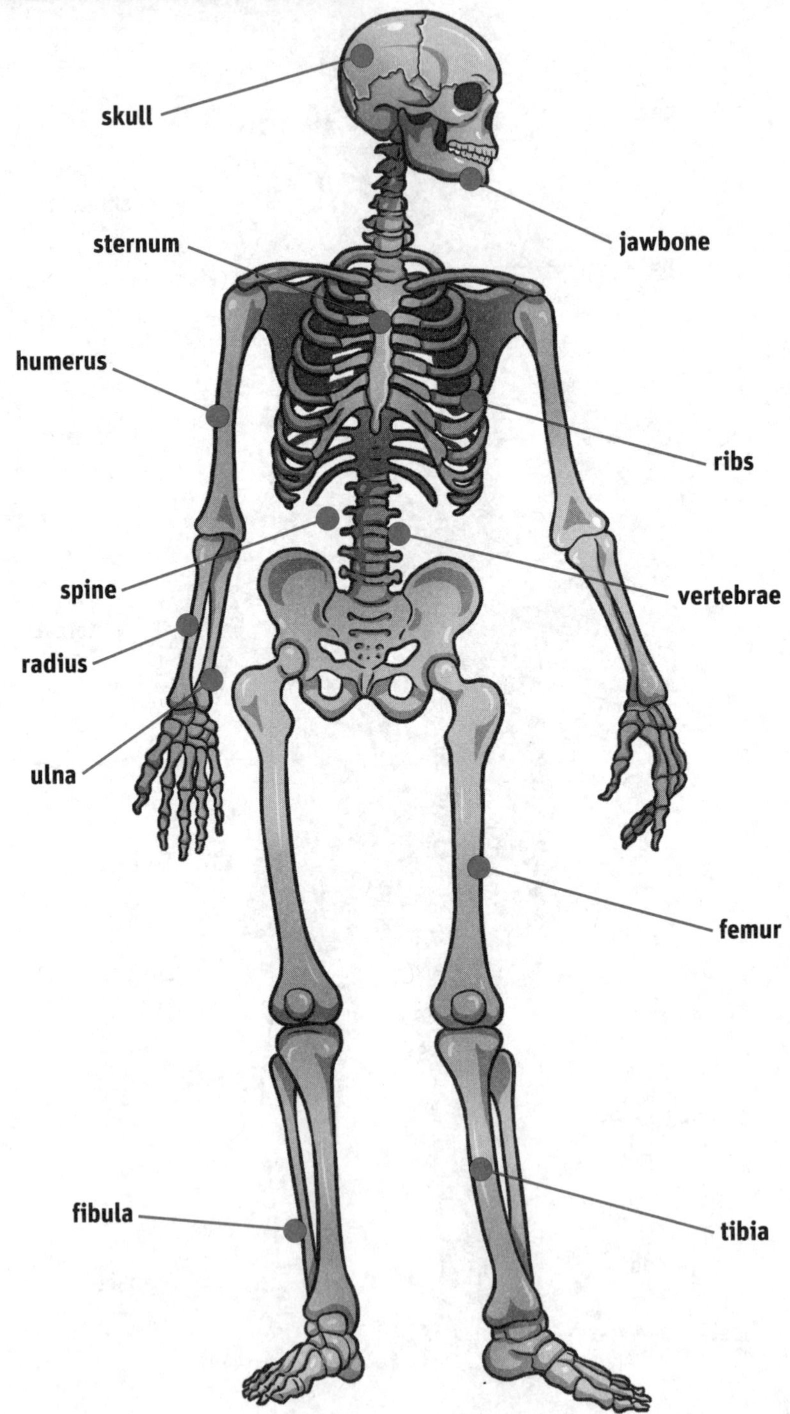

the muscular system

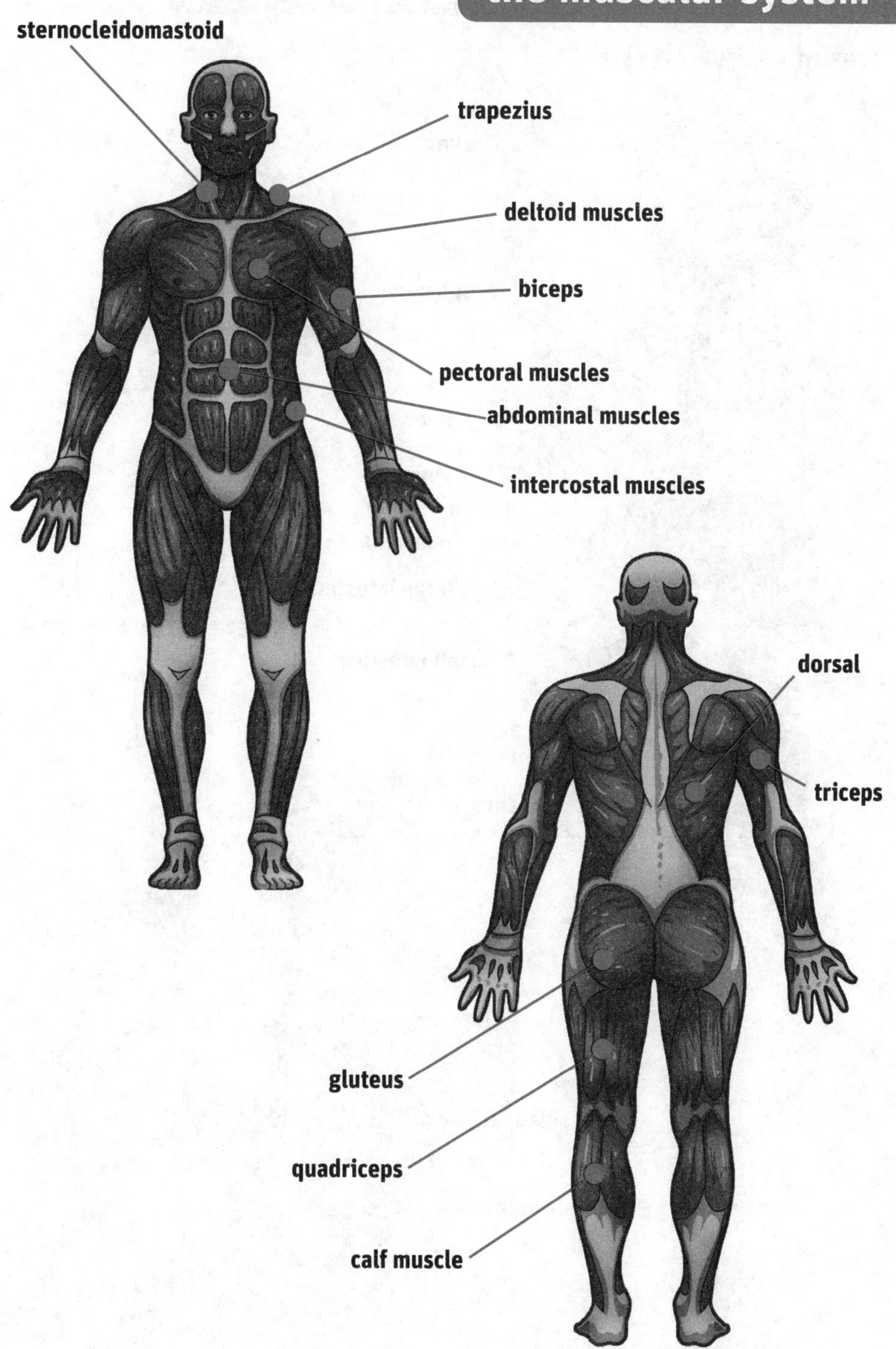

the digestive and excretory systems

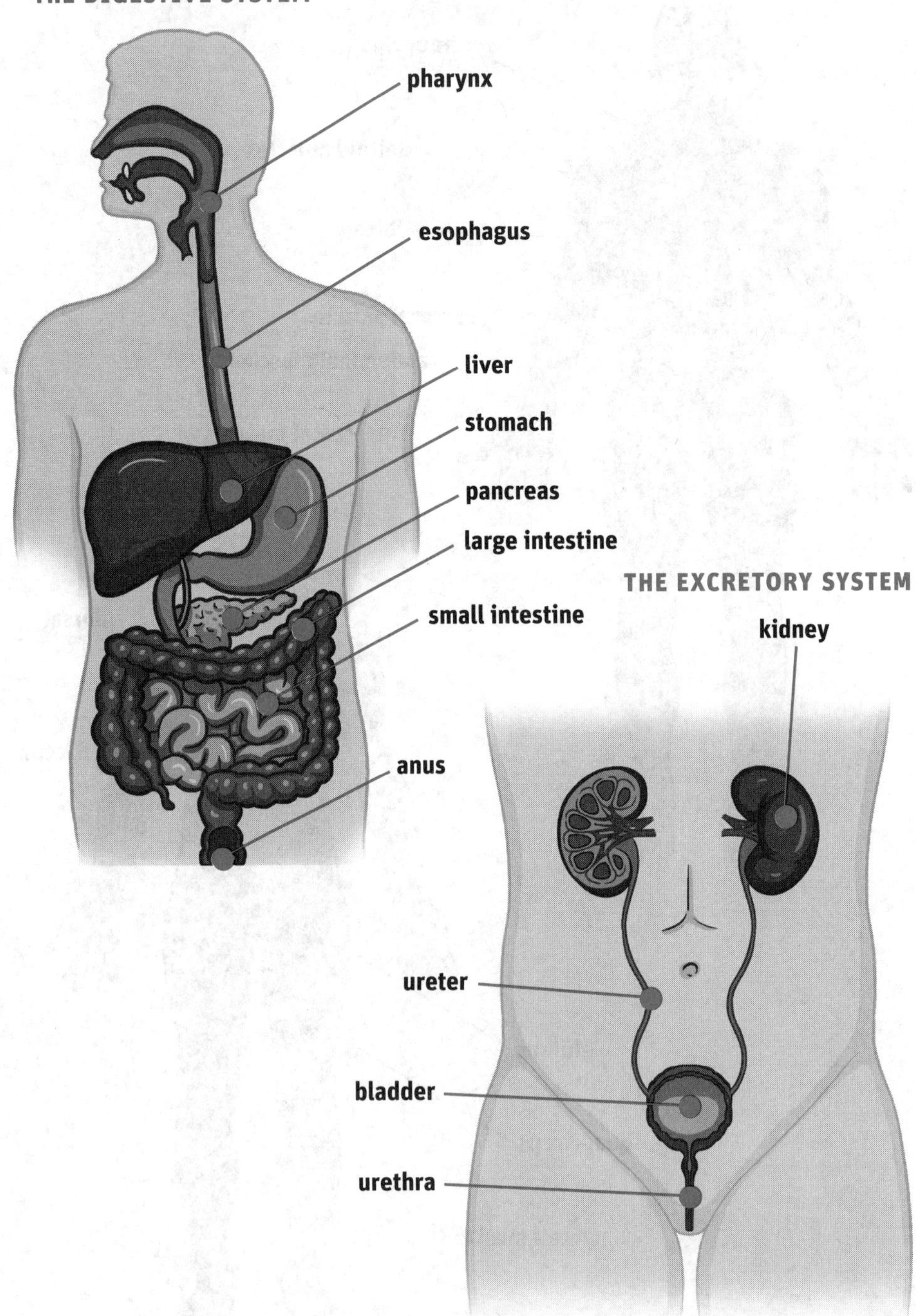

the respiratory and reproductive systems

THE RESPIRATORY SYSTEM

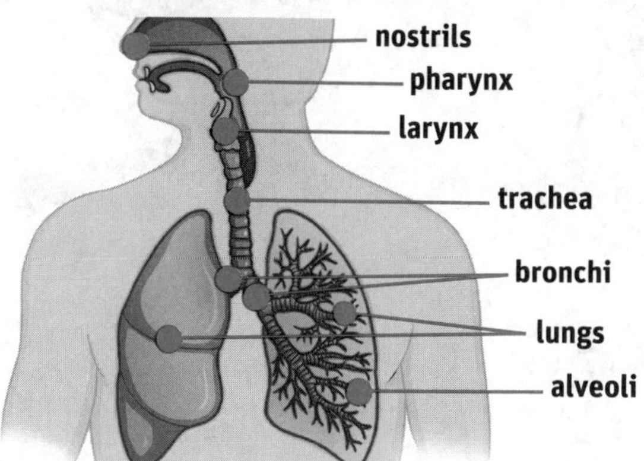

THE FEMALE REPRODUCTIVE SYSTEM

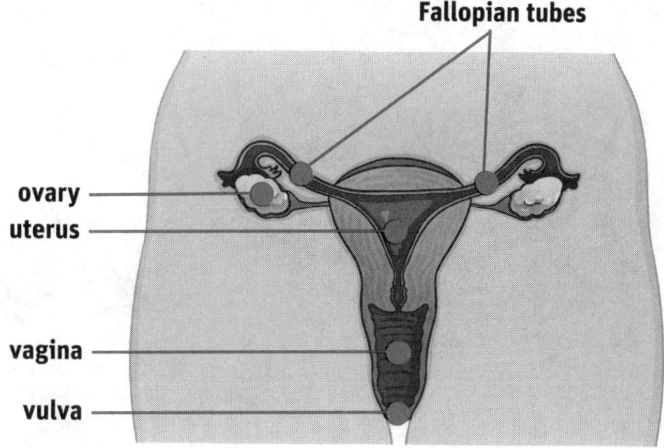

THE MALE REPRODUCTIVE SYSTEM

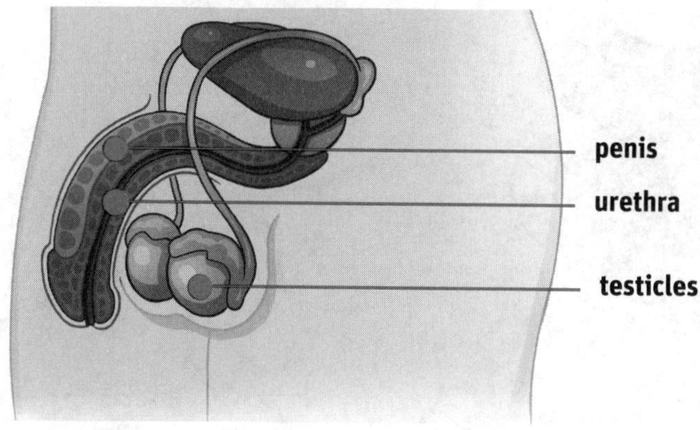

animal groups

mammals

birds

fish

reptiles

amphibians

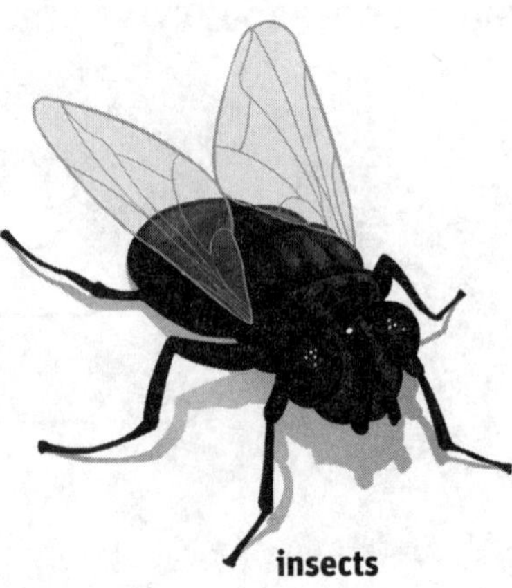

insects

animal groups

vertebrates

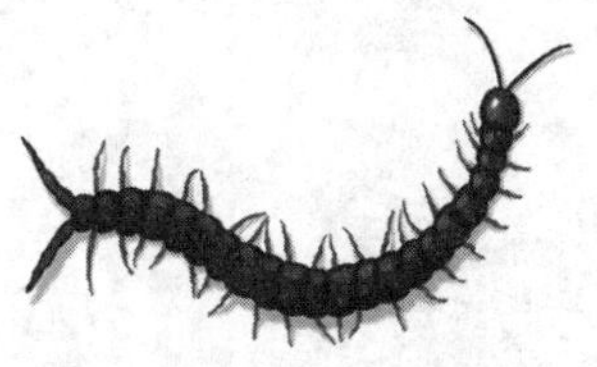

invertebrates

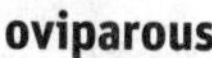

oviparous

viviparous

herbivores

carnivores

omnivores

mammals

tiger
lion
giraffe
elephant
donkey
sheep
cow
zebra
bear
monkey
kangaroo
rabbit
goat
dolphin
leopard
lamb
squirrel
wolf
deer
seal
panther
pig
camel
hippopotamus

penguin

duck

hen

parrot

turkey

flamingo

pigeon

peacock

budgerigar

goose

seagull

fish and reptiles

FISH

sardine

salmon

tuna

shark

trout

REPTILES

tortoise

crocodile

chameleon

snake

lizard

turtle

amphibians and insects

AMPHIBIANS

frog

salamander

INSECTS

spider

ladybird

ant

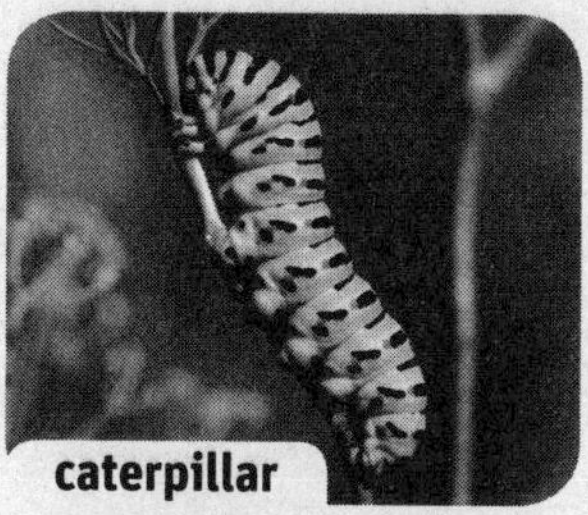

caterpillar

fly

grasshopper

butterfly

bee

beetle

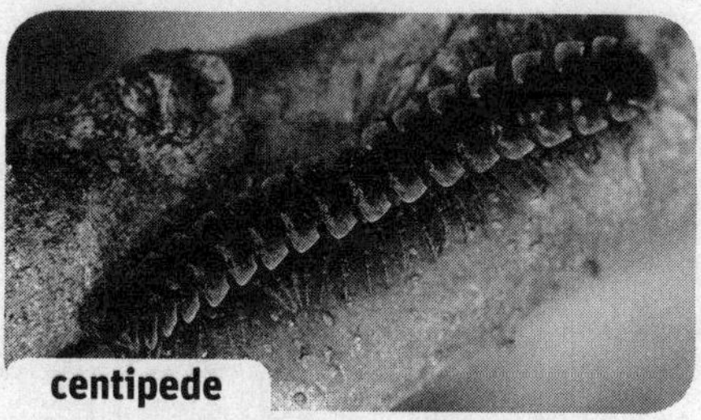

centipede

cricket

plants

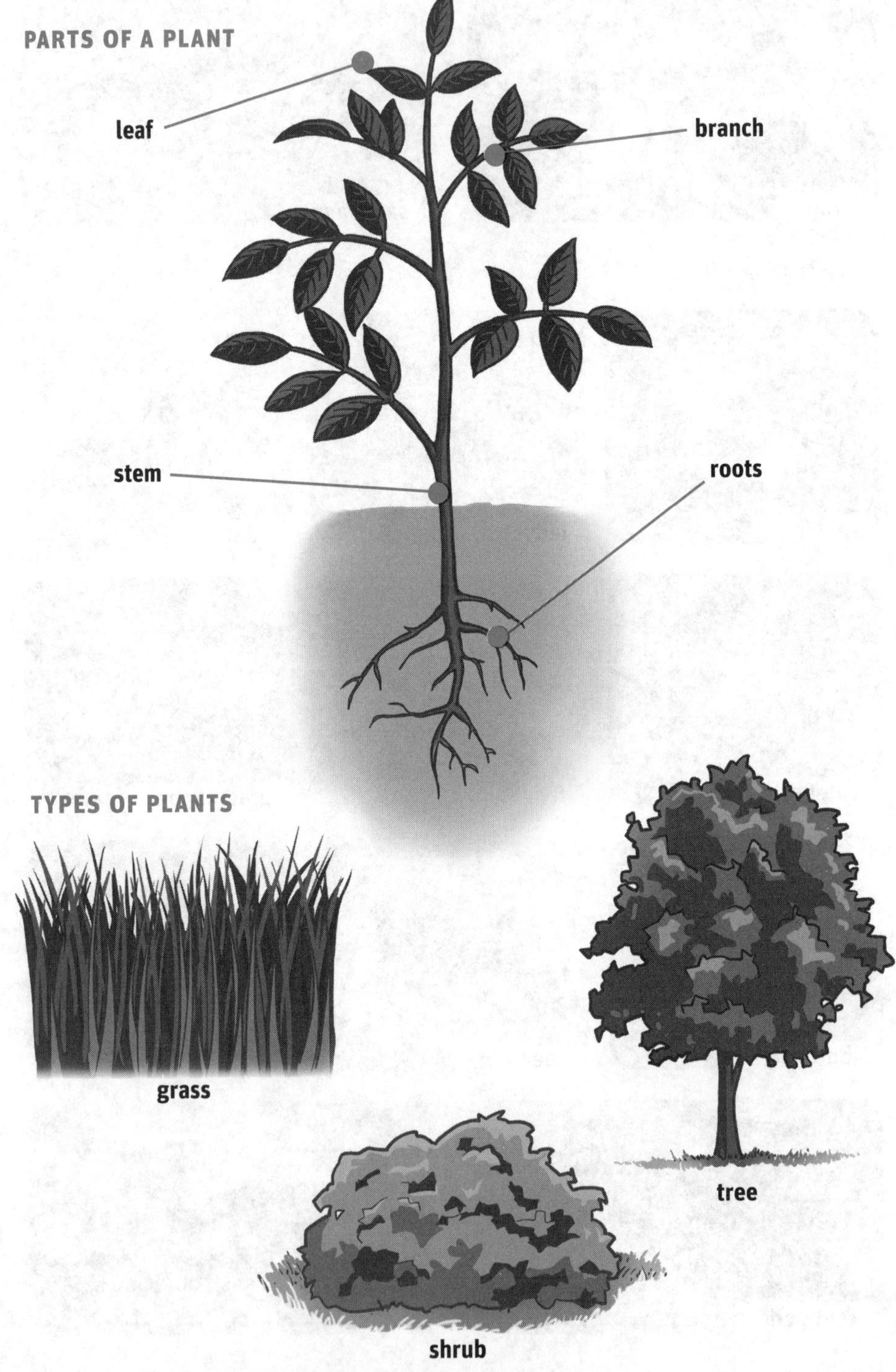
PARTS OF A PLANT
leaf
branch
stem
roots
TYPES OF PLANTS
grass
tree
shrub

PARTS OF A FLOWER

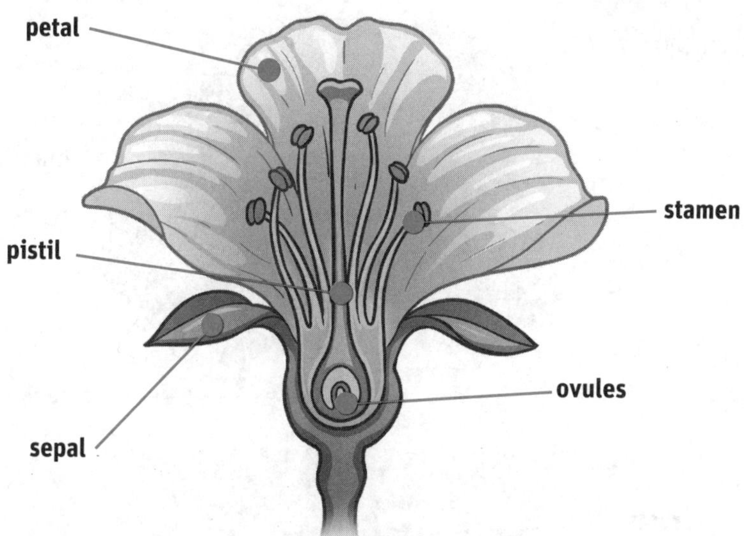

petal
stamen
pistil
ovules
sepal

FLOWERS

geranium
tulip
sunflower
orchid
rose
poppy
carnation

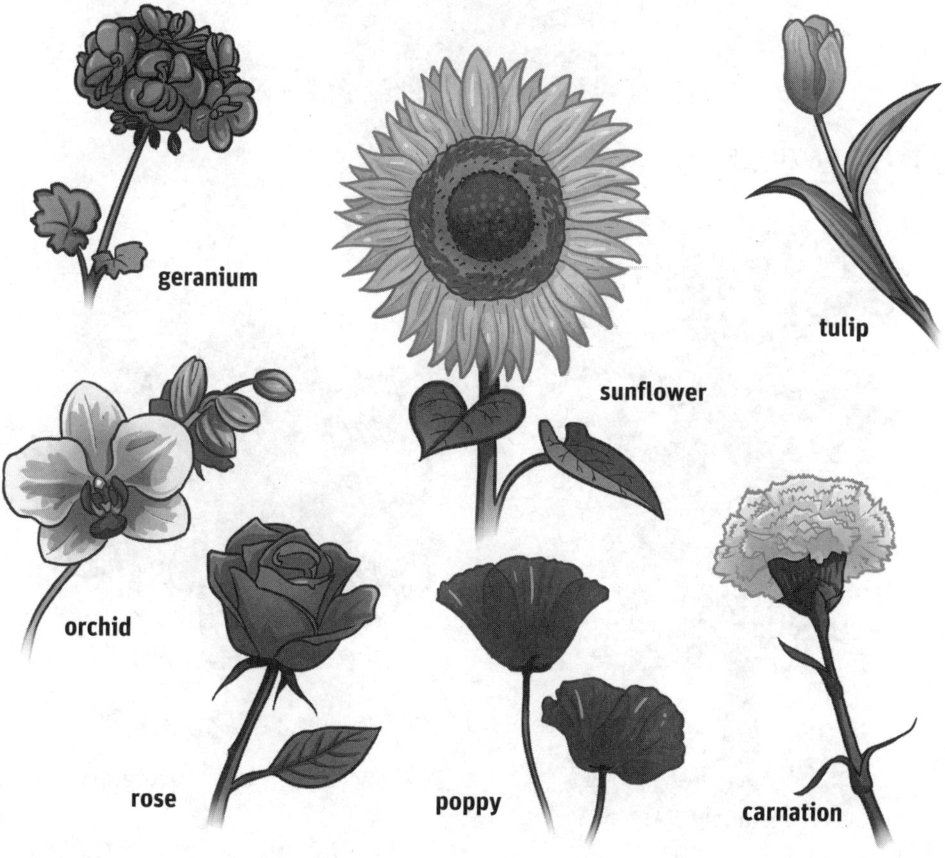

trees

PARTS OF A TREE

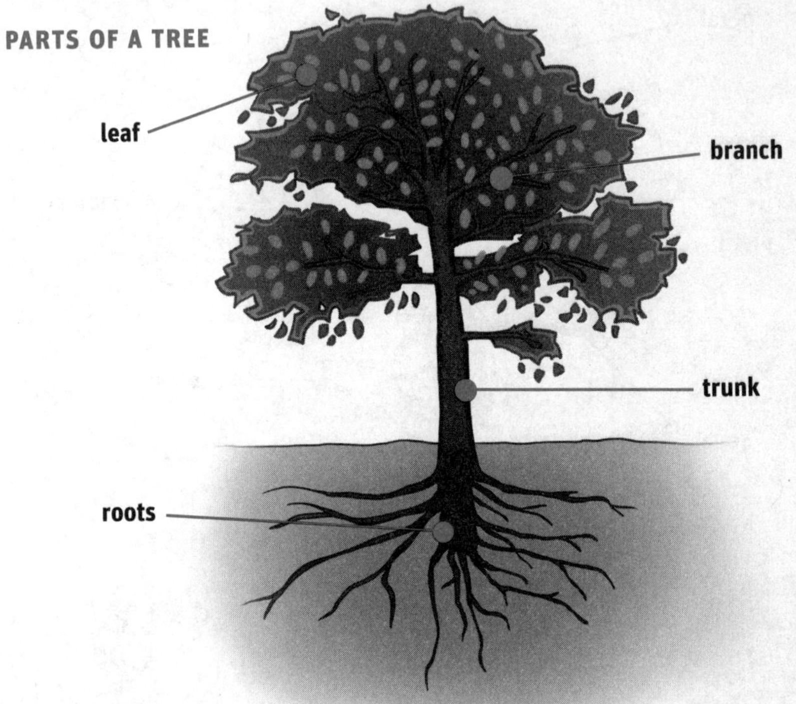

TYPES OF TREES

trees

almond tree

elm tree

pine tree

fir tree

oak tree

palm tree

coconut palm

banana tree

apple tree

orange tree

fruits

grape
raspberry
strawberry
orange
lemon
grapefruit
pear
apple
cherry
mango
pineapple
coconut
banana
fig
plum
peach
melon
watermelon

vegetables

lettuce

cabbage

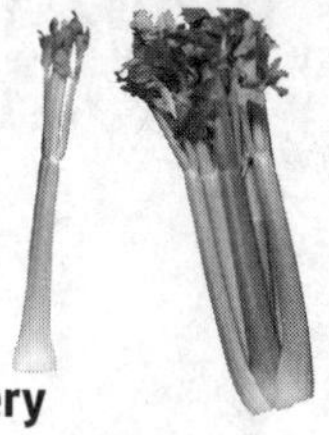

celery

carrot

radish

courgette

broccoli

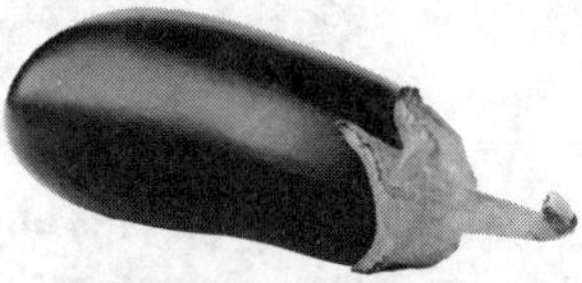

aubergine

spinach

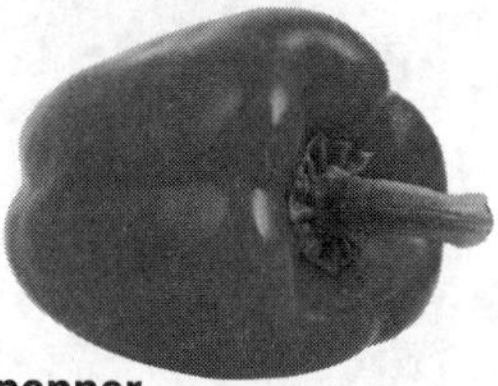

pepper

asparagus

potato

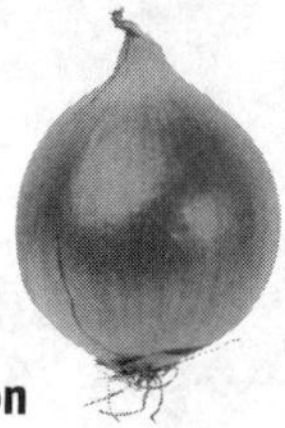

onion

tomato

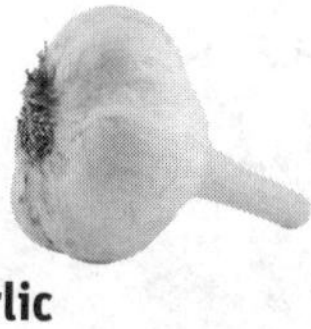

garlic

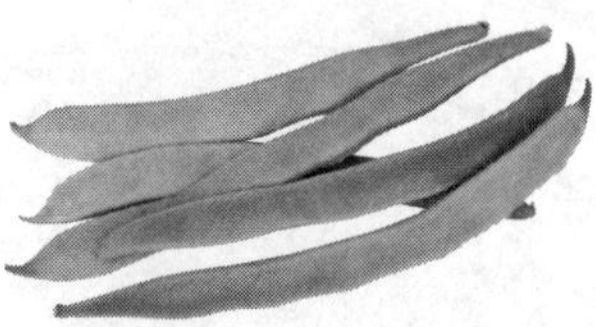

beans

mushroom

peas

the water cycle

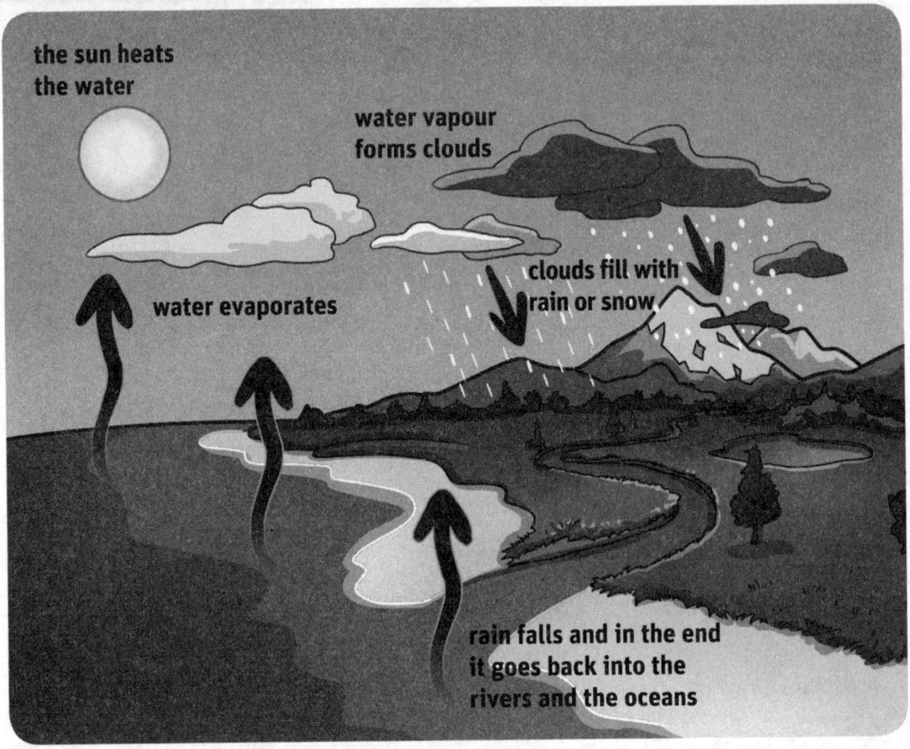

the sun heats
the water
water vapour
forms clouds
clouds fill with
rain or snow
water evaporates
rain falls and in the end
it goes back into the
rivers and the oceans

melting
evaporation
solid
liquid
gas
solidification
condensation

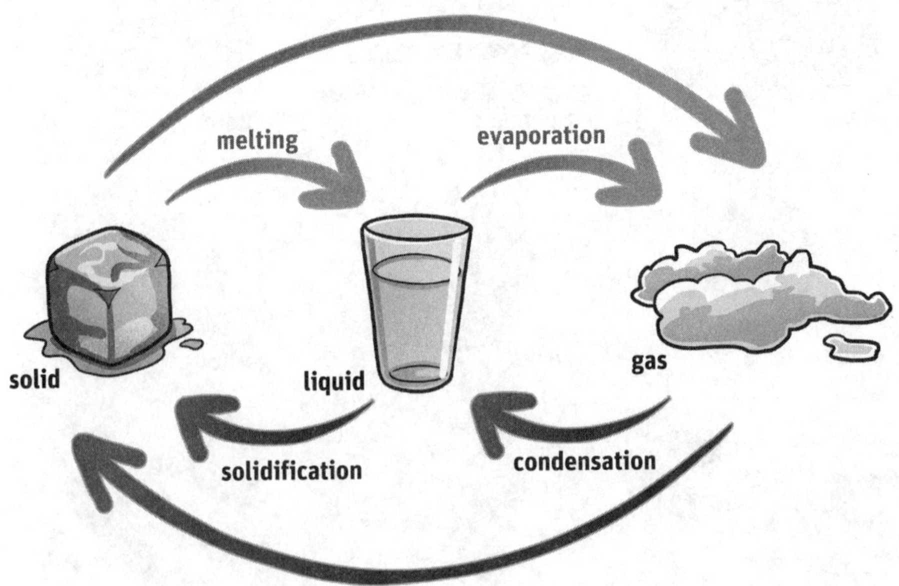

sources of energy

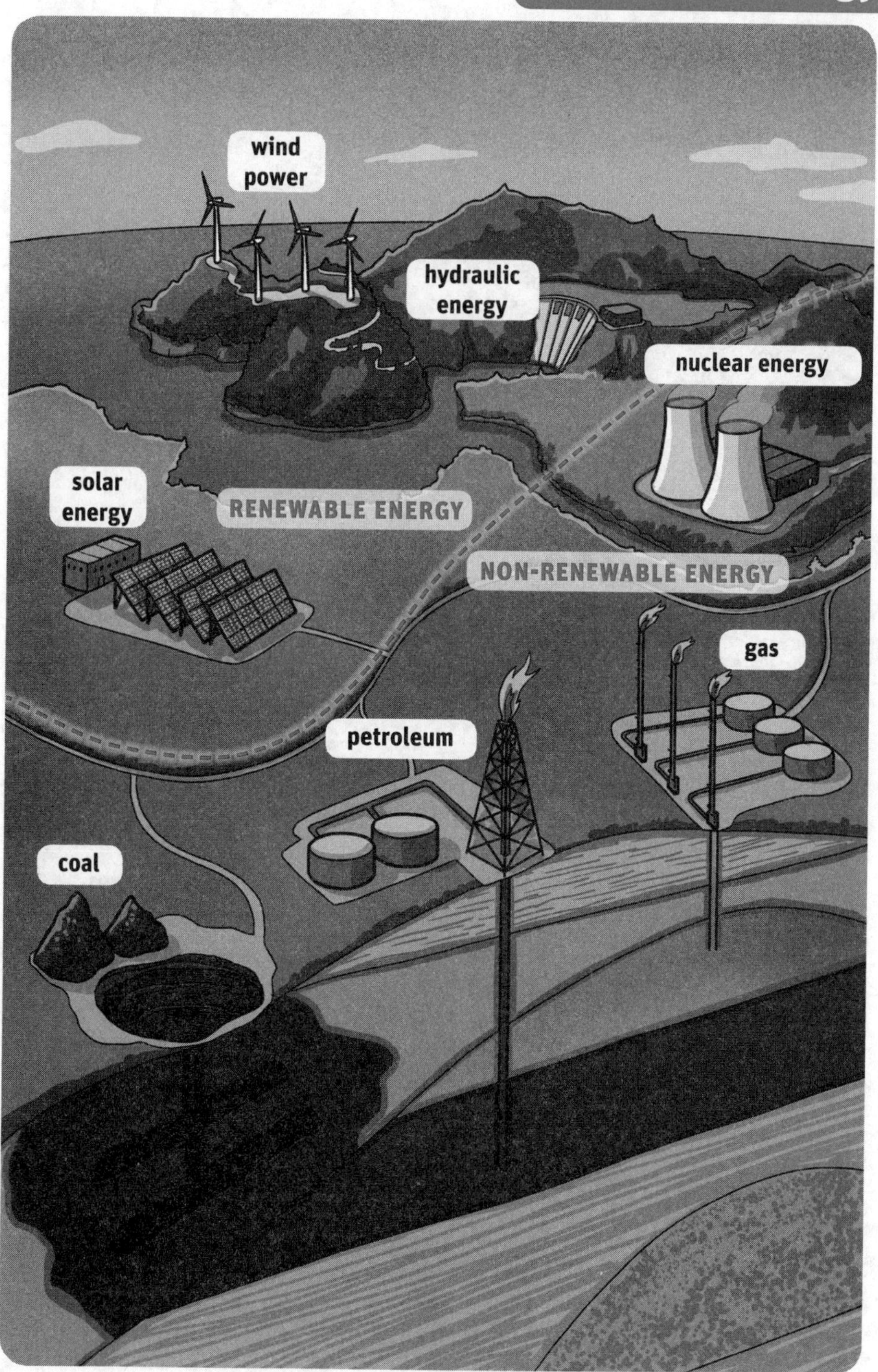

laboratory

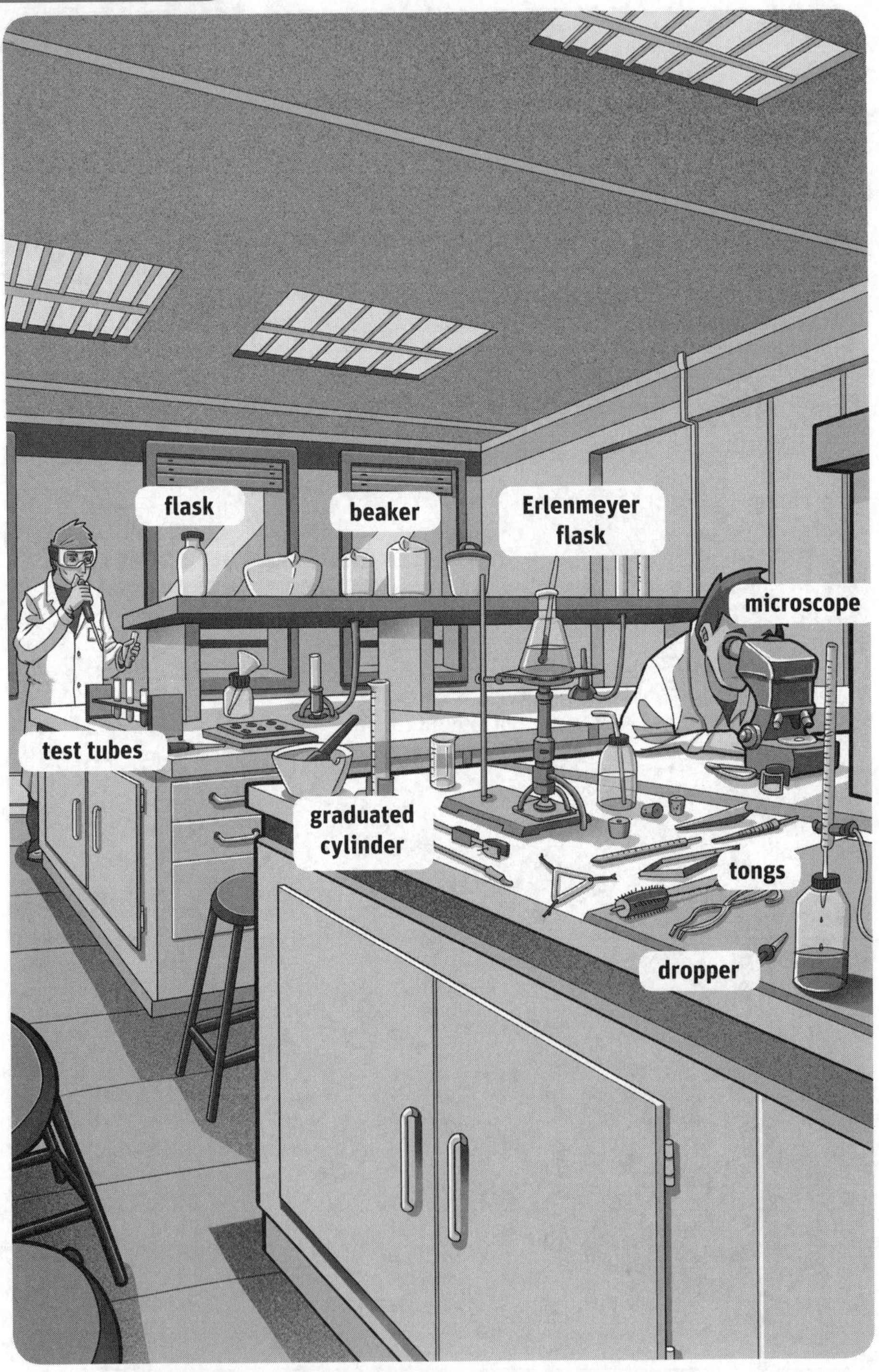
flask
beaker
Erlenmeyer flask
microscope
test tubes
graduated cylinder
tongs
dropper

bicycle and car

BICYCLE

CAR

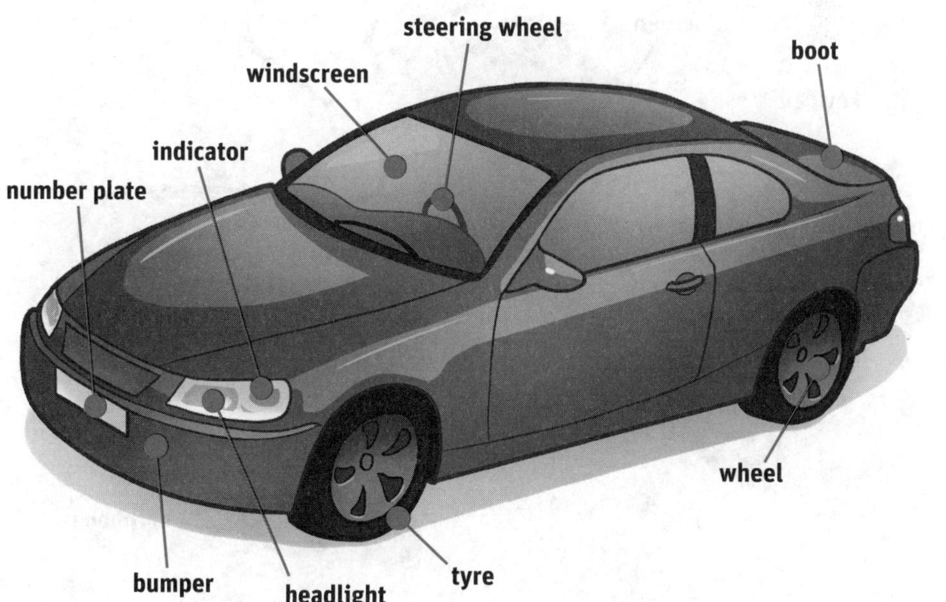

electronics

COMPUTER

MOBILE PHONE

inventions

printing press

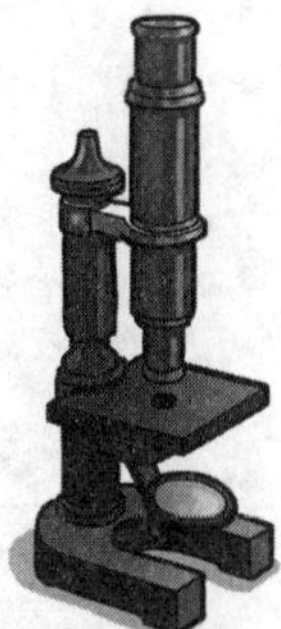
microscope

telephone

steam engine

television

gramophone

radio

mobile phone

computer

coastal landscape

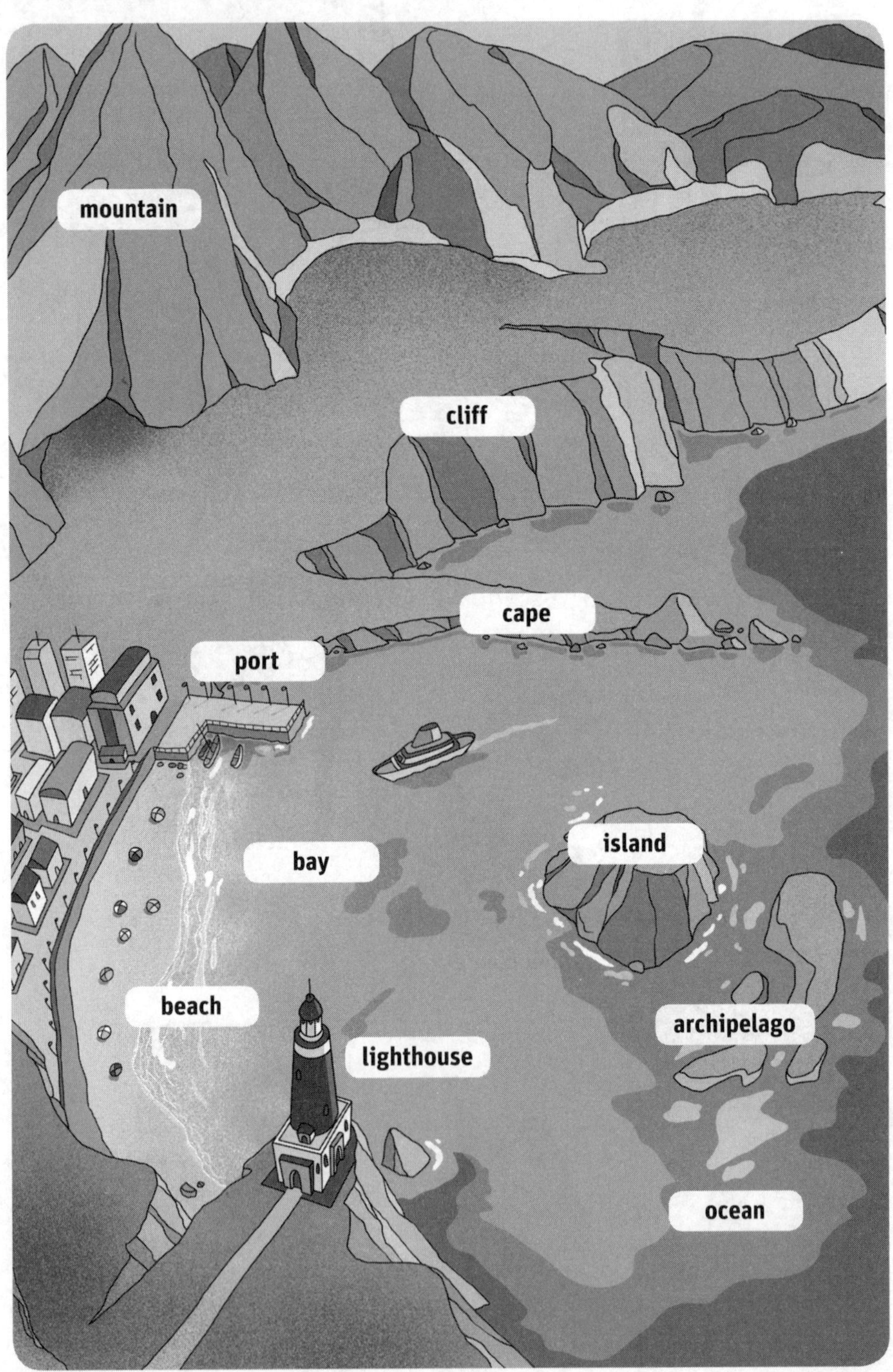

mountain landscape

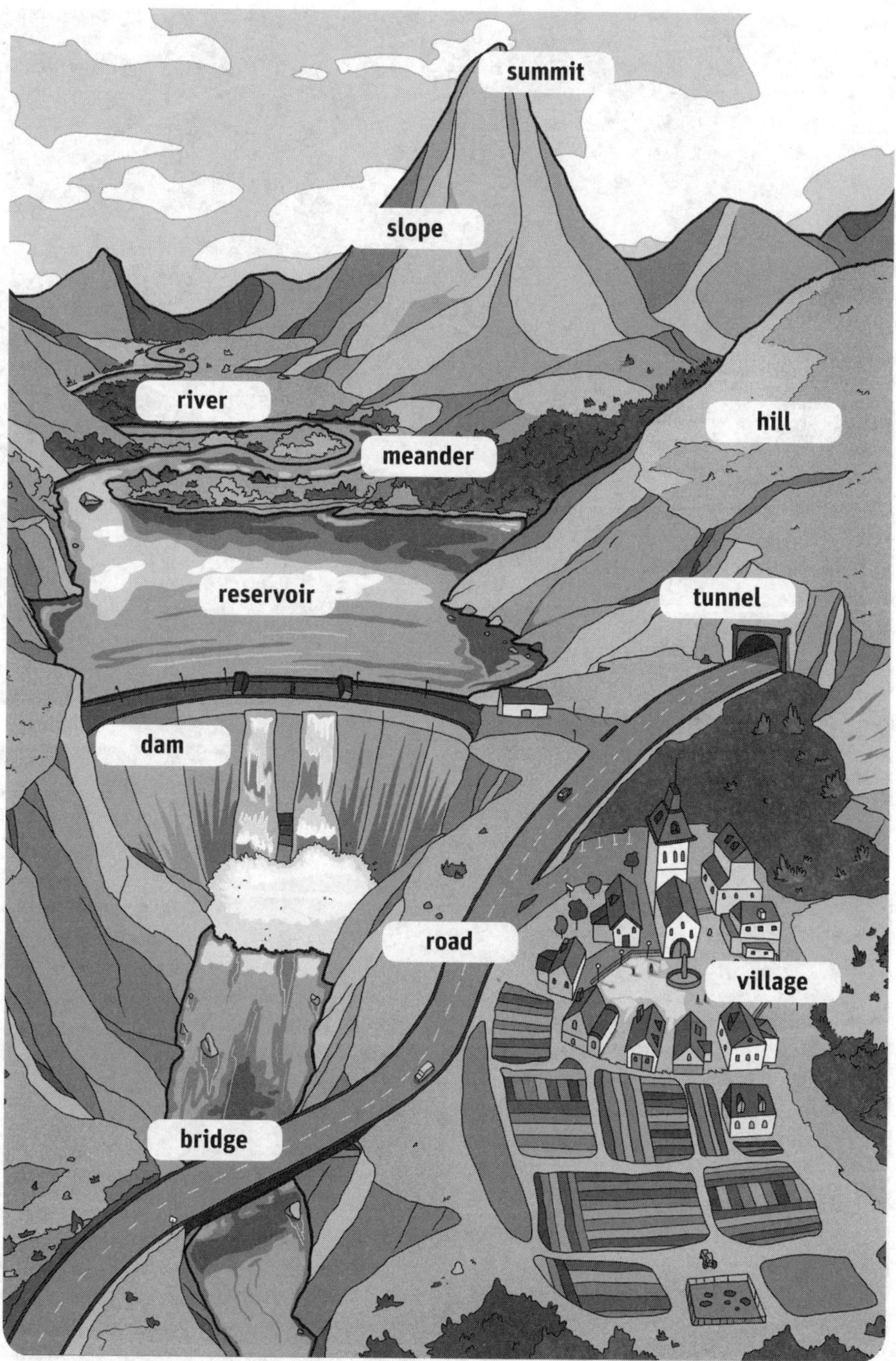

the Solar system

the Solar system

the movement of the Earth

THE MOVEMENT OF THE EARTH

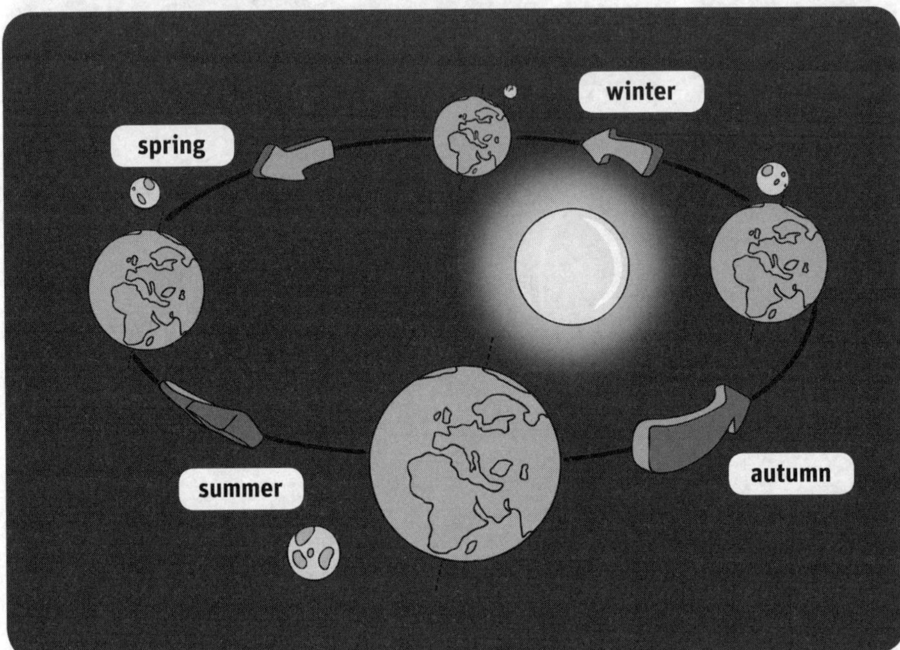

THE MOON

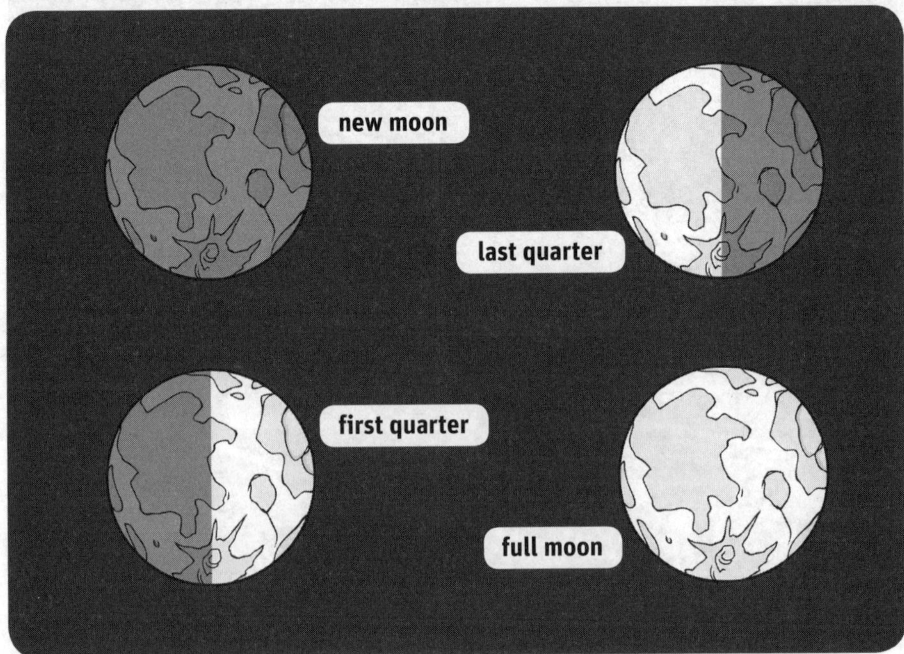

ATMOSPHERE

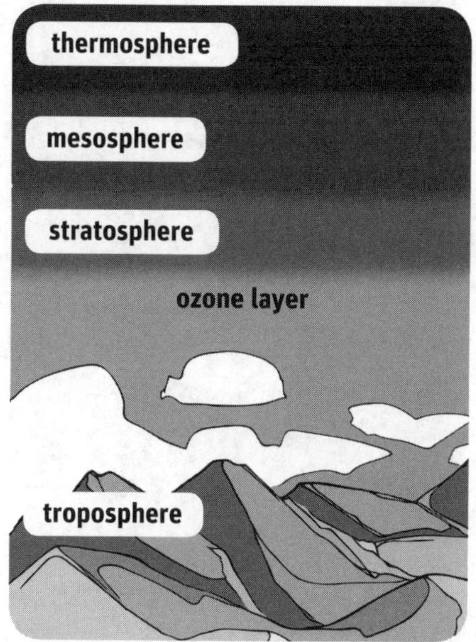

GEOSPHERE

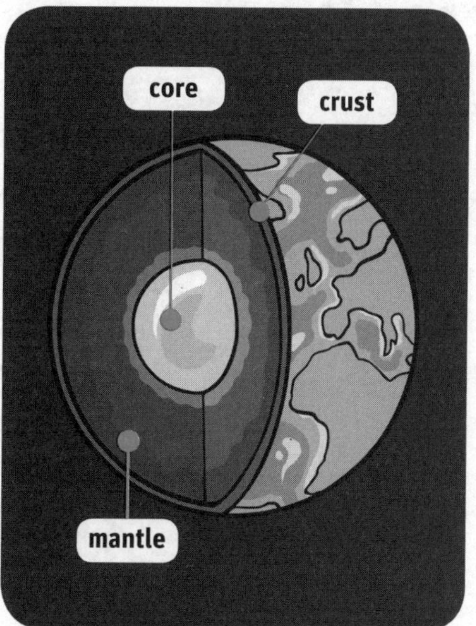

HEMISPHERE

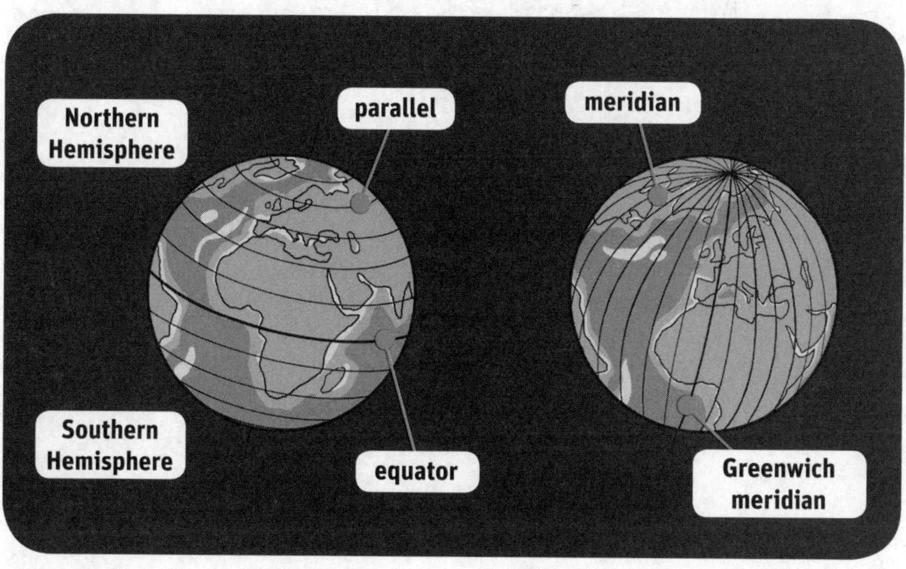

US and Canada relief map

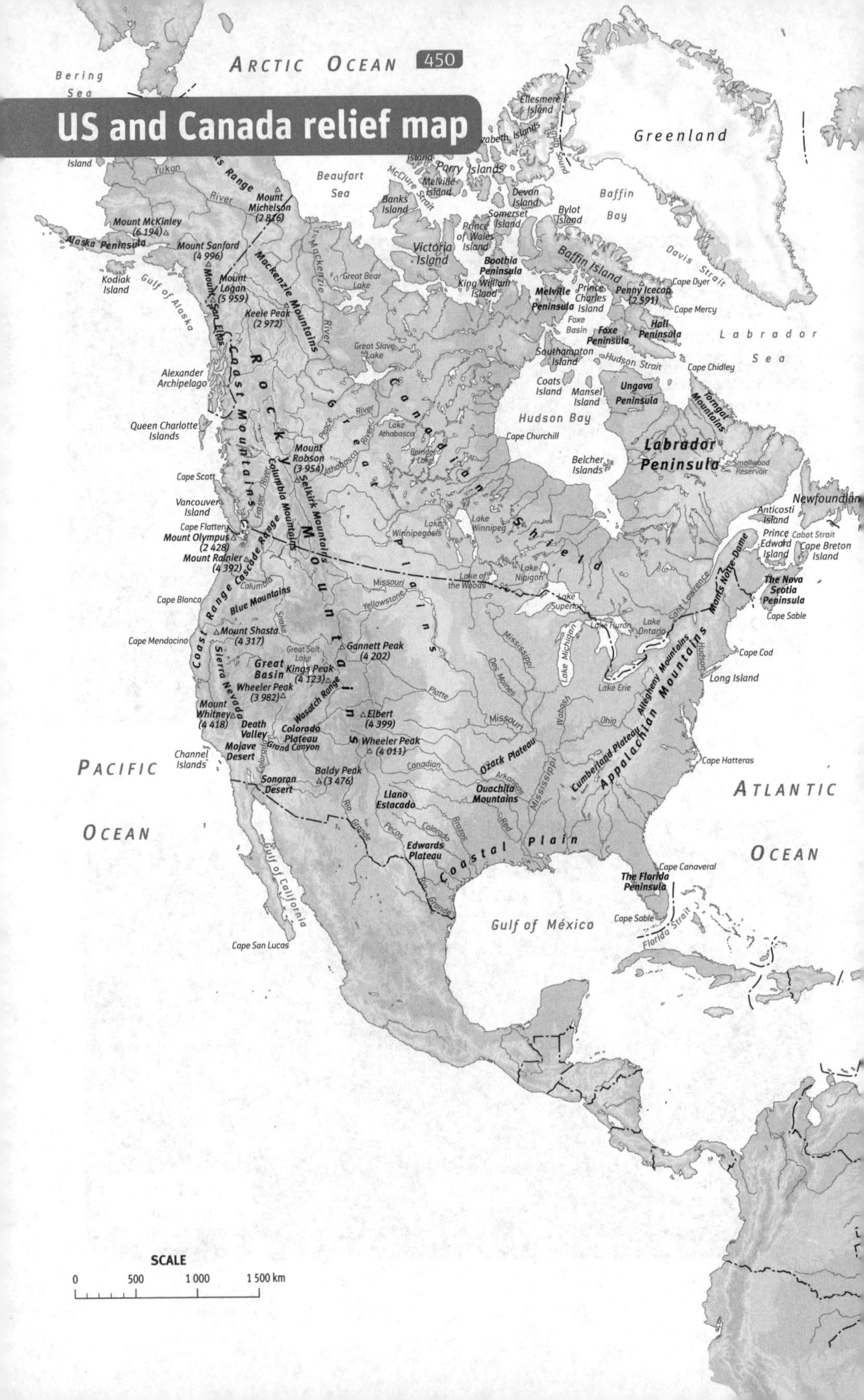

ARCTIC OCEAN
Bering Sea
Island
Yukon
River
Range
Mount Michelson (2 816)
Mount McKinley (6 194)
Alaska Peninsula
Mount Sanford (4 996)
Kodiak Island
Gulf of Alaska
Mount Logan (5 959)
Mount San Elias
Mackenzie Mountains
Keele Peak (2 972)
Mackenzie River
Great Bear Lake
Great Slave Lake
Alexander Archipelago
Coast Mountains
Rocky Mountains
Queen Charlotte Islands
Mount Robson (3 954)
Columbia Mountains
Selkirk Mountains
Cape Scott
Fraser River
Vancouver Island
Cape Flattery
Mount Olympus (2 428)
Mount Rainier (4 392)
Cascade Range
Columbia
Cape Blanco
Blue Mountains
Snake
Coast Range
Mount Shasta (4 317)
Cape Mendocino
Sierra Nevada
Great Salt Lake
Great Basin
Gannett Peak (4 202)
Kings Peak (4 123)
Wheeler Peak (3 982)
Wasatch Range
Mount Whitney (4 418)
Death Valley
Colorado Plateau
Grand Canyon
Elbert (4 399)
Wheeler Peak (4 011)
Mojave Desert
Colorado
Channel Islands
PACIFIC OCEAN
Sonoran Desert
Baldy Peak (3 476)
Llano Estacado
Rio Grande
Pecos
Edwards Plateau
Gulf of California
Cape San Lucas
Beaufort Sea
McClure Strait
Banks Island
Parry Islands
Melville Island
Victoria Island
Prince of Wales Island
Somerset Island
Devon Island
Ellesmere Island
Elizabeth Islands
Smith Sound
Greenland
Baffin Bay
Bylot Island
Boothia Peninsula
King William Island
Baffin Island
Davis Strait
Melville Peninsula
Prince Charles Island
Penny Icecap (2 591)
Cape Dyer
Cape Mercy
Foxe Basin
Foxe Peninsula
Hall Peninsula
Labrador Sea
Southampton Island
Hudson Strait
Cape Chidley
Coats Island
Mansel Island
Ungava Peninsula
Torngat Mountains
Hudson Bay
Cape Churchill
Labrador Peninsula
Smallwood Reservoir
Belcher Islands
Peace River
Athabasca River
Lake Athabasca
Reindeer Lake
Canadian Shield
Great Plains
Lake Winnipegosis
Lake Winnipeg
Newfoundland
Anticosti Island
Cabot Strait
Prince Edward Island
Cape Breton Island
Monts Notre-Dame
The Nova Scotia Peninsula
Cape Sable
Lake of the Woods
Lake Nipigon
Lake Superior
Missouri
Yellowstone
Saint Lawrence
Lake Huron
Lake Ontario
Lake Michigan
Mississippi
Des Moines
Allegheny Mountains
Appalachian Mountains
Hudson
Cape Cod
Long Island
Lake Erie
Platte
Missouri
Wabash
Ohio
Cumberland Plateau
Ozark Plateau
Canadian
Arkansas
Ouachita Mountains
Mississippi
Cape Hatteras
ATLANTIC OCEAN
Red
Brazos
Colorado
Coastal Plain
Cape Canaveral
The Florida Peninsula
Cape Sable
Florida Strait
Gulf of México
SCALE
0
500
1 000
1 500 km

US and Canada political map

ALASKA (U.S.A.)
Barrow
Bethel
Fairbanks
Homer
Anchorage
Dawson
YUKON TERRITORY
Whitehorse
Juneau
Inuvik
Kugluktuk (Coppermine)
Norman Wells
NORTHWEST TERRITORIES
Fort Providence
Yellowknife
NUNAVUT
Iqaluit
Fort Nelson
Arviat
Hazelton
Prince Rupert
Kitimat
BRITISH COLUMBIA
Prince George
Fort Vermilion
Uranium City
Dawson Creek
Fort McMurray
ALBERTA
Edmonton
Calgary
La Ronge
SASKATCHEWAN
Saskatoon
Yorkton
Regina
CANADA
Churchill
MANITOBA
Winnipeg
Kuujjuaq (Fort Chimo)
NEWFOUNDLAND AND LABRADOR
Goose Bay
Schefferville
St. John's
QUEBEC
Sept-Îles
Moosonee
ONTARIO
Kapuskasing
Timmins
Thunder Bay
Sudbury
Chicoutimi
Quebec
Richmond
Montreal
Ottawa
Toronto
Windsor
PRINCE EDWARD
Charlottetown
NEW BRUNSWICK
Fredericton
Moncton
Halifax
NOVA SCOTIA
Victoria
Vancouver
WASHINGTON
Seattle
Olimpia
Portland
Salem
Spokane
OREGON
Helena
MONTANA
Billings
Boise
IDAHO
Idaho Falls
NORTH DAKOTA
Bismarck
Grand Forks
Fargo
Duluth
MINNESOTA
Minneapolis
St. Paul
WISCONSIN
Green Bay
Madison
Milwaukee
MICHIGAN
Lansing
Detroit
Rapid City
Pierre
SOUTH DAKOTA
Sioux Falls
WYOMING
Cheyenne
NEVADA
Reno
Carson City
Sacramento
San Francisco
San Jose
Fresno
CALIFORNIA
Bakersfield
Los Angeles
San Diego
Las Vegas
Salt Lake City
UTAH
UNITED STATES
Denver
Colorado Springs
Pueblo
COLORADO
NEBRASKA
Omaha
Lincoln
IOWA
Des Moines
Waterloo
Chicago
Springfield
KANSAS
Topeka
Wichita
Kansas City
Saint Louis
Jefferson City
MISSOURI
ILLINOIS
INDIANA
Indianapolis
OHIO
Cleveland
Columbus
Buffalo
Albany
NEW YORK
New York
PENNSYLVANIA
Harrisburg
Philadelphia
MAINE
Augusta
Montpelier
Portland
Concord
Boston
Hartford
VERMONT
NEW HAMPSHIRE
MASSACHUSETTS
RHODE ISLAND (Providence)
CONNECTICUT
NEW JERSEY (Trenton)
DELAWARE (Dover)
MARYLAND (Annapolis)
Washington DISTRICT OF COLUMBIA
WEST VIRGINIA
Charleston
Richmond
Norfolk
VIRGINIA
Frankfort
KENTUCKY
Nashville
TENNESSEE
Memphis
NORTH CAROLINA
Raleigh
Charlotte
Greenville
Columbia
SOUTH CAROLINA
Charleston
Atlanta
Augusta
Columbus
Savannah
GEORGIA
Birmingham
Montgomery
ALABAMA
MISSISSIPPI
Jackson
Little Rock
ARKANSAS
LOUISIANA
Baton Rouge
New Orleans
Tallahassee
Jacksonville
FLORIDA
Orlando
Tampa
Cape Coral
Miami
Santa Fe
Albuquerque
NEW MEXICO
ARIZONA
Phoenix
Tucson
Tulsa
Oklahoma City
OKLAHOMA
Amarillo
Lubbock
El Paso
Fort Worth
Dallas
TEXAS
Waco
Austin
Houston
San Antonio
Laredo
Corpus Christi
PACIFIC OCEAN
ATLANTIC OCEAN
Honolulu
HAWAII

SCALE
0 500 1 000 1 500 km

international boundary
national boundary
capital city
city or town

World political map

Abbreviation of states and the capital cities

A. Albania (Tirana)
A. and B. Antigua and Barbuda (Saint John's)
Au. Austria (Viena)
B. and H. Bosnia-Herzegovina (Sarajevo)
Bel. Belgium (Brussels)
C. Croatia (Zagreb)
C. and N. St. Kitts and Nevis (Basseterre)
Cy. Cyprus (Nicosia)
D. Dominica (Roseau)
G. Grenada (Saint Georges)
H. Hungary (Budapest)
L. Liechtenstein (Vaduz)

World political map
Svalbard (Nor.)
Zemlya Frantsa-Iosifa
Severnaya Zemlya
Novaya Zemlya
Barents Sea
Russian Federation
Alaska (U.S.A.)
Sea of Okhotsk
Bering Sea
Aleutian Is. (U.S.A.)
Finland
Helsinki
Tallinn
Estonia
Riga
Latvia
Lithuania
Vilnius
R.F.
Minsk
Belarus
Moscow
Warsaw
Kiev
Ukraine
Moldova
Chisinau
Romania
Bucharest
Bulgaria
Sofia
Black Sea
Greece
Athens
Turkey
Ankara
Georgia
T'bilisi
Armenia
Yerevan
Azerbaijan
Baku
Caspian Sea
Kazakhstan
Astana
Uzbekistan
Tashkent
Turkmenistan
Ashgabat
Kyrgyzstan
Bishkek
Tajikistan
Dushanbe
Mongolia
Ulan Bator
China
Beijing
N. Korea
P'yongyang
S. Korea
Seoul
Japan
Tokyo
Cy.
Syria
Lebanon
Beirut
Damascus
Israel
Jerusalem
Amman
Jordan
Iraq
Baghdad
Iran
Tehran
Afghanistan
Kabul
Islamabad
Pakistan
Kuwait
Bahrain
Manama
Qatar
Doha
Abu Dhabi
U.A.E.
Muscat
Oman
Riyadh
Saudi Arabia
Cairo
Egypt
Red Sea
Nepal
Kathmandu
Thimbu
Bhutan
New Delhi
India
Dhaka
Bangladesh
Myanmar
Ha Noi
Laos
Vientiane
Thailand
Vietnam
Rangoon
Bangkok
Cambodia
Phnom Penh
Pacific Ocean
Ryukyu Islands (Jap.)
Philippines
Manila
Philippine Sea
Northern Mariana Islands (U.S.A.)
Guam (U.S.A.)
Marshall Islands
Delap-Uliga-Djarrit
Palikir
Federated States of Micronesia
Koror
Palau
Bairiki
Kiribati
Yaren
Nauru
Arabian Sea
Socotra (Yem.)
Andaman Is. (India)
Gulf of Bengala
Sri Lanka
Sri Jayawardenepura
Maldives
Male
Brunei
Bandar Seri Begawan
Malaysia
Kuala Lumpur
Singapore
Indonesia
Jakarta
Papua New Guinea
Port Moresby
Dili
East Timor
Solomon Islands
Honiara
Funafuti
Tuvalu
Samoa
Apia
Wallis and Futuna (Fra.)
Port Vila
Vanuatu
Coral Sea
Suva
Fiji
Tonga
Nuku'Alofa
New Caledonia (Fra.)
Libya
Chad
Ndjamena
Sudan
Khartoum
Eritrea
Asmara
Sanaa
Yemen
Djibouti
Addis Ababa
Ethiopia
South Sudan
Juba
Somalia
Mogadishu
Central African Republic
Bangui
Uganda
Kampala
Kenya
Nairobi
Rwanda
Kigali
Bujumbura
Burundi
Dem. Rep. of Congo
Tanzania
Dodoma
Seychelles
Victoria
British Indian Ocean Territory
Cocos Islands (Aut.)
Christmas Island (Aut.)
Moroni
Comoros
Mayotte (Fra.)
Zambia
Lusaka
Lilongwe
Malawi
Harare
Zimbabwe
Mozambique
Madagascar
Antananarivo
Mauritius
Port Louis
Reunión (Fra.)
Botswana
Gaborone
Pretoria
Maputo
Mbabane
Swaziland
Bloemfontein
Maseru
Lesotho
Republic of South Africa
Indian Ocean
Australia
Canberra
Tasman Sea
New Zealand
Wellington
Ile Amsterdam (Fra.)
Ile Saint Paul (Fra.)
Prince Edward Island (R.S.)
Iles Crozet (Fra.)
Iles Kerguelen (Fra.)
Heard Island (Aut.)
Ocean
international boundary
capital city
Lu. Luxembourg (Luxembourg)
M. Macedonia (Skopje)
Mon. Montenegro (Podgorica)
Neth. Netherlands (Amsterdam)
Cz. R. Czech Republic (Prague)
R. F. Russian Federation (Moscow)
S. Serbia (Belgrade)
S. L. St. Lucia (Castries)
Sl. Slovenia (Ljubljana)
Sla. Slovakia (Bratislava)
Sw. Switzerland (Bern)
S. M. San Marino (San Marino)

the English-speaking world

ARCTIC
ALASKA (U.S.A.)
CANADA
Quebec
UNITED KINGDOM
REPUBLIC OF IRELAND
UNITED STATES OF AMERICA
ATLANTIC OCEAN
GIBRALTAR (U.K.)
Bermuda (U.K.)
BAHAMAS
Hawaiian Islands (U.S.A.)
PUERTO RICO (U.S.A.)
BELIZE
JAMAICA
GAMBIA
PACIFIC OCEAN
GUAYANA
SIERRA LEONE
LIBERIA
GHANA
KIRIBATI
AMERICAN SAMOA
Falkland Islands (U.K.)
Scale
0 1 000 2 000 3 000 4 000 km
ANTARCTIC

The English-speaking world

- Countries and territories where English is official language and mother tongue
- Countries and territories where English is one of the official languages

the English-speaking world

OCEAN

MALTA

PACIFIC OCEAN

Midway (U.S.A.)

PAKISTAN

INDIA

HONG KONG

NORTHERN MARIANA IS. (U.S.A.)

GUAM (U.S.A.)

SRI LANKA

PALAU

MARSHALL ISLANDS

SOUTH SUDAN

CAMEROON

UGANDA

SINGAPORE

KENYA

NAURU

SEYCHELLES

TANZANIA

PAPUA NEW GUINEA

SOLOMON ISLANDS

TUVALU

ZAMBIA

MALAWI

WESTERN SAMOA

INDIAN OCEAN

VANUATU

FIJI

ZIMBABWE

MAURITIUS

BOTSWANA

TONGA

SWAZILAND

AUSTRALIA

SOUTH AFRICA

LESOTHO

NEW ZEALAND

OCEAN

drawing tools

shapes

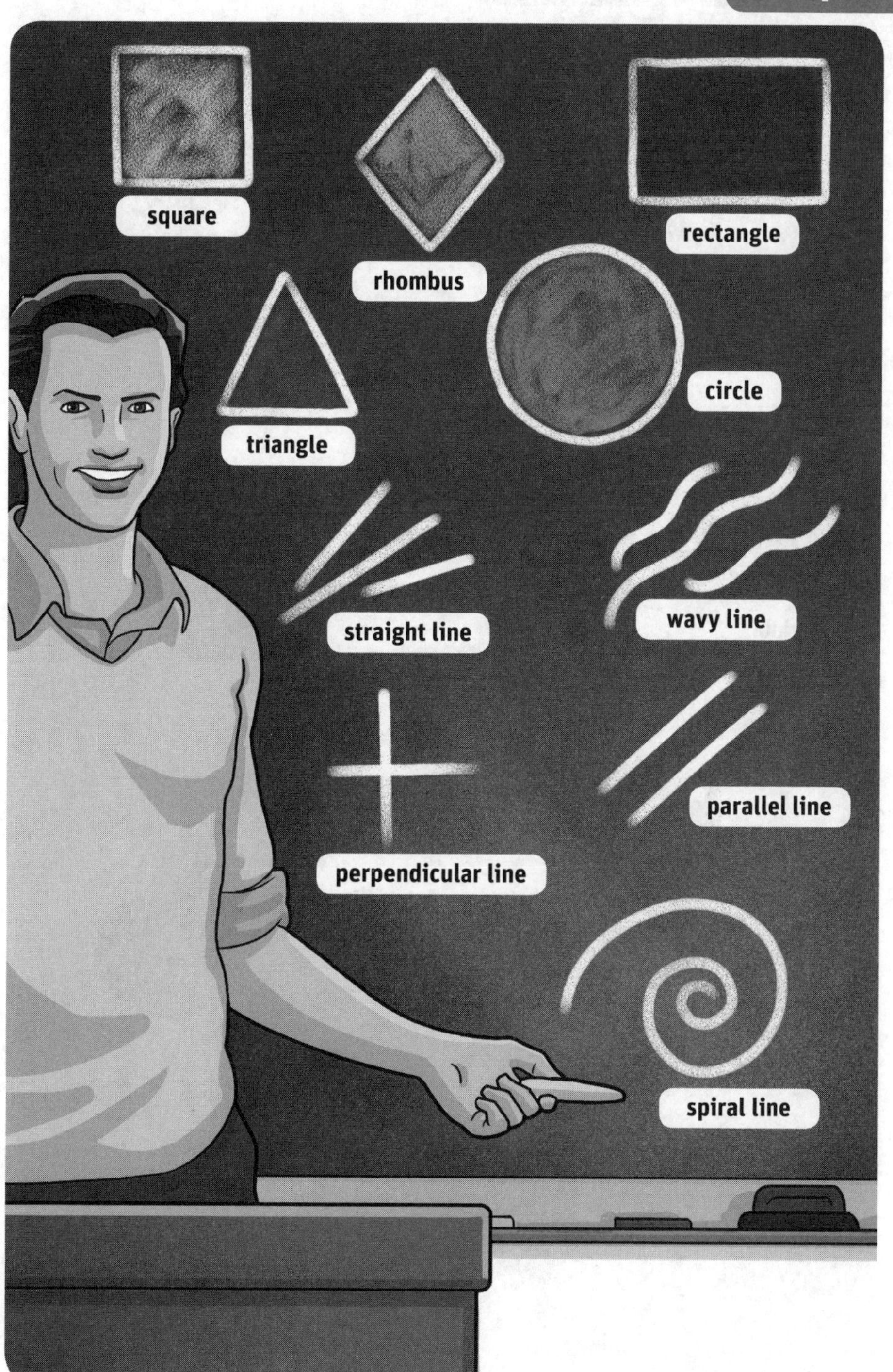
square
rhombus
rectangle
triangle
circle
straight line
wavy line
perpendicular line
parallel line
spiral line

musical instruments

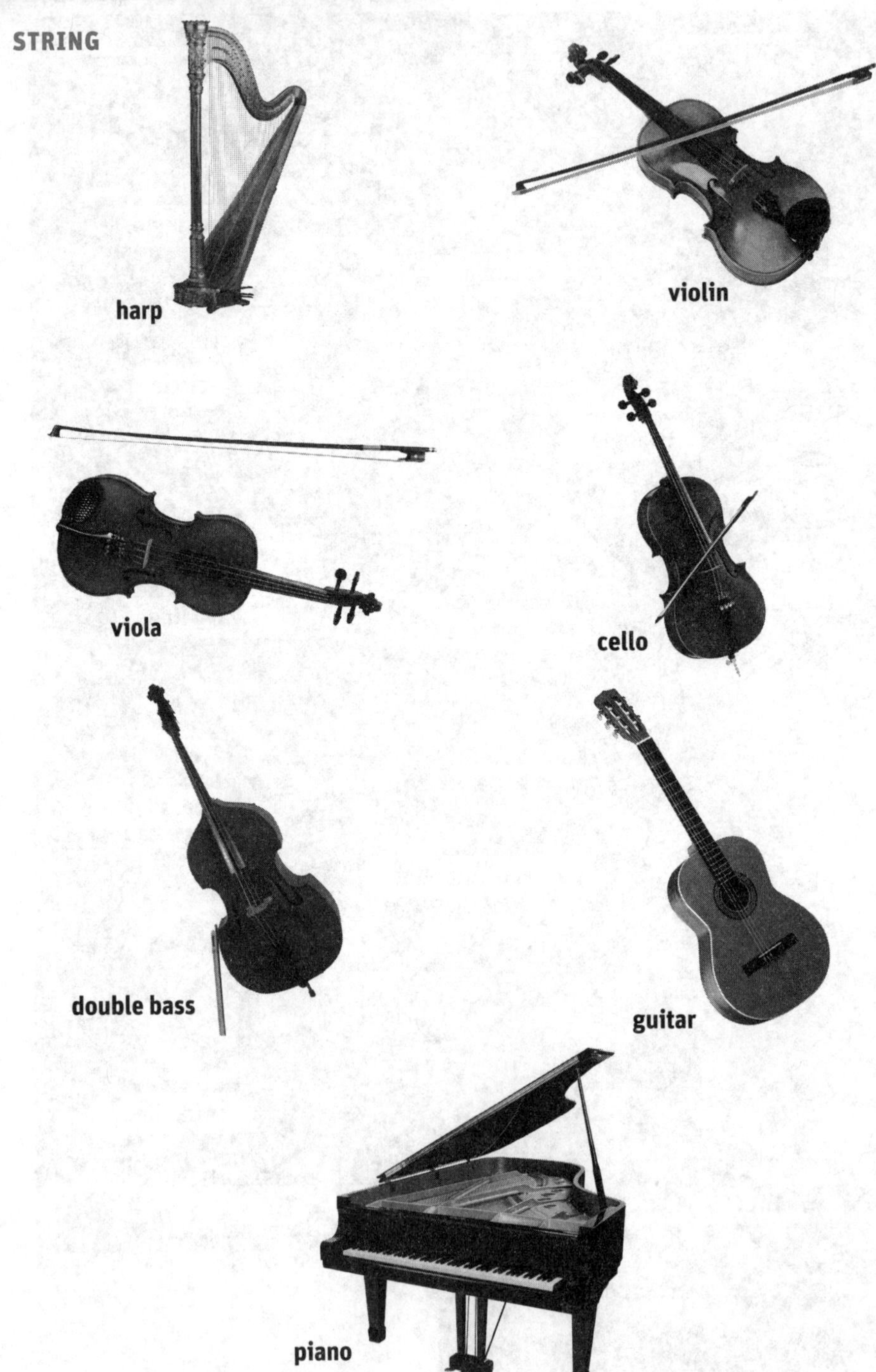

musical instruments

PERCUSSION

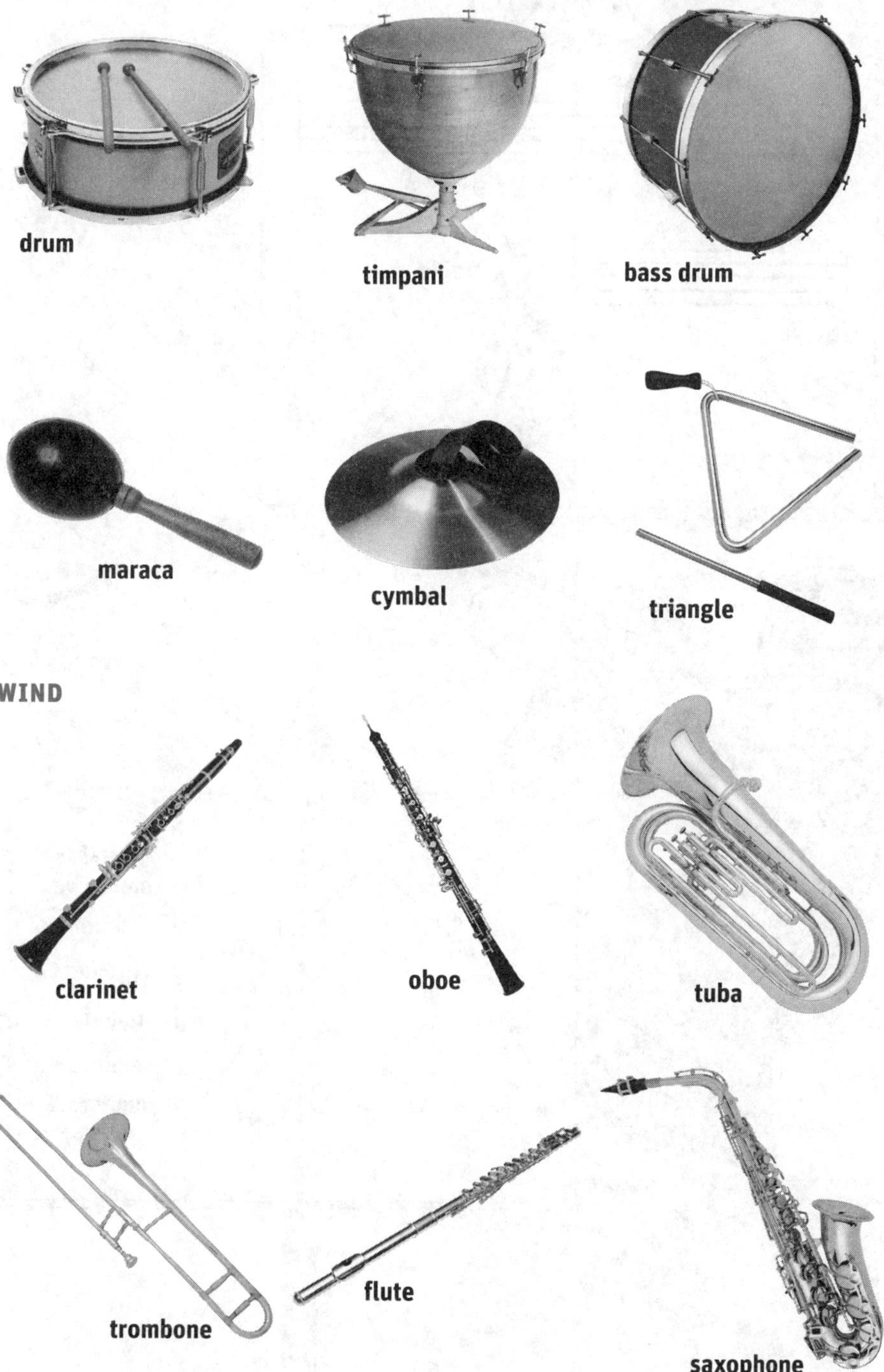

musical symbols

CONVERSATION GUIDE

The weather

What's the weather like?

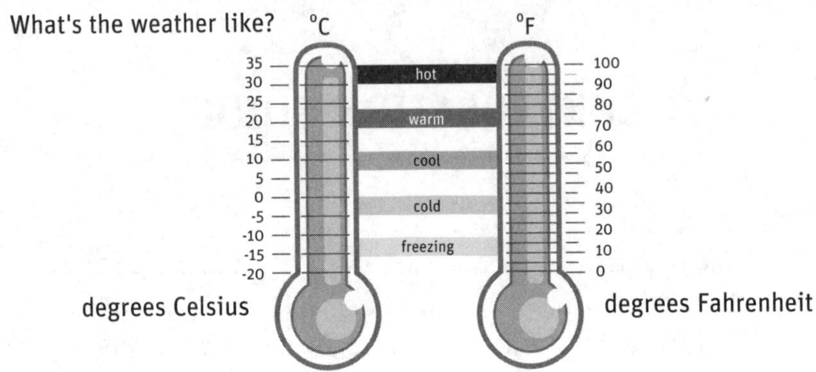

Glossary

weather forecast	thick / dense fog
sunny	storm
clear	heavy shower
unpleasant	drizzle
cloudy	rainbow
windy	foggy
snowy	It's pouring down.
rainy	It looks like rain.

Conversations

- It's hot today, isn't it?
- Yes, it is. Do you think it will last?
- I hope not. I'm roasting.

- What a lovely warm day! / Isn't it a nice day?
- Yes, it is. We've been lucky with the weather this week.

- It's windy today, isn't it?
- It certainly is. Is it always this windy here?
- No, it's blowing a real gale today.

- It's very cloudy today. Is it raining?
- No, just drizzling. It won't last long.
- Do you think the sun will come out later?
- Maybe. The forecast says it will clear up inthe afternoon, but they're usually wrong.

- What a gray day! Do you think it is going to rain?
- I think so. / Probably. The forecast is heavy showers.
- I've been here two weeks and I haven't seen the sun yet! The weather's been awful.

- It's pouring down!
- Yes, I'm soaked. Does it usually rain so much?
- It rains quite a lot here, but we've had particularly bad weather this month.

- It's cold today, isn't it?
- I'm freezing. / It's freezing. I'm not used to this.
- Yes, it's not very pleasant, is it? We get an easterly wind that brings in the cold from ...

In class

Glossary

to mean	to take an exam
to do the homework	to pass
to underline	to fail
to summarize	to get an A, B, C, D, E
to study	subject
to check / go over	

Asking the teacher

- What does ________ mean?
- How do you say ________ in English?
- How do you pronounce that word?
- I don't understand you. Could you repeat that sentence, please?
- Could you speak more slowly, please?
- I'm sorry, I don't understand.
- Could / Would you please spell it for me?
- Is this correct, please?
- May I go to the restroom?
- How much time do we still have before the bell rings?

Introductions

Introducing yourself

Introducing someone

INFORMAL

FORMAL

Let me introduce you. Sara, this is Robert. Robert, this is Sara.

How do you do. Pleased to meet you.

How do you do. Pleased to meet you.

Greetings, congratulations

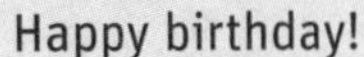

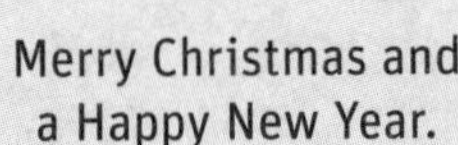

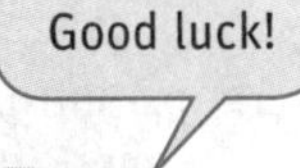

Sorry! Excuse me... Pardon?

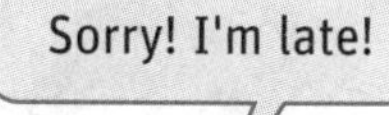

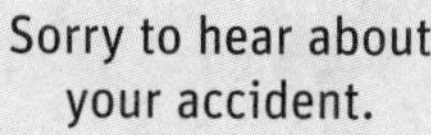

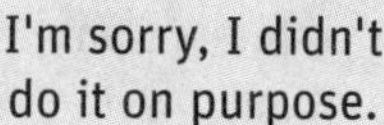

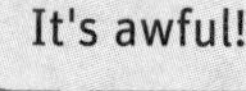

Directions

Glossary

intersection	stop sign
opposite	yield
traffic circle	crosswalk
straight ahead	cul-de-sac
to carry on	hill / slope
to turn	sidewalk
stoplights	perpendicular
turning	U-turn

Asking directions

- Excuse me, can you tell me where the ________ is?
- Excuse me, can you tell me the way to ________ , please?

Giving directions

- It's up there, on the right.
- Certainly. You go straight ahead until you get to the stoplights, and then turn left ...
- Carry on down this road and take the second turn on the right. Then when you pass the next intersection, it'll be on your left.
- Sorry, I don't live here.

Asking "How far...?"

- Is it far? / How far is it?
- How long will it take to get there?
- It's about a ten-minute walk.
- It's just around the corner.
- How are you going? On foot or by car?
- When you get to the intersection, ask again.
- It's a long way. You need to take the bus.

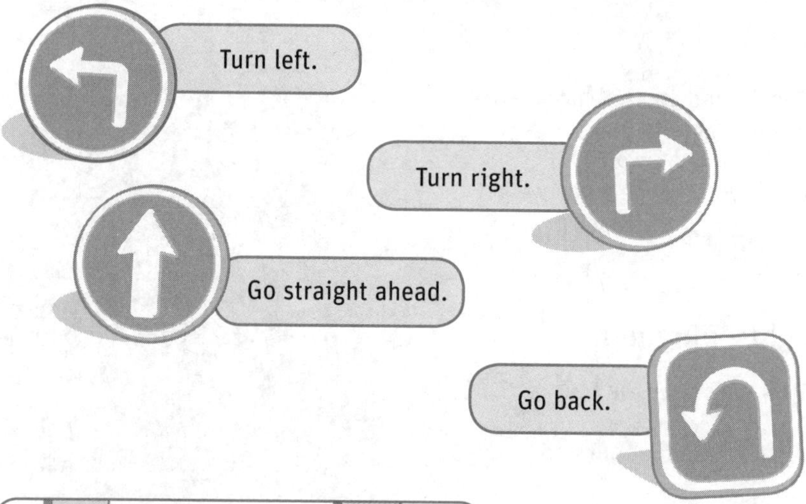

Turn left.

Turn right.

Go straight ahead.

Go back.

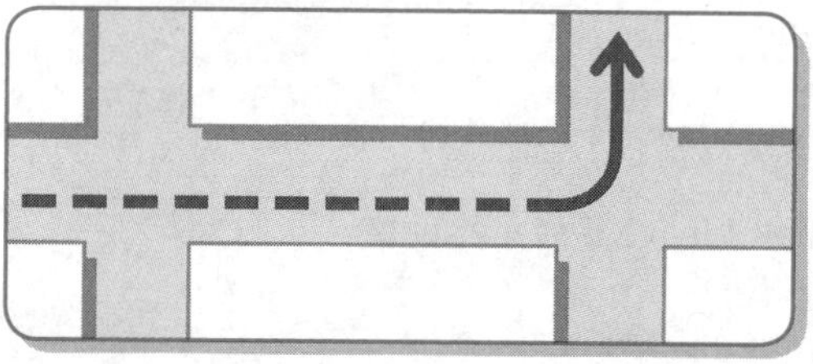

The second turn on the left.

Transportation

Asking about transportation

- What's the best way to go / get to ________ ? By bus or by subway?
- Is there a direct bus / train to ________ ?
- No, you need to take a bus / train to ________ and then change.
- Where is the railway station, please?
- Where can I get / catch a bus to ________ ?
- What number bus do I need to go to ________ ?

On the bus

- How much is it to ________ ?
- Does this bus go to ________ ?
- Can / could you tell me where / when to get off, please?
- Could you tell me when we get to ________ , please?

Sightseeing tours

- How long does the tour last?
- Where does the tour end?
- Which sights are included in the tour?
- May I get off and get on as many times as I want to?
- May I keep the brochure or shall I leave it at my seat?

At the railway / bus station

- Where is the ticket office, please?
- Can I have a single / return ticket to ________, please?
- 1st class or 2nd class?
- Returning when?
- Can I have a weekly pass, please?
- For what zones?
- What zone is Fisherman's Wharf in?

The subway

- Where's the nearest subway station, please?
- What time is the last train back, please?
- Where are the elevators / escalators?
- What line is it on?
- It's on the Museum of Natural History line.
- Do I have to change lines?
- Please watch your step when getting off. Be sure you do not step between the car and the platform.

On the train

- Mind the gap! / Mind the doors!
- Madam, you may have my seat.
- We apologize for the delay.
- Next stop = Change here for the Circle line.
- End of line!
- I have to change at the next station.

Restaurant

Ordering

Are you ready to order?

Yes, to begin I'd like a salad. And for my main course I'll have a steak.

Could we see the menu, please?

And for dessert, an ice cream.

How would you like your steak: rare, medium or well-done?

Paying

- Could we have the bill, please?
- Please pay at the register.
- How are you going to pay, in cash or by credit card?
- Here's your change.

At a fast food restaurant / take out

Ordering

- A large burger and french fries, please.
- Large fries or small? Any drinks?
- Yes, do you have bottled water? / What kinds of soda do you have?
- To take away or to eat here? That will be five dollars and thirty-five cents, please.

At the table

- Put the tray over there.
- Can you pass me the salt?
- Mmm! This is delicious.
- Do you have any mayonnaise for the burger?

Glossary

tray	cash register
soda / soft drink	bill
takeout food	change
large / small (french) fries	to pay in cash
well-done / medium-rare hamburger	to pay by (credit) card

Shopping for clothes

Glossary

receipt	dryer
size	iron
wool	delicate garment
cotton	tight-fitting
fiber	tailored / fitted (shirt)
to wash it by hand	fitted / tight (jacket, dress)

- I'm looking for a red sweater. / Can you show me a red sweater?
- We don't have anything in red.
- Do you have one in blue?
- What size do you wear?

Sizes

USA	United Kingdom	Latin America and Spain
Shoes		
5	3 ½	36
6	4 ½	37
6 ½	5	38
7 ½	6	39
8	6 ½	40
8 ½	7	41
9	8	42
10	9	43
11	10	44
Clothes		
6	8	36
8	10	38
10	12	40
14	14	42
14	16	44
16	18	46
18	20	48

- This is too small.
  Can you bring me one in a larger size?

- This is too big.
  Can you bring me one in a smaller size?

- OK, I'll take it. Where do I pay?
- How much is this? /
  How much are these?
- How much is it?
- Is it machine-washable?
- Can I have a receipt, please?
- Here's your dress and
  here's the receipt.

Talking on the phone

Glossary

a call	to pick up the phone
voice mail	to put someone through
beep	to call back
to ring	collect call
to phone	missed call
to dial	text / message
to hang up	MMS picture
Hold on.	signal
to be busy	battery

land line

cellphone / mobile (phone)

Making a call

- Hello.
- Hello. This is Rosa. Is John there, please?
- I think you have the wrong number.

- Can I speak to John, please?
- John's out, I'm afraid. Can I take a message?
- Can you tell him that Rosa called?

More telephone language

- I'm in the car. I'll call you back later.
- This is the voice mail of Diana Williams. I'm not available at the moment. You can leave a message and I'll get back to you as soon as possible.
- Hold on, I'll put you through.
- Can you speak a bit louder? It's a bad connection.
- Can you call back later? The line is busy.

Talking about making a call

- Did you speak to John this morning?
- No, his number was busy. I'll try again tonight.
- Did you speak to Mary?
- No, I called her, but she did not answer.
- What's the cheapest time to call abroad?
- How can I make a collect call?
- What is Sally's number?

Call me when you get here. Just let it ring once and I'll come down.

I'll send you a text where to meet.

I just got your message. I had no signal.

My battery's going. I'll have to put it on charge.

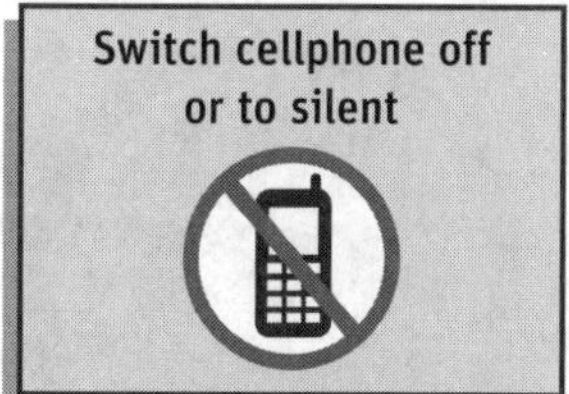

Please switch off cellphones during the movie.

I'd put it on silent so I missed your call.

Telling the time

Asking the time

- What time is it?
- What's the time, please?
- Could you tell me the time, please?

- It's 12 o'clock.
- I'm sorry. I don't have a watch.

What time is it?

- When it's exactly on the hour, we say:
  It's ________ o'clock.

It's two o'clock.

- When it's 15 minutes past, we say:
  It's (a) quarter past ________
  (or It's ________ fifteen).

It's quarter past two
(It's two fifteen).

- When it's 30 minutes past, we say:
  It's ________ thirty.

It's two thirty.

- For any time between o'clock and 30 minutes past, we say:
It's ________ past ________ .

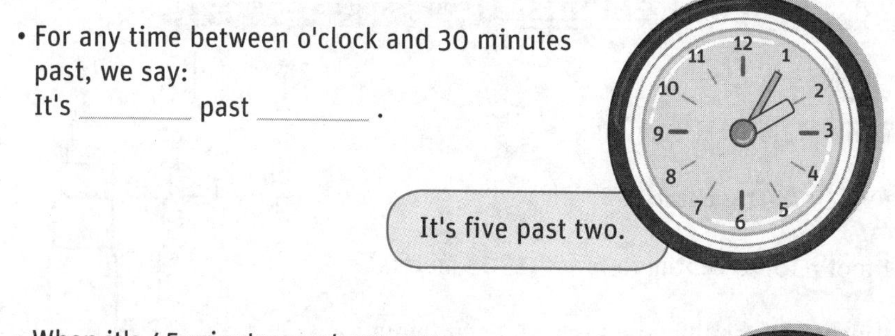

- When it's 45 minutes past, we say:
It's quarter to ________ [the next hour].
(or It's ________ forty-five).

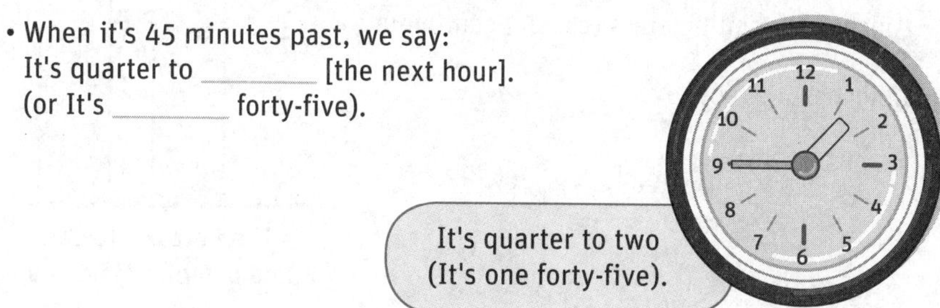

- For any time between 30 minutes past and o'clock, we say the number of minutes remaining to the next hour.

Morning or afternoon / evening

The 24-hour clock is not used in spoken English (it is mainly used in bus and train timetables and the armed forces). To distinguish between 08.00 and 20.00 hours, we say:

- It's eight (o'clock) in the morning.

- It's eight (o'clock) in the evening.

Measurements

Length

- 1 mile = 1.609 kilometers
- 1 yard= 0.914 meters
- 1 foot= 30.48 centimeters (or 0.305 meters)
- 1 inch = 25.4 millimeters (or 2.54 centimeters)
- 12 inches = 1 foot
- 3 feet = 1 yard

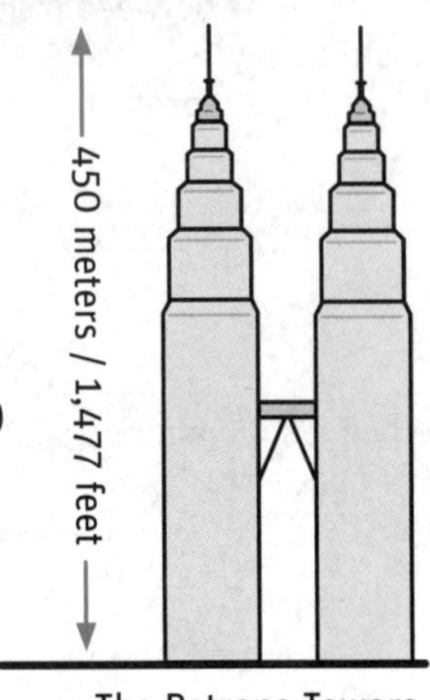

The Petrona Towers, Kuala Lumpur, Malaysia

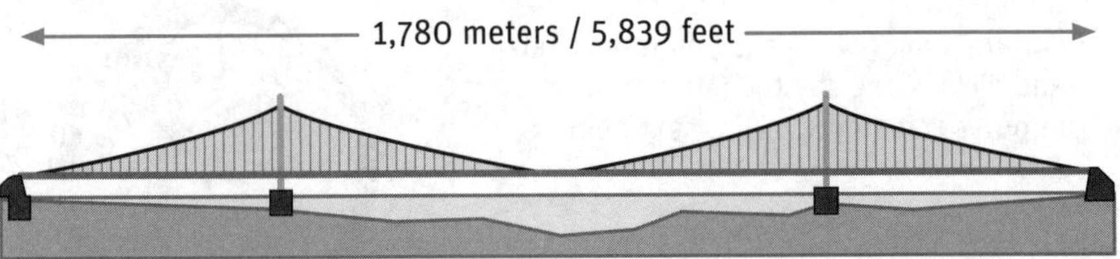

Akashi-Kaikyo Bridge, Japan

Capacity

- 1 pint = 0.568 liter
- 1 gallon = 8 pints = 4.546 liter

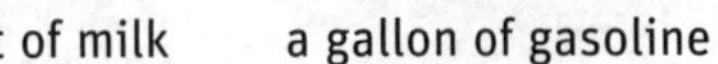

a pint of milk

a gallon of gasoline

Weight

- 1 ounce = 28.35 grams
- 1 pound = 0.454 kilograms
- 16 ounces = 1 pound

Temperature

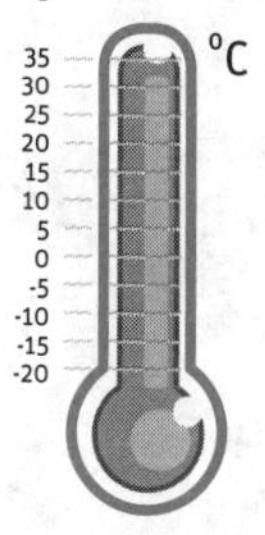

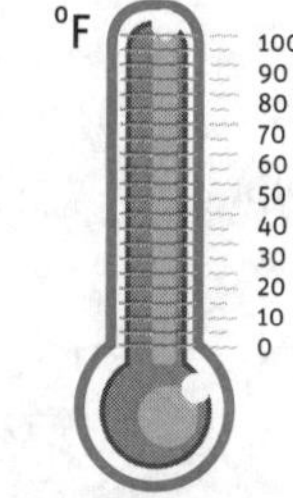

degrees Celsius degrees Fahrenheit

- From °F to °C:
  subtract 32, multiply by 5 and divide by 9.
- From °C to °F:
  multiply by 9, divide by 5 and add 32.

100 °C or 212 °F
boiling point of water

37 °C or 98.4 °F
body temperature

0 °C or 32 °F
freezing point

-273,15 °C or -459.67 °F
absolute zero

Measuring instruments

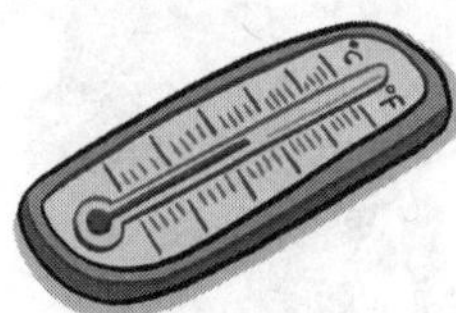

thermometer

bathroom scale

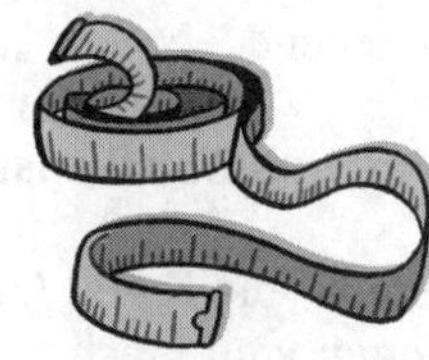

tape measure

ruler

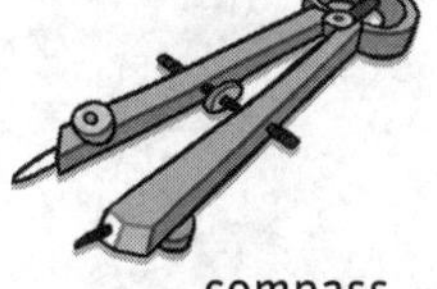

compass

set square / triangle

Daily routine

Getting up

Leaving for school

- What do you want to eat for breakfast? Breakfast is the most important meal of theday since it brings you all the energy you need.
- Hurry up. You'll miss the bus.
- Brush your teeth. And don't forget your lunch.
- Have you put all of your books in your backpack?

Coming home

- How was your day at school? Do you have much homework?

- Mom, may I go to the neighbor's before dinner? I have finished my homework.

- Ana, Carlos, clean up your room and put your clothes in the laundry basket before going to bed.

- Carlos likes to read in bed before going to sleep. The books he likes most are adventure stories.

- Don't forget to set the alarm for seven o'clock.

- Sleep well. Good night and sweet dreams.

Going shopping

At the newsstand

Glossary

newspaper
magazine
weekly
monthly

At the office supply store

- Do you have any baseball cards?
- How much is this compass?
- Do you have notebooks with ruled paper?
- Do you have any ring binders?
- Do you have a Spanish-English bilingual dictionary?

Glossary

ruler
eraser
marker
pencil
paperclips
thumbtacks

At the supermarket

- Did we bring the shopping list?
- Please get a shopping basket or even better a shopping cart.
- Please, Tom, help me put the groceries away in the cabinets, the pantry, and the fridge.

Music

piano

guitar

violin

viola

cello (violoncello)

double bass

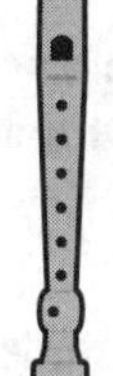

flute

saxophone

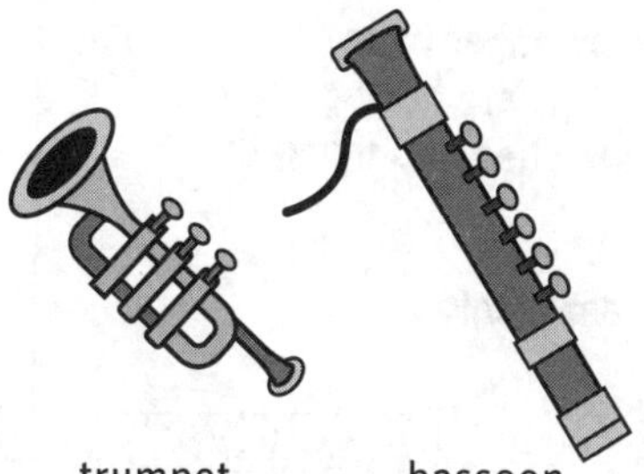

trumpet

bassoon

clarinet

drums

Glossary

- to play an instrument
- sol-fa class
- music
- notes
- work
- composer
- orchestra
- conductor
- performance
- festival

Writing letters and notes

An informal letter

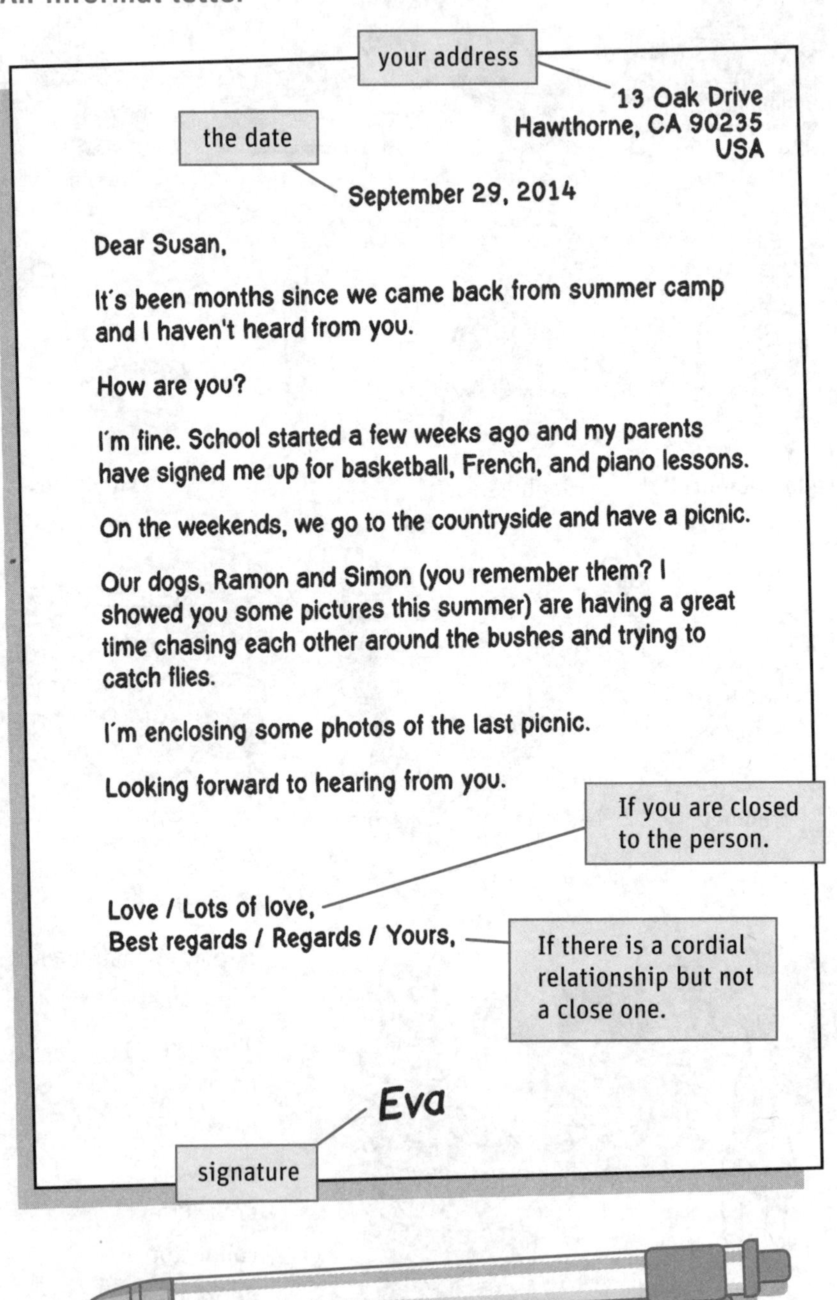

your address

13 Oak Drive
Hawthorne, CA 90235
USA

the date

September 29, 2014

Dear Susan,

It´s been months since we came back from summer camp and I haven't heard from you.

How are you?

I´m fine. School started a few weeks ago and my parents have signed me up for basketball, French, and piano lessons.

On the weekends, we go to the countryside and have a picnic.

Our dogs, Ramon and Simon (you remember them? I showed you some pictures this summer) are having a great time chasing each other around the bushes and trying to catch flies.

I´m enclosing some photos of the last picnic.

Looking forward to hearing from you.

Love / Lots of love,
Best regards / Regards / Yours,

If you are closed to the person.

If there is a cordial relationship but not a close one.

Eva

signature

Notes

Hey Pepe!

You're invited to my birthday. It will be in our backyard next Saturday at 5.

There'll be snacks, balloons, and games.

Bye,

Danny

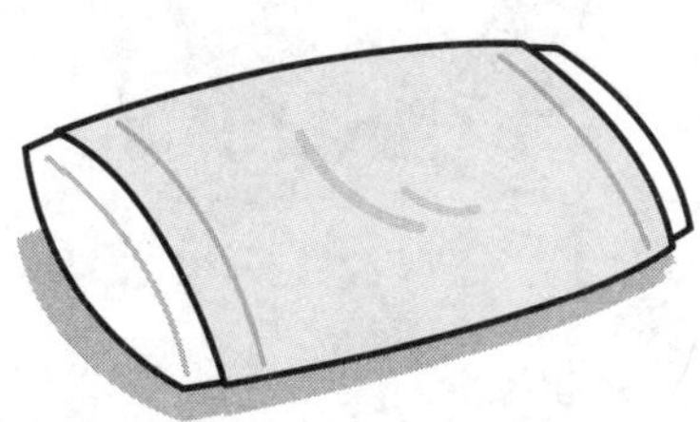

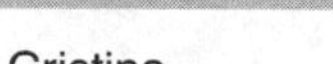

Dear Cristina,

You're invited to a sleepover at my house. Paula and Irene are coming too.

My mom's letting us have a slumber party.

See you Friday.

Bye,

Rachel

Dear Sarah,

Thanks for asking me to your birthday barbecue.

I couldn't come because I had to go to my cousin's graduation.

Here's your present.

Happy birthday!

Robert

Sports

Glossary

training / practice	trainer / coach
game / match	competition
championship	
prize	
league	
cup	
medal	
changing room	
showers	
discipline	
physical effort	
sports drink	
tracksuit	

Soccer

goal	corner	offside
to score a goal	soccer boots	yellow / red card
to send off	penalty	foul
		ban
		referee
		to blow the whistle
		linesman / lineswoman
		goalkeeper
		forward
		midfield player
		defender
		stadium
		anthem

Ballet

- ballet shoes
- tights
- bun
- tutu
- barre
- mirror

Basketball

- basket
- ball
- to make / score / shoot a basket

Golf

- club
- ball
- hole
- tee
- golf course
- hit balls at the driving range
- handicap

Tennis

- tennis court
- racket
- tennis ball
- net
- sneakers

Other sports

- football
- volleyball
- baseball

The laboratory

Weekend activities with the family

- Going for a walk in the countryside: we put our rubber boots on, the raincoat, a scarf and the woolen cap.

- Going to have lunch at my grandparents': for dessert they always have cheesecake.

- My dad drives me to the league game next Sunday. It is exciting to see the flags and to hear how the fans sing our team's anthem.

- When the weather is bad, we can go to the movies, to the theater, and to a museum as well. Nevertheless, if we stay at home, it is fun when we all sit around the fireplace to watch a movie and drink a hot chocolate.

GRAMMAR SUMMARY

GRAMMAR SUMMARY

1 ARTICLES

- We use the **indefinite articles** ***A / AN:***

  - When we don't specify the person, animal or object we are talking about.
    - *There's **a cat** on that roof.*
      *The dog has **an apple** in its mouth.*

  - With the names of professions and jobs.
    - *My mother is **a doctor**.*

- We use the **definite article** ***THE:***

  - When we refer to a specific person, animal or object.
    - *I get on well with **all the girls in my class**.*

  - With the names of musical instruments.
    - *My brother plays **the Piano**.*

  - With the names of rivers, seas and regions.
    - ***the Mississippi***
    - ***the Atlantic Ocean***
    - ***the South Pole***

- **NO article:**

  - When we talk about things in general.
    - *I don't watch **TV** often.*
    - ***Animals** are classified in **mammals, birds, fishes, reptiles, amphibians** and **insects**.*

  - When we talk about some places (*church, college, prison, school, university, work*).
    - *I have to study after **school**.*

  - With the sports names.
    - *She likes playing **soccer.***

  - With meals.
    - *I always have **lunch** at one o'clock.*

2 NOUNS

2.1 PLURAL NOUNS

- **Countable nouns**

– Countable nouns (those which can be counted) usually form their plural by adding **-s** to the singular form.

a car → *two car**s*** *a boy* → *some boy**s***

– The ones ending in *-ch*, *-sh*, *-s*, *-x* or *-z* add ***-es*** to the singular form.

a watch → *two watch**es*** *a box* → *four box**es***
a bus → *three bus**es*** *a quiz* → *two quiz**zes***

– The ones ending in *-y* preceded by a consonant form their plural by changing the '*y*' to '***i***' and adding ***-es***.

a baby → *two bab**ies*** *a city* → *two cit**ies***

– The ones ending in *-f* or *-fe* form their plural by changing the '*f*' to '***v***' and adding ***-es*** or ***-s*** respectively.

a thief → *two thie**ves*** *a knife* → *two kni**ves***

– Some nouns ending in *-o* form their plural by adding ***-es***.

a potato → *two potato**es*** *a tomato* → *two tomato**es***

– Irregular plurals.

child → *children* *foot* → *feet*
man → *men* *tooth* → *teeth*
woman → *women* *goose* → *geese*
person → *people* *mouse* → *mice*

Note: The irregular plurals never end in *-s*.

- **Uncountable nouns**

Uncountable nouns (those which cannot be counted) do not have plural form and they never take *a*, *an* or a number.

I need ~~a~~ money. → *I need money.*
Drink ~~one~~ water. → *Drink some water.*
They give me ~~an~~ advice. → *They give me a piece of advice.*

2.2 COMMON AND PROPER NOUNS

- **Common nouns**

A common noun is a word that names people, objects or ideas in general.

· *This **city** is the capital of Mexico.*

- **Proper nouns**

A proper noun is a word that names individual persons or things. These nouns begin with a capital letter.

· ***Edinburgh** is the capital of Scotland.*

3 ADJECTIVES

3.1 USUAL WORD ORDER OF ADJECTIVES

- Adjectives always go before nouns or after *to be*.

  *my **little** sister.*
  *Peter is **tall**.*

- When a noun is preceded by more than one adjective, they are arranged in a particular order.

general opinion	*specific opinion*	*size*	*shape*	*age*	*color*	*nacionality*	*material*

- For example:
  - size + color:
    *Pamela has **short brown** hair.*
  - color + material:
    *She is carrying a **blue plastic** bag.*

3.2 COMPARATIVE AND SUPERLATIVE FORMS

- We add **-er, -est** to all the adjectives with one syllable and those with two syllables ending in -y.

	Comparative	*Superlative*
tall	*taller*	*the tallest*
nice	*nicer*	*the nicest*
big	*bigger*	*the biggest*
easy	*easier*	*the easiest*

- We add **more , most** to the other adjectives with two syllables and all the adjectives with more than two.

	Comparative	*Superlative*
boring	*more boring*	*the most boring*

- **Irregular forms.**

	Comparative	*Superlative*
good *bad* *little* *much / many* *far*	*better* *worse* *less* *more* *farther / further*	*best* *worst* *least* *most* *farthest / furthest*

4 PRONOUNS

4.1 PERSONAL PRONOUNS

	Subject	Objet
1st person singular	I	me
2nd person singular	you	you
3rd person singular	he	him
	she	her
	it	it
1st person plural	we	us
2nd person plural	you	you
3rd person plural	they	them

- A subject pronoun (*I, you, he, she, it, we, you, they*) functions as the subject of a clause or sentence.
    - ***I** went to New York yesterday.*
    - ***She** is a lawyer.*
    - ***They** often go to the movies on the weekend.*

- A object pronoun (*me, you, him, her, it, us, you, them*) functions as the object of a clause or sentence.
    - *Don't give the money to **me**, give it to **him**.*
    - *If you speak to **us**, we'll explain everything.*
    - *The kids must be here, I saw **them** earlier.*

4.2 REFLEXIVE PRONOUNS

Subject	Reflexive
I	myself
you	yourself
he	himself
she	herself
it	itself
we	ourselves
you	youselves
they	themselves

- Reflexive pronouns are used:
  - When the subject and object of the clause or sentence are the same person.
    - *Be careful! Don't hurt **yourself** with the scissors!*
    - *Don't pay attention to me! **I'm** talking to **myself**.*
  - To put emphasis on a particular noun that precedes them.
    - *He **himself** told me the truth.*
    - *They ate all the cakes **themselves**.*

4.3 POSSESSIVE PRONOUNS AND ADJECTIVES

Subject	Object	Possessive		Reflexive
		Adjective	Pronoun	
I	me	my	mine	myself
you	you	your	yours	yourself
he	him	his	his	himself
she	her	her	hers	herself
it	it	its	its	itself
we	us	our	ours	ourselves
you	you	your	yours	yourselves
they	them	their	theirs	themselves

4.4 INTERROGATIVE PRONOUNS AND ADVERBS

- **which:** asking about choice, when there are limited alternatives.
  - *Which is the correct answer: A or B?*
- **what:** asking for information about something.
  - *What is your favorite color?*
- **who:** asking which person.
  - *Who is the lady with the hat?*
- **where:** asking in or at what place.
  - *Where are you?*
- **when:** asking about time.
  - *When is your birthday?*
- **how:** asking about manner or condition.
  - *How did you get there?*
- **how much:** asking about quantity (uncountable) or prices.
  - *How much money do you have?*
  - *How much is this car?*
- **how many:** asking about quantity (countable).
  - *How many candies do you have?*

5 POSSESSIVE APOSTROPHE

The apostrophe used to express possession is named **possessive (*'s*)**.

- There are different cases:

  – When we talk about an item or person that belongs or relates to someone.
  - ***Linda's*** *car*
  - ***Anne and Jim's*** *neighbor*

  Note: It's not necessary to indicate the item or person when it appeared in the previous clause or sentence.
  - *Whose* ***book*** *is this? It's John's.*

  – When we talk about time expressions.
  - ***today's*** *newspaper*

  – When we talk about organizations, countries or cities.
  - ***the team's*** *uniform*
  - ***China's*** *most important city*

  – When we talk about workplaces.
  - *I went to the* ***doctor's****.*

- Forms:

  – Adding **'s** to the singular nouns.
  - *my brother**'s** computer*

  – Adding **'s** to the plural nouns that don't end in -*s*.
  - *the children**'s** room*

  – Adding **'** to the plural nouns that end in -*s*.
  - *my brothers**'** computer*
  - *my parents**'** house*

6 VERBS

6.1 AUXILIARY VERBS: *BE / DO / HAVE*

- **BE** is used with:
  - Progressive tenses: *be* + the *'-ing'* form of the main verb.
    - *I **was walking** through the park when I found a ring.*
  - Passive voice: *be* + the past participle of the main verb.
    - *English **is spoken** in Australia.*
  - Short forms: when we don't want to repeat all the previous sentence.
    - *Was Jim at the party? No, he **wasn't.***
- **DO** is used with:
  - Simple present (interrogative and negative sentences):
    - *I **don't drink** coffee.*
    - ***Do** you **want** an apple?*
  - Simple past (interrogative and negative sentences):
    - *I **didn't understand** that movie.*
    - ***Did** you **have** a good time?*
  - Short forms:
    - *Does your mother speak English? Yes, she **does**.*
  - Question tags:
    - *She usually comes back at 6 pm, **doesn't** she?*
- **HAVE** is used with:
  - Present perfect:
    - *I should **have studied** harder.*
  - Present perfect progressive:
    - *We **have been looking** for you.*
  - Past perfect:
    - *Susan **had left** when I arrived home.*
  - Past perfect progressive:
    - *He told me he **had been waiting** for a long time.*
  - Short forms:
    - *Have you done your homework? Yes, I **have**.*
  - Questions tags:
    - *He hasn't seen her today, **has** he?*

6.2 MODAL VERBS

- The modal verbs are:

can	*could*
may	*might*
must	
will	*would*
shall	
should	*ought to*

– They do not have infinitive forms.
  · ~~*to*~~ *can* ~~*to*~~ *would* ~~*to*~~ *shall*

– They do not add -s to the 3rd person singular of the simple present.
  · *Sam **can** drive.*
  · *Jane **must** finish her homework.*

– They are always followed by an infinitive without to.
  · *It might **rain** this weekend.*
  · *Don't worry about Andrew. He can **do** it.*

Note: The verb ought is always followed by **to**.
  · We **ought to** work harder if we want to win the game.

6.3 IRREGULAR VERBS

Infinitive	Past Simple	Past Participle
arise	arose	arisen
awake	awoke (*US tb* awaked)	awoken
be	was/were	been
bear	bore	borne (*US tb* born)
beat	beat	beaten (*US tb* beat)
become	became	become
begin	began	begun
bend	bent	bent
bet	bet, betted	bet, betted
bid	bid, bade	bid, bidden
bite	bit	bitten
bleed	bled	bled
bless	blessed	blest
blow	blew	blown
break	broke	broken
breed	bred	bred
bring	brought	brought
broadcast	broadcast (*US tb* broadcasted)	broadcast (*US tb* broadcasted)
build	built	built
burn	burnt, burned	burnt, burned
bust	bust (*US* busted)	bust (*US* busted)
buy	bought	bought
catch	caught	caught
choose	chose	chosen
come	came	come
cost	cost, costed	cost, costed
creep	crept	crept
cut	cut	cut
deal	dealt	dealt
dig	dug	dug
dive	dived (*US tb* dove)	dived
do	did	done
draw	drew	drawn
dream	dreamed, dreamt	dreamed, dreamt
drink	drank	drunk
drive	drove	driven
eat	ate	eaten
fall	fell	fallen
feed	fed	fed
feel	felt	felt
fight	fought	fought
find	found	found
fly	flew	flown
forbid	forbade, forbad	forbidden
forget	forgot	forgotten
forgive	forgave	forgiven
freeze	froze	frozen
get	got	got (*US tb* gotten)
give	gave	given

Infinitive	Past Simple	Past Participle
go	went	gone
grow	grew	grown
hang	hung, hanged	hung, hanged
have	had	had
hear	heard	heard
hide	hid	hidden
hit	hit	hit
hold	held	held
hurt	hurt	hurt
keep	kept	kept
knit	knitted, knit	knitted, knit
lay	laid	laid
lead	led	led
lean	leaned (*UK tb* leant)	leaned (*UK tb* leant)
learn	learned (*UK tb* learnt)	learned (*UK tb* learnt)
leave	left	left
lend	lent	lent
let	let	let
lie	lay, lied	lain, lied
light	lit, lighted	lit, lighted
lose	lost	lost
make	made	made
mean	mean	meant
meet	met	met
mimic	mimicked	mimicked
mistake	mistook	mistaken
misunderstand	misunderstood	misunderstood
outdo	outdid	outdone
overcome	overcame	overcome
oversleep	overslept	overslept
overtake	overtook	overtaken
pay	paid	paid
plead	pleaded (*US tb* pled)	pleaded (*US tb* pled)
prove	proved	proved, proven
put	put	put
quit	quit, quitted	quit, quitted
read	read	read
rewind	rewound	rewound
rid	rid	rid
ride	rode	ridden
ring	rang	rung
rise	rose	risen
run	ran	run
saw	sawed	sawn (*US tb* sawed)
say	said	said
see	saw	seen
seek	sought	sought
sell	sold	sold
send	sent	sent
set	set	set
sew	sewed	sewn, sewed

Infinitive	Past Simple	Past Participle
shake	shook	shaken
shine	shone	shone
shoot	shot	shot
show	showed	shown
shut	shut	shut
sing	sang	sung
sink	sank	sunk
sit	sat	sat
sleep	slept	slept
slide	slid	slid
smell	smelled (*UK tb* smelt)	smelled (*UK tb* smelt)
sow	sowed	sown, sowed
speak	spoke	spoken
speed	sped, speeded	sped, speeded
spell	spelled (*UK tb* spelt)	spelled (*UK tb* spelt)
spend	spent	spent
spill	spilled (*UK tb* spilt)	spilled (*UK tb* spilt)
spin	spun	spun
spit	spat (*US tb* spit)	spat (*US tb* spit)
split	split	split
spoil	spoiled, spoilt	spoiled, spoilt
spread	spread	spread
spring	sprang	sprung
stand	stood	stood
steal	stole	stolen
stick	stuck	stuck
sting	stung	stung
stink	stank (*US tb* stunk)	stunk
strike	struck	struck (*US tb* stricken)
swear	swore	sworn
sweep	swept	swept
swell	swelled	swollen, swelled
swim	swam	swum
swing	swung	swung
take	took	taken
teach	taught	taught
tear	tore	torn
tell	told	told
think	thought	thought
throw	threw	thrown
thrust	thrust	thrust
understand	understood	understood
undo	undid	undone
upset	upset	upset
wake	woke	woken
wear	wore	worn
wet	wet, wetted	wet, wetted
win	won	won
wind	wound	wound
withstand	withstood	withstood
write	wrote	written

6.4 PHRASAL VERBS

- A phrasal verb is a combination of a verb plus a particle which has a different meaning from the original verb.

  – **verb + adverb**
  throw away (reject)

  – **verb + preposition**
  take off (depart, remove: clothing)

  – **verb + adverb + preposition**
  be up to (be capable of/ be engaged in suspicious activity)

- Some common phrasal verbs are:

  – ***break down*** *(analyze)*
  – ***break up*** *(finish a relationship)*
  – ***bring up*** *(vomit)*
  – ***call back*** *(recall)*
  – ***call off*** *(cancel)*
  – ***come by*** *(visit)*
  – ***come out*** *(be published)*
  – ***do with*** *(need)*
  – ***fall for*** *(be in loved with)*
  – ***get away*** *(escape)*
  – ***get in*** *(enter: car, taxi)*
  – ***get on*** *(enter: bus, train)*
  – ***give back*** *(reimburse)*
  – ***go away*** *(leave)*
  – ***go on*** *(continue)*
  – ***hang up*** *(put the phone down)*
  – ***keep off*** *(avoid)*
  – ***keep up*** *(continue)*
  – ***look after*** *(care for)*
  – ***look for*** *(search)*
  – ***look forward to*** *(hope for)*
  – ***make out*** *(recognize)*
  – ***put on*** *(wear)*
  – ***put up*** *(build)*
  – ***shut up*** *(be quiet)*
  – ***sit down*** *(have a sit)*
  – ***stand up*** *(arise)*
  – ***take up*** *(start)*
  – ***turn down*** *(lower volume)*
  – ***turn off*** *(stop functioning)*
  – ***turn on*** *(start functioning)*
  – ***turn up*** *(increase volume)*

  · *I **broke up** with my girlfriend after two years.*
  (I finished my relationship after two years.).

  · *You should **go on** studying English.*
  (You should continue studying English).

  · *I love this song! **Turn** it **up**, please!*
  (I love this song! Increase the volume, please!).

7 VERB TENSES

7.1 SIMPLE TENSES

AFFIRMATIVE FORM	NEGATIVE FORM	INTERROGATIVE FORM
PRESENT SIMPLE		
I study English every day. *She studies English every day.* *I read every night.* *He reads every night.*	*I don't study English every day.* *She doesn't study English every day.* *I don't read every night.* *He doesn't read every night.*	*Do you study English every day?* *Does she study English every day?* *Do you read every night?* *Does he read every night?*
PAST SIMPLE		
I studied English last week. *Last year, he read every night.*	*I didn't study English last week.* *Last year, he didn't read every night.*	*Did you study English last week?* *Did you read every night last year?*
FUTURE SIMPLE		
She will study English next summer. *From now on, I will read every night.*	*She won't study English next summer.* *From now on, I won't read every night.*	*Will she study English next summer?* *Will you read from now on every night?*

7.2 COMPOUND TENSES

AFFIRMATIVE FORM	NEGATIVE FORM	INTERROGATIVE FORM
PRESENT PERFECT		
I have studied English for two years.	*I haven't studied English since last week.*	*Have you ever studied English?*
She has studied English for two years.	*She hasn't studied English since last week.*	*Has she ever studied English?*
I have already read that book.	*I haven't read that book yet.*	*Have you read that book yet?*
She has already read that book.	*She hasn't read that book yet.*	*Has she read that book yet?*
PAST PERFECT		
I had already studied English when she arrived.	*I hadn't studied English yet when she arrived.*	*Had you studied English when she arrived?*
She had already read that book.	*She hadn't read that book yet*	*Had she read that book yet?*
FUTURE PERFECT		
By the time she arrives, I will have already studied English.	*By the time she arrives, I won't have studied English yet.*	*Will you have studied English by the time she arrives?*
She will have already read that book by the end of June.	*She won't have read that book yet by the end of June.*	*Will she have read that book by the end of June?*

7.3 PROGRESSIVE TENSES

AFFIRMATIVE FORM	NEGATIVE FORM	INTERROGATIVE FORM
PRESENT PROGRESSIVE		
I am studying English now. *You are studying English now.* *He is studying English now.*	*I am not studying English now.* *You are not studying English now.* *He is not studying English now.*	*Am I studying English now?* *Are you studying English now?* *Is he studying English now?*
PAST PROGRESSIVE		
I was studying English when she arrived. *You were studying English when she arrived.* *He was studying English when she arrived.*	*I wasn't studying English when she arrived.* *You weren't studying English when she arrived.* *He wasn't studying English when she arrived.*	*Was I studying English when she arrived?* *Were you studying English when she arrived?* *Was he studying English when she arrived?*
PRESENT PERFECT PROGRESSIVE		
I have been studying English since 3 o'clock. *He has been studying English since 3 o'clock.*	*I haven't been studying English for too long.* *He hasn't been studying English for too long.*	*Have you been studying English since 3 o'clock?* *Has he been studying English since 3 o'clock?*
PAST PERFECT PROGRESSIVE		
I had been studying English when she arrived.	*I hadn't been studying English when she arrived.*	*Had you been studying English when she arrived?*

CONDITIONAL SENTENCES

Conditionals are sentences with two clauses ('if clause + main clause) that are closely related. There are three different types:

- **FIRST CONDITIONAL**

It is used to express:

– real and possible situations.

– advices and promises.

	conditional sentence	main sentence
If	present	will / can / may / might / must + infinitive without to

– ***If*** *you need help, you* ***can call*** *me.*

– ***If*** *he calls me, I'****ll go*** *to the movies with him.*

- **SECOND CONDITIONAL**

It is used to express unreal or unlikely situations in the present or in the future.

	conditional sentence	main sentence
If	past perfect	would / could / might + infinitive without *to*

– ***If*** *I* ***had*** *a plane, I* ***would travel*** *around the world.*

- **THIRD CONDITIONAL**

It is used to express an action in the past that did not happen.

	conditional sentence	main sentence
If	past perfect	would have / could have / might have + past participle

– ***If*** *we* ***hadn't*** *go lost, we* ***would have arrived*** *on time.*

– ***If*** *you* ***had made*** *the reservations, we* ***could have slept*** *in that hotel.*

9 IDIOMS AND PHRASES

- An idiom or phrase is a combination of words that has a peculiar meaning owing to its common usage and it cannot be understood from the individual meanings of its elements.

- Some common idioms and phrases are:

– ***as easy as pie:*** very easy and simple.
  · *I passed the final exam! I studied all the night so it was as easy as pie.*

– ***to add fuel to the fire:*** to make a bad problem even worse.
  · *He added fuel to the fire by bringing up old grudges while they were arguing.*

– ***to be head over heels in love:*** to be very much in love with someone.
  · *John is head over heels in love with Mary. They are going to get married soon.*

– ***to be in the chips***: to get suddenly a lot of money.
  · *Apparently his uncle has left him everything, so he's really in the chips.*

– ***to be on one's last leg***: to be very tired, especially after a lot of physical activity or work.
  · *She was on her last leg after the race.*

– ***to bend over backwards:*** to try very hard to do something, especially to help or please someone else.
  · *Banks are bending over backwards to help those in difficulties.*

– ***to drive somebody up the wall***: to annoy or irritate someone.
  · *Stop whistling that tune. You're driving me up the wall.*

– ***to drop someone a line***: to write a short letter to someone.
  · *We really do like hearing from you, so drop us a line and let us know how you are.*

– ***to eat one's heart out:*** to be envious or jealous.
  · *Eat your heart out Frank, I'm going to Paris!*

– ***to face the music:*** to accept the (unpleasant) consequences of what you have done.
  · *After years of bad decision making, the CEO finally had to face the music.*

– ***to go bananas:*** to become very angry.
  · *She'll go bananas if she sees the room in this state.*

– ***to have a change of heart***: to go against one's previous decision.
  · *She's had a change of heart and she is inviting her sister after all.*

– ***to know something like the back of your hand***: to be very familiar with something.
  · *He knew East London like the back of his hand.*

– ***to let the cat out the bag:*** to reveal a secret or a surprise by accident.
  · *I tried to keep the party a secret, but Jim went and let the cat out of the bag.*

– ***neck and neck:*** very close, as in a race.
  · *The two candidates were running neck and neck a month before the election.*

– ***to pull somebody's leg:*** to tell someone something that is not true as a way of joking with them.
  · *Is he really angry with me or do you think he's just pulling my leg?*

– ***to save money for a rainy day:*** to reserve something for some future need.
  · *I've saved a little money for a rainy day.*

– ***to see eye to eye on something:*** to have a similar opinion on something.
  · *Despite their differences, the two candidates actually see eye to eye on most issues.*

– ***to shake in one's boots:*** to be afraid of something.
  · *I was shaking in my boots because I had to go to my manager's office for being late.*

– ***to take it easy:*** to be calm and not get too excited or angry.
  · *I know you're upset, but you just take it easy, I'll make you some tea, and you can tell me all about it.*